Less managing. More teaching. Greater learning.

 INSTRUCTORS...

Would you like your **students** to show up for class **more prepared**? *(Let's face it, class is much more fun if everyone is engaged and prepared...)*

Want an **easy way to assign** homework online and track student **progress**? *(Less time grading means more time teaching...)*

Want an **instant view** of student or class performance relative to learning objectives? *(No more wondering if students understand...)*

Need to **collect data and generate reports** required for administration or accreditation? *(Say goodbye to manually tracking student learning outcomes...)*

Want to **record and post your lectures** for students to view online?

 With **McGraw-Hill's *Connect*™ *Plus Accounting*,**

INSTRUCTORS GET:

- Simple **assignment management**, allowing you to spend more time teaching.

- **Auto-graded** assignments, quizzes, and tests.

- **Detailed Visual Reporting** where student and section results can be viewed and analyzed.

- Sophisticated **online testing** capability.

- A **filtering and reporting** function that allows you to easily assign and report on materials that are correlated to accreditation standards, learning outcomes, and Bloom's taxonomy.

- An easy-to-use **lecture capture** tool.

- The option to **upload course documents** for student access.

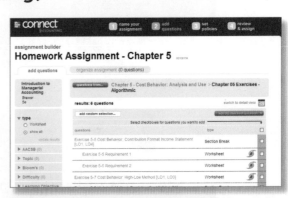

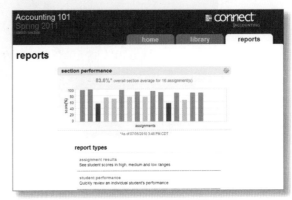

Want an online, **searchable version** of your textbook?

Wish your textbook could be **available online** while you're doing your assignments?

 ### *Connect™ Plus Accounting* eBook

If you choose to use *Connect™ Plus Accounting*, you have an affordable and searchable online version of your book integrated with your other online tools.

Connect™ Plus Accounting eBook offers features like:

- Topic search
- Direct links from assignments
- Adjustable text size
- Jump to page number
- Print by section

 Want to get more **value** from your textbook purchase?

Think learning accounting should be a bit more **interesting**?

 ### Check out the STUDENT RESOURCES section under the *Connect™* Library tab.

Here you'll find a wealth of resources designed to help you achieve your goals in the course. You'll find things like **quizzes, PowerPoints, and Internet activities** to help you study. Every student has different needs, so explore the STUDENT RESOURCES to find the materials best suited to you.

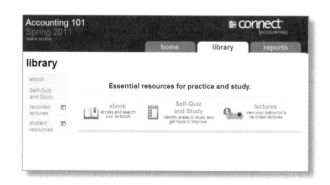

Fundamental Accounting Principles

20th edition

Volume 2, Chapters 12–25

John J. Wild
University of Wisconsin at Madison

Ken W. Shaw
University of Missouri at Columbia

Barbara Chiappetta
Nassau Community College

McGraw-Hill
Irwin

To my students and family, especially **Kimberly, Jonathan, Stephanie,** and **Trevor.**
To my wife **Linda** and children, **Erin, Emily,** and **Jacob.**
To my mother, husband **Bob,** and sons **Michael** and **David.**

FUNDAMENTAL ACCOUNTING PRINCIPLES

Published by McGraw-Hill/Irwin, a business unit of The McGraw-Hill Companies, Inc., 1221 Avenue of the Americas, New York, NY, 10020. Copyright © 2011, 2009, 2007, 2005, 2002, 1999, 1996, 1993, 1990, 1987, 1984, 1981, 1978, 1975, 1972, 1969, 1966, 1963, 1959, 1955 by The McGraw-Hill Companies, Inc. All rights reserved. No part of this publication may be reproduced or distributed in any form or by any means, or stored in a database or retrieval system, without the prior written consent of The McGraw-Hill Companies, Inc., including, but not limited to, in any network or other electronic storage or transmission, or broadcast for distance learning.

Some ancillaries, including electronic and print components, may not be available to customers outside the United States.

This book is printed on acid-free paper.

3 4 5 6 7 8 9 0 DOW/DOW 1 0 9 8 7 6 5 4 3 2

ISBN-13: 978-0-07-811087-0 (combined edition)
ISBN-10: 0-07-811087-4 (combined edition)
ISBN-13: 978-0-07-733825-1 (volume 1, chapters 1-12)
ISBN-10: 0-07-733825-1 (volume 1, chapters 1-12)
ISBN-13: 978-0-07-733824-4 (volume 2, chapters 12-25)
ISBN-10: 0-07-733824-3 (volume 2, chapters 12-25)
ISBN-13: 978-0-07-733826-8 (with working papers volume 1, chapters 1-12)
ISBN-10: 0-07-733826-X (with working papers volume 1, chapters 1-12)
ISBN-13: 978-0-07-733827-5 (with working papers volume 2, chapters 12-25)
ISBN-10: 0-07-733827-8 (with working papers volume 2, chapters 12-25)
ISBN-13: 978-0-07-733823-7 (principles, chapters 1-17)
ISBN-10: 0-07-733823-5 (principles, chapters 1-17)

Vice president and editor-in-chief: *Brent Gordon*
Editorial director: *Stewart Mattson*
Publisher: *Tim Vertovec*
Executive editor: *Steve Schuetz*
Director of development: *Ann Torbert*
Senior development editor: *Christina A. Sanders*
Vice president and director of marketing: *Robin J. Zwettler*
Marketing director: *Brad Parkins*
Marketing manager: *Michelle Heaster*
Vice president of editing, design, and production: *Sesha Bolisetty*
Managing editor: *Lori Koetters*

Senior buyer: *Carol A. Bielski*
Lead designer: *Matthew Baldwin*
Senior photo research coordinator: *Jeremy Cheshareck*
Photo researcher: *Sarah Evertson*
Lead media project manager: *Brian Nacik*
Media project manager: *Ron Nelms*
Interior and cover design: *Laurie Entringer*
Cover image: © *Getty Images*
Typeface: *10.5/12 Times Roman*
Compositor: *Aptara®, Inc.*
Printer: *R. R. Donnelley*

The Library of Congress has cataloged the single volume edition of this work as follows

Wild, John J.
    Fundamental accounting principles / John J. Wild, Ken W. Shaw, Barbara Chiappetta.—20th ed.
      p. cm.
    Includes index.
    ISBN-13: 978-0-07-811087-0 (combined edition : alk. paper)
    ISBN-10: 0-07-811087-4 (combined edition : alk. paper)
    ISBN-13: 978-0-07-733825-1 (volume 1 ch. 1-12 : alk. paper)
    ISBN-10: 0-07-733825-1 (volume 1 ch. 1-12 : alk. paper)
    [etc.]
    1. Accounting. I. Shaw, Ken W. II. Chiappetta, Barbara. III. Title.
HF5636.W675 2011
657—dc22

                            2010026205

www.mhhe.com

Dear Colleagues/Friends,

As we roll out the new edition of *Fundamental Accounting Principles*, we thank each of you who provided suggestions to improve our textbook. As teachers, we know how important it is to select the right book for our course. This new edition reflects the advice and wisdom of many dedicated reviewers, symposium and workshop participants, students, and instructors. Our book consistently rates number one in customer loyalty because of you. Together, we have created the most readable, concise, current, accurate, and innovative accounting book available today.

Throughout the writing process, we steered this book in the manner you directed. Reviewers, instructors, and students say this book's enhanced presentation, graphics, and technology cater to different learning styles and helps students better understand accounting. *Connect Accounting Plus* offers new features to improve student learning and to assist instructor teaching and grading. Our iPod content lets students study on the go, while our Algorithmic Test Bank provides an infinite variety of exam problems. You and your students will find all these tools easy to apply.

We owe the success of this book to our colleagues who graciously took time to help us focus on the changing needs of today's instructors and students. We feel fortunate to have witnessed our profession's extraordinary devotion to teaching. Your feedback and suggestions are reflected in everything we write. Please accept our heartfelt thanks for your dedication in helping today's students learn, understand, and appreciate accounting.

With kindest regards,

John J. Wild   *Ken W. Shaw*   *Barbara Chiappetta*

iii

About the Authors

JOHN J. WILD is a distinguished professor of accounting at the University of Wisconsin at Madison. He previously held appointments at Michigan State University and the University of Manchester in England. He received his BBA, MS, and PhD from the University of Wisconsin.

Professor Wild teaches accounting courses at both the undergraduate and graduate levels. He has received numerous teaching honors, including the Mabel W. Chipman Excellence-in-Teaching Award, the departmental Excellence-in-Teaching Award, and the Teaching Excellence Award from the 2003 and 2005 business graduates at the University of Wisconsin. He also received the Beta Alpha Psi and Roland F. Salmonson Excellence-in-Teaching Award from Michigan State University. Professor Wild has received several research honors and is a past KPMG Peat Marwick National Fellow and is a recipient of fellowships from the American Accounting Association and the Ernst and Young Foundation.

Professor Wild is an active member of the American Accounting Association and its sections. He has served on several committees of these organizations, including the Outstanding Accounting Educator Award, Wildman Award, National Program Advisory, Publications, and Research Committees. Professor Wild is author of Financial Accounting, Managerial Accounting, and College Accounting, each published by McGraw-Hill/Irwin. His research articles on accounting and analysis appear in The Accounting Review, Journal of Accounting Research, Journal of Accounting and Economics, Contemporary Accounting Research, Journal of Accounting, Auditing and Finance, Journal of Accounting and Public Policy, and other journals. He is past associate editor of Contemporary Accounting Research and has served on several editorial boards including The Accounting Review.

In his leisure time, Professor Wild enjoys hiking, sports, travel, people, and spending time with family and friends.

KEN W. SHAW is an associate professor of accounting and the Deloitte Professor at the University of Missouri. He previously was on the faculty at the University of Maryland at College Park. He received an accounting degree from Bradley University and an MBA and PhD from the University of Wisconsin. He is a Certified Public Accountant with work experience in public accounting.

Professor Shaw teaches financial accounting at the undergraduate and graduate levels. He received the Williams-Keepers LLC Teaching Excellence award in 2007, was voted the "Most Influential Professor" by the 2005, 2006, and 2010 School of Accountancy graduating classes, and is a two-time recipient of the O'Brien Excellence in Teaching Award. He is the advisor to his School's chapter of the Association of Certified Fraud Examiners.

Professor Shaw is an active member of the American Accounting Association and its sections. He has served on many committees of these organizations and presented his research papers at national and regional meetings. Professor Shaw's research appears in The Accounting Review; Journal of Accounting Research; Contemporary Accounting Research; Journal of Financial and Quantitative Analysis; Journal of the American Taxation Association; Journal of Accounting, Auditing, and Finance; Journal of Financial Research; Research in Accounting Regulation; and other journals. He has served on the editorial boards of Issues in Accounting Education, the Journal of Business Research, and Research in Accounting Regulation. Professor Shaw is co-author of Financial and Managerial Accounting and College Accounting, both published by McGraw-Hill.

In his leisure time, Professor Shaw enjoys tennis, cycling, music, and coaching his children's sports teams.

BARBARA CHIAPPETTA received her BBA in Accountancy and MS in Education from Hofstra University and is a tenured full professor at Nassau Community College. For the past two decades, she has been an active executive board member of the Teachers of Accounting at Two-Year Colleges (TACTYC), serving 10 years as vice president and as president from 1993 through 1999. As an active member of the American Accounting Association, she has served on the Northeast Regional Steering Committee, chaired the Curriculum Revision Committee of the Two-Year Section, and participated in numerous national committees. Professor Chiappetta has been inducted into the American Accounting Association Hall of Fame for the Northeast Region. She had also received the Nassau Community College dean of instruction's Faculty Distinguished Achievement Award. Professor Chiappetta was honored with the State University of New York Chancellor's Award for Teaching Excellence in 1997. As a confirmed believer in the benefits of the active learning pedagogy, Professor Chiappetta has authored Student Learning Tools, an active learning workbook for a first-year accounting course, published by McGraw-Hill/Irwin.

In her leisure time, Professor Chiappetta enjoys tennis and participates on a U.S.T.A. team. She also enjoys the challenge of bridge. Her husband, Robert, is an entrepreneur in the leisure sport industry. She has two sons—Michael, a lawyer, specializing in intellectual property law in New York, and David, a composer, pursuing a career in music for film in Los Angeles.

Helping Students Achieve Peak Performance

Fundamental Accounting Principles 20e

Great performances result from pushing the limits through quality practices and reinforcing feedback to strengthen abilities and motivation. Assist your students in achieving their peak performance by giving them what they need to succeed in today's accounting principles course.

Whether the goal is to become an accountant or a businessperson, or simply to be an informed consumer of accounting information, *Fundamental Accounting Principles (FAP)* has helped generations of students succeed by giving them support in the form of leading-edge accounting content that engages students, paired with state-of-the-art technology that elevates their understanding of key accounting principles.

With *FAP* on your side, you'll be provided with **engaging content** in a **motivating style** to help students see the relevance of accounting. Students are motivated when reading materials that are clear and pertinent. *FAP* excels at engaging students. Its chapter-opening vignettes showcase dynamic, successful entrepreneurial individuals and companies guaranteed to **interest and excite students**. This edition's featured companies—**Research In Motion** (maker of BlackBerry), **Apple**, **Nokia**, and **Palm**—captivate students with their products and annual reports, which are a pathway for learning financial statements. Further, this book's coverage of the accounting cycle fundamentals is widely praised for its clarity and effectiveness.

FAP also delivers innovative technology to help student performance. ***Connect Accounting*** provides students with instant grading and feedback for assignments that are completed online. ***Connect Accounting Plus*** integrates an online version of the textbook with *Connect Accounting*. Our algorithmic test bank offers infinite variations of numerical test bank questions. The Self-Quiz and Study, Interactive Presentations, and LearnSmart all provide additional support to help reinforce concepts and keep students motivated.

We're confident you'll agree that ***FAP* will help your students achieve peak performance**.

Your Students' Connection to

McGraw-Hill *Connect Accounting* is an online assignment and assessment solution that connects your students with the tools and resources needed to achieve success through faster learning, more efficient studying, and higher retention of knowledge.

Online Assignments: *Connect Accounting* helps students learn more efficiently by providing feedback and practice material when they need it, where they need it. *Connect* grades homework automatically and gives immediate feedback on any questions students may have missed.

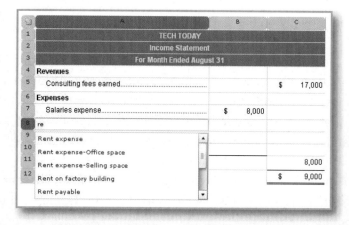

Interactive Presentations: The interactive presentations provide engaging narratives of all chapter learning objectives in an interactive online format. The presentations are tied specifically to *Fundamental Accounting Principles*, 20e. They follow the structure of the text and are organized to match the learning objectives within each chapter. While the interactive presentations are not meant to replace the textbook in this course, they provide additional explanation and enhancement of material from the text chapter, allowing students to learn, study, and practice with instant feedback at their own pace.

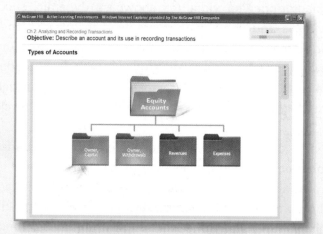

Student Resource Library: The *Connect Accounting* Student Study Center gives access to additional resources such as recorded lectures, online practice materials, an eBook, and more.

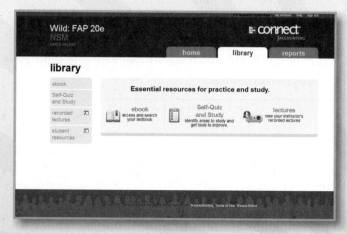

Reach Peak Performance!

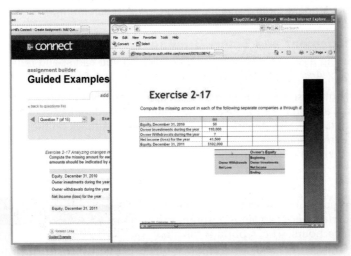

Guided Examples: The Guided Examples in *Connect Accounting* provide a narrated, animated, step-by-step walk-through of select exercises similar to those assigned. These short presentations provide reinforcement when students need it most.

LearnSmart: LearnSmart adaptive self-study technology within *Connect Accounting* helps students make the best use of their study time. LearnSmart provides a seamless combination of practice, assessment, and remediation for every concept in the textbook. LearnSmart's intelligent software adapts to students by supplying questions on a new concept when they are ready to learn it. With LearnSmart, students will spend less time on topics they understand and practice more on those they have yet to master.

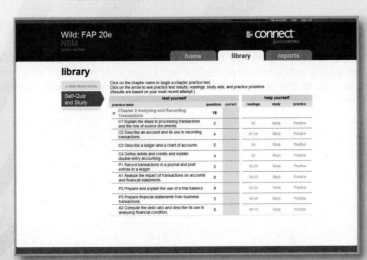

Self-Quiz and Study: The Self-Quiz and Study (SQS) connects students to the learning resources students need to succeed in the course. For each chapter, students can take a practice quiz and immediately see how well they performed. A study plan then recommends specific readings from the text, supplemental study material, and practice exercises that will improve students' understanding and mastery of each learning objective.

Connect Accounting

Connect Accounting offers a number of powerful tools and features to make managing assignments easier, so faculty can spend more time teaching. With *Connect Accounting*, students can engage with their coursework anytime and anywhere, making the learning process more accessible and efficient. (Please see previous page for a description of the student tools available within *Connect Accounting*.)

Simple Assignment Management and Smart Grading

With *Connect Accounting,* creating assignments is easier than ever, so you can spend more time teaching and less time managing. *Connect Accounting* enables you to:

- Create and deliver assignments easily with select end-of-chapter questions and test bank items.
- Go paperless with the eBook and online submission and grading of student assignments.
- Have assignments scored automatically, giving students immediate feedback on their work and side-by-side comparisons with correct answers.
- Reinforce classroom concepts with practice tests and instant quizzes.

Student Reporting

Connect Accounting keeps instructors informed about how each student, section, and class is performing, allowing for more productive use of lecture and office hours. The reporting function enables you to:

- View scored work immediately and track individual or group performance with assignment and grade reports.
- Access an instant view of student or class performance relative to learning objectives.
- Collect data and generate reports required by many accreditation organizations, such as AACSB and AICPA.

Instructor Library

The *Connect Accounting* Instructor Library is your repository for additional resources to improve student engagement in and out of class. You can select and use any asset that enhances your lecture. The *Connect Accounting* Instructor Library includes: access to the eBook version of the text, PowerPoint files, Solutions Manual, Instructor Resource Manual, and Test Bank.

Tools for Instructors

McGraw-Hill *Connect Plus Accounting*

McGraw-Hill reinvents the textbook learning experience for the modern student with *Connect Plus Accounting*. A seamless integration of an eBook and *Connect Accounting, Connect Plus Accounting* provides all of the *Connect Accounting* features plus:

- An integrated eBook, allowing for anytime, anywhere access to the textbook.
- Dynamic links between the problems or questions you assign to your students and the location in the eBook where that problem or question is covered.
- A powerful search function to pinpoint and connect key concepts in a snap.

For more information about *Connect*, go to **www.mcgrawhillconnect.com**, or contact your local McGraw-Hill sales representative.

Tegrity Campus: Lectures 24/7

Tegrity Campus is a service that makes class time available 24/7 by automatically capturing every lecture. With a simple one-click start-and-stop process, you capture all computer screens and corresponding audio in a format that is easily searchable, frame by frame. Students can replay any part of any class with easy-to-use browser-based viewing on a PC or Mac, an iPod, or other mobile device.

Educators know that the more students can see, hear, and experience class resources, the better they learn. In fact, studies prove it. Tegrity Campus's unique search feature helps students efficiently find what they need, when they need it, across an entire semester of class recordings. Help turn your students' study time into learning moments immediately supported by your lecture. With Tegrity Campus, you also increase intent listening and class participation by easing students' concerns about note-taking. Lecture Capture will make it more likely you will see students' faces, not the tops of their heads.

To learn more about Tegrity watch a two-minute Flash demo at **http://tegritycampus.mhhe.com**.

McGraw-Hill Customer Care Contact Information

At McGraw-Hill, we understand that getting the most from new technology can be challenging. That's why our services don't stop after you purchase our products. You can e-mail our Product Specialists 24 hours a day to get product training online. Or you can search our knowledge bank of Frequently Asked Questions on our support Website. For Customer Support, call 800-331-5094 or visit **www.mhhe.com/support**. One of our Technical Support Analysts will be able to assist you in a timely fashion.

How Can Text-Related Web Resources Enrich My Course?

Online Learning Center (OLC)

© Okea; iStockphoto

We offer an Online Learning Center (OLC) that follows *Fundamental Accounting Principles* chapter by chapter. It doesn't require any building or maintenance on your part. It's ready to go the moment you and your students type in the URL: *www.mhhe.com/wildFAP20e*

As students study and learn from *Fundamental Accounting Principles*, they can visit the Student Edition of the OLC Website to work with a multitude of helpful tools:

- Generic Template Working Papers
- Chapter Learning Objectives
- Interactive Chapter Quizzes
- PowerPoint® Presentations

- Narrated PowerPoint® Presentations*
- Video Library
- Excel Template Assignments
- iPod Content*

* indicates Premium Content

A secured Instructor Edition stores essential course materials to save you prep time before class. Everything you need to run a lively classroom and an efficient course is included. All resources available to students, plus . . .

- Instructor's Resource Manual
- Solutions Manual
- Solutions to Excel Template Assignments
- Test Bank
- Solutions to CYGL, Peachtree, and QuickBooks templates

The OLC Website also serves as a doorway to other technology solutions, like course management systems.

> "There are numerous materials and resources available for the instructor. I love how everything is on one Website and there is no need for a CD or different supplements/materials that need to be carried around."
>
> **—Jeanine Metzler, Northampton Community College, on the OLC**

www.blackboard.com

Online Course Management

No matter what online course management system you use (WebCT, BlackBoard, or eCollege), we have a course content ePack available for *FAP* 20e. Our new ePacks are specifically designed to make it easy for students to navigate and access content online. They are easier than ever to install on the latest version of the course management system available today.

Don't forget that you can count on the highest level of service from McGraw-Hill. Our online course management specialists are ready to assist you with your online course needs. They provide training and will answer any questions you have throughout the life of your adoption. So try our new ePack for *FAP* 20e and make online course content delivery easy and fun.

x

CourseSmart

CourseSmart is a new way to find and buy eTextbooks. CourseSmart has the largest selection of eTextbooks available anywhere, offering thousands of the most commonly adopted textbooks from a wide variety of higher education publishers. CourseSmart eTextbooks are available in one standard online reader with full text search, notes, and highlighting, and email tools for sharing between classmates. Visit **www.CourseSmart.com** for more information on ordering.

How Students Can Study On the Go Using Their iPods

iPod Content

Harness the power of one of the most popular technology tools students use today—the Apple iPod. Our innovative approach allows students to download audio and video presentations right into their iPod and take learning materials with them wherever they go. Students just need to visit the Online Learning Center at **www.mhhe.com/wildFAP20e** to download our iPod content. For each chapter of the book they will be able to download audio narrated lecture presentations for use on various versions of iPods. iPod Touch users can even access self-quizzes.

It makes review and study time as easy as putting on headphones.

How Can McGraw-Hill Help Teach My Course Online?

Improve Student Learning Outcomes and Save Instructor Time with ALEKS®

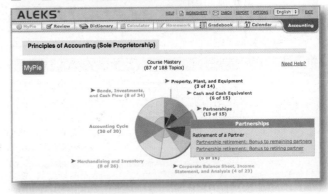

ALEKS is an assessment and learning program that provides individualized instruction in accounting. Available online in partnership with McGraw-Hill/Irwin, ALEKS interacts with students much like a skilled human tutor, with the ability to assess precisely a student's knowledge and provide instruction on the exact topics the student is most ready to learn. By providing topics to meet individual students' needs, allowing students to move between explanation and practice, correcting and analyzing errors, and defining terms, ALEKS helps students to master course content quickly and easily.

ALEKS also includes an Instructor Module with powerful, assignment-driven features and extensive content flexibility. The complimentary Instructor Module provides a course calendar, a customizable gradebook with automatically graded homework, textbook integration, and dynamic reports to monitor student and class progress. ALEKS simplifies course management and allows instructors to spend less time with administrative tasks and more time directing student learning.

To learn more about ALEKS, visit **www.aleks.com/highered/business**.

ALEKS is a registered trademark of ALEKS Corporation.

Innovative Textbook Features

Using Accounting for Decisions

Whether we prepare, analyze, or apply accounting information, one skill remains essential: decision-making. To help develop good decision-making habits and to illustrate the relevance of accounting, our book uses a unique pedagogical framework we call the Decision Center. This framework is comprised of a variety of approaches and subject areas, giving students insight into every aspect of business decision-making; see three examples to the right and one below. Answers to Decision Maker and Ethics boxes are at the end of each chapter.

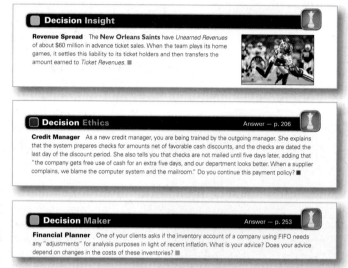

Decision Insight

Revenue Spread The **New Orleans Saints** have *Unearned Revenues* of about $60 million in advance ticket sales. When the team plays its home games, it settles this liability to its ticket holders and then transfers the amount earned to *Ticket Revenues.* ∎

Decision Ethics   Answer — p. 206

Credit Manager As a new credit manager, you are being trained by the outgoing manager. She explains that the system prepares checks for amounts net of favorable cash discounts, and the checks are dated the last day of the discount period. She also tells you that checks are not mailed until five days later, adding that "the company gets free use of cash for an extra five days, and our department looks better. When a supplier complains, we blame the computer system and the mailroom." Do you continue this payment policy? ∎

Decision Maker   Answer — p. 253

Financial Planner One of your clients asks if the inventory account of a company using FIFO needs any "adjustments" for analysis purposes in light of recent inflation. What is your advice? Does your advice depend on changes in the costs of these inventories? ∎

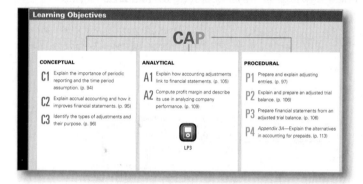

CAP Model

The Conceptual/Analytical/Procedural (CAP) Model allows courses to be specially designed to meet your teaching needs or those of a diverse faculty. This model identifies learning objectives, textual materials, assignments, and test items by C, A, or P, allowing different instructors to teach from the same materials, yet easily customize their courses toward a conceptual, analytical, or procedural approach (or a combination thereof) based on personal preferences.

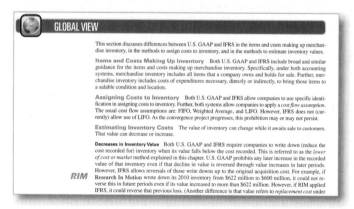

New Global View

This section explains international accounting practices relating to the material covered in that chapter. This section is purposefully located at the end of each chapter so that each instructor can decide what emphasis, if at all, is to be assigned to it. The aim of this Global View section is to describe accounting practices and to identify the similarities and differences in international accounting practices versus that in the U.S. As we move toward global convergence in accounting practices, and as we witness the likely conversion of U.S. GAAP to IFRS, the importance of student familiarity with international accounting grows. This innovative section helps us begin down that path of learning and teaching global accounting practices.

"...the chapter openers are absolutely excellent and include entrepreneurs that the students can easily relate to. This helps the students understand the need/importance of accounting in a small business."

— Michelle Grant, Bossier Parish Community College

Bring Accounting To Life

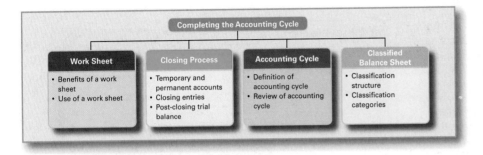

Chapter Preview With Flowchart

This feature provides a handy textual/visual guide at the start of every chapter. Students can now begin their reading with a clear understanding of what they will learn and when, allowing them to stay more focused and organized along the way.

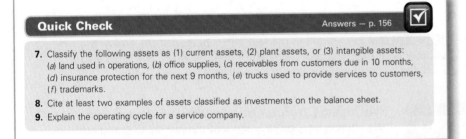

Quick Check   Answers — p. 156

7. Classify the following assets as (1) current assets, (2) plant assets, or (3) intangible assets: (a) land used in operations, (b) office supplies, (c) receivables from customers due in 10 months, (d) insurance protection for the next 9 months, (e) trucks used to provide services to customers, (f) trademarks.
8. Cite at least two examples of assets classified as investments on the balance sheet.
9. Explain the operating cycle for a service company.

Quick Check

These short question/answer features reinforce the material immediately preceding them. They allow the reader to pause and reflect on the topics described, then receive immediate feedback before going on to new topics. Answers are provided at the end of each chapter.

"The author(s) are doing an excellent job of using learning and study aids. The examples are real-world and easy to understand. I cannot think of anything else that I would add."

—**Shirly Kleiner, Johnson County Community College**

g transactions is to post journal entries to ledger is up-to-date, entries are posted as en time permits. All entries must be posted to ensure that account balances are up-to-bits in journal entries are transferred into

Point: Computerized systems often provide a code beside a balance such as *dr.* or *cr.* to identify its balance. Posting is automatic and immediate with accounting software.

Marginal Student Annotations

These annotations provide students with additional hints, tips, and examples to help them more fully understand the concepts and retain what they have learned. The annotations also include notes on global implications of accounting and further examples.

Outstanding Assignment Material

Once a student has finished reading the chapter, how well he or she retains the material can depend greatly on the questions, exercises, and problems that reinforce it. This book leads the way in comprehensive, accurate assignments.

Demonstration Problems present both a problem and a complete solution, allowing students to review the entire problem-solving process and achieve success.

Chapter Summaries provide students with a review organized by learning objectives. Chapter Summaries are a component of the CAP model (see page xii), which recaps each conceptual, analytical, and procedural objective.

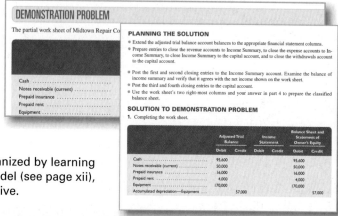

Key Terms are bolded in the text and repeated at the end of the chapter with page numbers indicating their location. The book also includes a complete Glossary of Key Terms.

Multiple Choice Quiz Questions quickly test chapter knowledge before a student moves on to complete Quick Studies, Exercises, and Problems.

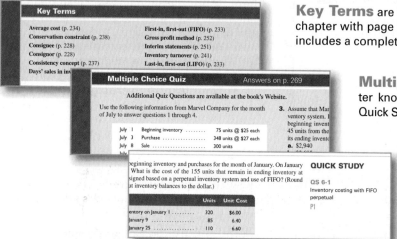

Quick Study assignments are short exercises that often focus on one learning objective. Most are included in *Connect Accounting*. There are usually 8-10 Quick Study assignments per chapter.

Exercises are one of this book's many strengths and a competitive advantage. There are about 10-15 per chapter and most are included in *Connect Accounting*.

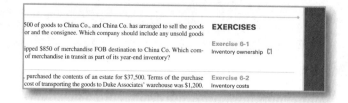

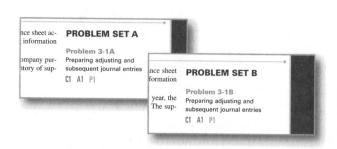

Problem Sets A & B are proven problems that can be assigned as homework or for in-class projects. All problems are coded according to the CAP model (see page xii), and Set A is included in *Connect Accounting*.

PUT AWAY YOUR RED PEN!

We pride ourselves on the accuracy of this book's assignment materials. Independent research reports that instructors and reviewers point to the accuracy of this book's assignment materials as one of its key competitive advantages.

Helps Students Master Key Concepts

Beyond the Numbers exercises ask students to use accounting figures and understand their meaning. Students also learn how accounting applies to a variety of business situations. These creative and fun exercises are all new or updated, and are divided into sections:

- Reporting in Action
- Comparative Analysis
- Ethics Challenge
- Communicating in Practice
- Taking It To The Net
- Teamwork in Action
- Hitting the Road
- Entrepreneurial Decision
- Global Decision

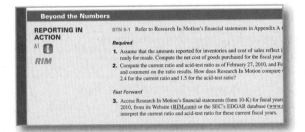

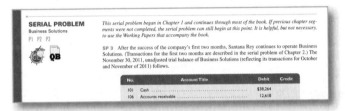

Serial Problem uses a continuous running case study to illustrate chapter concepts in a familiar context. The Serial Problem can be followed continuously from the first chapter or picked up at any later point in the book; enough information is provided to ensure students can get right to work.

> "Well planned, and very organized. A very thorough coverage of all topics. Easy to read and comprehend."
>
> **— Linda Bolduc, Mount Wachusett Community College**

The End of the Chapter Is Only the Beginning Our valuable and proven assignments aren't just confined to the book. From problems that require technological solutions to materials found exclusively online, this book's end-of-chapter material is fully integrated with its technology package.

 connect |ACCOUNTING
- Quick Studies, Exercises, and Problems available in *Connect* are marked with an icon.

- Problems supported by the General Ledger Application Software, Peachtree, or Quickbooks are marked with an icon.

- Online Learning Center (OLC) includes Interactive Quizzes, Excel template assignments, and more.

 e**X**cel
mhhe.com/wildFAP20e
- Problems supported with Microsoft Excel template assignments are marked with an icon.

- Material that receives additional coverage (slide shows, videos, audio, etc.) available in iPod ready format are marked with an icon.

- Assignments that focus on global accounting practices and companies are often identified with an icon.

The authors extend a special thanks to accuracy checkers Barbara Schnathorst, The Write Solution, Inc.; Helen Roybark, Radford University; Beth Woods, CPA, Accuracy Counts; and David Krug, Johnson County Community College.

Enhancements in This Edition

This edition's revisions are driven by instructors and students. General revisions to the entire book follow (including chapter-by-chapter revisions):

- Revised and updated assignments throughout
- Updated ratio (tool) analyses for each chapter
- New material on International Financial Reporting Standards (IFRS) in most chapters, including global examples
- New and revised entrepreneurial examples and elements
- Revised serial problem through nearly all chapters
- New art program, visual info-graphics and text layout

- New Research In Motion (maker of BlackBerry) annual report with comparisons to Apple, Palm, and Nokia (IFRS) with new assignments
- Updated graphics added to each chapter's analysis section
- New technology content integrated and referenced in the book
- New Global View section in each chapter referencing international accounting including examples using global companies
- New assignments covering international accounting

Chapter 1

Facebook NEW opener with new entrepreneurial assignment
Streamlined and consolidated learning objectives
New section on International Standards and convergence
Revised section on accounting principles, assumptions, and constraints
New visual layouts for conceptual framework and the building blocks of GAAP
New discussion of conceptual framework linked to IFRSs
New graphic discussing fraud control in accounting
Updated compensation data in exhibit

Chapter 2

CitySlips NEW opener with new entrepreneurial assignment
Reorganized and streamlined learning objectives
Revised introduction of double-entry accounting
New 4-step process for analyzing, recording, and posting transactions
Revised layout for transaction analysis
New discussion on accounting quality

Chapter 3

Cheezburger Network NEW opener with new entrepreneurial assignment
Updated 3-step process for adjusting accounts
Enhanced and streamlined presentation of accounting adjustments
Revised info-graphics for adjusting entries
Enhanced exhibit on steps in preparing financial statements
Expanded discussion of global accounting

Chapter 4

Gamer Grub NEW opener with new entrepreneurial assignment
Slightly revised steps 1 and 2 of work sheet

Enhanced graphics for closing process
Enhanced details for general ledger after the closing process
Updated color-coded work sheet

Chapter 5

Heritage Link Brands NEW opener with new entrepreneurial assignment
Streamlined learning objectives
New 2-step presentation for recording merchandise sales and its costs
Revised presentation on purchase returns
New discussion on fraud and invoices
Revised discussion of gross margin

Chapter 6

Fitness Anywhere NEW opener with new entrepreneurial assignment
Streamlined presentation for lower of cost or market (LCM)
Color-coded graphic for introducing cost flow assumptions
Enhanced graphics for learning inventory errors
Expanded discussion on inventory controls
Expanded explanation of inventory accounting under IFRS

Chapter 7

New Belgium Brewing Company NEW opener with new entrepreneurial assignment
Streamlined learning objectives
Enhanced graphics for special journals
Detailed four benefits from subsidiary ledgers
Updated ERP presentation
Revised discussion of segment returns

Chapter 8

Dylan's Candy Bar REVISED opener with new entrepreneurial assignment
Enhanced SOX discussion of controls, including the role of COSO
Streamlined learning objectives
New material on drivers of human fraud

New graphic introducing a bank reconciliation with links to bank and book balances
Updated graphic on frequent cyber frauds
New graphic on drivers of financial misconduct

Chapter 9

LaserMonks NEW opener with new entrepreneurial assignment
Streamlined learning objectives
Reorganized recording of credit sales
Further clarification of interest formula
Enhanced graphics for bad debts estimation

Chapter 10

Games2U NEW opener with new entrepreneurial assignment
Reorganized learning objectives
Added entry to record impairment
Enhanced discussion of asset sales
Expanded explanation of asset valuation under IFRS
Updated all real world examples and graphics

Chapter 11

SnorgTees NEW opener with new entrepreneurial assignment
Updated tax illustrations and assignments using most recent government rates
New data on frauds involving employee payroll
New entry to reclassify long- to short-term debt
Updated all real world examples and graphics

Chapter 12

Kids Konserve NEW opener with new entrepreneurial assignment
New 3-step process for partnership liquidation
New *statement of liquidation* introduced
Enhanced discussion of partnership liquidation

For Better Learning

Chapter 13

Clean Air Lawn Care NEW opener with new entrepreneurial assignment
Streamlined learning objectives
Inserted numerous key margin computations for entries involving equity
Updated statement of stockholders' equity
Updated all real world examples and graphics
Explained accounting for equity under IFRS

Chapter 14

CakeLove NEW opener with new entrepreneurial assignment
Enhanced graphics for bonds and notes
Revised discussion of debt-to-equity
Enhanced explanation of how U.S. GAAP and IFRS determine fair value
New arrow lines linking effective interest amortization tables to journal entries

Chapter 15

Blackboard NEW opener with new entrepreneurial assignment
Streamlined learning objectives
Phrase "fair value" used in lieu of "market value"
Enhanced exhibit summarizing accounting for securities
Revised explanation of investments in securities with significant influence
New, enhanced section on comprehensive income

Chapter 16

Animoto NEW opener with new entrepreneurial assignment
Streamlined learning objectives
Enhanced graphics on cash inflows and outflows involving operating, investing, and financing
Highlighted 5-step process to prepare the statement of cash flows
New discussion of different classifications for certain cash flows under IFRS
Increased number and range of assignments

Chapter 17

Motley Fool REVISED opener with new entrepreneurial assignment
Streamlined learning objectives
New companies—Research In Motion, Apple, Palm and Nokia—data throughout the chapter, exhibits, and illustrations

Enhanced horizontal and vertical analysis using new company and industry data
Enhanced discussion of common-size graphics
Enhanced ratio analysis using new company and industry data

Chapter 18

Hot Box Cookies NEW opener with new entrepreneurial assignment
Revised learning objectives
Enhanced discussion of trends in managerial accounting, including e-commerce and role of services
New exhibit and discussion of the value chain
Discussion of fraud and ethics in managerial accounting moved to earlier in chapter
New discussion of global trends in managerial accounting

Chapter 19

Liberty Tax Service NEW opener with new entrepreneurial assignment
Enhanced explanation of events in job order costing, including new 3-step process
Added new arrow lines to exhibits as learning aids
Enhanced discussion of adjusting factory overhead
New factory overhead T-account exhibit
New exhibit on entries to adjust factory overhead account
Added several new assignments

Chapter 20

IdeaPaint NEW opener with new entrepreneurial assignment
Streamlined learning objectives
Updated list of companies applying process operations
Enhanced several exhibits for better learning
New section on trends in process operations, including discussion of just-in-time, automation, role of services, and customer focus
Increased number and range of assignments

Chapter 21

Skullcandy NEW opener with new entrepreneurial assignment
Streamlined learning objectives
Enhanced activity-based costing exhibits
Revised discussion and exhibits for comparisons between activity-based costing and two-stage cost allocation
Added summary of cost allocation methods with exhibit

Deleted section on departmental reporting and analysis
Added Serial Problem to end of chapter assignments

Chapter 22

Johnny Cupcakes NEW opener with new entrepreneurial assignment
Streamlined learning objectives
Revised cost exhibits for added clarity and learning
New discussion on global use of contribution margin

Chapter 23

Smathers and Branson NEW opener with new entrepreneurial assignment
Reorganized learning objectives
New discussion on potential outcomes of participatory budgeting
Enhanced discussion and exhibits for cash budgets
New exhibit on general formula for preparing the cash budget
Added Decision Insight box on Apple's cash cushion
Enhanced discussion of computing cash disbursements for purchases, including new exhibit
Increased number and range of assignments

Chapter 24

SewWhat? NEW opener with new entrepreneurial assignment
Streamlined learning objectives
Simplified presentation of overhead variances to focus on controllable and volume variances
Moved detailed overhead variances and standard cost system journal entries to (new) Appendix 24A
Increased number and range of assignments

Chapter 25

Dogswell NEW opener with new entrepreneurial assignment
Streamlined learning objectives
Updated graphic on industry cost of capital estimates
Added section and assignments on decision to keep or replace equipment
Increased number and range of assignments

Instructor Supplements

Instructor's Resource CD-ROM
Chapters 1-25
ISBN13: 978007338107
ISBN10: 0077338103

This is your all-in-one resource. It allows you to create custom presentations from your own materials or from the following text-specific materials provided in the CD's asset library:

- **Instructor's Resource Manual**

  Written by Barbara Chiappetta, Nassau Community College, and Patricia Walczak, Lansing Community College.

  This manual contains (for each chapter) a Lecture Outline, a chart linking all assignment materials to Learning Objectives, a list of relevant active learning activities, and additional visuals with transparency masters.

- **Solutions Manual**
- **Test Bank, Computerized Test Bank**
- **PowerPoint® Presentations**
  Prepared by Jon Booker, Charles Caldwell, Cindy Rooney, and Susan Galbreth.

  Presentations allow for revision of lecture slides, and includes a viewer, allowing screens to be shown with or without the software.

- **Link to PageOut**

Test Bank
Vol. 1, Chapters 1-12
ISBN13: 9780077338183
ISBN10: 0077338189

Vol. 2, Chapters 13-25
ISBN13: 9780077338190
ISBN10: 0077338197

Revised by Barbara Gershowitz, Nashville State Technical Community College.

Solutions Manual
Vol. 1, Chapters 1-12
ISBN13: 9780077338152
ISBN10: 0077338154

Vol. 2, Chapters 13-25
ISBN13: 9780077338145
ISBN10: 0077338146

Written by John J. Wild, Ken W. Shaw, and Anita Kroll, University of Wisconsin–Madison.

Student Supplements

Excel Working Papers CD
ISBN13: 9780077338084
ISBN10: 0077338081

Written by John J. Wild.

Working Papers (for Chapters 1-25) delivered in Excel spreadsheets. These Excel Working Papers are available on CD-ROM and can be bundled with the printed Working Papers; see your representative for information.

Working Papers
Vol. 1, Chapters 1-12
ISBN13: 9780077338220
ISBN10: 0077338227

Vol. 2, Chapters 12-25
ISBN13: 9780077338206
ISBN10: 0077338200

Principles of Financial Accounting
Chapters 1-17
ISBN13: 9780077338213
ISBN10: 0077338219

Written by John J. Wild.

Study Guide
Vol. 1, Chapters 1-12
ISBN13: 9780077338169
ISBN10: 0077338162

Vol. 2, Chapters 12-25
ISBN13: 9780077338176
ISBN10: 0077338170

Written by Barbara Chiapetta, Nassau Community College, and Patricia Walczak, Lansing Community College.

Covers each chapter and appendix with reviews of the learning objectives, outlines of the chapters, summaries of chapter materials, and additional problems with solutions.

Carol Yacht's General Ledger CD-ROM
ISBN13: 9780077338039
ISBN10: 0077338030

The CD-ROM includes fully functioning versions of McGraw-Hill's own General Ledger Application software. Problem templates prepared by Carol Yacht and student user guides are included that allow you to assign text problems for working in Yacht's General Ledger or Peachtree.

QuickBooks Pro 2011 Student Guide and Templates
ISBN13: 9780077455309
ISBN10: 0077455304

Prepared by Carol Yacht.

To better prepare students for accounting in the real world, select end-of-chapter material in the text is tied to QuickBooks software. The accompanying student guide provides a step-by-step walkthrough for students on how to complete the problem in the software.

Assurance of Learning Ready

Many educational institutions today are focused on the notion of assurance of learning, an important element of some accreditation standards. *Fundamental Accounting Principles* is designed specifically to support your assurance of learning initiatives with a simple, yet powerful solution. Each test bank question for *Fundamental Accounting Principles* maps to a specific chapter learning objective listed in the text. You can use our test bank software, EZ Test and EZ Test Online, or *Connect Accounting* to easily query for learning objectives that directly relate to the learning objectives for your course. You can then use the reporting features of EZ Test to aggregate student results in similar fashion, making the collection and presentation of assurance of learning data simple and easy.

> "Best on the market! Great examples, complete coverage of principle's topics, and great resources!"
>
> — David Alldredge, Salt Lake Community College

AACSB Statement

The McGraw-Hill Companies is a proud corporate member of AACSB International. Understanding the importance and value of AACSB accreditation, *Fundamental Accounting Principles* recognizes the curricula guidelines detailed in the AACSB standards for business accreditation by connecting selected questions in the test bank to the six general knowledge and skill guidelines in the AACSB standards. The statements contained in *Fundamental Accounting Principles* are provided only as a guide for the users of this textbook. The AACSB leaves content coverage and assessment within the purview of individual schools, the mission of the school, and the faculty. While *Fundamental Accounting Principles* and the teaching package make no claim of any specific AACSB qualification or evaluation, we have within *Fundamental Accounting Principles* labeled select questions according to the six general knowledge and skills areas.

The authors extend a special thanks to our contributing and technology supplement authors:

Contributing Author: Anita Kroll, University of Wisconsin–Madison
LearnSmart Authors: Anna Boulware, St. Charles Community College; Brenda Mattison, Tri County Technical College; and Dominique Svarc, William Rainey Harper College
Online Quizzes: Gina Jones, Aims County Community College
Connect Self-Quiz and Study: Jeannine Metzler, Northampton Community College
Interactive Presentations: Kathleen O'Donnell, Onongada Community College, and Jeannie Folk, College of DuPage

Acknowledgments

John J. Wild, Ken W. Shaw, Barbara Chiappetta, and McGraw-Hill/Irwin would like to recognize the following instructors for their valuable feedback and involvement in the development of *Fundamental Accounting Principles* 20e. We are thankful for their suggestions, counsel, and encouragement.

Nelson Alino, Quinnipiac University

David Alldredge, Salt Lake Community College

Sheila Ammons, Austin Community College

Victoria Badura, Chadron State College

Susan Baker, University of Michigan-Dearborn

Charles Scott Barhight, Northampton Community College

Robert Beebe, Morrisville State University

Teri Bernstein, Santa Monica College

Swati Bhandarkar, University of Georgia

Jaswinder Bhangal, Chabot College

Linda Bolduc, Mount Wachusett Community College

Anna Boulware, St. Charles Community College

Philip Brown, Harding University

Jay Buchanon, Burlington County College-Pemberton

Mary Burnell, Fairmont State University

Nathaniel Calloway, University of Maryland

Sal Cardiel, Chaffey College

Lloyd Carroll, Borough of Manhattan Community College

Hong Chen, Northeastern Illinois University

Stanley Chu, Borough of Manhattan Community College

Kwang-Hyun Chung, Pace University

Shiefei Chung, Rowan University

Robert Churchman, Harding University

Marilyn Ciolino, Delgado Community College

Lisa Cole, Johnson County Community College

Howard A. Collins, SUNY at Stony Brook

William Cooper, North Carolina A &T University

Suzie Cordes, Johnson County Community College

James Cosby, John Tyler Community College

Richard Culp, Ball State University

Alan Czyzewski, Indiana State University-Terre Haute

Judy Daulton, Piedmont Technical College

Walter DeAguero, Saddleback College

Mike Deschamps, Mira Costa College

Rosemond Desir, Colorado State University

Vincent Dicalogero, Suffolk County Community College

Roger Dorsey, University of Arkansas-Little Rock

Jap Efendi, University of Texas-Arlington

Terry Elliott Morehead State University

James M. Emig, Villanova University

Steven Englert, Ivy Tech Community College

Caroline Falconetti, Nassau Community College

Stephanie Farewell, University of Arkansas-Little Rock

Laura Farrell, Wagner College

Charles Fazzi, Saint Vincent College

Ronald A. Feinberg, Suffolk Community College

Kathleen Fitzpatrick, University of Toledo-Scott Park

Jeannie Folk, College of DuPage

Mary Foster, Illinois Central College

Mitchell Franklin, Syracuse University

Paul Franklin, Kaplan University Online

Kim Gatzke, Delgado Community College

Rich Geglien, Ivy Tech Community College

Barbara Gershowitz, Nashville State Technical Community College

Richard Gordon, Columbia Southern

Michelle Grant, Bossier Parish Community College

Richard P. Green II, Texas A& M University

Tony Greig, Purdue University

Joyce Griffin, Kansas City Kansas Community College

Lillian Grose, Delgado Community College

Denise Guest, Germanna Community College

Amy Haas, Kingsborough Community College

Betty Habiger, New Mexico State University

Francis Haggerty, Lee College

Betty Harper, Middle Tennessee State University

Jeannie Harrington, Middle Tennessee State University

John L. Haverty, St. Joseph's University

Laurie Hays, Western Michigan University

Shelley Henke, Fox Valley Technical College

Geoffrey Heriot, Greenville Technical College

Lyle Hicks, Danville Area Community College

Cecil Hill, Jackson State University

Patricia Holmes, Des Moines Area Community College

Margaret Houston, Wright State University

Constance Hylton, George Mason University

Gary Allen Hypes, Mount Aloysius College

Catherine Jeppson, Caifornia State University–Northridge

Gina M. Jones, Aims Community College

Rita Jones, Columbus State University

Christine Jonick, Gainesville State College

Thomas Kam, Hawaii Pacific University

Jack Karbens, Hawaii Pacific University

Connie Kelt, San Juan College

Karen Kettelson, Western Technical College

Randy Kidd, Longview Community College

Irene Kim, George Washington University

James Kinard, Ohio State University-Columbus

Rita Kingery-Cook, University of Delaware

Frank Klaus, Cleveland State University

Shirly A. Kleiner, Johnson County Community College

Robert F. Koch, Saint Peter's College

Phillip Korb, University of Baltimore

David Krug, Johnson County Community College

Jill Kolody, Anne Arundel Community College

Charles Lacey, Henry Ford Community College

Tara Laken, Joliet Junior College

Beth Lasky, Delgado Community College

Phillip Lee, Nashville State Technical Community College

Jerry Lehman, Madison Area Technical College

Frederic Lerner, New York University

Roger Lewis, West Virginia University-Parkersburg

Eric Lindquist, Lansing Community College

Jeannie Liu, Chaffey College

Rebecca Lohmann, Southeast Missouri State University

Debra Luna, El Paso Community College

Sylvester A. Maorino, SUNY Westchester Community College

Thomas S. Marsh, Northern Virginia Community College-Annadale

Stacie Mayes, Rose State College

Brenda Mattison, Tri-County Technical College

Jeanine Metzler, Northampton Community College

Kathleen Michele, Prairieville University

Tim Miller, El Camino College

Roger L. Moore, Arkansas State University-Beebe

Robbie Morse, Ivy Tech Community College

Linda Muren, Cuyahoga Community College—West Campus

Andrea Murowski, Brookdale Community College

Ramesh Narasimhan, Montclair State University

Mary Beth Nelson, North Shore Community College

Deborah Niemer, Oakland Community College

Kathleen O'Donnell, Onongada Community College

Ahmed Omar, Burlington County College

Deborah Pauly, Loras College

Joel Peralto, Hawaii Community College

Yvonne Phang, Borough of Manhattan Community College

Gary Pieroni, Diablo Valley College

Susan Pope, University of Akron

Jean Price, Marshall University

Debbie Rankin, Lincoln University

Susan Reeves, University of South Carolina

Jenny Resnick, Santa Monica College

Ruthie Reynolds, Howard University

Carla Rich, Pensacola Junior College

Paul Rivers, Bunker Hill Community College

Jill Roberts, Campbellsville University

Karen Robinson, Morgan State University

Richard Roding, Red Rocks Community College

Joel Rosenfeld, New York University

Pamela Rouse, Butler University

Helen Roybark, Radford University

Alphonse Ruggiero, Suffolk County Community College

Martin Sabo, Community College of Denver

Judith Sage, Texas A&M International University

Nathaniel Samba, Ivy Tech Community College

Linda Schain, Hoefstra University

Christine Schalow, University of Wisconsin-Stevens Point

Bunney Schmidt, Keiser University

Geeta Shankhar, University of Dayton

Regina Shea, Community College of Baltimore County—Essex

Jay Siegel, Union County College

Lois Slutsky, Broward College-South

Gerald Smith, University of Northern Iowa

Kathleen Sobieralski, University of Maryland

Charles Spector, State University of New York College

Jane Stam, Onondaga Community College

Douglas P. Stives, Monmouth University

Jacqueline Stoute, Baruch University

Beverly Strachan, Troy University

John Suckow, Lansing Community College

Dominique Svarc, William Rainey Harper College

Anthony Teng, Saddleback College

Sue Terizan, Wright State University

Leslie Thysell, John Tyler Community College

Michael Ulinski, Pace University-Pleasantville

Bob Urell, Irvine Valley College

Alonda Vaughn, Strayer University-Tampa East

Ari Vega, Fashion Institute of Technology

Adam Vitalis, University of Wisconsin

Patricia Walczak, Lansing Community College

Li Wang, University of Akron

Doris Warmflash, SUNY Westchester Community College

David Welch, Franklin University

Jean Wells, Howard University

Robert A. Widman, Brooklyn College CUNY

Christopher Widmer, Tidewater Community College

Jane Wiese, Valencia Community College

Kenneth L. Wild, University of London

Scott Williams, County College of Morris

Wanda Wong, Chabot College

Darryl Woolley, University of Idaho

Gloria Worthy, Southwest Tennessee Community College-Macon

Lorenzo Ybarra, West Los Angeles College

Laura Young, University of Central Arkansas

Judy Zander, Grossmont College

In addition to the helpful and generous colleagues listed above, we thank the entire McGraw-Hill/Irwin *Fundamental Accounting Principles* 20e team, including Stewart Mattson, Tim Vertovec, Steve Schuetz, Christina Sanders, Aaron Downey of Matrix Productions, Lori Koetters, Matthew Baldwin, Carol Bielski, Patricia Plumb, and Brian Nacik. We also thank the great marketing and sales support staff, including Michelle Heaster, Kathleen Klehr, and Simi Dutt. Many talented educators and professionals worked hard to create the supplements for this book, and for their efforts we're grateful. Finally, many more people we either did not meet or whose efforts we did not personally witness nevertheless helped to make this book everything that it is, and we thank them all.

John J. Wild   *Ken W. Shaw*   *Barbara Chiappetta*

Brief Contents

Contents

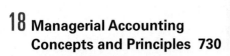

20 Process Cost Accounting 812

21 Cost Allocation and Performance Measurement 856

22 Cost-Volume-Profit Analysis 906

23 Master Budgets and Planning 944

24 Flexible Budgets and Standard Costs 988

25 Capital Budgeting and Managerial Decisions 1034

Fundamental Accounting Principles

Volume 2, Chapters 12–25

12

Accounting for Partnerships

A Look Back

Chapter 11 focused on how current liabilities are identified, computed, recorded, and reported. Attention was directed at notes, payroll, sales taxes, warranties, employee benefits, and contingencies.

A Look at This Chapter

This chapter explains the partnership form of organization. Important partnership characteristics are described along with the accounting concepts and procedures for its most fundamental transactions.

A Look Ahead

Chapter 13 extends our discussion to the corporate form of organization. We describe the accounting and reporting for stock issuances, dividends, and other equity transactions.

Learning Objectives

CONCEPTUAL

C1 Identify characteristics of partnerships and similar organizations. (p. 480)

ANALYTICAL

A1 Compute partner return on equity and use it to evaluate partnership performance. (p. 492)

LP12

PROCEDURAL

P1 Prepare entries for partnership formation. (p. 483)

P2 Allocate and record income and loss among partners. (p. 483)

P3 Account for the admission and withdrawal of partners. (p. 486)

P4 Prepare entries for partnership liquidation. (p. 490)

Let's Do Eco-Lunch

"We are making a difference"
—CHANCE CLAXTON AND LYNN JULIAN

PHOENIX—Believe it or not, nearly 20,000 pounds of trash is generated annually from the typical elementary school. "When we researched it," explains Chance Claxton, "We discovered that 67 pounds of lunchtime trash is created by each schoolage child each school year." Armed with that evidence, and as mothers of young children, Chance, along with partner Lynn Julian, felt an urgent need to respond. The result is **Kids Konserve (KidsKonserve.com),** a start-up partnership that sells reusable and recycled food kits. "With waste from snack and lunch breaks at an all-time high," says Chance, "Kids Konserve is empowering parents and kids with information and a reusable product that will help . . . decrease waste in community landfills."

While Chance focuses on the design and sales side, Lynn's focus is on the accounting, marketing, and financial side of Kids Konserve. Her knowledge of partnerships and their financial implications are important to Kid Konserve's success. Lynn explains that she is working on a model for fund-raising opportunities to further expand their product opportunities. Both partners stress the importance of attending to partnership

formation, partnership agreements, and financial reports to stay afloat. They refer to the partners' return on equity and establishing the proper organizational form as key inputs to partnership strategies and decisions.

Success is causing their partnership to evolve, but the partners adhere to an eco-focused mentality. "The best part of being a 'mompreneur' is that I am doing something for myself, for others, for my family, and for the earth," insists Chance. "It is a great feeling to have my children watch me work."

The partners continue to apply strict accounting fundamentals. Lynn explains that their partnership cannot survive unless the business is profitable, even with their noble agenda. To that end, both partners review their accounting results and regularly assess the partnership's costs and revenues. Nevertheless, Lynn emphasizes their greater goal: "We're delivering a program that reduces waste on campus. I'd say that deserves an A+."

[Sources: *Kids Konserve Website,* January 2011; *Entrepreneur,* October 2009; *MomBites.com,* September 2009; *Daily Grommet,* September 2009]

The three basic types of business organizations are proprietorships, partnerships, and corporations. Partnerships are similar to proprietorships, except they have more than one owner. This chapter explains partnerships and looks at several variations of them such as limited partnerships, limited liability partnerships, S corporations, and limited liability companies. Understanding the advantages and disadvantages of the partnership form of business organization is important for making informed business decisions.

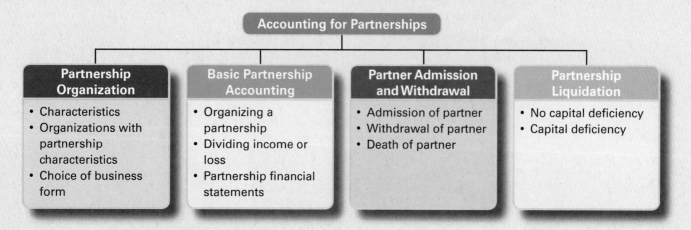

PARTNERSHIP FORM OF ORGANIZATION

C1 Identify characteristics of partnerships and similar organizations.

A **partnership** is an unincorporated association of two or more people to pursue a business for profit as co-owners. Many businesses are organized as partnerships. They are especially common in small retail and service businesses. Many professional practitioners, including physicians, lawyers, investors, and accountants, also organize their practices as partnerships.

Characteristics of Partnerships

Partnerships are an important type of organization because they offer certain advantages with their unique characteristics. We describe these characteristics in this section.

Voluntary Association   A partnership is a voluntary association between partners. Joining a partnership increases the risk to one's personal financial position. Some courts have ruled that partnerships are created by the actions of individuals even when there is no *express agreement* to form one.

Partnership Agreement   Forming a partnership requires that two or more legally competent people (who are of age and of sound mental capacity) agree to be partners. Their agreement becomes a **partnership contract,** also called *articles of copartnership.* Although it should be in writing, the contract is binding even if it is only expressed verbally. Partnership agreements normally include details of the partners' (1) names and contributions, (2) rights and duties, (3) sharing of income and losses, (4) withdrawal arrangement, (5) dispute procedures, (6) admission and withdrawal of partners, and (7) rights and duties in the event a partner dies.

Point: When a new partner is admitted, all parties usually must agree to the admission.

Limited Life   The life of a partnership is limited. Death, bankruptcy, or any event taking away the ability of a partner to enter into or fulfill a contract ends a partnership. Any one of the partners can also terminate a partnership at will.

Point: The end of a partnership is referred to as its *dissolution.*

Taxation   A partnership is not subject to taxes on its income. The income or loss of a partnership is allocated to the partners according to the partnership agreement, and it is included in determining the taxable income for each partner's tax return. Partnership income or loss is allocated each year whether or not cash is distributed to partners.

Point: Partners are taxed on their share of partnership income, not on their withdrawals.

Mutual Agency   Mutual agency implies that each partner is a fully authorized agent of the partnership. As its agent, a partner can commit or bind the partnership to any contract within the scope of the partnership business. For instance, a partner in a merchandising business can sign contracts binding the partnership to buy merchandise, lease a store building, borrow money, or hire employees. These activities are all within the scope of a merchandising firm. A partner in a law firm, acting alone, however, cannot bind the other partners to a contract to buy snowboards for resale or rent an apartment for parties. These actions are outside the normal scope of a law firm's business. Partners also can agree to limit the power of any one or more of the partners to negotiate contracts for the partnership. This agreement is binding on the partners and on outsiders who know it exists. It is not binding on outsiders who do not know it exists. Outsiders unaware of the agreement have the right to assume each partner has normal agency powers for the partnership. Mutual agency exposes partners to the risk of unwise actions by any one partner.

Unlimited Liability   **Unlimited liability** implies that each partner can be called on to pay a partnership's debts. When a partnership cannot pay its debts, creditors usually can apply their claims to partners' *personal* assets. If a partner does not have enough assets to meet his or her share of the partnership debt, the creditors can apply their claims to the assets of the other partners. A partnership in which all partners have *mutual agency* and *unlimited liability* is called a **general partnership.** Mutual agency and unlimited liability are two main reasons that most general partnerships have only a few members.

Co-Ownership of Property   Partnership assets are owned jointly by all partners. Any investment by a partner becomes the joint property of all partners. Partners have a claim on partnership assets based on their capital account and the partnership contract.

Organizations with Partnership Characteristics

Organizations exist that combine certain characteristics of partnerships with other forms of organizations. We discuss several of these forms in this section.

Limited Partnerships   Some individuals who want to invest in a partnership are unwilling to accept the risk of unlimited liability. Their needs can be met with a **limited partnership.** This type of organization is identified in its name with the words "Limited Partnership" or "Ltd." or "LP." A limited partnership has two classes of partners, general and limited. At least one partner must be a **general partner,** who assumes management duties and unlimited liability for the debts of the partnership. The **limited partners** have no personal liability beyond the amounts they invest in the partnership. Limited partners have no active role except as specified in the partnership agreement. A limited partnership agreement often specifies unique procedures for allocating income and losses between general and limited partners. The accounting procedures are similar for both limited and general partnerships.

Decision Insight

Nutty Partners   The Hawaii-based **ML Macadamia Orchards LP** is one of the world's largest growers of macadamia nuts. It reported the following partners' capital balances ($ 000s) in its balance sheet: ■

General Partner	$ 81
Limited Partners	$43,560

Limited Liability Partnerships   Most states allow individuals to form a **limited liability partnership.** This is identified in its name with the words "Limited Liability Partnership" or by "LLP." This type of partnership is designed to protect innocent partners from malpractice or negligence claims resulting from the acts of another partner. When a partner provides service resulting in a malpractice claim, that partner has personal liability for the claim. The remaining partners who were not responsible for the actions resulting in the claim are not personally liable for it. However, most states hold all partners personally liable for other partnership debts. Accounting for a limited liability partnership is the same as for a general partnership.

S Corporations   Certain corporations with 100 or fewer stockholders can elect to be treated as a partnership for income tax purposes. These corporations are called *Sub-Chapter S* or simply **S corporations.** This distinguishes them from other corporations, called *Sub-Chapter C* or simply **C corporations.** S corporations provide stockholders the same limited liability feature that C corporations do. The advantage of an S corporation is that it does not pay income taxes. If stockholders work for an S corporation, their salaries are treated as expenses of the corporation. The remaining income or loss of the corporation is allocated to stockholders for inclusion on their personal tax returns. Except for C corporations having to account for income tax expenses and liabilities, the accounting procedures are the same for both S and C corporations.

Limited Liability Companies   A relatively new form of business organization is the **limited liability company.** The names of these businesses usually include the words "Limited Liability Company" or an abbreviation such as "LLC" or "LC." This form of business has certain features similar to a corporation and others similar to a limited partnership. The owners, who are called *members,* are protected with the same limited liability feature as owners of corporations. While limited partners cannot actively participate in the management of a limited partnership, the members of a limited liability company can assume an active management role. A limited liability company usually has a limited life. For income tax purposes, a limited liability company is typically treated as a partnership. This treatment depends on factors such as whether the members' equity interests are freely transferable and whether the company has continuity of life. A limited liability company's accounting system is designed to help management comply with the dictates of the articles of organization and company regulations adopted by its members. The accounting system also must provide information to support the company's compliance with state and federal laws, including taxation.

Point: The majority of proprietorships and partnerships that are organized today are set up as LLCs.

Point: Accounting for LLCs is similar to that for partnerships (and proprietorships). One difference is that Owner (Partner), Capital is usually called *Members, Capital* for LLCs.

Choosing a Business Form

Choosing the proper business form is crucial. Many factors should be considered, including taxes, liability risk, tax and fiscal year-end, ownership structure, estate planning, business risks, and earnings and property distributions. The following table summarizes several important characteristics of business organizations:

	Proprietorship	Partnership	LLP	LLC	S Corp.	Corporation
Business entity	Yes	Yes	Yes	Yes	Yes	Yes
Legal entity	No	No	No	Yes	Yes	Yes
Limited liability	No	No	Limited*	Yes	Yes	Yes
Business taxed	No	No	No	No	No	Yes
One owner allowed	Yes	No	No	Yes	Yes	Yes

* A partner's personal liability for LLP debts is limited. Most LLPs carry insurance to protect against malpractice.

Point: The Small Business Administration provides suggestions and information on setting up the proper form for your organization—see **SBA.gov**.

We must remember that this table is a summary, not a detailed list. Many details underlie each of these business forms, and several details differ across states. Also, state and federal laws change, and a body of law is still developing around LLCs. Business owners should look at these details and consider unique business arrangements such as organizing various parts of their businesses in different forms.

Quick Check   Answers — p. 495

1. A partnership is terminated in the event (*a*) a partnership agreement is not in writing, (*b*) a partner dies, (*c*) a partner exercises mutual agency.
2. What does the term *unlimited liability* mean when applied to a general partnership?
3. Which of the following forms of organization do not provide limited liability to *all* of its owners? (*a*) S corporation, (*b*) limited liability company, (*c*) limited partnership.

BASIC PARTNERSHIP ACCOUNTING

Since ownership rights in a partnership are divided among partners, partnership accounting

- Uses a capital account for each partner.
- Uses a withdrawals account for each partner.
- Allocates net income or loss to partners according to the partnership agreement.

This section describes partnership accounting for organizing a partnership, distributing income and loss, and preparing financial statements.

Organizing a Partnership

When partners invest in a partnership, their capital accounts are credited for the invested amounts. Partners can invest both assets and liabilities. Each partner's investment is recorded at an agreed-on value, normally the market values of the contributed assets and liabilities at the date of contribution. To illustrate, Kayla Zayn and Hector Perez organize a partnership on January 11 called BOARDS that offers year-round facilities for skateboarding and snowboarding. Zayn's initial net investment in BOARDS is $30,000, made up of cash ($7,000), boarding facilities ($33,000), and a note payable reflecting a bank loan for the new business ($10,000). Perez's initial investment is cash of $10,000. These amounts are the values agreed on by both partners. The entries to record these investments follow.

P1	Prepare entries for partnership formation.

Zayn's Investment

Jan. 11	Cash	7,000	
	Boarding facilities	33,000	
	Note payable		10,000
	K. Zayn, Capital		30,000
	To record the investment of Zayn.		

Assets = Liabilities + Equity
+7,000   +10,000   +30,000
+33,000

Perez's Investment

Jan. 11	Cash	10,000	
	H. Perez, Capital		10,000
	To record the investment of Perez.		

Assets = Liabilities + Equity
+10,000   +10,000

In accounting for a partnership, the following additional relations hold true: (1) Partners' withdrawals are debited to their own separate withdrawals accounts. (2) Partners' capital accounts are credited (or debited) for their shares of net income (or net loss) when closing the accounts at the end of a period. (3) Each partner's withdrawals account is closed to that partner's capital account. Separate capital and withdrawals accounts are kept for each partner.

Point: Both equity and cash are reduced when a partner withdraws cash from a partnership.

Decision Insight

Broadway Partners Big River Productions is a partnership that owns the rights to the play *Big River*. The play is performed on tour and periodically on Broadway. For a recent year-end, its Partners' Capital was approximately $300,000, and it was distributed in its entirety to the partners. ■

Dividing Income or Loss

Partners are not employees of the partnership but are its owners. If partners devote their time and services to their partnership, they are understood to do so for profit, not for salary. This means there are no salaries to partners that are reported as expenses on the partnership income statement. However, when net income or loss of a partnership is allocated among partners, the partners can agree to allocate "salary allowances" reflecting the relative value of services

P2	Allocate and record income and loss among partners.

provided. Partners also can agree to allocate "interest allowances" based on the amount invested. For instance, since Zayn contributes three times the investment of Perez, it is only fair that this be considered when allocating income between them. Like salary allowances, these interest allowances are not expenses on the income statement.

Partners can agree to any method of dividing income or loss. In the absence of an agreement, the law says that the partners share income or loss of a partnership equally. If partners agree on how to share income but say nothing about losses, they share losses the same way they share income. Three common methods to divide income or loss use (1) a stated ratio basis, (2) the ratio of capital balances, or (3) salary and interest allowances and any remainder according to a fixed ratio. We explain each of these methods in this section.

Point: Partners can agree on a ratio to divide income and another ratio to divide a loss.

Point: The fractional basis can be stated as a proportion, ratio, or percent. For example, a 3:2 basis is the same as ⅗ and ⅖, or 60% and 40%.

Allocation on Stated Ratios   The *stated ratio* (also called the *income-and-loss-sharing ratio,* the *profit and loss ratio,* or the *P&L ratio*) method of allocating partnership income or loss gives each partner a fraction of the total. Partners must agree on the fractional share each receives. To illustrate, assume the partnership agreement of K. Zayn and H. Perez says Zayn receives two-thirds and Perez one-third of partnership income and loss. If their partnership's net income is $60,000, it is allocated to the partners when the Income Summary account is closed as follows.

Assets = Liabilities + Equity
                       −60,000
                       +40,000
                       +20,000

Dec. 31	Income Summary	60,000	
	K. Zayn, Capital		40,000
	H. Perez, Capital		20,000
	To allocate income and close Income Summary.		

Point: To determine the percent of income received by each partner, divide an individual partner's share by total net income.

Allocation on Capital Balances   The *capital balances* method of allocating partnership income or loss assigns an amount based on the ratio of each partner's relative capital balance. If Zayn and Perez agree to share income and loss on the ratio of their beginning capital balances—Zayn's $30,000 and Perez's $10,000—Zayn receives three-fourths of any income or loss ($30,000/$40,000) and Perez receives one-fourth ($10,000/$40,000). The journal entry follows the same format as that using stated ratios (see the preceding entries).

Allocation on Services, Capital, and Stated Ratios   The *services, capital, and stated ratio* method of allocating partnership income or loss recognizes that service and capital contributions of partners often are not equal. Salary allowances can make up for differences in service contributions. Interest allowances can make up for unequal capital contributions. Also, the allocation of income and loss can include *both* salary and interest allowances. To illustrate, assume that the partnership agreement of K. Zayn and H. Perez reflects differences in service and capital contributions as follows: (1) annual salary allowances of $36,000 to Zayn and $24,000 to Perez, (2) annual interest allowances of 10% of a partner's beginning-year capital balance, and (3) equal share of any remaining balance of income or loss. These salaries and interest allowances are *not* reported as expenses on the income statement. They are simply a means of dividing partnership income or loss. The remainder of this section provides two illustrations using this three-point allocation agreement.

Illustration when income exceeds allowance.   If BOARDS has first-year net income of $70,000, and Zayn and Perez apply the three-point partnership agreement described in the prior paragraph, income is allocated as shown in Exhibit 12.1. Zayn gets $42,000 and Perez gets $28,000 of the $70,000 total.

Point: When allowances exceed income, the amount of this negative balance often is referred to as a *sharing agreement loss* or *deficit.*

Illustration when allowances exceed income.   The sharing agreement between Zayn and Perez must be followed even if net income is less than the total of the allowances. For example, if BOARDS' first-year net income is $50,000 instead of $70,000, it is allocated to the partners as shown in Exhibit 12.2. Computations for salaries and interest are identical to those in Exhibit 12.1. However, when we apply the total allowances against income, the balance of income is negative. This $(14,000) negative balance is allocated equally to the partners per their sharing agreement. This means that a negative $(7,000) is allocated to each partner. In this case, Zayn ends up with $32,000 and Perez with $18,000. If BOARDS had experienced a net loss, Zayn and Perez would share it in the same manner as the $50,000 income. The only difference is that they would have begun with a negative amount because of the loss. Specifically, the partners would still have been

Point: Check to make sure the sum of the dollar amounts allocated to each partner equals net income or loss.

EXHIBIT 12.1

Dividing Income When Income Exceeds Allowances

	Zayn	Perez	Total
Net income			**$70,000**
Salary allowances			
Zayn	$ 36,000		
Perez		$ 24,000	
Interest allowances			
Zayn (10% × $30,000)	3,000		
Perez (10% × $10,000)		1,000	
Total salaries and interest	39,000	25,000	64,000
Balance of income			6,000
Balance allocated equally			
Zayn	3,000 ←		
Perez		3,000 ←	
Total allocated			6,000
Balance of income			$ 0
Income of each partner	**$42,000**	**$28,000**	

EXHIBIT 12.2

Dividing Income When Allowances Exceed Income

	Zayn	Perez	Total
Net income			**$50,000**
Salary allowances			
Zayn	$ 36,000		
Perez		$ 24,000	
Interest allowances			
Zayn (10% × $30,000)	3,000		
Perez (10% × $10,000)		1,000	
Total salaries and interest	39,000	25,000	64,000
Balance of income			(14,000)
Balance allocated equally			
Zayn	(7,000) ←		
Perez		(7,000) ←	
Total allocated			(14,000)
Balance of income			$ 0
Income of each partner	**$32,000**	**$18,000**	

allocated their salary and interest allowances, further adding to the negative balance of the loss. This *total* negative balance *after* salary and interest allowances would have been allocated equally between the partners. These allocations would have been applied against the positive numbers from any allowances to determine each partner's share of the loss.

Point: When a loss occurs, it is possible for a specific partner's capital to increase (when closing income summary) if that partner's allowance is in excess of his or her share of the negative balance. This implies that decreases to the capital balances of other partners exceed the partnership's loss amount.

Quick Check   Answer — p. 495

4. Denzel and Shantell form a partnership by contributing $70,000 and $35,000, respectively. They agree to an interest allowance equal to 10% of each partner's capital balance at the beginning of the year, with the remaining income shared equally. Allocate first-year income of $40,000 to each partner.

Partnership Financial Statements

Partnership financial statements are similar to those of other organizations. The **statement of partners' equity,** also called *statement of partners' capital,* is one exception. It shows *each* partner's beginning capital balance, additional investments, allocated income or loss, withdrawals, and ending capital balance. To illustrate, Exhibit 12.3 shows the statement of partners' equity for BOARDS prepared using the sharing agreement of Exhibit 12.1. Recall that BOARDS' income was $70,000; also, assume that Zayn withdrew $20,000 and Perez $12,000 at year-end.

EXHIBIT 12.3

Statement of Partners' Equity

	Zayn		Perez		Total
BOARDS					
Statement of Partners' Equity					
For Year Ended December 31, 2011					
Beginning capital balances		$ 0		$ 0	$ 0
Plus					
Investments by owners		30,000		10,000	40,000
Net income					
Salary allowances	$36,000		$24,000		
Interest allowances	3,000		1,000		
Balance allocated	3,000		3,000		
Total net income		42,000		28,000	70,000
		72,000		38,000	110,000
Less partners' withdrawals		(20,000)		(12,000)	(32,000)
Ending capital balances		**$52,000**		**$26,000**	**$78,000**

The equity section of the balance sheet of a partnership usually shows the separate capital account balance of each partner. In the case of BOARDS, both K. Zayn, Capital, and H. Perez, Capital, are listed in the equity section along with their balances of $52,000 and $26,000, respectively.

> ### Decision Insight
>
> **Gambling Partners**   **Trump Entertainment Resorts LP** and subsidiaries operate three casino hotel properties in Atlantic City: Trump Taj Mahal Casino Resort ("Trump Taj Mahal"), Trump Plaza Hotel and Casino ("Trump Plaza"), and Trump Marina Hotel Casino ("Trump Marina"). Its recent statement of partners' equity reports $1,020,000 in partners' withdrawals, leaving $605,314,000 in partners' capital balances. ∎
>
>

ADMISSION AND WITHDRAWAL OF PARTNERS

P3 Account for the admission and withdrawal of partners.

A partnership is based on a contract between individuals. When a partner is admitted or withdraws, the present partnership ends. Still, the business can continue to operate as a new partnership consisting of the remaining partners. This section considers how to account for the admission and withdrawal of partners.

Admission of a Partner

A new partner is admitted in one of two ways: by purchasing an interest from one or more current partners or by investing cash or other assets in the partnership.

Purchase of Partnership Interest   The purchase of partnership interest is a *personal transaction between one or more current partners and the new partner.* To become a partner, the current partners must accept the purchaser. Accounting for the purchase of partnership interest involves reallocating current partners' capital to reflect the transaction. To illustrate, at the end of BOARDS' first year, H. Perez sells one-half of his partnership interest to Tyrell Rasheed for $18,000. This means that Perez gives up a $13,000 recorded interest ($26,000 × 1/2) in the partnership (see the ending capital balance in Exhibit 12.3). The partnership records this January 4 transaction as follows.

Assets = Liabilities + Equity
                         −13,000
                         +13,000

Jan. 4	H. Perez, Capital	13,000	
	T. Rasheed, Capital		13,000
	To record admission of Rasheed by purchase.		

After this entry is posted, BOARDS' equity shows K. Zayn, Capital; H. Perez, Capital; and T. Rasheed, Capital, and their respective balances of $52,000, $13,000, and $13,000.

Two aspects of this transaction are important. First, the partnership does *not* record the $18,000 Rasheed paid Perez. The partnership's assets, liabilities, and *total equity* are unaffected by this transaction among partners. Second, Zayn and Perez must agree that Rasheed is to become a partner. If they agree to accept Rasheed, a new partnership is formed and a new contract with a new income-and-loss-sharing agreement is prepared. If Zayn or Perez refuses to accept Rasheed as a partner, then (under the Uniform Partnership Act) Rasheed gets Perez's sold share of partnership income and loss. If the partnership is liquidated, Rasheed gets Perez's sold share of partnership assets. Rasheed gets no voice in managing the company unless Rasheed is admitted as a partner.

Point: Partners' withdrawals are not constrained by the partnership's annual income or loss.

Investing Assets in a Partnership   Admitting a partner by accepting assets is a *transaction between the new partner and the partnership.* The invested assets become partnership property. To illustrate, if Zayn (with a $52,000 interest) and Perez (with a $26,000 interest) agree to accept Rasheed as a partner in BOARDS after an investment of $22,000 cash, this is recorded as follows.

Jan. 4	Cash	22,000	
	T. Rasheed, Capital		22,000
	To record admission of Rasheed by investment.		

Assets = Liabilities + Equity
+22,000   +22,000

After this entry is posted, both assets (cash) and equity (T. Rasheed, Capital) increase by $22,000. Rasheed now has a 22% equity in the assets of the business, computed as $22,000 divided by the entire partnership equity ($52,000 + $26,000 + $22,000). Rasheed does not necessarily have a right to 22% of income. Dividing income and loss is a separate matter on which partners must agree.

Bonus to old partners.   When the current value of a partnership is greater than the recorded amounts of equity, the partners usually require a new partner to pay a bonus for the privilege of joining. To illustrate, assume that Zayn and Perez agree to accept Rasheed as a partner with a 25% interest in BOARDS if Rasheed invests $42,000. Recall that the partnership's accounting records show that Zayn's recorded equity in the business is $52,000 and Perez's recorded equity is $26,000 (see Exhibit 12.3). Rasheed's equity is determined as follows.

Equities of existing partners ($52,000 + $26,000)	$ 78,000
Investment of new partner	42,000
Total partnership equity	$120,000
Equity of Rasheed (25% × $120,000)	$ 30,000

Although Rasheed invests $42,000, the equity attributed to Rasheed in the new partnership is only $30,000. The $12,000 difference is called a *bonus* and is allocated to existing partners (Zayn and Perez) according to their income-and-loss-sharing agreement. A bonus is shared in this way because it is viewed as reflecting a higher value of the partnership that is not yet reflected in income. The entry to record this transaction follows.

Jan. 4	Cash	42,000	
	T. Rasheed, Capital		30,000
	K. Zayn, Capital ($12,000 × ½)		6,000
	H. Perez, Capital ($12,000 × ½)		6,000
	To record admission of Rasheed and bonus.		

Assets = Liabilities + Equity
+42,000   +30,000
                        +6,000
                        +6,000

Bonus to new partner.   Alternatively, existing partners can grant a bonus to a new partner. This usually occurs when they need additional cash or the new partner has exceptional talents. The bonus to the new partner is in the form of a larger share of equity than the amount invested. To illustrate, assume that Zayn and Perez agree to accept Rasheed as a partner with a

25% interest in the partnership, but they require Rasheed to invest only $18,000. Rasheed's equity is determined as follows.

Equities of existing partners ($52,000 + $26,000)	$78,000
Investment of new partner	18,000
Total partnership equity	$96,000
Equity of Rasheed (25% × $96,000)	$24,000

The old partners contribute the $6,000 bonus (computed as $24,000 minus $18,000) to Rasheed according to their income-and-loss-sharing ratio. Moreover, Rasheed's 25% equity does not necessarily entitle Rasheed to 25% of future income or loss. This is a separate matter for agreement by the partners. The entry to record the admission and investment of Rasheed is

Assets = Liabilities + Equity
+18,000   −3,000
                 −3,000
                 +24,000

Jan. 4	Cash	18,000	
	K. Zayn, Capital ($6,000 × ½)	3,000	
	H. Perez, Capital ($6,000 × ½)	3,000	
	T. Rasheed, Capital		24,000
	To record Rasheed's admission and bonus.		

Withdrawal of a Partner

A partner generally withdraws from a partnership in one of two ways. (1) First, the withdrawing partner can sell his or her interest to another person who pays for it in cash or other assets. For this, we need only debit the withdrawing partner's capital account and credit the new partner's capital account. (2) The second case is when cash or other assets of the partnership are distributed to the withdrawing partner in settlement of his or her interest. To illustrate these cases, assume that Perez withdraws from the partnership of BOARDS in some future period. The partnership shows the following capital balances at the date of Perez's withdrawal: K. Zayn, $84,000; H. Perez, $38,000; and T. Rasheed, $38,000. The partners (Zayn, Perez, and Rasheed) share income and loss equally. Accounting for Perez's withdrawal depends on whether a bonus is paid. We describe three possibilities.

No Bonus If Perez withdraws and takes cash equal to Perez's capital balance, the entry is

Assets = Liabilities + Equity
−38,000   −38,000

Oct. 31	H. Perez, Capital	38,000	
	Cash		38,000
	To record withdrawal of Perez from partnership		
	with no bonus.		

Perez can take any combination of assets to which the partners agree to settle Perez's equity. Perez's withdrawal creates a new partnership between the remaining partners. A new partnership contract and a new income-and-loss-sharing agreement are required.

Bonus to Remaining Partners A withdrawing partner is sometimes willing to take less than the recorded value of his or her equity to get out of the partnership or because the recorded value is overstated. Whatever the reason, when this occurs, the withdrawing partner in effect gives the remaining partners a bonus equal to the equity left behind. The remaining partners share this unwithdrawn equity according to their income-and-loss-sharing ratio. To illustrate, if Perez withdraws and agrees to take $34,000 cash in settlement of Perez's capital balance, the entry is

Assets = Liabilities + Equity
−34,000   −38,000
                 +2,000
                 +2,000

Oct. 31	H. Perez, Capital	38,000	
	Cash		34,000
	K. Zayn, Capital		2,000
	T. Rasheed, Capital		2,000
	To record withdrawal of Perez and bonus to		
	remaining partners.		

Perez withdrew $4,000 less than Perez's recorded equity of $38,000. This $4,000 is divided between Zayn and Rasheed according to their income-and-loss-sharing ratio.

Bonus to Withdrawing Partner   A withdrawing partner may be able to receive more than his or her recorded equity for at least two reasons. First, the recorded equity may be understated. Second, the remaining partners may agree to remove this partner by giving assets of greater value than this partner's recorded equity. In either case, the withdrawing partner receives a bonus. The remaining partners reduce their equity by the amount of this bonus according to their income-and-loss-sharing ratio. To illustrate, if Perez withdraws and receives $40,000 cash in settlement of Perez's capital balance, the entry is

Oct. 31	H. Perez, Capital	38,000	
	K. Zayn, Capital	1,000	
	T. Rasheed, Capital	1,000	
	Cash		40,000
	To record Perez's withdrawal from partnership with a bonus to Perez.		

Assets	= Liabilities +	Equity
−40,000		−38,000
		−1,000
		−1,000

Falcon Cable Communications set up a partnership withdrawal agreement. Falcon owns and operates cable television systems and had two managing general partners. The partnership agreement stated that either partner "can offer to sell to the other partner the offering partner's entire partnership interest . . . for a negotiated price. If the partner receiving such an offer rejects it, the offering partner may elect to cause [the partnership] . . . to be liquidated and dissolved."

Death of a Partner

A partner's death dissolves a partnership. A deceased partner's estate is entitled to receive his or her equity. The partnership contract should contain provisions for settlement in this case. These provisions usually require (1) closing the books to determine income or loss since the end of the previous period and (2) determining and recording current market values for both assets and liabilities. The remaining partners and the deceased partner's estate then must agree to a settlement of the deceased partner's equity. This can involve selling the equity to remaining partners or to an outsider, or it can involve withdrawing assets.

◼ Decision Ethics   Answer — p. 495

Financial Planner   You are hired by the two remaining partners of a three-member partnership after the third partner's death. The partnership agreement states that a deceased partner's estate is entitled to a "share of partnership assets equal to the partner's relative equity balance" (partners' equity balances are equal). The estate argues that it is entitled to one-third of the current value of partnership assets. The remaining partners say the distribution should use asset book values, which are 75% of current value. They also point to partnership liabilities, which equal 40% of total asset book value and 30% of current value. How would you resolve this situation? ◼

LIQUIDATION OF A PARTNERSHIP

When a partnership is liquidated, its business ends and four concluding steps are required.

P4 Prepare entries for partnership liquidation.

1. Record the sale of noncash assets for cash and any gain or loss from their liquidation.
2. Allocate any gain or loss from liquidation of the assets in step 1 to the partners *using their income-and-loss-sharing ratio.*
3. Pay or settle all partner liabilities.
4. Distribute any remaining cash to partners *based on their capital balances.*

Partnership liquidation usually falls into one of two cases, as described in this section.

No Capital Deficiency

No capital deficiency means that all partners have a zero or credit balance in their capital accounts for final distribution of cash. To illustrate, assume that Zayn, Perez, and Rasheed operate their partnership in BOARDS for several years, sharing income and loss equally. The partners then decide to liquidate. On the liquidation date, the current period's income or loss is transferred to the partners' capital accounts according to the sharing agreement. After that transfer, assume the partners' recorded account balances (immediately prior to liquidation) are:

Cash	$178,000	Accounts payable	$20,000	H. Perez, Capital	$66,000
Land	40,000	K. Zayn, Capital	70,000	T. Rasheed, Capital	62,000

We apply three steps for liquidation. ① *The partnership sells its noncash assets, and any losses or gains from liquidation are shared among partners according to their income-and-loss-sharing agreement* (equal for these partners). Assume that BOARDS sells its noncash assets consisting of $40,000 in land for $46,000 cash, yielding a net gain of $6,000. In a liquidation, gains or losses usually result from the sale of noncash assets, which are called *losses and gains from liquidation*. The entry to sell its assets for $46,000 follows.

Assets = Liabilities + Equity
−40,000   +6,000
+46,000

Jan. 15	Cash	46,000	
	Land		40,000
	Gain from Liquidation		6,000
	Sold noncash assets at a gain.		

Allocation of the gain from liquidation per the partners' income-and-loss-sharing agreement follows.

Assets = Liabilities + Equity
                  −6,000
                  +2,000
                  +2,000
                  +2,000

Jan. 15	Gain from Liquidation	6,000	
	K. Zayn, Capital		2,000
	H. Perez, Capital		2,000
	T. Rasheed, Capital		2,000
	To allocate liquidation gain to partners.		

② *The partnership pays its liabilities, and any losses or gains from liquidation of liabilities are shared among partners according to their income-and-loss-sharing agreement.* BOARDS' only liability is $20,000 in accounts payable, and no gain or loss occurred.

Assets = Liabilities + Equity
−20,000 −20,000

Jan. 15	Accounts Payable	20,000	
	Cash		20,000
	To pay claims of creditors.		

After step 2, we have the following capital balances along with the remaining cash balance.

K. Zayn			H. Perez, Capital			T. Rasheed, Capital			Cash			
	Bal.	70,000		Bal.	66,000		Bal.	62,000	Bal.	178,000	(3)	20,000
	(2)	2,000		(2)	2,000		(2)	2,000	(1)	46,000		
	Bal.	72,000		Bal.	68,000		Bal.	64,000	Bal.	204,000		

③ *Any remaining cash is divided among the partners **according to their capital account balances.*** The entry to record the final distribution of cash to partners follows.

Assets = Liabilities + Equity
−204,000   −72,000
                  −68,000
                  −64,000

Jan. 15	K. Zayn, Capital	72,000	
	H. Perez, Capital	68,000	
	T. Rasheed, Capital	64,000	
	Cash		204,000
	To distribute remaining cash to partners.		

It is important to remember that the final cash payment is distributed to partners according to their capital account balances, whereas gains and losses from liquidation are allocated according to the income-and-loss-sharing ratio. The following *statement of liquidation* summarizes the three steps in this section.

Statement of Liquidation	Cash	Noncash Assets	=	Liabilities	K. Zayn, Capital	H. Perez, Capital	T. Rasheed, Capital
Balances prior to liquidation....	$178,000	$ 40,000		$ 20,000	$ 70,000	$66,000	$62,000
① Sale of noncash assets	46,000	(40,000)			2,000	2,000	2,000
② Payment of liabilities	(20,000)			(20,000)	0	0	0
Balances for distribution	204,000				72,000	68,000	64,000
③ Distribution of cash to partners	(204,000)				(72,000)	(68,000)	(64,000)

Capital Deficiency

Capital deficiency means that at least one partner has a debit balance in his or her capital account at the point of final cash distribution (during step ③ as explained in the prior section). This can arise from liquidation losses, excessive withdrawals before liquidation, or recurring losses in prior periods. A partner with a capital deficiency must, if possible, cover the deficit by paying cash into the partnership.

To illustrate, assume that Zayn, Perez, and Rasheed operate their partnership in BOARDS for several years, sharing income and losses equally. The partners then decide to liquidate. Immediately prior to the final distribution of cash, the partners' recorded capital balances are Zayn, $19,000; Perez, $8,000; and Rasheed, $(3,000). Rasheed's capital deficiency means that Rasheed owes the partnership $3,000. Both Zayn and Perez have a legal claim against Rasheed's personal assets. The final distribution of cash in this case depends on how this capital deficiency is handled. Two possibilities exist: the partner pays the deficiency or the partner cannot pay the deficiency.

Partner Pays Deficiency Rasheed is obligated to pay $3,000 into the partnership to cover the deficiency. If Rasheed is willing and able to pay, the entry to record receipt of payment from Rasheed follows.

Jan. 15	Cash	3,000	
	T. Rasheed, Capital		3,000
	To record payment of deficiency by Rasheed.		

Assets = Liabilities + Equity
+3,000   +3,000

After the $3,000 payment, the partners' capital balances are Zayn, $19,000; Perez, $8,000; and Rasheed, $0. The entry to record the final cash distributions to partners is

Jan. 15	K. Zayn, Capital	19,000	
	H. Perez, Capital	8,000	
	Cash		27,000
	To distribute remaining cash to partners.		

Assets = Liabilities + Equity
−27,000   −19,000
                             −8,000

Partner Cannot Pay Deficiency The remaining partners with credit balances absorb any partner's unpaid deficiency according to their income-and-loss-sharing ratio. To illustrate, if Rasheed is unable to pay the $3,000 deficiency, Zayn and Perez absorb it. Since they share income and loss equally, Zayn and Perez each absorb $1,500 of the deficiency. This is recorded as follows.

Jan. 15	K. Zayn, Capital	1,500	
	H. Perez, Capital	1,500	
	T. Rasheed, Capital		3,000
	To transfer Rasheed deficiency to Zayn and Perez.		

Assets = Liabilities + Equity
                             −1,500
                             −1,500
                             +3,000

After Zayn and Perez absorb Rasheed's deficiency, the capital accounts of the partners are Zayn, $17,500; Perez, $6,500; and Rasheed, $0. The entry to record the final cash distribution to the partners is

Jan. 15	K. Zayn, Capital	17,500	
	H. Perez, Capital	6,500	
	Cash		24,000
	To distribute remaining cash to partners.		

Assets = Liabilities + Equity
−24,000   −17,500
                             −6,500

Rasheed's inability to cover this deficiency does not relieve Rasheed of the liability. If Rasheed becomes able to pay at a future date, Zayn and Perez can each collect $1,500 from Rasheed.

GLOBAL VIEW

Partnership accounting according to U.S. GAAP is similar, but not identical, to that under IFRS. This section discusses broad differences in partnership accounting, organization, admission, withdrawal, and liquidation.

Both U.S. GAAP and IFRS include broad and similar guidance for partnership accounting. Further, partnership organization is similar worldwide; however, different legal and tax systems dictate different implications and motivations for how a partnership is effectively set up.

The accounting for partnership admission, withdrawal, and liquidation is likewise similar worldwide. Specifically, procedures for admission, withdrawal, and liquidation depend on the partnership agreements constructed by all parties involved. However, different legal and tax systems impact those agreements and their implications to the parties.

Decision Analysis ■■■   Partner Return on Equity

A1 Compute partner return on equity and use it to evaluate partnership performance.

An important role of partnership financial statements is to aid current and potential partners in evaluating partnership success compared with other opportunities. One measure of this success is the **partner return on equity** ratio:

$$\text{Partner return on equity} = \frac{\text{Partner net income}}{\text{Average partner equity}}$$

This measure is separately computed for each partner. To illustrate, Exhibit 12.4 reports selected data from the **Boston Celtics LP**. The return on equity for the *total* partnership is computed as $\$216/[(\$85 + \$253)/2] = 127.8\%$. However, return on equity is quite different across the partners. For example, the **Boston Celtics LP I** partner return on equity is computed as $\$44/[(\$122 + \$166)/2] = 30.6\%$, whereas the **Celtics LP** partner return on equity is computed as $\$111/[(\$270 + \$333)/2] = 36.8\%$. Partner return on equity provides *each* partner an assessment of its return on its equity invested in the partnership. A specific partner often uses this return to decide whether additional investment or withdrawal of resources is best for that partner. Exhibit 12.4 reveals that the year shown produced good returns for all partners (the Boston Celtics LP II return is not computed because its average equity is negative due to an unusual and large distribution in the prior year).

EXHIBIT 12.4

Selected Data from Boston Celtics LP

($ thousands)	Total*	Boston Celtics LP I	Boston Celtics LP II	Celtics LP
Beginning-year balance	$ 85	$122	$(307)	$270
Net income (loss) for year	216	44	61	111
Cash distribution	(48)	—	—	(48)
Ending-year balance	$253	$166	$(246)	$333
Partner return on equity	127.8%	30.6%	n.a.	36.8%

* Totals may not add up due to rounding.

DEMONSTRATION PROBLEM

The following transactions and events affect the partners' capital accounts in several successive partnerships. Prepare a table with six columns, one for each of the five partners along with a total column to show the effects of the following events on the five partners' capital accounts.

Part 1

4/13/2009   Ries and Bax create R&B Company. Each invests $10,000, and they agree to share income and losses equally.

12/31/2009   R&B Co. earns $15,000 in income for its first year. Ries withdraws $4,000 from the partnership, and Bax withdraws $7,000.

1/1/2010   Royce is made a partner in RB&R Company after contributing $12,000 cash. The partners agree that a 10% interest allowance will be given on each partner's beginning-year capital balance. In addition, Bax and Royce are to receive $5,000 salary allowances. The remainder of the income or loss is to be divided evenly.

12/31/2010   The partnership's income for the year is $40,000, and withdrawals at year-end are Ries, $5,000; Bax, $12,500; and Royce, $11,000.

1/1/2011   Ries sells her interest for $20,000 to Murdock, whom Bax and Royce accept as a partner in the new BR&M Co. Income or loss is to be shared equally after Bax and Royce receive $25,000 salary allowances.

12/31/2011   The partnership's income for the year is $35,000, and year-end withdrawals are Bax, $2,500, and Royce, $2,000.

1/1/2012   Elway is admitted as a partner after investing $60,000 cash in the new Elway & Associates partnership. He is given a 50% interest in capital after the other partners transfer $3,000 to his account from each of theirs. A 20% interest allowance (on the beginning-year capital balances) will be used in sharing any income or loss, there will be no salary allowances, and Elway will receive 40% of the remaining balance—the other three partners will each get 20%.

12/31/2012   Elway & Associates earns $127,600 in income for the year, and year-end withdrawals are Bax, $25,000; Royce, $27,000; Murdock, $15,000; and Elway, $40,000.

1/1/2013   Elway buys out Bax and Royce for the balances of their capital accounts after a revaluation of the partnership assets. The revaluation gain is $50,000, which is divided in using a 1:1:1:2 ratio (Bax:Royce:Murdock:Elway). Elway pays the others from personal funds. Murdock and Elway will share income on a 1:9 ratio.

2/28/2013   The partnership earns $10,000 of income since the beginning of the year. Murdock retires and receives partnership cash equal to her capital balance. Elway takes possession of the partnership assets in his own name, and the partnership is dissolved.

Part 2

Journalize the events affecting the partnership for the year ended December 31, 2010.

PLANNING THE SOLUTION

- Evaluate each transaction's effects on the capital accounts of the partners.
- Each time a new partner is admitted or a partner withdraws, allocate any bonus based on the income-or-loss-sharing agreement.
- Each time a new partner is admitted or a partner withdraws, allocate subsequent net income or loss in accordance with the new partnership agreement.
- Prepare entries to (1) record Royce's initial investment; (2) record the allocation of interest, salaries, and remainder; (3) show the cash withdrawals from the partnership; and (4) close the withdrawal accounts on December 31, 2010.

SOLUTION TO DEMONSTRATION PROBLEM

Part 1

Event	Ries	Bax	Royce	Murdock	Elway	Total
4/13/2009						
Initial investment	$10,000	$10,000				$ 20,000
12/31/2009						
Income (equal)	7,500	7,500				15,000
Withdrawals	(4,000)	(7,000)				(11,000)
Ending balance	$13,500	$10,500				$ 24,000
1/1/2010						
New investment			$12,000			$ 12,000
12/31/2010						
10% interest	1,350	1,050	1,200			3,600
Salaries		5,000	5,000			10,000
Remainder (equal)	8,800	8,800	8,800			26,400
Withdrawals	(5,000)	(12,500)	(11,000)			(28,500)
Ending balance	$18,650	$12,850	$16,000			$ 47,500

[continued on next page]

[continued from previous page]

Event	Ries	Bax	Royce	Murdock	Elway	Total
1/1/2011						
Transfer interest	(18,650)			$18,650		$ 0
12/31/2011						
Salaries		25,000	25,000			50,000
Remainder (equal)		(5,000)	(5,000)	(5,000)		(15,000)
Withdrawals		(2,500)	(2,000)			(4,500)
Ending balance	$ 0	$30,350	$34,000	$13,650		$ 78,000
1/1/2012						
New investment					$ 60,000	60,000
Bonuses to Elway		(3,000)	(3,000)	(3,000)	9,000	0
Adjusted balance		$27,350	$31,000	$10,650	$ 69,000	$138,000
12/31/2012						
20% interest..............		5,470	6,200	2,130	13,800	27,600
Remainder (1:1:1:2)		20,000	20,000	20,000	40,000	100,000
Withdrawals..............		(25,000)	(27,000)	(15,000)	(40,000)	(107,000)
Ending balance		$27,820	$30,200	$17,780	$ 82,800	$158,600
1/1/2013						
Gain (1:1:1:2)		10,000	10,000	10,000	20,000	50,000
Adjusted balance		$37,820	$40,200	$27,780	$102,800	$208,600
Transfer interests		(37,820)	(40,200)		78,020	0
Adjusted balance		$ 0	$ 0	$27,780	$180,820	$208,600
2/28/2013						
Income (1:9)..............				1,000	9,000	10,000
Adjusted balance				$28,780	$189,820	$218,600
Settlements				(28,780)	(189,820)	(218,600)
Final balance..............				$ 0	$ 0	$ 0

Part 2

2010			
Jan. 1	Cash	12,000	
	Royce, Capital		12,000
	To record investment of Royce.		
Dec. 31	Income Summary	40,000	
	Ries, Capital		10,150
	Bax, Capital		14,850
	Royce, Capital		15,000
	To allocate interest, salaries, and remainders.		
Dec. 31	Ries, Withdrawals	5,000	
	Bax, Withdrawals	12,500	
	Royce, Withdrawals	11,000	
	Cash		28,500
	To record cash withdrawals by partners.		
Dec. 31	Ries, Capital	5,000	
	Bax, Capital	12,500	
	Royce, Capital	11,000	
	Ries, Withdrawals		5,000
	Bax, Withdrawals		12,500
	Royce, Withdrawals		11,000
	To close withdrawal accounts.		

Summary

C1 Identify characteristics of partnerships and similar organizations. Partnerships are voluntary associations, involve partnership agreements, have limited life, are not subject to income tax, include mutual agency, and have unlimited liability. Organizations that combine selected characteristics of partnerships and corporations include limited partnerships, limited liability partnerships, S corporations, and limited liability companies.

A1 Compute partner return on equity and use it to evaluate partnership performance. Partner return on equity provides each partner an assessment of his or her return on equity invested in the partnership.

P1 Prepare entries for partnership formation. A partner's initial investment is recorded at the market value of the assets contributed to the partnership.

P2 Allocate and record income and loss among partners. A partnership agreement should specify how to allocate partnership income or loss among partners. Allocation can be based on a stated ratio, capital balances, or salary and interest allowances to compensate partners for differences in their service and capital contributions.

P3 Account for the admission and withdrawal of partners. When a new partner buys a partnership interest directly from one or more existing partners, the amount of cash paid from one partner to another does not affect the partnership total recorded equity. When a new partner purchases equity by investing additional assets in the partnership, the new partner's investment can yield a bonus either to existing partners or to the new partner. The entry to record a withdrawal can involve payment from either (1) the existing partners' personal assets or (2) partnership assets. The latter can yield a bonus to either the withdrawing or remaining partners.

P4 Prepare entries for partnership liquidation. When a partnership is liquidated, losses and gains from selling partnership assets are allocated to the partners according to their income-and-loss-sharing ratio. If a partner's capital account has a deficiency that the partner cannot pay, the other partners share the deficit according to their relative income-and-loss-sharing ratio.

Guidance Answers to Decision Ethics

Financial Planner The partnership agreement apparently fails to mention liabilities or use the term *net assets*. To give the estate one-third of total assets is not fair to the remaining partners because if the partner had lived and the partners had decided to liquidate, the liabilities would need to be paid out of assets before any liquidation. Also, a settlement based on the deceased partner's recorded equity would fail to recognize excess of current value over book value. This value increase would be realized if the partnership were liquidated. A fair settlement would seem to be a payment to the estate for the balance of the deceased partner's equity based on the *current value of net assets*.

Guidance Answers to Quick Checks

1. (*b*)
2. *Unlimited liability* means that the creditors of a partnership require each partner to be personally responsible for all partnership debts.
3. (*c*)

4.

	Denzel	Shantell	Total
Net income			$40,000
Interest allowance (10%)	$ 7,000	$ 3,500	10,500
Balance of income			$29,500
Balance allocated equally	14,750	14,750	29,500
Balance of income			$ 0
Income of partners	$21,750	$18,250	

Key Terms   mhhe.com/wildFAP20e

C corporation (p. 482)	Limited partners (p. 481)	Partnership contract (p. 480)
General partner (p. 481)	Limited partnership (p. 481)	Partnership liquidation (p. 489)
General partnership (p. 481)	Mutual agency (p. 480)	S corporation (p. 482)
Limited liability company (LLC) (p. 482)	Partner return on equity (p. 492)	Statement of partners' equity (p. 485)
Limited liability partnership (p. 481)	Partnership (p. 480)	Unlimited liability (p. 481)

Multiple Choice Quiz   Answers on p. 505   mhhe.com/wildFAP20e

Additional Quiz Questions are available at the book's Website.

1. Stokely and Leder are forming a partnership. Stokely invests a building that has a market value of $250,000; and the partnership assumes responsibility for a $50,000 note secured by a mortgage on that building. Leder invests $100,000 cash. For the partnership, the amounts recorded for the building and for Stokely's Capital account are these:
   a. Building, $250,000; Stokely, Capital, $250,000.
   b. Building, $200,000; Stokely, Capital, $200,000.
   c. Building, $200,000; Stokely, Capital, $100,000.
   d. Building, $200,000; Stokely, Capital, $250,000.
   e. Building, $250,000; Stokely, Capital, $200,000.

2. Katherine, Alliah, and Paulina form a partnership. Katherine contributes $150,000, Alliah contributes $150,000, and Paulina contributes $100,000. Their partnership agreement calls for the income or loss division to be based on the ratio of capital invested. If the partnership reports income of $90,000 for its first year of operations, what amount of income is credited to Paulina's capital account?
   a. $22,500
   b. $25,000
   c. $45,000
   d. $30,000
   e. $90,000

3. Jamison and Blue form a partnership with capital contributions of $600,000 and $800,000, respectively. Their partnership agreement calls for Jamison to receive $120,000 per year in salary. Also, each partner is to receive an interest allowance equal to 10% of the partner's beginning capital contributions, with any remaining income or loss divided equally. If net income for its initial year is $270,000, then Jamison's and Blue's respective shares are
   a. $135,000; $135,000.
   b. $154,286; $115,714.
   c. $120,000; $150,000.
   d. $185,000; $85,000.
   e. $85,000; $185,000.

4. Hansen and Fleming are partners and share equally in income or loss. Hansen's current capital balance in the partnership is $125,000 and Fleming's is $124,000. Hansen and Fleming agree to accept Black with a 20% interest. Black invests $75,000 in the partnership. The bonus granted to Hansen and Fleming equals
   a. $13,000 each.
   b. $5,100 each.
   c. $4,000 each.
   d. $5,285 to Hansen; $4,915 to Fleming.
   e. $0; Hansen and Fleming grant a bonus to Black.

5. Mee Su is a partner in Hartford Partners, LLC. Her partnership capital balance at the beginning of the current year was $110,000, and her ending balance was $124,000. Her share of the partnership income is $10,500. What is her partner return on equity?
   a. 8.97%
   b. 1060.00%
   c. 9.54%
   d. 1047.00%
   e. 8.47%

Icon denotes assignments that involve decision making.

Discussion Questions

1. If a partnership contract does not state the period of time the partnership is to exist, when does the partnership end?

2. What does the term *mutual agency* mean when applied to a partnership?

3. Can partners limit the right of a partner to commit their partnership to contracts? Would such an agreement be binding (*a*) on the partners and (*b*) on outsiders?

4. Assume that Amey and Lacey are partners. Lacey dies, and her son claims the right to take his mother's place in the partnership. Does he have this right? Why or why not?

5. Assume that the Barnes and Ardmore partnership agreement provides for a two-third/one-third sharing of income but says nothing about losses. The first year of partnership operation resulted in a loss, and Barnes argues that the loss should be shared equally because the partnership agreement said nothing about sharing losses. Is Barnes correct? Explain.

6. Allocation of partnership income among the partners appears on what financial statement?

7. What does the term *unlimited liability* mean when it is applied to partnership members?

8. How does a general partnership differ from a limited partnership?

9. George, Burton, and Dillman have been partners for three years. The partnership is being dissolved. George is leaving the firm, but Burton and Dillman plan to carry on the business. In the final settlement, George places a $75,000 salary claim against the partnership. He contends that he has a claim for a salary of $25,000 for each year because he devoted all of his time for three years to the affairs of the partnership. Is his claim valid? Why or why not?

10. Kay, Kat, and Kim are partners. In a liquidation, Kay's share of partnership losses exceeds her capital account balance. Moreover, she is unable to meet the deficit from her personal assets, and her partners shared the excess losses. Does this relieve Kay of liability?

11. After all partnership assets have been converted to cash and all liabilities paid, the remaining cash should equal the sum of the balances of the partners' capital accounts. Why?

12. Assume a partner withdraws from a partnership and receives assets of greater value than the book value of his equity. Should the remaining partners share the resulting reduction in their equities in the ratio of their relative capital balances or according to their income-and-loss-sharing ratio?

connect™

Kent and Davis are partners in operating a store. Without consulting Kent, Davis enters into a contract to purchase merchandise for the store. Kent contends that he did not authorize the order and refuses to pay for it. The vendor sues the partners for the contract price of the merchandise. (*a*) Must the partnership pay for the merchandise? Why? (*b*) Does your answer differ if Kent and Davis are partners in a public accounting firm? Explain.

QS 12-1
Partnership liability

C1

Lamb organized a limited partnership and is the only general partner. Maxi invested $20,000 in the partnership and was admitted as a limited partner with the understanding that she would receive 10% of the profits. After two unprofitable years, the partnership ceased doing business. At that point, partnership liabilities were $85,000 larger than partnership assets. How much money can the partnership's creditors obtain from Maxi's personal assets to satisfy the unpaid partnership debts?

QS 12-2
Liability in limited partnerships

P1

Ann Keeley and Susie Norton are partners in a business they started two years ago. The partnership agreement states that Keeley should receive a salary allowance of $40,000 and that Norton should receive a $30,000 salary allowance. Any remaining income or loss is to be shared equally. Determine each partner's share of the current year's net income of $210,000.

QS 12-3
Partnership income allocation

P2

Jake and Ness are partners who agree that Jake will receive a $60,000 salary allowance and that any remaining income or loss will be shared equally. If Ness's capital account is credited for $1,000 as his share of the net income in a given period, how much net income did the partnership earn in that period?

QS 12-4
Partnership income allocation

P2

Jones and Bordan are partners, each with $30,000 in their partnership capital accounts. Holly is admitted to the partnership by investing $30,000 cash. Make the entry to show Holly's admission to the partnership.

QS 12-5
Admission of a partner

P3

Mintz agrees to pay Bogg and Heyer $10,000 each for a one-third (33⅓%) interest in the Bogg and Heyer partnership. Immediately prior to Mintz's admission, each partner had a $30,000 capital balance. Make the journal entry to record Mintz's purchase of the partners' interest.

QS 12-6
Partner admission through purchase of interest

P3

The Red, White & Blue partnership was begun with investments by the partners as follows: Red, $175,000; White, $220,000; and Blue, $205,000. The operations did not go well, and the partners eventually decided to liquidate the partnership, sharing all losses equally. On August 31, after all assets were converted to cash and all creditors were paid, only $60,000 in partnership cash remained.

1. Compute the capital account balance of each partner after the liquidation of assets and the payment of creditors.

2. Assume that any partner with a deficit agrees to pay cash to the partnership to cover the deficit. Present the journal entries on August 31 to record (*a*) the cash receipt from the deficient partner(s) and (*b*) the final disbursement of cash to the partners.

3. Assume that any partner with a deficit is not able to reimburse the partnership. Present journal entries (*a*) to transfer the deficit of any deficient partners to the other partners and (*b*) to record the final disbursement of cash to the partners.

QS 12-7
Liquidation of partnership

P4

Check   (1) Red, $(5,000)

Gilson and Lott's company is organized as a partnership. At the prior year-end, partnership equity totaled $300,000 ($200,000 from Gilson and $100,000 from Lott). For the current year, partnership net income is $50,000 ($40,000 allocated to Gilson and $10,000 allocated to Lott), and year-end total partnership equity is $400,000 ($280,000 from Gilson and $120,000 from Lott). Compute the total partnership return on equity *and* the individual partner return on equity ratios.

QS 12-8
Partner return on equity

A1

■ connect™

EXERCISES

Exercise 12-1
Forms of organization

C1

For each of the following separate cases, recommend a form of business organization. With each recommendation, explain how business income would be taxed if the owners adopt the form of organization recommended. Also list several advantages that the owners will enjoy from the form of business organization that you recommend.

a. Milan has been out of school for about six years and has become quite knowledgeable about the residential real estate market. He would like to organize a company that buys and sells real estate. Milan believes he has the expertise to manage the company but needs funds to invest in residential property.

b. Dr. Langholz and Dr. Clark are recent graduates from medical residency programs. Both are family practice physicians and would like to open a clinic in an underserved rural area. Although neither has any funds to bring to the new venture, an investor has expressed interest in making a loan to provide start-up funds for their practice.

c. Ross, Jenks and Keim are recent college graduates in computer science. They want to start a Website development company. They all have college debts and currently do not own any substantial computer equipment needed to get the company started.

Exercise 12-2
Characteristics of partnerships

C1

Next to the following list of eight characteristics of business organizations, enter a brief description of how each characteristic applies to general partnerships.

Characteristic	Application to General Partnerships
1. Ease of formation	
2. Transferability of ownership	
3. Ability to raise large amounts of capital	
4. Life	
5. Owners' liability	
6. Legal status	
7. Tax status of income	
8. Owners' authority	

Exercise 12-3
Journalizing partnership formation

P2

Anita Kroll and Aaron Rogers organize a partnership on January 1. Kroll's initial net investment is $60,000, consisting of cash ($14,000), equipment ($66,000), and a note payable reflecting a bank loan for the new business ($20,000). Rogers's initial investment is cash of $25,000. These amounts are the values agreed on by both partners. Prepare journal entries to record (1) Kroll's investment and (2) Rogers's investment.

Exercise 12-4
Journalizing partnership transactions

P2

On March 1, 2011, Abbey and Dames formed a partnership. Abbey contributed $88,000 cash and Dames contributed land valued at $70,000 and a building valued at $100,000. The partnership also assumed responsibility for Dames's $80,000 long-term note payable associated with the land and building. The partners agreed to share income as follows: Abbey is to receive an annual salary allowance of $30,000, both are to receive an annual interest allowance of 10% of their beginning-year capital investment, and any remaining income or loss is to be shared equally. On October 20, 2011, Abbey withdrew $32,000 cash and Dames withdrew $25,000 cash. After the adjusting and closing entries are made to the revenue and expense accounts at December 31, 2011, the Income Summary account had a credit balance of $79,000.

1. Prepare journal entries to record (*a*) the partners' initial capital investments, (*b*) their cash withdrawals, and (*c*) the December 31 closing of both the Withdrawals and Income Summary accounts.

Check (2) Dames, $89,600

2. Determine the balances of the partners' capital accounts as of December 31, 2011.

Exercise 12-5
Income allocation in a partnership

P2

Cosmo and Ellis began a partnership by investing $50,000 and $75,000, respectively. During its first year, the partnership earned $165,000. Prepare calculations showing how the $165,000 income should be allocated to the partners under each of the following three separate plans for sharing income and loss: (1) the partners failed to agree on a method to share income; (2) the partners agreed to share income and loss in proportion to their initial investments (round amounts to the nearest dollar); and (3) the partners agreed to share income by granting a $55,000 per year salary allowance to Cosmo, a $45,000 per year salary allowance to Ellis, 10% interest on their initial capital investments, and the remaining balance shared equally.

Check Plan 3, Cosmo, $86,250

Assume that the partners of Exercise 12-5 agreed to share net income and loss by granting annual salary allowances of $55,000 to Cosmo and $45,000 to Ellis, 10% interest allowances on their investments, and any remaining balance shared equally.

1. Determine the partners' shares of Cosmo and Ellis given a first-year net income of $94,400.

2. Determine the partners' shares of Cosmo and Ellis given a first-year net loss of $15,700.

Exercise 12-6
Income allocation in a partnership
P2

Check (2) Cosmo, $(4,100)

The partners in the Biz Partnership have agreed that partner Mona may sell her $90,000 equity in the partnership to Seal, for which Seal will pay Mona $75,000. Present the partnership's journal entry to record the sale of Mona's interest to Seal on September 30.

Exercise 12-7
Sale of partnership interest
P3

The Treed Partnership has total partners' equity of $510,000, which is made up of Elm, Capital, $400,000, and Oak, Capital, $110,000. The partners share net income and loss in a ratio of 80% to Elm and 20% to Oak. On November 1, Ash is admitted to the partnership and given a 15% interest in equity and a 15% share in any income and loss. Prepare the journal entry to record the admission of Ash under each of the following separate assumptions: Ash invests cash of (1) $90,000; (2) $125,000; and (3) $60,000.

Exercise 12-8
Admission of new partner
P3

Holland, Flowers, and Tulip have been partners while sharing net income and loss in a 5:3:2 ratio. On January 31, the date Tulip retires from the partnership, the equities of the partners are Holland, $350,000; Flowers, $240,000; and Tulip, $180,000. Present journal entries to record Tulip's retirement under each of the following separate assumptions: Tulip is paid for her equity using partnership cash of (1) $180,000; (2) $200,000; and (3) $150,000.

Exercise 12-9
Retirement of partner
P3

Tuttle, Ritter, and Lee are partners who share income and loss in a 1:4:5 ratio. After lengthy disagreements among the partners and several unprofitable periods, the partners decide to liquidate the partnership. Immediately before liquidation, the partnership balance sheet shows total assets, $116,000; total liabilities, $88,000; Tuttle, Capital, $1,200; Ritter, Capital, $11,700; and Lee, Capital, $15,100. The cash proceeds from selling the assets were sufficient to repay all but $24,000 to the creditors. (*a*) Calculate the loss from selling the assets. (*b*) Allocate the loss to the partners. (*c*) Determine how much of the remaining liability should be paid by each partner.

Exercise 12-10
Liquidation of partnership
P4

Check (b) Lee, Capital after allocation, $(10,900)

Assume that the Tuttle, Ritter, and Lee partnership of Exercise 12-10 is a limited partnership. Tuttle and Ritter are general partners and Lee is a limited partner. How much of the remaining $24,000 liability should be paid by each partner? (Round amounts to the nearest dollar.)

Exercise 12-11
Liquidation of limited partnership
P4

Hunt Sports Enterprises LP is organized as a limited partnership consisting of two individual partners: Soccer LP and Football LP. Both partners separately operate a minor league soccer team and a semipro football team. Compute partner return on equity for each limited partnership (and the total) for the year ended June 30, 2011, using the following selected data on partner capital balances from Hunt Sports Enterprises LP.

Exercise 12-12
Partner return on equity
A1

	Soccer LP	Football LP	Total
Balance at 6/30/2010	$378,000	$1,516,000	$1,894,000
Annual net income	44,268	891,796	936,064
Cash distribution	—	(100,000)	(100,000)
Balance at 6/30/2011	$422,268	$2,307,796	$2,730,064

PROBLEM SET A

Problem 12-1A

Allocating partnership income

P2

Check　(3) Thomas, Capital, $48,900

Kim Ries, Tere Bax, and Josh Thomas invested $40,000, $56,000, and $64,000, respectively, in a partnership. During its first calendar year, the firm earned $124,500.

Required

Prepare the entry to close the firm's Income Summary account as of its December 31 year-end and to allocate the $124,500 net income to the partners under each of the following separate assumptions: The partners (1) have no agreement on the method of sharing income and loss; (2) agreed to share income and loss in the ratio of their beginning capital investments; and (3) agreed to share income and loss by providing annual salary allowances of $33,000 to Ries, $28,000 to Bax, and $40,000 to Thomas; granting 10% interest on the partners' beginning capital investments; and sharing the remainder equally.

Problem 12-2A

Allocating partnership income and loss; sequential years

P2

mhhe.com/wildFAP20e

Rex Baker and Ty Farney are forming a partnership to which Baker will devote one-half time and Farney will devote full time. They have discussed the following alternative plans for sharing income and loss: (*a*) in the ratio of their initial capital investments, which they have agreed will be $21,000 for Baker and $31,500 for Farney; (*b*) in proportion to the time devoted to the business; (*c*) a salary allowance of $3,000 per month to Farney and the balance in accordance with the ratio of their initial capital investments; or (*d*) a salary allowance of $3,000 per month to Farney, 10% interest on their initial capital investments, and the balance shared equally. The partners expect the business to perform as follows: year 1, $18,000 net loss; year 2, $45,000 net income; and year 3, $75,000 net income.

Required

Prepare three tables with the following column headings.

Income (Loss) Sharing Plan	Calculations	Year ———		
			Baker	Farney

Check　Plan d, year 1, Farney's share, $9,525

Complete the tables, one for each of the first three years, by showing how to allocate partnership income or loss to the partners under each of the four plans being considered. (Round answers to the nearest whole dollar.)

Problem 12-3A

Partnership income allocation, statement of partners' equity, and closing entries

P2

mhhe.com/wildFAP20e

Will Beck, Ron Beck, and Barb Beck formed the BBB Partnership by making capital contributions of $183,750, $131,250, and $210,000, respectively. They predict annual partnership net income of $225,000 and are considering the following alternative plans of sharing income and loss: (*a*) equally; (*b*) in the ratio of their initial capital investments; or (*c*) salary allowances of $40,000 to Will, $30,000 to Ron, and $45,000 to Barb; interest allowances of 10% on their initial capital investments; and the balance shared equally.

Required

1. Prepare a table with the following column headings.

Income (Loss) Sharing Plan	Calculations	Will	Ron	Barb	Total

Check　(2) Barb, Ending Capital, $223,000

Use the table to show how to distribute net income of $225,000 for the calendar year under each of the alternative plans being considered. (Round answers to the nearest whole dollar.)

2. Prepare a statement of partners' equity showing the allocation of income to the partners assuming they agree to use plan (*c*), that income earned is $104,500, and that Will, Ron, and Barb withdraw $17,000, $24,000, and $32,000, respectively, at year-end.

3. Prepare the December 31 journal entry to close Income Summary assuming they agree to use plan (*c*) and that net income is $104,500. Also close the withdrawals accounts.

Part 1. Goering, Zarcus, and Schmit are partners and share income and loss in a 3:2:5 ratio. The partnership's capital balances are as follows: Goering, $84,000; Zarcus, $69,000; and Schmit, $147,000. Zarcus decides to withdraw from the partnership, and the partners agree to not have the assets revalued upon Zarcus's retirement. Prepare journal entries to record Zarcus's February 1 withdrawal from the partnership under each of the following separate assumptions: Zarcus (a) sells her interest to Getz for $80,000 after Goering and Schmit approve the entry of Getz as a partner; (b) gives her interest to a son-in-law, Swanson, and thereafter Goering and Schmit accept Swanson as a partner; (c) is paid $69,000 in partnership cash for her equity; (d) is paid $107,000 in partnership cash for her equity; and (e) is paid $15,000 in partnership cash plus equipment recorded on the partnership books at $35,000 less its accumulated depreciation of $11,600.

Part 2. Assume that Zarcus does not retire from the partnership described in Part 1. Instead, Ford is admitted to the partnership on February 1 with a 25% equity. Prepare journal entries to record Ford's entry into the partnership under each of the following separate assumptions: Ford invests (a) $100,000; (b) $74,000; and (c) $131,000.

Problem 12-4A
Partner withdrawal
and admission
P3

Check   (1e) Cr. Schmit, Capital,
$19,125

(2c) Cr. Zarcus, Capital,
$4,650

Quick, Drake, and Sage share income and loss in a 3:2:1 ratio. The partners have decided to liquidate their partnership. On the day of liquidation their balance sheet appears as follows.

Problem 12-5A
Liquidation of a partnership
P4

QUICK, DRAKE, AND SAGE Balance Sheet May 31			
Assets		**Liabilities and Equity**	
Cash	$ 90,400	Accounts payable	$122,750
Inventory	268,600	Quick, Capital	46,500
		Drake, Capital	106,250
		Sage, Capital	83,500
Total assets	$359,000	Total liabilities and equity	$359,000

Required

Prepare journal entries for (a) the sale of inventory, (b) the allocation of its gain or loss, (c) the payment of liabilities at book value, and (d) the distribution of cash in each of the following separate cases: Inventory is sold for (1) $300,000; (2) $250,000; (3) $160,000 and any partners with capital deficits pay in the amount of their deficits; and (4) $125,000 and the partners have no assets other than those invested in the partnership. (Round to the nearest dollar.)

Check   (4) Cash distribution: Sage,
$51,134

Matt Albin, Ryan Peters and Seth Ramsey invested $82,000, $49,200 and $32,800, respectively, in a partnership. During its first calendar year, the firm earned $135,000.

PROBLEM SET B

Problem 12-1B
Allocating partnership income
P2

Required

Prepare the entry to close the firm's Income Summary account as of its December 31 year-end and to allocate the $135,000 net income to the partners under each of the following separate assumptions. (Round answers to whole dollars.) The partners (1) have no agreement on the method of sharing income and loss; (2) agreed to share income and loss in the ratio of their beginning capital investments; and (3) agreed to share income and loss by providing annual salary allowances of $48,000 to Albin, $36,000 to Peters, and $25,000 to Ramsey; granting 10% interest on the partners' beginning capital investments; and sharing the remainder equally.

Check   (3) Ramsey, Capital,
$31,480

Maria Karto and J.R. Black are forming a partnership to which Karto will devote one-third time and Black will devote full time. They have discussed the following alternative plans for sharing income and loss: (a) in the ratio of their initial capital investments, which they have agreed will be $52,000 for Karto and $78,000 for Black; (b) in proportion to the time devoted to the business; (c) a salary allowance of $2,000 per month to Black and the balance in accordance with the ratio of their initial capital investments; or

Problem 12-2B
Allocating partnership income
and loss; sequential years
P2

(*d*) a salary allowance of $2,000 per month to Black, 10% interest on their initial capital investments, and the balance shared equally. The partners expect the business to perform as follows: year 1, $18,000 net loss; year 2, $38,000 net income; and year 3, $94,000 net income.

Required

Prepare three tables with the following column headings.

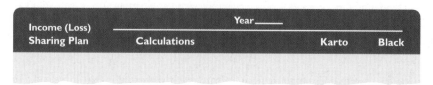

Check Plan d, year 1, Black's share, $4,300

Complete the tables, one for each of the first three years, by showing how to allocate partnership income or loss to the partners under each of the four plans being considered. (Round answers to the nearest whole dollar.)

Problem 12-3B

Partnership income allocation, statement of partners' equity, and closing entries

P2

Staci Cook, Lin Xi, and Kevin Schwartz formed the CXS Partnership by making capital contributions of $72,000, $108,000, and $60,000, respectively. They predict annual partnership net income of $120,000 and are considering the following alternative plans of sharing income and loss: (*a*) equally; (*b*) in the ratio of their initial capital investments; or (*c*) salary allowances of $20,000 to Cook, $15,000 to Xi, and $40,000 to Schwartz; interest allowances of 12% on their initial capital investments; and the balance shared equally.

Required

1. Prepare a table with the following column headings.

Check (2) Schwartz, Ending Capital, $75,200

Use the table to show how to distribute net income of $120,000 for the calendar year under each of the alternative plans being considered. (Round answers to the nearest whole dollar.)

2. Prepare a statement of partners' equity showing the allocation of income to the partners assuming they agree to use plan (*c*), that income earned is $43,800, and that Cook, Xi, and Schwartz withdraw $9,000, $19,000, and $12,000, respectively, at year-end.

3. Prepare the December 31 journal entry to close Income Summary assuming they agree to use plan (*c*) and that net income is $43,800. Also close the withdrawals accounts.

Problem 12-4B

Partner withdrawal and admission

P3

Part 1. Gibbs, Mier, and Hill are partners and share income and loss in a 5:1:4 ratio. The partnership's capital balances are as follows: Gibbs, $303,000; Mier, $74,000; and Hill, $223,000. Gibbs decides to withdraw from the partnership, and the partners agree not to have the assets revalued upon Gibbs's retirement. Prepare journal entries to record Gibbs's April 30 withdrawal from the partnership under each of the following separate assumptions: Gibbs (*a*) sells her interest to Brady for $250,000 after Mier and Hill approve the entry of Brady as a partner; (*b*) gives her interest to a daughter-in-law, Cannon, and thereafter Mier and Hill accept Cannon as a partner; (*c*) is paid $303,000 in partnership cash for her equity; (*d*) is paid $175,000 in partnership cash for her equity; and (*e*) is paid $100,000 in partnership cash plus manufacturing equipment recorded on the partnership books at $269,000 less its accumulated depreciation of $168,000.

Check (1*e*) Cr. Hill, Capital, $81,600

Part 2. Assume that Gibbs does not retire from the partnership described in Part 1. Instead, Brise is admitted to the partnership on April 30 with a 20% equity. Prepare journal entries to record the entry of Brise under each of the following separate assumptions: Brise invests (*a*) $150,000; (*b*) $98,000; and (*c*) $213,000.

Check (2*c*) Cr. Mier, Capital, $5,040

Asure, Ramirez, and Soney, who share income and loss in a 2:1:2 ratio, plan to liquidate their partnership. At liquidation, their balance sheet appears as follows.

Problem 12-5B
Liquidation of a partnership
P4

ASURE, RAMIREZ, AND SONEY			
Balance Sheet			
January 18			
Assets		**Liabilities and Equity**	
Cash	$174,300	Accounts payable	$171,300
Equipment	308,600	Asure, Capital	150,200
		Ramirez, Capital	97,900
		Soney, Capital	63,500
Total assets	$482,900	Total liabilities and equity	$482,900

Required

Prepare journal entries for (*a*) the sale of equipment, (*b*) the allocation of its gain or loss, (*c*) the payment of liabilities at book value, and (*d*) the distribution of cash in each of the following separate cases: Equipment is sold for (1) $325,000; (2) $265,000; (3) $100,000 and any partners with capital deficits pay in the amount of their deficits; and (4) $75,000 and the partners have no assets other than those invested in the partnership. (Round amounts to the nearest dollar.)

Check   (4) Cash distribution: Asure, $36,800

(This serial problem began in Chapter 1 and continues through most of the book. If previous chapter segments were not completed, the serial problem can begin at this point. It is helpful, but not necessary, to use the Working Papers that accompany the book.)

SERIAL PROBLEM
Business Solutions
P3

SP 12   At the start of 2012, Santana Rey is considering adding a partner to her business. She envisions the new partner taking the lead in generating sales of both services and merchandise for Business Solutions. S. Rey's equity in Business Solutions as of January 1, 2012, is reflected in the following capital balance.

S. Rey, Capital $80,360

Required

1. S. Rey is evaluating whether the prospective partner should be an equal partner with respect to capital investment and profit sharing (1:1) or whether the agreement should be 4:1 with Rey retaining four-fifths interest with rights to four-fifths of the net income or loss. What factors should she consider in deciding which partnership agreement to offer?

2. Prepare the January 1, 2012, journal entry(ies) necessary to admit a new partner to Business Solutions through the purchase of a partnership interest for each of the following two separate cases: (*a*) 1:1 sharing agreement and (*b*) 4:1 sharing agreement.

3. Prepare the January 1, 2012, journal entry(ies) required to admit a new partner if the new partner invests cash of $20,090.

4. After posting the entry in part 3, what would be the new partner's equity percentage?

Beyond the Numbers

BTN 12-1   Take a step back in time and imagine **Research In Motion** in its infancy as a company. The year is 1984.

REPORTING IN ACTION
C1

RIM

Required

1. Read the history of Research In Motion at **www.RIM.com**. Identify the two partners that founded the company.

2. Assume that Research In Motion was originally organized as a partnership. RIM's income statement in Appendix A varies in several key ways from what it would look like for a partnership. Identify at least two ways in which a corporate income statement differs from a partnership income statement.

3. Compare the Research In Motion balance sheet in Appendix A to what a partnership balance sheet would have shown. Identify and explain any account differences we would anticipate.

COMPARATIVE ANALYSIS

C1

RIM

Apple

BTN 12-2 Over the years **Research In Motion** and **Apple** have evolved into large corporations. Today it is difficult to imagine them as fledgling start-ups. Research each company's history online.

Required

1. Which company is older?
2. In what years did each company first achieve $1,000,000,000 in sales?
3. In what years did each company have its first public offering of stock?

ETHICS CHALLENGE

P2

BTN 12-3 Doctors Maben, Orlando, and Clark have been in a group practice for several years. Maben and Orlando are family practice physicians, and Clark is a general surgeon. Clark receives many referrals for surgery from his family practice partners. Upon the partnership's original formation, the three doctors agreed to a two-part formula to share income. Every month each doctor receives a salary allowance of $3,000. Additional income is divided according to a percent of patient charges the doctors generate for the month. In the current month, Maben generated 10% of the billings, Orlando 30%, and Clark 60%. The group's income for this month is $50,000. Clark has expressed dissatisfaction with the income-sharing formula and asks that income be split entirely on patient charge percents.

Required

1. Compute the income allocation for the current month using the original agreement.
2. Compute the income allocation for the current month using Clark's proposed agreement.
3. Identify the ethical components of this partnership decision for the doctors.

COMMUNICATING IN PRACTICE

C1

BTN 12-4 Assume that you are studying for an upcoming accounting exam with a good friend. Your friend says that she has a solid understanding of general partnerships but is less sure that she understands organizations that combine certain characteristics of partnerships with other forms of business organization. You offer to make some study notes for your friend to help her learn about limited partnerships, limited liability partnerships, S corporations, and limited liability companies. Prepare a one-page set of well-organized, complete study notes on these four forms of business organization.

TAKING IT TO THE NET

P1   P2

BTN 12-5 Access the March 29, 2010, filing of the December 31, 2009, 10-K of **America First Tax Exempt Investors LP**. This company deals with tax-exempt mortgage revenue bonds that, among other things, finance student housing properties.

1. Locate its December 31, 2009, balance sheet and list the account titles reported in the equity section of the balance sheet.
2. Locate its statement of partners' capital and comprehensive income (loss). How many units of limited partnership (known as "beneficial unit certificate holders") are outstanding at December 31, 2009?
3. What is the partnership's largest asset and its amount at December 31, 2009?

TEAMWORK IN ACTION

P2

BTN 12-6 This activity requires teamwork to reinforce understanding of accounting for partnerships.

Required

1. Assume that Baker, Warner, and Rice form the BWR Partnership by making capital contributions of $200,000, $300,000, and $500,000, respectively. BWR predicts annual partnership net income of $600,000. The partners are considering various plans for sharing income and loss. Assign a different team member to compute how the projected $600,000 income would be shared under each of the following separate plans:
   a. Shared equally.
   b. In the ratio of the partners' initial capital investments.
   c. Salary allowances of $50,000 to Baker, $60,000 to Warner, and $70,000 to Rice, with the remaining balance shared equally.
   d. Interest allowances of 10% on the partners' initial capital investments, with the remaining balance shared equally.

2. In sequence, each member is to present his or her income-sharing calculations with the team.

3. As a team, identify and discuss at least one other possible way that income could be shared.

BTN 12-7   Recall the chapter's opening feature involving Chance Claxton and Lynn Julian, and their company, **Kids Konserve**. Assume that Chance and Lynn, partners in Kids Konserve, decide to expand their business with the help of general partners.

ENTREPRENEURIAL DECISION

C1

Required

1. What details should Chance, Lynn, and their future partners specify in the general partnership agreements?

2. What advantages should Chance, Lynn, and their future partners be aware of with respect to organizing as a general partnership?

3. What disadvantages should Chance, Lynn, and their future partners be aware of with respect to organizing as a general partnership?

BTN 12-8   Access **Nokia**'s Website (www.Nokia.com) and research the company's history.

GLOBAL DECISION

C1

NOKIA

1. When was the company founded?

2. What three companies merged to create Nokia Corporation?

3. What are some of the companies that are part of Nokia?

ANSWERS TO MULTIPLE CHOICE QUIZ

1. e; Capital = $250,000 − $50,000

2. a; $90,000 × [$100,000/($150,000 + $150,000 + $100,000)]
     = $22,500

3. d;

	Jamison	Blue	Total
Net income			$ 270,000
Salary allowance	$120,000		(120,000)
Interest allowance	60,000	$80,000	(140,000)
Balance of income			10,000
Balance divided equally	5,000	5,000	(10,000)
Totals	$185,000	$85,000	$ 0

4. b; Total partnership equity = $125,000 + $124,000 + $75,000
     = $324,000
     Equity of Black = $324,000 × 20% = $64,800
     Bonus to old partners = $75,000 − $64,800 = $10,200, split equally

5. a; $10,500/[($110,000 + $124,000)/2] = 8.97%

13

Accounting for Corporations

A Look Back

Chapter 12 focused on the partnership form of organization. We described crucial characteristics of partnerships and the accounting and reporting of their important transactions.

A Look at This Chapter

This chapter emphasizes details of the corporate form of organization. The accounting concepts and procedures for equity transactions are explained. We also describe how to report and analyze income, earnings per share, and retained earnings.

A Look Ahead

Chapter 14 focuses on long-term liabilities. We explain how to value, record, amortize, and report these liabilities in financial statements.

Learning Objectives

CAP

CONCEPTUAL

C1 Identify characteristics of corporations and their organization. (p. 508)

C2 Explain characteristics of, and distribute dividends between, common and preferred stock. (p. 519)

C3 Explain the items reported in retained earnings. (p. 524)

ANALYTICAL

A1 Compute earnings per share and describe its use. (p. 527)

A2 Compute price-earnings ratio and describe its use in analysis. (p. 527)

A3 Compute dividend yield and explain its use in analysis. (p. 528)

A4 Compute book value and explain its use in analysis. (p. 528)

LP13

PROCEDURAL

P1 Record the issuance of corporate stock. (p. 512)

P2 Record transactions involving cash dividends, stock dividends, and stock splits. (p. 515)

P3 Record purchases and sales of treasury stock and the retirement of stock. (p. 522)

Decision Insight

Greener Lawns

"Every part of our business is . . . profitable"
—KELLY GIARD

FORT COLLINS, CO—According to the U.S. Environmental Protection Agency, a gas-powered lawn mower produces as much air pollution as 43 new cars each driven 12,000 miles. "At least 5 percent of pollution is caused by gas-powered maintenance equipment," explains Kelly Giard, owner of **Clean Air Lawn Care (CleanAirLawnCare.com).** "This is one of the last dirty frontiers in America that can be easily solved."

Kelly launched his business four years ago, which is a full-service sustainable lawn care company dedicated to using clean electrical and biodiesel powered equipment. His equipment is charged by solar panels during the day and by wind power overnight. "I started [it] out of my garage mostly for fun," says Kelly. "And business took off."

Kelly explains that his success would not have been possible without equity financing and knowledge of business operations. To make it happen, says Kelly, he studied corporate formation, equity issuance, stock types, retaining earnings, and dividend policies. After that analysis, Kelly set up Clean Air Lawn Care as a corporation, which had several benefits given his business

goals and strategies. With his corporate structure in place, Kelly was ready to attack the market. "Only about 1% of the country uses an electrical mower," says Kelly. "That's awful, and that's something we're committed to changing."

The success of Kelly's corporate structure and his equity financing brings both opportunities and challenges. The positive is being part of the green movement, yielding "a ripple effect where there's profit, happy customers and an environmental benefit." The challenge is effectively using accounting for equity as a tool to achieve those objectives. That includes his knowledge of corporate formation, stock types, and equity transactions. "This is critical to us doing well in the long term," explains Kelly. Still, the focus remains on the environment. "We want [consumers] to have a choice when they hire a service: sustainable vs. dirty."

[Sources: *Clean Air Lawn Care Website,* January 2011; *Entrepreneur,* January 2010; *Lawn & Landscape,* April 2010; *Charles & Hudson Website,* 2010]

This chapter focuses on equity transactions. The first part of the chapter describes the basics of the corporate form of organization and explains the accounting for common and preferred stock. We then focus on several special financing transactions, including cash and stock dividends, stock splits, and treasury stock. The final section considers accounting for retained earnings, including prior period adjustments, retained earnings restrictions, and reporting guidelines.

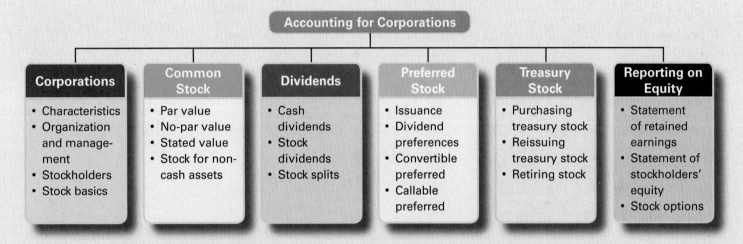

Accounting for Corporations

Corporations	Common Stock	Dividends	Preferred Stock	Treasury Stock	Reporting on Equity
• Characteristics • Organization and management • Stockholders • Stock basics	• Par value • No-par value • Stated value • Stock for non-cash assets	• Cash dividends • Stock dividends • Stock splits	• Issuance • Dividend preferences • Convertible preferred • Callable preferred	• Purchasing treasury stock • Reissuing treasury stock • Retiring stock	• Statement of retained earnings • Statement of stockholders' equity • Stock options

CORPORATE FORM OF ORGANIZATION

C1 Identify characteristics of corporations and their organization.

A **corporation** is an entity created by law that is separate from its owners. It has most of the rights and privileges granted to individuals. Owners of corporations are called *stockholders* or *shareholders*. Corporations can be separated into two types. A *privately held* (or *closely held*) corporation does not offer its stock for public sale and usually has few stockholders. A *publicly held* corporation offers its stock for public sale and can have thousands of stockholders. *Public sale* usually refers to issuance and trading on an organized stock market.

Characteristics of Corporations

Corporations represent an important type of organization. Their unique characteristics offer advantages and disadvantages.

Advantages of Corporate Characteristics

- **Separate legal entity:** A corporation conducts its affairs with the same rights, duties, and responsibilities of a person. It takes actions through its agents, who are its officers and managers.

- **Limited liability of stockholders:** Stockholders are liable for neither corporate acts nor corporate debt.

Point: The *business entity assumption* requires a corporation to be accounted for separately from its owners (shareholders).

- **Transferable ownership rights:** The transfer of shares from one stockholder to another usually has no effect on the corporation or its operations except when this causes a change in the directors who control or manage the corporation.

- **Continuous life:** A corporation's life continues indefinitely because it is not tied to the physical lives of its owners.

Global: U.S., U.K., and Canadian corporations finance much of their operations with stock issuances, but companies in countries such as France, Germany, and Japan finance mainly with note and bond issuances.

- **Lack of mutual agency for stockholders:** A corporation acts through its agents, who are its officers and managers. Stockholders, who are not its officers and managers, do not have the power to bind the corporation to contracts—referred to as *lack of mutual agency.*

- **Ease of capital accumulation:** Buying stock is attractive to investors because (1) stockholders are not liable for the corporation's acts and debts, (2) stocks usually are transferred easily, (3) the life of the corporation is unlimited, and (4) stockholders are not corporate agents. These advantages enable corporations to accumulate large amounts of capital from the combined investments of many stockholders.

Disadvantages of Corporate Characteristics

- **Government regulation:** A corporation must meet requirements of a state's incorporation laws, which subject the corporation to state regulation and control. Proprietorships and partnerships avoid many of these regulations and governmental reports.

- **Corporate taxation:** Corporations are subject to the same property and payroll taxes as proprietorships and partnerships plus *additional* taxes. The most burdensome of these are federal and state income taxes that together can take 40% or more of corporate pretax income. Moreover, corporate income is usually taxed a second time as part of stockholders' personal income when they receive cash distributed as dividends. This is called *double taxation*. (The usual dividend tax is 15%; however, it is less than 15% for lower income taxpayers, and in some cases zero.)

Decision Insight

Stock Financing   Marc Andreessen cofounded **Netscape** at age 22, only four months after earning his degree. One year later, he and friends issued Netscape shares to the public. The stock soared, making Andreessen a multimillionaire. ■

Corporate Organization and Management

This section describes the incorporation, costs, and management of corporate organizations.

Incorporation   A corporation is created by obtaining a charter from a state government. A charter application usually must be signed by the prospective stockholders called *incorporators* or *promoters* and then filed with the proper state official. When the application process is complete and fees paid, the charter is issued and the corporation is formed. Investors then purchase the corporation's stock, meet as stockholders, and elect a board of directors. Directors oversee a corporation's affairs.

Organization Expenses   Organization expenses (also called *organization costs*) are the costs to organize a corporation; they include legal fees, promoters' fees, and amounts paid to obtain a charter. The corporation records (debits) these costs to an expense account called *Organization Expenses*. Organization costs are expensed as incurred because it is difficult to determine the amount and timing of their future benefits.

Management of a Corporation   The ultimate control of a corporation rests with stockholders who control a corporation by electing its *board of directors*, or simply, *directors*. Each stockholder usually has one vote for each share of stock owned. This control relation is shown in Exhibit 13.1. Directors are responsible for and have final authority for managing corporate activities. A board can act only as a collective body and usually limits its actions to setting general policy.

A corporation usually holds a stockholder meeting at least once a year to elect directors and transact business as its bylaws require. A group of stockholders owning or controlling votes of more than a 50% share of a corporation's stock can elect the board and control the corporation. Stockholders who do not attend stockholders' meetings must have an opportunity to delegate their voting rights to an agent by signing a **proxy,** a document that gives a designated agent the right to vote the stock.

Day-to-day direction of corporate business is delegated to executive officers appointed by the board. A corporation's chief executive officer (CEO) is often its president. Several vice presidents, who report to the president, are commonly assigned specific areas of management responsibility such as finance, production, and marketing. One person often has the dual role

EXHIBIT 13.1

Corporate Structure

Stockholders
↓
Board of Directors
↓
President, Vice President, and Other Officers
↓
Employees of the Corporation

Point: Proprietorships and partnerships are not subject to income taxes. Their income is taxed as the personal income of their owners.

Point: Double taxation is less severe when a corporation's owner-manager collects a salary that is taxed only once as part of his or her personal income.

Point: A corporation is not required to have an office in its state of incorporation.

Point: *Bylaws* are guidelines that govern the behavior of individuals employed by and managing the corporation.

of chairperson of the board of directors and CEO. In this case, the president is usually designated the chief operating officer (COO).

Decision Insight

Seed Money   Sources for start-up money include (1) "angel" investors such as family, friends, or anyone who believes in a company, (2) employees, investors, and even suppliers who can be paid with stock, and (3) venture capitalists (investors) who have a record of entrepreneurial success. See the National Venture Capital Association (**NVCA.org**) for information. ■

Stockholders of Corporations

This section explains stockholder rights, stock purchases and sales, and the role of registrar and transfer agents.

Rights of Stockholders   When investors buy stock, they acquire all *specific* rights the corporation's charter grants to stockholders. They also acquire *general* rights granted stockholders by the laws of the state in which the company is incorporated. When a corporation has only one class of stock, it is identified as **common stock.** State laws vary, but common stockholders usually have the general right to

1. Vote at stockholders' meetings.
2. Sell or otherwise dispose of their stock.
3. Purchase their proportional share of any common stock later issued by the corporation. This **preemptive right** protects stockholders' proportionate interest in the corporation. For example, a stockholder who owns 25% of a corporation's common stock has the first opportunity to buy 25% of any new common stock issued.
4. Receive the same dividend, if any, on each common share of the corporation.
5. Share in any assets remaining after creditors and preferred stockholders are paid when, and if, the corporation is liquidated. Each common share receives the same amount.

Stockholders also have the right to receive timely financial reports.

Stock Certificates and Transfer   Investors who buy a corporation's stock, sometimes receive a *stock certificate* as proof of share ownership. Many corporations issue only one certificate for each block of stock purchased. A certificate can be for any number of shares. Exhibit 13.2 shows a stock certificate of the **Green Bay Packers**. A certificate shows the company name, stockholder name, number of shares, and other crucial information. Issuance of certificates is becoming less common. Instead, many stockholders maintain accounts with the corporation or their stockbrokers and never receive actual certificates.

EXHIBIT 13.2

Stock Certificate

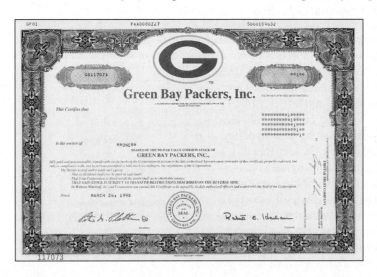

Registrar and Transfer Agents   If a corporation's stock is traded on a major stock exchange, the corporation must have a registrar and a transfer agent. A *registrar* keeps stockholder records and prepares official lists of stockholders for stockholder meetings and dividend payments. A *transfer agent* assists with purchases and sales of shares by receiving and issuing certificates as necessary. Registrars and transfer agents are usually large banks or trust companies with computer facilities and staff to do this work.

Decision Insight

Pricing Stock   A prospectus accompanies a stock's initial public offering (IPO), giving financial information about the company issuing the stock. A prospectus should help answer these questions to price an IPO: (1) Is the underwriter reliable? (2) Is there growth in revenues, profits, and cash flows? (3) What is management's view of operations? (4) Are current owners selling? (5) What are the risks? ■

Basics of Capital Stock

Capital stock is a general term that refers to any shares issued to obtain capital (owner financing). This section introduces terminology and accounting for capital stock.

Authorized Stock   **Authorized stock** is the number of shares that a corporation's charter allows it to sell. The number of authorized shares usually exceeds the number of shares issued (and outstanding), often by a large amount. (*Outstanding stock* refers to issued stock held by stockholders.) No formal journal entry is required for stock authorization. A corporation must apply to the state for a change in its charter if it wishes to issue more shares than previously authorized. A corporation discloses the number of shares authorized in the equity section of its balance sheet or notes. **Apple**'s balance sheet in Appendix A reports 1.8 billion common shares authorized as of the start of its 2010 fiscal year.

Subcategories of Authorized Stock

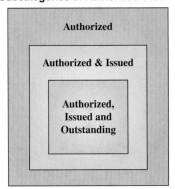

Selling (Issuing) Stock   A corporation can sell stock directly or indirectly. To *sell directly,* it advertises its stock issuance to potential buyers. This type of issuance is most common with privately held corporations. To *sell indirectly,* a corporation pays a brokerage house (investment banker) to issue its stock. Some brokerage houses *underwrite* an indirect issuance of stock; that is, they buy the stock from the corporation and take all gains or losses from its resale.

Market Value of Stock   **Market value per share** is the price at which a stock is bought and sold. Expected future earnings, dividends, growth, and other company and economic factors influence market value. Traded stocks' market values are available daily in newspapers such as *The Wall Street Journal* and online. The current market value of previously issued shares (for example, the price of stock in trades between investors) does not impact the issuing corporation's stockholders' equity.

Classes of Stock   When all authorized shares have the same rights and characteristics, the stock is called *common stock.* A corporation is sometimes authorized to issue more than one class of stock, including preferred stock and different classes of common stock. **American Greetings**, for instance, has two types of common stock: Class A stock has 1 vote per share and Class B stock has 10 votes per share.

Par Value Stock   **Par value stock** is stock that is assigned a **par value,** which is an amount assigned per share by the corporation in its charter. For example, **Palm**'s common stock has a par value of $0.001. Other commonly assigned par values are $10, $5, $1 and $0.01. There is no restriction on the assigned par value. In many states, the par value of a stock establishes **minimum legal capital,** which refers to the least amount that the buyers of stock must contribute to the corporation or be subject to paying at a future date. For example, if a corporation issues 1,000 shares of $10 par value stock, the corporation's minimum legal capital in these states would be $10,000. Minimum legal capital is intended to protect a corporation's creditors. Since creditors cannot demand payment from stockholders' personal assets, their claims are limited to the corporation's assets and any minimum legal capital. At liquidation, creditor claims are paid before any amounts are distributed to stockholders.

Point: Managers are motivated to set a low par value when minimum legal capital or state issuance taxes are based on par value.

Point: Minimum legal capital was intended to protect creditors by requiring a minimum level of net assets.

No-Par Value Stock   **No-par value stock,** or simply *no-par stock,* is stock *not* assigned a value per share by the corporate charter. Its advantage is that it can be issued at any price without the possibility of a minimum legal capital deficiency.

Point: Par, no-par, and stated value do *not* set the stock's market value.

EXHIBIT 13.3

Equity Composition

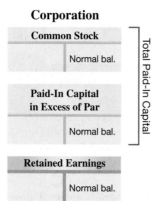

Corporation

Common Stock

| | Normal bal. |

Paid-In Capital in Excess of Par

| | Normal bal. |

Retained Earnings

| | Normal bal. |

Total Paid-In Capital

Point: Paid-in capital comes from stock-related transactions, whereas retained earnings comes from operations.

Stated Value Stock   **Stated value stock** is no-par stock to which the directors assign a "stated" value per share. Stated value per share becomes the minimum legal capital per share in this case.

Stockholders' Equity   A corporation's equity is known as **stockholders' equity,** also called *shareholders' equity* or *corporate capital.* Stockholders' equity consists of (1) paid-in (or contributed) capital and (2) retained earnings; see Exhibit 13.3. **Paid-in capital** is the total amount of cash and other assets the corporation receives from its stockholders in exchange for its stock. **Retained earnings** is the cumulative net income (and loss) not distributed as dividends to its stockholders.

Decision Insight

Stock Quote   The **Best Buy** stock quote is interpreted as (left to right): **Hi,** highest price in past 52 weeks; **Lo,** lowest price in past 52 weeks;

52 Weeks				Yld		Vol				Net
Hi	Lo	Sym	Div	%	PE	mil.	Hi	Lo	Close	Chg
54.15	41.85	BBY	0.13	0.98	19	7.2	53.14	52.36	52.91	+0.20

Sym, company exchange symbol; **Div,** dividends paid per share in past year; **Yld %,** dividend divided by closing price; **PE,** stock price per share divided by earnings per share; **Vol mil.,** number (in millions) of shares traded; **Hi,** highest price for the day; **Lo,** lowest price for the day; **Close,** closing price for the day; **Net Chg,** change in closing price from prior day. ■

Quick Check

Answers — p. 533

1. Which of the following is *not* a characteristic of the corporate form of business? (*a*) Ease of capital accumulation, (*b*) Stockholder responsibility for corporate debts, (*c*) Ease in transferability of ownership rights, or (*d*) Double taxation.
2. Why is a corporation's income said to be taxed twice?
3. What is a proxy?

COMMON STOCK

 P1   Record the issuance of corporate stock.

Accounting for the issuance of common stock affects only paid-in (contributed) capital accounts; no retained earnings accounts are affected.

Issuing Par Value Stock

Par value stock can be issued at par, at a premium (above par), or at a discount (below par). In each case, stock can be exchanged for either cash or noncash assets.

Issuing Par Value Stock at Par   When common stock is issued at par value, we record amounts for both the asset(s) received and the par value stock issued. To illustrate, the entry to record Dillon Snowboards' issuance of 30,000 shares of $10 par value stock for $300,000 cash on June 5, 2011, follows.

Assets   = Liabilities +   Equity
+300,000   +300,000

$10 par value × 30,000 shares

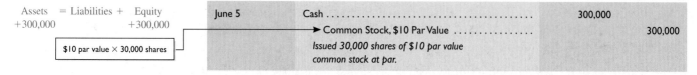

June 5	Cash	300,000	
	Common Stock, $10 Par Value		300,000
	Issued 30,000 shares of $10 par value		
	common stock at par.		

Exhibit 13.4 shows the stockholders' equity of Dillon Snowboards at year-end 2011 (its first year of operations) after income of $65,000 and no dividend payments.

EXHIBIT 13.4

Stockholders' Equity for Stock
Issued at Par

Stockholders' Equity	
Common Stock—$10 par value; 50,000 shares authorized;	
30,000 shares issued and outstanding	$300,000
Retained earnings	65,000
Total stockholders' equity	$365,000

Issuing Par Value Stock at a Premium   A **premium on stock** occurs when a corporation sells its stock for more than par (or stated) value. To illustrate, if Dillon Snowboards issues its $10 par value common stock at $12 per share, its stock is sold at a $2 per share premium. The premium, known as **paid-in capital in excess of par value,** is reported as part of equity; it is not revenue and is not listed on the income statement. The entry to record Dillon Snowboards' issuance of 30,000 shares of $10 par value stock for $12 per share on June 5, 2011, follows

Point: A *premium* is the amount by which issue price exceeds par (or stated) value. It is recorded in the "Paid-In Capital in Excess of Par Value, Common Stock" account; also called "Additional Paid-In Capital, Common Stock."

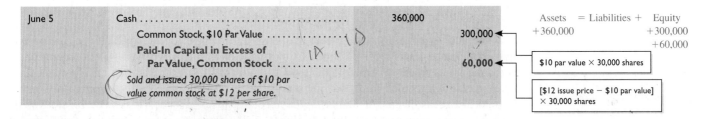

The Paid-In Capital in Excess of Par Value account is added to the par value of the stock in the equity section of the balance sheet as shown in Exhibit 13.5.

Point: The *Paid-In Capital* terminology is interchangeable with *Contributed Capital.*

EXHIBIT 13.5

Stockholders' Equity for Stock
Issued at a Premium

Stockholders' Equity	
Common Stock—$10 par value; 50,000 shares authorized;	
30,000 shares issued and outstanding	$300,000
Paid-in capital in excess of par value, common stock	60,000
Retained earnings	65,000
Total stockholders' equity	$425,000

Issuing Par Value Stock at a Discount   A **discount on stock** occurs when a corporation sells its stock for less than par (or stated) value. Most states prohibit the issuance of stock at a discount. In states that allow stock to be issued at a discount, its buyers usually become contingently liable to creditors for the discount. If stock is issued at a discount, the amount by which issue price is less than par is debited to a *Discount on Common Stock* account, a contra to the common stock account, and its balance is subtracted from the par value of stock in the equity section of the balance sheet. This discount is not an expense and does not appear on the income statement.

Point: Retained earnings can be negative, reflecting accumulated losses. Amazon.com had an accumulated deficit of $730 million at the start of 2009.

Issuing No-Par Value Stock

When no-par stock is issued and is not assigned a stated value, the amount the corporation receives becomes legal capital and is recorded as Common Stock. This means that the entire proceeds are credited to a no-par stock account. To illustrate, a corporation records its October 20 issuance of 1,000 shares of no-par stock for $40 cash per share as follows.

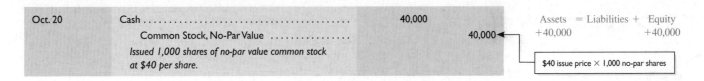

Frequency of Stock Types

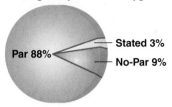

Par 88%   — Stated 3%
           — No-Par 9%

Issuing Stated Value Stock

When no-par stock is issued and assigned a stated value, its stated value becomes legal capital and is credited to a stated value stock account. Assuming that stated value stock is issued at an amount in excess of stated value (the usual case), the excess is credited to Paid-In Capital in Excess of Stated Value, Common Stock, which is reported in the stockholders' equity section. To illustrate, a corporation that issues 1,000 shares of no-par common stock having a stated value of $40 per share in return for $50 cash per share records this as follows.

Assets = Liabilities + Equity
+50,000   +40,000
                        +10,000

$40 stated value × 1,000 shares

[$50 issue price − $40 stated value] × 1,000 shares

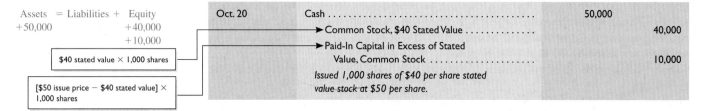

Oct. 20	Cash	50,000	
	➤ Common Stock, $40 Stated Value		40,000
	➤ Paid-In Capital in Excess of Stated		
	Value, Common Stock		10,000
	Issued 1,000 shares of $40 per share stated value stock at $50 per share.		

Issuing Stock for Noncash Assets

Point: Stock issued for noncash assets should be recorded at the market value of either the stock or the noncash asset, whichever is more clearly determinable.

A corporation can receive assets other than cash in exchange for its stock. (It can also assume liabilities on the assets received such as a mortgage on property received.) The corporation records the assets received at their market values as of the date of the transaction. The stock given in exchange is recorded at its par (or stated) value with any excess recorded in the Paid-In Capital in Excess of Par (or Stated) Value account. (If no-par stock is issued, the stock is recorded at the assets' market value.) To illustrate, the entry to record receipt of land valued at $105,000 in return for issuance of 4,000 shares of $20 par value common stock on June 10 is

Assets   = Liabilities + Equity
+105,000   +80,000
                         +25,000

$20 par value × 4,000 shares

$105,000 asset value − $80,000 stock value

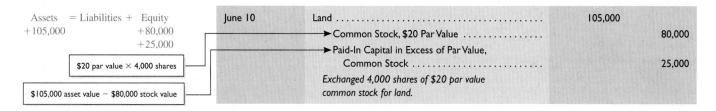

June 10	Land	105,000	
	➤ Common Stock, $20 Par Value		80,000
	➤ Paid-In Capital in Excess of Par Value,		
	Common Stock		25,000
	Exchanged 4,000 shares of $20 par value common stock for land.		

Point: Any type of stock can be issued for noncash assets.

A corporation sometimes gives shares of its stock to promoters in exchange for their services in organizing the corporation, which the corporation records as **Organization Expenses.** The entry to record receipt of services valued at $12,000 in organizing the corporation in return for 600 shares of $15 par value common stock on June 5 is

Assets = Liabilities + Equity
                       −12,000
                       +9,000
                       +3,000

$15 par value × 600 shares

$12,000 services value − $9,000 stock value

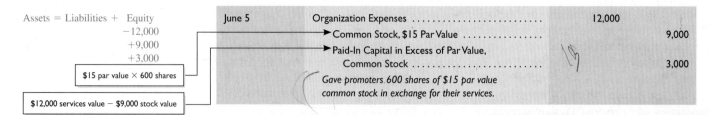

June 5	Organization Expenses	12,000	
	➤ Common Stock, $15 Par Value		9,000
	➤ Paid-In Capital in Excess of Par Value,		
	Common Stock		3,000
	Gave promoters 600 shares of $15 par value common stock in exchange for their services.		

Quick Check   Answers — p. 533 ☑

4. A company issues 7,000 shares of its $10 par value common stock in exchange for equipment valued at $105,000. The entry to record this transaction includes a credit to (*a*) Paid-In Capital in Excess of Par Value, Common Stock, for $35,000. (*b*) Retained Earnings for $35,000. (*c*) Common Stock, $10 Par Value, for $105,000.

5. What is a premium on stock issuance?

6. Who is intended to be protected by minimum legal capital?

DIVIDENDS

This section describes both cash and stock dividend transactions.

Cash Dividends

The decision to pay cash dividends rests with the board of directors and involves more than evaluating the amounts of retained earnings and cash. The directors, for instance, may decide to keep the cash to invest in the corporation's growth, to meet emergencies, to take advantage of unexpected opportunities, or to pay off debt. Alternatively, many corporations pay cash dividends to their stockholders at regular dates. These cash flows provide a return to investors and almost always affect the stock's market value.

P2 Record transactions involving cash dividends, stock dividends, and stock splits.

Accounting for Cash Dividends Dividend payment involves three important dates: declaration, record, and payment. **Date of declaration** is the date the directors vote to declare and pay a dividend. This creates a legal liability of the corporation to its stockholders. **Date of record** is the future date specified by the directors for identifying those stockholders listed in the corporation's records to receive dividends. The date of record usually follows the date of declaration by at least two weeks. Persons who own stock on the date of record receive dividends. **Date of payment** is the date when the corporation makes payment; it follows the date of record by enough time to allow the corporation to arrange checks, money transfers, or other means to pay dividends.

Percent of Corporations Paying Dividends

Cash Dividend to Common **75%**

Cash Dividend to Preferred **22%**

0%   20%   40%   60%   80%   100%

To illustrate, the entry to record a January 9 declaration of a $1 per share cash dividend by the directors of Z-Tech, Inc., with 5,000 outstanding shares is

Date of Declaration

Jan. 9	Retained Earnings	5,000	
	Common Dividend Payable		5,000
	Declared $1 per common share cash dividend.[1]		

Assets = Liabilities + Equity
    +5,000   −5,000

$1 per share declared dividend × 5,000 shares

Common Dividend Payable is a current liability. The date of record for the Z-Tech dividend is January 22. *No formal journal entry is needed on the date of record.* The February 1 date of payment requires an entry to record both the settlement of the liability and the reduction of the cash balance, as follows:

Date of Payment

Feb. 1	Common Dividend Payable	5,000	
	Cash		5,000
	Paid $1 per common share cash dividend.		

Assets = Liabilities + Equity
−5,000   −5,000

Deficits and Cash Dividends A corporation with a debit (abnormal) balance for retained earnings is said to have a **retained earnings deficit,** which arises when a company incurs cumulative losses and/or pays more dividends than total earnings from current and prior years. A deficit is reported as a deduction on the balance sheet, as shown in Exhibit 13.6. Most states prohibit a corporation with a deficit from paying a cash dividend to its stockholders. This legal restriction is designed to protect creditors by preventing distribution of assets to stockholders when the company may be in financial difficulty.

Point: It is often said a dividend is a distribution of retained earnings, but it is more precise to describe a dividend as a distribution of assets to satisfy stockholder claims.

Point: The Retained Earnings Deficit account is also called *Accumulated Deficit.*

---

[1] An alternative entry is to debit Dividends instead of Retained Earnings. The balance in Dividends is then closed to Retained Earnings at the end of the reporting period. The effect is the same: Retained Earnings is decreased and a Dividend Payable is increased. For simplicity, all assignments in this chapter use the Retained Earnings account to record dividend declarations.

EXHIBIT 13.6

Stockholders' Equity
with a Deficit

Common stock—$10 par value, 5,000 shares authorized, issued, and outstanding	$50,000
Retained earnings deficit	(6,000)
Total stockholders' equity	$44,000

Some state laws allow cash dividends to be paid by returning a portion of the capital contributed by stockholders. This type of dividend is called a **liquidating cash dividend,** or simply *liquidating dividend,* because it returns a part of the original investment back to the stockholders. This requires a debit entry to one of the contributed capital accounts instead of Retained Earnings at the declaration date.

Point: Amazon.com has never declared a cash dividend.

Quick Check
Answers — p. 534

7. What type of an account is the Common Dividend Payable account?

8. What three crucial dates are involved in the process of paying a cash dividend?

9. When does a dividend become a company's legal obligation?

Stock Dividends

A **stock dividend,** declared by a corporation's directors, is a distribution of additional shares of the corporation's own stock to its stockholders without the receipt of any payment in return. Stock dividends and cash dividends are different. A stock dividend does not reduce assets and equity but instead transfers a portion of equity from retained earnings to contributed capital.

Reasons for Stock Dividends Stock dividends exist for at least two reasons. First, directors are said to use stock dividends to keep the market price of the stock affordable. For example, if a corporation continues to earn income but does not issue cash dividends, the price of its common stock likely increases. The price of such a stock may become so high that it discourages some investors from buying the stock (especially in lots of 100 and 1,000). When a corporation has a stock dividend, it increases the number of outstanding shares and lowers the per share stock price. Another reason for a stock dividend is to provide evidence of management's confidence that the company is doing well and will continue to do well.

Accounting for Stock Dividends A stock dividend affects the components of equity by transferring part of retained earnings to contributed capital accounts, sometimes described as *capitalizing* retained earnings. Accounting for a stock dividend depends on whether it is a small or large stock dividend. A **small stock dividend** is a distribution of 25% or less of previously outstanding shares. It is recorded by capitalizing retained earnings for an amount equal to the market value of the shares to be distributed. A **large stock dividend** is a distribution of more than 25% of previously outstanding shares. A large stock dividend is recorded by capitalizing retained earnings for the minimum amount required by state law governing the corporation. Most states require capitalizing retained earnings equal to the par or stated value of the stock.

To illustrate stock dividends, we use the equity section of Quest's balance sheet shown in Exhibit 13.7 just *before* its declaration of a stock dividend on December 31.

EXHIBIT 13.7

Stockholders' Equity *before*
Declaring a Stock Dividend

Stockholders' Equity (before dividend)	
Common stock—$10 par value, 15,000 shares authorized,	
10,000 shares issued and outstanding	$100,000
Paid-in capital in excess of par value, common stock	8,000
Retained earnings	35,000
Total stockholders' equity	$143,000

Recording a small stock dividend.   Assume that Quest's directors declare a 10% stock dividend on December 31. This stock dividend of 1,000 shares, computed as 10% of its 10,000 issued and outstanding shares, is to be distributed on January 20 to the stockholders of record on January 15. Since the market price of Quest's stock on December 31 is $15 per share, this small stock dividend declaration is recorded as follows:

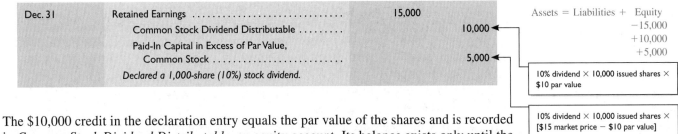

Date of Declaration—Small Stock Dividend

Dec. 31	Retained Earnings	15,000	
	Common Stock Dividend Distributable		10,000
	Paid-In Capital in Excess of Par Value,		
	Common Stock		5,000
	Declared a 1,000-share (10%) stock dividend.		

Assets = Liabilities + Equity
−15,000
+10,000
+5,000

10% dividend × 10,000 issued shares × $10 par value

10% dividend × 10,000 issued shares × [$15 market price − $10 par value]

The $10,000 credit in the declaration entry equals the par value of the shares and is recorded in *Common Stock Dividend Distributable,* an equity account. Its balance exists only until the shares are issued. The $5,000 credit equals the amount by which market value exceeds par value. This amount increases the Paid-In Capital in Excess of Par Value account in anticipation of the issuance of shares. In general, the balance sheet changes in three ways when a stock dividend is declared. First, the amount of equity attributed to common stock increases; for Quest, from $100,000 to $110,000 for 1,000 additional declared shares. Second, paid-in capital in excess of par increases by the excess of market value over par value for the declared shares. Third, retained earnings decreases, reflecting the transfer of amounts to both common stock and paid-in capital in excess of par. The stockholders' equity of Quest is shown in Exhibit 13.8 *after* its 10% stock dividend is declared on December 31—the items impacted are in bold.

EXHIBIT 13.8

Stockholders' Equity *after* Declaring a Stock Dividend

Stockholders' Equity (after dividend)	
Common stock—$10 par value, 15,000 shares authorized,	
10,000 shares issued and outstanding	$100,000
Common stock dividend distributable—1,000 shares	**10,000**
Paid-in capital in excess of par value, common stock	**13,000**
Retained earnings	**20,000**
Total stockholders' equity	$143,000

No entry is made on the date of record for a stock dividend. On January 20, the date of payment, Quest distributes the new shares to stockholders and records this entry:

Date of Payment—Small Stock Dividend

Jan. 20	Common Stock Dividend Distributable	10,000	
	Common Stock, $10 Par Value		10,000
	To record issuance of common stock dividend.		

Assets = Liabilities + Equity
−10,000
+10,000

The combined effect of these stock dividend entries is to transfer (or capitalize) $15,000 of retained earnings to paid-in capital accounts. The amount of capitalized retained earnings equals the market value of the 1,000 issued shares ($15 × 1,000 shares). A stock dividend has no effect on the ownership percent of individual stockholders.

Recording a large stock dividend.   A corporation capitalizes retained earnings equal to the minimum amount required by state law for a large stock dividend. For most states, this amount is the par or stated value of the newly issued shares. To illustrate, suppose Quest's board declares a stock dividend of 30% instead of 10% on December 31. Since this dividend is more than 25%, it is treated as a large stock dividend. Thus, the par value of the 3,000 dividend shares is capitalized at the date of declaration with this entry:

Date of Declaration—Large Stock Dividend

Assets = Liabilities + Equity
        −30,000
        +30,000

Dec. 31	Retained Earnings	30,000	
	Common Stock Dividend Distributable		30,000
	Declared a 3,000-share (30%) stock dividend.		

30% dividend × 10,000 issued shares × $10 par value

This transaction decreases retained earnings and increases contributed capital by $30,000. On the date of payment the company debits Common Stock Dividend Distributable and credits Common Stock for $30,000. The effects from a large stock dividend on balance sheet accounts are similar to those for a small stock dividend except for the absence of any effect on paid-in capital in excess of par.

Stock Splits

Before 5:1 Split: 1 share, $50 par

After 5:1 Split: 5 shares, $10 par

Point: Berkshire Hathaway has resisted a stock split. Its recent stock price was $150,000 per share.

Point: A reverse stock split is the opposite of a stock split. It increases both the market value per share and the par or stated value per share with a split ratio less than 1-for-1, such as 1-for-2. A reverse split results in fewer shares.

A **stock split** is the distribution of additional shares to stockholders according to their percent ownership. When a stock split occurs, the corporation "calls in" its outstanding shares and issues more than one new share in exchange for each old share. Splits can be done in any ratio, including 2-for-1, 3-for-1, or higher. Stock splits reduce the par or stated value per share. The reasons for stock splits are similar to those for stock dividends.

To illustrate, CompTec has 100,000 outstanding shares of $20 par value common stock with a current market value of $88 per share. A 2-for-1 stock split cuts par value in half as it replaces 100,000 shares of $20 par value stock with 200,000 shares of $10 par value stock. Market value is reduced from $88 per share to about $44 per share. The split does not affect any equity amounts reported on the balance sheet or any individual stockholder's percent ownership. Both the Paid-In Capital and Retained Earnings accounts are unchanged by a split, and *no journal entry is made*. The only effect on the accounts is a change in the stock account description. CompTec's 2-for-1 split on its $20 par value stock means that after the split, it changes its stock account title to Common Stock, $10 Par Value. This stock's description on the balance sheet also changes to reflect the additional authorized, issued, and outstanding shares and the new par value.

The difference between stock splits and large stock dividends is often blurred. Many companies report stock splits in their financial statements without calling in the original shares by simply changing their par value. This type of "split" is really a large stock dividend and results in additional shares issued to stockholders by capitalizing retained earnings or transferring other paid-in capital to Common Stock. This approach avoids administrative costs of splitting the stock. **Harley-Davidson** recently declared a 2-for-1 stock split executed in the form of a 100% stock dividend.

Decision Maker   Answer — p. 533

Entrepreneur   A company you cofounded and own stock in announces a 50% stock dividend. Has the value of your stock investment increased, decreased, or remained the same? Would it make a difference if it was a 3-for-2 stock split executed in the form of a dividend? ■

Quick Check   Answers — p. 534

10. How does a stock dividend impact assets and retained earnings?
11. What distinguishes a large stock dividend from a small stock dividend?
12. What amount of retained earnings is capitalized for a small stock dividend?

PREFERRED STOCK

C2 Explain characteristics of, and distribute dividends between, common and preferred stock.

A corporation can issue two basic kinds of stock, common and preferred. **Preferred stock** has special rights that give it priority (or senior status) over common stock in one or more areas. Special rights typically include a preference for receiving dividends and for the distribution of assets if the corporation is liquidated. Preferred stock carries all rights of common stock unless the corporate charter nullifies them. Most preferred stock, for instance, does not confer the right to vote. Exhibit 13.9 shows that preferred stock is issued by about one-fourth of corporations. All corporations issue common stock.

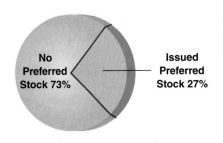

EXHIBIT 13.9

Corporations and
Preferred Stock

Issuance of Preferred Stock

Preferred stock usually has a par value. Like common stock, it can be sold at a price different from par. Preferred stock is recorded in its own separate capital accounts. To illustrate, if Dillon Snowboards issues 50 shares of $100 par value preferred stock for $6,000 cash on July 1, 2011, the entry is

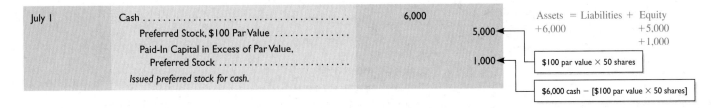

July 1	Cash	6,000	
	Preferred Stock, $100 Par Value		5,000
	Paid-In Capital in Excess of Par Value,		
	Preferred Stock		1,000
	Issued preferred stock for cash.		

Assets = Liabilities + Equity
+6,000   +5,000
                              +1,000

$100 par value × 50 shares

$6,000 cash − [$100 par value × 50 shares]

The equity section of the year-end balance sheet for Dillon Snowboards, including preferred stock, is shown in Exhibit 13.10. (This exhibit assumes that common stock was issued at par.) Issuing no-par preferred stock is similar to issuing no-par common stock. Also, the entries for issuing preferred stock for noncash assets are similar to those for common stock.

Stockholders' Equity	
Common stock—$10 par value; 50,000 shares authorized;	
30,000 shares issued and outstanding	$300,000
Preferred stock—$100 par value; 1,000 shares authorized;	
50 shares issued and outstanding	5,000
Paid-in capital in excess of par value, preferred stock	1,000
Retained earnings	65,000
Total stockholders' equity	$371,000

EXHIBIT 13.10

Stockholders' Equity with
Common and Preferred Stock

Dividend Preference of Preferred Stock

Preferred stock usually carries a preference for dividends, meaning that preferred stockholders are allocated their dividends before any dividends are allocated to common stockholders. The dividends allocated to preferred stockholders are usually expressed as a dollar amount per share or a percent applied to par value. A preference for dividends does *not* ensure dividends. If the directors do not declare a dividend, neither the preferred nor the common stockholders receive one.

Cumulative or Noncumulative Dividend Most preferred stocks carry a cumulative dividend right. **Cumulative preferred stock** has a right to be paid both the current and all prior periods' unpaid dividends before any dividend is paid to common stockholders. When preferred stock is cumulative and the directors either do not declare a dividend to preferred stockholders or declare one that does not cover the total amount of cumulative dividend, the unpaid dividend amount is called **dividend in arrears.** Accumulation of dividends in arrears on cumulative preferred stock does not guarantee they will be paid. **Noncumulative preferred stock** confers no right to prior periods' unpaid dividends if they were not declared in those prior periods.

To illustrate the difference between cumulative and noncumulative preferred stock, assume that a corporation's outstanding stock includes (1) 1,000 shares of $100 par, 9% preferred

Point: Dividend preference does not imply that preferred stockholders receive more dividends than common stockholders, nor does it guarantee a dividend.

stock—yielding $9,000 per year in potential dividends, and (2) 4,000 shares of $50 par value common stock. During 2010, the first year of operations, the directors declare cash dividends of $5,000. In year 2011, they declare cash dividends of $42,000. See Exhibit 13.11 for the allocation of dividends for these two years. Allocation of year 2011 dividends depends on whether the preferred stock is noncumulative or cumulative. With noncumulative preferred, the preferred stockholders never receive the $4,000 skipped in 2010. If the preferred stock is cumulative, the $4,000 in arrears is paid in 2011 before any other dividends are paid.

EXHIBIT 13.11

Allocation of Dividends (noncumulative vs. cumulative preferred stock)

Example: What dividends do cumulative preferred stockholders receive in 2011 if the corporation paid only $2,000 of dividends in 2010? How does this affect dividends to common stockholders in 2011?
Answers: $16,000 ($7,000 dividends in arrears, plus $9,000 current preferred dividends). Dividends to common stockholders decrease to $26,000.

	Preferred	Common
Preferred Stock Is Noncumulative		
Year 2010	$ 5,000	$ 0
Year 2011		
Step 1: Current year's preferred dividend	$ 9,000	
Step 2: Remainder to common		$33,000
Preferred Stock Is Cumulative		
Year 2010	$ 5,000	$ 0
Year 2011		
Step 1: Dividend in arrears	$ 4,000	
Step 2: Current year's preferred dividend	9,000	
Step 3: Remainder to common		$29,000
Totals for year 2011	$13,000	$29,000

A liability for a dividend does not exist until the directors declare a dividend. If a preferred dividend date passes and the corporation's board fails to declare the dividend on its cumulative preferred stock, the dividend in arrears is not a liability. The *full-disclosure principle* requires a corporation to report (usually in a note) the amount of preferred dividends in arrears as of the balance sheet date.

Participating or Nonparticipating Dividend Nonparticipating preferred stock has a feature that limits dividends to a maximum amount each year. This maximum is often stated as a percent of the stock's par value or as a specific dollar amount per share. Once preferred stockholders receive this amount, the common stockholders receive any and all additional dividends. **Participating preferred stock** has a feature allowing preferred stockholders to share with common stockholders in any dividends paid in excess of the percent or dollar amount stated on the preferred stock. This participation feature does not apply until common stockholders receive dividends equal to the preferred stock's dividend percent. Many corporations are authorized to issue participating preferred stock but rarely do, and most managers never expect to issue it.[2]

Convertible Preferred Stock

Preferred stock is more attractive to investors if it carries a right to exchange preferred shares for a fixed number of common shares. **Convertible preferred stock** gives holders the option to

---

[2] Participating preferred stock is usually authorized as a defense against a possible corporate *takeover* by an "unfriendly" investor (or a group of investors) who intends to buy enough voting common stock to gain control. Taking a term from spy novels, the financial world refers to this type of plan as a *poison pill* that a company swallows if enemy investors threaten its capture. A poison pill usually works as follows: A corporation's common stockholders on a given date are granted the right to purchase a large amount of participating preferred stock at a very low price. This right to purchase preferred shares is *not* transferable. If an unfriendly investor buys a large block of common shares (whose right to purchase participating preferred shares does *not* transfer to this buyer), the board can issue preferred shares at a low price to the remaining common shareholders who retained the right to purchase. Future dividends are then divided between the newly issued participating preferred shares and the common shares. This usually transfers value from common shares to preferred shares, causing the unfriendly investor's common stock to lose much of its value and reduces the potential benefit of a hostile takeover.

exchange their preferred shares for common shares at a specified rate. When a company prospers and its common stock increases in value, convertible preferred stockholders can share in this success by converting their preferred stock into more valuable common stock.

Callable Preferred Stock

Callable preferred stock gives the issuing corporation the right to purchase (retire) this stock from its holders at specified future prices and dates. The amount paid to call and retire a preferred share is its **call price**, or *redemption value,* and is set when the stock is issued. The call price normally includes the stock's par value plus a premium giving holders additional return on their investment. When the issuing corporation calls and retires a preferred stock, the terms of the agreement often require it to pay the call price *and* any dividends in arrears.

 IFRS

Like U.S. GAAP, IFRS requires that preferred stocks be classified as debt or equity based on analysis of the stock's contractual terms. However, IFRS uses different criteria for such classification. ■

Reasons for Issuing Preferred Stock

Corporations issue preferred stock for several reasons. One is to raise capital without sacrificing control. For example, suppose a company's organizers have $100,000 cash to invest and organize a corporation that needs $200,000 of capital to start. If they sell $200,000 worth of common stock (with $100,000 to the organizers), they would have only 50% control and would need to negotiate extensively with other stockholders in making policy. However, if they issue $100,000 worth of common stock to themselves and sell outsiders $100,000 of 8%, cumulative preferred stock with no voting rights, they retain control.

A second reason to issue preferred stock is to boost the return earned by common stockholders. To illustrate, suppose a corporation's organizers expect to earn an annual after-tax income of $24,000 on an investment of $200,000. If they sell and issue $200,000 worth of common stock, the $24,000 income produces a 12% return on the $200,000 of common stockholders' equity. However, if they issue $100,000 of 8% preferred stock to outsiders and $100,000 of common stock to themselves, their own return increases to 16% per year, as shown in Exhibit 13.12.

Net (after-tax) income	$24,000
Less preferred dividends at 8%	(8,000)
Balance to common stockholders	$16,000
Return to common stockholders ($16,000/$100,000)	16%

EXHIBIT 13.12

Return to Common Stockholders When Preferred Stock Is Issued

Common stockholders earn 16% instead of 12% because assets contributed by preferred stockholders are invested to earn $12,000 while the preferred dividend is only $8,000. Use of preferred stock to increase return to common stockholders is an example of **financial leverage** (also called *trading on the equity*). As a general rule, when the dividend rate on preferred stock is less than the rate the corporation earns on its assets, the effect of issuing preferred stock is to increase (or *lever*) the rate earned by common stockholders.

Other reasons for issuing preferred stock include its appeal to some investors who believe that the corporation's common stock is too risky or that the expected return on common stock is too low.

Point: The issuing corporation has the right, or option, to retire its callable preferred stock.

Point: Financial leverage also occurs when debt is issued and the interest rate paid on it is less than the rate earned from using the assets the creditors lend the company.

Decision Maker
Answer — p. 533

Concert Organizer Assume that you alter your business strategy from organizing concerts targeted at under 1,000 people to those targeted at between 5,000 to 20,000 people. You also incorporate because of increased risk of lawsuits and a desire to issue stock for financing. It is important that you control the company for decisions on whom to schedule. What types of stock do you offer? ■

13. In what ways does preferred stock often have priority over common stock?

14. Increasing the return to common stockholders by issuing preferred stock is an example of (*a*) Financial leverage. (*b*) Cumulative earnings. (*c*) Dividend in arrears.

15. A corporation has issued and outstanding (i) 9,000 shares of $50 par value, 10% cumulative, nonparticipating preferred stock and (ii) 27,000 shares of $10 par value common stock. No dividends have been declared for the two prior years. During the current year, the corporation declares $288,000 in dividends. The amount paid to common shareholders is (*a*) $243,000. (*b*) $153,000. (*c*) $135,000.

TREASURY STOCK

P3	Record purchases and sales of treasury stock and the retirement of stock.

Corporations acquire shares of their own stock for several reasons: (1) to use their shares to acquire another corporation, (2) to purchase shares to avoid a hostile takeover of the company, (3) to reissue them to employees as compensation, and (4) to maintain a strong market for their stock or to show management confidence in the current price.

A corporation's reacquired shares are called **treasury stock,** which is similar to unissued stock in several ways: (1) neither treasury stock nor unissued stock is an asset, (2) neither receives cash dividends or stock dividends, and (3) neither allows the exercise of voting rights. However, treasury stock does differ from unissued stock in one major way: The corporation can resell treasury stock at less than par without having the buyers incur a liability, provided it was originally issued at par value or higher. Treasury stock purchases also require management to exercise ethical sensitivity because funds are being paid to specific stockholders instead of all stockholders. Managers must be sure the purchase is in the best interest of all stockholders. These concerns cause companies to fully disclose treasury stock transactions.

Corporations and Treasury Stock

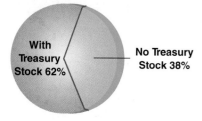

With Treasury Stock 62%

No Treasury Stock 38%

Purchasing Treasury Stock

Purchasing treasury stock reduces the corporation's assets and equity by equal amounts. (We describe the *cost method* of accounting for treasury stock, which is the most widely used method. The *par value* method is another method explained in advanced courses.) To illustrate, Exhibit 13.13 shows Cyber Corporation's account balances *before* any treasury stock purchase (Cyber has no liabilities).

EXHIBIT 13.13

Account Balances *before* Purchasing Treasury Stock

Assets		**Stockholders' Equity**	
Cash	$ 30,000	Common stock—$10 par; 10,000 shares	
Other assets	95,000	authorized, issued, and outstanding	$100,000
		Retained earnings	25,000
Total assets	$125,000	Total stockholders' equity	$125,000

Cyber then purchases 1,000 of its own shares for $11,500 on May 1, which is recorded as follows.

Assets = Liabilities + Equity
−11,500   −11,500

$11.50 cost per share × 1,000 shares

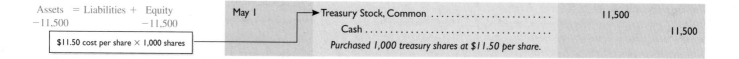

May 1	Treasury Stock, Common	11,500	
	Cash		11,500
	Purchased 1,000 treasury shares at $11.50 per share.		

This entry reduces equity through the debit to the Treasury Stock account, which is a contra equity account. Exhibit 13.14 shows account balances *after* this transaction.

EXHIBIT 13.14

Account Balances *after* Purchasing Treasury Stock

Assets		Stockholders' Equity	
Cash	$ 18,500	Common stock—$10 par; 10,000 shares authorized and issued; 1,000 shares in treasury	$100,000
Other assets	95,000	Retained earnings, $11,500 restricted by treasury stock purchase	25,000
		Less cost of treasury stock	**(11,500)**
Total assets	$113,500	Total stockholders' equity	$113,500

The treasury stock purchase reduces Cyber's cash, total assets, and total equity by $11,500 but does not reduce the balance of either the Common Stock or the Retained Earnings account. The equity reduction is reported by deducting the cost of treasury stock in the equity section. Also, two disclosures are evident. First, the stock description reveals that 1,000 issued shares are in treasury, leaving only 9,000 shares still outstanding. Second, the description for retained earnings reveals that it is partly restricted.

Point: The Treasury Stock account is *not* an asset. Treasury stock does not carry voting or dividend rights.

Point: A treasury stock purchase is also called a *stock buyback*.

Reissuing Treasury Stock

Treasury stock can be reissued by selling it at cost, above cost, or below cost.

Selling Treasury Stock at Cost   If treasury stock is reissued at cost, the entry is the reverse of the one made to record the purchase. For instance, if on May 21 Cyber reissues 100 of the treasury shares purchased on May 1 at the same $11.50 per share cost, the entry is

May 21	Cash	1,150	
	Treasury Stock, Common		1,150
	Received $11.50 per share for 100 treasury shares costing $11.50 per share.		

Assets = Liabilities + Equity
+1,150   +1,150

$11.50 cost per share × 100 shares

Selling Treasury Stock *above* Cost   If treasury stock is sold for more than cost, the amount received in excess of cost is credited to the Paid-In Capital, Treasury Stock account. This account is reported as a separate item in the stockholders' equity section. No gain is ever reported from the sale of treasury stock. To illustrate, if Cyber receives $12 cash per share for 400 treasury shares costing $11.50 per share on June 3, the entry is

Point: Treasury stock does not represent ownership. A company cannot own a part of itself.

June 3	Cash	4,800	
	Treasury Stock, Common		4,600
	Paid-In Capital, Treasury Stock		200
	Received $12 per share for 400 treasury shares costing $11.50 per share.		

Assets = Liabilities + Equity
+4,800   +4,600
                                 +200

$11.50 cost per share × 400 shares

[$12 issue price − $11.50 cost per share] × 400 shares

Selling Treasury Stock *below* Cost   When treasury stock is sold below cost, the entry to record the sale depends on whether the Paid-In Capital, Treasury Stock account has a credit balance. If it has a zero balance, the excess of cost over the sales price is debited to Retained Earnings. If the Paid-In Capital, Treasury Stock account has a credit balance, it is debited for the excess of the cost over the selling price but not to exceed the balance in this account. When the credit balance in this paid-in capital account is eliminated, any remaining difference between the cost and selling price is debited to Retained Earnings. To illustrate, if Cyber sells its remaining 500 shares of treasury stock at $10 per share on July 10, equity is

Point: The phrase *treasury stock* is believed to arise from the fact that reacquired stock is held in a corporation's treasury.

Point: The Paid-In Capital, Treasury Stock account can have a zero or credit balance but never a debit balance.

reduced by $750 (500 shares × $1.50 per share excess of cost over selling price), as shown in this entry:

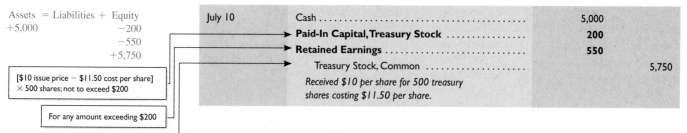

Assets = Liabilities + Equity
+5,000   −200
                  −550
                  +5,750

[$10 issue price − $11.50 cost per share] × 500 shares; not to exceed $200

For any amount exceeding $200

$11.50 cost per share × 500 shares

July 10	Cash	5,000	
	Paid-In Capital, Treasury Stock	200	
	Retained Earnings	550	
	Treasury Stock, Common		5,750
	Received $10 per share for 500 treasury shares costing $11.50 per share.		

This entry eliminates the $200 credit balance in the paid-in capital account created on June 3 and then reduces the Retained Earnings balance by the remaining $550 excess of cost over selling price. A company never reports a loss (or gain) from the sale of treasury stock.

Retiring Stock

A corporation can purchase its own stock and retire it. Retiring stock reduces the number of issued shares. Retired stock is the same as authorized and unissued shares. Purchases and retirements of stock are permissible under state law only if they do not jeopardize the interests of creditors and stockholders. When stock is purchased for retirement, we remove all capital amounts related to the retired shares. If the purchase price exceeds the net amount removed, this excess is debited to Retained Earnings. If the net amount removed from all capital accounts exceeds the purchase price, this excess is credited to the Paid-In Capital from Retirement of Stock account. A company's assets and equity are always reduced by the amount paid for the retiring stock.

Quick Check   Answers — p. 534

16. Purchase of treasury stock (*a*) has no effect on assets; (*b*) reduces total assets and total equity by equal amounts; or (*c*) is recorded with a debit to Retained Earnings.

17. Southern Co. purchases shares of Northern Corp. Should either company classify these shares as treasury stock?

18. How does treasury stock affect the authorized, issued, and outstanding shares?

19. When a company purchases treasury stock, (*a*) retained earnings are restricted by the amount paid; (*b*) Retained Earnings is credited; or (*c*) it is retired.

REPORTING OF EQUITY

C3 Explain the items reported in retained earnings.

Statement of Retained Earnings

Retained earnings generally consist of a company's cumulative net income less any net losses and dividends declared since its inception. Retained earnings are part of stockholders' claims on the company's net assets, but this does *not* imply that a certain amount of cash or other assets is available to pay stockholders. For example, **Research In Motion** has $5,274,365 thousand in retained earnings, but only $1,550,861 thousand in cash. This section describes events and transactions affecting retained earnings and how retained earnings are reported.

Restrictions and Appropriations   The term **restricted retained earnings** refers to both statutory and contractual restrictions. A common *statutory* (or *legal*) *restriction* is to limit treasury stock purchases to the amount of retained earnings. The balance sheet in Exhibit 13.14 provides an example. A common *contractual restriction* involves loan agreements that restrict paying dividends beyond a specified amount or percent of retained earnings. Restrictions are usually described in the notes. The term **appropriated retained earnings** refers to a voluntary transfer of amounts from the Retained Earnings account to the Appropriated Retained Earnings account to inform users of special activities that require funds.

Prior Period Adjustments   **Prior period adjustments** are corrections of material errors in prior period financial statements. These errors include arithmetic mistakes, unacceptable accounting, and missed facts. Prior period adjustments are reported in the *statement of retained earnings* (or the statement of stockholders' equity), net of any income tax effects. Prior period adjustments result in changing the beginning balance of retained earnings for events occurring prior to the earliest period reported in the current set of financial statements. To illustrate, assume that ComUS makes an error in a 2009 journal entry for the purchase of land by incorrectly debiting an expense account. When this is discovered in 2011, the statement of retained earnings includes a prior period adjustment, as shown in Exhibit 13.15. This exhibit also shows the usual format of the statement of retained earnings.

Point: If a year 2009 error is discovered in 2010, the company records the adjustment in 2010. But if the financial statements include 2009 and 2010 figures, the statements report the correct amounts for 2009, and a note describes the correction.

ComUS Statement of Retained Earnings For Year Ended December 31, 2011	
Retained earnings, Dec. 31, 2010, as previously reported	$4,745,000
Prior period adjustment	
Cost of land incorrectly expensed (net of $63,000 income taxes)	147,000
Retained earnings, Dec. 31, 2010, as adjusted	4,892,000
Plus net income	1,224,300
Less cash dividends declared	(301,800)
Retained earnings, Dec. 31, 2011	$5,814,500

EXHIBIT 13.15

Statement of Retained Earnings with a Prior Period Adjustment

Many items reported in financial statements are based on estimates. Future events are certain to reveal that some of these estimates were inaccurate even when based on the best data available at the time. These inaccuracies are *not* considered errors and are *not* reported as prior period adjustments. Instead, they are identified as **changes in accounting estimates** and are accounted for in current and future periods. To illustrate, we know that depreciation is based on estimated useful lives and salvage values. As time passes and new information becomes available, managers may need to change these estimates and the resulting depreciation expense for current and future periods.

Point: Accounting for changes in estimates is sometimes criticized as two wrongs to make a right. Consider a change in an asset's life. Depreciation neither before nor after the change is the amount computed if the revised estimate were originally selected. Regulators chose this approach to avoid restating prior period numbers.

Closing Process   The closing process was explained earlier in the book as: (1) Close credit balances in revenue accounts to Income Summary, (2) Close debit balances in expense accounts to Income Summary, and (3) Close Income Summary to Retained Earnings. If dividends are recorded in a Dividends account, and not as an immediate reduction to Retained Earnings (as shown in this chapter), a fourth step is necessary to close the Dividends account to Retained Earnings.

Statement of Stockholders' Equity

Instead of a separate statement of retained earnings, companies commonly report a statement of stockholders' equity that includes changes in retained earnings. A **statement of stockholders' equity** lists the beginning and ending balances of key equity accounts and describes the changes that occur during the period. The companies in Appendix A report such a statement. The usual format is to provide a column for each component of equity and use the rows to describe events occurring in the period. Exhibit 13.16 shows a condensed statement for **Apple**.

Reporting Stock Options

The majority of corporations whose shares are publicly traded issue **stock options,** which are rights to purchase common stock at a fixed price over a specified period. As the stock's price rises, the option's value increases. **Starbucks** and **Home Depot** offer stock options to both full- and part-time employees. Stock options are said to motivate managers and employees to

EXHIBIT 13.16

Statement of Stockholders' Equity

Apple

APPLE Statement of Stockholders' Equity					
($ millions, shares in thousands)	Common Stock Shares	Common Stock Amount	Retained Earnings	Other	Total Equity
Balance, Sept. 27, 2008	888,326	$7,177	$15,129	$(9)	$22,297
Net income	—	—	8,235	—	8,235
Issuance of Common Stock	11,480	404	(11)	—	393
Other	—	629	—	86	715
Cash Dividends ($0.00 per share)	—	—	—	—	—
Balance, Sept. 26, 2009	899,806	$8,210	$23,353	$77	$31,640

(1) focus on company performance, (2) take a long-run perspective, and (3) remain with the company. A stock option is like having an investment with no risk ("a carrot with no stick").

To illustrate, Quantum grants each of its employees the option to purchase 100 shares of its $1 par value common stock at its current market price of $50 per share anytime within the next 10 years. If the stock price rises to $70 per share, an employee can exercise the option at a gain of $20 per share (acquire a $70 stock at the $50 option price). With 100 shares, a single employee would have a total gain of $2,000, computed as $20 × 100 shares. Companies report the cost of stock options in the income statement. Measurement of this cost is explained in advanced courses.

GLOBAL VIEW

This section discusses similarities and differences between U.S. GAAP and IFRS in accounting and reporting for equity.

Accounting for Common Stock   The accounting for and reporting of common stock under U.S. GAAP and IFRS are similar. Specifically, procedures for issuing common stock at par, at a premium, at a discount, and for noncash assets are similar across the two systems. However, we must be aware of legal and cultural differences across the world that can impact the rights and responsibilities of common shareholders. **Nokia**'s terminology is a bit different as it uses the phrase "share capital" in reference to what U.S. GAAP would title "common shares" (see Appendix A). It also discloses that it has issued (and outstanding) shares of 3,744,956,052.

NOKIA

Accounting for Dividends   Accounting for and reporting of dividends under U.S. GAAP and IFRS are consistent. This applies to cash dividends, stock dividends, and stock splits. For **Nokia**, a "dividend of EUR 0.40 per share is to be paid out on the shares of the Company." Nokia, like many other companies, follows a dividend policy set by management and its board.

Accounting for Preferred Stock   Accounting and reporting for preferred stock are similar for U.S. GAAP and IFRS, but there are some important differences. First, preferred stock that is redeemable at the option of the preferred stockholders is reported *between* liabilities and equity in U.S. GAAP balance sheets. However, that same stock is reported as a liability in IFRS balance sheets. Second, the issue price of convertible preferred stock (and bonds) is recorded entirely under preferred stock (or bonds) *and none is assigned to the conversion feature* under U.S. GAAP. However, IFRS requires that a portion of the issue price be allocated to the conversion feature when it exists. Nokia has no preferred stock.

Accounting for Treasury Stock   Both U.S. GAAP and IFRS apply the principle that companies do not record gains or losses on transactions involving their own stock. This applies to purchases, reissuances, and retirements of treasury stock. Consequently, the accounting for treasury stock explained in this chapter is consistent with that under IFRS. However, IFRS in this area is less detailed than that of U.S. GAAP. **Nokia**'s policy regarding treasury stock follows: "[It] recognizes acquired treasury shares as a deduction from equity at their acquisition cost."

Earnings per Share

The income statement reports **earnings per share,** also called *EPS* or *net income per share,* which is the amount of income earned per each share of a company's outstanding common stock. The **basic earnings per share** formula is shown in Exhibit 13.17. When a company has no preferred stock, then preferred dividends are zero. The weighted-average common shares outstanding is measured over the income reporting period; its computation is explained in advanced courses.

 A1 Compute earnings per share and describe its use.

$$\text{Basic earnings per share} = \frac{\text{Net income} - \text{Preferred dividends}}{\text{Weighted-average common shares outstanding}}$$

EXHIBIT 13.17

Basic Earnings per Share

To illustrate, assume that Quantum Co. earns $40,000 net income in 2011 and declares dividends of $7,500 on its noncumulative preferred stock. (If preferred stock is *non*cumulative, the income available [numerator] is the current period net income less any preferred dividends *declared* in that same period. If preferred stock is cumulative, the income available [numerator] is the current period net income less the preferred dividends whether declared or not.) Quantum has 5,000 weighted-average common shares outstanding during 2011. Its basic EPS[3] is

$$\text{Basic earnings per share} = \frac{\$40,000 - \$7,500}{5,000 \text{ shares}} = \$6.50$$

Price-Earnings Ratio

A stock's market value is determined by its *expected* future cash flows. A comparison of a company's EPS and its market value per share reveals information about market expectations. This comparison is traditionally made using a **price-earnings (or PE) ratio,** expressed also as *price earnings, price to earnings,* or *PE.* Some analysts interpret this ratio as what price the market is willing to pay for a company's current earnings stream. Price-earnings ratios can differ across companies that have similar earnings because of either higher or lower expectations of future earnings. The price-earnings ratio is defined in Exhibit 13.18.

A2 Compute price-earnings ratio and describe its use in analysis.

Point: The average PE ratio of stocks in the 1950–2010 period is about 14.

$$\text{Price-earnings ratio} = \frac{\text{Market value (price) per share}}{\text{Earnings per share}}$$

EXHIBIT 13.18

Price-Earnings Ratio

This ratio is often computed using EPS from the most recent period (for Amazon, its PE is 52; for Altria, its PE is 13). However, many users compute this ratio using *expected* EPS for the next period.

Some analysts view stocks with high PE ratios (higher than 20 to 25) as more likely to be overpriced and stocks with low PE ratios (less than 5 to 8) as more likely to be underpriced. These investors prefer to sell or avoid buying stocks with high PE ratios and to buy or hold stocks with low PE ratios. However, investment decision making is rarely so simple as to rely on a single ratio. For instance, a stock with a high PE ratio can prove to be a good investment if its earnings continue to increase beyond current expectations. Similarly, a stock with a low PE ratio can prove to be a poor investment if its earnings decline below expectations.

Point: Average PE ratios for U.S. stocks increased over the past two decades. Some analysts interpret this as a signal the market is overpriced. But higher ratios can at least partly reflect accounting changes that have reduced reported earnings.

---

[3] A corporation can be classified as having either a simple or complex capital structure. The term **simple capital structure** refers to a company with only common stock and nonconvertible preferred stock outstanding. The term **complex capital structure** refers to companies with dilutive securities. **Dilutive securities** include options, rights to purchase common stock, and any bonds or preferred stock that are convertible into common stock. A company with a complex capital structure must often report two EPS figures: basic and diluted. **Diluted earnings per share** is computed by adding all dilutive securities to the denominator of the basic EPS computation. It reflects the decrease in basic EPS *assuming* that all dilutive securities are converted into common shares.

◻ Decision Maker   Answer — p. 533

Answer — p. 533

Money Manager   You plan to invest in one of two companies identified as having identical future prospects. One has a PE of 19 and the other a PE of 25. Which do you invest in? Does it matter if your *estimate* of PE for these two companies is 29 as opposed to 22? ■

Dividend Yield

A3 Compute dividend yield and explain its use in analysis.

Investors buy shares of a company's stock in anticipation of receiving a return from either or both cash dividends and stock price increases. Stocks that pay large dividends on a regular basis, called *income stocks,* are attractive to investors who want recurring cash flows from their investments. In contrast, some stocks pay little or no dividends but are still attractive to investors because of their expected stock price increases. The stocks of companies that distribute little or no cash but use their cash to finance expansion are called *growth stocks.* One way to help identify whether a stock is an income stock or a growth stock is to analyze its dividend yield. **Dividend yield,** defined in Exhibit 13.19, shows the annual amount of cash dividends distributed to common shares relative to their market value.

EXHIBIT 13.19

Dividend Yield

$$\text{Dividend yield} = \frac{\text{Annual cash dividends per share}}{\text{Market value per share}}$$

Dividend yield can be computed for current and prior periods using actual dividends and stock prices and for future periods using expected values. Exhibit 13.20 shows recent dividend and stock price data for **Amazon** and **Altria Group** to compute dividend yield.

EXHIBIT 13.20

Dividend and Stock Price Information

Company	Cash Dividends per Share	Market Value per Share	Dividend Yield
Amazon	$0.00	$80	0.0%
Altria Group	1.68	20	8.4

Point: The *payout ratio* equals cash dividends declared on common stock divided by net income. A low payout ratio suggests that a company is retaining earnings for future growth.

Dividend yield is zero for Amazon, implying it is a growth stock. An investor in Amazon would look for increases in stock prices (and eventual cash from the sale of stock). Altria has a dividend yield of 8.4%, implying it is an income stock for which dividends are important in assessing its value.

Book Value per Share

A4 Compute book value and explain its use in analysis.

Case 1: Common Stock (Only) Outstanding. **Book value per common share,** defined in Exhibit 13.21, reflects the amount of equity applicable to *common* shares on a per share basis. To illustrate, we use Dillon Snowboards' data from Exhibit 13.4. Dillon has 30,000 outstanding common shares, and the stockholders' equity applicable to common shares is $365,000. Dillon's book value per common share is $12.17, computed as $365,000 divided by 30,000 shares.

EXHIBIT 13.21

Book Value per Common Share

$$\text{Book value per common share} = \frac{\text{Stockholders' equity applicable to common shares}}{\text{Number of common shares outstanding}}$$

Point: Book value per share is also referred to as *stockholders' claim to assets on a per share basis.*

Case 2: Common and Preferred Stock Outstanding. To compute book value when both common and preferred shares are outstanding, we allocate total equity between the two types of shares. The **book value per preferred share** is computed first; its computation is shown in Exhibit 13.22.

EXHIBIT 13.22

Book Value per Preferred Share

$$\text{Book value per preferred share} = \frac{\text{Stockholders' equity applicable to preferred shares}}{\text{Number of preferred shares outstanding}}$$

The equity applicable to preferred shares equals the preferred share's call price (or par value if the preferred is not callable) plus any cumulative dividends in arrears. The remaining equity is the portion applicable to common shares. To illustrate, consider LTD's equity in Exhibit 13.23. Its preferred stock is callable at $108 per share, and two years of cumulative preferred dividends are in arrears.

EXHIBIT 13.23

Stockholders' Equity with Preferred and Common Stock

Stockholders' Equity

Preferred stock—$100 par value, 7% cumulative, 2,000 shares authorized, 1,000 shares issued and outstanding	$100,000
Common stock—$25 par value, 12,000 shares authorized, 10,000 shares issued and outstanding	250,000
Paid-in capital in excess of par value, common stock	15,000
Retained earnings	82,000
Total stockholders' equity	$447,000

The book value computations are in Exhibit 13.24. Equity is first allocated to preferred shares before the book value of common shares is computed.

EXHIBIT 13.24

Computing Book Value per Preferred and Common Share

Total stockholders' equity		$447,000
Less equity applicable to preferred shares		
Call price (1,000 shares × $108)	$108,000	
Dividends in arrears ($100,000 × 7% × 2 years)	14,000	(122,000)
Equity applicable to common shares		$325,000
Book value per preferred share ($122,000/1,000 shares)		**$122.00**
Book value per common share ($325,000/10,000 shares)		**$ 32.50**

Book value per share reflects the value per share if a company is liquidated at balance sheet amounts. Book value is also the starting point in many stock valuation models, merger negotiations, price setting for public utilities, and loan contracts. The main limitation in using book value is the potential difference between recorded value and market value for assets and liabilities. Investors often adjust their analysis for estimates of these differences.

Decision Maker   Answer — p. 533

Investor You are considering investing in **BMX**, whose book value per common share is $4 and price per common share on the stock exchange is $7. From this information, are BMX's net assets priced higher or lower than its recorded values? ■

DEMONSTRATION PROBLEM 1

Barton Corporation began operations on January 1, 2010. The following transactions relating to stockholders' equity occurred in the first two years of the company's operations.

2010

Jan. 1  Authorized the issuance of 2 million shares of $5 par value common stock and 100,000 shares of $100 par value, 10% cumulative, preferred stock.

Jan. 2 Issued 200,000 shares of common stock for $12 cash per share.

Jan. 3 Issued 100,000 shares of common stock in exchange for a building valued at $820,000 and merchandise inventory valued at $380,000.

Jan. 4 Paid $10,000 cash to the company's founders for organization activities.

Jan. 5 Issued 12,000 shares of preferred stock for $110 cash per share.

2011

June 4 Issued 100,000 shares of common stock for $15 cash per share.

Required

1. Prepare journal entries to record these transactions.

2. Prepare the stockholders' equity section of the balance sheet as of December 31, 2010, and December 31, 2011, based on these transactions.

3. Prepare a table showing dividend allocations and dividends per share for 2010 and 2011 assuming Barton declares the following cash dividends: 2010, $50,000, and 2011, $300,000.

4. Prepare the January 2, 2010, journal entry for Barton's issuance of 200,000 shares of common stock for $12 cash per share assuming

  a. Common stock is no-par stock without a stated value.

  b. Common stock is no-par stock with a stated value of $10 per share.

PLANNING THE SOLUTION

- Record journal entries for the transactions for 2010 and 2011.
- Determine the balances for the 2010 and 2011 equity accounts for the balance sheet.
- Prepare the contributed capital portion of the 2010 and 2011 balance sheets.
- Prepare a table similar to Exhibit 13.11 showing dividend allocations for 2010 and 2011.
- Record the issuance of common stock under both specifications of no-par stock.

SOLUTION TO DEMONSTRATION PROBLEM 1

1. Journal entries.

2010			
Jan. 2	Cash	2,400,000	
	Common Stock, $5 Par Value		1,000,000
	Paid-In Capital in Excess of Par Value, Common Stock		1,400,000
	Issued 200,000 shares of common stock.		
Jan. 3	Building	820,000	
	Merchandise Inventory	380,000	
	Common Stock, $5 Par Value		500,000
	Paid-In Capital in Excess of Par Value, Common Stock		700,000
	Issued 100,000 shares of common stock.		
Jan. 4	Organization Expenses	10,000	
	Cash		10,000
	Paid founders for organization costs.		
Jan. 5	Cash	1,320,000	
	Preferred Stock, $100 Par Value		1,200,000
	Paid-In Capital in Excess of Par Value, Preferred Stock		120,000
	Issued 12,000 shares of preferred stock.		
2011			
June 4	Cash	1,500,000	
	Common Stock, $5 Par Value		500,000
	Paid-In Capital in Excess of Par Value, Common Stock		1,000,000
	Issued 100,000 shares of common stock.		

2. Balance sheet presentations (at December 31 year-end).

	2011	2010
Stockholders' Equity		
Preferred stock—$100 par value, 10% cumulative, 100,000 shares authorized, 12,000 shares issued and outstanding	$1,200,000	$1,200,000
Paid-in capital in excess of par value, preferred stock	120,000	120,000
Total paid-in capital by preferred stockholders	1,320,000	1,320,000
Common stock—$5 par value, 2,000,000 shares authorized, 300,000 shares issued and outstanding in 2010, and 400,000 shares issued and outstanding in 2011	2,000,000	1,500,000
Paid-in capital in excess of par value, common stock	3,100,000	2,100,000
Total paid-in capital by common stockholders	5,100,000	3,600,000
Total paid-in capital	$6,420,000	$4,920,000

3. Dividend allocation table.

	Common	Preferred
2010 ($50,000)		
Preferred—current year (12,000 shares × $10 = $120,000)	$ 0	$ 50,000
Common—remainder (300,000 shares outstanding)	0	0
Total for the year	$ 0	$ 50,000
2011 ($300,000)		
Preferred—dividend in arrears from 2010 ($120,000 − $50,000)	$ 0	$ 70,000
Preferred—current year	0	120,000
Common—remainder (400,000 shares outstanding)	110,000	0
Total for the year	$110,000	$190,000
Dividends per share		
2010	$ 0.00	$ 4.17
2011	$ 0.28	$ 15.83

4. Journal entries.

a. For 2010 (no-par stock without a stated value):

Jan. 2	Cash	2,400,000	
	Common Stock, No-Par Value		2,400,000
	Issued 200,000 shares of no-par common		
	stock at $12 per share.		

b. For 2010 (no-par stock with a stated value):

Jan. 2	Cash	2,400,000	
	Common Stock, $10 Stated Value		2,000,000
	Paid-In Capital in Excess of		
	Stated Value, Common Stock		400,000
	Issued 200,000 shares of $10 stated value		
	common stock at $12 per share.		

DEMONSTRATION PROBLEM 2

Precision Company began year 2011 with the following balances in its stockholders' equity accounts.

Common stock—$10 par, 500,000 shares authorized, 200,000 shares issued and outstanding	$2,000,000
Paid-in capital in excess of par, common stock	1,000,000
Retained earnings	5,000,000
Total	$8,000,000

All outstanding common stock was issued for $15 per share when the company was created. Prepare journal entries to account for the following transactions during year 2011.

Jan. 10 The board declared a $0.10 cash dividend per share to shareholders of record Jan. 28.
Feb. 15 Paid the cash dividend declared on January 10.
Mar. 31 Declared a 20% stock dividend. The market value of the stock is $18 per share.
May 1 Distributed the stock dividend declared on March 31.
July 1 Purchased 30,000 shares of treasury stock at $20 per share.
Sept. 1 Sold 20,000 treasury shares at $26 cash per share.
Dec. 1 Sold the remaining 10,000 shares of treasury stock at $7 cash per share.

PLANNING THE SOLUTION

- Calculate the total cash dividend to record by multiplying the cash dividend declared by the number of shares as of the date of record.
- Decide whether the stock dividend is a small or large dividend. Then analyze each event to determine the accounts affected and the appropriate amounts to be recorded.

SOLUTION TO DEMONSTRATION PROBLEM 2

Jan. 10	Retained Earnings	20,000	
	Common Dividend Payable		20,000
	Declared a $0.10 per share cash dividend.		
Feb. 15	Common Dividend Payable	20,000	
	Cash		20,000
	Paid $0.10 per share cash dividend.		
Mar. 31	Retained Earnings	720,000	
	Common Stock Dividend Distributable		400,000
	Paid-In Capital in Excess of		
	Par Value, Common Stock		320,000
	Declared a small stock dividend of 20% or		
	40,000 shares; market value is $18 per share.		
May 1	Common Stock Dividend Distributable	400,000	
	Common Stock		400,000
	Distributed 40,000 shares of common stock.		
July 1	Treasury Stock, Common	600,000	
	Cash		600,000
	Purchased 30,000 common shares at $20 per share.		
Sept. 1	Cash	520,000	
	Treasury Stock, Common		400,000
	Paid-In Capital, Treasury Stock		120,000
	Sold 20,000 treasury shares at $26 per share.		
Dec. 1	Cash	70,000	
	Paid-In Capital, Treasury Stock	120,000	
	Retained Earnings	10,000	
	Treasury Stock, Common		200,000
	Sold 10,000 treasury shares at $7 per share.		

Summary

C1 **Identify characteristics of corporations and their organization.** Corporations are legal entities whose stockholders are not liable for its debts. Stock is easily transferred, and the life of a corporation does not end with the incapacity of a stockholder. A corporation acts through its agents, who are its officers and managers. Corporations are regulated and subject to income taxes. Authorized stock is the stock that a corporation's charter authorizes it to sell. Issued stock is the portion of authorized shares sold. Par value stock is a value per share assigned by the charter. No-par value stock is stock *not* assigned a value per share by the charter. Stated value stock is no-par stock to which the directors assign a value per share.

C2 **Explain characteristics of, and distribute dividends between, common and preferred stock.** Preferred stock has a priority (or senior status) relative to common stock in one or more areas, usually (1) dividends and (2) assets in case of liquidation. Preferred stock usually does not carry voting rights and can be convertible or callable. Convertibility permits the holder to convert preferred to common. Callability permits the issuer to buy back preferred stock under specified conditions. Preferred stockholders usually hold the right to dividend distributions before common stockholders. When preferred stock is cumulative and in arrears, the amount in arrears must be distributed to preferred before any dividends are distributed to common.

C3 **Explain the items reported in retained earnings.** Stockholders' equity is made up of (1) paid-in capital and (2) retained earnings. Paid-in capital consists of funds raised by stock issuances. Retained earnings consists of cumulative net income (losses) not distributed. Many companies face statutory and contractual restrictions on retained earnings. Corporations can voluntarily appropriate retained earnings to inform others about their disposition. Prior period adjustments are corrections of errors in prior financial statements.

A1 **Compute earnings per share and describe its use.** A company with a simple capital structure computes basic EPS by dividing net income less any preferred dividends by the weighted-average number of outstanding common shares. A company with a complex capital structure must usually report both basic and diluted EPS.

A2 **Compute price-earnings ratio and describe its use in analysis.** A common stock's price-earnings (PE) ratio is computed by dividing the stock's market value (price) per share by its EPS. A stock's PE is based on expectations that can prove to be better or worse than eventual performance.

A3 **Compute dividend yield and explain its use in analysis.** Dividend yield is the ratio of a stock's annual cash dividends per share to its market value (price) per share. Dividend yield can be compared with the yield of other companies to determine whether the stock is expected to be an income or growth stock.

A4 **Compute book value and explain its use in analysis.** Book value per common share is equity applicable to common shares divided by the number of outstanding common shares. Book value per preferred share is equity applicable to preferred shares divided by the number of outstanding preferred shares.

P1 **Record the issuance of corporate stock.** When stock is issued, its par or stated value is credited to the stock account and any excess is credited to a separate contributed capital account. If a stock has neither par nor stated value, the entire proceeds are credited to the stock account. Stockholders must contribute assets equal to minimum legal capital or be potentially liable for the deficiency.

P2 **Record transactions involving cash dividends, stock dividends, and stock splits.** Cash dividends involve three events. On the date of declaration, the directors bind the company to pay the dividend. A dividend declaration reduces retained earnings and creates a current liability. On the date of record, recipients of the dividend are identified. On the date of payment, cash is paid to stockholders and the current liability is removed. Neither a stock dividend nor a stock split alters the value of the company. However, the value of each share is less due to the distribution of additional shares. The distribution of additional shares is according to individual stockholders' ownership percent. Small stock dividends ($\leq 25\%$) are recorded by capitalizing retained earnings equal to the market value of distributed shares. Large stock dividends ($>25\%$) are recorded by capitalizing retained earnings equal to the par or stated value of distributed shares. Stock splits do not necessitate journal entries but do necessitate changes in the description of stock.

P3 **Record purchases and sales of treasury stock and the retirement of stock.** When a corporation purchases its own previously issued stock, it debits the cost of these shares to Treasury Stock. Treasury stock is subtracted from equity in the balance sheet. If treasury stock is reissued, any proceeds in excess of cost are credited to Paid-In Capital, Treasury Stock. If the proceeds are less than cost, they are debited to Paid-In Capital, Treasury Stock to the extent a credit balance exists. Any remaining amount is debited to Retained Earnings. When stock is retired, all accounts related to the stock are removed.

Guidance Answers to Decision Maker and Decision Ethics

Entrepreneur The 50% stock dividend provides you no direct income. A stock dividend often reveals management's optimistic expectations about the future and can improve a stock's marketability by making it affordable to more investors. Accordingly, a stock dividend usually reveals "good news" and because of this, it likely increases (slightly) the market value for your stock. The same conclusions apply to the 3-for-2 stock split.

Concert Organizer You have two basic options: (1) different classes of common stock or (2) common and preferred stock. Your objective is to issue to yourself stock that has all or a majority of the voting power. The other class of stock would carry limited or no voting rights. In this way, you maintain control and are able to raise the necessary funds.

Money Manager Since one company requires a payment of $19 for each $1 of earnings, and the other requires $25, you would prefer the stock with the PE of 19; it is a better deal given identical prospects. You should make sure these companies' earnings computations are roughly the same, for example, no extraordinary items, unusual events, and so forth. Also, your PE estimates for these companies do matter. If you are willing to pay $29 for each $1 of earnings for these companies, you obviously expect both to exceed current market expectations.

Investor Book value reflects recorded values. BMX's book value is $4 per common share. Stock price reflects the market's expectation of net asset value (both tangible and intangible items). BMX's market value is $7 per common share. Comparing these figures suggests BMX's market value of net assets is higher than its recorded values (by an amount of $7 versus $4 per share).

Guidance Answers to Quick Checks

1. (*b*)

2. A corporation pays taxes on its income, and its stockholders normally pay personal income taxes (at the 15% rate or lower) on any cash dividends received from the corporation.

3. A proxy is a legal document used to transfer a stockholder's right to vote to another person.

4. (*a*)

5. A stock premium is an amount in excess of par (or stated) value paid by purchasers of newly issued stock.

6. Minimum legal capital intends to protect creditors of a corporation by obligating stockholders to some minimum level of equity financing and by constraining a corporation from excessive payments to stockholders.

7. Common Dividend Payable is a current liability account.

8. The date of declaration, date of record, and date of payment.

9. A dividend is a legal liability at the date of declaration, on which date it is recorded as a liability.

10. A stock dividend does not transfer assets to stockholders, but it does require an amount of retained earnings to be transferred to a contributed capital account(s).

11. A small stock dividend is 25% or less of the previous outstanding shares. A large stock dividend is more than 25%.

12. Retained earnings equal to the distributable shares' market value should be capitalized for a small stock dividend.

13. Typically, preferred stock has a preference in receipt of dividends and in distribution of assets.

14. (a)

15. (b)

Total cash dividend	$288,000
To preferred shareholders	135,000*
Remainder to common shareholders	$153,000

* 9,000 × $50 × 10% × 3 years = $135,000.

16. (b)

17. No. The shares are an investment for Southern Co. and are issued and outstanding shares for Northern Corp.

18. Treasury stock does not affect the number of authorized or issued shares, but it reduces the outstanding shares.

19. (a)

Key Terms

mhhe.com/wildFAP20e

Appropriated retained earnings (p. 525)
Authorized stock (p. 511)
Basic earnings per share (p. 527)
Book value per common share (p. 528)
Book value per preferred share (p. 528)
Call price (p. 521)
Callable preferred stock (p. 521)
Capital stock (p. 511)
Changes in accounting estimates (p. 525)
Common stock (p. 510)
Complex capital structure (p. 527)
Convertible preferred stock (p. 520)
Corporation (p. 508)
Cumulative preferred stock (p. 519)
Date of declaration (p. 515)
Date of payment (p. 515)
Date of record (p. 515)
Diluted earnings per share (p. 527)
Dilutive securities (p. 527)

Discount on stock (p. 513)
Dividend in arrears (p. 519)
Dividend yield (p. 528)
Earnings per share (EPS) (p. 527)
Financial leverage (p. 521)
Large stock dividend (p. 516)
Liquidating cash dividend (p. 516)
Market value per share (p. 511)
Minimum legal capital (p. 511)
Noncumulative preferred stock (p. 519)
Nonparticipating preferred stock (p. 520)
No-par value stock (p. 511)
Organization expenses (p. 509)
Paid-in capital (p. 512)
Paid-in capital in excess of par value (p. 513)
Participating preferred stock (p. 520)
Par value (p. 511)
Par value stock (p. 511)

Preemptive right (p. 510)
Preferred stock (p. 518)
Premium on stock (p. 513)
Price-earnings (PE) ratio (p. 527)
Prior period adjustments (p. 525)
Proxy (p. 509)
Restricted retained earnings (p. 524)
Retained earnings (p. 512)
Retained earnings deficit (p. 515)
Reverse stock split (p. 518)
Simple capital structure (p. 527)
Small stock dividend (p. 516)
Stated value stock (p. 512)
Statement of stockholders' equity (p. 525)
Stock dividend (p. 516)
Stock options (p. 525)
Stock split (p. 518)
Stockholders' equity (p. 512)
Treasury stock (p. 522)

Multiple Choice Quiz

Answers on p. 549

mhhe.com/wildFAP20e

Additional Quiz Questions are available at the book's Website.

1. A corporation issues 6,000 shares of $5 par value common stock for $8 cash per share. The entry to record this transaction includes:

  a. A debit to Paid-In Capital in Excess of Par Value for $18,000.

  b. A credit to Common Stock for $48,000.

  c. A credit to Paid-In Capital in Excess of Par Value for $30,000.

  d. A credit to Cash for $48,000.

  e. A credit to Common Stock for $30,000.

2. A company reports net income of $75,000. Its weighted-average common shares outstanding is 19,000. It has no other stock outstanding. Its earnings per share is:

  a. $4.69

  b. $3.95

  c. $3.75

  d. $2.08

  e. $4.41

3. A company has 5,000 shares of $100 par preferred stock and 50,000 shares of $10 par common stock outstanding. Its total stockholders' equity is $2,000,000. Its book value per common share is:

- **a.** $100.00
- **b.** $ 10.00
- **c.** $ 40.00
- **d.** $ 30.00
- **e.** $ 36.36

4. A company paid cash dividends of $0.81 per share. Its earnings per share is $6.95 and its market price per share is $45.00. Its dividend yield is:

- **a.** 1.8%
- **b.** 11.7%
- **c.** 15.4%
- **d.** 55.6%
- **e.** 8.6%

5. A company's shares have a market value of $85 per share. Its net income is $3,500,000, and its weighted-average common shares outstanding is 700,000. Its price-earnings ratio is:

- **a.** 5.9
- **b.** 425.0
- **c.** 17.0
- **d.** 10.4
- **e.** 41.2

Icon denotes assignments that involve decision making.

Discussion Questions

1. What are organization expenses? Provide examples.

2. How are organization expenses reported?

3. Who is responsible for directing a corporation's affairs?

4. What is the preemptive right of common stockholders?

5. List the general rights of common stockholders.

6. What is the difference between authorized shares and outstanding shares?

7. Why would an investor find convertible preferred stock attractive?

8. What is the difference between the market value per share and the par value per share?

9. What is the difference between the par value and the call price of a share of preferred stock?

10. Identify and explain the importance of the three dates relevant to corporate dividends.

11. Why is the term *liquidating dividend* used to describe cash dividends debited against paid-in capital accounts?

12. How does declaring a stock dividend affect the corporation's assets, liabilities, and total equity? What are the effects of the eventual distribution of that stock?

13. What is the difference between a stock dividend and a stock split?

14. Courts have ruled that a stock dividend is not taxable income to stockholders. What justifies this decision?

15. How does the purchase of treasury stock affect the purchaser's assets and total equity?

16. Why do laws place limits on treasury stock purchases?

17. How are EPS results computed for a corporation with a simple capital structure?

18. What is a stock option?

19. How is book value per share computed for a corporation with no preferred stock? What is the main limitation of using book value per share to value a corporation?

20. Review the 2009 balance sheet for Nokia in Appendix A and list the amounts for treasury shares and retained earnings. **NOKIA**

21. Refer to **Research In Motion**'s 2010 balance sheet in Appendix A. How many shares of common stock are authorized? How many shares of voting common stock are issued? **RIM**

22. Refer to the 2009 balance sheet for **Palm** in Appendix A. What is the par value per share of its common stock? Suggest a rationale for the amount of par value it assigned. **Palm**

23. Refer to the financial statements for **Apple** in Appendix A. What are its cash proceeds from issuance of common stock *and* its cash repurchases of common stock for the year ended September 26, 2009? Explain. **Apple**

---

connect _____

Of the following statements, which are true for the corporate form of organization?

1. Owners are not agents of the corporation.

2. It is a separate legal entity.

3. It has a limited life.

4. Capital is more easily accumulated than with most other forms of organization.

5. Corporate income that is distributed to shareholders is usually taxed twice.

6. Owners have unlimited liability for corporate debts.

7. Ownership rights cannot be easily transferred.

QUICK STUDY

QS 13-1
Characteristics of corporations
C1

QS 13-2

Issuance of common stock

P1

Prepare the journal entry to record Channel One Company's issuance of 100,000 shares of $0.50 par value common stock assuming the shares sell for:

a. $0.50 cash per share.

b. $2 cash per share.

QS 13-3

Issuance of no-par common stock

P1

Prepare the journal entry to record Selectist Company's issuance of 104,000 shares of no-par value common stock assuming the shares:

a. Sell for $15 cash per share.

b. Are exchanged for land valued at $1,560,000.

QS 13-4

Issuance of par and stated value common stock

P1

Prepare the journal entry to record Typist Company's issuance of 250,000 shares of its common stock assuming the shares have a:

a. $1 par value and sell for $10 cash per share.

b. $1 stated value and sell for $10 cash per share.

QS 13-5

Issuance of common stock

P1

Prepare the issuer's journal entry for each separate transaction. (*a*) On March 1, Edgar Co. issues 44,500 shares of $4 par value common stock for $255,000 cash. (*b*) On April 1, GT Co. issues no-par value common stock for $50,000 cash. (*c*) On April 6, MTV issues 2,000 shares of $20 par value common stock for $35,000 of inventory, $135,000 of machinery, and acceptance of an $84,000 note payable.

QS 13-6

Issuance of preferred stock

P1 P2

a. Prepare the journal entry to record Stefan Company's issuance of 12,000 shares of $50 par value 6% cumulative preferred stock for $75 cash per share.

b. Assuming the facts in part 1, if Stefan declares a year-end cash dividend, what is the amount of dividend paid to preferred shareholders? (Assume no dividends in arrears.)

QS 13-7

Accounting for cash dividends

P2

Prepare journal entries to record the following transactions for Emerson Corporation.

April 15   Declared a cash dividend payable to common stockholders of $40,000.
May 15   Date of record is May 15 for the cash dividend declared on April 15.
May 31   Paid the dividend declared on April 15.

QS 13-8

Dividend allocation between classes of shareholders

C2

Stockholders' equity of STIX Company consists of 75,000 shares of $5 par value, 8% cumulative preferred stock and 200,000 shares of $1 par value common stock. Both classes of stock have been outstanding since the company's inception. STIX did not declare any dividends in the prior year, but it now declares and pays a $108,000 cash dividend at the current year-end. Determine the amount distributed to each class of stockholders for this two-year-old company.

QS 13-9

Accounting for small stock dividend

P2

The stockholders' equity section of Zacman Company's balance sheet as of April 1 follows. On April 2, Zacman declares and distributes a 10% stock dividend. The stock's per share market value on April 2 is $25 (prior to the dividend). Prepare the stockholders' equity section immediately after the stock dividend.

Common stock—$5 par value, 375,000 shares authorized, 150,000 shares issued and outstanding	$ 750,000
Paid-in capital in excess of par value, common stock	352,500
Retained earnings	633,000
Total stockholders' equity	$1,735,500

QS 13-10

Accounting for changes in estimates; error adjustments

C3

Answer the following questions related to a company's activities for the current year:

1. After using an expected useful life of 20 years and no salvage value to depreciate its office equipment over the preceding 15 years, the company decided early this year that the equipment will last only two more years. How should the effects of this decision be reported in the current year financial statements?

2. A review of the notes payable files discovers that two years ago the company reported the entire amount of a payment (principal and interest) on an installment note payable as interest expense. This mistake had a material effect on the amount of income in that year. How should the correction be reported in the current year financial statements?

On May 3, Lassman Corporation purchased 3,000 shares of its own stock for $27,000 cash. On November 4, Lassman reissued 750 shares of this treasury stock for $7,080. Prepare the May 3 and November 4 journal entries to record Lassman's purchase and reissuance of treasury stock.

QS 13-11
Purchase and sale of treasury stock P3

Barnes Company earned net income of $450,000 this year. The number of common shares outstanding during the entire year was 200,000, and preferred shareholders received a $10,000 cash dividend. Compute Barnes Company's basic earnings per share.

QS 13-12
Basic earnings per share A1

Campbell Company reports net income of $1,200,000 for the year. It has no preferred stock, and its weighted-average common shares outstanding is 300,000 shares. Compute its basic earnings per share.

QS 13-13
Basic earnings per share A1

Compute Fox Company's price-earnings ratio if its common stock has a market value of $30.75 per share and its EPS is $4.10. Would an analyst likely consider this stock potentially over- or underpriced? Explain.

QS 13-14
Price-earnings ratio A2

Fiona Company expects to pay a $2.10 per share cash dividend this year on its common stock. The current market value of Fiona stock is $28.50 per share. Compute the expected dividend yield on the Fiona stock. Would you classify the Fiona stock as a growth or an income stock? Explain.

QS 13-15
Dividend yield A3

The stockholders' equity section of Axel Company's balance sheet follows. The preferred stock's call price is $30. Determine the book value per share of the common stock.

QS 13-16
Book value per common share

A4

Preferred stock—5% cumulative, $10 par value, 10,000 shares authorized, issued and outstanding	$100,000
Common stock—$5 par value, 100,000 shares authorized, 75,000 shares issued and outstanding	375,000
Retained earnings	445,000
Total stockholders' equity	$920,000

Air France-KLM reports the following equity information for its fiscal year ended March 31, 2009 (euros in millions). Prepare its journal entry, using its account titles, to record the issuance of capital stock assuming that its entire par value stock was issued on March 31, 2009, for cash.

QS 13-17
International equity disclosures

P1

March 31	2009
Issued capital	€2,552
Additional paid-in capital	765

connect

Describe how each of the following characteristics of organizations applies to corporations.

1. Duration of life	5. Owner authority and control
2. Owner liability	6. Ease of formation
3. Legal status	7. Transferability of ownership
4. Tax status of income	8. Ability to raise large capital amounts

EXERCISES

Exercise 13-1
Characteristics of corporations

C1

Aloha Corporation issues 6,000 shares of its common stock for $144,000 cash on February 20. Prepare journal entries to record this event under each of the following separate situations.
1. The stock has neither par nor stated value.
2. The stock has a $20 par value.
3. The stock has an $8 stated value.

Exercise 13-2
Accounting for par, stated, and no-par stock issuances

P1

Exercise 13-3
Recording stock issuances
P1

Prepare journal entries to record the following four separate issuances of stock.

1. A corporation issued 2,000 shares of no-par common stock to its promoters in exchange for their efforts, estimated to be worth $30,000. The stock has no stated value.

2. A corporation issued 2,000 shares of no-par common stock to its promoters in exchange for their efforts, estimated to be worth $30,000. The stock has a $1 per share stated value.

3. A corporation issued 4,000 shares of $10 par value common stock for $70,000 cash.

4. A corporation issued 1,000 shares of $100 par value preferred stock for $120,000 cash.

Exercise 13-4
Stock issuance for noncash assets
P1

Soku Company issues 36,000 shares of $9 par value common stock in exchange for land and a building. The land is valued at $225,000 and the building at $360,000. Prepare the journal entry to record issuance of the stock in exchange for the land and building.

Exercise 13-5
Identifying characteristics of preferred stock
C2

Match each description 1 through 6 with the characteristic of preferred stock that it best describes by writing the letter of that characteristic in the blank next to each description.

A. Cumulative   **B.** Noncumulative   **C.** Convertible

D. Callable   **E.** Nonparticipating   **F.** Participating

_____ **1.** Holders of the stock lose any dividends that are not declared in the current year.

_____ **2.** The issuing corporation can retire the stock by paying a prespecified price.

_____ **3.** Holders of the stock can receive dividends exceeding the stated rate under certain conditions.

_____ **4.** Holders of the stock are not entitled to receive dividends in excess of the stated rate.

_____ **5.** Holders of this stock can exchange it for shares of common stock.

_____ **6.** Holders of the stock are entitled to receive current and all past dividends before common stockholders receive any dividends.

Exercise 13-6
Stock dividends and splits
P2

On June 30, 2011, Quinn Corporation's common stock is priced at $31 per share before any stock dividend or split, and the stockholders' equity section of its balance sheet appears as follows.

Common stock—$10 par value, 60,000 shares authorized, 25,000 shares issued and outstanding	$250,000
Paid-in capital in excess of par value, common stock	100,000
Retained earnings	330,000
Total stockholders' equity	$680,000

1. Assume that the company declares and immediately distributes a 100% stock dividend. This event is recorded by capitalizing retained earnings equal to the stock's par value. Answer these questions about stockholders' equity as it exists *after* issuing the new shares.

    a. What is the retained earnings balance?

Check   (1*b*) $680,000

    b. What is the amount of total stockholders' equity?

    c. How many shares are outstanding?

2. Assume that the company implements a 2-for-1 stock split instead of the stock dividend in part 1. Answer these questions about stockholders' equity as it exists *after* issuing the new shares.

    (2*a*) $330,000

    a. What is the retained earnings balance?

    b. What is the amount of total stockholders' equity?

    c. How many shares are outstanding?

3. Explain the difference, if any, to a stockholder from receiving new shares distributed under a large stock dividend versus a stock split.

Exercise 13-7
Stock dividends and per share book values
P2

The stockholders' equity of Whiz.com Company at the beginning of the day on February 5 follows.

Common stock—$25 par value, 150,000 shares authorized, 60,000 shares issued and outstanding	$1,500,000
Paid-in capital in excess of par value, common stock	525,000
Retained earnings	675,000
Total stockholders' equity	$2,700,000

On February 5, the directors declare a 20% stock dividend distributable on February 28 to the February 15 stockholders of record. The stock's market value is $40 per share on February 5 before the stock dividend. The stock's market value is $34 per share on February 28.

1. Prepare entries to record both the dividend declaration and its distribution.

2. One stockholder owned 750 shares on February 5 before the dividend. Compute the book value per share and total book value of this stockholder's shares immediately before *and* after the stock dividend of February 5.

3. Compute the total market value of the investor's shares in part 2 as of February 5 and February 28.

Check (2) Book value per share: before, $45; after, $37.50

Wade's outstanding stock consists of 40,000 shares of *noncumulative* 7.5% preferred stock with a $10 par value and also 100,000 shares of common stock with a $1 par value. During its first four years of operation, the corporation declared and paid the following total cash dividends.

2011	$ 10,000
2012	24,000
2013	100,000
2014	196,000

Determine the amount of dividends paid each year to each of the two classes of stockholders: preferred and common. Also compute the total dividends paid to each class for the four years combined.

Exercise 13-8
Dividends on common and noncumulative preferred stock
C2

Check 4-year total paid to preferred, $94,000

Use the data in Exercise 13-8 to determine the amount of dividends paid each year to each of the two classes of stockholders assuming that the preferred stock is *cumulative*. Also determine the total dividends paid to each class for the four years combined.

Exercise 13-9
Dividends on common and cumulative preferred stock C2

On October 10, the stockholders' equity of Noble Systems appears as follows.

Common stock—$10 par value, 36,000 shares authorized, issued, and outstanding	$360,000
Paid-in capital in excess of par value, common stock	108,000
Retained earnings	432,000
Total stockholders' equity	$900,000

1. Prepare journal entries to record the following transactions for Noble Systems.

a. Purchased 4,500 shares of its own common stock at $30 per share on October 11.

b. Sold 1,200 treasury shares on November 1 for $36 cash per share.

c. Sold all remaining treasury shares on November 25 for $25 cash per share.

2. Explain how the company's equity section changes after the October 11 treasury stock purchase, and prepare the revised equity section of its balance sheet at that date.

Exercise 13-10
Recording and reporting treasury stock transactions
P3

Check (1c) Dr. Retained Earnings, $9,300

The following information is available for Ballard Company for the year ended December 31, 2011.

a. Balance of retained earnings, December 31, 2010, prior to discovery of error, $850,000.

b. Cash dividends declared and paid during 2011, $15,000.

c. It neglected to record 2009 depreciation expense of $55,600, which is net of $5,500 in income taxes.

d. The company earned $205,000 in 2011 net income.

Prepare a 2011 statement of retained earnings for Ballard Company.

Exercise 13-11
Preparing a statement of retained earnings
C3

Guess Company reports $648,500 of net income for 2011 and declares $102,500 of cash dividends on its preferred stock for 2011. At the end of 2011, the company had 260,000 weighted-average shares of common stock.

1. What amount of net income is available to common stockholders for 2011?

2. What is the company's basic EPS for 2011?

Exercise 13-12
Earnings per share
A1

Check (2) $2.10

Exercise 13-13
Earnings per share
A1

Check (2) $3.56

Franklin Company reports $698,000 of net income for 2011 and declares $75,500 of cash dividends on its preferred stock for 2011. At the end of 2011, the company had 175,000 weighted-average shares of common stock.

1. What amount of net income is available to common stockholders for 2011?

2. What is the company's basic EPS for 2011? Round your answer to the nearest whole cent.

Exercise 13-14
Dividend yield computation and interpretation
A3

Compute the dividend yield for each of these four separate companies. Which company's stock would probably *not* be classified as an income stock? Explain.

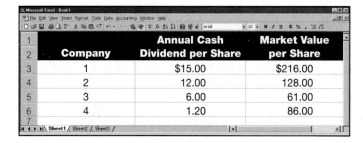

Company	Annual Cash Dividend per Share	Market Value per Share
1	$15.00	$216.00
2	12.00	128.00
3	6.00	61.00
4	1.20	86.00

Exercise 13-15
Price-earnings ratio computation and interpretation
A2

Compute the price-earnings ratio for each of these four separate companies. Which stock might an analyst likely investigate as being potentially undervalued by the market? Explain.

Company	Earnings per Share	Market Value per Share
1	$10.00	$166.00
2	9.00	90.00
3	6.50	84.50
4	40.00	240.00

Exercise 13-16
Book value per share
A4

The equity section of Webster Corporation's balance sheet shows the following.

Preferred stock—5% cumulative, $10 par value, $15 call price, 10,000 shares issued and outstanding	$100,000
Common stock—$10 par value, 55,000 shares issued and outstanding	550,000
Retained earnings	267,500
Total stockholders' equity	$917,500

Determine the book value per share of the preferred and common stock under two separate situations.

Check (1) Book value of common, $13.95

1. No preferred dividends are in arrears.

2. Three years of preferred dividends are in arrears.

Exercise 13-17
Accounting for equity under IFRS
C3 P1

Unilever Group reports the following equity information for the years ended December 31, 2007 and 2008 (euros in millions).

December 31	2008	2007
Share capital	€ 484	€ 484
Share premium	121	153
Other reserves	(6,469)	(3,412)
Retained profit	15,812	15,162
Shareholders' equity	€ 9,948	€12,387

1. For each of the three account titles *share capital, share premium,* and *retained profit,* match it with the usual account title applied under U.S. GAAP from the following options:

   a. Paid-in capital in excess of par value, common stock

   b. Retained earnings

   c. Common stock, par value

2. Prepare Unilever's journal entry, using its account titles, to record the issuance of capital stock assuming that its entire par value stock was issued on December 31, 2007, for cash.

3. What were Unilever's 2008 dividends assuming that only dividends and income impacted retained profit for 2008 and that its 2008 income totaled €2,692?

Kroll Corporation reports the following components of stockholders' equity on December 31, 2011.

Exercise 13-18
Cash dividends, treasury stock, and statement of retained earnings

C3 P2 P3

Common stock—$25 par value, 40,000 shares authorized, 30,000 shares issued and outstanding	$ 750,000
Paid-in capital in excess of par value, common stock	50,000
Retained earnings	260,000
Total stockholders' equity	$1,060,000

In year 2012, the following transactions affected its stockholders' equity accounts.

Jan. 2 Purchased 2,000 shares of its own stock at $25 cash per share.
Jan. 7 Directors declared a $2 per share cash dividend payable on Feb. 28 to the Feb. 9 stockholders of record.
Feb. 28 Paid the dividend declared on January 7.
July 9 Sold 500 of its treasury shares at $30 cash per share.
Aug. 27 Sold 1,500 of its treasury shares at $23 cash per share.
Sept. 9 Directors declared a $2 per share cash dividend payable on October 22 to the September 23 stockholders of record.
Oct. 22 Paid the dividend declared on September 9.
Dec. 31 Closed the $8,000 credit balance (from net income) in the Income Summary account to Retained Earnings.

Required

1. Prepare journal entries to record each of these transactions for 2012.
2. Prepare a statement of retained earnings for the year ended December 31, 2012.
3. Prepare the stockholders' equity section of the company's balance sheet as of December 31, 2012.

connect

Oxygen Co. is incorporated at the beginning of this year and engages in a number of transactions. The following journal entries impacted its stockholders' equity during its first year of operations.

PROBLEM SET A

Problem 13-1A
Stockholders' equity transactions and analysis

C2 P1

a.	Cash	150,000	
	Common Stock, $25 Par Value		125,000
	Paid-In Capital in Excess of Par Value, Common Stock		25,000
b.	Organization Expenses	75,000	
	Common Stock, $25 Par Value		62,500
	Paid-In Capital in Excess of Par Value, Common Stock		12,500
c.	Cash	21,500	
	Accounts Receivable	7,500	
	Building	30,000	
	Notes Payable		19,000
	Common Stock, $25 Par Value		25,000
	Paid-In Capital in Excess of Par Value, Common Stock		15,000

[continued on next page]

[continued from previous page]

d.			
	Cash	60,000	
	Common Stock, $25 Par Value		37,500
	Paid-In Capital in Excess of		
	Par Value, Common Stock		22,500

Required

1. Explain the transaction(s) underlying each journal entry (*a*) through (*d*).

Check   (2) 10,000 shares

(3) $250,000

(4) $325,000

2. How many shares of common stock are outstanding at year-end?
3. What is the amount of minimum legal capital (based on par value) at year-end?
4. What is the total paid-in capital at year-end?
5. What is the book value per share of the common stock at year-end if total paid-in capital plus retained earnings equals $347,500?

Problem 13-2A

Cash dividends, treasury stock, and statement of retained earnings

C3 P2 P3

Context Corporation reports the following components of stockholders' equity on December 31, 2011.

Common stock—$10 par value, 50,000 shares authorized,		
20,000 shares issued and outstanding	$200,000	
Paid-in capital in excess of par value, common stock	30,000	
Retained earnings	135,000	
Total stockholders' equity	$365,000	

In year 2012, the following transactions affected its stockholders' equity accounts.

Jan.   1   Purchased 2,000 shares of its own stock at $20 cash per share.
Jan.   5   Directors declared a $2 per share cash dividend payable on Feb. 28 to the Feb. 5 stockholders of record.
Feb. 28   Paid the dividend declared on January 5.
July   6   Sold 750 of its treasury shares at $24 cash per share.
Aug. 22   Sold 1,250 of its treasury shares at $17 cash per share.
Sept.   5   Directors declared a $2 per share cash dividend payable on October 28 to the September 25 stockholders of record.
Oct. 28   Paid the dividend declared on September 5.
Dec. 31   Closed the $194,000 credit balance (from net income) in the Income Summary account to Retained Earnings.

Required

1. Prepare journal entries to record each of these transactions for 2012.

Check   (2) Retained earnings, Dec. 31, 2012, $252,250.

2. Prepare a statement of retained earnings for the year ended December 31, 2012.
3. Prepare the stockholders' equity section of the company's balance sheet as of December 31, 2012.

Problem 13-3A

Equity analysis—journal entries and account balances

P2

At September 30, the end of Excel Company's third quarter, the following stockholders' equity accounts are reported.

Common stock, $12 par value	$720,000
Paid-in capital in excess of par value, common stock	180,000
Retained earnings	640,000

In the fourth quarter, the following entries related to its equity are recorded.

Oct. 2	Retained Earnings	120,000	
	Common Dividend Payable		120,000
Oct. 25	Common Dividend Payable	120,000	
	Cash		120,000
Oct. 31	Retained Earnings	150,000	
	Common Stock Dividend Distributable		72,000
	Paid-In Capital in Excess of		
	Par Value, Common Stock		78,000

[continued on next page]

[continued from previous page]

Nov. 5	Common Stock Dividend Distributable	72,000	
	Common Stock, $12 Par Value		72,000
Dec. 1	Memo—Change the title of the common stock account to reflect the new par value of $4.		
Dec. 31	Income Summary	420,000	
	Retained Earnings		420,000

Required

1. Explain the transaction(s) underlying each journal entry.
2. Complete the following table showing the equity account balances at each indicated date (include the balances from September 30).

	Oct. 2	Oct. 25	Oct. 31	Nov. 5	Dec. 1	Dec. 31
Common stock	$____	$____	$____	$____	$____	$____
Common stock dividend distributable	____	____	____	____	____	____
Paid-in capital in excess of par, common stock	____	____	____	____	____	____
Retained earnings	____	____	____	____	____	____
Total equity	$____	$____	$____	$____	$____	$____

Check Total equity: Oct. 2, $1,420,000; Dec. 31, $1,840,000

The equity sections from Salazar Group's 2011 and 2012 year-end balance sheets follow.

Problem 13-4A
Analysis of changes in stockholders' equity accounts

C3 P2 P3

Stockholders' Equity (December 31, 2011)

Common stock—$4 par value, 50,000 shares authorized, 20,000 shares issued and outstanding	$ 80,000
Paid-in capital in excess of par value, common stock	60,000
Retained earnings	160,000
Total stockholders' equity	$300,000

Stockholders' Equity (December 31, 2012)

Common stock—$4 par value, 50,000 shares authorized, 23,700 shares issued, 1,500 shares in treasury	$ 94,800
Paid-in capital in excess of par value, common stock	89,600
Retained earnings ($15,000 restricted by treasury stock)	200,000
	384,400
Less cost of treasury stock	(15,000)
Total stockholders' equity	$369,400

The following transactions and events affected its equity during year 2012.

Jan. 5   Declared a $0.50 per share cash dividend, date of record January 10.
Mar. 20   Purchased treasury stock for cash.
Apr. 5   Declared a $0.50 per share cash dividend, date of record April 10.
July 5   Declared a $0.50 per share cash dividend, date of record July 10.
July 31   Declared a 20% stock dividend when the stock's market value is $12 per share.
Aug. 14   Issued the stock dividend that was declared on July 31.
Oct. 5   Declared a $0.50 per share cash dividend, date of record October 10.

Required

1. How many common shares are outstanding on each cash dividend date?
2. What is the total dollar amount for each of the four cash dividends?
3. What is the amount of the capitalization of retained earnings for the stock dividend?
4. What is the per share cost of the treasury stock purchased?
5. How much net income did the company earn during year 2012?

Check (3) $44,400
(4) $10
(5) $124,000

Problem 13-5A

Computation of book values and
dividend allocations

C2 A4

Razz Corporation's common stock is currently selling on a stock exchange at $170 per share, and its current balance sheet shows the following stockholders' equity section.

Preferred stock—5% cumulative, $___ par value, 1,000 shares authorized, issued, and outstanding	$100,000
Common stock—$___ par value, 4,000 shares authorized, issued, and outstanding	160,000
Retained earnings	300,000
Total stockholders' equity	$560,000

Required (Round per share amounts to cents.)

1. What is the current market value (price) of this corporation's common stock?
2. What are the par values of the corporation's preferred stock and its common stock?
3. If no dividends are in arrears, what are the book values per share of the preferred stock and the common stock?

Check (4) Book value of common, $112.50

4. If two years' preferred dividends are in arrears, what are the book values per share of the preferred stock and the common stock?

(5) Book value of common, $110

5. If two years' preferred dividends are in arrears and the preferred stock is callable at $110 per share, what are the book values per share of the preferred stock and the common stock?

(6) Dividends per common share, $1.25

6. If two years' preferred dividends are in arrears and the board of directors declares cash dividends of $20,000, what total amount will be paid to the preferred and to the common shareholders? What is the amount of dividends per share for the common stock?

Analysis Component

7. What are some factors that can contribute to a difference between the book value of common stock and its market value (price)?

PROBLEM SET B

Problem 13-1B

Stockholders' equity
transactions and analysis

C2 P1

Nilson Company is incorporated at the beginning of this year and engages in a number of transactions. The following journal entries impacted its stockholders' equity during its first year of operations.

a.	Cash	60,000	
	Common Stock, $1 Par Value		1,500
	Paid-In Capital in Excess of Par Value, Common Stock		58,500
b.	Organization Expenses	20,000	
	Common Stock, $1 Par Value		500
	Paid-In Capital in Excess of Par Value, Common Stock		19,500
c.	Cash	6,650	
	Accounts Receivable	4,000	
	Building	12,500	
	Notes Payable		3,150
	Common Stock, $1 Par Value		400
	Paid-In Capital in Excess of Par Value, Common Stock		19,600
d.	Cash	30,000	
	Common Stock, $1 Par Value		600
	Paid-In Capital in Excess of Par Value, Common Stock		29,400

Required

1. Explain the transaction(s) underlying each journal entry (a) through (d).

Check (2) 3,000 shares

2. How many shares of common stock are outstanding at year-end?

(3) $3,000

3. What is the amount of minimum legal capital (based on par value) at year-end?

4. What is the total paid-in capital at year-end?

5. What is the book value per share of the common stock at year-end if total paid-in capital plus retained earnings equals $141,500?

(4) $130,000

Baycore Corp. reports the following components of stockholders' equity on December 31, 2011.

Problem 13-2B
Cash dividends, treasury stock, and statement of retained earnings

C3 P2 P3

Common stock—$1 par value, 160,000 shares authorized, 100,000 shares issued and outstanding	$ 100,000
Paid-in capital in excess of par value, common stock	700,000
Retained earnings	1,080,000
Total stockholders' equity	$1,880,000

It completed the following transactions related to stockholders' equity in year 2012.

Jan. 10   Purchased 20,000 shares of its own stock at $12 cash per share.

Mar. 2   Directors declared a $1.50 per share cash dividend payable on March 31 to the March 15 stockholders of record.

Mar. 31   Paid the dividend declared on March 2.

Nov. 11   Sold 12,000 of its treasury shares at $13 cash per share.

Nov. 25   Sold 8,000 of its treasury shares at $9.50 cash per share.

Dec. 1   Directors declared a $2.50 per share cash dividend payable on January 2 to the December 10 stockholders of record.

Dec. 31   Closed the $536,000 credit balance (from net income) in the Income Summary account to Retained Earnings.

Required

1. Prepare journal entries to record each of these transactions for 2012.

2. Prepare a statement of retained earnings for the year ended December 31, 2012.

3. Prepare the stockholders' equity section of the company's balance sheet as of December 31, 2012.

Check   (2) Retained earnings, Dec. 31, 2012, $1,238,000

At December 31, the end of Intertec Communication's third quarter, the following stockholders' equity accounts are reported.

Problem 13-3B
Equity analysis—journal entries and account balances

P2

Common stock, $10 par value	$480,000
Paid-in capital in excess of par value, common stock	192,000
Retained earnings	800,000

In the fourth quarter, the following entries related to its equity are recorded.

Jan. 17	Retained Earnings	48,000	
	Common Dividend Payable		48,000
Feb. 5	Common Dividend Payable	48,000	
	Cash		48,000
Feb. 28	Retained Earnings	126,000	
	Common Stock Dividend Distributable		60,000
	Paid-In Capital in Excess of Par Value, Common Stock		66,000
Mar. 14	Common Stock Dividend Distributable	60,000	
	Common Stock, $10 Par Value		60,000
Mar. 25	Memo—Change the title of the common stock account to reflect the new par value of $5.		
Mar. 31	Income Summary	360,000	
	Retained Earnings		360,000

Required

1. Explain the transaction(s) underlying each journal entry.

2. Complete the following table showing the equity account balances at each indicated date (include the balances from December 31).

	Jan. 17	Feb. 5	Feb. 28	Mar. 14	Mar. 25	Mar. 31
Common stock	$____	$____	$____	$____	$____	$____
Common stock dividend distributable	____	____	____	____	____	____
Paid-in capital in excess of par, common stock	____	____	____	____	____	____
Retained earnings	____	____	____	____	____	____
Total equity	$____	$____	$____	$____	$____	$____

Check Total equity: Jan. 17, $1,424,000; Mar. 31, $1,784,000

Problem 13-4B
Analysis of changes in stockholders' equity accounts

C3 P2 P3

The equity sections from Jetta Corporation's 2011 and 2012 balance sheets follow.

Stockholders' Equity (December 31, 2011)

Common stock—$20 par value, 15,000 shares authorized, 8,500 shares issued and outstanding	$170,000
Paid-in capital in excess of par value, common stock	30,000
Retained earnings	135,000
Total stockholders' equity	$335,000

Stockholders' Equity (December 31, 2012)

Common stock—$20 par value, 15,000 shares authorized, 9,500 shares issued, 500 shares in treasury	$190,000
Paid-in capital in excess of par value, common stock	52,000
Retained earnings ($20,000 restricted by treasury stock)	147,600
	389,600
Less cost of treasury stock	(20,000)
Total stockholders' equity	$369,600

The following transactions and events affected its equity during year 2012.

Feb. 15   Declared a $0.40 per share cash dividend, date of record five days later.
Mar. 2   Purchased treasury stock for cash.
May 15   Declared a $0.40 per share cash dividend, date of record five days later.
Aug. 15   Declared a $0.40 per share cash dividend, date of record five days later.
Oct. 4   Declared a 12.5% stock dividend when the stock's market value is $42 per share.
Oct. 20   Issued the stock dividend that was declared on October 4.
Nov. 15   Declared a $0.40 per share cash dividend, date of record five days later.

Required

1. How many common shares are outstanding on each cash dividend date?
2. What is the total dollar amount for each of the four cash dividends?
3. What is the amount of the capitalization of retained earnings for the stock dividend?
4. What is the per share cost of the treasury stock purchased?
5. How much net income did the company earn during year 2012?

Check (3) $42,000
(4) $40
(5) $68,000

Problem 13-5B
Computation of book values and dividend allocations

C2 A4

Scotch Company's common stock is currently selling on a stock exchange at $45 per share, and its current balance sheet shows the following stockholders' equity section.

Preferred stock—8% cumulative, $___ par value, 1,500 shares authorized, issued, and outstanding	$ 187,500
Common stock—$___ par value, 18,000 shares authorized, issued, and outstanding	450,000
Retained earnings	562,500
Total stockholders' equity	$1,200,000

Required (Round per share amounts to cents.)

1. What is the current market value (price) of this corporation's common stock?

2. What are the par values of the corporation's preferred stock and its common stock?

3. If no dividends are in arrears, what are the book values per share of the preferred stock and the common stock? (Round per share values to the nearest cent.)

4. If two years' preferred dividends are in arrears, what are the book values per share of the preferred stock and the common stock? (Round per share values to the nearest cent.)

5. If two years' preferred dividends are in arrears and the preferred stock is callable at $140 per share, what are the book values per share of the preferred stock and the common stock? (Round per share values to the nearest cent.)

6. If two years' preferred dividends are in arrears and the board of directors declares cash dividends of $50,000, what total amount will be paid to the preferred and to the common shareholders? What is the amount of dividends per share for the common stock? (Round per share values to the nearest cent.)

Check (4) Book value of common, $54.58

(5) Book value of common, $53.33

(6) Dividends per common share, $0.28

Analysis Component

7. Discuss why the book value of common stock is not always a good estimate of its market value.

(This serial problem began in Chapter 1 and continues through most of the book. If previous chapter segments were not completed, the serial problem can begin at this point. It is helpful, but not necessary, to use the Working Papers that accompany the book.)

SERIAL PROBLEM
Business Solutions
P1 C1 C2

SP 13 Santana Rey created Business Solutions on October 1, 2011. The company has been successful, and Santana plans to expand her business. She believes that an additional $86,000 is needed and is investigating three funding sources.

a. Santana's sister Cicely is willing to invest $86,000 in the business as a common shareholder. Since Santana currently has about $129,000 invested in the business, Cicely's investment will mean that Santana will maintain about 60% ownership, and Cicely will have 40% ownership of Business Solutions.

b. Santana's uncle Marcello is willing to invest $86,000 in the business as a preferred shareholder. Marcello would purchase 860 shares of $100 par value, 7% preferred stock.

c. Santana's banker is willing to lend her $86,000 on a 7%, 10-year note payable. She would make monthly payments of $1,000 per month for 10 years.

Required

1. Prepare the journal entry to reflect the initial $86,000 investment under each of the options (a), (b), and (c).

2. Evaluate the three proposals for expansion, providing the pros and cons of each option.

3. Which option do you recommend Santana adopt? Explain.

Beyond the Numbers

BTN 13-1 Refer to **Research In Motion**'s financial statements in Appendix A to answer the following.

REPORTING IN ACTION

C2 A1 A4

1. How many shares of common stock are issued and outstanding at February 27, 2010, and February 28, 2009? How do these numbers compare with the basic weighted-average common shares outstanding at February 27, 2010, and February 28, 2009?

RIM

2. What is the book value of its entire common stock at February 27, 2010?

3. What is the total amount of cash dividends paid to common stockholders for the years ended February 27, 2010, and February 28, 2009?

4. Identify and compare basic EPS amounts across fiscal years 2010, 2009, and 2008. Identify and comment on any notable changes.

5. How many shares does Research In Motion hold in treasury stock, if any, as of February 27, 2010? As of February 28, 2009?

Fast Forward

6. Access Research In Motion's financial statements for fiscal years ending after February 27, 2010, from its Website (**RIM.com**) or the SEC's EDGAR database (**www.sec.gov**). Has the number of common shares outstanding increased since that date? Has the company increased the total amount of cash dividends paid compared to the total amount for fiscal year 2010?

COMPARATIVE ANALYSIS

A1 A2 A3 A4

RIM

Palm

Apple

BTN 13-2   Key comparative figures for **Research In Motion**, **Palm**, and **Apple** follow.

Key Figures	Research In Motion	Palm	Apple
Net income (in millions)	$2,457	$ (753)	$8,235
Cash dividends declared per common share	$ —	$ —	$ —
Common shares outstanding (in millions)	557	140	900
Weighted-average common shares outstanding (in mil.)	564	116	893
Market value (price) per share	$69.76	$12.19	$184.40
Equity applicable to common shares (in millions)	$7,603	$ (414)	$31,640

Required

1. Compute the book value per common share for each company using these data.
2. Compute the basic EPS for each company using these data.
3. Compute the dividend yield for each company using these data. Does the dividend yield of any of the companies characterize it as an income or growth stock? Explain.
4. Compute, compare, and interpret the price-earnings ratio for each company using these data.

ETHICS CHALLENGE

C3

BTN 13-3   Gianna Tuck is an accountant for Post Pharmaceuticals. Her duties include tracking research and development spending in the new product development division. Over the course of the past six months, Gianna notices that a great deal of funds have been spent on a particular project for a new drug. She hears "through the grapevine" that the company is about to patent the drug and expects it to be a major advance in antibiotics. Gianna believes that this new drug will greatly improve company performance and will cause the company's stock to increase in value. Gianna decides to purchase shares of Post in order to benefit from this expected increase.

Required

What are Gianna's ethical responsibilities, if any, with respect to the information she has learned through her duties as an accountant for Post Pharmaceuticals? What are the implications to her planned purchase of Post shares?

COMMUNICATING IN PRACTICE

A1 A2

Hint: Make a transparency of each team's memo for a class discussion.

BTN 13-4   Teams are to select an industry, and each team member is to select a different company in that industry. Each team member then is to acquire the selected company's financial statements (or Form 10-K) from the SEC site (www.SEC.gov). Use these data to identify basic EPS. Use the financial press (or finance.yahoo.com) to determine the market price of this stock, and then compute the price-earnings ratio. Communicate with teammates via a meeting, e-mail, or telephone to discuss the meaning of this ratio, how companies compare, and the industry norm. The team must prepare a single memorandum reporting the ratio for each company and identifying the team conclusions or consensus of opinion. The memorandum is to be duplicated and distributed to the instructor and teammates.

TAKING IT TO THE NET

C1 C3

BTN 13-5   Access the February 26, 2010, filing of the 2009 calendar-year 10-K report of **McDonald's**, (ticker MCD) from www.SEC.gov.

Required

1. Review McDonald's balance sheet and identify how many classes of stock it has issued.
2. What are the par values, number of authorized shares, and issued shares of the classes of stock you identified in part 1?
3. Review its statement of cash flows and identify what total amount of cash it paid in 2009 to purchase treasury stock.
4. What amount did McDonald's pay out in common stock cash dividends for 2009?

TEAMWORK IN ACTION

P3

Hint: Instructor should be sure each team accurately completes part 1 before proceeding.

BTN 13-6   This activity requires teamwork to reinforce understanding of accounting for treasury stock.

1. Write a brief team statement (*a*) generalizing what happens to a corporation's financial position when it engages in a stock "buyback" and (*b*) identifying reasons why a corporation would engage in this activity.
2. Assume that an entity acquires 100 shares of its $100 par value common stock at a cost of $134 cash per share. Discuss the entry to record this acquisition. Next, assign *each* team member to prepare *one* of the following entries (assume each entry applies to all shares):

    a. Reissue treasury shares at cost.

    b. Reissue treasury shares at $150 per share.

c. Reissue treasury shares at $120 per share; assume the paid-in capital account from treasury shares has a $1,500 balance.

d. Reissue treasury shares at $120 per share; assume the paid-in capital account from treasury shares has a $1,000 balance.

e. Reissue treasury shares at $120 per share; assume the paid-in capital account from treasury shares has a zero balance.

3. In sequence, each member is to present his/her entry to the team and explain the *similarities* and *differences* between that entry and the previous entry.

ENTREPRENEURIAL DECISION

C2 P2

BTN 13-7 Assume that Kelly Giard of **Clean Air Lawn Care** decides to launch a new retail chain to market electrical mowers. This chain, named Mow Green, requires $500,000 of start-up capital. Kelly contributes $375,000 of personal assets in return for 15,000 shares of common stock, but he must raise another $125,000 in cash. There are two alternative plans for raising the additional cash. *Plan A* is to sell 3,750 shares of common stock to one or more investors for $125,000 cash. *Plan B* is to sell 1,250 shares of cumulative preferred stock to one or more investors for $125,000 cash (this preferred stock would have a $100 par value, an annual 8% dividend rate, and be issued at par).

1. If the new business is expected to earn $72,000 of after-tax net income in the first year, what rate of return on beginning equity will Kelly earn under each alternative plan? Which plan will provide the higher expected return?

2. If the new business is expected to earn $16,800 of after-tax net income in the first year, what rate of return on beginning equity will Kelly earn under each alternative plan? Which plan will provide the higher expected return?

3. Analyze and interpret the differences between the results for parts 1 and 2.

HITTING THE ROAD

A1 A2 A3

BTN 13-8 Review 30 to 60 minutes of financial news programming on television. Take notes on companies that are catching analysts' attention. You might hear reference to over- and undervaluation of firms and to reports about PE ratios, dividend yields, and earnings per share. Be prepared to give a brief description to the class of your observations.

GLOBAL DECISION

A1 C3

NOKIA

BTN 13-9 Financial information for **Nokia Corporation** (www.nokia.com) follows.

Net income (in millions)	€ 260
Cash dividends declared (in millions)	€ 1,481
Cash dividends declared per share	€ 0.40
Number of shares outstanding (in millions)*	3,708
Equity applicable to shares (in millions)	€14,749

* Assume that for Nokia the year-end number of shares outstanding approximates the weighted-average shares outstanding.

Required

1. Compute book value per share for Nokia.

2. Compute earnings per share (EPS) for Nokia.

3. Compare Nokia's dividends per share with its EPS. Is Nokia paying out a large or small amount of its income as dividends? Explain.

ANSWERS TO MULTIPLE CHOICE QUIZ

1. e; Entry to record this stock issuance is:

Cash (6,000 × $8)	48,000	
Common Stock (6,000 × $5)		30,000
Paid-In Capital in Excess of Par Value, Common Stock		18,000

2. b; $75,000/19,000 shares = $3.95 per share

3. d; Preferred stock = 5,000 × $100 = $500,000
Book value per share = ($2,000,000 − $500,000)/50,000 shares = $30 per common share

4. a; $0.81/$45.00 = 1.8%

5. c; Earnings per share = $3,500,000/700,000 shares = $5 per share
PE ratio = $85/$5 = 17.0

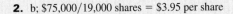

14

Long-Term Liabilities

A Look Back

Chapter 13 focused on corporate equity transactions, including stock issuances and dividends. We also explained how to report and analyze income, earnings per share, and retained earnings.

A Look at This Chapter

This chapter describes the accounting for and analysis of bonds and notes. We explain their characteristics, payment patterns, interest computations, retirement, and reporting requirements. An appendix to this chapter introduces leases and pensions.

A Look Ahead

Chapter 15 focuses on how to classify, account for, and report investments in both debt and equity securities. We also describe accounting for transactions listed in a foreign currency.

Learning Objectives

CAP

CONCEPTUAL

C1 Explain the types and payment patterns of notes. (p. 562)

C2 *Appendix 14A*—Explain and compute the present value of an amount(s) to be paid at a future date(s). (p. 570)

C3 *Appendix 14C*—Describe interest accrual when bond payment periods differ from accounting periods. (p. 574)

C4 *Appendix 14D*—Describe accounting for leases and pensions. (p. 576)

ANALYTICAL

A1 Compare bond financing with stock financing. (p. 552)

A2 Assess debt features and their implications. (p. 566)

A3 Compute the debt-to-equity ratio and explain its use. (p. 566)

LP14

PROCEDURAL

P1 Prepare entries to record bond issuance and interest expense. (p. 554)

P2 Compute and record amortization of bond discount. (p. 555)

P3 Compute and record amortization of bond premium. (p. 558)

P4 Record the retirement of bonds. (p. 561)

P5 Prepare entries to account for notes. (p. 564)

Decision Insight

Love At First Bite

"Each individual problem you face is totally surmountable"
—WARREN BROWN

WASHINGTON, DC—Warren Brown started baking cakes in his apartment after work each evening. He sold his sweet concoctions mostly to coworkers and friends, and even held a cake open house at the local art gallery. But Warren was determined to grow his business. He took a course in entrepreneurship at his local community college, and there he discovered the importance of financial reporting and accounting.

Launching his fledgling cake business presented Warren with many challenges. He needed to especially focus on the important task of managing liabilities for payroll, baking supplies, employee benefits, training, and taxes. Warren insists that effective management of liabilities, especially long-term financing from sources such as bonds and notes, is crucial to business success. "Everything feels like a disaster when it's right in your face," says Warren. "You just have to be calm, look at what you're doing, and fix the problem."

Warren fixed the problems and unveiled his business called **Cake Love (CakeLove.com),** funded with short- and long-term notes. "I opened up this tiny retail, walk-up bakery . . . [to sell] goodies that are baked from scratch," Warren explains. Today Cake Love entices the neighborhood with a gentle scent of fresh bakery and a sidewalk view into the kitchen. Warmly painted walls, comfy window seats, and free wireless Internet encourage customers to lounge for hours. "I want it to be relaxed and comfortable," says Warren. "People can bring their work, their kids, their friends, and just relax."

Warren continues to monitor liabilities and their payment patterns, and he is not shy about striving to better learn the accounting side. "I'm always getting better, improving my skills," he explains. Warren insists that accounting for and monitoring liabilities of long-term financing are important ingredients to a successful start-up. His company now generates sufficient income to pay for liabilities of interest and principal on long-term debt and still produces revenue growth for expansion. He shows a keen appetite for using accounting information to make good business decisions. "But," says Warren, "I love eating what I make more."

"The bigger message of Cake Love is finding your passion and working to reach your goals," explains Warren. That's a slice of advice worth more than any amount of dough.

[Sources: *Cake Love Website,* January 2011; *Black Enterprise,* September 2004; *Georgetown Voice,* March 2005; *National Public Radio (NPR) Website,* May 2005; *Inc.com,* April 2005]

Individuals, companies, and governments issue bonds to finance their activities. In return for financing, bonds promise to repay the lender with interest. This chapter explains the basics of bonds and the accounting for their issuance and retirement. The chapter also describes long-term notes as another financing source. We explain how present value concepts impact both the accounting for and reporting of bonds and notes. Appendixes to this chapter discuss present value concepts applicable to liabilities, effective interest amortization, and the accounting for leases and pensions.

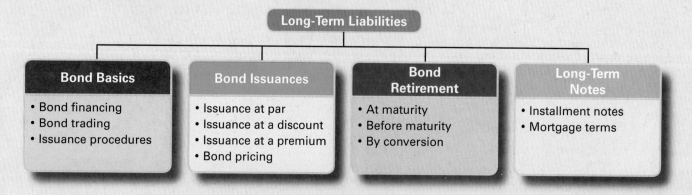

Long-Term Liabilities

Bond Basics
- Bond financing
- Bond trading
- Issuance procedures

Bond Issuances
- Issuance at par
- Issuance at a discount
- Issuance at a premium
- Bond pricing

Bond Retirement
- At maturity
- Before maturity
- By conversion

Long-Term Notes
- Installment notes
- Mortgage terms

BASICS OF BONDS

This section explains the basics of bonds and a company's motivation for issuing them.

Bond Financing

A1 Compare bond financing with stock financing.

Projects that demand large amounts of money often are funded from bond issuances. (Both for-profit and nonprofit companies, as well as governmental units, such as nations, states, cities, and school districts, issue bonds.) A **bond** is its issuer's written promise to pay an amount identified as the par value of the bond with interest. The **par value of a bond,** also called the *face amount* or *face value,* is paid at a specified future date known as the bond's *maturity date.* Most bonds also require the issuer to make semiannual interest payments. The amount of interest paid each period is determined by multiplying the par value of the bond by the bond's contract rate of interest for that same period. This section explains both advantages and disadvantages of bond financing.

Advantages of Bonds   There are three main advantages of bond financing:

1. *Bonds do not affect owner control.* Equity financing reflects ownership in a company, whereas bond financing does not. A person who contributes $1,000 of a company's $10,000 equity financing typically controls one-tenth of all owner decisions. A person who owns a $1,000, 11%, 20-year bond has no ownership right. This person, or bond-holder, is to receive from the bond issuer 11% interest, or $110, each year the bond is outstanding and $1,000 when it matures in 20 years.

2. *Interest on bonds is tax deductible.* Bond interest payments are tax deductible for the issuer, but equity payments (distributions) to owners are not. To illustrate, assume that a corporation with no bond financing earns $15,000 in income *before* paying taxes at a 40% tax rate, which amounts to $6,000 ($15,000 × 40%) in taxes. If a portion of its financing is in bonds, however, the resulting bond interest is deducted in computing taxable income. That is, if bond interest expense is $10,000, the taxes owed would be $2,000 ([$15,000 − $10,000] × 40%), which is less than the $6,000 owed with no bond financing.

3. *Bonds can increase return on equity.* A company that earns a higher return with borrowed funds than it pays in interest on those funds increases its return on equity. This process is called *financial leverage* or *trading on the equity.*

Point: Financial leverage reflects issuance of bonds, notes, or preferred stock.

To illustrate the third point, consider Magnum Co., which has $1 million in equity and is planning a $500,000 expansion to meet increasing demand for its product. Magnum predicts the

$500,000 expansion will yield $125,000 in additional income before paying any interest. It currently earns $100,000 per year and has no interest expense. Magnum is considering three plans. Plan A is to not expand. Plan B is to expand and raise $500,000 from equity financing. Plan C is to expand and issue $500,000 of bonds that pay 10% annual interest ($50,000). Exhibit 14.1 shows how these three plans affect Magnum's net income, equity, and return on equity (net income/equity). The owner(s) will earn a higher return on equity if expansion occurs. Moreover, the preferred expansion plan is to issue bonds. Projected net income under Plan C ($175,000) is smaller than under Plan B ($225,000), but the return on equity is larger because of less equity investment. Plan C has another advantage if income is taxable. This illustration reflects a general rule: *Return on equity increases when the expected rate of return from the new assets is higher than the rate of interest expense on the debt financing.*

Example: Compute return on equity for all three plans if Magnum currently earns $150,000 instead of $100,000.
Answer ($ 000s):
Plan A = 15%   ($150/$1,000)
Plan B = 18.3%   ($275/$1,500)
Plan C = 22.5%   ($225/$1,000)

EXHIBIT 14.1

Financing with Bonds versus Equity

	Plan A: Do Not Expand	Plan B: Equity Financing	Plan C: Bond Financing
Income before interest expense	$ 100,000	$ 225,000	$ 225,000
Interest expense	—	—	(50,000)
Net income	**$ 100,000**	**$ 225,000**	**$ 175,000**
Equity	$1,000,000	$1,500,000	$1,000,000
Return on equity	**10.0%**	**15.0%**	**17.5%**

Disadvantages of Bonds   The two main disadvantages of bond financing are these:

1. *Bonds can decrease return on equity.* When a company earns a lower return with the borrowed funds than it pays in interest, it decreases its return on equity. This downside risk of financial leverage is more likely to arise when a company has periods of low income or net losses.

2. *Bonds require payment of both periodic interest and the par value at maturity.* Bond payments can be especially burdensome when income and cash flow are low. Equity financing, in contrast, does not require any payments because cash withdrawals (dividends) are paid at the discretion of the owner (or board).

Point: Debt financing is desirable when interest is tax deductible, when owner control is preferred, and when return on equity exceeds the debt's interest rate.

A company must weigh the risks and returns of the disadvantages and advantages of bond financing when deciding whether to issue bonds to finance operations.

Bond Trading

Bonds are securities that can be readily bought and sold. A large number of bonds trade on both the New York Exchange and the American Exchange. A bond *issue* consists of a number of bonds, usually in denominations of $1,000 or $5,000, and is sold to many different lenders. After bonds are issued, they often are bought and sold by investors, meaning that any particular bond probably has a number of owners before it matures. Since bonds are exchanged (bought and sold) in the market, they have a market value (price). For convenience, bond market values are expressed as a percent of their par (face) value. For example, a company's bonds might be trading at 103½, meaning they can be bought or sold for 103.5% of their par value. Bonds can also trade below par value. For instance, if a company's bonds are trading at 95, they can be bought or sold at 95% of their par value.

Decision Insight

Quotes   The **IBM** bond quote here is interpreted (left to right) as **Bonds**, issuer name; **Rate**, contract interest rate (7%); **Mat,** matures in year 2025 when

Bonds	Rate	Mat	Yld	Vol	Close	Chg
IBM	7	25	5.9	130	119¼	+1¼

principal is paid; **Yld,** yield rate (5.9%) of bond at current price; **Vol,** daily dollar worth ($130,000) of trades (in 1,000s); **Close,** closing price (119.25) for the day as percentage of par value; **Chg,** change (+1.25) in closing price from prior day's close. ∎

Bond-Issuing Procedures

State and federal laws govern bond issuances. Bond issuers also want to ensure that they do not violate any of their existing contractual agreements when issuing bonds. Authorization of bond issuances includes the number of bonds authorized, their par value, and the contract interest rate. The legal document identifying the rights and obligations of both the bondholders and the issuer is called the **bond indenture,** which is the legal contract between the issuer and the bondholders. A bondholder may also receive a bond certificate as evidence of the company's debt. A **bond certificate,** such as that shown in Exhibit 14.2, includes specifics such as the issuer's name, the par value, the contract interest rate, and the maturity date. Many companies reduce costs by not issuing paper certificates to bondholders.[1]

EXHIBIT 14.2

Bond Certificate

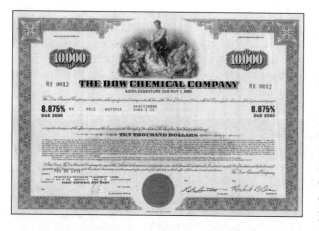

Point: *Indenture* refers to a bond's legal contract; *debenture* refers to an unsecured bond.

BOND ISSUANCES

This section explains accounting for bond issuances at par, below par (discount), and above par (premium). It also describes how to amortize a discount or premium and record bonds issued between interest payment dates.

Issuing Bonds at Par

P1 Prepare entries to record bond issuance and interest expense.

To illustrate an issuance of bonds at par value, suppose a company receives authorization to issue $800,000 of 9%, 20-year bonds dated January 1, 2011, that mature on December 31, 2030, and pay interest semiannually on each June 30 and December 31. After accepting the bond indenture on behalf of the bondholders, the trustee can sell all or a portion of the bonds to an underwriter. If all bonds are sold at par value, the issuer records the sale as follows.

Assets = Liabilities + Equity
+800,000   +800,000

2011			
Jan. 1	Cash	800,000	
	Bonds Payable		800,000
	Sold bonds at par.		

This entry reflects increases in the issuer's cash *and* long-term liabilities.

The issuer records the first semiannual interest payment as follows.

Assets = Liabilities + Equity
−36,000   −36,000

2011			
June 30	Bond Interest Expense	36,000	
	Cash		36,000
	Paid semiannual interest (9% × $800,000 × ½ year).		

Point: The *spread* between the dealer's cost and what buyers pay can be huge. Dealers earn more than $25 billion in annual spread revenue.

Global: In the United Kingdom, government bonds are called *gilts*— short for gilt-edged investments.

---

[1] The issuing company normally sells its bonds to an investment firm called an *underwriter,* which resells them to the public. An issuing company can also sell bonds directly to investors. When an underwriter sells bonds to a large number of investors, a *trustee* represents and protects the bondholders' interests. The trustee monitors the issuer to ensure that it complies with the obligations in the bond indenture. Most trustees are large banks or trust companies. The trustee writes and accepts the terms of a bond indenture before it is issued. When bonds are offered to the public, called *floating an issue,* they must be registered with the Securities and Exchange Commission (SEC). SEC registration requires the issuer to file certain financial information. Most company bonds are issued in par value units of $1,000 or $5,000. *A baby bond* has a par value of less than $1,000, such as $100.

The issuer pays and records its semiannual interest obligation every six months until the bonds mature. When they mature, the issuer records its payment of principal as follows.

2030			
Dec. 31	Bonds Payable	800,000	
	Cash		800,000
	Paid bond principal at maturity.		

Assets = Liabilities + Equity
−800,000   −800,000

Bond Discount or Premium

The bond issuer pays the interest rate specified in the indenture, the **contract rate,** also referred to as the *coupon rate, stated rate,* or *nominal rate.* The annual interest paid is determined by multiplying the bond par value by the contract rate. The contract rate is usually stated on an annual basis, even if interest is paid semiannually. For example, if a company issues a $1,000, 8% bond paying interest semiannually, it pays annual interest of $80 (8% × $1,000) in two semiannual payments of $40 each.

The contract rate sets the amount of interest the issuer pays in *cash,* which is not necessarily the *bond interest expense* actually incurred by the issuer. Bond interest expense depends on the bond's market value at issuance, which is determined by market expectations of the risk of lending to the issuer. The bond's **market rate** of interest is the rate that borrowers are willing to pay and lenders are willing to accept for a particular bond and its risk level. As the risk level increases, the rate increases to compensate purchasers for the bonds' increased risk. Also, the market rate is generally higher when the time period until the bond matures is longer due to the risk of adverse events occurring over a longer time period.

Many bond issuers try to set a contract rate of interest equal to the market rate they expect as of the bond issuance date. When the contract rate and market rate are equal, a bond sells at par value, but when they are not equal, a bond does not sell at par value. Instead, it is sold at a *premium* above par value or at a *discount* below par value. Exhibit 14.3 shows the relation between the contract rate, market rate, and a bond's issue price.

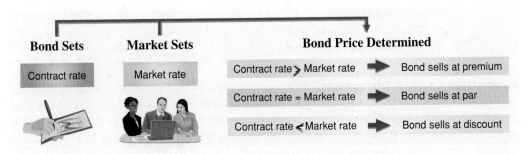

EXHIBIT 14.3

Relation between Bond Issue Price, Contract Rate, and Market Rate

Quick Check   Answers — p. 579

1. A company issues $10,000 of 9%, 5-year bonds dated January 1, 2011, that mature on December 31, 2015, and pay interest semiannually on each June 30 and December 31. Prepare the entry to record this bond issuance and the first semiannual interest payment.
2. How do you compute the amount of interest a bond issuer pays in cash each year?
3. When the contract rate is above the market rate, do bonds sell at a premium or a discount? Do purchasers pay more or less than the par value of the bonds?

Issuing Bonds at a Discount

A **discount on bonds payable** occurs when a company issues bonds with a contract rate less than the market rate. This means that the issue price is less than par value. To illustrate, assume that **Fila** announces an offer to issue bonds with a $100,000 par value, an 8% annual contract rate (paid semiannually), and a two-year life. Also assume that the market rate for Fila bonds is

P2 Compute and record amortization of bond discount.

10%. These bonds then will sell at a discount since the contract rate is less than the market rate. The exact issue price for these bonds is stated as 96.454 (implying 96.454% of par value, or $96,454); we show how to compute this issue price later in the chapter. These bonds obligate the issuer to pay two separate types of future cash flows:

1. Par value of $100,000 cash at the end of the bonds' two-year life.
2. Cash interest payments of $4,000 (4% × $100,000) at the end of each semiannual period during the bonds' two-year life.

The exact pattern of cash flows for the Fila bonds is shown in Exhibit 14.4.

EXHIBIT 14.4

Cash Flows for Fila Bonds

When Fila accepts $96,454 cash for its bonds on the issue date of December 31, 2011, it records the sale as follows.

Assets	=	Liabilities	+	Equity
+96,454		+100,000		
		−3,546		

Dec. 31	Cash..	96,454	
	Discount on Bonds Payable	3,546	
	Bonds Payable		100,000
	Sold bonds at a discount on their issue date.		

These bonds are reported in the long-term liability section of the issuer's December 31, 2011, balance sheet as shown in Exhibit 14.5. A discount is deducted from the par value of bonds to yield the **carrying (book) value of bonds.** Discount on Bonds Payable is a contra liability account.

EXHIBIT 14.5

Balance Sheet Presentation of Bond Discount

Long-term liabilities		
Bonds payable, 8%, due December 31, 2013	$100,000	
Less discount on bonds payable	3,546	$96,454

Amortizing a Bond Discount Fila receives $96,454 for its bonds; in return it must pay bondholders $100,000 after two years (plus semiannual interest payments). The $3,546 discount is paid to bondholders at maturity and is part of the cost of using the $96,454 for two years. The upper portion of panel A in Exhibit 14.6 shows that total bond interest expense of $19,546 is the difference between the total amount repaid to bondholders ($116,000) and the amount borrowed from bondholders ($96,454). Alternatively, we can compute total bond interest expense as the sum of the four interest payments and the bond discount. This alternative computation is shown in the lower portion of panel A.

The total $19,546 bond interest expense must be allocated across the four semiannual periods in the bonds' life, and the bonds' carrying value must be updated at each balance sheet date. This is accomplished using the straight-line method (or the effective interest method in Appendix 14B). Both methods systematically reduce the bond discount to zero over the two-year life. This process is called *amortizing a bond discount.*

Straight-Line Method The **straight-line bond amortization** method allocates an equal portion of the total bond interest expense to each interest period. To apply the straight-line method to Fila's bonds, we divide the total bond interest expense of $19,546 by 4 (the number of semiannual periods in the bonds' life). This gives a bond interest expense of $4,887 per period, which is $4,886.5 rounded to the nearest dollar per period (all computations, including those for assignments, are rounded to the nearest whole dollar). Alternatively, we can find this number by first dividing the $3,546 discount by 4, which yields the $887 amount of discount to be amortized each interest period. When the $887 is added to the $4,000 cash payment, the bond

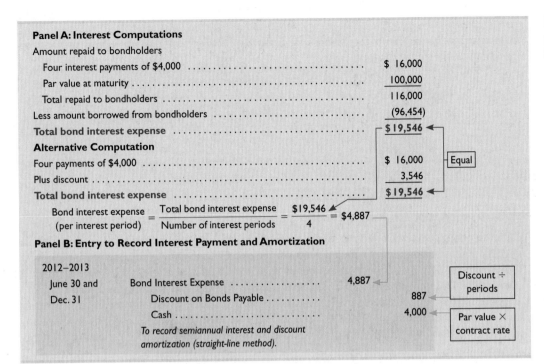

EXHIBIT 14.6

Interest Computation and Entry for Bonds Issued at a Discount

Panel A: Interest Computations

Amount repaid to bondholders	
Four interest payments of $4,000	$ 16,000
Par value at maturity	100,000
Total repaid to bondholders	116,000
Less amount borrowed from bondholders	(96,454)
Total bond interest expense	**$19,546**
Alternative Computation	
Four payments of $4,000	$ 16,000
Plus discount	3,546
Total bond interest expense	**$19,546**

Equal

$$\text{Bond interest expense (per interest period)} = \frac{\text{Total bond interest expense}}{\text{Number of interest periods}} = \frac{\$19,546}{4} = \$4,887$$

Panel B: Entry to Record Interest Payment and Amortization

2012–2013			
June 30 and	Bond Interest Expense	4,887	
Dec. 31	Discount on Bonds Payable		887
	Cash		4,000
	To record semiannual interest and discount amortization (straight-line method).		

Discount ÷ periods

Par value × contract rate

interest expense for each period is $4,887. Panel B of Exhibit 14.6 shows how the issuer records bond interest expense and updates the balance of the bond liability account at the end of *each* of the four semiannual interest periods (June 30, 2012, through December 31, 2013).

Exhibit 14.7 shows the pattern of decreases in the Discount on Bonds Payable account and the pattern of increases in the bonds' carrying value. The following points summarize the discount bonds' straight-line amortization:

1. At issuance, the $100,000 par value consists of the $96,454 cash received by the issuer plus the $3,546 discount.

2. During the bonds' life, the (unamortized) discount decreases each period by the $887 amortization ($3,546/4), and the carrying value (par value less unamortized discount) increases each period by $887.

3. At maturity, the unamortized discount equals zero, and the carrying value equals the $100,000 par value that the issuer pays the holder.

EXHIBIT 14.7

Straight-Line Amortization of Bond Discount

Semiannual Period-End	Unamortized Discount*	Carrying Value†
(0) 12/31/2011	$3,546	$ 96,454
(1) 6/30/2012	2,659	97,341
(2) 12/31/2012	1,772	98,228
(3) 6/30/2013	885	99,115
(4) 12/31/2013	0‡	100,000

The two columns always sum to par value for a discount bond.

* Total bond discount (of $3,546) less accumulated periodic amortization ($887 per semiannual interest period).

† Bond par value (of $100,000) less unamortized discount.

‡ Adjusted for rounding.

We see that the issuer incurs a $4,887 bond interest expense each period but pays only $4,000 cash. The $887 unpaid portion of this expense is added to the bonds' carrying value. (The total $3,546 unamortized discount is "paid" when the bonds mature; $100,000 is paid at maturity but only $96,454 was received at issuance.)

Decision Insight

Ratings Game Many bond buyers rely on rating services to assess bond risk. The best known are **Standard & Poor's, Moody's,** and **Fitch.** These services focus on the issuer's financial statements and other factors in setting ratings. Standard & Poor's ratings, from best quality to default, are AAA, AA, A, BBB, BB, B, CCC, CC, C, and D. Ratings can include a plus (+) or minus (−) to show relative standing within a category. ∎

Quick Check   Answers — p. 579

Five-year, 6% bonds with a $100,000 par value are issued at a price of $91,893. Interest is paid semiannually, and the bonds' market rate is 8% on the issue date. Use this information to answer the following questions:

4. Are these bonds issued at a discount or a premium? Explain your answer.

5. What is the issuer's journal entry to record the issuance of these bonds?

6. What is the amount of bond interest expense recorded at the first semiannual period using the straight-line method?

Issuing Bonds at a Premium

P3 Compute and record amortization of bond premium.

When the contract rate of bonds is higher than the market rate, the bonds sell at a price higher than par value. The amount by which the bond price exceeds par value is the **premium on bonds.** To illustrate, assume that **Adidas** issues bonds with a $100,000 par value, a 12% annual contract rate, semiannual interest payments, and a two-year life. Also assume that the market rate for Adidas bonds is 10% on the issue date. The Adidas bonds will sell at a premium because the contract rate is higher than the market rate. The issue price for these bonds is stated as 103.546 (implying 103.546% of par value, or $103,546); we show how to compute this issue price later in the chapter. These bonds obligate the issuer to pay out two separate future cash flows:

1. Par value of $100,000 cash at the end of the bonds' two-year life.
2. Cash interest payments of $6,000 (6% × $100,000) at the end of each semiannual period during the bonds' two-year life.

The exact pattern of cash flows for the Adidas bonds is shown in Exhibit 14.8.

EXHIBIT 14.8

Cash Flows for Adidas Bonds

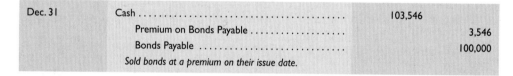

When Adidas accepts $103,546 cash for its bonds on the issue date of December 31, 2011, it records this transaction as follows.

Assets	=	Liabilities	+ Equity
+103,546		+100,000	
		+3,546	

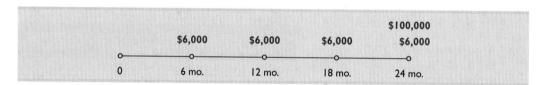

Dec. 31	Cash	103,546	
	Premium on Bonds Payable		3,546
	Bonds Payable		100,000
	Sold bonds at a premium on their issue date.		

These bonds are reported in the long-term liability section of the issuer's December 31, 2011, balance sheet as shown in Exhibit 14.9. A premium is added to par value to yield the carrying (book) value of bonds. Premium on Bonds Payable is an adjunct (also called *accretion*) liability account.

EXHIBIT 14.9

Balance Sheet Presentation of Bond Premium

Long-term liabilities		
Bonds payable, 12%, due December 31, 2013	$100,000	
Plus premium on bonds payable	3,546	$103,546

Amortizing a Bond Premium   Adidas receives $103,546 for its bonds; in return, it pays bondholders $100,000 after two years (plus semiannual interest payments). The $3,546 premium not repaid to issuer's bondholders at maturity goes to reduce the issuer's expense of using the $103,546 for two years. The upper portion of panel A of Exhibit 14.10 shows that total bond interest expense of $20,454 is the difference between the total amount repaid to bondholders ($124,000) and the amount borrowed from bondholders ($103,546). Alternatively, we can compute total bond interest expense as the sum of the four interest payments less the bond premium. The premium is

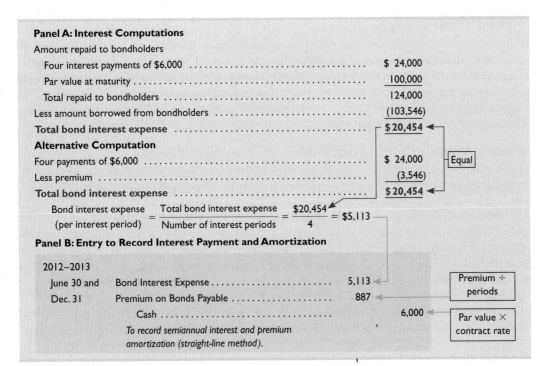

EXHIBIT 14.10

Interest Computation and Entry for Bonds Issued at a Premium

subtracted because it will not be paid to bondholders when the bonds mature; see the lower portion of panel A. Total bond interest expense must be allocated over the four semiannual periods using the straight-line method (or the effective interest method in Appendix 14B).

Straight-Line Method   The straight-line method allocates an equal portion of total bond interest expense to each of the bonds' semiannual interest periods. To apply this method to Adidas bonds, we divide the two years' total bond interest expense of $20,454 by 4 (the number of semiannual periods in the bonds' life). This gives a total bond interest expense of $5,113 per

Point: A premium decreases Bond Interest Expense; a discount increases it.

period, which is $5,113.5 rounded down so that the journal entry balances and for simplicity in presentation (alternatively, one could carry cents). Panel B of Exhibit 14.10 shows how the issuer records bond interest expense and updates the balance of the bond liability account for *each* semiannual period (June 30, 2012, through December 31, 2013).

Exhibit 14.11 shows the pattern of decreases in the unamortized Premium on Bonds Payable account and in the bonds' carrying value. The following points summarize straight-line amortization of the premium bonds:

Semiannual Period-End	Unamortized Premium*	Carrying Value†
(0) 12/31/2011	$3,546	$103,546
(1) 6/30/2012	2,659	102,659
(2) 12/31/2012	1,772	101,772
(3) 6/30/2013	885	100,885
(4) 12/31/2013	0‡	100,000

* Total bond premium (of $3,546) less accumulated periodic amortization ($887 per semiannual interest period).

† Bond par value (of $100,000) plus unamortized premium.

‡ Adjusted for rounding.

EXHIBIT 14.11

Straight-Line Amortization of Bond Premium

During the bond life, carrying value is adjusted to par and the amortized premium to zero.

1. At issuance, the $100,000 par value plus the $3,546 premium equals the $103,546 cash received by the issuer.

2. During the bonds' life, the (unamortized) premium decreases each period by the $887 amortization ($3,546/4), and the carrying value decreases each period by the same $887.

3. At maturity, the unamortized premium equals zero, and the carrying value equals the $100,000 par value that the issuer pays the holder.

The next section describes bond pricing. An instructor can choose to cover bond pricing or not. Assignments requiring the next section are Quick Study 14-5, and Exercises 14-9 & 14-10.

Bond Pricing

Prices for bonds traded on an organized exchange are often published in newspapers and through online services. This information normally includes the bond price (called *quote*), its contract rate, and its current market (called *yield*) rate. However, only a fraction of bonds are traded on organized exchanges. To compute the price of a bond, we apply present value concepts. This section explains how to use *present value concepts* to price the Fila discount bond and the Adidas premium bond described earlier.

Point: InvestingInBonds.com is a bond research and learning source.

Point: A bond's market value (price) at issuance equals the present value of its future cash payments, where the interest (discount) rate used is the bond's market rate.

Point: Many calculators have present value functions for computing bond prices.

Present Value of a Discount Bond   The issue price of bonds is found by computing the present value of the bonds' cash payments, discounted at the bonds' market rate. When computing the present value of the Fila bonds, we work with *semiannual* compounding periods because this is the time between interest payments; the annual market rate of 10% is considered a semiannual rate of 5%. Also, the two-year bond life is viewed as four semiannual periods. The price computation is twofold: (1) Find the present value of the $100,000 par value paid at maturity and (2) find the present value of the series of four semiannual payments of $4,000 each; see Exhibit 14.4. These present values can be found by using *present value tables*. Appendix B at the end of this book shows present value tables and describes their use. Table B.1 at the end of Appendix B is used for the single $100,000 maturity payment, and Table B.3 in Appendix B is used for the $4,000 series of interest payments. Specifically, we go to Table B.1, row 4, and across to the 5% column to identify the present value factor of 0.8227 for the maturity payment. Next, we go to Table B.3, row 4, and across to the 5% column, where the present value factor is 3.5460 for the series of interest payments. We compute bond price by multiplying the cash flow payments by their corresponding present value factors and adding them together; see Exhibit 14.12.

EXHIBIT 14.12

Computing Issue Price for the Fila Discount Bonds

Cash Flow	Table	Present Value Factor	Amount	Present Value
$100,000 par (maturity) value	B.1	0.8227	× $100,000 =	$ 82,270
$4,000 interest payments	B.3	3.5460	× 4,000 =	14,184
Price of bond				$96,454

Present Value of a Premium Bond   We find the issue price of the Adidas bonds by using the market rate to compute the present value of the bonds' future cash flows. When computing the present value of these bonds, we again work with *semiannual* compounding periods because this is the time between interest payments. The annual 10% market rate is applied as a semiannual rate of 5%, and the two-year bond life is viewed as four semiannual periods. The computation is twofold: (1) Find the present value of the $100,000 par value paid at maturity and (2) find the present value of the series of four payments of $6,000 each; see Exhibit 14.8. These present values can be found by using present value tables. First, go to Table B.1, row 4, and across to the 5% column where the present value factor is 0.8227 for the maturity payment. Second, go to Table B.3, row 4, and across to the 5% column, where the present value factor is 3.5460 for the series of interest payments. The bonds' price is computed by multiplying the cash flow payments by their corresponding present value factors and adding them together; see Exhibit 14.13.

Point: There are nearly 5 million individual U.S. bond issues, ranging from huge treasuries to tiny municipalities. This compares to about 12,000 individual U.S. stocks that are traded.

EXHIBIT 14.13

Computing Issue Price for the Adidas Premium Bonds

Cash Flow	Table	Present Value Factor	Amount	Present Value
$100,000 par (maturity) value	B.1	0.8227	× $100,000 =	$ 82,270
$6,000 interest payments	B.3	3.5460	× 6,000 =	21,276
Price of bond				$103,546

On December 31, 2010, a company issues 16%, 10-year bonds with a par value of $100,000. Interest is paid on June 30 and December 31. The bonds are sold to yield a 14% annual market rate at an issue price of $110,592. Use this information to answer questions 7 through 9:

7. Are these bonds issued at a discount or a premium? Explain your answer.

8. Using the straight-line method to allocate bond interest expense, the issuer records the second interest payment (on December 31, 2011) with a debit to Premium on Bonds Payable in the amount of (a) $7,470, (b) $530, (c) $8,000, or (d) $400.

9. How are these bonds reported in the long-term liability section of the issuer's balance sheet as of December 31, 2011?

BOND RETIREMENT

This section describes the retirement of bonds (1) at maturity, (2) before maturity, and (3) by conversion to stock.

P4 Record the retirement of bonds.

Bond Retirement at Maturity

The carrying value of bonds at maturity always equals par value. For example, both Exhibits 14.7 (a discount) and 14.11 (a premium) show that the carrying value of bonds at the end of their lives equals par value ($100,000). The retirement of these bonds at maturity, assuming interest is already paid and entered, is recorded as follows:

2013			
Dec. 31	Bonds Payable	100,000	
	Cash		100,000
	To record retirement of bonds at maturity.		

Assets = Liabilities + Equity
−100,000   −100,000

Bond Retirement before Maturity

Issuers sometimes wish to retire some or all of their bonds prior to maturity. For instance, if interest rates decline greatly, an issuer may wish to replace high-interest-paying bonds with new low-interest bonds. Two common ways to retire bonds before maturity are to (1) exercise a call option or (2) purchase them on the open market. In the first instance, an issuer can reserve the right to retire bonds early by issuing callable bonds. The bond indenture can give the issuer an option to *call* the bonds before they mature by paying the par value plus a *call premium* to bondholders. In the second case, the issuer retires bonds by repurchasing them on the open market at their current price. Whether bonds are called or repurchased, the issuer is unlikely to pay a price that exactly equals their carrying value. When a difference exists between the bonds' carrying value and the amount paid, the issuer records a gain or loss equal to the difference.

To illustrate the accounting for retiring callable bonds, assume that a company issued callable bonds with a par value of $100,000. The call option requires the issuer to pay a call premium of $3,000 to bondholders in addition to the par value. Next, assume that after the June 30, 2011, interest payment, the bonds have a carrying value of $104,500. Then on July 1, 2011, the issuer calls these bonds and pays $103,000 to bondholders. The issuer recognizes a $1,500 gain from the difference between the bonds' carrying value of $104,500 and the retirement price of $103,000. The issuer records this bond retirement as follows.

Point: Bond retirement is also referred to as *bond redemption*.

Point: Gains and losses from retiring bonds were *previously* reported as extraordinary items. New standards require that they now be judged by the "unusual and infrequent" criteria for reporting purposes.

July 1	Bonds Payable	100,000	
	Premium on Bonds Payable	4,500	
	Gain on Bond Retirement		1,500
	Cash		103,000
	To record retirement of bonds before maturity.		

Assets = Liabilities + Equity
−103,000   −100,000   +1,500
            −4,500

An issuer usually must call all bonds when it exercises a call option. However, to retire as many or as few bonds as it desires, an issuer can purchase them on the open market. If it retires less than the entire class of bonds, it recognizes a gain or loss for the difference between the carrying value of those bonds retired and the amount paid to acquire them.

Bond Retirement by Conversion

Convertible Bond

Holders of convertible bonds have the right to convert their bonds to stock. When conversion occurs, the bonds' carrying value is transferred to equity accounts and no gain or loss is recorded. (We further describe convertible bonds in the Decision Analysis section of this chapter.)

To illustrate, assume that on January 1 the $100,000 par value bonds of **Converse**, with a carrying value of $100,000, are converted to 15,000 shares of $2 par value common stock. The entry to record this conversion follows (the market prices of the bonds and stock are *not* relevant to this entry; the material in Chapter 13 is helpful in understanding this transaction):

Assets = Liabilities + Equity
−100,000   +30,000
                    +70,000

Jan. 1	Bonds Payable	100,000	
	Common Stock		30,000
	Paid-In Capital in Excess of Par Value		70,000
	To record retirement of bonds by conversion.		

Decision Insight

Junk Bonds   Junk bonds are company bonds with low credit ratings due to a higher than average likelihood of default. On the upside, the high risk of junk bonds can yield high returns if the issuer survives and repays its debt. ■

Quick Check   Answer — p. 579

10. Six years ago, a company issued $500,000 of 6%, eight-year bonds at a price of 95. The current carrying value is $493,750. The company decides to retire 50% of these bonds by buying them on the open market at a price of 102½. What is the amount of gain or loss on the retirement of these bonds?

LONG-TERM NOTES PAYABLE

C1   Explain the types and payment patterns of notes.

Like bonds, notes are issued to obtain assets such as cash. Unlike bonds, notes are typically transacted with a *single* lender such as a bank. An issuer initially records a note at its selling price—that is, the note's face value minus any discount or plus any premium. Over the note's life, the amount of interest expense allocated to each period is computed by multiplying the market rate (at issuance of the note) by the beginning-of-period note balance. The note's carrying (book) value at any time equals its face value minus any unamortized discount or plus any unamortized premium; carrying value is also computed as the present value of all remaining payments, discounted using the market rate at issuance.

Installment Notes

An **installment note** is an obligation requiring a series of payments to the lender. Installment notes are common for franchises and other businesses when lenders and borrowers agree to spread payments over several periods. To illustrate, assume that Foghog borrows $60,000 from a bank to purchase equipment. It signs an 8% installment note requiring six annual payments of principal plus interest and it records the note's issuance at January 1, 2011, as follows.

Jan. 1	Cash	60,000	
	Notes Payable		60,000
	Borrowed $60,000 by signing an 8%, six-year installment note.		

Assets = Liabilities + Equity
+60,000   +60,000

Payments on an installment note normally include the accrued interest expense plus a portion of the amount borrowed (the *principal*). This section describes an installment note with equal payments.

The equal total payments pattern consists of changing amounts of both interest and principal. To illustrate, assume that Foghog borrows $60,000 by signing a $60,000 note that requires six *equal payments* of $12,979 at the end of each year. (The present value of an annuity of six annual payments of $12,979, discounted at 8%, equals $60,000; we show this computation in footnote 2 on the next page.) The $12,979 includes both interest and principal, the amounts of which change with each payment. Exhibit 14.14 shows the pattern of equal total payments and its two parts, interest and principal. Column A shows the note's beginning balance. Column B shows accrued interest for each year at 8% of the beginning note balance. Column C shows the impact on the note's principal, which equals the difference between the total payment in column D and the interest expense in column B. Column E shows the note's year-end balance.

Years
2011 2012 2013 2014 2015 2016

$12,979 $12,979 $12,979 $12,979 $12,979 $12,979

Point: Most consumer notes are installment notes that require equal total payments.

EXHIBIT 14.14

Installment Note: Equal Total Payments

			Payments		
Period Ending Date	**(A)** Beginning Balance	**(B)** Debit Interest Expense 8% × (A)	+ **(C)** Debit Notes Payable (D) − (B)	= **(D)** Credit Cash (computed)	**(E)** Ending Balance (A) − (C)
(1) 12/31/2011	$60,000	$ 4,800	$ 8,179	$12,979	$51,821
(2) 12/31/2012	51,821	4,146	8,833	12,979	42,988
(3) 12/31/2013	42,988	3,439	9,540	12,979	33,448
(4) 12/31/2014	33,448	2,676	10,303	12,979	23,145
(5) 12/31/2015	23,145	1,852	11,127	12,979	12,018
(6) 12/31/2016	12,018	961	12,018	12,979	0
		$17,874	$60,000	$77,874	

Interest ▨   Principal ▢

	Decreasing Accrued Interest ↓	Increasing Principal Component ↓	Equal Total Payments ↓
2011	$4,800	$8,179	
2012	$4,146	$8,833	
2013	$3,439	$9,540	
2014	$2,676	$10,303	
2015	$1,852	$11,127	
2016	$961	$12,018	

End of Year

0    $2,500 $5,000 $7,500 $10,000 $12,500 $15,000
Cash Payment Pattern

> ### ◼ Decision Insight
>
> **Hidden Debt** A study reports that 13% of employees in finance and accounting witnessed the falsifying or manipulating of accounting information in the past year (KPMG 2009). This is of special concern with long-term liabilities. For example, Enron violated GAAP to keep debt off its balance sheet. This concern extends to hidden environment liabilities. That same study reports 27% of employees in quality, safety, and environmental areas observed violations of environmental standards, which can yield massive liabilities. ◼

P5 Prepare entries to account for notes.

Although the six cash payments are equal, accrued interest decreases each year because the principal balance of the note declines. As the amount of interest decreases each year, the portion of each payment applied to principal increases. This pattern is graphed in the lower part of Exhibit 14.14. Foghog uses the amounts in Exhibit 14.14 to record its first two payments (for years 2011 and 2012) as follows:

Assets = Liabilities + Equity
−12,979   −8,179   −4,800

2011		
Dec. 31	Interest Expense	4,800	
	Notes Payable	8,179	
	Cash		12,979
	To record first installment payment.		

Assets = Liabilities + Equity
−12,979   −8,833   −4,146

2012		
Dec. 31	Interest Expense	4,146	
	Notes Payable	8,833	
	Cash		12,979
	To record second installment payment.		

Foghog records similar entries but with different amounts for each of the remaining four payments. After six years, the Notes Payable account balance is zero.[2]

Mortgage Notes and Bonds

Point: The Truth-in-Lending Act requires lenders to provide information about loan costs including finance charges and interest rate.

A **mortgage** is a legal agreement that helps protect a lender if a borrower fails to make required payments on notes or bonds. A mortgage gives the lender a right to be paid from the cash proceeds of the sale of a borrower's assets identified in the mortgage. A legal document, called a *mortgage contract,* describes the mortgage terms.

Mortgage notes carry a mortgage contract pledging title to specific assets as security for the note. Mortgage notes are especially popular in the purchase of homes and the acquisition of plant assets. Less common *mortgage bonds* are backed by the issuer's assets. Accounting for mortgage notes and bonds is similar to that for unsecured notes and bonds, except that the mortgage agreement must be disclosed. For example, **TIBCO Software** reports that its "mortgage note payable ... is collateralized by the commercial real property acquired [corporate headquarters]."

Global: Countries vary in the preference given to debtholders vs. stockholders when a company is in financial distress. Some countries such as Germany, France, and Japan give preference to stockholders over debtholders.

---

[2] Table B.3 in Appendix B is used to compute the dollar amount of the six payments that equal the initial note balance of $60,000 at 8% interest. We go to Table B.3, row 6, and across to the 8% column, where the present value factor is 4.6229. The dollar amount is then computed by solving this relation:

Table	Present Value Factor	Dollar Amount		Present Value
B.3	4.6229	× ?	=	$60,000

The dollar amount is computed by dividing $60,000 by 4.6229, yielding $12,979.

Example: Suppose the $60,000 installment loan has an 8% interest rate with eight equal annual payments. What is the annual payment? *Answer* (using Table B.3): $60,000/5.7466 = $10,441

Decision Maker   Answer — p. 579

Entrepreneur   You are an electronics retailer planning a holiday sale on a custom stereo system that requires no payments for two years. At the end of two years, buyers must pay the full amount. The system's suggested retail price is $4,100, but you are willing to sell it today for $3,000 cash. What is your holiday sale price if payment will not occur for two years and the market interest rate is 10%? ■

Quick Check   Answers — p. 579

11. Which of the following is true for an installment note requiring a series of equal total cash payments? (*a*) Payments consist of increasing interest and decreasing principal; (*b*) payments consist of changing amounts of principal but constant interest; or (*c*) payments consist of decreasing interest and increasing principal.

12. How is the interest portion of an installment note payment computed?

13. When a borrower records an interest payment on an installment note, how are the balance sheet and income statement affected?

GLOBAL VIEW

This section discusses similarities and differences between U.S. GAAP and IFRS in accounting and reporting for long-term liabilities such as bonds and notes.

Accounting for Bonds and Notes   The definitions and characteristics of bonds and notes are broadly similar for both U.S. GAAP and IFRS. Although slight differences exist, accounting for bonds and notes under U.S. GAAP and IFRS is similar. Specifically, the accounting for issuances (including recording discounts and premiums), market pricing, and retirement of both bonds and notes follows the procedures in this chapter. **Nokia** describes its accounting for bonds, which follows the amortized cost approach explained in this chapter (and in Appendix 14B), as follows: Loans payable [bonds] are recognized initially at fair value, net of transaction costs incurred. In the subsequent periods, they are stated at amortized cost.

NOKIA

Both U.S. GAAP and IFRS allow companies to account for bonds and notes using fair value (different from the amortized value described in this chapter). This method is referred to as the **fair value option**. This method is similar to that applied in measuring and accounting for debt and equity securities. *Fair value* is the amount a company would receive if it settled a liability (or sold an asset) in an orderly transaction as of the balance sheet date. Companies can use several sources of inputs to determine fair value, and those inputs fall into three classes (ranked in order of preference):

Level 1: Observable quoted market prices in active markets for identical items.
Level 2: Observable inputs other than those in Level 1 such as prices from inactive markets or from similar, but not identical, items.
Level 3: Unobservable inputs reflecting a company's assumptions about value.

The exact procedures for marking liabilities to fair value at each balance sheet date are in advanced courses.

Accounting for Leases and Pensions   Both U.S. GAAP and IFRS require companies to distinguish between operating leases and capital leases; the latter is referred to as *finance leases* under IFRS. The accounting and reporting for leases are broadly similar for both U.S. GAAP and IFRS. The main difference is the criteria for identifying a lease as a capital lease are more general under IFRS. However, the basic approach applies. **Nokia** describes its accounting for operating leases as follows: the payments . . . are treated as rentals and recognized in the profit and loss account.

For pensions, both U.S. GAAP and IFRS require companies to record costs of retirement benefits as employees work and earn them. The basic methods are similar in accounting and reporting for pensions.

Collateral agreements can reduce the risk of loss for both bonds and notes. Unsecured bonds and notes are riskier because the issuer's obligation to pay interest and principal has the same priority as all other unsecured liabilities in the event of bankruptcy. If a company is unable to pay its debts in full, the unsecured creditors (including the holders of debentures) lose all or a portion of their balances. These types of legal agreements and other characteristics of long-term liabilities are crucial for effective business decisions. The first part of this section describes the different types of features sometimes included with bonds and notes. The second part explains and applies the debt-to-equity ratio.

A2 Assess debt features and their implications.

Features of Bonds and Notes

This section describes common features of debt securities.

Secured Debt   **Unsecured Debt**

Secured or Unsecured   Secured bonds (and notes) have specific assets of the issuer pledged (or *mortgaged*) as collateral. This arrangement gives holders added protection against the issuer's default. If the issuer fails to pay interest or par value, the secured holders can demand that the collateral be sold and the proceeds used to pay the obligation. **Unsecured bonds** (and notes), also called *debentures,* are backed by the issuer's general credit standing. Unsecured debt is riskier than secured debt. *Subordinated debentures* are liabilities that are not repaid until the claims of the more senior, unsecured (and secured) liabilities are settled.

Term or Serial   **Term bonds** (and notes) are scheduled for maturity on one specified date. **Serial bonds** (and notes) mature at more than one date (often in series) and thus are usually repaid over a number of periods. For instance, $100,000 of serial bonds might mature at the rate of $10,000 each year from 6 to 15 years after they are issued. Many bonds are **sinking fund bonds,** which to reduce the holder's risk require the issuer to create a *sinking fund* of assets set aside at specified amounts and dates to repay the bonds.

Registered or Bearer   Bonds issued in the names and addresses of their holders are **registered bonds.** The issuer makes bond payments by sending checks (or cash transfers) to registered holders. A registered holder must notify the issuer of any ownership change. Registered bonds offer the issuer the practical advantage of not having to actually issue bond certificates. Bonds payable to whoever holds them (the *bearer*) are called **bearer bonds** or *unregistered bonds.* Sales or exchanges might not be recorded, so the holder of a bearer bond is presumed to be its rightful owner. As a result, lost bearer bonds are difficult to replace. Many bearer bonds are also **coupon bonds.** This term reflects interest coupons that are attached to the bonds. When each coupon matures, the holder presents it to a bank or broker for collection. At maturity, the holder follows the same process and presents the bond certificate for collection. Issuers of coupon bonds cannot deduct the related interest expense for taxable income. This is to prevent abuse by taxpayers who own coupon bonds but fail to report interest income on their tax returns.

Convertible Debt   **Callable Debt**

Convertible and/or Callable   Convertible bonds (and notes) can be exchanged for a fixed number of shares of the issuing corporation's common stock. Convertible debt offers holders the potential to participate in future increases in stock price. Holders still receive periodic interest while the debt is held and the par value if they hold the debt to maturity. In most cases, the holders decide whether and when to convert debt to stock. **Callable bonds** (and notes) have an option exercisable by the issuer to retire them at a stated dollar amount before maturity.

▢ **Decision Insight**

Munis   More than a million municipal bonds, or "munis," exist, and many are tax exempt. Munis are issued by state, city, town, and county governments to pay for public projects including schools, libraries, roads, bridges, and stadiums. ■

A3 Compute the debt-to-equity ratio and explain its use.

Debt-to-Equity Ratio

Beyond assessing different characteristics of debt as just described, we want to know the level of debt, especially in relation to total equity. Such knowledge helps us assess the risk of a company's financing structure. A company financed mainly with debt is more risky because liabilities must be repaid—usually with periodic interest—whereas equity financing does not. A measure to assess the risk of a company's financing structure is the **debt-to-equity ratio** (see Exhibit 14.15).

$$\text{Debt-to-equity} = \frac{\text{Total liabilities}}{\text{Total equity}}$$

EXHIBIT 14.15

Debt-to-Equity Ratio

The debt-to-equity ratio varies across companies and industries. Industries that are more variable tend to have lower ratios, while more stable industries are less risky and tend to have higher ratios. To apply the debt-to-equity ratio, let's look at this measure for **Cedar Fair** in Exhibit 14.16.

EXHIBIT 14.16

Cedar Fair's Debt-to-Equity Ratio

($ millions)	2009	2008	2007	2006	2005
Total liabilities	$2,017.577	$2,079.297	$2,133.576	$2,100.306	$590.560
Total equity	$ 127.862	$ 106.786	$ 285.092	$ 410.615	$434.234
Debt-to-equity	15.8	19.5	7.5	5.1	1.4
Industry debt-to-equity	11.4	10.3	5.7	3.2	1.2

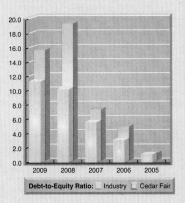

Cedar Fair's 2009 debt-to-equity ratio is 15.8, meaning that debtholders contributed $15.8 for each $1 contributed by equityholders. This implies a fairly risky financing structure for Cedar Fair. A similar concern is drawn from a comparison of Cedar Fair with its competitors, where the 2009 industry ratio is 11.4. Analysis across the years shows that Cedar Fair's financing structure has grown increasingly risky in recent years. Given its sluggish revenues and increasing operating expenses in recent years (see its annual report), Cedar Fair is increasingly at risk of financial distress.

Decision Maker   Answer — p. 579

Bond Investor   You plan to purchase debenture bonds from one of two companies in the same industry that are similar in size and performance. The first company has $350,000 in total liabilities, and $1,750,000 in equity. The second company has $1,200,000 in total liabilities, and $1,000,000 in equity. Which company's debenture bonds are less risky based on the debt-to-equity ratio? ■

DEMONSTRATION PROBLEM

Water Sports Company (WSC) patented and successfully test-marketed a new product. To expand its ability to produce and market the new product, WSC needs to raise $800,000 of financing. On January 1, 2011, the company obtained the money in two ways:

a. WSC signed a $400,000, 10% installment note to be repaid with five equal annual installments to be made on December 31 of 2011 through 2015.

b. WSC issued five-year bonds with a par value of $400,000. The bonds have a 12% annual contract rate and pay interest on June 30 and December 31. The bonds' annual market rate is 10% as of January 1, 2011.

Required

1. For the installment note, (a) compute the size of each annual payment, (b) prepare an amortization table such as Exhibit 14.14, and (c) prepare the journal entry for the first payment.

2. For the bonds, (a) compute their issue price; (b) prepare the January 1, 2011, journal entry to record their issuance; (c) prepare an amortization table using the straight-line method; (d) prepare the June 30, 2011, journal entry to record the first interest payment; and (e) prepare a journal entry to record retiring the bonds at a $416,000 call price on January 1, 2013.

3.[B]Redo parts 2(c), 2(d), and 2(e) assuming the bonds are amortized using the effective interest method.

PLANNING THE SOLUTION

- For the installment note, divide the borrowed amount by the annuity factor (from Table B.3) using the 10% rate and five payments to compute the amount of each payment. Prepare a table similar to Exhibit 14.14 and use the numbers in the table's first line for the journal entry.
- Compute the bonds' issue price by using the market rate to find the present value of their cash flows (use tables found in Appendix B). Then use this result to record the bonds' issuance. Next, prepare an amortization table like Exhibit 14.11 (and Exhibit 14B.2) and use it to get the numbers needed for the journal entry. Also use the table to find the carrying value as of the date of the bonds' retirement that you need for the journal entry.

SOLUTION TO DEMONSTRATION PROBLEM

Part 1: Installment Note

a. Annual payment = Note balance/Annuity factor = $400,000/3.7908 = $105,519 (The annuity factor is for five payments and a rate of 10%.)

b. An amortization table follows.

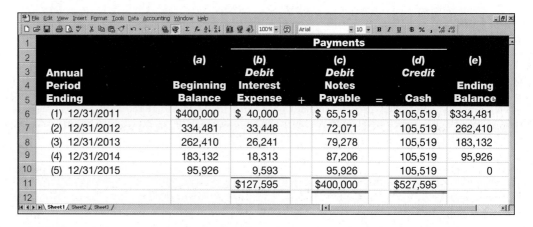

Annual Period Ending	(a) Beginning Balance	(b) Debit Interest Expense	+	(c) Debit Notes Payable	=	(d) Credit Cash	(e) Ending Balance
(1) 12/31/2011	$400,000	$ 40,000		$ 65,519		$105,519	$334,481
(2) 12/31/2012	334,481	33,448		72,071		105,519	262,410
(3) 12/31/2013	262,410	26,241		79,278		105,519	183,132
(4) 12/31/2014	183,132	18,313		87,206		105,519	95,926
(5) 12/31/2015	95,926	9,593		95,926		105,519	0
		$127,595		$400,000		$527,595	

c. Journal entry for December 31, 2011, payment.

Dec. 31	Interest Expense	40,000	
	Notes Payable	65,519	
	Cash		105,519
	To record first installment payment.		

Part 2: Bonds (Straight-Line Amortization)

a. Compute the bonds' issue price.

Cash Flow	Table	Present Value Factor*	Amount	Present Value
Par (maturity) value	B.1 in App. B (PV of 1)	0.6139	× 400,000	= $245,560
Interest payments	B.3 in App. B (PV of annuity)	7.7217	× 24,000	= 185,321
Price of bond				$430,881

* Present value factors are for 10 payments using a semiannual market rate of 5%.

b. Journal entry for January 1, 2011, issuance.

Jan. 1	Cash	430,881	
	Premium on Bonds Payable		30,881
	Bonds Payable		400,000
	Sold bonds at a premium.		

c. Straight-line amortization table for premium bonds.

Semiannual Period-End	Unamortized Premium	Carrying Value
(0) 1/1/2011	$30,881	$430,881
(1) 6/30/2011	27,793	427,793
(2) 12/31/2011	24,705	424,705
(3) 6/30/2012	21,617	421,617
(4) 12/31/2012	18,529	418,529
(5) 6/30/2013	15,441	415,441
(6) 12/31/2013	12,353	412,353
(7) 6/30/2014	9,265	409,265
(8) 12/31/2014	6,177	406,177
(9) 6/30/2015	3,089	403,089
(10) 12/31/2015	0*	400,000

* Adjusted for rounding.

d. Journal entry for June 30, 2011, bond payment.

June 30	Bond Interest Expense	20,912	
	Premium on Bonds Payable	3,088	
	Cash		24,000
	Paid semiannual interest on bonds.		

e. Journal entry for January 1, 2013, bond retirement.

Jan. 1	Bonds Payable	400,000	
	Premium on Bonds Payable	18,529	
	Cash		416,000
	Gain on Retirement of Bonds		2,529
	To record bond retirement (carrying value as of Dec. 31, 2012).		

Part 3: Bonds (Effective Interest Amortization)[B]

c. The effective interest amortization table for premium bonds.

Semiannual Interest Period	(A) Cash Interest Paid 6% × $400,000	(B) Interest Expense 5% × Prior (E)	(C) Premium Amortization (A) – (B)	(D) Unamortized Premium Prior (D) – (C)	(E) Carrying Value $400,000 + (D)
(0) 1/1/2011				$30,881	$430,881
(1) 6/30/2011	$ 24,000	$ 21,544	$ 2,456	28,425	428,425
(2) 12/31/2011	24,000	21,421	2,579	25,846	425,846
(3) 6/30/2012	24,000	21,292	2,708	23,138	423,138
(4) 12/31/2012	24,000	21,157	2,843	20,295	420,295
(5) 6/30/2013	24,000	21,015	2,985	17,310	417,310
(6) 12/31/2013	24,000	20,866	3,134	14,176	414,176
(7) 6/30/2014	24,000	20,709	3,291	10,885	410,885
(8) 12/31/2014	24,000	20,544	3,456	7,429	407,429
(9) 6/30/2015	24,000	20,371	3,629	3,800	403,800
(10) 12/31/2015	24,000	20,200*	3,800	0	400,000
	$240,000	$209,119	$30,881		

* Adjusted for rounding

d. Journal entry for June 30, 2011, bond payment.

June 30	Bond Interest Expense	21,544	
	Premium on Bonds Payable	2,456	
	Cash		24,000
	Paid semiannual interest on bonds.		

e. Journal entry for January 1, 2013, bond retirement.

Jan. 1	Bonds Payable	400,000	
	Premium on Bonds Payable	20,295	
	Cash		416,000
	Gain on Retirement of Bonds		4,295
	To record bond retirement (carrying value		
	as of December 31, 2012).		

APPENDIX

14A   Present Values of Bonds and Notes

This appendix explains how to apply present value techniques to measure a long-term liability when it is created and to assign interest expense to the periods until it is settled. Appendix B at the end of the book provides additional discussion of present value concepts.

> **C2** Explain and compute the present value of an amount(s) to be paid at a future date(s).

Present Value Concepts   The basic present value concept is that cash paid (or received) in the future has less value now than the same amount of cash paid (or received) today. To illustrate, if we must pay $1 one year from now, its present value is less than $1. To see this, assume that we borrow $0.9259 today that must be paid back in one year with 8% interest. Our interest expense for this loan is computed as $0.9259 × 8%, or $0.0741. When the $0.0741 interest is added to the $0.9259 borrowed, we get the $1 payment necessary to repay our loan with interest. This is formally computed in Exhibit 14A.1. The $0.9259 borrowed is the present value of the $1 future payment. More generally, an amount borrowed equals the present value of the future payment. (This same interpretation applies to an investment. If $0.9259 is invested at 8%, it yields $0.0741 in revenue after one year. This amounts to $1, made up of principal and interest.)

EXHIBIT 14A.1

Components of a
One-Year Loan

Amount borrowed	$0.9259
Interest for one year at 8%	0.0741
Amount owed after 1 year	$ 1.0000

> **Point:** Benjamin Franklin is said to have described compounding as "the money, money makes, makes more money."

To extend this example, assume that we owe $1 two years from now instead of one year, and the 8% interest is compounded annually. *Compounded* means that interest during the second period is based on the total of the amount borrowed plus the interest accrued from the first period. The second period's interest is then computed as 8% multiplied by the sum of the amount borrowed plus interest earned in the first period. Exhibit 14A.2 shows how we compute the present value of $1 to be paid in two years. This amount is $0.8573. The first year's interest of $0.0686 is added to the principal so that the second year's interest is based on $0.9259. Total interest for this two-year period is $0.1427, computed as $0.0686 plus $0.0741.

EXHIBIT 14A.2

Components of a Two-Year Loan

Amount borrowed	$0.8573
Interest for first year ($0.8573 × 8%)	0.0686
Amount owed after 1 year	0.9259
Interest for second year ($0.9259 × 8%)	0.0741
Amount owed after 2 years	$ 1.0000

Present Value Tables The present value of $1 that we must repay at some future date can be computed by using this formula: $1/(1 + i)^n$. The symbol i is the interest rate per period and n is the number of periods until the future payment must be made. Applying this formula to our two-year loan, we get $1/(1.08)^2$, or $0.8573. This is the same value shown in Exhibit 14A.2. We can use this formula to find any present value. However, a simpler method is to use a *present value table,* which lists present values computed with this formula for various interest rates and time periods. Many people find it helpful in learning present value concepts to first work with the table and then move to using a calculator.

Exhibit 14A.3 shows a present value table for a future payment of 1 for up to 10 periods at three different interest rates. Present values in this table are rounded to four decimal places. This table is drawn from the larger and more complete Table B.1 in Appendix B at the end of the book. Notice that the first value in the 8% column is 0.9259, the value we computed earlier for the present value of a $1 loan for one year at 8% (see Exhibit 14A.1). Go to the second row in the same 8% column and find the present value of 1 discounted at 8% for two years, or 0.8573. This $0.8573 is the present value of our obligation to repay $1 after two periods at 8% interest (see Exhibit 14A.2).

EXHIBIT 14A.3

Present Value of 1

Periods	Rate		
	6%	8%	10%
1	0.9434	**0.9259**	0.9091
2	0.8900	**0.8573**	0.8264
3	0.8396	0.7938	0.7513
4	0.7921	0.7350	0.6830
5	0.7473	0.6806	0.6209
6	0.7050	0.6302	0.5645
7	0.6651	0.5835	0.5132
8	0.6274	0.5403	0.4665
9	0.5919	0.5002	0.4241
10	0.5584	0.4632	0.3855

Example: Use Exhibit 14A.3 to find the present value of $1 discounted for 2 years at 6%. *Answer:* $0.8900

Applying a Present Value Table To illustrate how to measure a liability using a present value table, assume that a company plans to borrow cash and repay it as follows: $2,000 after one year, $3,000 after two years, and $5,000 after three years. How much does this company receive today if the interest rate on this loan is 10%? To answer, we need to compute the present value of the three future payments, discounted at 10%. This computation is shown in Exhibit 14A.4 using present values from Exhibit 14A.3. The company can borrow $8,054 today at 10% interest in exchange for its promise to make these three payments at the scheduled dates.

EXHIBIT 14A.4

Present Value of a Series of Unequal Payments

Periods	Payments	Present Value of 1 at 10%	Present Value of Payments
1	$2,000	0.9091	$ 1,818
2	3,000	0.8264	2,479
3	5,000	0.7513	3,757
Present value of all payments			**$8,054**

Present Value of an Annuity The $8,054 present value for the loan in Exhibit 14A.4 equals the sum of the present values of the three payments. When payments are not equal, their combined present value is best computed by adding the individual present values as shown in Exhibit 14A.4. Sometimes payments follow an **annuity,** which is a series of *equal* payments at equal time intervals. The present value of an annuity is readily computed.

To illustrate, assume that a company must repay a 6% loan with a $5,000 payment at each year-end for the next four years. This loan amount equals the present value of the four payments discounted at 6%. Exhibit 14A.5 shows how to compute this loan's present value of $17,326 by multiplying each payment by its matching present value factor taken from Exhibit 14A.3.

However, the series of $5,000 payments is an annuity, so we can compute its present value with either of two shortcuts. First, the third column of Exhibit 14A.5 shows that the sum of the present values of 1 at 6% for periods 1 through 4 equals 3.4651. One shortcut is to multiply this total of 3.4651 by the $5,000 annual payment to get the combined present value of $17,326. It requires one multiplication instead of four.

EXHIBIT 14A.5

Present Value of a Series of Equal Payments (Annuity) by Discounting Each Payment

Periods	Payments	Present Value of 1 at 6%	Present Value of Payments
1	$5,000	0.9434	$ 4,717
2	5,000	0.8900	4,450
3	5,000	0.8396	4,198
4	5,000	0.7921	3,961
Present value of all payments		**3.4651**	**$17,326**

EXHIBIT 14A.6

Present Value of an Annuity of 1

Periods	Rate		
	6%	8%	10%
1	0.9434	0.9259	0.9091
2	1.8334	1.7833	1.7355
3	2.6730	2.5771	2.4869
4	**3.4651**	3.3121	3.1699
5	4.2124	3.9927	3.7908
6	4.9173	4.6229	4.3553
7	5.5824	5.2064	4.8684
8	6.2098	5.7466	5.3349
9	6.8017	6.2469	5.7590
10	7.3601	6.7101	6.1446

Example: Use Exhibit 14A.6 to find the present value of an annuity of eight $15,000 payments with an 8% interest rate. *Answer:* $15,000 × 5.7466 = $86,199

Example: If this borrower makes five semiannual payments of $8,000, what is the present value of this annuity at a 12% rate? *Answer:* 4.2124 × $8,000 = $33,699

The second shortcut uses an *annuity table* such as the one shown in Exhibit 14A.6, which is drawn from the more complete Table B.3 in Appendix B. We go directly to the annuity table to get the present value factor for a specific number of payments and interest rate. We then multiply this factor by the amount of the payment to find the present value of the annuity. Specifically, find the row for four periods and go across to the 6% column, where the factor is 3.4651. This factor equals the present value of an annuity with four payments of 1, discounted at 6%. We then multiply 3.4651 by $5,000 to get the $17,326 present value of the annuity.

Compounding Periods Shorter Than a Year

The present value examples all involved periods of one year. In many situations, however, interest is compounded over shorter periods. For example, the interest rate on bonds is usually stated as an annual rate but interest is often paid every six months (semiannually). This means that the present value of interest payments from such bonds must be computed using interest periods of six months.

Assume that a borrower wants to know the present value of a series of 10 *semiannual payments* of $4,000 made over five years at an *annual interest rate* of 12%. The interest rate is stated as an annual rate of 12%, but it is actually a rate of 6% per semiannual interest period. To compute the present value of this series of $4,000 payments, go to row 10 of Exhibit 14A.6 and across to the 6% column to find the factor 7.3601. The present value of this annuity is $29,440 (7.3601 × $4,000).

Appendix B further describes present value concepts and includes more complete present value tables and assignments.

Quick Check

Answers — p. 579

14. A company enters into an agreement to make four annual year-end payments of $1,000 each, starting one year from now. The annual interest rate is 8%. The present value of these four payments is (a) $2,923, (b) $2,940, or (c) $3,312.

15. Suppose a company has an option to pay either (a) $10,000 after one year or (b) $5,000 after six months and another $5,000 after one year. Which choice has the lower present value?

APPENDIX

14B

Effective Interest Amortization

Effective Interest Amortization of a Discount Bond   The straight-line method yields changes in the bonds' carrying value while the amount for bond interest expense remains constant. This gives the impression of a changing interest rate when users divide a constant bond interest expense over a changing carrying value. As a result, accounting standards allow use of the straight-line method only when its results do not differ materially from those obtained using the effective interest method. The **effective interest method,** or simply *interest method,* allocates total bond interest expense over the bonds' life in a way that yields a constant rate of interest. This constant rate of interest is the market rate at the issue date. Thus, bond interest expense for a period equals the carrying value of the bond at the beginning of that period multiplied by the market rate when issued.

Point: The effective interest method computes bond interest expense using the market rate at issuance. This rate is applied to a changing carrying value.

Exhibit 14B.1 shows an effective interest amortization table for the Fila bonds (as described in Exhibit 14.4). The key difference between the effective interest and straight-line methods lies in computing bond interest expense. Instead of assigning an equal amount of bond interest expense to each period, the effective interest method assigns a bond interest expense amount that increases over the life of a discount bond. **Both methods allocate the *same* $19,546 of total bond interest expense to the bonds' life, but in different patterns.** Specifically, the amortization table in Exhibit 14B.1 shows that the balance of the discount (column D) is amortized until it reaches zero. Also, the bonds' carrying value (column E) changes each period until it equals par value at maturity. Compare columns D and E to the corresponding columns in Exhibit 14.7 to see the amortization patterns. Total bond interest expense is $19,546, consisting of $16,000 of semiannual cash payments and $3,546 of the original bond discount, the same for both methods.

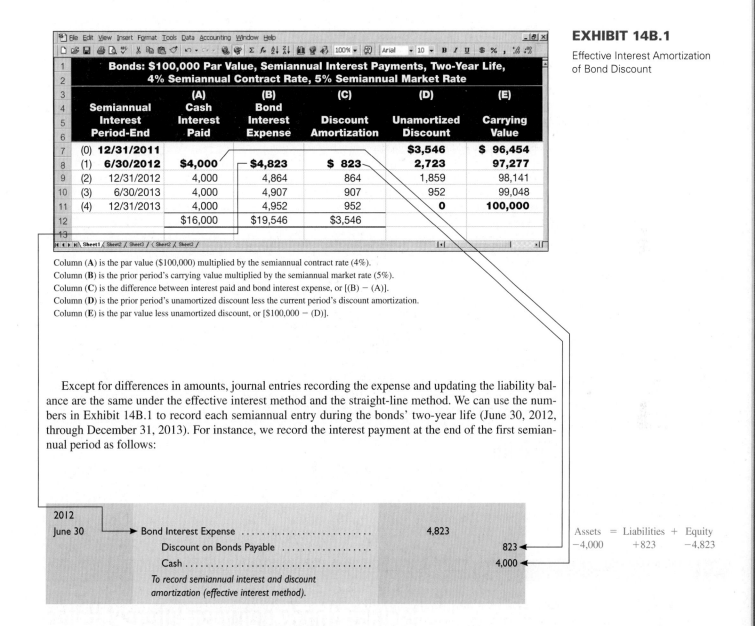

EXHIBIT 14B.1

Effective Interest Amortization of Bond Discount

Bonds: $100,000 Par Value, Semiannual Interest Payments, Two-Year Life, 4% Semiannual Contract Rate, 5% Semiannual Market Rate					
Semiannual Interest Period-End	(A) Cash Interest Paid	(B) Bond Interest Expense	(C) Discount Amortization	(D) Unamortized Discount	(E) Carrying Value
(0) 12/31/2011				$3,546	$ 96,454
(1) 6/30/2012	$4,000	$4,823	$ 823	2,723	97,277
(2) 12/31/2012	4,000	4,864	864	1,859	98,141
(3) 6/30/2013	4,000	4,907	907	952	99,048
(4) 12/31/2013	4,000	4,952	952	0	100,000
	$16,000	$19,546	$3,546		

Column (**A**) is the par value ($100,000) multiplied by the semiannual contract rate (4%).
Column (**B**) is the prior period's carrying value multiplied by the semiannual market rate (5%).
Column (**C**) is the difference between interest paid and bond interest expense, or [(B) − (A)].
Column (**D**) is the prior period's unamortized discount less the current period's discount amortization.
Column (**E**) is the par value less unamortized discount, or [$100,000 − (D)].

Except for differences in amounts, journal entries recording the expense and updating the liability balance are the same under the effective interest method and the straight-line method. We can use the numbers in Exhibit 14B.1 to record each semiannual entry during the bonds' two-year life (June 30, 2012, through December 31, 2013). For instance, we record the interest payment at the end of the first semiannual period as follows:

2012			
June 30	Bond Interest Expense	4,823	
	Discount on Bonds Payable		823
	Cash		4,000
	To record semiannual interest and discount amortization (effective interest method).		

Assets = Liabilities + Equity
−4,000   +823   −4,823

Effective Interest Amortization of a Premium Bond   Exhibit 14B.2 shows the amortization table using the effective interest method for the Adidas bonds (as described in Exhibit 14.8). Column A lists the semiannual cash payments. Column B shows the amount of bond interest expense, computed as the 5% semiannual market rate at issuance multiplied by the beginning-of-period carrying value. The amount of cash paid in column A is larger than the bond interest expense because the cash payment is based on the higher 6% semiannual contract rate. The excess cash payment over the interest expense reduces the principal. These amounts are shown in column C. Column E shows the carrying value after

EXHIBIT 14B.2

Effective Interest Amortization
of Bond Premium

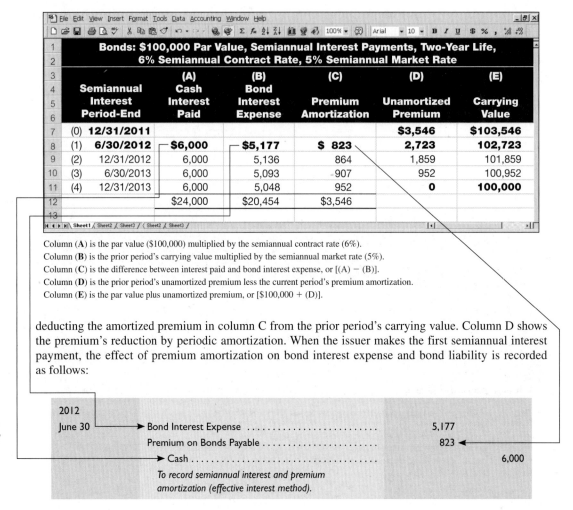

Column (**A**) is the par value ($100,000) multiplied by the semiannual contract rate (6%).
Column (**B**) is the prior period's carrying value multiplied by the semiannual market rate (5%).
Column (**C**) is the difference between interest paid and bond interest expense, or [(A) − (B)].
Column (**D**) is the prior period's unamortized premium less the current period's premium amortization.
Column (**E**) is the par value plus unamortized premium, or [$100,000 + (D)].

deducting the amortized premium in column C from the prior period's carrying value. Column D shows the premium's reduction by periodic amortization. When the issuer makes the first semiannual interest payment, the effect of premium amortization on bond interest expense and bond liability is recorded as follows:

Assets	=	Liabilities	+	Equity
−6,000		−823		−5,177

2012			
June 30	Bond Interest Expense	5,177	
	Premium on Bonds Payable	823	
	Cash		6,000
	To record semiannual interest and premium		
	amortization (effective interest method).		

Similar entries with different amounts are recorded at each payment date until the bond matures at the end of 2013. The effective interest method yields decreasing amounts of bond interest expense and increasing amounts of premium amortization over the bonds' life.

🌐 IFRS

Unlike U.S. GAAP, IFRS requires that interest expense be computed using the effective interest method with *no exemptions*. ■

APPENDIX

14C

Issuing Bonds between Interest Dates

C3 Describe interest accrual when bond payment periods differ from accounting periods.

An issuer can sell bonds at a date other than an interest payment date. When this occurs, the buyers normally pay the issuer the purchase price plus any interest accrued since the prior interest payment date. This accrued interest is then repaid to these buyers on the next interest payment date. To illustrate, suppose **Avia** sells $100,000 of its 9% bonds at par on March 1, 2011, 60 days after the stated issue date. The interest on Avia bonds is payable semiannually on each June 30 and December 31. Since 60 days have passed, the issuer collects accrued interest from the buyers at the time of issuance. This amount is $1,500 ($100,000 × 9% × 60/360 year). This case is reflected in Exhibit 14C.1.

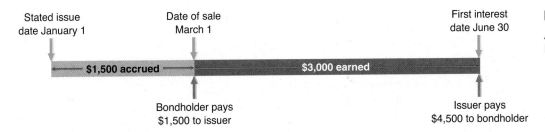

EXHIBIT 14C.1

Accruing Interest between Interest Payment Dates

Avia records the issuance of these bonds on March 1, 2011, as follows:

Mar. 1	Cash	101,500	
	Interest Payable		1,500
	Bonds Payable.............................		100,000
	Sold bonds at par with accrued interest.		

Assets   =   Liabilities   +   Equity
+101,500   +100,000
                      +1,500

Liabilities for interest payable and bonds payable are recorded in separate accounts. When the June 30, 2011, semiannual interest date arrives, Avia pays the full semiannual interest of $4,500 ($100,000 × 9% × ½ year) to the bondholders. This payment includes the four months' interest of $3,000 earned by the bondholders from March 1 to June 30 *plus* the repayment of the 60 days' accrued interest collected by Avia when the bonds were sold. Avia records this first semiannual interest payment as follows:

Example: How much interest is collected from a buyer of $50,000 of Avia bonds sold at par 150 days after the contract issue date? *Answer:* $1,875 (computed as $50,000 × 9% × $^{150}/_{360}$ year)

June 30	Interest Payable	1,500	
	Bond Interest Expense........................	3,000	
	Cash		4,500
	Paid semiannual interest on the bonds.		

Assets   =   Liabilities   +   Equity
−4,500   −1,500   −3,000

The practice of collecting and then repaying accrued interest with the next interest payment is to simplify the issuer's administrative efforts. To explain, suppose an issuer sells bonds on 15 or 20 different dates between the stated issue date and the first interest payment date. If the issuer does not collect accrued interest from buyers, it needs to pay different amounts of cash to each of them according to the time that passed after purchasing the bonds. The issuer needs to keep detailed records of buyers and the dates they bought bonds. Issuers avoid this recordkeeping by having each buyer pay accrued interest at purchase. Issuers then pay the full semiannual interest to all buyers, regardless of when they bought bonds.

Accruing Bond Interest Expense   If a bond's interest period does not coincide with the issuer's accounting period, an adjusting entry is needed to recognize bond interest expense accrued since the most recent interest payment. To illustrate, assume that the stated issue date for Adidas bonds described in Exhibit 14.10 is September 1, 2011, instead of December 31, 2011, and that the bonds are sold on September 1, 2011. As a result, four months' interest (and premium amortization) accrue before the end of the 2011 calendar year. Interest for this period equals $3,409, or ⅔ of the first six months' interest of $5,113. Also, the premium amortization is $591, or ⅔ of the first six months' amortization of $887. The sum of the bond interest expense and the amortization is $4,000 ($3,409 + $591), which equals ⅔ of the $6,000 cash payment due on February 28, 2012. Adidas records these effects with an adjusting entry at December 31, 2011.

Point: Computation of accrued bond interest may use months instead of days for simplicity purposes. For example, the accrued interest computation for the Adidas bonds is based on months.

Dec. 31	Bond Interest Expense	3,409	
	Premium on Bonds Payable	591	
	Interest Payable		4,000
	To record four months' accrued interest and premium amortization.		

Assets   =   Liabilities   +   Equity
                    −591   −3,409
                  +4,000

Similar entries are made on each December 31 throughout the bonds' two-year life. When the $6,000 cash payment occurs on each February 28 interest payment date, Adidas must recognize bond interest expense and amortization for January and February. It must also eliminate the interest payable liability created by the December 31 adjusting entry. For example, Adidas records its payment on February 28, 2012, as follows:

Assets = Liabilities + Equity
−6,000   −4,000   −1,704
              −296

Feb. 28	Interest Payable	4,000	
	Bond Interest Expense ($5,113 × ⅔)	1,704	
	Premium on Bonds Payable ($887 × ⅔)	296	
	Cash		6,000
	To record 2 months' interest and amortization, and		
	eliminate accrued interest liability.		

The interest payments made each August 31 are recorded as usual because the entire six-month interest period is included within this company's calendar-year reporting period.

Decision Maker   Answer — p. 579

Bond Rater   You must assign a rating to a bond that reflects its risk to bondholders. Identify factors you consider in assessing bond risk. Indicate the likely levels (relative to the norm) for the factors you identify for a bond that sells at a discount. ■

Quick Check   Answer — p. 579

16. On May 1, a company sells 9% bonds with a $500,000 par value that pay semiannual interest on each January 1 and July 1. The bonds are sold at par plus interest accrued since January 1. The issuer records the first semiannual interest payment on July 1 with (*a*) a debit to Interest Payable for $15,000, (*b*) a debit to Bond Interest Expense for $22,500, or (*c*) a credit to Interest Payable for $7,500.

14D   Leases and Pensions

This appendix briefly explains the accounting and analysis for both leases and pensions.

C4 Describe accounting for leases and pensions.

Lease Liabilities   A **lease** is a contractual agreement between a *lessor* (asset owner) and a *lessee* (asset renter or tenant) that grants the lessee the right to use the asset for a period of time in return for cash (rent) payments. Nearly one-fourth of all equipment purchases are financed with leases. The advantages of lease financing include the lack of an immediate large cash payment and the potential to deduct rental payments in computing taxable income. From an accounting perspective, leases can be classified as either operating or capital leases.

Point: Home Depot reports that its rental expenses from operating leases total more than $900 million.

Operating Leases   **Operating leases** are short-term (or cancelable) leases in which the lessor retains the risks and rewards of ownership. Examples include most car and apartment rental agreements. The lessee records such lease payments as expenses; the lessor records them as revenue. The lessee does not report the leased item as an asset or a liability (it is the lessor's asset). To illustrate, if an employee of Amazon leases a car for $300 at an airport while on company business, Amazon (lessee) records this cost as follows:

Assets = Liabilities + Equity
−300   −300

July 4	Rental Expense	300	
	Cash		300
	To record lease rental payment.		

Capital Leases **Capital leases** are long-term (or noncancelable) leases by which the lessor transfers substantially all risks and rewards of ownership to the lessee.[3] Examples include most leases of airplanes and department store buildings. The lessee records the leased item as its own asset along with a lease liability at the start of the lease term; the amount recorded equals the present value of all lease payments. To illustrate, assume that K2 Co. enters into a six-year lease of a building in which it will sell sporting equipment. The lease transfers all building ownership risks and rewards to K2 (the present value of its $12,979 annual lease payments is $60,000). K2 records this transaction as follows:

2011			
Jan. 1	Leased Asset—Building	60,000	
	Lease Liability		60,000
	To record leased asset and lease liability.		

Assets = Liabilities + Equity
+60,000   +60,000

K2 reports the leased asset as a plant asset and the lease liability as a long-term liability. The portion of the lease liability expected to be paid in the next year is reported as a current liability.[4] At each year-end, K2 records depreciation on the leased asset (assume straight-line depreciation, six-year lease term, and no salvage value) as follows:

Point: Home Depot reports *"certain locations . . . are leased under capital leases."* The net present value of this Lease Liability is about $400 million.

Dec. 31	Depreciation Expense—Building	10,000	
	Accumulated Depreciation—Building		10,000
	To record depreciation on leased asset.		

Assets = Liabilities + Equity
−10,000   −10,000

K2 also accrues interest on the lease liability at each year-end. Interest expense is computed by multiplying the remaining lease liability by the interest rate on the lease. Specifically, K2 records its annual interest expense as part of its annual lease payment ($12,979) as follows (for its first year):

2011			
Dec. 31	Interest Expense	4,800	
	Lease Liability	8,179	
	Cash		12,979
	*To record first annual lease payment.**		

Assets = Liabilities + Equity
−12,979   −8,179   −4,800

* These numbers are computed from a *lease payment schedule*. For simplicity, we use the same numbers from Exhibit 14.14 for this lease payment schedule—with different headings as follows:

			Payments		
	(A)	(B)	(C)	(D)	(E)
		Debit	*Debit*	*Credit*	
Period Ending Date	Beginning Balance of Lease Liability	Interest on Lease Liability 8% × (A)	+ Lease Liability (D) − (B)	= Cash Lease Payment	Ending Balance of Lease Liability (A) − (C)
12/31/2011	$60,000	$ 4,800	$ 8,179	$12,979	$51,821
12/31/2012	51,821	4,146	8,833	12,979	42,988
12/31/2013	42,988	3,439	9,540	12,979	33,448
12/31/2014	33,448	2,676	10,303	12,979	23,145
12/31/2015	23,145	1,852	11,127	12,979	12,018
12/31/2016	12,018	961	12,018	12,979	0
		$17,874	$60,000	$77,874	

---

[3] A *capital lease* meets any one or more of four criteria: (1) transfers title of leased asset to lessee, (2) contains a bargain purchase option, (3) has a lease term that is 75% or more of the leased asset's useful life, or (4) has a present value of lease payments that is 90% or more of the leased asset's market value.

[4] Most lessees try to keep leased assets and lease liabilities off their balance sheets by failing to meet any one of the four criteria of a capital lease. This is because a lease liability increases a company's total liabilities, making it more difficult to obtain additional financing. The acquisition of assets without reporting any related liabilities (or other asset outflows) on the balance sheet is called **off-balance-sheet financing.**

Point: Fringe benefits are often 40% or more of salaries and wages, and pension benefits make up nearly 15% of fringe benefits.

Pension Liabilities   A **pension plan** is a contractual agreement between an employer and its employees for the employer to provide benefits (payments) to employees after they retire. Most employers pay the full cost of the pension, but sometimes employees pay part of the cost. An employer records its payment into a pension plan with a debit to Pension Expense and a credit to Cash. A *plan administrator* receives payments from the employer, invests them in pension assets, and makes benefit payments to *pension recipients* (retired employees). Insurance and trust companies often serve as pension plan administrators.

Point: Two types of pension plans are (1) *defined benefit plan*—the retirement benefit is defined and the employer estimates the contribution necessary to pay these benefits—and (2) *defined contribution plan*—the pension contribution is defined and the employer and/or employee contributes amounts specified in the pension agreement.

Many pensions are known as *defined benefit plans* that define future benefits; the employer's contributions vary, depending on assumptions about future pension assets and liabilities. Several disclosures are necessary in this case. Specifically, a pension liability is reported when the accumulated benefit obligation is *more than* the plan assets, a so-called *underfunded plan.* The accumulated benefit obligation is the present value of promised future pension payments to retirees. *Plan assets* refer to the market value of assets the plan administrator holds. A pension asset is reported when the accumulated benefit obligation is *less than* the plan assets, a so-called *overfunded plan.* An employer reports pension expense when it receives the benefits from the employees' services, which is sometimes decades before it pays pension benefits to employees. (*Other Postretirement Benefits* refer to nonpension benefits such as health care and life insurance benefits. Similar to a pension, costs of these benefits are estimated and liabilities accrued when the employees earn them.)

Summary

C1 **Explain the types and payment patterns of notes.** Notes repaid over a period of time are called *installment notes* and usually follow one of two payment patterns: (1) decreasing payments of interest plus equal amounts of principal or (2) equal total payments. Mortgage notes also are common.

C2^A **Explain and compute the present value of an amount(s) to be paid at a future date(s).** The basic concept of present value is that an amount of cash to be paid or received in the future is worth less than the same amount of cash to be paid or received today. Another important present value concept is that interest is compounded, meaning interest is added to the balance and used to determine interest for succeeding periods. An annuity is a series of equal payments occurring at equal time intervals. An annuity's present value can be computed using the present value table for an annuity (or a calculator).

C3^C **Describe interest accrual when bond payment periods differ from accounting periods.** Issuers and buyers of debt record the interest accrued when issue dates or accounting periods do not coincide with debt payment dates.

C4^D **Describe accounting for leases and pensions.** A lease is a rental agreement between the lessor and the lessee. When the lessor retains the risks and rewards of asset ownership (an *operating lease*), the lessee debits Rent Expense and credits Cash for its lease payments. When the lessor substantially transfers the risks and rewards of asset ownership to the lessee (a *capital lease*), the lessee capitalizes the leased asset and records a lease liability. Pension agreements can result in either pension assets or pension liabilities.

A1 **Compare bond financing with stock financing.** Bond financing is used to fund business activities. Advantages of bond financing versus stock include (1) no effect on owner control, (2) tax savings, and (3) increased earnings due to financial leverage. Disadvantages include (1) interest and principal payments and (2) amplification of poor performance.

A2 **Assess debt features and their implications.** Certain bonds are secured by the issuer's assets; other bonds, called *debentures,* are unsecured. Serial bonds mature at different points in time;

term bonds mature at one time. Registered bonds have each bondholder's name recorded by the issuer; bearer bonds are payable to the holder. Convertible bonds are exchangeable for shares of the issuer's stock. Callable bonds can be retired by the issuer at a set price. Debt features alter the risk of loss for creditors.

A3 **Compute the debt-to-equity ratio and explain its use.** Both creditors and equity holders are concerned about the relation between the amount of liabilities and the amount of equity. A company's financing structure is at less risk when the debt-to-equity ratio is lower, as liabilities must be paid and usually with periodic interest.

P1 **Prepare entries to record bond issuance and interest expense.** When bonds are issued at par, Cash is debited and Bonds Payable is credited for the bonds' par value. At bond interest payment dates (usually semiannual), Bond Interest Expense is debited and Cash credited—the latter for an amount equal to the bond par value multiplied by the bond contract rate.

P2 **Compute and record amortization of bond discount.** Bonds are issued at a discount when the contract rate is less than the market rate, making the issue (selling) price less than par. When this occurs, the issuer records a credit to Bonds Payable (at par) and debits both Discount on Bonds Payable and Cash. The amount of bond interest expense assigned to each period is computed using either the straight-line or effective interest method.

P3 **Compute and record amortization of bond premium.** Bonds are issued at a premium when the contract rate is higher than the market rate, making the issue (selling) price greater than par. When this occurs, the issuer records a debit to Cash and credits both Premium on Bonds Payable and Bonds Payable (at par). The amount of bond interest expense assigned to each period is computed using either the straight-line or effective interest method. The Premium on Bonds Payable is allocated to reduce bond interest expense over the life of the bonds.

P4 **Record the retirement of bonds.** Bonds are retired at maturity with a debit to Bonds Payable and a credit to Cash at par value. The issuer can retire the bonds early by exercising a call option or purchasing them in the market. Bondholders can also re-tire bonds early by exercising a conversion feature on convertible bonds. The issuer recognizes a gain or loss for the difference between the amount paid and the bond carrying value.

P5 **Prepare entries to account for notes.** Interest is allocated to each period in a note's life by multiplying its beginning-period carrying value by its market rate at issuance. If a note is repaid with equal payments, the payment amount is computed by dividing the borrowed amount by the present value of an annuity factor (taken from a present value table) using the market rate and the number of payments.

Guidance Answers to Decision Maker

Entrepreneur This is a "present value" question. The market interest rate (10%) and present value ($3,000) are known, but the payment required two years later is unknown. This amount ($3,630) can be computed as $3,000 \times 1.10 \times 1.10$. Thus, the sale price is $3,630 when no payments are received for two years. The $3,630 received two years from today is equivalent to $3,000 cash today.

Bond Investor The debt-to-equity ratio for the first company is 0.2 ($350,000/$1,750,000) and for the second company is 1.2 ($1,200,000/$1,000,000), suggesting that the financing structure of the second company is more risky than that of the first company. Consequently, as a buyer of unsecured debenture bonds, you prefer the first company (all else equal).

Bond Rater Bonds with longer repayment periods (life) have higher risk. Also, bonds issued by companies in financial difficulties or facing higher than normal uncertainties have higher risk. Moreover, companies with higher than normal debt and large fluctuations in earnings are considered of higher risk. Discount bonds are more risky on one or more of these factors.

Guidance Answers to Quick Checks

1.

2011			
Jan. 1	Cash	10,000	
	Bonds Payable		10,000
June 30	Bond Interest Expense	450	
	Cash		450

2. Multiply the bond's par value by its contract rate of interest.

3. Bonds sell at a premium when the contract rate exceeds the market rate and the purchasers pay more than their par value.

4. The bonds are issued at a discount, meaning that issue price is less than par value. A discount occurs because the bond contract rate (6%) is less than the market rate (8%).

5.

Cash	91,893	
Discount on Bonds Payable	8,107	
Bonds Payable		100,000

6. $3,811 (total bond interest expense of $38,107 divided by 10 periods; or the $3,000 semiannual cash payment plus the $8,107 discount divided by 10 periods).

7. The bonds are issued at a premium, meaning issue price is higher than par value. A premium occurs because the bonds' contract rate (16%) is higher than the market rate (14%).

8. (b) For each semiannual period: $10,592/20 periods = $530 premium amortization.

9.

Bonds payable, 16%, due 12/31/2020	$100,000	
Plus premium on bonds payable	9,532*	$109,532

* Original premium balance of $10,592 less $530 and $530 amortized on 6/30/2011 and 12/31/2011, respectively.

10. $9,375 loss, computed as the difference between the repurchase price of $256,250 [50% of ($500,000 × 102.5%)] and the carrying value of $246,875 (50% of $493,750).

11. (c)

12. The interest portion of an installment payment equals the period's beginning loan balance multiplied by the market interest rate at the time of the note's issuance.

13. On the balance sheet, the account balances of the related liability (note payable) and asset (cash) accounts are decreased. On the income statement, interest expense is recorded.

14. (c), computed as 3.3121 × $1,000 = $3,312.

15. The option of paying $10,000 after one year has a lower present value. It postpones paying the first $5,000 by six months. More generally, the present value of a further delayed payment is always lower than a less delayed payment.

16. (a) Reflects payment of accrued interest recorded back on May 1; $500,000 × 9% × ⅟₁₂ = $15,000.

Convertible bonds (p. 566)
Coupon bonds (p. 566)
Debt-to-equity ratio (p. 567)
Discount on bonds payable (p. 555)
Effective interest method (p. 572)
Fair value option (p. 565)
Installment note (p. 562)
Lease (p. 576)

Market rate (p. 555)
Mortgage (p. 564)
Off-balance-sheet financing (p. 577)
Operating leases (p. 576)
Par value of a bond (p. 552)
Pension plan (p. 578)
Premium on bonds (p. 558)
Registered bonds (p. 566)

Secured bonds (p. 566)
Serial bonds (p. 566)
Sinking fund bonds (p. 566)
Straight-line bond amortization (p. 556)
Term bonds (p. 566)
Unsecured bonds (p. 566)

Multiple Choice Quiz   Answers on p. 593   mhhe.com/wildFAP20e

Additional Quiz Questions are available at the book's Website.

1. A bond traded at 97½ means that
  a. The bond pays 97½% interest.
  b. The bond trades at $975 per $1,000 bond.
  c. The market rate of interest is below the contract rate of interest for the bond.
  d. The bonds can be retired at $975 each.
  e. The bond's interest rate is 2½%.

2. A bondholder that owns a $1,000, 6%, 15-year bond has
  a. The right to receive $1,000 at maturity.
  b. Ownership rights in the bond issuing entity.
  c. The right to receive $60 per month until maturity.
  d. The right to receive $1,900 at maturity.
  e. The right to receive $600 per year until maturity.

3. A company issues 8%, 20-year bonds with a par value of $500,000. The current market rate for the bonds is 8%. The amount of interest owed to the bondholders for each semiannual interest payment is
  a. $40,000.
  b. $0.
  c. $20,000.

  d. $800,000.
  e. $400,000.

4. A company issued 5-year, 5% bonds with a par value of $100,000. The company received $95,735 for the bonds. Using the straight-line method, the company's interest expense for the first semiannual interest period is
  a. $2,926.50.
  b. $5,853.00.
  c. $2,500.00.
  d. $5,000.00.
  e. $9,573.50.

5. A company issued 8-year, 5% bonds with a par value of $350,000. The company received proceeds of $373,745. Interest is payable semiannually. The amount of premium amortized for the first semiannual interest period, assuming straight-line bond amortization, is
  a. $2,698.
  b. $23,745.
  c. $8,750.
  d. $9,344.
  e. $1,484.

B(C,D) *Superscript letter B(C, D) denotes assignments based on Appendix 14B (14C, 14D).*
⬛ Icon denotes assignments that involve decision making.

Discussion Questions

1. What is the main difference between a bond and a share of stock?

2. What is the main difference between notes payable and bonds payable?

3. ⬛ What is the advantage of issuing bonds instead of obtaining financing from the company's owners?

4. What are the duties of a trustee for bondholders?

5. What is a bond indenture? What provisions are usually included in it?

6. What are the *contract* rate and the *market* rate for bonds?

7. ⬛ What factors affect the market rates for bonds?

8.ᴮ⬛ Does the straight-line or effective interest method produce an interest expense allocation that yields a constant rate of interest over a bond's life? Explain.

9.ᶜWhy does a company that issues bonds between interest dates collect accrued interest from the bonds' purchasers?

10. ⬛ If you know the par value of bonds, the contract rate, and the market rate, how do you compute the bonds' price?

11. What is the issue price of a $2,000 bond sold at 98¼? What is the issue price of a $6,000 bond sold at 101½?

12. Describe the debt-to-equity ratio and explain how creditors and owners would use this ratio to evaluate a company's risk.

13. 🚹 What obligation does an entrepreneur (owner) have to investors that purchase bonds to finance the business?

14. Refer to **Research In Motion**'s annual report in Appendix A. Is there any indication that RIM has issued bonds?   *RIM*

15. By what amount did **Palm**'s long-term debt increase or decrease in 2009?   Palm

16. Refer to the statement of cash flows for **Nokia** in Appendix A. For the year ended December 31, 2009, what was the amount for repayment of bank loans?   **NOKIA**

17. Refer to the annual report for **Apple** in Appendix A. For the year ended September 26, 2009, what is its debt-to-equity ratio? What does this ratio tell us?   *Apple*

18.ᴰ When can a lease create both an asset and a liability for the lessee?

19.ᴰ Compare and contrast an operating lease with a capital lease.

20.ᴰ Describe the two basic types of pension plans.

🖥 connect

Round dollar amounts to the nearest whole dollar.

Enter the letter of the description A through H that best fits each term or phrase 1 through 8.

A. Records and tracks the bondholders' names.
B. Is unsecured; backed only by the issuer's credit standing.
C. Has varying maturity dates for amounts owed.
D. Identifies rights and responsibilities of the issuer and the bondholders.
E. Can be exchanged for shares of the issuer's stock.
F. Is unregistered; interest is paid to whoever possesses them.
G. Maintains a separate asset account from which bondholders are paid at maturity.
H. Pledges specific assets of the issuer as collateral.

1. _____ Debenture
2. _____ Bond indenture
3. _____ Bearer bond
4. _____ Registered bond
5. _____ Sinking fund bond
6. _____ Convertible bond
7. _____ Secured bond
8. _____ Serial bond

QUICK STUDY

QS 14-1
Bond features and terminology
A2

Alberto Company issues 8%, 10-year bonds with a par value of $350,000 and semiannual interest payments. On the issue date, the annual market rate for these bonds is 10%, which implies a selling price of 87½. The straight-line method is used to allocate interest expense.

1. What are the issuer's cash proceeds from issuance of these bonds?
2. What total amount of bond interest expense will be recognized over the life of these bonds?
3. What is the amount of bond interest expense recorded on the first interest payment date?

QS 14-2
Bond computations—
straight-line
P1 P2

Sanchez Company issues 10%, 15-year bonds with a par value of $120,000 and semiannual interest payments. On the issue date, the annual market rate for these bonds is 8%, which implies a selling price of 117¼. The effective interest method is used to allocate interest expense.

1. What are the issuer's cash proceeds from issuance of these bonds?
2. What total amount of bond interest expense will be recognized over the life of these bonds?
3. What amount of bond interest expense is recorded on the first interest payment date?

QS 14-3ᴮ
Bond computations—
effective interest
P1 P3

Prepare the journal entries for the issuance of the bonds in both QS 14-2 and QS 14-3. Assume that both bonds are issued for cash on January 1, 2011.

QS 14-4
Journalize bond issuance   P1

Using the bond details in both QS 14-2 and QS 14-3, confirm that the bonds' selling prices given in each problem are approximately correct. Use the present value tables B.1 and B.3 in Appendix B.

QS 14-5
Computing bond price   P2 P3

QS 14-6

Recording bond issuance and discount amortization   **P1 P2**

Bellvue Company issues 10%, five-year bonds, on December 31, 2010, with a par value of $100,000 and semiannual interest payments. Use the following straight-line bond amortization table and prepare journal entries to record (*a*) the issuance of bonds on December 31, 2010; (*b*) the first interest payment on June 30, 2011; and (*c*) the second interest payment on December 31, 2011.

Semiannual Period-End		Unamortized Discount	Carrying Value
(0)	12/31/2010	$7,360	$92,640
(1)	6/30/2011	6,624	93,376
(2)	12/31/2011	5,888	94,112

QS 14-7

Bond retirement by call option

P4

On July 1, 2011, Jackson Company exercises a $5,000 call option (plus par value) on its outstanding bonds that have a carrying value of $208,000 and par value of $200,000. The company exercises the call option after the semiannual interest is paid on June 30, 2011. Record the entry to retire the bonds.

QS 14-8

Bond retirement by stock conversion   **P4**

On January 1, 2011, the $1,000,000 par value bonds of Gruden Company with a carrying value of $1,000,000 are converted to 500,000 shares of $0.50 par value common stock. Record the entry for the conversion of the bonds.

QS 14-9

Computing payments for an installment note   **C1**

Valdez Company borrows $170,000 cash from a bank and in return signs an installment note for five annual payments of equal amount, with the first payment due one year after the note is signed. Use Table B.3 in Appendix B to compute the amount of the annual payment for each of the following annual market rates: (*a*) 4%, (*b*) 8%, and (*c*) 12%.

QS 14-10

Debt-to-equity ratio

A2

Compute the debt-to-equity ratio for each of the following companies. Which company appears to have a riskier financing structure? Explain.

	Canal Company	Sears Company
Total liabilities	$492,000	$ 384,000
Total equity	656,000	1,200,000

QS 14-11[C]

Issuing bonds between interest dates   **P1**

Kemper Company plans to issue 6% bonds on January 1, 2011, with a par value of $1,000,000. The company sells $900,000 of the bonds on January 1, 2011. The remaining $100,000 sells at par on March 1, 2011. The bonds pay interest semiannually as of June 30 and December 31. Record the entry for the March 1 cash sale of bonds.

QS 14-12[D]

Recording operating leases   **C4**

Lauren Wright, an employee of ETrain.com, leases a car at O'Hare airport for a three-day business trip. The rental cost is $350. Prepare the entry by ETrain.com to record Lauren's short-term car lease cost.

QS 14-13[D]

Recording capital leases   **C4**

Juicyfruit, Inc., signs a five-year lease for office equipment with Office Solutions. The present value of the lease payments is $20,859. Prepare the journal entry that Juicyfruit records at the inception of this capital lease.

QS 14-14

International liabilities disclosures

P1 P2

Vodafone Group Plc reports the following information among its bonds payable as of March 31, 2009 (pounds in millions).

Financial Long-Term Liabilities Measured at Amortised Cost			
(£ millions)	Nominal (par) Value	Carrying Value	Fair Value
4.625% (US dollar 500 million) bond due July 2018	£350	£392	£315

a. What is the par value of the 4.625% bond issuance? What is its book (carrying) value?

b. Was the 4.625% bond sold at a discount or a premium? Explain.

Refer to the information in QS 14-14 for **Vodafone Group Plc**. The following price quotes (from Yahoo! Finance Bond Center) relate tó its bonds payable as of late 2009. For example, the price quote indicates that the 4.625% bonds have a market price of 98.0 (98.0% of par value), resulting in a yield to maturity of 4.899%.

QS 14-15
International liabilities disclosures and interpretations

P1 P2

Price	Contract Rate (coupon)	Maturity Date	Market Rate (YTM)
98.0	4.625%	15-Jul-2018	4.899%

a. Assuming that the 4.625% bonds were originally issued at par value, what does the market price reveal about interest rate changes since bond issuance? (Assume that Vodafone's credit rating has remained the same.)

b. Does the change in market rates since the issuance of these bonds affect the amount of interest expense reported on Vodafone's income statement? Explain.

c. How much cash would Vodafone need to pay to repurchase the 4.625% bonds at the quoted market price of 98.0? (Assume no interest is owed when the bonds are repurchased.)

d. Assuming that the 4.625% bonds remain outstanding until maturity, at what market price will the bonds sell on the due date in 2018?

Mc Graw Hill connect

> Round dollar amounts to the nearest whole dollar. Assume no reversing entries are used.

EXERCISES

On January 1, 2011, Kidman Enterprises issues bonds that have a $1,700,000 par value, mature in 20 years, and pay 9% interest semiannually on June 30 and December 31. The bonds are sold at par.

1. How much interest will Kidman pay (in cash) to the bondholders every six months?

2. Prepare journal entries to record (*a*) the issuance of bonds on January 1, 2011; (*b*) the first interest payment on June 30, 2011; and (*c*) the second interest payment on December 31, 2011.

3. Prepare the journal entry for issuance assuming the bonds are issued at (*a*) 98 and (*b*) 102.

Exercise 14-1
Recording bond issuance and interest

P1

Moss issues bonds with a par value of $90,000 on January 1, 2011. The bonds' annual contract rate is 8%, and interest is paid semiannually on June 30 and December 31. The bonds mature in three years. The annual market rate at the date of issuance is 10%, and the bonds are sold for $85,431.

1. What is the amount of the discount on these bonds at issuance?

2. How much total bond interest expense will be recognized over the life of these bonds?

3. Prepare an amortization table like the one in Exhibit 14.7 for these bonds; use the straight-line method to amortize the discount.

Exercise 14-2
Straight-line amortization of bond discount

P2

Welch issues bonds dated January 1, 2011, with a par value of $250,000. The bonds' annual contract rate is 9%, and interest is paid semiannually on June 30 and December 31. The bonds mature in three years. The annual market rate at the date of issuance is 12%, and the bonds are sold for $231,570.

1. What is the amount of the discount on these bonds at issuance?

2. How much total bond interest expense will be recognized over the life of these bonds?

3. Prepare an amortization table like the one in Exhibit 14B.1 for these bonds; use the effective interest method to amortize the discount.

Exercise 14-3ᴮ
Effective interest amortization of bond discount

P2

Prairie Dunes Co. issues bonds dated January 1, 2011, with a par value of $800,000. The bonds' annual contract rate is 13%, and interest is paid semiannually on June 30 and December 31. The bonds mature in three years. The annual market rate at the date of issuance is 12%, and the bonds are sold for $819,700.

1. What is the amount of the premium on these bonds at issuance?

2. How much total bond interest expense will be recognized over the life of these bonds?

3. Prepare an amortization table like the one in Exhibit 14.11 for these bonds; use the straight-line method to amortize the premium.

Exercise 14-4
Straight-line amortization of bond premium

P3

Exercise 14-5ᴮ
Effective interest amortization of bond premium   P3

Refer to the bond details in Exercise 14-4 and prepare an amortization table like the one in Exhibit 14B.2 for these bonds using the effective interest method to amortize the premium.

Exercise 14-6
Recording bond issuance and premium amortization
P1   P3

Jobbs Company issues 10%, five-year bonds, on December 31, 2010, with a par value of $100,000 and semiannual interest payments. Use the following straight-line bond amortization table and prepare journal entries to record (*a*) the issuance of bonds on December 31, 2010; (*b*) the first interest payment on June 30, 2011; and (*c*) the second interest payment on December 31, 2011.

Semiannual Period-End	Unamortized Premium	Carrying Value
(0) 12/31/2010	$8,111	$108,111
(1) 6/30/2011	7,300	107,300
(2) 12/31/2011	6,489	106,489

Exercise 14-7
Recording bond issuance and discount amortization
P1   P2

Matchbox Company issues 6%, four-year bonds, on December 31, 2011, with a par value of $100,000 and semiannual interest payments. Use the following straight-line bond amortization table and prepare journal entries to record (*a*) the issuance of bonds on December 31, 2011; (*b*) the first interest payment on June 30, 2012; and (*c*) the second interest payment on December 31, 2012.

Semiannual Period-End	Unamortized Discount	Carrying Value
(0) 12/31/2011	$6,733	$93,267
(1) 6/30/2012	5,891	94,109
(2) 12/31/2012	5,049	94,951

Exercise 14-8
Recording bond issuance and discount amortization
P1   P2

Oneil Company issues 5%, two-year bonds, on December 31, 2011, with a par value of $100,000 and semiannual interest payments. Use the following straight-line bond amortization table and prepare journal entries to record (*a*) the issuance of bonds on December 31, 2011; (*b*) the first through fourth interest payments on each June 30 and December 31; and (*c*) the maturity of the bond on December 31, 2013.

Semiannual Period-End	Unamortized Discount	Carrying Value
(0) 12/31/2011	$6,000	$ 94,000
(1) 6/30/2012	4,500	95,500
(2) 12/31/2012	3,000	97,000
(3) 6/30/2013	1,500	98,500
(4) 12/31/2013	0	100,000

Exercise 14-9
Computing bond interest and price; recording bond issuance
P2

Jester Company issues bonds with a par value of $600,000 on their stated issue date. The bonds mature in 10 years and pay 6% annual interest in semiannual payments. On the issue date, the annual market rate for the bonds is 8%.

1. What is the amount of each semiannual interest payment for these bonds?
2. How many semiannual interest payments will be made on these bonds over their life?
3. Use the interest rates given to determine whether the bonds are issued at par, at a discount, or at a premium.

Check (4) $518,465

4. Compute the price of the bonds as of their issue date.
5. Prepare the journal entry to record the bonds' issuance.

Exercise 14-10
Computing bond interest and price; recording bond issuance
P3

Metro Company issues bonds with a par value of $75,000 on their stated issue date. The bonds mature in five years and pay 10% annual interest in semiannual payments. On the issue date, the annual market rate for the bonds is 8%.

1. What is the amount of each semiannual interest payment for these bonds?
2. How many semiannual interest payments will be made on these bonds over their life?
3. Use the interest rates given to determine whether the bonds are issued at par, at a discount, or at a premium.

4. Compute the price of the bonds as of their issue date.

5. Prepare the journal entry to record the bonds' issuance.

Check (4) $81,086

On January 1, 2011, Steadman issues $350,000 of 10%, 15-year bonds at a price of 97¾. Six years later, on January 1, 2017, Steadman retires 20% of these bonds by buying them on the open market at 104½. All interest is accounted for and paid through December 31, 2016, the day before the purchase. The straight-line method is used to amortize any bond discount.

Exercise 14-11
Bond computations, straight-line amortization, and bond retirement
P2 P4

1. How much does the company receive when it issues the bonds on January 1, 2011?

2. What is the amount of the discount on the bonds at January 1, 2011?

3. How much amortization of the discount is recorded on the bonds for the entire period from January 1, 2011, through December 31, 2016?

4. What is the carrying (book) value of the bonds as of the close of business on December 31, 2016? What is the carrying value of the 20% soon-to-be-retired bonds on this same date?

5. How much did the company pay on January 1, 2017, to purchase the bonds that it retired?

6. What is the amount of the recorded gain or loss from retiring the bonds?

Check (6) $4,095 loss

7. Prepare the journal entry to record the bond retirement at January 1, 2017.

On May 1, 2011, Fellenger Enterprises issues bonds dated January 1, 2011, that have a $1,700,000 par value, mature in 20 years, and pay 9% interest semiannually on June 30 and December 31. The bonds are sold at par plus four months' accrued interest.

Exercise 14-12^C
Recording bond issuance with accrued interest
C4 P1

1. How much accrued interest do the bond purchasers pay Fellenger on May 1, 2011?

2. Prepare Fellenger's journal entries to record (*a*) the issuance of bonds on May 1, 2011; (*b*) the first interest payment on June 30, 2011; and (*c*) the second interest payment on December 31, 2011.

Check (1) $51,000

Simon issues four-year bonds with a $50,000 par value on June 1, 2011, at a price of $47,974. The annual contract rate is 7%, and interest is paid semiannually on November 30 and May 31.

Exercise 14-13
Straight-line amortization and accrued bond interest expense
P1 P2

1. Prepare an amortization table like the one in Exhibit 14.7 for these bonds. Use the straight-line method of interest amortization.

2. Prepare journal entries to record the first two interest payments and to accrue interest as of December 31, 2011.

On January 1, 2011, Randa borrows $25,000 cash by signing a four-year, 7% installment note. The note requires four equal total payments of accrued interest and principal on December 31 of each year from 2011 through 2014.

Exercise 14-14
Installment note with equal total payments C1 P5

Check (1) $7,381

1. Compute the amount of each of the four equal total payments.

2. Prepare an amortization table for this installment note like the one in Exhibit 14.14.

Use the information in Exercise 14-14 to prepare the journal entries for Randa to record the loan on January 1, 2011, and the four payments from December 31, 2011, through December 31, 2014.

Exercise 14-15
Installment note entries P5

Ramirez Company is considering a project that will require a $500,000 loan. It presently has total liabilities of $220,000, and total assets of $620,000.

Exercise 14-16
Applying debt-to-equity ratio
A3

1. Compute Ramirez's (*a*) present debt-to-equity ratio and (*b*) the debt-to-equity ratio assuming it borrows $500,000 to fund the project.

2. Evaluate and discuss the level of risk involved if Ramirez borrows the funds to pursue the project.

Indicate whether the company in each separate case 1 through 3 has entered into an operating lease or a capital lease.

Exercise 14-17^D
Identifying capital and operating leases
C4

1. The present value of the lease payments is 95% of the leased asset's market value, and the lease term is 70% of the leased asset's useful life.

2. The title is transferred to the lessee, the lessee can purchase the asset for $1 at the end of the lease, and the lease term is five years. The leased asset has an expected useful life of six years.

3. The lessor retains title to the asset, and the lease term is three years on an asset that has a five-year useful life.

Exercise 14-18ᴰ
Accounting for capital lease

C4

Flyer (lessee) signs a five-year capital lease for office equipment with a $20,000 annual lease payment. The present value of the five annual lease payments is $82,000, based on a 7% interest rate.

1. Prepare the journal entry Flyer will record at inception of the lease.
2. If the leased asset has a five-year useful life with no salvage value, prepare the journal entry Flyer will record each year to recognize depreciation expense related to the leased asset.

Exercise 14-19ᴰ
Analyzing lease options

C2 C3 C4

General Motors advertised three alternatives for a 25-month lease on a new Blazer: (1) zero dollars down and a lease payment of $1,750 per month for 25 months, (2) $5,000 down and $1,500 per month for 25 months, or (3) $38,500 down and no payments for 25 months. Use the present value Table B.3 in Appendix B to determine which is the best alternative (assume you have enough cash to accept any alternative and the annual interest rate is 12% compounded monthly).

Exercise 14-20
Accounting for long-term liabilities under IFRS

P1 P2 P3

Heineken N.V. reports the following information for its Loans and Borrowings as of December 31, 2008, including proceeds and repayments for the year ended December 31, 2008 (euros in millions).

Loans and borrowings (noncurrent liabilities)	
Loans and borrowings, December 31, 2008	€ 9,084
Proceeds (cash) from issuances of loans and borrowings	6,361
Repayments (in cash) of loans and borrowings	(2,532)

1. Prepare Heineken's journal entry to record its cash proceeds from issuances of its loans and borrowings for 2008. Assume that the par value of these issuances is €6,000.
2. Prepare Heineken's journal entry to record its cash repayments of its loans and borrowings for 2008. Assume that the par value of these issuances is €2,400, and the premium on them is €32.
3. Compute the discount or premium on its loans and borrowings as of December 31, 2008, assuming that the par value of these liabilities is €9,000.
4. Given the facts in part 3 and viewing the entirety of loans and borrowings as one issuance, was the contract rate on these loans and borrowings higher or lower than the market rate at the time of issuance? Explain. (Assume that Heineken's credit rating has remained the same.)

ᴹᶜGʳᵃʷHⁱˡˡ connect

PROBLEM SET A

Round dollar amounts to the nearest whole dollar. Assume no reversing entries are used.

Problem 14-1A
Computing bond price and recording issuance

P1 P2 P3

Check (1) Premium, $2,718

(3) Discount, $2,294

Stowers Research issues bonds dated January 1, 2011, that pay interest semiannually on June 30 and December 31. The bonds have a $20,000 par value and an annual contract rate of 10%, and they mature in 10 years.

Required

For each of the following three separate situations, (*a*) determine the bonds' issue price on January 1, 2011, and (*b*) prepare the journal entry to record their issuance.

1. The market rate at the date of issuance is 8%.
2. The market rate at the date of issuance is 10%.
3. The market rate at the date of issuance is 12%.

Problem 14-2A
Straight-line amortization of bond discount

P1 P2

mhhe.com/wildFAP20e

Check (3) $2,071,776

(4) 12/31/2012 carrying value, $1,764,460

Heathrow issues $2,000,000 of 6%, 15-year bonds dated January 1, 2011, that pay interest semiannually on June 30 and December 31. The bonds are issued at a price of $1,728,224.

Required

1. Prepare the January 1, 2011, journal entry to record the bonds' issuance.
2. For each semiannual period, compute (*a*) the cash payment, (*b*) the straight-line discount amortization, and (*c*) the bond interest expense.
3. Determine the total bond interest expense to be recognized over the bonds' life.
4. Prepare the first two years of an amortization table like Exhibit 14.7 using the straight-line method.
5. Prepare the journal entries to record the first two interest payments.

Refer to the bond details in Problem 14-2A, *except* assume that the bonds are issued at a price of $2,447,990.

Problem 14-3A
Straight-line amortization of bond premium
P1 P3

Required

1. Prepare the January 1, 2011, journal entry to record the bonds' issuance.
2. For each semiannual period, compute (*a*) the cash payment, (*b*) the straight-line premium amortization, and (*c*) the bond interest expense.
3. Determine the total bond interest expense to be recognized over the bonds' life.
4. Prepare the first two years of an amortization table like Exhibit 14.7 using the straight-line method.
5. Prepare the journal entries to record the first two interest payments.

Check (3) $1,352,010

(4) 12/31/2012 carrying value, $2,388,258

Saturn issues 6.5%, five-year bonds dated January 1, 2011, with a $500,000 par value. The bonds pay interest on June 30 and December 31 and are issued at a price of $510,666. The annual market rate is 6% on the issue date.

Problem 14-4A
Straight-line amortization of bond premium
P1 P3   e**X**cel

mhhe.com/wildFAP20e

Required

1. Calculate the total bond interest expense over the bonds' life.
2. Prepare a straight-line amortization table like Exhibit 14.11 for the bonds' life.
3. Prepare the journal entries to record the first two interest payments.

Check (2) 6/30/2013 carrying value, $505,331

Refer to the bond details in Problem 14-4A.

Problem 14-5A[B]
Effective interest amortization of bond premium; computing bond price P1 P3

Required

1. Compute the total bond interest expense over the bonds' life.
2. Prepare an effective interest amortization table like the one in Exhibit 14B.2 for the bonds' life.
3. Prepare the journal entries to record the first two interest payments.
4. Use the market rate at issuance to compute the present value of the remaining cash flows for these bonds as of December 31, 2013. Compare your answer with the amount shown on the amortization table as the balance for that date (from part 2) and explain your findings.

Check (2) 6/30/2013 carrying value, $505,728

(4) $504,653

Patton issues $650,000 of 5%, four-year bonds dated January 1, 2011, that pay interest semiannually on June 30 and December 31. They are issued at $584,361 and their market rate is 8% at the issue date.

Problem 14-6A
Straight-line amortization of bond discount
P1 P2

Required

1. Prepare the January 1, 2011, journal entry to record the bonds' issuance.
2. Determine the total bond interest expense to be recognized over the bonds' life.
3. Prepare a straight-line amortization table like the one in Exhibit 14.7 for the bonds' first two years.
4. Prepare the journal entries to record the first two interest payments.

Check (2) $195,639

(3) 12/31/2012 carrying value, $617,181

Analysis Component

5. Assume the market rate on January 1, 2011, is 4% instead of 8%. Without providing numbers, describe how this change affects the amounts reported on Patton's financial statements.

Refer to the bond details in Problem 14-6A.

Problem 14-7A[B]
Effective interest amortization of bond discount P1 P2

Required

1. Prepare the January 1, 2011, journal entry to record the bonds' issuance.
2. Determine the total bond interest expense to be recognized over the bonds' life.
3. Prepare an effective interest amortization table like the one in Exhibit 14B.1 for the bonds' first two years.
4. Prepare the journal entries to record the first two interest payments.

Check (2) $195,639

(3) 12/31/2012 carrying value, $614,614

e**X**cel

mhhe.com/wildFAP20e

Problem 14-8A[B]

Effective interest amortization of bond premium; retiring bonds

P1 P3 P4

Check   (3) 6/30/2012 carrying value, $91,224

(5) $2,635 gain

mhhe.com/wildFAP20e

McFad issues $90,000 of 11%, three-year bonds dated January 1, 2011, that pay interest semiannually on June 30 and December 31. They are issued at $92,283. Their market rate is 10% at the issue date.

Required

1. Prepare the January 1, 2011, journal entry to record the bonds' issuance.
2. Determine the total bond interest expense to be recognized over the bonds' life.
3. Prepare an effective interest amortization table like Exhibit 14B.2 for the bonds' first two years.
4. Prepare the journal entries to record the first two interest payments.
5. Prepare the journal entry to record the bonds' retirement on January 1, 2013, at 98.

Analysis Component

6. Assume that the market rate on January 1, 2011, is 12% instead of 10%. Without presenting numbers, describe how this change affects the amounts reported on McFad's financial statements.

Problem 14-9A

Installment notes

C1 P5

Check   (2) 10/31/2015 ending balance, $92,759

On November 1, 2011, Leetch Ltd. borrows $400,000 cash from a bank by signing a five-year installment note bearing 8% interest. The note requires equal total payments each year on October 31.

Required

1. Compute the total amount of each installment payment.
2. Complete an amortization table for this installment note similar to the one in Exhibit 14.14.
3. Prepare the journal entries in which Leetch records (a) accrued interest as of December 31, 2011 (the end of its annual reporting period), and (b) the first annual payment on the note.

Problem 14-10A

Applying the debt-to-equity ratio

A3

At the end of the current year, the following information is available for both Kumar Company and Asher Company.

	Kumar Company	Asher Company
Total assets	$2,254,500	$1,123,500
Total liabilities	904,500	598,500
Total equity	1,350,000	525,000

Required

1. Compute the debt-to-equity ratios for both companies.
2. Comment on your results and discuss the riskiness of each company's financing structure.

Problem 14-11A[D]

Capital lease accounting

C4

Check   (1) $79,854

(3) Year 3 ending balance, $35,664

Montana Company signs a five-year capital lease with Elway Company for office equipment. The annual lease payment is $20,000, and the interest rate is 8%.

Required

1. Compute the present value of Montana's five-year lease payments.
2. Prepare the journal entry to record Montana's capital lease at its inception.
3. Complete a lease payment schedule for the five years of the lease with the following headings. Assume that the beginning balance of the lease liability (present value of lease payments) is $79,854. (*Hint:* To find the amount allocated to interest in year 1, multiply the interest rate by the beginning-of-year lease liability. The amount of the annual lease payment not allocated to interest is allocated to principal. Reduce the lease liability by the amount allocated to principal to update the lease liability at each year-end.)

Period Ending Date	Beginning Balance of Lease Liability	Interest on Lease Liability	Reduction of Lease Liability	Cash Lease Payment	Ending Balance of Lease Liability

4. Use straight-line depreciation and prepare the journal entry to depreciate the leased asset at the end of year 1. Assume zero salvage value and a five-year life for the office equipment.

> Round dollar amounts to the nearest whole dollar. Assume no reversing entries are used.

Sedona Systems issues bonds dated January 1, 2011, that pay interest semiannually on June 30 and December 31. The bonds have a $45,000 par value and an annual contract rate of 12%, and they mature in five years.

Problem 14-1B
Computing bond price and recording issuance
P1 P2 P3

Required

For each of the following three separate situations, (a) determine the bonds' issue price on January 1, 2011, and (b) prepare the journal entry to record their issuance.

1. The market rate at the date of issuance is 10%.

2. The market rate at the date of issuance is 12%.

3. The market rate at the date of issuance is 14%.

Check   (1) Premium, $3,475

(3) Discount, $3,162

ParFour issues $1,700,000 of 10%, 10-year bonds dated January 1, 2011, that pay interest semiannually on June 30 and December 31. The bonds are issued at a price of $1,505,001.

Problem 14-2B
Straight-line amortization of bond discount
P1 P2

Required

1. Prepare the January 1, 2011, journal entry to record the bonds' issuance.

2. For each semiannual period, compute (a) the cash payment, (b) the straight-line discount amortization, and (c) the bond interest expense.

3. Determine the total bond interest expense to be recognized over the bonds' life.

4. Prepare the first two years of an amortization table like Exhibit 14.7 using the straight-line method.

5. Prepare the journal entries to record the first two interest payments.

Check   (3) $1,894,999

(4) 6/30/2012 carrying value, $1,534,251

Refer to the bond details in Problem 14-2B, *except* assume that the bonds are issued at a price of $2,096,466.

Problem 14-3B
Straight-line amortization of bond premium
P1 P3

Required

1. Prepare the January 1, 2011, journal entry to record the bonds' issuance.

2. For each semiannual period, compute (a) the cash payment, (b) the straight-line premium amortization, and (c) the bond interest expense.

3. Determine the total bond interest expense to be recognized over the bonds' life.

4. Prepare the first two years of an amortization table like Exhibit 14.7 using the straight-line method.

5. Prepare the journal entries to record the first two interest payments.

Check   (3) $1,303,534

(4) 6/30/2012 carrying value, $2,036,997

Zooba Company issues 9%, five-year bonds dated January 1, 2011, with a $160,000 par value. The bonds pay interest on June 30 and December 31 and are issued at a price of $166,494. Their annual market rate is 8% on the issue date.

Problem 14-4B
Straight-line amortization of bond premium
P1 P3

Required

1. Calculate the total bond interest expense over the bonds' life.

2. Prepare a straight-line amortization table like Exhibit 14.11 for the bonds' life.

3. Prepare the journal entries to record the first two interest payments.

Check   (2) 6/30/2013 carrying value, $163,249

Refer to the bond details in Problem 14-4B.

Problem 14-5B[B]
Effective interest amortization of bond premium; computing bond price   P1 P3

Required

1. Compute the total bond interest expense over the bonds' life.

2. Prepare an effective interest amortization table like the one in Exhibit 14B.2 for the bonds' life.

3. Prepare the journal entries to record the first two interest payments.

4. Use the market rate at issuance to compute the present value of the remaining cash flows for these bonds as of December 31, 2013. Compare your answer with the amount shown on the amortization table as the balance for that date (from part 2) and explain your findings.

Check   (2) 6/30/2013 carrying value, $163,568

(4) $162,903

Problem 14-6B
Straight-line amortization of
bond discount

P1 P2

Check (2) $128,753

(3) 6/30/2012 carrying
value, $101,323

Roney issues $120,000 of 6%, 15-year bonds dated January 1, 2011, that pay interest semiannually on June 30 and December 31. They are issued at $99,247, and their market rate is 8% at the issue date.

Required

1. Prepare the January 1, 2011, journal entry to record the bonds' issuance.
2. Determine the total bond interest expense to be recognized over the life of the bonds.
3. Prepare a straight-line amortization table like the one in Exhibit 14.7 for the bonds' first two years.
4. Prepare the journal entries to record the first two interest payments.

Problem 14-7B[B]
Effective interest amortization of
bond discount

P1 P2

Check (2) $128,753;
(3) 6/30/2012 carrying
value, $100,402

Refer to the bond details in Problem 14-6B.

Required

1. Prepare the January 1, 2011, journal entry to record the bonds' issuance.
2. Determine the total bond interest expense to be recognized over the bonds' life.
3. Prepare an effective interest amortization table like the one in Exhibit 14B.1 for the bonds' first two years.
4. Prepare the journal entries to record the first two interest payments.

Problem 14-8B[B]
Effective interest amortization of
bond premium; retiring bonds

P1 P3 P4

Check (3) 6/30/2012 carrying value,
$958,406

(5) $6,174 loss

Hutton issues $900,000 of 13%, four-year bonds dated January 1, 2011, that pay interest semiannually on June 30 and December 31. They are issued at $987,217, and their market rate is 10% at the issue date.

Required

1. Prepare the January 1, 2011, journal entry to record the bonds' issuance.
2. Determine the total bond interest expense to be recognized over the bonds' life.
3. Prepare an effective interest amortization table like the one in Exhibit 14B.2 for the bonds' first two years.
4. Prepare the journal entries to record the first two interest payments.
5. Prepare the journal entry to record the bonds' retirement on January 1, 2013, at 106.

Analysis Component

6. Assume that the market rate on January 1, 2011, is 14% instead of 10%. Without presenting numbers, describe how this change affects the amounts reported on Hutton's financial statements.

Problem 14-9B
Installment notes

C1 P5

Check (2) 9/30/2013 ending
balance, $109,673

On October 1, 2011, Milan Enterprises borrows $300,000 cash from a bank by signing a three-year installment note bearing 10% interest. The note requires equal total payments each year on September 30.

Required

1. Compute the total amount of each installment payment.
2. Complete an amortization table for this installment note similar to the one in Exhibit 14.14.
3. Prepare the journal entries to record (*a*) accrued interest as of December 31, 2011 (the end of its annual reporting period) and (*b*) the first annual payment on the note.

Problem 14-10B
Applying the debt-to-equity ratio

A3

At the end of the current year, the following information is available for both West Elm Company and East Park Company.

	West Elm Company	East Park Company
Total assets	$396,396	$1,650,000
Total liabilities	178,596	1,237,500
Total equity	217,800	412,500

Required

1. Compute the debt-to-equity ratios for both companies.
2. Comment on your results and discuss what they imply about the relative riskiness of these companies.

Preston Company signs a five-year capital lease with Starbuck Company for office equipment. The annual lease payment is $10,000, and the interest rate is 10%.

Required

1. Compute the present value of Preston's lease payments.
2. Prepare the journal entry to record Preston's capital lease at its inception.
3. Complete a lease payment schedule for the five years of the lease with the following headings. Assume that the beginning balance of the lease liability (present value of lease payments) is $37,908. (*Hint:* To find the amount allocated to interest in year 1, multiply the interest rate by the beginning-of-year lease liability. The amount of the annual lease payment not allocated to interest is allocated to principal. Reduce the lease liability by the amount allocated to principal to update the lease liability at each year-end.)

Check (1) $37,908

(3) Year 3 ending balance, $17,356

Period Ending Date	Beginning Balance of Lease Liability	Interest on Lease Liability	Reduction of Lease Liability	Cash Lease Payment	Ending Balance of Lease Liability

4. Use straight-line depreciation and prepare the journal entry to depreciate the leased asset at the end of year 1. Assume zero salvage value and a five-year life for the office equipment.

(This serial problem began in Chapter 1 and continues through most of the book. If previous chapter segments were not completed, the serial problem can begin at this point. It is helpful, but not necessary, to use the Working Papers that accompany the book.)

SERIAL PROBLEM
Business Solutions
A1   A3

SP 14   Santana Rey has consulted with her local banker and is considering financing an expansion of her business by obtaining a long-term bank loan. Selected account balances at March 31, 2012, for Business Solutions follow.

Total assets	$120,268	Total liabilities	$875	Total equity	$119,393

Required

1. The bank has offered a long-term secured note to Business Solutions. The bank's loan procedures require that a client's debt-to-equity ratio not exceed 0.8. As of March 31, 2012, what is the maximum amount that Business Solutions could borrow from this bank (rounded to nearest dollar)?
2. If Business Solutions borrows the maximum amount allowed from the bank, what percentage of assets would be financed (*a*) by debt and (*b*) by equity?
3. What are some factors Santana Rey should consider before borrowing the funds?

Check (1) $94,639

Beyond the Numbers

BTN 14-1   Refer to **Research In Motion**'s financial statements in Appendix A to answer the following.

REPORTING IN ACTION
A1   A2

RIM

1. Identify the items, if any, that make up RIM's long-term debt as reported on its balance sheet at February 27, 2010.
2. Assume that RIM has $402,000 thousand in convertible debentures that carry a 2.25% contract rate of interest. How much annual cash interest must be paid on those convertible debentures?
3. How much cash did it generate from issuance of debt for the year-ended February 27, 2010? How much cash did it use for repayments of debt for that same year?

Fast Forward

4. Access Research In Motion's financial statements for the years ending after February 27, 2010, from its Website (**RIM.com**) or the SEC's EDGAR database (**www.sec.gov**). Has it issued additional long-term debt since the year-end February 27, 2010? If yes, identify the amount(s).

COMPARATIVE ANALYSIS

A3

RIM

Apple

BTN 14-2 Key figures for **Research In Motion** and **Apple** follow.

($ millions)	Research In Motion		Apple	
	Current Year	Prior Year	Current Year	Prior Year
Total assets	$10,204	$8,101	$47,501	$36,171
Total liabilities	2,602	2,227	15,861	13,874
Total equity	7,603	5,874	31,640	22,297

Required

1. Compute the debt-to-equity ratios for Research In Motion and Apple for both the current year and the prior year.

2. Use the ratios you computed in part 1 to determine which company's financing structure is least risky. Assume an industry average of 0.64 for debt-to-equity.

ETHICS CHALLENGE

C4 A1

BTN 14-3 Holly County needs a new county government building that would cost $24 million. The politicians feel that voters will not approve a municipal bond issue to fund the building since it would increase taxes. They opt to have a state bank issue $24 million of tax-exempt securities to pay for the building construction. The county then will make yearly lease payments (of principal and interest) to repay the obligation. Unlike conventional municipal bonds, the lease payments are not binding obligations on the county and, therefore, require no voter approval.

Required

1. Do you think the actions of the politicians and the bankers in this situation are ethical?

2. How do the tax-exempt securities used to pay for the building compare in risk to a conventional municipal bond issued by Holly County?

COMMUNICATING IN PRACTICE

P3

BTN 14-4 Your business associate mentions that she is considering investing in corporate bonds currently selling at a premium. She says that since the bonds are selling at a premium, they are highly valued and her investment will yield more than the going rate of return for the risk involved. Reply with a memorandum to confirm or correct your associate's interpretation of premium bonds.

TAKING IT TO THE NET

A2

BTN 14-5 Access the March 25, 2010, filing of the 10-K report of **Home Depot** for the year ended January 31, 2010, from www.SEC.gov (Ticker: HD). Refer to Home Depot's balance sheet, including its note 4 (on debt).

Required

1. Identify Home Depot's long-term liabilities and the amounts for those liabilities from Home Depot's balance sheet at January 31, 2010.

2. Review Home Depot's note 5. The note reports that as of January 31, 2010, it had $2.96 billion of "5.875% Senior Notes; due December 16, 2036; interest payable semiannually on June 16 and December 16." These notes have a face value of $3.0 billion and were originally issued at $2.958 billion.

   a. Why would Home Depot issue $3.0 billion of its notes for only $2.958 billion?

   b. How much cash interest must Home Depot pay each June 16 and December 16 on these notes?

TEAMWORK IN ACTION

P2 P3

BTN 14-6[B] Break into teams and complete the following requirements related to effective interest amortization for a premium bond.

1. Each team member is to independently prepare a blank table with proper headings for amortization of a bond premium. When all have finished, compare tables and ensure that all are in agreement.

Parts 2 and 3 require use of these facts: On January 1, 2010, Caleb issues $100,000, 9%, five-year bonds at 104.1. The market rate at issuance is 8%. Caleb pays interest semiannually on June 30 and December 31.

2. In rotation, *each* team member must explain how to complete *one* line of the bond amortization table, including all computations for his or her line. (Round amounts to the nearest dollar.) All members are to fill in their tables during this process. You need not finish the table; stop after all members have explained a line.

3. In rotation, *each* team member is to identify a separate column of the table and indicate what the final number in that column will be and explain the reasoning.

4. Reach a team consensus as to what the total bond interest expense on this bond issue will be if the bond is not retired before maturity.

5. As a team, prepare a list of similarities and differences between the amortization table just prepared and the amortization table if the bond had been issued at a discount.

Hint: Rotate teams to report on parts 4 and 5. Consider requiring entries for issuance and interest payments.

BTN 14-7 Warren Brown is the founder of **Cake Love**. Assume that his company currently has $250,000 in equity, and he is considering a $100,000 expansion to meet increased demand. The $100,000 expansion would yield $16,000 in additional annual income before interest expense. Assume that the business currently earns $40,000 annual income before interest expense of $10,000, yielding a return on equity of 12% ($30,000/$250,000). To fund the expansion, he is considering the issuance of a 10-year, $100,000 note with annual interest payments (the principal due at the end of 10 years).

ENTREPRENEURIAL DECISION

A1

Required

1. Using return on equity as the decision criterion, show computations to support or reject the expansion if interest on the $100,000 note is (*a*) 10%, (*b*) 15%, (*c*) 16%, (*d*) 17%, and (*e*) 20%.

2. What general rule do the results in part 1 illustrate?

BTN 14-8 Visit your city or county library. Ask the librarian to help you locate the recent financial records of your city or county government. Examine those records.

HITTING THE ROAD

A1

Required

1. Determine the amount of long-term bonds and notes currently outstanding.

2. Read the supporting information to your municipality's financial statements and record

   a. The market interest rate(s) when the bonds and/or notes were issued.

   b. The date(s) when the bonds and/or notes will mature.

   c. Any rating(s) on the bonds and/or notes received from **Moody's, Standard & Poor's**, or another rating agency.

BTN 14-9 Nokia (**www.Nokia.com**), **Research In Motion**, and **Apple** are competitors in the global marketplace. Selected results from these companies follow.

GLOBAL DECISION

A3

NOKIA

RIM

Apple

Key Figures	Nokia (EURm)		Research In Motion ($ millions)		Apple ($ millions)	
	Current Year	Prior Year	Current Year	Prior Year	Current Year	Prior Year
Total assets	€35,738	€39,582	$10,204	$8,101	$47,501	$36,171
Total liabilities	20,989	23,072	2,602	2,227	15,861	13,874
Total equity	14,749	16,510	7,603	5,874	31,640	22,297
Debt-to-equity ratio	?	?	0.34	0.38	0.50	0.62

Required

1. Compute Nokia's debt-to-equity ratios for the current year and the prior year.

2. Use the data provided and the ratios computed in part 1 to determine which company's financing structure is least risky.

ANSWERS TO MULTIPLE CHOICE QUIZ

1. b

2. a

3. c; $500,000 × 0.08 × ½ year = $20,000

4. a; Cash interest paid = $100,000 × 5% × ½ year = $2,500
Discount amortization = ($100,000 − $95,735)/10 periods = $426.50
Interest expense = $2,500.00 + $426.50 = $2,926.50

5. e; ($373,745 − $350,000)/16 periods = $1,484

15

Investments and International Operations

A Look Back

Chapter 14 focused on long-term liabilities—a main part of most companies' financing. We explained how to value, record, amortize, and report these liabilities in financial statements.

A Look at This Chapter

This chapter focuses on investments in securities. We explain how to identify, account for, and report investments in both debt and equity securities. We also explain accounting for transactions listed in a foreign currency.

A Look Ahead

Chapter 16 focuses on reporting and analyzing a company's cash flows. Special emphasis is directed at the statement of cash flows reported under the indirect method.

Learning Objectives

CAP

CONCEPTUAL

C1 Distinguish between debt and equity securities and between short-term and long-term investments. (p. 596)

C2 Describe how to report equity securities with controlling influence. (p. 603)

C3 *Appendix 15A*—Explain foreign exchange rates and record transactions listed in a foreign currency. (p. 610)

ANALYTICAL

A1 Compute and analyze the components of return on total assets. (p. 605)

LP15

PROCEDURAL

P1 Account for trading securities. (p. 599)

P2 Account for held-to-maturity securities. (p. 600)

P3 Account for available-for-sale securities. (p. 600)

P4 Account for equity securities with significant influence. (p. 602)

Schooling the Market

"There's this whole new emerging category of academic technology"

—**MICHAEL CHASEN**

WASHINGTON, DC—Michael Chasen and Matthew Pittinsky had just finished college—Michael earning a degree in accounting and Matthew Pittinsky in education. Both took jobs at KPMG. "Matthew and I had decided to leave KPMG and start an e-learning business, which we called **Blackboard (Blackboard.com),**" explains Michael. "Campuses nationwide were beginning to connect to the Internet but had no way to put courses online."

What Michael and Matthew did was leverage online technology to enhance education and learning for both students and instructors. "[Students and instructors] want improved ease of use," insists Michael. "They want the teaching and learning kept not just inside the class, but outside the classroom." Michael and Matthew have been so successful that their company's operations now extend over many countries. "We not only continue to expand within higher education but we are expanding internationally," says Michael. "I travel all over the world for Blackboard."

This broad reach has led to business challenges involving both investments and international operations. "I am asked a lot of questions about . . . education on the Internet," explains Michael. "[Investments are] often one of the better ways to deploy capital."

Blackboard's annual report states: "[We] pursue strategic relationships with, acquisitions of, and investments in, companies that would enhance the technological features of our products, offer complementary products, services and technologies, or broaden the scope of our product offerings." Also, investments in international operations require them to translate their performance into U.S. dollars for financial reporting. Those tasks require knowledge of accounting and reporting requirements for investments, including investments in securities of other companies.

Blackboard's annual report reveals that it has "a variety of marketable investments." It reports that "for those investments in entities where the Company has significant influence over operations . . . [it] follows the equity method of accounting." It also explains that Blackboard "consolidates investments where it has a controlling financial interest." Still, Michael insists that their investment in the future of learning is the key. "We are very much focused on innovation," says Michael. "[The market's] ripe for a technology explosion in e-learning."

[Sources: *Blackboard Website,* January 2011; *Entrepreneur,* March 2009; *The New York Times,* November 2009; *The Washington Post,* August 2007; *Washington Business Journal,* October 2008]

This chapter's main focus is investments in securities. Many companies have investments, and many of these are in the form of debt and equity securities issued by other companies. We describe investments in these securities and how to account for them. An increasing number of companies also invest in international operations. We explain how to account for and report international transactions listed in foreign currencies.

Investments and International Operations

Basics of Investments	Noninfluential Investments	Influential Investments
• Motivation for investments • Short-term versus long-term • Classification and reporting • Accounting basics	• Trading securities • Held-to-maturity securities • Available-for-sale securities	• Securities with significant influence • Securities with controlling influence • Accounting summary

BASICS OF INVESTMENTS

C1 Distinguish between debt and equity securities and between short-term and long-term investments.

This section describes the motivation for investments, the distinction between short- and long-term investments, and the different classes of investments.

Motivation for Investments

Companies make investments for at least three reasons. First, companies transfer *excess cash* into investments to produce higher income. Second, some entities, such as mutual funds and pension funds, are set up to produce income from investments. Third, companies make investments for strategic reasons. Examples are investments in competitors, suppliers, and even customers. Exhibit 15.1 shows short-term (S-T) and long-term (L-T) investments as a percent of total assets for several companies.

EXHIBIT 15.1

Investments of Selected Companies

Pfizer	S-T 19% L-T 4%
Gap	S-T 2% L-T 1%
Starbucks	S-T 3% L-T 5%
Coca-Cola	S-T 1% L-T 18%

0%   25%

Percent of total assets

Short-Term Investments Cash equivalents are investments that are both readily converted to known amounts of cash and mature within three months. Many investments, however, mature between 3 and 12 months. These investments are **short-term investments**, also called *temporary investments* and *marketable securities*. Specifically, short-term investments are securities that (1) management intends to convert to cash within one year or the operating cycle, whichever is longer, and (2) are readily convertible to cash. Short-term investments are reported under current assets and serve a purpose similar to cash equivalents.

Long-Term Investments **Long-term investments** in securities are defined as those securities that are not readily convertible to cash or are not intended to be converted into cash in the short term. Long-term investments can also include funds earmarked for a special purpose, such as bond sinking funds and investments in land or other assets not used in the company's operations. Long-term investments are reported in the noncurrent section of the balance sheet, often in its own separate line titled *Long-Term Investments*.

Debt Securities versus Equity Securities Investments in securities can include both debt and equity securities. *Debt securities* reflect a creditor relationship such as investments in notes, bonds, and certificates of deposit; they are issued by governments, companies, and individuals. *Equity securities* reflect an owner relationship such as shares of stock issued by companies.

Classification and Reporting

Accounting for investments in securities depends on three factors: (1) security type, either debt or equity, (2) the company's intent to hold the security either short term or long term, and (3) the company's (investor's) percent ownership in the other company's (investee's) equity securities. Exhibit 15.2 identifies five classes of securities using these three factors. It describes each of these five classes of securities and the standard reporting required under each class.

EXHIBIT 15.2

Investments in Securities

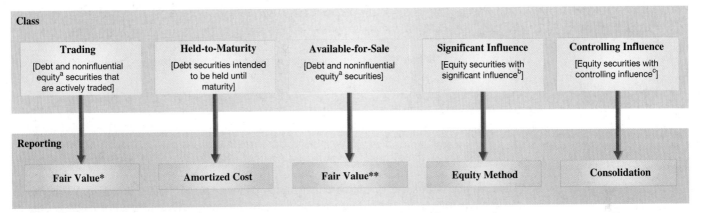

Class

Trading	Held-to-Maturity	Available-for-Sale	Significant Influence	Controlling Influence
[Debt and noninfluential equity[a] securities that are actively traded]	[Debt securities intended to be held until maturity]	[Debt and noninfluential equity[a] securities]	[Equity securities with significant influence[b]]	[Equity securities with controlling influence[c]]

Reporting

Fair Value*	Amortized Cost	Fair Value**	Equity Method	Consolidation

[a] Holding less than 20% of voting stock (equity securities only).   [b] Holding 20% or more, but not more than 50%, of voting stock.
[c] Holding more than 50% of voting stock.
* Unrealized gains and losses reported on the income statement.
** Unrealized gains and losses reported in the equity section of the balance sheet and in comprehensive income.

Debt Securities: Accounting Basics

This section explains the accounting basics for *debt securities,* including that for acquisition, disposition, and any interest.

Acquisition.   Debt securities are recorded at cost when purchased. To illustrate, assume that Music City paid $29,500 plus a $500 brokerage fee on September 1, 2010, to buy Dell's 7%, two-year bonds payable with a $30,000 par value. The bonds pay interest semiannually on August 31 and February 28. Music City intends to hold the bonds until they mature on August 31, 2012; consequently, they are classified as held-to-maturity (HTM) securities. The entry to record this purchase follows. (If the maturity of the securities was short term, and management's intent was to hold them until they mature, then they would be classified as Short-Term Investments—HTM.)

2010			
Sept. 1	Long-Term Investments—HTM (Dell)	30,000	
	Cash		30,000
	Purchased bonds to be held to maturity.		

Assets = Liabilities + Equity
+30,000
−30,000

Interest earned.   Interest revenue for investments in debt securities is recorded when earned. To illustrate, on December 31, 2010, at the end of its accounting period, Music City accrues interest receivable as follows.

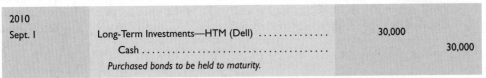

Dec. 31	Interest Receivable	700	
	Interest Revenue		700
	Accrued interest earned ($30,000 × 7% × 1/12).		

Assets = Liabilities + Equity
+700   +700

The $700 reflects 4/6 of the semiannual cash receipt of interest—the portion Music City earned as of December 31. Relevant sections of Music City's financial statements at December 31, 2010, are shown in Exhibit 15.3.

EXHIBIT 15.3

Financial Statement Presentation
of Debt Securities

On the income statement for year 2010:	
Interest revenue	$ 700
On the December 31, 2010, balance sheet:	
Long-term investments—Held-to-maturity securities (at amortized cost)	$30,000

On February 28, 2011, Music City records receipt of semiannual interest.

Feb. 28	Cash	1,050	
	Interest Receivable		700
	Interest Revenue		350
	Received six months' interest on Dell bonds.		

Assets = Liabilities + Equity
+1,050   +350
−700

Disposition.   When the bonds mature, the proceeds (not including the interest entry) are recorded as:

2012			
Aug. 31	Cash	30,000	
	Long-Term Investments—HTM (Dell).		30,000
	Received cash from matured bonds.		

Assets = Liabilities + Equity
+30,000
−30,000

The cost of a debt security can be either higher or lower than its maturity value. When the investment is long term, the difference between cost and maturity value is amortized over the remaining life of the security. We assume for ease of computations that the cost of a long-term debt security equals its maturity value.

Equity Securities: Accounting Basics

This section explains the accounting basics for *equity securities,* including that for acquisition, dividends, and disposition.

Example: What is cost per share?
Answer: Cost per share is the total cost of acquisition, including broker fees, divided by number of shares acquired.

Acquisition.   Equity securities are recorded at cost when acquired, including commissions or brokerage fees paid. To illustrate, assume that Music City purchases 1,000 shares of Intex common stock at par value for $86,000 on October 10, 2010. It records this purchase of available-for-sale (AFS) securities as follows.

Oct. 10	Long-Term Investments—AFS (Intex)	86,000	
	Cash		86,000
	Purchased 1,000 shares of Intex.		

Assets = Liabilities + Equity
+86,000
−86,000

Dividend earned.   Any cash dividends received are credited to Dividend Revenue and reported in the income statement. To illustrate, on November 2, Music City receives a $1,720 quarterly cash dividend on the Intex shares, which it records as:

Nov. 2	Cash	1,720	
	Dividend Revenue		1,720
	Received dividend of $1.72 per share.		

Assets = Liabilities + Equity
+1,720   +1,720

Disposition.   When the securities are sold, sale proceeds are compared with the cost, and any gain or loss is recorded. To illustrate, on December 20, Music City sells 500 of the Intex shares for $45,000 cash and records this sale as:

Dec. 20	Cash	45,000	
	Long-Term Investments—AFS (Intex)		43,000
	Gain on Sale of Long-Term Investments		2,000
	Sold 500 Intex shares ($86,000 × 500/1,000).		

Assets = Liabilities + Equity
+45,000   +2,000
−43,000

REPORTING OF NONINFLUENTIAL INVESTMENTS

Companies must value and report most noninfluential investments at *fair value*. The exact reporting requirements depend on whether the investments are classified as (1) trading, (2) held-to-maturity, or (3) available-for-sale.

Trading Securities

Trading securities are *debt and equity securities* that the company intends to actively manage and trade for profit. Frequent purchases and sales are expected and are made to earn profits on short-term price changes. Trading securities are *always* reported as current assets.

P1	Account for trading securities.

Valuing and reporting trading securities. The entire portfolio of trading securities is reported at its fair value; this requires a "fair value adjustment" from the cost of the portfolio. The term *portfolio* refers to a group of securities. Any unrealized gain (or loss) from a change in the fair value of the portfolio of trading securities is reported on the income statement. Most users believe accounting reports are more useful when changes in fair value for trading securities are reported in income.

To illustrate, TechCom's portfolio of trading securities had a total cost of $11,500 and a fair value of $13,000 on December 31, 2010, the first year it held trading securities. The difference between the $11,500 cost and the $13,000 fair value reflects a $1,500 gain. It is an unrealized gain because it is not yet confirmed by actual sales. The fair value adjustment for trading securities is recorded with an adjusting entry at the end of each period to equal the difference between the portfolio's cost and its fair value. TechCom records this gain as follows.

Point: '*Unrealized gain (or loss)*' refers to a change in fair value that is not yet realized through actual sale.

Point: 'Fair Value Adjustment—Trading' is a *permanent account*, shown as a deduction or addition to 'Short-Term Investments—Trading.'

Dec. 31	Fair Value Adjustment—Trading	1,500	
	Unrealized Gain—Income		1,500
	To reflect an unrealized gain in fair values		
	of trading securities.		

Assets = Liabilities + Equity
+1,500   +1,500

The **Unrealized Gain (or Loss)** is reported in the Other Revenues and Gains (or Expenses and Losses) section on the income statement. Unrealized Gain (or Loss)—Income is a *temporary* account that is closed to Income Summary at the end of each period. Fair Value Adjustment—Trading is a *permanent* account, which adjusts the reported value of the trading securities portfolio from its prior period fair value to the current period fair value. The total cost of the trading securities portfolio is maintained in one account, and the fair value adjustment is recorded in a separate account. For example, TechCom's investment in trading securities is reported in the current assets section of its balance sheet as follows.

Example: If TechCom's trading securities have a cost of $14,800 and a fair value of $16,100 at Dec. 31, 2011, its adjusting entry is
Unrealized Loss—Income 200
    Fair Value Adj.—Trading 200
This is computed as: $1,500 Beg. Dr. bal. + $200 Cr. = $1,300 End. Dr. bal.

Current Assets		
Short-term investments—Trading (at cost)	$11,500	
Fair Value adjustment—Trading	1,500	
Short-term investments—Trading (at fair value)		$13,000
or simply		
Short-term investments—Trading (at fair value; cost is $11,500)		$13,000

Selling trading securities. When individual trading securities are sold, the difference between the net proceeds (sale price less fees) and the cost of the individual trading securities that are sold is recognized as a gain or a loss. Any prior period fair value adjustment to the portfolio is *not* used to compute the gain or loss from sale of individual trading securities. For example, if TechCom sold some of its trading securities that had cost $1,000 for $1,200 cash on January 9, 2011, it would record the following.

Point: Reporting securities at fair value is referred to as *mark-to-market* accounting.

Assets = Liabilities + Equity
+1,200   +200
−1,000

Jan. 9	Cash	1,200	
	Short-Term Investments—Trading		1,000
	Gain on Sale of Short-Term Investments		200
	Sold trading securities costing $1,000 for $1,200 cash.		

A gain is reported in the Other Revenues and Gains section on the income statement, whereas a loss is shown in Other Expenses and Losses. When the period-end fair value adjustment for the portfolio of trading securities is computed, it excludes the cost and fair value of any securities sold.

Held-to-Maturity Securities

P2 Account for held-to-maturity securities.

Held-to-maturity (HTM) securities are *debt* securities a company intends and is able to hold until maturity. They are reported in current assets if their maturity dates are within one year or the operating cycle, whichever is longer. HTM securities are reported in long-term assets when the maturity dates extend beyond one year or the operating cycle, whichever is longer. All HTM securities are recorded at cost when purchased, and interest revenue is recorded when earned.

The portfolio of HTM securities is usually reported at (amortized) cost, which is explained in advanced courses. There is no fair value adjustment to the portfolio of HTM securities—neither to the short-term nor long-term portfolios. The basics of accounting for HTM securities were described earlier in this chapter.

Point: Only debt securities can be classified as *held-to-maturity;* equity securities have no maturity date.

Decision Maker   Answer — p. 613

Money Manager You expect interest rates to sharply fall within a few weeks and remain at this lower rate. What is your strategy for holding investments in fixed-rate bonds and notes? ■

Available-for-Sale Securities

P3 Account for available-for-sale securities.

Available-for-sale (AFS) securities are *debt and equity securities* not classified as trading or held-to-maturity securities. AFS securities are purchased to yield interest, dividends, or increases in fair value. They are not actively managed like trading securities. If the intent is to sell AFS securities within the longer of one year or operating cycle, they are classified as short-term investments. Otherwise, they are classified as long-term.

Valuing and reporting available-for-sale securities. As with trading securities, companies adjust the cost of the portfolio of AFS securities to reflect changes in fair value. This is done with a fair value adjustment to its total portfolio cost. However, any unrealized gain or loss for the portfolio of AFS securities is *not* reported on the income statement. Instead, it is reported in the equity section of the balance sheet (and is part of *comprehensive income,* explained later). To illustrate, assume that Music City had no prior period investments in available-for-sale securities other than those purchased in the current period. Exhibit 15.4 shows both the cost and fair value of those investments on December 31, 2010, the end of its reporting period.

Example: If fair value in Exhibit 15.4 is $70,000 (instead of $74,550), what entry is made? *Answer:*
Unreal. Loss—Equity 3,000
    Fair Value Adj.—AFS. . .   3,000

EXHIBIT 15.4

Cost and Fair Value of Available-for-Sale Securities

	Cost	Fair Value	Unrealized Gain (Loss)
Improv bonds	$30,000	$29,050	$ (950)
Intex common stock, 500 shares	43,000	45,500	2,500
Total	$73,000	$74,550	$1,550

The year-end adjusting entry to record the fair value of these investments follows.

Assets = Liabilities + Equity
+1,550   +1,550

Dec. 31	Fair Value Adjustment—Available-for-Sale (LT)	1,550	
	Unrealized Gain—Equity		1,550
	To record adjustment to fair value of available-for-sale securities.		

Exhibit 15.5 shows the December 31, 2010, balance sheet presentation—it assumes these investments are long term, but they can also be short term. It is also common to combine the cost of investments with the balance in the Fair Value Adjustment account and report the net as a single amount.

Point: 'Unrealized Loss—Equity' and 'Unrealized Gain—Equity' are *permanent* (balance sheet) equity *accounts*.

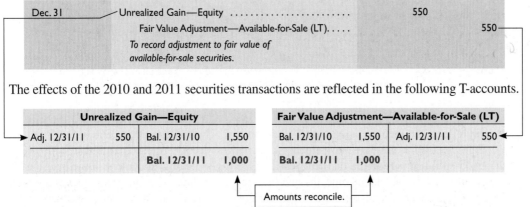

Assets

Long-term investments—Available-for-sale (at cost)	$73,000	
Fair value adjustment—Available-for-sale	1,550	
Long-term investments—Available-for-sale (at fair value)		$74,550

or simply

Long-term investments—Available-for-sale (at fair value; cost is $73,000)	$74,550

Equity

... consists of usual equity accounts ...

Add unrealized gain on available-for-sale securities*	$ 1,550

(Reconciled)

EXHIBIT 15.5

Balance Sheet Presentation of Available-for-Sale Securities

* Often included under the caption Accumulated Other Comprehensive Income.

Let's extend this illustration and assume that at the end of its next calendar year (December 31, 2011), Music City's portfolio of long-term AFS securities has an $81,000 cost and an $82,000 fair value. It records the adjustment to fair value as follows.

Point: Income can be window-dressed upward by selling AFS securities with unrealized gains; income is reduced by selling those with unrealized losses.

Dec. 31	Unrealized Gain—Equity	550	
	Fair Value Adjustment—Available-for-Sale (LT).....		550
	To record adjustment to fair value of available-for-sale securities.		

Assets = Liabilities + Equity
−550   −550

The effects of the 2010 and 2011 securities transactions are reflected in the following T-accounts.

Example: If cost is $83,000 and fair value is $82,000 at Dec. 31, 2011, it records the following adjustment:
Unreal. Gain—Equity 1,550
Unreal. Loss—Equity 1,000
    Fair Value Adj.—AFS .. 2,550

Unrealized Gain—Equity			
Adj. 12/31/11	550	Bal. 12/31/10	1,550
		Bal. 12/31/11	1,000

Fair Value Adjustment—Available-for-Sale (LT)			
Bal. 12/31/10	1,550	Adj. 12/31/11	550
Bal. 12/31/11	1,000		

Amounts reconcile.

Selling available-for-sale securities.   Accounting for the sale of individual AFS securities is identical to that described for the sale of trading securities. When individual AFS securities are sold, the difference between the cost of the individual securities sold and the net proceeds (sale price less fees) is recognized as a gain or loss.

Point: 'Fair Value Adjustment—Available-for-Sale' is a permanent account, shown as a deduction or addition to the Investment account.

Quick Check   Answers — p. 613

1. How are short-term held-to-maturity securities reported (valued) on the balance sheet?
2. How are trading securities reported (valued) on the balance sheet?
3. Where are unrealized gains and losses on available-for-sale securities reported?
4. Where are unrealized gains and losses on trading securities reported?

Alert   *Both U.S. GAAP (and IFRS) permit companies to use fair value in reporting financial assets (referred to as the fair value option). This option allows companies to report any financial asset at fair value and recognize value changes in income. This method was previously reserved only for trading securities, but is now an option for available-for-sale and held-to-maturity securities (and other 'financial assets and liabilities' such as accounts and notes receivable, accounts and notes payable, and bonds). U.S. standards also set a 3-level system to determine fair value:*
—Level 1: Use quoted market values
—Level 2: Use observable values from related assets or liabilities
—Level 3: Use unobservable values from estimates or assumptions
To date, a fairly small set of companies has chosen to broadly apply the fair value option—but, we continue to monitor its use...

REPORTING OF INFLUENTIAL INVESTMENTS

Investment in Securities with Significant Influence

P4 Account for equity securities with significant influence.

A long-term investment classified as **equity securities with significant influence** implies that the investor can exert significant influence over the investee. An investor that owns 20% or more (but not more than 50%) of a company's voting stock is usually presumed to have a significant influence over the investee. In some cases, however, the 20% test of significant influence is overruled by other, more persuasive, evidence. This evidence can either lower the 20% requirement or increase it. The **equity method** of accounting and reporting is used for long-term investments in equity securities with significant influence, which is explained in this section.

Long-term investments in equity securities with significant influence are recorded at cost when acquired. To illustrate, Micron Co. records the purchase of 3,000 shares (30%) of Star Co. common stock at a total cost of $70,650 on January 1, 2010, as follows.

Assets = Liabilities + Equity
+70,650
−70,650

Jan. 1	Long-Term Investments—Star	70,650	
	Cash		70,650
	To record purchase of 3,000 Star shares.		

The investee's (Star) earnings increase both its net assets and the claim of the investor (Micron) on the investee's net assets. Thus, when the investee reports its earnings, the investor records its share of those earnings in its investment account. To illustrate, assume that Star reports net income of $20,000 for 2010. Micron then records its 30% share of those earnings as follows.

Assets = Liabilities + Equity
+6,000   +6,000

Dec. 31	Long-Term Investments—Star	6,000	
	Earnings from Long-Term Investment		6,000
	To record 30% equity in investee earnings.		

The debit reflects the increase in Micron's equity in Star. The credit reflects 30% of Star's net income. Earnings from Long-Term Investment is a *temporary* account (closed to Income Summary at each period-end) and is reported on the investor's (Micron's) income statement. If the investee incurs a net loss instead of a net income, the investor records its share of the loss and reduces (credits) its investment account. The investor closes this earnings or loss account to Income Summary.

The receipt of cash dividends is not revenue under the equity method because the investor has already recorded its share of the investee's earnings. Instead, cash dividends received by an investor from an investee are viewed as a conversion of one asset to another; that is, dividends reduce the balance of the investment account. To illustrate, Star declares and pays $10,000 in cash dividends on its common stock. Micron records its 30% share of these dividends received on January 9, 2011, as:

Assets = Liabilities + Equity
+3,000
−3,000

Jan. 9	Cash	3,000	
	Long-Term Investments—Star		3,000
	To record share of dividend paid by Star.		

The book value of an investment under the equity method equals the cost of the investment plus (minus) the investor's equity in the *undistributed* (*distributed*) earnings of the investee. Once Micron records these transactions, its Long-Term Investments account appears as in Exhibit 15.6.

EXHIBIT 15.6

Investment in Star Common Stock (Ledger Account)

Long-Term Investment—Star			
1/ 1/2010 Investment acquisition	70,650		
12/31/2010 Share of earnings	6,000		
12/31/2010 Balance	76,650		
		1/ 9/2011 Share of dividend	3,000
1/ 9/2011 Balance	73,650		

Micron's account balance on January 9, 2011, for its investment in Star is $73,650. This is the investment's cost *plus* Micron's equity in Star's earnings since its purchase *less* Micron's equity in Star's cash dividends since its purchase. When an investment in equity securities is sold, the gain or loss is computed by comparing proceeds from the sale with the book value of the investment on the date of sale. If Micron sells its Star stock for $80,000 on January 10, 2011, it records the sale as:

Point: Security prices are sometimes listed in fractions. For example, a debt security with a price of $22\frac{1}{4}$ is the same as $22.25.

Jan. 10	Cash	80,000	
	Long-Term Investments—Star		73,650
	Gain on Sale of Investment		6,350
	Sold 3,000 shares of stock for $80,000.		

Assets = Liabilities + Equity
+80,000   +6,350
−73,650

Investment in Securities with Controlling Influence

A long-term investment classified as **equity securities with controlling influence** implies that the investor can exert a controlling influence over the investee. An investor who owns more than 50% of a company's voting stock has control over the investee. This investor can dominate all other shareholders in electing the corporation's board of directors and has control over the investee's management. In some cases, controlling influence can extend to situations of less than 50% ownership. Exhibit 15.7 summarizes the accounting for investments in equity securities based on an investor's ownership in the stock.

The *equity method with consolidation* is used to account for long-term investments in equity securities with controlling influence. The investor reports *consolidated financial statements* when owning such securities. The controlling investor is called the **parent,** and the investee is called the **subsidiary.** Many companies are parents with subsidiaries. Examples are (1) **McGraw-Hill**, the parent of J.D. Power and Associates, Standard & Poor's, and Platt's; (2) **Gap, Inc.**, the parent of Gap, Old Navy, and Banana Republic; and (3) **Brunswick**, the parent of Mercury Marine, Sea Ray, and U.S. Marine. A company owning all the outstanding stock of a subsidiary can, if it desires, take over the subsidiary's assets, retire the subsidiary's stock, and merge the subsidiary into the parent. However, there often are financial, legal, and tax advantages if a business operates as a parent controlling one or more subsidiaries. When a company operates as a parent with subsidiaries, each entity maintains separate accounting records. From a legal viewpoint, the parent and each subsidiary are separate entities with all rights, duties, and responsibilities of individual companies.

Consolidated financial statements show the financial position, results of operations, and cash flows of all entities under the parent's control, including all subsidiaries. These statements are prepared as if the business were organized as one entity. The parent uses the equity method in its accounts, but the investment account is *not* reported on the parent's financial statements. Instead, the individual assets and liabilities of the parent and its subsidiaries are combined on one balance sheet. Their revenues and expenses also are combined on one income statement, and their cash flows are combined on one statement of cash flows. The procedures for preparing consolidated financial statements are in advanced courses.

C2 Describe how to report equity securities with controlling influence.

EXHIBIT 15.7

Accounting for Equity Investments by Percent of Ownership

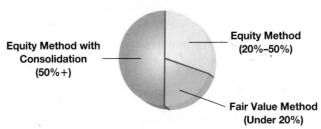

Equity Method with Consolidation (50%+)

Equity Method (20%–50%)

Fair Value Method (Under 20%)

🌐 IFRS

Unlike U.S. GAAP, IFRS requires uniform accounting policies be used throughout the group of consolidated subsidiaries. Also, unlike U.S. GAAP, IFRS offers no detailed guidance on valuation procedures. ■

Accounting Summary for Investments in Securities

Exhibit 15.8 summarizes the standard accounting for investments in securities. Recall that many investment securities are classified as either short term or long term depending on management's intent and ability to convert them in the future. Understanding the accounting for these investments enables us to draw better conclusions from financial statements in making business decisions.

EXHIBIT 15.8

Accounting for Investments
in Securities

Classification	Accounting
Short-Term Investment in Securities	
Held-to-maturity (debt) securities	Cost (without any discount or premium amortization)
Trading (debt and equity) securities	**Fair value** (with fair value adjustment to income)
Available-for-sale (debt and equity) securities	**Fair value** (with fair value adjustment to equity)
Long-Term Investment in Securities	
Held-to-maturity (debt) securities	Cost (with any discount or premium amortization)
Available-for-sale (debt and equity) securities	**Fair value** (with fair value adjustment to equity)
Equity securities with significant influence	Equity method
Equity securities with controlling influence	Equity method (with consolidation)

Comprehensive Income   **Comprehensive income** is defined as all changes in equity during a period except those from owners' investments and dividends. Specifically, comprehensive income is computed by adding or subtracting *other comprehensive income* to net income:

Net income	$ #
Other comprehensive income	#
Comprehensive income	$ #

Other comprehensive income includes unrealized gains and losses on available-for-sale securities, foreign currency adjustments, and pension adjustments. (*Accumulated other comprehensive income* is defined as the cumulative impact of *other comprehensive income.*)

Comprehensive income can be reported in financial statements:

1. As part of the statement of stockholders' equity
2. On the income statement
3. In a statement of comprehensive income

Apple   Option 1 is the most common. **Apple**, for example, reports comprehensive income as part of its statement of shareholders' equity in Appendix A near the end of the book as follows ($ millions):

Net income	$8,235
Change in foreign currency translation	(14)
Change in unrealized loss on AFS securities	118
Change in unrealized gain on derivatives	(18)
Comprehensive income	$8,321

Other comprehensive income

The 2009 *cumulative* total of Apple's *other comprehensive income* from all prior periods is $77, which is reported in its statement of shareholders' equity and is its *accumulated other comprehensive income*. That total is carried over to the equity section of its balance sheet as follows:

Common stock	$ 8,210
Retained earnings	23,353
Accumulated other comprehensive income	77
Total shareholders' equity	$31,640

Point: Some users believe that since AFS securities are not actively traded, reporting fair value changes in income would unnecessarily increase income variability and decrease usefulness.

Quick Check   Answers — p. 613

5. Give at least two examples of assets classified as long-term investments.
6. What are the requirements for an equity security to be listed as a long-term investment?
7. Identify similarities and differences in accounting for long-term investments in debt securities that are held-to-maturity versus those available-for-sale.
8. What are the three possible classifications of long-term equity investments? Describe the criteria for each class and the method used to account for each.

GLOBAL VIEW

This section discusses similarities and differences for the accounting and reporting of investments when financial statements are prepared under U.S. GAAP vis-à-vis IFRS.

Accounting for Noninfluential Securities   The accounting for noninfluential securities is broadly similar between U.S. GAAP and IFRS. *Trading securities* are accounted for using fair values with unrealized gains and losses reported in net income as fair values change. *Available-for-sale securities* are accounted for using fair values with unrealized gains and losses reported in other comprehensive income as fair values change (and later in net income when realized). *Held-to-maturity securities* are accounted for using amortized cost. Similarly, companies have the option under both systems to apply the fair value option for available-for-sale and held-to-maturity securities. Also, both systems review held-to-maturity securities for impairment. There are some differences in terminology under IFRS: (1) trading securities are commonly referred to as *financial assets at fair value through profit and loss,* and (2) available-for-sale securities are commonly referred to as *available-for-sale financial assets.* NOKIA reports the following categories for noninfluential securities: (1) ***Financial assets at fair value through profit or loss,*** consisting of financial assets held for trading and financial assets designated upon initial recognition as at fair value through profit or loss, (2) ***Available-for-sale financial assets,*** which are measured at fair value.

NOKIA

Accounting for Influential Securities   The accounting for influential securities is broadly similar across U.S. GAAP and IFRS. Specifically, under the *equity method,* the share of investee's net income is reported in the investor's income in the same period the investee earns that income; also, the investment account equals the acquisition cost plus the share of investee income less the share of investee dividends (minus amortization of excess on purchase price above fair value of identifiable, limited-life assets). Under the *consolidation method,* investee and investor revenues and expenses are combined, absent intercompany transactions, and subtracting noncontrolling interests. Also, nonintercompany assets and liabilities are similarly combined (eliminating the need for an investment account), and noncontrolling interests are subtracted from equity. There are some differences in terminology: (1) U.S. GAAP companies commonly refer to earnings from long-term investments as *equity in earnings of affiliates* whereas IFRS companies commonly use *equity in earnings of associated (or associate) companies,* (2) U.S. GAAP companies commonly refer to noncontrolling interests in consolidated subsidiaries as *minority interests* whereas IFRS companies commonly use *noncontrolling interests.*

| Components of Return on Total Assets | **Decision Analysis** |

A company's **return on total assets** (or simply *return on assets*) is important in assessing financial performance. The return on total assets can be separated into two components, profit margin and total asset turnover, for additional analyses. Exhibit 15.9 shows how these two components determine return on total assets.

A1 Compute and analyze the components of return on total assets.

$$\text{Return on total assets} = \text{Profit margin} \times \text{Total asset turnover}$$

$$\frac{\text{Net income}}{\text{Average total assets}} = \frac{\text{Net income}}{\text{Net sales}} \times \frac{\text{Net sales}}{\text{Average total assets}}$$

EXHIBIT 15.9

Components of Return on Total Assets

Profit margin reflects the percent of net income in each dollar of net sales. Total asset turnover reflects a company's ability to produce net sales from total assets. All companies desire a high return on total assets. By considering these two components, we can often discover strengths and weaknesses not revealed by return on total assets alone. This improves our ability to assess future performance and company strategy.

To illustrate, consider return on total assets and its components for **Gap Inc.** in Exhibit 15.10.

EXHIBIT 15.10

Gap's Components of Return on
Total Assets

Fiscal Year	Return on Total Assets	=	Profit Margin	×	Total Asset Turnover
2009	12.6%	=	6.66%	×	1.89
2008	10.2*	=	5.28	×	1.92
2007	9.0	=	4.9	×	1.84
2006	11.8*	=	6.9	×	1.70
2005	11.1	=	7.1	×	1.57

* Differences due to rounding.

At least three findings emerge. First, Gap's return on total assets improved from 9.0% in 2007 to 12.6% in 2009. Second, total asset turnover has slightly improved over this period, from 1.84 to 1.89. Third, Gap's profit margin steadily increased over this period, from 4.9% in 2007 to 6.66% in 2009. These components reveal the dual role of profit margin and total asset turnover in determining return on total assets. They also reveal that the driver of Gap's recent improvement in return on total assets is not total asset turnover but profit margin.

Generally, if a company is to maintain or improve its return on total assets, it must meet any decline in either profit margin or total asset turnover with an increase in the other. If not, return on assets will decline. Companies consider these components in planning strategies. A component analysis can also reveal where a company is weak and where changes are needed, especially in a competitor analysis. If asset turnover is lower than the industry norm, for instance, a company should focus on raising asset turnover at least to the norm. The same applies to profit margin.

Decision Maker   Answer — p. 613

Retailer You are an entrepreneur and owner of a retail sporting goods store. The store's recent annual performance reveals (industry norms in parentheses): return on total assets = 11% (11.2%); profit margin = 4.4% (3.5%); and total asset turnover = 2.5 (3.2). What does your analysis of these figures reveal? ■

DEMONSTRATION PROBLEM—1

Garden Company completes the following selected transactions related to its short-term investments during 2011.

May 8   Purchased 300 shares of FedEx stock as a short-term investment in available-for-sale securities at $40 per share plus $975 in broker fees.

Sept. 2   Sold 100 shares of its investment in FedEx stock at $47 per share and held the remaining 200 shares; broker's commission was $225.

Oct. 2   Purchased 400 shares of Ajay stock for $60 per share plus $1,600 in commissions. The stock is held as a short-term investment in available-for-sale securities.

Required

1. Prepare journal entries for the above transactions of Garden Company for 2011.

2. Prepare an adjusting journal entry as of December 31, 2011, if the fair values of the equity securities held by Garden Company are $48 per share for FedEx and $55 per share for Ajay. (Year 2011 is the first year Garden Company acquired short-term investments.)

SOLUTION TO DEMONSTRATION PROBLEM—1

1.

May 8	Short-Term Investments—AFS (FedEx)	12,975	
	Cash		12,975
	Purchased 300 shares of FedEx stock		
	(300 × $40) + $975.		

[continued on next page]

[continued from previous page]

Sept. 2	Cash	4,475	
	Gain on Sale of Short-Term Investment		150
	Short-Term Investments—AFS (FedEx)		4,325
	Sold 100 shares of FedEx for $47 per share less a $225 commission. The original cost is ($12,975 × 100/300).		
Oct. 2	Short-Term Investments—AFS (Ajay)	25,600	
	Cash		25,600
	Purchased 400 shares of Ajay for $60 per share plus $1,600 in commissions.		

2. Computation of unrealized gain or loss follows.

Short-Term Investments in Available-for-Sale Securities	Shares	Cost per Share	Total Cost	Fair Value per Share	Total Fair Value	Unrealized Gain (Loss)
FedEx	200	$43.25	$ 8,650	$48.00	$ 9,600	
Ajay	400	64.00	25,600	55.00	22,000	
Totals			$34,250		$31,600	$(2,650)

The adjusting entry follows.

Dec. 31	Unrealized Loss—Equity	2,650	
	Fair Value Adjustment—Available-for-Sale (ST)		2,650
	To reflect an unrealized loss in fair values of available-for-sale securities.		

DEMONSTRATION PROBLEM—2

The following transactions relate to Brown Company's long-term investments during 2010 and 2011. Brown did not own any long-term investments prior to 2010. Show (1) the appropriate journal entries and (2) the relevant portions of each year's balance sheet and income statement that reflect these transactions for both 2010 and 2011.

2010

Sept. 9 Purchased 1,000 shares of Packard, Inc., common stock for $80,000 cash. These shares represent 30% of Packard's outstanding shares.

Oct. 2 Purchased 2,000 shares of AT&T common stock for $60,000 cash as a long-term investment. These shares represent less than a 1% ownership in AT&T.

   17 Purchased as a long-term investment 1,000 shares of Apple Computer common stock for $40,000 cash. These shares are less than 1% of Apple's outstanding shares.

Nov. 1 Received $5,000 cash dividend from Packard.

   30 Received $3,000 cash dividend from AT&T.

Dec. 15 Received $1,400 cash dividend from Apple.

   31 Packard's net income for this year is $70,000.

   31 Fair values for the investments in equity securities are Packard, $84,000; AT&T, $48,000; and Apple Computer, $45,000.

   31 For preparing financial statements, note the following post-closing account balances: Common Stock, $500,000, and Retained Earnings, $350,000.

2011

Jan. 1 Sold Packard, Inc., shares for $108,000 cash.

May 30 Received $3,100 cash dividend from AT&T.

June 15 Received $1,600 cash dividend from Apple.

Aug. 17 Sold the AT&T stock for $52,000 cash.
     19 Purchased 2,000 shares of Coca-Cola common stock for $50,000 cash as a long-term invest-ment. The stock represents less than a 5% ownership in Coca-Cola.
Dec. 15 Received $1,800 cash dividend from Apple.
     31 Fair values of the investments in equity securities are Apple, $39,000, and Coca-Cola, $48,000.
     31 For preparing financial statements, note the following post-closing account balances: Common Stock, $500,000, and Retained Earnings, $410,000.

PLANNING THE SOLUTION

- Account for the investment in Packard under the equity method.
- Account for the investments in AT&T, Apple, and Coca-Cola as long-term investments in available-for-sale securities.
- Prepare the information for the two years' balance sheets by including the relevant asset and equity accounts, and the two years' income statements by identifying the relevant revenues, earnings, gains, and losses.

SOLUTION TO DEMONSTRATION PROBLEM—2

1. Journal entries for 2010.

Sept. 9	Long-Term Investments—Packard	80,000	
	Cash		80,000
	Acquired 1,000 shares, representing a 30% equity in Packard.		
Oct. 2	Long-Term Investments—AFS (AT&T)	60,000	
	Cash		60,000
	Acquired 2,000 shares as a long-term investment in available-for-sale securities.		
Oct. 17	Long-Term Investments—AFS (Apple)	40,000	
	Cash		40,000
	Acquired 1,000 shares as a long-term investment in available-for-sale securities.		
Nov. 1	Cash	5,000	
	Long-Term Investments—Packard		5,000
	Received dividend from Packard.		
Nov. 30	Cash	3,000	
	Dividend Revenue		3,000
	Received dividend from AT&T.		
Dec. 15	Cash	1,400	
	Dividend Revenue		1,400
	Received dividend from Apple.		
Dec. 31	Long-Term Investments—Packard	21,000	
	Earnings from Investment (Packard)		21,000
	To record 30% share of Packard's annual earnings of $70,000.		
Dec. 31	Unrealized Loss—Equity	7,000	
	Fair Value Adjustment—Available-for-Sale (LT)* ...		7,000
	To record change in fair value of long-term available-for-sale securities.		

* Fair value adjustment computations:

	Cost	Fair Value	Unrealized Gain (Loss)
AT&T	$ 60,000	$48,000	$(12,000)
Apple	40,000	45,000	5,000
Total	$100,000	$93,000	$ (7,000)

Required balance of the Fair Value Adjustment—Available-for-Sale (LT) account (credit)	$(7,000)
Existing balance	0
Necessary adjustment (credit)	$(7,000)

2. The December 31, 2010, selected balance sheet items appear as follows.

Assets	
Long-term investments	
Available-for-sale securities (at fair value; cost is $100,000)	$ 93,000
Investment in equity securities	96,000
Total long-term investments	189,000
Stockholders' Equity	
Common stock	500,000
Retained earnings	350,000
Unrealized loss—Equity	(7,000)

The relevant income statement items for the year ended December 31, 2010, follow.

Dividend revenue	$ 4,400
Earnings from investment	21,000

1. Journal entries for 2011.

Jan. 1	Cash	108,000	
	Long-Term Investments—Packard		96,000
	Gain on Sale of Long-Term Investments		12,000
	Sold 1,000 shares for cash.		
May 30	Cash	3,100	
	Dividend Revenue		3,100
	Received dividend from AT&T.		
June 15	Cash	1,600	
	Dividend Revenue		1,600
	Received dividend from Apple.		
Aug. 17	Cash	52,000	
	Loss on Sale of Long-Term Investments	8,000	
	Long-Term Investments—AFS (AT&T)		60,000
	Sold 2,000 shares for cash.		
Aug. 19	Long-Term Investments—AFS (Coca-Cola)	50,000	
	Cash		50,000
	Acquired 2,000 shares as a long-term investment in available-for-sale securities.		
Dec. 15	Cash	1,800	
	Dividend Revenue		1,800
	Received dividend from Apple.		
Dec. 31	Fair Value Adjustment—Available-for-Sale (LT)*	4,000	
	Unrealized Loss—Equity		4,000
	To record change in fair value of long-term available-for-sale securities.		

* Fair value adjustment computations:

	Cost	Fair Value	Unrealized Gain (Loss)		Required balance of the Fair Value Adjustment—Available-for-Sale	
					(LT) account (credit)	$(3,000)
Apple	$40,000	$39,000	$(1,000)		Existing balance (credit)	(7,000)
Coca-Cola	50,000	48,000	(2,000)		Necessary adjustment (debit)	$ 4,000
Total	$90,000	$87,000	$(3,000)			

2. The December 31, 2011, balance sheet items appear as follows.

Assets	
Long-term investments	
Available-for-sale securities (at fair value; cost is $90,000)	$ 87,000
Stockholders' Equity	
Common stock	500,000
Retained earnings	410,000
Unrealized loss—Equity	(3,000)

The relevant income statement items for the year ended December 31, 2011, follow.

Dividend revenue	$ 6,500
Gain on sale of long-term investments.	12,000
Loss on sale of long-term investments	(8,000)

15A
Investments in International Operations

Many entities from small entrepreneurs to large corporations conduct business internationally. Some entities' operations occur in so many different countries that the companies are called **multinationals.** Many of us think of **Coca-Cola** and **McDonald's,** for example, as primarily U.S. companies, but most of their sales occur outside the United States. Exhibit 15A.1 shows the percent of international sales and income for selected U.S. companies. Managing and accounting for multinationals present challenges. This section describes some of these challenges and how to account for and report these activities.

EXHIBIT 15A.1

International Sales and Income as a Percent of Their Totals

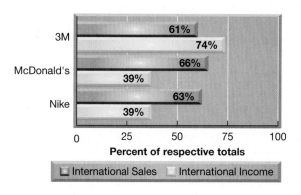

Percent of respective totals

☐ International Sales   ☐ International Income

Two major accounting challenges that arise when companies have international operations relate to transactions that involve more than one currency. The first is to account for sales and purchases listed in a foreign currency. The second is to prepare consolidated financial statements with international subsidiaries. For ease in this discussion, we use companies with a U.S. base of operations and assume the need to prepare financial statements in U.S. dollars. This means the *reporting currency* of these companies is the U.S. dollar.

Point: Transactions *listed* or *stated* in a foreign currency are said to be *denominated* in that currency.

C3 Explain foreign exchange rates and record transactions listed in a foreign currency.

Point: To convert currency, see XE.com

Exchange Rates between Currencies   Markets for the purchase and sale of foreign currencies exist all over the world. In these markets, U.S. dollars can be exchanged for Canadian dollars, British pounds, Japanese yen, Euros, or any other legal currencies. The price of one currency stated in terms of another currency is called a **foreign exchange rate.** Exhibit 15A.2 lists recent exchange rates for selected currencies. The exchange rate for British pounds and U.S. dollars is $1.8980, meaning 1 British pound could be purchased for $1.8980. On that same day, the exchange rate between Mexican pesos and U.S. dollars is $0.0925, or 1 Mexican peso can be purchased for $0.0925. Exchange rates fluctuate due to changing economic and political conditions, including the supply and demand for currencies and expectations about future events.

■ Decision Insight

Rush to Russia   Investors are still eager to buy Russian equities even in the face of rampant crime, corruption, and slow economic growth. Why? Many argue Russia remains a bargain-priced, if risky, bet on future growth. Some analysts argue that natural-resource-rich Russia is one of the least expensive emerging markets. ■

Source (unit)	Price in $U.S.	Source (unit)	Price in $U.S.
Britain (pound)	$1.8980	Canada (dollar)	$0.9793
Mexico (peso)	0.0925	Japan (yen)	0.0090
Taiwan (dollar)	0.0305	Europe (Euro)	1.2920

EXHIBIT 15A.2

Foreign Exchange Rates for Selected Currencies*

* Rates will vary over time based on economic, political, and other changes.

Sales and Purchases Listed in a Foreign Currency

When a U.S. company makes a credit sale to an international customer, accounting for the sale and the account receivable is straightforward if sales terms require the international customer's payment in U.S. dollars. If sale terms require (or allow) payment in a foreign currency, however, the U.S. company must account for the sale and the account receivable in a different manner.

Sales in a Foreign Currency   To illustrate, consider the case of the U.S.-based manufacturer Boston Company, which makes credit sales to London Outfitters, a British retail company. A sale occurs on December 12, 2010, for a price of £10,000 with payment due on February 10, 2011. Boston Company keeps its accounting records in U.S. dollars. To record the sale, Boston Company must translate the sales price from pounds to dollars. This is done using the exchange rate on the date of the sale. Assuming the exchange rate on December 12, 2010, is $1.80, Boston records this sale as follows.

Dec. 12	Accounts Receivable—London Outfitters	18,000	
	Sales*		18,000
	To record a sale at £10,000, when the exchange rate equals $1.80. * (£10,000 × $1.80/£)		

Assets = Liabilities + Equity
+18,000   +18,000

When Boston Company prepares its annual financial statements on December 31, 2010, the current exchange rate is $1.84. Thus, the current dollar value of Boston Company's receivable is $18,400 (£10,000 × $1.84/£). This amount is $400 higher than the amount recorded on December 12. Accounting principles require a receivable to be reported in the balance sheet at its current dollar value. Thus, Boston Company must make the following entry to record the increase in the dollar value of this receivable at year-end.

Dec. 31	Accounts Receivable—London Outfitters	400	
	Foreign Exchange Gain		400
	To record the increased value of the British pound for the receivable.		

Assets = Liabilities + Equity
+400   +400

On February 10, 2011, Boston Company receives London Outfitters' payment of £10,000. It immediately exchanges the pounds for U.S. dollars. On this date, the exchange rate for pounds is $1.78. Thus, Boston Company receives only $17,800 (£10,000 × $1.78/£). It records the cash receipt and the loss associated with the decline in the exchange rate as follows.

Point: Foreign exchange gains are credits, and foreign exchange losses are debits.

Feb. 10	Cash	17,800	
	Foreign Exchange Loss	600	
	Accounts Receivable—London Outfitters		18,400
	Received foreign currency payment of an account and converted it into dollars.		

Assets = Liabilities + Equity
+17,800   −600
−18,400

Gains and losses from foreign exchange transactions are accumulated in the Foreign Exchange Gain (or Loss) account. After year-end adjustments, the balance in the Foreign Exchange Gain (or Loss) account is reported on the income statement and closed to the Income Summary account.

Purchases in a Foreign Currency   Accounting for credit purchases from an international seller is similar to the case of a credit sale to an international customer. In particular, if the U.S. company is required to make payment in a foreign currency, the account payable must be translated into dollars before the U.S. company can record it. If the exchange rate is different when preparing financial statements and when paying for the purchase, the U.S. company must recognize a foreign exchange gain or loss at those dates. To illustrate, assume NC Imports, a U.S. company, purchases products costing €20,000 (euros) from

Example: Assume that a U.S. company makes a credit purchase from a British company for £10,000 when the exchange rate is $1.62. At the balance sheet date, this rate is $1.72. Does this imply a gain or loss for the U.S. company? *Answer:* A loss.

Hamburg Brewing on January 15, when the exchange rate is $1.20 per euro. NC records this transaction as follows.

Assets = Liabilities + Equity
+24,000   +24,000

Jan. 15	Inventory	24,000	
	Accounts Payable—Hamburg Brewing		24,000
	To record a €20,000 purchase when exchange rate *is $1.20 (€20,000 × $1.20/€)*		

NC Imports makes payment in full on February 14 when the exchange rate is $1.25 per euro, which is recorded as follows.

Assets = Liabilities + Equity
−25,000   −24,000   −1,000

Feb. 14	Accounts Payable—Hamburg Brewing	24,000	
	Foreign Exchange Loss	1,000	
	Cash		25,000
	To record cash payment towards €20,000 account *when exchange rate is $1.25 (€20,000 × $1.25/€).*		

Decision Insight

Global Greenback   What do changes in foreign exchange rates mean? A decline in the price of the U.S. dollar against other currencies usually yields increased international sales for U.S. companies, without hiking prices or cutting costs, and puts them on a stronger competitive footing abroad. At home, they can raise prices without fear that foreign rivals will undercut them. ■

Consolidated Statements with International Subsidiaries   A second challenge in accounting for international operations involves preparing consolidated financial statements when the parent company has one or more international subsidiaries. Consider a U.S.-based company that owns a controlling interest in a French subsidiary. The reporting currency of the U.S. parent is the dollar. The French subsidiary maintains its financial records in euros. Before preparing consolidated statements, the parent must translate financial statements of the French company into U.S. dollars. After this translation is complete (including that for accounting differences), it prepares consolidated statements the same as for domestic subsidiaries. Procedures for translating an international subsidiary's account balances depend on the nature of the subsidiary's operations. The process requires the parent company to select appropriate foreign exchange rates and to apply those rates to the foreign subsidiary's account balances. This is described in advanced courses.

Global: A weaker U.S. dollar often increases global sales for U.S. companies.

Decision Maker   Answer — p. 613

Entrepreneur   You are a U.S. home builder that purchases lumber from mills in both the U.S. and Canada. The price of the Canadian dollar in terms of the U.S. dollar jumps from US$0.70 to US$0.80. Are you now more or less likely to buy lumber from Canadian or U.S. mills? ■

Summary

C1 **Distinguish between debt and equity securities and between short-term and long-term investments.** *Debt securities* reflect a creditor relationship and include investments in notes, bonds, and certificates of deposit. *Equity securities* reflect an owner relationship and include shares of stock issued by other companies. Short-term investments in securities are current assets that meet two criteria: (1) They are expected to be converted into cash within one year or the current operating cycle of the business, whichever is longer and (2) they are readily convertible to cash, or *marketable*. All other investments in securities are long-term. Long-term investments also include assets not used in operations and those held for special purposes, such as land for expansion.

Investments in securities are classified into one of five groups: (1) trading securities, which are always short-term, (2) debt securities held-to-maturity, (3) debt and equity securities available-for-sale, (4) equity securities in which an investor has a significant influence over the investee, and (5) equity securities in which an investor has a controlling influence over the investee.

C2 **Describe how to report equity securities with controlling influence.** If an investor owns more than 50% of another company's voting stock and controls the investee, the investor's financial reports are prepared on a consolidated basis. These reports are prepared as if the company were organized as one entity.

C3A **Explain foreign exchange rates and record transactions listed in a foreign currency.** A foreign exchange rate is the price of one currency stated in terms of another. An entity with transactions in a foreign currency when the exchange rate changes between the transaction dates and their settlement will experience exchange gains or losses. When a company makes a credit sale to a foreign customer and sales terms call for payment in a foreign currency, the company must translate the foreign currency into dollars to record the receivable. If the exchange rate changes before payment is received, exchange gains or losses are recognized in the year they occur. The same treatment is used when a company makes a credit purchase from a foreign supplier and is required to make payment in a foreign currency.

A1 **Compute and analyze the components of return on total assets.** Return on total assets has two components: profit margin and total asset turnover. A decline in one component must be met with an increase in another if return on assets is to be maintained. Component analysis is helpful in assessing company performance compared to that of competitors and its own past.

P1 **Account for trading securities.** Investments are initially recorded at cost, and any dividend or interest from these investments is recorded in the income statement. Investments classified as trading securities are reported at fair value. Unrealized gains and losses on trading securities are reported in income. When investments are sold, the difference between the net proceeds from the sale and the cost of the securities is recognized as a gain or loss.

P2 **Account for held-to-maturity securities.** Debt securities held-to-maturity are reported at cost when purchased. Interest revenue is recorded as it accrues. The cost of long-term held-to-maturity securities is adjusted for the amortization of any difference between cost and maturity value.

P3 **Account for available-for-sale securities.** Debt and equity securities available-for-sale are recorded at cost when purchased. Available-for-sale securities are reported at their fair values on the balance sheet with unrealized gains or losses shown in the equity section. Gains and losses realized on the sale of these investments are reported in the income statement.

P4 **Account for equity securities with significant influence.** The equity method is used when an investor has a significant influence over an investee. This usually exists when an investor owns 20% or more of the investee's voting stock but not more than 50%. The equity method means an investor records its share of investee earnings with a debit to the investment account and a credit to a revenue account. Dividends received reduce the investment account balance.

Guidance Answers to Decision Maker

Money Manager If you have investments in fixed-rate bonds and notes when interest rates fall, the value of your investments increases. This is so because the bonds and notes you hold continue to pay the same (high) rate while the market is demanding a new lower interest rate. Your strategy is to continue holding your investments in bonds and notes, and, potentially, to increase these holdings through additional purchases.

Retailer Your store's return on assets is 11%, which is similar to the industry norm of 11.2%. However, disaggregation of return on assets reveals that your store's profit margin of 4.4% is much higher than the norm of 3.5%, but your total asset turnover of 2.5 is much lower than the norm of 3.2. These results suggest that, as compared with competitors, you are less efficient in using assets. You need to focus on increasing sales or reducing assets. You might consider reducing prices to increase sales, provided such a strategy does not reduce your return on assets. For instance, you could reduce your profit margin to 4% to increase sales. If total asset turnover increases to more than 2.75 when profit margin is lowered to 4%, your overall return on assets is improved.

Entrepreneur You are now less likely to buy Canadian lumber because it takes more U.S. money to buy a Canadian dollar (and lumber). For instance, the purchase of lumber from a Canadian mill with a $1,000 (Canadian dollars) price would have cost the U.S. builder $700 (U.S. dollars, computed as C$1,000 × US$0.70) before the rate change, and $800 (US dollars, computed as C$1,000 × US$0.80) after the rate change.

Guidance Answers to Quick Checks

1. Short-term held-to-maturity securities are reported at cost.
2. Trading securities are reported at fair value.
3. The equity section of the balance sheet (and in comprehensive income).
4. The income statement.
5. Long-term investments include (1) long-term funds earmarked for a special purpose, (2) debt and equity securities that do not meet current asset requirements, and (3) long-term assets not used in the regular operations of the business.
6. An equity investment is classified as long term if it is not marketable or, if marketable, it is not held as an available source of cash to meet the needs of current operations.
7. Debt securities held-to-maturity and debt securities available-for-sale are both recorded at cost. Also, interest on both is accrued as earned. However, only long-term securities held-to-maturity require amortization of the difference between cost and maturity value. In addition, only securities available-for-sale require a period-end adjustment to fair value.
8. Long-term equity investments are placed in one of three categories and accounted for as follows: (a) **available-for-sale** (noninfluential, less than 20% of outstanding stock)—fair value; (b) **significant influence** (20% to 50% of outstanding stock)—equity method; and (c) **controlling influence** (holding more than 50% of outstanding stock)—equity method with consolidation.

Key Terms

mhhe.com/wildFAP20e

Available-for-sale (AFS) securities (p. 600)

Comprehensive income (p. 604)

Consolidated financial statements (p. 603)

Equity method (p. 602)

Equity securities with controlling influence (p. 603)

Equity securities with significant influence (p. 602)

Foreign exchange rate (p. 610)

Held-to-maturity (HTM) securities (p. 600)

Long-term investments (p. 596)

Multinational (p. 610)

Other comprehensive income (p. 604)

Parent (p. 603)

Return on total assets (p. 605)

Short-term investments (p. 596)

Subsidiary (p. 603)

Trading securities (p. 599)

Unrealized gain (loss) (p. 599)

Multiple Choice Quiz

Answers on p. 629   mhhe.com/wildFAP20e

Additional Quiz Questions are available at the book's Website.

1. A company purchased $30,000 of 5% bonds for investment purposes on May 1. The bonds pay interest on February 1 and August 1. The amount of interest revenue accrued at December 31 (the company's year-end) is:
   a. $1,500
   b. $1,375
   c. $1,000
   d. $625
   e. $300

2. Earlier this period, Amadeus Co. purchased its only available-for-sale investment in the stock of Bach Co. for $83,000. The period-end fair value of this stock is $84,500. Amadeus records a:
   a. Credit to Unrealized Gain—Equity for $1,500.
   b. Debit to Unrealized Loss—Equity for $1,500.
   c. Debit to Investment Revenue for $1,500.
   d. Credit to Fair Value Adjustment—Available-for-Sale for $3,500.
   e. Credit to Cash for $1,500.

3. Mozart Co. owns 35% of Melody Inc. Melody pays $50,000 in cash dividends to its shareholders for the period. Mozart's entry to record the Melody dividend includes a:
   a. Credit to Investment Revenue for $50,000.
   b. Credit to Long-Term Investments for $17,500.

   c. Credit to Cash for $17,500.
   d. Debit to Long-Term Investments for $17,500.
   e. Debit to Cash for $50,000.

4. A company has net income of $300,000, net sales of $2,500,000, and total assets of $2,000,000. Its return on total assets equals:
   a. 6.7%
   b. 12.0%
   c. 8.3%
   d. 80.0%
   e. 15.0%

5. A company had net income of $80,000, net sales of $600,000, and total assets of $400,000. Its profit margin and total asset turnover are:

	Profit Margin	Total Asset Turnover
a.	1.5%	13.3
b.	13.3%	1.5
c.	13.3%	0.7
d.	7.0%	13.3
e.	10.0%	26.7

^A Superscript A denotes assignments based on Appendix 15A.

[I] Icon denotes assignments that involve decision making.

Discussion Questions

1. Under what two conditions should investments be classified as current assets?

2. [I] On a balance sheet, what valuation must be reported for short-term investments in trading securities?

3. If a short-term investment in available-for-sale securities costs $6,780 and is sold for $7,500, how should the difference between these two amounts be recorded?

4. Identify the three classes of noninfluential and two classes of influential investments in securities.

5. Under what conditions should investments be classified as current assets? As long-term assets?

6. If a company purchases its only long-term investments in available-for-sale debt securities this period and their fair value is below cost at the balance sheet date, what entry is required to recognize this unrealized loss?

7. On a balance sheet, what valuation must be reported for debt securities classified as available-for-sale?

8. Under what circumstances are long-term investments in debt securities reported at cost and adjusted for amortization of any difference between cost and maturity value?

9. For investments in available-for-sale securities, how are unrealized (holding) gains and losses reported?

10. In accounting for investments in equity securities, when should the equity method be used?

11. Under what circumstances does a company prepare consolidated financial statements?

12.^A What are two major challenges in accounting for international operations?

13.^A Assume a U.S. company makes a credit sale to a foreign customer that is required to make payment in its foreign currency. In the current period, the exchange rate is $1.40 on the date of the sale and is $1.30 on the date the customer pays the receivable. Will the U.S. company record an exchange gain or loss?

14.^A If a U.S. company makes a credit sale to a foreign customer required to make payment in U.S. dollars, can the U.S. company have an exchange gain or loss on this sale?

15. Refer to **Apple**'s statement of changes in shareholders' equity in Appendix A. What is the amount of foreign currency translation adjustment for the year ended September 26, 2009? Is this adjustment an unrealized gain or an unrealized loss? **Apple**

16. Refer to **Palm**'s statement of stockholders' equity. What was the amount of its fiscal 2009 unrealized gain or loss on securities? **Palm**

17. Refer to the balance sheet of **Nokia** in Appendix A. How can you tell that Nokia uses the consolidated method of accounting? **NOKIA**

18. Refer to the financial statements of **Research In Motion** in Appendix A. Compute its return on total assets for the year ended February 27, 2010. **RIM**

connect

Complete the following descriptions by filling in the blanks.

1. Accrual of interest on bonds held as long-term investments requires a credit to _____ _____.

2. The controlling investor (more than 50% ownership) is called the _____, and the investee company is called the _____.

3. Trading securities are classified as _____ assets.

4. Equity securities giving an investor significant influence are accounted for using the _____ _____.

5. Available-for-sale debt securities are reported on the balance sheet at _____ _____.

QUICK STUDY

QS 15-1
Describing investments in securities
C1 C2

Which of the following statements are true of long-term investments?

a. They can include investments in trading securities.

b. They are always easily sold and therefore qualify as being marketable.

c. They can include debt and equity securities available-for-sale.

d. They are held as an investment of cash available for current operations.

e. They can include debt securities held-to-maturity.

f. They can include bonds and stocks not intended to serve as a ready source of cash.

g. They can include funds earmarked for a special purpose, such as bond sinking funds.

QS 15-2
Identifying long-term investments
C1

On April 18, Dice Co. made a short-term investment in 500 common shares of XLT Co. The purchase price is $45 per share and the broker's fee is $150. The intent is to actively manage these shares for profit. On May 30, Dice Co. receives $1 per share from XLT in dividends. Prepare the April 18 and May 30 journal entries to record these transactions.

QS 15-3
Short-term equity investments P1

Fender Co. purchased short-term investments in available-for-sale securities at a cost of $100,000 on November 25, 2011. At December 31, 2011, these securities had a fair value of $94,000. This is the first and only time the company has purchased such securities.

1. Prepare the December 31, 2011, year-end adjusting entry for the securities' portfolio.

2. For each account in the entry for part 1, explain how it is reported in financial statements.

3. Prepare the April 6, 2012, entry when Fender sells one-half of these securities for $52,000.

QS 15-4
Available-for-sale securities
P3

Prepare Hoffman Company's journal entries to reflect the following transactions for the current year.

May 7   Purchases 100 shares of Lov stock as a short-term investment in available-for-sale securities at a cost of $25 per share plus $200 in broker fees.

June 6   Sells 100 shares of its investment in Lov stock at $28 per share. The broker's commission on this sale is $75.

QS 15-5
Available-for-sale securities
P3

QS 15-6

Available-for-sale securities

P3

Galaxy Company completes the following transactions during the current year.

May 9 Purchases 400 shares of X&O stock as a short-term investment in available-for-sale securities at a cost of $50 per share plus $400 in broker fees.

June 2 Sells 200 shares of its investment in X&O stock at $56 per share. The broker's commission on this sale is $180.

Dec. 31 The closing market price (fair value) of the X&O stock is $46 per share.

Prepare the May 9 and June 2 journal entries and the December 31 adjusting entry. This is the first and only time the company purchased such securities.

QS 15-7

Recording equity securities

P3

On May 20, 2011, Alexis Co. paid $750,000 to acquire 25,000 common shares (10%) of TKR Corp. as a long-term investment. On August 5, 2012, Alexis sold one-half of these shares for $475,000. What valuation method should be used to account for this stock investment? Prepare entries to record both the acquisition and the sale of these shares.

QS 15-8

Equity method transactions

P4

Assume the same facts as in QS 15-7 except that the stock acquired represents 40% of TKR Corp.'s outstanding stock. Also assume that TKR Corp. paid a $125,000 dividend on November 1, 2011, and reported a net income of $550,000 for 2011. Prepare the entries to record (*a*) the receipt of the dividend and (*b*) the December 31, 2011, year-end adjustment required for the investment account.

QS 15-9

Debt securities transactions

P2

On February 1, 2011, Charo Mendez purchased 6% bonds issued by CR Utilities at a cost of $30,000, which is their par value. The bonds pay interest semiannually on July 31 and January 31. For 2011, prepare entries to record Mendez's July 31 receipt of interest and its December 31 year-end interest accrual.

QS 15-10

Recording fair value adjustment for securities

P3

During the current year, Patton Consulting Group acquired long-term available-for-sale securities at a $35,000 cost. At its December 31 year-end, these securities had a fair value of $29,000. This is the first and only time the company purchased such securities.

1. Prepare the necessary year-end adjusting entry related to these securities.

2. Explain how each account used in part 1 is reported in the financial statements.

QS 15-11

Return on total assets   A1

The return on total assets is the focus of analysts, creditors, and other users of financial statements.

1. How is the return on total assets computed?

2. What does this important ratio reflect?

QS 15-12

Component return on total assets   A1

Return on total assets can be separated into two important components.

1. Write the formula to separate the return on total assets into its two basic components.

2. Explain how these components of the return on total assets are helpful to financial statement users for business decisions.

QS 15-13ᴬ

Foreign currency transactions

C3

A U.S. company sells a product to a British company with the transaction listed in British pounds. On the date of the sale, the transaction total of $16,000 is billed as £10,000, reflecting an exchange rate of 1.60 (that is, $1.60 per pound). Prepare the entry to record (1) the sale and (2) the receipt of payment in pounds when the exchange rate is 1.50.

QS 15-14ᴬ

Foreign currency transactions

C3

On March 1, 2011, a U.S. company made a credit sale requiring payment in 30 days from a Malaysian company, Hamac Sdn. Bhd., in 20,000 Malaysian ringgits. Assuming the exchange rate between Malaysian ringgits and U.S. dollars is $0.6811 on March 1 and $0.6985 on March 31, prepare the entries to record the sale on March 1 and the cash receipt on March 31.

QS 15-15

Equity securities with controlling influence

C2

Complete the following descriptions by filling in the blanks.

1. A long-term investment classified as equity securities with controlling influence implies that the investor can exert a _____ influence over the investee.

2. The controlling investor is called the _____, and the investee is called the _____.

The **Carrefour Group** reports the following description of its trading securities (titled "financial assets reported at fair value in the income statement").

> These are financial assets held by the Group in order to make a short-term profit on the sale. These assets are valued at their fair value with variations in value recognized in the income statement.

Note 10 to Carrefour's 2008 financial statements reports €117 million in unrealized gains for 2008 and €63 million in unrealized losses for 2008, both included in the fair value of those financial assets held for trading. What amount of these unrealized gains and unrealized losses, if any, are reported in its 2008 income statement? Explain.

connect

Prepare journal entries to record the following transactions involving the short-term securities investments of Maxwell Co., all of which occurred during year 2011.

a. On February 15, paid $100,000 cash to purchase FTR's 90-day short-term debt securities ($100,000 principal), dated February 15, that pay 8% interest (categorized as held-to-maturity securities).

b. On May 16, received a check from FTR in payment of the principal and 90 days' interest on the debt securities purchased in transaction *a*.

Prepare journal entries to record the following transactions involving the short-term securities investments of Smart Co., all of which occurred during year 2011.

a. On March 22, purchased 700 shares of FIX Company stock at $30 per share plus a $150 brokerage fee. These shares are categorized as trading securities.

b. On September 1, received a $1.00 per share cash dividend on the FIX Company stock purchased in transaction *a*.

c. On October 8, sold 350 shares of FIX Co. stock for $40 per share, less a $140 brokerage fee.

Prepare journal entries to record the following transactions involving the short-term securities investments of Prairie Co., all of which occurred during year 2011.

a. On August 1, paid $60,000 cash to purchase Better Buy's 10% debt securities ($60,000 principal), dated July 30, 2011, and maturing January 30, 2012 (categorized as available-for-sale securities).

b. On October 30, received a check from Better Buy for 90 days' interest on the debt securities purchased in transaction *a*.

Exercise 15-3
Accounting for short-term
available-for-sale securities

P3

Complete the following descriptions by filling in the blanks.

1. Short-term investments are securities that (1) management intends to convert to cash within ___ ___ or the ___ ___ whichever is longer, and (2) are readily convertible to ___.

2. Long-term investments in securities are defined as those securities that are ___ ___ convertible to cash or are ___ ___ to be converted into cash in the short term.

3. Debt securities reflect a _____ relationship such as investments in notes, bonds, and certificates of deposit.

4. Equity securities reflect an _____ relationship such as shares of stock issued by companies.

Exercise 15-4
Debt and equity securities and
short- and long-term investments

C1

Complete the following descriptions by filling in the blanks.

1. The equity method with _____ is used to account for long-term investments in equity securities with controlling influence.

2. Consolidated _____ _____ show the financial position, results of operations, and cash flows of all entities under the parent's control, including all subsidiaries.

Forex Co. purchases various investments in trading securities at a cost of $56,000 on December 27, 2011. (This is its first and only purchase of such securities.) At December 31, 2011, these securities had a fair value of $66,000.

1. Prepare the December 31, 2011, year-end adjusting entry for the trading securities' portfolio.

2. Explain how each account in the entry of part 1 is reported in financial statements.

3. Prepare the January 3, 2012, entry when Forex sells a portion of its trading securities (that had originally cost $28,000) for $30,000.

Exercise 15-7

Adjusting available-for-sale securities to fair value

P3

Check Unrealized loss, $100

On December 31, 2011, Rollo Company held the following short-term investments in its portfolio of available-for-sale securities. Rollo had no short-term investments in its prior accounting periods. Prepare the December 31, 2011, adjusting entry to report these investments at fair value.

	Cost	Fair Value
Vicks Corporation bonds payable	$79,600	$90,600
Pace Corporation notes payable	60,600	52,900
Lake Lugano Company common stock	85,500	82,100

Exercise 15-8

Transactions in short-term and long-term investments

P1 P2 P3

Prepare journal entries to record the following transactions involving both the short-term and long-term investments of Sophia Corp., all of which occurred during calendar year 2011. Use the account Short-Term Investments for any transactions that you determine are short term.

a. On February 15, paid $150,000 cash to purchase American General's 120-day short-term notes at par, which are dated February 15 and pay 10% interest (classified as held-to-maturity).

b. On March 22, bought 700 shares of Frain Industries common stock at $25 cash per share plus a $250 brokerage fee (classified as long-term available-for-sale securities).

c. On June 15, received a check from American General in payment of the principal and 120 days' interest on the notes purchased in transaction *a*.

d. On July 30, paid $50,000 cash to purchase MP3 Electronics' 8% notes at par, dated July 30, 2011, and maturing on January 30, 2012 (classified as trading securities).

e. On September 1, received a $0.50 per share cash dividend on the Frain Industries common stock purchased in transaction *b*.

f. On October 8, sold 350 shares of Frain Industries common stock for $32 cash per share, less a $175 brokerage fee.

g. On October 30, received a check from MP3 Electronics for three months' interest on the notes purchased in transaction *d*.

Exercise 15-9

Fair value adjustment to available-for-sale securities

P3

On December 31, 2011, Manhattan Co. held the following short-term available-for-sale securities.

	Cost	Fair Value
Nintendo Co. common stock	$68,900	$75,300
Atlantic bonds payable	24,500	22,800
Kellogg Co. notes payable	50,000	47,200
McDonald's Corp. common stock	91,400	86,600

Manhattan had no short-term investments prior to the current period. Prepare the December 31, 2011, year-end adjusting entry to record the fair value adjustment for these securities.

Exercise 15-10

Fair value adjustment to available-for-sale securities

P3

Berroa Co. began operations in 2010. The cost and fair values for its long-term investments portfolio in available-for-sale securities are shown below. Prepare Berroa's December 31, 2011, adjusting entry to reflect any necessary fair value adjustment for these investments.

	Cost	Fair Value
December 31, 2010	$79,483	$72,556
December 31, 2011	85,120	90,271

Exercise 15-11

Multiyear fair value adjustments to available-for-sale securities

P3

Ticker Services began operations in 2009 and maintains long-term investments in available-for-sale securities. The year-end cost and fair values for its portfolio of these investments follow. Prepare journal entries to record each year-end fair value adjustment for these securities.

	Cost	Fair Value
December 31, 2009	$374,000	$362,560
December 31, 2010	426,900	453,200
December 31, 2011	580,700	686,450
December 31, 2012	875,500	778,800

Information regarding Central Company's individual investments in securities during its calendar-year 2011, along with the December 31, 2011, fair values, follows.

a. Investment in Beeman Company bonds: $418,500 cost, $455,000 fair value. Central intends to hold these bonds until they mature in 2016.

b. Investment in Baybridge common stock: 29,500 shares; $332,450 cost; $361,375 fair value. Central owns 32% of Baybridge's voting stock and has a significant influence over Baybridge.

c. Investment in Carroll common stock: 12,000 shares; $169,750 cost; $183,000 fair value. This investment amounts to 3% of Carroll's outstanding shares, and Central's goal with this investment is to earn dividends over the next few years.

d. Investment in Newtech common stock: 3,500 shares; $95,300 cost; $93,625 fair value. Central's goal with this investment is to reap an increase in fair value of the stock over the next three to five years. Newtech has 30,000 common shares outstanding.

e. Investment in Flock common stock: 16,300 shares; $102,860 cost; $109,210 fair value. This stock is marketable and is held as an investment of cash available for operations.

Required

1. Identify whether each investment should be classified as a short-term or long-term investment. For each long-term investment, indicate in which of the long-term investment classifications it should be placed.

2. Prepare a journal entry dated December 31, 2011, to record the fair value adjustment of the long-term investments in available-for-sale securities. Central had no long-term investments prior to year 2011.

Exercise 15-12
Classifying investments in securities; recording fair values
C1 P2 P3 P4

Check (2) Unrealized gain, $11,575

Prepare journal entries to record the following transactions and events of Kash Company.

2011

| Jan. | 2 | Purchased 30,000 shares of Bushtex Co. common stock for $204,000 cash plus a broker's fee of $3,480 cash. Bushtex has 90,000 shares of common stock outstanding and its policies will be significantly influenced by Kash. |

Sept. 1 Bushtex declared and paid a cash dividend of $3.10 per share.
Dec. 31 Bushtex announced that net income for the year is $624,900.
Dec 31 Kash sold 10,000 Shares of Bushtex for $500,000

2012

June 1 Bushtex declared and paid a cash dividend of $3.60 per share.
Dec. 31 Bushtex announced that net income for the year is $699,750.
Dec. 31 Kash sold 10,000 shares of Bushtex for $162,500 cash.

Exercise 15-13
Securities transactions; equity method
P4

The following information is available from the financial statements of Wright Industries. Compute Wright's return on total assets for 2011 and 2012. (Round returns to one-tenth of a percent.) Comment on the company's efficiency in using its assets in 2011 and 2012.

Exercise 15-14
Return on total assets
A1

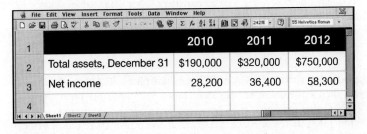

	2010	2011	2012
Total assets, December 31	$190,000	$320,000	$750,000
Net income	28,200	36,400	58,300

Desi of New York sells its products to customers in the United States and the United Kingdom. On December 16, 2011, Desi sold merchandise on credit to Bronson Ltd. of London at a price of 17,000 pounds. The exchange rate on that day for £1 was $1.5238. On December 31, 2011, when Desi prepared its financial statements, the rate was £1 for $1.4990. Bronson paid its bill in full on January 15, 2012, at which time the exchange rate was £1 for $1.5156. Desi immediately exchanged the 17,000 pounds for U.S. dollars. Prepare Desi's journal entries on December 16, December 31, and January 15 (round to the nearest dollar).

Exercise 15-15[A]
Foreign currency transactions
C3

Exercise 15-16ᴬ
Computing foreign exchange
gains and losses on receivables

C3

On May 8, 2011, Jett Company (a U.S. company) made a credit sale to Lopez (a Mexican company). The terms of the sale required Lopez to pay 800,000 pesos on February 10, 2012. Jett prepares quarterly financial statements on March 31, June 30, September 30, and December 31. The exchange rates for pesos during the time the receivable is outstanding follow.

May 8, 2011	$0.1984
June 30, 2011	0.2013
September 30, 2011	0.2029
December 31, 2011	0.1996
February 10, 2012	0.2047

Compute the foreign exchange gain or loss that Jett should report on each of its quarterly income statements for the last three quarters of 2011 and the first quarter of 2012. Also compute the amount reported on Jett's balance sheets at the end of each of its last three quarters of 2011.

Exercise 15-17
International accounting
for investments

P3

The **Carrefour Group** reports the following description of its financial assets available-for-sale.

> Assets available for sale are . . . valued at fair value. Unrealized . . . gains or losses are recorded as shareholders' equity until they are sold.

Note 10 to Carrefour's 2008 financial statements reports €6 million in *net* unrealized losses (net of unrealized gains) for 2008, which is included in the fair value of its available-for-sale securities reported on the balance sheet.

1. What amount of the €6 million net unrealized losses, if any, is reported in its 2008 income statement? Explain.

2. If the €6 million net unrealized losses are not reported in the income statement, in which statement are they reported, if any? Explain.

⬛ connect

PROBLEM SET A

Problem 15-1A
Recording transactions and
fair value adjustments for
trading securities

P1

 QB

Ryder Company, which began operations in 2011, invests its idle cash in trading securities. The following transactions are from its short-term investments in its trading securities.

2011

Jan. 20   Purchased 900 shares of Ford Motor Co. at $36 per share plus a $125 commission.
Feb. 9   Purchased 4,400 shares of Lucent at $10 per share plus a $200 commission.
Oct. 12   Purchased 500 shares of Z-Seven at $8 per share plus a $100 commission.

2012

Apr. 15   Sold 900 shares of Ford Motor Co. at $39 per share less a $185 commission.
July   5   Sold 500 shares of Z-Seven at $10.25 per share less a $100 commission.
July 22   Purchased 800 shares of Hunt Corp. at $30 per share plus a $225 commission.
Aug. 19   Purchased 1,000 shares of Donna Karan at $12 per share plus a $100 commission.

2013

Feb. 27   Purchased 3,400 shares of HCA at $22 per share plus a $220 commission.
Mar. 3   Sold 800 shares of Hunt at $25 per share less a $125 commission.
June 21   Sold 4,400 shares of Lucent at $8 per share less a $180 commission.
June 30   Purchased 1,000 shares of Black & Decker at $47.50 per share plus a $195 commission.
Nov. 1   Sold 1,000 shares of Donna Karan at $22 per share less a $208 commission.

Required

1. Prepare journal entries to record these short-term investment activities for the years shown. (Ignore any year-end adjusting entries.)

Check   (2) Dr. Fair Value
Adjustment—Trading $2,385

2. On December 31, 2013, prepare the adjusting entry to record any necessary fair value adjustment for the portfolio of trading securities when HCA's share price is $24 and Black & Decker's share price is $43.50. (Assume the Fair Value Adjustment—Trading account had an unadjusted balance of zero.)

Perry Company had no short-term investments prior to year 2011. It had the following transactions involving short-term investments in available-for-sale securities during 2011.

Apr. 16   Purchased 8,000 shares of Gem Co. stock at $24.25 per share plus a $360 brokerage fee.

May   1   Paid $200,000 to buy 90-day U.S. Treasury bills (debt securities): $200,000 principal amount, 6% interest, securities dated May 1.

July   7   Purchased 4,000 shares of PepsiCo stock at $49.25 per share plus a $350 brokerage fee.

      20   Purchased 2,000 shares of Xerox stock at $16.75 per share plus a $410 brokerage fee.

Aug.   3   Received a check for principal and accrued interest on the U.S. Treasury bills that matured on July 29.

      15   Received an $0.85 per share cash dividend on the Gem Co. stock.

      28   Sold 4,000 shares of Gem Co. stock at $30 per share less a $450 brokerage fee.

Oct.   1   Received a $1.90 per share cash dividend on the PepsiCo shares.

Dec. 15   Received a $1.05 per share cash dividend on the remaining Gem Co. shares.

      31   Received a $1.30 per share cash dividend on the PepsiCo shares.

Required

1. Prepare journal entries to record the preceding transactions and events.

2. Prepare a table to compare the year-end cost and fair values of Perry's short-term investments in available-for-sale securities. The year-end fair values per share are: Gem Co., $26.50; PepsiCo, $46.50; and Xerox, $13.75.

3. Prepare an adjusting entry, if necessary, to record the year-end fair value adjustment for the portfolio of short-term investments in available-for-sale securities.

Analysis Component

4. Explain the balance sheet presentation of the fair value adjustment for Perry's short-term investments.

5. How do these short-term investments affect Perry's (*a*) income statement for year 2011 and (*b*) the equity section of its balance sheet at year-end 2011?

Problem 15-2A

Recording, adjusting, and reporting short-term available-for-sale securities

P3

Check   (2) Cost = $328,440

(3) Dr. Unrealized Loss—Equity $8,940

Shaq Security, which began operations in 2011, invests in long-term available-for-sale securities. Following is a series of transactions and events determining its long-term investment activity.

2011

Jan. 20   Purchased 900 shares of Johnson & Johnson at $18.75 per share plus a $590 commission.

Feb.   9   Purchased 2,200 shares of Sony at $46.88 per share plus a $2,578 commission.

June 12   Purchased 500 shares of Mattel at $55.50 per share plus an $832 commission.

Dec. 31   Per share fair values for stocks in the portfolio are Johnson & Johnson, $20.38; Mattel, $57.25; Sony, $39.

2012

Apr. 15   Sold 900 shares of Johnson & Johnson at $21.75 per share less a $685 commission.

July   5   Sold 500 shares of Mattel at $49.13 per share less a $491 commission.

July 22   Purchased 1,600 shares of Sara Lee at $36.25 per share plus a $1,740 commission.

Aug. 19   Purchased 1,800 shares of Eastman Kodak at $28 per share plus a $1,260 commission.

Dec. 31   Per share fair values for stocks in the portfolio are: Kodak, $31.75; Sara Lee, $30.00; Sony, $36.50.

2013

Feb. 27   Purchased 3,400 shares of Microsoft at $23.63 per share plus a $1,606 commission.

June 21   Sold 2,200 shares of Sony at $40.00 per share less a $2,640 commission.

June 30   Purchased 1,200 shares of Black & Decker at $47.50 per share plus a $1,995 commission.

Aug.   3   Sold 1,600 shares of Sara Lee at $31.25 per share less a $1,750 commission.

Nov.   1   Sold 1,800 shares of Eastman Kodak at $42.75 per share less a $2,309 commission.

Dec. 31   Per share fair values for stocks in the portfolio are: Black & Decker, $56.50; Microsoft, $28.

Required

1. Prepare journal entries to record these transactions and events and any year-end fair value adjustments to the portfolio of long-term available-for-sale securities.

Problem 15-3A

Recording, adjusting, and reporting long-term available-for-sale securities

P3

Check (2b) Fair Value Adjustment bal.: 12/31/11, $(18,994); 12/31/12; $(31,664)

(3b) Unrealized Gain at 12/31/2013, $22,057

2. Prepare a table that summarizes the (*a*) total cost, (*b*) total fair value adjustment, and (*c*) total fair value of the portfolio of long-term available-for-sale securities at each year-end.

3. Prepare a table that summarizes (*a*) the realized gains and losses and (*b*) the unrealized gains or losses for the portfolio of long-term available-for-sale securities at each year-end.

Problem 15-4A
Long-term investment transactions; unrealized and realized gains and losses
C2 P3 P4

Park Co.'s long-term available-for-sale portfolio at December 31, 2010, consists of the following.

Available-for-Sale Securities	Cost	Fair Value
80,000 shares of Company A common stock	$1,070,600	$ 980,000
14,000 shares of Company B common stock	318,750	308,000
35,000 shares of Company C common stock	1,325,500	1,281,875

Park enters into the following long-term investment transactions during year 2011.

Jan. 29 Sold 7,000 shares of Company B common stock for $158,375 less a brokerage fee of $3,100.

Apr. 17 Purchased 20,000 shares of Company W common stock for $395,000 plus a brokerage fee of $3,500. The shares represent a 30% ownership in Company W.

July 6 Purchased 9,000 shares of Company X common stock for $253,125 plus a brokerage fee of $3,500. The shares represent a 10% ownership in Company X.

Aug. 22 Purchased 100,000 shares of Company Y common stock for $750,000 plus a brokerage fee of $8,200. The shares represent a 51% ownership in Company Y.

Nov. 13 Purchased 17,000 shares of Company Z common stock for $533,800 plus a brokerage fee of $6,900. The shares represent a 5% ownership in Company Z.

Dec. 9 Sold 80,000 shares of Company A common stock for $1,030,000 less a brokerage fee of $4,100.

The fair values of its investments at December 31, 2011, are: B, $162,750; C, $1,220,625; W, $382,500; X, $236,250; Y, $1,062,500; and Z, $557,600.

Required

1. Determine the amount Park should report on its December 31, 2011, balance sheet for its long-term investments in available-for-sale securities.

Check (2) Cr. Unrealized Loss—Equity, $40,000

2. Prepare any necessary December 31, 2011, adjusting entry to record the fair value adjustment for the long-term investments in available-for-sale securities.

3. What amount of gains or losses on transactions relating to long-term investments in available-for-sale securities should Park report on its December 31, 2011, income statement?

Problem 15-5A
Accounting for long-term investments in securities; with and without significant influence
P3 P4

Pillar Steel Co., which began operations on January 4, 2011, had the following subsequent transactions and events in its long-term investments.

2011

Jan. 5 Pillar purchased 30,000 shares (20% of total) of Kildaire's common stock for $780,000.

Oct. 23 Kildaire declared and paid a cash dividend of $1.60 per share.

Dec. 31 Kildaire's net income for 2011 is $582,000, and the fair value of its stock at December 31 is $27.75 per share.

2012

Oct. 15 Kildaire declared and paid a cash dividend of $1.30 per share.

Dec. 31 Kildaire's net income for 2012 is $738,000, and the fair value of its stock at December 31 is $30.45 per share.

2013

Jan. 2 Pillar sold all of its investment in Kildaire for $947,000 cash.

Part 1

Assume that Pillar has a significant influence over Kildaire with its 20% share of stock.

Required

1. Prepare journal entries to record these transactions and events for Pillar.

Check (2) Carrying value per share, $31.90

2. Compute the carrying (book) value per share of Pillar's investment in Kildaire common stock as reflected in the investment account on January 1, 2013.

3. Compute the net increase or decrease in Pillar's equity from January 5, 2011, through January 2, 2013, resulting from its investment in Kildaire.

Part 2

Assume that although Pillar owns 20% of Kildaire's outstanding stock, circumstances indicate that it does not have a significant influence over the investee and that it is classified as an available-for-sale security investment.

Required

1. Prepare journal entries to record the preceding transactions and events for Pillar. Also prepare an entry dated January 2, 2013, to remove any balance related to the fair value adjustment.
2. Compute the cost per share of Pillar's investment in Kildaire common stock as reflected in the investment account on January 1, 2013.
3. Compute the net increase or decrease in Pillar's equity from January 5, 2011, through January 2, 2013, resulting from its investment in Kildaire.

(1) 1/2/2013 Dr. Unrealized Gain—Equity $133,500

(3) Net increase, $254,000

Roundtree Company, a U.S. corporation with customers in several foreign countries, had the following selected transactions for 2011 and 2012.

Problem 15-6A[A]
Foreign currency transactions

C3

2011

Apr. 8   Sold merchandise to Salinas & Sons of Mexico for $7,938 cash. The exchange rate for pesos is $0.1323 on this day.

July 21   Sold merchandise on credit to Sumito Corp. in Japan. The price of 1.5 million yen is to be paid 120 days from the date of sale. The exchange rate for yen is $0.0096 on this day.

Oct. 14   Sold merchandise for 19,000 pounds to Smithers Ltd. of Great Britain, payment in full to be received in 90 days. The exchange rate for pounds is $1.5181 on this day.

Nov. 18   Received Sumito's payment in yen for its July 21 purchase and immediately exchanged the yen for dollars. The exchange rate for yen is $0.0091 on this day.

Dec. 20   Sold merchandise for 17,000 ringgits to Hamid Albar of Malaysia, payment in full to be received in 30 days. On this day, the exchange rate for ringgits is $0.6852.

Dec. 31   Recorded adjusting entries to recognize exchange gains or losses on Roundtree's annual financial statements. Rates for exchanging foreign currencies on this day follow.

Pesos (Mexico)	$0.1335
Yen (Japan)	0.0095
Pounds (Britain)	1.5235
Ringgits (Malaysia)	0.6807

2012

Jan. 12   Received full payment in pounds from Smithers for the October 14 sale and immediately exchanged the pounds for dollars. The exchange rate for pounds is $1.5314 on this day.

Jan. 19   Received Hamid Albar's full payment in ringgits for the December 20 sale and immediately exchanged the ringgits for dollars. The exchange rate for ringgits is $0.6771 on this day.

Required

1. Prepare journal entries for the Roundtree transactions and adjusting entries (round amounts to the nearest dollar).
2. Compute the foreign exchange gain or loss to be reported on Roundtree's 2011 income statement.

Check   (2) 2011 total foreign exchange loss, $723

Analysis Component

3. What actions might Roundtree consider to reduce its risk of foreign exchange gains or losses?

Deal Company, which began operations in 2011, invests its idle cash in trading securities. The following transactions relate to its short-term investments in its trading securities.

PROBLEM SET B

Problem 15-1B
Recording transactions and fair value adjustments for trading securities   P1

2011

Mar. 10   Purchased 1,200 shares of AOL at $59.15 per share plus a $773 commission.
May 7   Purchased 2,500 shares of MTV at $36.25 per share plus a $1,428 commission.
Sept. 1   Purchased 600 shares of UPS at $57.25 per share plus a $625 commission.

2012

Apr. 26   Sold 2,500 shares of MTV at $34.50 per share less a $1,025 commission.
Apr. 27   Sold 600 shares of UPS at $60.50 per share less an $894 commission.

June   2   Purchased 1,800 shares of SPW at $172 per share plus a $1,625 commission.
June 14   Purchased 450 shares of Walmart at $50.25 per share plus a $541.50 commission.

2013

Jan. 28   Purchased 1,000 shares of PepsiCo at $43 per share plus a $1,445 commission.
Jan. 31   Sold 1,800 shares of SPW at $168 per share less a $1,020 commission.
Aug. 22   Sold 1,200 shares of AOL at $56.75 per share less a $1,240 commission.
Sept. 3   Purchased 750 shares of Vodaphone at $40.50 per share plus an $840 commission.
Oct.   9   Sold 450 shares of Walmart at $53.75 per share less a $610.50 commission.

Required

1. Prepare journal entries to record these short-term investment activities for the years shown. (Ignore any year-end adjusting entries.)

Check (2) Cr. Fair Value
Adjustment—Trading $6,910

2. On December 31, 2013, prepare the adjusting entry to record any necessary fair value adjustment for the portfolio of trading securities when PepsiCo's share price is $41 and Vodaphone's share price is $37. (Assume the Fair Value Adjustment—Trading account had an unadjusted balance of zero.)

Problem 15-2B
Recording, adjusting, and reporting short-term available-for-sale securities

P3

Day Systems had no short-term investments prior to 2011. It had the following transactions involving short-term investments in available-for-sale securities during 2011.

Feb.   6   Purchased 1,700 shares of Nokia stock at $41.25 per share plus a $1,500 brokerage fee.
      15   Paid $10,000 to buy six-month U.S. Treasury bills (debt securities): $10,000 principal amount, 6% interest, securities dated February 15.
Apr.   7   Purchased 600 shares of Dell Co. stock at $39.50 per share plus a $627 brokerage fee.
June   2   Purchased 1,250 shares of Merck stock at $72.50 per share plus a $1,945 brokerage fee.
      30   Received a $0.19 per share cash dividend on the Nokia shares.
Aug. 11   Sold 425 shares of Nokia stock at $46 per share less a $525 brokerage fee.
      16   Received a check for principal and accrued interest on the U.S. Treasury bills purchased February 15.
      24   Received a $0.10 per share cash dividend on the Dell shares.
Nov.   9   Received a $0.20 per share cash dividend on the remaining Nokia shares.
Dec. 18   Received a $0.15 per share cash dividend on the Dell shares.

Required

1. Prepare journal entries to record the preceding transactions and events.

Check (2) Cost = $170,616

2. Prepare a table to compare the year-end cost and fair values of the short-term investments in available-for-sale securities. The year-end fair values per share are: Nokia, $40.25; Dell, $41; and Merck, $59.

(3) Dr. Unrealized Loss—
Equity, $20,947

3. Prepare an adjusting entry, if necessary, to record the year-end fair value adjustment for the portfolio of short-term investments in available-for-sale securities.

Analysis Component

4. Explain the balance sheet presentation of the fair value adjustment to Day's short-term investments.

5. How do these short-term investments affect (*a*) its income statement for year 2011 and (*b*) the equity section of its balance sheet at the 2011 year-end?

Problem 15-3B
Recording, adjusting, and reporting long-term available-for-sale securities

P3

Venice Enterprises, which began operations in 2011, invests in long-term available-for-sale securities. Following is a series of transactions and events involving its long-term investment activity.

2011

Mar. 10   Purchased 2,400 shares of Apple at $33.25 per share plus $1,995 commission.
Apr.   7   Purchased 5,000 shares of Ford at $17.50 per share plus $2,625 commission.
Sept. 1   Purchased 1,200 shares of Polaroid at $49.00 per share plus $1,176 commission.
Dec. 31   Per share fair values for stocks in the portfolio are: Apple, $35.50; Ford, $17.00; Polaroid, $51.75.

2012

Apr. 26   Sold 5,000 shares of Ford at $16.38 per share less a $2,237 commission.
June   2   Purchased 3,600 shares of Duracell at $18.88 per share plus a $2,312 commission.
June 14   Purchased 900 shares of Sears at $24.50 per share plus a $541 commission.
Nov. 27   Sold 1,200 shares of Polaroid at $52 per share less a $1,672 commission.
Dec. 31   Per share fair values for stocks in the portfolio are: Apple, $35.50; Duracell, $18.00; Sears, $26.00.

2013

Jan. 28   Purchased 2,000 shares of Coca-Cola Co. at $41 per share plus a $3,280 commission.
Aug. 22   Sold 2,400 shares of Apple at $29.75 per share less a $2,339 commission.
Sept. 3   Purchased 1,500 shares of Motorola at $29 per share plus a $870 commission.
Oct.   9   Sold 900 shares of Sears at $27.50 per share less a $619 commission.
Oct. 31   Sold 3,600 shares of Duracell at $16.00 per share less a $1,496 commission.
Dec. 31   Per share fair values for stocks in the portfolio are: Coca-Cola, $46.00; Motorola, $22.00.

Required

1. Prepare journal entries to record these transactions and events and any year-end fair value adjustments to the portfolio of long-term available-for-sale securities.

2. Prepare a table that summarizes the (*a*) total cost, (*b*) total fair value adjustment, and (*c*) total fair value for the portfolio of long-term available-for-sale securities at each year-end.

3. Prepare a table that summarizes (*a*) the realized gains and losses and (*b*) the unrealized gains or losses for the portfolio of long-term available-for-sale securities at each year-end.

Check (2b) Fair Value Adjustment
bal.: 12/31/11, $404; 12/31/12, $(1,266)

(3b) Unrealized Loss at
12/31/2013, $4,650

Capollo's long-term available-for-sale portfolio at December 31, 2010, consists of the following.

Problem 15-4B
Long-term investment
transactions; unrealized and
realized gains and losses

C2 P3 P4

Available-for-Sale Securities	Cost	Fair Value
45,000 shares of Company R common stock	$1,118,250	$1,198,125
17,000 shares of Company S common stock	616,760	586,500
22,000 shares of Company T common stock	294,470	303,600

Capollo enters into the following long-term investment transactions during year 2011.

Jan. 13   Sold 4,250 shares of Company S stock for $144,500 less a brokerage fee of $2,390.
Mar. 24   Purchased 31,000 shares of Company U common stock for $565,750 plus a brokerage fee of $9,900. The shares represent a 62% ownership interest in Company U.
Apr. 5   Purchased 85,000 shares of Company V common stock for $267,750 plus a brokerage fee of $4,500. The shares represent a 10% ownership in Company V.
Sept. 2   Sold 22,000 shares of Company T common stock for $313,500 less a brokerage fee of $5,400.
Sept. 27   Purchased 5,000 shares of Company W common stock for $101,000 plus a brokerage fee of $2,100. The shares represent a 25% ownership interest in Company W.
Oct. 30   Purchased 10,000 shares of Company X common stock for $97,500 plus a brokerage fee of $2,340. The shares represent a 13% ownership interest in Company X.

The fair values of its investments at December 31, 2011, are: R, $1,136,250; S, $420,750; U, $545,600; V, $269,875; W, $109,375; and X, $91,250.

Required

1. Determine the amount Capollo should report on its December 31, 2011, balance sheet for its long-term investments in available-for-sale securities.

2. Prepare any necessary December 31, 2011, adjusting entry to record the fair value adjustment of the long-term investments in available-for-sale securities.

3. What amount of gains or losses on transactions relating to long-term investments in available-for-sale securities should Capollo report on its December 31, 2011, income statement?

Check (2) Dr. Unrealized Loss—
Equity, $34,785; Cr. Fair Value
Adjustment—AFS (LT), $93,530

Bengal Company, which began operations on January 3, 2011, had the following subsequent transactions and events in its long-term investments.

Problem 15-5B
Accounting for long-term
investments in securities; with
and without significant influence

P3 P4

2011

Jan. 5   Bengal purchased 15,000 shares (25% of total) of Bloch's common stock for $187,500.
Aug. 1   Bloch declared and paid a cash dividend of $0.95 per share.
Dec. 31   Bloch's net income for 2011 is $92,000, and the fair value of its stock is $12.90 per share.

2012

Aug. 1   Bloch declared and paid a cash dividend of $1.25 per share.
Dec. 31   Bloch's net income for 2012 is $76,000, and the fair value of its stock is $13.55 per share.

2013

Jan.   8   Bengal sold all of its investment in Bloch for $204,750 cash.

Part 1

Assume that Bengal has a significant influence over Bloch with its 25% share.

Required

Check   (2) Carrying value per share, $13.10

1. Prepare journal entries to record these transactions and events for Bengal.
2. Compute the carrying (book) value per share of Bengal's investment in Bloch common stock as reflected in the investment account on January 7, 2013.
3. Compute the net increase or decrease in Bengal's equity from January 5, 2011, through January 8, 2013, resulting from its investment in Bloch.

Part 2

Assume that although Bengal owns 25% of Bloch's outstanding stock, circumstances indicate that it does not have a significant influence over the investee and that it is classified as an available-for-sale security investment.

Required

(1) 1/8/2013 Dr. Unrealized Gain—Equity $15,750

1. Prepare journal entries to record these transactions and events for Bengal. Also prepare an entry dated January 8, 2013, to remove any balance related to the fair value adjustment.
2. Compute the cost per share of Bengal's investment in Bloch common stock as reflected in the investment account on January 7, 2013.

(3) Net increase, $50,250

3. Compute the net increase or decrease in Bengal's equity from January 5, 2011, through January 8, 2013, resulting from its investment in Bloch.

Problem 15-6B[A]
Foreign currency transactions

C3

Datamix, a U.S. corporation with customers in several foreign countries, had the following selected transactions for 2011 and 2012.

2011

May 26   Sold merchandise for 6.5 million yen to Fuji Company of Japan, payment in full to be received in 60 days. On this day, the exchange rate for yen is $0.0094.

June   1   Sold merchandise to Fordham Ltd. of Great Britain for $72,613 cash. The exchange rate for pounds is $1.5277 on this day.

July 25   Received Fuji's payment in yen for its May 26 purchase and immediately exchanged the yen for dollars. The exchange rate for yen is $0.0090 on this day.

Oct. 15   Sold merchandise on credit to Martinez Brothers of Mexico. The price of 373,000 pesos is to be paid 90 days from the date of sale. On this day, the exchange rate for pesos is $0.1340.

Dec.   6   Sold merchandise for 242,000 yuans to Chi-Ying Company of China, payment in full to be received in 30 days. The exchange rate for yuans is $0.1975 on this day.

Dec. 31   Recorded adjusting entries to recognize exchange gains or losses on Datamix's annual financial statements. Rates of exchanging foreign currencies on this day follow.

Yen (Japan)	$0.0094
Pounds (Britain)	1.5318
Pesos (Mexico)	0.1560
Yuans (China)	0.2000

2012

Jan.   5   Received Chi-Ying's full payment in yuans for the December 6 sale and immediately exchanged the yuans for dollars. The exchange rate for yuans is $0.2060 on this day.

Jan. 13   Received full payment in pesos from Martinez for the October 15 sale and immediately exchanged the pesos for dollars. The exchange rate for pesos is $0.1420 on this day.

Required

1. Prepare journal entries for the Datamix transactions and adjusting entries.

Check   (2) 2011 total foreign exchange gain, $6,211

2. Compute the foreign exchange gain or loss to be reported on Datamix's 2011 income statement.

Analysis Component

3. What actions might Datamix consider to reduce its risk of foreign exchange gains or losses?

(This serial problem began in Chapter 1 and continues through most of the book. If previous chapter segments were not completed, the serial problem can begin at this point. It is helpful, but not necessary, to use the Working Papers that accompany the book.)

SP 15   While reviewing the March 31, 2012, balance sheet of Business Solutions, Santana Rey notes that the business has built a large cash balance of $68,057. Its most recent bank money market statement shows that the funds are earning an annualized return of 0.75%. S. Rey decides to make several investments with the desire to earn a higher return on the idle cash balance. Accordingly, in April 2012, Business Solutions makes the following investments in trading securities:

April 16   Purchases 400 shares of Johnson & Johnson stock at $50 per share plus $300 commission.
April 30   Purchases 200 shares of Starbucks Corporation at $22 per share plus $250 commission.

On June 30, 2012, the per share market price (fair value) of the Johnson & Johnson shares is $55 and the Starbucks shares is $19.

Required

1. Prepare journal entries to record the April purchases of trading securities by Business Solutions.

2. On June 30, 2012, prepare the adjusting entry to record any necessary fair value adjustment to its portfolio of trading securities.

Beyond the Numbers

BTN 15-1   Refer to **Research In Motion**'s financial statements in Appendix A to answer the following.
1. Are Research In Motion's financial statements consolidated? How can you tell?
2. What is Research In Motion's *comprehensive income* for the year ended February 27, 2010?
3. Does Research In Motion have any foreign operations? How can you tell?
4. Compute Research In Motion's return on total assets for the year ended February 27, 2010.

**REPORTING IN
ACTION**

C3 A1

RIM

Fast Forward

5. Access Research In Motion's annual report for a fiscal year ending after February 27, 2010, from either its Website (**RIM.com**) or the SEC's database (**www.SEC.gov**). Recompute Research In Motion's return on total assets for the years subsequent to February 27, 2010.

BTN 15-2   Key figures for **Research In Motion** and **Apple** follow.

**COMPARATIVE
ANALYSIS**

A1

RIM
Apple

($ millions)	Research In Motion			Apple		
	Current Year	I Year Prior	2 Years Prior	Current Year	I Year Prior	2 Years Prior
Net income	$ 2,457	$1,893	$1,294	$ 8,235	$ 6,119	$ 3,495
Net sales	12,536	9,411	4,914	42,905	37,491	24,578
Total assets	10,204	8,101	5,511	47,501	36,171	25,347

Required

1. Compute return on total assets for Research In Motion and Apple for the two most recent years.

2. Separate the return on total assets computed in part 1 into its components for both companies and both years according to the formula in Exhibit 15.9.

3. Which company has the highest total return on assets? The highest profit margin? The highest total asset turnover? What does this comparative analysis reveal? (Assume an industry average of 10.0% for return on assets.)

BTN 15-3   Kendra Wecker is the controller for Wildcat Company, which has numerous long-term investments in debt securities. Wildcat's investments are mainly in 10-year bonds. Wecker is preparing its year-end financial statements. In accounting for long-term debt securities, she knows that each long-term investment must be designated as a held-to-maturity or an available-for-sale security. Interest rates rose

ETHICS CHALLENGE

P2 P3

sharply this past year causing the portfolio's fair value to substantially decline. The company does not intend to hold the bonds for the entire 10 years. Wecker also earns a bonus each year, which is computed as a percent of net income.

Required

1. Will Wecker's bonus depend in any way on the classification of the debt securities? Explain.
2. What criteria must Wecker use to classify the securities as held-to-maturity or available-for-sale?
3. Is there likely any company oversight of Wecker's classification of the securities? Explain.

COMMUNICATING IN PRACTICE

P4

BTN 15-4   Assume that you are Jackson Company's accountant. Company owner Abel Terrio has reviewed the 2011 financial statements you prepared and questions the $6,000 loss reported on the sale of its investment in Blackhawk Co. common stock. Jackson acquired 50,000 shares of Blackhawk's common stock on December 31, 2009, at a cost of $500,000. This stock purchase represented a 40% interest in Blackhawk. The 2010 income statement reported that earnings from all investments were $126,000. On January 3, 2011, Jackson Company sold the Blackhawk stock for $575,000. Blackhawk did not pay any dividends during 2010 but reported a net income of $202,500 for that year. Terrio believes that because the Blackhawk stock purchase price was $500,000 and was sold for $575,000, the 2011 income statement should report a $75,000 gain on the sale.

Required

Draft a one-half page memorandum to Terrio explaining why the $6,000 loss on sale of Blackhawk stock is correctly reported.

TAKING IT TO THE NET

C1

BTN 15-5   Access the July 30, 2009, 10-K filing (for year-end June 30, 2009) of **Microsoft (MSFT)** at **www.SEC.gov**. Review its note 4, "Investments."

Required

1. How does the "cost-basis" total amount for its investments as of June 30, 2009, compare to the prior year-end amount?
2. Identify at least eight types of short-term investments held by Microsoft as of June 30, 2009.
3. What were Microsoft's unrealized gains and its unrealized losses from its investments for 2009?
4. Was the cost or fair value ("recorded basis") of the investments higher as of June 30, 2009?

TEAMWORK IN ACTION

C1 C2 P1 P2 P3 P4

BTN 15-6   Each team member is to become an expert on a specific classification of long-term investments. This expertise will be used to facilitate other teammates' understanding of the concepts and procedures relevent to the classification chosen.

1. Each team member must select an area for expertise by choosing one of the following classifications of long-term investments.
    a. Held-to-maturity debt securities
    b. Available-for-sale debt and equity securities
    c. Equity securities with significant influence
    d. Equity securities with controlling influence
2. Learning teams are to disburse and expert teams are to be formed. Expert teams are made up of those who select the same area of expertise. The instructor will identify the location where each expert team will meet.
3. Expert teams will collaborate to develop a presentation based on the following requirements. Students must write the presentation in a format they can show to their learning teams in part (4).

Requirements for Expert Presentation

    a. Write a transaction for the acquisition of this type of investment security. The transaction description is to include all necessary data to reflect the chosen classification.
    b. Prepare the journal entry to record the acquisition.
    [*Note:* The expert team on equity securities with controlling influence will substitute requirements (*d*) and (*e*) with a discussion of the reporting of these investments.]

c. Identify information necessary to complete the end-of-period adjustment for this investment.

d. Assuming that this is the only investment owned, prepare any necessary year-end entries.

e. Present the relevant balance sheet section(s).

4. Re-form learning teams. In rotation, experts are to present to their teams the presentations they developed in part 3. Experts are to encourage and respond to questions.

BTN 15-7^A Refer to the opening feature in this chapter about Michael Chasen and Matthew Pittinsky and their company, **Blackboard**. Assume that they must acquire the Japanese rights to certain educational software that will then be produced for sale to U.S. consumers. Assume Blackboard acquires those rights on January 1, 2011, from a Japanese distributor and agrees to pay 12,000,000 yen per year for those rights. Quarterly payments are due March 31, June 30, September 30, and December 31 each year. On January 1, 2011, the yen is worth $0.00891.

ENTREPRENEURIAL DECISION

C3

Required

1. Prepare the journal entry to record the rights purchased on January 1, 2011.

2. Prepare the journal entries to record the payments on March 31, June 30, September 30, and December 31, 2011. The value of the yen on those dates follows.

March 31	$0.00893
June 30	0.00901
September 30	0.00902
December 31	0.00897

3. How can Blackboard protect itself from unanticipated gains and losses from currency translation if all of the payments are specified to be paid in yen?

BTN 15-8^A Assume that you are planning a spring break trip to Europe. Identify three locations where you can find exchange rates for the dollar relative to the Euro or other currencies.

HITTING THE ROAD

C3

BTN 15-9 **Nokia, Research In Motion,** and **Apple** are competitors in the global marketplace. Following are selected data from each company.

GLOBAL DECISION

A1

NOKIA

RIM

Apple

| Key Figure | Nokia (Euro millions) | | | Research In Motion | | Apple | |
	Current Year	One Year Prior	Two Years Prior	Current Year	Prior Year	Current Year	Prior Year
Net income	€ 260	€ 3,889	€ 6,746	—	—	—	—
Net sales	40,984	50,710	51,058	—	—	—	—
Total assets	35,738	39,582	37,599	—	—	—	—
Profit margin	?	?	—	19.6%	20.1%	19.2%	16.3%
Total asset turnover	?	?	—	1.37	1.38	1.03	1.22

Required

1. Compute Nokia's return on total assets, and its components of profit margin and total asset turnover, for the most recent two years using the data provided.

2. Which of these three companies has the highest return on total assets? Highest profit margin? Highest total asset turnover? Interpret these results.

ANSWERS TO MULTIPLE CHOICE QUIZ

1. d; $30,000 × 5% × 5/12 = $625

2. a; Unrealized gain = $84,500 − $83,000 = $1,500

3. b; $50,000 × 35% = $17,500

4. e; $300,000/$2,000,000 = 15%

5. b; Profit margin = $80,000/$600,000 = 13.3%
   Total asset turnover = $600,000/$400,000 = 1.5

16

Reporting the Statement of Cash Flows

A Look Back

Chapter 15 focused on how to identify, account for, and report investments in securities. We also accounted for transactions listed in a foreign currency.

A Look at This Chapter

This chapter focuses on reporting and analyzing cash inflows and cash outflows. We emphasize how to prepare and interpret the statement of cash flows.

A Look Ahead

Chapter 17 focuses on tools to help us analyze financial statements. We also describe comparative analysis and the application of ratios for financial analysis.

Learning Objectives

CAP

CONCEPTUAL

C1 Distinguish between operating, investing, and financing activities, and describe how noncash investing and financing activities are disclosed. (p. 633)

ANALYTICAL

A1 Analyze the statement of cash flows and apply the cash flow on total assets ratio. (p. 650)

LP16

PROCEDURAL

P1 Prepare a statement of cash flows. (p. 636)

P2 Compute cash flows from operating activities using the indirect method. (p. 639)

P3 Determine cash flows from both investing and financing activities. (p. 645)

P4 *Appendix 16A*—Illustrate use of a spreadsheet to prepare a statement of cash flows. (p. 654)

P5 *Appendix 16B*—Compute cash flows from operating activities using the direct method. (p. 657)

Shape Up Your Images

"We feel like we have a great competitive advantage"
—BRAD JEFFERSON

NEW YORK—"I don't know about you, but I get shown so many boring slideshows of my friends' trips," admits Jason Hsiao. "It's like 20 minutes, and you're like, 'Kill me now.'" However, unlike the rest of us, Jason decided to do something about it. He, along with childhood buddies Brad Jefferson, Stevie Clifton, and Tom Clifton, launched **Animoto (Animoto.com).** Its Website describes their service as "a web application that automatically . . . analyzes and combines user-selected images, video clips, and music."

"We want to help users create professional-quality content," explains Jason. "So it doesn't matter what you give us, we'll take that and put it in our magic black box, and in a couple minutes, we'll deliver something that . . . you never could have dreamed of doing on your own." The owners point out that they can create a 30-second video for free. This has cash flow implications. "We decided that we would make a *freemium* model, which allows people to get a taste of the Animoto service for free," says Brad. However, longer videos and videos with more user-options require cash payments, which generate positive cash inflows.

User traffic at Animoto has grown to over 1 million per month. That type of growth has obvious cash implications for technology support, accounting, and other operating and investing cash outflows. The owners emphasize the importance of monitoring and tracking cash inflows and cash outflows. Jason admits, "There's

no possible way we could handle [growth] . . . without quickly digging ourselves into a multimillion dollar hole!"

Accordingly, the young owners learned to monitor and control cash flows for each of their operating, investing, and financing activities. Their focus on controlling cash flows led them to apply *cloud computing,* which is a pay-as-you-go model. "[We] could not have existed . . . without cloud computing," admits Jason. A review of Animoto's statement of cash flows, and its individual cash inflows and outflows, led them to this cash flow model. Explains Brad, "We use Amazon . . . for all IT infrastructure . . . PayPal and Google . . . for billing/payment . . . SaaS for email and sales." This model highlights those activities that generate the most cash and those that are cash drains. Adds Jason, "The only real asset we have in our office [is] . . . a fancy espresso machine!"

Yet cash management has not curtailed the team's fun-loving approach. Their Website describes themselves as "a bunch of techies . . . who decided to lock themselves in a room together and nerd out!" Adds Brad, "We're going through the process of figuring out where we want the future to take us."

[Sources: *Animoto Website,* January 2011; *Entrepreneur,* January 2009; *Fast Company,* September 2008; *Bellevue Reporter,* May 2008]

A company cannot achieve or maintain profits without carefully managing cash. Managers and other users of information pay attention to a company's cash position and the events and transactions affecting cash. This chapter explains how we prepare, analyze, and interpret a statement of cash flows. It also discusses the importance of cash flow information for predicting future performance and making managerial decisions. More generally, effectively using the statement of cash flows is crucial for managing and analyzing the operating, investing, and financing activities of businesses.

Reporting the Statement of Cash Flows

Basics of Cash Flow Reporting	Cash Flows from Operating	Cash Flows from Investing	Cash Flows from Financing
• Purpose • Importance • Measurement • Classification • Noncash activities • Format and preparation	• Indirect and direct methods of reporting • Application of indirect method of reporting • Summary of indirect method adjustments	• Three-stage process of analysis • Analysis of noncurrent assets • Analysis of other assets	• Three-stage process of analysis • Analysis of non-current liabilities • Analysis of equity

BASICS OF CASH FLOW REPORTING

This section describes the basics of cash flow reporting, including its purpose, measurement, classification, format, and preparation.

Purpose of the Statement of Cash Flows

The purpose of the **statement of cash flows** is to report cash receipts (inflows) and cash payments (outflows) during a period. This includes separately identifying the cash flows related to operating, investing, and financing activities. The statement of cash flows does more than simply report changes in cash. It is the detailed disclosure of individual cash flows that makes this statement useful to users. Information in this statement helps users answer questions such as these:

- How does a company obtain its cash?
- Where does a company spend its cash?
- What explains the change in the cash balance?

Point: Internal users rely on the statement of cash flows to make investing and financing decisions. External users rely on this statement to assess the amount and timing of a company's cash flows.

The statement of cash flows addresses important questions such as these by summarizing, classifying, and reporting a company's cash inflows and cash outflows for each period.

Importance of Cash Flows

Information about cash flows can influence decision makers in important ways. For instance, we look more favorably at a company that is financing its expenditures with cash from operations than one that does it by selling its assets. Information about cash flows helps users decide whether a company has enough cash to pay its existing debts as they mature. It is also relied upon to evaluate a company's ability to meet unexpected obligations and pursue unexpected opportunities. External information users especially want to assess a company's ability to take advantage of new business opportunities. Internal users such as managers use cash flow information to plan day-to-day operating activities and make long-term investment decisions.

Macy's striking turnaround is an example of how analysis and management of cash flows can lead to improved financial stability. Several years ago Macy's obtained temporary protection from bankruptcy, at which time it desperately needed to improve its cash flows. It did so by engaging in aggressive cost-cutting measures. As a result, Macy's annual cash flow rose to $210 million, up from a negative cash flow of $38.9 million in the prior year. Macy's eventually met its financial obligations and then successfully merged with **Federated Department Stores**.

The case of **W. T. Grant Co.** is a classic example of the importance of cash flow information in predicting a company's future performance and financial strength. Grant reported net income of more than $40 million per year for three consecutive years. At that same time, it was experiencing an alarming decrease in cash provided by operations. For instance, net cash outflow was more than $90 million by the end of that three-year period. Grant soon went bankrupt. Users who relied solely on Grant's income numbers were unpleasantly surprised. This reminds us that cash flows as well as income statement and balance sheet information are crucial in making business decisions.

Measurement of Cash Flows

Cash flows are defined to include both *cash* and *cash equivalents*. The statement of cash flows explains the difference between the beginning and ending balances of cash and cash equivalents. We continue to use the phrases *cash flows* and the *statement of cash flows,* but we must remember that both phrases refer to cash and cash equivalents. Recall that a cash equivalent must satisfy two criteria: (1) be readily convertible to a known amount of cash and (2) be sufficiently close to its maturity so its market value is unaffected by interest rate changes. In most cases, a debt security must be within three months of its maturity to satisfy these criteria. Companies must disclose and follow a clear policy for determining cash and cash equivalents and apply it consistently from period to period. **American Express**, for example, defines its cash equivalents as "time deposits and other highly liquid investments with original maturities of 90 days or less."

Classification of Cash Flows

Since cash and cash equivalents are combined, the statement of cash flows does not report transactions between cash and cash equivalents such as cash paid to purchase cash equivalents and cash received from selling cash equivalents. However, all other cash receipts and cash payments are classified and reported on the statement as operating, investing, or financing activities. Individual cash receipts and payments for each of these three categories are labeled to identify their originating transactions or events. A net cash inflow (source) occurs when the receipts in a category exceed the payments. A net cash outflow (use) occurs when the payments in a category exceed the receipts.

C1 Distinguish between operating, investing, and financing activities, and describe how noncash investing and financing activities are disclosed.

Operating Activities **Operating activities** include those transactions and events that determine net income. Examples are the production and purchase of merchandise, the sale of goods and services to customers, and the expenditures to administer the business. Not all items in income, such as unusual gains and losses, are operating activities (we discuss these exceptions later in the chapter). Exhibit 16.1 lists the more common cash inflows and outflows from operating activities. (Although cash receipts and cash payments from buying and selling trading

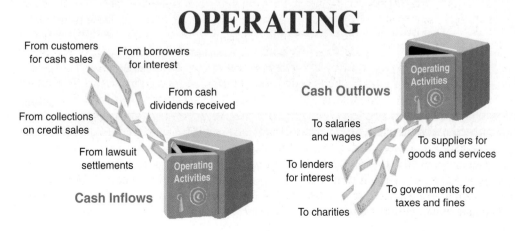

OPERATING

Cash Inflows

From customers for cash sales

From borrowers for interest

From cash dividends received

From collections on credit sales

From lawsuit settlements

Operating Activities

Cash Outflows

Operating Activities

To salaries and wages

To lenders for interest

To suppliers for goods and services

To governments for taxes and fines

To charities

EXHIBIT 16.1

Cash Flows from Operating Activities

securities are often reported under operating activities, new standards require that these receipts and payments be classified based on the nature and purpose of those securities.)

Investing Activities   **Investing activities** generally include those transactions and events that affect long-term assets—namely, the purchase and sale of long-term assets. They also include (1) the purchase and sale of short-term investments in the securities of other entities, other than cash equivalents and trading securities and (2) lending and collecting money for notes receivable. Exhibit 16.2 lists examples of cash flows from investing activities. Proceeds from collecting the principal amounts of notes deserve special mention. If the note results from sales to customers, its cash receipts are classed as operating activities whether short-term or long-term. If the note results from a loan to another party apart from sales, however, the cash receipts from collecting the note principal are classed as an investing activity. The FASB requires that the collection of interest on loans be reported as an operating activity.

Point: The FASB requires that *cash dividends received* and *cash interest received* be reported as operating activities.

EXHIBIT 16.2

Cash Flows from
Investing Activities

Financing Activities   **Financing activities** include those transactions and events that affect long-term liabilities and equity. Examples are (1) obtaining cash from issuing debt and repaying the amounts borrowed and (2) receiving cash from or distributing cash to owners. These activities involve transactions with a company's owners and creditors. They also often involve borrowing and repaying principal amounts relating to both short- and long-term debt. GAAP requires that payments of interest expense be classified as operating activities. Also, cash payments to settle credit purchases of merchandise, whether on account or by note, are operating activities. Exhibit 16.3 lists examples of cash flows from financing activities.

EXHIBIT 16.3

Cash Flows from
Financing Activities

FINANCING

From issuing its own
equity stock

From contributions
by owners

From issuing short-
and long-term debt

Cash Outflows   Financing
Activities

To repay
cash loans

To pay dividends
to shareholders

To pay
withdrawals
by owners

To purchase
treasury stock

From issuing
notes and bonds   Financing
Activities

Cash Inflows

Point: Interest payments on a loan are classified as operating activities, but payments of loan principal are financing activities.

Decision Insight

Cash Monitoring   Cash flows can be delayed or accelerated at the end of a period to improve or reduce current period cash flows. Also, cash flows can be misclassified. Cash outflows reported under operations are interpreted as expense payments. However, cash outflows reported under investing activities are interpreted as a positive sign of growth potential. Thus, managers face incentives to misclassify cash flows. For these reasons, cash flow reporting warrants our scrutiny. ∎

Noncash Investing and Financing

When important investing and financing activities do not affect cash receipts or payments, they are still disclosed at the bottom of the statement of cash flows or in a note to the statement because of their importance and the *full-disclosure principle*. One example of such a transaction is the purchase of long-term assets using a long-term note payable (loan). This transaction involves both investing and financing activities but does not affect any cash inflow or outflow and is not reported in any of the three sections of the statement of cash flows. This disclosure rule also extends to transactions with partial cash receipts or payments.

To illustrate, assume that Goorin purchases land for $12,000 by paying $5,000 cash and trading in used equipment worth $7,000. The investing section of the statement of cash flows reports only the $5,000 cash outflow for the land purchase. The $12,000 investing transaction is only partially described in the body of the statement of cash flows, yet this information is potentially important to users because it changes the makeup of assets. Goorin could either describe the transaction in a footnote or include information at the bottom of its statement that lists the $12,000 land purchase along with the cash financing of $5,000 and a $7,000 trade-in of equipment. As another example, Borg Co. acquired $900,000 of assets in exchange for $200,000 cash and a $700,000 long-term note, which should be reported as follows:

Point: A stock dividend transaction involving a transfer from retained earnings to common stock or a credit to contributed capital is *not* considered a noncash investing and financing activity because the company receives no consideration for shares issued.

Fair value of assets acquired	$900,000
Less cash paid	200,000
Liabilities incurred or assumed	$700,000

Exhibit 16.4 lists transactions commonly disclosed as noncash investing and financing activities.

- Retirement of debt by issuing equity stock.
- Conversion of preferred stock to common stock.
- Lease of assets in a capital lease transaction.
- Purchase of long-term assets by issuing a note or bond.
- Exchange of noncash assets for other noncash assets.
- Purchase of noncash assets by issuing equity or debt.

EXHIBIT 16.4

Examples of Noncash Investing and Financing Activities

Format of the Statement of Cash Flows

Accounting standards require companies to include a statement of cash flows in a complete set of financial statements. This statement must report information about a company's cash receipts and cash payments during the period. Exhibit 16.5 shows the usual format. A company must report cash flows from three activities: operating, investing, and financing. The statement

EXHIBIT 16.5

Format of the Statement of Cash Flows

COMPANY NAME Statement of Cash Flows For *period* Ended *date*	
Cash flows from operating activities	
[List of individual inflows and outflows]	
Net cash provided (used) by operating activities	$ #
Cash flows from investing activities	
[List of individual inflows and outflows]	
Net cash provided (used) by investing activities	#
Cash flows from financing activities	
[List of individual inflows and outflows]	
Net cash provided (used) by financing activities	#
Net increase (decrease) in cash	$ #
Cash (and equivalents) balance at prior period-end	#
Cash (and equivalents) balance at current period-end	$ #

Separate schedule or note disclosure of any "noncash investing and financing transactions" is required.

explains how transactions and events impact the prior period-end cash (and cash equivalents) balance to produce its current period-end balance.

◻ Decision Maker   Answer — p. 662

Entrepreneur   You are considering purchasing a start-up business that recently reported a $110,000 annual net loss and a $225,000 annual net cash inflow. How are these results possible? ■

☑ Quick Check   Answers — p. 662

1. Does a statement of cash flows report the cash payments to purchase cash equivalents? Does it report the cash receipts from selling cash equivalents?
2. Identify the three categories of cash flows reported separately on the statement of cash flows.
3. Identify the cash activity category for each transaction: (*a*) purchase equipment for cash, (*b*) cash payment of wages, (*c*) sale of common stock for cash, (*d*) receipt of cash dividends from stock investment, (*e*) cash collection from customers, (*f*) notes issued for cash.

Preparing the Statement of Cash Flows

P1   Prepare a statement of cash flows.

Preparing a statement of cash flows involves five steps: ①compute the net increase or decrease in cash; ②compute and report the net cash provided or used by operating activities (using either the direct or indirect method; both are explained); ③compute and report the net cash provided or used by investing activities; ④compute and report the net cash provided or used by financing activities; and ⑤compute the net cash flow by combining net cash provided or used by operating, investing, and financing activities and then *prove it* by adding it to the beginning cash balance to show that it equals the ending cash balance.

Step ① Compute net increase or decrease in cash

Step ② Compute net cash from operating activities

Step ③ Compute net cash from investing activities

Step ④ Compute net cash from financing activities

Step ⑤ Prove and report beginning and ending cash balances

Point: View the change in cash as a *target* number that we will fully explain and prove in the statement of cash flows.

Computing the net increase or net decrease in cash is a simple but crucial computation. It equals the current period's cash balance minus the prior period's cash balance. This is the *bottom-line* figure for the statement of cash flows and is a check on accuracy. The information we need to prepare a statement of cash flows comes from various sources including comparative balance sheets at the beginning and end of the period, and an income statement for the period. There are two alternative approaches to preparing the statement: (1) analyzing the Cash account and (2) analyzing noncash accounts.

Analyzing the Cash Account   A company's cash receipts and cash payments are recorded in the Cash account in its general ledger. The Cash account is therefore a natural place to look for information about cash flows from operating, investing, and financing activities. To illustrate, review the summarized Cash T-account of Genesis, Inc., in Exhibit 16.6. Individual cash transactions are summarized in this Cash account according to the major types of cash receipts and cash payments. For instance, only the total of cash receipts from all customers is listed. Individual cash transactions underlying these totals can number in the thousands. Accounting software is available to provide summarized cash accounts.

Preparing a statement of cash flows from Exhibit 16.6 requires determining whether an individual cash inflow or outflow is an operating, investing, or financing activity, and then listing each by

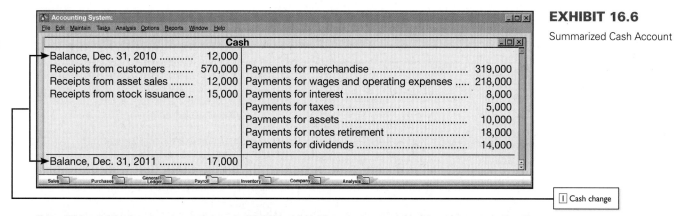

EXHIBIT 16.6

Summarized Cash Account

activity. This yields the statement shown in Exhibit 16.7. However, preparing the statement of cash flows from an analysis of the summarized Cash account has two limitations. First, most companies have many individual cash receipts and payments, making it difficult to review them all. Accounting software minimizes this burden, but it is still a task requiring professional judgment for many transactions. Second, the Cash account does not usually carry an adequate description of each cash transaction, making assignment of all cash transactions according to activity difficult.

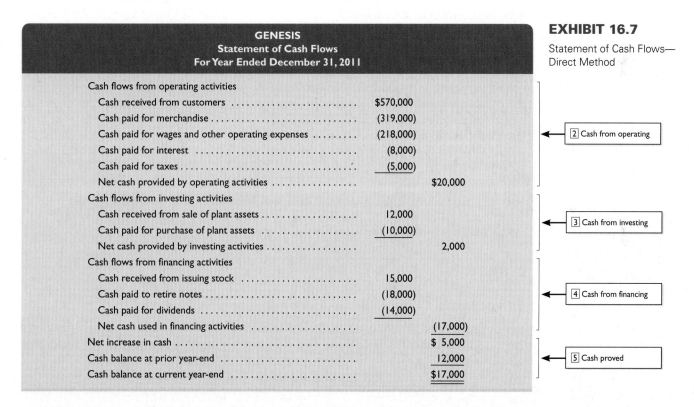

EXHIBIT 16.7

Statement of Cash Flows—Direct Method

Analyzing Noncash Accounts   A second approach to preparing the statement of cash flows is analyzing noncash accounts. This approach uses the fact that when a company records cash inflows and outflows with debits and credits to the Cash account (see Exhibit 16.6), it also records credits and debits in noncash accounts (reflecting double-entry accounting). Many of these noncash accounts are balance sheet accounts—for instance, from the sale of land for cash. Others are revenue and expense accounts that are closed to equity. For instance, the sale of services for cash yields a credit to Services Revenue that is closed to Retained Earnings for a corporation. In sum, *all cash transactions eventually affect noncash balance sheet accounts*. Thus, we can determine cash inflows and outflows by analyzing changes in noncash balance sheet accounts.

Exhibit 16.8 uses the accounting equation to show the relation between the Cash account and the noncash balance sheet accounts. This exhibit starts with the accounting equation at the

EXHIBIT 16.8

Relation between Cash and
Noncash Accounts

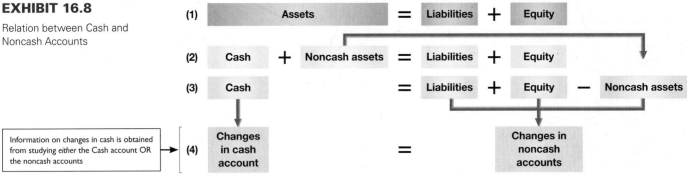

Information on changes in cash is obtained
from studying *either* the Cash account OR
the noncash accounts

top. It is then expanded in line (2) to separate cash from noncash asset accounts. Line (3) moves noncash asset accounts to the right-hand side of the equality where they are subtracted. This shows that cash equals the sum of the liability and equity accounts *minus* the noncash asset accounts. Line (4) points out that *changes* on one side of the accounting equation equal *changes* on the other side. It shows that we can explain changes in cash by analyzing changes in the noncash accounts consisting of liability accounts, equity accounts, and noncash asset accounts. By analyzing noncash balance sheet accounts and any related income statement accounts, we can prepare a statement of cash flows.

Information to Prepare the Statement   Information to prepare the statement of cash flows usually comes from three sources: (1) comparative balance sheets, (2) the current income statement, and (3) additional information. Comparative balance sheets are used to compute changes in noncash accounts from the beginning to the end of the period. The current income statement is used to help compute cash flows from operating activities. Additional information often includes details on transactions and events that help explain both the cash flows and noncash investing and financing activities.

Decision Insight

e-Cash   Every credit transaction on the Net leaves a trail that a hacker or a marketer can pick up. Enter e-cash—or digital money. The encryption of e-cash protects your money from snoops and thieves and cannot be traced, even by the issuing bank. ■

CASH FLOWS FROM OPERATING

Indirect and Direct Methods of Reporting

Cash flows provided (used) by operating activities are reported in one of two ways: the *direct method* or the *indirect method*. **These two different methods apply only to the operating activities section.**

The **direct method** separately lists each major item of operating cash receipts (such as cash received from customers) and each major item of operating cash payments (such as cash paid for merchandise). The cash payments are subtracted from cash receipts to determine the net cash provided (used) by operating activities. The operating activities section of Exhibit 16.7 reflects the direct method of reporting operating cash flows.

The **indirect method** reports net income and then adjusts it for items necessary to obtain net cash provided or used by operating activities. It does *not* report individual items of cash inflows and cash outflows from operating activities. Instead, the indirect method reports the necessary adjustments to reconcile net income to net cash provided or used by operating activities. The operating activities section for Genesis prepared under the indirect method is shown in Exhibit 16.9. **The net cash amount provided by operating activities is *identical* under both the direct and indirect methods.**

Cash flows from operating activities

Net income		$ 38,000
Adjustments to reconcile net income to net cash provided by operating activities		
Increase in accounts receivable	(20,000)	
Increase in merchandise inventory	(14,000)	
Increase in prepaid expenses	(2,000)	
Decrease in accounts payable	(5,000)	
Decrease in interest payable	(1,000)	
Increase in income taxes payable	10,000	
Depreciation expense	24,000	
Loss on sale of plant assets	6,000	
Gain on retirement of notes	(16,000)	
Net cash provided by operating activities		**$20,000**

EXHIBIT 16.9

Operating Activities Section—Indirect Method

This equality always exists. The difference in these methods is with the computation and presentation of this amount. The FASB recommends the direct method, but because it is not required and the indirect method is arguably easier to compute, nearly all companies report operating cash flows using the indirect method.

To illustrate, we prepare the operating activities section of the statement of cash flows for Genesis. Exhibit 16.10 shows the December 31, 2010 and 2011, balance sheets of Genesis along with its 2011 income statement. We use this information to prepare a statement of cash flows that explains the $5,000 increase in cash for 2011 as reflected in its balance sheets. This $5,000 is computed as Cash of $17,000 at the end of 2011 minus Cash of $12,000 at the end of 2010. Genesis discloses additional information on its 2011 transactions:

a. The accounts payable balances result from merchandise inventory purchases.

b. Purchased $70,000 in plant assets by paying $10,000 cash and issuing $60,000 of notes payable.

c. Sold plant assets with an original cost of $30,000 and accumulated depreciation of $12,000 for $12,000 cash, yielding a $6,000 loss.

d. Received $15,000 cash from issuing 3,000 shares of common stock.

e. Paid $18,000 cash to retire notes with a $34,000 book value, yielding a $16,000 gain.

f. Declared and paid cash dividends of $14,000.

> *The next section describes the indirect method. Appendix 16B describes the direct method. An instructor can choose to cover either one or both methods. Neither section depends on the other.*

Application of the Indirect Method of Reporting

Net income is computed using accrual accounting, which recognizes revenues when earned and expenses when incurred. Revenues and expenses do not necessarily reflect the receipt and payment of cash. The indirect method of computing and reporting net cash flows from operating activities involves adjusting the net income figure to obtain the net cash provided or used by operating activities. This includes subtracting noncash increases (credits) from net income and adding noncash charges (debits) back to net income.

To illustrate, the indirect method begins with Genesis's net income of $38,000 and adjusts it to obtain net cash provided by operating activities of $20,000. Exhibit 16.11 shows the results of the indirect method of reporting operating cash flows, which adjusts net income for three types of adjustments. There are adjustments ① to reflect changes in noncash current assets and current liabilities related to operating activities, ② to income statement items involving operating activities that do not affect cash inflows or outflows, and ③ to eliminate gains and losses resulting from investing and financing activities (not part of operating activities). This section describes each of these adjustments.

Point: To better understand the direct and indirect methods of reporting operating cash flows, identify similarities and differences between Exhibits 16.7 and 16.11.

P2 Compute cash flows from operating activities using the indirect method.

Point: *Noncash credits* refer to *revenue* amounts reported on the income statement that are *not collected in cash* this period. *Noncash charges* refer to *expense* amounts reported on the income statement that are *not paid* this period.

EXHIBIT 16.10

Financial Statements

GENESIS Income Statement For Year Ended December 31, 2011		
Sales		$590,000
Cost of goods sold	$300,000	
Wages and other operating expenses ..	216,000	
Interest expense	7,000	
Depreciation expense	24,000	(547,000)
		43,000
Other gains (losses)		
Gain on retirement of notes	16,000	
Loss on sale of plant assets	(6,000)	10,000
Income before taxes		53,000
Income taxes expense		(15,000)
Net income		$ 38,000

GENESIS Balance Sheets December 31, 2011 and 2010		
	2011	**2010**
Assets		
Current assets		
Cash	$ 17,000	$ 12,000
Accounts receivable	60,000	40,000
Merchandise inventory	84,000	70,000
Prepaid expenses	6,000	4,000
Total current assets	167,000	126,000
Long-term assets		
Plant assets	250,000	210,000
Accumulated depreciation	(60,000)	(48,000)
Total assets	$357,000	$288,000
Liabilities		
Current liabilities		
Accounts payable	$ 35,000	$ 40,000
Interest payable	3,000	4,000
Income taxes payable	22,000	12,000
Total current liabilities	60,000	56,000
Long-term notes payable	90,000	64,000
Total liabilities	150,000	120,000
Equity		
Common stock, $5 par	95,000	80,000
Retained earnings	112,000	88,000
Total equity	207,000	168,000
Total liabilities and equity	$357,000	$288,000

① **Adjustments for Changes in Current Assets and Current Liabilities** This section describes adjustments for changes in noncash current assets and current liabilities.

Adjustments for changes in noncash current assets. Changes in noncash current assets normally result from operating activities. Examples are sales affecting accounts receivable and building usage affecting prepaid rent. Decreases in noncash current assets yield the following adjustment:

> **Decreases in noncash current assets are added to net income.**

To see the logic for this adjustment, consider that a decrease in a noncash current asset such as accounts receivable suggests more available cash at the end of the period compared to the beginning. This is so because a decrease in accounts receivable implies higher cash receipts than reflected in sales. We add these higher cash receipts (from decreases in noncash current assets) to net income when computing cash flow from operations.

In contrast, an increase in noncash current assets such as accounts receivable implies less cash receipts than reflected in sales. As another example, an increase in prepaid rent indicates that more cash is paid for rent than is deducted as rent expense. Increases in noncash current assets yield the following adjustment:

> **Increases in noncash current assets are subtracted from net income.**

To illustrate, these adjustments are applied to the noncash current assets in Exhibit 16.10.

Accounts receivable. Accounts receivable *increase* $20,000, from a beginning balance of $40,000 to an ending balance of $60,000. This increase implies that Genesis collects less cash than is reported in sales. That is, some of these sales were in the form of accounts receivable and that amount increased during the period. To see this it is helpful to use *account analysis.* This usually involves setting up a T-account and reconstructing its major entries to compute cash receipts or payments. The following reconstructed Accounts Receivable T-account reveals that cash receipts are less than sales:

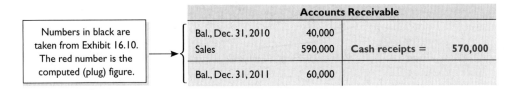

Accounts Receivable			
Bal., Dec. 31, 2010	40,000		
Sales	590,000	Cash receipts =	570,000
Bal., Dec. 31, 2011	60,000		

Numbers in black are taken from Exhibit 16.10. The red number is the computed (plug) figure.

We see that sales are $20,000 greater than cash receipts. This $20,000—as reflected in the $20,000 increase in Accounts Receivable—is subtracted from net income when computing cash provided by operating activities (see Exhibit 16.11).

Merchandise inventory. Merchandise inventory *increases* by $14,000, from a $70,000 beginning balance to an $84,000 ending balance. This increase implies that Genesis had greater cash purchases than cost of goods sold. This larger amount of cash purchases is in the form of inventory, as reflected in the following account analysis:

Merchandise Inventory			
Bal., Dec. 31, 2010	70,000		
Purchases =	314,000	Cost of goods sold	300,000
Bal., Dec. 31, 2011	84,000		

EXHIBIT 16.11

Statement of Cash Flows—Indirect Method

GENESIS Statement of Cash Flows For Year Ended December 31, 2011		
Cash flows from operating activities		
Net income	$ 38,000	
Adjustments to reconcile net income to net cash provided by operating activities		
① Increase in accounts receivable.	(20,000)	
Increase in merchandise inventory	(14,000)	
Increase in prepaid expenses	(2,000)	
Decrease in accounts payable.	(5,000)	
Decrease in interest payable.	(1,000)	
Increase in income taxes payable	10,000	
② { Depreciation expense	24,000	
③ Loss on sale of plant assets.	6,000	
Gain on retirement of notes.	(16,000)	
Net cash provided by operating activities		$20,000
Cash flows from investing activities		
Cash received from sale of plant assets	12,000	
Cash paid for purchase of plant assets	(10,000)	
Net cash provided by investing activities		2,000
Cash flows from financing activities		
Cash received from issuing stock	15,000	
Cash paid to retire notes	(18,000)	
Cash paid for dividends.	(14,000)	
Net cash used in financing activities		(17,000)
Net increase in cash		$ 5,000
Cash balance at prior year-end.		12,000
Cash balance at current year-end		$17,000

Point: Refer to Exhibit 16.10 and identify the $5,000 change in cash. This change is what the statement of cash flows explains; it serves as a check.

The amount by which purchases exceed cost of goods sold—as reflected in the $14,000 increase in inventory—is subtracted from net income when computing cash provided by operating activities (see Exhibit 16.11).

Prepaid expenses. Prepaid Expenses *increase* $2,000, from a $4,000 beginning balance to a $6,000 ending balance, implying that Genesis's cash payments exceed its recorded prepaid expenses. These higher cash payments increase the amount of Prepaid Expenses, as reflected in its reconstructed T-account:

Prepaid Expenses			
Bal., Dec. 31, 2010	4,000		
Cash payments =	218,000	Wages and other operating exp.	216,000
Bal., Dec. 31, 2011	6,000		

The amount by which cash payments exceed the recorded operating expenses—as reflected in the $2,000 increase in Prepaid Expenses—is subtracted from net income when computing cash provided by operating activities (see Exhibit 16.11).

Adjustments for changes in current liabilities.   Changes in current liabilities normally result from operating activities. An example is a purchase that affects accounts payable. Increases in current liabilities yield the following adjustment to net income when computing operating cash flows:

Increases in current liabilities are added to net income.

To see the logic for this adjustment, consider that an increase in the Accounts Payable account suggests that cash payments are less than the related (cost of goods sold) expense. As another example, an increase in wages payable implies that cash paid for wages is less than the recorded wages expense. Since the recorded expense is greater than the cash paid, we add the increase in wages payable to net income to compute net cash flow from operations.

Conversely, when current liabilities decrease, the following adjustment is required:

Decreases in current liabilities are subtracted from net income.

To illustrate, these adjustments are applied to the current liabilities in Exhibit 16.10.

Accounts payable. Accounts payable *decrease* $5,000, from a beginning balance of $40,000 to an ending balance of $35,000. This decrease implies that cash payments to suppliers exceed purchases by $5,000 for the period, which is reflected in the reconstructed Accounts Payable T-account:

Accounts Payable			
		Bal., Dec. 31, 2010	40,000
Cash payments =	319,000	Purchases	314,000
		Bal., Dec. 31, 2011	35,000

The amount by which cash payments exceed purchases—as reflected in the $5,000 decrease in Accounts Payable—is subtracted from net income when computing cash provided by operating activities (see Exhibit 16.11).

Interest payable. Interest payable *decreases* $1,000, from a $4,000 beginning balance to a $3,000 ending balance. This decrease indicates that cash paid for interest exceeds interest expense by $1,000, which is reflected in the Interest Payable T-account:

Interest Payable			
		Bal., Dec. 31, 2010	4,000
Cash paid for interest =	8,000	Interest expense	7,000
		Bal., Dec. 31, 2011	3,000

The amount by which cash paid exceeds recorded expense—as reflected in the $1,000 decrease in Interest Payable—is subtracted from net income (see Exhibit 16.11).

Income taxes payable. Income taxes payable *increase* $10,000, from a $12,000 beginning balance to a $22,000 ending balance. This increase implies that reported income taxes exceed the cash paid for taxes, which is reflected in the Income Taxes Payable T-account:

Income Taxes Payable			
		Bal., Dec. 31, 2010	12,000
Cash paid for taxes =	5,000	Income taxes expense	15,000
		Bal., Dec. 31, 2011	22,000

The amount by which cash paid falls short of the reported taxes expense—as reflected in the $10,000 increase in Income Taxes Payable—is added to net income when computing cash provided by operating activities (see Exhibit 16.11).

② **Adjustments for Operating Items Not Providing or Using Cash**   The income statement usually includes some expenses that do not reflect cash outflows in the period. Examples are depreciation, amortization, depletion, and bad debts expense. The indirect method for reporting operating cash flows requires that

Expenses with no cash outflows are added back to net income.

To see the logic of this adjustment, recall that items such as depreciation, amortization, depletion, and bad debts originate from debits to expense accounts and credits to noncash accounts. These entries have *no* cash effect, and we add them back to net income when computing net cash flows from operations. Adding them back cancels their deductions.

Similarly, when net income includes revenues that do not reflect cash inflows in the period, the indirect method for reporting operating cash flows requires that

Revenues with no cash inflows are subtracted from net income.

We apply these adjustments to the Genesis operating items that do not provide or use cash.

Depreciation.   Depreciation expense is the only Genesis operating item that has no effect on cash flows in the period. We must add back the $24,000 depreciation expense to net income when computing cash provided by operating activities. (We later explain that any cash outflow to acquire a plant asset is reported as an investing activity.)

③ **Adjustments for Nonoperating Items**   Net income often includes losses that are not part of operating activities but are part of either investing or financing activities. Examples are a loss from the sale of a plant asset and a loss from retirement of notes payable. The indirect method for reporting operating cash flows requires that

Nonoperating losses are added back to net income.

To see the logic, consider that items such as a plant asset sale and a notes retirement are normally recorded by recognizing the cash, removing all plant asset or notes accounts, and recognizing any loss or gain. The cash received or paid is not part of operating activities but is part of either investing or financing activities. *No* operating cash flow effect occurs. However, because the nonoperating loss is a deduction in computing net income, we need to add it back to net income when computing cash flow from operations. Adding it back cancels the deduction.

Similarly, when net income includes gains not part of operating activities, the indirect method for reporting operating cash flows requires that

Nonoperating gains are subtracted from net income.

To illustrate these adjustments, we consider the nonoperating items of Genesis.

Summary Adjustments for Changes in Current Assets and Current Liabilities		
Account	**Increases**	**Decreases**
Noncash current assets	Deduct from NI	Add to NI
Current liabilities	Add to NI	Deduct from NI

Point: An income statement reports revenues, gains, expenses, and losses on an accrual basis. The statement of cash flows reports cash received and cash paid for operating, financing, and investing activities.

Loss on sale of plant assets.   Genesis reports a $6,000 loss on sale of plant assets as part of net income. This loss is a proper deduction in computing income, but it is *not part of operating activities*. Instead, a sale of plant assets is part of investing activities. Thus, the $6,000 nonoperating loss is added back to net income (see Exhibit 16.11). Adding it back cancels the loss. We later explain how to report the cash inflow from the asset sale in investing activities.

Gain on retirement of debt.   A $16,000 gain on retirement of debt is properly included in net income, but it is *not part of operating activities*. This means the $16,000 nonoperating gain must be subtracted from net income to obtain net cash provided by operating activities (see Exhibit 16.11). Subtracting it cancels the recorded gain. We later describe how to report the cash outflow to retire debt.

Summary of Adjustments for Indirect Method

Exhibit 16.12 summarizes the most common adjustments to net income when computing net cash provided or used by operating activities under the indirect method.

EXHIBIT 16.12

Summary of Selected Adjustments for Indirect Method

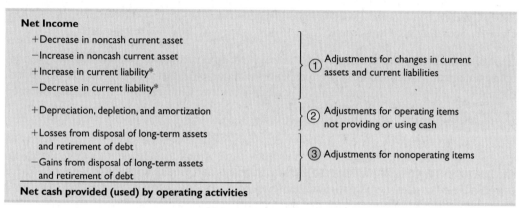

* Excludes current portion of long-term debt and any (nonsales-related) short-term notes payable—both are financing activities.

The computations in determining cash provided or used by operating activities are different for the indirect and direct methods, but the result is identical. Both methods yield the same $20,000 figure for cash from operating activities for Genesis; see Exhibits 16.7 and 16.11.

Decision Insight

Cash or Income   The difference between net income and operating cash flows can be large and sometimes reflects on the quality of earnings. This bar chart shows the net income and operating cash flows of three companies. Operating cash flows can be either higher or lower than net income. ■

Quick Check   Answers — p. 662

 4. Determine the net cash provided or used by operating activities using the following data: net income, $74,900; decrease in accounts receivable, $4,600; increase in inventory, $11,700; decrease in accounts payable, $1,000; loss on sale of equipment, $3,400; payment of cash dividends, $21,500.

 5. Why are expenses such as depreciation and amortization added to net income when cash flow from operating activities is computed by the indirect method?

 6. A company reports net income of $15,000 that includes a $3,000 gain on the sale of plant assets. Why is this gain subtracted from net income in computing cash flow from operating activities using the indirect method?

CASH FLOWS FROM INVESTING

The third major step in preparing the statement of cash flows is to compute and report cash flows from investing activities. We normally do this by identifying changes in (1) all noncurrent asset accounts and (2) the current accounts for both notes receivable and investments in securities (excluding trading securities). We then analyze changes in these accounts to determine their effect, if any, on cash and report the cash flow effects in the investing activities section of the statement of cash flows. **Reporting of investing activities is identical under the direct method and indirect method.**

Three-Stage Process of Analysis

Information to compute cash flows from investing activities is usually taken from beginning and ending balance sheets and the income statement. We use a three-stage process to determine cash provided or used by investing activities: (1) identify changes in investing-related accounts, (2) explain these changes using reconstruction analysis, and (3) report their cash flow effects.

P3 Determine cash flows from both investing and financing activities.

Analysis of Noncurrent Assets

Information about the Genesis transactions provided earlier reveals that the company both purchased and sold plant assets during the period. Both transactions are investing activities and are analyzed for their cash flow effects in this section.

Plant Asset Transactions The first stage in analyzing the Plant Assets account and its related Accumulated Depreciation is to identify any changes in these accounts from comparative balance sheets in Exhibit 16.10. This analysis reveals a $40,000 increase in plant assets from $210,000 to $250,000 and a $12,000 increase in accumulated depreciation from $48,000 to $60,000.

Point: Investing activities include (1) purchasing and selling long-term assets, (2) lending and collecting on notes receivable, and (3) purchasing and selling short-term investments other than cash equivalents and trading securities.

The second stage is to explain these changes. Items *b* and *c* of the additional information for Genesis (page 639) are relevant in this case. Recall that the Plant Assets account is affected by both asset purchases and sales, while its Accumulated Depreciation account is normally increased from depreciation and decreased from the removal of accumulated depreciation in asset sales. To explain changes in these accounts and to identify their cash flow effects, we prepare *reconstructed entries* from prior transactions; *they are not the actual entries by the preparer.*

Point: Financing and investing info is available in ledger accounts to help explain changes in comparative balance sheets. Post references lead to relevant entries and explanations.

To illustrate, item *b* reports that Genesis purchased plant assets of $70,000 by issuing $60,000 in notes payable to the seller and paying $10,000 in cash. The reconstructed entry for analysis of item *b* follows:

Reconstruction	Plant Assets	70,000	
	Notes Payable		60,000
	Cash		**10,000**

This entry reveals a $10,000 cash outflow for plant assets and a $60,000 noncash investing and financing transaction involving notes exchanged for plant assets.

Next, item *c* reports that Genesis sold plant assets costing $30,000 (with $12,000 of accumulated depreciation) for $12,000 cash, resulting in a $6,000 loss. The reconstructed entry for analysis of item *c* follows:

Reconstruction	**Cash**	**12,000**	
	Accumulated Depreciation	12,000	
	Loss on Sale of Plant Assets	6,000	
	Plant Assets		30,000

This entry reveals a $12,000 cash inflow from assets sold. The $6,000 loss is computed by comparing the asset book value to the cash received and does not reflect any cash inflow or outflow. We also reconstruct the entry for Depreciation Expense using information from the income statement.

Reconstruction	Depreciation Expense	24,000
	Accumulated Depreciation	24,000

This entry shows that Depreciation Expense results in no cash flow effect. These three reconstructed entries are reflected in the following plant asset and related T-accounts.

Plant Assets				
Bal., Dec. 31, 2010	210,000			
Purchase	70,000	Sale	30,000	
Bal., Dec. 31, 2011	250,000			

Accumulated Depreciation—Plant Assets				
		Bal., Dec. 31, 2010	48,000	
Sale	12,000	Depr. expense	24,000	
		Bal., Dec. 31, 2011	60,000	

This reconstruction analysis is complete in that the change in plant assets from $210,000 to $250,000 is fully explained by the $70,000 purchase and the $30,000 sale. Also, the change in accumulated depreciation from $48,000 to $60,000 is fully explained by depreciation expense of $24,000 and the removal of $12,000 in accumulated depreciation from an asset sale. (Preparers of the statement of cash flows have the entire ledger and additional information at their disposal, but for brevity reasons only the information needed for reconstructing accounts is given.)

The third stage looks at the reconstructed entries for identification of cash flows. The two identified cash flow effects are reported in the investing section of the statement as follows (also see Exhibit 16.7 or 16.11):

Cash flows from investing activities	
Cash received from sale of plant assets	$12,000
Cash paid for purchase of plant assets	(10,000)

The $60,000 portion of the purchase described in item *b* and financed by issuing notes is a noncash investing and financing activity. It is reported in a note or in a separate schedule to the statement as follows:

Noncash investing and financing activity	
Purchased plant assets with issuance of notes	$60,000

Analysis of Other Assets

Many other asset transactions (including those involving current notes receivable and investments in certain securities) are considered investing activities and can affect a company's cash flows. Since Genesis did not enter into other investing activities impacting assets, we do not need to extend our analysis to these other assets. If such transactions did exist, we would analyze them using the same three-stage process illustrated for plant assets.

Quick Check   Answer — p. 662

7. Equipment costing $80,000 with accumulated depreciation of $30,000 is sold at a loss of $10,000. What is the cash receipt from this sale? In what section of the statement of cash flows is this transaction reported?

CASH FLOWS FROM FINANCING

The fourth major step in preparing the statement of cash flows is to compute and report cash flows from financing activities. We normally do this by identifying changes in all noncurrent liability accounts (including the current portion of any notes and bonds) and the equity accounts. These accounts include long-term debt, notes payable, bonds payable, common stock, and retained earnings. Changes in these accounts are then analyzed using available information to determine their effect, if any, on cash. Results are reported in the financing activities section of the statement. **Reporting of financing activities is identical under the direct method and indirect method.**

Three-Stage Process of Analysis

We again use a three-stage process to determine cash provided or used by financing activities: (1) identify changes in financing-related accounts, (2) explain these changes using reconstruction analysis, and (3) report their cash flow effects.

Analysis of Noncurrent Liabilities

Information about Genesis provided earlier reveals two transactions involving noncurrent liabilities. We analyzed one of those, the $60,000 issuance of notes payable to purchase plant assets. This transaction is reported as a significant noncash investing and financing activity in a footnote or a separate schedule to the statement of cash flows. The other remaining transaction involving noncurrent liabilities is the cash retirement of notes payable.

Point: Financing activities generally refer to changes in the noncurrent liability and the equity accounts. Examples are (1) receiving cash from issuing debt or repaying amounts borrowed and (2) receiving cash from or distributing cash to owners.

Notes Payable Transactions   The first stage in analysis of notes is to review the comparative balance sheets from Exhibit 16.10. This analysis reveals an increase in notes payable from $64,000 to $90,000.

The second stage explains this change. Item *e* of the additional information for Genesis (page 639) reports that notes with a carrying value of $34,000 are retired for $18,000 cash, resulting in a $16,000 gain. The reconstructed entry for analysis of item *e* follows:

Reconstruction	Notes Payable	34,000	
	Gain on retirement of debt		16,000
	Cash		**18,000**

This entry reveals an $18,000 cash outflow for retirement of notes and a $16,000 gain from comparing the notes payable carrying value to the cash received. This gain does not reflect any cash inflow or outflow. Also, item *b* of the additional information reports that Genesis purchased plant assets costing $70,000 by issuing $60,000 in notes payable to the seller and paying $10,000 in cash. We reconstructed this entry when analyzing investing activities: It showed a $60,000 increase to notes payable that is reported as a noncash investing and financing transaction. The Notes Payable account reflects (and is fully explained by) these reconstructed entries as follows:

Notes Payable			
		Bal., Dec. 31, 2010	64,000
Retired notes	**34,000**	**Issued notes**	**60,000**
		Bal., Dec. 31, 2011	90,000

The third stage is to report the cash flow effect of the notes retirement in the financing section of the statement as follows (also see Exhibit 16.7 or 16.11):

Cash flows from financing activities	
Cash paid to retire notes	$(18,000)

Analysis of Equity

The Genesis information reveals two transactions involving equity accounts. The first is the issuance of common stock for cash. The second is the declaration and payment of cash dividends. We analyze both.

Common Stock Transactions The first stage in analyzing common stock is to review the comparative balance sheets from Exhibit 16.10, which reveal an increase in common stock from $80,000 to $95,000.

The second stage explains this change. Item *d* of the additional information (page 639) reports that 3,000 shares of common stock are issued at par for $5 per share. The reconstructed entry for analysis of item *d* follows:

Reconstruction	Cash	15,000	
	Common Stock		15,000

This entry reveals a $15,000 cash inflow from stock issuance and is reflected in (and explains) the Common Stock account as follows:

Common Stock	
Bal., Dec. 31, 2010	80,000
Issued stock	**15,000**
Bal., Dec. 31, 2011	95,000

The third stage discloses the cash flow effect from stock issuance in the financing section of the statement as follows (also see Exhibit 16.7 or 16.11):

Cash flows from financing activities
Cash received from issuing stock $15,000

Retained Earnings Transactions The first stage in analyzing the Retained Earnings account is to review the comparative balance sheets from Exhibit 16.10. This reveals an increase in retained earnings from $88,000 to $112,000.

The second stage explains this change. Item *f* of the additional information (page 639) reports that cash dividends of $14,000 are paid. The reconstructed entry follows:

Reconstruction	Retained Earnings	14,000	
	Cash		14,000

This entry reveals a $14,000 cash outflow for cash dividends. Also see that the Retained Earnings account is impacted by net income of $38,000. (Net income was analyzed under the operating section of the statement of cash flows.) The reconstructed Retained Earnings account follows:

	Retained Earnings		
		Bal., Dec. 31, 2010	88,000
Cash dividend	**14,000**	**Net income**	**38,000**
		Bal., Dec. 31, 2011	112,000

Point: Financing activities not affecting cash flow include *declaration* of a cash dividend, *declaration* of a stock dividend, payment of a stock dividend, and a stock split.

The third stage reports the cash flow effect from the cash dividend in the financing section of the statement as follows (also see Exhibit 16.7 or 16.11):

Cash flows from financing activities
Cash paid for dividends.................... $(14,000)

Global: There are no requirements to separate domestic and international cash flows, leading some users to ask, "Where in the world is cash flow?"

We now have identified and explained all of the Genesis cash inflows and cash outflows and one noncash investing and financing transaction. Specifically, our analysis has reconciled changes in all noncash balance sheet accounts.

Proving Cash Balances

The fifth and final step in preparing the statement is to report the beginning and ending cash balances and prove that the *net change in cash* is explained by operating, investing, and financing cash flows. This step is shown here for Genesis.

Net cash provided by operating activities	$20,000
Net cash provided by investing activities	2,000
Net cash used in financing activities	(17,000)
Net increase in cash	**$ 5,000**
Cash balance at 2010 year-end	12,000
Cash balance at 2011 year-end	$17,000

The preceding table shows that the $5,000 net increase in cash, from $12,000 at the beginning of the period to $17,000 at the end, is reconciled by net cash flows from operating ($20,000 inflow), investing ($2,000 inflow), and financing ($17,000 outflow) activities. This is formally reported at the bottom of the statement of cash flows as shown in both Exhibits 16.7 and 16.11.

■ Decision Maker   Answer — p. 662

Reporter   Management is in labor contract negotiations and grants you an interview. It highlights a recent $600,000 net loss that involves a $930,000 extraordinary loss and a total net cash outflow of $550,000 (which includes net cash outflows of $850,000 for investing activities and $350,000 for financing activities). What is your assessment of this company? ■

GLOBAL VIEW

The statement of cash flows, which explains changes in cash (including cash equivalents) from period to period, is required under both U.S. GAAP and IFRS. This section discusses similarities and differences between U.S. GAAP and IFRS in reporting that statement.

Reporting Cash Flows from Operating   Both U.S. GAAP and IFRS permit the reporting of cash flows from operating activities using either the direct or indirect method. Further, the basic requirements underlying the application of both methods are fairly consistent across these two accounting systems. Appendix A shows that **Nokia** reports its cash flows from operating activities using the indirect method, and in a manner similar to that explained in this chapter. Further, the definition of cash and cash equivalents is roughly similar for U.S. GAAP and IFRS.

NOKIA

There are, however, some differences between U.S. GAAP and IFRS in reporting operating cash flows. We mention two of the more notable. First, U.S. GAAP requires cash inflows from interest revenue and dividend revenue be classified as operating, whereas IFRS permits classification under operating or investing provided that this classification is consistently applied across periods. Nokia reports its cash from interest received under operating, consistent with U.S. GAAP (no mention is made of any dividends received). Second, U.S. GAAP requires cash outflows for interest expense be classified as operating, whereas IFRS again permits classification under operating or financing provided that it is consistently applied across periods. (Some believe that interest payments, like dividends payments, are better classified as financing because they represent payments to financiers.) Nokia reports cash outflows for interest under operating, which is consistent with U.S. GAAP and acceptable under IFRS.

Reporting Cash Flows from Investing and Financing   U.S. GAAP and IFRS are broadly similar in computing and classifying cash flows from investing and financing activities. A quick review of these two sections for **Nokia**'s statement of cash flows shows a structure similar to that explained in this chapter. One notable exception is that U.S. GAAP requires cash outflows for income tax be classified as operating, whereas IFRS permits the splitting of those cash flows among operating, investing, and financing depending on the sources of that tax. Nokia reports its cash outflows for income tax under operating, which is similar to U.S. GAAP.

Decision Analysis ▢▢▢   Cash Flow Analysis

Analyzing Cash Sources and Uses

A1 Analyze the statement of cash flows and apply the cash flow on total assets ratio.

Most managers stress the importance of understanding and predicting cash flows for business decisions. Creditors evaluate a company's ability to generate cash before deciding whether to lend money. Investors also assess cash inflows and outflows before buying and selling stock. Information in the statement of cash flows helps address these and other questions such as (1) How much cash is generated from or used in operations? (2) What expenditures are made with cash from operations? (3) What is the source of cash for debt payments? (4) What is the source of cash for distributions to owners? (5) How is the increase in investing activities financed? (6) What is the source of cash for new plant assets? (7) Why is cash flow from operations different from income? (8) How is cash from financing used?

To effectively answer these questions, it is important to separately analyze investing, financing, and operating activities. To illustrate, consider data from three different companies in Exhibit 16.13. These companies operate in the same industry and have been in business for several years.

EXHIBIT 16.13

Cash Flows of Competing Companies

($ thousands)	BMX	ATV	Trex
Cash provided (used) by operating activities	$90,000	$40,000	$(24,000)
Cash provided (used) by investing activities			
Proceeds from sale of plant assets			26,000
Purchase of plant assets	(48,000)	(25,000)	
Cash provided (used) by financing activities			
Proceeds from issuance of debt			13,000
Repayment of debt	(27,000)		
Net increase (decrease) in cash	$15,000	$15,000	$ 15,000

Each company generates an identical $15,000 net increase in cash, but its sources and uses of cash flows are very different. BMX's operating activities provide net cash flows of $90,000, allowing it to purchase plant assets of $48,000 and repay $27,000 of its debt. ATV's operating activities provide $40,000 of cash flows, limiting its purchase of plant assets to $25,000. Trex's $15,000 net cash increase is due to selling plant assets and incurring additional debt. Its operating activities yield a net cash outflow of $24,000. Overall, analysis of these cash flows reveals that BMX is more capable of generating future cash flows than is ATV or Trex.

▢ **Decision Insight**

Free Cash Flows   Many investors use cash flows to value company stock. However, cash-based valuation models often yield different stock values due to differences in measurement of cash flows. Most models require cash flows that are "free" for distribution to shareholders. These *free cash flows* are defined as cash flows available to shareholders after operating asset reinvestments and debt payments. Knowledge of the statement of cash flows is key to proper computation of free cash flows. A company's growth and financial flexibility depend on adequate free cash flows. ■

Cash Flow on Total Assets

Cash flow information has limitations, but it can help measure a company's ability to meet its obligations, pay dividends, expand operations, and obtain financing. Users often compute and analyze a cash-based ratio similar to return on total assets except that its numerator is net cash flows from operating activities. The **cash flow on total assets** ratio is in Exhibit 16.14.

EXHIBIT 16.14

Cash Flow on Total Assets

$$\text{Cash flow on total assets} = \frac{\text{Cash flow from operations}}{\text{Average total assets}}$$

This ratio reflects actual cash flows and is not affected by accounting income recognition and measurement. It can help business decision makers estimate the amount and timing of cash flows when planning and analyzing operating activities.

To illustrate, the 2009 cash flow on total assets ratio for Nike is 13.5%—see Exhibit 16.15. Is a 13.5% ratio good or bad? To answer this question, we compare this ratio with the ratios of prior years (we could also compare its ratio with those of its competitors and the market). Nike's cash flow on total assets ratio for several prior years is in the second column of Exhibit 16.15. Results show that its 13.5% return is the lowest return over the past several years. This is probably reflective of the recent recessionary period.

EXHIBIT 16.15

Nike's Cash Flow on Total Assets

Year	Cash Flow on Total Assets	Return on Total Assets
2009.........	13.5%	11.6%
2008.........	16.7	16.3
2007.........	18.3	14.5
2006.........	17.9	14.9
2005.........	18.8	14.5

As an indicator of *earnings quality,* some analysts compare the cash flow on total assets ratio to the return on total assets ratio. Nike's return on total assets is provided in the third column of Exhibit 16.15. Nike's cash flow on total assets ratio exceeds its return on total assets in each of the five years, leading some analysts to infer that Nike's earnings quality is high for that period because more earnings are realized in the form of cash.

Decision Insight

Cash Flow Ratios Analysts use various other cash-based ratios, including the following two:

$$(1) \quad \text{Cash coverage of growth} = \frac{\text{Operating cash flow}}{\text{Cash outflow for plant assets}}$$

where a low ratio (less than 1) implies cash inadequacy to meet asset growth, whereas a high ratio implies cash adequacy for asset growth.

$$(2) \quad \text{Operating cash flow to sales} = \frac{\text{Operating cash flow}}{\text{Net sales}}$$

When this ratio substantially and consistently differs from the operating income to net sales ratio, the risk of accounting improprieties increases. ■

Point: The following ratio helps assess whether operating cash flow is adequate to meet long-term obligations:
Cash coverage of debt = Cash flow from operations ÷ Noncurrent liabilities. A low ratio suggests a higher risk of insolvency; a high ratio suggests a greater ability to meet long-term obligations.

DEMONSTRATION PROBLEM

Umlauf's comparative balance sheets, income statement, and additional information follow.

UMLAUF COMPANY
Balance Sheets
December 31, 2011 and 2010

	2011	2010
Assets		
Cash	$ 43,050	$ 23,925
Accounts receivable	34,125	39,825
Merchandise inventory	156,000	146,475
Prepaid expenses	3,600	1,650
Equipment	135,825	146,700
Accum. depreciation—Equipment	(61,950)	(47,550)
Total assets	$310,650	$311,025
Liabilities and Equity		
Accounts payable	$ 28,800	$ 33,750
Income taxes payable	5,100	4,425
Dividends payable	0	4,500
Bonds payable	0	37,500
Common stock, $10 par	168,750	168,750
Retained earnings	108,000	62,100
Total liabilities and equity	$310,650	$311,025

UMLAUF COMPANY
Income Statement
For Year Ended December 31, 2011

Sales		$446,100
Cost of goods sold	$222,300	
Other operating expenses	120,300	
Depreciation expense	25,500	(368,100)
		78,000
Other gains (losses)		
Loss on sale of equipment	3,300	
Loss on retirement of bonds ..	825	(4,125)
Income before taxes		73,875
Income taxes expense		(13,725)
Net income		$ 60,150

Additional Information

a. Equipment costing $21,375 with accumulated depreciation of $11,100 is sold for cash.

b. Equipment purchases are for cash.

c. Accumulated Depreciation is affected by depreciation expense and the sale of equipment.

d. The balance of Retained Earnings is affected by dividend declarations and net income.

e. All sales are made on credit.

f. All merchandise inventory purchases are on credit.

g. Accounts Payable balances result from merchandise inventory purchases.

h. Prepaid expenses relate to "other operating expenses."

Required

1. Prepare a statement of cash flows using the indirect method for year 2011.

2.[B] Prepare a statement of cash flows using the direct method for year 2011.

PLANNING THE SOLUTION

- Prepare two blank statements of cash flows with sections for operating, investing, and financing activities using the (1) indirect method format and (2) direct method format.

- Compute the cash paid for equipment and the cash received from the sale of equipment using the additional information provided along with the amount for depreciation expense and the change in the balances of equipment and accumulated depreciation. Use T-accounts to help chart the effects of the sale and purchase of equipment on the balances of the Equipment account and the Accumulated Depreciation account.

- Compute the effect of net income on the change in the Retained Earnings account balance. Assign the difference between the change in retained earnings and the amount of net income to dividends declared. Adjust the dividends declared amount for the change in the Dividends Payable balance.

- Compute cash received from customers, cash paid for merchandise, cash paid for other operating expenses, and cash paid for taxes as illustrated in the chapter.

- Enter the cash effects of reconstruction entries to the appropriate section(s) of the statement.

- Total each section of the statement, determine the total net change in cash, and add it to the beginning balance to get the ending balance of cash.

SOLUTION TO DEMONSTRATION PROBLEM

Supporting computations for cash receipts and cash payments.

(1)	*Cost of equipment sold	$ 21,375
	Accumulated depreciation of equipment sold	(11,100)
	Book value of equipment sold	10,275
	Loss on sale of equipment	(3,300)
	Cash received from sale of equipment	$ 6,975
	Cost of equipment sold	$ 21,375
	Less decrease in the equipment account balance	(10,875)
	Cash paid for new equipment	$ 10,500
(2)	Loss on retirement of bonds	$ 825
	Carrying value of bonds retired	37,500
	Cash paid to retire bonds	$ 38,325
(3)	Net income	$ 60,150
	Less increase in retained earnings	45,900
	Dividends declared	14,250
	Plus decrease in dividends payable	4,500
	Cash paid for dividends	$ 18,750
(4)[B]	Sales	$ 446,100
	Add decrease in accounts receivable	5,700
	Cash received from customers	$451,800

[continued on next page]

[continued from previous page]

(5)B Cost of goods sold	$ 222,300
Plus increase in merchandise inventory	9,525
Purchases	231,825
Plus decrease in accounts payable	4,950
Cash paid for merchandise	$236,775
(6)B Other operating expenses	$ 120,300
Plus increase in prepaid expenses	1,950
Cash paid for other operating expenses	$122,250
(7)B Income taxes expense	$ 13,725
Less increase in income taxes payable	(675)
Cash paid for income taxes	$ 13,050

* Supporting T-account analysis for part 1 follows:

Equipment			
Bal., Dec. 31, 2010	146,700		
Cash purchase	10,500	Sale	21,375
Bal., Dec. 31, 2011	135,825		

Accumulated Depreciation—Equipment			
		Bal., Dec. 31, 2010	47,550
Sale	11,100	Depr. expense	25,500
		Bal., Dec. 31, 2011	61,950

UMLAUF COMPANY
Statement of Cash Flows (Indirect Method)
For Year Ended December 31, 2011

Cash flows from operating activities		
Net income	$60,150	
Adjustments to reconcile net income to net cash provided by operating activities		
Decrease in accounts receivable	5,700	
Increase in merchandise inventory	(9,525)	
Increase in prepaid expenses	(1,950)	
Decrease in accounts payable	(4,950)	
Increase in income taxes payable	675	
Depreciation expense	25,500	
Loss on sale of plant assets	3,300	
Loss on retirement of bonds	825	
Net cash provided by operating activities		$79,725
Cash flows from investing activities		
Cash received from sale of equipment	6,975	
Cash paid for equipment	(10,500)	
Net cash used in investing activities		(3,525)
Cash flows from financing activities		
Cash paid to retire bonds payable	(38,325)	
Cash paid for dividends	(18,750)	
Net cash used in financing activities		(57,075)
Net increase in cash		$19,125
Cash balance at prior year-end		23,925
Cash balance at current year-end		$43,050

UMLAUF COMPANY
Statement of Cash Flows (Direct Method)
For Year Ended December 31, 2011

Cash flows from operating activities		
Cash received from customers	$451,800	
Cash paid for merchandise	(236,775)	
Cash paid for other operating expenses	(122,250)	
Cash paid for income taxes	(13,050)	
Net cash provided by operating activities		$79,725
Cash flows from investing activities		
Cash received from sale of equipment	6,975	
Cash paid for equipment	(10,500)	
Net cash used in investing activities		(3,525)
Cash flows from financing activities		
Cash paid to retire bonds payable	(38,325)	
Cash paid for dividends	(18,750)	
Net cash used in financing activities		(57,075)
Net increase in cash		$19,125
Cash balance at prior year-end		23,925
Cash balance at current year-end		$43,050

(handwritten note: Cash paid for interest)

APPENDIX

16A

Spreadsheet Preparation of the Statement of Cash Flows

This appendix explains how to use a spreadsheet to prepare the statement of cash flows under the indirect method.

P4 Illustrate use of a spreadsheet to prepare a statement of cash flows.

Preparing the Indirect Method Spreadsheet   Analyzing noncash accounts can be challenging when a company has a large number of accounts and many operating, investing, and financing transactions. A *spreadsheet,* also called *work sheet* or *working paper,* can help us organize the information needed to prepare a statement of cash flows. A spreadsheet also makes it easier to check the accuracy of our work. To illustrate, we return to the comparative balance sheets and income statement shown in Exhibit 16.10. We use the following identifying letters *a* through *g* to code changes in accounts, and letters *h* through *m* for additional information, to prepare the statement of cash flows:

a. Net income is $38,000.

b. Accounts receivable increase by $20,000.

c. Merchandise inventory increases by $14,000.

d. Prepaid expenses increase by $2,000.

e. Accounts payable decrease by $5,000.

f. Interest payable decreases by $1,000.

g. Income taxes payable increase by $10,000.

h. Depreciation expense is $24,000.

i. Plant assets costing $30,000 with accumulated depreciation of $12,000 are sold for $12,000 cash. This yields a loss on sale of assets of $6,000.

j. Notes with a book value of $34,000 are retired with a cash payment of $18,000, yielding a $16,000 gain on retirement.

k. Plant assets costing $70,000 are purchased with a cash payment of $10,000 and an issuance of notes payable for $60,000.

l. Issued 3,000 shares of common stock for $15,000 cash.

m. Paid cash dividends of $14,000.

Exhibit 16A.1 shows the indirect method spreadsheet for Genesis. We enter both beginning and ending balance sheet amounts on the spreadsheet. We also enter information in the Analysis of Changes columns (keyed to the additional information items *a* through *m*) to explain changes in the accounts and determine the cash flows for operating, investing, and financing activities. Information about noncash investing and financing activities is reported near the bottom.

EXHIBIT 16A.1

Spreadsheet for Preparing Statement of Cash Flows— Indirect Method

	Dec. 31, 2010		Analysis of Changes Debit		Analysis of Changes Credit	Dec. 31, 2011
GENESIS — Spreadsheet for Statement of Cash Flows—Indirect Method — For Year Ended December 31, 2011						
Balance Sheet—Debit Bal. Accounts						
Cash	$ 12,000					$ 17,000
Accounts receivable	40,000	(b)	$ 20,000			60,000
Merchandise inventory	70,000	(c)	14,000			84,000
Prepaid expenses	4,000	(d)	2,000			6,000
Plant assets	210,000	(k1)	70,000	(i)	$ 30,000	250,000
	$336,000					$417,000
Balance Sheet—Credit Bal. Accounts						
Accumulated depreciation	$ 48,000	(i)	12,000	(h)	24,000	$ 60,000
Accounts payable	40,000	(e)	5,000			35,000
Interest payable	4,000	(f)	1,000			3,000
Income taxes payable	12,000			(g)	10,000	22,000
Notes payable	64,000	(j)	34,000	(k2)	60,000	90,000
Common stock, $5 par value	80,000			(l)	15,000	95,000
Retained earnings	88,000	(m)	14,000	(a)	38,000	112,000
	$336,000					$417,000
Statement of Cash Flows						
Operating activities						
Net income		(a)	38,000			
Increase in accounts receivable				(b)	20,000	
Increase in merchandise inventory				(c)	14,000	
Increase in prepaid expenses				(d)	2,000	
Decrease in accounts payable				(e)	5,000	
Decrease in interest payable				(f)	1,000	
Increase in income taxes payable		(g)	10,000			
Depreciation expense		(h)	24,000			
Loss on sale of plant assets		(i)	6,000			
Gain on retirement of notes				(j)	16,000	
Investing activities						
Receipts from sale of plant assets		(i)	12,000			
Payment for purchase of plant assets				(k1)	10,000	
Financing activities						
Payment to retire notes				(j)	18,000	
Receipts from issuing stock		(l)	15,000			
Payment of cash dividends				(m)	14,000	
Noncash Investing and Financing Activities						
Purchase of plant assets with notes		(k2)	60,000	(k1)	60,000	
			$337,000		$337,000	

Sheet1 / Sheet2 / Sheet3 /

Entering the Analysis of Changes on the Spreadsheet   The following sequence of procedures is used to complete the spreadsheet after the beginning and ending balances of the balance sheet accounts are entered:

① Enter net income as the first item in the Statement of Cash Flows section for computing operating cash inflow (debit) and as a credit to Retained Earnings.

② In the Statement of Cash Flows section, adjustments to net income are entered as debits if they increase cash flows and as credits if they decrease cash flows. Applying this same rule, adjust net income for the change in each noncash current asset and current liability account related to operating activities. For each adjustment to net income, the offsetting debit or credit must help reconcile the beginning and ending balances of a current asset or current liability account.

③ Enter adjustments to net income for income statement items not providing or using cash in the period. For each adjustment, the offsetting debit or credit must help reconcile a noncash balance sheet account.

④ Adjust net income to eliminate any gains or losses from investing and financing activities. Because the cash from a gain must be excluded from operating activities, the gain is entered as a credit in the operating activities section. Losses are entered as debits. For each adjustment, the related debit and/or credit must help reconcile balance sheet accounts and involve reconstructed entries to show the cash flow from investing or financing activities.

⑤ After reviewing any unreconciled balance sheet accounts and related information, enter the remaining reconciling entries for investing and financing activities. Examples are purchases of plant assets, issuances of long-term debt, stock issuances, and dividend payments. Some of these may require entries in the noncash investing and financing section of the spreadsheet (reconciled).

⑥ Check accuracy by totaling the Analysis of Changes columns and by determining that the change in each balance sheet account has been explained (reconciled).

Point: Analysis of the changes on the spreadsheet are summarized here:

1. Cash flows from operating activities generally affect net income, current assets, and current liabilities.

2. Cash flows from investing activities generally affect noncurrent asset accounts.

3. Cash flows from financing activities generally affect noncurrent liability and equity accounts.

We illustrate these steps in Exhibit 16A.1 for Genesis:

Step	Entries
①·········	(a)
②·········	(b) through (g)
③·········	(h)
④·········	(i) through (j)
⑤·········	(k) through (m)

Since adjustments *i, j,* and *k* are more challenging, we show them in the following debit and credit format. These entries are for purposes of our understanding; they are *not* the entries actually made in the journals. Changes in the Cash account are identified as sources or uses of cash.

i.	Loss from sale of plant assets	6,000	
	Accumulated depreciation	12,000	
	Receipt from sale of plant assets **(source of cash)**	12,000	
	Plant assets		30,000
	To describe sale of plant assets.		
j.	Notes payable	34,000	
	Payments to retire notes **(use of cash)**		18,000
	Gain on retirement of notes		16,000
	To describe retirement of notes.		
k1.	Plant assets	70,000	
	Payment to purchase plant assets **(use of cash)**		10,000
	Purchase of plant assets financed by notes		60,000
	To describe purchase of plant assets.		
k2.	Purchase of plant assets financed by notes	60,000	
	Notes payable		60,000
	To issue notes for purchase of assets.		

Direct Method of Reporting Operating Cash Flows   # 16B

We compute cash flows from operating activities under the direct method by adjusting accrual-based income statement items to the cash basis. The usual approach is to adjust income statement accounts related to operating activities for changes in their related balance sheet accounts as follows:

P5 Compute cash flows from operating activities using the direct method.

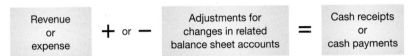

The framework for reporting cash receipts and cash payments for the operating section of the cash flow statement under the direct method is shown in Exhibit 16B.1. We consider cash receipts first and then cash payments.

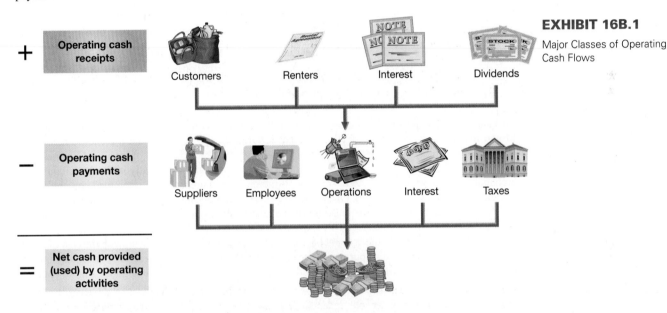

EXHIBIT 16B.1

Major Classes of Operating Cash Flows

Operating Cash Receipts   A review of Exhibit 16.10 and the additional information reported by Genesis suggests only one potential cash receipt: sales to customers. This section, therefore, starts with sales to customers as reported on the income statement and then adjusts it as necessary to obtain cash received from customers to report on the statement of cash flows.

Cash Received from Customers   If all sales are for cash, the amount received from customers equals the sales reported on the income statement. When some or all sales are on account, however, we must adjust the amount of sales for the change in Accounts Receivable. It is often helpful to use *account analysis* to do this. This usually involves setting up a T-account and reconstructing its major entries, with emphasis on cash receipts and payments. To illustrate, we use a T-account that includes accounts receivable balances for Genesis on December 31, 2010 and 2011. The beginning balance is $40,000 and the ending balance is $60,000. Next, the income statement shows sales of $590,000, which we enter on the debit side of this account. We now can reconstruct the Accounts Receivable account to determine the amount of cash received from customers as follows:

Point: An accounts receivable increase implies that cash received from customers is less than sales (the converse is also true).

Accounts Receivable			
Bal., Dec. 31, 2010	40,000		
Sales	590,000	Cash receipts =	570,000
Bal., Dec. 31, 2011	60,000		

This T-account shows that the Accounts Receivable balance begins at $40,000 and increases to $630,000 from sales of $590,000, yet its ending balance is only $60,000. This implies that cash receipts from customers are $570,000, computed as $40,000 + $590,000 − [?] = $60,000. This computation can be rearranged to express cash received as equal to sales of $590,000 minus a $20,000 increase in accounts receivable. This computation is summarized as a general rule in Exhibit 16B.2. The statement of cash flows in Exhibit 16.7 reports the $570,000 cash received from customers as a cash inflow from operating activities.

EXHIBIT 16B.2

Formula to Compute Cash Received from Customers—Direct Method

$$\text{Cash received from customers} = \text{Sales} - \left[\begin{array}{l} + \text{ Decrease in accounts receivable} \\ \qquad\qquad\qquad \text{or} \\ - \text{ Increase in accounts receivable} \end{array} \right.$$

Other Cash Receipts   While Genesis's cash receipts are limited to collections from customers, we often see other types of cash receipts, most commonly cash receipts involving rent, interest, and dividends. We compute cash received from these items by subtracting an increase in their respective receivable or adding a decrease. For instance, if rent receivable increases in the period, cash received from renters is less than rent revenue reported on the income statement. If rent receivable decreases, cash received is more than reported rent revenue. The same logic applies to interest and dividends. The formulas for these computations are summarized later in this appendix.

Operating Cash Payments   A review of Exhibit 16.10 and the additional Genesis information shows four operating expenses: cost of goods sold; wages and other operating expenses; interest expense; and taxes expense. We analyze each expense to compute its cash amounts for the statement of cash flows. (We then examine depreciation and the other losses and gains.)

Cash Paid for Merchandise   We compute cash paid for merchandise by analyzing both cost of goods sold and merchandise inventory. If all merchandise purchases are for cash and the ending balance of Merchandise Inventory is unchanged from the beginning balance, the amount of cash paid for merchandise equals cost of goods sold—an uncommon situation. Instead, there normally is some change in the Merchandise Inventory balance. Also, some or all merchandise purchases are often made on credit, and this yields changes in the Accounts Payable balance. When the balances of both Merchandise Inventory and Accounts Payable change, we must adjust the cost of goods sold for changes in both accounts to compute cash paid for merchandise. This is a two-step adjustment.

First, we use the change in the account balance of Merchandise Inventory, along with the cost of goods sold amount, to compute cost of purchases for the period. An increase in merchandise inventory implies that we bought more than we sold, and we add this inventory increase to cost of goods sold to compute cost of purchases. A decrease in merchandise inventory implies that we bought less than we sold, and we subtract the inventory decrease from cost of goods sold to compute purchases. We illustrate the *first step* by reconstructing the Merchandise Inventory account of Genesis:

Merchandise Inventory			
Bal., Dec. 31, 2010	70,000		
Purchases =	314,000	Cost of goods sold	300,000
Bal., Dec. 31, 2011	84,000		

The beginning balance is $70,000, and the ending balance is $84,000. The income statement shows that cost of goods sold is $300,000, which we enter on the credit side of this account. With this information, we determine the amount for cost of purchases to be $314,000. This computation can be rearranged to express cost of purchases as equal to cost of goods sold of $300,000 plus the $14,000 increase in inventory.

The second step uses the change in the balance of Accounts Payable, and the amount of cost of purchases, to compute cash paid for merchandise. A decrease in accounts payable implies that we paid for more goods than we acquired this period, and we would then add the accounts payable decrease to cost of purchases to compute cash paid for merchandise. An increase in accounts payable implies that we paid for less than the amount of goods acquired, and we would subtract the accounts payable increase from purchases to compute cash paid for merchandise. The *second step* is applied to Genesis by reconstructing its Accounts Payable account:

Accounts Payable			
		Bal., Dec. 31, 2010	40,000
Cash payments =	319,000	Purchases	314,000
		Bal., Dec. 31, 2011	35,000

Its beginning balance of $40,000 plus purchases of $314,000 minus an ending balance of $35,000 yields cash paid of $319,000 (or $40,000 + $314,000 − [?] = $35,000). Alternatively, we can express cash paid for merchandise as equal to purchases of $314,000 plus the $5,000 decrease in accounts payable. The $319,000 cash paid for merchandise is reported on the statement of cash flows in Exhibit 16.7 as a cash outflow under operating activities.

We summarize this two-step adjustment to cost of goods sold to compute cash paid for merchandise inventory in Exhibit 16B.3.

Example: If the ending balances of Inventory and Accounts Payable are $60,000 and $50,000, respectively (instead of $84,000 and $35,000), what is cash paid for merchandise? *Answer:* $280,000

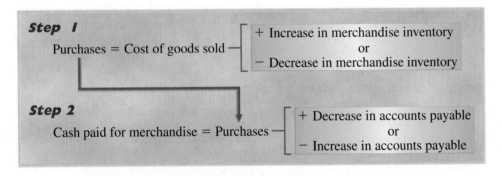

EXHIBIT 16B.3

Two Steps to Compute Cash Paid for Merchandise—Direct Method

Cash Paid for Wages and Operating Expenses (Excluding Depreciation)   The income statement of Genesis shows wages and other operating expenses of $216,000 (see Exhibit 16.10). To compute cash paid for wages and other operating expenses, we adjust this amount for any changes in their related balance sheet accounts. We begin by looking for any prepaid expenses and accrued liabilities related to wages and other operating expenses in the balance sheets of Genesis in Exhibit 16.10. The balance sheets show prepaid expenses but no accrued liabilities. Thus, the adjustment is limited to the change in prepaid expenses. The amount of adjustment is computed by assuming that all cash paid for wages and other operating expenses is initially debited to Prepaid Expenses. This assumption allows us to reconstruct the Prepaid Expenses account:

Prepaid Expenses			
Bal., Dec. 31, 2010	4,000		
Cash payments =	218,000	Wages and other operating exp.	216,000
Bal., Dec. 31, 2011	6,000		

Prepaid Expenses increase by $2,000 in the period, meaning that cash paid for wages and other operating expenses exceeds the reported expense by $2,000. Alternatively, we can express cash paid for wages and other operating expenses as equal to its reported expenses of $216,000 plus the $2,000 increase in prepaid expenses.[1]

Exhibit 16B.4 summarizes the adjustments to wages (including salaries) and other operating expenses. The Genesis balance sheet did not report accrued liabilities, but we include them in the formula to explain the adjustment to cash when they do exist. A decrease in accrued liabilities implies that we paid cash for more goods or services than received this period, so we add the decrease in accrued liabilities to the expense amount to obtain cash paid for these goods or services. An increase in accrued liabilities implies that we paid cash for less than what was acquired, so we subtract this increase in accrued liabilities from the expense amount to get cash paid.

Point: A decrease in prepaid expenses implies that reported expenses include an amount(s) that did not require a cash outflow in the period.

---

[1] The assumption that all cash payments for wages and operating expenses are initially debited to Prepaid Expenses is not necessary for our analysis to hold. If cash payments are debited directly to the expense account, the total amount of cash paid for wages and other operating expenses still equals the $216,000 expense plus the $2,000 increase in Prepaid Expenses (which arise from end-of-period adjusting entries).

EXHIBIT 16B.4

Formula to Compute Cash Paid for
Wages and Operating
Expenses—Direct Method

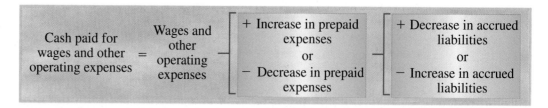

Cash paid for interest and income taxes   Computing operating cash flows for interest and taxes is similar to that for operating expenses. Both require adjustments to their amounts reported on the income statement for changes in their related balance sheet accounts. We begin with the Genesis income statement showing interest expense of $7,000 and income taxes expense of $15,000. To compute the cash paid, we adjust interest expense for the change in interest payable and then the income taxes expense for the change in income taxes payable. These computations involve reconstructing both liability accounts:

Interest Payable		
	Bal., Dec. 31, 2010	4,000
Cash paid for interest = **8,000**	Interest expense	7,000
	Bal., Dec. 31, 2011	3,000

Income Taxes Payable		
	Bal., Dec. 31, 2010	12,000
Cash paid for taxes = **5,000**	Income taxes expense	15,000
	Bal., Dec. 31, 2011	22,000

These accounts reveal cash paid for interest of $8,000 and cash paid for income taxes of $5,000. The formulas to compute these amounts are in Exhibit 16B.5. Both of these cash payments are reported as operating cash outflows on the statement of cash flows in Exhibit 16.7.

EXHIBIT 16B.5

Formulas to Compute Cash
Paid for Both Interest and Taxes—
Direct Method

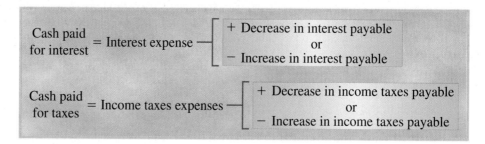

Analysis of Additional Expenses, Gains, and Losses   Genesis has three additional items reported on its income statement: depreciation, loss on sale of assets, and gain on retirement of debt. We must consider each for its potential cash effects.

Depreciation Expense   Depreciation expense is $24,000. It is often called a *noncash expense* because depreciation has no cash flows. Depreciation expense is an allocation of an asset's depreciable cost. The cash outflow with a plant asset is reported as part of investing activities when it is paid for. Thus, depreciation expense is *never* reported on a statement of cash flows using the direct method; nor is depletion or amortization expense.

Loss on Sale of Assets   Sales of assets frequently result in gains and losses reported as part of net income, but the amount of recorded gain or loss does *not* reflect any cash flows in these transactions. Asset sales result in cash inflow equal to the cash amount received, regardless of whether the asset was sold at a gain or a loss. This cash inflow is reported under investing activities. Thus, the loss or gain on a sale of assets is *never* reported on a statement of cash flows using the direct method.

Gain on Retirement of Debt   Retirement of debt usually yields a gain or loss reported as part of net income, but that gain or loss does *not* reflect cash flow in this transaction. Debt retirement results in cash outflow equal to the cash paid to settle the debt, regardless of whether the debt is retired at a gain or loss.

This cash outflow is reported under financing activities; the loss or gain from retirement of debt is *never* reported on a statement of cash flows using the direct method.

Summary of Adjustments for Direct Method   Exhibit 16B.6 summarizes common adjustments for net income to yield net cash provided (used) by operating activities under the direct method.

EXHIBIT 16B.6

Summary of Selected Adjustments for Direct Method

Item	From Income Statement	Adjustments to Obtain Cash Flow Numbers	
Receipts			
From sales	Sales Revenue	+ Decrease in Accounts Receivable − Increase in Accounts Receivable	
From rent	Rent Revenue	+ Decrease in Rent Receivable − Increase in Rent Receivable	
From interest	Interest Revenue	+ Decrease in Interest Receivable − Increase in Interest Receivable	
From dividends	Dividend Revenue	+ Decrease in Dividends Receivable − Increase in Dividends Receivable	
Payments			
To suppliers	Cost of Goods Sold	+ Increase in Inventory − Decrease in Inventory	+ Decrease in Accounts Payable − Increase in Accounts Payable
For operations	Operating Expense	+ Increase in Prepaids − Decrease in Prepaids	+ Decrease in Accrued Liabilities − Increase in Accrued Liabilities
To employees	Wages (Salaries) Expense	+ Decrease in Wages (Salaries) Payable − Increase in Wages (Salaries) Payable	
For interest	Interest Expense	+ Decrease in Interest Payable − Increase in Interest Payable	
For taxes	Income Tax Expense	+ Decrease in Income Tax Payable − Increase in Income Tax Payable	

Direct Method Format of Operating Activities Section   Exhibit 16.7 shows the Genesis statement of cash flows using the direct method. Major items of cash inflows and cash outflows are listed separately in the operating activities section. The format requires that operating cash outflows be subtracted from operating cash inflows to get net cash provided (used) by operating activities. The FASB recommends that the operating activities section of the statement of cash flows be reported using the direct method, which is considered more useful to financial statement users. *However, the FASB requires a reconciliation of net income to net cash provided (used) by operating activities when the direct method is used* (which can be reported in the notes). This reconciliation is similar to preparation of the operating activities section of the statement of cash flows using the indirect method.

Point: Some preparers argue that it is easier to prepare a statement of cash flows using the indirect method. This likely explains its greater frequency in financial statements.

 IFRS _____

Like U.S. GAAP, IFRS allows cash flows from operating activities to be reported using either the indirect method or the direct method. ■

Quick Check   Answers — p. 662

8. Net sales in a period are $590,000, beginning accounts receivable are $120,000, and ending accounts receivable are $90,000. What cash amount is collected from customers in the period?

9. The Merchandise Inventory account balance decreases in the period from a beginning balance of $32,000 to an ending balance of $28,000. Cost of goods sold for the period is $168,000. If the Accounts Payable balance increases $2,400 in the period, what is the cash amount paid for merchandise inventory?

10. This period's wages and other operating expenses total $112,000. Beginning-of-period prepaid expenses totaled $1,200, and its ending balance is $4,200. There were no beginning-of-period accrued liabilities, but end-of-period wages payable equal $5,600. How much cash is paid for wages and other operating expenses?

Summary

C1 **Distinguish between operating, investing, and financing activities, and describe how noncash investing and financing activities are disclosed.** The purpose of the statement of cash flows is to report major cash receipts and cash payments relating to operating, investing, or financing activities. Operating activities include transactions and events that determine net income. Investing activities include transactions and events that mainly affect long-term assets. Financing activities include transactions and events that mainly affect long-term liabilities and equity. Noncash investing and financing activities must be disclosed in either a note or a separate schedule to the statement of cash flows. Examples are the retirement of debt by issuing equity and the exchange of a note payable for plant assets.

A1 **Analyze the statement of cash flows and apply the cash flow on total assets ratio.** To understand and predict cash flows, users stress identification of the sources and uses of cash flows by operating, investing, and financing activities. Emphasis is on operating cash flows since they derive from continuing operations. The cash flow on total assets ratio is defined as operating cash flows divided by average total assets. Analysis of current and past values for this ratio can reflect a company's ability to yield regular and positive cash flows. It is also viewed as a measure of earnings quality.

P1 **Prepare a statement of cash flows.** Preparation of a statement of cash flows involves five steps: (1) Compute the net increase or decrease in cash; (2) compute net cash provided or used by operating activities (*using either the direct or indirect method*); (3) compute net cash provided or used by investing activities; (4) compute net cash

provided or used by financing activities; and (5) report the beginning and ending cash balance and prove that it is explained by net cash flows. Noncash investing and financing activities are also disclosed.

P2 **Compute cash flows from operating activities using the indirect method.** The indirect method for reporting net cash provided or used by operating activities starts with net income and then adjusts it for three items: (1) changes in noncash current assets and current liabilities related to operating activities, (2) revenues and expenses not providing or using cash, and (3) gains and losses from investing and financing activities.

P3 **Determine cash flows from both investing and financing activities.** Cash flows from both investing and financing activities are determined by identifying the cash flow effects of transactions and events affecting each balance sheet account related to these activities. All cash flows from these activities are identified when we can explain changes in these accounts from the beginning to the end of the period.

P4^A **Illustrate use of a spreadsheet to prepare a statement of cash flows.** A spreadsheet is a useful tool in preparing a statement of cash flows. Six key steps (see Appendix 16A) are applied when using the spreadsheet to prepare the statement.

P5^B **Compute cash flows from operating activities using the direct method.** The direct method for reporting net cash provided or used by operating activities lists major operating cash inflows less cash outflows to yield net cash inflow or outflow from operations.

Guidance Answers to Decision Maker

Entrepreneur Several factors might explain an increase in net cash flows when a net loss is reported, including (1) early recognition of expenses relative to revenues generated (such as research and development), (2) cash advances on long-term sales contracts not yet recognized in income, (3) issuances of debt or equity for cash to finance expansion, (4) cash sale of assets, (5) delay of cash payments, and (6) cash prepayment on sales. Analysis needs to focus on the components of both the net loss and the net cash flows and their implications for future performance.

Reporter Your initial reaction based on the company's $600,000 loss with a $550,000 decrease in net cash flows is not positive. However, closer scrutiny reveals a more positive picture of this company's performance. Cash flow from operating activities is $650,000, computed as [?] − $850,000 − $350,000 = $(550,000). You also note that net income *before* the extraordinary loss is $330,000, computed as [?] − $930,000 = $(600,000).

Guidance Answers to Quick Checks

1. No to both. The statement of cash flows reports changes in the sum of cash plus cash equivalents. It does not report transfers between cash and cash equivalents.

2. The three categories of cash inflows and outflows are operating activities, investing activities, and financing activities.

3. **a.** Investing   **c.** Financing   **e.** Operating
   b. Operating   **d.** Operating   **f.** Financing

4. $74,900 + $4,600 − $11,700 − $1,000 + $3,400 = $70,200

5. Expenses such as depreciation and amortization do not require current cash outflows. Therefore, adding these expenses back to

net income eliminates these noncash items from the net income number, converting it to a cash basis.

6. A gain on the sale of plant assets is subtracted from net income because a sale of plant assets is not an operating activity; it is an investing activity for the amount of cash received from its sale. Also, such a gain yields no cash effects.

7. $80,000 − $30,000 − $10,000 = $40,000 cash receipt. The $40,000 cash receipt is reported as an investing activity.

8. $590,000 + ($120,000 − $90,000) = $620,000

9. $168,000 − ($32,000 − $28,000) − $2,400 = $161,600

10. $112,000 + ($4,200 − $1,200) − $5,600 = $109,400

Key Terms

Cash flow on total assets (p. 650)   Indirect method (p. 638)   Operating activities (p. 633)

Direct method (p. 638)   Investing activities (p. 634)   Statement of cash flows (p. 632)

Financing activities (p. 634)

Multiple Choice Quiz   Answers on p. 683   mhhe.com/wildFAP20e

Additional Quiz Questions are available at the book's Website.

1. A company uses the indirect method to determine its cash flows from operating activities. Use the following information to determine its net cash provided or used by operating activities.

Net income	$15,200
Depreciation expense	10,000
Cash payment on note payable	8,000
Gain on sale of land	3,000
Increase in inventory	1,500
Increase in accounts payable	2,850

   a. $23,550 used by operating activities

   b. $23,550 provided by operating activities

   c. $15,550 provided by operating activities

   d. $42,400 provided by operating activities

   e. $20,850 provided by operating activities

2. A machine with a cost of $175,000 and accumulated depreciation of $94,000 is sold for $87,000 cash. The amount reported as a source of cash under cash flows from investing activities is

   a. $81,000.

   b. $6,000.

   c. $87,000.

   d. Zero; this is a financing activity.

   e. Zero; this is an operating activity.

3. A company settles a long-term note payable plus interest by paying $68,000 cash toward the principal amount and $5,440 cash for interest. The amount reported as a use of cash under cash flows from financing activities is

   a. Zero; this is an investing activity.

   b. Zero; this is an operating activity.

   c. $73,440.

   d. $68,000.

   e. $5,440.

4. The following information is available regarding a company's annual salaries and wages. What amount of cash is paid for salaries and wages?

Salaries and wages expense	$255,000
Salaries and wages payable, prior year-end	8,200
Salaries and wages payable, current year-end	10,900

   a. $252,300

   b. $257,700

   c. $255,000

   d. $274,100

   e. $235,900

5. The following information is available for a company. What amount of cash is paid for merchandise for the current year?

Cost of goods sold	$545,000
Merchandise inventory, prior year-end	105,000
Merchandise inventory, current year-end	112,000
Accounts payable, prior year-end	98,500
Accounts payable, current year-end	101,300

   a. $545,000

   b. $554,800

   c. $540,800

   d. $535,200

   e. $549,200

$^{A(B)}$ *Superscript letter A (B) denotes assignments based on Appendix 16A (16B).*

🔲 Icon denotes assignments that involve decision making.

Discussion Questions

1. What is the reporting purpose of the statement of cash flows? Identify at least two questions that this statement can answer.

2. Describe the direct method of reporting cash flows from operating activities.

3. When a statement of cash flows is prepared using the direct method, what are some of the operating cash flows?

4. Describe the indirect method of reporting cash flows from operating activities.

5. What are some investing activities reported on the statement of cash flows?

6. What are some financing activities reported on the statement of cash flows?

7. Where on the statement of cash flows is the payment of cash dividends reported?

8. Assume that a company purchases land for $100,000, paying $20,000 cash and borrowing the remainder with a long-term note payable. How should this transaction be reported on a statement of cash flows?

9. On June 3, a company borrows $50,000 cash by giving its bank a 160-day, interest-bearing note. On the statement of cash flows, where should this be reported?

10. If a company reports positive net income for the year, can it also show a net cash outflow from operating activities? Explain.

11. Is depreciation a source of cash flow?

12. Refer to **Research In Motion**'s statement of cash flows in Appendix A. (a) Which method is used **RIM** to compute its net cash provided by operating activities?

(b) While its balance sheet shows an increase in working capital (current assets less current liabilities) from fiscal years 2009 to 2010, why is this increase in working capital subtracted when computing net cash provided by operating activities for the year ended February 27, 2010?

13. Refer to **Palm**'s statement of cash flows in Appendix A. What are its cash flows from financing **Palm** activities for the year ended May 31, 2009? List items and amounts.

14. Refer to **Nokia**'s statement of cash flows in Appendix A. List its cash flows from operating **NOKIA** activities, investing activities, and financing activities.

15. Refer to **Apple**'s statement of cash flows in Appendix A. What investing activities result in cash **Apple** outflows for the year ended September 26, 2009? List items and amounts.

---

connect

QUICK STUDY

QS 16-1

Transaction classification by activity

C1

Classify the following cash flows as operating, investing, or financing activities.

1. Paid cash for property taxes on building.

2. Paid cash dividends.

3. Paid cash for wages and salaries.

4. Purchased inventories for cash.

5. Received cash payments from customers.

6. Received cash from sale of land at a loss.

7. Received cash interest on a note.

8. Paid cash interest on outstanding notes.

9. Issued common stock for cash.

10. Sold long-term investments for cash.

QS 16-2

Statement of cash flows

C1

The statement of cash flows is one of the four primary financial statements.

1. Describe the content and layout of a statement of cash flows, including its three sections.

2. List at least three transactions classified as significant noncash financing and investing activities in the statement of cash flows.

3. List at least three transactions classified as financing activities in a statement of cash flows.

4. List at least three transactions classified as investing activities in a statement of cash flows.

QS 16-3

Computing cash from operations (indirect)

P2

Use the following information to determine this company's cash flows from operating activities using the indirect method.

LING COMPANY
Selected Balance Sheet Information
December 31, 2011 and 2010

	2011	2010
Current assets		
Cash	$338,600	$107,200
Accounts receivable	100,000	128,000
Inventory	240,000	216,400
Current liabilities		
Accounts payable	121,600	102,800
Income taxes payable	8,200	8,800

LING COMPANY
Income Statement
For Year Ended December 31, 2011

Sales		$2,060,000
Cost of goods sold		1,326,400
Gross profit		733,600
Operating expenses		
Depreciation expense	$144,000	
Other expenses	486,000	630,000
Income before taxes		103,600
Income taxes expense		30,800
Net income		$ 72,800

The following selected information is from Mooney Company's comparative balance sheets.

QS 16-4
Computing cash from asset sales
P3

At December 31	2011	2010
Furniture	$155,000	$ 260,000
Accumulated depreciation—Furniture	(74,400)	(121,400)

The income statement reports depreciation expense for the year of $36,000. Also, furniture costing $105,000 was sold for its book value. Compute the cash received from the sale of furniture.

The following selected information is from the Teeter Company's comparative balance sheets.

QS 16-5
Computing financing cash flows
P3

At December 31	2011	2010
Common stock, $10 par value	$ 310,000	$300,000
Paid-in capital in excess of par	1,134,000	684,000
Retained earnings	627,000	575,000

The company's net income for the year ended December 31, 2011, was $196,000.
1. Compute the cash received from the sale of its common stock during 2011.
2. Compute the cash paid for dividends during 2011.

For each of the following separate cases, compute cash flows from operations. The list includes all balance sheet accounts related to operating activities.

QS 16-6
Computing cash flows from
operations (indirect)
P2

	Case A	Case B	Case C
Net income	$ 20,000	$125,000	$105,000
Depreciation expense	60,000	16,000	48,000
Accounts receivable increase (decrease)	80,000	40,000	(8,000)
Inventory increase (decrease)	(40,000)	(20,000)	21,000
Accounts payable increase (decrease)	28,000	(44,000)	16,000
Accrued liabilities increase (decrease)	(88,000)	10,000	(16,000)

Compute cash flows from investing activities using the following company information.

QS 16-7
Computing cash flows from
investing
P3

Sale of short-term investments	$16,000
Cash collections from customers	44,000
Purchase of used equipment	10,000
Depreciation expense	6,000

Compute cash flows from financing activities using the following company information.

QS 16-8
Computing cash flows from
financing
P3

Additional short-term borrowings	$88,000
Purchase of short-term investments	25,000
Cash dividends paid	32,000
Interest paid	17,000

QS 16-9

Computing cash from operations (indirect) P2

Use the following balance sheets and income statement to answer QS 16-9 through QS 16-14.

Use the indirect method to prepare the cash provided or used from operating activities section only of the statement of cash flows for this company.

ORWELL, INC. Comparative Balance Sheets December 31, 2011		
	2011	**2010**
Assets		
Cash	$ 95,800	$ 25,000
Accounts receivable, net	42,000	52,000
Inventory	86,800	96,800
Prepaid expenses	6,400	5,200
Furniture	110,000	120,000
Accum. depreciation—Furniture	(18,000)	(10,000)
Total assets	$323,000	$289,000
Liabilities and Equity		
Accounts payable	$ 16,000	$ 22,000
Wages payable	10,000	6,000
Income taxes payable	2,400	3,600
Notes payable (long-term)	30,000	70,000
Common stock, $5 par value	230,000	180,000
Retained earnings	34,600	7,400
Total liabilities and equity	$323,000	$289,000

ORWELL, INC. Income Statement For Year Ended December 31, 2011		
Sales		$468,000
Cost of goods sold		312,000
Gross profit		156,000
Operating expenses		
Depreciation expense	$38,600	
Other expenses	57,000	95,600
Income before taxes		60,400
Income taxes expense		24,600
Net income		$ 35,800

QS 16-10

Computing cash from asset sales

P3

Refer to the data in QS 16-9.
Furniture costing $54,000 is sold at its book value in 2011. Acquisitions of furniture total $44,000 cash, on which no depreciation is necessary because it is acquired at year-end. What is the cash inflow related to the sale of furniture?

QS 16-11

Computing financing cash outflows P3

Refer to the data in QS 16-9.
1. Assume that all common stock is issued for cash. What amount of cash dividends is paid during 2011?
2. Assume that no additional notes payable are issued in 2011. What cash amount is paid to reduce the notes payable balance in 2011?

QS 16-12ᴮ

Computing cash received from customers P5

Refer to the data in QS 16-9.
1. How much cash is received from sales to customers for year 2011?
2. What is the net increase or decrease in cash for year 2011?

QS 16-13ᴮ

Computing operating cash outflows P5

Refer to the data in QS 16-9.
1. How much cash is paid to acquire merchandise inventory during year 2011?
2. How much cash is paid for operating expenses during year 2011?

QS 16-14ᴮ

Computing cash from operations (direct) P5

Refer to the data in QS 16-9.
Use the direct method to prepare the cash provided or used from operating activities section only of the statement of cash flows for this company.

QS 16-15

Analyses of sources and uses of cash A1

Financial data from three competitors in the same industry follow.
1. Which of the three competitors is in the strongest position as shown by its statement of cash flows?
2. Analyze and compare the strength of Z-Best's cash flow on total assets ratio to that of Lopez.

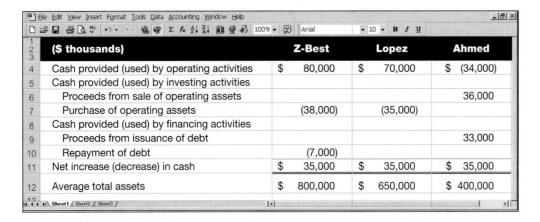

($ thousands)	Z-Best	Lopez	Ahmed
Cash provided (used) by operating activities	$ 80,000	$ 70,000	$ (34,000)
Cash provided (used) by investing activities			
Proceeds from sale of operating assets			36,000
Purchase of operating assets	(38,000)	(35,000)	
Cash provided (used) by financing activities			
Proceeds from issuance of debt			33,000
Repayment of debt	(7,000)		
Net increase (decrease) in cash	$ 35,000	$ 35,000	$ 35,000
Average total assets	$ 800,000	$ 650,000	$ 400,000

When a spreadsheet for a statement of cash flows is prepared, all changes in noncash balance sheet accounts are fully explained on the spreadsheet. Explain how these noncash balance sheet accounts are used to fully account for cash flows on a spreadsheet.

QS 16-16ᴬ
Noncash accounts on a spreadsheet P4

Use the following financial statements and additional information to (1) prepare a statement of cash flows for the year ended December 31, 2012, using the *indirect method,* and (2) analyze and briefly discuss the statement prepared in part 1 with special attention to operating activities and to the company's cash level.

QS 16-17
Preparation of statement of cash flows (indirect)
P1

KRUG INC.
Comparative Balance Sheets
December 31, 2012 and 2011

	2012	2011
Assets		
Cash	$ 26,400	$ 30,550
Accounts receivable, net	14,050	12,150
Inventory	90,100	70,150
Equipment	49,900	44,500
Accum. depreciation—Equipment	(22,500)	(18,300)
Total assets	$157,950	$139,050
Liabilities and Equity		
Accounts payable	$ 23,350	$ 25,400
Salaries payable	1,050	600
Common stock, no par value	107,000	100,000
Retained earnings	26,550	13,050
Total liabilities and equity	$157,950	$139,050

KRUG INC.
Income Statement
For Year Ended December 31, 2012

Sales		$47,575
Cost of goods sold		(17,950)
Gross profit		29,625
Operating expenses		
Depreciation expense	$4,200	
Other expenses	8,550	
Total operating expense		12,750
Income before taxes		16,875
Income tax expense		3,375
Net income		$13,500

Additional Information

a. No dividends are declared or paid in 2012.

b. Issued additional stock for $7,000 cash in 2012.

c. Purchased equipment for cash in 2012; no equipment was sold in 2012.

Answer each of the following related to international accounting standards.

1. Which method, indirect or direct, is acceptable for reporting operating cash flows under IFRS?

2. For each of the following four cash flows, identify whether it is reported under the operating, investing, or financing section (or some combination) within the indirect format of the statement of cash flows reported under IFRS and under U.S. GAAP.

QS 16-18
International cash flow disclosures
C1

Cash Flow Source	US GAAP Reporting	IFRS Reporting
a. Interest paid		
b. Dividends paid		
c. Interest received		
d. Dividends received		

EXERCISES

Exercise 16-1

Cash flow from operations (indirect)

P2

Rasheed Company reports net income of $390,000 for the year ended December 31, 2011. It also reports $70,000 depreciation expense and a $10,000 gain on the sale of machinery. Its comparative balance sheets reveal a $30,000 increase in accounts receivable, $16,000 increase in accounts payable, $8,000 decrease in prepaid expenses, and $12,000 decrease in wages payable.

Required

Prepare only the operating activities section of the statement of cash flows for 2011 using the *indirect method*.

Exercise 16-2

Cash flow classification (indirect)

C1

The following transactions and events occurred during the year. Assuming that this company uses the *indirect method* to report cash provided by operating activities, indicate where each item would appear on its statement of cash flows by placing an *x* in the appropriate column.

	Statement of Cash Flows			Noncash Investing and Financing Activities	Not Reported on Statement or in Notes
	Operating Activities	Investing Activities	Financing Activities		
a. Accounts receivable decreased in the year	___	___	___	___	___
b. Purchased land by issuing common stock	___	___	___	___	___
c. Paid cash to purchase inventory	___	___	___	___	___
d. Sold equipment for cash, yielding a loss	___	___	___	___	___
e. Accounts payable decreased in the year	___	___	___	___	___
f. Income taxes payable increased in the year	___	___	___	___	___
g. Declared and paid a cash dividend	___	___	___	___	___
h. Recorded depreciation expense	___	___	___	___	___
i. Paid cash to settle long-term note payable	___	___	___	___	___
j. Prepaid expenses increased in the year	___	___	___	___	___

Exercise 16-3^B

Cash flow classification (direct)

C1 P5

The following transactions and events occurred during the year. Assuming that this company uses the *direct method* to report cash provided by operating activities, indicate where each item would appear on the statement of cash flows by placing an *x* in the appropriate column.

	Statement of Cash Flows			Noncash Investing and Financing Activities	Not Reported on Statement or in Notes
	Operating Activities	Investing Activities	Financing Activities		
a. Accepted six-month note receivable in exchange for plant assets	___	___	___	___	___
b. Recorded depreciation expense	___	___	___	___	___
c. Paid cash to acquire treasury stock	___	___	___	___	___
d. Collected cash from sales	___	___	___	___	___
e. Borrowed cash from bank by signing a nine-month note payable	___	___	___	___	___
f. Paid cash to purchase a patent	___	___	___	___	___
g. Retired long-term notes payable by issuing common stock	___	___	___	___	___
h. Paid cash toward accounts payable	___	___	___	___	___
i. Sold inventory for cash	___	___	___	___	___
j. Paid cash dividend that was declared in a prior period	___	___	___	___	___

Roney Company's calendar-year 2011 income statement shows the following: Net Income, $364,000; Depreciation Expense, $45,000; Amortization Expense, $8,200; Gain on Sale of Plant Assets, $7,000. An examination of the company's current assets and current liabilities reveals the following changes (all from operating activities): Accounts Receivable decrease, $18,100; Merchandise Inventory decrease, $52,000; Prepaid Expenses increase, $3,700; Accounts Payable decrease, $9,200; Other Payables increase, $1,400. Use the *indirect method* to compute cash flow from operating activities.

Exercise 16-4

Cash flows from operating activities (indirect)

P2

For each of the following three separate cases, use the information provided about the calendar-year 2012 operations of Sahim Company to compute the required cash flow information.

Exercise 16-5^B

Computation of cash flows (direct)

P5

Case A: Compute cash received from customers:	
Sales	$510,000
Accounts receivable, December 31, 2011	25,200
Accounts receivable, December 31, 2012	34,800
Case B: Compute cash paid for rent:	
Rent expense	$140,800
Rent payable, December 31, 2011	8,800
Rent payable, December 31, 2012	7,200
Case C: Compute cash paid for merchandise:	
Cost of goods sold	$528,000
Merchandise inventory, December 31, 2011	159,600
Accounts payable, December 31, 2011	67,800
Merchandise inventory, December 31, 2012	131,400
Accounts payable, December 31, 2012	84,000

Use the following income statement and information about changes in noncash current assets and current liabilities to prepare only the cash flows from operating activities section of the statement of cash flows using the *indirect* method.

Exercise 16-6

Cash flows from operating activities (indirect)

P2

BEKHAM COMPANY		
Income Statement		
For Year Ended December 31, 2011		
Sales		$1,818,000
Cost of goods sold		891,000
Gross profit		927,000
Operating expenses		
Salaries expense	$248,535	
Depreciation expense	43,200	
Rent expense	48,600	
Amortization expenses—Patents	5,400	
Utilities expense	19,125	364,860
		562,140
Gain on sale of equipment		7,200
Net income		$ 569,340

Changes in current asset and current liability accounts for the year that relate to operations follow.

Accounts receivable	$40,500 increase	Accounts payable	$13,500 decrease
Merchandise inventory	27,000 increase	Salaries payable	4,500 decrease

Refer to the information about Bekham Company in Exercise 16-6.
Use the *direct method* to prepare only the cash provided or used by operating activities section of the statement of cash flows for this company.

Exercise 16-7^B

Cash flows from operating activities (direct) P5

Exercise 16-8

Cash flows from investing activities

P3

Use the following information to determine this company's cash flows from investing activities.

a. Sold land costing $315,000 for $400,000 cash, yielding a gain of $15,000.

b. Paid $106,000 cash for a new truck.

c. Equipment with a book value of $80,500 and an original cost of $165,000 was sold at a loss of $34,000.

d. Long-term investments in stock were sold for $94,700 cash, yielding a gain of $15,750.

Exercise 16-9

Cash flows from financing activities

P3

Use the following information to determine this company's cash flows from financing activities.

a. Net income was $472,000.

b. Issued common stock for $75,000 cash.

c. Paid cash dividend of $13,000.

d. Paid $120,000 cash to settle a note payable at its $120,000 maturity value.

e. Paid $118,000 cash to acquire its treasury stock.

f. Purchased equipment for $92,000 cash.

Exercise 16-10

Preparation of statement of cash flows (indirect)   P1

Use the following financial statements and additional information to (1) prepare a statement of cash flows for the year ended June 30, 2011, using the *indirect method,* and (2) compute the company's cash flow on total assets ratio for its fiscal year 2011.

GECKO INC.		
Comparative Balance Sheets		
June 30, 2011 and 2010		
	2011	**2010**
Assets		
Cash	$ 85,800	$ 45,000
Accounts receivable, net	70,000	52,000
Inventory	66,800	96,800
Prepaid expenses	5,400	5,200
Equipment	130,000	120,000
Accum. depreciation—Equipment	(28,000)	(10,000)
Total assets	$330,000	$309,000
Liabilities and Equity		
Accounts payable	$ 26,000	$ 32,000
Wages payable	7,000	16,000
Income taxes payable	2,400	3,600
Notes payable (long term)	40,000	70,000
Common stock, $5 par value	230,000	180,000
Retained earnings	24,600	7,400
Total liabilities and equity	$330,000	$309,000

GECKO INC.	
Income Statement	
For Year Ended June 30, 2011	
Sales	$668,000
Cost of goods sold	412,000
Gross profit	256,000
Operating expenses	
Depreciation expense	$58,600
Other expenses	67,000
Total operating expenses	125,600
	130,400
Other gains (losses)	
Gain on sale of equipment	2,000
Income before taxes	132,400
Income taxes expense	45,640
Net income	$ 86,760

Additional Information

a. A $30,000 note payable is retired at its $30,000 carrying (book) value in exchange for cash.

b. The only changes affecting retained earnings are net income and cash dividends paid.

c. New equipment is acquired for $58,600 cash.

d. Received cash for the sale of equipment that had cost $48,600, yielding a $2,000 gain.

e. Prepaid Expenses and Wages Payable relate to Other Expenses on the income statement.

f. All purchases and sales of merchandise inventory are on credit.

Check   (b) Cash dividends, $69,560

(d) Cash from equip. sale, $10,000

Refer to the data in Exercise 16-10.

Using the *direct method,* prepare the statement of cash flows for the year ended June 30, 2011.

Exercise 16-11B

Preparation of statement of cash flows (direct)

P1

Use the following information about the cash flows of Kansas Company to prepare a complete statement of cash flows (*direct method*) for the year ended December 31, 2011. Use a note disclosure for any noncash investing and financing activities.

Exercise 16-12B

Preparation of statement of cash flows (direct) and supporting note

P1

Cash and cash equivalents balance, December 31, 2010	$ 25,000
Cash and cash equivalents balance, December 31, 2011	70,000
Cash received as interest	2,500
Cash paid for salaries	72,500
Bonds payable retired by issuing common stock (no gain or loss on retirement)	187,500
Cash paid to retire long-term notes payable	125,000
Cash received from sale of equipment	61,250
Cash received in exchange for six-month note payable	25,000
Land purchased by issuing long-term note payable	106,250
Cash paid for store equipment	23,750
Cash dividends paid	15,000
Cash paid for other expenses	40,000
Cash received from customers	485,000
Cash paid for merchandise	252,500

The following summarized Cash T-account reflects the total debits and total credits to the Cash account of Texas Corporation for calendar year 2011.

(1) Use this information to prepare a complete statement of cash flows for year 2011. The cash provided or used by operating activities should be reported using the *direct method.*

(2) Refer to the statement of cash flows prepared for part 1 to answer the following questions *a* through *d*: (*a*) Which section—operating, investing, or financing—shows the largest cash (i) inflow and (ii) outflow? (*b*) What is the largest individual item among the investing cash outflows? (*c*) Are the cash proceeds larger from issuing notes or issuing stock? (*d*) Does the company have a net cash inflow or outflow from borrowing activities?

Exercise 16-13B

Preparation of statement of cash flows (direct) from Cash T-account

P1

Accounting System:		_ □ ×
File Edit Maintain Tasks Analysis Options Reports Window Help		

Cash			_ □ ×
Balance, Dec. 31, 2010	135,200		
Receipts from customers	6,000,000	Payments for merchandise	1,590,000
Receipts from dividends	208,400	Payments for wages	550,000
Receipts from land sale	220,000	Payments for rent	320,000
Receipts from machinery sale	710,000	Payments for interest	218,000
Receipts from issuing stock	1,540,000	Payments for taxes	450,000
Receipts from borrowing	2,600,000	Payments for machinery	2,236,000
		Payments for long-term investments	2,260,000
		Payments for note payable	386,000
		Payments for dividends	500,000
		Payments for treasury stock	218,000
Balance, Dec. 31, 2011	$?		

Sales   Purchases   General Ledger   Payroll   Inventory   Company   Analysis

Exercise 16-14

Reporting cash flows from operations (indirect)

P2

Harold Company reports the following information for its recent calendar year.

Sales	$70,000
Expenses	
Cost of goods sold	40,000
Salaries expense	12,000
Depreciation expense	6,000
Net income	$12,000
Accounts receivable increase	$ 9,000
Inventory decrease	3,000
Salaries payable increase	800

Required

Prepare the operating activities section of the statement of cash flows for Harold Company using the indirect method.

Exercise 16-15

Reporting and interpreting cash flows from operations (indirect)

P2

Oregon Company disclosed the following information for its recent calendar year.

Revenues	$100,000
Expenses	
Salaries expense	68,000
Utilities expense	28,000
Depreciation expense	29,200
Other expenses	6,800
Net loss	$ (32,000)
Accounts receivable decrease	$ 28,000
Purchased a machine	20,000
Salaries payable increase	26,000
Other accrued liabilities decrease	16,000

Required

1. Prepare the operating activities section of the statement of cash flows using the indirect method.
2. What were the major reasons that this company was able to report a net loss but positive cash flow from operations?
3. Of the potential causes of differences between cash flow from operations and net income, which are the most important to investors?

Exercise 16-16

Analyses of cash flow on total assets   A1

A company reported average total assets of $248,000 in 2010 and $302,000 in 2011. Its net operating cash flow in 2010 was $20,575 and $27,750 in 2011. Calculate its cash flow on total assets ratio for both years. Comment on the results and any change in performance.

Exercise 16-17

Cash flows spreadsheet (indirect method)

P4

Complete the following spreadsheet in preparation of the statement of cash flows. (The statement of cash flows is not required.) Prepare the spreadsheet as in Exhibit 16A.1; report operating activities under the indirect method. Identify the debits and credits in the Analysis of Changes columns with letters that correspond to the following transactions *a* through *e*.

a. Net income for the year was $30,000.

b. Dividends of $10,000 cash were declared and paid.

c. Stylish's only noncash expense was $50,000 of depreciation.

d. The company purchased plant assets for $70,000 cash.

e. Notes payable of $40,000 were issued for $40,000 cash.

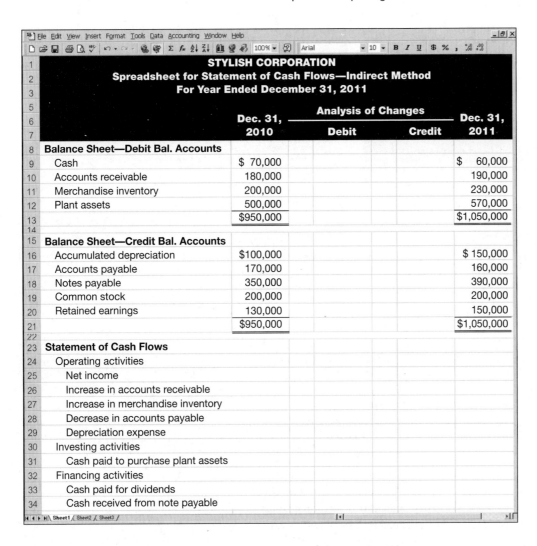

| | | | |

STYLISH CORPORATION
Spreadsheet for Statement of Cash Flows—Indirect Method
For Year Ended December 31, 2011

| | | Dec. 31, 2010 | Analysis of Changes | | Dec. 31, 2011 |
			Debit	Credit	
8	**Balance Sheet—Debit Bal. Accounts**				
9	Cash	$ 70,000			$ 60,000
10	Accounts receivable	180,000			190,000
11	Merchandise inventory	200,000			230,000
12	Plant assets	500,000			570,000
13		$950,000			$1,050,000
14					
15	**Balance Sheet—Credit Bal. Accounts**				
16	Accumulated depreciation	$100,000			$ 150,000
17	Accounts payable	170,000			160,000
18	Notes payable	350,000			390,000
19	Common stock	200,000			200,000
20	Retained earnings	130,000			150,000
21		$950,000			$1,050,000
22					
23	**Statement of Cash Flows**				
24	Operating activities				
25	Net income				
26	Increase in accounts receivable				
27	Increase in merchandise inventory				
28	Decrease in accounts payable				
29	Depreciation expense				
30	Investing activities				
31	Cash paid to purchase plant assets				
32	Financing activities				
33	Cash paid for dividends				
34	Cash received from note payable				

Peugeot S.A. reports the following financial information for the year ended December 31, 2008 (euros in millions). Prepare its statement of cash flows under the indirect method.

Exercise 16-18
Statement of cash flows
under IFRS (indirect)

P1

Net loss	€ 500	Cash from sales of treasury stock and other	€ 812
Depreciation and amortization	3,679	Cash paid for dividends	361
Gains on disposals and other	(362)	Cash from disposal of plant assets and intangibles	88
Net increase in current assets	(417)	Cash paid for plant assets and intangibles	(3,331)
Net decrease in current liabilities ...	(2,338)	Cash and cash equivalents, December 31, 2007	5,937

connect

Kazaam Company, a merchandiser, recently completed its calendar-year 2011 operations. For the year, (1) all sales are credit sales, (2) all credits to Accounts Receivable reflect cash receipts from customers, (3) all purchases of inventory are on credit, (4) all debits to Accounts Payable reflect cash payments for inventory, and (5) Other Expenses are paid in advance and are initially debited to Prepaid Expenses. The company's balance sheets and income statement follow.

PROBLEM SET A

Problem 16-1A
Statement of cash flows
(indirect method)

A1 P1 P2 P3

KAZAAM COMPANY
Comparative Balance Sheets
December 31, 2011 and 2010

	2011	2010
Assets		
Cash	$ 53,875	$ 76,625
Accounts receivable	65,000	49,625
Merchandise inventory	273,750	252,500
Prepaid expenses	5,375	6,250
Equipment	159,500	110,000
Accum. depreciation—Equipment	(34,625)	(44,000)
Total assets	$522,875	$451,000
Liabilities and Equity		
Accounts payable	$ 88,125	$116,625
Short-term notes payable	10,000	6,250
Long-term notes payable	93,750	53,750
Common stock, $5 par value	168,750	156,250
Paid-in capital in excess of par, common stock	32,500	0
Retained earnings	129,750	118,125
Total liabilities and equity	$522,875	$451,000

KAZAAM COMPANY
Income Statement
For Year Ended December 31, 2011

Sales		$496,250
Cost of goods sold		250,000
Gross profit		246,250
Operating expenses		
Depreciation expense	$ 18,750	
Other expenses.................	136,500	155,250
Other gains (losses)		
Loss on sale of equipment		5,125
Income before taxes		85,875
Income taxes expense		12,125
Net income		$ 73,750

Additional Information on Year 2011 Transactions

a. The loss on the cash sale of equipment was $5,125 (details in *b*).

b. Sold equipment costing $46,875, with accumulated depreciation of $28,125, for $13,625 cash.

c. Purchased equipment costing $96,375 by paying $25,000 cash and signing a long-term note payable for the balance.

d. Borrowed $3,750 cash by signing a short-term note payable.

e. Paid $31,375 cash to reduce the long-term notes payable.

f. Issued 2,500 shares of common stock for $18 cash per share.

g. Declared and paid cash dividends of $62,125.

Required

Check Cash from operating activities, $33,375

1. Prepare a complete statement of cash flows; report its operating activities using the *indirect method*. Disclose any noncash investing and financing activities in a note.

Analysis Component

2. Analyze and discuss the statement of cash flows prepared in part 1, giving special attention to the wisdom of the cash dividend payment.

Problem 16-2A[B]
Statement of cash flows (direct method) P1 P3 P5

Check Cash used in financing activities, $(44,750)

Refer to Kazaam Company's financial statements and related information in Problem 16-1A.

Required

Prepare a complete statement of cash flows; report its operating activities according to the *direct method*. Disclose any noncash investing and financing activities in a note.

Problem 16-3A[A]
Cash flows spreadsheet (indirect method)

P1 P2 P3 P4

Refer to the information reported about Kazaam Company in Problem 16-1A.

Required

Prepare a complete statement of cash flows using a spreadsheet as in Exhibit 16A.1; report its operating activities using the indirect method. Identify the debits and credits in the Analysis of Changes columns with letters that correspond to the following list of transactions and events.

a. Net income was $73,750.

b. Accounts receivable increased.

c. Merchandise inventory increased.

d. Prepaid expenses decreased.

e. Accounts payable decreased.

f. Depreciation expense was $18,750.

g. Sold equipment costing $46,875, with accumulated depreciation of $28,125, for $13,625 cash. This yielded a loss of $5,125.

h. Purchased equipment costing $96,375 by paying $25,000 cash and **(i.)** by signing a long-term note payable for the balance.

j. Borrowed $3,750 cash by signing a short-term note payable.

k. Paid $31,375 cash to reduce the long-term notes payable.

l. Issued 2,500 shares of common stock for $18 cash per share.

m. Declared and paid cash dividends of $62,125.

Check Analysis of Changes column totals, $515,375

Galley Corp., a merchandiser, recently completed its 2011 operations. For the year, (1) all sales are credit sales, (2) all credits to Accounts Receivable reflect cash receipts from customers, (3) all purchases of inventory are on credit, (4) all debits to Accounts Payable reflect cash payments for inventory, (5) Other Expenses are all cash expenses, and (6) any change in Income Taxes Payable reflects the accrual and cash payment of taxes. The company's balance sheets and income statement follow.

Problem 16-4A
Statement of cash flows (indirect method)
P1 P2 P3

mhhe.com/wildFAP20e

GALLEY CORPORATION
Comparative Balance Sheets
December 31, 2011 and 2010

	2011	2010
Assets		
Cash	$ 174,000	$117,000
Accounts receivable	93,000	81,000
Merchandise inventory	609,000	534,000
Equipment	333,000	297,000
Accum. depreciation—Equipment	(156,000)	(102,000)
Total assets	$1,053,000	$927,000
Liabilities and Equity		
Accounts payable	$ 69,000	$ 96,000
Income taxes payable	27,000	24,000
Common stock, $2 par value	582,000	558,000
Paid-in capital in excess of par value, common stock	198,000	162,000
Retained earnings	177,000	87,000
Total liabilities and equity	$1,053,000	$927,000

GALLEY CORPORATION
Income Statement
For Year Ended December 31, 2011

Sales		$1,992,000
Cost of goods sold		1,194,000
Gross profit		798,000
Operating expenses		
Depreciation expense	$ 54,000	
Other expenses	501,000	555,000
Income before taxes		243,000
Income taxes expense		42,000
Net income		$ 201,000

Additional Information on Year 2011 Transactions

a. Purchased equipment for $36,000 cash.

b. Issued 12,000 shares of common stock for $5 cash per share.

c. Declared and paid $111,000 in cash dividends.

Required

Prepare a complete statement of cash flows; report its cash inflows and cash outflows from operating activities according to the *indirect method*.

Check Cash from operating activities, $144,000

Refer to Galley Corporation's financial statements and related information in Problem 16-4A.

Required

Prepare a complete statement of cash flows; report its cash flows from operating activities according to the *direct method*.

Problem 16-5A[B]
Statement of cash flows (direct method) P1 P3 P5

mhhe.com/wildFAP20e

Check Cash used in financing activities, $(51,000)

Problem 16-6A[A]
Cash flows spreadsheet
(indirect method)

P1 P2 P3 P4

mhhe.com/wildFAP20e

Refer to the information reported about Galley Corporation in Problem 16-4A.

Required

Prepare a complete statement of cash flows using a spreadsheet as in Exhibit 16A.1; report operating activities under the indirect method. Identify the debits and credits in the Analysis of Changes columns with letters that correspond to the following list of transactions and events.

a. Net income was $201,000.

b. Accounts receivable increased.

c. Merchandise inventory increased.

d. Accounts payable decreased.

e. Income taxes payable increased.

f. Depreciation expense was $54,000.

g. Purchased equipment for $36,000 cash.

Check Analysis of Changes column totals, $579,000

h. Issued 12,000 shares at $5 cash per share.

i. Declared and paid $111,000 of cash dividends.

Problem 16-7A
Computing cash flows from operations (indirect)

P2

Rapture Company's 2011 income statement and selected balance sheet data at December 31, 2010 and 2011, follow ($ thousands).

RAPTURE COMPANY Selected Balance Sheet Accounts		
At December 31	2011	2010
Accounts receivable	$380	$390
Inventory	99	77
Accounts payable...........	120	130
Salaries payable	44	35
Utilities payable	11	8
Prepaid insurance	13	14
Prepaid rent	11	9

RAPTURE COMPANY Income Statement For Year Ended December 31, 2011	
Sales revenue	$58,600
Expenses	
Cost of goods sold	21,000
Depreciation expense	6,000
Salaries expense	11,000
Rent expense	2,500
Insurance expense	1,900
Interest expense	1,800
Utilities expense	1,400
Net income	$13,000

Required

Check Cash from operating activities, $18,989

Prepare the cash flows from operating activities section only of the company's 2011 statement of cash flows using the indirect method.

Problem 16-8A[B]
Computing cash flows from operations (direct)

P5

Refer to the information in Problem 16-7A.

Required

Prepare the cash flows from operating activities section only of the company's 2011 statement of cash flows using the direct method.

PROBLEM SET B

Problem 16-1B
Statement of cash flows
(indirect method)

A1 P1 P2 P3

Kite Corporation, a merchandiser, recently completed its calendar-year 2011 operations. For the year, (1) all sales are credit sales, (2) all credits to Accounts Receivable reflect cash receipts from customers, (3) all purchases of inventory are on credit, (4) all debits to Accounts Payable reflect cash payments for inventory, and (5) Other Expenses are paid in advance and are initially debited to Prepaid Expenses. The company's balance sheets and income statement follow.

KITE CORPORATION
Comparative Balance Sheets
December 31, 2011 and 2010

	2011	2010
Assets		
Cash	$136,500	$ 71,550
Accounts receivable	74,100	90,750
Merchandise inventory	454,500	490,200
Prepaid expenses	17,100	19,200
Equipment	278,250	216,000
Accum. depreciation—Equipment	(108,750)	(93,000)
Total assets	$851,700	$794,700
Liabilities and Equity		
Accounts payable	$117,450	$123,450
Short-term notes payable	17,250	11,250
Long-term notes payable	112,500	82,500
Common stock, $5 par	465,000	450,000
Paid-in capital in excess of par, common stock	18,000	0
Retained earnings	121,500	127,500
Total liabilities and equity	$851,700	$794,700

KITE CORPORATION
Income Statement
For Year Ended December 31, 2011

Sales		$1,083,000
Cost of goods sold		585,000
Gross profit		498,000
Operating expenses		
Depreciation expense	$ 36,600	
Other expenses	392,850	
Total operating expenses		429,450
		68,550
Other gains (losses)		
Loss on sale of equipment		2,100
Income before taxes		66,450
Income taxes expense		9,450
Net income		$ 57,000

Additional Information on Year 2011 Transactions

a. The loss on the cash sale of equipment was $2,100 (details in *b*).

b. Sold equipment costing $51,000, with accumulated depreciation of $20,850, for $28,050 cash.

c. Purchased equipment costing $113,250 by paying $38,250 cash and signing a long-term note payable for the balance.

d. Borrowed $6,000 cash by signing a short-term note payable.

e. Paid $45,000 cash to reduce the long-term notes payable.

f. Issued 3,000 shares of common stock for $11 cash per share.

g. Declared and paid cash dividends of $63,000.

Required

1. Prepare a complete statement of cash flows; report its operating activities using the *indirect method*. Disclose any noncash investing and financing activities in a note.

Check Cash from operating activities, $144,150

Analysis Component

2. Analyze and discuss the statement of cash flows prepared in part 1, giving special attention to the wisdom of the cash dividend payment.

Refer to Kite Corporation's financial statements and related information in Problem 16-1B.

Required

Prepare a complete statement of cash flows; report its operating activities according to the *direct method*. Disclose any noncash investing and financing activities in a note.

Problem 16-2B[B]
Statement of cash flows
(direct method) P1 P3 P5

Check Cash used in financing activities, $(69,000)

Refer to the information reported about Kite Corporation in Problem 16-1B.

Required

Prepare a complete statement of cash flows using a spreadsheet as in Exhibit 16A.1; report its operating activities using the *indirect method*. Identify the debits and credits in the Analysis of Changes columns with letters that correspond to the following list of transactions and events.

Problem 16-3B[A]
Cash flows spreadsheet
(indirect method)

P1 P2 P3 P4

a. Net income was $57,000.

b. Accounts receivable decreased.

c. Merchandise inventory decreased.

d. Prepaid expenses decreased.

e. Accounts payable decreased.

f. Depreciation expense was $36,600.

g. Sold equipment costing $51,000, with accumulated depreciation of $20,850, for $28,050 cash. This yielded a loss of $2,100.

h. Purchased equipment costing $113,250 by paying $38,250 cash and **(i.)** by signing a long-term note payable for the balance.

j. Borrowed $6,000 cash by signing a short-term note payable.

k. Paid $45,000 cash to reduce the long-term notes payable.

Check Analysis of Changes column totals, $540,300

l. Issued 3,000 shares of common stock for $11 cash per share.

m. Declared and paid cash dividends of $63,000.

Problem 16-4B
Statement of cash flows
(indirect method)

P1 P2 P3

Taurasi Company, a merchandiser, recently completed its 2011 operations. For the year, (1) all sales are credit sales, (2) all credits to Accounts Receivable reflect cash receipts from customers, (3) all purchases of inventory are on credit, (4) all debits to Accounts Payable reflect cash payments for inventory, (5) Other Expenses are cash expenses, and (6) any change in Income Taxes Payable reflects the accrual and cash payment of taxes. The company's balance sheets and income statement follow.

TAURASI COMPANY
Comparative Balance Sheets
December 31, 2011 and 2010

	2011	2010
Assets		
Cash	$ 53,925	$ 31,800
Accounts receivable	19,425	23,250
Merchandise inventory	175,350	139,875
Equipment	105,450	76,500
Accum. depreciation—Equipment	(48,300)	(30,600)
Total assets	$305,850	$240,825
Liabilities and Equity		
Accounts payable	$ 38,475	$ 35,625
Income taxes payable	4,500	6,750
Common stock, $2 par value	165,000	150,000
Paid-in capital in excess		
of par, common stock	42,000	15,000
Retained earnings	55,875	33,450
Total liabilities and equity	$305,850	$240,825

TAURASI COMPANY
Income Statement
For Year Ended December 31, 2011

Sales		$609,750
Cost of goods sold		279,000
Gross profit		330,750
Operating expenses		
Depreciation expense	$ 17,700	
Other expenses...............	179,775	197,475
Income before taxes		133,275
Income taxes expense		44,850
Net income		$ 88,425

Additional Information on Year 2011 Transactions

a. Purchased equipment for $28,950 cash.

b. Issued 3,000 shares of common stock for $14 cash per share.

c. Declared and paid $66,000 of cash dividends.

Required

Check Cash from operating activities, $75,075

Prepare a complete statement of cash flows; report its cash inflows and cash outflows from operating activities according to the *indirect method*.

Problem 16-5B[B]
Statement of cash flows
(direct method)   P1 P3 P5

Check Cash used by financing activities, $(24,000)

Refer to Taurasi Company's financial statements and related information in Problem 16-4B.

Required

Prepare a complete statement of cash flows; report its cash flows from operating activities according to the *direct method*.

Refer to the information reported about Taurasi Company in Problem 16-4B.

Required

Prepare a complete statement of cash flows using a spreadsheet as in Exhibit 16A.1; report operating activities under the *indirect method*. Identify the debits and credits in the Analysis of Changes columns with letters that correspond to the following list of transactions and events.

a. Net income was $88,425.

b. Accounts receivable decreased.

c. Merchandise inventory increased.

d. Accounts payable increased.

e. Income taxes payable decreased.

f. Depreciation expense was $17,700.

g. Purchased equipment for $28,950 cash.

h. Issued 3,000 shares at $14 cash per share.

i. Declared and paid $66,000 of cash dividends.

Problem 16-6B[A]
Cash flows spreadsheet
(indirect method)

P1 P2 P3 P4

Check Analysis of Changes
column totals, $287,475

Tyra Company's 2011 income statement and selected balance sheet data at December 31, 2010 and 2011, follow ($ thousands).

Problem 16-7B
Computing cash flows from
operations (indirect)

P2

TYRA COMPANY
Income Statement
For Year Ended December 31, 2011

Sales revenue	$412,000
Expenses	
Cost of goods sold	244,000
Depreciation expense	64,000
Salaries expense	30,000
Rent expense	20,000
Insurance expense	5,200
Interest expense	4,800
Utilities expense	4,000
Net income	$ 40,000

TYRA COMPANY
Selected Balance Sheet Accounts

At December 31	2011	2010
Accounts receivable	$820	$700
Inventory	272	296
Accounts payable	480	520
Salaries payable	280	220
Utilities payable	40	0
Prepaid insurance	28	36
Prepaid rent	40	60

Required

Prepare the cash flows from operating activities section only of the company's 2011 statement of cash flows using the indirect method.

Check Cash from operating
activities, $103,992

Refer to the information in Problem 16-7B.

Required

Prepare the cash flows from operating activities section only of the company's 2011 statement of cash flows using the direct method.

Problem 16-8B[B]
Computing cash flows from
operations (direct)

P5

(This serial problem began in Chapter 1 and continues through most of the book. If previous chapter segments were not completed, the serial problem can begin at this point. It is helpful, but not necessary, to use the Working Papers that accompany the book.)

SERIAL PROBLEM
Business Solutions

P1 P2 P3

SP 16 Santana Rey, owner of Business Solutions, decides to prepare a statement of cash flows for her business. (Although the serial problem allowed for various ownership changes in earlier chapters, we will prepare the statement of cash flows using the following financial data.)

<table>
<tr><td colspan="3">

BUSINESS SOLUTIONS
Comparative Balance Sheets
December 31, 2011, and March 31, 2012

</td></tr>
</table>

	2012	2011
Assets		
Cash	$ 68,057	$48,372
Accounts receivable	22,867	5,668
Merchandise inventory	704	0
Computer supplies	2,005	580
Prepaid insurance	1,110	1,665
Prepaid rent	825	825
Office equipment	8,000	8,000
Accumulated depreciation—Office equipment	(800)	(400)
Computer equipment	20,000	20,000
Accumulated depreciation— Computer equipment	(2,500)	(1,250)
Total assets	$120,268	$83,460
Liabilities and Equity		
Accounts payable	$ 0	$ 1,100
Wages payable	875	500
Unearned computer service revenue	0	1,500
Common stock	98,000	73,000
Retained earnings	21,393	7,360
Total liabilities and equity	$120,268	$83,460

<table>
<tr><td colspan="2">

BUSINESS SOLUTIONS
Income Statement
For Three Months Ended March 31, 2012

</td></tr>
</table>

Computer services revenue		$25,307
Net sales		18,693
Total revenue.....................		44,000
Cost of goods sold	$14,052	
Depreciation expense— Office equipment	400	
Depreciation expense— Computer equipment	1,250	
Wages expense	3,250	
Insurance expense	555	
Rent expense	2,475	
Computer supplies expense	1,305	
Advertising expense	600	
Mileage expense	320	
Repairs expense—Computer	960	
Total expenses		25,167
Net income		$18,833

Required

Check Cash flows used by operations: $(515)

Prepare a statement of cash flows for Business Solutions using the *indirect method* for the three months ended March 31, 2012. Recall that the owner Santana Rey contributed $25,000 to the business in exchange for additional stock in the first quarter of 2012 and has received $4,800 in cash dividends.

Beyond the Numbers

REPORTING IN ACTION

A1

RIM

BTN 16-1 Refer to **Research In Motion**'s financial statements in Appendix A to answer the following.

1. Is Research In Motion's statement of cash flows prepared under the direct method or the indirect method? How do you know?
2. For each fiscal year 2010, 2009, and 2008, is the amount of cash provided by operating activities more or less than the cash paid for dividends?
3. What is the largest amount in reconciling the difference between net income and cash flow from operating activities in 2010? In 2009? In 2008?
4. Identify the largest cash inflow and outflow for investing *and* for financing activities in 2010 and in 2009.

Fast Forward

5. Obtain Research In Motion's financial statements for a fiscal year ending after February 27, 2010, from either its Website (**RIM.com**) or the SEC's database (**www.sec.gov**). Since February 27, 2010, what are Research In Motion's largest cash outflows and cash inflows in the investing and in the financing sections of its statement of cash flows?

BTN 16-2   Key figures for **Research In Motion** and **Apple** follow.

COMPARATIVE
ANALYSIS

A1

RIM

Apple

($ millions)	Research In Motion			Apple		
	Current Year	I Year Prior	2 Years Prior	Current Year	I Year Prior	2 Years Prior
Operating cash flows	$ 3,035	$1,452	$1,577	$10,159	$ 9,596	$ 5,470
Total assets	10,204	8,101	5,511	47,501	36,171	25,347

**COMPARATIVE
ANALYSIS**

A1

RIM

Apple

Required

1. Compute the recent two years' cash flow on total assets ratios for Research In Motion and Apple.
2. What does the cash flow on total assets ratio measure?
3. Which company has the highest cash flow on total assets ratio for the periods shown?
4. Does the cash flow on total assets ratio reflect on the quality of earnings? Explain.

BTN 16-3   Lisa Gish is preparing for a meeting with her banker. Her business is finishing its fourth year of operations. In the first year, it had negative cash flows from operations. In the second and third years, cash flows from operations were positive. However, inventory costs rose significantly in year 4, and cash flows from operations will probably be down 25%. Gish wants to secure a line of credit from her banker as a financing buffer. From experience, she knows the banker will scrutinize operating cash flows for years 1 through 4 and will want a projected number for year 5. Gish knows that a steady progression upward in operating cash flows for years 1 through 4 will help her case. She decides to use her discretion as owner and considers several business actions that will turn her operating cash flow in year 4 from a decrease to an increase.

ETHICS CHALLENGE

C1 A1

Required

1. Identify two business actions Gish might take to improve cash flows from operations.
2. Comment on the ethics and possible consequences of Gish's decision to pursue these actions.

BTN 16-4   Your friend, Jessica Willard, recently completed the second year of her business and just received annual financial statements from her accountant. Willard finds the income statement and balance sheet informative but does not understand the statement of cash flows. She says the first section is especially confusing because it contains a lot of additions and subtractions that do not make sense to her. Willard adds, "The income statement tells me the business is more profitable than last year and that's most important. If I want to know how cash changes, I can look at comparative balance sheets."

**COMMUNICATING
IN PRACTICE**

C1

Required

Write a half-page memorandum to your friend explaining the purpose of the statement of cash flows. Speculate as to why the first section is so confusing and how it might be rectified.

BTN 16-5   Access the March 19, 2010, filing of the 10-K report (for fiscal year ending January 30, 2010) of **J. Crew Group, Inc.** (ticker JCG), at www.sec.gov.

**TAKING IT TO
THE NET**

A1

Required

1. Does J. Crew use the direct or indirect method to construct its consolidated statement of cash flows?
2. For the fiscal year ended January 30, 2010, what is the largest item in reconciling the net income to net cash provided by operating activities?
3. In the recent three years, has the company been more successful in generating operating cash flows or in generating net income? Identify the figures to support the answer.
4. In the year ended January 30, 2010, what was the largest cash outflow for investing activities *and* for financing activities?
5. What item(s) does J. Crew report as supplementary cash flow information?
6. Does J. Crew report any noncash financing activities for fiscal year 2010? Identify them, if any.

TEAMWORK IN ACTION

C1 A1 P2 P5

BTN 16-6   Team members are to coordinate and independently answer one question within each of the following three sections. Team members should then report to the team and confirm or correct teammates' answers.

1. Answer *one* of the following questions about the statement of cash flows.

   a. What are this statement's reporting objectives?

   b. What two methods are used to prepare it? Identify similarities and differences between them.

   c. What steps are followed to prepare the statement?

   d. What types of analyses are often made from this statement's information?

2. Identify and explain the adjustment from net income to obtain cash flows from operating activities using the indirect method for *one* of the following items.

   a. Noncash operating revenues and expenses.

   b. Nonoperating gains and losses.

   c. Increases and decreases in noncash current assets.

   d. Increases and decreases in current liabilities.

Note: For teams of more than four, some pairing within teams is necessary. Use as an in-class activity or as an assignment. If used in class, specify a time limit on each part. Conclude with reports to the entire class, using team rotation. Each team can prepare responses on a transparency.

3.ᴮIdentify and explain the formula for computing cash flows from operating activities using the direct method for *one* of the following items.

   a. Cash receipts from sales to customers.

   b. Cash paid for merchandise inventory.

   c. Cash paid for wages and operating expenses.

   d. Cash paid for interest and taxes.

ENTREPRENEURIAL DECISION

C1 A1

BTN 16-7   Review the chapter's opener involving **Animoto** and its four young entrepreneurial owners.

Required

1. In a business such as Animoto, monitoring cash flow is always a priority. Even though Animoto now has thousands in annual sales and earns a positive net income, explain how cash flow can lag behind earnings.

2. Animoto is a closely held corporation. What are potential sources of financing for its future expansion?

C1 A1

BTN 16-8   Jenna and Matt Wilder are completing their second year operating Mountain High, a downhill ski area and resort. Mountain High reports a net loss of $(10,000) for its second year, which includes an $85,000 extraordinary loss from fire. This past year also involved major purchases of plant assets for renovation and expansion, yielding a year-end total asset amount of $800,000. Mountain High's net cash outflow for its second year is $(5,000); a summarized version of its statement of cash flows follows:

Net cash flow provided by operating activities	$295,000
Net cash flow used by investing activities	(310,000)
Net cash flow provided by financing activities	10,000

Required

Write a one-page memorandum to the Wilders evaluating Mountain High's current performance and assessing its future. Give special emphasis to cash flow data and their interpretation.

HITTING THE ROAD

C1

BTN 16-9   Visit **The Motley Fool**'s Website (**Fool.com**). Enter the *Fool's School* (at *Fool.com/School*). Identify and select the link *How to Value Stocks*.

Required

1. Click on *Introduction to Valuation Methods,* and then *Cash-Flow-Based Valuations.* How does the Fool's school define cash flow? What is the school's reasoning for this definition?

2. Per the school's instruction, why do analysts focus on earnings before interest and taxes (EBIT)?

3. Visit other links at this Website that interest you such as "How to Read a Balance Sheet," or find out what the "Fool's Ratio" is. Write a half-page report on what you find.

BTN 16-10   Key comparative information for **Nokia** (www.Nokia.com), which is a leading global manufacturer of mobile devices and services, follows (in EUR).

GLOBAL DECISION

C1

NOKIA
RIM
Apple

(Euro millions)	Current Year	1 Year Prior	2 Years Prior
Operating cash flows	3,247	3,197	7,882
Total assets	35,738	39,582	37,599

Required

1. Compute the recent two years' cash flow on total assets ratio for Nokia.
2. How does Nokia's ratio compare to Research In Motion's and Apple's ratios from BTN 16-2?

ANSWERS TO MULTIPLE CHOICE QUIZ

1. b;

Net income	$15,200
Depreciation expense	10,000
Gain on sale of land	(3,000)
Increase in inventory	(1,500)
Increase in accounts payable	2,850
Net cash provided by operations	$23,550

2. c; cash received from sale of machine is reported as an investing activity.

3. d; FASB requires cash interest paid to be reported under operating.

4. a; Cash paid for salaries and wages = $255,000 + $8,200 − $10,900 = $252,300

5. e; Increase in inventory = $112,000 − $105,000 = $7,000
Increase in accounts payable = $101,300 − $98,500 = $2,800
Cash paid for merchandise = $545,000 + $7,000 − $2,800 = $549,200

17

Analysis of Financial Statements

A Look Back

Chapter 16 focused on reporting and analyzing cash inflows and cash outflows. We explained how to prepare, analyze, and interpret the statement of cash flows.

A Look at This Chapter

This chapter emphasizes the analysis and interpretation of financial statement information. We learn to apply horizontal, vertical, and ratio analyses to better understand company performance and financial condition.

A Look Ahead

Chapter 18 introduces us to managerial accounting. We discuss its purposes, concepts, and roles in helping managers gather and organize information for decisions. We also explain basic management principles.

Learning Objectives

CAP

CONCEPTUAL

C1 Explain the purpose and identify the building blocks of analysis. (p. 686)

C2 Describe standards for comparisons in analysis. (p. 688)

ANALYTICAL

A1 Summarize and report results of analysis. (p. 706)

A2 *Appendix 17A*—Explain the form and assess the content of a complete income statement. (p. 710)

LP17

PROCEDURAL

P1 Explain and apply methods of horizontal analysis. (p. 688)

P2 Describe and apply methods of vertical analysis. (p. 693)

P3 Define and apply ratio analysis. (p. 696)

Motley Fool

"What goes on at The Motley Fool . . . is similar to what goes on in a library"

—**TOM GARDNER** (DAVID GARDNER ON LEFT)

ALEXANDRIA, VA—In Shakespeare's Elizabethan comedy *As You Like It,* only the fool could speak truthfully to the King without getting his head lopped off. Inspired by Shakespeare's stage character, Tom and David Gardner vowed to become modern-day fools who tell it like it is. With under $10,000 in start-up money, the brothers launched **The Motley Fool (Fool.com).** And befitting of a Shakespearean play, the two say they are "dedicated to educating, amusing, and enriching individuals in search of the truth."

The Gardners do not fear the wrath of any King, real or fictional. They are intent on exposing the truth, as they see it, "that the financial world preys on ignorance and fear." As Tom explains, "There is such a great need in the general populace for financial information." Who can argue, given their brilliant success through practically every medium, including their Website, radio shows, newspaper columns, online store, investment newsletters, and global expansion.

Despite the brothers' best efforts, however, ordinary people still do not fully use information contained in financial state-

ments. For instance, discussions keep appearing on The Motley Fool's online bulletin board that can be easily resolved using reliable and available accounting data. So, it would seem that the Fools must continue their work of "educating and enriching" individuals and showing them the advantages of financial statement analysis.

Following The Motley Fool's objectives, this chapter introduces horizontal and vertical analyses—tools used to reveal crucial trends and insights from financial information. It also expands on ratio analysis, which gives insight into a company's financial condition and performance. By arming ourselves with the information contained in this chapter and the investment advice of The Motley Fool, *we* can be sure to not play the fool in today's financial world.

[Sources: *Motley Fool Website,* January 2011; *Entrepreneur,* July 1997; *What to Do with Your Money Now,* June 2002; *USA Weekend,* July 2004; *Washington Post,* November 2007; *Money after 40,* April 2007]

This chapter shows how we use financial statements to evaluate a company's financial performance and condition. We explain financial statement analysis, its basic building blocks, the information available, standards for comparisons, and tools of analysis. Three major analysis tools are presented: horizontal analysis, vertical analysis, and ratio analysis. We apply each of these tools using **Research In Motion**'s financial statements, and we introduce comparative analysis using **Apple** and **Nokia** (and sometimes **Palm**). This chapter expands and organizes the ratio analyses introduced at the end of each chapter.

Analysis of Financial Statements

Basics of Analysis
- Purpose
- Building blocks
- Information
- Standards for comparisons
- Tools

Horizontal Analysis
- Comparative balance sheets
- Comparative income statements
- Trend analysis

Vertical Analysis
- Common-size balance sheet
- Common-size income statement
- Common-size graphics

Ratio Analysis
- Liquidity and efficiency
- Solvency
- Profitability
- Market prospects
- Ratio summary

BASICS OF ANALYSIS

C1 Explain the purpose and identify the building blocks of analysis.

Financial statement analysis applies analytical tools to general-purpose financial statements and related data for making business decisions. It involves transforming accounting data into more useful information. Financial statement analysis reduces our reliance on hunches, guesses, and intuition as well as our uncertainty in decision making. It does not lessen the need for expert judgment; instead, it provides us an effective and systematic basis for making business decisions. This section describes the purpose of financial statement analysis, its information sources, the use of comparisons, and some issues in computations.

Purpose of Analysis

Internal users of accounting information are those involved in strategically managing and operating the company. They include managers, officers, internal auditors, consultants, budget directors, and market researchers. The purpose of financial statement analysis for these users is to provide strategic information to improve company efficiency and effectiveness in providing products and services.

External users of accounting information are *not* directly involved in running the company. They include shareholders, lenders, directors, customers, suppliers, regulators, lawyers, brokers, and the press. External users rely on financial statement analysis to make better and more informed decisions in pursuing their own goals.

Point: Financial statement analysis tools are also used for personal financial investment decisions.

We can identify other uses of financial statement analysis. Shareholders and creditors assess company prospects to make investing and lending decisions. A board of directors analyzes financial statements in monitoring management's decisions. Employees and unions use financial statements in labor negotiations. Suppliers use financial statement information in establishing credit terms. Customers analyze financial statements in deciding whether to establish supply relationships. Public utilities set customer rates by analyzing financial statements. Auditors use financial statements in assessing the "fair presentation" of their clients' financial results. Analyst services such as **Dun & Bradstreet**, **Moody's**, and **Standard & Poor's** use financial statements in making buy-sell recommendations and in setting credit ratings. The common goal of these users is to evaluate company performance and financial condition. This includes evaluating (1) past and current performance, (2) current financial position, and (3) future performance and risk.

Point: Financial statement analysis is a topic on the CPA, CMA, CIA, and CFA exams.

Building Blocks of Analysis

Financial statement analysis focuses on one or more elements of a company's financial condition or performance. Our analysis emphasizes four areas of inquiry—with varying degrees of importance. These four areas are described and illustrated in this chapter and are considered the *building blocks* of financial statement analysis:

- **Liquidity** and **efficiency**—ability to meet short-term obligations and to efficiently generate revenues.
- **Solvency**—ability to generate future revenues and meet long-term obligations.
- **Profitability**—ability to provide financial rewards sufficient to attract and retain financing.
- **Market prospects**—ability to generate positive market expectations.

Applying the building blocks of financial statement analysis involves determining (1) the objectives of analysis and (2) the relative emphasis among the building blocks. We distinguish among these four building blocks to emphasize the different aspects of a company's financial condition or performance, yet we must remember that these areas of analysis are interrelated. For instance, a company's operating performance is affected by the availability of financing and short-term liquidity conditions. Similarly, a company's credit standing is not limited to satisfactory short-term liquidity but depends also on its profitability and efficiency in using assets. Early in our analysis, we need to determine the relative emphasis of each building block. Emphasis and analysis can later change as a result of evidence collected.

▐ Decision Insight

Chips and Brokers The phrase *blue chips* refers to stock of big, profitable companies. The phrase comes from poker; where the most valuable chips are blue. The term *brokers* refers to those who execute orders to buy or sell stock. The term comes from wine retailers—individuals who broach (break) wine casks. ▪

Information for Analysis

Some users, such as managers and regulatory authorities, are able to receive special financial reports prepared to meet their analysis needs. However, most users must rely on **general-purpose financial statements** that include the (1) income statement, (2) balance sheet, (3) statement of stockholders' equity (or statement of retained earnings), (4) statement of cash flows, and (5) notes to these statements.

  Financial reporting refers to the communication of financial information useful for making investment, credit, and other business decisions. Financial reporting includes not only general-purpose financial statements but also information from SEC 10-K or other filings, press releases, shareholders' meetings, forecasts, management letters, auditors' reports, and Webcasts.

  Management's Discussion and Analysis (MD&A) is one example of useful information outside traditional financial statements. **Research In Motion**'s MD&A (available at **RIM.com**), for example, begins with an overview, followed by critical accounting policies and restatements of previous statements. It then discusses operating results followed by financial condition (liquidity, capital resources, and cash flows). The final few parts discuss legal proceedings, market risk of financial instruments, disclosure controls, and internal controls. The MD&A is an excellent starting point in understanding a company's business activities.

▐ Decision Insight

Analysis Online Many Websites offer free access and screening of companies by key numbers such as earnings, sales, and book value. For instance, **Standard & Poor's** has information for more than 10,000 stocks (**www.standardandpoors.com**). ▪

C2 Describe standards for comparisons in analysis.

Standards for Comparisons

When interpreting measures from financial statement analysis, we need to decide whether the measures indicate good, bad, or average performance. To make such judgments, we need standards (benchmarks) for comparisons that include the following:

- *Intracompany*—The company under analysis can provide standards for comparisons based on its own prior performance and relations between its financial items. **Research In Motion**'s current net income, for instance, can be compared with its prior years' net income and in relation to its revenues or total assets.
- *Competitor*—One or more direct competitors of the company being analyzed can provide standards for comparisons. **Coca-Cola**'s profit margin, for instance, can be compared with **PepsiCo**'s profit margin.
- *Industry*—Industry statistics can provide standards of comparisons. Such statistics are available from services such as **Dun & Bradstreet**, **Standard & Poor's**, and **Moody's**.
- *Guidelines (rules of thumb)*—General standards of comparisons can develop from experience. Examples are the 2:1 level for the current ratio or 1:1 level for the acid-test ratio. Guidelines, or rules of thumb, must be carefully applied because context is crucial.

Point: Each chapter's *Reporting in Action* problems engage students in *intracompany* analysis, whereas *Comparative Analysis* problems require competitor analysis (RIM vs. Apple and often vs. Palm).

All of these comparison standards are useful when properly applied, yet measures taken from a selected competitor or group of competitors are often best. Intracompany and industry measures are also important. Guidelines or rules of thumb should be applied with care, and then only if they seem reasonable given past experience and industry norms.

Tools of Analysis

Three of the most common tools of financial statement analysis are

1. **Horizontal analysis**—Comparison of a company's financial condition and performance across time.
2. **Vertical analysis**—Comparison of a company's financial condition and performance to a base amount.
3. **Ratio analysis**—Measurement of key relations between financial statement items.

The remainder of this chapter describes these analysis tools and how to apply them.

Quick Check   Answers — p. 713

1. Who are the intended users of general-purpose financial statements?
2. General-purpose financial statements consist of what information?
3. Which of the following is *least* useful as a basis for comparison when analyzing ratios? (*a*) Company results from a different economic setting. (*b*) Standards from past experience. (*c*) Rule-of-thumb standards. (*d*) Industry averages.
4. What is the preferred basis of comparison for ratio analysis?

HORIZONTAL ANALYSIS

Analysis of any single financial number is of limited value. Instead, much of financial statement analysis involves identifying and describing relations between numbers, groups of numbers, and changes in those numbers. Horizontal analysis refers to examination of financial statement data *across time*. [The term *horizontal analysis* arises from the left-to-right (or right-to-left) movement of our eyes as we review comparative financial statements across time.]

Comparative Statements

P1 Explain and apply methods of horizontal analysis.

Comparing amounts for two or more successive periods often helps in analyzing financial statements. **Comparative financial statements** facilitate this comparison by showing financial amounts in side-by-side columns on a single statement, called a *comparative format*. Using figures from **Research In Motion**'s financial statements, this section explains how to compute dollar changes and percent changes for comparative statements.

Computation of Dollar Changes and Percent Changes   Comparing financial statements over relatively short time periods—two to three years—is often done by analyzing changes in line items. A change analysis usually includes analyzing absolute dollar amount changes and percent changes. Both analyses are relevant because dollar changes can yield large percent changes inconsistent with their importance. For instance, a 50% change from a base figure of $100 is less important than the same percent change from a base amount of $100,000 in the same statement. Reference to dollar amounts is necessary to retain a proper perspective and to assess the importance of changes. We compute the *dollar change* for a financial statement item as follows:

Example: What is a more significant change, a 70% increase on a $1,000 expense or a 30% increase on a $400,000 expense? *Answer:* The 30% increase.

$$\text{Dollar change} = \text{Analysis period amount} - \text{Base period amount}$$

Analysis period is the point or period of time for the financial statements under analysis, and *base period* is the point or period of time for the financial statements used for comparison purposes. The prior year is commonly used as a base period. We compute the *percent change* by dividing the dollar change by the base period amount and then multiplying this quantity by 100 as follows:

$$\text{Percent change} (\%) = \frac{\text{Analysis period amount} - \text{Base period amount}}{\text{Base period amount}} \times 100$$

We can always compute a dollar change, but we must be aware of a few rules in working with percent changes. To illustrate, look at four separate cases in this chart:

Case	Analysis Period	Base Period	Change Analysis Dollar	Change Analysis Percent
A	$ 1,500	$(4,500)	$ 6,000	—
B	(1,000)	2,000	(3,000)	—
C	8,000	—	8,000	—
D	0	10,000	(10,000)	(100%)

When a negative amount appears in the base period and a positive amount in the analysis period (or vice versa), we cannot compute a meaningful percent change; see cases A and B. Also, when no value is in the base period, no percent change is computable; see case C. Finally, when an item has a value in the base period and zero in the analysis period, the decrease is 100 percent; see case D.

Example: When there is a value in the base period and zero in the analysis period, the decrease is 100%. Why isn't the reverse situation an increase of 100%? *Answer:* A 100% increase of zero is still zero.

It is common when using horizontal analysis to compare amounts to either average or median values from prior periods (average and median values smooth out erratic or unusual fluctuations).[1] We also commonly round percents and ratios to one or two decimal places, but practice on this matter is not uniform. Computations are as detailed as necessary, which is judged by whether rounding potentially affects users' decisions. Computations should not be excessively detailed so that important relations are lost among a mountain of decimal points and digits.

Comparative Balance Sheets   Comparative balance sheets consist of balance sheet amounts from two or more balance sheet dates arranged side by side. Its usefulness is often improved by showing each item's dollar change and percent change to highlight large changes.

Analysis of comparative financial statements begins by focusing on items that show large dollar or percent changes. We then try to identify the reasons for these changes and, if possible, determine whether they are favorable or unfavorable. We also follow up on items with small changes when we expected the changes to be large.

Point: Spreadsheet programs can help with horizontal, vertical, and ratio analyses, including graphical depictions of financial relations.

[1] *Median* is the middle value in a group of numbers. For instance, if five prior years' incomes are (in 000s) $15, $19, $18, $20, and $22, the median value is $19. When there are two middle numbers, we can take their average. For instance, if four prior years' sales are (in 000s) $84, $91, $96, and $93, the median is $92 (computed as the average of $91 and $93).

EXHIBIT 17.1

Comparative Balance Sheets

RIM

RESEARCH IN MOTION Comparative Balance Sheets February 27, 2010 and February 28, 2009				
($ thousands)	2010	2009	Dollar Change	Percent Change
Assets				
Cash and cash equivalents	$ 1,550,861	$ 835,546	$ 715,315	85.6%
Short-term investments	360,614	682,666	(322,052)	(47.2)
Accounts receivable, net	2,593,742	2,112,117	481,625	22.8
Other receivables	206,373	157,728	48,645	30.8
Inventories	621,611	682,400	(60,789)	(8.9)
Other current assets.........................	285,539	187,257	98,282	52.5
Deferred income tax asset	193,916	183,872	10,044	5.5
Total current assets.....................	5,812,656	4,841,586	971,070	20.1
Long-term investments	958,248	720,635	237,613	33.0
Property, plant and equipment, net	1,956,581	1,334,648	621,933	46.6
Intangible assets, net	1,326,363	1,066,527	259,836	24.4
Goodwill	150,561	137,572	12,989	9.4
Deferred income tax asset	0	404	(404)	(100.0)
Total assets	$10,204,409	$8,101,372	$2,103,037	26.0
Liabilities				
Accounts payable	$ 615,620	$ 448,339	$ 167,281	37.3%
Accrued liabilities	1,638,260	1,238,602	399,658	32.3
Income taxes payable	95,650	361,460	(265,810)	(73.5)
Deferred revenue	67,573	53,834	13,739	25.5
Deferred income tax liability	14,674	13,116	1,558	11.9
Total current liabilities......................	2,431,777	2,115,351	316,426	15.0
Deferred income tax liability	141,382	87,917	53,465	60.8
Income taxes payable	28,587	23,976	4,611	19.2
Total liabilities	2,601,746	2,227,244	374,502	16.8
Shareholders' Equity				
Capital stock	2,207,609	2,208,235	(626)	0.0
Treasury stock..............................	(94,463)	0	(94,463)	—
Retained earnings	5,274,365	3,545,710	1,728,655	48.8
Additional paid-in capital	164,060	119,726	44,334	37.0
Accumulated other comprehensive income	51,092	457	50,635	11,079
Total stockholders' equity	7,602,663	5,874,128	1,728,535	29.4
Total liabilities and stockholders' equity	$10,204,409	$8,101,372	$2,103,037	26.0

Point: Business consultants use comparative statement analysis to provide management advice.

Exhibit 17.1 shows comparative balance sheets for **Research In Motion** (RIM). A few items stand out. Many asset categories substantially increase, which is probably not surprising because RIM is a growth company. Much of the increase in current assets is from the 85.6% increase in cash and equivalents and the 22.8% increase in accounts receivable; although the 47.2% decline in short-term investments dampened this growth. The long-term assets of property, plant and equipment, intangible assets, and long-term investments also markedly increased. Of course, its sizeable total asset growth of 26.0% must be accompanied by future income to validate RIM's growth strategy.

We likewise see substantial increases on the financing side, the most notable ones (in amount) being accounts payable and accrued liabilities totaling $566,939 thousand. The increase in these items is probably related to the recessionary period covering this report. RIM also reinvested much of its income as reflected in the $1,728,655 thousand increase in retained earnings. Again, we must monitor these increases in investing and financing activities to be sure they are reflected in increased operating performance.

Comparative Income Statements Comparative income statements are prepared similarly to comparative balance sheets. Amounts for two or more periods are placed side by side, with additional columns for dollar and percent changes. Exhibit 17.2 shows Research In Motion's comparative income statements.

RESEARCH IN MOTION Comparative Income Statements For Years Ended February 27, 2010 and February 28, 2009				
($ thousands, except per share data)	2010	2009	Dollar Change	Percent Change
Revenue..........................	$14,953,224	$11,065,186	$3,888,038	35.1%
Cost of sales	8,368,958	5,967,888	2,401,070	40.2
Gross profit	6,584,266	5,097,298	1,486,968	29.2
Research and development.................	964,841	684,702	280,139	40.9
Selling, marketing, and administration	1,907,398	1,495,697	411,701	27.5
Amortization.........................	310,357	194,803	115,554	59.3
Litigation	163,800	—	163,800	—
Income from operations	3,237,870	2,722,096	515,774	18.9
Investment income	28,640	78,267	(49,627)	(63.4)
Income before income taxes	3,266,510	2,800,363	466,147	16.6
Provision for income taxes	809,366	907,747	(98,381)	(10.8)
Net income..........................	$ 2,457,144	$ 1,892,616	564,528	29.8
Basic earnings per share	$ 4.35	$ 3.35	$ 1.00	29.9
Diluted earnings per share	$ 4.31	$ 3.30	$ 1.01	30.6

EXHIBIT 17.2

Comparative Income Statements

RIM

RIM has substantial revenue growth of 35.1% in 2010. This finding helps support management's growth strategy as reflected in the comparative balance sheets. RIM evidences some ability to control costs of selling, marketing, and administration, which increased 27.5% (versus the 35.1% revenue increase). However, cost of sales increased 40.2% and other expenses also increased at a rate more than that for sales. RIM's net income growth of 29.8% on revenue growth of 35.1% is still good.

Point: Percent change can also be computed by dividing the current period by the prior period and subtracting 1.0. For example, the 35.1% revenue increase of Exhibit 17.2 is computed as: ($14,953,224/$11,065,186) − 1.

Trend Analysis

Trend analysis, also called *trend percent analysis* or *index number trend analysis,* is a form of horizontal analysis that can reveal patterns in data across successive periods. It involves computing trend percents for a series of financial numbers and is a variation on the use of percent changes. The difference is that trend analysis does not subtract the base period amount in the numerator. To compute trend percents, we do the following:

1. Select a *base period* and assign each item in the base period a weight of 100%.
2. Express financial numbers as a percent of their base period number.

Specifically, a *trend percent,* also called an *index number,* is computed as follows:

Financial Results

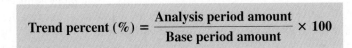

$$\text{Trend percent (\%)} = \frac{\text{Analysis period amount}}{\text{Base period amount}} \times 100$$

Point: *Index* refers to the comparison of the analysis period to the base period. Percents determined for each period are called *index numbers.*

To illustrate trend analysis, we use the **Research In Motion** data shown in Exhibit 17.3.

(in thousands)	2010	2009	2008	2007	2006
Revenue	$14,953,224	$11,065,186	$6,009,395	$3,037,103	$2,065,845
Cost of sales	8,368,958	5,967,888	2,928,814	1,379,301	925,598
Operating expenses	3,346,396	2,375,202	1,349,422	850,974	523,155

EXHIBIT 17.3

Revenue and Expenses

These data are from RIM's current and prior financial statements. The base period is 2006 and the trend percent is computed in each subsequent year by dividing that year's amount by its 2006 amount. For instance, the revenue trend percent for 2010 is 723.8%, computed as $14,953,224/$2,065,845. The trend percents—using the data from Exhibit 17.3—are shown in Exhibit 17.4.

EXHIBIT 17.4

Trend Percents for Revenue and Expenses

	2010	2009	2008	2007	2006
Revenue	723.8%	535.6%	290.9%	147.0%	100.0%
Cost of sales	904.2	644.8	316.4	149.0	100.0
Operating expenses	639.7	454.0	257.9	162.7	100.0

Point: Trend analysis expresses a percent of base, not a percent of change.

Graphical depictions often aid analysis of trend percents. Exhibit 17.5 shows the trend percents from Exhibit 17.4 in a *line graph,* which can help us identify trends and detect changes in direction or magnitude. It reveals that the trend line for revenue consistently falls short of

EXHIBIT 17.5

Trend Percent Lines for Revenue and Expenses of Research In Motion

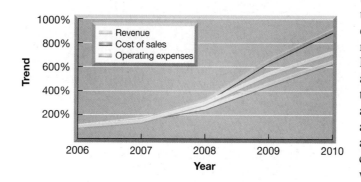

that for cost of sales. Moreover, the magnitude of that difference has slightly grown. This result does not bode well for RIM because its cost of sales are by far its largest cost, and the company fails to show an ability to control these expenses as it expands. The line graph also reveals a consistent increase in each of these accounts, which is typical of growth companies. The trend line for operating expenses is more encouraging because it falls short of the revenue trend line in 2008, 2009 and 2010. Still, the bad news is that much of the shift in cost of sales occurred in the most recent two years. Management must try to better control those costs in future years.

EXHIBIT 17.6

Trend Percent Lines—Research In Motion, Apple and Palm

RIM

Apple

Palm

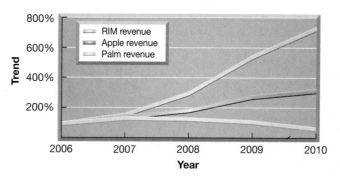

Exhibit 17.6 compares **RIM**'s revenue trend line to that of **Apple** and **Palm** for this same period. RIM's revenues sharply increased over this time period while those of Apple exhibited less growth, and those for Palm were declining. These data indicate that RIM's products and services have met with considerable consumer acceptance.

Trend analysis of financial statement items can include comparisons of relations between items on different financial statements. For instance, Exhibit 17.7 compares RIM's revenue and total assets. The rate of increase in total assets (440.9%) is less than the increase in revenues (723.8%) since 2006. Is this result favorable or not? The answer is that RIM was *more* efficient in using its assets in 2010. Management has generated revenues sufficient to compensate for this asset growth.

EXHIBIT 17.7

Revenue and Asset Data for Research In Motion

($ thousands)	2010	2006	Trend Percent (2010 vs. 2006)
Revenue	$14,953,224	$2,065,845	723.8%
Total assets	10,204,409	2,314,349	440.9

Overall we must remember that an important role of financial statement analysis is identifying questions and areas of interest, which often direct us to important factors bearing on a company's future. Accordingly, financial statement analysis should be seen as a continuous process of refining our understanding and expectations of company performance and financial condition.

◼ Decision Maker   Answer — p. 712

Auditor   Your tests reveal a 3% increase in sales from $200,000 to $206,000 and a 4% decrease in expenses from $190,000 to $182,400. Both changes are within your "reasonableness" criterion of ±5%, and thus you don't pursue additional tests. The audit partner in charge questions your lack of follow-up and mentions the *joint relation* between sales and expenses. To what is the partner referring? ◼

VERTICAL ANALYSIS

Vertical analysis is a tool to evaluate individual financial statement items or a group of items in terms of a specific base amount. We usually define a key aggregate figure as the base, which for an income statement is usually revenue and for a balance sheet is usually total assets. This section explains vertical analysis and applies it to **Research In Motion**. [The term *vertical analysis* arises from the up-down (or down-up) movement of our eyes as we review common-size financial statements. Vertical analysis is also called *common-size analysis*.]

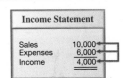

Common-Size Statements

The comparative statements in Exhibits 17.1 and 17.2 show the change in each item over time, but they do not emphasize the relative importance of each item. We use **common-size financial statements** to reveal changes in the relative importance of each financial statement item. All individual amounts in common-size statements are redefined in terms of common-size percents. A *common-size percent* is measured by dividing each individual financial statement amount under analysis by its base amount:

P2   Describe and apply methods of vertical analysis.

$$\text{Common-size percent }(\%) = \frac{\text{Analysis amount}}{\text{Base amount}} \times 100$$

Common-Size Balance Sheets   Common-size statements express each item as a percent of a *base amount,* which for a common-size balance sheet is usually total assets. The base amount is assigned a value of 100%. (This implies that the total amount of liabilities plus equity equals 100% since this amount equals total assets.) We then compute a common-size percent for each asset, liability, and equity item using total assets as the base amount. When we present a company's successive balance sheets in this way, changes in the mixture of assets, liabilities, and equity are apparent.

Point: The *base* amount in common-size analysis is an *aggregate* amount from that period's financial statement.

Exhibit 17.8 shows common-size comparative balance sheets for RIM. Some relations that stand out on both a magnitude and percentage basis include (1) a 4.9% point increase in cash and equivalents, which is likely balanced with a 4.9% point decline in short-term investments, (2) a 2.3% point decline in inventories, (3) a 2.7% point increase in net property, plant and equipment, (4) a 3.6% point decline in taxes payable, and (5) a marked increase in retained earnings. Many of these changes are characteristic of a growth/stable company. The concern, if any, is whether RIM can continue to generate sufficient revenue and income to support its asset buildup within a very competitive industry.

Point: Common-size statements often are used to compare two or more companies in the same industry.

Point: Common-size statements are also useful in comparing firms that report in different currencies.

Common-Size Income Statements   Analysis also benefits from use of a common-size income statement. Revenue is usually the base amount, which is assigned a value of 100%. Each common-size income statement item appears as a percent of revenue. If we think of the 100%

EXHIBIT 17.8

Common-Size Comparative
Balance Sheets

RIM

			Common-Size Percents*	
RESEARCH IN MOTION Common-Size Comparative Balance Sheets February 27, 2010 and February 28, 2009				
(in thousands)	2010	2009	2010	2009
Assets				
Cash and cash equivalents	$ 1,550,861	$ 835,546	15.2%	10.3%
Short-term investments	360,614	682,666	3.5	8.4
Accounts receivable, net	2,593,742	2,112,117	25.4	26.1
Other receivables	206,373	157,728	2.0	1.9
Inventories	621,611	682,400	6.1	8.4
Other current assets	285,539	187,257	2.8	2.3
Deferred income tax asset	193,916	183,872	1.9	2.3
Total current assets	5,812,656	4,841,586	57.0	59.8
Long-term investments	958,248	720,635	9.4	8.9
Property, plant and equipment, net	1,956,581	1,334,648	19.2	16.5
Intangible assets, net	1,326,363	1,066,527	13.0	13.2
Goodwill	150,561	137,572	1.5	1.7
Deferred income tax asset	0	404	0.0	0.0
Total assets	$10,204,409	$8,101,372	100.0%	100.0%
Liabilities				
Accounts payable	$ 615,620	$ 448,339	6.0%	5.5%
Accrued liabilities	1,638,260	1,238,602	16.1	15.3
Income taxes payable	95,650	361,460	0.9	4.5
Deferred revenue	67,573	53,834	0.7	0.7
Deferred income tax liability	14,674	13,116	0.1	0.2
Total current liabilities	2,431,777	2,115,351	23.8	26.1
Deferred income tax liability	141,382	87,917	1.4	1.1
Income taxes payable	28,587	23,976	0.3	0.3
Total liabilities	2,601,746	2,227,244	25.5	27.5
Shareholders' Equity				
Capital stock	2,207,609	2,208,235	21.6	27.3
Treasury stock	(94,463)	0	(0.9)	0.0
Retained earnings............................	5,274,365	3,545,710	51.7	43.8
Additional paid-in capital	164,060	119,726	1.6	1.5
Accumulated other comprehensive income	51,092	457	0.5	0.0
Total stockholders' equity	7,602,663	5,874,128	74.5	72.5
Total liabilities and stockholders' equity	$10,204,409	$8,101,372	100.0%	100.0%

* Percents are rounded to tenths and thus may not exactly sum to totals and subtotals.

revenue amount as representing one sales dollar, the remaining items show how each revenue dollar is distributed among costs, expenses, and income.

Exhibit 17.9 shows common-size comparative income statements for each dollar of RIM's revenue. The past two years' common-size numbers are similar with a few exceptions. The bad news is that RIM has given up 0.7 cent in earnings per revenue dollar—evidenced by the 17.1% to 16.4% decline in earnings as a percentage of revenue. This implies that management is not effectively controlling costs. Much of this is attributed to the rise in cost of sales from 53.9% to 56.0% as a percentage of revenue. This is a concern given the price-competitive smartphone market. Some good news is apparent with the decline in selling, marketing, and administration expenses as a percentage of revenue. Analysis here shows that common-size percents for successive income statements can uncover potentially important changes in a company's expenses. Evidence of no changes, especially when changes are expected, is also informative.

EXHIBIT 17.9

Common-Size Comparative
Income Statements

RIM

RESEARCH IN MOTION Common-Size Comparative Income Statements For Years Ended February 27, 2010 and February 28, 2009			Common-Size Percents*	
($ thousands)	2010	2009	2010	2009
Revenue	$14,953,224	$11,065,186	100.0%	100.0%
Cost of sales	8,368,958	5,967,888	56.0	53.9
Gross margin	6,584,266	5,097,298	44.0	46.1
Research and development	964,841	684,702	6.5	6.2
Selling, marketing, and administration	1,907,398	1,495,697	12.8	13.5
Amortization	310,357	194,803	2.1	1.8
Litigation	163,800	—	1.1	0.0
Income from operations	3,237,870	2,722,096	21.7	24.6
Investment income	28,640	78,267	0.2	0.7
Income before income taxes	3,266,510	2,800,363	21.8	25.3
Provision for income taxes	809,366	907,747	5.4	8.2
Net income	$ 2,457,144	$ 1,892,616	16.4%	17.1%

* Percents are rounded to tenths and thus may not exactly sum to totals and subtotals.

Common-Size Graphics

Two of the most common tools of common-size analysis are trend analysis of common-size statements and graphical analysis. The trend analysis of common-size statements is similar to that of comparative statements discussed under vertical analysis. It is not illustrated here because the only difference is the substitution of common-size percents for trend percents. Instead, this section discusses graphical analysis of common-size statements.

An income statement readily lends itself to common-size graphical analysis. This is so because revenues affect nearly every item in an income statement. Exhibit 17.10 shows **RIM**'s 2010 common-size income statement in graphical form. This pie chart highlights the contribution of each cost component of revenue for net income, excluding investment income.

EXHIBIT 17.10

Common-Size Graphic of
Income Statement

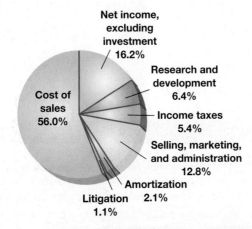

Exhibit 17.11 previews more complex graphical analyses available and the insights they provide. The data for this exhibit are taken from **RIM**'s *Segments* footnote. RIM has at least two reportable segments: (1) United States, and (2) outside the United States (titled Non-U.S.).

EXHIBIT 17.11

Revenue and Total Asset
Breakdown by Segment

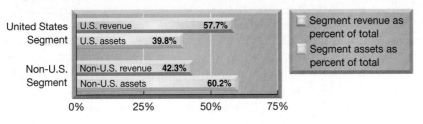

EXHIBIT 17.12

Common-Size Graphic of
Asset Components

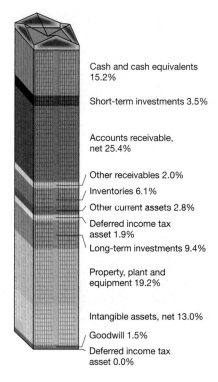

Cash and cash equivalents
15.2%

Short-term investments 3.5%

Accounts receivable,
net 25.4%

Other receivables 2.0%

Inventories 6.1%

Other current assets 2.8%

Deferred income tax
asset 1.9%

Long-term investments 9.4%

Property, plant and
equipment 19.2%

Intangible assets, net 13.0%

Goodwill 1.5%

Deferred income tax
asset 0.0%

The upper set of bars in Exhibit 17.11 shows the percent of revenues from, and the assets invested in, its U.S. segment. Its U.S. segment generates 57.7% of its revenue, while only 39.8% of its assets are in the United States. The lower set of bars shows that 42.3% of its revenue is generated outside the United States, while 60.2% of its assets are outside the United States. This can lead to questions about the revenue generated per assets invested across different countries. This type of information can help users in determining strategic analyses and actions.

Graphical analysis is also useful in identifying (1) sources of financing including the distribution among current liabilities, noncurrent liabilities, and equity capital and (2) focuses of investing activities, including the distribution among current and noncurrent assets. To illustrate, Exhibit 17.12 shows a common-size graphical display of RIM's assets. Common-size balance sheet analysis can be extended to examine the composition of these subgroups. For instance, in assessing liquidity of current assets, knowing what proportion of *current* assets consists of inventories is usually important, and not simply what proportion inventories are of *total* assets.

Common-size financial statements are also useful in comparing different companies. Exhibit 17.13 shows common-size graphics of **RIM**, **Apple** and **Nokia** on financing sources. This graphic highlights the larger percent of equity financing for RIM and Apple than for Nokia. It also highlights the much larger noncurrent (debt) financing of Nokia and Apple versus RIM. Comparison of a company's common-size statements with competitors' or industry common-size statistics alerts us to differences in the structure or distribution of its financial statements but not to their dollar magnitude.

EXHIBIT 17.13

Common-Size Graphic of Financing
Sources—Competitor Analysis

RIM

Apple

NOKIA

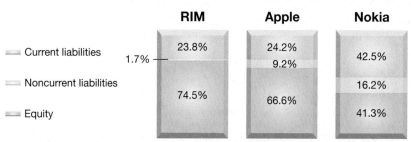

	RIM	Apple	Nokia
Current liabilities	23.8%	24.2%	42.5%
Noncurrent liabilities	1.7%	9.2%	16.2%
Equity	74.5%	66.6%	41.3%

Quick Check   Answers — p. 713

5. Which of the following is true for common-size comparative statements? (*a*) Each item is expressed as a percent of a base amount. (*b*) Total assets often are assigned a value of 100%. (*c*) Amounts from successive periods are placed side by side. (*d*) All are true. (*e*) None is true.

6. What is the difference between the percents shown on a comparative income statement and those shown on a common-size comparative income statement?

7. Trend percents are (*a*) shown on comparative income statements and balance sheets, (*b*) shown on common-size comparative statements, or (*c*) also called *index numbers*.

RATIO ANALYSIS

P3 Define and apply ratio analysis.

Ratios are among the more widely used tools of financial analysis because they provide clues to and symptoms of underlying conditions. A ratio can help us uncover conditions and trends difficult to detect by inspecting individual components making up the ratio. Ratios, like other analysis tools, are usually future oriented; that is, they are often adjusted for their probable future trend and magnitude, and their usefulness depends on skillful interpretation.

A ratio expresses a mathematical relation between two quantities. It can be expressed as a percent, rate, or proportion. For instance, a change in an account balance from $100 to $250 can be expressed as (1) 150% increase, (2) 2.5 times, or (3) 2.5 to 1 (or 2.5:1). Computation of a ratio is a simple arithmetic operation, but its interpretation is not. To be meaningful, a ratio must refer to an economically important relation. For example, a direct and crucial relation exists between an item's sales price and its cost. Accordingly, the ratio of cost of goods sold to sales is meaningful. In contrast, no obvious relation exists between freight costs and the balance of long-term investments.

This section describes an important set of financial ratios and its application. The selected ratios are organized into the four building blocks of financial statement analysis: (1) liquidity and efficiency, (2) solvency, (3) profitability, and (4) market prospects. All of these ratios were explained at relevant points in prior chapters. The purpose here is to organize and apply them under a summary framework. We use four common standards, in varying degrees, for comparisons: intracompany, competitor, industry, and guidelines.

Point: Some sources for industry norms are *Annual Statement Studies* by Robert Morris Associates, *Industry Norms & Key Business Ratios* by Dun & Bradstreet, *Standard & Poor's Industry Surveys*, and Reuters.com/finance.

Liquidity and Efficiency

Liquidity refers to the availability of resources to meet short-term cash requirements. It is affected by the timing of cash inflows and outflows along with prospects for future performance. Analysis of liquidity is aimed at a company's funding requirements. *Efficiency* refers to how productive a company is in using its assets. Efficiency is usually measured relative to how much revenue is generated from a certain level of assets.

Both liquidity and efficiency are important and complementary. If a company fails to meet its current obligations, its continued existence is doubtful. Viewed in this light, all other measures of analysis are of secondary importance. Although accounting measurements assume the company's continued existence, our analysis must always assess the validity of this assumption using liquidity measures. Moreover, inefficient use of assets can cause liquidity problems. A lack of liquidity often precedes lower profitability and fewer opportunities. It can foretell a loss of owner control. To a company's creditors, lack of liquidity can yield delays in collecting interest and principal payments or the loss of amounts due them. A company's customers and suppliers of goods and services also are affected by short-term liquidity problems. Implications include a company's inability to execute contracts and potential damage to important customer and supplier relationships. This section describes and illustrates key ratios relevant to assessing liquidity and efficiency.

Working Capital and Current Ratio The amount of current assets less current liabilities is called **working capital,** or *net working capital.* A company needs adequate working capital to meet current debts, to carry sufficient inventories, and to take advantage of cash discounts. A company that runs low on working capital is less likely to meet current obligations or to continue operating. When evaluating a company's working capital, we must not only look at the dollar amount of current assets less current liabilities, but also at their ratio. The *current ratio* is defined as follows (see Chapter 3 for additional explanation):

$$\text{Current ratio} = \frac{\text{Current assets}}{\text{Current liabilities}}$$

Drawing on information in Exhibit 17.1, **RIM**'s working capital and current ratio for both 2010 and 2009 are shown in Exhibit 17.14. Also, **Apple** (2.74), **Palm** (1.03), and the Industry's current ratio (2.4) are shown in the margin. RIM's 2010 ratio (2.39) is between the competitors' ratios, and it does not appear in danger of defaulting on loan payments. A high current ratio suggests a strong liquidity position and an ability to meet current obligations. A company can, however, have a current ratio that is too high. An excessively high current ratio means that the company has invested too much in current assets compared to its current obligations.

($ thousands)	2010	2009
Current assets	$ 5,812,656	$ 4,841,586
Current liabilities	2,431,777	2,115,351
Working capital	**$3,380,879**	**$2,726,235**
Current ratio		
$5,812,656/$2,431,777 =	2.39 to 1	
$4,841,586/$2,115,351 =		2.29 to 1

EXHIBIT 17.14

RIM's Working Capital and Current Ratio

Current ratio
Apple = 2.74
Palm = 1.03
Industry = 2.4

An excessive investment in current assets is not an efficient use of funds because current assets normally generate a low return on investment (compared with long-term assets).

Many users apply a guideline of 2:1 (or 1.5:1) for the current ratio in helping evaluate a company's debt-paying ability. A company with a 2:1 or higher current ratio is generally thought to be a good credit risk in the short run. Such a guideline or any analysis of the current ratio must recognize at least three additional factors: (1) type of business, (2) composition of current assets, and (3) turnover rate of current asset components.

Type of business.   A service company that grants little or no credit and carries few inventories can probably operate on a current ratio of less than 1:1 if its revenues generate enough cash to pay its current liabilities. On the other hand, a company selling high-priced clothing or furniture requires a higher ratio because of difficulties in judging customer demand and cash receipts. For instance, if demand falls, inventory may not generate as much cash as expected. Accordingly, analysis of the current ratio should include a comparison with ratios from successful companies in the same industry and from prior periods. We must also recognize that a company's accounting methods, especially choice of inventory method, affect the current ratio. For instance, when costs are rising, a company using LIFO tends to report a smaller amount of current assets than when using FIFO.

Point: When a firm uses LIFO in a period of rising costs, the standard for an adequate current ratio usually is lower than if it used FIFO.

Composition of current assets.   The composition of a company's current assets is important to an evaluation of short-term liquidity. For instance, cash, cash equivalents, and short-term investments are more liquid than accounts and notes receivable. Also, short-term receivables normally are more liquid than inventory. Cash, of course, can be used to immediately pay current debts. Items such as accounts receivable and inventory, however, normally must be converted into cash before payment is made. An excessive amount of receivables and inventory weakens a company's ability to pay current liabilities. The acid-test ratio (see below) can help with this assessment.

Turnover rate of assets.   Asset turnover measures a company's efficiency in using its assets. One relevant measure of asset efficiency is the revenue generated. A measure of total asset turnover is revenues divided by total assets, but evaluation of turnover for individual assets is also useful. We discuss both receivables turnover and inventory turnover on the next page.

■ Decision Maker   Answer — p. 713

Banker   A company requests a one-year, $200,000 loan for expansion. This company's current ratio is 4:1, with current assets of $160,000. Key competitors carry a current ratio of about 1.9:1. Using this information, do you approve the loan application? Does your decision change if the application is for a 10-year loan? ■

Acid-Test Ratio   Quick assets are cash, short-term investments, and current receivables. These are the most liquid types of current assets. The *acid-test ratio,* also called *quick ratio,* and introduced in Chapter 5, reflects on a company's short-term liquidity.

$$\text{Acid-test ratio} = \frac{\text{Cash + Short-term investments + Current receivables}}{\text{Current liabilities}}$$

RIM's acid-test ratio is computed in Exhibit 17.15. RIM's 2010 acid-test ratio (1.94) is between that for Apple (2.33) and Palm (0.94), and greater than the 1:1 common guideline for an

EXHIBIT 17.15

Acid-Test Ratio

($ thousands)	2010	2009
Cash and equivalents	$1,550,861	$ 835,546
Short-term investments	360,614	682,666
Current receivables	2,800,115	2,269,845
Total quick assets	$4,711,590	$3,788,057
Current liabilities	$2,431,777	$2,115,351
Acid-test ratio		
$4,711,590/$2,431,777	1.94 to 1	
$3,788,057/$2,115,351		1.79 to 1

Acid-test ratio
Apple = 2.33
Palm = 0.94
Industry = 1.5

acceptable acid-test ratio. The ratios for both RIM and Apple exceed the 1.5 industry norm. As with analysis of the current ratio, we need to consider other factors. For instance, the frequency with which a company converts its current assets into cash affects its working capital requirements. This implies that analysis of short-term liquidity should also include an analysis of receivables and inventories, which we consider next.

Accounts Receivable Turnover We can measure how frequently a company converts its receivables into cash by computing the *accounts receivable turnover*. This ratio is defined as follows (see Chapter 9 for additional explanation):

$$\text{Accounts receivable turnover} = \frac{\text{Net sales}}{\text{Average accounts receivable, net}}$$

Short-term receivables from customers are often included in the denominator along with accounts receivable. Also, accounts receivable turnover is more precise if credit sales are used for the numerator, but external users generally use net sales (or net revenues) because information about credit sales is typically not reported. RIM's 2010 accounts receivable turnover is computed as follows ($ millions).

$$\frac{14,953,224}{(\$2,593,742 + \$2,112,117)/2} = 6.4 \text{ times}$$

Accounts receivable turnover
Apple = 14.8
Palm = 8.0
Industry = 6.6

RIM's value of 6.4 is between that of Apple's 14.8 and Palm's 8.0. Accounts receivable turnover is high when accounts receivable are quickly collected. A high turnover is favorable because it means the company need not commit large amounts of funds to accounts receivable. However, an accounts receivable turnover can be too high; this can occur when credit terms are so restrictive that they negatively affect sales volume.

Inventory Turnover How long a company holds inventory before selling it will affect working capital requirements. One measure of this effect is *inventory turnover,* also called *merchandise turnover* or *merchandise inventory turnover,* which is defined as follows (see Chapter 6 for additional explanation):

$$\text{Inventory turnover} = \frac{\text{Cost of goods sold}}{\text{Average inventory}}$$

Using RIM's cost of goods sold and inventories information, we compute its inventory turnover for 2010 as follows (if the beginning and ending inventories for the year do not represent the usual inventory amount, an average of quarterly or monthly inventories can be used).

Inventory turnover
Apple = 53.28
Palm = 13.22
Industry = 10.1

$$\frac{\$8,368,958}{(\$621,611 + \$682,400)/2} = 12.84 \text{ times}$$

RIM's inventory turnover of 12.84 is less than Apple's 53.28, but similar to Palm's 13.22, and the industry's 10.1. A company with a high turnover requires a smaller investment in inventory than one producing the same sales with a lower turnover. Inventory turnover can be too high, however, if the inventory a company keeps is so small that it restricts sales volume.

Days' Sales Uncollected Accounts receivable turnover provides insight into how frequently a company collects its accounts. Days' sales uncollected is one measure of this activity, which is defined as follows (Chapter 8 provides additional explanation):

$$\text{Days' sales uncollected} = \frac{\text{Accounts receivable, net}}{\text{Net sales}} \times 365$$

Any short-term notes receivable from customers are normally included in the numerator.

RIM's 2010 days' sales uncollected follows.

Day's sales uncollected
Apple = 28.59
Palm = 32.96

$$\frac{\$2,593,742}{\$14,953,224} \times 365 = 63.31 \text{ days}$$

Both Apple's days' sales uncollected of 28.59 days and Palm's 32.96 days are less than the 63.31 days for RIM. Days' sales uncollected is more meaningful if we know company credit terms. A rough guideline states that days' sales uncollected should not exceed $1\frac{1}{3}$ times the days in its (1) credit period, *if* discounts are not offered or (2) discount period, *if* favorable discounts are offered.

Days' Sales in Inventory   *Days' sales in inventory* is a useful measure in evaluating inventory liquidity. Days' sales in inventory is linked to inventory in a way that days' sales uncollected is linked to receivables. We compute days' sales in inventory as follows (Chapter 6 provides additional explanation).

$$\textbf{Days' sales in inventory} = \frac{\textbf{Ending inventory}}{\textbf{Cost of goods sold}} \times \textbf{365}$$

RIM's days' sales in inventory for 2010 follows.

Days' sales in inventory
Apple = 6.5
Palm = 12.5
Industry = 25

$$\frac{\$621,611}{\$8,368,958} \times 365 = 27.1 \text{ days}$$

Point: *Average collection period is estimated by dividing 365 by the accounts receivable turnover ratio. For example, 365 divided by an accounts receivable turnover of 6.1 indicates a 60-day average collection period.*

If the products in RIM's inventory are in demand by customers, this formula estimates that its inventory will be converted into receivables (or cash) in 27.1 days. If all of RIM's sales were credit sales, the conversion of inventory to receivables in 27.1 days *plus* the conversion of receivables to cash in 63.31 days implies that inventory will be converted to cash in about 90.41 days (27.1 + 63.31).

Total Asset Turnover   *Total asset turnover* reflects a company's ability to use its assets to generate sales and is an important indication of operating efficiency. The definition of this ratio follows (Chapter 10 offers additional explanation).

$$\textbf{Total asset turnover} = \frac{\textbf{Net sales}}{\textbf{Average total assets}}$$

RIM's total asset turnover for 2010 follows and is greater than that for both Apple (1.03) and Palm (0.81).

Total asset turnover
Apple = 1.03
Palm = 0.81
Industry = 1.0

$$\frac{\$14,953,224}{(\$10,204,409 + \$8,101,372)/2} = 1.63 \text{ times}$$

Quick Check

Answers — p. 713

8. Information from Paff Co. at Dec. 31, 2010, follows: cash, $820,000; accounts receivable, $240,000; inventories, $470,000; plant assets, $910,000; accounts payable, $350,000; and income taxes payable, $180,000. Compute its (a) current ratio and (b) acid-test ratio.

9. On Dec. 31, 2011, Paff Company (see question 8) had accounts receivable of $290,000 and inventories of $530,000. During 2011, net sales amounted to $2,500,000 and cost of goods sold was $750,000. Compute (a) accounts receivable turnover, (b) days' sales uncollected, (c) inventory turnover, and (d) days' sales in inventory.

Solvency

Solvency refers to a company's long-run financial viability and its ability to cover long-term obligations. All of a company's business activities—financing, investing, and operating—affect its solvency. Analysis of solvency is long term and uses less precise but more encompassing measures than liquidity. One of the most important components of solvency analysis is the composition of a company's capital structure. *Capital structure* refers to a company's financing sources. It ranges from relatively permanent equity financing to riskier or more temporary short-term financing. Assets represent security for financiers, ranging from loans secured by specific assets to the assets available as general security to unsecured creditors. This section describes the tools of solvency analysis. Our analysis focuses on a company's ability to both meet its obligations and provide security to its creditors *over the long run.* Indicators of this ability include *debt* and *equity* ratios, the relation between *pledged assets and secured liabilities,* and the company's capacity to earn sufficient income to *pay fixed interest charges.*

Debt and Equity Ratios   One element of solvency analysis is to assess the portion of a company's assets contributed by its owners and the portion contributed by creditors. This relation is reflected in the debt ratio (also described in Chapter 2). The *debt ratio* expresses total liabilities as a percent of total assets. The **equity ratio** provides complementary information by expressing total equity as a percent of total assets. **RIM**'s debt and equity ratios follow.

($ thousands)	2010	Ratios	
Total liabilities	$ 2,601,746	25.5%	[Debt ratio]
Total equity	7,602,663	74.5	[Equity ratio]
Total liabilities and equity	$10,204,409	100.0%	

Debt ratio :: Equity ratio
Apple = 33.4% :: 66.6%
Industry = 40% :: 60%

RIM's financial statements reveal more equity than debt. A company is considered less risky if its capital structure (equity and long-term debt) contains more equity. One risk factor is the required payment for interest and principal when debt is outstanding. Another factor is the greater the stockholder financing, the more losses a company can absorb through equity before the assets become inadequate to satisfy creditors' claims. From the stockholders' point of view, if a company earns a return on borrowed capital that is higher than the cost of borrowing, the difference represents increased income to stockholders. The inclusion of debt is described as *financial leverage* because debt can have the effect of increasing the return to stockholders. Companies are said to be highly leveraged if a large portion of their assets is financed by debt.

Debt-to-Equity Ratio   The ratio of total liabilities to equity is another measure of solvency. We compute the ratio as follows (Chapter 14 offers additional explanation).

$$\text{Debt-to-equity ratio} = \frac{\text{Total liabilities}}{\text{Total equity}}$$

RIM's debt-to-equity ratio for 2010 is

$$\$2,601,746/\$7,602,663 = 0.34$$

Debt-to-equity
Apple = 0.50
Industry = 0.7

RIM's 0.34 debt-to-equity ratio is less than the 0.50 ratio for Apple, and less than the industry ratio of 0.7. Consistent with our inferences from the debt ratio, RIM's capital structure has more equity than debt, which decreases risk. Recall that debt must be repaid with interest, while equity does not. These debt requirements can be burdensome when the industry and/or the economy experience a downturn. A larger debt-to-equity ratio also implies less opportunity to expand through use of debt financing.

Times Interest Earned   The amount of income before deductions for interest expense and income taxes is the amount available to pay interest expense. The following *times interest earned* ratio reflects the creditors' risk of loan repayments with interest (see Chapter 11 for additional explanation).

$$\text{Times interest earned} = \frac{\text{Income before interest expense and income taxes}}{\text{Interest expense}}$$

The larger this ratio, the less risky is the company for creditors. One guideline says that creditors are reasonably safe if the company earns its fixed interest expense two or more times each year. RIM's times interest earned ratio follows; its value suggests that its creditors have little risk of nonrepayment.

Times interest earned
Apple = n.a.

$$\frac{\$2,457,144 + \sim\$0 \text{ (see RIM note \#16)} + \$809,366}{\sim\$0} = \text{"infinite" (not applicable)}$$

Decision Insight

Bears and Bulls   A *bear market* is a declining market. The phrase comes from bear-skin jobbers who often sold the skins before the bears were caught. The term *bear* was then used to describe investors who sold shares they did not own in anticipation of a price decline. A *bull market* is a rising market. This phrase comes from the once popular sport of bear and bull baiting. The term *bull* came to mean the opposite of *bear*. ■

Profitability

We are especially interested in a company's ability to use its assets efficiently to produce profits (and positive cash flows). *Profitability* refers to a company's ability to generate an adequate return on invested capital. Return is judged by assessing earnings relative to the level and sources of financing. Profitability is also relevant to solvency. This section describes key profitability measures and their importance to financial statement analysis.

Profit Margin   A company's operating efficiency and profitability can be expressed by two components. The first is *profit margin,* which reflects a company's ability to earn net income from sales (Chapter 3 offers additional explanation). It is measured by expressing net income as a percent of sales (*sales* and *revenues* are similar terms). **RIM**'s profit margin follows.

Profit margin
Apple = 19.2%
Industry = 3%

$$\text{Profit margin} = \frac{\text{Net income}}{\text{Net sales}} = \frac{\$2,457,144}{\$14,953,224} = 16.4\%$$

To evaluate profit margin, we must consider the industry. For instance, an appliance company might require a profit margin between 10% and 15%; whereas a retail supermarket might require a profit margin of 1% or 2%. Both profit margin and *total asset turnover* make up the two basic components of operating efficiency. These ratios reflect on management because managers are ultimately responsible for operating efficiency. The next section explains how we use both measures to analyze return on total assets.

Return on Total Assets   *Return on total assets* is defined as follows.

$$\text{Return on total assets} = \frac{\text{Net income}}{\text{Average total assets}}$$

RIM's 2010 return on total assets is

Return on total assets
Apple = 19.7%
Industry = 4%

$$\frac{\$2,457,144}{(\$10,204,409 + \$8,101,372)/2} = 26.8\%$$

RIM's 26.8% return on total assets is higher than that for many businesses and is higher than Apple's return of 19.7% and the industry's 4% return. We also should evaluate any trend in the rate of return.

Point: Many analysts add back *Interest expense* × (1 − *Tax rate*) to net income in computing return on total assets.

The following equation shows the important relation between profit margin, total asset turnover, and return on total assets.

$$\textbf{Profit margin} \times \textbf{Total asset turnover} = \textbf{Return on total assets}$$

or

$$\frac{\textbf{Net income}}{\textbf{Net sales}} \times \frac{\textbf{Net sales}}{\textbf{Average total assets}} = \frac{\textbf{Net income}}{\textbf{Average total assets}}$$

Both profit margin and total asset turnover contribute to overall operating efficiency, as measured by return on total assets. If we apply this formula to RIM, we get

$$16.4\% \times 1.63 = 26.8\% \text{ (with rounding error)}$$

Apple: 19.2% × 1.03 = 19.7%
(with rounding)

This analysis shows that RIM's superior return on assets versus that of Apple is driven mainly by its higher total asset turnover.

Return on Common Stockholders' Equity   Perhaps the most important goal in operating a company is to earn net income for its owner(s). *Return on common stockholders' equity* measures a company's success in reaching this goal and is defined as follows.

$$\textbf{Return on common stockholders' equity} = \frac{\textbf{Net income} - \textbf{Preferred dividends}}{\textbf{Average common stockholders' equity}}$$

RIM's 2010 return on common stockholders' equity is computed as follows:

$$\frac{\$2,457,144 - \$0}{(\$5,874,128 + \$7,602,663)/2} = 36.5\%$$

Return on common equity
Apple = 30.5%
Industry = 6%

The denominator in this computation is the book value of common equity (minority interest is often included in common equity for this ratio). In the numerator, the dividends on cumulative preferred stock are subtracted whether they are declared or are in arrears. If preferred stock is noncumulative, its dividends are subtracted only if declared.

▮ Decision **Insight**

Wall Street   *Wall Street* is synonymous with financial markets, but its name comes from the street location of the original New York Stock Exchange. The street's name derives from stockades built by early settlers to protect New York from pirate attacks. ▪

Market Prospects

Market measures are useful for analyzing corporations with publicly traded stock. These market measures use stock price, which reflects the market's (public's) expectations for the company. This includes expectations of both company return and risk—as the market perceives it.

Price-Earnings Ratio   Computation of the *price-earnings ratio* follows (Chapter 13 provides additional explanation).

$$\textbf{Price-earnings ratio} = \frac{\textbf{Market price per common share}}{\textbf{Earnings per share}}$$

Predicted earnings per share for the next period is often used in the denominator of this computation. Reported earnings per share for the most recent period is also commonly used. In both cases, the ratio is used as an indicator of the future growth and risk of a company's earnings as perceived by the stock's buyers and sellers.

The market price of RIM's common stock at the start of fiscal year 2010 was $50.84. Using RIM's $4.35 basic earnings per share, we compute its price-earnings ratio as follows (some analysts compute this ratio using the median of the low and high stock price).

$$\frac{\$50.84}{\$4.35} = 11.7$$

PE (year-end)
Apple = 13.9

RIM's price-earnings ratio is less than that for Apple, but is slightly higher than the norm for the recessionary period 2009–2010. (Palm's ratio is negative due to its abnormally low earnings.) RIM's middle-of-the-pack ratio likely reflects investors' expectations of stagnant growth but normal earnings.

Dividend Yield   *Dividend yield* is used to compare the dividend-paying performance of different investment alternatives. We compute dividend yield as follows (Chapter 13 offers additional explanation).

$$\text{Dividend yield} = \frac{\textbf{Annual cash dividends per share}}{\textbf{Market price per share}}$$

RIM's dividend yield, based on its fiscal year-end market price per share of $50.84 and its policy of $0.00 cash dividends per share, is computed as follows.

$$\frac{\$0.00}{\$50.84} = 0.0\%$$

Dividend yield
Apple = 0.0%
Palm = 0.0%

Some companies do not declare and pay dividends because they wish to reinvest the cash.

Summary of Ratios

Exhibit 17.16 summarizes the major financial statement analysis ratios illustrated in this chapter and throughout the book. This summary includes each ratio's title, its formula, and the purpose for which it is commonly used.

Decision Insight

Ticker Prices   *Ticker prices* refer to a band of moving data on a monitor carrying up-to-the-minute stock prices. The phrase comes from *ticker tape,* a 1-inch-wide strip of paper spewing stock prices from a printer that ticked as it ran. Most of today's investors have never seen actual ticker tape, but the phrase survives. ■

Quick Check   Answers — p. 713

10. Which ratio best reflects a company's ability to meet immediate interest payments? (*a*) Debt ratio. (*b*) Equity ratio. (*c*) Times interest earned.

11. Which ratio best measures a company's success in earning net income for its owner(s)? (*a*) Profit margin. (*b*) Return on common stockholders' equity. (*c*) Price-earnings ratio. (*d*) Dividend yield.

12. If a company has net sales of $8,500,000, net income of $945,000, and total asset turnover of 1.8 times, what is its return on total assets?

EXHIBIT 17.16

Financial Statement Analysis Ratios*

Ratio	Formula	Measure of
Liquidity and Efficiency		
Current ratio	$= \dfrac{\text{Current assets}}{\text{Current liabilities}}$	Short-term debt-paying ability
Acid-test ratio	$= \dfrac{\text{Cash} + \text{Short-term investments} + \text{Current receivables}}{\text{Current liabilities}}$	Immediate short-term debt-paying ability
Accounts receivable turnover	$= \dfrac{\text{Net sales}}{\text{Average accounts receivable, net}}$	Efficiency of collection
Inventory turnover	$= \dfrac{\text{Cost of goods sold}}{\text{Average inventory}}$	Efficiency of inventory management
Days' sales uncollected	$= \dfrac{\text{Accounts receivable, net}}{\text{Net sales}} \times 365$	Liquidity of receivables
Days' sales in inventory	$= \dfrac{\text{Ending inventory}}{\text{Cost of goods sold}} \times 365$	Liquidity of inventory
Total asset turnover	$= \dfrac{\text{Net sales}}{\text{Average total assets}}$	Efficiency of assets in producing sales
Solvency		
Debt ratio	$= \dfrac{\text{Total liabilities}}{\text{Total assets}}$	Creditor financing and leverage
Equity ratio	$= \dfrac{\text{Total equity}}{\text{Total assets}}$	Owner financing
Debt-to-equity ratio	$= \dfrac{\text{Total liabilities}}{\text{Total equity}}$	Debt versus equity financing
Times interest earned	$= \dfrac{\text{Income before interest expense and income taxes}}{\text{Interest expense}}$	Protection in meeting interest payments
Profitability		
Profit margin ratio	$= \dfrac{\text{Net income}}{\text{Net sales}}$	Net income in each sales dollar
Gross margin ratio	$= \dfrac{\text{Net sales} - \text{Cost of goods sold}}{\text{Net sales}}$	Gross margin in each sales dollar
Return on total assets	$= \dfrac{\text{Net income}}{\text{Average total assets}}$	Overall profitability of assets
Return on common stockholders' equity	$= \dfrac{\text{Net income} - \text{Preferred dividends}}{\text{Average common stockholders' equity}}$	Profitability of owner investment
Book value per common share	$= \dfrac{\text{Shareholders' equity applicable to common shares}}{\text{Number of common shares outstanding}}$	Liquidation at reported amounts
Basic earnings per share	$= \dfrac{\text{Net income} - \text{Preferred dividends}}{\text{Weighted-average common shares outstanding}}$	Net income per common share
Market Prospects		
Price-earnings ratio	$= \dfrac{\text{Market price per common share}}{\text{Earnings per share}}$	Market value relative to earnings
Dividend yield	$= \dfrac{\text{Annual cash dividends per share}}{\text{Market price per share}}$	Cash return per common share

* Additional ratios also examined in previous chapters included credit risk ratio; plant asset useful life; plant asset age; days' cash expense coverage; cash coverage of growth; cash coverage of debt; free cash flow; cash flow on total assets; and payout ratio.

GLOBAL VIEW

The analysis and interpretation of financial statements is, of course, impacted by the accounting system in effect. This section discusses similarities and differences for analysis of financial statements when prepared under U.S. GAAP vis-à-vis IFRS.

Horizontal and Vertical Analyses   Horizontal and vertical analyses help eliminate many differences between U.S. GAAP and IFRS when analyzing and interpreting financial statements. Financial numbers are converted to percentages that are, in the best case scenario, consistently applied across and within periods. This enables users to effectively compare companies across reporting regimes. However, when fundamental differences in reporting regimes impact financial statements, such as with certain recognition rule differences, the user must exercise caution when drawing conclusions. Some users will reformulate one set of numbers to be more consistent with the other system to enable comparative analysis. This reformulation process is covered in advanced courses. The important point is that horizontal and vertical analyses help strip away differences between the reporting regimes, but several key differences sometimes remain and require adjustment of the numbers. **Nokia** reports the following partial vertical analysis to its shareholders as part of its MD&A report.

NOKIA

As a Percentage of Revenue	2010
Research and development	6.5%
Selling, marketing and administration	12.8
Amortization	2.1
Litigation	1.1
Total operating expenses	22.5%

Ratio Analysis   Ratio analysis of financial statement numbers has many of the advantages and disadvantages of horizontal and vertical analyses discussed above. Importantly, ratio analysis is useful for business decisions, with some possible changes in interpretation depending on what is and what is not included in accounting measures across U.S. GAAP and IFRS. Still, we must take care in drawing inferences from a comparison of ratios across reporting regimes because what a number measures can differ across regimes. **Nokia** offers the following example of its own ratio analysis applied to gross margin: "Consolidated gross margin increased by $1.48 billion, or 29.2%, to $6.58 billion, or 44.0% of revenue, in fiscal 2010, compared to $5.10 billion, or 46.1% of revenue, in fiscal 2009. The decrease of 2.1% in consolidated gross margin percentage was primarily due to a decrease in the blended device margins."

Decision Insight

Not Created Equal   Financial regulation has several goals. Two of them are to ensure adequate accounting disclosure and to strengthen corporate governance. For disclosure purposes, companies must now provide details of related-party transactions and material off-balance-sheet agreements. This is motivated by several major frauds. For corporate governance, the CEO and CFO must now certify the fairness of financial statements and the effectiveness of internal controls. Yet, concerns remain. A study reports that 23% of management and administrative employees observed activities that posed a conflict of interest in the past year (KPMG 2009). Another 12% witnessed the falsifying or manipulating of accounting information. The bottom line: All financial statements are not of equal quality. ■

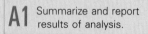

Decision Analysis   ▢▢▢   Analysis Reporting

A1 Summarize and report results of analysis.

Understanding the purpose of financial statement analysis is crucial to the usefulness of any analysis. This understanding leads to efficiency of effort, effectiveness in application, and relevance in focus. The purpose of most financial statement analyses is to reduce uncertainty in business decisions through a rigorous and sound evaluation. A *financial statement analysis report* helps by directly addressing the building blocks of analysis and by identifying weaknesses in inference by requiring explanation: It forces us to organize our reasoning and to verify its flow and logic. A report also serves as a communication link with readers, and the writing process reinforces our judgments and vice versa. Finally, the report helps us (re)evaluate evidence and refine conclusions on key building blocks. A good analysis report usually consists of six sections:

1. **Executive summary**—brief focus on important analysis results and conclusions.
2. **Analysis overview**—background on the company, its industry, and its economic setting.
3. **Evidential matter**—financial statements and information used in the analysis, including ratios, trends, comparisons, statistics, and all analytical measures assembled; often organized under the building blocks of analysis.
4. **Assumptions**—identification of important assumptions regarding a company's industry and economic environment, and other important assumptions for estimates.
5. **Key factors**—list of important favorable and unfavorable factors, both quantitative and qualitative, for company performance; usually organized by areas of analysis.
6. **Inferences**—forecasts, estimates, interpretations, and conclusions drawing on all sections of the report.

We must remember that the user dictates relevance, meaning that the analysis report should include a brief table of contents to help readers focus on those areas most relevant to their decisions. All irrelevant matter must be eliminated. For example, decades-old details of obscure transactions and detailed miscues of the analysis are irrelevant. Ambiguities and qualifications to avoid responsibility or hedging inferences must be eliminated. Finally, writing is important. Mistakes in grammar and errors of fact compromise the report's credibility.

■ Decision Insight

Short Selling   *Short selling* refers to selling stock before you buy it. Here's an example: You borrow 100 shares of Nike stock, sell them at $40 each, and receive money from their sale. You then wait. You hope that Nike's stock price falls to, say, $35 each and you can replace the borrowed stock for less than you sold it for, reaping a profit of $5 each less any transaction costs. ■

DEMONSTRATION PROBLEM

Use the following financial statements of Precision Co. to complete these requirements.

1. Prepare comparative income statements showing the percent increase or decrease for year 2011 in comparison to year 2010.
2. Prepare common-size comparative balance sheets for years 2011 and 2010.
3. Compute the following ratios as of December 31, 2011, or for the year ended December 31, 2011, and identify its building block category for financial statement analysis.
    a. Current ratio
    b. Acid-test ratio
    c. Accounts receivable turnover
    d. Days' sales uncollected
    e. Inventory turnover
    f. Debt ratio
    g. Debt-to-equity ratio
    h. Times interest earned
    i. Profit margin ratio
    j. Total asset turnover
    k. Return on total assets
    l. Return on common stockholders' equity

PRECISION COMPANY Comparative Income Statements For Years Ended December 31, 2011 and 2010		
	2011	**2010**
Sales	$2,486,000	$2,075,000
Cost of goods sold	1,523,000	1,222,000
Gross profit	963,000	853,000
Operating expenses		
Advertising expense	145,000	100,000
Sales salaries expense	240,000	280,000
Office salaries expense	165,000	200,000
Insurance expense	100,000	45,000
Supplies expense	26,000	35,000
Depreciation expense	85,000	75,000
Miscellaneous expenses	17,000	15,000
Total operating expenses	778,000	750,000
Operating income	185,000	103,000
Interest expense	44,000	46,000
Income before taxes	141,000	57,000
Income taxes	47,000	19,000
Net income	$ 94,000	$ 38,000
Earnings per share	$ 0.99	$ 0.40

PRECISION COMPANY Comparative Balance Sheets December 31, 2011 and 2010		
	2011	**2010**
Assets		
Current assets		
Cash	$ 79,000	$ 42,000
Short-term investments	65,000	96,000
Accounts receivable, net	120,000	100,000
Merchandise inventory	250,000	265,000
Total current assets	514,000	503,000
Plant assets		
Store equipment, net	400,000	350,000
Office equipment, net	45,000	50,000
Buildings, net	625,000	675,000
Land	100,000	100,000
Total plant assets	1,170,000	1,175,000
Total assets	$1,684,000	$1,678,000
Liabilities		
Current liabilities		
Accounts payable	$ 164,000	$ 190,000
Short-term notes payable	75,000	90,000
Taxes payable	26,000	12,000
Total current liabilities	265,000	292,000
Long-term liabilities		
Notes payable (secured by mortgage on buildings)	400,000	420,000
Total liabilities	665,000	712,000
Stockholders' Equity		
Common stock, $5 par value	475,000	475,000
Retained earnings	544,000	491,000
Total stockholders' equity	1,019,000	966,000
Total liabilities and equity	$1,684,000	$1,678,000

PLANNING THE SOLUTION

- Set up a four-column income statement; enter the 2011 and 2010 amounts in the first two columns and then enter the dollar change in the third column and the percent change from 2010 in the fourth column.
- Set up a four-column balance sheet; enter the 2011 and 2010 year-end amounts in the first two columns and then compute and enter the amount of each item as a percent of total assets.
- Compute the required ratios using the data provided. Use the average of beginning and ending amounts when appropriate (see Exhibit 17.16 for definitions).

SOLUTION TO DEMONSTRATION PROBLEM

1.

PRECISION COMPANY Comparative Income Statements For Years Ended December 31, 2011 and 2010				
			Increase (Decrease) in 2011	
	2011	**2010**	**Amount**	**Percent**
Sales	$2,486,000	$2,075,000	$411,000	19.8%
Cost of goods sold	1,523,000	1,222,000	301,000	24.6
Gross profit	963,000	853,000	110,000	12.9

[continued on next page]

[continued from previous page]

Operating expenses				
Advertising expense	145,000	100,000	45,000	45.0
Sales salaries expense	240,000	280,000	(40,000)	(14.3)
Office salaries expense	165,000	200,000	(35,000)	(17.5)
Insurance expense	100,000	45,000	55,000	122.2
Supplies expense	26,000	35,000	(9,000)	(25.7)
Depreciation expense	85,000	75,000	10,000	13.3
Miscellaneous expenses	17,000	15,000	2,000	13.3
Total operating expenses	778,000	750,000	28,000	3.7
Operating income	185,000	103,000	82,000	79.6
Interest expense	44,000	46,000	(2,000)	(4.3)
Income before taxes	141,000	57,000	84,000	147.4
Income taxes	47,000	19,000	28,000	147.4
Net income	$ 94,000	$ 38,000	$ 56,000	147.4
Earnings per share	$ 0.99	$ 0.40	$ 0.59	147.5

2.

PRECISION COMPANY Common-Size Comparative Balance Sheets December 31, 2011 and 2010				
	December 31		**Common-Size Percents**	
	2011	**2010**	**2011***	**2010***
Assets				
Current assets				
Cash	$ 79,000	$ 42,000	4.7%	2.5%
Short-term investments	65,000	96,000	3.9	5.7
Accounts receivable, net	120,000	100,000	7.1	6.0
Merchandise inventory	250,000	265,000	14.8	15.8
Total current assets	514,000	503,000	30.5	30.0
Plant assets				
Store equipment, net	400,000	350,000	23.8	20.9
Office equipment, net	45,000	50,000	2.7	3.0
Buildings, net	625,000	675,000	37.1	40.2
Land	100,000	100,000	5.9	6.0
Total plant assets	1,170,000	1,175,000	69.5	70.0
Total assets	$1,684,000	$1,678,000	100.0	100.0
Liabilities				
Current liabilities				
Accounts payable	$ 164,000	$ 190,000	9.7%	11.3%
Short-term notes payable	75,000	90,000	4.5	5.4
Taxes payable	26,000	12,000	1.5	0.7
Total current liabilities	265,000	292,000	15.7	17.4
Long-term liabilities				
Notes payable (secured by mortgage on buildings)	400,000	420,000	23.8	25.0
Total liabilities	665,000	712,000	39.5	42.4
Stockholders' equity				
Common stock, $5 par value	475,000	475,000	28.2	28.3
Retained earnings	544,000	491,000	32.3	29.3
Total stockholders' equity	1,019,000	966,000	60.5	57.6
Total liabilities and equity	$1,684,000	$1,678,000	100.0	100.0

* Columns do not always exactly add to 100 due to rounding.

3. Ratios for 2011:

   a. Current ratio: $514,000/$265,000 = 1.9:1 (liquidity and efficiency)

   b. Acid-test ratio: ($79,000 + $65,000 + $120,000)/$265,000 = 1.0:1 (liquidity and efficiency)

   c. Average receivables: ($120,000 + $100,000)/2 = $110,000
      Accounts receivable turnover: $2,486,000/$110,000 = 22.6 times (liquidity and efficiency)

   d. Days' sales uncollected: ($120,000/$2,486,000) $\times$ 365 = 17.6 days (liquidity and efficiency)

   e. Average inventory: ($250,000 + $265,000)/2 = $257,500
      Inventory turnover: $1,523,000/$257,500 = 5.9 times (liquidity and efficiency)

   f. Debt ratio: $665,000/$1,684,000 = 39.5% (solvency)

   g. Debt-to-equity ratio: $665,000/$1,019,000 = 0.65 (solvency)

   h. Times interest earned: $185,000/$44,000 = 4.2 times (solvency)

   i. Profit margin ratio: $94,000/$2,486,000 = 3.8% (profitability)

   j. Average total assets: ($1,684,000 + $1,678,000)/2 = $1,681,000
      Total asset turnover: $2,486,000/$1,681,000 = 1.48 times (liquidity and efficiency)

   k. Return on total assets: $94,000/$1,681,000 = 5.6% or 3.8% $\times$ 1.48 = 5.6% (profitability)

   l. Average total common equity: ($1,019,000 + $966,000)/2 = $992,500
      Return on common stockholders' equity: $94,000/$992,500 = 9.5% (profitability)

APPENDIX

17A

Sustainable Income

| A2 | Explain the form and assess the content of a complete income statement. |

When a company's revenue and expense transactions are from normal, continuing operations, a simple income statement is usually adequate. When a company's activities include income-related events not part of its normal, continuing operations, it must disclose information to help users understand these events and predict future performance. To meet these objectives, companies separate the income statement into continuing operations, discontinued segments, extraordinary items, comprehensive income, and earnings per share. For illustration, Exhibit 17A.1 shows such an income statement for ComUS. These separate distinctions help us measure *sustainable income,* which is the income level most likely to continue into the future. Sustainable income is commonly used in PE ratios and other market-based measures of performance.

Continuing Operations   The first major section (①) shows the revenues, expenses, and income from continuing operations. Users especially rely on this information to predict future operations. Many users view this section as the most important. Earlier chapters explained the items comprising income from continuing operations.

Discontinued Segments   A **business segment** is a part of a company's operations that serves a particular line of business or class of customers. A segment has assets, liabilities, and financial results of operations that can be distinguished from those of other parts of the company. A company's gain or loss from selling or closing down a segment is separately reported. Section ② of Exhibit 17A.1 reports both (1) income from operating the discontinued segment for the current period prior to its disposal and (2) the loss from disposing of the segment's net assets. The income tax effects of each are reported separately from the income taxes expense in section ①.

Extraordinary Items   Section ③ reports **extraordinary gains and losses,** which are those that are *both unusual* and *infrequent.* An **unusual gain or loss** is abnormal or otherwise unrelated to the company's regular activities and environment. An **infrequent gain or loss** is not expected to recur given the company's operating environment. Reporting extraordinary items in a separate category helps users predict future performance, absent the effects of extraordinary items. Items usually considered extraordinary include (1) expropriation (taking away) of property by a foreign government, (2) condemning of property by a domestic government body, (3) prohibition against using an asset by a newly enacted law, and (4) losses and gains from an unusual and infrequent calamity ("act of God"). Items *not* considered extraordinary include (1) write-downs of inventories and write-offs of receivables, (2) gains and losses from disposing of segments, and (3) financial effects of labor strikes.

EXHIBIT 17A.1

Income Statement (all-inclusive)
for a Corporation

ComUS
Income Statement
For Year Ended December 31, 2011

Net sales		$8,478,000
Operating expenses		
Cost of goods sold	$5,950,000	
Depreciation expense	35,000	
Other selling, general, and administrative expenses	515,000	
Interest expense	20,000	
① Total operating expenses		(6,520,000)
Other gains (losses)		
Loss on plant relocation		(45,000)
Gain on sale of surplus land		72,000
Income from continuing operations before taxes		1,985,000
Income taxes expense		(595,500)
Income from continuing operations		1,389,500
Discontinued segment		
② Income from operating Division A (net of $180,000 taxes)	420,000	
Loss on disposal of Division A (net of $66,000 tax benefit)	(154,000)	266,000
Income before extraordinary items		1,655,500
Extraordinary items		
③ Gain on land expropriated by state (net of $85,200 taxes)	198,800	
Loss from earthquake damage (net of $270,000 tax benefit)	(630,000)	(431,200)
Net income		$1,224,300
Earnings per common share (200,000 outstanding shares)		
Income from continuing operations		$ 6.95
Discontinued operations		1.33
④ Income before extraordinary items		8.28
Extraordinary items		(2.16)
Net income (basic earnings per share)		$ 6.12

Gains and losses that are neither unusual nor infrequent are reported as part of continuing operations. Gains and losses that are *either* unusual *or* infrequent, but *not* both, are reported as part of continuing operations *but* after the normal revenues and expenses.

Decision Maker   Answer — p. 713

Small Business Owner   You own an orange grove near Jacksonville, Florida. A bad frost destroys about one-half of your oranges. You are currently preparing an income statement for a bank loan. Can you claim the loss of oranges as extraordinary? ■

Earnings per Share   The final section ④ of the income statement in Exhibit 17A.1 reports earnings per share for each of the three subcategories of income (continuing operations, discontinued segments, and extraordinary items) when they exist. Earnings per share is discussed in Chapter 13.

Changes in Accounting Principles   The *consistency concept* directs a company to apply the same accounting principles across periods. Yet a company can change from one acceptable accounting principle (such as FIFO, LIFO, or weighted-average) to another as long as the change improves the usefulness of information in its financial statements. A footnote would describe the accounting change and why it is an improvement.

    Changes in accounting principles require retrospective application to prior periods' financial statements. *Retrospective application* involves applying a different accounting principle to prior periods as if that principle had always been used. Retrospective application enhances the consistency of financial information between periods, which improves the usefulness of information, especially with comparative

Point: Changes in principles are sometimes required when new accounting standards are issued.

analyses. (Prior to 2005, the cumulative effect of changes in accounting principles was recognized in net income in the period of the change.) Accounting standards also require that *a change in depreciation, amortization, or depletion method for long-term operating assets is accounted for as a change in accounting estimate*—that is, prospectively over current and future periods. This reflects the notion that an entity should change its depreciation, amortization, or depletion method only with changes in estimated asset benefits, the pattern of benefit usage, or information about those benefits.

Quick Check

Answers — p. 713

13. Which of the following is an extraordinary item? (*a*) a settlement paid to a customer injured while using the company's product, (*b*) a loss to a plant from damages caused by a meteorite, or (*c*) a loss from selling old equipment.
14. Identify the four major sections of an income statement that are potentially reportable.
15. A company using FIFO for the past 15 years decides to switch to LIFO. The effect of this event on prior years' net income is (*a*) reported as if the new method had always been used; (*b*) ignored because it is a change in an accounting estimate; or (*c*) reported on the current year income statement.

Summary

C1 **Explain the purpose and identify the building blocks of analysis.** The purpose of financial statement analysis is to help users make better business decisions. Internal users want information to improve company efficiency and effectiveness in providing products and services. External users want information to make better and more informed decisions in pursuing their goals. The common goals of all users are to evaluate a company's (1) past and current performance, (2) current financial position, and (3) future performance and risk. Financial statement analysis focuses on four "building blocks" of analysis: (1) liquidity and efficiency—ability to meet short-term obligations and efficiently generate revenues; (2) solvency—ability to generate future revenues and meet long-term obligations; (3) profitability—ability to provide financial rewards sufficient to attract and retain financing; and (4) market prospects—ability to generate positive market expectations.

C2 **Describe standards for comparisons in analysis.** Standards for comparisons include (1) intracompany—prior performance and relations between financial items for the company under analysis; (2) competitor—one or more direct competitors of the company; (3) industry—industry statistics; and (4) guidelines (rules of thumb)—general standards developed from past experiences and personal judgments.

A1 **Summarize and report results of analysis.** A financial statement analysis report is often organized around the building blocks of analysis. A good report separates interpretations and conclusions of analysis from the information underlying them. An analysis report often consists of six sections: (1) executive summary, (2) analysis overview, (3) evidential matter, (4) assumptions, (5) key factors, and (6) inferences.

A2^A **Explain the form and assess the content of a complete income statement.** An income statement has four *potential* sections: (1) continuing operations, (2) discontinued segments, (3) extraordinary items, and (4) earnings per share.

P1 **Explain and apply methods of horizontal analysis.** Horizontal analysis is a tool to evaluate changes in data across time. Two important tools of horizontal analysis are comparative statements and trend analysis. Comparative statements show amounts for two or more successive periods, often with changes disclosed in both absolute and percent terms. Trend analysis is used to reveal important changes occurring from one period to the next.

P2 **Describe and apply methods of vertical analysis.** Vertical analysis is a tool to evaluate each financial statement item or group of items in terms of a base amount. Two tools of vertical analysis are common-size statements and graphical analyses. Each item in common-size statements is expressed as a percent of a base amount. For the balance sheet, the base amount is usually total assets, and for the income statement, it is usually sales.

P3 **Define and apply ratio analysis.** Ratio analysis provides clues to and symptoms of underlying conditions. Ratios, properly interpreted, identify areas requiring further investigation. A ratio expresses a mathematical relation between two quantities such as a percent, rate, or proportion. Ratios can be organized into the building blocks of analysis: (1) liquidity and efficiency, (2) solvency, (3) profitability, and (4) market prospects.

Guidance Answers to Decision Maker

Auditor The *joint relation* referred to is the combined increase in sales and the decrease in expenses yielding more than a 5% increase in income. Both *individual* accounts (sales and expenses) yield percent changes within the ±5% acceptable range. However, a joint analysis suggests a different picture. For example, consider a joint analysis using the profit margin ratio. The client's profit margin is 11.46% ($206,000 − $182,400/$206,000) for the current year compared with 5.0% ($200,000 − $190,000/$200,000) for the prior year—yielding a 129% increase in profit margin! This is what concerns the partner, and it suggests expanding audit tests to verify or refute the client's figures.

Banker Your decision on the loan application is positive for at least two reasons. First, the current ratio suggests a strong ability to meet short-term obligations. Second, current assets of $160,000 and a current ratio of 4:1 imply current liabilities of $40,000 (one-fourth of current assets) and a working capital excess of $120,000. This working capital excess is 60% of the loan amount. However, if the application is for a 10-year loan, our decision is less optimistic. The

current ratio and working capital suggest a good safety margin, but indications of inefficiency in operations exist. In particular, a 4:1 current ratio is more than double its key competitors' ratio. This is characteristic of inefficient asset use.

Small Business Owner The frost loss is probably not extraordinary. Jacksonville experiences enough recurring frost damage to make it difficult to argue this event is both unusual and infrequent. Still, you want to highlight the frost loss and hope the bank views this uncommon event separately from continuing operations.

Guidance Answers to Quick Checks

1. General-purpose financial statements are intended for a variety of users interested in a company's financial condition and performance—users without the power to require specialized financial reports to meet their specific needs.

2. General-purpose financial statements include the income statement, balance sheet, statement of stockholders' (owners') equity, and statement of cash flows plus the notes related to these statements.

3. *a*

4. Data from one or more direct competitors are usually preferred for comparative purposes.

5. *d*

6. Percents on comparative income statements show the increase or decrease in each item from one period to the next. On common-size comparative income statements, each item is shown as a percent of net sales for that period.

7. *c*

8. (*a*) ($820,000 + $240,000 + $470,000)/
($350,000 + $180,000) = 2.9 to 1.

(*b*) ($820,000 + $240,000)/($350,000 + $180,000) = 2:1.

9. (*a*) $2,500,000/[($290,000 + $240,000)/2] = 9.43 times.

(*b*) ($290,000/$2,500,000) × 365 = 42 days.

(*c*) $750,000/[($530,000 + $470,000)/2] = 1.5 times.

(*d*) ($530,000/$750,000) × 365 = 258 days.

10. *c*

11. *b*

12. $\text{Profit margin} \times \dfrac{\text{Total asset}}{\text{turnover}} = \dfrac{\text{Return on}}{\text{total assets}}$

$\dfrac{\$945,000}{\$8,500,000} \times 1.8 = 20\%$

13. (*b*)

14. The four (potentially reportable) major sections are income from continuing operations, discontinued segments, extraordinary items, and earnings per share.

15. (*a*); known as retrospective application.

Key Terms

mhhe.com/wildFAP20e

Business segment (p. 710)
Common-size financial statement (p. 693)
Comparative financial statements (p. 688)
Efficiency (p. 687)
Equity ratio (p. 701)
Extraordinary gains and losses (p. 710)
Financial reporting (p. 687)

Financial statement analysis (p. 686)
General-purpose financial
statements (p. 687)
Horizontal analysis (p. 688)
Infrequent gain or loss (p. 710)
Liquidity (p. 687)
Market prospects (p. 687)

Profitability (p. 687)
Ratio analysis (p. 688)
Solvency (p. 687)
Unusual gain or loss (p. 710)
Vertical analysis (p. 688)
Working capital (p. 697)

Multiple Choice Quiz

Answers on p. 729   mhhe.com/wildFAP20e

Additional Quiz Questions are available at the book's Website.

1. A company's sales in 2010 were $300,000 and in 2011 were $351,000. Using 2010 as the base year, the sales trend percent for 2011 is:

a. 17%

b. 85%

c. 100%

d. 117%

e. 48%

Use the following information for questions 2 through 5.

GALLOWAY COMPANY
Balance Sheet
December 31, 2011

Assets

Cash.........................	$ 86,000
Accounts receivable	76,000
Merchandise inventory	122,000
Prepaid insurance	12,000
Long-term investments	98,000
Plant assets, net	436,000
Total assets	$830,000

Liabilities and Equity

Current liabilities..............	$124,000
Long-term liabilities............	90,000
Common stock	300,000
Retained earnings	316,000
Total liabilities and equity	$830,000

2. What is Galloway Company's current ratio?
   a. 0.69
   b. 1.31
   c. 3.88
   d. 6.69
   e. 2.39

3. What is Galloway Company's acid-test ratio?
   a. 2.39
   b. 0.69
   c. 1.31
   d. 6.69
   e. 3.88

4. What is Galloway Company's debt ratio?
   a. 25.78%
   b. 100.00%
   c. 74.22%
   d. 137.78%
   e. 34.74%

5. What is Galloway Company's equity ratio?
   a. 25.78%
   b. 100.00%
   c. 34.74%
   d. 74.22%
   e. 137.78%

A   *Superscript letter A denotes assignments based on Appendix 17A.*
🔘 Icon denotes assignments that involve decision making.

Discussion Questions

1. What is the difference between comparative financial statements and common-size comparative statements?

2. Which items are usually assigned a 100% value on (*a*) a common-size balance sheet and (*b*) a common-size income statement?

3. Explain the difference between financial reporting and financial statements.

4. 🔘 What three factors would influence your evaluation as to whether a company's current ratio is good or bad?

5. 🔘 Suggest several reasons why a 2:1 current ratio might not be adequate for a particular company.

6. 🔘 Why is working capital given special attention in the process of analyzing balance sheets?

7. 🔘 What does the number of days' sales uncollected indicate?

8. 🔘 What does a relatively high accounts receivable turnover indicate about a company's short-term liquidity?

9. 🔘 Why is a company's capital structure, as measured by debt and equity ratios, important to financial statement analysts?

10. 🔘 How does inventory turnover provide information about a company's short-term liquidity?

11. 🔘 What ratios would you compute to evaluate management performance?

12. 🔘 Why would a company's return on total assets be different from its return on common stockholders' equity?

13. Where on the income statement does a company report an unusual gain not expected to occur more often than once every two years or so?

14. Use **Research In Motion**'s financial statements in Appendix A to compute its return on total assets for **RIM** fiscal years ended February 27, 2010, and February 28, 2009. Total assets at March 1, 2008, were $5,511,187 (in thousands).

15. Refer to **Palm**'s financial statements in Appendix A to compute its equity ratio as of May 31, 2009 and **Palm** May 31, 2008.

16. Refer to **Nokia**'s financial statements in Appendix A. Compute its debt ratio as of December 31, **NOKIA** 2009, and December 31, 2008.

17. Refer to **Apple**'s financial statements in Appendix A. Compute its profit margin for the fiscal year **Apple** ended September 26, 2009.

■■connect

Which of the following items (1) through (9) are part of financial reporting but are *not* included as part of general-purpose financial statements? (1) stock price information and analysis, (2) statement of cash flows, (3) management discussion and analysis of financial performance, (4) income statement, (5) company news releases, (6) balance sheet, (7) financial statement notes, (8) statement of shareholders' equity, (9) prospectus.

QUICK STUDY

QS 17-1
Financial reporting C1

What are four possible standards of comparison used to analyze financial statement ratios? Which of these is generally considered to be the most useful? Which one is least likely to provide a good basis for comparison?

QS 17-2
Standard of comparison C2

Use the following information for Tipster Corporation to determine the 2010 and 2011 trend percents for net sales using 2010 as the base year.

QS 17-3
Trend percents

P1

($ thousands)	2011	2010
Net sales	$201,600	$114,800
Cost of goods sold	109,200	60,200

Refer to the information in QS 17-3. Use that information for Tipster Corporation to determine the 2010 and 2011 common-size percents for cost of goods sold using net sales as the base.

QS 17-4
Common-size analysis P2

Compute the annual dollar changes and percent changes for each of the following accounts.

QS 17-5
Horizontal analysis

P1

	2011	2010
Short-term investments	$217,800	$165,000
Accounts receivable	42,120	48,000
Notes payable	57,000	0

For each ratio listed, identify whether the change in ratio value from 2010 to 2011 is usually regarded as favorable or unfavorable.

QS 17-6
Ratio interpretation

P3

Ratio	2011	2010	Ratio	2011	2010
1. Profit margin	8%	6%	5. Accounts receivable turnover	5.4	6.6
2. Debt ratio	45%	40%	6. Basic earnings per share	$1.24	$1.20
3. Gross margin	33%	45%	7. Inventory turnover	3.5	3.3
4. Acid-test ratio	0.99	1.10	8. Dividend yield	1%	0.8%

The following information is available for Silverado Company and Titan Company, similar firms operating in the same industry. Write a half-page report comparing Silverado and Titan using the available information. Your discussion should include their ability to meet current obligations and to use current assets efficiently.

QS 17-7
Analysis of short-term financial condition

A1

Microsoft Excel - Book1						
	Silverado			**Titan**		
	2012	**2011**	**2010**	**2012**	**2011**	**2010**
Current ratio	1.6	1.7	2.0	3.1	2.6	1.8
Acid-test ratio	0.9	1.0	1.1	2.7	2.4	1.5
Accounts receivable turnover	29.5	24.2	28.2	15.4	14.2	15.0
Merchandise inventory turnover	23.2	20.9	16.1	13.5	12.0	11.6
Working capital	$60,000	$48,000	$42,000	$121,000	$93,000	$68,000

Team Project: Assume that the two companies apply for a one-year loan from the team. Identify additional information the companies must provide before the team can make a loan decision.

QS 17-8ᴬ
Error adjustments
A2

A review of the notes payable files discovers that three years ago the company reported the entire amount of a payment (principal and interest) on an installment note payable as interest expense. This mistake had a material effect on the amount of income in that year. How should the correction be reported in the current year financial statements?

QS 17-9
International ratio analysis
C2

Answer each of the following related to international accounting and analysis.

a. Identify an advantage to using horizontal and vertical analyses when examining companies reporting under different currencies.

b. Identify a limitation to using ratio analysis when examining companies reporting under different accounting systems such as IFRS versus U.S. GAAP.

EXERCISES

Exercise 17-1
Building blocks of analysis
C1

Match the ratio to the building block of financial statement analysis to which it best relates.

A. Liquidity and efficiency   **C.** Profitability
B. Solvency   **D.** Market prospects

1. _____ Book value per common share   **6.** _____ Gross margin ratio
2. _____ Days' sales in inventory   **7.** _____ Acid-test ratio
3. _____ Accounts receivable turnover   **8.** _____ Equity ratio
4. _____ Debt-to-equity   **9.** _____ Return on total assets
5. _____ Times interest earned   **10.** _____ Dividend yield

Exercise 17-2
Identifying financial ratios
C2

1. Which two short-term liquidity ratios measure how frequently a company collects its accounts?
2. What measure reflects the difference between current assets and current liabilities?
3. Which two ratios are key components in measuring a company's operating efficiency? Which ratio summarizes these two components?

Exercise 17-3
Computation and analysis of trend percents
P1

Compute trend percents for the following accounts, using 2009 as the base year. State whether the situation as revealed by the trends appears to be favorable or unfavorable for each account.

	2013	2012	2011	2010	2009
Sales	$283,880	$271,800	$253,680	$235,560	$151,000
Cost of goods sold	129,200	123,080	116,280	107,440	68,000
Accounts receivable	19,100	18,300	17,400	16,200	10,000

Exercise 17-4
Determination of income effects from common-size and trend percents
P1 P2

Common-size and trend percents for Aziz Company's sales, cost of goods sold, and expenses follow. Determine whether net income increased, decreased, or remained unchanged in this three-year period.

	Common-Size Percents			Trend Percents		
	2012	2011	2010	2012	2011	2010
Sales	100.0%	100.0%	100.0%	104.4%	103.2%	100.0%
Cost of goods sold	62.4	60.9	58.1	102.0	108.1	100.0
Total expenses	14.3	13.8	14.1	105.9	101.0	100.0

Express the following comparative income statements in common-size percents and assess whether or not this company's situation has improved in the most recent year.

Exercise 17-5
Common-size percent computation and interpretation

P2

GERALDO CORPORATION		
Comparative Income Statements		
For Years Ended December 31, 2011 and 2010		
	2011	2010
Sales	$720,000	$535,000
Cost of goods sold	475,200	280,340
Gross profit	244,800	254,660
Operating expenses	151,200	103,790
Net income	$ 93,600	$150,870

Rolf Company and Kent Company are similar firms that operate in the same industry. Kent began operations in 2011 and Rolf in 2008. In 2013, both companies pay 7% interest on their debt to creditors. The following additional information is available.

Exercise 17-6
Analysis of efficiency and financial leverage

A1

	Rolf Company			Kent Company		
	2013	2012	2011	2013	2012	2011
Total asset turnover	3.0	2.7	2.9	1.6	1.4	1.1
Return on total assets	8.9%	9.5%	8.7%	5.8%	5.5%	5.2%
Profit margin ratio	2.3%	2.4%	2.2%	2.7%	2.9%	2.8%
Sales	$400,000	$370,000	$386,000	$200,000	$160,000	$100,000

Write a half-page report comparing Rolf and Kent using the available information. Your analysis should include their ability to use assets efficiently to produce profits. Also comment on their success in employing financial leverage in 2013.

Sanderson Company's year-end balance sheets follow. Express the balance sheets in common-size percents. Round amounts to the nearest one-tenth of a percent. Analyze and comment on the results.

Exercise 17-7
Common-size percents

P2

At December 31	2012	2011	2010
Assets			
Cash	$ 30,800	$ 35,625	$ 36,800
Accounts receivable, net	88,500	62,500	49,200
Merchandise inventory	111,500	82,500	53,000
Prepaid expenses	9,700	9,375	4,000
Plant assets, net	277,500	255,000	229,500
Total assets	$518,000	$445,000	$372,500
Liabilities and Equity			
Accounts payable	$128,900	$ 75,250	$ 49,250
Long-term notes payable secured by mortgages on plant assets	97,500	102,500	82,500
Common stock, $10 par value	162,500	162,500	162,500
Retained earnings	129,100	104,750	78,250
Total liabilities and equity	$518,000	$445,000	$372,500

Refer to Sanderson Company's balance sheets in Exercise 17-7. Analyze its year-end short-term liquidity position at the end of 2012, 2011, and 2010 by computing (1) the current ratio and (2) the acid-test ratio. Comment on the ratio results. (Round ratio amounts to two decimals.)

Exercise 17-8
Liquidity analysis

P3

Exercise 17-9

Liquidity analysis and interpretation

P3

Refer to the Sanderson Company information in Exercise 17-7. The company's income statements for the years ended December 31, 2012 and 2011, follow. Assume that all sales are on credit and then compute: (1) days' sales uncollected, (2) accounts receivable turnover, (3) inventory turnover, and (4) days' sales in inventory. Comment on the changes in the ratios from 2011 to 2012. (Round amounts to one decimal.)

For Year Ended December 31	2012		2011	
Sales		$672,500		$530,000
Cost of goods sold	$410,225		$344,500	
Other operating expenses	208,550		133,980	
Interest expense	11,100		12,300	
Income taxes	8,525		7,845	
Total costs and expenses		638,400		498,625
Net income		$ 34,100		$ 31,375
Earnings per share		$ 2.10		$ 1.93

Exercise 17-10

Risk and capital structure analysis   P3

Refer to the Sanderson Company information in Exercises 17-7 and 17-9. Compare the company's long-term risk and capital structure positions at the end of 2012 and 2011 by computing these ratios: (1) debt and equity ratios, (2) debt-to-equity ratio, and (3) times interest earned. Comment on these ratio results.

Exercise 17-11

Efficiency and profitability analysis   P3

Refer to Sanderson Company's financial information in Exercises 17-7 and 17-9. Evaluate the company's efficiency and profitability by computing the following for 2012 and 2011: (1) profit margin ratio, (2) total asset turnover, and (3) return on total assets. Comment on these ratio results.

Exercise 17-12

Profitability analysis

P3

Refer to Sanderson Company's financial information in Exercises 17-7 and 17-9. Additional information about the company follows. To help evaluate the company's profitability, compute and interpret the following ratios for 2012 and 2011: (1) return on common stockholders' equity, (2) price-earnings ratio on December 31, and (3) dividend yield.

Common stock market price, December 31, 2012	$15.00
Common stock market price, December 31, 2011	14.00
Annual cash dividends per share in 2012	0.30
Annual cash dividends per share in 2011	0.15

Exercise 17-13ᴬ

Income statement categories

A2

In 2011, Jin Merchandising, Inc., sold its interest in a chain of retail outlets, taking the company completely out of the retailing business. The company still operates its wholesale outlets. A listing of the major sections of an income statement follows:

A. Income (loss) from continuing operations

B. Income (loss) from operating, or gain (loss) from disposing, a discontinued segment

C. Extraordinary gain (loss)

Indicate where each of the following income-related items for this company appears on its 2011 income statement by writing the letter of the appropriate section in the blank beside each item.

Section	Item	Debit	Credit
_____	1. Net sales		$3,000,000
_____	2. Gain on state's condemnation of company property (net of tax)		330,000
_____	3. Salaries expense	$ 640,000	
_____	4. Income taxes expense	117,000	
_____	5. Depreciation expense	432,500	
_____	6. Gain on sale of retail business segment (net of tax)		875,000
_____	7. Loss from operating retail business segment (net of tax)	544,000	
_____	8. Cost of goods sold	1,580,000	

Use the financial data for Jin Merchandising, Inc., in Exercise 17-13 to prepare its income statement for calendar year 2011. (Ignore the earnings per share section.)

Exercise 17-14ᴬ
Income statement presentation
A2

Nintendo Company, Ltd., reports the following financial information as of, or for the year ended, March 31, 2008. Nintendo reports its financial statements in both Japanese yen and U.S. dollars as shown (amounts in millions).

Exercise 17-15
Ratio analysis under different currencies

P3

Current assets	¥1,646,834	$16,468.348
Total assets	1,802,490	18,024.903
Current liabilities	567,222	5,672.229
Net sales	1,672,423	16,724.230
Net income	257,342	2,573.426

1. Compute Nintendo's current ratio, net profit margin, and sales-to-total-assets using the financial information reported in (a) yen and (b) dollars.
2. What can we conclude from a review of the results for part 1?

connect

Selected comparative financial statements of Bennington Company follow.

PROBLEM SET A

Problem 17-1A
Ratios, common-size statements, and trend percents

P1 P2 P3

mhhe.com/wildFAP20e

BENNINGTON COMPANY Comparative Income Statements For Years Ended December 31, 2012, 2011, and 2010			
	2012	2011	2010
Sales	$444,000	$340,000	$236,000
Cost of goods sold	267,288	212,500	151,040
Gross profit	176,712	127,500	84,960
Selling expenses	62,694	46,920	31,152
Administrative expenses	40,137	29,920	19,470
Total expenses	102,831	76,840	50,622
Income before taxes	73,881	50,660	34,338
Income taxes	13,764	10,370	6,962
Net income	$ 60,117	$ 40,290	$ 27,376

BENNINGTON COMPANY Comparative Balance Sheets December 31, 2012, 2011, and 2010			
	2012	2011	2010
Assets			
Current assets	$ 48,480	$ 37,924	$ 50,648
Long-term investments	0	500	3,720
Plant assets, net	90,000	96,000	57,000
Total assets	$138,480	$134,424	$111,368
Liabilities and Equity			
Current liabilities	$ 20,200	$ 19,960	$ 19,480
Common stock	72,000	72,000	54,000
Other paid-in capital	9,000	9,000	6,000
Retained earnings	37,280	33,464	31,888
Total liabilities and equity	$138,480	$134,424	$111,368

Required

1. Compute each year's current ratio. (Round ratio amounts to one decimal.)
2. Express the income statement data in common-size percents. (Round percents to two decimals.)

3. Express the balance sheet data in trend percents with 2010 as the base year. (Round percents to two decimals.)

Analysis Component

4. Comment on any significant relations revealed by the ratios and percents computed.

Problem 17-2A

Calculation and analysis of trend percents

A1 P1

Selected comparative financial statements of Sugo Company follow.

SUGO COMPANY **Comparative Income Statements** **For Years Ended December 31, 2012–2006**							
($ thousands)	2012	2011	2010	2009	2008	2007	2006
Sales	$1,594	$1,396	$1,270	$1,164	$1,086	$1,010	$828
Cost of goods sold	1,146	932	802	702	652	610	486
Gross profit	448	464	468	462	434	400	342
Operating expenses	340	266	244	180	156	154	128
Net income	$ 108	$ 198	$ 224	$ 282	$ 278	$ 246	$214

SUGO COMPANY **Comparative Balance Sheets** **December 31, 2012–2006**							
($ thousands)	2012	2011	2010	2009	2008	2007	2006
Assets							
Cash	$ 68	$ 88	$ 92	$ 94	$ 98	$ 96	$ 99
Accounts receivable, net	480	504	456	350	308	292	206
Merchandise inventory	1,738	1,264	1,104	932	836	710	515
Other current assets	46	42	24	44	38	38	19
Long-term investments	0	0	0	136	136	136	136
Plant assets, net	2,120	2,114	1,852	1,044	1,078	960	825
Total assets	$4,452	$4,012	$3,528	$2,600	$2,494	$2,232	$1,800
Liabilities and Equity							
Current liabilities	$1,120	$ 942	$ 618	$ 514	$ 446	$ 422	$ 272
Long-term liabilities	1,194	1,040	1,012	470	480	520	390
Common stock	1,000	1,000	1,000	840	840	640	640
Other paid-in capital	250	250	250	180	180	160	160
Retained earnings	888	780	648	596	548	490	338
Total liabilities and equity	$4,452	$4,012	$3,528	$2,600	$2,494	$2,232	$1,800

Required

1. Compute trend percents for all components of both statements using 2006 as the base year. (Round percents to one decimal.)

Analysis Component

2. Analyze and comment on the financial statements and trend percents from part 1.

Problem 17-3A

Transactions, working capital, and liquidity ratios

P3

mhhe.com/wildFAP20e

Park Corporation began the month of May with $650,000 of current assets, a current ratio of 2.50:1, and an acid-test ratio of 1.10:1. During the month, it completed the following transactions (the company uses a perpetual inventory system).

May 2 Purchased $75,000 of merchandise inventory on credit.
    8 Sold merchandise inventory that cost $58,000 for $103,000 cash.
  10 Collected $19,000 cash on an account receivable.
  15 Paid $21,000 cash to settle an account payable.

17 Wrote off a $3,000 bad debt against the Allowance for Doubtful Accounts account.

22 Declared a $1 per share cash dividend on its 40,000 shares of outstanding common stock.

26 Paid the dividend declared on May 22.

27 Borrowed $75,000 cash by giving the bank a 30-day, 10% note.

28 Borrowed $90,000 cash by signing a long-term secured note.

29 Used the $165,000 cash proceeds from the notes to buy new machinery.

Check May 22: Current ratio, 2.12; Acid-test ratio, 1.04

May 29: Current ratio, 1.82; Working capital, $320,000

Required

Prepare a table showing Park's (1) current ratio, (2) acid-test ratio, and (3) working capital, after each transaction. Round ratios to two decimals.

Selected year-end financial statements of McCord Corporation follow. (All sales were on credit; selected balance sheet amounts at December 31, 2010, were inventory, $32,400; total assets, $182,400; common stock, $90,000; and retained earnings, $31,300.)

Problem 17-4A

Calculation of financial statement ratios

P3

mhhe.com/wildFAP20e

McCORD CORPORATION Income Statement For Year Ended December 31, 2011	
Sales	$348,600
Cost of goods sold	229,150
Gross profit	119,450
Operating expenses	52,500
Interest expense	3,100
Income before taxes	63,850
Income taxes	15,800
Net income	$ 48,050

McCORD CORPORATION Balance Sheet December 31, 2011			
Assets		**Liabilities and Equity**	
Cash	$ 9,000	Accounts payable	$ 16,500
Short-term investments	7,400	Accrued wages payable	2,200
Accounts receivable, net	28,200	Income taxes payable	2,300
Notes receivable (trade)*	3,500	Long-term note payable, secured	
Merchandise inventory	31,150	by mortgage on plant assets	62,400
Prepaid expenses	1,650	Common stock	90,000
Plant assets, net	152,300	Retained earnings	59,800
Total assets	$233,200	Total liabilities and equity	$233,200

* These are short-term notes receivable arising from customer (trade) sales.

Required

Compute the following: (1) current ratio, (2) acid-test ratio, (3) days' sales uncollected, (4) inventory turnover, (5) days' sales in inventory, (6) debt-to-equity ratio, (7) times interest earned, (8) profit margin ratio, (9) total asset turnover, (10) return on total assets, and (11) return on common stockholders' equity.

Check Acid-test ratio, 2.3 to 1: Inventory turnover, 7.2

Summary information from the financial statements of two companies competing in the same industry follows.

Problem 17-5A

Comparative ratio analysis

A1 P3

	Ryan Company	Priest Company		Ryan Company	Priest Company
Data from the current year-end balance sheets			**Data from the current year's income statement**		
Assets			Sales	$660,000	$780,200
Cash	$ 18,500	$ 33,000	Cost of goods sold	485,100	532,500
Accounts receivable, net	36,400	56,400	Interest expense	6,900	11,000
Current notes receivable (trade)	8,100	6,200	Income tax expense	12,800	19,300
Merchandise inventory	83,440	131,500	Net income	67,770	105,000
Prepaid expenses	4,000	5,950	Basic earnings per share	1.94	2.56
Plant assets, net	284,000	303,400			
Total assets	$434,440	$536,450			
			Beginning-of-year balance sheet data		
Liabilities and Equity			Accounts receivable, net	$ 28,800	$ 53,200
Current liabilities	$ 60,340	$ 92,300	Current notes receivable (trade)	0	0
Long-term notes payable	79,800	100,000	Merchandise inventory	54,600	106,400
Common stock, $5 par value	175,000	205,000	Total assets	388,000	372,500
Retained earnings	119,300	139,150	Common stock, $5 par value	175,000	205,000
Total liabilities and equity	$434,440	$536,450	Retained earnings	94,300	90,600

Required

Check   (1) Priest: Accounts receivable turnover, 13.5; Inventory turnover, 4.5

     (2) Ryan: Profit margin, 10.3%; PE, 12.9

1. For both companies compute the (*a*) current ratio, (*b*) acid-test ratio, (*c*) accounts (including notes) receivable turnover, (*d*) inventory turnover, (*e*) days' sales in inventory, and (*f*) days' sales uncollected. Identify the company you consider to be the better short-term credit risk and explain why.

2. For both companies compute the (*a*) profit margin ratio, (*b*) total asset turnover, (*c*) return on total assets, and (*d*) return on common stockholders' equity. Assuming that each company paid cash dividends of $1.50 per share and each company's stock can be purchased at $25 per share, compute their (*e*) price-earnings ratios and (*f*) dividend yields. Identify which company's stock you would recommend as the better investment and explain why.

Problem 17-6A[A]

Income statement computations and format

A2

Selected account balances from the adjusted trial balance for Zen Corporation as of its calendar year-end December 31, 2011, follow.

	Debit	Credit
a. Income taxes expense	$?	
b. Correction of overstatement of prior year's sales (pretax)	17,000	
c. Loss on sale of machinery	26,850	
d. Loss from settlement of lawsuit	24,750	
e. Other operating expenses	107,400	
f. Accumulated depreciation—Machinery		$ 72,600
g. Gain from settlement of lawsuit		45,000
h. Accumulated depreciation—Buildings		175,500
i. Loss from operating a discontinued segment (pretax)	19,250	
j. Gain on insurance recovery of tornado damage (pretax and extraordinary)		30,120
k. Net sales		999,500
l. Depreciation expense—Buildings	53,000	
m. Depreciation expense—Machinery	35,000	
n. Gain on sale of discontinued segment's assets (pretax)		35,000
o. Accounts payable		45,000
p. Interest revenue		15,000
q. Cost of goods sold	483,500	

Required

Answer each of the following questions by providing supporting computations.

1. Assume that the company's income tax rate is 30% for all items. Identify the tax effects and after-tax amounts of the four items labeled pretax.
2. What is the amount of income from continuing operations before income taxes? What is the amount of the income taxes expense? What is the amount of income from continuing operations?
3. What is the total amount of after-tax income (loss) associated with the discontinued segment?
4. What is the amount of income (loss) before the extraordinary items?
5. What is the amount of net income for the year?

Check   (3) $11,025

(4) $241,325

(5) $262,409

Selected comparative financial statement information of Sawgrass Corporation follows.

PROBLEM SET B

Problem 17-1B
Ratios, common-size statements, and trend percents

P1 P2 P3

SAWGRASS CORPORATION			
Comparative Income Statements			
For Years Ended December 31, 2012, 2011, and 2010			
	2012	2011	2010
Sales	$199,800	$167,000	$144,800
Cost of goods sold	109,890	87,175	67,200
Gross profit	89,910	79,825	77,600
Selling expenses	23,680	20,790	19,000
Administrative expenses	17,760	15,610	16,700
Total expenses	41,440	36,400	35,700
Income before taxes	48,470	43,425	41,900
Income taxes	5,050	4,910	4,300
Net income	$ 43,420	$ 38,515	$ 37,600

SAWGRASS CORPORATION			
Comparative Balance Sheets			
December 31, 2012, 2011, and 2010			
	2012	2011	2010
Assets			
Current assets	$ 55,860	$ 33,660	$ 37,300
Long-term investments	0	2,700	11,600
Plant assets, net	113,810	114,660	80,000
Total assets	$169,670	$151,020	$128,900
Liabilities and Equity			
Current liabilities	$ 23,370	$ 20,180	$ 17,500
Common stock	47,500	47,500	38,000
Other paid-in capital	14,850	14,850	12,300
Retained earnings	83,950	68,490	61,100
Total liabilities and equity	$169,670	$151,020	$128,900

Required

1. Compute each year's current ratio. (Round ratio amounts to one decimal.)
2. Express the income statement data in common-size percents. (Round percents to two decimals.)
3. Express the balance sheet data in trend percents with 2010 as the base year. (Round percents to two decimals.)

Check   (3) 2012, Total assets trend, 131.63%

Analysis Component

4. Comment on any significant relations revealed by the ratios and percents computed.

Problem 17-2B
Calculation and analysis of trend percents

A1 P1

Selected comparative financial statements of Deuce Company follow.

DEUCE COMPANY Comparative Income Statements For Years Ended December 31, 2012–2006							
($ thousands)	2012	2011	2010	2009	2008	2007	2006
Sales	$660	$710	$730	$780	$840	$870	$960
Cost of goods sold	376	390	394	414	440	450	480
Gross profit	284	320	336	366	400	420	480
Operating expenses	184	204	212	226	240	244	250
Net income	$100	$116	$124	$140	$160	$176	$230

DEUCE COMPANY Comparative Balance Sheets December 31, 2012–2006							
($ thousands)	2012	2011	2010	2009	2008	2007	2006
Assets							
Cash	$ 34	$ 36	$ 42	$ 44	$ 50	$ 52	$ 58
Accounts receivable, net	120	126	130	134	140	144	150
Merchandise inventory	156	162	168	170	176	180	198
Other current assets	24	24	26	28	28	30	30
Long-term investments	26	20	16	100	100	100	100
Plant assets, net	410	414	420	312	320	328	354
Total assets	$770	$782	$802	$788	$814	$834	$890
Liabilities and Equity							
Current liabilities	$138	$146	$176	$180	$200	$250	$270
Long-term liabilities	82	110	132	138	184	204	250
Common stock	150	150	150	150	150	150	150
Other paid-in capital	60	60	60	60	60	60	60
Retained earnings	340	316	284	260	220	170	160
Total liabilities and equity	$770	$782	$802	$788	$814	$834	$890

Required

Check (1) 2012, Total assets trend, 86.5%

1. Compute trend percents for all components of both statements using 2006 as the base year. (Round percents to one decimal.)

Analysis Component

2. Analyze and comment on the financial statements and trend percents from part 1.

Problem 17-3B
Transactions, working capital, and liquidity ratios P3

Check June 1: Current ratio, 3.19; Acid-test ratio, 2.21

June 30: Working capital, $59,000; Current ratio, 1.19

Ready Corporation began the month of June with $280,000 of current assets, a current ratio of 2.8:1, and an acid-test ratio of 1.2:1. During the month, it completed the following transactions (the company uses a perpetual inventory system).

June 1 Sold merchandise inventory that cost $62,000 for $101,000 cash.
  3 Collected $78,000 cash on an account receivable.
  5 Purchased $130,000 of merchandise inventory on credit.
  7 Borrowed $90,000 cash by giving the bank a 60-day, 10% note.
  10 Borrowed $180,000 cash by signing a long-term secured note.
  12 Purchased machinery for $280,000 cash.
  15 Declared a $1 per share cash dividend on its 60,000 shares of outstanding common stock.
  19 Wrote off a $7,000 bad debt against the Allowance for Doubtful Accounts account.
  22 Paid $11,000 cash to settle an account payable.
  30 Paid the dividend declared on June 15.

Required

Prepare a table showing the company's (1) current ratio, (2) acid-test ratio, and (3) working capital after each transaction. Round ratios to two decimals.

Selected year-end financial statements of Overland Corporation follow. (All sales were on credit; selected balance sheet amounts at December 31, 2010, were inventory, $16,400; total assets, $95,900; common stock, $41,500; and retained earnings, $19,800.)

Problem 17-4B
Calculation of financial statement ratios

P3

OVERLAND CORPORATION
Income Statement
For Year Ended December 31, 2011

Sales	$215,500
Cost of goods sold	136,100
Gross profit	79,400
Operating expenses	50,200
Interest expense	1,200
Income before taxes	28,000
Income taxes	2,200
Net income	$ 25,800

OVERLAND CORPORATION
Balance Sheet
December 31, 2011

Assets		Liabilities and Equity	
Cash	$ 5,100	Accounts payable	$ 10,500
Short-term investments	5,900	Accrued wages payable	2,300
Accounts receivable, net	11,100	Income taxes payable	1,600
Notes receivable (trade)*	2,000	Long-term note payable, secured	
Merchandise inventory	12,500	by mortgage on plant assets	25,000
Prepaid expenses	1,000	Common stock, $5 par value	41,000
Plant assets, net	72,900	Retained earnings	30,100
Total assets	$110,500	Total liabilities and equity	$110,500

* These are short-term notes receivable arising from customer (trade) sales.

Required

Compute the following: (1) current ratio, (2) acid-test ratio, (3) days' sales uncollected, (4) inventory turnover, (5) days' sales in inventory, (6) debt-to-equity ratio, (7) times interest earned, (8) profit margin ratio, (9) total asset turnover, (10) return on total assets, and (11) return on common stockholders' equity.

Check   Acid-test ratio, 1.7 to 1; Inventory turnover, 9.4

Summary information from the financial statements of two companies competing in the same industry follows.

Problem 17-5B
Comparative ratio analysis

A1 P3

	Loud Company	Clear Company		Loud Company	Clear Company
Data from the current year-end balance sheets			**Data from the current year's income statement**		
Assets			Sales	$395,600	$669,500
Cash	$ 22,000	$ 38,500	Cost of goods sold	292,600	482,000
Accounts receivable, net	79,100	72,500	Interest expense	7,900	12,400
Current notes receivable (trade)	13,600	11,000	Income tax expense	7,700	14,300
Merchandise inventory	88,800	84,000	Net income	35,850	63,700
Prepaid expenses	11,700	12,100	Basic earnings per share	1.33	2.23
Plant assets, net	178,900	254,300			
Total assets	$394,100	$472,400			
			Beginning-of-year balance sheet data		
Liabilities and Equity			Accounts receivable, net	$ 74,200	$ 75,300
Current liabilities	$ 92,500	$ 99,000	Current notes receivable (trade)	0	0
Long-term notes payable	95,000	95,300	Merchandise inventory	107,100	82,500
Common stock, $5 par value	135,000	143,000	Total assets	385,400	445,000
Retained earnings	71,600	135,100	Common stock, $5 par value	135,000	143,000
Total liabilities and equity	$394,100	$472,400	Retained earnings	51,100	111,700

Required

1. For both companies compute the (*a*) current ratio, (*b*) acid-test ratio, (*c*) accounts (including notes) receivable turnover, (*d*) inventory turnover, (*e*) days' sales in inventory, and (*f*) days' sales uncollected. Identify the company you consider to be the better short-term credit risk and explain why.

2. For both companies compute the (*a*) profit margin ratio, (*b*) total asset turnover, (*c*) return on total assets, and (*d*) return on common stockholders' equity. Assuming that each company paid cash dividends of $3.00 per share and each company's stock can be purchased at $25 per share, compute their (*e*) price-earnings ratios and (*f*) dividend yields. Identify which company's stock you would recommend as the better investment and explain why.

Check (1) Loud: Accounts receivable turnover, 4.7; Inventory turnover, 3.0

(2) Clear: Profit margin, 9.5%; PE, 11.2

Problem 17-6B^A

Income statement computations and format

A2

Selected account balances from the adjusted trial balance for Halogen Corp. as of its calendar year-end December 31, 2011, follow.

	Debit	Credit
a. Other operating expenses	$ 338,000	
b. Depreciation expense—Buildings	110,000	
c. Loss from settlement of lawsuit	46,000	
d. Income taxes expense	?	
e. Loss on hurricane damage (pretax and extraordinary)	74,000	
f. Accumulated depreciation—Buildings		$ 230,000
g. Accumulated depreciation—Equipment		410,000
h. Interest revenue		30,000
i. Net sales		2,650,000
j. Gain from settlement of lawsuit		78,000
k. Loss on sale of building	34,000	
l. Loss from operating a discontinued segment (pretax)	130,000	
m. Accounts payable		142,000
n. Correction of overstatement of prior year's expense (pretax)		58,000
o. Cost of goods sold	1,050,000	
p. Loss on sale of discontinued segment's assets (pretax)	190,000	
q. Depreciation expense—Equipment	166,000	

Required

Answer each of the following questions by providing supporting computations.

1. Assume that the company's income tax rate is 25% for all items. Identify the tax effects and after-tax amounts of the four items labeled pretax.

2. What is the amount of income from continuing operations before income taxes? What is the amount of income taxes expense? What is the amount of income from continuing operations?

Check (3) $(240,000)

(4) $520,500

(5) $465,000

3. What is the total amount of after-tax income (loss) associated with the discontinued segment?

4. What is the amount of income (loss) before the extraordinary items?

5. What is the amount of net income for the year?

SERIAL PROBLEM
Business Solutions

P3

(This serial problem began in Chapter 1 and continues through most of the book. If previous chapter segments were not completed, the serial problem can begin at this point. It is helpful, but not necessary, to use the Working Papers that accompany the book.)

SP 17   Use the following selected data from Business Solutions' income statement for the three months ended March 31, 2012, and from its March 31, 2012, balance sheet to complete the requirements below: computer services revenue, $25,307; net sales (of goods), $18,693; total sales and revenue, $44,000; cost of goods sold, $14,052; net income, $18,833; quick assets, $90,924; current assets, $95,568; total assets, $120,268; current liabilities, $875; total liabilities, $875; and total equity, $119,393.

Required

1. Compute the gross margin ratio (both with and without services revenue) and net profit margin ratio.

2. Compute the current ratio and acid-test ratio.

3. Compute the debt ratio and equity ratio.

4. What percent of its assets are current? What percent are long term?

Beyond the Numbers

REPORTING IN ACTION

A1 P1 P2

RIM

BTN 17-1 Refer to **Research In Motion** financial statements in Appendix A to answer the following.

1. Using fiscal 2008 as the base year, compute trend percents for fiscal years 2008, 2009, and 2010 for revenues, cost of sales, operating expenses, income taxes, and net income. (Round percents to one decimal.)

2. Compute common-size percents for fiscal years 2009 and 2010 for the following categories of assets: (*a*) total current assets, (*b*) property and equipment, net, and (*c*) intangible assets. (Round to the nearest tenth of a percent.)

3. Comment on any notable changes across the years for the income statement trends computed in part 1 and the balance sheet percents computed in part 2.

Fast Forward

4. Access Research In Motion's financial statements for fiscal years ending after February 27, 2010, from its Website (**RIM.com**) or the SEC database (**www.sec.gov**). Update your work for parts 1, 2, and 3 using the new information accessed.

BTN 17-2 Key figures for **Research In Motion** and **Apple** follow.

COMPARATIVE ANALYSIS

C2 P2

RIM

Apple

($ millions)	Research In Motion	Apple
Cash and equivalents	$ 1,551	$ 5,263
Accounts receivable, net	2,594	3,361
Inventories	622	455
Retained earnings	5,274	23,353
Cost of sales	8,369	25,683
Revenues	14,953	42,905
Total assets	10,204	47,501

Required

1. Compute common-size percents for each of the companies using the data provided. (Round percents to one decimal.)

2. Which company retains a higher portion of cumulative net income in the company?

3. Which company has a higher gross margin ratio on sales?

4. Which company holds a higher percent of its total assets as inventory?

BTN 17-3 As Baldwin Company controller, you are responsible for informing the board of directors about its financial activities. At the board meeting, you present the following information.

ETHICS CHALLENGE

A1

	2011	2010	2009
Sales trend percent	147.0%	135.0%	100.0%
Selling expenses to sales	10.1%	14.0%	15.6%
Sales to plant assets ratio	3.8 to 1	3.6 to 1	3.3 to 1
Current ratio	2.9 to 1	2.7 to 1	2.4 to 1
Acid-test ratio	1.1 to 1	1.4 to 1	1.5 to 1
Inventory turnover	7.8 times	9.0 times	10.2 times
Accounts receivable turnover	7.0 times	7.7 times	8.5 times
Total asset turnover	2.9 times	2.9 times	3.3 times
Return on total assets	10.4%	11.0%	13.2%
Return on stockholders' equity.........	10.7%	11.5%	14.1%
Profit margin ratio	3.6%	3.8%	4.0%

After the meeting, the company's CEO holds a press conference with analysts in which she mentions the following ratios.

	2011	2010	2009
Sales trend percent	147.0%	135.0%	100.0%
Selling expenses to sales	10.1%	14.0%	15.6%
Sales to plant assets ratio	3.8 to 1	3.6 to 1	3.3 to 1
Current ratio	2.9 to 1	2.7 to 1	2.4 to 1

Required

1. Why do you think the CEO decided to report 4 ratios instead of the 11 prepared?
2. Comment on the possible consequences of the CEO's reporting of the ratios selected.

COMMUNICATING IN PRACTICE

A1 P3

BTN 17-4 Each team is to select a different industry, and each team member is to select a different company in that industry and acquire its financial statements. Use those statements to analyze the company, including at least one ratio from each of the four building blocks of analysis. When necessary, use the financial press to determine the market price of its stock. Communicate with teammates via a meeting, e-mail, or telephone to discuss how different companies compare to each other and to industry norms. The team is to prepare a single one-page memorandum reporting on its analysis and the conclusions reached.

TAKING IT TO THE NET

P3

BTN 17-5 Access the February 19, 2010, filing of the December 31, 2009, 10-K report of **The Hershey Company** (ticker HSY) at **www.SEC.gov** and complete the following requirements.

Required

Compute or identify the following profitability ratios of Hershey for its years ending December 31, 2009, *and* December 31, 2008. Interpret its profitability using the results obtained for these two years.

1. Profit margin ratio.
2. Gross profit ratio.
3. Return on total assets. (Total assets at year-end 2007 were $4,247,113,000.)
4. Return on common stockholders' equity. (Total shareholders' equity at year-end 2007 was $592,922,000.)
5. Basic net income per common share.

TEAMWORK IN ACTION

P1 P2 P3

BTN 17-6 A team approach to learning financial statement analysis is often useful.

Required

1. Each team should write a description of horizontal and vertical analysis that all team members agree with and understand. Illustrate each description with an example.
2. *Each* member of the team is to select *one* of the following categories of ratio analysis. Explain what the ratios in that category measure. Choose one ratio from the category selected, present its formula, and explain what it measures.

   a. Liquidity and efficiency   **c.** Profitability
   b. Solvency   **d.** Market prospects

3. Each team member is to present his or her notes from part 2 to teammates. Team members are to confirm or correct other teammates' presentation.

Hint: Pairing within teams may be necessary for part 2. Use as an in-class activity or as an assignment. Consider presentations to the entire class using team rotation with transparencies.

ENTREPRENEURIAL DECISION

A1 P1 P2 P3

BTN 17-7 Assume that David and Tom Gardner of **The Motley Fool** (**Fool.com**) have impressed you since you first heard of their rather improbable rise to prominence in financial circles. You learn of a staff opening at The Motley Fool and decide to apply for it. Your resume is successfully screened from the thousands received and you advance to the interview process. You learn that the interview consists of analyzing the following financial facts and answering analysis questions. (*Note:* The data are taken from a small merchandiser in outdoor recreational equipment.)

	2010	2009	2008
Sales trend percents	137.0%	125.0%	100.0%
Selling expenses to sales	9.8%	13.7%	15.3%
Sales to plant assets ratio	3.5 to 1	3.3 to 1	3.0 to 1
Current ratio	2.6 to 1	2.4 to 1	2.1 to 1
Acid-test ratio	0.8 to 1	1.1 to 1	1.2 to 1
Merchandise inventory turnover	7.5 times	8.7 times	9.9 times
Accounts receivable turnover	6.7 times	7.4 times	8.2 times
Total asset turnover	2.6 times	2.6 times	3.0 times
Return on total assets	8.8%	9.4%	11.1%
Return on equity	9.75%	11.50%	12.25%
Profit margin ratio	3.3%	3.5%	3.7%

Required

Use these data to answer each of the following questions with explanations.

1. Is it becoming easier for the company to meet its current liabilities on time and to take advantage of any available cash discounts? Explain.

2. Is the company collecting its accounts receivable more rapidly? Explain.

3. Is the company's investment in accounts receivable decreasing? Explain.

4. Is the company's investment in plant assets increasing? Explain.

5. Is the owner's investment becoming more profitable? Explain.

6. Did the dollar amount of selling expenses decrease during the three-year period? Explain.

BTN 17-8 You are to devise an investment strategy to enable you to accumulate $1,000,000 by age 65. Start by making some assumptions about your salary. Next compute the percent of your salary that you will be able to save each year. If you will receive any lump-sum monies, include those amounts in your calculations. Historically, stocks have delivered average annual returns of 10–11%. Given this history, you should probably not assume that you will earn above 10% on the money you invest. It is not necessary to specify exactly what types of assets you will buy for your investments; just assume a rate you expect to earn. Use the future value tables in Appendix B to calculate how your savings will grow. Experiment a bit with your figures to see how much less you have to save if you start at, for example, age 25 versus age 35 or 40. (For this assignment, do not include inflation in your calculations.)

HITTING THE ROAD

C1 P3

BTN 17-9 **Nokia (www.Nokia.com),** which is a leading manufacturer of mobile devices and services, along with **Research In Motion** and **Apple** are competitors in the global marketplace. Key figures for Nokia follow (in Euro millions).

GLOBAL DECISION

A1

NOKIA

RIM

Apple

Cash and equivalents	1,142
Accounts receivable, net	7,981
Inventories	1,865
Retained earnings	10,132
Cost of sales	27,720
Revenues	40,984
Total assets	35,738

Required

1. Compute common-size percents for Nokia using the data provided. (Round percents to one decimal.)

2. Compare the results with Research In Motion and Apple from BTN 17-2.

ANSWERS TO MULTIPLE CHOICE QUIZ

1. d; ($351,000/$300,000) × 100 = 117%

2. e; ($86,000 + $76,000 + $122,000 + $12,000)/$124,000 = 2.39

3. c; ($86,000 + $76,000)/$124,000 = 1.31

4. a; ($124,000 + $90,000)/$830,000 = 25.78%

5. d; ($300,000 + $316,000)/$830,000 = 74.22%

18

Managerial Accounting Concepts and Principles

A Look Back

Chapter 17 described the analysis and interpretation of financial statement information. We applied horizontal, vertical, and ratio analyses to better understand company performance and financial condition.

A Look at This Chapter

We begin our study of managerial accounting by explaining its purpose and describing its major characteristics. We also discuss cost concepts and describe how they help managers gather and organize information for making decisions. The reporting of manufacturing activities is also discussed.

A Look Ahead

The remaining chapters discuss the types of decisions managers must make and how managerial accounting helps with those decisions. The first of these chapters, Chapter 19, considers how we measure costs assigned to certain types of projects.

Learning Objectives

CAP

CONCEPTUAL

C1 Explain the purpose and nature of, and the role of ethics in, managerial accounting. (p. 732)

C2 Describe accounting concepts useful in classifying costs. (p. 736)

C3 Define product and period costs and explain how they impact financial statements. (p. 738)

C4 Explain how balance sheets and income statements for manufacturing and merchandising companies differ. (p. 740)

C5 Explain manufacturing activities and the flow of manufacturing costs. (p. 744)

C6 Describe trends in managerial accounting. (p. 747)

ANALYTICAL

A1 Compute cycle time and cycle efficiency, and explain their importance to production management (p. 749)

PROCEDURAL

P1 Compute cost of goods sold for a manufacturer. (p. 741)

P2 Prepare a manufacturing statement and explain its purpose and links to financial statements. (p. 745)

LP18

Decision Insight

Hot Late Nights

"I didn't know I was a baker . . ."

—COREY RIMMEL

COLUMBIA, MO—Hanging out in a friend's basement one night, college students Corey Rimmel, Adam Hendin, and David Melnick thought a late-night bakery would be the perfect recipe for their hunger. But, the enterprising trio's thoughts weren't just on eating cookies but also on starting a business. "At first we were just joking, kicking the idea around," Corey says. "Before long, we were in the library every night doing research. One day we said, 'Well, let's just see if we can do it.'" After weeks of research, talking to entrepreneurs, writing a business plan, and setting up a managerial accounting system, the friends started **Hot Box Cookies (HotBoxCookies.com).**

Hot Box Cookies focuses on meeting individual customer's tastes. Starting with homemade dough in four flavors, the company's bakers mix in whatever the customer wants—chocolate chips, Reese's pieces, candy bars. After placing their orders, customers can play board games or surf the Internet in the Hot Box store or have their fresh cookies delivered. The owners say their biggest surprise is how incredibly busy they were from the very beginning of their business. "We haven't had time to work our way through our marketing plan . . . we've just been too busy," explains Corey.

The owners insist college is a great time to start a new business. Risk is low, and "if the owners are passionate and have a good plan, banks will lend money to get the business going," says Corey. "It's nice having something to call our own," Adam says. "A lot of people want to own a business, but they don't." But the trio, two of whom are accounting majors, emphasize that understanding basic managerial principles, product and period costs, manufacturing statements, and cost flow is crucial. The owners use managerial accounting information from the baking process to monitor and control costs and to assess what cookies are most popular and profitable. Success has enabled the business to expand and grow into other product lines such as catering, coffee, and "Dough on the Go" sold in local markets.

Corey, Adam, and David believe that entrepreneurs fill a void by creating a niche. "I've always had it in my mind that I would work for myself," says Corey. However, financial success depends on monitoring and controlling operations to best meet customer needs. By staying focused and applying sound managerial accounting principles and concepts to their business, the owners hope to expand to other college campuses across the country. Ah, the sweet smell of success.

Sources: *Hot Box Cookies* Website, January 2011; *Columbia Missourian,* October 2008; *The MOVE Magazine,* October 2008; *Columbia Business Times,* August 2008; *Columbia Tribune,* November 2008.

Managerial accounting, like financial accounting, provides information to help users make better decisions. However, managerial accounting and financial accounting differ in important ways, which this chapter explains. This chapter also compares the accounting and reporting practices used by manufacturing and merchandising companies. A merchandising company sells products without changing their condition. A manufacturing company buys raw materials and turns them into finished products for sale to customers. A third type of company earns revenues by providing services rather than products. The skills, tools, and techniques developed for measuring a manufacturing company's activities apply to service companies as well. The chapter concludes by explaining the flow of manufacturing activities and preparing the manufacturing statement.

Managerial Accounting Concepts and Principles

Managerial Accounting Basics	Managerial Cost Concepts	Reporting Manufacturing Activities
• Purpose of managerial accounting • Nature of managerial accounting • Managerial decisions • Fraud and ethics in managerial accounting	• Types of cost classifications • Identification of cost classifications • Cost concepts for service companies	• Balance sheet • Income statement • Flow of activities • Manufacturing statement • Trends in managerial accounting

MANAGERIAL ACCOUNTING BASICS

Managerial accounting is an activity that provides financial and nonfinancial information to an organization's managers and other internal decision makers. This section explains the purpose of managerial accounting (also called *management accounting*) and compares it with financial accounting. The main purpose of the financial accounting system is to prepare general-purpose financial statements. That information is incomplete for internal decision makers who manage organizations.

Purpose of Managerial Accounting

C1 Explain the purpose and nature of, and the role of ethics in, managerial accounting.

The purpose of both managerial accounting and financial accounting is providing useful information to decision makers. They do this by collecting, managing, and reporting information in demand by their users. Both areas of accounting also share the common practice of reporting monetary information, although managerial accounting includes the reporting of nonmonetary information. They even report some of the same information. For instance, a company's financial statements contain information useful for both its managers (insiders) and other persons interested in the company (outsiders).

The remainder of this book looks carefully at managerial accounting information, how to gather it, and how managers use it. We consider the concepts and procedures used to determine the costs of products and services as well as topics such as budgeting, break-even analysis, product costing, profit planning, and cost analysis. Information about the costs of products and services is important for many decisions that managers make. These decisions include predicting the future costs of a product or service. Predicted costs are used in product pricing, profitability analysis, and in deciding whether to make or buy a product or component. More generally, much of managerial accounting involves gathering information about costs for planning and control decisions.

Point: Nonfinancial information, also called nonmonetary information, includes customer and employee satisfaction data, the percentage of on-time deliveries, and product defect rates.

Point: Costs are important to managers because they impact both the financial position and profitability of a business. Managerial accounting assists in analysis, planning, and control of costs.

Planning is the process of setting goals and making plans to achieve them. Companies formulate long-term strategic plans that usually span a 5- to 10-year horizon and then refine them with medium-term and short-term plans. Strategic plans usually set a firm's long-term direction by developing a road map based on opportunities such as new products, new markets, and capital investments. A strategic plan's goals and objectives are broadly defined given its long-term orientation. Medium- and short-term plans are more operational in nature. They translate the strategic plan into actions. These plans are more concrete and consist of better defined objectives and goals. A short-term plan often covers a one-year period that, when translated in monetary terms, is known as a budget.

Control is the process of monitoring planning decisions and evaluating an organization's activities and employees. It includes the measurement and evaluation of actions, processes, and outcomes. Feedback provided by the control function allows managers to revise their plans. Measurement of actions and processes also allows managers to take corrective actions to avoid undesirable outcomes. For example, managers periodically compare actual results with planned results. Exhibit 18.1 portrays the important management functions of planning and control.

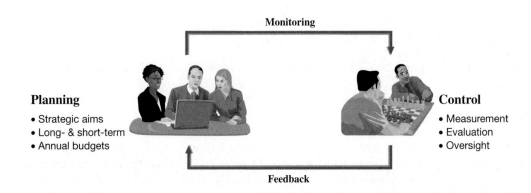

EXHIBIT 18.1

Planning and Control (including monitoring and feedback)

Managers use information to plan and control business activities. In later chapters, we explain how managers also use this information to direct and improve business operations.

Nature of Managerial Accounting

Managerial accounting has its own special characteristics. To understand these characteristics, we compare managerial accounting to financial accounting; they differ in at least seven important ways. These differences are summarized in Exhibit 18.2. This section discusses each of these characteristics.

EXHIBIT 18.2

Key Differences between Managerial Accounting and Financial Accounting

	Financial Accounting	Managerial Accounting
1. Users and decision makers	Investors, creditors, and other users external to the organization	Managers, employees, and decision makers internal to the organization
2. Purpose of information	Assist external users in making investment, credit, and other decisions	Assist managers in making planning and control decisions
3. Flexibility of practice	Structured and often controlled by GAAP	Relatively flexible (no GAAP constraints)
4. Timeliness of information	Often available only after an audit is complete	Available quickly without the need to wait for an audit
5. Time dimension	Focus on historical information with some predictions	Many projections and estimates; historical information also presented
6. Focus of information	Emphasis on whole organization	Emphasis on an organization's projects, processes, and subdivisions
7. Nature of information	Monetary information	Mostly monetary; but also nonmonetary information

Users and Decision Makers   Companies accumulate, process, and report financial accounting and managerial accounting information for different groups of decision makers. Financial accounting information is provided primarily to external users including investors, creditors, analysts, and regulators. External users rarely have a major role in managing a company's daily activities. Managerial accounting information is provided primarily to internal users who are responsible for making and implementing decisions about a company's business activities.

Purpose of Information   Investors, creditors, and other external users of financial accounting information must often decide whether to invest in or lend to a company. If they have already done so, they must decide whether to continue owning the company or carrying the loan. Internal decision makers must plan a company's future. They seek to take advantage of opportunities or to overcome obstacles. They also try to control activities and ensure their effective and efficient implementation. Managerial accounting information helps these internal users make both planning and control decisions.

Flexibility of Practice   External users compare companies by using financial reports and need protection against false or misleading information. Accordingly, financial accounting relies on accepted principles that are enforced through an extensive set of rules and guidelines, or GAAP. Internal users need managerial accounting information for planning and controlling their company's activities rather than for external comparisons. They require different types of information depending on the activity. This makes standardizing managerial accounting systems across companies difficult. Instead, managerial accounting systems are flexible. The design of a company's managerial accounting system depends largely on the nature of the business and the arrangement of its internal operations. Managers can decide for themselves what information they want and how they want it reported. Even within a single company, different managers often design their own systems to meet their special needs. The important question a manager must ask is whether the information being collected and reported is useful for planning, decision making, and control purposes.

Timeliness of Information   Formal financial statements reporting past transactions and events are not immediately available to outside parties. Independent certified public accountants often must *audit* a company's financial statements before it provides them to external users. Thus, because audits often take several weeks to complete, financial reports to outsiders usually are not available until well after the period-end. However, managers can quickly obtain managerial accounting information. External auditors need not review it. Estimates and projections are acceptable. To get information quickly, managers often accept less precision in reports. As an example, an early internal report to management prepared right after the year-end could report net income for the year between $4.2 and $4.8 million. An audited income statement could later show net income for the year at $4.6 million. The internal report is not precise, but its information can be more useful because it is available earlier.

    Internal auditing plays an important role in managerial accounting. Internal auditors evaluate the flow of information not only inside but also outside the company. Managers are responsible for preventing and detecting fraudulent activities in their companies.

Time Dimension   To protect external users from false expectations, financial reports deal primarily with results of both past activities and current conditions. While some predictions such as service lives and salvage values of plant assets are necessary, financial accounting avoids predictions whenever possible. Managerial accounting regularly includes predictions of conditions and events. As an example, one important managerial accounting report is a budget, which predicts revenues, expenses, and other items. If managerial accounting reports were restricted to the past and present, managers would be less able to plan activities and less effective in managing and evaluating current activities.

EXHIBIT 18.3

Focus of External Reports

Focus of Information   Companies often organize into divisions and departments, but investors rarely can buy shares in one division or department. Nor do creditors lend money to a company's single division or department. Instead, they own shares in or make loans to the entire company. Financial accounting focuses primarily on a company as a whole as depicted in Exhibit 18.3. The focus of managerial accounting is different. While top-level managers are responsible for managing the whole company, most other managers are responsible for much smaller sets of activities. These middle-level and lower-level managers need managerial accounting reports dealing with specific activities, projects, and subdivisions for which they are responsible. For instance, division sales managers are directly responsible only for the results achieved in their divisions. Accordingly, division sales managers need information about results achieved in their own divisions to improve their performance. This information includes the level of success achieved by each individual, product, or department in each division as depicted in Exhibit 18.4.

EXHIBIT 18.4

Focus of Internal Reports

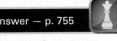

Nature of Information Both financial and managerial accounting systems report monetary information. Managerial accounting systems also report considerable nonmonetary information. Monetary information is an important part of managerial decisions, and nonmonetary information plays a crucial role, especially when monetary effects are difficult to measure. Common examples of nonmonetary information are the quality and delivery criteria of purchasing decisions.

Decision Ethics   Answer — p. 755

Production Manager   You invite three friends to a restaurant. When the dinner check arrives, David, a self-employed entrepreneur, picks it up saying, "Here, let me pay. I'll deduct it as a business expense on my tax return." Denise, a salesperson, takes the check from David's hand and says, "I'll put this on my company's credit card. It won't cost us anything." Derek, a factory manager for a company, laughs and says, "Neither of you understands. I'll put this on my company's credit card and call it overhead on a cost-plus contract my company has with a client." (*A cost-plus contract means the company receives its costs plus a percent of those costs.*) Adds Derek, "That way, my company pays for dinner *and* makes a profit." Who should pay the bill? Why? ∎

Managerial Decision Making

The previous section emphasized differences between financial and managerial accounting, but they are not entirely separate. Similar information is useful to both external and internal users. For instance, information about costs of manufacturing products is useful to all users in making decisions. Also, both financial and managerial accounting affect peoples' actions. For example, **Trek**'s design of a sales compensation plan affects the behavior of its salesforce when selling its manufactured bikes. It also must estimate the dual effects of promotion and sales compensation plans on buying patterns of customers. These estimates impact the equipment purchase decisions for manufacturing and can affect the supplier selection criteria established by purchasing. Thus, financial and managerial accounting systems do more than measure; they also affect people's decisions and actions.

Fraud and Ethics in Managerial Accounting

Fraud, and the role of ethics in reducing fraud, are important factors in running business operations. Fraud involves the use of one's job for personal gain through the deliberate misuse of the employer's assets. Examples include theft of the employer's cash or other assets, overstating reimbursable expenses, payroll schemes, and financial statement fraud. Fraud affects all business and it is costly: A 2008 *Report to the Nation* from the Association of Certified Fraud Examiners estimates the average U.S. business loses 7% of its annual revenues to fraud.

The most common type of fraud, where employees steal or misuse the employer's resources, results in an average loss of $175,000 per occurrence. For example, in a billing fraud, an employee sets up a bogus supplier. The employee then prepares bills from the supplier and pays these bills from the employer's checking account. The employee cashes the checks sent to the bogus supplier and uses them for his or her own personal benefit.

More generally, although there are many types of fraud schemes, all fraud:

- Is done to provide direct or indirect benefit to the employee.
- Violates the employee's obligations to the employer.
- Costs the employer money or loss of other assets.
- Is hidden from the employer.

Implications for Managerial Accounting   Fraud increases a business's costs. Left undetected, these inflated costs can result in poor pricing decisions, an improper product mix, and faulty performance evaluations. Management can develop accounting systems to closely track costs and identify deviations from expected amounts. In addition, managers rely on an **internal control system** to monitor and control business activities. An internal control system is the policies and procedures managers use to:

- Urge adherence to company policies.
- Promote efficient operations.
- Ensure reliable accounting.
- Protect assets.

Combating fraud and other dilemmas requires ethics in accounting. **Ethics** are beliefs that distinguish right from wrong. They are accepted standards of good and bad behavior. Identifying the ethical path can be difficult. The preferred path is a course of action that avoids casting doubt on one's decisions.

Point: The IMA also issues the Certified Management Accountant (CMA) and the Certified Financial Manager (CFM) certifications. Employees with the CMA or CFM certifications typically earn higher salaries than those without.

Point: The **Sarbanes-Oxley Act** requires each issuer of securities to disclose whether it has adopted a code of ethics for its senior officers and the content of that code.

The **Institute of Management Accountants** (IMA), the professional association for management accountants, has issued a code of ethics to help accountants involved in solving ethical dilemmas. The IMA's Statement of Ethical Professional Practice requires that management accountants be competent, maintain confidentiality, act with integrity, and communicate information in a fair and credible manner.

The IMA provides a "road map" for resolving ethical conflicts. It suggests that an employee follow the company's policies on how to resolve such conflicts. If the conflict remains unresolved, an employee should contact the next level of management (such as the immediate supervisor) who is not involved in the ethical conflict.

Quick Check   Answers — p. 756

1. Managerial accounting produces information (*a*) to meet internal users' needs, (*b*) to meet a user's specific needs, (*c*) often focusing on the future, or (*d*) all of these.
2. What is the difference between the intended users of financial and managerial accounting?
3. Do generally accepted accounting principles (GAAP) control and dictate managerial accounting?

MANAGERIAL COST CONCEPTS

C2 Describe accounting concepts useful in classifying costs.

An organization incurs many different types of costs that are classified differently, depending on management needs (different costs for different purposes). We can classify costs on the basis of their (1) behavior, (2) traceability, (3) controllability, (4) relevance, and (5) function. This section explains each concept for assigning costs to products and services.

Types of Cost Classifications

Classification by Behavior   At a basic level, a cost can be classified as fixed or variable. A **fixed cost** does not change with changes in the volume of activity (within a range of activity known as an activity's *relevant range*). For example, straight-line depreciation on equipment is a fixed cost. A **variable cost** changes in proportion to changes in the volume of activity. Sales commissions computed as a percent of sales revenue are variable costs. Additional examples of fixed and variable costs for a bike manufacturer are provided in Exhibit 18.5. When cost items are combined, total cost can be fixed, variable, or mixed. *Mixed* refers to a combination of fixed and variable costs. Equipment rental often includes a fixed cost for some minimum amount and a variable cost based on amount of usage. Classification of costs by behavior is helpful in cost-volume-profit analyses and short-term decision making. We discuss these in Chapters 22 and 25.

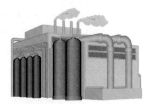

Fixed Cost: Rent for Rocky Mountain Bikes' building is $22,000, and it doesn't change with the number of bikes produced.

Variable Cost: Cost of bicycle tires is variable with the number of bikes produced—this cost is $15 per pair.

EXHIBIT 18.5

Fixed and Variable Costs

Classification by Traceability A cost is often traced to a **cost object,** which is a product, process, department, or customer to which costs are assigned. **Direct costs** are those traceable to a single cost object. For example, if a product is a cost object, its material and labor costs are usually directly traceable. **Indirect costs** are those that cannot be easily and cost–beneficially traced to a single cost object. An example of an indirect cost is a maintenance plan that benefits two or more departments. Exhibit 18.6 identifies examples of both direct and indirect costs for the maintenance department in a manufacturing plant. Thus, salaries of Rocky Mountain Bikes' maintenance department employees are considered indirect if the cost object is bicycles and direct if the cost object is the maintenance department. Classification of costs by traceability is useful for cost allocation. This is discussed in Chapter 21.

EXHIBIT 18.6

Direct and Indirect Costs of a Maintenance Department

Direct Costs		Indirect Costs	
• Salaries of maintenance department employees	• Materials purchased by maintenance department	• Factory accounting	• Factory light and heat
• Equipment purchased by maintenance department	• Maintenance department equipment depreciation	• Factory administration	• Factory internal audit
		• Factory rent	• Factory intranet
		• Factory manager's salary	• Insurance on factory

Decision Maker   Answer — p. 755

Entrepreneur You wish to trace as many of your assembly department's direct costs as possible. You can trace 90% of them in an economical manner. To trace the other 10%, you need sophisticated and costly accounting software. Do you purchase this software? ■

Classification by Controllability A cost can be defined as **controllable** or **not controllable.** Whether a cost is controllable or not depends on the employee's responsibilities, as shown in Exhibit 18.7. This is referred to as *hierarchical levels* in management, or *pecking order.* For example, investments in machinery are controllable by upper-level managers but not lower-level managers. Many daily operating expenses such as overtime often are controllable by lower-level managers. Classification of costs by controllability is especially useful for assigning responsibility to and evaluating managers.

Senior Manager Controls costs of investments in land, buildings, and equipment.

Supervisor Controls daily expenses such as supplies, maintenance, and overtime.

EXHIBIT 18.7

Controllability of Costs

Classification by Relevance   A cost can be classified by relevance by identifying it as either a sunk cost or an out-of-pocket cost. A **sunk cost** has already been incurred and cannot be avoided or changed. It is irrelevant to future decisions. One example is the cost of a company's office equipment previously purchased. An **out-of-pocket cost** requires a future outlay of cash and is relevant for decision making. Future purchases of equipment involve out-of-pocket costs. A discussion of relevant costs must also consider opportunity costs. An **opportunity cost** is the potential benefit lost by choosing a specific action from two or more alternatives. One example is a student giving up wages from a job to attend evening classes. Consideration of opportunity cost is important when, for example, an insurance company must decide whether to outsource its payroll function or maintain it internally. This is discussed in Chapter 25.

C3	Define product and period costs and explain how they impact financial statements.

Classification by Function   Another cost classification (for manufacturers) is capitalization as inventory or to expense as incurred. Costs capitalized as inventory are called **product costs,** which refer to expenditures necessary and integral to finished products. They include direct materials, direct labor, and indirect manufacturing costs called *overhead costs*. Product costs pertain to activities carried out to manufacture the product. Costs expensed are called **period costs,** which refer to expenditures identified more with a time period than with finished products. They include selling and general administrative expenses. Period costs pertain to activities that are not part of the manufacturing process. A distinction between product and period costs is important because period costs are expensed in the income statement and product costs are assigned to inventory on the balance sheet until that inventory is sold. An ability to understand and identify product costs and period costs is crucial to using and interpreting a *manufacturing statement* described later in this chapter.

Exhibit 18.8 shows the different effects of product and period costs. Period costs flow directly to the current income statement as expenses. They are not reported as assets. Product costs are first assigned to inventory. Their final treatment depends on when inventory is sold or disposed of. Product costs assigned to finished goods that are sold in year 2011 are reported on the 2011 income statement as part of cost of goods sold. Product costs assigned to unsold inventory are carried forward on the balance sheet at the end of year 2011. If this inventory is sold in year 2012 product costs assigned to it are reported as part of cost of goods sold in that year's income statement.

The difference between period and product costs explains why the year 2011 income statement does not report operating expenses related to either factory workers' wages or depreciation on factory buildings and equipment. Instead, both costs are combined with the cost of raw materials to compute the product cost of finished goods. A portion of these manufacturing costs

EXHIBIT 18.8

Period and Product Costs in Financial Statements

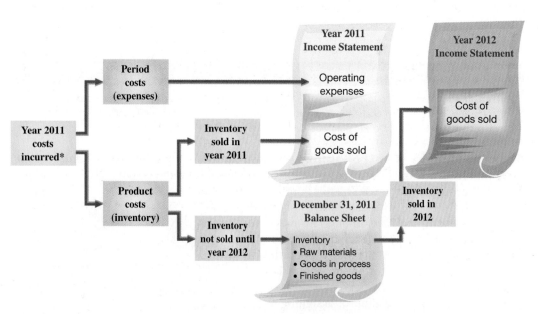

* This diagram excludes costs to acquire assets other than inventory.

(related to the goods sold) is reported in the year 2011 income statement as part of Cost of Goods Sold. The other portion is reported on the balance sheet at the end of that year as part of Inventory. The portion assigned to inventory could be included in any or all of raw materials, goods in process, or finished goods inventories.

Point: For a team approach to identifying period and product costs, see *Teamwork in Action* in the *Beyond the Numbers* section.

Decision Maker   Answer — p. 756

Purchase Manager   You are evaluating two potential suppliers of seats for the manufacturing of motorcycles. One supplier (A) quotes a $145 price per seat and ensures 100% quality standards and on-time delivery. The second supplier (B) quotes a $115 price per seat but does not give any written assurances on quality or delivery. You decide to contract with the second supplier (B), saving $30 per seat. Does this decision have opportunity costs? ■

Identification of Cost Classifications

It is important to understand that a cost can be classified using any one (or combination) of the five different means described here. To do this we must understand costs and operations. Specifically, for the five classifications, we must be able to identify the *activity* for behavior, *cost object* for traceability, *management hierarchical level* for controllability, *opportunity cost* for relevance, and *benefit period* for function. Factory rent, for instance, can be classified as a product cost; it is fixed with respect to number of units produced, it is indirect with respect to the product, and it is not controllable by a production supervisor. Potential multiple classifications are shown in Exhibit 18.9 using different cost items incurred in manufacturing mountain bikes. The finished bike is the cost object. Proper allocation of these costs and the managerial decisions based on cost data depend on a correct cost classification.

EXHIBIT 18.9

Examples of Multiple Cost Classifications

Cost Item	By Behavior	By Traceability	By Function
Bicycle tires	Variable	Direct	Product
Wages of assembly worker*	Variable	Direct	Product
Advertising	Fixed	Indirect	Period
Production manager's salary	Fixed	Indirect	Product
Office depreciation	Fixed	Indirect	Period

* Although an assembly worker's wages are classified as variable costs, their actual behavior depends on how workers are paid and whether their wages are based on a union contract (such as piece rate or monthly wages).

Cost Concepts for Service Companies

The cost concepts described are generally applicable to service organizations. For example, consider **Southwest Airlines**. Its cost of beverages for passengers is a variable cost based on number of passengers. The cost of leasing an aircraft is fixed with respect to number of passengers. We can also trace a flight crew's salary to a specific flight whereas we likely cannot trace wages for the ground crew to a specific flight. Classification by function (such as product versus period costs) is not relevant to service companies because services are not inventoried. Instead, costs incurred by a service firm are expensed in the reporting period when incurred.

Managers in service companies must understand and apply cost concepts. They seek and rely on accurate cost estimates for many decisions. For example, an airline manager must often decide between canceling or rerouting flights. The manager must also be able to estimate costs saved by canceling a flight versus rerouting. Knowledge of fixed costs is equally important. We explain more about the cost requirements for these and other managerial decisions in Chapter 25.

Point: All expenses of service companies are period costs because these companies do not have inventory.

Service Costs
- Beverages and snacks
- Cleaning fees
- Pilot and copilot salaries
- Attendant salaries
- Fuel and oil costs
- Travel agent fees
- Ground crew salaries

Quick Check   Answers — p. 756

4. Which type of cost behavior increases total costs when volume of activity increases?

5. How could traceability of costs improve managerial decisions?

REPORTING MANUFACTURING ACTIVITIES

Companies with manufacturing activities differ from both merchandising and service companies. The main difference between merchandising and manufacturing companies is that merchandisers buy goods ready for sale while manufacturers produce goods from materials and labor. **Payless** is an example of a merchandising company. It buys and sells shoes without physically changing them. **Adidas** is primarily a manufacturer of shoes, apparel, and accessories. It purchases materials such as leather, cloth, dye, plastic, rubber, glue, and laces and then uses employees' labor to convert these materials to products. **Southwest Airlines** is a service company that transports people and items.

Manufacturing activities differ from both selling merchandise and providing services. Also, the financial statements for manufacturing companies differ slightly. This section considers some of these differences and compares them to accounting for a merchandising company.

Manufacturer's Balance Sheet

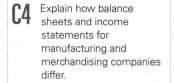

C4 Explain how balance sheets and income statements for manufacturing and merchandising companies differ.

Manufacturers carry several unique assets and usually have three inventories instead of the single inventory that merchandisers carry. Exhibit 18.10 shows three different inventories in the current asset section of the balance sheet for Rocky Mountain Bikes, a manufacturer. The three inventories are raw materials, goods in process, and finished goods.

Point: Reducing the size of inventories saves storage costs and frees money for other uses.

Raw Materials Inventory **Raw materials inventory** refers to the goods a company acquires to use in making products. It uses raw materials in two ways: directly and indirectly. Most raw materials physically become part of a product and are identified with specific units or batches of a product. Raw materials used directly in a product are called *direct materials*. Other materials used to support production processes are sometimes not as clearly identified with specific units or batches of product. These materials are called **indirect materials** because they are not clearly identified with specific product units or batches. Items used as indirect materials often appear on a balance sheet as factory supplies or are included in raw materials. Some direct materials are classified as indirect materials when their costs are low (insignificant). Examples include screws and nuts used in assembling mountain bikes and staples and glue used in manufacturing shoes. Using

EXHIBIT 18.10

Balance Sheet for a Manufacturer

ROCKY MOUNTAIN BIKES			
Balance Sheet			
December 31, 2011			
Assets		**Liabilities and Equity**	
Current assets		Current liabilities	
Cash	$ 11,000	Accounts payable	$ 14,000
Accounts receivable, net	30,150	Wages payable	540
Raw materials inventory	9,000	Interest payable	2,000
Goods in process inventory	7,500	Income taxes payable	32,600
Finished goods inventory	10,300	Total current liabilities	49,140
Factory supplies	350		
Prepaid insurance	300	Long-term liabilities	
Total current assets	68,600	Long-term notes payable	50,000
Plant assets		Total liabilities	99,140
Small tools, net	1,100		
Delivery equipment, net	5,000	Stockholders' equity	
Office equipment, net	1,300	Common stock, $1.2 par	24,000
Factory machinery, net	65,500	Paid-in capital	76,000
Factory building, net	86,700	Retained earnings	49,760
Land	9,500	Total stockholders' equity	149,760
Total plant assets, net	169,100		
Intangible assets (patents), net	11,200	Total liabilities and equity	$248,900
Total assets	$248,900		

the *materiality principle*, individually tracing the costs of each of these materials and classifying them separately as direct materials does not make much economic sense. For instance, keeping detailed records of the amount of glue used to manufacture one shoe is not cost beneficial.

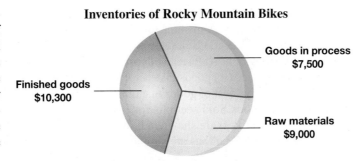

Inventories of Rocky Mountain Bikes

Goods in process
$7,500

Finished goods
$10,300

Raw materials
$9,000

Goods in Process Inventory   Another inventory held by manufacturers is **goods in process inventory,** also called *work in process inventory.* It consists of products in the process of being manufactured but not yet complete. The amount of goods in process inventory depends on the type of production process. If the time required to produce a unit of product is short, the goods in process inventory is likely small; but if weeks or months are needed to produce a unit, the goods in process inventory is usually larger.

Finished Goods Inventory   A third inventory owned by a manufacturer is **finished goods inventory,** which consists of completed products ready for sale. This inventory is similar to merchandise inventory owned by a merchandising company. Manufacturers also often own unique plant assets such as small tools, factory buildings, factory equipment, and patents to manufacture products. The balance sheet in Exhibit 18.10 shows that Rocky Mountain Bikes owns all of these assets. Some manufacturers invest millions or even billions of dollars in production facilities and patents. **Briggs & Stratton**'s recent balance sheet shows about $1 billion net investment in land, buildings, machinery and equipment, much of which involves production facilities. It manufactures more racing engines than any other company in the world.

Manufacturer's Income Statement

The main difference between the income statement of a manufacturer and that of a merchandiser involves the items making up cost of goods sold. Exhibit 18.11 compares the components of cost of goods sold for a manufacturer and a merchandiser. A merchandiser adds cost of goods purchased to beginning merchandise inventory and then subtracts ending merchandise inventory to get cost of goods sold. A manufacturer adds cost of goods manufactured to beginning finished goods inventory and then subtracts ending finished goods inventory to get cost of goods sold.

P1   Compute cost of goods sold for a manufacturer.

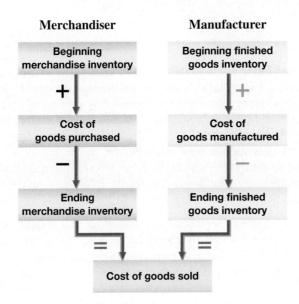

Merchandiser

Beginning merchandise inventory

+

Cost of goods purchased

−

Ending merchandise inventory

=

Manufacturer

Beginning finished goods inventory

+

Cost of goods manufactured

−

Ending finished goods inventory

=

Cost of goods sold

EXHIBIT 18.11

Cost of Goods Sold Computation

A merchandiser often uses the term *merchandise* inventory; a manufacturer often uses the term *finished goods* inventory. A manufacturer's inventories of raw materials and goods in process are not included in finished goods because they are not available for sale. A manufacturer also shows cost of goods *manufactured* instead of cost of goods *purchased*. This difference occurs because a manufacturer produces its goods instead of purchasing them ready for sale. We show later in this chapter how to derive cost of goods manufactured from the manufacturing statement.

The Cost of Goods Sold sections for both a merchandiser (Tele-Mart) and a manufacturer (Rocky Mountain Bikes) are shown in Exhibit 18.12 to highlight these differences. The remaining income statement sections are similar.

EXHIBIT 18.12

Cost of Goods Sold for a Merchandiser and Manufacturer

Merchandising (Tele-Mart) Company		Manufacturing (Rocky Mtn. Bikes) Company	
Cost of goods sold		Cost of goods sold	
Beginning *merchandise* inventory	$ 14,200	Beginning *finished goods* inventory	$ 11,200
Cost of merchandise *purchased*	234,150	Cost of goods *manufactured**	170,500
Goods available for sale	248,350	Goods available for sale	181,700
Less ending *merchandise* inventory	12,100	Less ending *finished goods* inventory	10,300
Cost of goods sold	$236,250	Cost of goods sold	$171,400

* Cost of goods manufactured is reported in the income statement of Exhibit 18.14.

Although the cost of goods sold computations are similar, the numbers in these computations reflect different activities. A merchandiser's cost of goods purchased is the cost of buying products to be sold. A manufacturer's cost of goods manufactured is the sum of direct materials, direct labor, and factory overhead costs incurred in producing products. The remainder of this section further explains these three manufacturing costs and describes prime and conversion costs.

Direct Materials **Direct materials** are tangible components of a finished product. **Direct material costs** are the expenditures for direct materials that are separately and readily traced through the manufacturing process to finished goods. Examples of direct materials in manufacturing a mountain bike include its tires, seat, frame, pedals, brakes, cables, gears, and handlebars. The chart in the margin shows that direct materials generally make up about 45% of manufacturing costs in today's products, but this amount varies across industries and companies.

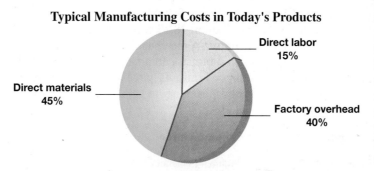

Typical Manufacturing Costs in Today's Products

Direct labor 15%
Direct materials 45%
Factory overhead 40%

Direct Labor **Direct labor** refers to the efforts of employees who physically convert materials to finished product. **Direct labor costs** are the wages and salaries for direct labor that are separately and readily traced through the manufacturing process to finished goods. Examples of direct labor in manufacturing a mountain bike include operators directly involved in converting raw materials into finished products (welding, painting, forming) and assembly workers who attach materials such as tires, seats, pedals, and brakes to the bike frames. Costs of other workers on the assembly line who assist direct laborers are classified as **indirect labor costs.** **Indirect labor** refers to manufacturing workers' efforts not linked to specific units or batches of the product.

Point: Indirect labor costs are part of factory overhead.

Factory Overhead **Factory overhead** consists of all manufacturing costs that are not direct materials or direct labor. **Factory overhead costs** cannot be separately or readily traced to finished goods. These costs include indirect materials and indirect labor, costs not directly traceable to the product. Overtime paid to direct laborers is also included in overhead because overtime is due to delays, interruptions, or constraints not necessarily identifiable to a specific product or batches of product. Factory overhead costs also include maintenance of the mountain bike

Point: Factory overhead is also called *manufacturing overhead.*

factory, supervision of its employees, repairing manufacturing equipment, factory utilities (water, gas, electricity), production manager's salary, factory rent, depreciation on factory buildings and equipment, factory insurance, property taxes on factory buildings and equipment, and factory accounting and legal services. Factory overhead does *not* include selling and administrative expenses because they are not incurred in manufacturing products. These expenses are called *period costs* and are recorded as expenses on the income statement when incurred.

Prime and Conversion Costs Direct material costs and direct labor costs are also called **prime costs**—expenditures directly associated with the manufacture of finished goods. Direct labor costs and overhead costs are called **conversion costs**—expenditures incurred in the process of converting raw materials to finished goods. Direct labor costs are considered both prime costs and conversion costs. Exhibit 18.13 conveys the relation between prime and conversion costs and their components of direct material, direct labor, and factory overhead.

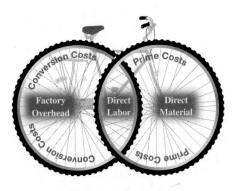

EXHIBIT 18.13

Prime and Conversion Costs and Their Makeup

Prime costs =
Direct materials + Direct labor.
Conversion costs =
Direct labor + Factory overhead.

Reporting Performance Exhibit 18.14 shows the income statement for Rocky Mountain Bikes. Its operating expenses include sales salaries, office salaries, and depreciation of delivery and office equipment. Operating expenses do not include manufacturing costs such as

EXHIBIT 18.14

Income Statement for a Manufacturer

ROCKY MOUNTAIN BIKES		
Income Statement		
For Year Ended December 31, 2011		
Sales...		$310,000
Cost of goods sold		
Finished goods inventory, Dec. 31, 2010	$ 11,200	
Cost of goods manufactured	170,500	
Goods available for sale	181,700	
Less finished goods inventory, Dec. 31, 2011	10,300	
Cost of goods sold		171,400
Gross profit......................................		138,600
Operating expenses		
Selling expenses		
Sales salaries expense	18,000	
Advertising expense	5,500	
Delivery wages expense	12,000	
Shipping supplies expense.......................	250	
Insurance expense—Delivery equipment	300	
Depreciation expense—Delivery equipment	2,100	
Total selling expenses		38,150
General and administrative expenses		
Office salaries expense	15,700	
Miscellaneous expense	200	
Bad debts expense	1,550	
Office supplies expense	100	
Depreciation expense—Office equipment	200	
Interest expense	4,000	
Total general and administrative expenses		21,750
Total operating expenses		59,900
Income before income taxes		78,700
Income taxes expense		32,600
Net income		$ 46,100

factory workers' wages and depreciation of production equipment and the factory buildings. These manufacturing costs are reported as part of cost of goods manufactured and included in cost of goods sold. We explained why and how this is done in the section "Classification by Function."

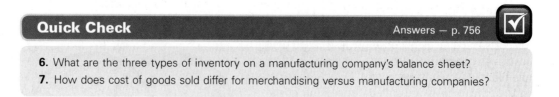

Quick Check   Answers — p. 756

6. What are the three types of inventory on a manufacturing company's balance sheet?
7. How does cost of goods sold differ for merchandising versus manufacturing companies?

Flow of Manufacturing Activities

C5 Explain manufacturing activities and the flow of manufacturing costs.

To understand manufacturing and its reports, we must first understand the flow of manufacturing activities and costs. Exhibit 18.15 shows the flow of manufacturing activities for a manufacturer. This exhibit has three important sections: *materials activity, production activity,* and *sales activity.* We explain each activity in this section.

EXHIBIT 18.15

Activities and Cost Flows in Manufacturing

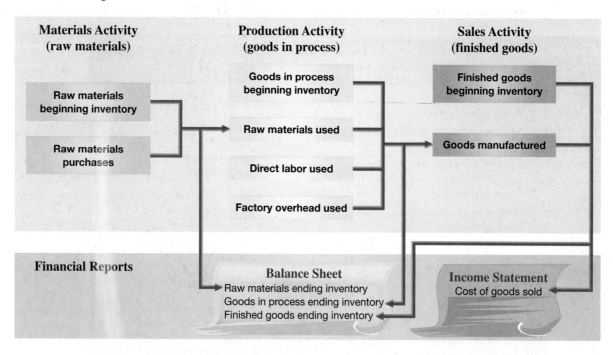

Materials Activity   The far left side of Exhibit 18.15 shows the flow of raw materials. Manufacturers usually start a period with some beginning raw materials inventory carried over from the previous period. The company then acquires additional raw materials in the current period. Adding these purchases to beginning inventory gives total raw materials available for use in production. These raw materials are then either used in production in the current period or remain in inventory at the end of the period for use in future periods.

Production Activity   The middle section of Exhibit 18.15 describes production activity. Four factors come together in production: beginning goods in process inventory, direct materials, direct labor, and overhead. Beginning goods in process inventory consists of partly assembled products from the previous period. Production activity results in products that are either finished or remain unfinished. The cost of finished products makes up the cost of goods manufactured for the current period. Unfinished products are identified as ending goods in process inventory. The cost of unfinished products consists of direct materials, direct labor, and factory overhead, and is reported on the current period's balance sheet. The costs of both finished goods manufactured and goods in process are *product costs*.

Sales Activity   The company's sales activity is portrayed in the far right side of Exhibit 18.15. Newly completed units are combined with beginning finished goods inventory to make up total finished goods available for sale in the current period. The cost of finished products sold is reported on the income statement as cost of goods sold. The cost of products not sold is reported on the current period's balance sheet as ending finished goods inventory.

Manufacturing Statement

A company's manufacturing activities are described in a **manufacturing statement,** also called the *schedule of manufacturing activities* or the *schedule of cost of goods manufactured.* The manufacturing statement summarizes the types and amounts of costs incurred in a company's manufacturing process. Exhibit 18.16 shows the manufacturing statement for Rocky Mountain Bikes. The statement is divided into four parts: *direct materials, direct labor, overhead,* and *computation of cost of goods manufactured.* We describe each of these parts in this section.

P2 Prepare a manufacturing statement and explain its purpose and links to financial statements.

① The manufacturing statement begins by computing direct materials used. We start by adding beginning raw materials inventory of $8,000 to the current period's purchases of $86,500. This yields $94,500 of total raw materials available for use. A physical count of inventory shows $9,000 of ending raw materials inventory. This implies a total cost of raw materials used during the period of $85,500 ($94,500 total raw materials available for use − $9,000 ending inventory). (*Note:* All raw materials are direct materials for Rocky Mountain Bikes.)

EXHIBIT 18.16

Manufacturing Statement

ROCKY MOUNTAIN BIKES
Manufacturing Statement
For Year Ended December 31, 2011

Direct materials			
①	Raw materials inventory, Dec. 31, 2010	$ 8,000	
	Raw materials purchases	86,500	
	Raw materials available for use	94,500	
	Less raw materials inventory, Dec. 31, 2011	9,000	
	Direct materials used		$ 85,500
②	**Direct labor**		60,000
	Factory overhead		
③	Indirect labor	9,000	
	Factory supervision	6,000	
	Factory utilities	2,600	
	Repairs—Factory equipment	2,500	
	Property taxes—Factory building	1,900	
	Factory supplies used	600	
	Factory insurance expired	1,100	
	Depreciation expense—Small tools	200	
	Depreciation expense—Factory equipment	3,500	
	Depreciation expense—Factory building	1,800	
	Amortization expense—Patents	800	
	Total factory overhead		30,000
	Total manufacturing costs		175,500
	Add goods in process inventory, Dec. 31, 2010		2,500
④	Total cost of goods in process		178,000
	Less goods in process inventory, Dec. 31, 2011		7,500
	Cost of goods manufactured		$170,500

② The second part of the manufacturing statement reports direct labor costs. Rocky Mountain Bikes had total direct labor costs of $60,000 for the period. This amount includes payroll taxes and fringe benefits.

③ The third part of the manufacturing statement reports overhead costs. The statement lists each important factory overhead item and its cost. Total factory overhead cost for the period is $30,000. Some companies report only *total* factory overhead on the manufacturing statement and attach a separate schedule listing individual overhead costs.

④ The final section of the manufacturing statement computes and reports the *cost of goods manufactured*. (Total manufacturing costs for the period are $175,500 [$85,500 + $60,000 + $30,000], the sum of direct materials used and direct labor and overhead costs incurred.) This amount is first added to beginning goods in process inventory. This gives the total goods in process inventory of $178,000 ($175,500 + $2,500). We then compute the current period's cost of goods manufactured of $170,500 by taking the $178,000 total goods in process and subtracting the $7,500 cost of ending goods in process inventory that consists of direct materials, direct labor, and factory overhead. The cost of goods manufactured amount is also called *net cost of goods manufactured* or *cost of goods completed*. Exhibit 18.14 shows that this item and amount are listed in the Cost of Goods Sold section of Rocky Mountain Bikes' income statement and the balance sheet.

A managerial accounting system records costs and reports them in various reports that eventually determine financial statements. Exhibit 18.17 shows how overhead costs flow through the system: from an initial listing of specific costs, to a section of the manufacturing statement, to the reporting on the income statement and the balance sheet.

Management uses information in the manufacturing statement to plan and control the company's manufacturing activities. To provide timely information for decision making, the

EXHIBIT 18.17

Overhead Cost Flows across Accounting Reports

Rocky Mountain Bikes
Factory Overhead Costs
For Year Ended December 31, 2011

Indirect labor	$ 9,000
Supervision	6,000
Other overhead items*	15,000
Total overhead	$30,000

*Overhead items are listed in Exhibit 18.16.

Rocky Mountain Bikes
Manufacturing Statement
For Year Ended December 31, 2011

Direct materials	$ 85,500
Direct labor	60,000
Factory overhead	30,000
Total manuf. costs	175,500
Beg. goods in process	2,500
Total goods in process	178,000
End. goods in process	(7,500)
Cost of goods manuf.	$170,500

Rocky Mountain Bikes
Income Statement
For Year Ended December 31, 2011

Sales	$310,000
Cost of goods sold	
Beg. finished goods	11,200
Cost of goods manuf.	170,500
End. finished goods	(10,300)
Cost of goods sold	171,400
Gross profit	138,600
Expenses	59,900
Income taxes	32,600
Net income	$ 46,100

Rocky Mountain Bikes
Balance Sheet–PARTIAL
December 31, 2011

Cash	$11,000
Accounts receivable, net	30,150
Raw materials inventory	9,000
Goods in process inventory	7,500
Finished goods inventory	10,300
Factory supplies	350
Prepaid insurance	300
Total current assets	$68,600

statement is often prepared monthly, weekly, or even daily. In anticipation of release of its much-hyped iPad, **Apple** grew its inventory of critical components, and its finished goods inventory. The manufacturing statement contains information useful to external users but is not a general-purpose financial statement. Companies rarely publish the manufacturing statement because managers view this information as proprietary and potentially harmful to them if released to competitors.

Quick Check Answers — p. 756

8. A manufacturing statement (*a*) computes cost of goods manufactured for the period, (*b*) computes cost of goods sold for the period, or (*c*) reports operating expenses incurred for the period.
9. Are companies required to report a manufacturing statement?
10. How are both beginning and ending goods in process inventories reported on a manufacturing statement?

Trends in Managerial Accounting

The analytical tools and techniques of managerial accounting have always been useful, and their relevance and importance continue to increase. This is so because of changes in the business environment. This section describes some of these changes and their impact on managerial accounting.

C6 Describe trends in managerial accounting.

Customer Orientation There is an increased emphasis on *customers* as the most important constituent of a business. Customers expect to derive a certain value for the money they spend to buy products and services. Specifically, they expect that their suppliers will offer them the right service (or product) at the right time and the right price. This implies that companies accept the notion of **customer orientation,** which means that employees understand the changing needs and wants of their customers and align their management and operating practices accordingly.

Global Economy Our *global economy* expands competitive boundaries and provides customers more choices. The global economy also produces changes in business activities. One notable case that reflects these changes in customer demand and global competition is auto manufacturing. The top three Japanese auto manufacturers (**Honda, Nissan,** and **Toyota**) once controlled more than 40% of the U.S. auto market. Customers perceived that Japanese auto manufacturers provided value not available from other manufacturers. Many European and North American auto manufacturers responded to this challenge and regained much of the lost market share.

E-Commerce People have become increasingly interconnected via smartphones, text messaging, and other electronic applications. Consumers thus expect and demand to be able to buy items electronically, whenever and wherever they want. Many businesses have enhanced their Websites to allow for online transactions. Online sales now make up over 7% of total retail sales.

Service Economy Businesses that provide services, such as telecommunications and health care, constitute an ever-growing part of our economy. In developed economies like the United States, service businesses typically account for over 60% to 70% of total economic activity.

Companies must be alert to these and other factors. Many companies have responded by adopting the **lean business model,** whose goal is to *eliminate waste* while "satisfying the customer" and "providing a positive return" to the company.

Lean Practices **Continuous improvement** rejects the notions of "good enough" or "acceptable" and challenges employees and managers to continuously experiment with new and improved business practices. This has led companies to adopt practices such as total quality management (TQM) and just-in-time (JIT) manufacturing. The philosophy underlying both practices is continuous improvement; the difference is in the focus.

Total quality management focuses on quality improvement and applies this standard to all aspects of business activities. In doing so, managers and employees seek to uncover waste in business activities including accounting activities such as payroll and disbursements. To encourage an emphasis on quality, the U.S. Congress established the Malcolm Baldrige National Quality Award (MBNQA). Entrants must conduct a thorough analysis and evaluation of their business using guidelines from the Baldrige committee. **Ritz Carlton Hotel** is a recipient of the Baldrige award in the service category. The company applies a core set of values, collectively called *The Gold Standards,* to improve customer service.

Just-in-time manufacturing is a system that acquires inventory and produces only when needed. An important aspect of JIT is that companies manufacture products only after they receive an order (a *demand-pull* system) and then deliver the customer's requirements on time. This means that processes must be aligned to eliminate any delays and inefficiencies including inferior inputs and outputs. Companies must also establish good relations and communications with their suppliers. On the downside, JIT is more susceptible to disruption than traditional systems. As one example, several **General Motors** plants were temporarily shut down due to a strike at an assembly division; the plants supplied components *just in time* to the assembly division.

Value Chain The **value chain** refers to the series of activities that add value to a company's products or services. Exhibit 18.18 illustrates a possible value chain for a retail cookie company. Companies can use lean practices to increase efficiency and profits.

Point: Goals of a TQM process include reduced waste, better inventory control, fewer defects, and continuous improvement. Just-in-time concepts have similar goals.

Point: The time between buying raw materials and selling finished goods is called *throughput time.*

EXHIBIT 18.18

Typical Value Chain (Cookie Retailer)

Acquire raw materials → Baking → Sales → Service

Decision Insight

Global Lean **Toyota Motor Corporation** pioneered lean manufacturing, and it has since spread to other manufacturers throughout the world. The goals include improvements in quality, reliability, inventory turnover, productivity, exports, and—above all—sales and income. ■

"My boss wants us to appeal to a younger and hipper crowd. So, I'd like to get a tattoo that says-- 'Accounting rules!'"

Copyright © Jerry King. www.artizans.com

Implications for Managerial Accounting Adopting the lean business model can be challenging because to foster its implementation, all systems and procedures that a company follows must be realigned. Managerial accounting has an important role to play by providing accurate cost and performance information. Companies must understand the nature and sources of cost and must develop systems that capture costs accurately. Developing such a system is important to measuring the "value" provided to customers. The price that customers pay for acquiring goods and services is an important determinant of value. In turn, the costs a company incurs are key determinants of price. All else being equal, the better a company is at controlling its costs, the better its performance.

Decision Insight

Balanced Scorecard The *balanced scorecard* aids continuous improvement by augmenting financial measures with information on the "drivers" (indicators) of future financial performance along four dimensions: (1) *financial*—profitability and risk, (2) *customer*—value creation and product and service differentiation, (3) *internal business processes*—business activities that create customer and owner satisfaction, and (4) *learning and growth*—organizational change, innovation, and growth. ∎

GLOBAL VIEW

Managerial accounting is more flexible than financial accounting and does not follow a set of strict rules. However, many international businesses use the managerial accounting concepts and principles described in this chapter.

Customer Focus Nestlé, one of the world's leading nutrition and wellness companies, adopts a customer focus and strives to understand its customers' tastes. For example, Nestlé employees spent three days living with people in Lima, Peru, to understand their motivations, routines, buying habits, and everyday lives. This allowed Nestlé to adjust its products to suit local tastes.

Reporting Manufacturing Activities Nestlé must classify and report costs. In reporting inventory, Nestlé includes direct production costs, production overhead, and factory depreciation. A recent Nestlé annual report shows the following:

(in millions of Swiss francs)	Ending Inventory	Beginning Inventory
Raw materials, work in progress, and sundry supplies	3,708	3,590
Finished goods	5,901	3,590

Nestlé managers use this information, along with the more detailed information found in a manufacturing statement, to plan and control manufacturing activities.

Cycle Time and Cycle Efficiency **Decision Analysis**

As lean manufacturing practices help companies move toward just-in-time manufacturing, it is important for these companies to reduce the time to manufacture their products and to improve manufacturing efficiency. One metric that measures that time element is **cycle time (CT).** A definition of cycle time is in Exhibit 18.19.

A1 Compute cycle time and cycle efficiency, and explain their importance to production management.

$$\text{Cycle time} = \text{Process time} + \text{Inspection time} + \text{Move time} + \text{Wait time}$$

EXHIBIT 18.19
Cycle Time

Process time is the time spent producing the product. *Inspection time* is the time spent inspecting (1) raw materials when received, (2) goods in process while in production, and (3) finished goods prior to shipment. *Move time* is the time spent moving (1) raw materials from storage to production and (2) goods in process from one factory location to another factory location. *Wait time* is the time that an order or job sits with no production applied to it; this can be due to order delays, bottlenecks in production, and poor scheduling.

Process time is considered **value-added time** because it is the only activity in cycle time that adds value to the product from the customer's perspective. The other three time activities are considered **non-value-added time** because they add no value to the customer.

Companies strive to reduce non-value-added time to improve **cycle efficiency (CE).** Cycle efficiency is the ratio of value-added time to total cycle time—see Exhibit 18.20.

EXHIBIT 18.20

Cycle Efficiency

$$\text{Cycle efficiency} = \frac{\text{Value-added time}}{\text{Cycle time}}$$

To illustrate, assume that Rocky Mountain Bikes receives and produces an order for 500 Tracker® mountain bikes. Assume that the following times were measured during production of this order.

Process time... 1.8 days   **Inspection time... 0.5 days**   **Move time... 0.7 days**   **Wait time... 3.0 days**

In this case, cycle time is 6.0 days, computed as 1.8 days + 0.5 days + 0.7 days + 3.0 days. Also, cycle efficiency is 0.3, or 30%, computed as 1.8 days divided by 6.0 days. This means that Rocky Mountain Bikes spends 30% of its time working on the product (value-added time). The other 70% is spent on non-value-added activities.

If a company has a CE of 1, it means that its time is spent entirely on value-added activities. If the CE is low, the company should evaluate its production process to see if it can identify ways to reduce non-value-added activities. The 30% CE for Rocky Mountain Bikes is low and its management should look for ways to reduce non-value-added activities.

DEMONSTRATION PROBLEM 1: COST BEHAVIOR AND CLASSIFICATION

Understanding the classification and assignment of costs is important. Consider a company that manufactures computer chips. It incurs the following costs in manufacturing chips and in operating the company.

1. Plastic board used to mount the chip, $3.50 each.
2. Assembly worker pay of $15 per hour to attach chips to plastic board.
3. Salary for factory maintenance workers who maintain factory equipment.
4. Factory supervisor pay of $55,000 per year to supervise employees.
5. Real estate taxes paid on the factory, $14,500.
6. Real estate taxes paid on the company office, $6,000.
7. Depreciation costs on machinery used by workers, $30,000.
8. Salary paid to the chief financial officer, $95,000.
9. Advertising costs of $7,800 paid to promote products.
10. Salespersons' commissions of $0.50 for each assembled chip sold.
11. Management has the option to rent the manufacturing plant to six local hospitals to store medical records instead of producing and assembling chips.

Classify each cost in the following table according to the categories listed in the table header. A cost can be classified under more than one category. For example, the plastic board used to mount chips is classified as a direct material product cost and as a direct unit cost.

| Cost | Period Costs | Product Costs | | | Unit Cost Classification | | Sunk Cost | Opportunity Cost |
	Selling and Administrative	Direct Material (Prime Cost)	Direct Labor (Prime and Conversion)	Factory Overhead (Conversion Cost)	Direct	Indirect		
1. Plastic board used to mount the chip, $3.50 each		✔			✔			

SOLUTION TO DEMONSTRATION PROBLEM 1

| Cost* | Period Costs | Product Costs | | | Unit Cost Classification | | Sunk Cost | Opportunity Cost |
	Selling and Administrative	Direct Material (Prime Cost)	Direct Labor (Prime and Conversion)	Factory Overhead (Conversion Cost)	Direct	Indirect		
1.		✔			✔			
2.			✔		✔			
3.				✔		✔		
4.				✔		✔		
5.				✔		✔		
6.	✔							
7.				✔		✔	✔	
8.	✔							
9.	✔							
10.	✔							
11.								✔

* Costs 1 through 11 refer to the 11 cost items described at the beginning of the problem.

DEMONSTRATION PROBLEM 2: REPORTING FOR MANUFACTURERS

A manufacturing company's balance sheet and income statement differ from those for a merchandising or service company.

Required

1. Fill in the [BLANK] descriptors on the partial balance sheets for both the manufacturing company and the merchandising company. Explain why a different presentation is required.

Manufacturing Company

ADIDAS GROUP Partial Balance Sheet December 31, 2011	
Current assets	
Cash.....................	$10,000
[BLANK]	8,000
[BLANK]	5,000
[BLANK]	7,000
Supplies	500
Prepaid insurance	500
Total current assets	$31,000

Merchandising Company

PAYLESS SHOE OUTLET Partial Balance Sheet December 31, 2011	
Current assets	
Cash.....................	$ 5,000
[BLANK]	12,000
Supplies	500
Prepaid insurance	500
Total current assets	$18,000

2. Fill in the [BLANK] descriptors on the income statements for the manufacturing company and the merchandising company. Explain why a different presentation is required.

Manufacturing Company

ADIDAS GROUP Partial Income Statement For Year Ended December 31, 2011	
Sales..	$200,000
Cost of goods sold	
Finished goods inventory, Dec. 31, 2010	10,000
[BLANK]	120,000
Goods available for sale	130,000
Finished goods inventory, Dec. 31, 2011	(7,000)
Cost of goods sold	123,000
Gross profit................................	$ 77,000

Merchandising Company

PAYLESS SHOE OUTLET Partial Income Statement For Year Ended December 31, 2011	
Sales..	$190,000
Cost of goods sold	
Merchandise inventory, Dec. 31, 2010	8,000
[BLANK]	108,000
Goods available for sale	116,000
Merchandise inventory, Dec. 31, 2011	(12,000)
Cost of goods sold	104,000
Gross profit................................	$ 86,000

3. A manufacturer's cost of goods manufactured is the sum of (a) _____, (b) _____, and (c) _____ costs incurred in producing the product.

SOLUTION TO DEMONSTRATION PROBLEM 2

1. Inventories for a manufacturer and for a merchandiser.

Manufacturing Company

ADIDAS GROUP Partial Balance Sheet December 31, 2011	
Current assets	
Cash	$10,000
Raw materials inventory	8,000
Goods in process inventory	5,000
Finished goods inventory	7,000
Supplies	500
Prepaid insurance	500
Total current assets	$31,000

Merchandising Company

PAYLESS SHOE OUTLET Partial Balance Sheet December 31, 2011	
Current assets	
Cash	$ 5,000
Merchandise inventory	12,000
Supplies	500
Prepaid insurance	500
Total current assets	$18,000

Explanation: A manufacturing company must control and measure three types of inventories: raw materials, goods in process, and finished goods. In the sequence of making a product, the raw materials move into production—called *goods in process inventory*—and then to finished goods. All raw materials and goods in process inventory at the end of each accounting period are considered current assets. All unsold finished inventory is considered a current asset at the end of each accounting period. The merchandising company must control and measure only one type of inventory, purchased goods.

2. Cost of goods sold for a manufacturer and for a merchandiser.

Manufacturing Company

ADIDAS GROUP Partial Income Statement For Year Ended December 31, 2011	
Sales	$200,000
Cost of goods sold	
Finished goods inventory, Dec. 31, 2010	10,000
Cost of goods manufactured	120,000
Goods available for sale	130,000
Finished goods inventory, Dec. 31, 2011	(7,000)
Cost of goods sold	123,000
Gross profit	$ 77,000

Merchandising Company

PAYLESS SHOE OUTLET Partial Income Statement For Year Ended December 31, 2011	
Sales	$190,000
Cost of goods sold	
Merchandise inventory, Dec. 31, 2010	8,000
Cost of purchases	108,000
Goods available for sale	116,000
Merchandise inventory, Dec. 31, 2011	(12,000)
Cost of goods sold	104,000
Gross profit	$ 86,000

Explanation: Manufacturing and merchandising companies use different reporting terms. In particular, the terms *finished goods* and *cost of goods manufactured* are used to reflect the production of goods, yet the concepts and techniques of reporting cost of goods sold for a manufacturing company and merchandising company are similar.

3. A manufacturer's cost of goods manufactured is the sum of (a) *direct material,* (b) *direct labor,* and (c) *factory overhead* costs incurred in producing the product.

DEMONSTRATION PROBLEM 3: MANUFACTURING STATEMENT

The following account balances and other information are from SUNN Corporation's accounting records for year-end December 31, 2011. Use this information to prepare (1) a table listing factory overhead costs, (2) a manufacturing statement (show only the total factory overhead cost), and (3) an income statement.

Advertising expense	$ 85,000	Goods in process inventory, Dec. 31, 2010	$ 8,000
Amortization expense—Factory Patents	16,000	Goods in process inventory, Dec. 31, 2011	9,000
Bad debts expense	28,000	Income taxes	53,400
Depreciation expense—Office equipment	37,000	Indirect labor	26,000
Depreciation expense—Factory building	133,000	Interest expense	25,000
Depreciation expense—Factory equipment	78,000	Miscellaneous expense	55,000
Direct labor	250,000	Property taxes on factory equipment	14,000
Factory insurance expired	62,000	Raw materials inventory, Dec. 31, 2010	60,000
Factory supervision	74,000	Raw materials inventory, Dec. 31, 2011	78,000
Factory supplies used	21,000	Raw materials purchases	313,000
Factory utilities	115,000	Repairs expense—Factory equipment	31,000
Finished goods inventory, Dec. 31, 2010	15,000	Salaries expense	150,000
Finished goods inventory, Dec. 31, 2011	12,500	Sales	1,630,000

PLANNING THE SOLUTION

● Analyze the account balances and select those that are part of factory overhead costs.

● Arrange these costs in a table that lists factory overhead costs for the year.

● Analyze the remaining costs and select those related to production activity for the year; selected costs should include the materials and goods in process inventories and direct labor.

● Prepare a manufacturing statement for the year showing the calculation of the cost of materials used in production, the cost of direct labor, and the total factory overhead cost. When presenting overhead cost on this statement, report only total overhead cost from the table of overhead costs for the year. Show the costs of beginning and ending goods in process inventory to determine cost of goods manufactured.

● Organize the remaining revenue and expense items into the income statement for the year. Combine cost of goods manufactured from the manufacturing statement with the finished goods inventory amounts to compute cost of goods sold for the year.

SOLUTION TO DEMONSTRATION PROBLEM 3

SUNN CORPORATION
Factory Overhead Costs
For Year Ended December 31, 2011

Amortization expense—Factory patents	$ 16,000
Depreciation expense—Factory building	133,000
Depreciation expense—Factory equipment	78,000
Factory insurance expired	62,000
Factory supervision	74,000
Factory supplies used	21,000
Factory utilities	115,000
Indirect labor	26,000
Property taxes on factory equipment	14,000
Repairs expense—Factory equipment	31,000
Total factory overhead	$570,000

SUNN CORPORATION
Manufacturing Statement
For Year Ended December 31, 2011

Direct materials		
Raw materials inventory, Dec. 31, 2010	$ 60,000	
Raw materials purchase	313,000	
Raw materials available for use	373,000	
Less raw materials inventory, Dec. 31, 2011	78,000	
Direct materials used	295,000	
Direct labor	250,000	
Factory overhead	570,000	
Total manufacturing costs	1,115,000	
Goods in process inventory, Dec. 31, 2010	8,000	
Total cost of goods in process	1,123,000	
Less goods in process inventory, Dec. 31, 2011	9,000	
Cost of goods manufactured	$1,114,000	

SUNN CORPORATION
Income Statement
For Year Ended December 31, 2011

Sales		$1,630,000
Cost of goods sold		
Finished goods inventory, Dec. 31, 2010	$ 15,000	
Cost of goods manufactured	1,114,000	
Goods available for sale	1,129,000	
Less finished goods inventory, Dec. 31, 2011	12,500	
Cost of goods sold		1,116,500
Gross profit		513,500
Operating expenses		
Advertising expense	85,000	
Bad debts expense	28,000	
Depreciation expense—Office equipment	37,000	
Interest expense	25,000	
Miscellaneous expense	55,000	
Salaries expense	150,000	
Total operating expenses		380,000
Income before income taxes		133,500
Income taxes		53,400
Net income		$ 80,100

Summary

C1 Explain the purpose and nature of, and the role of ethics in, managerial accounting. The purpose of managerial accounting is to provide useful information to management and other internal decision makers. It does this by collecting, managing, and reporting both monetary and nonmonetary information in a manner useful to internal users. Major characteristics of managerial accounting include (1) focus on internal decision makers, (2) emphasis on planning and control, (3) flexibility, (4) timeliness, (5) reliance on forecasts and estimates, (6) focus on segments and projects, and (7) reporting both monetary and nonmonetary information. Ethics are beliefs that distinguish right from wrong. Ethics can be important in reducing fraud in business operations.

C2 Describe accounting concepts useful in classifying costs. We can classify costs on the basis of their (1) behavior—fixed vs. variable, (2) traceability—direct vs. indirect, (3) controllability—controllable vs. uncontrollable, (4) relevance—sunk vs. out of pocket, and (5) function—product vs. period. A cost can be classified in more than one way, depending on the purpose for which the cost is being determined. These classifications help us understand cost patterns, analyze performance, and plan operations.

C3 Define product and period costs and explain how they impact financial statements. Costs that are capitalized because they are expected to have future value are called *product costs;* costs that are expensed are called *period costs.* This classification is important because it affects the amount of costs expensed in the income statement and the amount of costs assigned to inventory on the balance sheet. Product costs are commonly made up of direct materials, direct labor, and overhead. Period costs include selling and administrative expenses.

C4 Explain how balance sheets and income statements for manufacturing and merchandising companies differ. The main difference is that manufacturers usually carry three inventories on their balance sheets—raw materials, goods in process, and finished goods—instead of one inventory that merchandisers carry. The main difference between income statements of manufacturers and merchandisers is the items making up cost of goods sold. A merchandiser adds beginning merchandise inventory to cost of goods purchased and then subtracts ending merchandise inventory to get cost of goods sold. A manufacturer adds beginning finished goods inventory to cost of goods manufactured and then subtracts ending finished goods inventory to get cost of goods sold.

C5 Explain manufacturing activities and the flow of manufacturing costs. Manufacturing activities consist of materials, production, and sales activities. The materials activity consists of the purchase and issuance of materials to production. The production activity consists of converting materials into finished goods. At this stage in the process, the materials, labor, and overhead costs have been incurred and the manufacturing statement is prepared. The sales activity consists of selling some or all of finished goods available for sale. At this stage, the cost of goods sold is determined.

C6 Describe trends in managerial accounting. Important trends in managerial accounting include an increased focus on satisfying customers, the impact of a global economy, and the growing presence of e-commerce and service-based businesses. The lean business model, designed to eliminate waste and satisfy customers, can be useful in responding to recent trends. Concepts such as total quality management, just-in-time production, and the value chain often aid in application of the lean business model.

A1 Compute cycle time and cycle efficiency, and explain their importance to production management. It is important for companies to reduce the time to produce their products and to improve manufacturing efficiency. One measure of that time is cycle time (CT), defined as Process time + Inspection time + Move time + Wait time. Process time is value-added time; the others are non-value-added time. Cycle efficiency (CE) is the ratio of value-added time to total cycle time. If CE is low, management should evaluate its production process to see if it can reduce non-value-added activities.

P1 Compute cost of goods sold for a manufacturer. A manufacturer adds beginning finished goods inventory to cost of goods manufactured and then subtracts ending finished goods inventory to get cost of goods sold.

P2 Prepare a manufacturing statement and explain its purpose and links to financial statements. The manufacturing statement reports computation of cost of goods manufactured for the period. It begins by showing the period's costs for direct materials, direct labor, and overhead and then adjusts these numbers for the beginning and ending inventories of the goods in process to yield cost of goods manufactured.

Guidance Answers to Decision Maker and Decision Ethics

Production Manager It appears that all three friends want to pay the bill with someone else's money. David is using money belonging to the tax authorities, Denise is taking money from her company, and Derek is defrauding the client. To prevent such practices, companies have internal audit mechanisms. Many companies also adopt ethical codes of conduct to help guide employees. We must recognize that some entertainment expenses are justifiable and even encouraged. For example, the tax law allows certain deductions for entertainment that have a business purpose. Corporate policies also sometimes allow and encourage reimbursable spending for social activities, and contracts can include entertainment as allowable costs.

Nevertheless, without further details, payment for this bill should be made from personal accounts.

Entrepreneur Tracing all costs directly to cost objects is always desirable, but you need to be able to do so in an economically feasible manner. In this case, you are able to trace 90% of the assembly department's direct costs. It may not be economical to spend more money on a new software to trace the final 10% of costs. You need to make a cost–benefit trade-off. If the software offers benefits beyond tracing the remaining 10% of the assembly department's costs, your decision should consider this.

Purchase Manager Opportunity costs relate to the potential quality and delivery benefits given up by not choosing supplier (A). Selecting supplier (B) might involve future costs of poor-quality seats (inspection, repairs, and returns). Also, potential delivery delays could interrupt work and increase manufacturing costs. Your company could also incur sales losses if the product quality of supplier (B) is low. As purchase manager, you are responsible for these costs and must consider them in making your decision.

Guidance Answers to Quick Checks

1. *d*

2. Financial accounting information is intended for users external to an organization such as investors, creditors, and government authorities. Managerial accounting focuses on providing information to managers, officers, and other decision makers within the organization.

3. No, GAAP do not control the practice of managerial accounting. Unlike external users, the internal users need managerial accounting information for planning and controlling business activities rather than for external comparison. Different types of information are required, depending on the activity. Therefore it is difficult to standardize managerial accounting.

4. Variable costs increase when volume of activity increases.

5. By being able to trace costs to cost objects (say, to products and departments), managers better understand the total costs associated with a cost object. This is useful when managers consider making changes to the cost object (such as when dropping the product or expanding the department).

6. Raw materials inventory, goods in process inventory, and finished goods inventory.

7. The cost of goods sold for merchandising companies includes all costs of acquiring the merchandise; the cost of goods sold for manufacturing companies includes the three costs of manufacturing: direct materials, direct labor, and overhead.

8. *a*

9. No; companies rarely report a manufacturing statement.

10. Beginning goods in process inventory is added to total manufacturing costs to yield total goods in process. Ending goods in process inventory is subtracted from total goods in process to yield cost of goods manufactured for the period.

Key Terms   mhhe.com/wildFAP20e

Continuous improvement (p. 748)
Control (p. 733)
Controllable or not controllable cost (p. 737)
Conversion costs (p. 743)
Cost object (p. 737)
Customer orientation (p. 747)
Cycle efficiency (CE) (p. 750)
Cycle time (CT) (p. 749)
Direct costs (p. 737)
Direct labor (p. 742)
Direct labor costs (p. 742)
Direct material (p. 742)
Direct material costs (p. 742)
Ethics (p. 736)

Factory overhead (p. 742)
Factory overhead costs (p. 742)
Finished goods inventory (p. 741)
Fixed cost (p. 736)
Goods in process inventory (p. 741)
Indirect costs (p. 737)
Indirect labor (p. 742)
Indirect labor costs (p. 742)
Indirect material (p. 740)
Institute of Management Accountants (IMA) (p. 736)
Internal control system (p. 736)
Just-in-time (JIT) manufacturing (p. 748)
Lean business model (p. 747)
Managerial accounting (p. 732)

Manufacturing statement (p. 745)
Non-value-added time (p. 750)
Opportunity cost (p. 738)
Out-of-pocket cost (p. 738)
Period costs (p. 738)
Planning (p. 732)
Prime costs (p. 743)
Product costs (p. 738)
Raw materials inventory (p. 740)
Sunk cost (p. 738)
Total quality management (TQM) (p. 748)
Value-added time (p. 750)
Value chain (p. 748)
Variable cost (p. 736)

Multiple Choice Quiz   Answers on p. 773   mhhe.com/wildFAP20e

Additional Quiz Questions are available at the book's Website.

1. Continuous improvement
  a. Is used to reduce inventory levels.
  b. Is applicable only in service businesses.
  c. Rejects the notion of "good enough."
  d. Is used to reduce ordering costs.
  e. Is applicable only in manufacturing businesses.

2. A direct cost is one that is
   a. Variable with respect to the cost object.
   b. Traceable to the cost object.
   c. Fixed with respect to the cost object.
   d. Allocated to the cost object.
   e. A period cost.

3. Costs that are incurred as part of the manufacturing process, but are not clearly traceable to the specific unit of product or batches of product, are called
   a. Period costs.
   b. Factory overhead.
   c. Sunk costs.
   d. Opportunity costs.
   e. Fixed costs.

4. The three major cost components of manufacturing a product are
   a. Direct materials, direct labor, and factory overhead.
   b. Period costs, product costs, and sunk costs.

   c. Indirect labor, indirect materials, and fixed expenses.
   d. Variable costs, fixed costs, and period costs.
   e. Opportunity costs, sunk costs, and direct costs.

5. A company reports the following for the current year.

Finished goods inventory, beginning year	$6,000
Finished goods inventory, ending year	3,200
Cost of goods sold	7,500

Its cost of goods manufactured for the current year is
   a. $1,500.
   b. $1,700.
   c. $7,500.
   d. $2,800.
   e. $4,700.

[I] Icon denotes assignments that involve decision making.

Discussion Questions

1. Describe the managerial accountant's role in business planning, control, and decision making.

2. Distinguish between managerial and financial accounting on
   a. Users and decision makers. **b.** Purpose of information.
   c. Flexibility of practice.   **d.** Time dimension.
   e. Focus of information.   **f.** Nature of information.

3. [I] Identify the usual changes that a company must make when it adopts a customer orientation.

4. Distinguish between direct material and indirect material.

5. Distinguish between direct labor and indirect labor.

6. Distinguish between (a) factory overhead and (b) selling and administrative overhead.

7. What product cost is listed as both a prime cost and a conversion cost?

8. [I] Assume that you tour **Apple**'s factory where it makes its products. List three direct costs and three indirect costs that you are likely to see.   Apple

9. [I] Should we evaluate a manager's performance on the basis of controllable or noncontrollable costs? Why?

10. [I] Explain why knowledge of cost behavior is useful in product performance evaluation.

11. Explain why product costs are capitalized but period costs are expensed in the current accounting period.

12. [I] Explain how business activities and inventories for a manufacturing company, a merchandising company, and a service company differ.

13. [I] Why does managerial accounting often involve working with numerous predictions and estimates?

14. How do an income statement and a balance sheet for a manufacturing company and a merchandising company differ?

15. Besides inventories, what other assets often appear on manufacturers' balance sheets but not on merchandisers' balance sheets?

16. Why does a manufacturing company require three different inventory categories?

17. Manufacturing activities of a company are described in the _____. This statement summarizes the types and amounts of costs incurred in its manufacturing _____.

18. What are the three categories of manufacturing costs?

19. List several examples of factory overhead.

20. [I] List the four components of a manufacturing statement and provide specific examples of each for **Apple**.   Apple

21. [I] Prepare a proper title for the annual "manufacturing statement" of **Palm**. Does the date match the balance sheet or income statement? Why?   Palm

22. [I] Describe the relations among the income statement, the manufacturing statement, and a detailed listing of factory overhead costs.

23. [I] Define and describe *cycle time* and identify the components of cycle time.

24. [I] Explain the difference between value-added time and non-value-added time.

25. Define and describe *cycle efficiency*.

26. [I] Can management of a company such as **Research In Motion** use cycle time and cycle efficiency as useful measures of performance? Explain.   RIM

27. Access **Dell**'s annual report (10-K) for the fiscal year ended January 29, 2010, at the SEC's EDGAR database (**SEC.gov**) or its Website (**Dell.com**). From its financial statement notes, identify the titles and amounts of its inventory components.

QUICK STUDY

QS 18-1

Managerial accounting versus financial accounting

C1

Identify whether each description most likely applies to managerial or financial accounting.

1. _____ Its primary focus is on the organization as a whole.

2. _____ Its principles and practices are very flexible.

3. _____ It is directed at external users in making investment, credit, and other decisions.

4. _____ Its primary users are company managers.

5. _____ Its information is often available only after an audit is complete.

QS 18-2

Managerial accounting defined

C1

Managerial accounting (choose one)

1. Must follow generally accepted accounting principles.

2. Provides information to aid management in planning and controlling business activities.

3. Is directed at reporting aggregate data on the company as a whole.

4. Provides information that is widely available to all interested parties.

QS 18-3

Fixed and variable costs

C2

Which of these statements is true regarding fixed and variable costs?

1. Fixed costs increase and variable costs decrease in total as activity volume decreases.

2. Fixed costs stay the same and variable costs increase in total as activity volume increases.

3. Both fixed and variable costs increase as activity volume increases.

4. Both fixed and variable costs stay the same in total as activity volume increases.

QS 18-4

Direct and indirect costs

C2

Kasey Anthony Company produces sporting equipment, including basketballs. Identify each of the following costs as direct or indirect if the cost object is a basketball produced by Kasey Anthony.

1. Materials used to produce basketballs.

2. Electricity used in the production plant.

3. Labor used on the basketball production line.

4. Salary of manager who supervises the entire plant.

5. Depreciation on equipment used to produce basketballs.

QS 18-5

Product and period costs

C3

Which of these statements is true regarding product and period costs?

1. Sales commission is a product cost and factory rent is a period cost.

2. Factory wages are a product cost and direct material is a period cost.

3. Factory maintenance is a product cost and sales commission is a period cost.

4. Sales commission is a product cost and depreciation on factory equipment is a product cost.

QS 18-6

Inventory reporting for manufacturers C4

Three inventory categories are reported on a manufacturing company's balance sheet: (i) raw materials, (ii) goods in process, and (iii) finished goods. Identify the usual order in which these inventory items are reported on the balance sheet.

1. (i)(ii)(iii)   **2.** (ii)(i)(iii)   **3.** (ii)(iii)(i)   **4.** (iii)(ii)(i)

QS 18-7

Cost of goods sold   P1

A company has year-end cost of goods manufactured of $5,000, beginning finished goods inventory of $700, and ending finished goods inventory of $850. Its cost of goods sold is

1. $4,250   **2.** $4,000   **3.** $4,850   **4.** $6,550

QS 18-8

Manufacturing flows identified

C5

Identify the usual sequence of manufacturing activities by filling in the blank (with i, ii or iii) corresponding to its order: _____ Production activities; _____ sales activities; _____ materials activities.

Match each lean business concept with its best description by entering its letter in the blank.

1. _____ Customer orientation

2. _____ Total quality management

3. _____ Just-in-time manufacturing

4. _____ Continuous improvements

A. Inventory is acquired or produced only as needed.

B. Flexible product designs can be modified to accommodate customer choices.

C. Every manager and employee constantly looks for ways to improve company operations.

D. Focuses on quality throughout the production process.

QS 18-9
Lean business concepts
C6

Compute cost of goods sold for year 2011 using the following information.

Finished goods inventory, Dec. 31, 2010	$321,500
Goods in process inventory, Dec. 31, 2010	74,550
Goods in process inventory, Dec. 31, 2011	81,200
Cost of goods manufactured, year 2011	972,345
Finished goods inventory, Dec. 31, 2011	297,200

QS 18-10
Cost of goods sold
P1

Prepare the 2011 manufacturing statement for Carmichael Company using the following information.

Direct materials	$192,500
Direct labor	65,150
Factory overhead costs	26,000
Goods in process, Dec. 31, 2010	159,600
Goods in process, Dec. 31, 2011	144,750

QS 18-11
Cost of goods manufactured
P2

Compute and interpret (*a*) manufacturing cycle time and (*b*) manufacturing cycle efficiency using the following information from a manufacturing company.

Process time	15 minutes
Inspection time	2 minutes
Move time	6.4 minutes
Wait time	36.6 minutes

QS 18-12
Manufacturing cycle time and efficiency
A1

Nestlé reports beginning raw materials inventory of 3,590 and ending raw materials inventory of 3,708 (both numbers in millions of Swiss francs). If Nestlé purchased 12,000 (in millions of Swiss francs) of raw materials during the year, what is the amount of raw materials it used during the year?

QS 18-13
Direct materials used
C5

連 connect

Both managerial accounting and financial accounting provide useful information to decision makers. Indicate in the following chart the most likely source of information for each business decision (a decision can require major input from both sources, in which case both can be marked).

	Primary Information Source	
Business Decision	**Managerial**	**Financial**
1. Plan the budget for next quarter	_____	_____
2. Measure profitability of all individual stores	_____	_____
3. Prepare financial reports according to GAAP	_____	_____
4. Determine location and size for a new plant	_____	_____
5. Determine amount of dividends to pay stockholders	_____	_____
6. Evaluate a purchasing department's performance	_____	_____
7. Report financial performance to board of directors	_____	_____
8. Estimate product cost for a new line of shoes	_____	_____

EXERCISES

Exercise 18-1
Sources of accounting information
C1

Exercise 18-2

Characteristics of financial accounting and managerial accounting

C1

In the following chart, compare financial accounting and managerial accounting by describing how each differs for the items listed. Be specific in your responses.

	Financial Accounting	Managerial Accounting
1. Nature of information		
2. Flexibility of practice		
3. Focus of information		
4. Time dimension		
5. Users and decision makers		
6. Timeliness of information		
7. Purpose of information		

Exercise 18-3

Planning and control descriptions

C1

Complete the following statements by filling in the blanks.

1. _____ is the process of setting goals and making plans to achieve them.
2. _____ _____ usually covers a period of 5 to 10 years.
3. _____ _____ usually covers a period of one year.
4. _____ is the process of monitoring planning decisions and evaluating an organization's activities and employees.

Exercise 18-4

Cost analysis and identification

C3

Georgia Pacific, a manufacturer, incurs the following costs. (1) Classify each cost as either a product or a period cost. If a product cost, identify it as a prime and/or conversion cost. (2) Classify each product cost as either a direct cost or an indirect cost using the product as the cost object.

Prime DM or DL
Conversion FOH or DL

Cost	Product Cost Prime	Product Cost Conversion	Period Cost	Direct Cost	Indirect Cost
1. Office supplies used					
2. Bad debts expense					
3. Small tools used					
4. Factory utilities					
5. Advertising					
6. Amortization of patents on factory machine . . .					
7. Payroll taxes for production supervisor					
8. Accident insurance on factory workers					
9. Depreciation—Factory building					
10. State and federal income taxes					
11. Wages to assembly workers					
12. Direct materials used					

Exercise 18-5

Cost classifications C2

(1) Identify each of the five cost classifications discussed in the chapter. (2) List two purposes of identifying these separate cost classifications.

Exercise 18-6

Cost analysis and classification

C2

Listed here are product costs for the production of soccer balls. (1) Classify each cost (a) as either fixed or variable and (b) as either direct or indirect. (2) What pattern do you see regarding the relation between costs classified by behavior and costs classified by traceability?

Product Cost	Cost by Behavior Variable	Cost by Behavior Fixed	Cost by Traceability Direct	Cost by Traceability Indirect
1. Taxes on factory				
2. Machinery depreciation				
3. Coolants for machinery				
4. Wages of assembly workers				
5. Lace to hold leather together				
6. Leather covers for soccer balls				
7. Annual flat fee paid for office security				

Current assets for two different companies at calendar year-end 2011 are listed here. One is a manufacturer, Roller Blades Mfg., and the other, Sunny Foods, is a grocery distribution company. (1) Identify which set of numbers relates to the manufacturer and which to the merchandiser. (2) Prepare the current asset section for each company from this information. Discuss why the current asset section for these two companies is different.

Exercise 18-7
Balance sheet identification and preparation
C4

Account	Company 1	Company 2
Cash	$ 9,000	$ 7,000
Raw materials inventory	—	44,000
Merchandise inventory	47,000	—
Goods in process inventory	—	32,000
Finished goods inventory	—	52,000
Accounts receivable, net	64,000	77,000
Prepaid expenses	3,500	700

Compute cost of goods sold for each of these two companies for the year ended December 31, 2011.

Exercise 18-8
Cost of goods sold computation
P1

	Century Merchandising	New Homes Manufacturing
Beginning inventory		
Merchandise	$250,000	
Finished goods		$500,000
Cost of purchases	460,000	
Cost of goods manufactured		886,000
Ending inventory		
Merchandise	150,000	
Finished goods		144,000

Check Century Merchandising COGS, $560,000

Using the following data, compute (1) the cost of goods manufactured and (2) the cost of goods sold for both Canyon Company and Rossings Company.

Exercise 18-9
Cost of goods manufactured and cost of goods sold computation
P1 P2

	Canyon Company	Rossings Company
Beginning finished goods inventory	$14,000	$18,450
Beginning goods in process inventory	16,500	21,950
Beginning raw materials inventory	9,250	11,000
Rental cost on factory equipment	29,000	24,750
Direct labor	21,000	37,000
Ending finished goods inventory	19,650	15,300
Ending goods in process inventory	24,000	18,000
Ending raw materials inventory	7,300	9,200
Factory utilities	11,000	14,000
Factory supplies used	10,200	5,200
General and administrative expenses	23,000	45,000
Indirect labor	3,250	9,660
Repairs—Factory equipment	6,780	3,500
Raw materials purchases	35,000	54,000
Sales salaries	52,000	48,000

Check Canyon COGS, $105,030

Exercise 18-10
Components of accounting reports
P2

For each of the following accounts for a manufacturing company, place a ✔ in the appropriate column indicating that it appears on the balance sheet, the income statement, the manufacturing statement, and/or a detailed listing of factory overhead costs. Assume that the income statement shows the calculation of cost of goods sold and the manufacturing statement shows only the total amount of factory overhead. (An account can appear on more than one report.)

	Account	Balance Sheet	Income Statement	Manufacturing Statement	Overhead Report
3	Accounts receivable	$10,000			
4	Computer supplies used in office	$2,000			
5	Beginning finished goods inventory				
6	Beginning goods in process inventory				
7	Beginning raw materials inventory				
8	Cash				
9	Depreciation expense—Factory building				
10	Depreciation expense—Factory equipment				
11	Depreciation expense—Office building				
12	Depreciation expense—Office equipment				
13	Direct labor				
14	Ending finished goods inventory				
15	Ending goods in process inventory				
16	Ending raw materials inventory				
17	Factory maintenance wages				
18	Computer supplies used in factory				
19	Income taxes				
20	Insurance on factory building				
21	Rent cost on office building				
22	Office supplies used				
23	Property taxes on factory building				
24	Raw materials purchases				
25	Sales				

Exercise 18-11
Manufacturing statement preparation
P2

Given the following selected account balances of Randa Company, prepare its manufacturing statement for the year ended on December 31, 2011. Include a listing of the individual overhead account balances in this statement.

Sales	$1,252,000
Raw materials inventory, Dec. 31, 2010	39,000
Goods in process inventory, Dec. 31, 2010	55,900
Finished goods inventory, Dec. 31, 2010	64,750
Raw materials purchases	177,600
Direct labor	227,000
Factory computer supplies used	19,840
Indirect labor	49,000
Repairs—Factory equipment	7,250
Rent cost of factory building	59,000
Advertising expense	96,000
General and administrative expenses	131,300
Raw materials inventory, Dec. 31, 2011	44,700
Goods in process inventory, Dec. 31, 2011	43,500
Finished goods inventory, Dec. 31, 2011	69,300

Check Cost of goods manufactured, $546,390

Exercise 18-12
Income statement preparation
P2

Use the information in Exercise 18-11 to prepare an income statement for Randa Company (a manufacturer). Assume that its cost of goods manufactured is $546,390.

The following chart shows how costs flow through a business as a product is manufactured. Some boxes in the flowchart show cost amounts. Compute the cost amounts for the boxes that contain question marks.

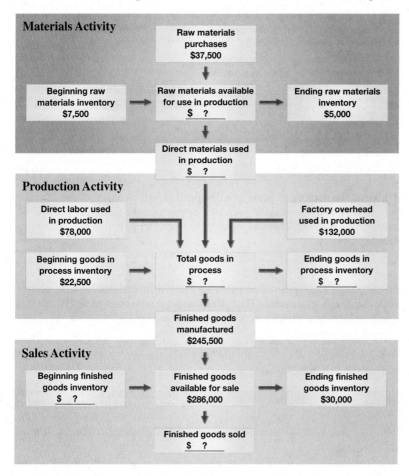

Customer orientation means that a company's managers and employees respond to customers' changing wants and needs. A manufacturer of metal parts has created a customer satisfaction survey that it asks each of its customers to complete. The survey asks about the following factors: (A) product performance; (B) price; (C) lead time; (D) delivery. Each factor is to be rated as unsatisfactory, marginal, average, satisfactory, or very satisfied.

a. Match the competitive forces 1 through 4 to the factors on the survey. A factor can be matched to more than one competitive force.

Survey Factor	Competitive Force
A. Product performance	_____ **1.** Cost
B. Price	_____ **2.** Time
C. Lead time	_____ **3.** Quality
D. Delivery	_____ **4.** Flexibility of service

b. How can managers of this company use the information from this customer satisfaction survey to better meet competitive forces and satisfy their customers?

Following are three separate events affecting the managerial accounting systems for different companies. Match the management concept(s) that the company is likely to adopt for the event identified. There is some overlap in the meaning of customer orientation and total quality management and, therefore, some responses can include more than one concept.

	Event	Management Concept
_____	1. The company starts measuring inventory turnover and discontinues elaborate inventory records. Its new focus is to pull inventory through the system.	a. Total quality management (TQM)
		b. Just-in-time (JIT) system
_____	2. The company starts reporting measures on customer complaints and product returns from customers.	c. Continuous improvement (CI)
		d. Customer orientation (CO)
_____	3. The company starts reporting measures such as the percent of defective products and the number of units scrapped.	

connect

PROBLEM SET A

Problem 18-1A
Managerial accounting role
C1

This chapter explained the purpose of managerial accounting in the context of the current business environment. Review the *automobile* section of your local newspaper; the Sunday paper is often best. Review advertisements of sport-utility vehicles and identify the manufacturers that offer these products and the factors on which they compete.

Required

Discuss the potential contributions and responsibilities of the managerial accounting professional in helping an automobile manufacturer succeed. (*Hint:* Think about information and estimates that a managerial accountant might provide new entrants into the sport-utility market.)

Problem 18-2A
Cost computation, classification, and analysis
C2 C3

Listed here are the total costs associated with the 2011 production of 1,000 drum sets manufactured by NeatBeat. The drum sets sell for $300 each.

		Cost by Behavior		Cost by Function	
	Costs	Variable	Fixed	Product	Period
1.	Plastic for casing—$12,000.	$12,000		$12,000	
2.	Wages of assembly workers—$60,000.				
3.	Property taxes on factory—$6,000				
4.	Accounting staff salaries—$45,000				
5.	Drum stands (1,000 stands outsourced)—$25,000				
6.	Rent cost of equipment for sales staff—$7,000				
7.	Upper management salaries—$100,000				
8.	Annual flat fee for maintenance service—$9,000				
9.	Sales commissions—$10 per unit				
10.	Machinery depreciation—$10,000				

Required

Check (1) Total variable
manufacturing cost, $97,000

1. Classify each cost and its amount as (*a*) either fixed or variable and (*b*) either product or period. (The first cost is completed as an example.)

2. Compute the manufacturing cost per drum set.

Analysis Component

3. Assume that 1,200 drum sets are produced in the next year. What do you predict will be the total cost of plastic for the casings and the per unit cost of the plastic for the casings? Explain.

4. Assume that 1,200 drum sets are produced in the next year. What do you predict will be the total cost of property taxes and the per unit cost of the property taxes? Explain.

Problem 18-3A
Cost classification
and explanation
C2 C3

Assume that you must make a presentation to the marketing staff explaining the difference between product and period costs. Your supervisor tells you the marketing staff would also like clarification regarding prime and conversion costs and an explanation of how these terms fit with product and period cost. You are told that many on the staff are unable to classify costs in their merchandising activities.

Required

Prepare a one-page memorandum to your supervisor outlining your presentation to the marketing staff.

Refer to *Decision Maker,* **Purchase Manager,** in this chapter. Assume that you are the motorcycle manu-facturer's managerial accountant. The purchasing manager asks you about preparing an estimate of the related costs for buying motorcycle seats from supplier (B). She tells you this estimate is needed because unless dollar estimates are attached to nonfinancial factors, such as lost production time, her supervisor will not give it full attention. The manager also shows you the following information.

Problem 18-4A
Opportunity cost estimation and application

C1   C2

- Production output is 3,000 motorcycles per year based on 250 production days a year.
- Production time per day is 8 hours at a cost of $2,000 per hour to run the production line.
- Lost production time due to poor quality is 1%.
- Satisfied customers purchase, on average, three motorcycles during a lifetime.
- Satisfied customers recommend the product, on average, to 10 other people.
- Marketing predicts that using seat (B) will result in 10 lost customers per year from repeat business and referrals.
- Average gross profit per motorcycle is $3,000.

Required

Estimate the costs (including opportunity costs) of buying motorcycle seats from supplier (B). This prob-lem requires that you think creatively and make reasonable estimates; thus there could be more than one correct answer. (*Hint:* Reread the answer to *Decision Maker* and compare the cost savings for buying from supplier [B] to the sum of lost customer revenue from repeat business and referrals and the cost of lost production time.)

Check   Estimated cost of lost production time, $40,000

Shepler Boot Company makes specialty boots for the rodeo circuit. On December 31, 2010, the company had (*a*) 500 pairs of boots in finished goods inventory and (*b*) 1,500 heels at a cost of $5 each in raw ma-terials inventory. During 2011, the company purchased 50,000 additional heels at $5 each and manufac-tured 20,000 pairs of boots.

Problem 18-5A
Ending inventory computation and evaluation

C4

Required

1. Determine the unit and dollar amounts of raw materials inventory in heels at December 31, 2011.

Check   (1) Ending (heel) inventory, 11,500 units; $57,500

Analysis Component

2. Write a one-half page memorandum to the production manager explaining why a just-in-time inventory system for heels should be considered. Include the amount of working capital that can be reduced at December 31, 2011, if the ending heel raw material inventory is cut by half.

Shown here are annual financial data at December 31, 2011, taken from two different companies.

Problem 18-6A
Inventory computation and reporting

C4   P1

mhhe.com/wildFAP20e

	Pinnacle Retail	Slope Board Manufacturing
Beginning inventory		
Merchandise	$150,000	
Finished goods		$300,000
Cost of purchases	250,000	
Cost of goods manufactured		586,000
Ending inventory		
Merchandise	100,000	
Finished goods		200,000

Required

1. Compute the cost of goods sold section of the income statement at December 31, 2011, for each com-pany. Include the proper title and format in the solution.

2. Write a half-page memorandum to your instructor (*a*) identifying the inventory accounts and (*b*) de-scribing where each is reported on the income statement and balance sheet for both companies.

Check   (1) Slope Board's cost of goods sold, $686,000

Problem 18-7A

Lean business concepts

C6

Many fast-food restaurants compete on lean business concepts. Match each of the following activities at a fast-food restaurant with the lean business concept it strives to achieve. Some activities might relate to more than one lean business concept.

_____ **1.** Clean tables and floors

_____ **2.** Orders filled within three minutes

_____ **3.** Standardized food making processes

_____ **4.** Courteous employees

_____ **5.** Food produced to order

_____ **6.** New product development

_____ **7.** Customer satisfaction surveys

_____ **8.** Continually changing menus

_____ **9.** Drive-through windows

_____ **10.** Standardized menus from location to location

a. Just-in-time (JIT)

b. Continuous improvement (CI)

c. Total quality management (TQM)

3A

Problem 18-8A

Manufacturing and income statements; inventory analysis P2

The following calendar year-end information is taken from the December 31, 2011, adjusted trial balance and other records of Plaza Company.

Advertising expense	$ 30,750	Direct labor	$ 677,480
Depreciation expense—Office equipment	9,250	Income taxes expense	235,725
Depreciation expense—Selling equipment	10,600	Indirect labor	58,875
Depreciation expense—Factory equipment	35,550	Miscellaneous production costs	10,425
Factory supervision	104,600	Office salaries expense	65,000
Factory supplies used	9,350	Raw materials purchases	927,000
Factory utilities	35,000	Rent expense—Office space	24,000
Inventories		Rent expense—Selling space	28,100
Raw materials, December 31, 2010	168,850	Rent expense—Factory building	78,800
Raw materials, December 31, 2011	184,000	Maintenance expense—Factory equipment	37,400
Goods in process, December 31, 2010	17,700	Sales	4,527,000
Goods in process, December 31, 2011	21,380	Sales discounts	64,500
Finished goods, December 31, 2010	169,350	Sales salaries expense	394,560
Finished goods, December 31, 2011	138,490		

Work

Required

Check (1) Cost of goods manufactured, $1,955,650

1. Prepare the company's 2011 manufacturing statement.

2. Prepare the company's 2011 income statement that reports separate categories for (_a_) selling expenses and (_b_) general and administrative expenses.

Analysis Component

3. Compute the (_a_) inventory turnover, defined as cost of goods sold divided by average inventory, and (_b_) days' sales in inventory, defined as 365 times ending inventory divided by cost of goods sold, for both its raw materials inventory and its finished goods inventory. (To compute turnover and days' sales in inventory for raw materials, use raw materials used rather than cost of goods sold.) Discuss some possible reasons for differences between these ratios for the two types of inventories. Round answers to one decimal place.

Problem 18-9A

Manufacturing cycle time and efficiency

A1

White Maple Company produces maple bookcases to customer order. It received an order from a customer to produce 15,000 bookcases. The following information is available for the production of the bookcases.

Process time	16.0 days
Inspection time	0.5 days
Move time	5.5 days
Wait time	18.0 days

Required

1. Compute the company's manufacturing cycle time.

2. Compute the company's manufacturing cycle efficiency. Interpret your answer.

Check (2) Manufacturing cycle efficiency, 0.40

Analysis Component

3. Assume that White Maple wishes to increase its manufacturing cycle efficiency to 0.75. What are some ways that it can accomplish this?

This chapter described the purpose of managerial accounting in the context of the current business environment. Review the *home electronics* section of your local newspaper; the Sunday paper is often best. Review advertisements of home electronics and identify the manufacturers that offer these products and the factors on which they compete.

Required

Discuss the potential contributions and responsibilities of the managerial accounting professional in helping a home electronics manufacturer succeed. (*Hint:* Think about information and estimates that a managerial accountant might provide new entrants into the home electronics market.)

PROBLEM SET B

Problem 18-1B
Managerial accounting role

C1

Listed here are the total costs associated with the 2011 production of 10,000 Blu-ray Discs (BDs) manufactured by Hip-Hop. The BDs sell for $15 each.

Problem 18-2B
Cost computation, classification, and analysis

C2 C3

Costs	Cost by Behavior		Cost by Function	
	Variable	Fixed	Product	Period
1. Plastic for BDs—$1,000	$1,000		$1,000	
2. Wages of assembly workers—$20,000				
3. Cost of factory rent—$4,500				
4. Systems staff salaries—$10,000				
5. Labeling (outsourced)—$2,500				
6. Cost of office equipment rent—$700				
7. Upper management salaries—$100,000				
8. Annual fixed fee for cleaning service—$3,000				
9. Sales commissions—$0.50 per BD				
10. Machinery depreciation—$15,000				

Required

1. Classify each cost and its amount as (*a*) either fixed or variable and (*b*) either product or period. (The first cost is completed as an example.)

2. Compute the manufacturing cost per BD.

Check (2) Total variable manufacturing cost, $23,500

Analysis Component

3. Assume that 15,000 BDs are produced in the next year. What do you predict will be the total cost of plastic for the BDs and the per unit cost of the plastic for the BDs? Explain.

4. Assume that 15,000 BDs are produced in the next year. What do you predict will be the total cost of factory rent and the per unit cost of the factory rent? Explain.

Assume that you must make a presentation to a client explaining the difference between prime and conversion costs. The client makes and sells 50,000 cookies per week. The client tells you that her sales staff also would like a clarification regarding product and period costs. She tells you that most of the staff lack training in managerial accounting.

Problem 18-3B
Cost classification and explanation

C2 C3

Required

Prepare a one-page memorandum to your client outlining your planned presentation to her sales staff.

Problem 18-4B
Opportunity cost estimation
and application

C1 C2

Refer to *Decision Maker,* **Purchase Manager,** in this chapter. Assume that you are the motorcycle manufacturer's managerial accountant. The purchasing manager asks you about preparing an estimate of the related costs for buying motorcycle seats from supplier (B). She tells you this estimate is needed because unless dollar estimates are attached to nonfinancial factors such as lost production time, her supervisor will not give it full attention. The manager also shows you the following information.

- Production output is 2,000 motorcycles per year based on 250 production days a year.
- Production time per day is 8 hours at a cost of $500 per hour to run the production line.
- Lost production time due to poor quality is 1%.
- Satisfied customers purchase, on average, three motorcycles during a lifetime.
- Satisfied customers recommend the product, on average, to 10 other people.
- Marketing predicts that using seat (B) will result in 8 lost customers per year from repeat business and referrals.
- Average gross profit per motorcycle is $4,000.

Required

Check   Cost of lost gross profit,
$32,000

Estimate the costs (including opportunity costs) of buying motorcycle seats from supplier (B). This problem requires that you think creatively and make reasonable estimates; thus there could be more than one correct answer. (*Hint:* Reread the answer to *Decision Maker,* and compare the cost savings for buying from supplier [B] to the sum of lost customer revenue from repeat business and referrals and the cost of lost production time.)

Problem 18-5B
Ending inventory computation
and evaluation

C4

The Edge Company makes specialty skates for the ice skating circuit. On December 31, 2010, the company had (*a*) 500 skates in finished goods inventory and (*b*) 2,000 blades at a cost of $15 each in raw materials inventory. During 2011, Edge Company purchased 45,000 additional blades at $15 each and manufactured 20,000 pairs of skates.

Required

Check   (1) Ending (blade) inventory,
7,000 units; $105,000

1. Determine the unit and dollar amounts of raw materials inventory in blades at December 31, 2011.

Analysis Component

2. Write a one-half page memorandum to the production manager explaining why a just-in-time inventory system for blades should be considered. Include the amount of working capital that can be reduced at December 31, 2011, if the ending blade raw material inventory is cut in half.

Problem 18-6B
Inventory computation and
reporting

C4 P1

Shown here are annual financial data at December 31, 2011, taken from two different companies.

	Cardinal Drug (Retail)	Nandina (Manufacturing)
Beginning inventory		
Merchandise	$ 50,000	
Finished goods		$200,000
Cost of purchases	350,000	
Cost of goods manufactured		686,000
Ending inventory		
Merchandise	25,000	
Finished goods		300,000

Required

Check   (1) Cardinal Drug cost of
goods sold, $375,000

1. Compute the cost of goods sold section of the income statement at December 31, 2011, for each company. Include the proper title and format in the solution.

2. Write a half-page memorandum to your instructor (*a*) identifying the inventory accounts and (*b*) identifying where each is reported on the income statement and balance sheet for both companies.

Eastman-Kodak manufactures digital cameras and must compete on lean manufacturing concepts. Match each of the following activities that it engages in with the lean manufacturing concept it strives to achieve. (Some activities might relate to more than one lean manufacturing concept.)

_____ **1.** Kodak monitors the market to determine what features its competitors are offering on digital cameras.

_____ **2.** Kodak asks production workers for ideas to improve production.

_____ **3.** Lenses are received daily based on customer orders.

_____ **4.** Customers receive a satisfaction survey with each camera purchased.

_____ **5.** The manufacturing process is standardized and documented.

_____ **6.** Cameras are produced in small lots, and only to customer order.

_____ **7.** Manufacturing facilities are arranged to reduce move time and wait time.

_____ **8.** Kodak conducts focus groups to determine new features that customers want in digital cameras.

_____ **9.** Orders received are filled within two business days.

_____ **10.** Kodak works with suppliers to reduce inspection time of incoming materials.

a. Just-in-time (JIT)

b. Continuous improvement (CI)

c. Total quality management (TQM)

The following calendar year-end information is taken from the December 31, 2011, adjusted trial balance and other records of Firethorn Furniture.

Advertising expense	$ 22,250	Direct labor	$ 564,500
Depreciation expense—Office equipment	10,440	Income taxes expense	138,700
Depreciation expense—Selling equipment	12,125	Indirect labor	61,000
Depreciation expense—Factory equipment	37,400	Miscellaneous production costs	10,440
Factory supervision	123,500	Office salaries expense	72,875
Factory supplies used	8,060	Raw materials purchases	896,375
Factory utilities	39,500	Rent expense—Office space	25,625
Inventories		Rent expense—Selling space	29,000
Raw materials, December 31, 2010	42,375	Rent expense—Factory building	95,500
Raw materials, December 31, 2011	72,430	Maintenance expense—Factory equipment	32,375
Goods in process, December 31, 2010	14,500	Sales	5,002,000
Goods in process, December 31, 2011	16,100	Sales discounts	59,375
Finished goods, December 31, 2010	179,200	Sales salaries expense	297,300
Finished goods, December 31, 2011	143,750		

Required

1. Prepare the company's 2011 manufacturing statement.

2. Prepare the company's 2011 income statement that reports separate categories for (_a_) selling expenses and (_b_) general and administrative expenses.

Check (1) Cost of goods manufactured, $1,836,995

Analysis Component

3. Compute the (_a_) inventory turnover, defined as cost of goods sold divided by average inventory, and (_b_) days' sales in inventory, defined as 365 times ending inventory divided by cost of goods sold, for both its raw materials inventory and its finished goods inventory. (To compute turnover and days' sales in inventory for raw materials, use raw materials used rather than cost of goods sold.) Discuss some possible reasons for differences between these ratios for the two types of inventories. Round answers to one decimal place.

Problem 18-9B
Manufacturing cycle time and
efficiency

A1

Quick Dry Ink produces ink-jet printers for personal computers. It received an order for 600 printers from a customer. The following information is available for this order.

Process time	16.0 hours
Inspection time	3.4 hours
Move time	9.0 hours
Wait time	21.6 hours

Required

1. Compute the company's manufacturing cycle time.

2. Compute the company's manufacturing cycle efficiency. Interpret your answer.

Analysis Component

3. Assume that Quick Dry Ink wishes to increase its manufacturing cycle efficiency to 0.80. What are some ways that it can accomplish this?

SERIAL PROBLEM
Business Solutions

C2   C4   P2

(This serial problem begins in Chapter 1 and continues through most of the book. If previous chapter segments were not completed, the serial problem can begin at this point. It is helpful, but not necessary, to use the Working Papers that accompany the book.)

SP 18   Santana Rey, owner of Business Solutions, decides to diversify her business by also manufacturing computer workstation furniture.

Required

1. Classify the following manufacturing costs of Business Solutions by behavior and traceability.

	Cost by Behavior		Cost by Traceability	
Product Costs	**Variable**	**Fixed**	**Direct**	**Indirect**
1. Monthly flat fee to clean workshop	____	____	____	____
2. Laminate coverings for desktops	____	____	____	____
3. Taxes on assembly workshop	____	____	____	____
4. Glue to assemble workstation component parts	____	____	____	____
5. Wages of desk assembler	____	____	____	____
6. Electricity for workshop	____	____	____	____
7. Depreciation on tools	____	____	____	____

2. Prepare a manufacturing statement for Business Solutions for the month ended January 31, 2012. Assume the following manufacturing costs:

Direct materials: $2,200

Factory overhead: $490

Direct labor: $900

Beginning goods in process: none (December 31, 2011)

Ending goods in process: $540 (January 31, 2012)

Beginning finished goods inventory: none (December 31, 2011)

Ending finished goods inventory: $350 (January 31, 2012)

Check (3) COGS, $2,700

3. Prepare the cost of goods sold section of a partial income statement for Business Solutions for the month ended January 31, 2012.

Beyond the Numbers

BTN 18-1   Managerial accounting is more than recording, maintaining, and reporting financial results. Managerial accountants must provide managers with both financial and nonfinancial information including estimates, projections, and forecasts. There are many accounting estimates that management accountants must make, and **Research In Motion** must notify shareholders of these estimates.

REPORTING IN ACTION

C1

RIM

Required

1. Access and read Research In Motion's "Use of Estimates" section of the "Summary of Significant Accounting Policies" footnote to its financial statements, from Appendix A. What are some of the accounting estimates that Research In Motion made in preparing its financial statements? What are some of the effects if the company's actual results differ from its estimates?

2. What is the management accountant's role in determining those estimates?

Fast Forward

3. Access **Research In Motion**'s annual report for a fiscal year ending after February 27, 2010, from either its Website [**RIM.com**] or the SEC's EDGAR database [**www.sec.gov**]. Answer the questions in parts (1) and (2) after reading the current "Summary of Significant Accounting Policies". Identify any major changes.

BTN 18-2   Manufacturing companies must decide whether to operate their own manufacturing facilities or instead outsource the manufacturing function to a third-party (outside) company. This decision impacts both company managers and also financial statement items. Access the annual report or 10-K for both **Research In Motion** (RIM) and **Apple**. The RIM report is for the year ended February 27, 2010 and the Apple report is for the year ended September 26, 2009.

COMPARATIVE ANALYSIS

C1

RIM
Apple

Required

1. Determine whether RIM operates its own manufacturing facilities or outsources the manufacturing function. (*Hint:* Search for "Manufacturing Capacity.")

2. Determine whether Apple operates its own manufacturing facilities or outsources the manufacturing function. (*Hint:* Search for "product manufacturing.")

3. For both companies, determine the amounts they report for (a) raw materials inventory, (b) work-in-process inventory, and (c) finished goods inventory. Explain how the decision on outsourcing (or not) of manufacturing operations is related to the components of inventory.

BTN 18-3   Assume that you are the managerial accountant at Infostore, a manufacturer of hard drives, CDs, and DVDs. Its reporting year-end is December 31. The chief financial officer is concerned about having enough cash to pay the expected income tax bill because of poor cash flow management. On November 15, the purchasing department purchased excess inventory of CD raw materials in anticipation of rapid growth of this product beginning in January. To decrease the company's tax liability, the chief financial officer tells you to record the purchase of this inventory as part of supplies and expense it in the current year; this would decrease the company's tax liability by increasing expenses.

ETHICS CHALLENGE

C1 C3

Required

1. In which account should the purchase of CD raw materials be recorded?

2. How should you respond to this request by the chief financial officer?

BTN 18-4   Write a one-page memorandum to a prospective college student about salary expectations for graduates in business. Compare and contrast the expected salaries for accounting (including different subfields such as public, corporate, tax, audit, and so forth), marketing, management, and finance majors. Prepare a graph showing average starting salaries (and those for experienced professionals in those fields if available). To get this information, stop by your school's career services office; libraries also have this information. The Website **JobStar.org** (click on *Salary Info*) also can get you started.

COMMUNICATING IN PRACTICE

C6

**TAKING IT TO
THE NET**

C1

BTN 18-5   Managerial accounting professionals follow a code of ethics. As a member of the Institute of Management Accountants, the managerial accountant must comply with Standards of Ethical Conduct.

Required

1. Identify, print, and read the *Statement of Ethical Professional Practice* posted at **www.IMAnet.org**. (Search using "ethical professional practice.")
2. What four overarching ethical principles underlie the IMA's statement?
3. Describe the courses of action the IMA recommends in resolving ethical conflicts.

**TEAMWORK IN
ACTION**

C5 P2

BTN 18-6   The following calendar-year information is taken from the December 31, 2011, adjusted trial balance and other records of Azalea Company.

Advertising expense	$ 19,125	Direct labor	$ 650,750
Depreciation expense—Office equipment	8,750	Indirect labor	60,000
Depreciation expense—Selling equipment	10,000	Miscellaneous production costs	8,500
Depreciation expense—Factory equipment	32,500	Office salaries expense	100,875
Factory supervision	122,500	Raw materials purchases	872,500
Factory supplies used	15,750	Rent expense—Office space	21,125
Factory utilities	36,250	Rent expense—Selling space	25,750
Inventories		Rent expense—Factory building	79,750
Raw materials, December 31, 2010	177,500	Maintenance expense—Factory equipment	27,875
Raw materials, December 31, 2011	168,125	Sales	3,275,000
Goods in process, December 31, 2010	15,875	Sales discounts	57,500
Goods in process, December 31, 2011	14,000	Sales salaries expense	286,250
Finished goods, December 31, 2010	164,375		
Finished goods, December 31, 2011	129,000		

Required

1. *Each* team member is to be responsible for computing **one** of the following amounts. You are not to duplicate your teammates' work. Get any necessary amounts from teammates. Each member is to explain the computation to the team in preparation for reporting to class.

  a. Materials used.   **d.** Total cost of goods in process.
  b. Factory overhead.   **e.** Cost of goods manufactured.
  c. Total manufacturing costs.

2. Check your cost of goods manufactured with the instructor. If it is correct, proceed to part (3).
3. *Each* team member is to be responsible for computing **one** of the following amounts. You are not to duplicate your teammates' work. Get any necessary amounts from teammates. Each member is to explain the computation to the team in preparation for reporting to class.

  a. Net sales.   **d.** Total operating expenses.
  b. Cost of goods sold.   **e.** Net income or loss before taxes.
  c. Gross profit.

Point: Provide teams with transparencies and markers for presentation purposes.

**ENTREPRENEURIAL
DECISION**

C1 C2 C6

BTN 18-7   Corey Rimmel, Adam Hendin, and David Melnick of **Hot Box Cookies** must understand manufacturing costs to effectively operate and succeed as a profitable and efficient business.

Required

1. What are the three main categories of manufacturing costs the owners must monitor and control? Provide examples of each.

2. How can the owners make Hot Box Cookies' manufacturing process more cost-effective? Provide examples of two useful managerial measures of time and efficiency.

3. What are four goals of a total quality management process? How can Hot Box Cookies use TQM to improve its business activities?

BTN 18-8   Visit your favorite fast-food restaurant. Observe its business operations.

HITTING THE ROAD

C1 C2

Required

1. Describe all business activities from the time a customer arrives to the time that customer departs.

2. List all costs you can identify with the separate activities described in part 1.

3. Classify each cost from part 2 as fixed or variable, and explain your classification.

BTN 18-9   Access Nokia's Website (www.nokia.com/about-nokia) and select "Corporate Governance" and then select "Overview." Read the section dealing with the responsibilities of its board of directors.

GLOBAL DECISION

C1

NOKIA

Required

1. Identify the responsibilities of Nokia's board of directors.

2. How would management accountants be involved in assisting the board of directors in carrying out their responsibilities? Explain.

ANSWERS TO MULTIPLE CHOICE QUIZ

1. c

2. b

3. b

4. a

5. Beginning finished goods + Cost of goods manufactured (COGM) − Ending finished goods = Cost of goods sold

$6,000 + COGM − $3,200 = $7,500

COGM = $4,700

19

Job Order Cost Accounting

A Look Back

Chapter 18 introduced managerial accounting and explained basic cost concepts. We also described the lean business model and the reporting of manufacturing activities, including the manufacturing statement.

A Look at This Chapter

We begin this chapter by describing a cost accounting system. We then explain the procedures used to determine costs using a job order costing system. We conclude with a discussion of over- and underapplied overhead.

A Look Ahead

Chapter 20 focuses on measuring costs in process production companies. We explain process production, describe how to assign costs to processes, and compute and analyze cost per equivalent unit.

Learning Objectives

CAP

CONCEPTUAL

C1 Describe important features of job order production. (p. 776)

C2 Explain job cost sheets and how they are used in job order cost accounting. (p. 778)

ANALYTICAL

A1 Apply job order costing in pricing services. (p. 789)

LP19

PROCEDURAL

P1 Describe and record the flow of materials costs in job order cost accounting. (p. 780)

P2 Describe and record the flow of labor costs in job order cost accounting. (p. 782)

P3 Describe and record the flow of overhead costs in job order cost accounting. (p. 783)

P4 Determine adjustments for overapplied and underapplied factory overhead. (p. 788)

Decision Insight

Riding the Wavers

VIRGINIA BEACH, VA—Don't be surprised if we find Uncle Sam and Lady Liberty waving to us around tax time. Use of these characters to market tax services is the brainchild of John Hewitt, founder of **Liberty Tax Service (LibertyTax.com),** a tax return preparation service. On street corners across America, Uncle Sam and Lady Liberty wave, dance, do cartwheels, and play air guitar, all to draw customers into Liberty's stores. This unconventional marketing scheme has helped Liberty become the fastest growing retail tax business ever.

The company started humbly, finalizing its business plan in a spare bedroom and renting a tiny office for a business address. John explains that one of his key tasks was developing a cost accounting system. Manufacturers of custom products, and providers of custom services like Liberty Tax Services, use state-of-the-art job order cost accounting to track costs. This includes tracking the cost of materials, labor, and overhead and managing those expenses. With job order costing, a company tracks costs separately for each job. If a job's cost is too high,

the company must reduce any future costs and perhaps also increase its selling price. Job order costing systems allow entrepreneurs such as John to better isolate costs and avoid the run-away costs often experienced by start-ups that fail to use costing techniques.

John's mission is simple: Set the standard, improve each day, and have some fun. While Uncle Sam and Lady Liberty get customers in the door, the company's fanatical focus on customer satisfaction and retention drive its growth. John continually works to improve services and adapt to market trends and competitors. With every successful customer contact his company approaches its ultimate goal: To be the largest tax preparation company in the universe. With Uncle Sam on air guitar, Liberty expects to ride the wave of growth.

[Sources: *Liberty Tax Service Website,* January 2011; *The Wall Street Journal,* April 17, 2006; *Hampton Roads Website,* February 2007]

This chapter introduces a system for assigning costs to the flow of goods through a production process. We then describe the details of a *job order cost accounting system.* Job order costing is frequently used by manufacturers of custom products or providers of custom services. Manufacturers that use job order costing typically base it on a perpetual inventory system, which provides a continuous record of materials, goods in process, and finished goods inventories.

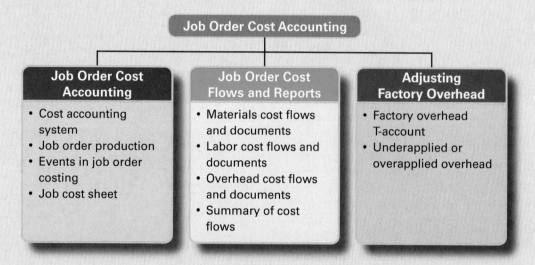

Job Order Cost Accounting		
Job Order Cost Accounting	**Job Order Cost Flows and Reports**	**Adjusting Factory Overhead**
• Cost accounting system • Job order production • Events in job order costing • Job cost sheet	• Materials cost flows and documents • Labor cost flows and documents • Overhead cost flows and documents • Summary of cost flows	• Factory overhead T-account • Underapplied or overapplied overhead

JOB ORDER COST ACCOUNTING

This section describes a cost accounting system and job order production and costing.

Cost Accounting System

Point: Cost accounting systems accumulate costs and then assign them to products and services.

An ever-increasing number of companies use a cost accounting system to generate timely and accurate inventory information. A **cost accounting system** records manufacturing activities using a *perpetual* inventory system, which continuously updates records for costs of materials, goods in process, and finished goods inventories. A cost accounting system also provides timely information about inventories and manufacturing costs per unit of product. This is especially helpful for managers' efforts to control costs and determine selling prices. (A **general accounting system** records manufacturing activities using a *periodic* inventory system. Some companies still use a general accounting system, but its use is declining as competitive forces and customer demands have increased pressures on companies to better manage inventories.)

The two basic types of cost accounting systems are *job order cost accounting* and *process cost accounting.* We describe job order cost accounting in this chapter. Process cost accounting is explained in the next chapter.

Job Order Production

C1 Describe important features of job order production.

Many companies produce products individually designed to meet the needs of a specific customer. Each customized product is manufactured separately and its production is called **job order production,** or *job order manufacturing* (also called *customized production,* which is the production of products in response to special orders). Examples of such products include synthetic football fields, special-order machines, a factory building, custom jewelry, wedding invitations, and artwork.

The production activities for a customized product represent a **job.** The principle of customization is equally applicable to both manufacturing *and* service companies. Most service companies meet customers' needs by performing a custom service for a specific customer. Examples of such services include an accountant auditing a client's financial statements, an interior designer remodeling an office, a wedding consultant planning and supervising a reception, and a lawyer defending a client. Whether the setting is manufacturing or services, job order operations involve meeting the needs of customers by producing or performing custom jobs.

Boeing's aerospace division is one example of a job order production system. Its primary business is twofold: (1) design, develop, and integrate space carriers and (2) provide systems engineering and integration of Department of Defense (DoD) systems. Many of its orders are customized and produced through job order operations.

When a job involves producing more than one unit of a custom product, it is often called a **job lot.** Products produced as job lots could include benches for a church, imprinted T-shirts for a 10K race or company picnic, or advertising signs for a chain of stores. Although these orders involve more than one unit, the volume of production is typically low, such as 50 benches, 200 T-shirts, or 100 signs. Another feature of job order production is the diversity, often called *heterogeneity,* of the products produced. Namely, each customer order is likely to differ from another in some important respect. These variations can be minor or major.

Events in Job Order Costing

The initial event in a normal job order operation is the receipt of a customer order for a custom product. This causes the company to begin work on a job. A less common case occurs when management decides to begin work on a job before it has a signed contract. This is referred to as *jobs produced on speculation.*

Step 1: Predict the cost to complete the job. This cost depends on the product design prepared by either the customer or the producer.

Step 2: Negotiate price and decide whether to pursue the job. Other than for government or other cost-plus contracts, the selling price is determined by market factors. Producers evaluate the market price, compare it to cost, and determine whether the profit on the job is reasonable. If the profit is not reasonable, the producer would determine a desired **target cost.**

Point: Some jobs are priced on a *cost-plus basis:* The customer pays the manufacturer for costs incurred on the job plus a negotiated amount or rate of profit.

Step 3: Schedule production of the job. This must meet the customer's needs and fit within the company's own production constraints. Preparation of this work schedule should consider workplace facilities including equipment, personnel, and supplies. Once this schedule is complete, the producer can place orders for raw materials. Production occurs as materials and labor are applied to the job.

An overview of job order production activity is shown in Exhibit 19.1. This exhibit shows the March production activity of Road Warriors, which installs security devices into cars and trucks. The company converts any vehicle by adding alarms, reinforced exterior, bulletproof glass, and bomb detectors. The company began by catering to high-profile celebrities, but it now caters to anyone who desires added security in a vehicle.

Job order production for Road Warriors requires materials, labor, and overhead costs. Recall that direct materials are goods used in manufacturing that are clearly identified with a particular job. Similarly, direct labor is effort devoted to a particular job. Overhead costs support production of more than one job. Common overhead items are depreciation on factory buildings and equipment, factory supplies, supervision, maintenance, cleaning, and utilities.

Exhibit 19.1 shows that materials, labor, and overhead are added to Jobs B15, B16, B17, B18, and B19, which were started during March. Special tires and bulletproof glass are added to Jobs B15 and B16, while Job B17 receives a reinforced exterior and bulletproof glass. Road Warriors completed Jobs B15, B16, and B17 in March and delivered Jobs B15 and B16 to customers. At the end of March, Jobs B18 and B19 remain in goods in process inventory and Job B17 is in finished goods inventory. Both labor and materials costs are also separated into their direct and indirect components. Their indirect amounts are added to overhead. Total overhead cost is then allocated to the various jobs.

Point: Many professional examinations including the CPA and CMA exams require knowledge of job order and process cost accounting.

EXHIBIT 19.1

Job Order Production Activities

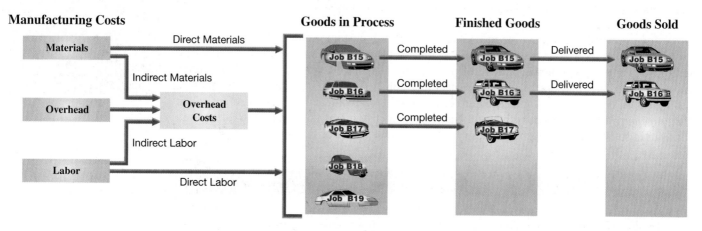

Decision Insight

Target Costing   Many producers determine a target cost for their jobs. Target cost is determined as follows: Expected selling price − Desired profit = Target cost. If the projected target cost of the job as determined by job costing is too high, the producer can apply *value engineering*, which is a method of determining ways to reduce job cost until the target cost is met. ■

Job Cost Sheet

C2 Explain job cost sheets and how they are used in job order cost accounting.

General ledger accounts usually do not provide the accounting information that managers of job order cost operations need to plan and control production activities. This is so because the needed information often requires more detailed data. Such detailed data are usually stored in subsidiary records controlled by general ledger accounts. Subsidiary records store information about raw materials, overhead costs, jobs in process, finished goods, and other items. This section describes the use of these records.

A major aim of a **job order cost accounting system** is to determine the cost of producing each job or job lot. In the case of a job lot, the system also aims to compute the cost per unit. The accounting system must include separate records for each job to accomplish this, and it must capture information about costs incurred and charge these costs to each job.

A **job cost sheet** is a separate record maintained for each job. Exhibit 19.2 shows a job cost sheet for an alarm system that Road Warriors produced for a customer. This job cost sheet identifies the customer, the job number assigned, the product, and key dates. Costs incurred on the job are immediately recorded on this sheet. When each job is complete, the supervisor enters the date of completion, records any remarks, and signs the sheet. The job cost sheet in Exhibit 19.2 classifies costs as direct materials, direct labor, or overhead. It shows that a total of $600 in direct materials is added to Job B15 on four different dates. It also shows seven entries for direct labor costs that total $1,000. Road Warriors *allocates* (also termed *applies, assigns,* or *charges*) factory overhead costs of $1,600 to this job using an allocation rate of 160% of direct labor cost (160% × $1,000)—we discuss overhead allocation later in this chapter.

Point: Factory overhead consists of costs (other than direct materials and direct labor) that ensure the production activities are carried out.

Cost Flows: During Production   While a job is being produced, its accumulated costs are kept in Goods in Process Inventory. The collection of job cost sheets for all jobs in process makes up a subsidiary ledger controlled by the Goods in Process Inventory account in the general ledger. Managers use job cost sheets to monitor costs incurred to date and to predict and control costs for each job.

EXHIBIT 19.2

Job Cost Sheet

Accounting System: Exhibit 19-2   _ □ ×

File   Edit   Maintain   Tasks   Analysis   Options   Reports   Window   Help

Road Warriors, Los Angeles, California   **JOB COST SHEET**

Customer's Name	Carroll Connor	Job No.	B15
Address	1542 High Point Dr.	City & State	Malibu, California
Job Description	Level 1 Alarm System on Ford Expedition		
Date promised	March 15	Date started	March 3	Date completed	March 11

Direct Materials			Direct Labor			Overhead		
Date	Requisition	Cost	Date	Time Ticket	Cost	Date	Rate	Cost
3/3/2011	R-4698	100.00	3/3/2011	L-3393	120.00	3/11/2011	160% of	1,600.00
3/7/2011	R-4705	225.00	3/4/2011	L-3422	150.00		Direct	
3/9/2011	R-4725	180.00	3/5/2011	L-3456	180.00		Labor	
3/10/2011	R-4777	95.00	3/8/2011	L-3479	60.00		Cost	
			3/9/2011	L-3501	90.00			
			3/10/2011	L-3535	240.00			
			3/11/2011	L-3559	160.00			
	Total	600.00		Total	1,000.00		Total	1,600.00

REMARKS: Completed job on March 11, and shipped to customer on March 15. Met all specifications and requirements.

SUMMARY:

Materials	600.00
Labor	1,000.00
Overhead	1,600.00

Signed: *C. Luther, Supervisor*

| Total cost | 3,200.00 |

Cost Flows: Job Completion   When a job is finished, its job cost sheet is completed and moved from the jobs in process file to the finished jobs file. This latter file acts as a subsidiary ledger controlled by the Finished Goods Inventory account.

Cost Flows: Job Delivery   When a finished job is delivered to a customer, the job cost sheet is moved to a permanent file supporting the total cost of goods sold. This permanent file contains records from both current and prior periods. When the job is finished, the company also prepares a journal entry that credits Sales and debits Cash (or Accounts Receivable).

Point: Documents (electronic and paper) are crucial in a job order system, and the job cost sheet is a cornerstone. Understanding it aids in grasping concepts of capitalizing product costs and product cost flow.

■ **Decision Maker**   Answer — p. 793

Management Consultant   One of your tasks is to control and manage costs for a consulting company. At the end of a recent month, you find that three consulting jobs were completed and two are 60% complete. Each unfinished job is estimated to cost $10,000 and to earn a revenue of $12,000. You are unsure how to recognize goods in process inventory and record costs and revenues. Do you recognize any inventory? If so, how much? How much revenue is recorded for unfinished jobs this month? ■

■ **Quick Check**   Answers — p. 793

1. Which of these products is likely to involve job order production? (*a*) inexpensive watches, (*b*) racing bikes, (*c*) bottled soft drinks, or (*d*) athletic socks.

2. What is the difference between a job and a job lot?

3. Which of these statements is correct? (*a*) The collection of job cost sheets for unfinished jobs makes up a subsidiary ledger controlled by the Goods in Process Inventory account, (*b*) Job cost sheets are financial statements provided to investors, or (*c*) A separate job cost sheet is maintained in the general ledger for each job in process.

4. What three costs are normally accumulated on job cost sheets?

JOB ORDER COST FLOWS AND REPORTS

Materials

P1	Describe and record the flow of materials costs in job order cost accounting.

Point: Some companies certify certain suppliers based on the quality of their materials. Goods received from these suppliers are not always inspected by the purchaser to save costs.

Materials Cost Flows and Documents

This section focuses on the flow of materials costs and the related documents in a job order cost accounting system. We begin analysis of the flow of materials costs by examining Exhibit 19.3. When materials are first received from suppliers, the employees count and inspect them and record the items' quantity and cost on a receiving report. The receiving report serves as the *source document* for recording materials received in both a materials ledger card and in the general ledger. In nearly all job order cost systems, **materials ledger cards** (or files) are perpetual records that are updated each time units are purchased and each time units are issued for use in production.

To illustrate the purchase of materials, Road Warriors acquired $450 of wiring and related materials on March 4, 2011. This purchase is recorded as follows.

Assets = Liabilities + Equity
+450   +450

Mar. 4	Raw Materials Inventory—M-347	450	
	Accounts Payable		450
	To record purchase of materials for production.		

EXHIBIT 19.3

Materials Cost Flows through Subsidiary Records

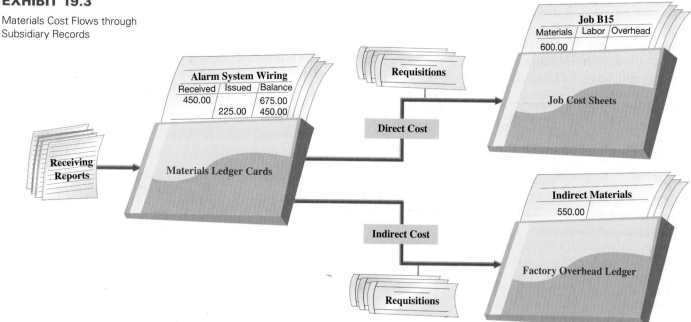

Exhibit 19.3 shows that materials can be requisitioned for use either on a specific job (direct materials) or as overhead (indirect materials). Cost of direct materials flows from the materials ledger card to the job cost sheet. The cost of indirect materials flows from the materials ledger card to the Indirect Materials account in the factory overhead ledger, which is a subsidiary ledger controlled by the Factory Overhead account in the general ledger.

Exhibit 19.4 shows a materials ledger card for material received and issued by Road Warriors. The card identifies the item as alarm system wiring and shows the item's stock number, its location in the storeroom, information about the maximum and minimum quantities that should be available, and the reorder quantity. For example, alarm system wiring is issued

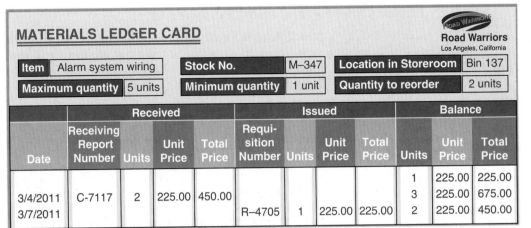

EXHIBIT 19.4

Materials Ledger Card

and recorded on March 7, 2011. The job cost sheet in Exhibit 19.2 showed that Job B15 used this wiring.

When materials are needed in production, a production manager prepares a **materials requisition** and sends it to the materials manager. The requisition shows the job number, the type of material, the quantity needed, and the signature of the manager authorized to make the requisition. Exhibit 19.5 shows the materials requisition for alarm system wiring for Job B15. To see how this requisition ties to the flow of costs, compare the information on the requisition with the March 7, 2011, data in Exhibits 19.2 and 19.4.

Point: Requisitions are often accumulated and recorded in one entry. The frequency of entries depends on the job, the industry, and management procedures.

MATERIALS REQUISITION   No. R-4705

Road Warriors
Los Angeles, California

Job No. _____ B15	Date _____ 3/7/2011
Material Stock No. _____ M-347	Material Description _____ Alarm system wiring
Quantity Requested _____ 1	Requested By _____ C. Luther
Quantity Provided _____ 1	Date Provided _____ 3/7/2011
Filled By _____ M. Bateman	Material Received By _____ C. Luther
Remarks _____	

EXHIBIT 19.5

Materials Requisition

The use of alarm system wiring on Job B15 yields the following entry (locate this cost item in the job cost sheet shown in Exhibit 19.2).

Mar. 7	Goods in Process Inventory—Job B15	225	
	Raw Materials Inventory—M-347		225
	To record use of material on Job B15.		

Assets = Liabilities + Equity
+225
−225

This entry is posted both to its general ledger accounts and to subsidiary records. Posting to subsidiary records includes a debit to a job cost sheet and a credit to a materials ledger card. (*Note:* An entry to record use of indirect materials is the same as that for direct materials *except* the debit is to Factory Overhead. In the subsidiary factory overhead ledger, this entry is posted to Indirect Materials.)

Labor

Labor Cost Flows and Documents

P2 Describe and record the
flow of labor costs in job
order cost accounting.

Exhibit 19.6 shows the flow of labor costs from clock cards and the Factory Payroll account to subsidiary records of the job order cost accounting system. Recall that costs in subsidiary records give detailed information needed to manage and control operations.

EXHIBIT 19.6

Labor Cost Flows through
Subsidiary Records

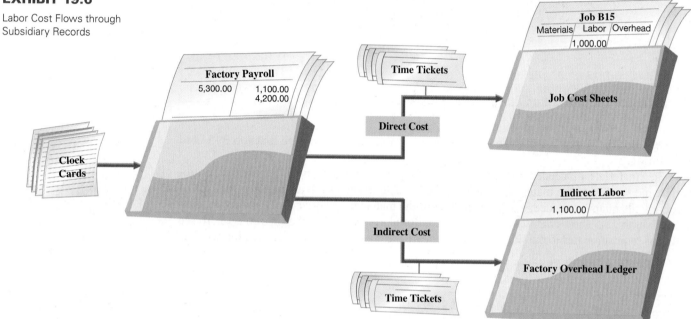

Point: Many employee fraud schemes involve payroll, including overstated hours on clock cards.

Point: In the accounting equation, we treat accounts such as Factory Payroll and Factory Overhead as temporary accounts, which hold various expenses until they are allocated to balance sheet or income statement accounts.

The flow of costs in Exhibit 19.6 begins with **clock cards.** Employees commonly use these cards to record the number of hours worked, and they serve as source documents for entries to record labor costs. Clock card data on the number of hours worked is used at the end of each pay period to determine total labor cost. This amount is then debited to the Factory Payroll account, a temporary account containing the total payroll cost (both direct and indirect). Payroll cost is later allocated to both specific jobs and overhead.

According to clock card data, workers earned $1,500 for the week ended March 5. Illustrating the flow of labor costs, the accrual and payment of these wages are recorded as follows.

Assets = Liabilities + Equity
−1,500   −1,500

Mar. 6	Factory Payroll	1,500	
	Cash		1,500
	To record the weekly payroll.		

*"It's on Corporate Standard Time...
It loses an hour of your pay every day."*

To assign labor costs to specific jobs and to overhead, we must know how each employee's time is used and its costs. Source documents called **time tickets** usually capture these data. Employees regularly fill out time tickets to report how much time they spent on each job. An employee who works on several jobs during a day completes a separate time ticket for each job. Tickets are also prepared for time charged to overhead as indirect labor. A supervisor signs an employee's time ticket to confirm its accuracy.

Exhibit 19.7 shows a time ticket reporting the time a Road Warrior employee spent working on Job B15. The employee's supervisor signed the ticket to confirm its accuracy. The hourly rate and total labor cost are computed after the time ticket is turned in. To see the effect of this time ticket on the job cost sheet, look at the entry dated March 8, 2011, in Exhibit 19.2.

EXHIBIT 19.7

Time Ticket

	No. L–3479
Road Warriors	**TIME TICKET** Date March 8 20 11
Los Angeles, California	

Employee Name	Employee Number	Job No.
T. Zeller	3969	B15

TIME AND RATE INFORMATION:

	Start Time	Finish Time	Elapsed Time	Hourly Rate
Remarks	9:00	12:00	3.0	$20.00
Approved By C. Luther			Total Cost	$60.00

When time tickets report labor used on a specific job, this cost is recorded as direct labor. The following entry records the data from the time ticket in Exhibit 19.7.

Mar. 8	Goods in Process Inventory—Job B15	60	
	Factory Payroll		60
	To record direct labor used on Job B15.		

Assets = Liabilities + Equity
+60   +60

The debit in this entry is posted both to the general ledger account and to the appropriate job cost sheet. (*Note:* An entry to record indirect labor is the same as for direct labor *except* that it debits Factory Overhead and credits Factory Payroll. In the subsidiary factory overhead ledger, the debit in this entry is posted to the Indirect Labor account.)

Overhead Cost Flows and Documents

Factory overhead (or simply overhead) cost flows are shown in Exhibit 19.8. Factory overhead includes all production costs other than direct materials and direct labor. Two sources of overhead costs are indirect materials and indirect labor. These costs are recorded from requisitions for indirect materials and time tickets for indirect labor. Two other sources of overhead are (1) vouchers authorizing payments for items such as supplies or utilities and (2) adjusting entries for costs such as depreciation on factory assets.

Overhead

P3   Describe and record the flow of overhead costs in job order cost accounting.

Factory overhead usually includes many different costs and, thus, a separate account for each is often maintained in a subsidiary factory overhead ledger. This ledger is controlled by the Factory Overhead account in the general ledger. Factory Overhead is a temporary account that accumulates costs until they are allocated to jobs.

Recording Overhead   Recall that overhead costs are recorded with debits to the Factory Overhead account and with credits to other accounts such as Cash, Accounts Payable, and

EXHIBIT 19.8

Overhead Cost Flows through Subsidiary Records

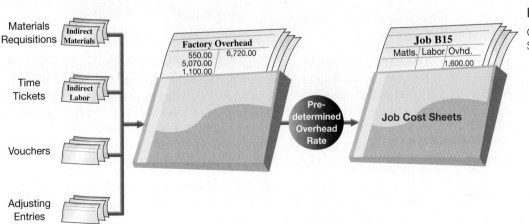

Accumulated Depreciation—Equipment. In the subsidiary factory overhead ledger, the debits are posted to their respective accounts such as Depreciation Expense—Equipment, Insurance Expense—Warehouse, or Amortization Expense—Patents.

To illustrate the recording of overhead, the following two entries reflect the depreciation of factory equipment and the accrual of utilities, respectively, for the week ended March 6.

Assets = Liabilities + Equity
−600   −600

Assets = Liabilities + Equity
         +250   −250

Mar. 6	Factory Overhead	600	
	Accumulated Depreciation—Equipment		600
	To record depreciation on factory equipment.		
Mar. 6	Factory Overhead	250	
	Utilities Payable		250
	To record the accrual of factory utilities.		

Exhibit 19.8 shows that overhead costs flow from the Factory Overhead account to job cost sheets. Because overhead is made up of costs not directly associated with specific jobs or job lots, we cannot determine the dollar amount incurred on a specific job. We know, however, that overhead costs represent a necessary part of business activities. If a job cost is to include all costs needed to complete the job, some amount of overhead must be included. Given the difficulty in determining the overhead amount for a specific job, however, we allocate overhead to individual jobs in some reasonable manner.

Overhead Allocation Bases We generally allocate overhead by linking it to another factor used in production, such as direct labor or machine hours. The factor to which overhead costs are linked is known as the *allocation base*. A manager must think carefully about how many and which allocation bases to use. This managerial decision influences the accuracy with which overhead costs are allocated to individual jobs. In turn, the cost of individual jobs might impact a manager's decisions for pricing or performance evaluation. In Exhibit 19.2, overhead is expressed as 160% of direct labor. We then allocate overhead by multiplying 160% by the estimated amount of direct labor on the jobs.

Point: The predetermined overhead rate is computed at the start of the period and is used throughout the period to allocate overhead to jobs.

Point: Predetermined overhead rates can be estimated using mathematical equations, statistical analysis, or professional experience.

Overhead Allocation Rates We cannot wait until the end of a period to allocate overhead to jobs because perpetual inventory records are part of the job order costing system (demanding up-to-date costs). Instead, we must predict overhead in advance and assign it to jobs so that a job's total costs can be estimated prior to its completion. This estimated cost is useful for managers in many decisions including setting prices and identifying costs that are out of control. Being able to estimate overhead in advance requires a **predetermined overhead rate,** also called *predetermined overhead allocation* (or *application*) *rate*. This rate requires an estimate of total overhead cost and an allocation factor such as total direct labor cost before the start of the period. Exhibit 19.9 shows the usual formula for computing a predetermined overhead rate (estimates are commonly based on annual amounts). This rate is used during the period to allocate overhead to jobs. It is common for companies to use multiple activity (allocation) bases and multiple predetermined overhead rates for different types of products and services.

EXHIBIT 19.9

Predetermined Overhead Allocation Rate Formula

$$\text{Predetermined overhead rate} = \frac{\text{Estimated overhead costs}}{\text{Estimated activity base}}$$

Example: If management predicts total direct labor costs of $100,000 and total overhead costs of $200,000, what is its predetermined overhead rate? *Answer:* 200% of direct labor cost.

Recording Allocated Overhead To illustrate, Road Warriors allocates overhead by linking it to direct labor. At the start of the current period, management predicts total direct labor costs of $125,000 and total overhead costs of $200,000. Using these estimates, management computes its predetermined overhead rate as 160% of direct labor cost ($200,000 ÷ $125,000). Specifically, reviewing the job order cost sheet in Exhibit 19.2, we see that $1,000 of direct labor went into Job B15. We then use the predetermined overhead rate of 160% to allocate $1,600 (equal to $1,000 × 1.60) of overhead to this job. The entry to record this allocation is

Assets = Liabilities + Equity
+1,600   +1,600

Mar. 11	Goods in Process Inventory—Job B15..............	1,600	
	Factory Overhead		1,600
	To assign overhead to Job B15.		

Since the allocation rate for overhead is estimated at the start of a period, the total amount assigned to jobs during a period rarely equals the amount actually incurred. We explain how this difference is treated later in this chapter.

Decision Ethics   Answer — p. 793

Web Consultant   You are working on seven client engagements. Two clients reimburse your firm for actual costs plus a 10% markup. The other five pay a fixed fee for services. Your firm's costs include overhead allocated at $47 per labor hour. The managing partner of your firm instructs you to record as many labor hours as possible to the two markup engagements by transferring labor hours from the other five. What do you do? ■

Summary of Cost Flows

We showed journal entries for charging Goods in Process Inventory (Job B15) with the cost of (1) direct materials requisitions, (2) direct labor time tickets, and (3) factory overhead. We made separate entries for each of these costs, but they are usually recorded in one entry. Specifically, materials requisitions are often collected for a day or a week and recorded with a single entry summarizing them. The same is done with labor time tickets. When summary entries are made, supporting schedules of the jobs charged and the types of materials used provide the basis for postings to subsidiary records.

Point: Study the flow of manufacturing costs through general ledger accounts and job cost sheets. Use Exhibit 19.11 as reinforcement.

To show all production cost flows for a period and their related entries, we again look at Road Warriors' activities. Exhibit 19.10 shows costs linked to all of Road Warriors' production activities for March. Road Warriors did not have any jobs in process at the beginning of March, but it did apply materials, labor, and overhead costs to five new jobs in March. Jobs B15 and B16 are completed and delivered to customers in March, Job B17 is completed but not delivered, and Jobs B18 and B19 are still in process. Exhibit 19.10 also shows purchases of raw materials for $2,750, labor costs incurred for $5,300, and overhead costs of $6,720.

EXHIBIT 19.10

Job Order Costs of All Production Activities

Explanation	Materials	Labor	Overhead Incurred	Overhead Allocated	Goods in Process	Finished Goods	Cost of Goods Sold
ROAD WARRIORS Job Order Manufacturing Costs For Month Ended March 31, 2011							
Job B15	$ 600	$1,000		$1,600			$3,200
Job B16	300	800		1,280			2,380
Job B17	500	1,100		1,760		$3,360	
Job B18	150	700		1,120	$1,970		
Job B19	250	600		960	1,810		
Total job costs	1,800	4,200		→$6,720	$3,780	$3,360	$5,580
Indirect materials	550		$ 550				
Indirect labor		1,100	1,100				
Other overhead			5,070				
Total costs used in production	2,350	$5,300	$6,720 ◄				
Ending materials inventory	1,400						
Materials available	3,750						
Less beginning materials inventory	(1,000)						
Materials purchased	$2,750						

The upper part of Exhibit 19.11 shows the flow of these costs through general ledger accounts and the end-of-month balances in key subsidiary records. Arrow lines are numbered to show the flows of costs for March. Each numbered cost flow reflects several entries made in March. The lower part of Exhibit 19.11 shows summarized job cost sheets and their status at the end of March. The sum of costs assigned to the jobs in process ($1,970 + $1,810) equals the

EXHIBIT 19.11

Job Order Cost Flows and Ending Job Cost Sheets

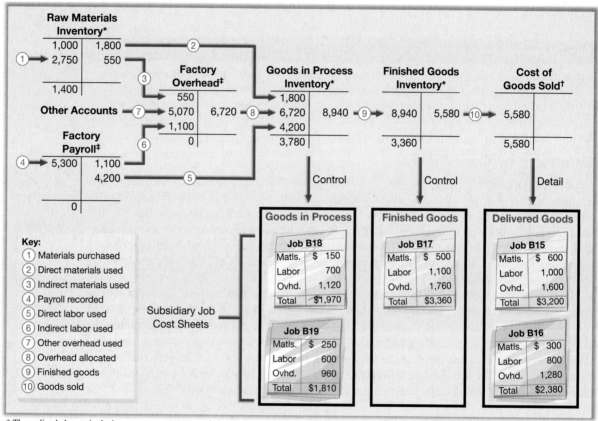

* The ending balances in the inventory accounts are carried to the balance sheet.

† The Cost of Goods Sold balance is carried to the income statement.

‡ Factory Payroll and Factory Overhead are considered temporary accounts; when these costs are allocated to jobs, the balances in these accounts are reduced.

$3,780 balance in Goods in Process Inventory shown in Exhibit 19.10. Also, costs assigned to Job B17 equal the $3,360 balance in Finished Goods Inventory. The sum of costs assigned to Jobs B15 and B16 ($3,200 + $2,380) equals the $5,580 balance in Cost of Goods Sold.

Exhibit 19.12 shows each cost flow with a single entry summarizing the actual individual entries made in March. Each entry is numbered to link with the arrow lines in Exhibit 19.11.

Decision Maker   Answer — p. 793

Entrepreneur   Competitors' prices on one of your product segments are lower than yours. Of the total product cost used in setting your prices, 53% is overhead allocated using direct labor hours. You believe that product costs are distorted and wonder whether there is a better way to allocate overhead and to set product price. What do you suggest? ■

Quick Check   Answers — p. 793

5. In job order cost accounting, which account is debited in recording a raw materials requisition? (*a*) Raw Materials Inventory, (*b*) Raw Materials Purchases, (*c*) Goods in Process Inventory if for a job, or (*d*) Goods in Process Inventory if they are indirect materials.

6. What are four sources of information for recording costs in the Factory Overhead account?

7. Why does job order cost accounting require a predetermined overhead rate?

8. What events result in a debit to Factory Payroll? What events result in a credit?

EXHIBIT 19.12

Entries for Job Order Production Costs*

①	Raw Materials Inventory	2,750
	Accounts Payable	2,750
	Acquired materials on credit for factory use.	
②	Goods in Process Inventory	1,800
	Raw Materials Inventory	1,800
	To assign costs of direct materials used.	
③	Factory Overhead	550
	Raw Materials Inventory	550
	To record use of indirect materials.	
④	Factory Payroll	5,300
	Cash (and other accounts)	5,300
	To record salaries and wages of factory workers (including various payroll liabilities).	
⑤	Goods in Process Inventory	4,200
	Factory Payroll	4,200
	To assign costs of direct labor used.	

⑥	Factory Overhead	1,100
	Factory Payroll	1,100
	To record indirect labor costs as overhead.	
⑦	Factory Overhead	5,070
	Cash (and other accounts)	5,070
	To record factory overhead costs such as insurance, utilities, rent, and depreciation.	
⑧	Goods in Process Inventory	6,720
	Factory Overhead	6,720
	To apply overhead at 160% of direct labor.	
⑨	Finished Goods Inventory	8,940
	Goods in Process Inventory	8,940
	To record completion of Jobs B15, B16, and B17.	
⑩	Cost of Goods Sold	5,580
	Finished Goods Inventory	5,580
	To record sale of Jobs B15 and B16.	

* Exhibit 19.12 provides summary journal entries. Remember, applied overhead is recorded *during* the period, while actual overhead is recorded at the end of the period. *Actual* overhead is debited to Factory Overhead. *Allocated* overhead is credited to Factory Overhead.

ADJUSTING FACTORY OVERHEAD

Refer to the debits in the Factory Overhead account in Exhibit 19.11 (or Exhibit 19.12). The total cost of factory overhead incurred during March is $6,720 ($550 + $5,070 + $1,100). The $6,720 exactly equals the amount assigned to goods in process inventory (see ⑧). Therefore, the overhead incurred equals the overhead applied in March. The amount of overhead incurred rarely equals the amount of overhead applied, however, because estimates rarely equal the exact amounts actually incurred. This section explains what we do when too much or too little overhead is applied to jobs.

Factory Overhead T-Account

Exhibit 19.13 shows a Factory Overhead T-account. The company applies overhead using a predetermined rate estimated at the beginning of the period. At the end of the period, the company receives bills for its actual overhead costs.

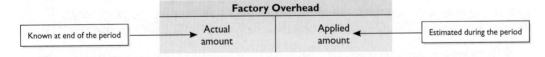

EXHIBIT 19.13

Factory Overhead T-account

Exhibit 19.14 shows what to do when actual overhead does not equal applied overhead. When less overhead is applied than is actually incurred, the remaining debit balance in the Factory Overhead account is called **underapplied overhead.** When the overhead applied in a period exceeds the overhead incurred, the resulting credit balance in the Factory Overhead account is called **overapplied overhead.** In either case, a journal entry is needed to adjust Factory Overhead and Cost of Goods Sold. Exhibit 19.14 summarizes this entry.

EXHIBIT 19.14

Adjusting Factory Overhead

Overhead Costs	Factory Overhead Balance Is	Overhead Is	Journal Entry Needed Is
Actual > Applied	Debit	Underapplied	Cost of Goods Sold ...... # Factory Overhead ..... #
Actual < Applied	Credit	Overapplied	Factory Overhead .... # Cost of Goods Sold .... #

Underapplied or Overapplied Overhead

To illustrate, assume that Road Warriors actually incurred *other overhead costs* of $5,550 instead of the $5,070 shown in Exhibit 19.11. This yields an actual total overhead cost of $7,200 in March. Since the amount of overhead applied was only $6,720, the Factory Overhead account is left with a $480 debit balance as shown in the ledger account in Exhibit 19.15.

EXHIBIT 19.15

Underapplied Overhead in the Factory Overhead Ledger Account

Factory Overhead				Acct. No. 540
Date	**Explanation**	**Debit**	**Credit**	**Balance**
Mar. 31	Indirect materials cost	550		550 Dr.
31	Indirect labor cost	1,100		1,650 Dr.
31	Other overhead cost	5,550		7,200 Dr.
31	Overhead costs applied to jobs		6,720	480 Dr.

Example: If we do not adjust for underapplied overhead, will net income be overstated or understated? *Answer:* Overstated.

Assets = Liabilities + Equity
       −480
       +480

The $480 debit balance reflects manufacturing costs not assigned to jobs. This means that the balances in Goods in Process Inventory, Finished Goods Inventory, and Cost of Goods Sold do not include all production costs incurred. When the underapplied overhead amount is immaterial, it is allocated (closed) to the Cost of Goods Sold account with the following adjusting entry.

Mar. 31	Cost of Goods Sold	480	
	Factory Overhead		480
	To adjust for underapplied overhead costs.		

The $480 debit (increase) to Cost of Goods Sold reduces income by $480. (When the underapplied (or overapplied) overhead is material, the amount is normally allocated to the Cost of Goods Sold, Finished Goods Inventory, and Goods in Process Inventory accounts. This process is covered in advanced courses.)

We treat overapplied overhead at the end of the period in the same way we treat underapplied overhead, except that we debit Factory Overhead and credit Cost of Good Sold for the amount.

Decision Insight

Job Order Education   Many companies invest in their employees, and the demand for executive education is strong. Annual spending on training and education exceeds $20 billion. Annual revenues for providers of executive education continue to rise, with about 40% of revenues coming from custom programs designed for one or a select group of companies. ■

Quick Check   Answers — p. 794

9. In a job order cost accounting system, why does the Factory Overhead account usually have an overapplied or underapplied balance at period-end?

10. When the Factory Overhead account has a debit balance at period-end, does this reflect overapplied or underapplied overhead?

GLOBAL VIEW

Porsche AG manufactures high-performance cars. Each car is built according to individual customer specifications. Customers can use the Internet to place orders for their dream cars. Porsche employs just-in-time inventory techniques to ensure a flexible production process that can respond rapidly to customer orders. For fiscal 2009, Porsche reported €33,781 million in costs of materials and €9,038 million in personnel costs, which helped generate €57,081 million in revenue.

A1 Apply job order costing in pricing services.

The chapter described job order costing mainly using a manufacturing setting. However, these concepts and procedures are applicable to a service setting. Consider AdWorld, an advertising agency that develops Web-based ads for small firms. Each of its customers has unique requirements, so costs for each individual job must be tracked separately.

AdWorld uses two types of labor: Web designers ($65 per hour) and computer staff ($50 per hour). It also incurs overhead costs that it assigns using two different predetermined overhead allocation rates: $125 per designer hour and $96 per staff hour. For each job, AdWorld must estimate the number of designer and staff hours needed. Then total costs pertaining to each job are determined using the procedures in the chapter. (*Note:* Most service firms have neither the category of materials cost nor inventory.)

To illustrate, a manufacturer of golf balls requested a quote from AdWorld for an advertising engagement. AdWorld estimates that the job will require 43 designer hours and 61 staff hours, with the following total estimated cost for this job.

Direct Labor		
Designers (43 hours × $65)	$ 2,795	
Staff (61 hours × $50)	3,050	
Total direct labor		$ 5,845
Overhead		
Designer related (43 hours × $125)	5,375	
Staff related (61 hours × $96)	5,856	
Total overhead		11,231
Total estimated job cost		$17,076

AdWorld can use this cost information to help determine the price quote for the job (see *Decision Maker, Sales Manager,* scenario in this chapter).

Another source of information that AdWorld must consider is the market, that is, how much competitors will quote for this job. Competitor information is often unavailable; therefore, AdWorld's managers must use estimates based on their assessment of the competitive environment.

▮ **Decision Maker**   Answer — p. 793

Sales Manager As AdWorld's sales manager, assume that you estimate costs pertaining to a proposed job as $17,076. Your normal pricing policy is to apply a markup of 18% from total costs. However, you learn that three other agencies are likely to bid for the same job, and that their quotes will range from $16,500 to $22,000. What price should you quote? What factors other than cost must you consider? ▪

DEMONSTRATION PROBLEM—JOB ORDER COSTING

The following information reflects Walczak Company's job order production activities for May.

Raw materials purchases	$16,000
Factory payroll cost	15,400
Overhead costs incurred	
Indirect materials	5,000
Indirect labor	3,500
Other factory overhead	9,500

Walczak's predetermined overhead rate is 150% of direct labor cost. Costs are allocated to the three jobs worked on during May as follows.

	Job 401	Job 402	Job 403
In-process balances on April 30			
Direct materials....................	$3,600		
Direct labor	1,700		
Applied overhead	2,550		
Costs during May			
Direct materials	3,550	$3,500	$1,400
Direct labor	5,100	6,000	800
Applied overhead	?	?	?
Status on May 31	**Finished (sold)**	**Finished (unsold)**	**In process**

Required

1. Determine the total cost of:
   a. The April 30 inventory of jobs in process.
   b. Materials used during May.
   c. Labor used during May.
   d. Factory overhead incurred and applied during May and the amount of any over- or underapplied overhead on May 31.
   e. Each job as of May 31, the May 31 inventories of both goods in process and finished goods, and the goods sold during May.

2. Prepare summarized journal entries for the month to record:
   a. Materials purchases (on credit), the factory payroll (paid with cash), indirect materials, indirect labor, and the other factory overhead (paid with cash).
   b. Assignment of direct materials, direct labor, and overhead costs to the Goods in Process Inventory account. (Use separate debit entries for each job.)
   c. Transfer of each completed job to the Finished Goods Inventory account.
   d. Cost of goods sold.
   e. Removal of any underapplied or overapplied overhead from the Factory Overhead account. (Assume the amount is not material.)

3. Prepare a manufacturing statement for May.

PLANNING THE SOLUTION

- Determine the cost of the April 30 goods in process inventory by totaling the materials, labor, and applied overhead costs for Job 401.
- Compute the cost of materials used and labor by totaling the amounts assigned to jobs and to overhead.
- Compute the total overhead incurred by summing the amounts for the three components. Compute the amount of applied overhead by multiplying the total direct labor cost by the predetermined overhead rate. Compute the underapplied or overapplied amount as the difference between the actual cost and the applied cost.
- Determine the total cost charged to each job by adding the costs incurred in April (if any) to the cost of materials, labor, and overhead applied during May.
- Group the costs of the jobs according to their completion status.
- Record the direct materials costs assigned to the three jobs, using a separate Goods in Process Inventory account for each job; do the same for the direct labor and the applied overhead.
- Transfer costs of Jobs 401 and 402 from Goods in Process Inventory to Finished Goods.
- Record the costs of Job 401 as cost of goods sold.
- Record the transfer of underapplied overhead from the Factory Overhead account to the Cost of Goods Sold account.
- On the manufacturing statement, remember to include the beginning and ending goods in process inventories and to deduct the underapplied overhead.

SOLUTION TO DEMONSTRATION PROBLEM

1. Total cost of

a. April 30 inventory of
jobs in process (Job 401).

Direct materials..........	$3,600
Direct labor	1,700
Applied overhead	2,550
Total cost	$7,850

b. Materials used during May.

Direct materials		
Job 401..................		$ 3,550
Job 402..................		3,500
Job 403..................		1,400
Total direct materials		8,450
Indirect materials		5,000
Total materials used		$13,450

c. Labor used during May.

Direct labor		
Job 401...............		$ 5,100
Job 402...............		6,000
Job 403...............		800
Total direct labor		11,900
Indirect labor		3,500
Total labor used..........		$15,400

d. Factory overhead incurred in May.

Actual overhead		
Indirect materials......................		$ 5,000
Indirect labor		3,500
Other factory overhead		9,500
Total actual overhead		18,000
Overhead applied (150% × $11,900)		17,850
Underapplied overhead		$ 150

e. Total cost of each job.

	401	402	403
In-process costs from April			
Direct materials................	$ 3,600		
Direct labor	1,700		
Applied overhead*	2,550		
Cost incurred in May			
Direct materials................	3,550	$ 3,500	$1,400
Direct labor	5,100	6,000	800
Applied overhead*	7,650	9,000	1,200
Total costs	$24,150	$18,500	$3,400

* Equals 150% of the direct labor cost.

Total cost of the May 31 inventory of goods in process (Job 403) = $3,400

Total cost of the May 31 inventory of finished goods (Job 402) = $18,500

Total cost of goods sold during May (Job 401) = $24,150

2. Journal entries.

a.

Raw Materials Inventory	16,000	
Accounts Payable		16,000
To record materials purchases.		
Factory Payroll	15,400	
Cash		15,400
To record factory payroll.		
Factory Overhead	5,000	
Raw Materials Inventory		5,000
To record indirect materials.		
Factory Overhead	3,500	
Factory Payroll		3,500
To record indirect labor.		
Factory Overhead	9,500	
Cash		9,500
To record other factory overhead.		

b. Assignment of costs to Goods in Process Inventory.

Goods in Process Inventory (Job 401)	3,550	
Goods in Process Inventory (Job 402)	3,500	
Goods in Process Inventory (Job 403)	1,400	
Raw Materials Inventory		8,450
To assign direct materials to jobs.		
Goods in Process Inventory (Job 401)	5,100	
Goods in Process Inventory (Job 402)	6,000	
Goods in Process Inventory (Job 403)	800	
Factory Payroll		11,900
To assign direct labor to jobs.		
Goods in Process Inventory (Job 401)	7,650	
Goods in Process Inventory (Job 402)	9,000	
Goods in Process Inventory (Job 403)	1,200	
Factory Overhead		17,850
To apply overhead to jobs.		

c. Transfer of completed jobs to Finished Goods Inventory.

Finished Goods Inventory	42,650	
Goods in Process Inventory (Job 401)		24,150
Goods in Process Inventory (Job 402)		18,500
To record completion of jobs.		

d.

Cost of Goods Sold	24,150	
Finished Goods Inventory		24,150
To record sale of Job 401.		

e.

Cost of Goods Sold	150	
Factory Overhead		150
To assign underapplied overhead.		

3.

WALCZAK COMPANY Manufacturing Statement For Month Ended May 31		
Direct materials		$ 8,450
Direct labor		11,900
Factory overhead		
Indirect materials	$5,000	
Indirect labor	3,500	
Other factory overhead	9,500	18,000
Total production costs		38,350
Add goods in process, April 30.........		7,850
Total cost of goods in process		46,200
Less goods in process, May 31		3,400
Less underapplied overhead		150
Cost of goods manufactured		$42,650

> Note how underapplied overhead is reported. Overapplied overhead is similarly reported, but is added.

Summary

C1 **Describe important features of job order production.** Certain companies called *job order manufacturers* produce custom-made products for customers. These customized products are produced in response to a customer's orders. A job order manufacturer produces products that usually are different and, typically, produced in low volumes. The production systems of job order companies are flexible and are not highly standardized.

C2 **Explain job cost sheets and how they are used in job order cost accounting.** In a job order cost accounting system, the costs of producing each job are accumulated on a separate job cost sheet. Costs of direct materials, direct labor, and overhead are accumulated separately on the job cost sheet and then added to determine the total cost of a job. Job cost sheets for jobs in process, finished jobs, and jobs sold make up subsidiary records controlled by general ledger accounts.

A1 **Apply job order costing in pricing services.** Job order costing can usefully be applied to a service setting. The resulting job cost estimate can then be used to help determine a price for services.

P1 **Describe and record the flow of materials costs in job order cost accounting.** Costs of materials flow from receiving reports to materials ledger cards and then to either job cost sheets or the Indirect Materials account in the factory overhead ledger.

P2 **Describe and record the flow of labor costs in job order cost accounting.** Costs of labor flow from clock cards to the Factory Payroll account and then to either job cost sheets or the Indirect Labor account in the factory overhead ledger.

P3 **Describe and record the flow of overhead costs in job order cost accounting.** Overhead costs are accumulated in the Factory Overhead account that controls the subsidiary factory overhead ledger. Then, using a predetermined overhead rate, overhead costs are charged to jobs.

P4 **Determine adjustments for overapplied and underapplied factory overhead.** At the end of each period, the Factory Overhead account usually has a residual debit (underapplied overhead) or credit (overapplied overhead) balance. If the balance is not material, it is transferred to Cost of Goods Sold, but if it is material, it is allocated to Goods in Process Inventory, Finished Goods Inventory, and Cost of Goods Sold.

Guidance Answers to Decision Maker and Decision Ethics

Management Consultant Service companies (such as this consulting firm) do not recognize goods in process inventory or finished goods inventory—an important difference between service and manufacturing companies. For the two jobs that are 60% complete, you could recognize revenues and costs at 60% of the total expected amounts. This means you could recognize revenue of $7,200 (0.60 × $12,000) and costs of $6,000 (0.60 × $10,000), yielding net income of $1,200 from each job.

Web Consultant The partner has a monetary incentive to *manage* the numbers and assign more costs to the two cost-plus engagements. This also would reduce costs on the fixed-price engagements. To act in such a manner is unethical. As a professional and an honest person, it is your responsibility to engage in ethical behavior. You must not comply with the partner's instructions. If the partner insists you act in an unethical manner, you should report the matter to a higher authority in the organization.

Entrepreneur An inadequate cost system can distort product costs. You should review overhead costs in detail. Once you know the different cost elements in overhead, you can classify them into groups such as material related, labor related, or machine related. Other groups can also be formed (we discuss this in Chapter 21). Once you have classified overhead items into groups, you can better establish overhead allocation bases and use them to compute predetermined overhead rates. These multiple rates and bases can then be used to assign overhead costs to products. This will likely improve product pricing.

Sales Manager The price based on AdWorld's normal pricing policy is $20,150 ($17,076 × 1.18), which is within the price range offered by competitors. One option is to apply normal pricing policy and quote a price of $20,150. On the other hand, assessing the competition, particularly in terms of their service quality and other benefits they might offer, would be useful. Although price is an input customers use to select suppliers, factors such as quality and timeliness (responsiveness) of suppliers are important. Accordingly, your price can reflect such factors.

Guidance Answers to Quick Checks

1. *b*

2. A job is a special order for a custom product. A job lot consists of a quantity of identical, special-order items.

3. *a*

4. Three costs normally accumulated on a job cost sheet are direct materials, direct labor, and factory overhead.

5. *c*

6. Four sources of factory overhead are materials requisitions, time tickets, vouchers, and adjusting entries.

7. Since a job order cost accounting system uses perpetual inventory records, overhead costs must be assigned to jobs before the end of a period. This requires the use of a predetermined overhead rate.

8. Debits are recorded when wages and salaries of factory employees are paid or accrued. Credits are recorded when direct labor costs are assigned to jobs and when indirect labor costs are transferred to the Factory Overhead account.

9. Overapplied or underapplied overhead usually exists at the end of a period because application of overhead is based on estimates

of overhead and another variable such as direct labor. Estimates rarely equal actual amounts incurred.

10. A debit balance reflects underapplied factory overhead.

Key Terms   mhhe.com/wildFAP20e

Clock card (p. 782)

Cost accounting system (p. 776)

Finished Goods Inventory (p. 779)

General accounting system (p. 776)

Goods in Process Inventory (p. 778)

Job (p. 776)

Job cost sheet (p. 778)

Job lot (p. 777)

Job order cost accounting system (p. 778)

Job order production (p. 776)

Materials ledger card (p. 780)

Materials requisition (p. 781)

Overapplied overhead (p. 787)

Predetermined overhead rate (p. 784)

Target cost (p. 777)

Time ticket (p. 782)

Underapplied overhead (p. 787)

Multiple Choice Quiz   Answers on p. 811   mhhe.com/wildFAP20e

Additional Quiz Questions are available at the book's Website.

1. A company's predetermined overhead allocation rate is 150% of its direct labor costs. How much overhead is applied to a job that requires total direct labor costs of $30,000?
   a. $15,000
   b. $30,000
   c. $45,000
   d. $60,000
   e. $75,000

2. A company's cost accounting system uses direct labor costs to apply overhead to goods in process and finished goods inventories. Its production costs for the period are: direct materials, $45,000; direct labor, $35,000; and overhead applied, $38,500. What is its predetermined overhead allocation rate?
   a. 10%
   b. 110%
   c. 86%
   d. 91%
   e. 117%

3. A company's ending inventory of finished goods has a total cost of $10,000 and consists of 500 units. If the overhead applied to these goods is $4,000, and the predetermined overhead rate is 80% of direct labor costs, how much direct materials cost was incurred in producing these 500 units?
   a. $10,000
   b. $ 6,000
   c. $ 4,000
   d. $ 5,000
   e. $ 1,000

4. A company's Goods in Process Inventory T-account follows.

Goods in Process Inventory			
Beginning balance	9,000		
Direct materials	94,200		
Direct labor	59,200	?	Finished goods
Overhead applied	31,600		
Ending balance	17,800		

The cost of units transferred to Finished Goods inventory is
   a. $193,000
   b. $211,800
   c. $185,000
   d. $144,600
   e. $176,200

5. At the end of its current year, a company learned that its overhead was underapplied by $1,500 and that this amount is not considered material. Based on this information, the company should
   a. Close the $1,500 to Finished Goods Inventory.
   b. Close the $1,500 to Cost of Goods Sold.
   c. Carry the $1,500 to the next period.
   d. Do nothing about the $1,500 because it is not material and it is likely that overhead will be overapplied by the same amount next year.
   e. Carry the $1,500 to the Income Statement as "Other Expense."

🔲 Icon denotes assignments that involve decision making.

Discussion Questions

1. Why must a company estimate the amount of factory overhead assigned to individual jobs or job lots?

2. 🔲 The chapter used a percent of labor cost to assign factory overhead to jobs. Identify another factor (or base) a company might reasonably use to assign overhead costs.

3. What information is recorded on a job cost sheet? How do management and employees use job cost sheets?

4. In a job order cost accounting system, what records serve as a subsidiary ledger for Goods in Process Inventory? For Finished Goods Inventory?

5. What journal entry is recorded when a materials manager receives a materials requisition and then issues materials (both direct and indirect) for use in the factory?

6. How does the materials requisition help safeguard a company's assets?

7. **Palm** uses a "time ticket" for some employees. What is the difference between a clock card and a time ticket?   **Palm**

8. What events cause debits to be recorded in the Factory Overhead account? What events cause credits to be recorded in the Factory Overhead account?

9. **Nokia** applies overhead to product costs. What account(s) is(are) used to eliminate overapplied   **NOKIA**

or underapplied overhead from the Factory Overhead account, assuming the amount is not material?

10. Assume that **Apple** produces a batch of 1,000 iPods. Does it account for this as 1,000 individual   **Apple** jobs or as a job lot? Explain (consider costs and benefits).

11. Why must a company prepare a predetermined overhead rate when using job order cost accounting?

12. How would a hospital apply job order costing? Explain.

13. **Harley-Davidson** manufactures 30 custom-made, **Harley-** luxury-model motorcycles. Does it account for these **Davidson** motorcycles as 30 individual jobs or as a job lot? Explain.

14. Assume **Research In Motion** will install and service a server to link all of a customer's employees' smart-   **RIM** phones to a centralized company server, for an upfront flat price. How can RIM use a job order costing system?

---

connect

Determine which products are most likely to be manufactured as a job and which as a job lot.

1. A hand-crafted table.

2. A 90-foot motor yacht.

3. Wedding dresses for a chain of stores.

4. A custom-designed home.

5. Hats imprinted with company logo.

6. Little League trophies.

QUICK STUDY

QS 19-1
Jobs and job lots   C1

List the three types of costs that are typically recorded on a job cost sheet. How can managers use job cost sheets?

QS 19-2
Job cost sheets   C2

During the current month, a company that uses a job order cost accounting system purchases $70,000 in raw materials for cash. It then uses $22,000 of raw materials indirectly as factory supplies and uses $42,000 of raw materials as direct materials. Prepare entries to record these three transactions.

QS 19-3
Direct materials journal entries
P1

During the current month, a company that uses a job order cost accounting system incurred a monthly factory payroll of $120,000, paid in cash. Of this amount, $30,000 is classified as indirect labor and the remainder as direct. Prepare entries to record these transactions.

QS 19-4
Direct labor journal entries   P2

A company incurred the following manufacturing costs this period: direct labor, $605,000; direct materials, $672,000; and factory overhead, $129,500. Compute its overhead cost as a percent of (1) direct labor and (2) direct materials. Express your answers as percents, rounded to one decimal place.

QS 19-5
Factory overhead rates   P3

During the current month, a company that uses a job order cost accounting system incurred a monthly factory payroll of $120,000, paid in cash. Of this amount, $30,000 is classified as indirect labor and the remainder as direct for the production of Job 65A. Factory overhead is applied at 150% of direct labor. Prepare the entry to apply factory overhead to this job lot.

QS 19-6
Factory overhead journal entries
P3

A company allocates overhead at a rate of 140% of direct labor cost. Actual overhead cost for the current period is $745,000, and direct labor cost is $500,000. Prepare the entry to close over- or underapplied overhead to cost of goods sold.

QS 19-7
Entry for over- or underapplied overhead   P4

A company's Factory Overhead T-account shows total debits of $325,000 and total credits of $331,000 at the end of a period. Prepare the journal entry to close the balance in the Factory Overhead account to Cost of Goods Sold.

QS 19-8
Entry for over- or underapplied overhead   P4

QS 19-9

Pricing services   A1

An advertising agency is estimating costs for advertising a music festival. The job will require 50 direct labor hours at a cost of $60 per hour. Overhead costs are applied at a rate of $95 per direct labor hour. What is the total estimated cost for this job?

QS 19-10

Predetermined overhead rate

P3

At the beginning of a period a company predicts total direct materials costs of $175,000 and total overhead costs of $218,750. If the company uses direct materials costs as its activity base to allocate overhead, what is the predetermined overhead rate it should use during the period?

QS 19-11

Job cost sheets   C2

Road Warriors' job cost sheet for job A75 shows that the cost to add security features to a car was $13,500. The car was delivered to the customer, who paid $18,900 in cash for the added features. What journal entries should Road Warriors record for the completion and delivery of job A75?

QS 19-12

Job order production   C1

Refer to this chapter's Global View. **Porsche AG** is the manufacturer of the Porsche automobile line. Does Porsche produce in jobs or in job lots? Explain.

McGraw Hill **connect**

EXERCISES

Exercise 19-1

Job order production

C1

Match the terms below with their definitions.

1. Job
2. Job order production
3. Job lot
4. Cost accounting system
5. Target cost
6. General accounting system

a. The expected selling price of a job minus its desired profit.
b. Production activities for a customized product.
c. A system that records manufacturing costs using a perpetual inventory system.
d. Production of products in response to customer orders.
e. Production of more than one unit of a custom product.
f. A system that records manufacturing costs using a periodic inventory system.

Exercise 19-2

Documents in job order cost accounting

P1   P2   P3

The left column lists the titles of documents and accounts used in job order cost accounting. The right column presents short descriptions of the purposes of the documents. Match each document in the left column to its numbered description in the right column.

A. Factory Payroll account
B. Materials ledger card
C. Time ticket
D. Voucher
E. Materials requisition
F. Factory Overhead account
G. Clock card

_____ **1.** Communicates the need for materials to complete a job.
_____ **2.** Shows only total time an employee works each day.
_____ **3.** Shows amount approved for payment of an overhead or other cost.
_____ **4.** Shows amount of time an employee works on a job.
_____ **5.** Temporarily accumulates the cost of incurred overhead until the cost is assigned to specific jobs.
_____ **6.** Temporarily accumulates incurred labor costs until they are assigned to specific jobs or to overhead.
_____ **7.** Perpetual inventory record of raw materials received, used, and available for use.

Exercise 19-3

Job cost computation

C2

The following information is from the materials requisitions and time tickets for Job 9-1005 completed by Wright Boats. The requisitions are identified by code numbers starting with the letter Q and the time tickets start with W. At the start of the year, management estimated that overhead cost would equal 140% of direct labor cost for each job. Determine the total cost on the job cost sheet for Job 9-1005.

Date	Document	Amount
7/1/2011	Q-4698	$1,350
7/1/2011	W-3393	700
7/5/2011	Q-4725	1,100
7/5/2011	W-3479	550
7/10/2011	W-3559	400

As of the end of June, the job cost sheets at Racing Wheels, Inc., show the following total costs accumulated on three custom jobs.

Exercise 19-4
Analysis of cost flows

C2 P1 P2 P3

	Job 102	Job 103	Job 104
Direct materials	$30,000	$66,000	$54,000
Direct labor	16,000	28,400	42,000
Overhead	8,000	14,200	21,000

Job 102 was started in production in May and the following costs were assigned to it in May: direct materials, $12,000; direct labor, $3,600; and overhead, $1,800. Jobs 103 and 104 are started in June. Overhead cost is applied with a predetermined rate based on direct labor cost. Jobs 102 and 103 are finished in June, and Job 104 is expected to be finished in July. No raw materials are used indirectly in June. Using this information, answer the following questions. (Assume this company's predetermined overhead rate did not change across these months).

1. What is the cost of the raw materials requisitioned in June for each of the three jobs?
2. How much direct labor cost is incurred during June for each of the three jobs?
3. What predetermined overhead rate is used during June?
4. How much total cost is transferred to finished goods during June?

Check (4) $162,600

In December 2010, Kent Computer's management establishes the year 2011 predetermined overhead rate based on direct labor cost. The information used in setting this rate includes estimates that the company will incur $756,000 of overhead costs and $540,000 of direct labor cost in year 2011. During March 2011, Kent began and completed Job No. 13-56.

Exercise 19-5
Overhead rate; costs assigned to jobs

P3

1. What is the predetermined overhead rate for year 2011?
2. Use the information on the following job cost sheet to determine the total cost of the job.

Check (2) $23,280

JOB COST SHEET

Customer's Name   Keiser Co.   **Job No.**   13-56

Job Description   5 color monitors—21 inch

	Direct Materials		Direct Labor		Overhead Costs Applied	
Date	Requisition No.	Amount	Time-Ticket No.	Amount	Rate	Amount
Mar. 8	4-129	$5,000	T-306	$ 640		
Mar. 11	4-142	7,050	T-432	1,280		
Mar. 18	4-167	3,550	T-456	1,280		
Totals						

Lopez Company uses a job order cost accounting system that charges overhead to jobs on the basis of direct material cost. At year-end, the Goods in Process Inventory account shows the following.

Exercise 19-6
Analysis of costs assigned to goods in process

P3

Accounting System   _ □ ×
File Edit Maintain Tasks Analysis Options Reports Window Help

Goods in Process Inventory   Acct. No. 121 _ □ ×

Date	Explanation	Debit	Credit	Balance
2011				
Dec. 31	Direct materials cost	1,500,000		1,500,000
31	Direct labor cost	240,000		1,740,000
31	Overhead costs	450,000		2,190,000
31	To finished goods		2,100,000	90,000

Sales   Purchases   General Ledger   Payroll   Inventory   Company   Analysis

1. Determine the overhead rate used (based on direct material cost).
2. Only one job remained in the goods in process inventory at December 31, 2011. Its direct materials cost is $30,000. How much direct labor cost and overhead cost are assigned to it?

Check (2) Direct labor cost, $51,000

Exercise 19-7
Cost flows in a job order cost system
P1 P2 P3 P4

The following information is available for Lock-Down Company, which produces special-order security products and uses a job order cost accounting system.

	April 30	May 31
Inventories		
Raw materials	$40,000	$ 50,000
Goods in process	9,600	19,500
Finished goods	60,000	33,200
Activities and information for May		
Raw materials purchases (paid with cash)		189,000
Factory payroll (paid with cash)		400,000
Factory overhead		
Indirect materials		12,000
Indirect labor		75,000
Other overhead costs		100,500
Sales (received in cash)		1,200,000
Predetermined overhead rate based on direct labor cost		65%

Compute the following amounts for the month of May.

1. Cost of direct materials used.
2. Cost of direct labor used.
3. Cost of goods manufactured.
4. Cost of goods sold.*
5. Gross profit.
6. Overapplied or underapplied overhead.

Check (3) $693,350

*Do not consider any underapplied or overapplied overhead.

Exercise 19-8
Journal entries for materials
P1

Use information in Exercise 19-7 to prepare journal entries for the following events for the month of May.

1. Raw materials purchases for cash.
2. Direct materials usage.
3. Indirect materials usage.

Exercise 19-9
Journal entries for labor
P2

Use information in Exercise 19-7 to prepare journal entries for the following events for the month of May.

1. Factory payroll costs in cash.
2. Direct labor usage.
3. Indirect labor usage.

Exercise 19-10
Journal entries for overhead
P3

Use information in Exercise 19-7 to prepare journal entries for the following events for the month of May.

1. Factory overhead excluding indirect materials and indirect labor (record credit to Other Accounts).
2. Application of overhead to goods in process.

Exercise 19-11
Adjusting factory overhead   P4

Refer to information in Exercise 19-7. Prepare the journal entry to allocate (close) overapplied or underapplied overhead to Cost of Goods Sold.

Exercise 19-12
Adjusting factory overhead
P4

Record the journal entry to close over- or underapplied factory overhead to Cost of Goods Sold for each of the independent cases below.

	JK Concert Promotions	EL Home Builders
Actual indirect materials costs	$12,000	$ 6,500
Actual indirect labor costs	56,000	46,500
Other overhead costs	17,000	49,000
Overhead applied	96,200	106,800

In December 2010, Ultravision established its predetermined overhead rate for movies produced during year 2011 by using the following cost predictions: overhead costs, $1,800,000, and direct labor costs, $450,000. At year end 2011, the company's records show that actual overhead costs for the year are $1,770,000. Actual direct labor cost had been assigned to jobs as follows.

Exercise 19-13
Factory overhead computed, applied, and adjusted
P3 P4

Movies completed and released	$400,000
Movies still in production	45,000
Total actual direct labor cost	$445,000

1. Determine the predetermined overhead rate for year 2011.

2. Set up a T-account for overhead and enter the overhead costs incurred and the amounts applied to movies during the year using the predetermined overhead rate.

3. Determine whether overhead is overapplied or underapplied (and the amount) during the year.

4. Prepare the adjusting entry to allocate any over- or underapplied overhead to Cost of Goods Sold.

Check (3) $10,000 overapplied

In December 2010, Perez Company established its predetermined overhead rate for jobs produced during year 2011 by using the following cost predictions: overhead costs, $600,000, and direct labor costs, $500,000. At year end 2011, the company's records show that actual overhead costs for the year are $680,000. Actual direct labor cost had been assigned to jobs as follows.

Exercise 19-14
Factory overhead computed, applied, and adjusted
P3 P4

Jobs completed and sold	$420,000
Jobs in finished goods inventory	84,000
Jobs in goods in process inventory	56,000
Total actual direct labor cost	$560,000

1. Determine the predetermined overhead rate for year 2011.

2. Set up a T-account for Factory Overhead and enter the overhead costs incurred and the amounts applied to jobs during the year using the predetermined overhead rate.

3. Determine whether overhead is overapplied or underapplied (and the amount) during the year.

4. Prepare the adjusting entry to allocate any over- or underapplied overhead to Cost of Goods Sold.

Red Wing Company applies factory overhead based on direct labor costs. The company incurred the following costs during 2011: direct materials costs, $637,500; direct labor costs, $2,500,000; and factory overhead costs applied, $1,000,000.

Exercise 19-15
Overhead rate calculation, allocation, and analysis
P3

1. Determine the company's predetermined overhead rate for year 2011.

2. Assuming that the company's $57,000 ending Goods in Process Inventory account for year 2011 had $18,000 of direct labor costs, determine the inventory's direct materials costs.

3. Assuming that the company's $337,485 ending Finished Goods Inventory account for year 2011 had $137,485 of direct materials costs, determine the inventory's direct labor costs and its overhead costs.

Check (3) $57,143 overhead costs

Vegas Company's ending Goods in Process Inventory account consists of 4,500 units of partially completed product, and its Finished Goods Inventory account consists of 11,700 units of product. The factory manager determines that Goods in Process Inventory includes direct materials cost of $10 per unit and direct labor cost of $7 per unit. Finished goods are estimated to have $12 of direct materials cost per unit and $9 of direct labor cost per unit. The company established the predetermined overhead rate using the following predictions: estimated direct labor cost, $300,000, and estimated factory overhead, $360,000. The company allocates factory overhead to its goods in process and finished goods inventories based on direct labor cost. During the period, the company incurred these costs: direct materials, $460,000; direct labor, $277,000; and factory overhead applied, $332,400.

Exercise 19-16
Costs allocated to ending inventories
P1 P2 P3

1. Determine the predetermined overhead rate.

2. Compute the total cost of the two ending inventories.

3. Compute cost of goods sold for the year (assume no beginning inventories and no underapplied or overapplied overhead).

Check (3) Cost of goods sold, $583,040

Exercise 19-17
Cost-based pricing

A1

Multiplex Corporation has requested bids from several architects to design its new corporate headquarters. Friesen Architects is one of the firms bidding on the job. Friesen estimates that the job will require the following direct labor.

	Labor	Estimated Hours	Hourly Rate
1			
2	Architects	200	$300
3	Staff	400	75
4	Clerical	700	20

Friesen applies overhead to jobs at 160% of direct labor cost. Friesen would like to earn at least $80,000 profit on the architectural job. Based on past experience and market research, it estimates that the competition will bid between $325,000 and $400,000 for the job.

Check   (1) $270,400

1. What is Friesen's estimated cost of the architectural job?

2. What bid would you suggest that Friesen submit?

Exercise 19-18
Direct materials journal entries

P1

A recent balance sheet for **Porsche AG** shows beginning raw materials inventory of €83 million and ending raw materials inventory of €85 million. Assume the company purchased raw materials (on account) for €3,108 million during the year. (1) Prepare journal entries to record (a) the purchase of raw materials and (b) the use of raw materials in production. (2) What do you notice about the € amounts in your journal entries?

PROBLEM SET A

Problem 19-1A
Production costs computed and recorded; reports prepared

C2 P1 P2 P3 P4

Winfrey Co.'s March 31 inventory of raw materials is $150,000. Raw materials purchases in April are $400,000, and factory payroll cost in April is $220,000. Overhead costs incurred in April are: indirect materials, $30,000; indirect labor, $14,000; factory rent, $20,000; factory utilities, $12,000; and factory equipment depreciation, $30,000. The predetermined overhead rate is 50% of direct labor cost. Job 306 is sold for $380,000 cash in April. Costs of the three jobs worked on in April follow.

	Job 306	Job 307	Job 308
Balances on March 31			
Direct materials............	$ 14,000	$ 18,000	
Direct labor	18,000	16,000	
Applied overhead...........	9,000	8,000	
Costs during April			
Direct materials............	100,000	170,000	$ 80,000
Direct labor	30,000	56,000	120,000
Applied overhead...........	?	?	?
Status on April 30............	Finished (sold)	Finished (unsold)	In process

Required

1. Determine the total of each production cost incurred for April (direct labor, direct materials, and applied overhead), and the total cost assigned to each job (including the balances from March 31).

2. Prepare journal entries for the month of April to record the following.

   a. Materials purchases (on credit), factory payroll (paid in cash), and actual overhead costs including indirect materials and indirect labor. (Factory rent and utilities are paid in cash.)

   b. Assignment of direct materials, direct labor, and applied overhead costs to the Goods in Process Inventory.

   c. Transfer of Jobs 306 and 307 to the Finished Goods Inventory.

   d. Cost of goods sold for Job 306.

   e. Revenue from the sale of Job 306.

Check   (2f) $3,000 underapplied

   f. Assignment of any underapplied or overapplied overhead to the Cost of Goods Sold account. (The amount is not material.)

(3) Cost of goods manufactured, $482,000

3. Prepare a manufacturing statement for April (use a single line presentation for direct materials and show the details of overhead cost).

4. Compute gross profit for April. Show how to present the inventories on the April 30 balance sheet.

Analysis Component

5. The over- or underapplied overhead is closed to Cost of Goods Sold. Discuss how this adjustment impacts business decision making regarding individual jobs or batches of jobs.

Thai Bay's computer system generated the following trial balance on December 31, 2011. The company's manager knows something is wrong with the trial balance because it does not show any balance for Goods in Process Inventory but does show balances for the Factory Payroll and Factory Overhead accounts.

Problem 19-2A
Source documents, journal entries, overhead, and financial reports

P1 P2 P3 P4

	Debit	Credit
Cash	$ 48,000	
Accounts receivable	42,000	
Raw materials inventory	26,000	
Goods in process inventory	0	
Finished goods inventory	9,000	
Prepaid rent	3,000	
Accounts payable		$ 10,500
Notes payable		13,500
Common stock		30,000
Retained earnings		87,000
Sales		180,000
Cost of goods sold	105,000	
Factory payroll	16,000	
Factory overhead	27,000	
Operating expenses	45,000	
Totals	$321,000	$321,000

After examining various files, the manager identifies the following six source documents that need to be processed to bring the accounting records up to date.

Materials requisition 21-3010:	$4,600 direct materials to Job 402
Materials requisition 21-3011:	$7,600 direct materials to Job 404
Materials requisition 21-3012:	$2,100 indirect materials
Labor time ticket 6052:	$5,000 direct labor to Job 402
Labor time ticket 6053:	$8,000 direct labor to Job 404
Labor time ticket 6054:	$3,000 indirect labor

Jobs 402 and 404 are the only units in process at year-end. The predetermined overhead rate is 200% of direct labor cost.

Required

1. Use information on the six source documents to prepare journal entries to assign the following costs.
   a. Direct materials costs to Goods in Process Inventory.
   b. Direct labor costs to Goods in Process Inventory.
   c. Overhead costs to Goods in Process Inventory.
   d. Indirect materials costs to the Factory Overhead account.
   e. Indirect labor costs to the Factory Overhead account.

2. Determine the revised balance of the Factory Overhead account after making the entries in part 1. Determine whether there is any under- or overapplied overhead for the year. Prepare the adjusting entry to allocate any over- or underapplied overhead to Cost of Goods Sold, assuming the amount is not material.

3. Prepare a revised trial balance.

4. Prepare an income statement for year 2011 and a balance sheet as of December 31, 2011.

Check (2) $6,100 underapplied overhead

(3) T. B. totals, $321,000

(4) Net income, $23,900

Analysis Component

5. Assume that the $2,100 on materials requisition 21-3012 should have been direct materials charged to Job 404. Without providing specific calculations, describe the impact of this error on the income statement for 2011 and the balance sheet at December 31, 2011.

Problem 19-3A

Source documents, journal entries, and accounts in job order cost accounting

P1 P2 P3

Westin Watercraft's predetermined overhead rate for year 2011 is 200% of direct labor. Information on the company's production activities during May 2011 follows.

a. Purchased raw materials on credit, $125,000.

b. Paid $84,000 cash for factory wages.

c. Paid $11,000 cash to a computer consultant to reprogram factory equipment.

d. Materials requisitions record use of the following materials for the month.

Job 136	$30,000
Job 137	20,000
Job 138	12,000
Job 139	14,000
Job 140	4,000
Total direct materials	80,000
Indirect materials	12,000
Total materials used	$92,000

e. Time tickets record use of the following labor for the month.

Job 136	$ 8,000
Job 137	7,000
Job 138	25,000
Job 139	26,000
Job 140	2,000
Total direct labor	68,000
Indirect labor	16,000
Total	$84,000

f. Applied overhead to Jobs 136, 138, and 139.

g. Transferred Jobs 136, 138, and 139 to Finished Goods.

h. Sold Jobs 136 and 138 on credit at a total price of $340,000.

i. The company incurred the following overhead costs during the month (credit Prepaid Insurance for expired factory insurance).

Depreciation of factory building	$37,000
Depreciation of factory equipment	21,000
Expired factory insurance	7,000
Accrued property taxes payable	31,000

j. Applied overhead at month-end to the Goods in Process (Jobs 137 and 140) using the predetermined overhead rate of 200% of direct labor cost.

Required

1. Prepare a job cost sheet for each job worked on during the month. Use the following simplified form.

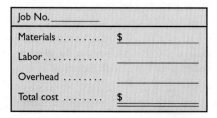

Check (2f) Cr. Factory Overhead, $118,000

2. Prepare journal entries to record the events and transactions *a* through *j*.

3. Set up T-accounts for each of the following general ledger accounts, each of which started the month with a zero balance: Raw Materials Inventory; Goods in Process Inventory; Finished Goods Inventory;

Factory Payroll; Factory Overhead; Cost of Goods Sold. Then post the journal entries to these T-accounts and determine the balance of each account.

4. Prepare a report showing the total cost of each job in process and prove that the sum of their costs equals the Goods in Process Inventory account balance. Prepare similar reports for Finished Goods Inventory and Cost of Goods Sold.

Check   (4) Finished Goods
Inventory, $92,000

In December 2010, Gomez Company's manager estimated next year's total direct labor cost assuming 50 persons working an average of 2,000 hours each at an average wage rate of $15 per hour. The manager also estimated the following manufacturing overhead costs for year 2011.

Problem 19-4A
Overhead allocation and adjustment using a predetermined overhead rate

P3 P4

mhhe.com/wildFAP20e

Indirect labor	$159,600
Factory supervision	120,000
Rent on factory building	70,000
Factory utilities	44,000
Factory insurance expired	34,000
Depreciation—Factory equipment	240,000
Repairs expense—Factory equipment	30,000
Factory supplies used	34,400
Miscellaneous production costs	18,000
Total estimated overhead costs	$750,000

At the end of 2011, records show the company incurred $725,000 of actual overhead costs. It completed and sold five jobs with the following direct labor costs: Job 201, $354,000; Job 202, $330,000; Job 203, $175,000; Job 204, $420,000; and Job 205, $184,000. In addition, Job 206 is in process at the end of 2011 and had been charged $10,000 for direct labor. No jobs were in process at the end of 2010. The company's predetermined overhead rate is based on direct labor cost.

Required

1. Determine the following.

 a. Predetermined overhead rate for year 2011.

 b. Total overhead cost applied to each of the six jobs during year 2011.

 c. Over- or underapplied overhead at year-end 2011.

2. Assuming that any over- or underapplied overhead is not material, prepare the adjusting entry to allocate any over- or underapplied overhead to Cost of Goods Sold at the end of year 2011.

Check   (1c) $11,500 overapplied
(2) Dr. Factory Overhead
$11,500

If the working papers that accompany this book are unavailable, do not attempt to solve this problem.
Sagrillo Company manufactures variations of its product, a technopress, in response to custom orders from its customers. On May 1, the company had no inventories of goods in process or finished goods but held the following raw materials.

Problem 19-5A
Production transactions, subsidiary records, and source documents

P1 P2 P3 P4

Material M	120 units @	$200 =		$24,000
Material R	80 units @	160 =		12,800
Paint	44 units @	72 =		3,168
Total cost				$39,968

On May 4, the company began working on two technopresses: Job 102 for Global Company and Job 103 for Rolf Company.

Required

Follow the instructions in this list of activities and complete the sheets provided in the working papers.

a. Purchased raw materials on credit and recorded the following information from receiving reports and invoices.

Receiving Report No. 426, Material M, 150 units at $200 each.
Receiving Report No. 427, Material R, 70 units at $160 each.

Instructions: Record these purchases with a single journal entry and post it to general ledger T-accounts, using the transaction letter *a* to identify the entry. Enter the receiving report information on the materials ledger cards.

b. Requisitioned the following raw materials for production.

> Requisition No. 35, for Job 102, 80 units of Material M.
> Requisition No. 36, for Job 102, 60 units of Material R.
> Requisition No. 37, for Job 103, 40 units of Material M.
> Requisition No. 38, for Job 103, 30 units of Material R.
> Requisition No. 39, for 12 units of paint.

Instructions: Enter amounts for direct materials requisitions on the materials ledger cards and the job cost sheets. Enter the indirect material amount on the materials ledger card and record a debit to the Indirect Materials account in the subsidiary factory overhead ledger. Do not record a journal entry at this time.

c. Received the following employee time tickets for work in May.

> Time tickets Nos. 1 to 10 for direct labor on Job 102, $40,000.
> Time tickets Nos. 11 to 30 for direct labor on Job 103, $32,000.
> Time tickets Nos. 31 to 36 for equipment repairs, $12,000.

Instructions: Record direct labor from the time tickets on the job cost sheets and then debit indirect labor to the Indirect Labor account in the subsidiary factory overhead ledger. Do not record a journal entry at this time.

d. Paid cash for the following items during the month: factory payroll, $84,000, and miscellaneous overhead items, $36,000.

Instructions: Record these payments with journal entries and then post them to the general ledger accounts. Also record a debit in the Miscellaneous Overhead account in the subsidiary factory overhead ledger.

e. Finished Job 102 and transferred it to the warehouse. The company assigns overhead to each job with a predetermined overhead rate equal to 70% of direct labor cost.

Instructions: Enter the allocated overhead on the cost sheet for Job 102, fill in the cost summary section of the cost sheet, and then mark the cost sheet "Finished." Prepare a journal entry to record the job's completion and its transfer to Finished Goods and then post it to the general ledger accounts.

f. Delivered Job 102 and accepted the customer's promise to pay $290,000 within 30 days.

Instructions: Prepare journal entries to record the sale of Job 102 and the cost of goods sold. Post them to the general ledger accounts.

g. Applied overhead to Job 103 based on the job's direct labor to date.

Instructions: Enter overhead on the job cost sheet but do not make a journal entry at this time.

Check (h) Dr. Goods in Process Inventory, $38,400

h. Recorded the total direct and indirect materials costs as reported on all the requisitions for the month.

Instructions: Prepare a journal entry to record these costs and post it to general ledger accounts.

i. Recorded the total direct and indirect labor costs as reported on all time tickets for the month.

Instructions: Prepare a journal entry to record these costs and post it to general ledger accounts.

j. Recorded the total overhead costs applied to jobs.

Check Balance in Factory Overhead, $1,536 Cr., overapplied

Instructions: Prepare a journal entry to record the allocation of these overhead costs and post it to general ledger accounts.

PROBLEM SET B

Problem 19-1B

Production costs computed and recorded; reports prepared

C2 P1 P2 P3 P4

Pak Co.'s August 31 inventory of raw materials is $16,000. Raw materials purchases in September are $60,000, and factory payroll cost in September is $68,000. Overhead costs incurred in September are: indirect materials, $6,000; indirect labor, $4,000; factory rent, $24,000; factory utilities, $22,000; and factory equipment depreciation, $25,000. The predetermined overhead rate is 130% of direct labor cost. Job 114 is sold for $100,000 cash in September. Costs for the three jobs worked on in September follow.

	Job 114	Job 115	Job 116
Balances on August 31			
Direct materials.............	$ 4,000	$ 6,000	
Direct labor................	2,000	2,200	
Applied overhead............	2,600	2,860	
Costs during September			
Direct materials.............	10,000	30,000	$16,000
Direct labor................	16,000	28,000	20,000
Applied overhead............	?	?	?
Status on September 30	Finished (sold)	Finished (unsold)	In process

Required

1. Determine the total of each production cost incurred for September (direct labor, direct materials, and applied overhead), and the total cost assigned to each job (including the balances from August 31).

2. Prepare journal entries for the month of September to record the following.

    a. Materials purchases (on credit), factory payroll (paid in cash), and actual overhead costs including indirect materials and indirect labor. (Factory rent and utilities are paid in cash.)

    b. Assignment of direct materials, direct labor, and applied overhead costs to Goods in Process Inventory.

    c. Transfer of Jobs 114 and 115 to the Finished Goods Inventory.

    d. Cost of Job 114 in the Cost of Goods Sold account.

    e. Revenue from the sale of Job 114.

    f. Assignment of any underapplied or overapplied overhead to the Cost of Goods Sold account. (The amount is not material.)

Check (2f) $2,200 overapplied

3. Prepare a manufacturing statement for September (use a single line presentation for direct materials and show the details of overhead cost).

(3) Cost of goods manufactured, $160,860

4. Compute gross profit for September. Show how to present the inventories on the September 30 balance sheet.

Analysis Component

5. The over- or underapplied overhead adjustment is closed to Cost of Goods Sold. Discuss how this adjustment impacts business decision making regarding individual jobs or batches of jobs.

Metro's computer system generated the following trial balance on December 31, 2011. The company's manager knows that the trial balance is wrong because it does not show any balance for Goods in Process Inventory but does show balances for the Factory Payroll and Factory Overhead accounts.

Problem 19-2B
Source documents, journal entries, overhead, and financial reports

P1 P2 P3 P4

	Debit	Credit
Cash............................	$ 40,000	
Accounts receivable	80,000	
Raw materials inventory	24,000	
Goods in process inventory	0	
Finished goods inventory	50,000	
Prepaid rent	4,000	
Accounts payable		$ 16,000
Notes payable		30,000
Common stock		60,000
Retained earnings		33,800
Sales...........................		250,000
Cost of goods sold	140,000	
Factory payroll	20,000	
Factory overhead	9,800	
Operating expenses	22,000	
Totals	$389,800	$389,800

After examining various files, the manager identifies the following six source documents that need to be processed to bring the accounting records up to date.

Materials requisition 94-231:	$ 5,000 direct materials to Job 603
Materials requisition 94-232:	$ 8,000 direct materials to Job 604
Materials requisition 94-233:	$ 1,500 indirect materials
Labor time ticket 765:	$ 6,000 direct labor to Job 603
Labor time ticket 766:	$12,000 direct labor to Job 604
Labor time ticket 777:	$ 2,000 indirect labor

Jobs 603 and 604 are the only units in process at year-end. The predetermined overhead rate is 80% of direct labor cost.

Required

1. Use information on the six source documents to prepare journal entries to assign the following costs.
   a. Direct materials costs to Goods in Process Inventory.
   b. Direct labor costs to Goods in Process Inventory.
   c. Overhead costs to Goods in Process Inventory.
   d. Indirect materials costs to the Factory Overhead account.
   e. Indirect labor costs to the Factory Overhead account.

Check (2) $1,100 overapplied overhead

(3) T. B. totals, $389,800

(4) Net income, $89,100

2. Determine the revised balance of the Factory Overhead account after making the entries in part 1. Determine whether there is under- or overapplied overhead for the year. Prepare the adjusting entry to allocate any over- or underapplied overhead to Cost of Goods Sold, assuming the amount is not material.
3. Prepare a revised trial balance.
4. Prepare an income statement for year 2011 and a balance sheet as of December 31, 2011.

Analysis Component

5. Assume that the $1,500 indirect materials on materials requisition 94-233 should have been direct materials charged to Job 604. Without providing specific calculations, describe the impact of this error on the income statement for 2011 and the balance sheet at December 31, 2011.

Problem 19-3B
Source documents, journal entries, and accounts in job order cost accounting

P1   P2   P3

Troupe Company's predetermined overhead rate is 90% of direct labor. Information on the company's production activities during September 2011 follows.
a. Purchased raw materials on credit, $57,000.
b. Paid $99,750 cash for factory wages.
c. Paid $11,250 cash for miscellaneous factory overhead costs.
d. Materials requisitions record use of the following materials for the month.

Job 487....................	$13,500
Job 488....................	9,000
Job 489....................	12,000
Job 490....................	10,500
Job 491....................	1,500
Total direct materials.........	46,500
Indirect materials............	3,750
Total materials used..........	$50,250

e. Time tickets record use of the following labor for the month.

Job 487.................	$16,500
Job 488.................	19,500
Job 489.................	25,500
Job 490.................	18,000
Job 491.................	7,500
Total direct labor.........	87,000
Indirect labor............	12,750
Total..................	$99,750

f. Allocated overhead to Jobs 487, 489, and 490.

g. Transferred Jobs 487, 489, and 490 to Finished Goods.

h. Sold Jobs 487 and 489 on credit for a total price of $225,000.

i. The company incurred the following overhead costs during the month (credit Prepaid Insurance for expired factory insurance).

Depreciation of factory building	$24,750
Depreciation of factory equipment	18,750
Expired factory insurance	2,250
Accrued property taxes payable	5,250

j. Applied overhead at month-end to the Goods in Process (Jobs 488 and 491) using the predetermined overhead rate of 90% of direct labor cost.

Required

1. Prepare a job cost sheet for each job worked on in the month. Use the following simplified form.

Job No. _____	
Materials	$ _____
Labor	_____
Overhead	_____
Total cost	$ _____

2. Prepare journal entries to record the events and transactions *a* through *j*.

3. Set up T-accounts for each of the following general ledger accounts, each of which started the month with a zero balance: Raw Materials Inventory, Goods in Process Inventory, Finished Goods Inventory, Factory Payroll, Factory Overhead, Cost of Goods Sold. Then post the journal entries to these T-accounts and determine the balance of each account.

4. Prepare a report showing the total cost of each job in process and prove that the sum of their costs equals the Goods in Process Inventory account balance. Prepare similar reports for Finished Goods Inventory and Cost of Goods Sold.

Check (2f) Cr. Factory Overhead, $54,000

(3) Finished goods inventory, $44,700

In December 2010, Monk Company's manager estimated next year's total direct labor cost assuming 40 persons working an average of 1,500 hours each at an average wage rate of $50 per hour. The manager also estimated the following manufacturing overhead costs for year 2011.

Indirect labor	$ 540,000
Factory supervision	450,000
Rent on factory building	360,000
Factory utilities	200,000
Factory insurance expired	60,000
Depreciation—Factory equipment	300,000
Repairs expense—Factory equipment	180,000
Factory supplies used	110,000
Miscellaneous production costs	200,000
Total estimated overhead costs	$2,400,000

Problem 19-4B
Overhead allocation and adjustment using a predetermined overhead rate

P3 P4

At the end of 2011, records show the company incurred $2,200,000 of actual overhead costs. It completed and sold five jobs with the following direct labor costs: Job 625, $300,000; Job 626, $225,000; Job 627, $975,000; Job 628, $240,000; and Job 629, $375,000. In addition, Job 630 is in process at the end of 2011 and had been charged $75,000 for direct labor. No jobs were in process at the end of 2010. The company's predetermined overhead rate is based on direct labor cost.

Required

1. Determine the following.

   a. Predetermined overhead rate for year 2011.

   b. Total overhead cost applied to each of the six jobs during year 2011.

   c. Over- or underapplied overhead at year-end 2011.

2. Assuming that any over- or underapplied overhead is not material, prepare the adjusting entry to allocate any over- or underapplied overhead to Cost of Goods Sold at the end of year 2011.

Problem 19-5B
Production transactions, subsidiary records, and source documents

P1　P2　P3　P4

If the working papers that accompany this book are unavailable, do not attempt to solve this problem.
Sim Company produces variations of its product, a megatron, in response to custom orders from its customers. On June 1, the company had no inventories of goods in process or finished goods but held the following raw materials.

Material M	150 units @ $ 40 =	$ 6,000
Material R	50 units @　160 =	8,000
Paint	20 units @　　20 =	400
Total cost		$14,400

On June 3, the company began working on two megatrons: Job 450 for Olivas Company and Job 451 for Ireland, Inc.

Required

Follow instructions in this list of activities and complete the sheets provided in the working papers.

a. Purchased raw materials on credit and recorded the following information from receiving reports and invoices.

> Receiving Report No. 20, Material M, 150 units at $40 each.
> Receiving Report No. 21, Material R, 200 units at $160 each.

Instructions: Record these purchases with a single journal entry and post it to general ledger T-accounts, using the transaction letter *a* to identify the entry. Enter the receiving report information on the materials ledger cards.

b. Requisitioned the following raw materials for production.

> Requisition No. 223, for Job 450, 60 units of Material M.
> Requisition No. 224, for Job 450, 100 units of Material R.
> Requisition No. 225, for Job 451, 30 units of Material M.
> Requisition No. 226, for Job 451, 75 units of Material R.
> Requisition No. 227, for 10 units of paint.

Instructions: Enter amounts for direct materials requisitions on the materials ledger cards and the job cost sheets. Enter the indirect material amount on the materials ledger card and record a debit to the Indirect Materials account in the subsidiary factory overhead ledger. Do not record a journal entry at this time.

c. Received the following employee time tickets for work in June.

> Time tickets Nos. 1 to 10 for direct labor on Job 450, $24,000.
> Time tickets Nos. 11 to 20 for direct labor on Job 451, $20,000.
> Time tickets Nos. 21 to 24 for equipment repairs, $4,000.

Instructions: Record direct labor from the time tickets on the job cost sheets and then debit indirect labor to the Indirect Labor account in the subsidiary factory overhead ledger. Do not record a journal entry at this time.

d. Paid cash for the following items during the month: factory payroll, $48,000, and miscellaneous overhead items, $47,000.

Instructions: Record these payments with journal entries and post them to the general ledger accounts. Also record a debit in the Miscellaneous Overhead account in the subsidiary factory overhead ledger.

e. Finished Job 450 and transferred it to the warehouse. The company assigns overhead to each job with a predetermined overhead rate equal to 120% of direct labor cost.

Instructions: Enter the allocated overhead on the cost sheet for Job 450, fill in the cost summary section of the cost sheet, and then mark the cost sheet "Finished." Prepare a journal entry to record the job's completion and its transfer to Finished Goods and then post it to the general ledger accounts.

f. Delivered Job 450 and accepted the customer's promise to pay $130,000 within 30 days.

Instructions: Prepare journal entries to record the sale of Job 450 and the cost of goods sold. Post them to the general ledger accounts.

g. Applied overhead cost to Job 451 based on the job's direct labor used to date.

Instructions: Enter overhead on the job cost sheet but do not make a journal entry at this time.

h. Recorded the total direct and indirect materials costs as reported on all the requisitions for the month.

Instructions: Prepare a journal entry to record these costs and post it to general ledger accounts.

Check   (h) Dr. Goods in Process Inventory, $31,600

i. Recorded the total direct and indirect labor costs as reported on all time tickets for the month.

Instructions: Prepare a journal entry to record these costs and post it to general ledger accounts.

j. Recorded the total overhead costs applied to jobs.

Instructions: Prepare a journal entry to record the allocation of these overhead costs and post it to general ledger accounts.

Check   Balance in Factory Overhead, $1,600 Cr., overapplied

(This serial problem began in Chapter 1 and continues through most of the book. If previous chapter segments were not completed, the serial problem can begin at this point. It is helpful, but not necessary, to use the Working Papers that accompany the book.)

SERIAL PROBLEM
Business Solutions
P1   P2   P3

SP 19   The computer workstation furniture manufacturing that Santana Rey started in January is progressing well. As of the end of June, Business Solutions' job cost sheets show the following total costs accumulated on three furniture jobs.

	Job 6.02	Job 6.03	Job 6.04
Direct materials.........	$1,500	$3,300	$2,700
Direct labor............	800	1,420	2,100
Overhead..............	400	710	1,050

Job 6.02 was started in production in May, and these costs were assigned to it in May: direct materials, $600; direct labor, $180; and overhead, $90. Jobs 6.03 and 6.04 were started in June. Overhead cost is applied with a predetermined rate based on direct labor costs. Jobs 6.02 and 6.03 are finished in June, and Job 6.04 is expected to be finished in July. No raw materials are used indirectly in June. (Assume this company's predetermined overhead rate did not change over these months).

Required

1. What is the cost of the raw materials used in June for each of the three jobs and in total?

2. How much total direct labor cost is incurred in June?

3. What predetermined overhead rate is used in June?

4. How much cost is transferred to finished goods inventory in June?

Check   (1) Total materials, $6,900

(3) 50%

Beyond the Numbers

BTN 19-1   **Research In Motion's** financial statements and notes in Appendix A provide evidence of growth potential in its sales.

REPORTING IN ACTION
C1

RIM

Required

1. Identify at least two types of costs that will predictably increase as a percent of sales with growth in sales.

2. Explain why you believe the types of costs identified for part 1 will increase, and describe how you might assess RIM's success with these costs. (*Hint:* You might consider the gross margin ratio.)

Fast Forward

3. Access RIM's annual report for a fiscal year ending after February 27, 2010, from its Website [RIM.com] or the SEC's EDGAR database [www.sec.gov]. Review and report its growth in sales along with its cost and income levels (including its gross margin ratio).

**COMPARATIVE
ANALYSIS**

C1

RIM

Apple

BTN 19-2   Retailers as well as manufacturers can apply just-in-time (JIT) to their inventory management. Both **Research In Motion** and **Apple** want to know the impact of a JIT inventory system for their operating cash flows. Review each company's statement of cash flows in Appendix A to answer the following. (For RIM, also review Note 16.)

Required

1. Identify the impact on operating cash flows (increase or decrease) for changes in inventory levels (increase or decrease) for both companies for each of the three most recent years.

2. What impact would a JIT inventory system have on both RIM's and Apple's operating income? Link the answer to your response for part 1.

3. Would the move to a JIT system have a one-time or recurring impact on operating cash flow?

ETHICS CHALLENGE

P3

Point: Students could compare responses and discuss differences in concerns with allocating overhead.

BTN 19-3   An accounting professional requires at least two skill sets. The first is to be technically competent. Knowing how to capture, manage, and report information is a necessary skill. Second, the ability to assess manager and employee actions and biases for accounting analysis is another skill. For instance, knowing how a person is compensated helps anticipate information biases. Draw on these skills and write a one-half page memo to the financial officer on the following practice of allocating overhead.

Background: Assume that your company sells portable housing to both general contractors and the government. It sells jobs to contractors on a bid basis. A contractor asks for three bids from different manufacturers. The combination of low bid and high quality wins the job. However, jobs sold to the government are bid on a cost-plus basis. This means price is determined by adding all costs plus a profit based on cost at a specified percent, such as 10%. You observe that the amount of overhead allocated to government jobs is higher than that allocated to contract jobs. These allocations concern you and motivate your memo.

**COMMUNICATING IN
PRACTICE**

C1 C2

Point: Have students present a mock interview, one assuming the role of the president of the company and the other the applicant.

BTN 19-4   Assume that you are preparing for a second interview with a manufacturing company. The company is impressed with your credentials but has indicated that it has several qualified applicants. You anticipate that in this second interview, you must show what you offer over other candidates. You learn the company currently uses a periodic inventory system and is not satisfied with the timeliness of its information and its inventory management. The company manufactures custom-order holiday decorations and display items. To show your abilities, you plan to recommend that it use a cost accounting system.

Required

In preparation for the interview, prepare notes outlining the following:

1. Your cost accounting system recommendation and why it is suitable for this company.

2. A general description of the documents that the proposed cost accounting system requires.

3. How the documents in part 2 facilitate the operation of the cost accounting system.

**TAKING IT TO
THE NET**

C1

BTN 19-5   Many contractors work on custom jobs that require a job order costing system.

Required

Access the Website **AMSI.com** and click on *Construction Management Software,* and then on STARBUILDER. Prepare a one-page memorandum for the CEO of a construction company providing information about the job order costing software this company offers. Would you recommend that the company purchase this software?

BTN 19-6   Consider the activities undertaken by a medical clinic in your area.

TEAMWORK IN ACTION

C1

Required

1. Do you consider a job order cost accounting system appropriate for the clinic?

2. Identify as many factors as possible to lead you to conclude that it uses a job order system.

BTN 19-7   Refer to the chapter opener regarding John Hewitt and his company, **Liberty Tax Service**. All successful businesses track their costs, and it is especially important for start-up businesses to monitor and control costs.

ENTREPRENEURIAL DECISION

C1

Required

1. Assume that Liberty Tax Service uses a job order costing system. For the basic cost category of direct materials, explain how a job cost sheet for Liberty Tax Service would differ from a job cost sheet for a manufacturing company.

2. For the basic cost categories of direct labor and overhead, provide examples of the types of costs that would fall into each category for Liberty Tax Service.

BTN 19-8   Job order cost accounting is frequently used by home builders.

HITTING THE ROAD

C2 P1 P2 P3

Required

1. You (or your team) are to prepare a job cost sheet for a single-family home under construction. List four items of both direct materials and direct labor. Explain how you think overhead should be applied.

2. Contact a builder and compare your job cost sheet to this builder's job cost sheet. If possible, speak to that company's accountant. Write your findings in a short report.

BTN 19-9   **Nokia** and **Palm** are competitors in the global marketplace. Access Nokia's annual report (www.Nokia.com) for the year ended December 31, 2009. The following information is available for Nokia.

GLOBAL DECISION

C1

NOKIA
Palm

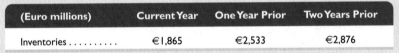

(Euro millions)	Current Year	One Year Prior	Two Years Prior
Inventories.........	€1,865	€2,533	€2,876

Required

1. Determine the change in Nokia's inventories for the last two years. Then identify the impact on net resources generated by operating activities (increase or decrease) for changes in inventory levels (increase or decrease) for Nokia for the last two years.

2. Would a move to a JIT system likely impact Nokia more than it would Palm? Explain.

ANSWERS TO MULTIPLE CHOICE QUIZ

1. c; $30,000 × 150% = $45,000

2. b; $38,500/$35,000 = 110%

3. e; Direct materials + Direct labor + Overhead = Total cost;
   Direct materials + ($4,000/.80) + $4,000 = $10,000
   Direct materials = $1,000

4. e; $9,000 + $94,200 + $59,200 + $31,600 − Finished goods = $17,800
   Thus, finished goods = $176,200

5. b

20

Process Cost Accounting

A Look Back

Chapter 18 introduced managerial accounting and described cost concepts and the reporting of manufacturing activities. Chapter 19 explained job order costing—an important cost accounting system for customized products and services.

A Look at This Chapter

This chapter focuses on how to measure and account for costs in process operations. We explain process production, describe how to assign costs to processes, and compute cost per equivalent unit for a process.

A Look Ahead

Chapter 21 explains how to allocate factory overhead costs to different products and introduces the activity-based costing method of overhead allocation. It also explains responsibility accounting and measures of departmental performance.

Learning Objectives

CAP

CONCEPTUAL

C1 Explain process operations and the way they differ from job order operations. (p. 814)

C2 Define and compute equivalent units and explain their use in process cost accounting. (p. 821)

C3 Define and prepare a process cost summary and describe its purposes. (p. 826)

C4 *Appendix 20A*—Explain and illustrate the accounting for production activity using FIFO. (p. 833)

ANALYTICAL

A1 Compare process cost accounting and job order cost accounting. (p. 817)

A2 Explain and illustrate a hybrid costing system. (p. 829)

LP20

PROCEDURAL

P1 Record the flow of direct materials costs in process cost accounting. (p. 818)

P2 Record the flow of direct labor costs in process cost accounting. (p. 819)

P3 Record the flow of factory overhead costs in process cost accounting. (p. 819)

P4 Record the transfer of completed goods to Finished Goods Inventory and Cost of Goods Sold. (p. 827)

Writing on Walls

"We're selling a dynamic environment. . . . it energizes you"
—**JEFF AVALLON**

CAMBRIDGE, MA—Brainstorming for a class, John Goscha and friends became frustrated with having to constantly erase a tiny whiteboard or hang paper all over their walls. Then, Goscha said, "Wouldn't it be great if we could have a dry erase board that just took up the entire wall?" John pursued the idea and started a company, **IdeaPaint (IdeaPaint.com),** bringing his friends Jeff Avallon and Morgen Newman on-board to help build the business. Their product is a paint that turns any wall into a dry-erase surface, at a lower cost than actually installing whiteboards.

Though the idea is simple, the process for turning their vision to reality was hard. The business partners spent time in their school's chemistry lab with all kinds of paint to develop a crude prototype. Two labs the group contacted gave up, concluding the idea was impossible. Finally, a third lab stumbled upon the proper chemistry and developed a paint from which markers can be wiped off.

IdeaPaint's production process offers clear advantages over those of companies that produce dry-erase whiteboards. Competitors use a host of raw materials, including wood, steel, and aluminum, and then use high-intensity ovens to make whiteboards. IdeaPaint is made in a process that combines paint pigment, additives, and water. IdeaPaint holds few materials in inventory, and as Jeff notes, IdeaPaint is "simply mixed and stirred." Still, entrepreneurs like Jeff, John, and Morgen rely on process cost summaries to help them monitor and control the costs of material, labor, and overhead applied to their production processes. Morgen admits that "every company has overhead to deal with," but IdeaPaint is able to beat competitors by saving on shipping and energy costs. Managerial accounting information provides insights into those production costs and aids in company decisions.

Having perfected their production process, the trio is now focused on the process of running their operation. "We assigned tasks based on who had slept more than four hours the past few days," says Morgen. Now, the partners each focus on different aspects of the business. As John explains, "We are learning how to take this from just an idea and paint in a can to a real business with distribution and sales." A focus on cost management minimizes their risk of bad decisions as the company pursues further expansion. With sales growing rapidly, the company recently raised over $3 million in venture-capital to finance entry into hospitals, schools, and retail stores. And, in addition to "working at their dream jobs" as Jeff puts it, they get to write on walls.

Sources: *IdeaPaint Company Website,* January 2011; *Inc.com; Businessweek.com,* September 2009; *CNNMoney.com,* March 2010.

The type of product or service a company offers determines its cost accounting system. Job order costing is used to account for custom products and services that meet the demands of a particular customer. Not all products are manufactured in this way; many carry standard designs so that one unit is no different than any other unit. Such a system often produces large numbers of units on a continuous basis, all of which pass through similar processes.

This chapter describes how to use a process cost accounting system to account for these types of products. It also explains how costs are accumulated for each process and then assigned to units passing through those processes. This information helps us understand and estimate the cost of each process as well as find ways to reduce costs and improve processes.

Process Cost Accounting

Process Operations	Process Cost Accounting	Equivalent Units of Production (EUP)	Process Costing Illustration
• Comparing job order and process operations • Organization of process operations • GenX Company—an illustration	• Direct and indirect costs • Accounting for materials costs • Accounting for labor costs • Accounting for factory overhead	• Accounting for goods in process • Differences between EUP for materials, labor, and overhead	• Physical flow of units • EUP • Cost per EUP • Cost reconciliation • Process cost summary • Transfers to finished goods and to cost of goods sold

PROCESS OPERATIONS

C1 Explain process operations and the way they differ from job order operations.

Process operations, also called *process manufacturing* or *process production,* is the mass production of products in a continuous flow of steps. This means that products pass through a series of sequential processes. Petroleum refining is a common example of process operations. Crude oil passes through a series of steps before it is processed into different grades of petroleum. **Exxon Mobil**'s oil activities reflect a process operation. An important characteristic of process operations is the high level of standardization necessary if the system is to produce large volumes of products. Process operations also extend to services. Examples include mail sorting in large post offices and order processing in large mail-order firms such as **L.L. Bean**. The common feature in these service organizations is that operations are performed in a sequential manner using a series of standardized processes. Other companies using process operations include:

Company	Product or Service	Company	Product or Service
Kellogg	Cereals	Heinz	Ketchup
Pfizer.	Pharmaceuticals	Penn	Tennis balls
Proctor & Gamble	Household products	Hershey	Chocolate
Coca-Cola	Soft drinks	Jiffy Lube	Oil changes

For virtual tours of process operations visit **PennRacquet.com/factory.html** (tennis balls) and **Hersheys.com/discover/tour_video.asp** (chocolate).

Each of these examples of products and services involves operations having a series of *processes,* or steps. Each process involves a different set of activities. A production operation that processes chemicals, for instance, might include the four steps shown in Exhibit 20.1. Understanding such processes for companies with process operations is crucial for measuring their costs. Increasingly, process operations use machines and automation to control product quality and reduce manufacturing costs.

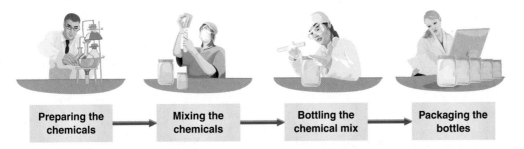

EXHIBIT 20.1

Process Operations: Chemicals

Comparing Job Order and Process Operations

Job order and process operations can be considered as two ends of a continuum. Important features of both systems are shown in Exhibit 20.2. We often describe job order and process operations with manufacturing examples, but both also apply to service companies. In a job order costing system, the measurement focus is on the individual job or batch. In a process costing system, the measurement focus is on the process itself and the standardized units produced.

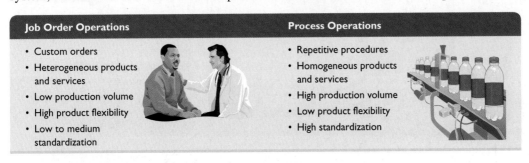

EXHIBIT 20.2

Comparing Job Order and Process Operations

Organization of Process Operations

In a process operation, each process is identified as a separate *production department, workstation,* or *work center.* With the exception of the first process or department, each receives the output from the prior department as a partially processed product. Depending on the nature of the process, a company applies direct labor, overhead, and, perhaps, additional direct materials to move the product toward completion. Only the final process or department in the series produces finished goods ready for sale to customers.

Tracking costs for several related departments can seem complex. Yet because process costing procedures are applied to the activity of each department or process separately, we need to consider only one process at a time. This simplifies the procedures.

When the output of one department becomes an input to another department, as is the case in sequential processing, we simply transfer the costs associated with those units from the first department into the next. We repeat these steps from department to department until the final process is complete. At that point the accumulated costs are transferred with the product from Goods in Process Inventory to Finished Goods Inventory. The next section illustrates a company with a single process, but the methods illustrated apply to a multiprocess scenario as each department's costs are handled separately for each department.

▮ Decision Insight

Accounting for Health Many service companies use process departments to perform specific tasks for consumers. Hospitals, for instance, have radiology and physical therapy facilities with special equipment and trained employees. When patients need services, they are processed through departments to receive prescribed care. Service companies need process cost accounting information as much as manufacturers to estimate costs of services, to plan future operations, to control costs, and to determine customer charges. ▪

GenX Company—An Illustration

The GenX Company illustrates process operations. It produces Profen®, an over-the-counter pain reliever for athletes. GenX sells Profen to wholesale distributors, who in turn sell it to

EXHIBIT 20.3

Floor Plan of GenX's Factory

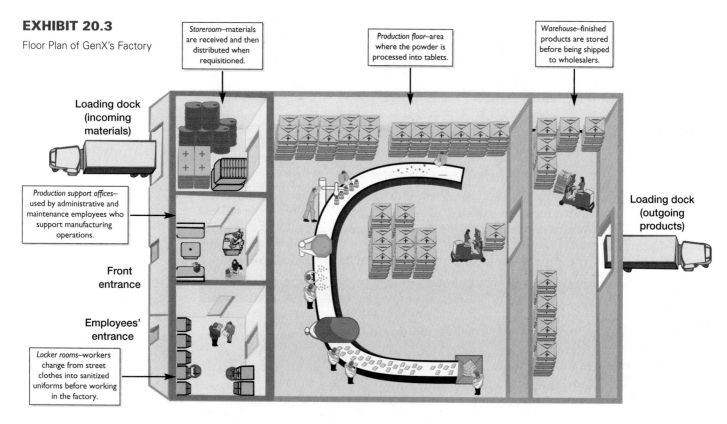

retailers. Profen is produced by mixing its active ingredient, Profelene, with flavorings and preservatives, molding it into Profen tablets, and packaging the tablets. Exhibit 20.3 shows a summary floor plan of the GenX factory, which has five areas.

The first step in process manufacturing is to decide when to produce a product. Management determines the types and quantities of materials and labor needed and then schedules the work. Unlike a job order process, where production often begins only after receipt of a custom order, managers of companies with process operations often forecast the demand expected for their products. Based on these plans, production begins. The flowchart in Exhibit 20.4 shows the production steps for GenX. The following sections explain how GenX uses a process cost accounting system to compute these costs. Many of the explanations refer to this exhibit and its numbered cost flows ① through ⑩. (*Hint:* The amounts for the numbered cost flows in Exhibit 20.4 are summarized in Exhibit 20.21. Those amounts are explained in the following pages, but it can help to refer to Exhibit 20.21 as we proceed through the explanations.)

Point: Electronic monitoring of operations is common in factories.

EXHIBIT 20.4

Process Operations and Costs: GenX

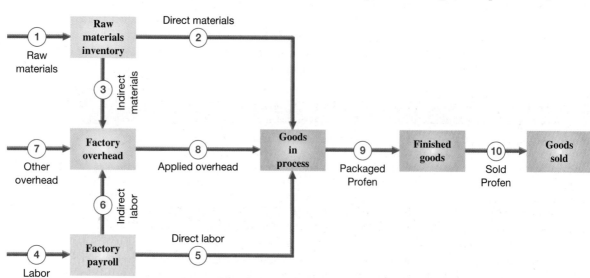

PROCESS COST ACCOUNTING

Comparing Job Order and Process Cost Accounting Systems

Process and job order operations are similar in that both combine materials, labor, and overhead in the process of producing products. They differ in how they are organized and managed. The measurement focus in a job order costing system is on the individual job or batch, whereas in a process costing system, it is on the individual process. Regardless of the measurement focus, we are ultimately interested in determining the cost per unit of product (or service) resulting from either system.

Specifically, the **job order cost accounting system** assigns direct materials, direct labor, and overhead to jobs. The total job cost is then divided by the number of units to compute a cost per unit for that job. The **process cost accounting system** assigns direct materials, direct labor, and overhead to specific processes (or departments). The total costs associated with each process are then divided by the number of units passing through that process to determine the cost per equivalent unit (defined later in the chapter) for that process. Differences in the way these two systems apply materials, labor, and overhead costs are highlighted in Exhibit 20.5.

A1 Compare process cost accounting and job order cost accounting.

Point: The cost object in a job order system is the specific job; the cost object in a process costing system is the process.

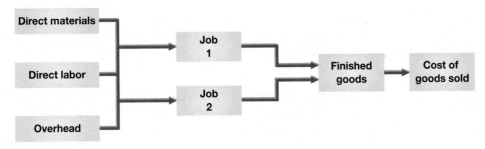

Job order systems

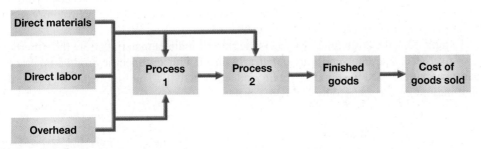

Process systems

EXHIBIT 20.5

Comparing Job Order and Process Cost Accounting Systems

Direct and Indirect Costs

Like job order operations, process cost accounting systems use the concepts of direct and indirect costs. If a cost can be traced to the cost object, it is direct; if it cannot, it is indirect. Materials and labor that can be traced to specific processes are assigned to those processes as direct costs. Materials and labor that cannot be traced to a specific process are indirect costs and are assigned to overhead. Some costs classified as overhead in a job order system may be classified as direct costs in process cost accounting. For example, depreciation of a machine used entirely by one process is a direct cost of that process.

Decision Insight

JIT Boon to Process Operations   Companies that adopt JIT manufacturing often organize their production system as a series of sequential processes. One survey found 60% of companies that converted to JIT used process operations; this compares to only 20% before converting to JIT. ■

P1	Record the flow of direct materials costs in process cost accounting.

Accounting for Materials Costs

In Exhibit 20.4, arrow line ① reflects the arrival of materials at GenX's factory. These materials include Profelene, flavorings, preservatives, and packaging. They also include supplies for the production support office. GenX uses a perpetual inventory system and makes all purchases on credit. The summary entry for receipts of raw materials in April follows (dates in journal entries numbered ① through ⑩ are omitted because they are summary entries, often reflecting two or more transactions or events).

Assets = Liabilities + Equity
+11,095   +11,095

①	Raw Materials Inventory	11,095	
	Accounts Payable		11,095
	Acquired materials on credit for factory use.		

Arrow line ② in Exhibit 20.4 reflects the flow of direct materials to production, where they are used to produce Profen. Most direct materials are physically combined into the finished product; the remaining direct materials include those used and clearly linked with a specific process. The manager of a process usually obtains materials by submitting a *materials requisition* to the materials storeroom manager. In some situations, materials move continuously from raw materials inventory through the manufacturing process. **Pepsi Bottling**, for instance, uses a process in which inventory moves continuously through the system. In these cases, a **materials consumption report** summarizes the materials used by a department during a reporting period and replaces materials requisitions. The entry to record the use of direct materials by GenX's production department in April follows.

Assets = Liabilities + Equity
+9,900
−9,900

②	Goods in Process Inventory	9,900	
	Raw Materials Inventory		9,900
	To assign costs of direct materials used in production.		

This entry transfers costs from one asset account to another asset account. (When two or more production departments exist, a company uses two or more Goods in Process Inventory accounts to separately accumulate costs incurred by each.)

In Exhibit 20.4, the arrow line ③ reflects the flow of indirect materials from the storeroom to factory overhead. These materials are not clearly linked with any specific production process or department but are used to support overall production activity. The following entry records the cost of indirect materials used by GenX in April.

Example: What types of materials might the flow of arrow line ③ in Exhibit 20.4 reflect? *Answer:* Goggles, gloves, protective clothing, recordkeeping supplies, and cleaning supplies.

Assets = Liabilities + Equity
−1,195   −1,195

③	Factory Overhead	1,195	
	Raw Materials Inventory		1,195
	To record indirect materials used in April.		

After the entries for both direct and indirect materials are posted, the Raw Materials Inventory account appears as shown in Exhibit 20.6. The April 30 balance sheet reports the $4,000 Raw Materials Inventory account as a current asset.

EXHIBIT 20.6

Raw Materials Inventory

Raw Materials Inventory				Acct. No. 132		
Date		Explanation		Debit	Credit	Balance
Mar.	31	Balance				4,000
Apr.	30	Materials purchases		11,095		15,095
	30	Direct materials usage			9,900	5,195
	30	Indirect materials usage			1,195	4,000

Accounting for Labor Costs

Exhibit 20.4 shows GenX factory payroll costs as reflected in arrow line ④. Total labor costs of $8,920 are paid in cash and are recorded in the Factory Payroll account.

④	Factory Payroll	8,920	
	Cash		8,920
	To record factory wages for April.		

Assets = Liabilities + Equity
−8,920   −8,920

Time reports from the production department and the production support office triggered this entry. (For simplicity, we do not separately identify withholdings and additional payroll taxes for employees.) In a process operation, the direct labor of a production department includes all labor used exclusively by that department. This is the case even if the labor is not applied to the product itself. If a production department in a process operation, for instance, has a full-time manager and a full-time maintenance worker, their salaries are direct labor costs of that process and are not factory overhead.

Arrow line ⑤ in Exhibit 20.4 shows GenX's use of direct labor in the production department. The following entry transfers April's direct labor costs from the Factory Payroll account to the Goods in Process Inventory account.

⑤	Goods in Process Inventory	5,700	
	Factory Payroll		5,700
	To assign costs of direct labor used in production.		

Assets = Liabilities + Equity
+5,700   +5,700

Arrow line ⑥ in Exhibit 20.4 reflects GenX's indirect labor costs. These employees provide clerical, maintenance, and other services that help produce Profen efficiently. For example, they order materials, deliver them to the factory floor, repair equipment, operate and program computers used in production, keep payroll and other production records, clean up, and move the finished goods to the warehouse. The following entry charges these indirect labor costs to factory overhead.

Point: A department's indirect labor cost might include an allocated portion of the salary of a manager who supervises two or more departments. Allocation of costs between departments is discussed in a later chapter.

⑥	Factory Overhead	3,220	
	Factory Payroll		3,220
	To record indirect labor as overhead.		

Assets = Liabilities + Equity
                                  −3,220
                                  +3,220

After these entries for both direct and indirect labor are posted, the Factory Payroll account appears as shown in Exhibit 20.7. The temporary Factory Payroll account is now closed to another temporary account, Factory Overhead, and is ready to receive entries for May. Next we show how to apply overhead to production and close the temporary Factory Overhead account.

Factory Payroll				Acct. No. 530	
Date		**Explanation**	**Debit**	**Credit**	**Balance**
Mar.	31	Balance			0
Apr.	30	Total payroll for April	8,920		8,920
	30	Direct labor costs		5,700	3,220
	30	Indirect labor costs		3,220	0

EXHIBIT 20.7

Factory Payroll

Accounting for Factory Overhead

Overhead costs other than indirect materials and indirect labor are reflected by arrow line ⑦ in Exhibit 20.4. These overhead items include the costs of insuring production assets, renting the factory building, using factory utilities, and depreciating equipment not directly related to a specific process. The following entry records overhead costs for April.

P2 Record the flow of direct labor costs in process cost accounting.

P3 Record the flow of factory overhead costs in process cost accounting.

Assets = Liabilities + Equity
−180   +645   −2,425
−750
−850

⑦	Factory Overhead	2,425	
	Prepaid Insurance		180
	Utilities Payable		645
	Cash		750
	Accumulated Depreciation—Factory Equipment ...		850
	To record overhead items incurred in April.		

After this entry is posted, the Factory Overhead account balance is $6,840, comprising indirect materials of $1,195, indirect labor of $3,220, and $2,425 of other overhead.

Arrow line ⑧ in Exhibit 20.4 reflects the application of factory overhead to production. Factory overhead is applied to processes by relating overhead cost to another variable such as direct labor hours or machine hours used. With increasing automation, companies with process operations are more likely to use machine hours to allocate overhead. In some situations, a single allocation basis such as direct labor hours (or a single rate for the entire plant) fails to provide useful allocations. As a result, management can use different rates for different production departments. Based on an analysis of its operations, GenX applies its April overhead at a rate of 120% of direct labor cost, as shown in Exhibit 20.8.

Point: The time it takes to process (cycle) products through a process is sometimes used to allocate costs.

EXHIBIT 20.8

Applying Factory Overhead
(Production Department)

> **Overhead applied = Direct labor cost × Predetermined rate**
> $6,840   = $5,700   ×   120%

GenX records its applied overhead with the following entry.

Assets = Liabilities + Equity
+6,840   +6,840

⑧	Goods in Process Inventory	6,840	
	Factory Overhead		6,840
	Allocated overhead costs to production at 120% of direct labor cost.		

After posting this entry, the Factory Overhead account appears as shown in Exhibit 20.9. For GenX, the amount of overhead applied equals the actual overhead incurred during April. In most cases, using a predetermined overhead rate leaves an overapplied or underapplied balance in the Factory Overhead account. At the end of the period, this overapplied or underapplied balance should be closed to the Cost of Goods Sold account, as described in the job order costing chapter.

EXHIBIT 20.9

Factory Overhead

Example: If applied overhead results in a $6,940 credit to the factory overhead account, does it yield an over- or underapplied overhead amount?
Answer: $100 overapplied overhead

	Factory Overhead				Acct. No. 540
Date		**Explanation**	**Debit**	**Credit**	**Balance**
Mar. 31		Balance			0
Apr. 30		Indirect materials usage	1,195		1,195
30		Indirect labor costs	3,220		4,415
30		Other overhead costs	2,425		6,840
30		Applied to production departments		6,840	0

Decision Ethics   Answer — p. 838

Budget Officer   You are working to identify the direct and indirect costs of a new processing department that has several machines. This department's manager instructs you to classify a majority of the costs as indirect to take advantage of the direct labor-based overhead allocation method so it will be charged a lower amount of overhead (because of its small direct labor cost). This would penalize other departments with higher allocations. It also will cause the performance ratings of managers in these other departments to suffer. What action do you take? ∎

1. A process operation (*a*) is another name for a job order operation, (*b*) does not use the concepts of direct materials or direct labor, or (*c*) typically produces large quantities of homogeneous products or services.
2. Under what conditions is a process cost accounting system more suitable for measuring production costs than a job order cost accounting system?
3. When direct materials are assigned and used in production, the entry to record their use includes (*a*) a credit to Goods in Process Inventory, (*b*) a debit to Goods in Process Inventory, or (*c*) a debit to Raw Materials Inventory.
4. What are the three cost categories incurred by both job order and process operations?
5. How many Goods in Process Inventory accounts are needed in a process cost system?

EQUIVALENT UNITS OF PRODUCTION

We explained how materials, labor, and overhead costs for a period are accumulated in the Goods in Process Inventory account, but we have not explained the arrow lines labeled ⑨ and ⑩ in Exhibit 20.4. These lines reflect the transfer of products from the production department to finished goods inventory, and from finished goods inventory to cost of goods sold. To determine the costs recorded for these flows, we must first determine the cost per unit of product and then apply this result to the number of units transferred.

> **C2** Define and compute equivalent units and explain their use in process cost accounting.

Accounting for Goods in Process

If a process has *no beginning and no ending goods in process inventory*, the unit cost of goods transferred out of a process is computed as follows.

$$\frac{\text{Total cost assigned to the process (direct materials, direct labor, and overhead)}}{\text{Total number of units started and finished in the period}}$$

If a process has a beginning or ending inventory of partially processed units (or both), then the total cost assigned to the process must be allocated to all completed and incomplete units worked on during the period. Therefore, the denominator must measure the entire production activity of the process for the period, called **equivalent units of production** (or **EUP**), a phrase that refers to the number of units that could have been started *and* completed given the cost incurred during a period. This measure is then used to compute the cost per equivalent unit and to assign costs to finished goods and goods in process inventory.

To illustrate, assume that GenX adds (or introduces) 100 units into its process during a period. Suppose at the end of that period, the production supervisor determines that those 100 units are 60% of the way through the process. Therefore, equivalent units of production for that period total 60 EUP (100 units × 60%). This means that with the resources used to put 100 units 60% of the way through the process, GenX could have started and completed 60 whole units.

> **Point:** For GenX, "units" might refer to individual Profen tablets. For a juice maker, units might refer to gallons.

Differences in Equivalent Units for Materials, Labor, and Overhead

In many processes, the equivalent units of production for direct materials are not the same with respect to direct labor and overhead. To illustrate, consider a five-step process operation shown in Exhibit 20.10.

EXHIBIT 20.10

An Illustrative Five-Step Process Operation

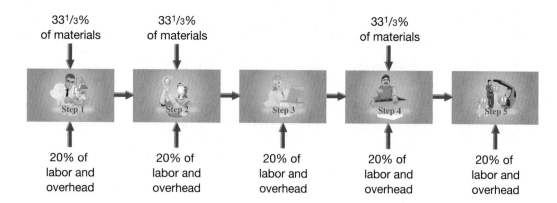

This exhibit shows that one-third of the direct material cost is added at each of three steps: 1, 2, and 4. One-fifth of the direct labor cost is added at each of the five steps. One-fifth of the overhead also is added at each step because overhead is applied as a percent of direct labor for this company.

When units finish step 1, they are one-third complete with respect to direct materials but only one-fifth complete with respect to direct labor and overhead. When they finish step 2, they are two-thirds complete with respect to direct materials but only two-fifths complete with respect to direct labor and overhead. When they finish step 3, they remain two-thirds complete with respect to materials but are now three-fifths complete with respect to labor and overhead. When they finish step 4, they are 100% complete with respect to materials (all direct materials have been added) but only four-fifths complete with respect to labor and overhead.

For example, if 300 units of product are started and processed through step 1 of Exhibit 20.10, they are said to be one-third complete *with respect to materials*. Expressed in terms of equivalent finished units, the processing of these 300 units is equal to finishing 100 EUP with respect to materials (300 units × 33⅓%). However, only one-fifth of direct labor and overhead has been applied to the 300 units at the end of step 1. This means that the equivalent units of production *with respect to labor and overhead* total 60 EUP (300 units × 20%).

Decision Insight

Process Services Customer interaction software is a hot item in customer service processes. Whether in insurance, delivery, or technology services, companies are finding that this software can turn their customer service process into an asset. How does it work? For starters, it cuts time spent on service calls because a customer describes a problem only once. It also yields a database of customer questions and complaints that gives insights into needed improvements. It recognizes incoming phone numbers and accesses previous dealings. ■

PROCESS COSTING ILLUSTRATION

This section applies process costing concepts and procedures to GenX. **This illustration uses the weighted-average method for inventory costs. The FIFO method is illustrated in Appendix 20A.** (Assume a weighted-average cost flow for all computations and assignments in this chapter unless explicitly stated differently. When using a just-in-time inventory system, different inventory methods yield similar results because inventories are immaterial.)

Exhibit 20.11 shows selected information from the production department for the month of April. Accounting for a department's activity for a period includes four steps involving analysis of (1) physical flow, (2) equivalent units, (3) cost per equivalent unit, and (4) cost assignment and reconciliation. The next sections describe each step.

Beginning goods in process inventory (March 31)	
Units of product	30,000 units
Percentage of completion—Direct materials	100%
Percentage of completion—Direct labor	65%
Direct materials costs	$ 3,300
Direct labor costs	$ 600
Factory overhead costs applied (120% of direct labor)	$ 720
Activities during the current period (April)	
Units started this period	90,000 units
Units transferred out (completed)	100,000 units
Direct materials costs	$ 9,900
Direct labor costs	$ 5,700
Factory overhead costs applied (120% of direct labor)	$ 6,840
Ending goods in process inventory (April 30)	
Units of product	20,000 units
Percentage of completion—Direct materials	100%
Percentage of completion—Direct labor	25%

EXHIBIT 20.11

Production Data

Step 1: Determine the Physical Flow of Units

A *physical flow reconciliation* is a report that reconciles (1) the physical units started in a period with (2) the physical units completed in that period. A physical flow reconciliation for GenX is shown in Exhibit 20.12 for April.

Units to Account For		Units Accounted For	
Beginning goods in process inventory	30,000 units	Units completed and transferred out	100,000 units
Units started this period	90,000 units	Ending goods in process inventory	20,000 units
Total units to account for	**120,000 units**	Total units accounted for	**120,000 units**

reconciled

EXHIBIT 20.12

Physical Flow Reconciliation

The weighted-average method does not require us to separately track the units in beginning work in process from those units started this period. Instead, the units are treated as part of a large pool with an average cost per unit.

Step 2: Compute Equivalent Units of Production

The second step is to compute *equivalent units of production* for direct materials, direct labor, and factory overhead for April. Overhead is applied using direct labor as the allocation base for GenX. This also implies that equivalent units are the same for both labor and overhead.

GenX used its direct materials, direct labor, and overhead to make finished units of Profen and to begin processing some units that are not yet complete. We must convert the physical units measure to equivalent units based on how each input has been used. Equivalent units are computed by multiplying the number of physical units by the percentage of completion for each input—see Exhibit 20.13.

Equivalent Units of Production	Direct Materials	Direct Labor	Factory Overhead
Equivalent units completed and transferred out (100,000 × 100%)	100,000 EUP	100,000 EUP	100,000 EUP
Equivalent units for ending goods in process			
Direct materials (20,000 × 100%)	20,000		
Direct labor (20,000 × 25%)		5,000	
Factory overhead (20,000 × 25%)			5,000
Equivalent units of production	120,000 EUP	105,000 EUP	105,000 EUP

EXHIBIT 20.13

Equivalent Units of Production— Weighted Average

The first row of Exhibit 20.13 reflects units transferred out in April. The production department entirely completed its work on the 100,000 units transferred out. These units have 100% of the materials, labor, and overhead required, or 100,000 equivalent units of each input (100,000 × 100%).

The second row references the ending goods in process, and rows three, four, and five break it down by materials, labor, and overhead. For direct materials, the units in ending goods in process inventory (20,000 physical units) include all materials required, so there are 20,000 equivalent units (20,000 × 100%) of materials in the unfinished physical units. Regarding labor, the units in ending goods in process inventory include 25% of the labor required, which implies 5,000 equivalent units of labor (20,000 × 25%). These units are only 25% complete and labor is used uniformly through the process. Overhead is applied on the basis of direct labor for GenX, so equivalent units for overhead are computed identically to labor (20,000 × 25%).

The final row reflects the whole units of product that could have been manufactured with the amount of inputs used to create some complete and some incomplete units. For GenX, the amount of inputs used to produce 100,000 complete units and to start 20,000 additional units is equivalent to the amount of direct materials in 120,000 whole units, the amount of direct labor in 105,000 whole units, and the amount of overhead in 105,000 whole units.

Step 3: Compute the Cost per Equivalent Unit

Equivalent units of production for each product (from step 2) is used to compute the average cost per equivalent unit. Under the **weighted-average method,** the computation of EUP does not separate the units in beginning inventory from those started this period; similarly, this method combines the costs of beginning goods in process inventory with the costs incurred in the current period. This process is illustrated in Exhibit 20.14.

EXHIBIT 20.14

Cost per Equivalent Unit of Production—Weighted Average

Cost per Equivalent Unit of Production	Direct Materials	Direct Labor	Factory Overhead
Costs of beginning goods in process inventory	$ 3,300	$ 600	$ 720
Costs incurred this period	9,900	5,700	6,840
Total costs	$13,200	$6,300	$7,560
÷ Equivalent units of production (from Step 2)	120,000 EUP	105,000 EUP	105,000 EUP
= Cost per equivalent unit of production	$0.11 per EUP*	$0.06 per EUP†	$0.072 per EUP‡

*$13,200 ÷ 120,000 EUP   †$6,300 ÷ 105,000 EUP   ‡$7,560 ÷ 105,000 EUP

For direct materials, the cost averages $0.11 per EUP, computed as the sum of direct materials cost from beginning goods in process inventory ($3,300) and the direct materials cost incurred in April ($9,900), and this sum ($13,200) is then divided by the 120,000 EUP for materials (from step 2). The costs per equivalent unit for labor and overhead are similarly computed. Specifically, direct labor cost averages $0.06 per EUP, computed as the sum of labor cost in beginning goods in process inventory ($600) and the labor costs incurred in April ($5,700), and this sum ($6,300) divided by 105,000 EUP for labor. Overhead costs averages $0.072 per EUP, computed as the sum of overhead cost in the beginning goods in process inventory ($720) and the overhead costs applied in April ($6,840), and this sum ($7,560) divided by 105,000 EUP for overhead.

Step 4: Assign and Reconcile Costs

The EUP from step 2 and the cost per EUP from step 3 are used in step 4 to assign costs to (a) units that production completed and transferred to finished goods and (b) units that remain in process. This is illustrated in Exhibit 20.15.

EXHIBIT 20.15

Report of Costs Accounted For—Weighted Average

Cost of units completed and transferred out		
Direct materials (100,000 EUP × $0.11 per EUP)	$11,000	
Direct labor (100,000 EUP × $0.06 per EUP)	6,000	
Factory overhead (100,000 EUP × $0.072 per EUP)	7,200	
Cost of units completed this period		$ 24,200
Cost of ending goods in process inventory		
Direct materials (20,000 EUP × $0.11 per EUP)	2,200	
Direct labor (5,000 EUP × $0.06 per EUP)	300	
Factory overhead (5,000 EUP × $0.072 per EUP)	360	
Cost of ending goods in process inventory		2,860
Total costs accounted for		**$27,060**

Cost of Units Completed and Transferred The 100,000 units completed and transferred to finished goods inventory required 100,000 EUP of direct materials. Thus, we assign $11,000 (100,000 EUP × $0.11 per EUP) of direct materials cost to those units. Similarly, those units had received 100,000 EUP of direct labor and 100,000 EUP of factory overhead (recall Exhibit 20.13). Thus, we assign $6,000 (100,000 EUP × $0.06 per EUP) of direct labor and $7,200 (100,000 EUP × $0.072 per EUP) of overhead to those units. The total cost of the 100,000 completed and transferred units is $24,200 ($11,000 + $6,000 + $7,200) and their average cost per unit is $0.242 ($24,200 ÷ 100,000 units).

Cost of Units for Ending Goods in Process There are 20,000 incomplete units in goods in process inventory at period-end. For direct materials, those units have 20,000 EUP of material (from step 2) at a cost of $0.11 per EUP (from step 3), which yields the materials cost of goods in process inventory of $2,200 (20,000 EUP × $0.11 per EUP). For direct labor, the in-process units have 25% of the required labor, or 5,000 EUP (from step 2). Using the $0.06 labor cost per EUP (from step 3) we obtain the labor cost of goods in process inventory of $300 (5,000 EUP × $0.06 per EUP). For overhead, the in-process units reflect 5,000 EUP (from step 2). Using the $0.072 overhead cost per EUP (from step 3) we obtain overhead costs with in-process inventory of $360 (5,000 EUP × $0.072 per EUP). Total cost of goods in process inventory at period-end is $2,860 ($2,200 + $300 + $360).

As a check, management verifies that total costs assigned to those units completed and transferred plus the costs of those in process (from Exhibit 20.15) equal the costs incurred by production. Exhibit 20.16 shows the costs incurred by production this period. We then reconcile the *costs accounted for* in Exhibit 20.15 with the *costs to account for* in Exhibit 20.16.

EXHIBIT 20.16

Report of Costs to Account For—Weighted Average

Cost of beginning goods in process inventory		
Direct materials	$3,300	
Direct labor	600	
Factory overhead	720	$ 4,620
Cost incurred this period		
Direct materials	9,900	
Direct labor	5,700	
Factory overhead	6,840	22,440
Total costs to account for		**$27,060**

At GenX, the production department manager is responsible for $27,060 in costs: $4,620 that is assigned to the goods in process at the start of the period plus $22,440 of materials, labor, and overhead incurred in the period. At period-end, that manager must show where these costs are assigned. The manager for GenX reports that $2,860 are assigned to units in process and $24,200 are assigned to units completed (per Exhibit 20.15). The sum of these amounts equals $27,060. Thus, the total *costs to account for* equal the total *costs accounted for* (minor differences can sometimes occur from rounding).

C3 Define and prepare a process cost summary and describe its purposes.

Point: Managers can examine changes in monthly costs per equivalent unit to help control the production process. When prices are set in a competitive market, managers can use process cost summary information to determine which costs should be cut to achieve a profit.

Process Cost Summary An important managerial accounting report for a process cost accounting system is the **process cost summary** (also called *production report*), which is prepared separately for each process or production department. Three reasons for the summary are to (1) help department managers control and monitor their departments, (2) help factory managers evaluate department managers' performances, and (3) provide cost information for financial statements. A process cost summary achieves these purposes by describing the costs charged to each department, reporting the equivalent units of production achieved by each department, and determining the costs assigned to each department's output. For our purposes, it is prepared using a combination of Exhibits 20.13, 20.14, 20.15, and 20.16.

The process cost summary for GenX is shown in Exhibit 20.17. The report is divided into three sections. Section ① lists the total costs charged to the department, including direct materials, direct labor, and overhead costs incurred, as well as the cost of the beginning goods in process inventory. Section ② describes the equivalent units of production for the department. Equivalent units for materials, labor, and overhead are in separate columns. It also reports direct

EXHIBIT 20.17

Process Cost Summary

GenX COMPANY
Process Cost Summary
For Month Ended April 30, 2011

Costs Charged to Production

Costs of beginning goods in process

Direct materials	$3,300	
Direct labor	600	
Factory overhead	720	$ 4,620

Costs incurred this period

Direct materials	9,900	
Direct labor	5,700	
Factory overhead	6,840	22,440
Total costs to account for		$27,060

Unit Cost Information

Units to account for:		Units accounted for:	
Beginning goods in process	30,000	Completed and transferred out	100,000
Units started this period	90,000	Ending goods in process	20,000
Total units to account for	120,000	Total units accounted for	120,000

Equivalent Units of Production (EUP)	Direct Materials	Direct Labor	Factory Overhead
Units completed and transferred out	100,000 EUP	100,000 EUP	100,000 EUP
Units of ending goods in process			
Direct materials (20,000 × 100%)	20,000		
Direct labor (20,000 × 25%)		5,000	
Factory overhead (20,000 × 25%)			5,000
Equivalent units of production	120,000 EUP	105,000 EUP	105,000 EUP

Cost per EUP	Direct Materials	Direct Labor	Factory Overhead
Costs of beginning goods in process	$ 3,300	$ 600	$ 720
Costs incurred this period	9,900	5,700	6,840
Total costs	$13,200	$6,300	$7,560
÷ EUP	120,000 EUP	105,000 EUP	105,000 EUP
Cost per EUP	$0.11 per EUP	$0.06 per EUP	$0.072 per EUP

Cost Assignment and Reconciliation

Costs transferred out (cost of goods manufactured)

Direct materials (100,000 EUP × $0.11 per EUP)	$11,000	
Direct labor (100,000 EUP × $0.06 per EUP)	6,000	
Factory overhead (100,000 EUP × $0.072 per EUP)	7,200	$ 24,200

Costs of ending goods in process

Direct materials (20,000 EUP × $0.11 per EUP)	2,200	
Direct labor (5,000 EUP × $0.06 per EUP)	300	
Factory overhead (5,000 EUP × $0.072 per EUP)	360	2,860
Total costs accounted for		$27,060

reconciled

materials, direct labor, and overhead costs per equivalent unit. Section ◇3◇ allocates total costs among units worked on in the period. The $24,200 is the total cost of goods transferred out of the department, and the $2,860 is the cost of partially processed ending inventory units. The assigned costs are then added to show that the total $27,060 cost charged to the department in section ◇1◇ is now assigned to the units in section ◇3◇.

Quick Check
Answers – p. 838

6. Equivalent units are (*a*) a measure of a production department's productivity in using direct materials, direct labor, or overhead; (*b*) units of a product produced by a foreign competitor that are similar to units produced by a domestic company; or (*c*) generic units of a product similar to brand name units of a product.

7. Interpret the meaning of a department's equivalent units with respect to direct labor.

8. A department began the period with 8,000 units that were one-fourth complete with respect to direct labor. It completed 58,000 units, and ended with 6,000 units that were one-third complete with respect to direct labor. What were its direct labor equivalent units for the period using the weighted-average method?

9. A process cost summary for a department has three sections. What information is presented in each of them?

Transfers to Finished Goods Inventory and Cost of Goods Sold

P4 Record the transfer of completed goods to Finished Goods Inventory and Cost of Goods Sold.

Arrow line ⑨ in Exhibit 20.4 reflects the transfer of completed products from production to finished goods inventory. The process cost summary shows that the 100,000 units of finished Profen are assigned a cost of $24,200. The entry to record this transfer follows.

⑨	Finished Goods Inventory	24,200	
	Goods in Process Inventory		24,200
	To record transfer of completed units.		

Assets = Liabilities + Equity
+24,200
−24,200

The credit to Goods in Process Inventory reduces that asset balance to reflect that 100,000 units are no longer in production. The cost of these units has been transferred to Finished Goods Inventory, which is recognized as a $24,200 increase in this asset. After this entry is posted, there remains a balance of $2,860 in the Goods in Process Inventory account, which is the amount computed in Step 4 previously. The cost of units transferred from Goods in Process Inventory to Finished Goods Inventory is called the **cost of goods manufactured.** Exhibit 20.18 reveals the activities in the Goods in Process Inventory account for this period. The ending balance of this account equals the cost assigned to the partially completed units in section ◇3◇ of Exhibit 20.17.

Goods in Process Inventory				Acct. No. 134
Date	Explanation	Debit	Credit	Balance
Mar. 31	Balance			4,620
Apr. 30	Direct materials usage	9,900		14,520
30	Direct labor costs incurred	5,700		20,220
30	Factory overhead applied	6,840		27,060
30	Transfer completed product to warehouse		24,200	2,860

EXHIBIT 20.18

Goods in Process Inventory

Arrow line ⑩ in Exhibit 20.4 reflects the sale of finished goods. Assume that GenX sold 106,000 units of Profen this period, and that its beginning inventory of finished goods consisted of 26,000 units with a cost of $6,292. Also assume that its ending finished goods inventory consists of 20,000 units at a cost of $4,840. Using this information, we can compute its cost of goods sold for April as shown in Exhibit 20.19.

Point: We omit the journal entry for sales, but it totals the number of units sold times price per unit.

EXHIBIT 20.19

Cost of Goods Sold

Beginning finished goods inventory................	$ 6,292
+ Cost of goods manufactured this period.........	24,200
= Cost of goods available for sale................	$30,492
− Ending finished goods inventory................	4,840
= Cost of goods sold...........................	$25,652

The summary entry to record cost of goods sold for this period follows.

Assets = Liabilities + Equity
−25,652   −25,652

⑩	Cost of Goods Sold.............................	25,652	
	Finished Goods Inventory.....................		25,652
	To record cost of goods sold for April.		

The Finished Goods Inventory account now appears as shown in Exhibit 20.20.

EXHIBIT 20.20

Finished Goods Inventory

Finished Goods Inventory			Acct. No. 135		
Date		**Explanation**	**Debit**	**Credit**	**Balance**
Mar.	31	Balance			6,292
Apr.	30	Transfer in cost of goods manufactured	24,200		30,492
	30	Cost of goods sold		25,652	4,840

Summary of Cost Flows Exhibit 20.21 shows GenX's manufacturing cost flows for April. Each of these cost flows and the entries to record them have been explained. The flow of costs through the accounts reflects the flow of production activities and products.

EXHIBIT 20.21*

Cost Flows through GenX

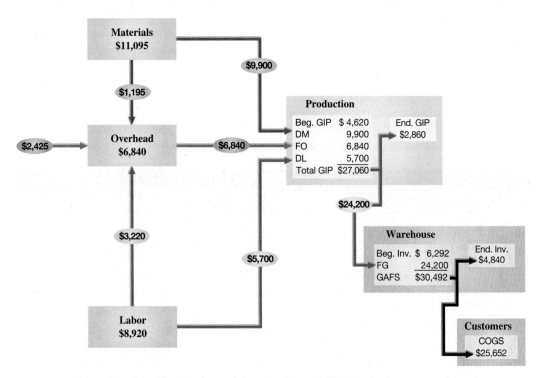

*Abbreviations: GIP (goods in process); DM (direct materials); DL (direct labor); FO (factory overhead); FG (finished goods); GAFS (goods available for sale); COGS (cost of goods sold).

Trends in Process Operations

Some of the recent trends in process operations are discussed in the following paragraphs.

Process Design   Management concerns with production efficiency can lead companies to entirely reorganize production processes. For example, instead of producing different types of computers in a series of departments, a separate work center for each computer can be established in one department. The process cost system is then changed to account for each work center's costs.

Just-in-Time Production   Companies are increasingly adopting just-in-time techniques. With a just-in-time inventory system, inventory levels can be minimal. If raw materials are not ordered or received until needed, a Raw Materials Inventory account might be unnecessary. Instead, materials cost is immediately debited to the Goods in Process Inventory account. Similarly, a Finished Goods Inventory account may not be needed. Instead, cost of finished goods may be immediately debited to the Cost of Goods Sold account.

Automation   Advances in technology increasingly enable companies to automate their production processes. This allows them to reduce direct labor costs. Reflecting this, some companies focus on **conversion costs per equivalent unit,** which is the combined costs of direct labor and factory overhead per equivalent unit.

Services   Service-based businesses are increasingly prevalent. For routine, standardized services like oil changes and simple tax returns, computing costs based on the process is simpler and more useful than a cost per individual job.

Customer Orientation   Focus on customer orientation also leads to improved processes. A manufacturer of control devices improved quality and reduced production time by forming teams to study processes and suggest improvements. An ice cream maker studied customer tastes to develop a more pleasing ice cream texture.

 GLOBAL VIEW

As part of a series of global environmental goals, the international giant **Anheuser-Busch InBev** set targets to reduce its water usage. The company uses massive amounts of water in beer production and in its cleaning and cooling processes. To meet these goals, the company followed recent trends in process operations. These included extensive redesign of production processes and the use of advanced technology to increase efficiency at wastewater treatment plants. As a result water usage decreased by almost 37 percent in its global operations.

Hybrid Costing System   **Decision Analysis**

This chapter explained the process costing system and contrasted it with the job order costing system. Many organizations use a *hybrid system* that contains features of both process and job order operations. A recent survey of manufacturers revealed that a majority use hybrid systems.

A2 Explain and illustrate a hybrid costing system.

To illustrate, consider a car manufacturer's assembly line. On one hand, the line resembles a process operation in that the assembly steps for each car are nearly identical. On the other hand, the specifications of most cars have several important differences. At the **Ford** Mustang plant, each car assembled on a given day can be different from the previous car and the next car. This means that the costs of materials (subassemblies or components) for each car can differ. Accordingly, while the conversion costs (direct labor and overhead) can be accounted for using a process costing system, the component costs (direct materials) are accounted for using a job order system (separately for each car or type of car).

A hybrid system of processes requires a *hybrid costing system* to properly cost products or services. In the Ford plant, the assembly costs per car are readily determined using process costing. The costs of additional components can then be added to the assembly costs to determine each car's total cost (as in job order costing). To illustrate, consider the following information for a daily assembly process at Ford.

Assembly process costs	
Direct materials	$10,600,000
Direct labor	$5,800,000
Factory overhead	$6,200,000
Number of cars assembled	1,000
Costs of three different types of steering wheels	$240, $330, $480
Costs of three different types of seats	$620, $840, $1,360

The assembly process costs $22,600 per car. Depending on the type of steering wheel and seats the customer requests, the cost of a car can range from $23,460 to $24,440 (a $980 difference).

Today companies are increasingly trying to standardize processes while attempting to meet individual customer needs. To the extent that differences among individual customers' requests are large, understanding the costs to satisfy those requests is important. Thus, monitoring and controlling both process and job order costs are important.

Decision Ethics   Answer — p. 838

Entrepreneur   You operate a process production company making similar products for three different customers. One customer demands 100% quality inspection of products at your location before shipping. The added costs of that inspection are spread across all customers, not just the one demanding it. If you charge the added costs to that customer, you could lose that customer and experience a loss. Moreover, your other two customers have agreed to pay 110% of full costs. What actions (if any) do you take? ■

DEMONSTRATION PROBLEM

Pennsylvania Company produces a product that passes through a single production process. Then completed products are transferred to finished goods in its warehouse. Information related to its manufacturing activities for July follows.

Raw Materials

Beginning inventory	$100,000
Raw materials purchased on credit	211,400
Direct materials used	(190,000)
Indirect materials used	(51,400)
Ending inventory	$ 70,000

Factory Payroll

Direct labor incurred	$ 55,500
Indirect labor incurred	50,625
Total payroll (paid in cash)	$106,125

Factory Overhead

Indirect materials used	$ 51,400
Indirect labor used	50,625
Other overhead costs	71,725
Total factory overhead incurred	$173,750

Factory Overhead Applied

Overhead applied (200% of direct labor)	$111,000

Production Department

Beginning goods in process inventory (units)	5,000
Percentage completed—Materials	100%
Percentage completed—Labor and overhead	60%
Beginning goods in process inventory (costs)	
Direct materials used	$ 20,000
Direct labor incurred	9,600
Overhead applied (200% of direct labor)	19,200
Total costs of beginning goods in process	$ 48,800
Units started this period	20,000
Units completed this period	17,000
Ending goods in process inventory (units)	8,000
Percentage completed—Materials	100%
Percentage completed—Labor and overhead	20%

Finished Goods Inventory

Beginning finished goods inventory	$ 96,400
Cost transferred in from production	321,300
Cost of goods sold	(345,050)
Ending finished goods inventory	$ 72,650

Required

1. Prepare a physical flow reconciliation for July as illustrated in Exhibit 20.12.
2. Compute the equivalent units of production in July for direct materials, direct labor, and factory overhead.
3. Compute the costs per equivalent units of production in July for direct materials, direct labor, and factory overhead.
4. Prepare a report of costs accounted for and a report of costs to account for.
5. Prepare summary journal entries to record the transactions and events of July for (a) raw materials purchases, (b) direct materials usage, (c) indirect materials usage, (d) factory payroll costs, (e) direct labor usage, (f) indirect labor usage, (g) other overhead costs (credit Other Accounts), (h) application of overhead to production, (i) transfer of finished goods from production, and (j) the cost of goods sold.

PLANNING THE SOLUTION

- Track the physical flow to determine the number of units completed in July.
- Compute the equivalent unit of production for direct materials, direct labor, and factory overhead.
- Compute the costs per equivalent unit of production with respect to direct materials, direct labor, and overhead; and determine the cost per unit for each.
- Compute the total cost of the goods transferred to production by using the equivalent units and unit costs. Determine (a) the cost of the beginning in-process inventory, (b) the materials, labor, and overhead costs added to the beginning in-process inventory, and (c) the materials, labor, and overhead costs added to the units started and completed in the month.
- Determine the cost of goods sold using balances in finished goods and cost of units completed this period.
- Use the information to record the summary journal entries for July.

SOLUTION TO DEMONSTRATION PROBLEM

1. Physical flow reconciliation.

Units to Account For		Units Accounted For	
Beginning goods in process inventory	5,000 units	Units completed and transferred out	17,000 units
Units started this period	20,000 units	Ending goods in process inventory.	8,000 units
Total units to account for	**25,000 units**	Total units accounted for	**25,000 units**

reconciled

2. Equivalent units of production.

Equivalent Units of Production	Direct Materials	Direct Labor	Factory Overhead
Equivalent units completed and transferred out	17,000 EUP	17,000 EUP	17,000 EUP
Equivalent units in ending goods in process			
Direct materials (8,000 × 100%)	8,000		
Direct labor (8,000 × 20%)		1,600	
Factory overhead (8,000 × 20%)			1,600
Equivalent units of production	25,000 EUP	18,600 EUP	18,600 EUP

3. Costs per equivalent unit of production.

Costs per Equivalent Unit of Production	Direct Materials	Direct Labor	Factory Overhead
Costs of beginning goods in process	$ 20,000	$ 9,600	$ 19,200
Costs incurred this period	190,000	55,500	111,000*
Total costs	$210,000	$65,100	$130,200
÷ Equivalent units of production (from part 2) . .	25,000 EUP	18,600 EUP	18,600 EUP
= Costs per equivalent unit of production	$8.40 per EUP	$3.50 per EUP	$7.00 per EUP

*Factory overhead applied

4. Reports of costs accounted for and of costs to account for

Report of Costs Accounted For		
Cost of units transferred out (cost of goods manufactured)		
Direct materials ($8.40 per EUP × 17,000 EUP)	$142,800	
Direct labor ($3.50 per EUP × 17,000 EUP)	59,500	
Factory overhead ($7.00 per EUP × 17,000 EUP)	119,000	
Cost of units completed this period		$ 321,300
Cost of ending goods in process inventory		
Direct materials ($8.40 per EUP × 8,000 EUP)	67,200	
Direct labor ($3.50 per EUP × 1,600 EUP)	5,600	
Factory overhead ($7.00 per EUP × 1,600 EUP)	11,200	
Cost of ending goods in process inventory		84,000
Total costs accounted for		**$405,300**

Report of Costs to Account For		
Cost of beginning goods in process inventory		
Direct materials	$ 20,000	
Direct labor	9,600	
Factory overhead	19,200	$ 48,800
Cost incurred this period		
Direct materials	190,000	
Direct labor	55,500	
Factory overhead	111,000	356,500
Total costs to account for		**$405,300**

reconciled

5. Summary journal entries for the transactions and events in July.

a.	Raw Materials Inventory	211,400		g.	Factory Overhead	71,725	
	Accounts Payable		211,400		Other Accounts		71,725
	To record raw materials purchases.				*To record other overhead costs.*		
b.	Goods in Process Inventory	190,000		h.	Goods in Process Inventory	111,000	
	Raw Materials Inventory		190,000		Factory Overhead		111,000
	To record direct materials usage.				*To record application of overhead.*		
c.	Factory Overhead	51,400		i.	Finished Goods Inventory	321,300	
	Raw Materials Inventory		51,400		Goods in Process Inventory		321,300
	To record indirect materials usage.				*To record transfer of finished goods*		
d.	Factory Payroll	106,125			*from production.*		
	Cash		106,125	j.	Cost of Goods Sold	345,050	
	To record factory payroll costs.				Finished Goods Inventory		345,050
e.	Goods in Process Inventory	55,500			*To record cost of goods sold.*		
	Factory Payroll		55,500				
	To record direct labor usage.						
f.	Factory Overhead	50,625					
	Factory Payroll		50,625				
	To record indirect labor usage.						

FIFO Method of Process Costing

20A

The **FIFO method** of process costing assigns costs to units assuming a first-in, first-out flow of product. The objectives, concepts, and journal entries (not amounts) are the same as for the weighted-average method, but computation of equivalent units of production and cost assignment are slightly different.

> **C4** Explain and illustrate the accounting for production activity using FIFO.

Exhibit 20A.1 shows selected information from GenX's production department for the month of April. Accounting for a department's activity for a period includes four steps: (1) determine physical flow, (2) compute equivalent units, (3) compute cost per equivalent unit, and (4) determine cost assignment and reconciliation. This appendix describes each of these steps using the FIFO method for process costing.

EXHIBIT 20A.1

Production Data

Beginning goods in process inventory (March 31)	
Units of product	30,000 units
Percentage of completion—Direct materials	100%
Percentage of completion—Direct labor	65%
Direct materials costs	$ 3,300
Direct labor costs	$ 600
Factory overhead costs applied (120% of direct labor)	$ 720
Activities during the current period (April)	
Units started this period	90,000 units
Units transferred out (completed)	100,000 units
Direct materials costs....................................	$ 9,900
Direct labor costs.......................................	$ 5,700
Factory overhead costs applied (120% of direct labor).........	$ 6,840
Ending goods in process inventory (April 30)	
Units of product	20,000 units
Percentage of completion—Direct materials	100%
Percentage of completion—Direct labor	25%

Step 1: Determine Physical Flow of Units   A *physical flow reconciliation* is a report that reconciles (1) the physical units started in a period with (2) the physical units completed in that period. The physical flow reconciliation for GenX is shown in Exhibit 20A.2 for April.

EXHIBIT 20A.2

Physical Flow Reconciliation

Units to Account For		Units Accounted For	
Beginning goods in process inventory	30,000 units	Units completed and transferred out	100,000 units
Units started this period	90,000 units	Ending goods in process inventory	20,000 units
Total units to account for	**120,000 units**	Total units accounted for	**120,000 units**

reconciled

FIFO assumes that the 100,000 units transferred to finished goods during April include the 30,000 units from the beginning goods in process inventory. The remaining 70,000 units transferred out are from units started in April. Of the total 90,000 units started in April, 70,000 were completed, leaving 20,000 units unfinished at period-end.

Step 2: Compute Equivalent Units of Production—FIFO   GenX used its direct materials, direct labor, and overhead both to make complete units of Profen and to start some units that are not yet complete. We need to convert the physical measure of units to equivalent units based on how much of each input has been used. We do this by multiplying the number of physical units by the percentage of processing applied to those units in the current period; this is done for each input (materials, labor, and overhead). The FIFO method accounts for cost flow in a sequential manner—earliest costs are the first to flow out. (This is different from the weighted-average method, which combines prior period costs—those in beginning Goods in Process Inventory—with costs incurred in the current period.)

Three distinct groups of units must be considered in determining the equivalent units of production under the FIFO method: (a) units in beginning Goods in Process Inventory that were completed this period, (b) units started *and* completed this period, and (c) units in ending Goods in Process Inventory. We must determine how much material, labor, and overhead are used for each of these unit groups. These computations are shown in Exhibit 20A.3. The remainder of this section explains these computations.

EXHIBIT 20A.3

Equivalent Units of
Production—FIFO

Equivalent Units of Production	Direct Materials	Direct Labor	Factory Overhead
(a) Equivalent units to complete beginning goods in process			
Direct materials (30,000 × 0%)	0 EUP		
Direct labor (30,000 × 35%)		10,500 EUP	
Factory overhead (30,000 × 35%)			10,500 EUP
(b) Equivalent units started and completed*	70,000	70,000	70,000
(c) Equivalent units in ending goods in process			
Direct materials (20,000 × 100%)	20,000		
Direct labor (20,000 × 25%)		5,000	
Factory overhead (20,000 × 25%)			5,000
Equivalent units of production	90,000 EUP	85,500 EUP	85,500 EUP

*Units completed this period .... 100,000 units
 Less units in beginning goods in process 30,000
 Units started and completed this period .... 70,000 units

(a) Beginning Goods in Process   Under FIFO, we assume that production first completes any units started in the prior period. There were 30,000 physical units in beginning goods in process inventory. Those units were 100% complete with respect to direct materials as of the end of the prior period. This means that no materials (0%) are needed in April to complete those 30,000 units. So the equivalent units of *materials* to complete beginning goods in process are zero (30,000 × 0%)—see first row under row "(a)" in Exhibit 20A.3. The units in process as of April 1 had already been through 65% of production prior to this period and need only go through the remaining 35% of production. The equivalent units of *labor* to complete the beginning goods in process are 10,500 (30,000 × 35%)—see the second row under row "(a)." This implies that the amount of labor required this period to complete the 30,000 units started in the prior period is the amount of labor needed to make 10,500 units, start-to-finish. Finally, overhead is applied based on direct labor costs, so GenX computes equivalent units for overhead as it would for direct labor.

(b) Units Started and Completed This Period   After completing any beginning goods in process, FIFO assumes that production begins on newly started units. GenX began work on 90,000 new units this period. Of those units, 20,000 remain incomplete at period-end. This means that 70,000 of the units started in April were completed in April. These complete units have received 100% of materials, labor, and overhead. Exhibit 20A.3 reflects this by including 70,000 equivalent units (70,000 × 100%) of materials, labor, and overhead in its equivalent units of production—see row "(b)."

(c) Ending Goods in Process   The 20,000 units started in April that GenX was not able to complete by period-end consumed materials, labor, and overhead. Specifically, those 20,000 units received 100% of materials and, therefore, the equivalent units of materials in ending goods in process inventory are 20,000 (20,000 × 100%)—see the first row under row "(c)." For labor and overhead, the units in ending goods in process were 25% complete in production. This means the equivalent units of labor and overhead for those units are 5,000 (20,000 × 25%) as GenX incurs labor and overhead costs uniformly throughout its production process. Finally, for each input (direct materials, direct labor, and factory overhead), the equivalent units for each of the unit groups (a), (b), and (c) are added to determine the total equivalent units of production with respect to each—see the final row in Exhibit 20A.3.

Step 3: Compute Cost per Equivalent Unit—FIFO   To compute cost per equivalent unit, we take the product costs (for each of direct materials, direct labor, and factory overhead from Exhibit 20A.1) added in April and divide by the equivalent units of production from step 2. Exhibit 20A.4 illustrates these computations.

EXHIBIT 20A.4

Cost per Equivalent Unit of
Production—FIFO

Cost per Equivalent Unit of Production	Direct Materials	Direct Labor	Factory Overhead
Costs incurred this period	$9,900	$5,700	$6,840
÷ Equivalent units of production (from Step 2)	90,000 EUP	85,500 EUP	85,500 EUP
Cost per equivalent unit of production	$0.11 per EUP	$0.067 per EUP	$0.08 per EUP

It is essential to compute costs per equivalent unit for *each* input because production inputs are added at different times in the process. The FIFO method computes the cost per equivalent unit based solely on this period's EUP and costs (unlike the weighted-average method, which adds in the costs of the beginning goods in process inventory).

Step 4: Assign and Reconcile Costs The equivalent units determined in step 2 and the cost per equivalent unit computed in step 3 are both used to assign costs (1) to units that the production department completed and transferred to finished goods and (2) to units that remain in process at period-end.

In Exhibit 20A.5, under the section for cost of units transferred out, we see that the cost of units completed in April includes the $4,620 cost carried over from March for work already applied to the 30,000 units that make up beginning Goods in Process Inventory, plus the $1,544 incurred in April to complete those units. This section also includes the $17,990 of cost assigned to the 70,000 units started and completed this period. Thus, the total cost of goods manufactured in April is $24,154 ($4,620 + $1,544 + $17,990). The average cost per unit for goods completed in April is $0.242 ($24,154 ÷ 100,000 completed units).

EXHIBIT 20A.5

Report of Costs Accounted For—FIFO

Cost of units transferred out (cost of goods manufactured)		
Cost of beginning goods in process inventory............................		$ 4,620
Cost to complete beginning goods in process		
Direct materials ($0.11 per EUP × 0 EUP)............................	$ 0	
Direct labor ($0.067 per EUP × 10,500 EUP)	704	
Factory overhead ($0.08 per EUP × 10,500 EUP)	840	1,544
Cost of units started and completed this period		
Direct materials ($0.11 per EUP × 70,000 EUP)	7,700	
Direct labor ($0.067 per EUP × 70,000 EUP)	4,690	
Factory overhead ($0.08 per EUP × 70,000 EUP)	5,600	17,990
Total cost of units finished this period		24,154
Cost of ending goods in process inventory		
Direct materials ($0.11 per EUP × 20,000 EUP)	2,200	
Direct labor ($0.067 per EUP × 5,000 EUP)	335	
Factory overhead ($0.08 per EUP × 5,000 EUP)	400	
Total cost of ending goods in process inventory		2,935
Total costs accounted for		**$27,089**

The computation for cost of ending goods in process inventory is in the lower part of Exhibit 20A.5. The cost of units in process includes materials, labor, and overhead costs corresponding to the percentage of these resources applied to those incomplete units in April. That cost of $2,935 ($2,200 + $335 + $400) also is the ending balance for the Goods in Process Inventory account.

Management verifies that the total costs assigned to units transferred out and units still in process equal the total costs incurred by production. We reconcile the costs accounted for (in Exhibit 20A.5) to the costs that production was charged for as shown in Exhibit 20A.6.

EXHIBIT 20A.6

Report of Costs to Account For—FIFO

Cost of beginning goods in process inventory		
Direct materials	$3,300	
Direct labor	600	
Factory overhead	720	$ 4,620
Costs incurred this period		
Direct materials	9,900	
Direct labor..	5,700	
Factory overhead	6,840	22,440
Total costs to account for		**$27,060**

The production manager is responsible for $27,060 in costs: $4,620 that had been assigned to the department's Goods in Process Inventory as of April 1 plus $22,440 of materials, labor, and overhead costs the department incurred in April. At period-end, the manager must identify where those costs were assigned. The production manager can report that $24,154 of cost was assigned to units completed in April and $2,935 was assigned to units still in process at period-end. The sum of these amounts is $29 different from the $27,060 total costs incurred by production due to rounding in step 3—rounding errors are common and not a concern.

The final report is the process cost summary, which summarizes key information from Exhibits 20A.3, 20A.4, 20A.5, and 20A.6. Reasons for the summary are to (1) help managers control and monitor costs, (2) help upper management assess department manager performance, and (3) provide cost information for financial reporting. The process cost summary, using FIFO, for GenX is in Exhibit 20A.7. Section ◇ lists

EXHIBIT 20A.7

Process Cost Summary

GenX COMPANY
Process Cost Summary
For Month Ended April 30, 2011

Costs charged to production

Costs of beginning goods in process inventory

Direct materials...	$3,300	
Direct labor..	600	
Factory overhead	720	$ 4,620

① Costs incurred this period

Direct materials	9,900	
Direct labor..	5,700	
Factory overhead	6,840	22,440
Total costs to account for		$27,060

Unit cost information

Units to account for		Units accounted for	
Beginning goods in process.........	30,000	Transferred out.................	100,000
Units started this period...........	90,000	Ending goods in process..........	20,000
Total units to account for..........	120,000	Total units accounted for	120,000

Equivalent units of production	Direct Materials	Direct Labor	Factory Overhead
Equivalent units to complete beginning goods in process			
Direct materials (30,000 × 0%)	0 EUP		
Direct labor (30,000 × 35%)		10,500 EUP	
② Factory overhead (30,000 × 35%)			10,500 EUP
Equivalent units started and completed	70,000	70,000	70,000
Equivalent units in ending goods in process			
Direct materials (20,000 × 100%)	20,000		
Direct labor (20,000 × 25%)		5,000	
Factory overhead (20,000 × 25%)			5000
Equivalent units of production	90,000 EUP	85,500 EUP	85,500 EUP

Cost per equivalent unit of production	Direct Materials	Direct Labor	Factory Overhead
Costs incurred this period	$9,900	$5,700	$6,840
÷ Equivalent units of production	90,000 EUP	85,500 EUP	85,500 EUP
Cost per equivalent unit of production	$0.11 per EUP	$0.067 per EUP	$0.08 per EUP

Cost assignment and reconciliation

(cost of units completed and transferred out)

Cost of beginning goods in process		$ 4,620
Cost to complete beginning goods in process		
Direct materials ($0.11 per EUP × 0 EUP)	$ 0	
Direct labor ($0.067 per EUP × 10,500 EUP).................................	704	
Factory overhead ($0.08 per EUP × 10,500 EUP)	840	1,544
Cost of units started and completed this period		
Direct materials ($0.11 per EUP × 70,000 EUP)	7,700	
③ Direct labor ($0.067 per EUP × 70,000 EUP).................................	4,690	
Factory overhead ($0.08 per EUP × 70,000 EUP)	5,600	17,990
Total cost of units finished this period		24,154

Cost of ending goods in process

Direct materials ($0.11 per EUP × 20,000 EUP)	2,200	
Direct labor ($0.067 per EUP × 5,000 EUP).................................	335	
Factory overhead ($0.08 per EUP × 5,000 EUP)	400	
Total cost of ending goods in process.....................................		2,935
Total costs accounted for		$27,089*

reconciled

*$29 difference due to rounding

the total costs charged to the department, including direct materials, direct labor, and overhead costs incurred, as well as the cost of the beginning goods in process inventory. Section ◇2◇ describes the equivalent units of production for the department. Equivalent units for materials, labor, and overhead are in separate columns. It also reports direct materials, direct labor, and overhead costs per equivalent unit. Section ◇3◇ allocates total costs among units worked on in the period.

□ Decision Maker   Answer — p. 838

Cost Manager   As cost manager for an electronics manufacturer, you apply a process costing system using FIFO. Your company plans to adopt a just-in-time system and eliminate inventories. What is the impact of the use of FIFO (versus the weighted-average method) given these plans? ■

Summary

C1 Explain process operations and the way they differ from job order operations. Process operations produce large quantities of similar products or services by passing them through a series of processes, or steps, in production. Like job order operations, they combine direct materials, direct labor, and overhead in the operations. Unlike job order operations that assign the responsibility for each job to a manager, process operations assign the responsibility for each *process* to a manager.

C2 Define and compute equivalent units and explain their use in process cost accounting. Equivalent units of production measure the activity of a process as the number of units that would be completed in a period if all effort had been applied to units that were started and finished. This measure of production activity is used to compute the cost per equivalent unit and to assign costs to finished goods and goods in process inventory. To compute equivalent units, determine the number of units that would have been finished if all materials (or labor or overhead) had been used to produce units that were started and completed during the period. The costs incurred by a process are divided by its equivalent units to yield cost per unit.

C3 Define and prepare a process cost summary and describe its purposes. A process cost summary reports on the activities of a production process or department for a period. It describes the costs charged to the department, the equivalent units of production for the department, and the costs assigned to the output. The report aims to (1) help managers control their departments, (2) help factory managers evaluate department managers' performances, and (3) provide cost information for financial statements. A process cost summary includes the physical flow of units, equivalent units of production, costs per equivalent unit, and a cost reconciliation. It reports the units and costs to account for during the period and how they were accounted for during the period. In terms of units, the summary includes the beginning goods in process inventory and the units started during the month. These units are accounted for in terms of the goods completed and transferred out, and the ending goods in process inventory. With respect to costs, the summary includes materials, labor, and overhead costs assigned to the process during the period. It shows how these costs are assigned to goods completed and transferred out, and to ending goods in process inventory.

C4 Explain and illustrate the accounting for production activity using FIFO. The FIFO method for process costing is applied and illustrated to (1) report the physical flow of units, (2) compute the equivalent units of production, (3) compute the cost per equivalent unit of production, and (4) assign and reconcile costs.

A1 Compare process cost accounting and job order cost accounting. Process and job order manufacturing operations are similar in that both combine materials, labor, and factory overhead to produce products or services. They differ in the way they are organized and managed. In job order operations, the job order cost accounting system assigns materials, labor, and overhead to specific jobs. In process operations, the process cost accounting system assigns materials, labor, and overhead to specific processes. The total costs associated with each process are then divided by the number of units passing through that process to get cost per equivalent unit. The costs per equivalent unit for all processes are added to determine the total cost per unit of a product or service.

A2 Explain and illustrate a hybrid costing system. A hybrid costing system contains features of both job order and process costing systems. Generally, certain direct materials are accounted for by individual products as in job order costing, but direct labor and overhead costs are accounted for similar to process costing.

P1 Record the flow of direct materials costs in process cost accounting. Materials purchased are debited to a Raw Materials Inventory account. As direct materials are issued to processes, they are separately accumulated in a Goods in Process Inventory account for that process.

P2 Record the flow of direct labor costs in process cost accounting. Direct labor costs are initially debited to the Factory Payroll account. The total amount in it is then assigned to the Goods in Process Inventory account pertaining to each process.

P3 Record the flow of factory overhead costs in process cost accounting. The different factory overhead items are first accumulated in the Factory Overhead account and are then allocated, using a predetermined overhead rate, to the different processes. The allocated amount is debited to the Goods in Process Inventory account pertaining to each process.

P4 Record the transfer of completed goods to Finished Goods Inventory and Cost of Goods Sold. As units complete the final process and are eventually sold, their accumulated cost is transferred to Finished Goods Inventory and finally to Cost of Goods Sold.

Guidance Answers to Decision Maker and Decision Ethics

Budget Officer   By instructing you to classify a majority of costs as indirect, the manager is passing some of his department's costs to a common overhead pool that other departments will partially absorb. Since overhead costs are allocated on the basis of direct labor for this company and the new department has a relatively low direct labor cost, the new department will be assigned less overhead. Such action suggests unethical behavior by this manager. You must object to such reclassification. If this manager refuses to comply, you must inform someone in a more senior position.

Entrepreneur   By spreading the added quality-related costs across three customers, the entrepreneur is probably trying to remain competitive with respect to the customer that demands the 100%

quality inspection. Moreover, the entrepreneur is partly covering the added costs by recovering two-thirds of them from the other two customers who are paying 110% of total costs. This act likely breaches the trust placed by the two customers in this entrepreneur's application of its costing system. The costing system should be changed, and the entrepreneur should consider renegotiating the pricing and/or quality test agreement with this one customer (at the risk of losing this currently loss-producing customer).

Cost Manager   Differences between the FIFO and weighted-average methods are greatest when large work in process inventories exist and when costs fluctuate. The method used if inventories are eliminated does not matter; both produce identical costs.

Guidance Answers to Quick Checks

1. *c*

2. When a company produces large quantities of similar products/services, a process cost system is often more suitable.

3. *b*

4. The costs are direct materials, direct labor, and overhead.

5. A goods in process inventory account is needed for *each* production department.

6. *a*

7. Equivalent units with respect to direct labor are the number of units that would have been produced if all labor had been used on units that were started and finished during the period.

8.

Units completed and transferred out	58,000 EUP
Units of ending goods in process	
Direct labor (6,000 × 1/3)	2,000 EUP
Units of production	60,000 EUP

9. The first section shows the costs charged to the department. The second section describes the equivalent units produced by the department. The third section shows the assignment of total costs to units worked on during the period.

Key Terms

mhhe.com/wildFAP20e

Conversion costs per equivalent unit (p. 829)

Cost of goods manufactured (p. 827)

Equivalent units of production (EUP) (p. 821)

FIFO method (p. 833)

Job order cost accounting system (p. 817)

Materials consumption report (p. 818)

Process cost accounting system (p. 817)

Process cost summary (p. 826)

Process operations (p. 814)

Weighted-average method (p. 824)

Multiple Choice Quiz

Answers on p. 855   mhhe.com/wildFAP20e

Additional Quiz Questions are available at the book's Website.

1. Equivalent units of production are equal to
  a. Physical units that were completed this period from all effort being applied to them.
  b. The number of units introduced into the process this period.
  c. The number of finished units actually completed this period.
  d. The number of units that could have been started and completed given the cost incurred.
  e. The number of units in the process at the end of the period.

2. Recording the cost of raw materials purchased for use in a process costing system includes a
  a. Credit to Raw Materials Inventory.
  b. Debit to Goods in Process Inventory.
  c. Debit to Factory Overhead.
  d. Credit to Factory Overhead.
  e. Debit to Raw Materials Inventory.

3. The production department started the month with a beginning goods in process inventory of $20,000. During the month, it was assigned the following costs: direct materials, $152,000; direct labor, $45,000; overhead applied at the rate of 40% of direct labor cost. Inventory with a cost of $218,000 was transferred to finished goods. The ending balance of goods in process inventory is
  a. $330,000.
  b. $ 17,000.
  c. $220,000.
  d. $112,000.
  e. $118,000.

4. A company's beginning work in process inventory consists of 10,000 units that are 20% complete with respect to direct labor costs. A total of 40,000 units are completed this period. There are 15,000 units in goods in process, one-third complete for direct labor, at period-end. The equivalent units of production (EUP) with respect to direct labor at period-end, assuming the weighted-average method, are
  a. 45,000 EUP.
  b. 40,000 EUP.
  c. 5,000 EUP.
  d. 37,000 EUP.
  e. 43,000 EUP.

5. Assume the same information as in question 4. Also assume that beginning work in process had $6,000 in direct labor cost and that $84,000 in direct labor is added during this period. What is the cost per EUP for labor?
  a. $0.50 per EUP
  b. $1.87 per EUP
  c. $2.00 per EUP
  d. $2.10 per EUP
  e. $2.25 per EUP

> *Assume the weighted-average inventory method is used for all assignments unless stated differently.*

^A *Superscript letter A denotes assignments based on Appendix 20A.*

🎲 Icon denotes assignments that involve decision making.

Discussion Questions

1. 🎲 Can services be delivered by means of process operations? Support your answer with an example.

2. 🎲 What is the main factor for a company in choosing between the job order costing and process costing accounting systems? Give two likely applications of each system.

3. Identify the control document for materials flow when a materials requisition slip is not used.

4. The focus in a job order costing system is the job or batch. Identify the main focus in process costing.

5. Are the journal entries that match cost flows to product flows in process costing primarily the same or much different than those in job order costing? Explain.

6. 🎲 Explain in simple terms the notion of equivalent units of production (EUP). Why is it necessary to use EUP in process costing?

7. 🎲 What are the two main inventory methods used in process costing? What are the differences between these methods?

8. 🎲 Why is it possible for direct labor in process operations to include the labor of employees who do not work directly on products or services?

9. Assume that a company produces a single product by processing it first through a single production department. Direct labor costs flow through what accounts in this company's process cost system?

10. After all labor costs for a period are allocated, what balance should remain in the Factory Payroll account?

11. 🎲 Is it possible to have under- or overapplied overhead costs in a process cost accounting system? Explain.

12. Explain why equivalent units of production for both direct labor and overhead can be the same as, and why they can be different from, equivalent units for direct materials.

13. Companies such as **Palm** apply process operations. List the four steps in accounting for production activity in a reporting period (for process operations). **Palm**

14. Companies such as **Nokia** commonly prepare a process cost summary. What purposes does a process cost summary serve? **NOKIA**

15. 🎲 Are there situations where **Research In Motion** can use process costing? Identify at least one and explain it. **RIM**

16. 🎲 **Apple** produces iMacs with a multiple production line. Identify and list some of its production processing steps and departments. **Apple**

🅼 **connect**

For each of the following products and services, indicate whether it is most likely produced in a process operation or in a job order operation.

1. Luxury cars   **3.** Apple juice

2. Vanilla ice cream   **4.** Tennis courts

QUICK STUDY

QS 20-1
Process vs. job order operations
C1

QS 20-2

Recording costs of direct materials   P1

Sturdy Packaging makes cardboard shipping cartons in a single operation. This period, Sturdy purchased $125,000 in raw materials. Its production department requisitioned $90,000 of those materials for use in producing cartons. Prepare journal entries to record its (1) purchase of raw materials and (2) requisition of direct materials.

QS 20-3

Recording costs of direct labor

P2

Refer to the information in QS 20-2. Sturdy Packaging incurred $165,000 in factory payroll costs, of which $110,000 was direct labor. Prepare journal entries to record its (1) total factory payroll incurred and (2) direct labor used in production.

QS 20-4

Recording costs of factory overhead

P3

Refer to the information in QS 20-2 and QS 20-3. Sturdy Packaging requisitioned $62,000 of indirect materials from its raw materials and used $55,000 of indirect labor in its production of boxes. Also, it incurred $220,000 of other factory overhead costs. It applies factory overhead at the rate of 130% of direct labor costs. Prepare journal entries to record its (1) indirect materials requisitioned, (2) indirect labor used in production, (3) other factory overhead costs incurred, and (4) application of overhead to production.

QS 20-5

Recording transfer of costs to finished goods   P4

Refer to the information in QS 20-2, QS 20-3, and QS 20-4. Sturdy Packaging completed 175,000 boxes costing $335,000 and transferred them to finished goods. Prepare its journal entry to record the transfer of the boxes from production to finished goods inventory.

QS 20-6

Computing equivalent units of production

C2

The following refers to units processed in Heath Printing's binding department in June. Compute the total equivalent units of production with respect to labor for June using the weighted-average inventory method.

	Units of Product	Percent of Labor Added
Beginning goods in process	150,000	85%
Goods started	310,000	100
Goods completed	340,000	100
Ending goods in process	120,000	25

QS 20-7

Computing EUP cost   C2

The cost of beginning inventory plus the costs added during the period should equal the cost of units _____ plus the cost of _____.

QS 20-8

Hybrid costing   A2

Explain how a car maintenance and repair garage might use a hybrid costing system.

QS 20-9A

Computing equivalent units—FIFO   C4

Refer to QS 20-6 and compute the total equivalent units of production with respect to labor for June using the FIFO inventory method.

QS 20-10

Steps in process costing

C3

Put the four steps in accounting for production activities in the order in which they would occur.

a. Assign and reconcile costs

b. Compute the cost per equivalent unit

c. Compute equivalent units of production

d. Determine physical flow of units

List the headings of the three major sections of a process cost summary. Refer to Exhibit 20.17.

QS 20-11
Process cost summary C3

Anheuser-Busch InBev is attempting to reduce its water usage. How could a company manager use a process cost summary to determine if the program to reduce water usage is successful?

QS 20-12
Process cost summary C3

Label each statement below as either true ("T") or false ("F").

1. Job order and process operations both combine materials, labor, and overhead in producing products or services.
2. Costs per job are computed in both job order and process costing systems.
3. Service companies are not able to use process costing.
4. The cost per equivalent unit is computed as the total costs of a process divided by the number of equivalent units passing through that process.

QS 20-13
Process vs. job order costing
A1

connect

Match each of the following items A through G with the best numbered description of its purpose.

A. Process cost summary
B. Equivalent units of production
C. Goods in Process Inventory account
D. Raw Materials Inventory account
E. Materials requisition
F. Finished Goods Inventory account
G. Factory Overhead account

_____ **1.** Holds costs of materials until they are used in production or as factory overhead.
_____ **2.** Holds costs of indirect materials, indirect labor, and similar costs until assigned to production.
_____ **3.** Holds costs of direct materials, direct labor, and applied overhead until products are transferred from production to finished goods (or another department).
_____ **4.** Standardizes partially completed units into equivalent completed units.
_____ **5.** Holds costs of finished products until sold to customers.
_____ **6.** Describes the activity and output of a production department for a period.
_____ **7.** Notifies the materials manager to send materials to a production department.

EXERCISES

Exercise 20-1
Terminology in process cost accounting
C1 A1 P1 P2 P3

Prepare journal entries to record its following production activities.

1. Purchased $80,000 of raw materials on credit.
2. Used $34,000 of direct materials in production.
3. Used $41,000 of indirect materials.

Exercise 20-2
Recording costs of materials
P1

Prepare journal entries to record the following production activities.

1. Incurred total labor cost of $77,000, which is paid in cash.
2. Used $58,000 of direct labor in production.
3. Used $19,000 of indirect labor.

Exercise 20-3
Recording costs of labor
P2

Refer to information in Exercise 20-3. Prepare journal entries to record the following production activities.

1. Paid overhead costs (other than indirect materials and indirect labor) of $22,000.
2. Applied overhead at 90% of direct labor costs.

Exercise 20-4
Recording overhead costs
P3

Prepare journal entries to record the following production activities.

1. Transferred completed products with a cost of $137,000 to finished goods inventory.
2. Sold $450,000 of products on credit. Their cost is $150,000.

Exercise 20-5
Recording cost of completed goods
P4

Exercise 20-6

Recording cost flows in a process cost system

P1 P2 P3 P4

Lowes Lumber produces bagged bark for use in landscaping. Production involves packaging bark chips in plastic bags in a bagging department. The following information describes production operations for October.

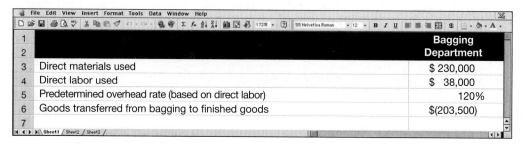

	Bagging Department
3 Direct materials used	$ 230,000
4 Direct labor used	$ 38,000
5 Predetermined overhead rate (based on direct labor)	120%
6 Goods transferred from bagging to finished goods	$(203,500)

Check (3) Cr. Factory Overhead, $45,600

The company's revenue for the month totaled $450,000 from credit sales, and its cost of goods sold for the month is $250,000. Prepare summary journal entries dated October 31 to record its October production activities for (1) direct material usage, (2) direct labor usage, (3) overhead allocation, (4) goods transfer from production to finished goods, and (5) sales.

Exercise 20-7

Interpretation of journal entries in process cost accounting

P1 P2 P3 P4

The following journal entries are recorded in Kiera Co.'s process cost accounting system. Kiera produces handbags and scarves. Overhead is applied to production based on direct labor cost for the period. Prepare a brief explanation (including any overhead rates applied) for each journal entry *a* through *j*.

a.	Raw Materials Inventory	54,000	
	Accounts Payable		54,000
b.	Goods in Process Inventory	44,000	
	Raw Materials Inventory		44,000
c.	Factory Payroll	36,000	
	Cash		36,000
d.	Goods in Process Inventory	28,000	
	Factory Payroll		28,000
e.	Factory Overhead	10,500	
	Cash		10,500
f.	Factory Overhead	3,000	
	Raw Materials Inventory		3,000

g.	Factory Overhead	8,000	
	Factory Payroll		8,000
h.	Goods in Process Inventory	35,000	
	Factory Overhead		35,000
i.	Finished Goods Inventory	98,000	
	Goods in Process Inventory		98,000
j.	Accounts Receivable	256,000	
	Sales		256,000
	Cost of Goods Sold	104,000	
	Finished Goods Inventory		104,000

Exercise 20-8

Computing equivalent units of production—weighted average

C2

During April, the production department of a process manufacturing system completed a number of units of a product and transferred them to finished goods. Of these transferred units, 37,500 were in process in the production department at the beginning of April and 150,000 were started and completed in April. April's beginning inventory units were 60% complete with respect to materials and 40% complete with respect to labor. At the end of April, 51,250 additional units were in process in the production department and were 80% complete with respect to materials and 30% complete with respect to labor.

1. Compute the number of units transferred to finished goods.

Check (2) EUP for materials, 228,500

2. Compute the number of equivalent units with respect to both materials used and labor used in the production department for April using the weighted-average method.

Exercise 20-9

Costs assigned to output and inventories—weighted average

C2 P4

The production department described in Exercise 20-8 had $531,480 of direct materials and $407,689 of direct labor cost charged to it during April. Also, its beginning inventory included $74,075 of direct materials cost and $28,493 of direct labor.

1. Compute the direct materials cost and the direct labor cost per equivalent unit for the department.

Check (1) $2.65 per EUP of direct materials

2. Using the weighted-average method, assign April's costs to the department's output—specifically, its units transferred to finished goods and its ending goods in process inventory.

Refer to the information in Exercise 20-8 to compute the number of equivalent units with respect to both materials used and labor used in the production department for April using the FIFO method.

Exercise 20-10ᴬ
Computing equivalent units of production—FIFO **C4**

Refer to the information in Exercise 20-8 and complete its parts (1) and (2) using the FIFO method.

Exercise 20-11ᴬ
Costs assigned to output—FIFO

C4 P4

The production department in a process manufacturing system completed 191,500 units of product and transferred them to finished goods during a recent period. Of these units, 31,500 were in process at the beginning of the period. The other 160,000 units were started and completed during the period. At period-end, 29,500 units were in process. Compute the department's equivalent units of production with respect to direct materials under each of three separate assumptions:

Exercise 20-12
Equivalent units computed—weighted average

C2

1. All direct materials are added to products when processing begins.
2. Direct materials are added to products evenly throughout the process. Beginning goods in process inventory was 40% complete, and ending goods in process inventory was 75% complete.
3. One-half of direct materials is added to products when the process begins and the other half is added when the process is 75% complete as to direct labor. Beginning goods in process inventory is 40% complete as to direct labor, and ending goods in process inventory is 60% complete as to direct labor.

Check   (3) EUP for materials, 206,250

Refer to the information in Exercise 20-12 and complete it for each of the three separate assumptions using the FIFO method for process costing.

Exercise 20-13ᴬ
Equivalent units computed—FIFO **C4**

Check   (3) EUP for materials, 190,500

The following flowchart shows the August production activity of the The Spade Company. Use the amounts shown on the flowchart to compute the missing four numbers identified by blanks.

Exercise 20-14
Flowchart of costs for a process operation P1 P2 P3 P4

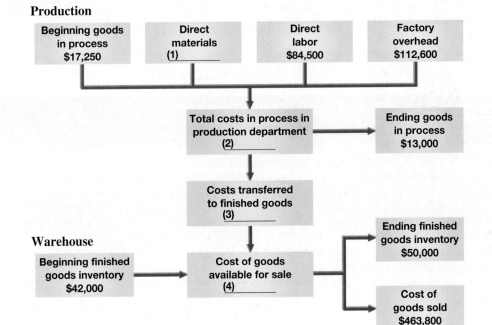

Exercise 20-15
Completing a process cost summary

C3

The following partially completed process cost summary describes the May production activities of Raman Company. Its production output is sent to its warehouse for shipping. Prepare its process cost summary using the weighted-average method.

Equivalent Units of Production	Direct Materials	Direct Labor	Factory Overhead
Units transferred out	128,000	128,000	128,000
Units of ending goods in process	10,000	6,000	6,000
Equivalent units of production	138,000	134,000	134,000

Costs per EUP	Direct Materials	Direct Labor	Factory Overhead
Costs of beginning goods in process	$ 37,100	$ 1,520	$ 3,040
Costs incurred this period	715,000	125,780	251,560
Total costs	$752,100	$127,300	$254,600

Units in beginning goods in process	8,000
Units started this period	130,000
Units completed and transferred out	128,000
Units in ending goods in process	10,000

Exercise 20-16
Process costing—weighted average   C3

Ebony Company uses the weighted-average method of process costing to assign production costs to its products. Information for April follows. Assume that all materials are added at the beginning of its production process, and that direct labor and factory overhead are added uniformly throughout the process.

Goods in process inventory, April 1 (4,000 units, 100% complete with respect to direct materials, 80% complete with respect to direct labor and overhead; includes $90,000 of direct material cost, $51,200 in direct labor cost, $61,440 overhead cost)	$202,640
Units started in April	56,000
Units completed and transferred to finished goods inventory	46,000
Goods in process inventory, April 30 (__?__ units, 100% complete with respect to direct materials, 40% complete with respect to direct labor and overhead)	?
Costs incurred in April	
Direct materials	$750,000
Direct labor	$310,000
Overhead applied at 120% of direct labor cost	?

Required

Fill in the blanks labeled *a* through *uu* in the following process cost summary.

EBONY COMPANY Process Cost Summary For Month Ended April 30		
Costs Charged to Production		
Costs of beginning goods in process		
Direct materials	$ 90,000	
Direct labor	51,200	
Factory overhead	61,440	$202,640
Costs incurred this period		
Direct materials	$750,000	
Direct labor	310,000	
Factory overhead	(a)_____	(b)_____
Total costs to account for		(c)_____

Check   (c) $1,634,640

[continued on next page]

[continued from previous page]

Unit Cost Information

Units to account for		Units accounted for	
Beginning goods in process	4,000	Completed and transferred out	46,000
Units started this period	56,000	Ending goods in process	(d)_____
Total units to account for	(e)_____	Total units accounted for	(f)_____

Equivalent Units of Production (EUP)

				Direct Materials	Direct Labor	Factory Overhead
Units completed and transferred out				(g)_____EUP	(h)_____EUP	(i)_____EUP
Units of ending goods in process						
Materials	(j)_____	×	100%	(k)_____EUP		
Direct labor	(l)_____	×	40%		(m)_____EUP	
Factory overhead	(n)_____	×	40%			(o)_____EUP
Equivalent units of production (EUP)				(p)_____EUP	(q)_____EUP	(r)_____EUP

Cost per EUP

	Direct Materials	Direct Labor	Factory Overhead
Costs of beginning goods in process	$ 90,000	$ 51,200	$61,440
Costs incurred this period	750,000	310,000	(s)_____
Total costs	$840,000	$361,200	(t)_____
÷ EUP	(u)_____	(v)_____	(w)_____
Cost per EUP	(x)_____	(y)_____	(z)_____

Check (z) $8.40 per EUP

Cost Assignment and Reconciliation

	Cost/EUP	×	EUP		
Costs transferred out					
Direct materials	(aa)_____	×	(bb)_____	(cc)_____	
Direct labor	(dd)_____	×	(ee)_____	(ff)_____	
Factory overhead	(gg)_____	×	(hh)_____	(ii)_____	
Costs of goods completed and transferred out					(jj)_____
Costs of ending goods in process					
Direct materials	(kk)_____	×	(ll)_____	(mm)_____	
Direct labor	(nn)_____	×	(oo)_____	(pp)_____	
Factory overhead	(qq)_____	×	(rr)_____	(ss)_____	
Costs of ending goods in process					(tt)_____
Total costs accounted for					(uu)_____

Exercise 20-17
Matching of product to cost accounting system
C1

For each of the following products and services, indicate whether it is most likely produced in a process operation or in a job order operation.

1. Door hardware
2. Cut flower arrangements
3. House paints
4. Concrete swimming pools
5. Custom tailored dresses
6. Grand pianos
7. Table lamps
8. Beach towels
9. Bolts and nuts
10. Lawn chairs
11. Headphones
12. Designed patio

Exercise 20-18
Compare process and job order operations
C1

Label each item *a* through *h* below as a feature of either a job order or process operation.

a. Routine, repetitive procedures
b. Custom orders
c. Low production volume
d. Heterogeneous products and services
e. Low product flexibility
f. Low product standardization
g. Focus on individual batch
h. Focus on standardized units

Exercise 20-19
Hybrid costing system
A2

Explain a hybrid costing system. Identify a product or service operation that might well fit a hybrid costing system.

PROBLEM SET A

Problem 20-1A
Production cost flow and
measurement; journal entries

P1 P2 P3 P4

Edison Company manufactures wool blankets and accounts for product costs using process costing. The
following information is available regarding its May inventories.

	Beginning Inventory	Ending Inventory
Raw materials inventory	$ 28,000	$ 25,500
Goods in process inventory	220,750	252,000
Finished goods inventory	319,000	277,000

The following additional information describes the company's production activities for May.

Raw materials purchases (on credit)	$ 135,000
Factory payroll cost (paid in cash)	791,500
Other overhead cost (Other Accounts credited)	43,000
Materials used	
Direct	$ 93,500
Indirect	31,000
Labor used	
Direct	$ 352,000
Indirect	439,500
Overhead rate as a percent of direct labor	110%
Sales (on credit)	$1,500,000

Check (1b) Cost of goods sold
$843,450

Required

1. Compute the cost of (a) products transferred from production to finished goods, and (b) goods sold.

2. Prepare summary journal entries dated May 31 to record the following production activities during
May: (a) raw materials purchases, (b) direct materials usage, (c) indirect materials usage, (d) payroll
costs, (e) direct labor costs, (f) indirect labor costs, (g) other overhead costs, (h) overhead applied,
(i) goods transferred from production to finished goods, and (j) sale of finished goods.

Problem 20-2A
Cost per equivalent unit; costs
assigned to products

C2 C3

mhhe.com/wildFAP20e

Fairfax Company uses weighted-average process costing to account for its production costs. Direct labor
is added evenly throughout the process. Direct materials are added at the beginning of the process. During
September, the company transferred 735,000 units of product to finished goods. At the end of September,
the goods in process inventory consists of 207,000 units that are 90% complete with respect to labor.
Beginning inventory had $244,920 of direct materials and $69,098 of direct labor cost. The direct labor
cost added in September is $1,312,852, and the direct materials cost added is $1,639,080.

Required

1. Determine the equivalent units of production with respect to (a) direct labor and (b) direct materials.

Check (2) Direct labor cost per
equivalent unit, $1.50

(3b) $693,450

2. Compute both the direct labor cost and the direct materials cost per equivalent unit.

3. Compute both direct labor cost and direct materials cost assigned to (a) units completed and transferred out, and (b) ending goods in process inventory.

Analysis Component

4. The company sells and ships all units to customers as soon as they are completed. Assume that an error
is made in determining the percentage of completion for units in ending inventory. Instead of being
90% complete with respect to labor, they are actually 65% complete. Write a one-page memo to the
plant manager describing how this error affects its September financial statements.

Li Company produces large quantities of a standardized product. The following information is available for its production activities for January.

Problem 20-3A
Journalizing in process costing; equivalent units and costs

C2 P1 P2 P3

Raw materials			Factory overhead incurred		
Beginning inventory		$ 26,000	Indirect materials used		$ 81,500
Raw materials purchased (on credit)		255,000	Indirect labor used		50,000
Direct materials used		(172,000)	Other overhead costs		159,308
Indirect materials used		(81,500)	Total factory overhead incurred		$290,808
Ending inventory		$ 27,500			
			Factory overhead applied		
Factory payroll			**(140% of direct labor cost)**		
Direct labor used		$207,720	Total factory overhead applied		$290,808
Indirect labor used		50,000			
Total payroll cost (paid in cash)		$257,720			

Additional information about units and costs of production activities follows.

Units		Costs		
Beginning goods in process inventory	2,200	Beginning goods in process inventory		
Started	30,000	Direct materials	$3,500	
Ending goods in process inventory	5,900	Direct labor	3,225	
		Factory overhead	4,515	$ 11,240
Status of ending goods in process inventory		Direct materials added		172,000
Materials—Percent complete	50%	Direct labor added		207,720
Labor and overhead—Percent complete	65%	Overhead applied (140% of direct labor)		290,808
		Total costs		$681,768
		Ending goods in process inventory		$ 82,128

During January, 55,000 units of finished goods are sold for $50 cash each. Cost information regarding finished goods follows.

Beginning finished goods inventory	$155,000
Cost transferred in	599,640
Cost of goods sold	(612,500)
Ending finished goods inventory	$142,140

Required

1. Prepare journal entries dated January 31 to record the following January activities: (a) purchase of raw materials, (b) direct materials usage, (c) indirect materials usage, (d) factory payroll costs, (e) direct labor costs used in production, (f) indirect labor costs, (g) other overhead costs—credit Other Accounts, (h) overhead applied, (i) goods transferred to finished goods, and (j) sale of finished goods.

2. Prepare a process cost summary report for this company, showing costs charged to production, units cost information, equivalent units of production, cost per EUP, and its cost assignment and reconciliation.

Check (2) Cost per equivalent unit: materials, $6.00; labor, $7.00; overhead, $9.80

Analysis Component

3. The company provides incentives to its department managers by paying monthly bonuses based on their success in controlling costs per equivalent unit of production. Assume that the production department underestimates the percentage of completion for units in ending inventory with the result that

its equivalent units of production in ending inventory for January are understated. What impact does this error have on the January bonuses paid to the production managers? What impact, if any, does this error have on February bonuses?

Problem 20-4A
Process cost summary; equivalent units

C2 C3 P4

mhhe.com/wildFAP20e

Easton Co. produces its product through a single processing department. Direct materials are added at the start of production, and direct labor and overhead are added evenly throughout the process. The company uses monthly reporting periods for its weighted-average process cost accounting system. Its Goods in Process Inventory account follows after entries for direct materials, direct labor, and overhead costs for October.

Goods in Process Inventory			Acct. No. 133		
Date		Explanation	Debit	Credit	Balance
Oct.	1	Balance			348,638
	31	Direct materials	104,090		452,728
	31	Direct labor	416,360		869,088
	31	Applied overhead	244,920		1,114,008

Its beginning goods in process consisted of $60,830 of direct materials, $176,820 of direct labor, and $110,988 of factory overhead. During October, the company started 280,000 units and transferred 306,000 units to finished goods. At the end of the month, the goods in process inventory consisted of 41,200 units that were 80% complete with respect to direct labor and factory overhead.

Required

Check (1) Costs transferred to finished goods, $1,002,150

1. Prepare the company's process cost summary for October using the weighted-average method.

2. Prepare the journal entry dated October 31 to transfer the cost of the completed units to finished goods inventory.

Problem 20-5A
Process cost summary, equivalent units, cost estimates

C2 C3 P4

Ogden Co. manufactures a single product in one department. All direct materials are added at the beginning of the manufacturing process. Direct labor and overhead are added evenly throughout the process. The company uses monthly reporting periods for its weighted-average process cost accounting. During October, the company completed and transferred 22,200 units of product to finished goods inventory. Its 3,000 units of beginning goods in process consisted of $9,900 of direct materials, $61,650 of direct labor, and $49,320 of factory overhead. It has 2,400 units (100% complete with respect to direct materials and 80% complete with respect to direct labor and overhead) in process at month-end. After entries to record direct materials, direct labor, and overhead for October, the company's Goods in Process Inventory account follows.

Goods in Process Inventory			Acct. No. 133		
Date		Explanation	Debit	Credit	Balance
Oct.	1	Balance			120,870
	31	Direct materials	248,400		369,270
	31	Direct labor	601,650		970,920
	31	Applied overhead	481,320		1,452,240

Required

Check (1) EUP for labor and overhead, 24,120 EUP

(2) Cost transferred to finished goods, $1,332,000

1. Prepare the company's process cost summary for October using the weighted-average method.

2. Prepare the journal entry dated October 31 to transfer the cost of completed units to finished goods inventory.

Analysis Components

3. The cost accounting process depends on numerous estimates.

 a. Identify two major estimates that determine the cost per equivalent unit.

 b. In what direction might you anticipate a bias from management for each estimate in part 3a (assume that management compensation is based on maintaining low inventory amounts)? Explain your answer.

Refer to the data in Problem 20-5A. Assume that Ogden uses the FIFO method to account for its process costing system. The following additional information is available:

● Beginning goods in process consisted of 3,000 units that were 100% complete with respect to direct materials and 40% complete with respect to direct labor and overhead.

● Of the 22,200 units completed, 3,000 were from beginning goods in process. The remaining 19,200 were units started and completed during October.

Required

1. Prepare the company's process cost summary for October using FIFO.

2. Prepare the journal entry dated October 31 to transfer the cost of completed units to finished goods inventory.

Problem 20-6Aᴬ
Process cost summary; equivalent units; cost estimates—FIFO

C3 C4 P4

Check (1) EUP for labor and overhead, 22,920 EUP

(2) Cost transferred to finished goods, $1,333,920

Tarick Toys Company manufactures video game consoles and accounts for product costs using process costing. The following information is available regarding its June inventories.

	Beginning Inventory	Ending Inventory
Raw materials inventory	$ 54,000	$ 82,500
Goods in process inventory	117,000	187,500
Finished goods inventory	120,000	148,500

The following additional information describes the company's production activities for June.

Raw materials purchases (on credit)	$150,000
Factory payroll cost (paid in cash)	300,000
Other overhead cost (Other Accounts credited)	127,875
Materials used	
Direct	$ 90,000
Indirect	31,500
Labor used	
Direct	$262,500
Indirect	37,500
Overhead rate as a percent of direct labor	75%
Sales (on credit)	$750,000

Required

1. Compute the cost of (a) products transferred from production to finished goods, and (b) goods sold.

2. Prepare journal entries dated June 30 to record the following production activities during June: (a) raw materials purchases, (b) direct materials usage, (c) indirect materials usage, (d) payroll costs, (e) direct labor costs, (f) indirect labor costs, (g) other overhead costs, (h) overhead applied, (i) goods transferred from production to finished goods, and (j) sale of finished goods.

PROBLEM SET B

Problem 20-1B
Production cost flow and measurement; journal entries

P1 P2 P3 P4

Check (1b) Cost of goods sold, $450,375

Eden Company uses process costing to account for its production costs. Direct labor is added evenly throughout the process. Direct materials are added at the beginning of the process. During April, the production department transferred 40,000 units of product to finished goods. Beginning goods in process had $116,000 of direct materials and $172,800 of direct labor cost. At the end of April, the goods in process inventory consists of 4,000 units that are 25% complete with respect to labor. The direct materials cost added in April is $1,424,000, and direct labor cost added is $3,960,000.

Problem 20-2B
Cost per equivalent unit; costs assigned to products

C2 C3

Required

1. Determine the equivalent units of production with respect to (a) direct labor and (b) direct materials.

2. Compute both the direct labor cost and the direct materials cost per equivalent unit.

3. Compute both direct labor cost and direct materials cost assigned to (a) units completed and transferred out, and (b) ending goods in process inventory.

Analysis Component

4. The company sells and ships all units to customers as soon as they are completed. Assume that an error is made in determining the percentage of completion for units in ending inventory. Instead of being 30% complete with respect to labor, they are actually 75% complete. Write a one-page memo to the plant manager describing how this error affects its April financial statements.

Problem 20-3B

Journalizing in process costing; equivalent units and costs

C2 P1 P2 P3 P4

Ying Company produces large quantities of a standardized product. The following information is available for its production activities for March.

Raw materials		Factory overhead incurred	
Beginning inventory	$ 16,000	Indirect materials used	$20,280
Raw materials purchased (on credit)	110,560	Indirect labor used	18,160
Direct materials used	(98,560)	Other overhead costs	17,216
Indirect materials used	(20,280)	Total factory overhead incurred	$55,656
Ending inventory	$ 7,720		
		Factory overhead applied	
Factory payroll		**(90% of direct labor cost)**	
Direct labor used	$ 61,840	Total factory overhead applied	$55,656
Indirect labor used	18,160		
Total payroll cost (paid in cash)	$ 80,000		

Additional information about units and costs of production activities follows.

Units		Costs		
Beginning goods in process inventory	8,000	Beginning goods in process inventory		
Started	24,000	Direct materials	$2,240	
Ending goods in process inventory	6,000	Direct labor	1,410	
		Factory overhead	1,269	$ 4,919
Status of ending goods in process inventory		Direct materials added		98,560
Materials—Percent complete	100%	Direct labor added		61,840
Labor and overhead—Percent complete	25%	Overhead applied (90% of direct labor) . . .		55,656
		Total costs		$220,975
		Ending goods in process inventory		$ 25,455

During March, 45,000 units of finished goods are sold for $25 cash each. Cost information regarding finished goods follows.

Beginning finished goods inventory	$ 74,200
Cost transferred in from production	195,520
Cost of goods sold	(225,000)
Ending finished goods inventory	$ 44,720

Required

1. Prepare journal entries dated March 31 to record the following March activities: (a) purchase of raw materials, (b) direct materials usage, (c) indirect materials usage, (d) factory payroll costs, (e) direct labor costs used in production, (f) indirect labor costs, (g) other overhead costs—credit Other Accounts, (h) overhead applied, (i) goods transferred to finished goods, and (j) sale of finished goods.

2. Prepare a process cost summary report for this company, showing costs charged to production, unit cost information, equivalent units of production, cost per EUP, and its cost assignment and reconciliation.

Analysis Component

3. This company provides incentives to its department managers by paying monthly bonuses based on their success in controlling costs per equivalent unit of production. Assume that production overestimates the percentage of completion for units in ending inventory with the result that its equivalent units of production in ending inventory for March are overstated. What impact does this error have on bonuses paid to the managers of the production department? What impact, if any, does this error have on these managers' April bonuses?

Basilex Company produces its product through a single processing department. Direct materials are added at the beginning of the process. Direct labor and overhead are added to the product evenly throughout the process. The company uses monthly reporting periods for its weighted-average process cost accounting. Its Goods in Process Inventory account follows after entries for direct materials, direct labor, and overhead costs for November.

Problem 20-4B
Process cost summary; equivalent units

C2 C3 P4

Goods in Process Inventory				Acct. No. 133
Date	Explanation	Debit	Credit	Balance
Nov. 1	Balance			10,650
30	Direct materials	58,200		68,850
30	Direct labor	213,400		282,250
30	Applied overhead	320,100		602,350

The 7,500 units of beginning goods in process consisted of $3,400 of direct materials, $2,900 of direct labor, and $4,350 of factory overhead. During November, the company finished and transferred 100,000 units of its product to finished goods. At the end of the month, the goods in process inventory consisted of 12,000 units that were 100% complete with respect to direct materials and 25% complete with respect to direct labor and factory overhead.

Required

1. Prepare the company's process cost summary for November using the weighted-average method.

2. Prepare the journal entry dated November 30 to transfer the cost of the completed units to finished goods inventory.

Check (1) Cost transferred to finished goods, $580,000

Oakley International Co. manufactures a single product in one department. Direct labor and overhead are added evenly throughout the process. Direct materials are added as needed. The company uses monthly reporting periods for its weighted-average process cost accounting. During March, Oakley completed and transferred 220,000 units of product to finished goods inventory. Its 10,000 units of beginning goods in process consisted of $16,800 of direct materials, $27,920 of direct labor, and $69,800 of factory overhead. 40,000 units (50% complete with respect to direct materials and 30% complete with respect to direct labor and overhead) are in process at month-end. After entries for direct materials, direct labor, and overhead for March, the company's Goods in Process Inventory account follows.

Problem 20-5B
Process cost summary; equivalent units; cost estimates

C2 C3 P4

Goods in Process Inventory				Acct. No. 133
Date	Explanation	Debit	Credit	Balance
Mar. 1	Balance			114,520
31	Direct materials	223,200		337,720
31	Direct labor	352,560		690,280
31	Applied overhead	881,400		1,571,680

Required

1. Prepare the company's process cost summary for March using the weighted-average method.

2. Prepare the journal entry dated March 31 to transfer the cost of completed units to finished goods inventory.

Check (1) EUP for labor and overhead, 232,000

(2) Cost transferred to finished goods, $1,482,800

Analysis Components

3. The cost accounting process depends on several estimates.

a. Identify two major estimates that affect the cost per equivalent unit.

b. In what direction might you anticipate a bias from management for each estimate in part 3a (assume that management compensation is based on maintaining low inventory amounts)? Explain your answer.

Problem 20-6B[A]
Process cost summary;
equivalent units; cost
estimates—FIFO

C3 C4 P4

Refer to the information in Problem 20-5B. Assume that Oakley International uses the FIFO method to account for its process costing system. The following additional information is available.

- Beginning goods in process consists of 10,000 units that were 75% complete with respect to direct materials and 60% complete with respect to direct labor and overhead.

- Of the 220,000 units completed, 10,000 were from beginning goods in process; the remaining 210,000 were units started and completed during March.

Required

Check (1) Labor and overhead EUP, 226,000

(2) Cost transferred, $1,486,960

1. Prepare the company's process cost summary for March using FIFO. Round cost per EUP to one-tenth of a cent.

2. Prepare the journal entry dated March 31 to transfer the cost of completed units to finished goods inventory.

SERIAL PROBLEM
Business Solutions

C1 A1

(This serial problem began in Chapter 1 and continues through most of the book. If previous chapter segments were not completed, the serial problem can begin at this point.)

SP 20 The computer workstation furniture manufacturing that Santana Rey started is progressing well. At this point, Santana is using a job order costing system to account for the production costs of this product line. Santana has heard about process costing and is wondering whether process costing might be a better method for her to keep track of and monitor her production costs.

Required

1. What are the features that distinguish job order costing from process costing?

2. Do you believe that Santana should continue to use job order costing or switch to process costing for her workstation furniture manufacturing? Explain.

COMPREHENSIVE PROBLEM

Major League Bat
Company
(Review of Chapters 2, 5, 18, 20)

CP 20 Major League Bat Company manufactures baseball bats. In addition to its goods in process inventories, the company maintains inventories of raw materials and finished goods. It uses raw materials as direct materials in production and as indirect materials. Its factory payroll costs include direct labor for production and indirect labor. All materials are added at the beginning of the process, and direct labor and factory overhead are applied uniformly throughout the production process.

Required

You are to maintain records and produce measures of inventories to reflect the July events of this company. Set up the following general ledger accounts and enter the June 30 balances: Raw Materials Inventory, $25,000; Goods in Process Inventory, $8,135 ($2,660 of direct materials, $3,650 of direct labor, and $1,825 of overhead); Finished Goods Inventory, $110,000; Sales, $0; Cost of Goods Sold, $0; Factory Payroll, $0; and Factory Overhead, $0.

1. Prepare journal entries to record the following July transactions and events.

a. Purchased raw materials for $125,000 cash (the company uses a perpetual inventory system).

b. Used raw materials as follows: direct materials, $52,440; and indirect materials, $10,000.

c. Incurred factory payroll cost of $227,250 paid in cash (ignore taxes).

d. Assigned factory payroll costs as follows: direct labor, $202,250; and indirect labor, $25,000.

e. Incurred additional factory overhead costs of $80,000 paid in cash.

f. Allocated factory overhead to production at 50% of direct labor costs.

Check (1f) Cr. Factory Overhead, $101,125

2. Information about the July inventories follows. Use this information with that from part 1 to prepare a process cost summary, assuming the weighted-average method is used.

Check   (2) EUP for overhead, 14,200

Units	
Beginning inventory	5,000 units
Started	14,000 units
Ending inventory	8,000 units
Beginning inventory	
Materials—Percent complete	100%
Labor and overhead—Percent complete	75%
Ending inventory	
Materials—Percent complete	100%
Labor and overhead—Percent complete	40%

3. Using the results from part 2 and the available information, make computations and prepare journal entries to record the following:

a. Total costs transferred to finished goods for July (label this entry g).

b. Sale of finished goods costing $265,700 for $625,000 in cash (label this entry h).

(3a) $271,150

4. Post entries from parts 1 and 3 to the ledger accounts set up at the beginning of the problem.

5. Compute the amount of gross profit from the sales in July. (*Note:* Add any underapplied overhead to, or deduct any overapplied overhead from, the cost of goods sold. Ignore the corresponding journal entry.)

Beyond the Numbers

BTN 20-1   Research In Motion reports in notes to its financial statements that, in addition to its merchandise sold, it includes the following costs (among others) in cost of goods sold: customer shipping and handling expenses, warranty expenses, and depreciation expense on assets used in manufacturing.

REPORTING IN ACTION

C2

RIM

Required

1. Why do you believe Research In Motion includes these costs in its cost of goods sold?

2. What effect does this cost accounting policy for its cost of goods sold have on Research In Motion's financial statements and any analysis of these statements? Explain.

Fast Forward

3. Access Research In Motion's financial statements for the fiscal years after February 27, 2010, from its Website (**RIM.com**) or the SEC's EDGAR Website (**sec.gov**). Review its footnote relating to Critical Accounting Policies and Estimates. Has Research In Motion changed its policy with respect to what costs are included in the cost of goods sold? Explain.

BTN 20-2   Manufacturers such as **Research In Motion, Apple,** and **Palm** usually work to maintain a high-quality and low-cost operation. One ratio routinely computed for this assessment is the cost of goods sold divided by total expenses. A decline in this ratio can mean that the company is spending too much on selling and administrative activities. An increase in this ratio beyond a reasonable level can mean that the company is not spending enough on selling activities. (Assume for this analysis that total expenses equal the cost of goods sold plus selling, general, and administrative expenses.)

COMPARATIVE ANALYSIS

C1

RIM

Apple

Palm

Required

1. For Research In Motion, Apple, and Palm refer to Appendix A and compute the ratios of cost of goods sold to total expenses for their two most recent fiscal years. (Record answers as percents, rounded to one decimal.)

2. Comment on the similarities or differences in the ratio results across both years among the companies.

ETHICS CHALLENGE

C1

BTN 20-3 Many accounting and accounting-related professionals are skilled in financial analysis, but most are not skilled in manufacturing. This is especially the case for process manufacturing environments (for example, a bottling plant or chemical factory). To provide professional accounting and financial services, one must understand the industry, product, and processes. We have an ethical responsibility to develop this understanding before offering services to clients in these areas.

Required

Write a one-page action plan, in memorandum format, discussing how you would obtain an understanding of key business processes of a company that hires you to provide financial services. The memorandum should specify an industry, a product, and one selected process and should draw on at least one reference, such as a professional journal or industry magazine.

COMMUNICATING IN PRACTICE

A1 C1 P1 P2

BTN 20-4 You hire a new assistant production manager whose prior experience is with a company that produced goods to order. Your company engages in continuous production of homogeneous products that go through various production processes. Your new assistant e-mails you questioning some cost classifications on an internal report—specifically why the costs of some materials that do not actually become part of the finished product, including some labor costs not directly associated with producing the product, are classified as direct costs. Respond to this concern via memorandum.

TAKING IT TO THE NET

C1

BTN 20-5 Many companies acquire software to help them monitor and control their costs and as an aid to their accounting systems. One company that supplies such software is **proDacapo** (**prodacapo.com**). There are many other such vendors. Access proDacapo's Website, click on "Prodacapo Process Management," and review the information displayed.

Required

How is process management software helpful to businesses? Explain with reference to costs, efficiency, and examples, if possible.

TEAMWORK IN ACTION

C1 P1 P2 P3 P4

BTN 20-6 The purpose of this team activity is to ensure that each team member understands process operations and the related accounting entries. Find the activities and flows identified in Exhibit 20.4 with numbers ①–⑩. Pick a member of the team to start by describing activity number ① in this exhibit, then verbalizing the related journal entry, and describing how the amounts in the entry are computed. The other members of the team are to agree or disagree; discussion is to continue until all members express understanding. Rotate to the next numbered activity and next team member until all activities and entries have been discussed. If at any point a team member is uncertain about an answer, the team member may pass and get back in the rotation when he or she can contribute to the team's discussion.

ENTREPRENEURIAL DECISION

C3 A2

BTN 20-7 This chapter's opener featured Jeff Avallon, John Goscha and Morgen Newman and their company **IdeaPaint**.

Required

1. How would a process cost summary differ between IdeaPaint and a competitor making dry-erase whiteboards?

2. How does not holding raw materials inventories reduce costs? If the items are not used in production, how can they impact profits? Explain.

3. Suppose IdeaPaint decides to allow customers to make their own unique paint colors. Why might the company then use a process costing system?

BTN 20-8 In process costing, the process is analyzed first and then a unit measure is computed in the form of equivalent units for direct materials, direct labor, overhead, and all three combined. The same analysis applies to both manufacturing and service processes.

HITTING THE ROAD

C2

Required

Visit your local **U.S. Mail** center. Look into the back room, and you will see several ongoing processes. Select one process, such as sorting, and list the costs associated with this process. Your list should include materials, labor, and overhead; be specific. Classify each cost as fixed or variable. At the bottom of your list, outline how overhead should be assigned to your identified process. The following format (with an example) is suggested.

Point: The class can compare and discuss the different processes studied and the answers provided.

Cost Description	Direct Material	Direct Labor	Overhead	Variable Cost	Fixed Cost
Manual sorting		X		X	
⋮					
Overhead allocation suggestions:					

BTN 20-9 **Nokia, Research In Motion, Apple,** and **Palm** are competitors in the global marketplace. Selected data for Nokia follow.

GLOBAL DECISION

C1

NOKIA

RIM

Apple

Palm

(millions of euros)	Current Year	Prior Year
Cost of goods sold	€27,720	€33,337
General, selling, and administrative expenses	5,078	5,664
Total expenses	€32,798	€39,001

Required

1. Review the discussion of the importance of the cost of goods sold divided by total expenses ratio in BTN 20-2. Compute the cost of goods sold to total expenses ratio for Nokia for the two years of data provided. (Record answers as percents, rounded to one decimal.)

2. Comment on the similarities or differences in the ratio results calculated in part 1 and in BTN 20-2 across years and companies. (Record answers as percents, rounded to one decimal.)

ANSWERS TO MULTIPLE CHOICE QUIZ

1. d

2. e

3. b; $20,000 + $152,000 + $45,000 + $18,000 − $218,000 = $17,000

4. a; 40,000 + (15,000 × 1/3) = 45,000 EUP

5. c; ($6,000 + $84,000) ÷ 45,000 EUP = $2 per EUP

21

Cost Allocation and Performance Measurement

A Look Back

Chapter 20 focused on how to measure and account for costs in process operations. It explained process production, described how to assign costs to processes, and computed cost per equivalent unit.

A Look at This Chapter

This chapter describes cost allocation and activity-based costing. It identifies managerial reports useful in directing a company's activities. It also describes responsibility accounting, measuring departmental performance, transfer pricing, and allocating common costs across departments.

A Look Ahead

Chapter 22 looks at cost behavior and explains how its identification is useful to managers in performing cost-volume-profit analyses. It also shows how to apply cost-volume-profit analysis for managerial decisions.

Learning Objectives

CAP

CONCEPTUAL

C1 Distinguish between direct and indirect expenses and identify bases for allocating indirect expenses to departments. (p. 865)

C2 Explain controllable costs and responsibility accounting. (p. 875)

C3 *Appendix 21A*—Explain transfer pricing and methods to set transfer prices. (p. 882)

C4 *Appendix 21B*—Describe allocation of joint costs across products. (p. 883)

ANALYTICAL

A1 Analyze investment centers using return on assets, residual income, and balanced scorecard. (p. 873)

A2 Analyze investment centers using profit margin and investment turnover. (p. 878)

LP21

PROCEDURAL

P1 Assign overhead costs using two-stage cost allocation. (p. 858)

P2 Assign overhead costs using activity-based costing. (p. 860)

P3 Prepare departmental income statements and contribution reports. (p. 867)

© MATTHEW TURLEY

Decision Insight

This Buds for You

"No good ideas come from sitting in an office"
—**RICK ALDEN**

PARK CITY, UT—Inspiration hit Rick Alden on a ski lift in Utah. While he was listening to music, his cell phone rang, and Rick fumbled around for the right device. Then a thought struck Rick: Why not make headphones that work together with cellphones and other mobile accessories? Why not target the 12 to 25 year-olds he saw snowboarding? Immediately getting to work, Rick designed headphones and earbuds in bright colors and skater patterns and came up with a cool name for his company.

Today, Rick's company **Skullcandy (SkullCandy.com)** is a fast-growing business that designs headphones, audio accessories, apparel, and audio-enabled lifestyle products like backpacks with built-in speakers and iPod controls. Skullcandy's product designs, drawn from hip-hop culture, let wearers show the world they are into the cool lifestyle of skiers, surfers, and skaters. The company also partners with brands like Burton Snowboards and users like Metallica and Snoop Dogg to stay cool. Skullcandy headquarters is a fun place to work, with surf retreats to reward good work, skateboards for traveling between offices, and a half-pipe behind the office. "The vibe is creative," says art director Kevin Horsburgh.

The company offers a diverse product line of edgy headphones, speaker-equipped backpacks and helmets, and mp3-equipped watches. This diversity of product offerings requires attention to cost management. Explaining that production factories were not willing to take a risk on his ideas, Rick laughs that "the first year we had to pay 100 percent of our costs upfront." Now, company managers monitor direct, indirect, and controllable costs and allocate them to departments and products. Understanding how its product lines are performing and their contribution margins helps Skullcandy plan for expansion. "We measure return on investment (ROI)," explains Rick. "We will expand as long as there are customers to win." Currently number two in its industry, the company hopes customer loyalty will propel it to number one.

As Skullcandy continues to grow, Rick critically focuses on contribution margins, investment turnover, and other performance indicators such as customer approval ratings and on-time delivery rates. But, to seek inspiration, Rick and his team "head to the mountain." "No good ideas ever come from sitting in an office," says Rick. "Not around here at least."

Sources: *Skullcandy Website,* January 2011; *Salt Lake Tribune,* April 20, 2009; *Entrepreneur,* January 2010; *Fortune,* December 30, 2008.

This chapter describes how to allocate costs shared by more than one product across those different products and how to allocate indirect costs of shared items such as utilities, advertising, and rent. The chapter also describes activity-based costing and how it traces the costs of individual activities. This knowledge helps managers better understand how to assign costs and assess company performance. The chapter also introduces additional managerial accounting reports useful in managing a company's activities and explains how and why management divides companies into departments.

Cost Allocation and Performance Measurement

Overhead Cost Allocation Methods	Departmental Accounting	Departmental Expense Allocation	Investment Centers	Responsibility Accounting
• Two-stage cost allocation • Activity-based cost allocation • Comparison of allocation methods	• Motivation for departmentalization • Departmental evaluation	• Direct and indirect expenses • Allocation of indirect expenses • Departmental income statements and contribution to overhead	• Financial performance measures • Nonfinancial performance measures	• Controllable versus direct costs • Responsibility accounting system • Transfer pricing

Section 1—Allocating Costs for Product Costing

Managers focus on different costs for different decisions. This requires different cost allocation methods to fit these decisions. This first of two sections in this chapter focuses on alternatives for allocation of costs to products and services. We explain and illustrate two basic methods: (1) traditional two-stage cost allocation and (2) activity-based cost allocation. The second section describes and illustrates the allocation of costs for performance evaluation.

OVERHEAD COST ALLOCATION METHODS

P1 Assign overhead costs using two-stage cost allocation.

Point: Use of a single overhead allocation rate is known as using a *plantwide rate*.

We previously explained how to assign overhead costs to jobs (and processes) by using a predetermined overhead rate per unit of an allocation base such as direct labor cost. When a single overhead rate is used on a companywide basis, all overhead is lumped together, and a predetermined overhead rate per unit of an allocation base is computed and used to assign overhead to jobs (and processes). The use of a single predetermined overhead rate suggests that this allocation process is simple. In reality, it can be complicated. This chapter explains the traditional two-stage cost allocation procedure and then introduces the activity-based cost allocation procedure.

Two-Stage Cost Allocation

An organization incurs overhead costs in many activities. These activities can be identified with various departments, which can be broadly classified as either operating or service departments. *Operating departments* perform an organization's main functions. For example, an accounting firm's main functions usually include auditing, tax, and advisory services. Similarly, the production and selling departments of a manufacturing firm perform its main functions and serve as operating departments. *Service departments* provide support to an organization's operating departments. Examples of service departments are payroll, human resource management, accounting, and executive management. Service departments do not engage in activities that generate revenues, yet their support is crucial for the operating departments' success. In this section, we apply a two-stage cost allocation procedure to assign (1) service department costs to operating departments and (2) operating department costs, including those assigned from service departments, to the organization's output.

Illustration of Two-Stage Cost Allocation   Exhibit 21.1 shows the two-stage cost allocation procedure. This exhibit uses data from **AutoGrand**, a custom automobile manufacturer. AutoGrand has five manufacturing-related departments: janitorial, maintenance, factory accounting, machining, and assembly. Expenses incurred by each of these departments are considered product costs. There are three service departments—janitorial, maintenance, and factory accounting; each incurs expenses of $10,000, $15,000 and $8,000, respectively. There are two operating departments, machining and assembly; they incur expenses of $10,000 and $18,000, respectively. As shown in Exhibit 21.1, the first stage of the two-stage procedure involves allocating the costs of the three service departments to the two operating departments (machining and assembly). The two operating departments use the resources of these service departments.

EXHIBIT 21.1

Two-Stage Cost Allocation

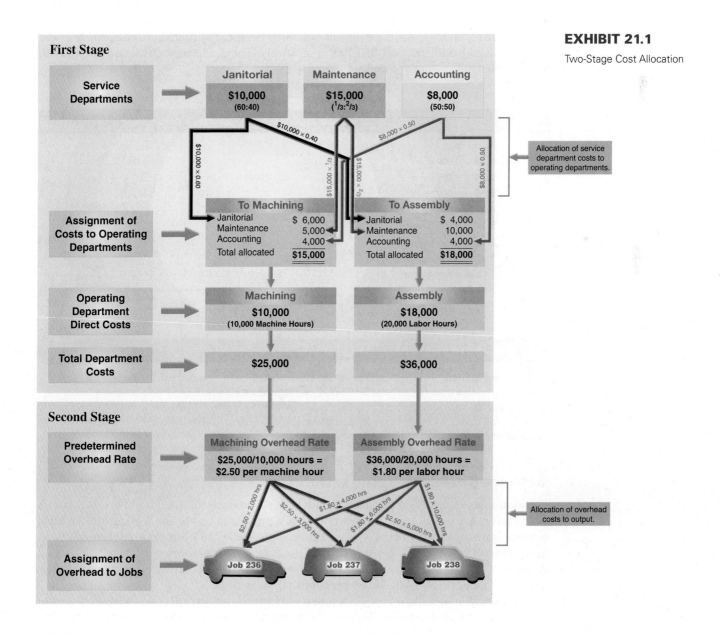

First Stage   To illustrate the first stage of cost allocation, we use the janitorial department. Its costs are allocated to machining and assembly in the ratio 60:40. This means that 60%, or $6,000, of janitorial costs are assigned to the machining department and 40%, or $4,000, to the assembly department. The expenses incurred by the maintenance and factory accounting departments are similarly assigned to machining and assembly. We then add the expenses directly incurred by each operating department to these assigned costs to determine the total expenses for each operating department. This yields total costs of $25,000 for machining and $36,000 for assembly.

Point: Use of a separate overhead allocation rate for each department is known as using *departmental rates.*

Second Stage   In the second stage, predetermined overhead rates are computed for each operating department. The allocation base is machine hours for machining and labor hours for assembly. The predetermined overhead rate is $2.50 per machine hour for the machining department and $1.80 per labor hour for the assembly department. These predetermined overhead rates are then used to assign overhead to output.

To illustrate this second stage, assume that three jobs were started and finished in a recent month. These jobs consumed resources as follows: Job 236—2,000 machine hours in machining and 4,000 labor hours in assembly; Job 237—3,000 machine hours and 6,000 labor hours; Job 238—5,000 machine hours and 10,000 labor hours. The overhead assigned to these three jobs is shown with the arrow lines in the bottom row of Exhibit 21.1.

Exhibit 21.2 summarizes these allocations. Total overhead allocated to Jobs 236, 237, and 238, is $12,200, $18,300, and $30,500, respectively. These allocated costs sum to $61,000, which is the total amount of overhead started with.

EXHIBIT 21.2

Assignment of Overhead Costs to Output

	Job 236	Job 237	Job 238	Department Totals
Machining				
$2.50 × 2,000 hours	$ 5,000			
$2.50 × 3,000 hours		$ 7,500		
$2.50 × 5,000 hours			$12,500	$25,000
Assembly				
$1.80 × 4,000 hours	7,200			
$1.80 × 6,000 hours		10,800		
$1.80 × 10,000 hours			18,000	36,000
Total overhead assigned	$12,200	$18,300	$30,500	$61,000

Decision Insight

Overhead Misled   **Futura Computer** outsourced a "money-losing" product to a Korean firm for manufacturing. Its own manufacturing facility was retooled to produce extra units of a "more profitable" product. Profits did not materialize, and losses grew to more than $20 million! What went wrong? It seems the better product was a loser and the losing product was a winner. Poor overhead allocations misled Futura's management. ■

Activity-Based Cost Allocation

P2 Assign overhead costs using activity-based costing.

For companies with only one product, or with multiple products that use about the same amount of indirect resources, using a single overhead cost rate based on volume is adequate. Multiple overhead rates can further improve on cost allocations. Yet, when a company has many products that consume different amounts of indirect resources, even the multiple overhead rate system based on volume is often inadequate. Such a system usually fails to reflect the products' different uses of indirect resources and often distorts products costs.

Specifically, low-volume complex products are usually undercosted, whereas high-volume simpler products are overcosted. This can cause companies to believe that their complex products

EXHIBIT 21.3

Activity-Based Cost Allocation

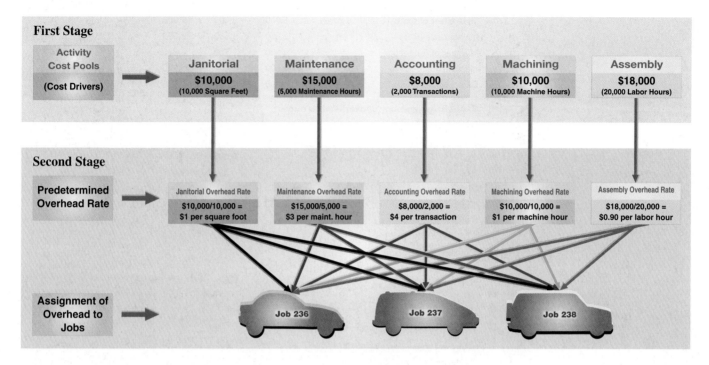

are more profitable than they really are, which can lead those companies to focus on them to the detriment of high-volume simpler products. This creates a demand for a better cost allocation system for these indirect (overhead) costs.

Activity-based costing (ABC) attempts to better allocate costs to the proper users of overhead by focusing on *activities*. Costs are traced to individual activities and then allocated to cost objects. Exhibit 21.3 shows the (two-stage) activity-based cost allocation method. The first stage identifies the activities involved in processing Jobs 236, 237, and 238 and forms activity cost *pools* by combining those activities. The second stage involves computing predetermined overhead cost rates for each cost pool and then assigning costs to jobs.

We begin our explanation at the top of Exhibit 21.3. The first stage identifies individual activities, which are pooled in a logical manner into homogenous groups, or *cost pools*. A homogenous cost pool consists of activities that belong to the same process and/or are caused by the same cost driver. An **activity cost driver,** or simply *cost driver,* is a factor that causes the cost of an activity to go up or down. For example, preparing an invoice, checking it, and dispatching it are activities of the "invoicing" process and can therefore be grouped in a single cost pool. Moreover, the number of invoices processed likely drives the costs of these activities.

An **activity cost pool** is a temporary account accumulating the costs a company incurs to support an identified set of activities. Costs accumulated in an activity cost pool include the variable and fixed costs of the activities in the pool. Variable costs pertain to resources acquired as needed (such as materials); fixed costs pertain to resources acquired in advance (such as equipment). An activity cost pool account is handled like a factory overhead account.

In the second stage, after all activity costs are accumulated in an activity cost pool account, overhead rates are computed. Then, costs are allocated to cost objects (users) based on cost drivers (allocation bases).

Illustration of Activity-Based Costing   To illustrate, let's return to AutoGrand's three jobs. Assume that resources used to complete Jobs 236, 237, and 238 are shown in panel A at the top of Exhibit 21.4.

Point: Activity-based costing is used in many settings. A study found that activity-based costing improves health care costing accuracy, enabling improved profitability analysis and decision making. However, identifying cost drivers in a health care setting is challenging.

Point: A cost driver is different from an allocation base. An allocation base is used as a basis for assigning overhead but need not have a cause-effect relation with the costs assigned. However, a cost driver has a cause-effect relation with the cost assigned.

EXHIBIT 21.4

Activity Resource Use and
Assignment of Overhead to Output

	Job 236	Job 237	Job 238	Activity Totals
Panel A: Resources Used				
Square feet of space	5,000	3,000	2,000	
Maintenance hours	2,500	1,500	1,000	
Number of transactions	500	700	800	
Machine hours	2,000	3,000	5,000	
Direct labor hours	4,000	6,000	10,000	
Panel B: Assignment of overhead to output				
Janitorial				
$1.00 × 5,000 sq. ft.	$ 5,000			
$1.00 × 3,000 sq. ft.		$ 3,000		
$1.00 × 2,000 sq. ft.			$ 2,000	$10,000
Maintenance				
$3.00 × 2,500 maint. hrs.	7,500			
$3.00 × 1,500 maint. hrs.		4,500		
$3.00 × 1,000 maint. hrs.			3,000	15,000
Factory Accounting				
$4.00 × 500 transactions	2,000			
$4.00 × 700 transactions		2,800		
$4.00 × 800 transactions			3,200	8,000
Machining				
$1.00 × 2,000 machine hrs.	2,000			
$1.00 × 3,000 machine hrs.		3,000		
$1.00 × 5,000 machine hrs.			5,000	10,000
Assembly				
$0.90 × 4,000 labor hrs.	3,600			
$0.90 × 6,000 labor hrs.		5,400		
$0.90 × 10,000 labor hrs.			9,000	18,000
Total overhead assigned	$20,100	$18,700	$22,200	$61,000

The $61,000 of total costs are assigned to these three jobs using activity-based costing as shown in panel B at the bottom of Exhibit 21.4 (rates are taken from the second stage of Exhibit 21.3).

From Exhibit 21.5, we see that the costs assigned to the three jobs vary markedly depending on whether two-stage (departmental) cost allocation or activity-based costing is used. Costs assigned to Job 236 go from $12,200 under two-stage cost allocation to $20,100 under activity-based costing. Costs assigned to Job 238 decline from $30,500 to $22,200. These differences in assigned amounts result from more accurately tracing costs to each job using activity-based costing where the allocation bases reflect actual cost drivers.

EXHIBIT 21.5

Comparing Overhead Costs
Assigned under Alternative
Methods

Overhead Assigned	Job 236	Job 237	Job 238	Total
Two-stage cost allocation (Exhibit 21.2)	$12,200	$18,300	$30,500	$61,000
Activity-based costing (Exhibit 21.4)	20,100	18,700	22,200	61,000

Decision Maker   Answer — p. 886

Director of Operations   Two department managers at your ad agency complain to you that overhead costs assigned to them are too high. Overhead is assigned on the basis of labor hours for designers. These managers argue that overhead depends not only on designers' hours but on many activities unrelated to these hours. What is your response? ■

Comparison of Two-Stage and Activity-Based Cost Allocation

Traditional cost systems capture overhead costs by individual department (or function) and accumulate these costs in one or more overhead accounts. Companies then assign these overhead costs using a single allocation base such as direct labor or multiple volume-based allocation bases. Unfortunately, traditional cost systems have tended to use allocation bases that are often not closely related to the way these costs are actually incurred.

In contrast, activity-based cost systems capture costs by individual activity. These activities and their costs are then accumulated into activity cost pools. A company selects a cost driver (allocation base) for each activity pool. It uses this cost driver to assign the accumulated activity costs to cost objects (such as jobs or products) benefiting from the activity. As shown in Exhibit 21.5, the activity-based costing (ABC) system can more accurately trace costs to individual jobs. More generally, we can conclude the following:

- ABC uses more allocation bases than a traditional cost system. For example, a Chicago-based manufacturer currently uses nearly 20 different activity cost drivers to assign overhead costs to its products. Exhibit 21.6 lists common examples of overhead cost pools and their usual cost drivers.

- ABC is especially effective when the same department or departments produce many different types of products. For instance, more complex products often require more help from service departments such as engineering, maintenance, and materials handling. If the same amount of direct labor is applied to the complex and simple products, a traditional overhead allocation system assigns the same overhead cost to both. With activity-based costing, however, the complex products are assigned a larger portion of overhead. The difference in overhead assigned can affect product pricing, make-or-buy, and other managerial decisions.

- ABC encourages managers to focus on *activities* as well as the use of those activities. For instance, assume AutoGrand can reduce the number of transactions processed in Factory Accounting to 1,500 (375 transactions for Job 236, 525 transactions for Job 237, and 600 transactions for Job 238) and that through continuous improvement it can reduce costs of processing those transactions to $4,500. The resulting rate to process a transaction is $3 per transaction ($4,500/1,500 transactions—down from $4 per Exhibit 21.3). The cost of transaction processing is reduced for all jobs (Job 236, $1,125; Job 237, $1,575; Job 238, $1,800). However, if those accounting costs were grouped in a single overhead cost pool, it is more difficult to identify cost savings and understand their effects on product costs.

- ABC requires managers to look at each item and encourages them to manage each cost to increase the benefit from each dollar spent. It also encourages managers to cooperate because it shows how their efforts are interrelated. This results in *activity-based management.*

Activity Cost Pool	Cost Driver
Materials purchasing	Number of purchase orders
Materials handling	Number of materials requisitions
Personnel processing	Number of employees hired or laid off
Equipment depreciation	Number of products produced or hours of use
Quality inspection	Number of units inspected
Indirect labor in setting up equipment	Number of setups required
Engineering costs for product modifications	Number of modifications (engineering change orders)

EXHIBIT 21.6

Cost Pools and Cost Drivers in Activity-Based Costing

Decision Ethics
Answer — p. 886

Accounting Officer   Your company produces expensive garments, whose production involves many complex and specialized activities. Your general manager recently learned about activity-based costing (ABC) and asks your advice. However, your supervisor does not want to disturb the existing cost system and instructs you to prepare a report stating that "implementation of ABC is a complicated process involving too many steps and not worth the effort." You believe ABC will actually help the company identify sources of costs and control them. What action do you take? ∎

Quick Check
Answers — p. 886

1. What is a cost driver?
2. When activity-based costing is used rather than traditional allocation methods, (a) managers must identify cost drivers for various items of overhead cost, (b) individual cost items in service departments are allocated directly to products or services, (c) managers can direct their attention to the activities that drive overhead cost, or (d) all of the above.

Section 2—Allocating Costs for Performance Evaluation

This second section of the chapter describes and illustrates allocation of costs for performance evaluation. We begin with departmental accounting and expense allocations and conclude with responsibility accounting.

DEPARTMENTAL ACCOUNTING

Companies are divided into *departments*, also called *subunits*, when they are too large to be managed effectively as a single unit. Managerial accounting for departments has two main goals. The first is to set up a **departmental accounting system** to provide information for managers to evaluate the profitability or cost effectiveness of each department's activities. The second goal is to set up a **responsibility accounting system** to control costs and expenses and evaluate managers' performances by assigning costs and expenses to the managers responsible for controlling them. Departmental and responsibility accounting systems are related and share much information.

Motivation for Departmentalization

Many companies are so large and complex that they are broken into separate divisions for efficiency and/or effectiveness purposes. Divisions then are usually organized into separate departments. When a company is departmentalized, each department is often placed under the direction of a manager. As a company grows, management often divides departments into new departments so that responsibilities for a department's activities do not overwhelm the manager's ability to oversee and control them. A company also creates departments to take advantage of the skills of individual managers. Departments are broadly classified as either operating or service departments.

Departmental Evaluation

Point: To improve profitability, **Sears, Roebuck & Co.** eliminated several departments, including its catalog division.

When a company is divided into departments, managers need to know how each department is performing. The accounting system must supply information about resources used and outputs achieved by each department. This requires a system to measure and accumulate revenue and expense information for each department whenever possible.

Departmental information is rarely distributed publicly because of its potential usefulness to competitors. Information about departments is prepared for internal managers to help control operations, appraise performance, allocate resources, and plan strategy. If a department is highly profitable, management may decide to expand its operations, or if a department is performing poorly, information about revenues or expenses can suggest useful changes.

More companies are emphasizing customer satisfaction as a main responsibility of many departments. This has led to changes in the measures reported. Increasingly, financial measurements are being supplemented with quality and customer satisfaction indexes. **Motorola**, for instance, uses two key measures: the number of defective parts per million parts produced and the percent of orders delivered on time to customers. (Note that some departments have only "internal customers.")

Financial information used to evaluate a department depends on whether it is evaluated as a profit center, cost center, or investment center. A **profit center** incurs costs and generates revenues; selling departments are often evaluated as profit centers. A **cost center** incurs costs without directly generating revenues. An **investment center** incurs costs and generates revenues, and is responsible for effectively using center assets. The manufacturing departments of a manufacturer and its service departments such as accounting, advertising, and purchasing, are all cost centers.

Evaluating managers' performance depends on whether they are responsible for profit centers, cost centers, or investment centers. Profit center managers are judged on their abilities to generate revenues in excess of the department's costs. They are assumed to influence both revenue generation and cost incurrence. Cost center managers are judged on their abilities to control costs by keeping them within a satisfactory range under an assumption that only they influence costs. Investment center managers are evaluated on their use of center assets to generate income.

Point: Selling departments are often treated as *revenue centers*; their managers are responsible for maximizing sales revenues.

Quick Check

Answers — p. 886

3. What is the difference between a departmental accounting system and a responsibility accounting system?
4. Service departments (*a*) manufacture products, (*b*) make sales directly to customers, (*c*) produce revenues, (*d*) assist operating departments.
5. Explain the difference between a cost center and a profit center. Cite an example of each.

DEPARTMENTAL EXPENSE ALLOCATION

When a company computes departmental profits, it confronts some accounting challenges that involve allocating its expenses across its operating departments.

C1 Distinguish between direct and indirect expenses and identify bases for allocating indirect expenses to departments.

Direct and Indirect Expenses

Direct expenses are costs readily traced to a department because they are incurred for that department's sole benefit. They require no allocation across departments. For example, the salary of an employee who works in only one department is a direct expense of that one department.

Indirect expenses are costs that are incurred for the joint benefit of more than one department and cannot be readily traced to only one department. For example, if two or more departments share a single building, all enjoy the benefits of the expenses for rent, heat, and light. Indirect expenses are allocated across departments benefiting from them when we need information about departmental profits. Ideally, we allocate indirect expenses by using a cause-effect relation. When we cannot identify cause-effect relations, we allocate each indirect expense on a basis approximating the relative benefit each department receives. Measuring the benefit for each department from an indirect expense can be difficult.

Point: Utility expense has elements of both direct and indirect expenses.

Illustration of Indirect Expense Allocation   To illustrate how to allocate an indirect expense, we consider a retail store that purchases janitorial services from an outside company. Management allocates this cost across the store's three departments according to the floor space each occupies. Costs of janitorial services for a recent month are $300. Exhibit 21.7 shows the square feet of floor space each department occupies. The store computes the percent of total square feet allotted to each department and uses it to allocate the $300 cost.

EXHIBIT 21.7

Indirect Expense Allocation

Department	Square Feet	Percent of Total	Allocated Cost
Jewelry	2,400	60%	$180
Watch repair	600	15	45
China and silver	1,000	25	75
Totals	4,000	100%	$300

Specifically, because the jewelry department occupies 60% of the floor space, 60% of the total $300 cost is assigned to it. The same procedure is applied to the other departments. When the allocation process is complete, these and other allocated costs are deducted from the gross profit for each department to determine net income for each. One consideration in allocating costs is to motivate managers and employees to behave as desired. As a result, a cost incurred in one department might be best allocated to other departments when one of the other departments caused the cost.

Allocation of Indirect Expenses

This section describes how to identify the bases used to allocate indirect expenses across departments. No standard rule identifies the best basis because expense allocation involves several factors, and the relative importance of these factors varies across departments and organizations. Judgment is required, and people do not always agree. Employee morale suffers when allocations are perceived as unfair. Thus, it is important to carefully design and explain the allocation of service department costs. In our discussion, note the parallels between activity-based costing and the departmental expense allocation procedures described here.

Wages and Salaries   Employee wages and salaries can be either direct or indirect expenses. If their time is spent entirely in one department, their wages are direct expenses of that department. However, if employees work for the benefit of more than one department, their wages are indirect expenses and must be allocated across the departments benefited. An employee's contribution to a department usually depends on the number of hours worked in contributing to that department. Thus, a reasonable basis for allocating employee wages and salaries is the *relative amount of time spent in each department*. In the case of a supervisor who manages more than one department, recording the time spent in each department may not always be practical. Instead, a company can allocate the supervisor's salary to departments on the basis of the number of employees in each department—a reasonable basis if a supervisor's main task is managing people. Another basis of allocation is on sales across departments, also a reasonable basis if a supervisor's job reflects on departmental sales.

Point: Some companies ask supervisors to estimate time spent supervising specific departments for purposes of expense allocation.

Rent and Related Expenses   Rent expense for a building is reasonably allocated to a department on the basis of floor space it occupies. Location can often make some floor space more valuable than other space. Thus, the allocation method can charge departments that occupy more valuable space a higher expense per square foot. Ground floor retail space, for instance, is often more valuable than basement or upper-floor space because all customers pass departments near the entrance but fewer go beyond the first floor. When no precise measures of floor space values exist, basing allocations on data such as customer traffic and real estate assessments is helpful. When a company owns its building, its expenses for depreciation, taxes, insurance, and other related building expenses are allocated like rent expense.

Advertising Expenses   Effective advertising of a department's products increases its sales and customer traffic. Moreover, advertising products for some departments usually helps other departments' sales because customers also often buy unadvertised products. Thus, many stores treat advertising as an indirect expense allocated on the basis of each department's proportion of total sales. For example, a department with 10% of a store's total sales is assigned 10% of advertising expense. Another method is to analyze each advertisement to compute the Web/ newspaper space or TV/radio time devoted to the products of a department and charge that department for the proportional costs of advertisements. Management must consider whether this more detailed and costly method is justified.

Equipment and Machinery Depreciation   Depreciation on equipment and machinery used only in one department is a direct expense of that department. Depreciation on equipment and machinery used by more than one department is an indirect expense to be allocated across departments. Accounting for each department's depreciation expense requires a company to keep records showing which departments use specific assets. The number of hours that a department uses equipment and machinery is a reasonable basis for allocating depreciation.

Utilities Expenses   Utilities expenses such as heating and lighting are usually allocated on the basis of floor space occupied by departments. This practice assumes their use is uniform across departments. When this is not so, a more involved allocation can be necessary, although there is often a trade-off between the usefulness of more precise allocations and the effort to compute them. Manufacturers often allocate electricity cost to departments on the basis of the horsepower of equipment located in each department.

Service Department Expenses   To generate revenues, operating departments require support services provided by departments such as personnel, payroll, advertising, and purchasing. Such service departments are typically evaluated as cost centers because they do not produce revenues. (Evaluating them as profit centers requires the use of a system that "charges" user departments a price that then serves as the "revenue" generated by service departments.) A departmental accounting system can accumulate and report costs incurred directly by each service department for this purpose. The system then allocates a service department's expenses to operating departments benefiting from them. This is often done, for example, using traditional two-stage cost allocation (see Exhibit 21.1). Exhibit 21.8 shows some commonly used bases for allocating service department expenses to operating departments.

Point: When a service department "charges" its user departments within a company, a *transfer pricing system* must be set up to determine the "revenue" from its services provided.

Service Department	Common Allocation Bases
Office expenses	Number of employees or sales in each department
Personnel expenses	Number of employees in each department
Payroll expenses	Number of employees in each department
Advertising expenses	Sales or amount of advertising charged directly to each department
Purchasing costs	Dollar amounts of purchases or number of purchase orders processed
Cleaning expenses	Square feet of floor space occupied
Maintenance expenses	Square feet of floor space occupied

EXHIBIT 21.8

Bases for Allocating Service Department Expenses

Departmental Income Statements

An income statement can be prepared for each operating department once expenses have been assigned to it. Its expenses include both direct expenses and its share of indirect expenses. For this purpose, compiling all expenses incurred in service departments before assigning them to operating departments is useful. We illustrate the steps to prepare departmental income statements using **A-1 Hardware** and its five departments. Two of them (office and purchasing) are service departments and the other three (hardware, housewares, and appliances) are operating (selling) departments. Allocating costs to operating departments and preparing departmental income statements involves four steps.

P3 Prepare departmental income statements and contribution reports.

1. Accumulating direct expenses by department.
2. Allocating indirect expenses across departments.
3. Allocating service department expenses to operating department.
4. Preparing departmental income statements.

Step 1   Step 1 accumulates direct expenses for each service and operating department as shown in Exhibit 21.9. Direct expenses include salaries, wages, and other expenses that each department incurs but does not share with any other department. This information is accumulated in departmental expense accounts.

EXHIBIT 21.9

Step 1: Direct Expense Accumulation

Accumulate Direct Expenses in Departmental Expense Accounts

Point: We sometimes allocate service department costs across other service departments before allocating them to operating departments. This "step-wise" process is in advanced courses.

Step 2   Step 2 allocates indirect expenses across all departments as shown in Exhibit 21.10. Indirect expenses can include items such as depreciation, rent, advertising, and any other expenses that cannot be directly assigned to a department. Indirect expenses are recorded in company expense accounts, an allocation base is identified for each expense, and costs are allocated using a *departmental expense allocation spreadsheet* described in step 3.

EXHIBIT 21.10

Step 2: Indirect Expense Allocation

Accumulate Indirect Expenses in Company Accounts and Allocate

Step 3   Step 3 allocates expenses of the service departments (office and purchasing) to the operating departments. Service department costs are not allocated to other service departments. Exhibit 21.11 reflects the allocation of service department expenses using the allocation base(s). All of the direct and indirect expenses of service departments are allocated to operating departments.[1]

EXHIBIT 21.11

Step 3: Service Department Expense Allocation to Operating Departments

General Office Department Expense Allocation

Purchasing Department Expense Allocation

Computations for both steps 2 and 3 are commonly made using a departmental expense allocation spreadsheet as shown in Exhibit 21.12. The first two sections of this spreadsheet list direct expenses and indirect expenses by department. The third section lists the service department expenses and their allocations to operating departments. The allocation bases are identified in the second column, and total expense amounts are reported in the third column.

Illustration of Steps 1, 2, and 3   The departmental expense allocation spreadsheet is useful in implementing the first three steps. To illustrate, first (step 1) the three direct expenses of salaries, depreciation, and supplies are accumulated in each of the five departments.

---

[1] In some cases we allocate a service department's expenses to other service departments when they use its services. For example, expenses of a payroll office benefit all service and operating departments and can be assigned to all departments. Nearly all examples and assignment materials in this book allocate service expenses only to operating departments for simplicity.

EXHIBIT 21.12

Departmental Expense Allocation Spreadsheet

			File Edit View Insert Format Tools Data Window Help					

A-1 HARDWARE
Departmental Expense Allocations
For Year Ended December 31, 2011

				Allocation of Expenses to Departments				
	Allocation Base	Expense Account Balance	General Office Dept.	Purchas- ing Dept.	Hard- ware Dept.	House- wares Dept.	Appli- ances Dept.
Direct expenses							
Salaries expense......................	Payroll records	$51,900	$13,300	$8,200	$15,600	$ 7,000	$ 7,800
Depreciation—Equipment......	Depreciation records	1,500	500	300	400	100	200
Supplies expense.....................	Requisitions..............................	900	200	100	300	200	100
Indirect expenses							
Rent expense	Amount and value of space..	12,000	600	600	4,860	3,240	2,700
Utilities expense......................	Floor space...............................	2,400	300	300	810	540	450
Advertising expense	Sales..	1,000			500	300	200
Insurance expense...................	Value of insured assets	2,500	400	200	900	600	400
Total department expenses		72,200	15,300	9,700	23,370	11,980	11,850
Service department expenses							
General office department.....	Sales..		(15,300)		7,650	4,590	3,060
Purchasing department	Purchase orders......................			(9,700)	3,880	2,630	3,190
Total expenses allocated to operating departments.............		$72,200	$ 0	$ 0	$34,900	$19,200	$18,100

Sheet1 / Sheet2 / Sheet3

Second (step 2), the four indirect expenses of rent, utilities, advertising, and insurance are allocated to all departments using the allocation bases identified. For example, consider rent allocation. Exhibit 21.13 lists the five departments' square footage of space occupied.

EXHIBIT 21.13

Departments' Allocation Bases

Department	Floor Space (Square Feet)	Value of Insured Assets ($)	Sales ($)	Number of Purchase Orders
General office	1,500	$ 38,000		—
Purchasing	1,500	19,000		—*
Hardware	4,050	85,500	$119,500	394
Housewares	2,700	57,000	71,700	267
Appliances	2,250	38,000	47,800	324
Total	12,000	$237,500	$239,000	985

* Purchasing department tracks purchase orders by department.

The two service departments (office and purchasing) occupy 25% of the total space (3,000 sq. feet/ 12,000 sq. feet). However, they are located near the back of the building, which is of lower value than space near the front that is occupied by operating departments. Management estimates that space near the back accounts for $1,200 of the total rent expense of $12,000. Exhibit 21.14 shows how we allocate the $1,200 rent expense between these two service departments in proportion to their square footage. Exhibit 21.14 shows a simple rule for cost

EXHIBIT 21.14

Allocating Indirect (Rent) Expense to Service Departments

Department	Square Feet	Percent of Total	Allocated Cost
General office	1,500	50.0%	$ 600
Purchasing	1,500	50.0	600
Totals	3,000	100.0%	$1,200

allocations: Allocated cost = Percentage of allocation base × Total cost. We then allocate the remaining $10,800 of rent expense to the three operating departments as shown in Exhibit 21.15.

EXHIBIT 21.15

Allocating Indirect (Rent) Expense to Operating Departments

Department	Square Feet	Percent of Total	Allocated Cost
Hardware	4,050	45.0%	$ 4,860
Housewares	2,700	30.0	3,240
Appliances	2,250	25.0	2,700
Totals	9,000	100.0%	$10,800

We continue step 2 by allocating the $2,400 of utilities expense to all departments based on the square footage occupied as shown in Exhibit 21.16.

EXHIBIT 21.16

Allocating Indirect (Utilities) Expense to All Departments

Department	Square Feet	Percent of Total	Allocated Cost
General office	1,500	12.50%	$ 300
Purchasing	1,500	12.50	300
Hardware	4,050	33.75	810
Housewares	2,700	22.50	540
Appliances	2,250	18.75	450
Totals	12,000	100.00%	$2,400

Exhibit 21.17 shows the allocation of $1,000 of advertising expense to the three operating departments on the basis of sales dollars. We exclude service departments from this allocation because they do not generate sales.

EXHIBIT 21.17

Allocating Indirect (Advertising) Expense to Operating Departments

Department	Sales	Percent of Total	Allocated Cost
Hardware	$119,500	50.0%	$ 500
Housewares	71,700	30.0	300
Appliances	47,800	20.0	200
Totals	$239,000	100.0%	$1,000

To complete step 2 we allocate insurance expense to each service and operating department as shown in Exhibit 21.18.

EXHIBIT 21.18

Allocating Indirect (Insurance) Expense to All Departments

Department	Value of Insured Assets	Percent of Total	Allocated Cost
General office	$ 38,000	16.0%	$ 400
Purchasing	19,000	8.0	200
Hardware	85,500	36.0	900
Housewares	57,000	24.0	600
Appliances	38,000	16.0	400
Total	$237,500	100.0%	$2,500

Third (step 3), total expenses of the two service departments are allocated to the three operating departments as shown in Exhibits 21.19 and 21.20.

EXHIBIT 21.19

Allocating Service Department (General Office) Expenses to Operating Departments

Department	Sales	Percent of Total	Allocated Cost
Hardware	$119,500	50.0%	$ 7,650
Housewares	71,700	30.0	4,590
Appliances	47,800	20.0	3,060
Total	$239,000	100.0%	$15,300

Department	Number of Purchase Orders	Percent of Total	Allocated Cost
Hardware	394	40.00%	$3,880
Housewares	267	27.11	2,630
Appliances	324	32.89	3,190
Total	985	100.00%	$9,700

EXHIBIT 21.20

Allocating Service Department (Purchasing) Expenses to Operating Departments

Step 4   The departmental expense allocation spreadsheet can now be used to prepare performance reports for the company's service and operating departments. The general office and purchasing departments are cost centers, and their managers will be evaluated on their control of costs. Actual amounts of service department expenses can be compared to budgeted amounts to help assess cost center manager performance.

Amounts in the operating department columns are used to prepare departmental income statements as shown in Exhibit 21.21. This exhibit uses the spreadsheet for its operating expenses; information on sales and cost of goods sold comes from departmental records.

Example: If the $15,300 general office expenses in Exhibit 21.12 are allocated equally across departments, what is net income for the hardware department and for the combined company? *Answer:* Hardware income, $13,350; combined income, $19,000.

EXHIBIT 21.21

Departmental Income Statements

A-1 HARDWARE Departmental Income Statements For Year Ended December 31, 2011	Hardware Department	Housewares Department	Appliances Department	Combined
Sales	$119,500	$71,700	$47,800	$239,000
Cost of goods sold	73,800	43,800	30,200	147,800
Gross profit	45,700	27,900	17,600	91,200
Operating expenses				
Salaries expense	15,600	7,000	7,800	30,400
Depreciation expense—Equipment	400	100	200	700
Supplies expense	300	200	100	600
Rent expense........................	4,860	3,240	2,700	10,800
Utilities expense	810	540	450	1,800
Advertising expense	500	300	200	1,000
Insurance expense....................	900	600	400	1,900
Share of general office expenses	7,650	4,590	3,060	15,300
Share of purchasing expenses	3,880	2,630	3,190	9,700
Total operating expenses	34,900	19,200	18,100	72,200
Net income (loss)	**$10,800**	**$8,700**	**$ (500)**	**$19,000**

Departmental Contribution to Overhead

Data from departmental income statements are not always best for evaluating each profit center's performance, especially when indirect expenses are a large portion of total expenses and when weaknesses in assumptions and decisions in allocating indirect expenses can markedly affect net income. In these and other cases, we might better evaluate profit center performance using the **departmental contribution to overhead,** which is a report of the amount of sales less *direct* expenses.[2] We can also examine cost center performance by focusing on control of direct expenses.

---

[2] A department's contribution is said to be "to overhead" because of the practice of considering all indirect expenses as overhead. Thus, the excess of a department's sales over direct expenses is a contribution toward at least a portion of its total overhead.

EXHIBIT 21.22

Departmental Contribution
to Overhead

A-1 HARDWARE Income Statement Showing Departmental Contribution to Overhead For Year Ended December 31, 2011				
	Hardware Department	Housewares Department	Appliances Department	Combined
Sales	$119,500	$ 71,700	$47,800	$239,000
Cost of goods sold	73,800	43,800	30,200	147,800
Gross profit	45,700	27,900	17,600	91,200
Direct expenses				
Salaries expense	15,600	7,000	7,800	30,400
Depreciation expense—Equipment	400	100	200	700
Supplies expense	300	200	100	600
Total direct expenses	16,300	7,300	8,100	31,700
Departmental contributions to overhead	**$29,400**	**$20,600**	**$ 9,500**	**$59,500**
Indirect expenses				
Rent expense				10,800
Utilities expense				1,800
Advertising expense				1,000
Insurance expense				1,900
General office department expense				15,300
Purchasing department expense				9,700
Total indirect expenses				40,500
Net income				**$ 19,000**
Contribution as percent of sales	24.6%	28.7%	19.9%	24.9%

Point: Net income is the same in Exhibits 21.21 and 21.22. The method of reporting indirect expenses in Exhibit 21.22 does not change total net income but does identify each department's contribution to overhead and net income.

The upper half of Exhibit 21.22 shows a departmental (profit center) contribution to overhead as part of an expanded income statement. This format is common when reporting departmental contributions to overhead. Using the information in Exhibits 21.21 and 21.22, we can evaluate the profitability of the three profit centers. For instance, let's compare the performance of the appliances department as described in these two exhibits. Exhibit 21.21 shows a $500 net loss resulting from this department's operations, but Exhibit 21.22 shows a $9,500 positive contribution to overhead, which is 19.9% of the appliance department's sales. The contribution of the appliances department is not as large as that of the other selling departments, but a $9,500 contribution to overhead is better than a $500 loss. This tells us that the appliances department is not a money loser. On the contrary, it is contributing $9,500 toward defraying total indirect expenses of $40,500.

Quick Check

Answers — p. 886

6. If a company has two operating (selling) departments (shoes and hats) and two service departments (payroll and advertising), which of the following statements is correct? (a) Wages incurred in the payroll department are direct expenses of the shoe department, (b) Wages incurred in the payroll department are indirect expenses of the operating departments, or (c) Advertising department expenses are allocated to the other three departments.

7. Which of the following bases can be used to allocate supervisors' salaries across operating departments? (a) Hours spent in each department, (b) number of employees in each department, (c) sales achieved in each department, or (d) any of the above, depending on which information is most relevant and accessible.

8. What three steps are used to allocate expenses to operating departments?

9. An income statement showing departmental contribution to overhead, (a) subtracts indirect expenses from each department's revenues, (b) subtracts only direct expenses from each department's revenues, or (c) shows net income for each department.

EVALUATING INVESTMENT CENTER PERFORMANCE

This section introduces both financial and nonfinancial measures of investment center performance.

Financial Performance Evaluation Measures

Investment center managers are typically evaluated using performance measures that combine income and assets. Consider the following data for ZTel, a company which operates two divisions: LCD and S-Phone. The LCD division manufactures liquid crystal display (LCD) touch-screen monitors and sells them for use in computers, cellular phones, and other products. The S-Phone division sells smartphones, mobile phones that also function as personal computers, MP3 players, cameras, and global positioning satellite (GPS) systems. Exhibit 21.23 shows current year income and assets for those divisions.

A1 Analyze investment centers using return on assets, residual income, and balanced scorecard.

	LCD	S-Phone
Net income	$ 526,500	$ 417,600
Average invested assets	2,500,000	1,850,000

EXHIBIT 21.23

Investment Center Income and Assets

Investment Center Return on Total Assets One measure to evaluate division performance is the **investment center return on total assets,** also called *return on investment* (ROI). This measure is computed as follows

$$\text{Return on investment} = \frac{\text{Investment center net income}}{\text{Investment center average invested assets}}$$

The return on investment for the LCD division is 21% (rounded), computed as $526,500/$2,500,000. The S-Phone division's return on investment is 23% (rounded), computed as $417,600/$1,850,000. Though the LCD division earned more dollars of net income, it was less efficient in using its assets to generate income compared to the S-Phone division.

Investment Center Residual Income Another way to evaluate division performance is to compute **investment center residual income,** which is computed as follows

$$\text{Residual income} = \frac{\text{Investment center}}{\text{net income}} - \frac{\text{Target investment center}}{\text{net income}}$$

Assume ZTel's top management sets target net income at 8% of divisional assets. For an investment center, this **hurdle rate** is typically the cost of obtaining financing. Applying this hurdle rate using the data from Exhibit 21.23 yields the residual income for ZTel's divisions in Exhibit 21.24.

	LCD	S-Phone
Net income	$526,500	$417,600
Less: Target net income		
$2,500,000 × 8%	200,000	
$1,850,000 × 8%		148,000
Investment center residual income	$326,500	$269,600

EXHIBIT 21.24

Investment Center Residual Income

Unlike return on assets, residual income is expressed in dollars. The LCD division outperformed the S-Phone division on the basis of residual income. However, this result is due in part to the LCD division having a larger asset base than the S-Phone division.

Using residual income to evaluate division performance encourages division managers to accept all opportunities that return more than the target net income, thus increasing company value. For example, the S-Phone division might not want to accept a new customer that will provide a 15% return on investment, since that will reduce the S-Phone division's overall return on investment (23% as shown above). However, the S-Phone division should accept this opportunity because the new customer would increase residual income by providing net income above the target net income.

Point: Residual income is also called *economic value added* (EVA).

Nonfinancial Performance Evaluation Measures

Evaluating performance solely on financial measures such as return on investment or residual income has limitations. For example, some investment center managers might forgo profitable opportunities to keep their return on investment high. Also, residual income is less useful when comparing investment centers of different size. And, both return on investment and residual income can encourage managers to focus too heavily on short-term financial goals.

In response to these limitations, companies consider nonfinancial measures. For example, a delivery company such as **FedEx** might track the percentage of on-time deliveries. The percentage of defective tennis balls manufactured can be used to assess performance of **Penn**'s production managers. **Walmart**'s credit card screens commonly ask customers at check-out whether the cashier was friendly or the store was clean. This kind of information can help division managers run their divisions and help top management evaluate division manager performance.

Balanced Scorecard   The **balanced scorecard** is a system of performance measures, including nonfinancial measures, used to assess company and division manager performance. The balanced scorecard requires managers to think of their company from four perspectives:

1. **Customer:** What do customers think of us?
2. **Internal processes:** Which of our operations are critical to meeting customer needs?
3. **Innovation and learning:** How can we improve?
4. **Financial:** What do our owners think of us?

Point: One survey indicates that nearly 60% of global companies use some form of a balanced scorecard.

The balanced scorecard collects information on several key performance indicators within each of the four perspectives. These key indicators vary across companies. Exhibit 21.25 lists common performance measures.

EXHIBIT 21.25

Balanced Scorecard Performance Indicators

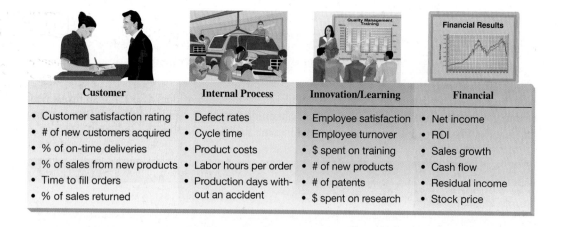

After selecting key performance indicators, companies collect data on each indicator and compare actual amounts to expected amounts to assess performance. For example, a company might have a goal of filling 98% of customer orders within two hours. Balanced scorecard reports are often presented in graphs or tables that can be updated frequently. Such timely information aids division managers in their decisions, and can be used by top management to evaluate division manager performance.

Customer Perspective	Actual	Goal
Checkout success	62%	↑
Orders returned	2.2%	↔
Customer satisfaction rating	9.5	↑
Number of customer complaints	142	↓

EXHIBIT 21.26

Balanced Scorecard Reporting:
Internet Retailer

Exhibit 21.26 is an example of balanced scorecard reporting on the customer perspective for an Internet retailer. This scorecard reports for example that the retailer is getting 62% of its potential customers successfully through the checkout process, and that 2.2% of all orders are returned. The *color* of the arrows in the right-most column reveals whether the company is exceeding its goal (green), barely meeting the goal (yellow), or not meeting the goal (red). The *direction* of the arrows reveals any trend in performance: an upward arrow indicates improvement, a downward arrow indicates declining performance, and an arrow pointing sideways indicates no change. A review of these arrows' color and direction suggests the retailer is meeting or exceeding its goals on checkout success, orders returned, and customer satisfaction. Further, checkout success and customer satisfaction are improving. The red arrow shows the company has received more customer complaints than was hoped for; however, the number of customer complaints is declining. A manager would combine this information with similar information on the internal process, innovation and learning, and financial perspectives to get an overall view of division performance.

■ **Decision Maker**   Answer — p. 886

Center Manager   Your center's usual return on total assets is 19%. You are considering two new investments for your center. The first requires a $250,000 average investment and is expected to yield annual net income of $50,000. The second requires a $1 million average investment with an expected annual net income of $175,000. Do you pursue either? ■

RESPONSIBILITY ACCOUNTING

Departmental accounting reports often provide data used to evaluate a department's performance, but are they useful in assessing how well a department *manager* performs? Neither departmental income nor its contribution to overhead may be useful because many expenses can be outside a manager's control. Instead, we often evaluate a manager's performance using responsibility accounting reports that describe a department's activities in terms of **controllable costs.**[3] A cost is controllable if a manager has the power to determine or at least significantly affect the amount incurred. **Uncontrollable costs** are not within the manager's control or influence.

C2 Explain controllable costs and responsibility accounting.

Controllable versus Direct Costs

Controllable costs are not always the same as direct costs. Direct costs are readily traced to a department, but the department manager might or might not control their amounts. For example, department managers often have little or no control over depreciation expense because

---

[3] The terms *cost* and *expense* are often used interchangeably in managerial accounting, but they are not necessarily the same. *Cost* often refers to the monetary outlay to acquire some resource that can have present and future benefit. *Expense* usually refers to an expired cost. That is, as the benefit of a resource expires, a portion of its cost is written off as an expense.

they cannot affect the amount of equipment assigned to their departments. Also, department managers rarely control their own salaries. However, they can control or influence items such as the cost of supplies used in their department. When evaluating managers' performances, we should use data reflecting their departments' outputs along with their controllable costs and expenses.

Distinguishing between controllable and uncontrollable costs depends on the particular manager and time period under analysis. For example, the cost of property insurance is usually not controllable at the department manager's level but by the executive responsible for obtaining the company's insurance coverage. Likewise, this executive might not control costs resulting from insurance policies already in force. However, when a policy expires, this executive can renegotiate a replacement policy and then controls these costs. Therefore, all costs are controllable at some management level if the time period is sufficiently long. We must use good judgment in identifying controllable costs.

Responsibility Accounting System

A *responsibility accounting system* uses the concept of controllable costs to assign managers the responsibility for costs and expenses under their control. Prior to each reporting period, a company prepares plans that identify costs and expenses under each manager's control. These plans are called **responsibility accounting budgets.** To ensure the cooperation of managers and the reasonableness of budgets, managers should be involved in preparing their budgets.

A responsibility accounting system also involves performance reports. A **responsibility accounting performance report** accumulates and reports costs and expenses that a manager is responsible for and their budgeted amounts. Management's analysis of differences between budgeted amounts and actual costs and expenses often results in corrective or strategic managerial actions. Upper-level management uses performance reports to evaluate the effectiveness of lower-level managers in controlling costs and expenses and keeping them within budgeted amounts.

A responsibility accounting system recognizes that control over costs and expenses belongs to several levels of management. We illustrate this by considering the organization chart in Exhibit 21.27. The lines in this chart connecting the managerial positions reflect channels of authority. For example, the four department managers of this consulting firm (benchmarking, cost management, outsourcing, and service) are responsible for controllable costs and expenses incurred in their departments, but these same costs are subject to the overall control of the vice president (VP) for operational consulting. Similarly, this VP's costs are subject to the control of the executive vice president (EVP) for operations, the president, and, ultimately, the board of directors.

At lower levels, managers have limited responsibility and relatively little control over costs and expenses. Performance reports for low-level management typically cover few controllable costs. Responsibility and control broaden for higher-level managers; therefore, their reports span a wider range of costs. However, reports to higher-level managers seldom contain the details reported to their subordinates but are summarized for two reasons: (1) lower-level managers are often responsible for these detailed costs and (2) detailed reports can obscure broader, more important issues facing a company.

Exhibit 21.28 shows summarized performance reports for the three management levels identified in Exhibit 21.27. Exhibit 21.28 shows that costs under the control of the benchmarking

EXHIBIT 21.27

Organizational Responsibility Chart

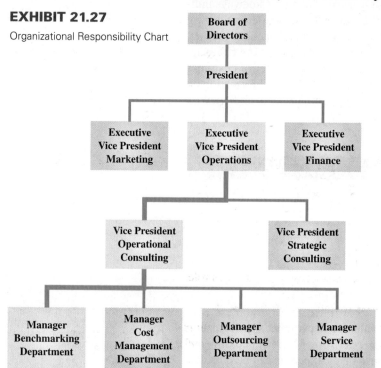

Point: Responsibility accounting does not place blame. Instead, responsibility accounting is used to identify opportunities for improving performance.

EXHIBIT 21.28

Responsibility Accounting
Performance Reports

Executive Vice President, Operations		For July	
Controllable Costs	**Budgeted Amount**	**Actual Amount**	**Over (Under) Budget**
Salaries, VPs	$ 80,000	$ 80,000	$ 0
Quality control costs	21,000	22,400	1,400
Office costs	29,500	28,800	(700)
Operational consulting	276,700	279,500	2,800
Strategic consulting	390,000	380,600	(9,400)
Totals	$ 797,200	$ 791,300	$ (5,900)

Vice President, Operational Consulting		For July	
Controllable Costs	**Budgeted Amount**	**Actual Amount**	**Over (Under) Budget**
Salaries, department managers	$ 75,000	$ 78,000	$ 3,000
Depreciation	10,600	10,600	0
Insurance	6,800	6,300	(500)
Benchmarking department	79,600	79,900	300
Cost management department	61,500	60,200	(1,300)
Outsourcing department	24,300	24,700	400
Service department	18,900	19,800	900
Totals	$276,700	$279,500	$2,800

Manager, Benchmarking Department		For July	
Controllable Costs	**Budgeted Amount**	**Actual Amount**	**Over (Under) Budget**
Salaries	$ 51,600	$ 52,500	$ 900
Supplies	8,000	7,800	(200)
Other controllable costs	20,000	19,600	(400)
Totals	$ 79,600	$ 79,900	$ 300

department manager are totaled and included among controllable costs of the VP for operational consulting. Also, costs under the control of the VP are totaled and included among controllable costs of the EVP for operations. In this way, a responsibility accounting system provides relevant information for each management level.

Technological advances increase our ability to produce vast amounts of information that often exceed our ability to use it. Good managers select relevant data for planning and controlling the areas under their responsibility. A good responsibility accounting system makes every effort to provide relevant information to the right person (the one who controls the cost) at the right time (before a cost is out of control).

Point: Responsibility accounting usually divides a company into subunits, or *responsibility centers*. A center manager is evaluated on how well the center performs, as reported in responsibility accounting reports.

Summary of Cost Allocation

Exhibit 21.29 summarizes the cost allocation techniques shown in this chapter. These methods focus on different types of costs, as managers need different information for different decisions.

EXHIBIT 21.29

Cost Allocation Methods

Cost Definition	Accounting Task	Managerial Decision
Overhead costs	Assign overhead to individual jobs	Product costing and pricing
Indirect expenses	Assign indirect expenses to departments	Evaluate department performance
Uncontrollable costs	Remove uncontrollable costs from responsibility accounting reports	Evaluate department manager performance

Quick Check

Answers — p. 886

10. Are the reports of departmental net income and the departmental contribution to overhead useful in assessing a department manager's performance? Explain.

11. Performance reports to evaluate managers should (a) include data about controllable expenses, (b) compare actual results with budgeted levels, or (c) both (a) and (b).

GLOBAL VIEW

L'Oreal is an international cosmetics company incorporated in France. With multiple brands and operations in over 100 countries, the company uses concepts of departmental accounting and controllable costs to evaluate performance. For example, a recent annual report shows the following for the major divisions in its Cosmetics branch:

Division	Operating Profit (€ millions)	
Consumer products	€1,578	
Professional products	519	
Luxury products	766	
Active cosmetics	259	
Other cosmetics	(12)	€3,110
Nonallocated costs		(502)
Cosmetics branch total		€2,608

For L'Oreal, nonallocated costs include costs that are not controllable by division managers, including fundamental research and development and costs of service operations like insurance and banking. Excluding noncontrollable costs enables L'Oreal to prepare more meaningful division performance evaluations.

Decision Analysis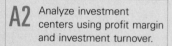

Investment Center Profit Margin and Investment Turnover

A2 Analyze investment centers using profit margin and investment turnover.

We can further examine investment center (division) performance by splitting return on investment into **profit margin** and **investment turnover** as follows

Return on investment	=	Profit margin	×	Investment turnover

$$\frac{\text{Investment center net income}}{\text{Investment center average assets}} = \frac{\text{Investment center net income}}{\text{Investment center sales}} \times \frac{\text{Investment center sales}}{\text{Investment center average assets}}$$

Profit margin measures the income earned per dollar of sales. **Investment turnover** measures how efficiently an investment center generates sales from its invested assets. Higher profit margin and higher investment turnover indicate better performance. To illustrate, consider **Best Buy** which reports in Exhibit 21.30 results for two divisions (segments): Domestic and International.

EXHIBIT 21.30

Best Buy Division Sales, Income, and Assets

($ millions)	Domestic	International
Sales	$37,314	$12,380
Net income	2,071	164
Average invested assets	9,745	7,319

Profit margin and investment turnover for its Domestic and International divisions are computed and shown in Exhibit 21.31:

($ millions)	Domestic	International
Profit Margin		
$2,071/$37,314	5.55%	
$164/$12,380		1.32%
Investment Turnover		
$37,314/9,745	3.83	
$12,380/$7,319		1.69

EXHIBIT 21.31

Best Buy Division Profit Margin and Investment Turnover

Best Buy's Domestic division generates 5.55 cents of profit per $1 of sales, while its International division generates only 1.32 cents of profit per dollar of sales. Its Domestic division also uses its assets more efficiently; its investment turnover of 3.83 is over twice that of its International division's 1.69. Top management can use profit margin and investment turnover to evaluate the performance of division managers. The measures can also aid management when considering further investment in its divisions.

Decision Maker 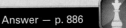 Answer — p. 886

Division Manager You manage a division in a highly competitive industry. You will receive a cash bonus if your division achieves an ROI above 12%. Your division's profit margin is 7%, equal to the industry average, and your division's investment turnover is 1.5. What actions can you take to increase your chance of receiving the bonus? ■

DEMONSTRATION PROBLEM

Management requests departmental income statements for Hacker's Haven, a computer store that has five departments. Three are operating departments (hardware, software, and repairs) and two are service departments (general office and purchasing).

	General Office	Purchasing	Hardware	Software	Repairs
Sales	—	—	$960,000	$600,000	$840,000
Cost of goods sold	—	—	500,000	300,000	200,000
Direct expenses					
Payroll	$60,000	$45,000	80,000	25,000	325,000
Depreciation	6,000	7,200	33,000	4,200	9,600
Supplies	15,000	10,000	10,000	2,000	25,000

The departments incur several indirect expenses. To prepare departmental income statements, the indirect expenses must be allocated across the five departments. Then the expenses of the two service departments must be allocated to the three operating departments. Total cost amounts and the allocation bases for each indirect expense follow.

Indirect Expense	Total Cost	Allocation Basis
Rent	$150,000	Square footage occupied
Utilities	50,000	Square footage occupied
Advertising	125,000	Dollars of sales
Insurance	30,000	Value of assets insured
Service departments		
General office	?	Number of employees
Purchasing	?	Dollars of cost of goods sold

The following additional information is needed for indirect expense allocations.

Department	Square Feet	Sales	Insured Assets	Employees	Cost of Goods Sold
General office	500		$ 60,000		
Purchasing	500		72,000		
Hardware............	4,000	$ 960,000	330,000	5	$ 500,000
Software............	3,000	600,000	42,000	5	300,000
Repairs	2,000	840,000	96,000	10	200,000
Totals	10,000	$2,400,000	$600,000	20	$1,000,000

Required

1. Prepare a departmental expense allocation spreadsheet for Hacker's Haven.
2. Prepare a departmental income statement reporting net income for each operating department and for all operating departments combined.

PLANNING THE SOLUTION

- Set up and complete four tables to allocate the indirect expenses—one each for rent, utilities, advertising, and insurance.
- Allocate the departments' indirect expenses using a spreadsheet like the one in Exhibit 21.12. Enter the given amounts of the direct expenses for each department. Then enter the allocated amounts of the indirect expenses that you computed.
- Complete two tables for allocating the general office and purchasing department costs to the three operating departments. Enter these amounts on the spreadsheet and determine the total expenses allocated to the three operating departments.
- Prepare departmental income statements like the one in Exhibit 21.21. Show sales, cost of goods sold, gross profit, individual expenses, and net income for each of the three operating departments and for the combined company.

SOLUTION TO DEMONSTRATION PROBLEM

Allocations of the four indirect expenses across the five departments.

Rent	Square Feet	Percent of Total	Allocated Cost
General office	500	5.0%	$ 7,500
Purchasing	500	5.0	7,500
Hardware............	4,000	40.0	60,000
Software	3,000	30.0	45,000
Repairs	2,000	20.0	30,000
Totals	10,000	100.0%	$150,000

Utilities	Square Feet	Percent of Total	Allocated Cost
General office	500	5.0%	$ 2,500
Purchasing	500	5.0	2,500
Hardware............	4,000	40.0	20,000
Software	3,000	30.0	15,000
Repairs	2,000	20.0	10,000
Totals	10,000	100.0%	$50,000

Advertising	Sales Dollars	Percent of Total	Allocated Cost
Hardware...........	$ 960,000	40.0%	$ 50,000
Software............	600,000	25.0	31,250
Repairs	840,000	35.0	43,750
Totals	$2,400,000	100.0%	$125,000

Insurance	Assets Insured	Percent of Total	Allocated Cost
General office	$ 60,000	10.0%	$ 3,000
Purchasing	72,000	12.0	3,600
Hardware	330,000	55.0	16,500
Software	42,000	7.0	2,100
Repairs	96,000	16.0	4,800
Totals	$600,000	100.0%	$30,000

1. Allocations of service department expenses to the three operating departments.

General Office Allocations to	Employees	Percent of Total	Allocated Cost
Hardware.............	5	25.0%	$23,500
Software.............	5	25.0	23,500
Repairs..............	10	50.0	47,000
Totals	20	100.0%	$94,000

Purchasing Allocations to	Cost of Goods Sold	Percent of Total	Allocated Cost
Hardware.............	$ 500,000	50.0%	$37,900
Software.............	300,000	30.0	22,740
Repairs	200,000	20.0	15,160
Totals	$1,000,000	100.0%	$75,800

HACKER'S HAVEN
Departmental Expense Allocations
For Year Ended December 31, 2011

	Allocation Base	Expense Account Balance	General Office Dept.	Purchasing Dept.	Hardware Dept.	Software Dept.	Repairs Dept.
Direct Expenses							
Payroll............................		$ 535,000	$ 60,000	$ 45,000	$ 80,000	$ 25,000	$ 325,000
Depreciation		60,000	6,000	7,200	33,000	4,200	9,600
Supplies		62,000	15,000	10,000	10,000	2,000	25,000
Indirect Expenses							
Rent	Square ft.	150,000	7,500	7,500	60,000	45,000	30,000
Utilities..........................	Square ft.	50,000	2,500	2,500	20,000	15,000	10,000
Advertising	Sales	125,000	—	—	50,000	31,250	43,750
Insurance	Assets	30,000	3,000	3,600	16,500	2,100	4,800
Total expenses		1,012,000	94,000	75,800	269,500	124,550	448,150
Service Department Expenses							
General office	Employees		(94,000)		23,500	23,500	47,000
Purchasing	Goods sold			(75,800)	37,900	22,740	15,160
Total expenses allocated to operating departments		$1,012,000	$ 0	$ 0	$330,900	$170,790	$510,310

2. Departmental income statements for Hacker's Haven.

HACKER'S HAVEN
Departmental Income Statements
For Year Ended December 31, 2011

	Hardware	Software	Repairs	Combined
Sales	$ 960,000	$ 600,000	$ 840,000	$2,400,000
Cost of goods sold	500,000	300,000	200,000	1,000,000
Gross profit	460,000	300,000	640,000	1,400,000
Expenses				
Payroll	80,000	25,000	325,000	430,000
Depreciation	33,000	4,200	9,600	46,800
Supplies	10,000	2,000	25,000	37,000
Rent	60,000	45,000	30,000	135,000
Utilities	20,000	15,000	10,000	45,000
Advertising	50,000	31,250	43,750	125,000
Insurance	16,500	2,100	4,800	23,400
Share of general office	23,500	23,500	47,000	94,000
Share of purchasing	37,900	22,740	15,160	75,800
Total expenses	330,900	170,790	510,310	1,012,000
Net income	$129,100	$129,210	$129,690	$ 388,000

21A

Transfer Pricing

C3 Explain transfer pricing and methods to set transfer prices.

Point: Transfer pricing can impact company profits when divisions are located in countries with different tax rates; this is covered in advanced courses.

Divisions in decentralized companies sometimes do business with one another. For example, a separate division of **Harley-Davidson** manufactures its plastic and fiberglass parts used in the company's motorcycles. **Anheuser-Busch**'s metal container division makes cans and lids used in its brewing operations, and also sells cans and lids to soft-drink companies. A division of **Prince** produces strings used in tennis rackets made by Prince and other manufacturers.

Determining the price that should be used to record transfers between divisions in the same company is the focus of this appendix. Because these transactions are transfers within the same company, the price to record them is called the **transfer price.** In decentralized organizations, division managers have input on or decide those prices. Transfer prices can be used in cost, profit, and investment centers. Since these transfers are not with customers outside the company, the transfer price has no direct impact on the company's overall profits. However, transfer prices can impact performance evaluations and, if set incorrectly, lead to bad decisions.

Alternative Transfer Prices Exhibit 21A.1 reports data on the LCD division of ZTel. LCD manufactures liquid crystal display (LCD) touch-screen monitors for use in ZTel's S-Phone division's smartphones, which sell for $400 each. The monitors can also be used in other products. So, LCD can sell its monitors to buyers other than S-Phone. Likewise, the S-Phone division can purchase monitors from suppliers other than LCD.

EXHIBIT 21A.1

LCD Division Manufacturing Information—Monitors

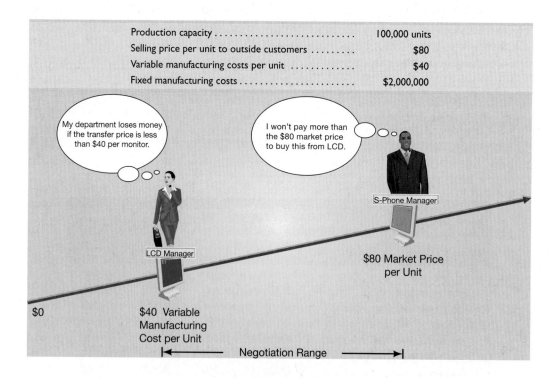

Production capacity	100,000 units
Selling price per unit to outside customers	$80
Variable manufacturing costs per unit	$40
Fixed manufacturing costs	$2,000,000

Exhibit 21A.1 reveals the range of transfer prices for transfers of monitors from LCD to S-Phone. The manager of LCD wants to report a division profit; thus, this manager will not accept a transfer price less than $40 (variable manufacturing cost per unit) because doing so would cause the division to lose money on each monitor transferred. The LCD manager will only consider transfer prices of $40 or more. On the other hand, the S-Phone division manager also wants to report a division profit. Thus, this manager will not pay more than $80 per monitor because similar monitors can be bought from outside suppliers at that price. The S-Phone manager will only consider transfer prices of $80 or less. As any transfer price between $40 and $80 per monitor is possible, how does ZTel determine the transfer price? The answer depends in part on whether the LCD division has excess capacity to manufacture monitors.

No Excess Capacity   Assume the LCD division can sell every monitor it produces, and thus is producing 100,000 units. In that case, a **market-based transfer price** of $80 per monitor is preferred. At that price, the LCD division manager is willing to either transfer monitors to S-Phone or sell to outside customers. The S-Phone manager cannot buy monitors for less than $80 from outside suppliers, so the $80 price is acceptable. Further, with a transfer price of $80 per monitor, top management of ZTel is indifferent to S-Phone buying from LCD or buying similar-quality monitors from outside suppliers.

With no excess capacity, the LCD manager will not accept a transfer price less than $80 per monitor. For example, suppose the S-Phone manager suggests a transfer price of $70 per monitor. At that price the LCD manager incurs an unnecessary *opportunity cost* of $10 per monitor (computed as $80 market price minus $70 transfer price). This would lower the LCD division's income and hurt its performance evaluation.

Excess Capacity   Assume that the LCD division has excess capacity. For example, the LCD division might currently be producing only 80,000 units. Because LCD has $2,000,000 of fixed manufacturing costs, both LCD and the top management of ZTel prefer that S-Phone purchases its monitors from LCD. For example, if S-Phone purchases its monitors from an outside supplier at the market price of $80 each, LCD manufactures no units. Then, LCD reports a division loss equal to its fixed costs, and ZTel overall reports a lower net income as its costs are higher. Consequently, with excess capacity, LCD should accept any transfer price of $40 per unit or greater and S-Phone should purchase monitors from LCD. This will allow LCD to recover some (or all) of its fixed costs and increase ZTel's overall profits. For example, if a transfer price of $50 per monitor is used, the S-Phone manager is pleased to buy from LCD, since that price is below the market price of $80. For each monitor transferred from LCD to S-Phone at $50, the LCD division receives a *contribution margin* of $10 (computed as $50 transfer price less $40 variable cost) to contribute towards recovering its fixed costs. This form of transfer pricing is called **cost-based transfer pricing.** Under this approach the transfer price might be based on variable costs, total costs, or variable costs plus a markup. Determining the transfer price under excess capacity is complex and is covered in advanced courses.

Additional Issues in Transfer Pricing   Several additional issues arise in determining transfer prices which include the following:

- **No market price exists.** Sometimes there is no market price for the product being transferred. The product might be a key component that requires additional conversion costs at the next stage and is not easily replicated by an outside company. For example, there is no market for a console for a **Nissan** Maxima and there is no substitute console **Nissan** can use in assembling a Maxima. In this case a market-based transfer price cannot be used.

- **Cost control.** To provide incentives for cost control, transfer prices might be based on standard, rather than actual costs. For example, if a transfer price of actual variable costs plus a markup of $20 per unit is used in the case above, LCD has no incentive to control its costs.

- **Division managers' negotiation.** With excess capacity, division managers will often negotiate a transfer price that lies between the variable cost per unit and the market price per unit. In this case, the **negotiated transfer price** and resulting departmental performance reports reflect, in part, the negotiating skills of the respective division managers. This might not be best for overall company performance.

- **Nonfinancial factors.** Factors such as quality control, reduced lead times, and impact on employee morale can be important factors in determining transfer prices.

Transfer Pricing Approaches Used by Companies

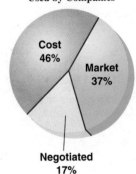

Cost 46%

Market 37%

Negotiated 17%

APPENDIX

Joint Costs and Their Allocation

21B

C4   Describe allocation of joint costs across products.

Most manufacturing processes involve **joint costs,** which refer to costs incurred to produce or purchase two or more products at the same time. A joint cost is like an indirect expense in the sense that more than one cost object share it. For example, a sawmill company incurs a joint cost when it buys logs that it cuts into lumber as shown in Exhibit 21B.1. The joint cost includes the logs (raw material) and its cutting (conversion) into boards classified as Clear, Select, No. 1 Common, No. 2 Common, No. 3 Common, and other types of lumber and by-products.

When a joint cost is incurred, a question arises as to whether to allocate it to different products resulting from it. The answer is that when management wishes to estimate the costs of individual products, joint

EXHIBIT 21B.1

Joint Products from Logs

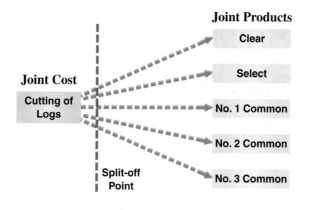

costs are included and must be allocated to these joint products. However, when management needs information to help decide whether to sell a product at a certain point in the production process or to process it further, the joint costs are ignored.

Financial statements prepared according to GAAP must assign joint costs to products. To do this, management must decide how to allocate joint costs across products benefiting from these costs. If some products are sold and others remain in inventory, allocating joint costs involves assigning costs to both cost of goods sold and ending inventory.

The two usual methods to allocate joint costs are the (1) *physical basis* and (2) the *value basis*. The physical basis typically involves allocating joint cost using physical characteristics such as the ratio of pounds, cubic feet, or gallons of each joint product to the total pounds, cubic feet, or gallons of all joint products flowing from the cost. This method is not preferred because the resulting cost allocations do not reflect the relative market values the joint cost generates. The preferred approach is the value basis, which allocates joint cost in proportion to the sales value of the output produced by the process at the "split-off point"; see Exhibit 21B.1.

Physical Basis Allocation of Joint Cost   To illustrate the physical basis of allocating a joint cost, we consider a sawmill that bought logs for $30,000. When cut, these logs produce 100,000 board feet of lumber in the grades and amounts shown in Exhibit 21B.2. The logs produce 20,000 board feet of No. 3 Common lumber, which is 20% of the total. With physical allocation, the No. 3 Common lumber is assigned 20% of the $30,000 cost of the logs, or $6,000 ($30,000 × 20%). Because this low-grade lumber sells for $4,000, this allocation gives a $2,000 loss from its production and sale. The physical basis for allocating joint costs does not reflect the extra value flowing into some products or the inferior value flowing into others. That is, the portion of a log that produces Clear and Select grade lumber is worth more than the portion used to produce the three grades of common lumber, but the physical basis fails to reflect this.

EXHIBIT 21B.2

Allocating Joint Costs on a Physical Basis

Grade of Lumber	Board Feet Produced	Percent of Total	Allocated Cost	Sales Value	Gross Profit
Clear and Select............	10,000	10.0%	$ 3,000	$12,000	$ 9,000
No. 1 Common	30,000	30.0	9,000	18,000	9,000
No. 2 Common	40,000	40.0	12,000	16,000	4,000
No. 3 Common	20,000	20.0	6,000	4,000	(2,000)
Totals	100,000	100.0%	$30,000	$50,000	$20,000

Value Basis Allocation of Joint Cost   Exhibit 21B.3 illustrates the value basis method of allocation. It determines the percents of the total costs allocated to each grade by the ratio of each grade's sales value to the total sales value of $50,000 (sales value is the unit selling price multiplied by the number of units produced). The Clear and Select lumber grades receive 24% of the total cost ($12,000/$50,000) instead of the 10% portion using a physical basis. The No. 3 Common lumber receives only 8% of the total cost, or $2,400, which is much less than the $6,000 assigned to it using the physical basis.

EXHIBIT 21B.3

Allocating Joint Costs on a Value Basis

Grade of Lumber	Sales Value	Percent of Total	Allocated Cost	Gross Profit
Clear and Select	$12,000	24.0%	$ 7,200	$ 4,800
No. 1 Common	18,000	36.0	10,800	7,200
No. 2 Common	16,000	32.0	9,600	6,400
No. 3 Common	4,000	8.0	2,400	1,600
Totals	$50,000	100.0%	$30,000	$20,000

An outcome of value basis allocation is that *each* grade produces exactly the same 40% gross profit at the split-off point. This 40% rate equals the gross profit rate from selling all the lumber made from the $30,000 logs for a combined price of $50,000.

> **Example:** Refer to Exhibit 21B.3. If the sales value of Clear and Select lumber is changed to $10,000, what is the revised ratio of the market value of No. I Common to the total? *Answer:* $18,000/$48,000 = 37.5%

Quick Check

Answers — p. 886

12. A company produces three products, B1, B2, and B3. The joint cost incurred for the current month for these products is $180,000. The following data relate to this month's production:

Product	Units Produced	Unit Sales Value
BI	96,000	$3.00
B2	64,000	6.00
B3	32,000	9.00

The amount of joint cost allocated to product B3 using the value basis allocation is (*a*) $30,000, (*b*) $54,000, or (*c*) $90,000.

Summary

C1 **Distinguish between direct and indirect expenses and identify bases for allocating indirect expenses to departments.** Direct expenses are traced to a specific department and are incurred for the sole benefit of that department. Indirect expenses benefit more than one department. Indirect expenses are allocated to departments when computing departmental net income. Ideally, we allocate indirect expenses by using a cause-effect relation for the allocation base. When a cause-effect relation is not identifiable, each indirect expense is allocated on a basis reflecting the relative benefit received by each department.

C2 **Explain controllable costs and responsibility accounting.** A controllable cost is one that is influenced by a specific management level. The total expenses of operating a department often include some items a department manager does not control. Responsibility accounting systems provide information for evaluating the performance of department managers. A responsibility accounting system's performance reports for evaluating department managers should include only the expenses (and revenues) that each manager controls.

C3 **Explain transfer pricing and methods to set transfer prices.** Transfer prices are used to record transfers of items between divisions of the same company. Transfer prices can be based on costs or market prices, or can be negotiated by division managers.

C4 **Describe allocation of joint costs across products.** A joint cost refers to costs incurred to produce or purchase two or more products at the same time. When income statements are prepared, joint costs are usually allocated to the resulting joint products using either a physical or value basis.

A1 **Analyze investment centers using return on assets, residual income, and balanced scorecard.** A financial measure often used to evaluate an investment center manager is the *investment center return on total assets,* also called *return on investment.* This measure is computed as the center's net income divided by the center's average total assets. Residual income, computed as investment center net income minus a target net income is an alternative

financial measure of investment center performance. A balanced scorecard uses a combination of financial and non-financial measures to evaluate performance.

A2 **Analyze investment centers using profit margin and investment turnover.** Return on investment can also be computed as profit margin times investment turnover. Profit margin (equal to net income/sales) measures the income earned per dollar of sales and investment turnover (equal to sales/assets) measures how efficiently a division uses its assets.

P1 **Assign overhead costs using two-stage cost allocation.** In the traditional two-stage cost allocation procedure, service department costs are first assigned to operating departments. Then, in the second stage, a predetermined overhead allocation rate is computed for each operating department and is used to assign overhead to output.

P2 **Assign overhead costs using activity-based costing.** In activity-based costing, the costs of related activities are collected and then pooled in some logical manner into activity cost pools. After all activity costs have been accumulated in an activity cost pool account, users of the activity, termed *cost objects,* are assigned a portion of the total activity cost using a cost driver (allocation base).

P3 **Prepare departmental income statements and contribution reports.** Each profit center (department) is assigned its expenses to yield its own income statement. These costs include its direct expenses and its share of indirect expenses. The departmental income statement lists its revenues and costs of goods sold to determine gross profit. Its operating expenses (direct expenses and its indirect expenses allocated to the department) are deducted from gross profit to yield departmental net income. The departmental contribution report is similar to the departmental income statement in terms of computing the gross profit for each department. Then the direct operating expenses for each department are deducted from gross profit to determine the contribution generated by each department. Indirect operating expenses are deducted *in total* from the company's combined contribution.

Guidance Answers to Decision Maker and Decision Ethics

Director of Operations   You should collect details on overhead items and review them to see whether direct labor drives these costs. If it does not, overhead might be improperly assigned to departments. The situation also provides an opportunity to consider other overhead allocation bases, including use of activity-based costing.

Accounting Officer   You should not author a report that you disagree with. You are responsible for ascertaining all the facts of ABC (implementation procedures, advantages and disadvantages, and costs). You should then approach your supervisor with these facts and suggest that you would like to modify the report to request, for example, a pilot test. The pilot test will allow you to further assess the suitability of ABC. Your suggestion might be rejected, at which time you may wish to speak with a more senior-level manager.

Center Manager   We must first realize that the two investment opportunities are not comparable on the basis of absolute dollars of income or on assets. For instance, the second investment provides a

higher income in absolute dollars but requires a higher investment. Accordingly, we need to compute return on total assets for each alternative: (1) $50,000 ÷ $250,000 = 20\%$, and (2) $175,000 ÷ \$1$ million $= 17.5\%$. Alternative 1 has the higher return and is preferred over alternative 2. Do you pursue one, both, or neither? Because alternative 1's return is higher than the center's usual return of 19%, it should be pursued, assuming its risks are acceptable. Also, since alternative 1 requires a small investment, top management is likely to be more agreeable to pursuing it. Alternative 2's return is lower than the usual 19% and is not likely to be acceptable.

Division Manager   Your division's ROI without further action is 10.5% (equal to $7\% \times 1.5$). In a highly competitive industry, it is difficult to increase profit margins by raising prices. Your division might be better able to control its costs to increase its profit margin. In addition, you might engage in a marketing program to increase sales without increasing your division's invested assets. Investment turnover and thus ROI will increase if the marketing campaign attracts customers.

Guidance Answers to Quick Checks

1. Cost drivers are the factors that have a cause-effect relation with costs (or activities that pertain to costs).

2. *d*

3. A departmental accounting system provides information used to evaluate the performance of *departments*. A responsibility accounting system provides information used to evaluate the performance of *department managers.*

4. *d*

5. A cost center, such as a service department, incurs costs without directly generating revenues. A profit center, such as a product division, incurs costs but also generates revenues.

6. *b*

7. *d*

8. (1) Assign the direct expenses to each department. (2) Allocate indirect expenses to all departments. (3) Allocate the service department expenses to the operating departments.

9. *b*

10. No, because many expenses that enter into these calculations are beyond the manager's control, and managers should not be evaluated using costs they do not control.

11. *c*

12. *b*; $180,000 \times ([32,000 \times \$9]/[96,000 \times \$3 + 64,000 \times \$6 + 32,000 \times \$9]) = \underline{\$54,000}$.

Key Terms

mhhe.com/wildFAP20e

Activity-based costing (ABC) (p. 861)	Direct expenses (p. 865)	Market-based transfer price (p. 883)
Activity cost driver (p. 861)	Hurdle rate (p. 873)	Negotiated transfer price (p. 883)
Activity cost pool (p. 861)	Indirect expenses (p. 865)	Profit center (p. 865)
Balanced scorecard (p. 874)	Investment center (p. 865)	Profit margin (p. 878)
Controllable costs (p. 875)	Investment center residual income (p. 873)	Responsibility accounting budget (p. 876)
Cost-based transfer pricing (p. 883)		Responsibility accounting performance report (p. 876)
Cost center (p. 865)	Investment center return on total assets (p. 873)	Responsibility accounting system (p. 864)
Departmental accounting system (p. 864)	Investment turnover (p. 878)	Transfer price (p. 882)
Departmental contribution to overhead (p. 871)	Joint cost (p. 883)	Uncontrollable costs (p. 875)

Additional Quiz Questions are available at the book's Website.

1. A retailer has three departments—housewares, appliances, and clothing—and buys advertising that benefits all departments. Advertising expense is $150,000 for the year, and departmental sales for the year follow: housewares, $356,250; appliances, $641,250; clothing, $427,500. How much advertising expense is allocated to appliances if allocation is based on departmental sales?
   a. $37,500
   b. $67,500
   c. $45,000
   d. $150,000
   e. $641,250

2. An activity-based costing system
   a. Does not require the level of detail that a traditional costing system requires.
   b. Does not enable the calculation of unit cost data.
   c. Allocates costs to products on the basis of activities performed on them.
   d. Cannot be used by a service company.
   e. Allocates costs to products based on the number of direct labor hours used.

3. A company produces two products, Grey and Red. The following information is available relating to those two products. Assume that the company's total setup cost is $162,000. Using activity-based costing, how much setup cost is allocated to each unit of Grey?

	Grey	Red
Units produced	500	40,000
Number of setups	50	100
Direct labor hours per unit	15	15

   a. $1,080
   b. $ 72
   c. $ 162
   d. $2,000
   e. $ 108

4. A company operates three retail departments as profit centers, and the following information is available for each. Which department has the largest dollar amount of departmental contribution to overhead and what is the dollar amount contributed?

Department	Sales	Cost of Goods Sold	Direct Expenses	Allocated Indirect Expenses
X	$500,000	$350,000	$50,000	$40,000
Y	200,000	75,000	20,000	50,000
Z	350,000	150,000	75,000	10,000

   a. Department Y, $ 55,000
   b. Department Z, $125,000
   c. Department X, $500,000
   d. Department Z, $200,000
   e. Department X, $ 60,000

5. Using the data in question 4, Department X's contribution to overhead as a percentage of sales is
   a. 20%
   b. 30%
   c. 12%
   d. 48%
   e. 32%

A(B) *Superscript letter A (B) denotes assignments based on Appendix 21A (21B).*
🔒 Icon denotes assignments that involve decision making.

Discussion Questions

1. Why are many companies divided into departments?
2. Complete the following for a traditional two-stage allocation system: In the first stage, service department costs are assigned to _____ departments. In the second stage, a predetermined overhead rate is computed for each operating department and used to assign overhead to _____.
3. What is the difference between operating departments and service departments?
4. What is activity-based costing? What is its goal?
5. 🔒 Identify at least four typical cost pools for activity-based costing in most organizations.
6. In activity-based costing, costs in a cost pool are allocated to _____ using predetermined overhead rates.

7. 🔒 What company circumstances especially encourage use of activity-based costing?
8. 🔒 What are two main goals in managerial accounting for reporting on and analyzing departments?
9. 🔒 Is it possible to evaluate a cost center's profitability? Explain.
10. What is the difference between direct and indirect expenses?
11. 🔒 Suggest a reasonable basis for allocating each of the following indirect expenses to departments: (a) salary of a supervisor who manages several departments, (b) rent, (c) heat, (d) electricity for lighting, (e) janitorial services, (f) advertising, (g) expired insurance on equipment, and (h) property taxes on equipment.

12. Research In Motion has many departments. How is **RIM** a department's contribution to overhead measured?

13. [i] What are controllable costs?

14. Controllable and uncontrollable costs must be identified with a particular _____ and a definite _____ period.

15. [i] Why should managers be closely involved in preparing their responsibility accounting budgets?

16. [i] **Nokia** aims to give its managers timely cost **NOKIA** reports. In responsibility accounting, who receives timely cost reports and specific cost information? Explain.

17.[A] What is a transfer price? Under what conditions is a market-based transfer price most likely to be used?

18.[B] What is a joint cost? How are joint costs usually allocated among the products produced from them?

19.[B] [i] Give two examples of products with joint costs.

20. [i] Each retail store of **Apple** has several depart- **Apple** ments. Why is it useful for its management to (a) collect accounting information about each department and (b) treat each department as a profit center?

21. [i] **Palm** delivers its products to locations around **Palm** the world. List three controllable and three uncontrollable costs for its delivery department.

---

connect

QUICK STUDY

QS 21-1

Allocation and measurement terms

C1

In each blank next to the following terms, place the identifying letter of its best description.

1. _____ Operating department

2. _____ Profit center

3. _____ Responsibility accounting system

4. _____ Cost center

5. _____ Investment center

6. _____ Departmental accounting system

7. _____ Service department

A. Holds manager responsible for revenues, costs, and investments.

B. Does not directly manufacture products but contributes to profitability of the entire company.

C. Incurs costs and also generates revenues.

D. Provides information used to evaluate the performance of a department.

E. Incurs costs without directly yielding revenues.

F. Provides information used to evaluate the performance of a department manager.

G. Engages directly in manufacturing or in making sales directly to customers.

QS 21-2

Basis for cost allocation

C1

For each of the following types of indirect expenses and service department expenses, identify one allocation basis that could be used to distribute it to the departments indicated.

1. Electric utility expenses of all departments.

2. General office department expenses of the operating departments.

3. Maintenance department expenses of the operating departments.

4. Computer service expenses of production scheduling for operating departments.

QS 21-3

Activity-based costing and overhead cost allocation

P2

The following is taken from Maxwell Co.'s internal records of its factory with two operating departments. The cost driver for indirect labor and supplies is direct labor costs, and the cost driver for the remaining overhead items is number of hours of machine use. Compute the total amount of overhead cost allocated to Operating Department 1 using activity-based costing.

	Direct Labor	Machine Use Hours
Operating department 1	$10,400	2,200
Operating department 2	9,600	3,000
Totals	$20,000	5,200
Factory overhead costs		
Rent and utilities	$ 7,100	
Indirect labor	3,700	
General office expense	2,700	
Depreciation—Equipment	4,500	
Supplies	300	
Total factory overhead	$18,300	

Check   Dept. 1 allocation, $8,130

Use the information in the following table to compute each department's contribution to overhead (both in dollars and as a percent). Which department contributes the largest dollar amount to total overhead? Which contributes the highest percent (as a percent of sales)? Round percents to one decimal.

QS 21-4
Departmental contribution to overhead
P3

	Dept. A	Dept. B	Dept. C
Sales	$53,000	$170,000	$84,000
Cost of goods sold	34,185	103,700	49,560
Gross profit	18,815	66,300	34,440
Total direct expenses	6,360	37,060	8,736
Contribution to overhead	$	$	$
Contribution percent	%	%	%

Compute return on assets for each of these **Best Buy** divisions (each is an investment center). Comment on the relative performance of each investment center. Round percents to one decimal.

QS 21-5
Investment center analysis
A1
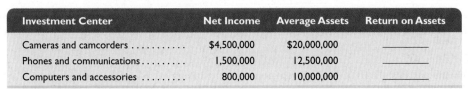

Investment Center	Net Income	Average Assets	Return on Assets
Cameras and camcorders	$4,500,000	$20,000,000	_____
Phones and communications	1,500,000	12,500,000	_____
Computers and accessories	800,000	10,000,000	_____

Refer to information in QS 21-5. Assume a target income of 12% of average invested assets. Compute residual income for each of Best Buy's divisions.

QS 21-6
Computing residual income
A1

A company's shipping division (an investment center) has sales of $4,700,000, net income of $916,000, and average invested assets of $3,000,000. Compute the division's profit margin and investment turnover.

QS 21-7
Computing performance measures A2

Fill in the blanks in the schedule below for two separate investment centers A and B.

QS 21-8
Performance measures
A1 A2

	Investment Center	
	A	B
Sales	$_____	$6,400,000
Net income	$ 252,000	$_____
Average invested assets	$1,400,000	_____
Profit margin	6%	____%
Investment turnover	_____	1.6
Return on assets	____%	10%

Classify each of the performance measures below into the most likely balanced scorecard perspective it relates to. Label your answers using C (customer), P (internal process), I (innovation and growth), or F (financial).

QS 21-9
Performance measures—balanced scorecard
A1

1. Number of new products introduced _____
2. Length of time raw materials are in inventory _____
3. Profit margin _____
4. Customer wait time _____
5. Change in market share _____
6. Employee training sessions attended _____
7. Number of days of employee absences _____
8. Customer satisfaction index _____

QS 21-10

Performance measures—
balanced scorecard

A1

Walt Disney reports the following information for its two Parks and Resorts divisions.

	East Coast		West Coast	
	Current year	Prior year	Current year	Prior year
Hotel occupancy rates	89%	86%	92%	93%

Assume Walt Disney uses a balanced scorecard and sets a target of 90% occupancy in its resorts. Using Exhibit 21.26 as a guide, show how the company's performance on hotel occupancy would appear on a balanced scorecard report.

QS 21-11[A]

Determining transfer prices
without excess capacity

C3

The Windshield division of Cargo Co. makes windshields for use in Cargo's Assembly division. The Windshield division incurs variable costs of $350 per windshield and has capacity to make 100,000 windshields per year. The market price is $600 per windshield. The Windshield division incurs total fixed costs of $3,000,000 per year. If the Windshield division is operating at full capacity, what transfer price should be used on transfers between the Windshield and Assembly divisions? Explain.

QS 21-12[A]

Determining transfer prices with
excess capacity   C3

Refer to information in QS 21-11. If the Windshield division has excess capacity, what is the range of possible transfer prices that could be used on transfers between the Windshield and Assembly divisions? Explain.

QS 21-13[B]

Joint cost allocation

C4

A company purchases a 10,000 square foot commercial building for $400,000 and spends an additional $65,000 to divide the space into two separate rental units and prepare it for rent. Unit A, which has the desirable location on the corner and contains 2,500 square feet, will be rented for $2.00 per square foot. Unit B contains 7,500 square feet and will be rented for $1.50 per square foot. How much of the joint cost should be assigned to Unit B using the value basis of allocation?

QS 21-14

Rent expense allocated
to departments

P1

Auto Market pays $128,000 rent each year for its two-story building. The space in this building is occupied by five departments as specified here.

Paint department	1,200 square feet of first-floor space
Engine department	3,600 square feet of first-floor space
Window department	1,920 square feet of second-floor space
Electrical department	1,056 square feet of second-floor space
Accessory department	1,824 square feet of second-floor space

Check   Allocated to Paint Dept., $20,800

The company allocates 65% of total rent expense to the first floor and 35% to the second floor, and then allocates rent expense for each floor to the departments occupying that floor on the basis of space occupied. Determine the rent expense to be allocated to each department. (Round percents to the nearest one-tenth and dollar amounts to the nearest whole dollar.)

QS 21-15

Return on investment

A1

For a recent year **L'Oreal** reported operating profit of €3,110 (in millions) for its Cosmetics division. Total assets were €11,314 at the beginning of the year and €12,988 (in millions) at the end of the year. Compute return on investment for the year. State your answer as a percent, rounded to one decimal.

---

connect

EXERCISES

Exercise 21-1
Departmental expense
allocations

P1

Won Han Co. has four departments: materials, personnel, manufacturing, and packaging. In a recent month, the four departments incurred three shared indirect expenses. The amounts of these indirect expenses and the bases used to allocate them follow.

Indirect Expense	Cost	Allocation Base
Supervision	$ 75,000	Number of employees
Utilities	60,000	Square feet occupied
Insurance	16,500	Value of assets in use
Total	$151,500	

Departmental data for the company's recent reporting period follow.

Department	Employees	Square Feet	Asset Values
Materials	18	27,000	$ 6,000
Personnel.............	6	4,500	1,200
Manufacturing	66	45,000	37,800
Packaging	30	13,500	15,000
Total	120	90,000	$60,000

(1) Use this information to allocate each of the three indirect expenses across the four departments.
(2) Prepare a summary table that reports the indirect expenses assigned to each of the four departments.

Check   (2) Total of $30,900 assigned to Materials Dept.

Pane Company produces two types of glass shelving, rounded edge and squared edge, on the same production line. For the current period, the company reports the following data.

Exercise 21-2
Activity-based costing of overhead

P2

	Rounded Edge	Squared Edge	Total
Direct materials..........................	$ 9,500	$21,600	$ 31,100
Direct labor	6,100	11,900	18,000
Overhead (300% of direct labor cost)	18,300	35,700	54,000
Total cost................................	$33,900	$69,200	$103,100
Quantity produced	10,500 ft.	14,100 ft.	
Average cost per ft.	$ 3.23	$ 4.91	

Pane's controller wishes to apply activity-based costing (ABC) to allocate the $54,000 of overhead costs incurred by the two product lines to see whether cost per foot would change markedly from that reported above. She has collected the following information.

Overhead Cost Category (Activity Cost Pool)	Cost
Supervision	$ 2,160
Depreciation of machinery	28,840
Assembly line preparation............................	23,000
Total overhead	$54,000

She has also collected the following information about the cost drivers for each category (cost pool) and the amount of each driver used by the two product lines.

Overhead Cost Category (Activity Cost Pool)	Driver	Usage		
		Rounded Edge	Squared Edge	Total
Supervision	Direct labor cost($)	$6,100	$11,900	$18,000
Depreciation of machinery	Machine hours	300 hours	700 hours	1,000 hours
Assembly line preparation	Setups (number)	31 times	94 times	125 times

Use this information to (1) assign these three overhead cost pools to each of the two products using ABC, (2) determine average cost per foot for each of the two products using ABC, and (3) compare the average cost per foot under ABC with the average cost per foot under the current method for each product. For part 3, explain why a difference between the two cost allocation methods exists.

Check   (2) Rounded edge, $2.92; Squared edge, $5.14

Below are departmental income statements for a guitar manufacturer. The manufacturer is considering dropping its electric guitar department since it has a net loss. The company classifies advertising, rent, and utilities expenses as indirect. (1) Prepare a departmental contribution report that shows each department's contribution to overhead. (2) Based on contribution to overhead, should the electric guitar department be eliminated?

Exercise 21-3
Departmental contribution report

P3

BEST GUITAR
Departmental Income Statements
For Year Ended December 31, 2011

	Acoustic	Electric
Sales	$101,500	$85,000
Cost of goods sold	45,675	46,750
Gross profit	55,825	38,250
Operating expenses		
Advertising expense	5,075	4,250
Depreciation expense-equipment	10,150	8,500
Salaries expense	20,300	17,000
Supplies expense	2,030	1,700
Rent expense	7,105	5,950
Utilities expense.....................	3,045	2,550
Total operating expenses	47,705	39,950
Net income (loss)	**$ 8,120**	**($1,700)**

Exercise 21-4
Departmental expense allocation spreadsheet

P1

Overroad Cycle Shop has two service departments (advertising and administration) and two operating departments (cycles and clothing). During 2011, the departments had the following direct expenses and occupied the following amount of floor space.

Department	Direct Expenses	Square Feet
Advertising	$ 16,000	1,088
Administrative	18,500	1,152
Cycles	101,600	6,336
Clothing	11,900	4,224

The advertising department developed and distributed 100 advertisements during the year. Of these, 76 promoted cycles and 24 promoted clothing. The store sold $300,000 of merchandise during the year. Of this amount, $225,000 is from the cycles department, and $75,000 is from the clothing department. The utilities expense of $64,000 is an indirect expense to all departments. Prepare a departmental expense allocation spreadsheet for Overroad Cycle Shop. The spreadsheet should assign (1) direct expenses to each of the four departments, (2) the $64,000 of utilities expense to the four departments on the basis of floor space occupied, (3) the advertising department's expenses to the two operating departments on the basis of the number of ads placed that promoted a department's products, and (4) the administrative department's expenses to the two operating departments based on the amount of sales. Provide supporting computations for the expense allocations.

Check   Total expenses allocated to Cycles Dept., $167,769

Exercise 21-5
Service department expenses allocated to operating departments   P3

The following is a partially completed lower section of a departmental expense allocation spreadsheet for Bookworm Bookstore. It reports the total amounts of direct and indirect expenses allocated to its five departments. Complete the spreadsheet by allocating the expenses of the two service departments (advertising and purchasing) to the three operating departments.

File   Edit   View   Insert   Format   Tools   Data   Window   Help

	Allocation Base	Expense Account Balance	Allocation of Expenses to Departments				
			Advertising Dept.	Purchasing Dept.	Books Dept.	Magazines Dept.	Newspapers Dept.
Total department expenses..........		$654,000	$22,000	$30,000	$425,000	$86,000	$91,000
Service department expenses							
Advertising department............Sales			?		?	?	?
Purchasing department............Purch. orders				?	?	?	?
Total expenses allocated to							
operating departments..............		?	$ 0	$ 0	?	?	?

Sheet1 / Sheet2 / Sheet3

Advertising and purchasing department expenses are allocated to operating departments on the basis of dollar sales and purchase orders, respectively. Information about the allocation bases for the three operating departments follows.

Department	Sales	Purchase Orders
Books..............	$448,000	424
Magazines...........	144,000	312
Newspapers.........	208,000	264
Total..............	$800,000	1,000

Check Total expenses allocated to Books Dept., $450,040

Monica Gellar works in both the jewelry department and the hosiery department of a retail store. Gellar assists customers in both departments and arranges and stocks merchandise in both departments. The store allocates Gellar's $30,000 annual wages between the two departments based on a sample of the time worked in the two departments. The sample is obtained from a diary of hours worked that Gellar kept in a randomly chosen two-week period. The diary showed the following hours and activities spent in the two departments. Allocate Gellar's annual wages between the two departments. (Round percents to one decimal.)

Exercise 21-6
Indirect payroll expense allocated to departments
C1

Selling in jewelry department...	64 hours
Arranging and stocking merchandise in jewelry department........................	6 hours
Selling in hosiery department	14 hours
Arranging and stocking merchandise in hosiery department	12 hours
Idle time spent waiting for a customer to enter one of the selling departments	4 hours

Check Assign $8,130 to Hosiery

Bob Daniels manages an auto dealership's service department. The recent month's income statement for his department follows. (1) Analyze the items on the income statement and identify those that definitely should be included on a performance report used to evaluate Daniels's performance. List them and explain why you chose them. (2) List and explain the items that should definitely be excluded. (3) List the items that are not definitely included or excluded and explain why they fall into that category.

Exercise 21-7
Managerial performance evaluation

C2

Revenues		
Sales of parts	$144,000	
Sales of services...........................	210,000	$354,000
Costs and expenses		
Cost of parts sold	60,000	
Building depreciation	18,600	
Income taxes allocated to department.........	17,400	
Interest on long-term debt	15,000	
Manager's salary............................	24,000	
Payroll taxes..............................	16,200	
Supplies	31,800	
Utilities..................................	8,800	
Wages (hourly)............................	32,000	
Total costs and expenses		223,800
Departmental net income		$130,200

You must prepare a return on investment analysis for the regional manager of Out-and-In Burgers. This growing chain is trying to decide which outlet of two alternatives to open. The first location (A) requires a $500,000 investment and is expected to yield annual net income of $80,000. The second location (B) requires a $200,000 investment and is expected to yield annual net income of $38,000. Compute the return on investment for each Out-and-In Burgers alternative and then make your recommendation in a one-half page memorandum to the regional manager. (The chain currently generates an 18% return on total assets.)

Exercise 21-8
Investment center analysis

A1

Exercise 21-9
Computing performance measures
A1

Comart, a retailer of consumer goods, provides the following information on two of its departments (each considered an investment center).

Investment Center	Sales	Net Income	Average Invested Assets
Electronics	$20,000,000	$1,500,000	$ 7,500,000
Sporting goods.	16,000,000	1,600,000	10,000,000

(1) Compute return on investment for each department. Using return on investment, which department is most efficient at using assets to generate returns for the company? (2) Assume a target income level of 12% of average invested assets. Compute residual income for each department. Which department generated the most residual income for the company? (3) Assume the Electronics department is presented with a new investment opportunity that will yield a 15% return on assets. Should the new investment opportunity be accepted? Explain.

Exercise 21-10
Computing performance measures   A2

Refer to information in Exercise 21-9. Compute profit margin and investment turnover for each department. Which department generates the most net income per dollar of sales? Which department is most efficient at generating sales from average invested assets?

Exercise 21-11
Performance measures—
balanced scorecard
A1

MidCoast Airlines uses the following performance measures. Classify each of the performance measures below into the most likely balanced scorecard perspective it relates to. Label your answers using C (customer), P (internal process), I (innovation and growth), or F (financial).

1. Flight attendant training sessions attended   ———
2. Customer complaints   ———
3. Percentage of on-time departures   ———
4. Market value   ———
5. Percentage of ground crew trained   ———
6. Return on investment   ———
7. On-time flight percentage   ———
8. Accidents or safety incidents per mile flown   ———
9. Number of reports of mishandled or lost baggage   ———
10. Cash flow from operations   ———
11. Time airplane is on ground between flights   ———
12. Airplane miles per gallon of fuel   ———
13. Revenue per seat   ———
14. Cost of leasing airplanes   ———

Exercise 21-12ᴬ
Determining transfer prices
C3

The Trailer department of Soni Bicycles makes bike trailers that attach to bicycles and can carry children or cargo. The trailers have a retail price of $100 each. Each trailer incurs $40 of variable manufacturing costs. The Trailer department has capacity for 40,000 trailers per year, and incurs fixed costs of $800,000 per year.

Required

1. Assume the Assembly division of Soni Bicycles wants to buy 10,000 trailers per year from the Trailer division. If the Trailer division can sell all of the trailers it manufactures to outside customers, what price should be used on transfers between Soni Bicycle's divisions? Explain.

2. Assume the Trailer division currently only sells 20,000 trailers to outside customers, and the Assembly division wants to buy 10,000 trailers per year from the Trailer division. What is the range of acceptable prices that could be used on transfers between Soni Bicycle's divisions? Explain.

3. Assume transfer prices of either $40 per trailer or $70 per trailer are being considered. Comment on the preferred transfer prices from the perspectives of the Trailer division manager, the Assembly division manager, and the top management of Soni Bicycles.

Exercise 21-13ᴮ
Joint real estate costs assigned
C4

Tidy Home Properties is developing a subdivision that includes 300 home lots. The 225 lots in the Garden section are below a ridge and do not have views of the neighboring gardens and hills; the 75 lots in the Premier section offer unobstructed views. The expected selling price for each Garden lot is $50,000 and for each Premier lot is $100,000. The developer acquired the land for $2,500,000 and spent another $2,000,000 on street and utilities improvements. Assign the joint land and improvement costs to the lots using the value basis of allocation and determine the average cost per lot.

Check Total Garden cost, $2,700,000

Pike Seafood Company purchases lobsters and processes them into tails and flakes. It sells the lobster tails for $20 per pound and the flakes for $15 per pound. On average, 100 pounds of lobster are processed into 57 pounds of tails and 24 pounds of flakes, with 19 pounds of waste. Assume that the company purchased 3,000 pounds of lobster for $6.00 per pound and processed the lobsters with an additional labor cost of $1,800. No materials or labor costs are assigned to the waste. If 1,510 pounds of tails and 710 pounds of flakes are sold, what is (1) the allocated cost of the sold items and (2) the allocated cost of the ending inventory? The company allocates joint costs on a value basis. (Round the dollar cost per pound to the nearest thousandth.)

Exercise 21-14[B]
Joint product costs assigned
C4

Check (2) Inventory cost, $1,826

L'Oreal reports the following for a recent year for the major divisions in its Cosmetics branch.

Exercise 21-15
Profit margin and investment turnover
A2

(€ millions)	Sales	Income	Total Assets End of Year	Total Assets Beginning of Year
Professional products	€ 2,472	€ 519	€ 2,516	€ 2,440
Consumer products	8,355	1,578	5,496	5,361
Luxury products	4,170	766	4,059	2,695
Active cosmetics	1,289	259	817	818
Total....................	€16,286	€3,122	€12,888	€11,314

1. Compute profit margin for each division. State your answers as percents, rounded to two decimal places. Which L'Oreal division has the highest profit margin?
2. Compute investment turnover for each division. Round your answers to two decimal places. Which L'Oreal division has the best investment turnover?

connect _____

City Bank has several departments that occupy both floors of a two-story building. The departmental accounting system has a single account, Building Occupancy Cost, in its ledger. The types and amounts of occupancy costs recorded in this account for the current period follow.

PROBLEM SET A

Problem 21-1A
Allocation of building occupancy costs to departments
P1

e**X**cel

mhhe.com/wildFAP20e

Depreciation—Building	$18,000
Interest—Building mortgage	27,000
Taxes—Building and land	8,000
Gas (heating) expense	2,500
Lighting expense	3,000
Maintenance expense	5,500
Total occupancy cost	$64,000

The building has 4,000 square feet on each floor. In prior periods, the accounting manager merely divided the $64,000 occupancy cost by 8,000 square feet to find an average cost of $8 per square foot and then charged each department a building occupancy cost equal to this rate times the number of square feet that it occupied.

Laura Diaz manages a first-floor department that occupies 1,000 square feet, and Lauren Wright manages a second-floor department that occupies 1,800 square feet of floor space. In discussing the departmental reports, the second-floor manager questions whether using the same rate per square foot for all departments makes sense because the first-floor space is more valuable. This manager also references a recent real estate study of average local rental costs for similar space that shows first-floor space worth $30 per square foot and second-floor space worth $20 per square foot (excluding costs for heating, lighting, and maintenance).

Required

1. Allocate occupancy costs to the Diaz and Wright departments using the current allocation method.
2. Allocate the depreciation, interest, and taxes occupancy costs to the Diaz and Wright departments in proportion to the relative market values of the floor space. Allocate the heating, lighting, and maintenance costs to the Diaz and Wright departments in proportion to the square feet occupied (ignoring floor space market values).

Check (1) Total allocated to Diaz and Wright, $22,400 (2) Total occupancy cost to Diaz, $9,330

Analysis Component

3. Which allocation method would you prefer if you were a manager of a second-floor department? Explain.

Problem 21-2A
Activity-based costing

P2

We Care is an outpatient surgical clinic that was profitable for many years, but Medicare has cut its reimbursements by as much as 50%. As a result, the clinic wants to better understand its costs. It decides to prepare an activity-based cost analysis, including an estimate of the average cost of both general surgery and orthopedic surgery. The clinic's three cost centers and their cost drivers follow.

Cost Center	Cost	Cost Driver	Driver Quantity
Professional salaries...............	$1,500,000	Professional hours	10,000
Patient services and supplies.........	25,000	Number of patients	500
Building cost	150,000	Square feet	1,500

The two main surgical units and their related data follow.

Service	Hours	Square Feet*	Patients
General surgery...........	2,500	500	400
Orthopedic surgery........	7,500	1,000	100

* Orthopedic surgery requires more space for patients, supplies, and equipment.

Required

1. Compute the cost per cost driver for each of the three cost centers.

Check (2) Average cost of general (orthopedic) surgery, $1,113 ($12,300) per patient

2. Use the results from part 1 to allocate costs from each of the three cost centers to both the general surgery and the orthopedic surgery units. Compute total cost and average cost per patient for both the general surgery and the orthopedic surgery units.

Analysis Component

3. Without providing computations, would the average cost of general surgery be higher or lower if all center costs were allocated based on the number of patients? Explain.

Problem 21-3A
Departmental income statements; forecasts

P3

Time-To-See Company began operations in January 2011 with two operating (selling) departments and one service (office) department. Its departmental income statements follow.

TIME-TO-SEE COMPANY Departmental Income Statements For Year Ended December 31, 2011			
	Clock	Mirror	Combined
Sales	$122,500	$52,500	$175,000
Cost of goods sold	60,000	32,000	92,000
Gross profit	62,500	20,500	83,000
Direct expenses			
Sales salaries	20,000	7,000	27,000
Advertising	1,200	500	1,700
Store supplies used	900	400	1,300
Depreciation—Equipment	1,500	300	1,800
Total direct expenses....................	23,600	8,200	31,800
Allocated expenses			
Rent expense..........................	7,020	3,780	10,800
Utilities expense	2,600	1,400	4,000
Share of office department expenses	10,500	4,500	15,000
Total allocated expenses	20,120	9,680	29,800
Total expenses	43,720	17,880	61,600
Net income	$ 18,780	$ 2,620	$ 21,400

Time-To-See plans to open a third department in January 2012 that will sell paintings. Management predicts that the new department will generate $35,000 in sales with a 55% gross profit margin and will require the following direct expenses: sales salaries, $8,000; advertising, $800; store supplies, $500; and equipment depreciation, $200. It will fit the new department into the current rented space by taking some square footage from the other two departments. When opened the new painting department will fill one-fifth of the space presently used by the clock department and one-sixth used by the mirror department. Management does not predict any increase in utilities costs, which are allocated to the departments in proportion to occupied space (or rent expense). The company allocates office department expenses to the operating departments in proportion to their sales. It expects the painting department to increase total office department expenses by $7,000. Since the painting department will bring new customers into the store, management expects sales in both the clock and mirror departments to increase by 7%. No changes for those departments' gross profit percents or their direct expenses are expected except for store supplies used, which will increase in proportion to sales.

Required

Prepare departmental income statements that show the company's predicted results of operations for calendar year 2012 for the three operating (selling) departments and their combined totals. (Round percents to the nearest one-tenth and dollar amounts to the nearest whole dollar.)

Check 2012 forecasted combined net income (sales), $29,869 ($222,250)

Becky Hoefer, the plant manager of Travel Far's Indiana plant, is responsible for all of that plant's costs other than her own salary. The plant has two operating departments and one service department. The camper and trailer operating departments manufacture different products and have their own managers. The office department, which Hoefer also manages, provides services equally to the two operating departments. A budget is prepared for each operating department and the office department. The company's responsibility accounting system must assemble information to present budgeted and actual costs in performance reports for each operating department manager and the plant manager. Each performance report includes only those costs that a particular operating department manager can control: raw materials, wages, supplies used, and equipment depreciation. The plant manager is responsible for the department managers' salaries, utilities, building rent, office salaries other than her own, and other office costs plus all costs controlled by the two operating department managers. The annual departmental budgets and actual costs for the two operating departments follow.

Problem 21-4A
Responsibility accounting performance reports; controllable and budgeted costs
C2

	Budget			Actual		
	Campers	**Trailers**	**Combined**	**Campers**	**Trailers**	**Combined**
Raw materials	$160,000	$250,000	$ 410,000	$159,400	$246,500	$ 405,900
Employee wages	99,000	191,000	290,000	102,300	193,700	296,000
Dept. manager salary	40,000	44,000	84,000	41,000	47,000	88,000
Supplies used	34,000	83,000	117,000	31,900	84,600	116,500
Depreciation—Equip.	58,000	110,000	168,000	58,000	110,000	168,000
Utilities..................	2,800	4,200	7,000	2,700	3,800	6,500
Building rent	5,000	8,000	13,000	4,800	7,200	12,000
Office department costs	56,000	56,000	112,000	54,450	54,450	108,900
Totals	$454,800	$746,200	$1,201,000	$454,550	$747,250	$1,201,800

The office department's annual budget and its actual costs follow.

	Budget	Actual
Plant manager salary	$ 60,000	$ 62,000
Other office salaries	30,000	27,700
Other office costs	22,000	19,200
Totals	$112,000	$108,900

Required

1. Prepare responsibility accounting performance reports like those in Exhibit 21.28 that list costs controlled by the following:

    a. Manager of the camper department.

    b. Manager of the trailer department.

    c. Manager of the Indiana plant.

In each report, include the budgeted and actual costs and show the amount that each actual cost is over or under the budgeted amount.

Analysis Component

2. Did the plant manager or the operating department managers better manage costs? Explain.

Problem 21-5A[B]
Allocation of joint costs

C4

Bloom Orchards produced a good crop of peaches this year. After preparing the following income statement, the company believes it should have given its No. 3 peaches to charity and saved its efforts.

BLOOM ORCHARDS **Income Statement** **For Year Ended December 31, 2011**				
	No. 1	**No. 2**	**No. 3**	**Combined**
Sales (by grade)				
No. 1: 300,000 lbs. @ $1.50/lb	$450,000			
No. 2: 300,000 lbs. @ $1.00/lb		$300,000		
No. 3: 750,000 lbs. @ $0.20/lb			$ 150,000	
Total sales				$900,000
Costs				
Tree pruning and care @ $0.20/lb	60,000	60,000	150,000	270,000
Picking, sorting, and grading @ $0.12/lb	36,000	36,000	90,000	162,000
Delivery costs $0.03/lb	9,000	9,000	22,500	40,500
Total costs	105,000	105,000	262,500	472,500
Net income (loss)	$345,000	$195,000	$(112,500)	$427,500

In preparing this statement, the company allocated joint costs among the grades on a physical basis as an equal amount per pound. The company's delivery cost records show that $30,000 of the $40,500 relates to crating the No. 1 and No. 2 peaches and hauling them to the buyer. The remaining $10,500 of delivery costs is for crating the No. 3 peaches and hauling them to the cannery.

Required

1. Prepare reports showing cost allocations on a sales value basis to the three grades of peaches. Separate the delivery costs into the amounts directly identifiable with each grade. Then allocate any shared delivery costs on the basis of the relative sales value of each grade.

2. Using your answers to part 1, prepare an income statement using the joint costs allocated on a sales value basis.

Analysis Component

3. Do you think delivery costs fit the definition of a joint cost? Explain.

PROBLEM SET B

Problem 21-1B
Allocation of building occupancy costs to departments

P1

Dixon's has several departments that occupy all floors of a two-story building that includes a basement floor. Dixon rented this building under a long-term lease negotiated when rental rates were low. The departmental accounting system has a single account, Building Occupancy Cost, in its ledger. The types and amounts of occupancy costs recorded in this account for the current period follow.

Building rent	$300,000
Lighting expense	24,000
Cleaning expense	16,000
Total occupancy cost	$340,000

The building has 7,500 square feet on each of the upper two floors but only 5,000 square feet in the base-ment. In prior periods, the accounting manager merely divided the $340,000 occupancy cost by 20,000 square feet to find an average cost of $17 per square foot and then charged each department a building occupancy cost equal to this rate times the number of square feet that it occupies.

Alex Ferrero manages a department that occupies 2,000 square feet of basement floor space. In dis-cussing the departmental reports with other managers, she questions whether using the same rate per square foot for all departments makes sense because different floor space has different values. Ferrero checked a recent real estate report of average local rental costs for similar space that shows first-floor space worth $40 per square foot, second-floor space worth $20 per square foot, and basement space worth $10 per square foot (excluding costs for lighting and cleaning).

Required

1. Allocate occupancy costs to Ferrero's department using the current allocation method.
2. Allocate the building rent cost to Ferrero's department in proportion to the relative market value of the floor space. Allocate to Ferrero's department the lighting and heating costs in proportion to the square feet occupied (ignoring floor space market values). Then, compute the total occupancy cost allocated to Ferrero's department.

Check   Total costs allocated to Ferrero's Dept., (1) $34,000; (2) Total occupancy cost to Ferrero $16,000

Analysis Component

3. Which allocation method would you prefer if you were a manager of a basement department?

Prairie Landscaping has enjoyed profits for many years, but new competition has cut service revenue by as much as 30%. As a result, the company wants to better understand its costs. It decides to prepare an activity-based cost analysis, including an estimate of the average cost of both general landscaping services and custom design landscaping services. The company's three cost centers and their cost drivers follow.

Problem 21-2B
Activity-based costing

P2

Cost Center	Cost	Cost Driver	Driver Quantity
Professional salaries	$500,000	Professional hours	10,000
Customer supplies	125,000	Number of customers	500
Building cost	150,000	Square feet	1,500

The two main landscaping units and their related data follow.

Service	Hours	Square Feet*	Customers
General landscaping..............	2,500	500	400
Custom design landscaping	7,500	1,000	100

* Custom design landscaping requires more space for equipment, supplies, and planning.

Required

1. Compute the cost per cost driver for each of the three cost centers.
2. Use the results from part 1 to allocate costs from each of the three cost centers to both the general landscaping and the custom design landscaping units. Compute total cost and average cost per cus-tomer for both the general landscaping and the custom design landscaping units.

Check   (2) Average cost of general (custom) landscaping, $687.50 ($5,000) per customer

Analysis Component

3. Without providing computations, would the average cost of general landscaping be higher or lower if all center costs were allocated based on the number of customers? Explain.

Hollywood Entertainment began operations in January 2011 with two operating (selling) departments and one service (office) department. Its departmental income statements follow.

Problem 21-3B
Departmental income statements; forecasts   P3

HOLLYWOOD ENTERTAINMENT Departmental Income Statements For Year Ended December 31, 2011			
	Movies	**Video Games**	**Combined**
Sales	$540,000	$180,000	$720,000
Cost of goods sold	378,000	138,600	516,600
Gross profit	162,000	41,400	203,400
Direct expenses			
Sales salaries	35,000	14,000	49,000
Advertising	10,500	5,500	16,000
Store supplies used	3,300	700	4,000
Depreciation—Equipment	4,200	2,800	7,000
Total direct expenses	53,000	23,000	76,000
Allocated expenses			
Rent expense	29,520	6,480	36,000
Utilities expense	4,100	900	5,000
Share of office department expenses	39,000	14,000	53,000
Total allocated expenses	72,620	21,380	94,000
Total expenses	125,620	44,380	170,000
Net income (loss)	$ 36,380	$ (2,980)	$ 33,400

The company plans to open a third department in January 2012 that will sell compact discs. Management predicts that the new department will generate $250,000 in sales with a 35% gross profit margin and will require the following direct expenses: sales salaries, $18,000; advertising, $10,000; store supplies, $1,500; and equipment depreciation, $1,000. The company will fit the new department into the current rented space by taking some square footage from the other two departments. When opened, the new compact disc department will fill one-fourth of the space presently used by the movie department and one-third of the space used by the video game department. Management does not predict any increase in utilities costs, which are allocated to the departments in proportion to occupied space (or rent expense). The company allocates office department expenses to the operating departments in proportion to their sales. It expects the compact disc department to increase total office department expenses by $8,000. Since the compact disc department will bring new customers into the store, management expects sales in both the movie and video game departments to increase by 10%. No changes for those departments' gross profit percents or for their direct expenses are expected, except for store supplies used, which will increase in proportion to sales.

Required

Check   2012 forecasted movies net income (sales), $64,885 ($594,000)

Prepare departmental income statements that show the company's predicted results of operations for calendar year 2012 for the three operating (selling) departments and their combined totals. (Round percents to the nearest one-tenth and dollar amounts to the nearest whole dollar.)

Problem 21-4B
Responsibility accounting performance reports; controllable and budgeted costs

C2

Aaron Braun, the plant manager of SOS Co.'s Chicago plant, is responsible for all of that plant's costs other than his own salary. The plant has two operating departments and one service department. The refrigerator and dishwasher operating departments manufacture different products and have their own managers. The office department, which Braun also manages, provides services equally to the two operating departments. A monthly budget is prepared for each operating department and the office department. The company's responsibility accounting system must assemble information to present budgeted and actual costs in performance reports for each operating department manager and the plant manager. Each performance report includes only those costs that a particular operating department manager can control: raw materials, wages, supplies used, and equipment depreciation. The plant manager is responsible for the department managers' salaries, utilities, building rent, office salaries other than his own, and other office costs plus all costs controlled by the two operating department managers. The April departmental budgets and actual costs for the two operating departments follow.

	Budget			Actual		
	Refrigerators	**Dishwashers**	**Combined**	**Refrigerators**	**Dishwashers**	**Combined**
Raw materials	$400,000	$200,000	$ 600,000	$375,000	$200,000	$ 575,000
Employee wages	172,000	80,000	252,000	174,700	76,800	251,500
Dept. manager salary	55,000	49,000	104,000	55,000	46,500	101,500
Supplies used	15,000	9,000	24,000	14,000	10,000	24,000
Depreciation—Equip.	53,000	37,000	90,000	53,000	37,000	90,000
Utilities......................	30,000	18,000	48,000	34,500	20,700	55,200
Building rent	63,000	17,000	80,000	61,000	15,000	76,000
Office department costs	70,500	70,500	141,000	75,000	75,000	150,000
Totals	$858,500	$480,500	$1,339,000	$842,200	$481,000	$1,323,200

The office department's budget and its actual costs for April follow.

	Budget	Actual
Plant manager salary	$ 80,000	$ 85,000
Other office salaries	40,000	35,200
Other office costs	21,000	29,800
Totals	$141,000	$150,000

Required

1. Prepare responsibility accounting performance reports like those in Exhibit 21.28 that list costs controlled by the following:

   a. Manager of the refrigerator department.

   b. Manager of the dishwasher department.

   c. Manager of the Chicago plant.

In each report, include the budgeted and actual costs for the month and show the amount by which each actual cost is over or under the budgeted amount.

Check   (1a) $23,300 total under budget

(1c) Chicago plant controllable costs, $20,800 total under budget

Analysis Component

2. Did the plant manager or the operating department managers better manage costs? Explain.

Sarah and Stew Salsa own and operate a tomato grove. After preparing the following income statement, Sarah believes they should have offered the No. 3 tomatoes to the public for free and saved themselves time and money.

Problem 21-5B[B]
Allocation of joint costs

C4

SARAH AND STEW SALSA Income Statement For Year Ended December 31, 2011				
	No. 1	**No. 2**	**No. 3**	**Combined**
Sales (by grade)				
No. 1: 400,000 lbs. @ $1.50/lb	$600,000			
No. 2: 300,000 lbs. @ $1.00/lb		$300,000		
No. 3: 100,000 lbs. @ $0.30/lb			$ 30,000	
Total sales				$930,000
Costs				
Land preparation, seeding, and cultivating @ $0.50/lb	200,000	150,000	50,000	400,000
Harvesting, sorting, and grading @ $0.02/lb	8,000	6,000	2,000	16,000
Delivery costs @ $0.01/lb	4,000	3,000	1,000	8,000
Total costs	212,000	159,000	53,000	424,000
Net income (loss)	$388,000	$141,000	$(23,000)	$506,000

In preparing this statement, Sarah and Stew allocated joint costs among the grades on a physical basis as an equal amount per pound. Also, their delivery cost records show that $7,000 of the $8,000 relates to crating the No. 1 and No. 2 tomatoes and hauling them to the buyer. The remaining $1,000 of delivery costs is for crating the No. 3 tomatoes and hauling them to the cannery.

Required

1. Prepare reports showing cost allocations on a sales value basis to the three grades of tomatoes. Separate the delivery costs into the amounts directly identifiable with each grade. Then allocate any shared delivery costs on the basis of the relative sales value of each grade. (Round percents to the nearest one-tenth and dollar amounts to the nearest whole dollar.)

2. Using your answers to part 1, prepare an income statement using the joint costs allocated on a sales value basis.

Analysis Component

3. Do you think delivery costs fit the definition of a joint cost? Explain.

SERIAL PROBLEM
Business Solutions

P1 P2

(*This serial problem began in Chapter 1 and continues through most of the book. If previous chapter segments were not completed, the serial problem can begin at this point. It is helpful, but not necessary, to use the Working Papers that accompany the book.*)

SP 21   After reading an article about activity-based costing in a trade journal for the furniture industry, Santana Rey wondered if it was time to critically analyze overhead costs at Business Solutions. In a recent month, Rey found that setup costs, inspection costs, and utility costs made up most of its overhead. Additional information about overhead follows.

Activity	Cost	Driver
Setting up machines	$20,000	25 batches
Inspecting components	$ 7,500	5,000 parts
Providing utilities	$10,000	5,000 machine hours

Overhead has been applied to output at a rate of 50% of direct labor costs. The following data pertain to Job 6.15.

Direct materials	$2,500	Number of parts	400 parts
Direct labor	$3,500	Machine hours	600 machine hours
Batches	2 batches		

Required

1. What is the total cost of Job 6.15 if Business Solutions applies overhead at 50% of direct labor cost?

2. What is the total cost of Job 6.15 if Business Solutions uses activity-based costing?

3. Which approach to assigning overhead gives a better representation of the costs incurred to produce Job 6.15? Explain.

Beyond the Numbers

REPORTING IN ACTION

C1

RIM

BTN 21-1   Review **Research In Motion**'s income statement in Appendix A and identify its revenues for the years ended February 27, 2010, February 28, 2009, and March 1, 2008. For the year ended February 27, 2010, Research In Motion reports the following product revenue mix. (Assume that its product revenue mix is the same for each of the three years reported when answering the requirements.)

Devices	Service	Software	Other
81%	14%	2%	3%

Required

1. Compute the amount of revenue from each of its product lines for the years ended February 27, 2010, February 28, 2009, and March 1, 2008.

2. If Research In Motion wishes to evaluate each of its product lines, how can it allocate its operating expenses to each of them to determine each product line's profitability?

Fast Forward

3. Access Research In Motion's annual report for a fiscal year ending after February 27, 2010, from its Website (**RIM.com**) or the SEC's EDGAR database (**sec.gov**). Compute its revenues for its product lines for the most recent year(s). Compare those results to those from part 1. How has its product mix changed?

BTN 21-2   **Research In Motion**, **Apple**, and **Palm** compete across the world in several markets.

Required

1. Design a three-tier responsibility accounting organizational chart assuming that you have available internal information for all three companies. Use Exhibit 21.27 as an example. The goal of this assignment is to design a reporting framework for the companies; numbers are not required. Limit your reporting framework to sales activity only.

2. Explain why it is important to have similar performance reports when comparing performance within a company (and across different companies). Be specific in your response.

COMPARATIVE ANALYSIS

P3

RIM

Apple

Palm

BTN 21-3   Senior Security Co. offers a range of security services for senior citizens. Each type of service is considered within a separate department. Mary Pincus, the overall manager, is compensated partly on the basis of departmental performance by staying within the quarterly cost budget. She often revises operations to make sure departments stay within budget. Says Pincus, "I will not go over budget even if it means slightly compromising the level and quality of service. These are minor compromises that don't significantly affect my clients, at least in the short term."

Required

1. Is there an ethical concern in this situation? If so, which parties are affected? Explain.
2. Can Mary Pincus take action to eliminate or reduce any ethical concerns? Explain.
3. What is Senior Security's ethical responsibility in offering professional services?

ETHICS CHALLENGE

P3

BTN 21-4   Home Station is a national home improvement chain with more than 100 stores throughout the country. The manager of each store receives a salary plus a bonus equal to a percent of the store's net income for the reporting period. The following net income calculation is on the Denver store manager's performance report for the recent monthly period.

COMMUNICATING IN PRACTICE

P3

Sales	$2,500,000
Cost of goods sold	800,000
Wages expense	500,000
Utilities expense	200,000
Home office expense	75,000
Net income	$ 925,000
Manager's bonus (0.5%)	$ 4,625

In previous periods, the bonus had also been 0.5%, but the performance report had not included any charges for the home office expense, which is now assigned to each store as a percent of its sales.

Required

Assume that you are the national office manager. Write a one-half page memorandum to your store managers explaining why home office expense is in the new performance report.

TAKING IT TO THE NET
P1

BTN 21-5 This chapter described and used spreadsheets to prepare various managerial reports (see Exhibit 21-12). You can download from Websites various tutorials showing how spreadsheets are used in managerial accounting and other business applications.

Required

1. Link to the Website **Lacher.com**. Select "Excel Examples." Identify and list three tutorials for review.

2. Describe in a one-half page memorandum to your instructor how the applications described in each tutorial are helpful in business and managerial decision making.

TEAMWORK IN ACTION
P2

BTN 21-6 Activity-based costing (ABC) is increasingly popular as a useful managerial tool to (1) measure the cost of resources consumed and (2) assign cost to products and services. This managerial tool has been available to accounting and business decision makers for more than 25 years.

Required

Break into teams and identify at least three likely reasons that activity-based costing has gained popularity in recent years. Be prepared to present your answers in a class discussion. (*Hint:* What changes have occurred in products and services over the past 25 years?)

ENTREPRENEURIAL DECISION
P3

BTN 21-7 **Skullcandy** sells headphones and other audio-mobile accessories and apparel. The company's plans call for continued expansion into other types of products.

Required

1. How can Skullcandy use departmental income statements to assist in understanding and controlling operations?

2. Are departmental income statements always the best measure of a department's performance? Explain.

3. Provide examples of nonfinancial performace indicators Skullcandy might use as part of a balanced scorecard system of performance evaluation.

HITTING THE ROAD
C1   C2

BTN 21-8 Visit a local movie theater and check out both its concession area and its showing areas. The manager of a theater must confront questions such as:

- How much return do we earn on concessions?
- What types of movies generate the greatest sales?
- What types of movies generate the greatest net income?

Required

Assume that you are the new accounting manager for a 16-screen movie theater. You are to set up a responsibility accounting reporting framework for the theater.

1. Recommend how to segment the different departments of a movie theater for responsibility reporting.

2. Propose an expense allocation system for heat, rent, insurance, and maintenance costs of the theater.

GLOBAL DECISION
P3

NOKIA

BTN 21-9 Selected product data from **Nokia** (www.Nokia.com) follow.

Product Segment for Year Ended (EURm)	Net Sales		Operating Income	
	December 31, 2009	December 31, 2008	December 31, 2009	December 31, 2008
Devices & Services	€27,841	€35,084	€3,314	€5,816
NAVTEQ	579	318	(344)	(153)
Nokia Siemens Networks	12,564	15,308	(1,639)	(301)

Required

1. Compute the percentage growth in net sales for each product line from fiscal year 2008 to 2009. Round percents to one decimal.
2. Which product line's net sales grew the fastest?
3. Which segment was the most profitable?
4. How can Nokia's managers use this information?

ANSWERS TO MULTIPLE CHOICE QUIZ

1. b; [$641,250/($356,250 + $641,250 + $427,500)] × $150,000 = $67,500

2. c;

3. e; $162,000 × 50/150 setups = $54,000; $54,000/500 units = $108 per Grey unit. (Red is $2.70 per unit.)

4. b;

	Department X	Department Y	Department Z
Sales	$500,000	$200,000	$350,000
Cost of goods sold	350,000	75,000	150,000
Gross profit	150,000	125,000	200,000
Direct expenses.	50,000	20,000	75,000
Departmental contribution.	$100,000	$105,000	$125,000

5. a; $100,000/$500,000 = 20%

22

Cost-Volume-Profit Analysis

A Look Back

Chapter 21 focused on cost allocation, activity-based costing, and performance measurement. We identified ways to measure and analyze company activities, its departments, and its managers.

A Look at This Chapter

This chapter shows how information on both costs and sales behavior is useful to managers in performing cost-volume-profit analysis. This analysis is an important part of successful management and sound business decisions.

A Look Ahead

Chapter 23 introduces and describes the budgeting process and its importance to management. It also explains the master budget and its usefulness to the planning of future company activities.

Learning Objectives

CAP

CONCEPTUAL

C1 Describe different types of cost behavior in relation to production and sales volume. (p. 908)

C2 Describe several applications of cost-volume-profit analysis. (p. 919)

ANALYTICAL

A1 Compute the contribution margin and describe what it reveals about a company's cost structure. (p. 914)

A2 Analyze changes in sales using the degree of operating leverage. (p. 924)

LP22

PROCEDURAL

P1 Determine cost estimates using the scatter diagram, high-low, and regression methods of estimating costs. (p. 911)

P2 Compute the break-even point for a single product company. (p. 915)

P3 Graph costs and sales for a single product company. (p. 916)

P4 Compute the break-even point for a multiproduct company. (p. 921)

Heeeere's Johnny!

"People ask for my autograph . . . it's unbelievable"
—JOHN EARLE

BOSTON, MS—Working at a music store, John Earle's co-workers coined new nicknames for him on an almost daily basis: Johnny Appleseed, Johnny Pancakes, Johnny Cupcakes. As a joke, John printed up a few t-shirts with the Johnny Cupcakes nickname for the heavy-metal band he played in. The shirts, based on a skull and crossbones design with a cupcake replacing the skull, drew attention, and John dropped his heavy-metal dreams to start his company, **Johnny Cupcakes, Inc. (JohnnyCupcakes.com).**

John was always a small-scale serial entrepreneur, operating lemonade stands, peddling glow sticks on the beach near his home, and selling packs of pranks and magic tricks. Like his itching powder prank that went awry at his school, "the Johnny Cupcakes brand started as a complete joke," admits John. One day John's mother Lorraine interrupted his band's tour to tell him he had a real business on his hands. Now, the company's designs—like a Statue of Liberty holding a cupcake, Marilyn Monroe with a tiny cupcake-shaped mole, and the cupcakes and crossbones motif—attract a cult following. By the time John opened his first store, over 500 people had lined up to get in (see photo above).

Though still a prankster, John knows that successful entrepreneurs must understand cost behavior to succeed. Identifying fixed and variable costs is key to understanding break-even points and maintaining the right mix of t-shirt choices. With t-shirts selling at prices between $40–$70 each, John focuses on making limited editions to keep demand high. In performing cost-volume-profit analyses, John's mother Lorraine, the company's chief financial officer, typically estimates sales at about half the amount John does. "A large gap between our estimates is pretty typical, but John is happy when we beat our break-even points and produce profits," says Lorraine. Johnny Cupcakes recently expanded into other product lines, including button-down shirts, jackets, sweaters, and baseball caps. With a diverse product line, an understanding of contribution margins and how costs relate to volume and profits become even more important.

From a handful of gag t-shirts made as a joke, Johnny Cupcakes now boasts sales of $3.4 million per year. "I never expected it to get this big," John says, encouraging potential entrepreneurs to get out and make it happen. "I work very hard," he says, "and I enjoy every minute of it."

[Sources: *Johnny Cupcakes Website,* January 2011; *Boston Globe,* October 2007; *Businessweek.com,* August 2008; *Inc magazine,* May 2010; *NPR.org,* August 2006]

This chapter describes different types of costs and shows how changes in a company's operating volume affect these costs. The chapter also analyzes a company's costs and sales to explain how different operating strategies affect profit or loss. Managers use this type of analysis to forecast what will happen if changes are made to costs, sales volume, selling prices, or product mix. They then use these forecasts to select the best business strategy for the company.

Cost-Volume-Profit Analysis

Identifying Cost Behavior
- Fixed costs
- Variable costs
- Mixed costs
- Step-wise costs
- Curvilinear costs

Measuring Cost Behavior
- Scatter diagrams
- High-low method
- Least-squares regression
- Comparison of cost estimation methods

Using Break-Even Analysis
- Computing contribution margin
- Computing break-even
- Preparing a cost-volume-profit chart
- Making assumptions in cost-volume-profit analysis

Applying Cost-Volume-Profit Analysis
- Computing income from sales and costs
- Computing sales for target income
- Computing margin of safety
- Using sensitivity analysis
- Computing multiproduct break-even

IDENTIFYING COST BEHAVIOR

Planning a company's future activities and events is a crucial phase in successful management. One of the first steps in planning is to predict the volume of activity, the costs to be incurred, sales to be made, and profit to be received. An important tool to help managers carry out this step is **cost-volume-profit (CVP) analysis,** which helps them predict how changes in costs and sales levels affect income. In its basic form, CVP analysis involves computing the sales level at which a company neither earns an income nor incurs a loss, called the *break-even point.* For this reason, this basic form of cost-volume-profit analysis is often called *break-even analysis.* Managers use variations of CVP analysis to answer questions such as these:

Point: *Profit* is another term for *income.*

- What sales volume is needed to earn a target income?
- What is the change in income if selling prices decline and sales volume increases?
- How much does income increase if we install a new machine to reduce labor costs?
- What is the income effect if we change the sales mix of our products or services?

Consequently, cost-volume-profit analysis is useful in a wide range of business decisions.

Conventional cost-volume-profit analysis requires management to classify all costs as either *fixed* or *variable* with respect to production or sales volume. The remainder of this section discusses the concepts of fixed and variable cost behavior as they relate to CVP analysis.

Decision Insight

No Free Lunch   Hardly a week goes by without a company advertising a free product with the purchase of another. Examples are a free printer with a digital camera purchase or a free monitor with a computer purchase. Can these companies break even, let alone earn profits? We are reminded of the *no-free-lunch* adage, meaning that companies expect profits from the companion or add-on purchase to make up for the free product. ■

Fixed Costs

C1 Describe different types of cost behavior in relation to production and sales volume.

A *fixed cost* remains unchanged in amount when the volume of activity varies from period to period within a relevant range. For example, $5,000 in monthly rent paid for a factory building remains the same whether the factory operates with a single eight-hour shift or around the clock with three shifts. This means that rent cost is the same each month at any level of output from zero to the plant's full productive capacity. Notice that while *total* fixed cost does not change as the level of production changes, the fixed cost *per unit* of output decreases as volume increases. For instance, if 20 units are produced when monthly rent is $5,000, the average rent cost per unit is $250 (computed as $5,000/20 units). When production increases to 100 units per month, the average cost per unit decreases to $50 (computed as $5,000/100 units). The average cost decreases to $10 per unit if production increases to 500 units per month. Common examples of fixed costs include depreciation, property taxes, office salaries, and many service department costs.

When production volume and costs are graphed, units of product are usually plotted on the *horizontal axis* and dollars of cost are plotted on the *vertical axis*. Fixed costs then are represented as a horizontal line because they remain constant at all levels of production. To illustrate, the graph in Exhibit 22.1 shows that fixed costs remain at $32,000 at all production levels up to the company's monthly capacity of 2,000 units of output. The *relevant range* for fixed costs in Exhibit 22.1 is 0 to 2,000 units. If the relevant range changes (that is, production capacity extends beyond this range), the amount of fixed costs will likely change.

Example: If the fixed cost line in Exhibit 22.1 is shifted upward, does the total cost line shift up, down, or remain in the same place? *Answer:* It shifts up by the same amount.

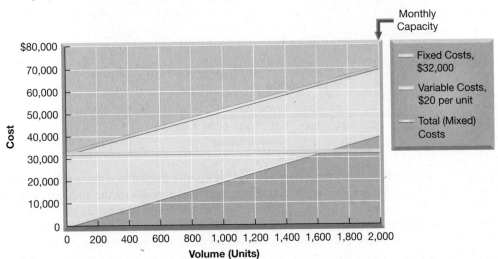

EXHIBIT 22.1

Relations of Fixed and Variable Costs to Volume

Example: If the level of fixed costs in Exhibit 22.1 changes, does the slope of the total cost line change? *Answer:* No, the slope doesn't change. The total cost line is simply shifted upward or downward.

Variable Costs

A *variable cost* changes in proportion to changes in volume of activity. The direct materials cost of a product is one example of a variable cost. If one unit of product requires materials costing $20, total materials costs are $200 when 10 units of product are manufactured, $400 for 20 units, $600 for 30 units, and so on. Notice that variable cost *per unit* remains constant but the *total* amount of variable cost changes with the level of production. In addition to direct materials, common variable costs include direct labor (if employees are paid per unit), sales commissions, shipping costs, and some overhead costs.

Point: Fixed costs are constant in total but vary (decline) per unit as more units are produced. Variable costs vary in total but are fixed per unit.

When variable costs are plotted on a graph of cost and volume, they appear as a straight line starting at the zero cost level. This straight line is upward (positive) sloping. The line rises as volume of activity increases. A variable cost line using a $20 per unit cost is graphed in Exhibit 22.1.

Mixed Costs

A **mixed cost** includes both fixed and variable cost components. For example, compensation for sales representatives often includes a fixed monthly salary and a variable commission based on sales. The total cost line in Exhibit 22.1 is a mixed cost. Like a fixed cost, it is greater than zero when volume is zero; but unlike a fixed cost, it increases steadily in proportion to increases in volume. The mixed cost line in Exhibit 22.1 starts on the vertical axis at the $32,000 fixed cost point. Thus, at the zero volume level, total cost equals the fixed costs. As the activity level increases, the mixed cost line increases at an amount equal to the variable cost per unit. This line is highest when volume of activity is at 2,000 units (the end point of the relevant range). In CVP analysis, mixed costs are often separated into fixed and variable components. The fixed component is added to other fixed costs, and the variable component is added to other variable costs.

Step-Wise Costs

A **step-wise cost** reflects a step pattern in costs. Salaries of production supervisors often behave in a step-wise manner in that their salaries are fixed within a *relevant range* of the current production volume. However, if production volume expands significantly (for example, with the addition of another shift), additional supervisors must be hired. This means that the total cost for supervisory salaries goes up by a lump-sum amount. Similarly, if volume takes another significant step up, supervisory salaries will increase by another lump sum. This behavior reflects a step-wise cost, also known as a *stair-step cost*, which is graphed in Exhibit 22.2. See how the step-wise cost line is flat within ranges (steps). Then, when volume significantly changes, it shifts to another level for that range (step).

EXHIBIT 22.2

Step-Wise and
Curvilinear Costs

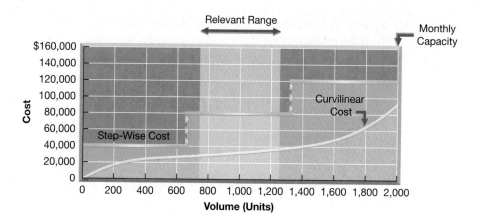

In a conventional CVP analysis, a step-wise cost is usually treated as either a fixed cost or a variable cost. This treatment involves manager judgment and depends on the width of the range and the expected volume. To illustrate, suppose after the production of every 25 snowboards, an operator lubricates the finishing machine. The cost of this lubricant reflects a step-wise pattern. Also, suppose that after the production of every 1,000 units, the snowboard cutting tool is replaced. Again, this is a step-wise cost. Note that the range of 25 snowboards is much narrower than the range of 1,000 snowboards. Some managers might treat the lubricant cost as a variable cost and the cutting tool cost as a fixed cost.

Curvilinear Costs

A variable cost, as explained, is a *linear* cost; that is, it increases at a constant rate as volume of activity increases. A **curvilinear cost,** also called a *nonlinear cost,* increases at a nonconstant rate as volume increases. When graphed, curvilinear costs appear as a curved line. Exhibit 22.2 shows a curvilinear cost beginning at zero when production is zero and then increasing at different rates.

An example of a curvilinear cost is total direct labor cost when workers are paid by the hour. At low to medium levels of production, adding more employees allows each of them to specialize by doing certain tasks repeatedly instead of doing several different tasks. This often yields additional units of output at lower costs. A point is eventually reached at which adding more employees creates inefficiencies. For instance, a large crew demands more time and effort in communicating and coordinating their efforts. While adding employees in this case increases output, the labor cost per unit increases, and the total labor cost goes up at a steeper slope. This pattern is seen in Exhibit 22.2 where the curvilinear cost curve starts at zero, rises, flattens out, and then increases at a faster rate as output nears the maximum.

Quick Check

Answers — p. 928

1. Which of the following statements is typically true? (*a*) Variable cost per unit increases as volume increases, (*b*) fixed cost per unit decreases as volume increases, or (*c*) a curvilinear cost includes both fixed and variable elements.

2. Describe the behavior of a fixed cost.

3. If cost per unit of activity remains constant (fixed), why is it called a variable cost?

MEASURING COST BEHAVIOR

Identifying and measuring cost behavior requires careful analysis and judgment. An important part of this process is to identify costs that can be classified as either fixed or variable, which often requires analysis of past cost behavior. Three methods are commonly used to analyze past costs: scatter diagrams, high-low method, and least-squares regression. Each method is discussed in this section using the unit and cost data shown in Exhibit 22.3, which are taken from a start-up company that uses units produced as the activity base in estimating cost behavior.

P1 Determine cost estimates using the scatter diagram, high-low, and regression methods of estimating costs.

Month	Units Produced	Total Cost
January	17,500	$20,500
February.	27,500	21,500
March	25,000	25,000
April	35,000	21,500
May.	47,500	25,500
June	22,500	18,500
July	30,000	23,500
August	52,500	28,500
September	37,500	26,000
October.	57,500	26,000
November	62,500	31,000
December	67,500	29,000

EXHIBIT 22.3

Data for Estimating Cost Behavior

Scatter Diagrams

Scatter diagrams display past cost and unit data in graphical form. In preparing a scatter diagram, units are plotted on the horizontal axis and cost is plotted on the vertical axis. Each individual point on a scatter diagram reflects the cost and number of units for a prior period. In Exhibit 22.4, the prior 12 months' costs and numbers of units are graphed. Each point reflects total costs incurred and units produced for one of those months. For instance, the point labeled March had units produced of 25,000 and costs of $25,000.

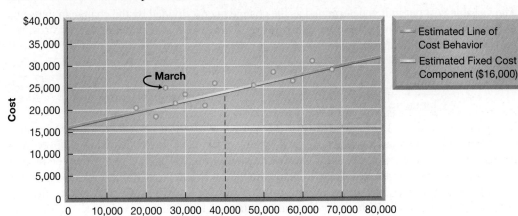

EXHIBIT 22.4

Scatter Diagram

The **estimated line of cost behavior** is drawn on a scatter diagram to reflect the relation between cost and unit volume. This line best visually "fits" the points in a scatter diagram. Fitting this line demands judgment. The line drawn in Exhibit 22.4 intersects the vertical axis at approximately $16,000, which reflects fixed cost. To compute variable cost per unit, or the slope, we perform three steps. First, we select any two points on the horizontal axis (units), say 0 and 40,000. Second, we draw a vertical line from each of these points to intersect the estimated line of cost behavior. The point on the vertical axis (cost) corresponding to the 40,000 units point that intersects the estimated line is roughly $24,000. Similarly, the cost corresponding to zero units is $16,000 (the fixed cost point). Third, we compute the slope of the line, or variable cost, as the change in cost divided by the change in units. Exhibit 22.5 shows this computation.

$$\frac{\text{Change in cost}}{\text{Change in units}} = \frac{\$24,000 - \$16,000}{40,000 - 0} = \frac{\$8,000}{40,000} = \$0.20 \text{ per unit}$$

Variable cost is $0.20 per unit. Thus, the cost equation that management will use to estimate costs for different unit levels is **$16,000 plus $0.20 per unit**.

High-Low Method

The **high-low method** is a way to estimate the cost equation by graphically connecting the two cost amounts at the highest and lowest unit volumes. In our case, the lowest number of units is 17,500, and the highest is 67,500. The costs corresponding to these unit volumes are $20,500 and $29,000, respectively (see the data in Exhibit 22.3). The estimated line of cost behavior for the high-low method is then drawn by connecting these two points on the scatter diagram corresponding to the lowest and highest unit volumes as follows.

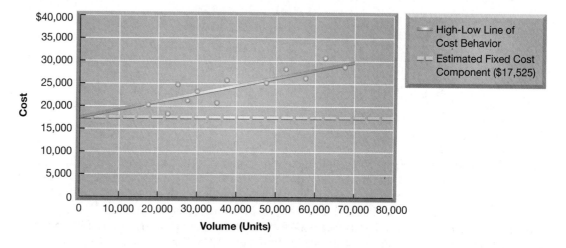

The variable cost per unit is determined as the change in cost divided by the change in units and uses the data from the high and low unit volumes. This results in a slope, or variable cost per unit, of $0.17 as computed in Exhibit 22.6.

$$\frac{\text{Change in cost}}{\text{Change in units}} = \frac{\$29,000 - \$20,500}{67,500 - 17,500} = \frac{\$8,500}{50,000} = \$0.17 \text{ per unit}$$

To estimate the fixed cost for the high-low method, we use the knowledge that total cost equals fixed cost plus variable cost per unit times the number of units. Then we pick either the high or low point to determine the fixed cost. This computation is shown in Exhibit 22.7—where we use the high point (67,500 units) in determining the fixed cost of $17,525. Use of the low point (17,500 units) yields the same fixed cost estimate: $20,500 = Fixed cost + ($0.17 per unit × 17,500), or Fixed cost = $17,525.

EXHIBIT 22.7

Fixed Cost (High-Low Method)

> **Total cost = Fixed cost + (Variable cost × Units)**
>
> $29,000 = Fixed cost + ($0.17 per unit × 67,500 units)
>
> Then,   Fixed cost = $17,525

Thus, the cost equation used to estimate costs at different units is **$17,525 plus $0.17 per unit**. This cost equation differs slightly from that determined from the scatter diagram method. A deficiency of the high-low method is that it ignores all cost points except the highest and lowest. The result is less precision because the high-low method uses the most extreme points rather than the more usual conditions likely to recur.

Least-Squares Regression

Least-squares regression is a statistical method for identifying cost behavior. For our purposes, we use the cost equation estimated from this method but leave the computational details for more advanced courses. Such computations for least-squares regression are readily done using most spreadsheet programs or calculators. We illustrate this using Excel® in Appendix 22A.

The regression cost equation for the data presented in Exhibit 22.3 is **$16,947 plus $0.19 per unit**; that is, the fixed cost is estimated as $16,947 and the variable cost at $0.19 per unit. Both costs are reflected in the following graph.

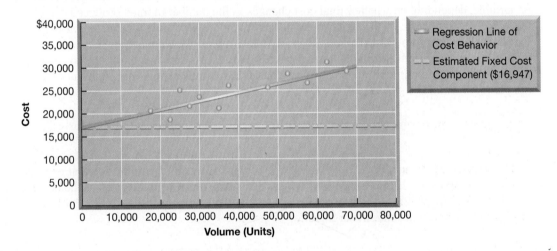

Comparison of Cost Estimation Methods

The three cost estimation methods result in slightly different estimates of fixed and variable costs as summarized in Exhibit 22.8. Estimates from the scatter diagram are based on a visual fit of the cost line and are subject to interpretation. Estimates from the high-low method use only two sets of values corresponding to the lowest and highest unit volumes. Estimates from least-squares regression use a statistical technique and all available data points.

EXHIBIT 22.8

Comparison of Cost
Estimation Methods

Estimation Method	Fixed Cost	Variable Cost
Scatter diagram	$16,000	$0.20 per unit
High-low method	17,525	0.17 per unit
Least-squares regression	16,947	0.19 per unit

We must remember that all three methods use *past data.* Thus, cost estimates resulting from these methods are only as good as the data used for estimation. Managers must establish that the data are reliable in deriving cost estimates for the future.

USING BREAK-EVEN ANALYSIS

Break-even analysis is a special case of cost-volume-profit analysis. This section describes break-even analysis by computing the break-even point and preparing a CVP (or break-even) chart.

Contribution Margin and Its Measures

A1 Compute the contribution margin and describe what it reveals about a company's cost structure.

We explained how managers classify costs by behavior. This often refers to classifying costs as being fixed or variable with respect to volume of activity. In manufacturing companies, volume of activity usually refers to the number of units produced. We then classify a cost as either fixed or variable, depending on whether total cost changes as the number of units produced changes. Once we separate costs by behavior, we can then compute a product's contribution margin. **Contribution margin per unit,** or *unit contribution margin,* is the amount by which a product's unit selling price exceeds its total unit variable cost. This excess amount contributes to covering fixed costs and generating profits on a per unit basis. Exhibit 22.9 shows the contribution margin per unit formula.

EXHIBIT 22.9

Contribution Margin per Unit

> **Contribution margin per unit = Sales price per unit − Total variable cost per unit**

The **contribution margin ratio,** which is the percent of a unit's selling price that exceeds total unit variable cost, is also useful for business decisions. It can be interpreted as the percent of each sales dollar that remains after deducting the total unit variable cost. Exhibit 22.10 shows the formula for the contribution margin ratio.

EXHIBIT 22.10

Contribution Margin Ratio

$$\text{Contribution margin ratio} = \frac{\text{Contribution margin per unit}}{\text{Sales price per unit}}$$

To illustrate the use of contribution margin, let's consider **Rydell,** which sells footballs for $100 per unit and incurs variable costs of $70 per unit sold. Its fixed costs are $24,000 per month with monthly capacity of 1,800 units (footballs). Rydell's contribution margin per unit is $30, which is computed as follows.

Selling price per unit	$100
Variable cost per unit	70
Contribution margin per unit	$ 30

Its contribution margin ratio is 30%, computed as $30/$100. This reveals that for each unit sold, Rydell has $30 that contributes to covering fixed cost and profit. If we consider sales in dollars, a contribution margin of 30% implies that for each $1 in sales, Rydell has $0.30 that contributes to fixed cost and profit.

Decision Maker   Answer — p. 927

Sales Manager   You are evaluating orders from two customers but can accept only one of the orders because of your company's limited capacity. The first order is for 100 units of a product with a contribution margin ratio of 60% and a selling price of $1,000. The second order is for 500 units of a product with a contribution margin ratio of 20% and a selling price of $800. The incremental fixed costs are the same for both orders. Which order do you accept? ∎

Computing the Break-Even Point

The **break-even point** is the sales level at which a company neither earns a profit nor incurs a loss. The concept of break-even is applicable to nearly all organizations, activities, and events. One of the most important items of information when launching a project is whether it will break even—that is, whether sales will at least cover total costs. The break-even point can be expressed in either units or dollars of sales.

> **P2**   Compute the break-even point for a single product company.

To illustrate the computation of break-even analysis, let's again look at Rydell, which sells footballs for $100 per unit and incurs $70 of variable costs per unit sold. Its fixed costs are $24,000 per month. Rydell breaks even for the month when it sells 800 footballs (sales volume of $80,000). We compute this break-even point using the formula in Exhibit 22.11. This formula uses the contribution margin per unit, which for Rydell is $30 ($100 − $70). From this we can compute the break-even sales volume as $24,000/$30, or 800 units per month.

$$\text{Break-even point in units} = \frac{\text{Fixed costs}}{\text{Contribution margin per unit}}$$

EXHIBIT 22.11

Formula for Computing Break-Even Sales (in Units)

At a price of $100 per unit, monthly sales of 800 units yield sales dollars of $80,000 (called *break-even sales dollars*). This $80,000 break-even sales can be computed directly using the formula in Exhibit 22.12.

$$\text{Break-even point in dollars} = \frac{\text{Fixed costs}}{\text{Contribution margin ratio}}$$

EXHIBIT 22.12

Formula for Computing Break-Even Sales (in Dollars)

Rydell's break-even point in dollars is computed as $24,000/0.30, or $80,000 of monthly sales. To verify that Rydell's break-even point equals $80,000 (or 800 units), we prepare a simplified income statement in Exhibit 22.13. It shows that the $80,000 revenue from sales of 800 units exactly equals the sum of variable and fixed costs.

Point: Even if a company operates at a level in excess of its break-even point, management may decide to stop operating because it is not earning a reasonable return on investment.

RYDELL COMPANY	
Contribution Margin Income Statement (at Break-Even)	
For Month Ended January 31, 2011	
Sales (800 units at $100 each)	$80,000
Variable costs (800 units at $70 each)	56,000
Contribution margin (800 Units at $30 each)	24,000
Fixed costs	24,000
Net income	$ 0

EXHIBIT 22.13

Contribution Margin Income Statement for Break-Even Sales

The statement in Exhibit 22.13 is called a *contribution margin income statement*. It differs in format from a conventional income statement in two ways. First, it separately classifies costs and expenses as variable or fixed. Second, it reports contribution margin (Sales − Variable costs). The contribution margin income statement format is used in this chapter's assignment materials because of its usefulness in CVP analysis.

Point: A contribution margin income statement is also referred to as a *variable costing income statement*. This differs from the traditional *absorption costing* approach where all product costs are assigned to units sold and to units in ending inventory. Recall that variable costing expenses all fixed product costs. Thus, income for the two approaches differs depending on the level of finished goods inventory; the lower inventory is, the more similar the two approaches are.

Preparing a Cost-Volume-Profit Chart

P3 Graph costs and sales for a single product company.

Exhibit 22.14 is a graph of Rydell's cost-volume-profit relations. This graph is called a **cost-volume-profit (CVP) chart,** or a *break-even chart* or *break-even graph*. The horizontal axis is the number of units produced and sold and the vertical axis is dollars of sales and costs. The lines in the chart depict both sales and costs at different output levels.

EXHIBIT 22.14

Cost-Volume-Profit Chart

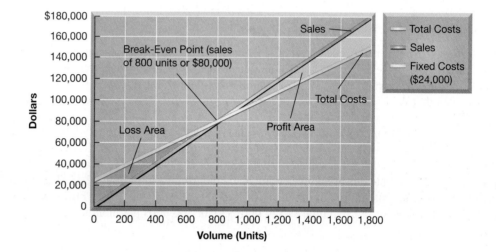

We follow three steps to prepare a CVP chart, which can also be drawn with computer programs that convert numeric data to graphs:

1. Plot fixed costs on the vertical axis ($24,000 for Rydell). Draw a horizontal line at this level to show that fixed costs remain unchanged regardless of output volume (drawing this fixed cost line is not essential to the chart).

2. Draw the total (variable plus fixed) costs line for a relevant range of volume levels. This line starts at the fixed costs level on the vertical axis because total costs equal fixed costs at zero volume. The slope of the total cost line equals the variable cost per unit ($70). To draw the line, compute the total costs for any volume level, and connect this point with the vertical axis intercept ($24,000). Do not draw this line beyond the productive capacity for the planning period (1,800 units for Rydell).

3. Draw the sales line. Start at the origin (zero units and zero dollars of sales) and make the slope of this line equal to the selling price per unit ($100). To sketch the line, compute dollar sales for any volume level and connect this point with the origin. Do not extend this line beyond the productive capacity. Total sales will be at the highest level at maximum capacity.

Example: In Exhibit 22.14, the sales line intersects the total cost line at 800 units. At what point would the two lines intersect if selling price is increased by 20% to $120 per unit? *Answer:* $24,000/($120 − $70) = 480 units

The total costs line and the sales line intersect at 800 units in Exhibit 22.14, which is the break-even point—the point where total dollar sales of $80,000 equals the sum of both fixed and variable costs ($80,000).

On either side of the break-even point, the vertical distance between the sales line and the total costs line at any specific volume reflects the profit or loss expected at that point. At volume levels to the left of the break-even point, this vertical distance is the amount of the expected loss because the total costs line is above the total sales line. At volume levels to the right of the break-even point, the vertical distance represents the expected profit because the total sales line is above the total costs line.

Decision Maker   Answer — p. 927

Operations Manager   As a start-up manufacturer, you wish to identify the behavior of manufacturing costs to develop a production cost budget. You know three methods can be used to identify cost behavior from past data, but past data are unavailable because this is a start-up. What do you do? ■

Making Assumptions in Cost-Volume-Profit Analysis

Cost-volume-profit analysis assumes that relations can normally be expressed as simple lines similar to those in Exhibits 22.4 and 22.14. Such assumptions allow users to answer several important questions, but the usefulness of the answers depends on the validity of three assumptions: (1) constant selling price per unit, (2) constant variable costs per unit, and (3) constant total fixed costs. These assumptions are not always realistic, but CVP analysis can be very useful for business decision making even when its assumptions are not strictly met. This section discusses these assumptions and other issues for CVP analysis.

Working with Assumptions   The behavior of individual costs and sales often is not perfectly consistent with CVP assumptions. If the expected costs and sales behavior differ from the assumptions, the results of CVP analysis can be limited. Still, we can perform useful analyses in spite of limitations with these assumptions for several reasons.

Summing costs can offset individual deviations.   Deviations from assumptions with individual costs are often minor when these costs are summed. That is, individual variable cost items may not be perfectly variable, but when we sum these variable costs, their individual deviations can offset each other. This means the assumption of variable cost behavior can be proper for total variable costs. Similarly, an assumption that total fixed costs are constant can be proper even when individual fixed cost items are not exactly constant.

CVP is applied to a relevant range of operations.   Sales, variable costs, and fixed costs often are reasonably reflected in straight lines on a graph when the assumptions are applied over a relevant range. The **relevant range of operations** is the normal operating range for a business. Except for unusually difficult or prosperous times, management typically plans for operations within a range of volume neither close to zero nor at maximum capacity. The relevant range excludes extremely high and low operating levels that are unlikely to occur. The validity of assuming that a specific cost is fixed or variable is more acceptable when operations are within the relevant range. As shown in Exhibit 22.2, a curvilinear cost can be treated as variable and linear if the relevant range covers volumes where it has a nearly constant slope. If the normal range of activity changes, some costs might need reclassification.

CVP analysis yields estimates.   CVP analysis yields approximate answers to questions about costs, volumes, and profits. These answers do not have to be precise because the analysis makes rough estimates about the future. As long as managers understand that CVP analysis gives estimates, it can be a useful tool for starting the planning process. Other qualitative factors also must be considered.

Working with Output Measures   CVP analysis usually describes the level of activity in terms of *sales volume,* which can be expressed in terms of either units sold or dollar sales. However, other measures of output exist. For instance, a manufacturer can use the number of units produced as a measure of output. Also, to simplify analysis, we sometimes assume that the production level is the same as the sales level. That is, inventory levels do not change. This often is justified by arguing that CVP analysis provides only approximations.

Example: If the selling price declines, what happens to the break-even point? *Answer:* It increases.

Quick Check   Answers — p. 928

7. Fixed cost divided by the contribution margin ratio yields the (a) break-even point in dollars, (b) contribution margin per unit, or (c) break-even point in units.

8. A company sells a product for $90 per unit with variable costs of $54 per unit. What is the contribution margin ratio?

9. Refer to Quick Check (8). If fixed costs for the period are $90,000, what is the break-even point in dollars?

10. What three basic assumptions are used in CVP analysis?

Working with Changes in Estimates Because CVP analysis uses estimates, knowing how changes in those estimates impact break-even is useful. For example, a manager might form three estimates for each of the components of break-even: optimistic, most likely, and pessimistic. Then ranges of break-even points in units can be computed using the formula in Exhibit 22.11.

To illustrate, assume Rydell's managers provide the set of estimates in Exhibit 22.15.

EXHIBIT 22.15

Alternative Estimates for Break-Even Analysis

	Selling Price per Unit	Variable Cost per Unit	Total Fixed Costs
Optimistic	$105	$68	$21,000
Most likely	100	70	24,000
Pessimistic	95	72	27,000

If, for example, Rydell's managers believe they can raise the selling price of a football to $105, without any change in variable or fixed costs, then the revised contribution margin per football is $35, and the revised break-even in units follows in Exhibit 22.16.

EXHIBIT 22.16

Revised Break-Even in Units

$$\text{Revised break-even point in units} = \frac{\$24,000}{\$35} = 686 \text{ units}$$

EXHIBIT 22.17

Scatter Diagrams—Break-Even Points for Alternative Estimates

Repeating this calculation using each of the other eight separate estimates above, and graphing the results, yields the three scatter diagrams in Exhibit 22.17.

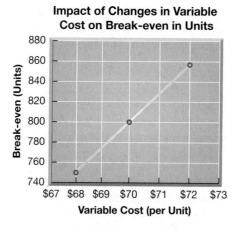

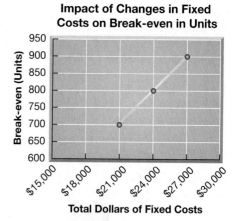

These scatter diagrams show how changes in selling prices, variable costs, and fixed costs impact break-even. When selling prices can be increased without impacting costs, break-even decreases. When competition drives selling prices down, and the company cannot reduce costs, break-even increases. Increases in either variable or fixed costs, if they cannot be passed on to customers via higher selling prices, will increase break-even. If costs can be reduced and selling prices held constant, the break-even decreases.

Point: This analysis changed only one estimate at a time; managers can examine how combinations of changes in estimates will impact break-even.

APPLYING COST-VOLUME-PROFIT ANALYSIS

Managers consider a variety of strategies in planning business operations. Cost-volume-profit analysis is useful in helping managers evaluate the likely effects of these strategies, which is the focus of this section.

Computing Income from Sales and Costs

An important question managers often need an answer to is "What is the predicted income from a predicted level of sales?" To answer this, we look at four variables in CVP analysis. These variables and their relations to income (pretax) are shown in Exhibit 22.18. We use these relations to compute expected income from predicted sales and cost levels.

 Describe several applications of cost-volume-profit analysis.

Sales
− Variable costs
Contribution margin
− Fixed costs
Income (pretax)

EXHIBIT 22.18

Income Relations in CVP Analysis

To illustrate, let's assume that Rydell's management expects to sell 1,500 units in January 2011. What is the amount of income if this sales level is achieved? Following Exhibit 22.18, we compute Rydell's expected income in Exhibit 22.19.

RYDELL COMPANY
Contribution Margin Income Statement
For Month Ended January 31, 2011

Sales (1,500 units at $100 each)	$150,000
Variable costs (1,500 units at $70 each)	105,000
Contribution margin (1500 units @ $30 each)	45,000
Fixed costs	24,000
Income (pretax)	$ 21,000

EXHIBIT 22.19

Computing Expected Pretax Income from Expected Sales

The $21,000 income is pretax. To find the amount of *after-tax* income from selling 1,500 units, management must apply the proper tax rate. Assume that the tax rate is 25%. Then we can prepare the after-tax income statement shown in Exhibit 22.20. We can also compute pretax income as after-tax income divided by (1 − tax rate); for Rydell, this is $15,750/(1 − 0.25), or $21,000.

RYDELL COMPANY
Contribution Margin Income Statement
For Month Ended January 31, 2011

Sales (1,500 units at $100 each)	$150,000
Variable costs (1,500 units at $70 each)	105,000
Contribution margin (1500 units @ $30 each)	45,000
Fixed costs	24,000
Pretax income	21,000
Income taxes (25%)	5,250
Net income (after tax)	$ 15,750

EXHIBIT 22.20

Computing Expected After-Tax Income from Expected Sales

Management then assesses whether this income is an adequate return on assets invested. Management should also consider whether sales and income can be increased by raising or lowering prices. CVP analysis is a good tool for addressing these kinds of "what-if" questions.

Computing Sales for a Target Income

Many companies' annual plans are based on certain income targets (sometimes called *budgets*). Rydell's income target for this year is to increase income by 10% over the prior year. When prior year income is known, Rydell easily computes its target income. CVP analysis helps to determine the sales level needed to achieve the target income. Computing this sales level is important because planning for the year is then based on this level. We use the formula shown in Exhibit 22.21 to compute sales for a target *after-tax* income.

"How many units must I sell to earn $50,000?"

EXHIBIT 22.21

Computing Sales (Dollars) for
a Target After-Tax Income

$$\text{Dollar sales at target after-tax income} = \frac{\text{Fixed costs} + \text{Target pretax income}}{\text{Contribution margin ratio}}$$

To illustrate, Rydell has monthly fixed costs of $24,000 and a 30% contribution margin ratio. Assume that it sets a target monthly after-tax income of $9,000 when the tax rate is 25%. This means the pretax income is targeted at $12,000 [$9,000/(1 − 0.25)] with a tax expense of $3,000. Using the formula in Exhibit 22.21, we find that $120,000 of sales are needed to produce a $9,000 after-tax income as shown in Exhibit 22.22.

EXHIBIT 22.22

Rydell's Dollar Sales for a
Target Income

$$\text{Dollar sales at target after-tax income} = \frac{\$24,000 + \$12,000}{30\%} = \$120,000$$

Point: Break-even is a special case
of the formulas in Exhibits 22.21 and
22.23; simply set target pretax income to
$0 and the formulas reduce to those in
Exhibits 22.11 and 22.12.

We can alternatively compute *unit sales* instead of dollar sales. To do this, we substitute *contribution margin per unit* for the contribution margin ratio in the denominator. This gives the number of units to sell to reach the target after-tax income. Exhibit 22.23 illustrates this for Rydell. The two computations in Exhibits 22.22 and 22.23 are equivalent because sales of 1,200 units at $100 per unit equal $120,000 of sales.

EXHIBIT 22.23

Computing Sales (Units)
for a Target After-Tax
Income

$$\text{Unit sales at target after-tax income} = \frac{\text{Fixed costs} + \text{Target pretax income}}{\text{Contribution margin per unit}}$$

$$= \frac{\$24,000 + \$12,000}{\$30} = 1,200 \text{ units}$$

Computing the Margin of Safety

All companies wish to sell more than the break-even number of units. The excess of expected sales over the break-even sales level is called a company's **margin of safety,** the amount that sales can drop before the company incurs a loss. It can be expressed in units, dollars, or even as a percent of the predicted level of sales. To illustrate, if Rydell's expected sales are $100,000, the margin of safety is $20,000 above break-even sales of $80,000. As a percent, the margin of safety is 20% of expected sales as shown in Exhibit 22.24.

EXHIBIT 22.24

Computing Margin of Safety
(in Percent)

$$\text{Margin of safety (in percent)} = \frac{\text{Expected sales} - \text{Break-even sales}}{\text{Expected sales}}$$

$$= \frac{\$100,000 - \$80,000}{\$100,000} = 20\%$$

Management must assess whether the margin of safety is adequate in light of factors such as sales variability, competition, consumer tastes, and economic conditions.

 **Decision Ethics**   Answer — p. 927

Supervisor   Your team is conducting a cost-volume-profit analysis for a new product. Different sales projections have different incomes. One member suggests picking numbers yielding favorable income because any estimate is "as good as any other." Another member points to a scatter diagram of 20 months' production on a comparable product and suggests dropping unfavorable data points for cost estimation. What do you do? ■

Using Sensitivity Analysis

Earlier we showed how changing one of the estimates in a CVP analysis impacts break-even. We can also examine strategies that impact several estimates in the CVP analysis. For instance, we might want to know what happens to income if we automate a currently manual process. We can use CVP analysis to predict income if we can describe how these changes affect a company's fixed costs, variable costs, selling price, and volume.

To illustrate, assume that Rydell Company is looking into buying a new machine that would increase monthly fixed costs from $24,000 to $30,000 but decrease variable costs from $70 per unit to $60 per unit. The machine is used to produce output whose selling price will remain unchanged at $100. This results in increases in both the unit contribution margin and the contribution margin ratio. The revised contribution margin per unit is $40 ($100 − $60), and the revised contribution margin ratio is 40% of selling price ($40/$100). Using CVP analysis, Rydell's revised break-even point in dollars would be $75,000 as computed in Exhibit 22.25.

Example: If fixed costs decline, what happens to the break-even point? *Answer:* It decreases.

$$\text{Revised break-even point in dollars} = \frac{\text{Revised fixed costs}}{\text{Revised contribution margin ratio}} = \frac{\$30,000}{40\%} = \$75,000$$

EXHIBIT 22.25

Revising Break-even When Changes Occur

The revised fixed costs and the revised contribution margin ratio can be used to address other issues including computation of (1) expected income for a given sales level and (2) the sales level needed to earn a target income. Once again, we can use sensitivity analysis to generate different sets of revenue and cost estimates that are *optimistic, pessimistic,* and *most likely.* Different CVP analyses based on these estimates provide different scenarios that management can analyze and use in planning business strategy.

Decision Insight

Eco-CVP Auto makers are increasingly offering hybrid cars, including the **Ford** Fusion, **Toyota** Prius, and **Nissan** Altima Hybrid. Hybrids yield better gas mileage and generate fewer greenhouse gases, but they are priced higher. Are hybrid models economically feasible for buyers? A study by **Edmunds.com** shows it take several years for consumers to break even (save enough money on gas to offset the higher purchase price) on most hybrid models. ■

Quick Check

Answers — p. 928

11. A company has fixed costs of $50,000 and a 25% contribution margin ratio. What dollar sales are necessary to achieve an after-tax net income of $120,000 if the tax rate is 20%? (*a*) $800,000, (*b*) $680,000, or (*c*) $600,000.

12. If a company's contribution margin ratio decreases from 50% to 25%, what can be said about the unit sales needed to achieve the same target income level?

13. What is a company's margin of safety?

Computing a Multiproduct Break-Even Point

To this point, we have looked only at cases where the company sells a single product or service. This was to keep the basic CVP analysis simple. However, many companies sell multiple products or services, and we can modify the CVP analysis for use in these cases. An important assumption in a multiproduct setting is that the sales mix of different products is known and remains constant during the planning period. **Sales mix** is the ratio (proportion) of the sales volumes for the various products. For instance, if a company normally sells 10,000 footballs, 5,000 softballs, and 4,000 basketballs per month, its sales mix can be expressed as 10:5:4 for footballs, softballs, and basketballs.

P4 Compute the break-even point for a multiproduct company.

To apply multiproduct CVP analysis, we can estimate the break-even point by using a **composite unit,** which consists of a specific number of units of each product in proportion to their expected sales mix. Multiproduct CVP analysis treats this composite unit as a single product. To illustrate, let's look at **Hair-Today,** a styling salon that offers three cuts: basic, ultra, and budget in the ratio of 4 basic units to 2 ultra units to 1 budget unit (expressed as 4:2:1). Management wants to estimate its break-even point for next year. Unit selling prices for these three cuts are basic, $20; ultra, $32; and budget, $16. Using the 4:2:1 sales mix, the selling price of a composite unit of the three products is computed as follows.

4 units of basic @ $20 per unit	$ 80
2 units of ultra @ $32 per unit	64
1 unit of budget @ $16 per unit	16
Selling price of a composite unit	**$160**

Point: Selling prices and variable costs are usually expressed in per unit amounts. Fixed costs are usually expressed in total amounts.

Hair-Today's fixed costs are $192,000 per year, and its variable costs of the three products are basic, $13; ultra, $18.00; and budget, $8.00. Variable costs for a composite unit of these products follow.

4 units of basic @ $13 per unit	$52
2 units of ultra @ $18 per unit	36
1 unit of budget @ $8 per unit	8
Variable costs of a composite unit	**$96**

Hair-Today's $64 contribution margin for a composite unit is computed by subtracting the variable costs of a composite unit ($96) from its selling price ($160). We then use the contribution margin to determine Hair-Today's break-even point in composite units in Exhibit 22.26.

EXHIBIT 22.26

Break-Even Point in Composite Units

$$\text{Break-even point in composite units} = \frac{\text{Fixed costs}}{\text{Contribution margin per composite unit}}$$

$$= \frac{\$192,000}{\$64} = 3,000 \text{ composite units}$$

Point: The break-even point in dollars for Exhibit 22.26 is $192,000/($64/$160) = $480,000.

This computation implies that Hair-Today breaks even when it sells 3,000 composite units. To determine how many units of each product it must sell to break even, we multiply the number of units of each product in the composite by 3,000 as follows.

Basic:	4 × 3,000	12,000 units
Ultra:	2 × 3,000	6,000 units
Budget:	1 × 3,000	3,000 units

Instead of computing contribution margin per composite unit, a company can compute a **weighted-average contribution margin.** Given the 4:2:1 product mix, basic cuts comprise 57.14% (computed as 4/7) of the company's haircuts, ultra makes up 28.57% of its business, and budget cuts comprise 14.29%. The weighted-average contribution margin follows in Exhibit 22.27.

EXHIBIT 22.27

Weighted-Average Contribution Margin

	Unit contribution margin	×	Percentage of sales mix	=	Weighted unit contribution margin
Basic.	$ 7		57.14%		$4.000
Ultra	14		28.57		4.000
Budget	8		14.29		1.143
Weighted-average contribution margin					**$9.143**

The company's break-even point in units is computed in Exhibit 22.28 as follows:

$$\text{Break-even point in units} = \frac{\text{Fixed costs}}{\text{Weighted-average contribution margin}}$$

$$= \frac{\$192,000}{\$9.143} = 21,000 \text{ units}$$

EXHIBIT 22.28

Break-Even in Units using Weighted-Average Contribution Margin

We see that the weighted-average contribution margin method yields 21,000 whole units as the break-even amount, the same total as the composite unit approach.

Exhibit 22.29 verifies the results for composite units by showing Hair-Today's sales and costs at this break-even point using a contribution margin income statement.

EXHIBIT 22.29

Multiproduct Break-Even Income Statement

HAIR-TODAY Forecasted Contribution Margin Income Statement (at Break-even)				
	Basic	Ultra	Budget	Totals
Sales				
Basic (12,000 @ $20)	$240,000			
Ultra (6,000 @ $32)		$192,000		
Budget (3,000 @ $16)			$48,000	
Total sales				$480,000
Variable costs				
Basic (12,000 @ $13)	156,000			
Ultra (6,000 @ $18)		108,000		
Budget (3,000 @ $8)			24,000	
Total variable costs				288,000
Contribution margin	$ 84,000	$ 84,000	$24,000	192,000
Fixed costs				192,000
Net income				$ 0

A CVP analysis using composite units can be used to answer a variety of planning questions. Once a product mix is set, all answers are based on the assumption that the mix remains constant at all relevant sales levels as other factors in the analysis do. We also can vary the sales mix to see what happens under alternative strategies.

Decision Maker   Answer — p. 928

Entrepreneur   A CVP analysis indicates that your start-up, which markets electronic products, will break even with the current sales mix and price levels. You have a target income in mind. What analysis might you perform to assess the likelihood of achieving this income? ■

Quick Check   Answers — p. 928

14. The sales mix of a company's two products, X and Y, is 2:1. Unit variable costs for both products are $2, and unit sales prices are $5 for X and $4 for Y. What is the contribution margin per composite unit? (a) $5, (b) $10, or (c) $8.

15. What additional assumption about sales mix must be made in doing a conventional CVP analysis for a company that produces and sells more than one product?

GLOBAL VIEW

Survey evidence shows that many German companies have elaborate and detailed cost accounting systems. Over 90 percent of companies surveyed report their systems focus on *contribution margin*. This focus helps German companies like **Volkswagen** control costs and plan their production levels. Recently, Volkswagen announced it expects its Spanish brand *Seat* to break even within five years. For 2009, the *Seat* brand lost €339 million on sales of 307, 502 units.

Decision Analysis ▪▪▫   Degree of Operating Leverage

A2 Analyze changes in sales using the degree of operating leverage.

CVP analysis is especially useful when management begins the planning process and wishes to predict outcomes of alternative strategies. These strategies can involve changes in selling prices, fixed costs, variable costs, sales volume, and product mix. Managers are interested in seeing the effects of changes in some or all of these factors.

One goal of all managers is to get maximum benefits from their fixed costs. Managers would like to use 100% of their output capacity so that fixed costs are spread over the largest number of units. This would decrease fixed cost per unit and increase income. The extent, or relative size, of fixed costs in the total cost structure is known as **operating leverage.** Companies having a higher proportion of fixed costs in their total cost structure are said to have higher operating leverage. An example of this is a company that chooses to automate its processes instead of using direct labor, increasing its fixed costs and lowering its variable costs. A useful managerial measure to help assess the effect of changes in the level of sales on income is the **degree of operating leverage (DOL)** defined in Exhibit 22.30.

EXHIBIT 22.30

Degree of Operating Leverage

$$\textbf{DOL = Total contribution margin (in dollars)/Pretax income}$$

To illustrate, let's return to Rydell Company. At a sales level of 1,200 units, Rydell's total contribution margin is \$36,000 (1,200 units × \$30 contribution margin per unit). Its pretax income, after subtracting fixed costs of \$24,000, is \$12,000 (\$36,000 − \$24,000). Rydell's degree of operating leverage at this sales level is 3.0, computed as contribution margin divided by pretax income (\$36,000/\$12,000). We then use DOL to measure the effect of changes in the level of sales on pretax income. For instance, suppose Rydell expects sales to increase by 10%. If this increase is within the relevant range of operations, we can expect this 10% increase in sales to result in a 30% increase in pretax income computed as DOL multiplied by the increase in sales (3.0 × 10%). Similar analyses can be done for expected decreases in sales.

DEMONSTRATION PROBLEM

Sport Caps Co. manufactures and sells caps for different sporting events. The fixed costs of operating the company are \$150,000 per month, and the variable costs for caps are \$5 per unit. The caps are sold for \$8 per unit. The fixed costs provide a production capacity of up to 100,000 caps per month.

Required

1. Use the formulas in the chapter to compute the following:
   a. Contribution margin per cap.
   b. Break-even point in terms of the number of caps produced and sold.
   c. Amount of net income at 30,000 caps sold per month (ignore taxes).
   d. Amount of net income at 85,000 caps sold per month (ignore taxes).

    e. Number of caps to be produced and sold to provide $45,000 of after-tax income, assuming an income tax rate of 25%.

2. Draw a CVP chart for the company, showing cap output on the horizontal axis. Identify (*a*) the break-even point and (*b*) the amount of pretax income when the level of cap production is 70,000. (Omit the fixed cost line.)

3. Use the formulas in the chapter to compute the

    a. Contribution margin ratio.

    b. Break-even point in terms of sales dollars.

    c. Amount of net income at $250,000 of sales per month (ignore taxes).

    d. Amount of net income at $600,000 of sales per month (ignore taxes).

    e. Dollars of sales needed to provide $45,000 of after-tax income, assuming an income tax rate of 25%.

PLANNING THE SOLUTION

- Identify the formulas in the chapter for the required items expressed in units and solve them using the data given in the problem.
- Draw a CVP chart that reflects the facts in the problem. The horizontal axis should plot the volume in units up to 100,000, and the vertical axis should plot the total dollars up to $800,000. Plot the total cost line as upward sloping, starting at the fixed cost level ($150,000) on the vertical axis and increasing until it reaches $650,000 at the maximum volume of 100,000 units. Verify that the break-even point (where the two lines cross) equals the amount you computed in part 1.
- Identify the formulas in the chapter for the required items expressed in dollars and solve them using the data given in the problem.

SOLUTION TO DEMONSTRATION PROBLEM

1. a. Contribution margin per cap   = Selling price per unit − Variable cost per unit
                                         = $8 − $5 = $\underline{\underline{\$3}}$

    b. Break-even point in caps $= \dfrac{\text{Fixed costs}}{\text{Contribution margin per cap}} = \dfrac{\$150,000}{\$3} = \underline{\underline{50,000 \text{ caps}}}$

    c. Net income at 30,000 caps sold   = (Units × Contribution margin per unit) − Fixed costs
                                           = (30,000 × $3) − $150,000 = $\underline{\underline{\$(60,000) \text{ loss}}}$

    d. Net income at 85,000 caps sold   = (Units × Contribution margin per unit) − Fixed costs
                                           = (85,000 × $3) − $150,000 = $\underline{\underline{\$105,000 \text{ profit}}}$

    e. Pretax income   = $45,000/(1 − 0.25) = $60,000
       Income taxes   = $60,000 × 25% = $15,000

       Units needed for $45,000 income $= \dfrac{\text{Fixed costs} + \text{Target pretax income}}{\text{Contribution margin per cap}}$

                                              $= \dfrac{\$150,000 + \$60,000}{\$3} = \underline{\underline{70,000 \text{ caps}}}$

2. CVP chart.

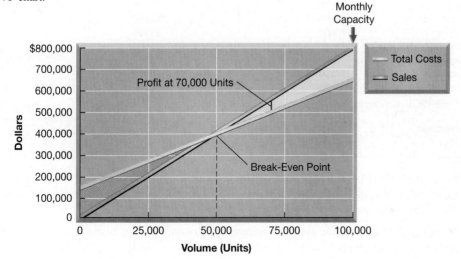

3. a. Contribution margin ratio $= \dfrac{\text{Contribution margin per unit}}{\text{Selling price per unit}} = \dfrac{\$3}{\$8} = \underline{\underline{0.375, \text{ or } 37.5\%}}$

   b. Break-even point in dollars $= \dfrac{\text{Fixed costs}}{\text{Contribution margin ratio}} = \dfrac{\$150,000}{37.5\%} = \underline{\underline{\$400,000}}$

   c. Net income at sales of \$250,000 $= (\text{Sales} \times \text{Contribution margin ratio}) - \text{Fixed costs}$
   $= (\$250,000 \times 37.5\%) - \$150,000 = \underline{\underline{\$(56,250) \text{ loss}}}$

   d. Net income at sales of \$600,000 $= (\text{Sales} \times \text{Contribution margin ratio}) - \text{Fixed costs}$
   $= (\$600,000 \times 37.5\%) - \$150,000 = \underline{\underline{\$75,000 \text{ income}}}$

   e. Dollars of sales to yield \$45,000 after-tax income $= \dfrac{\text{Fixed costs} + \text{Target pretax income}}{\text{Contribution margin ratio}}$
   $= \dfrac{\$150,000 + \$60,000}{37.5\%} = \underline{\underline{\$560,000}}$

APPENDIX

22A Using Excel to Estimate Least-Squares Regression

Microsoft Excel® 2007 and other spreadsheet software can be used to perform least-squares regressions to identify cost behavior. In Excel®, the INTERCEPT and SLOPE functions are used. The following screen shot reports the data from Exhibit 22.3 in cells A1 through C13 and shows the cell contents to find the intercept (cell B16) and slope (cell B17). Cell B16 uses Excel® to find the intercept from a least-squares regression of total cost (shown as C2:C13 in cell B16) on units produced (shown as B2:B13 in cell B16). Spreadsheet software is useful in understanding cost behavior when many data points (such as monthly total costs and units produced) are available.

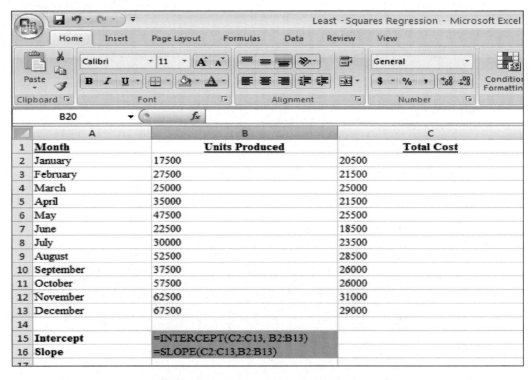

Excel® can also be used to create scatter diagrams such as that in Exhibit 22.4. In contrast to visually drawing a line that "fits" the data, Excel® more precisely fits the regression line. To draw a scatter diagram with a line of fit, follow these steps:

1. Highlight the data cells you wish to diagram; in this example, start from cell C13 and highlight through cell B2.

2. Then select "Insert" and "Scatter" from the drop-down menus. Selecting the chart type in the upper left corner of the choices under Scatter will produce a diagram that looks like that in Exhibit 22.4, without a line of fit.

3. To add a line of fit (also called trend line), select "Layout" and "Trendline" from the drop-down menus. Selecting "Linear Trendline" will produce a diagram that looks like that in Exhibit 22.4, including the line of fit.

Summary

C1 **Describe different types of cost behavior in relation to production and sales volume.** Cost behavior is described in terms of how its amount changes in relation to changes in volume of activity within a relevant range. Fixed costs remain constant to changes in volume. Total variable costs change in direct proportion to volume changes. Mixed costs display the effects of both fixed and variable components. Step-wise costs remain constant over a small volume range, then change by a lump sum and remain constant over another volume range, and so on. Curvilinear costs change in a nonlinear relation to volume changes.

C2 **Describe several applications of cost-volume-profit analysis.** Cost-volume-profit analysis can be used to predict what can happen under alternative strategies concerning sales volume, selling prices, variable costs, or fixed costs. Applications include "what-if" analysis, computing sales for a target income, and break-even analysis.

A1 **Compute the contribution margin and describe what it reveals about a company's cost structure.** Contribution margin per unit is a product's sales price less its total variable costs. Contribution margin ratio is a product's contribution margin per unit divided by its sales price. Unit contribution margin is the amount received from each sale that contributes to fixed costs and income. The contribution margin ratio reveals what portion of each sales dollar is available as contribution to fixed costs and income.

A2 **Analyze changes in sales using the degree of operating leverage.** The extent, or relative size, of fixed costs in a company's total cost structure is known as *operating leverage*. One tool useful in assessing the effect of changes in sales on income is the degree of operating leverage, or DOL. DOL is the ratio of contribution margin divided by pretax income. This ratio can be used to determine the expected percent change in income given a percent change in sales.

P1 **Determine cost estimates using the scatter diagram, high-low, and regression methods of estimating costs.** Three different methods used to estimate costs are the scatter diagram, the high-low method, and least-squares regression. All three methods use past data to estimate costs. Cost estimates from a scatter diagram are based on a visual fit of the cost line. Estimates from the high-low method are based only on costs corresponding to the lowest and highest sales. The least-squares regression method is a statistical technique and uses all data points.

P2 **Compute the break-even point for a single product company.** A company's break-even point for a period is the sales volume at which total revenues equal total costs. To compute a break-even point in terms of sales units, we divide total fixed costs by the contribution margin per unit. To compute a break-even point in terms of sales dollars, divide total fixed costs by the contribution margin ratio.

P3 **Graph costs and sales for a single product company.** The costs and sales for a company can be graphically illustrated using a CVP chart. In this chart, the horizontal axis represents the number of units sold and the vertical axis represents dollars of sales or costs. Straight lines are used to depict both costs and sales on the CVP chart.

P4 **Compute the break-even point for a multiproduct company.** CVP analysis can be applied to a multiproduct company by expressing sales volume in terms of composite units. A composite unit consists of a specific number of units of each product in proportion to their expected sales mix. Multiproduct CVP analysis treats this composite unit as a single product.

Guidance Answers to Decision Maker and Decision Ethics

Sales Manager   The contribution margin per unit for the first order is $600 (60% of $1,000); the contribution margin per unit for the second order is $160 (20% of $800). You are likely tempted to accept the first order based on its high contribution margin per unit, but you must compute the total contribution margin based on the number of units sold for each order. Total contribution margin is $60,000 ($600 per unit × 100 units) and $80,000 ($160 per unit × 500 units) for the two orders, respectively. The second order provides the largest return in absolute dollars and is the order you would accept. Another factor to consider in your selection is the potential for a long-term relationship with these customers including repeat sales and growth.

Operations Manager   Without the availability of past data, none of the three methods described in the chapter can be used to measure cost behavior. Instead, the manager must investigate whether data from similar manufacturers can be accessed. This is likely difficult due to the sensitive nature of such data. In the absence of data, the manager should develop a list of the different production inputs and identify input-output relations. This provides guidance to the manager in measuring cost behavior. After several months, actual cost data will be available for analysis.

Supervisor   Your dilemma is whether to go along with the suggestions to "manage" the numbers to make the project look like it will achieve sufficient profits. You should not succumb to these suggestions. Many people will likely be affected negatively if you manage the predicted numbers and the project eventually is unprofitable. Moreover, if it does fail, an investigation would likely reveal that data in the proposal were "fixed" to make it look good. Probably the only benefit from managing the numbers is the short-term payoff of pleasing those who proposed the product. One way to deal with this dilemma is to prepare several analyses showing results under different assumptions and then let senior management make the decision.

Entrepreneur   You must first compute the level of sales required to achieve the desired net income. Then you must conduct sensitivity analysis by varying the price, sales mix, and cost estimates. Results from the sensitivity analysis provide information you can use to assess the possibility of reaching the target sales level. For instance, you might have to pursue aggressive marketing strategies to push the high-margin products, or you might have to cut prices to increase sales and profits, or another strategy might emerge.

Guidance Answers to Quick Checks

1. *b*

2. A fixed cost remains unchanged in total amount regardless of output levels. However, fixed *cost per unit* declines with increased output.

3. Such a cost is considered variable because the *total* cost changes in proportion to volume changes.

4. *b*

5. The high-low method ignores all costs and sales (activity base) volume data points except the costs corresponding to the highest and lowest (most extreme) sales (activity base) volume.

6. *c*

7. *a*

8. ($90 − $54)/$90 = 40%

9. $90,000/40% = $225,000

10. Three basic CVP assumptions are that (1) selling price per unit is constant, (2) variable costs per unit are constant, and (3) total fixed costs are constant.

11. a; Two steps are required for explanation:
(1) Pretax income = $120,000/(1 − 0.20) = $150,000
(2) $\dfrac{\$50,000 + \$150,000}{25\%} = \$800,000$

12. If the contribution margin ratio decreases from 50% to 25%, unit sales would have to double.

13. A company's margin of safety is the excess of the predicted sales level over its break-even sales level.

14. *c*; Selling price of a composite unit:

2 units of X @ $5 per unit	$10
1 unit of Y @ $4 per unit	4
Selling price of a composite unit	$14

Variable costs of a composite unit:

2 units of X @ $2 per unit	$4
1 unit of Y @ $2 per unit	2
Variable costs of a composite unit	$6

Therefore, the contribution margin per composite unit is $8.

15. It must be assumed that the sales mix remains unchanged at all sales levels in the relevant range.

Key Terms   mhhe.com/wildFAP20e

Absorption costing (p. 915)

Break-even point (p. 915)

Composite unit (p. 922)

Contribution margin per unit (p. 914)

Contribution margin ratio (p. 914)

Cost-volume-profit (CVP) analysis (p. 908)

Cost-volume-profit (CVP) chart (p. 916)

Curvilinear cost (p. 910)

Degree of operating leverage (DOL) (p. 924)

Estimated line of cost behavior (p. 912)

High-low method (p. 912)

Least-squares regression (p. 913)

Margin of safety (p. 920)

Mixed cost (p. 909)

Operating leverage (p. 924)

Relevant range of operations (p. 917)

Sales mix (p. 921)

Scatter diagram (p. 911)

Step-wise cost (p. 910)

Variable costing income statement (p. 915)

Weighted-average contribution margin (p. 922)

Multiple Choice Quiz   Answers on p. 943   mhhe.com/wildFAP20e

Additional Quiz Questions are available at the book's Website.

1. A company's only product sells for $150 per unit. Its variable costs per unit are $100, and its fixed costs total $75,000. What is its contribution margin per unit?
   a. $50
   b. $250
   c. $100
   d. $150
   e. $25

2. Using information from question 1, what is the company's contribution margin ratio?
   a. 66⅔%
   b. 100%
   c. 50%
   d. 0%
   e. 33⅓%

3. Using information from question 1, what is the company's break-even point in units?
   a. 500 units
   b. 750 units
   c. 1,500 units
   d. 3,000 units
   e. 1,000 units
4. A company's forecasted sales are $300,000 and its sales at break-even are $180,000. Its margin of safety in dollars is
   a. $180,000.
   b. $120,000.
   c. $480,000.

   d. $60,000.
   e. $300,000.
5. A product sells for $400 per unit and its variable costs per unit are $260. The company's fixed costs are $840,000. If the company desires $70,000 pretax income, what is the required dollar sales?
   a. $2,400,000
   b. $200,000
   c. $2,600,000
   d. $2,275,000
   e. $1,400,000

A Superscript letter A denotes assignments based on Appendix 22A

🔲 Icon denotes assignments that involve decision making.

Discussion Questions

1. 🔲 How is cost-volume-profit analysis useful?
2. What is a variable cost? Identify two variable costs.
3. 🔲 When output volume increases, do variable costs per unit increase, decrease, or stay the same within the relevant range of activity? Explain.
4. 🔲 When output volume increases, do fixed costs per unit increase, decrease, or stay the same within the relevant range of activity? Explain.
5. How do step-wise costs and curvilinear costs differ?
6. Define and describe *contribution margin* per unit.
7. Define and explain the *contribution margin ratio*.
8. Describe the contribution margin ratio in layperson's terms.
9. In performing CVP analysis for a manufacturing company, what simplifying assumption is usually made about the volume of production and the volume of sales?
10. What two arguments tend to justify classifying all costs as either fixed or variable even though individual costs might not behave exactly as classified?
11. 🔲 How does assuming that operating activity occurs within a relevant range affect cost-volume-profit analysis?
12. List three methods to measure cost behavior.
13. How is a scatter diagram used to identify and measure the behavior of a company's costs?
14. In cost-volume-profit analysis, what is the estimated profit at the break-even point?

15. 🔲 Assume that a straight line on a CVP chart intersects the vertical axis at the level of fixed costs and has a positive slope that rises with each additional unit of volume by the amount of the variable costs per unit. What does this line represent?
16. **Palm** has both fixed and variable costs. Why are fixed costs depicted as a horizontal line on a CVP chart? **Palm**
17. 🔲 Each of two similar companies has sales of $20,000 and total costs of $15,000 for a month. Company A's total costs include $10,000 of variable costs and $5,000 of fixed costs. If Company B's total costs include $4,000 of variable costs and $11,000 of fixed costs, which company will enjoy more profit if sales double?
18. _____ of _____ reflects expected sales in excess of the level of break-even sales.
19. 🔲 **Apple** produces iPods for sale. Identify some of the variable and fixed product costs associated with that production. [*Hint:* Limit costs to product costs.] **Apple**
20. 🔲 Should **Research In Motion** use single product or multiproduct break-even analysis? Explain. **RIM**
21. 🔲 **Nokia** is thinking of expanding sales of its most popular cell-phone model by 65%. Do you **NOKIA** expect its variable and fixed costs for this model to stay within the relevant range? Explain.

Mc Graw Hill connect

Determine whether each of the following is best described as a fixed, variable, or mixed cost with respect to product units.

1. Maintenance of factory machinery.
2. Depreciation expense of warehouse.
3. Taxes on factory building.
4. Factory supervisor's salary.

5. Wages of an assembly-line worker paid on the basis of acceptable units produced.
6. Packaging expense.
7. Rubber used to manufacture athletic shoes.

QUICK STUDY

QS 22-1

Cost behavior identification

C1

QS 22-2

Cost behavior identification

C1

Listed here are four series of separate costs measured at various volume levels. Examine each series and identify whether it is best described as a fixed, variable, step-wise, or curvilinear cost. (It can help to graph the cost series.)

Volume (Units)	Series 1	Series 2	Series 3	Series 4
0	$ 0	$900	$ 400	$200
100	400	900	400	210
200	800	900	400	240
300	1,200	900	800	290
400	1,600	900	800	380
500	2,000	900	1,200	500
600	2,400	900	1,200	640

QS 22-3

Cost behavior estimation—scatter diagram

P1

This scatter diagram reflects past maintenance hours and their corresponding maintenance costs.

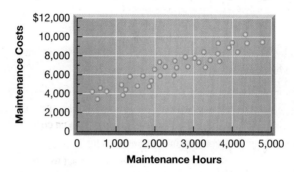

1. Draw an estimated line of cost behavior.
2. Estimate the fixed and variable components of maintenance costs.

QS 22-4

Cost behavior estimation—high-low method

P1

The following information is available for a company's maintenance cost over the last seven months. Using the high-low method, estimate both the fixed and variable components of its maintenance cost.

Month	Maintenance Hours	Maintenance Cost
June..............	20	$6,020
July	48	8,100
August	24	5,100
September	38	7,000
October	42	6,900
November	36	6,900
December	12	3,600

QS 22-5

Contribution margin ratio

A1

Compute and interpret the contribution margin ratio using the following data: sales, $150,000; total variable cost, $90,000.

QS 22-6

Contribution margin per unit and break-even units

P2

MCU Phone Company sells its cordless phone for $300 per unit. Fixed costs total $540,000, and variable costs are $120 per unit. Determine the (1) contribution margin per unit and (2) break-even point in units.

QS 22-7

Assumptions in CVP analysis

C2

Refer to the information from QS 22-6. How will the break-even point in units change in response to each of the following independent changes in selling price per unit, variable cost per unit, or total fixed costs? Use I for increase and D for decrease. (It is not necessary to compute new break-even points.)

Change	Break-even in Units Will
1. Total fixed cost to $520,000	_____
2. Variable cost to $134 per unit	_____
3. Selling price per unit to $290	_____
4. Variable cost to $100 per unit	_____
5. Total fixed cost to $544,000	_____
6. Selling price per unit to $320	_____

Refer to QS 22-6. Determine the (1) contribution margin ratio and (2) break-even point in dollars.

QS 22-8
Contribution margin ratio and break-even dollars   P2

Refer to QS 22-6. Assume that MCU Phone Co. is subject to a 30% income tax rate. Compute the units of product that must be sold to earn after-tax income of $504,000.

QS 22-9
CVP analysis and target income
P2

Which one of the following is an assumption that underlies cost-volume-profit analysis?

1. All costs have approximately the same relevant range.
2. The selling price per unit must change in proportion to the number of units sold.
3. For costs classified as variable, the costs per unit of output must change constantly.
4. For costs classified as fixed, the costs per unit of output must remain constant.

QS 22-10
CVP assumptions
C2

A high proportion of Company X's total costs are variable with respect to units sold; a high proportion of Company Y's total costs are fixed with respect to units sold. Which company is likely to have a higher degree of operating leverage (DOL)? Explain.

QS 22-11
Operating leverage analysis   A2

M-Mobile Company manufactures and sells two products, black phones and white phones, in the ratio of 5:3. Fixed costs are $85,000, and the contribution margin per composite unit is $170. What number of both black and white phones is sold at the break-even point?

QS 22-12
Multiproduct break-even   P4

Corme Company expects sales of $34 million (400,000 units). The company's total fixed costs are $17.5 million and its variable costs are $35 per unit. Prepare a CVP chart from this information.

QS 22-13
CVP graph   P3

A recent income statement for **Volkswagen** reports the following (in € millions). Assume 70 percent of the cost of sales and 70 percent of the selling and administrative costs are variable costs, and the remaining 30 percent of each is fixed. Compute the contribution margin (in € millions). (Round computations using percentages to the nearest whole euro.)

QS 22-14
Contribution margin   A1

Sales	€105,187
Cost of sales	91,608
Selling and administrative expenses	13,276

connect

A company reports the following information about its sales and its cost of sales. Each unit of its product sells for $500. Use these data to prepare a scatter diagram. Draw an estimated line of cost behavior and determine whether the cost appears to be variable, fixed, or mixed.

EXERCISES

Exercise 22-1
Measurement of cost behavior using a scatter diagram
P1

Period	Sales	Cost of Sales	Period	Sales	Cost of Sales
1..............	$15,000	$10,100	4..............	7,500	5,500
2..............	11,500	7,500	5..............	9,000	6,000
3..............	10,500	7,000	6..............	12,500	9,500

Exercise 22-2

Cost behavior in graphs

C1

Following are five graphs representing various cost behaviors. (1) Identify whether the cost behavior in each graph is mixed, step-wise, fixed, variable, or curvilinear. (2) Identify the graph (by number) that best illustrates each cost behavior: (a) Factory policy requires one supervisor for every 30 factory workers; (b) real estate taxes on factory; (c) electricity charge that includes the standard monthly charge plus a charge for each kilowatt hour; (d) commissions to salespersons; and (e) costs of hourly paid workers that provide substantial gains in efficiency when a few workers are added but gradually smaller gains in efficiency when more workers are added.

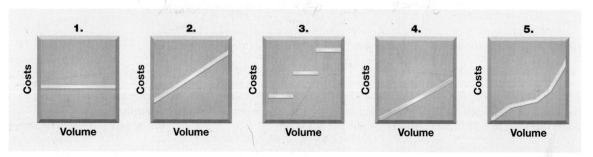

Exercise 22-3

Cost behavior defined

C1

The left column lists several cost classifications. The right column presents short definitions of those costs. In the blank space beside each of the numbers in the right column, write the letter of the cost best described by the definition.

A. Curvilinear cost

B. Step-wise cost

C. Fixed cost

D. Mixed cost

E. Variable cost

F. Total cost

_____ **1.** This cost increases in direct proportion to increases in volume; its amount is constant for each unit produced.

_____ **2.** This cost remains constant over a limited range of volume; when it reaches the end of its limited range, it changes by a lump sum and remains at that level until it exceeds another limited range.

_____ **3.** This cost has a component that remains the same over all volume levels and another component that increases in direct proportion to increases in volume.

_____ **4.** This cost increases when volume increases, but the increase is not constant for each unit produced.

_____ **5.** This cost remains constant over all volume levels within the productive capacity for the planning period.

_____ **6.** This cost is the combined amount of all the other costs.

Exercise 22-4

Cost behavior identification

C1

Following are five series of costs A through E measured at various volume levels. Examine each series and identify which is fixed, variable, mixed, step-wise, or curvilinear.

Volume (Units)	Series A	Series B	Series C	Series D	Series E
0	$ 0	$2,500	$ 0	$2,000	$4,000
200	3,600	3,100	6,000	2,000	4,000
400	7,200	3,700	6,600	4,000	4,000
600	10,800	4,300	7,200	4,000	4,000
800	14,400	4,900	8,200	6,000	4,000
1,000	18,000	5,500	9,600	6,000	4,000
1,200	21,600	6,100	13,500	8,000	4,000

Exercise 22-5

Predicting sales and variable costs using contribution margin

C2

Orlando Company management predicts that it will incur fixed costs of $250,000 and earn pretax income of $350,000 in the next period. Its expected contribution margin ratio is 60%. Use this information to compute the amounts of (1) total dollar sales and (2) total variable costs.

Use the following information about sales and costs to prepare a scatter diagram. Draw a cost line that reflects the behavior displayed by this cost. Determine whether the cost is variable, step-wise, fixed, mixed, or curvilinear.

Exercise 22-6
Scatter diagram and measurement of cost behavior

P1

Period	Sales	Costs	Period	Sales	Costs
1.............	$760	$590	9.............	$580	$390
2.............	800	560	10.............	320	240
3.............	200	230	11.............	240	230
4.............	400	400	12.............	720	550
5.............	480	390	13.............	280	260
6.............	620	550	14.............	440	410
7.............	680	590	15.............	380	260
8.............	540	430			

Felix & Co. reports the following information about its sales and cost of sales. Draw an estimated line of cost behavior using a scatter diagram, and compute fixed costs and variable costs per unit sold. Then use the high-low method to estimate the fixed and variable components of the cost of sales.

Exercise 22-7
Cost behavior estimation—scatter diagram and high-low

P1

Period	Units Sold	Cost of Sales	Period	Units Sold	Cost of Sales
1.............	0	$2,500	6.............	2,000	5,500
2.............	400	3,100	7.............	2,400	6,100
3.............	800	3,700	8.............	2,800	6,700
4.............	1,200	4,300	9.............	3,200	7,300
5.............	1,600	4,900	10.............	3,600	7,900

Refer to the information from Exercise 22-7. Use spreadsheet software to use ordinary least-squares regression to estimate the cost equation, including fixed and variable cost amounts.

Exercise 22-8[A]
Measurement of cost behavior using regression   P1

A pants maker is designing a new line of pants called the Redbird. The pants will sell for $325 per pair and cost $260 per pair in variable costs to make. (1) Compute the contribution margin per pair. (2) Compute the contribution margin ratio. (3) Describe what the contribution margin ratio reveals about this new pants line.

Exercise 22-9
Contribution margin

A2

Apollo Company manufactures a single product that sells for $168 per unit and whose total variable costs are $126 per unit. The company's annual fixed costs are $630,000. (1) Use this information to compute the company's (a) contribution margin, (b) contribution margin ratio, (c) break-even point in units, and (d) break-even point in dollars of sales.

Exercise 22-10
Contribution margin, break-even, and CVP chart   P2

Refer to the information in Exercise 22-10. Prepare a CVP chart for the company.

Exercise 22-11
CVP chart   P3

Refer to Exercise 22-10. (1) Prepare a contribution margin income statement for Apollo Company showing sales, variable costs, and fixed costs at the break-even point. (2) If the company's fixed costs increase by $135,000, what amount of sales (in dollars) is needed to break even? Explain.

Exercise 22-12
Income reporting and break-even analysis   C2

Apollo Company management (in Exercise 22-10) targets an annual after-tax income of $840,000. The company is subject to a 20% income tax rate. Assume that fixed costs remain at $630,000. Compute the (1) unit sales to earn the target after-tax net income and (2) dollar sales to earn the target after-tax net income.

Exercise 22-13
Computing sales to achieve target income   C2

Exercise 22-14

Forecasted income statement

C2

Check Forecasted income, $1,416,000

Apollo Company's sales manager (in Exercise 22-10) predicts that annual sales of the company's product will soon reach 40,000 units and its price will increase to $200 per unit. According to the production manager, the variable costs are expected to increase to $140 per unit but fixed costs will remain at $630,000. The income tax rate is 20%. What amounts of pretax and after-tax income can the company expect to earn from these predicted changes? (*Hint:* Prepare a forecasted contribution margin income statement as in Exhibit 22.20.)

Exercise 22-15

Predicting unit and dollar sales

C2

Greenspan Company management predicts $500,000 of variable costs, $800,000 of fixed costs, and a pretax income of $100,000 in the next period. Management also predicts that the contribution margin per unit will be $60. Use this information to compute the (1) total expected dollar sales for next period and (2) number of units expected to be sold next period.

Exercise 22-16

Computation of variable and fixed costs

C2

Cinquante Company expects to sell 100,000 units of its product next year, which would generate total sales of $12 million. Management predicts that pretax net income for next year will be $3,000,000 and that the contribution margin per unit will be $40. Use this information to compute next year's total expected (a) variable costs and (b) fixed costs.

Exercise 22-17

CVP analysis using composite units   P4

Check (3) 1,000 composite units

Home Builders sells windows and doors in the ratio of 8:2 (windows:doors). The selling price of each window is $100 and of each door is $250. The variable cost of a window is $62.50 and of a door is $175. Fixed costs are $450,000. Use this information to determine the (1) selling price per composite unit, (2) variable costs per composite unit, (3) break-even point in composite units, and (4) number of units of each product that will be sold at the break-even point.

Exercise 22-18

CVP analysis using weighted-average contribution margin

P4

Refer to the information from Exercise 22-17. Use the information to determine the (1) weighted-average contribution margin, (2) break-even point in units, and (3) number of units of each product that will be sold at the break-even point.

Exercise 22-19

CVP analysis using composite units

P4

Hubert Tax Service offers tax and consulting services to individuals and small businesses. Data for fees and costs of three types of tax returns follow. Hubert provides services in the ratio of 4:4:2 (easy, moderate, business). Fixed costs total $20,000 for the tax season. Use this information to determine the (1) selling price per composite unit, (2) variable costs per composite unit, (3) break-even point in composite units, and (4) number of units of each product that will be sold at the break-even point. Round answer to part (3) to two decimals.

Type of Return	Fee Charged	Variable Cost per Return
Easy (form 1040EZ)	$ 50	$ 30
Moderate (form 1040)	125	75
Business	275	100

Exercise 22-20

CVP analysis using weighted-average contribution margin

P4

Refer to the information from Exercise 22-19. Use the information to determine the (1) weighted-average contribution margin, (2) break-even point in units, and (3) number of units of each product that will be sold at the break-even point. Round answer to part (2) to one decimal.

Exercise 22-21

Operating leverage computed and applied

A2

Company A is a manufacturer with current sales of $3,000,000 and a 60% contribution margin. Its fixed costs equal $1,300,000. Company B is a consulting firm with current service revenues of $3,000,000 and a 25% contribution margin. Its fixed costs equal $250,000. Compute the degree of operating leverage (DOL) for each company. Identify which company benefits more from a 20% increase in sales and explain why.

connect

The following costs result from the production and sale of 4,000 drum sets manufactured by Vince Drum Company for the year ended December 31, 2011. The drum sets sell for $250 each. The company has a 25% income tax rate.

Variable production costs	
Plastic for casing	$ 68,000
Wages of assembly workers	328,000
Drum stands	104,000
Variable selling costs	
Sales commissions	60,000
Fixed manufacturing costs	
Taxes on factory	10,000
Factory maintenance	20,000
Factory machinery depreciation	80,000
Fixed selling and administrative costs	
Lease of equipment for sales staff..........	20,000
Accounting staff salaries	70,000
Administrative management salaries	150,000

PROBLEM SET A

Problem 22-1A
Contribution margin income statement and contribution margin ratio

A1

Required

1. Prepare a contribution margin income statement for the company.
2. Compute its contribution margin per unit and its contribution margin ratio.

Analysis Component

3. Interpret the contribution margin and contribution margin ratio from part 2.

Check (1) Net income, $67,500

Edge Equipment Co. manufactures and markets a number of rope products. Management is considering the future of Product XT, a special rope for hang gliding, that has not been as profitable as planned. Since Product XT is manufactured and marketed independently of the other products, its total costs can be precisely measured. Next year's plans call for a $150 selling price per 100 yards of XT rope. Its fixed costs for the year are expected to be $200,000, up to a maximum capacity of 550,000 yards of rope. Forecasted variable costs are $100 per 100 yards of XT rope.

Problem 22-2A
CVP analysis and charting

P2 P3

mhhe.com/wildFAP20e

Required

1. Estimate Product XT's break-even point in terms of (a) sales units and (b) sales dollars.
2. Prepare a CVP chart for Product XT like that in Exhibit 22.14. Use 5,500 units (550,000 yards/100 yards) as the maximum number of sales units on the horizontal axis of the graph, and $900,000 as the maximum dollar amount on the vertical axis.
3. Prepare a contribution margin income statement showing sales, variable costs, and fixed costs for Product XT at the break-even point.

Check (1) Break-even sales, 4,000 units

Alden Co.'s monthly sales and cost data for its operating activities of the past year follow. Management wants to use these data to predict future fixed and variable costs.

Problem 22-3A
Scatter diagram and cost behavior estimation

P1

Month	Sales	Total Cost	Month	Sales	Total Cost
1.............	$325,000	$162,500	7.............	$355,000	$242,000
2.............	170,000	106,250	8.............	275,000	156,750
3.............	270,000	210,600	9.............	75,000	60,000
4.............	210,000	105,000	10.............	155,000	135,625
5.............	295,000	206,500	11.............	99,000	99,000
6.............	195,000	117,000	12.............	105,000	76,650

Required

1. Prepare a scatter diagram for these data with sales volume (in $) plotted on the horizontal axis and total cost plotted on the vertical axis.

2. Estimate both the variable costs per sales dollar and the total monthly fixed costs using the high-low method. Draw the total costs line on the scatter diagram in part 1.

3. Use the estimated line of cost behavior and results from part 2 to predict future total costs when sales volume is (a) $380,000 and (b) $420,000.

Problem 22-4A

Break-even analysis; income targeting and forecasting

C2 P2 A1

Jetson Co. sold 20,000 units of its only product and incurred a $50,000 loss (ignoring taxes) for the current year as shown here. During a planning session for year 2012's activities, the production manager notes that variable costs can be reduced 50% by installing a machine that automates several operations. To obtain these savings, the company must increase its annual fixed costs by $150,000. The maximum output capacity of the company is 40,000 units per year.

JETSON COMPANY	
Contribution Margin Income Statement	
For Year Ended December 31, 2011	
Sales	$750,000
Variable costs	600,000
Contribution margin	150,000
Fixed costs	200,000
Net loss	$ (50,000)

Required

1. Compute the break-even point in dollar sales for year 2011.

2. Compute the predicted break-even point in dollar sales for year 2012 assuming the machine is installed and there is no change in the unit sales price.

3. Prepare a forecasted contribution margin income statement for 2012 that shows the expected results with the machine installed. Assume that the unit sales price and the number of units sold will not change, and no income taxes will be due.

4. Compute the sales level required in both dollars and units to earn $140,000 of after-tax income in 2012 with the machine installed and no change in the unit sales price. Assume that the income tax rate is 30%. (*Hint:* Use the procedures in Exhibits 22.21 and 22.23.)

5. Prepare a forecasted contribution margin income statement that shows the results at the sales level computed in part 4. Assume an income tax rate of 30%.

Problem 22-5A

Break-even analysis, different cost structures, and income calculations

C2 A1 P4

Letter Co. produces and sells two products, T and O. It manufactures these products in separate factories and markets them through different channels. They have no shared costs. This year, the company sold 50,000 units of each product. Sales and costs for each product follow.

	Product T	Product O
Sales	$800,000	$800,000
Variable costs..................	560,000	100,000
Contribution margin	240,000	700,000
Fixed costs.....................	100,000	560,000
Income before taxes	140,000	140,000
Income taxes (32% rate)	44,800	44,800
Net income	$ 95,200	$ 95,200

Required

1. Compute the break-even point in dollar sales for each product.

2. Assume that the company expects sales of each product to decline to 33,000 units next year with no change in unit sales price. Prepare forecasted financial results for next year following the format of the contribution margin income statement as just shown with columns for each of the two products (assume a 32% tax rate). Also, assume that any loss before taxes yields a 32% tax savings.

3. Assume that the company expects sales of each product to increase to 64,000 units next year with no change in unit sales price. Prepare forecasted financial results for next year following the format of the contribution margin income statement shown with columns for each of the two products (assume a 32% tax rate).

Analysis Component

4. If sales greatly decrease, which product would experience a greater loss? Explain.

5. Describe some factors that might have created the different cost structures for these two products.

Check   (2) After-tax income:
T, $39,712; O, $(66,640)

(3) After-tax income:
T, $140,896; O, $228,480

This year Cairo Company sold 35,000 units of its only product for $16 per unit. Manufacturing and selling the product required $120,000 of fixed manufacturing costs and $180,000 of fixed selling and administrative costs. Its per unit variable costs follow.

Material	$4.00
Direct labor (paid on the basis of completed units)..........	3.00
Variable overhead costs	0.40
Variable selling and administrative costs	0.20

Next year the company will use new material, which will reduce material costs by 60% and direct labor costs by 40% and will not affect product quality or marketability. Management is considering an increase in the unit sales price to reduce the number of units sold because the factory's output is nearing its annual output capacity of 40,000 units. Two plans are being considered. Under plan 1, the company will keep the price at the current level and sell the same volume as last year. This plan will increase income because of the reduced costs from using the new material. Under plan 2, the company will increase price by 25%. This plan will decrease unit sales volume by 10%. Under both plans 1 and 2, the total fixed costs and the variable costs per unit for overhead and for selling and administrative costs will remain the same.

Required

1. Compute the break-even point in dollar sales for both (a) plan 1 and (b) plan 2.

2. Prepare a forecasted contribution margin income statement with two columns showing the expected results of plan 1 and plan 2. The statements should report sales, total variable costs, contribution margin, total fixed costs, income before taxes, income taxes (30% rate), and net income.

Problem 22-6A
Analysis of price, cost, and volume changes for contribution margin and net income

P2 A1

mhhe.com/wildFAP20e

Check   (1) Break-even: Plan 1,
$400,000; Plan 2, $375,000

(2) Net income: Plan 1,
$84,000; Plan 2, $142,800

National Co. manufactures and sells three products: red, white, and blue. Their unit sales prices are red, $55; white, $85; and blue, $110. The per unit variable costs to manufacture and sell these products are red, $40; white, $60; and blue, $80. Their sales mix is reflected in a ratio of 5:4:2 (red:white:blue). Annual fixed costs shared by all three products are $150,000. One type of raw material has been used to manufacture all three products. The company has developed a new material of equal quality for less cost. The new material would reduce variable costs per unit as follows: red, by $10; white, by $20; and blue, by $10. However, the new material requires new equipment, which will increase annual fixed costs by $20,000. (Round answers to whole composite units.)

Required

1. If the company continues to use the old material, determine its break-even point in both sales units and sales dollars of each individual product.

2. If the company uses the new material, determine its new break-even point in both sales units and sales dollars of each individual product.

Analysis Component

3. What insight does this analysis offer management for long-term planning?

Problem 22-7A
Break-even analysis with composite units

P4

Check   (1) Old plan break-even,
639 composite units (rounded)

(2) New plan break-even,
442 composite units (rounded)

PROBLEM SET B

Problem 22-1B

Contribution margin income statement and contribution margin ratio

A1

The following costs result from the production and sale of 480,000 CD sets manufactured by Trace Company for the year ended December 31, 2011. The CD sets sell for $4.50 each. The company has a 25% income tax rate.

Variable manufacturing costs	
Plastic for CD sets	$ 43,200
Wages of assembly workers	600,000
Labeling	86,400
Variable selling costs	
Sales commissions	48,000
Fixed manufacturing costs	
Rent on factory	100,000
Factory cleaning service	75,000
Factory machinery depreciation	125,000
Fixed selling and administrative costs	
Lease of office equipment	120,000
Systems staff salaries	600,000
Administrative management salaries	300,000

Required

Check (1) Net income, $46,800

1. Prepare a contribution margin income statement for the company.
2. Compute its contribution margin per unit and its contribution margin ratio.

Analysis Component

3. Interpret the contribution margin and contribution margin ratio from part 2.

Problem 22-2B

CVP analysis and charting

P2   P3

Jammin Co. manufactures and markets several products. Management is considering the future of one product, electronic keyboards, that has not been as profitable as planned. Since this product is manufactured and marketed independently of the other products, its total costs can be precisely measured. Next year's plans call for a $225 selling price per unit. The fixed costs for the year are expected to be $30,000, up to a maximum capacity of 700 units. Forecasted variable costs are $150 per unit.

Required

Check (1) Break-even sales, 400 units

1. Estimate the keyboards' break-even point in terms of (a) sales units and (b) sales dollars.
2. Prepare a CVP chart for keyboards like that in Exhibit 22.14. Use 700 keyboards as the maximum number of sales units on the horizontal axis of the graph, and $180,000 as the maximum dollar amount on the vertical axis.
3. Prepare a contribution margin income statement showing sales, variable costs, and fixed costs for keyboards at the break-even point.

Problem 22-3B

Scatter diagram and cost behavior estimation

P1

Koto Co.'s monthly sales and costs data for its operating activities of the past year follow. Management wants to use these data to predict future fixed and variable costs.

Month	Sales	Total Cost	Month	Sales	Total Cost
1	$390	$194	7	$290	$186
2	250	174	8	370	210
3	210	146	9	270	170
4	310	178	10	170	116
5	190	162	11	350	190
6	430	220	12	230	158

Required

1. Prepare a scatter diagram for these data with sales volume (in $) plotted on the horizontal axis and total costs plotted on the vertical axis.

2. Estimate both the variable costs per sales dollar and the total monthly fixed costs using the high-low method. Draw the total costs line on the scatter diagram in part 1.

3. Use the estimated line of cost behavior and results from part 2 to predict future total costs when sales volume is (a) $150 and (b) $250.

Check   (2) Variable costs, $0.40 per sales dollar; fixed costs, $48

Caruso Co. sold 40,000 units of its only product and incurred a $100,000 loss (ignoring taxes) for the current year as shown here. During a planning session for year 2012's activities, the production manager notes that variable costs can be reduced 50% by installing a machine that automates several operations. To obtain these savings, the company must increase its annual fixed costs by $300,000. The maximum output capacity of the company is 80,000 units per year.

Problem 22-4B
Break-even analysis; income targeting and forecasting

C2 P2 A1

CARUSO COMPANY
Contribution Margin Income Statement
For Year Ended December 31, 2011

Sales	$1,500,000
Variable costs	1,200,000
Contribution margin	300,000
Fixed costs	400,000
Net loss	$ (100,000)

Required

1. Compute the break-even point in dollar sales for year 2011.

2. Compute the predicted break-even point in dollar sales for year 2012 assuming the machine is installed and no change occurs in the unit sales price. (Round the change in variable costs to a whole number.)

3. Prepare a forecasted contribution margin income statement for 2012 that shows the expected results with the machine installed. Assume that the unit sales price and the number of units sold will not change, and no income taxes will be due.

Check   (3) Net income, $200,000

4. Compute the sales level required in both dollars and units to earn $280,000 of after-tax income in 2012 with the machine installed and no change in the unit sales price. Assume that the income tax rate is 30%. (*Hint:* Use the procedures in Exhibits 22.21 and 22.23.)

(4) Required sales, $1,833,333 or 48,889 units

5. Prepare a forecasted contribution margin income statement that shows the results at the sales level computed in part 4. Assume an income tax rate of 30%.

Dominico Co. produces and sells two products, BB and TT. It manufactures these products in separate factories and markets them through different channels. They have no shared costs. This year, the company sold 120,000 units of each product. Sales and costs for each product follow.

Problem 22-5B
Break-even analysis, different cost structures, and income calculations

C2 P4 A1

	Product BB	Product TT
Sales	$3,000,000	$3,000,000
Variable costs	1,800,000	600,000
Contribution margin	1,200,000	2,400,000
Fixed costs	600,000	1,800,000
Income before taxes	600,000	600,000
Income taxes (35% rate)	210,000	210,000
Net income	$ 390,000	$ 390,000

Required

1. Compute the break-even point in dollar sales for each product.

2. Assume that the company expects sales of each product to decline to 104,000 units next year with no change in the unit sales price. Prepare forecasted financial results for next year following the format of the contribution margin income statement as shown here with columns for each of the two products (assume a 35% tax rate, and that any loss before taxes yields a 35% tax savings).

Check   (2) After-tax income: BB, $286,000; TT, $182,000

3. Assume that the company expects sales of each product to increase to 190,000 units next year with no change in the unit sales prices. Prepare forecasted financial results for next year following the format of the contribution margin income statement as shown here with columns for each of the two products (assume a 35% tax rate).

(3) After-tax income: BB, $845,000; TT, $1,300,000

Analysis Component

4. If sales greatly increase, which product would experience a greater increase in profit? Explain.

5. Describe some factors that might have created the different cost structures for these two products.

Problem 22-6B
Analysis of price, cost, and volume changes for contribution margin and net income

A1 P2

This year Jostens Company earned a disappointing 4.2% after-tax return on sales (Net income/Sales) from marketing 100,000 units of its only product. The company buys its product in bulk and repackages it for resale at the price of $25 per unit. Jostens incurred the following costs this year.

Total variable unit costs.............	$1,000,000
Total variable packaging costs	$ 100,000
Fixed costs......................	$1,250,000
Income tax rate	30%

The marketing manager claims that next year's results will be the same as this year's unless some changes are made. The manager predicts the company can increase the number of units sold by 80% if it reduces the selling price by 20% and upgrades the packaging. This change would increase variable packaging costs by 25%. Increased sales would allow the company to take advantage of a 20% quantity purchase discount on the cost of the bulk product. Neither the packaging change nor the volume discount would affect fixed costs, which provide an annual output capacity of 200,000 units.

Required

Check (1) Break-even sales for new strategy, $2,325,581

(2) Net income: Existing strategy, $105,000; new strategy, $479,500

1. Compute the break-even point in dollar sales under the (a) existing business strategy and (b) new strategy that alters both unit sales price and variable costs.

2. Prepare a forecasted contribution margin income statement with two columns showing the expected results of (a) the existing strategy and (b) changing to the new strategy. The statements should report sales, total variable costs (unit and packaging), contribution margin, fixed costs, income before taxes, income taxes, and net income. Also determine the after-tax return on sales for these two strategies.

Problem 22-7B
Break-even analysis with composite units

P4

Texon Co. manufactures and sells three products: product 1, product 2, and product 3. Their unit sales prices are product 1, $40; product 2, $30; and product 3, $14. The per unit variable costs to manufacture and sell these products are product 1, $30; product 2, $20; and product 3, $8. Their sales mix is reflected in a ratio of 6:3:5. Annual fixed costs shared by all three products are $200,000. One type of raw material has been used to manufacture products 1 and 2. The company has developed a new material of equal quality for less cost. The new material would reduce variable costs per unit as follows: product 1 by $10, and product 2, by $5. However, the new material requires new equipment, which will increase annual fixed costs by $50,000.

Required

Check (1) Old plan break-even, 1,667 composite units (rounded)

(2) New plan break-even, 1,282 composite units (rounded)

1. If the company continues to use the old material, determine its break-even point in both sales units and sales dollars of each individual product.

2. If the company uses the new material, determine its new break-even point in both sales units and sales dollars of each individual product.

Analysis Component

3. What insight does this analysis offer management for long-term planning?

SERIAL PROBLEM
Business Solutions

P4

(This serial problem began in Chapter 1 and continues through most of the book. If previous chapter segments were not completed, the serial problem can begin at this point. It is helpful, but not necessary, to use the working papers that accompany the book.)

SP 22 Business Solutions sells upscale modular desk units and office chairs in the ratio of 3:2 (desk unit:chair). The selling prices are $1,250 per desk unit and $500 per chair. The variable costs are $750 per desk unit and $250 per chair. Fixed costs are $120,000.

Required

1. Compute the selling price per composite unit.
2. Compute the variable costs per composite unit.
3. Compute the break-even point in composite units.
4. Compute the number of units of each product that would be sold at the break-even point.

Check (3) 60 composite units

Beyond the Numbers

BTN 22-1   **Research In Motion** offers services to Blackberry customers that allows them subscription access for wireless connectivity via a mobile carrier. As you complete the following requirements, assume that the Blackberry services department uses many of Research In Motion's existing resources such as its software, phone systems, account databases and buildings.

REPORTING IN ACTION

C1

RIM

Required

1. Identify several of the variable, mixed, and fixed costs that the Blackberry services department is likely to incur in carrying out its services.
2. Assume that Blackberry services revenues are expected to grow by 25% in the next year. How do you expect the costs identified in part 1 to change, if at all?
3. Based on your answer to part 2, can Research In Motion use the contribution margin ratio to predict how income will change in response to increases in Blackberry services revenues?

BTN 22-2   Both **Research In Motion** and **Apple** sell numerous hand-held consumer products, and each of these companies has a different product mix.

COMPARATIVE ANALYSIS

P2 A2

RIM

Apple

Required

1. Assume the following data are available for both companies. Compute each company's break-even point in unit sales. (Each company sells many hand-held consumer products at many different selling prices, and each has its own variable costs. This assignment assumes an *average* selling price per unit and an *average* cost per item.)

	Research In Motion	Apple
Average selling price per item sold	$350	$280
Average variable cost per item sold	$140	$110
Total fixed costs	$14,980 million	$12,580 million

2. If unit sales were to decline, which company would experience the larger decline in operating profit? Explain.

BTN 22-3   Labor costs of an auto repair mechanic are seldom based on actual hours worked. Instead, the amount paid a mechanic is based on an industry average of time estimated to complete a repair job. The repair shop bills the customer for the industry average amount of time at the repair center's billable cost per hour. This means a customer can pay, for example, $120 for two hours of work on a car when the actual time worked was only one hour. Many experienced mechanics can complete repair jobs faster than the industry average. The average data are compiled by engineering studies and surveys conducted in the auto repair business. Assume that you are asked to complete such a survey for a repair center. The survey calls for objective input, and many questions require detailed cost data and analysis. The mechanics and owners know you have the survey and encourage you to complete it in a way that increases the average billable hours for repair work.

ETHICS CHALLENGE

C1

Required

Write a one-page memorandum to the mechanics and owners that describes the direct labor analysis you will undertake in completing this survey.

COMMUNICATING IN PRACTICE

C2

BTN 22-4   Several important assumptions underlie CVP analysis. Assumptions often help simplify and focus our analysis of sales and costs. A common application of CVP analysis is as a tool to forecast sales, costs, and income.

Required

Assume that you are actively searching for a job. Prepare a one-half page report identifying (1) three assumptions relating to your expected revenue (salary) and (2) three assumptions relating to your expected costs for the first year of your new job. Be prepared to discuss your assumptions in class.

TAKING IT TO THE NET

C1

BTN 22-5   Access and review the entrepreneurial information at **Business Owner's Toolkit** [**Toolkit. cch.com**]. Access and review its *New Business Cash Needs Estimate* under the Business Tools/Business Finance menu bar or similar worksheets related to controls of cash and costs.

Required

Write a one-half page report that describes the information and resources available at the Business Owner's Toolkit to help the owner of a start-up business to control and monitor its costs.

TEAMWORK IN ACTION

C2

BTN 22-6   A local movie theater owner explains to you that ticket sales on weekends and evenings are strong, but attendance during the weekdays, Monday through Thursday, is poor. The owner proposes to offer a contract to the local grade school to show educational materials at the theater for a set charge per student during school hours. The owner asks your help to prepare a CVP analysis listing the cost and sales projections for the proposal. The owner must propose to the school's administration a charge per child. At a minimum, the charge per child needs to be sufficient for the theater to break even.

Required

Your team is to prepare two separate lists of questions that enable you to complete a reliable CVP analysis of this situation. One list is to be answered by the school's administration, the other by the owner of the movie theater.

ENTREPRENEURIAL DECISION

C1 A1

BTN 22-7   **Johnny Cupcakes**, launched by entrepreneur John Earle, produces t-shirts in unique styles and limited quantities. Selling prices typically range from $40 per shirt to $70 per shirt.

Required

1. Identify at least two fixed costs that will not change regardless of how many t-shirts Johnny Cupcakes produces.
2. How could overly optimistic sales estimates potentially hurt John Earle's business?
3. Explain how cost-volume-profit analysis can help John Earle manage Johnny Cupcakes.

HITTING THE ROAD

P4

BTN 22-8   Multiproduct break-even analysis is often viewed differently when actually applied in practice. You are to visit a local fast-food restaurant and count the number of items on the menu. To apply multiproduct break-even analysis to the restaurant, similar menu items must often be fit into groups. A reasonable approach is to classify menu items into approximately five groups. We then estimate average selling price and average variable cost to compute average contribution margin. (*Hint:* For fast-food restaurants, the highest contribution margin is with its beverages, at about 90%.)

Required

1. Prepare a one-year multiproduct break-even analysis for the restaurant you visit. Begin by establishing groups. Next, estimate each group's volume and contribution margin. These estimates are necessary to compute each group's contribution margin. Assume that annual fixed costs in total are $500,000 per year. (*Hint:* You must develop your own estimates on volume and contribution margin for each group to obtain the break-even point and sales.)

2. Prepare a one-page report on the results of your analysis. Comment on the volume of sales necessary to break even at a fast-food restaurant.

BTN 22-9   Access and review Nokia's Website (www.Nokia.com) to answer the following questions.

Required

1. Do you believe that Nokia's managers use single product CVP analysis or multiproduct break-even point analysis? Explain.

2. How does the addition of a new product line affect Nokia's CVP analysis?

GLOBAL DECISION

P4

NOKIA

ANSWERS TO MULTIPLE CHOICE QUIZ

1. a; $150 − $100 = $50
2. e; ($150 − $100)/$150 = 33⅓%
3. c; $75,000/$50 CM per unit = 1,500 units

4. b; $300,000 − $180,000 = $120,000
5. c; Contribution margin ratio = ($400 − $260)/$400 = 0.35
   Targeted sales = ($840,000 + $70,000)/0.35 = $2,600,000

23

Master Budgets and Planning

A Look Back

Chapter 22 looked at cost behavior and its use by managers in performing cost-volume-profit analysis. It also illustrated the application of cost-volume-profit analysis.

A Look at This Chapter

This chapter explains the importance of budgeting and describes the master budget and its preparation. It also discusses the value of the master budget to the planning of future business activities.

A Look Ahead

Chapter 24 focuses on flexible budgets, standard costs, and variance reporting. It explains the usefulness of these procedures and reports for business decisions.

Learning Objectives

CAP

CONCEPTUAL

C1 Describe the importance and benefits of budgeting and the process of budget administration. (p. 946)

C2 Describe a master budget and the process of preparing it. (p. 950)

ANALYTICAL

A1 Analyze expense planning using activity-based budgeting. (p. 960)

LP23

PROCEDURAL

P1 Prepare each component of a master budget and link each to the budgeting process. (p. 952)

P2 Link both operating and capital expenditures budgets to budgeted financial statements. (p. 956)

P3 *Appendix 23A*—Prepare production and manufacturing budgets. (p. 966)

Decision Insight

Not Grandma's Needlepoint

"This is incredible . . . people thought it was a foolish idea"
—**AUSTIN BRANSON**

Bethesda, MD—Peter Smathers Carter and Austin Branson's entrepreneurial adventure began with needlepoint belts they each received as gifts. Noting the interest the belts received, the duo began planning a company to manufacture cool hand-stitched belts. The result is **Smathers and Branson (SmathersAndBranson.com),** with annual sales now exceeding $2.5 million.

The company's products are best summed up as "not your grandmother's needlepoint." Belt designs include a string of banded beer cans, a "jolly roger" with skull and crossbones, and a martini-sipping pink elephant. As Austin explains, "we keep having random brainstorming sessions and adding good patterns." Yet their belts are more than just funky designs. Peter and Austin's belts are hand-stitched and use some of the best materials —the finest threads from Europe, full-grain leather tanned in Asia, and belt buckles from the United States.

Using top-quality materials and hand-stitching each belt rather than mass producing is not cheap, something the pair quickly realized in their budget planning process. Noting it takes about 40 to 50 hours to hand-stitch a single belt, Peter explains that "we calculated the materials and labor it cost our girlfriends to make the belts at around $300 per belt—more than the market would bear." The use of direct materials, direct labor, and factory overhead budgets led them to focus on reducing direct

labor costs as essential. Now, the company employs almost 2,000 stitchers in Vietnam, enabling the duo to sell their handcrafted belts at prices the market will pay. Sales, production, and manufacturing budgets help Peter and Austin continue to plan their use of materials, labor, and overhead.

As Austin puts it, "our original plan was to be finance majors. But the belts seemed more fun and unique and different." Keeping it fun and profitable however requires attention to plans. As the company continues to expand into additional product lines—dog collars, key fobs, wallets, headbands, wallets, and flasks—master budgets and the budgeting process become even more important. Budgets help formalize business plans and goals, and help direct and monitor employees. Peter and Austin also use budgeted income statements to determine how changes in the costs of material, labor, or overhead, impact the bottom line.

While linking budgeted data to budgeted financial statements and using that information to control costs is important, both Peter and Austin stress the importance of having fun and a passion for what they do as keys to their success. Austin explains "we're having a great time and growing rapidly."

[Sources: *Smathers and Branson Website*, January 2011; *Inc.com*, 2009; *Golfbusinesswire.com*; *Thrillist.com*]

Management seeks to turn its strategies into action plans. These action plans include financial details that are compiled in a master budget. The budgeting process serves several purposes, including motivating employees and communicating with them. The budget process also helps coordinate a company's activities toward common goals and is useful in evaluating results and management performance. This chapter explains how to prepare a master budget and use it as a formal plan of a company's future activities. The ability to prepare this type of plan is of enormous help in starting and operating a company. Such planning gives managers a glimpse into the future, and it can help translate ideas into actions.

Master Budgets and Planning

Budget Process
- Strategic budgeting
- Benchmarking budgets
- Budgeting and human behavior
- Budgeting as a management tool
- Budgeting communication

Budget Administration
- Budget committee
- Budget reporting
- Budget timing

Master Budget
- Master budget components
- Operating budgets
- Capital expenditures budget
- Financial budgets

BUDGET PROCESS

Strategic Budgeting

C1 Describe the importance and benefits of budgeting and the process of budget administration.

Most companies prepare long-term strategic plans spanning 5 to 10 years. They then fine-tune them in preparing medium-term and short-term plans. Strategic plans usually set a company's long-term direction. They provide a road map for the future about potential opportunities such as new products, markets, and investments. The strategic plan can be inexact, given its long-term focus. Medium- and short-term plans are more operational and translate strategic plans into actions. These action plans are fairly concrete and consist of defined objectives and goals.

Short-term financial plans are called *budgets* and typically cover a one-year period. A **budget** is a formal statement of a company's future plans. It is usually expressed in monetary terms because the economic or financial aspects of the business are the primary factors driving management's decisions. All managers should be involved in **budgeting,** the process of planning future business actions and expressing them as formal plans. Managers who plan carefully and formalize plans in a budgeting process increase the likelihood of both personal and company success. (Although most firms prepare annual budgets, it is not unusual for organizations to prepare three-year and five-year budgets that are revised at least annually.)

Companies Performing Annual Budgeting

Yes 91%   No* 9%

*Most of the 9% have eliminated annual budgeting in favor of rolling or continual budgeting.

The relevant focus of a budgetary analysis is the future. Management must focus on future transactions and events and the opportunities available. A focus on the future is important because the pressures of daily operating problems often divert management's attention and take precedence over planning. A good budgeting system counteracts this tendency by formalizing the planning process and demanding relevant input. Budgeting makes planning an explicit management responsibility.

Benchmarking Budgets

The control function requires management to evaluate (benchmark) business operations against some norm. Evaluation involves comparing actual results against one of two usual alternatives: (1) past performance or (2) expected performance.

An evaluation assists management in identifying problems and taking corrective actions if necessary. Evaluation using expected, or budgeted, performance is potentially superior to using past performance to decide whether actual results trigger a need for corrective actions. This is so because past performance fails to consider several changes that can affect current and future activities. Changes in economic conditions, shifts in competitive advantages within the industry, new product developments, increased or decreased advertising, and other factors reduce the usefulness of comparisons with past results. In hi-tech industries, for instance, increasing competition, technological advances, and other innovations often reduce the usefulness of performance comparisons across years.

Budgeted performance is computed after careful analysis and research that attempts to anticipate and adjust for changes in important company, industry, and economic factors. Therefore, budgets usually provide management an effective control and monitoring system.

Budgeting and Human Behavior

Budgeting provides standards for evaluating performance and can affect the attitudes of employees evaluated by them. It can be used to create a positive effect on employees' attitudes, but it can also create negative effects if not properly applied. Budgeted levels of performance, for instance, must be realistic to avoid discouraging employees. Personnel who will be evaluated should be consulted and involved in preparing the budget to increase their commitment to meeting it. Performance evaluations must allow the affected employees to explain the reasons for apparent performance deficiencies.

The budgeting process has three important guidelines: (1) Employees affected by a budget should be consulted when it is prepared (*participatory budgeting*), (2) goals reflected in a budget should be attainable, and (3) evaluations should be made carefully with opportunities to explain any failures. Budgeting can be a positive motivating force when these guidelines are followed. Budgeted performance levels can provide goals for employees to attain or even exceed as they carry out their responsibilities. This is especially important in organizations that consider the annual budget a "sacred" document.

Managers must also be aware of potential negative outcomes of budgeting. Under participatory budgeting, some employees might understate sales budgets and overstate expense budgets to allow them a cushion, or *budgetary slack,* to aid in meeting targets. For some businesses, pressure to meet budgeted results might lead employees to engage in unethical behavior or commit fraud. Finally, some employees might always spend their budgeted amounts, even on unnecessary items, to ensure their budgets aren't reduced for the next period.

Point: The practice of involving employees in the budgeting process is known as *participatory budgeting.*

Example: Assume a company's sales force receives a bonus when sales exceed the budgeted amount. How would this arrangement affect the participatory sales forecasts? *Answer:* Sales reps may understate their budgeted sales.

 **Decision Ethics** Answer — p. 968

Budget Staffer Your company's earnings for the current period will be far below the budgeted amount reported in the press. One of your superiors, who is aware of the upcoming earnings shortfall, has accepted a management position with a competitor. This superior is selling her shares of the company. What are your ethical concerns, if any? ■

Budgeting as a Management Tool

An important management objective in large companies is to ensure that activities of all departments contribute to meeting the company's overall goals. This requires coordination. Budgeting helps to achieve this coordination.

We describe later in this chapter that a company's budget, or operating plan, is based on its objectives. This operating plan starts with the sales budget, which drives all other budgets including production, materials, labor, and overhead. The budgeting process coordinates the activities of these various departments to meet the company's overall goals.

Budgeting Communication

Managers of small companies can adequately explain business plans directly to employees through conversations and other informal communications. However, conversations can create uncertainty and confusion if not supported by clear documentation of the plans. A written budget is preferred and can inform employees in all types of organizations about management's plans. The budget can also communicate management's specific action plans for the employees in the budget period.

Decision Insight

Budgets Exposed   When companies go public and their securities trade on an organized stock exchange, management usually develops specific future plans and budgets. For this purpose, companies often develop detailed six- to twelve-month budgets and less-detailed budgets spanning two to five years. ■

BUDGET ADMINISTRATION

Budget Committee

The task of preparing a budget should not be the sole responsibility of any one department. Similarly, the budget should not be simply handed down as top management's final word. Instead, budget figures and budget estimates developed through a *bottom-up* process

usually are more useful. This includes, for instance, involving the sales department in preparing sales estimates. Likewise, the production department should have initial responsibility for preparing its own expense budget. Without active employee involvement in preparing budget figures, there is a risk these employees will feel that the numbers fail to reflect their special problems and needs.

Most budgets should be developed by a bottom-up process, but the budgeting system requires central guidance. This guidance is supplied by a budget committee of department heads and other executives responsible for seeing that budgeted amounts are realistic and coordinated. If a de-

Point: In a large company, developing a budget through a bottom-up process can involve hundreds of employees and take several weeks to finalize.

partment submits initial budget figures not reflecting efficient performance, the budget committee should return them with explanatory comments on how to improve them. Then the originating department must either adjust its proposals or explain why they are acceptable. Communication between the originating department and the budget committee should continue as needed to ensure that both parties accept the budget as reasonable, attainable, and desirable.

The concept of continuous improvement applies to budgeting as well as production. For example, one of the world's largest energy companies streamlined its monthly budget report from a one-inch-thick stack of monthly control reports to a tidy, two-page flash report on monthly earnings and key production statistics. The key to this efficiency gain was the integration of new budgeting and cost allocation processes with its strategic planning process. Its controller explained the new role of the finance department with respect to the budgetary control process as follows: "there's less of an attitude that finance's job is to control. People really have come to see that our job is to help attain business objectives."

Budget Reporting

The budget period usually coincides with the accounting period. Most companies prepare at least an annual budget, which reflects the objectives for the next year. To provide specific guidance, the annual budget usually is separated into quarterly or monthly budgets. These short-term budgets allow management to periodically evaluate performance and take needed corrective action.

Managers can compare actual results to budgeted amounts in a report such as that shown in Exhibit 23.1. This report shows actual amounts, budgeted amounts, and their differences. A difference is called a *variance*. Management examines variances, particularly large ones, to identify areas for improvement and corrective action.

EXHIBIT 23.1

Comparing Actual Performance with Budgeted Performance

ECCENTRIC MUSIC Income Statement with Variances from Budget For Month Ended April 30, 2011			
	Actual	**Budget**	**Variance**
Net sales	$60,500	$57,150	$+3,350
Cost of goods sold	41,350	39,100	+2,250
Gross profit	19,150	18,050	+1,100
Operating expenses			
Selling expenses			
Sales salaries	6,250	6,000	+250
Advertising	900	800	+100
Store supplies	550	500	+50
Depreciation—Store equipment	1,600	1,600	
Total selling expenses	9,300	8,900	+400
General and administrative expenses			
Office salaries	2,000	2,000	
Office supplies used	165	150	+15
Rent	1,100	1,100	
Insurance	200	200	
Depreciation—Office equipment	100	100	
Total general and administrative expenses	3,565	3,550	+15
Total operating expenses	12,865	12,450	+415
Net income	$ 6,285	$ 5,600	$ +685

Example: Assume that you must explain variances to top management. Which variances in Exhibit 23.1 would you research and why? *Answer:* Sales and cost of goods sold—due to their large variances.

Budget Timing

The time period required for the annual budgeting process can vary considerably. For example, budgeting for 2012 can begin as early as January 2011 or as late as December 2011. Large, complex organizations usually require a longer time to prepare their budgets than do smaller organizations. This is so because considerable effort is required to coordinate the different units (departments) within large organizations.

Many companies apply **continuous budgeting** by preparing **rolling budgets.** As each monthly or quarterly budget period goes by, these companies revise their entire set of budgets for the months or quarters remaining and add new monthly or quarterly budgets to replace the ones that have lapsed. At any point in time, monthly or quarterly budgets are available for the next 12 months or four quarters. Exhibit 23.2 shows rolling budgets prepared at the end of five consecutive

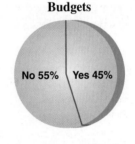

Companies Using Rolling Budgets

No 55%   Yes 45%

EXHIBIT 23.2

Rolling Budgets

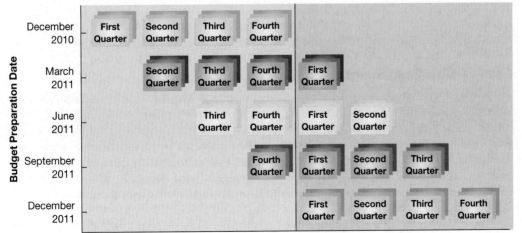

periods. The first set (at top) is prepared in December 2010 and covers the four calendar quarters of 2011. In March 2011, the company prepares another rolling budget for the next four quarters through March 2012. This same process is repeated every three months. As a result, management is continuously planning ahead.

Exhibit 23.2 reflects an annual budget composed of four quarters prepared four times per year using the most recent information available. For example, the budget for the fourth quarter of 2011 is prepared in December 2010 and revised in March, June, and September of 2011. When continuous budgeting is not used, the fourth-quarter budget is nine months old and perhaps out of date when applied.

Decision Insight

Budget Calendar   Many companies use long-range operating budgets. For large companies, three groups usually determine or influence the budgets: creditors, directors, and management. All three are interested in the companies' future cash flows and earnings. The annual budget process often begins six months or more before the budget is due to the board of directors. A typical budget calendar, shown here, provides insight into the budget process during a typical calendar year. ■

Quick Check

Answers — p. 968

1. What are the major benefits of budgeting?
2. What is the main responsibility of the budget committee?
3. What is the usual time period covered by a budget?
4. What are rolling budgets?

MASTER BUDGET

C2 Describe a master budget and the process of preparing it.

A **master budget** is a formal, comprehensive plan for a company's future. It contains several individual budgets that are linked with each other to form a coordinated plan.

Master Budget Components

The master budget typically includes individual budgets for sales, purchases, production, various expenses, capital expenditures, and cash. Managers often express the expected financial results of these planned activities with both a budgeted income statement for the budget period and a budgeted balance sheet for the end of the budget period. The usual number and types of budgets included in a master budget depend on the company's size and complexity. A master budget should include, at a minimum, the budgets listed in Exhibit 23.3. In addition to these individual budgets, managers often include supporting calculations and additional tables with the master budget.

Some budgets require the input of other budgets. For example, the merchandise purchases budget cannot be prepared until the sales budget has been prepared because the number of units

Operating budgets
- *Sales budget*
- For merchandisers add: *Merchandise purchases budget* (units to be purchased)
- For manufacturers add: *Production budget* (units to be produced)
  Manufacturing budget (manufacturing costs)
- *Selling expense budget*
- *General and administrative expense budget*

Capital expenditures budget (expenditures for plant assets)

Financial budgets
- *Cash budget* (cash receipts and disbursements)
- *Budgeted income statement*
- *Budgeted balance sheet*

EXHIBIT 23.3

Basic Components of a
Master Budget

to be purchased depends on how many units are expected to be sold. As a result, we often must sequentially prepare budgets within the master budget.

A typical sequence for a master budget consists of the five steps in Exhibit 23.4. Any stage in this budgeting process might reveal undesirable outcomes, so changes often must be made to prior budgets by repeating the previous steps. For instance, an early version of the cash budget could show an insufficient amount of cash unless cash outlays are reduced. This could yield a reduction in planned equipment purchases. A preliminary budgeted balance sheet could also reveal too much debt from an ambitious capital expenditures budget. Findings such as these often result in revised plans and budgets.

EXHIBIT 23.4

Master Budget Sequence

Prepare sales budget → Develop production budget → Prepare manufacturing, selling, and general and administrative expense budgets → Prepare capital expenditures budget → Consolidate operating and capital expenditures budgets into financial budgets:
- Cash budget
- Budgeted income statement
- Budgeted balance sheet

Operating Budgets   **Capital Expenditures Budget**   **Financial Budgets**

The remainder of this section explains how Hockey Den (HD), a retailer of youth hockey sticks, prepares its master budget. Its master budget includes operating, capital expenditures, and cash budgets for each month in each quarter. It also includes a budgeted income statement for each quarter and a budgeted balance sheet as of the last day of each quarter. We show how HD prepares budgets for October, November, and December 2011. Exhibit 23.5 presents HD's balance sheet at the start of this budgeting period, which we often refer to as we prepare the component budgets.

Decision Insight

Budgeting Targets   Budgeting is a crucial part of any acquisition. Analysis begins by projecting annual sales volume and prices. It then estimates cost of sales, expenses, and income for the next several years. Using the present value of this projected income stream, buyers determine an offer price. ■

EXHIBIT 23.5

Balance Sheet Prior to the Budgeting Periods

HOCKEY DEN		
Balance Sheet		
September 30, 2011		
Assets		
Cash		$ 20,000
Accounts receivable		42,000
Inventory (900 units @ $60)		54,000
Equipment*	$200,000	
Less accumulated depreciation	36,000	164,000
Total assets		$280,000
Liabilities and Equity		
Liabilities		
Accounts payable	$ 58,200	
Income taxes payable (due 10/31/2011)	20,000	
Note payable to bank	10,000	$ 88,200
Stockholders' equity		
Common stock	150,000	
Retained earnings	41,800	191,800
Total liabilities and equity		$280,000

* Equipment is depreciated on a straight-line basis over 10 years (salvage value is $20,000).

Operating Budgets

This section explains HD's preparation of operating budgets. Its operating budgets consist of the sales budget, merchandise purchases budget, selling expense budget, and general and administrative expense budget. HD does not prepare production and manufacturing budgets because it is a merchandiser. (The preparation of production budgets and manufacturing budgets is described in Appendix 23A.)

Sales Budget   The first step in preparing the master budget is planning the **sales budget,** which shows the planned sales units and the expected dollars from these sales. The sales budget is the starting point in the budgeting process because plans for most departments are linked to sales.

The sales budget should emerge from a careful analysis of forecasted economic and market conditions, business capacity, proposed selling expenses (such as advertising), and predictions of unit sales. A company's sales personnel are usually asked to develop predictions of sales for each territory and department because people normally feel a greater commitment to goals they help set. Another advantage to this participatory budgeting approach is that it draws on knowledge and experience of people involved in the activity.

To illustrate, in September 2011, HD sold 700 hockey sticks at $100 per unit. After considering sales predictions and market conditions, HD prepares its sales budget for the next quarter (three months) plus one extra month (see Exhibit 23.6). The sales budget includes

EXHIBIT 23.6

Sales Budget for Planned Unit and Dollar Sales

HOCKEY DEN			
Monthly Sales Budget			
October 2011–January 2012			
	Budgeted Unit Sales	**Budgeted Unit Price**	**Budgeted Total Sales**
September 2011 (actual)	700	$100	$ 70,000
October 2011	1,000	$100	$100,000
November 2011	800	100	80,000
December 2011	1,400	100	140,000
Totals for the quarter	3,200	100	$320,000
January 2012	900	100	$ 90,000

January 2012 because the purchasing department relies on estimated January sales to decide on December 2011 inventory purchases. The sales budget in Exhibit 23.6 includes forecasts of both unit sales and unit prices. Some sales budgets are expressed only in total sales dollars, but most are more detailed. Management finds it useful to know budgeted units and unit prices for many different products, regions, departments, and sales representatives.

Decision Maker   Answer — p. 968

Entrepreneur   You run a start-up that manufactures designer clothes. Business is seasonal, and fashions and designs quickly change. How do you prepare reliable annual sales budgets? ■

Merchandise Purchases Budget   Companies use various methods to help managers make inventory purchasing decisions. These methods recognize that the number of units added to inventory depends on budgeted sales volume. Whether a company manufactures or purchases the product it sells, budgeted future sales volume is the primary factor in most inventory management decisions. A company must also consider its inventory system and other factors that we discuss next.

Just-in-time inventory systems.   Managers of *just-in-time* (JIT) inventory systems use sales budgets for short periods (often as few as one or two days) to order just enough merchandise or materials to satisfy the immediate sales demand. This keeps the amount of inventory to a minimum (or zero in an ideal situation). A JIT system minimizes the costs of maintaining inventory, but it is practical only if customers are content to order in advance or if managers can accurately determine short-term sales demand. Suppliers also must be able and willing to ship small quantities regularly and promptly.

Point: Accurate estimates of future sales are crucial in a JIT system.

Safety stock inventory systems.   Market conditions and manufacturing processes for some products do not allow use of a just-in-time system. Companies in these cases maintain sufficient inventory to reduce the risk and cost of running short. This practice requires enough purchases to satisfy the budgeted sales amounts and to maintain a **safety stock,** a quantity of inventory that provides protection against lost sales caused by unfulfilled demands from customers or delays in shipments from suppliers.

Merchandise purchases budget preparation.   A merchandiser usually expresses a **merchandise purchases budget** in both units and dollars. Exhibit 23.7 shows the general layout for this budget in equation form. If this formula is expressed in units and only one product is involved, we can compute the number of dollars of inventory to be purchased for the budget by multiplying the units to be purchased by the cost per unit.

EXHIBIT 23.7

General Formula for a Merchandise Purchases Budget

To illustrate, after assessing the cost of keeping inventory along with the risk and cost of inventory shortages, HD decided that the number of units in its inventory at each month-end should equal 90% of next month's predicted sales. For example, inventory at the end of October should equal 90% of budgeted November sales, and the November ending inventory should equal 90% of budgeted December sales, and so on. Also, HD's suppliers expect the September 2011 per unit cost of $60 to remain unchanged through January 2012. This information along with knowledge of 900 units in inventory at September 30 (see Exhibit 23.5) allows the company to prepare the merchandise purchases budget shown in Exhibit 23.8.

The first three lines of HD's merchandise purchases budget determine the required ending inventories (in units). Budgeted unit sales are then added to the desired ending inventory to give the required units of available merchandise. We then subtract beginning inventory to

Example: Assume Hockey Den adopts a JIT system in purchasing merchandise. How will its sales budget differ from its merchandise purchases budget? *Answer:* The two budgets will be similar because future inventory should be near zero.

EXHIBIT 23.8

Merchandise Purchases Budget

HOCKEY DEN Merchandise Purchases Budget October 2011–December 2011	October	November	December
Next month's budgeted sales (units)	800	1,400	900
Ratio of inventory to future sales	× 90%	× 90%	× 90%
Budgeted ending inventory (units)	720	1,260	810
Add budgeted sales (units)	1,000	800	1,400
Required units of available merchandise	1,720	2,060	2,210
Deduct beginning inventory (units)	900	720	1,260
Units to be purchased	820	1,340	950
Budgeted cost per unit	$ 60	$ 60	$ 60
Budgeted cost of merchandise purchases	$49,200	$80,400	$57,000

Example: If ending inventory in Exhibit 23.8 is required to equal 80% of next month's predicted sales, how many units must be purchased each month? *Answer:* Budgeted ending inventory: Oct. = 640 units; Nov. = 1,120 units; Dec. = 720 units. Required purchases: Oct. = 740 units; Nov. = 1,280 units; Dec. = 1,000 units.

determine the budgeted number of units to be purchased. The last line is the budgeted cost of the purchases, computed by multiplying the number of units to be purchased by the predicted cost per unit.

We already indicated that some budgeting systems describe only the total dollars of budgeted sales. Likewise, a system can express a merchandise purchases budget only in terms of the total cost of merchandise to be purchased, omitting the number of units to be purchased. This method assumes a constant relation between sales and cost of goods sold. HD, for instance, might assume the expected cost of goods sold to be 60% of sales, computed from the budgeted unit cost of $60 and the budgeted sales price of $100. However, it still must consider the effects of changes in beginning and ending inventories in determining the amounts to be purchased.

Selling Expense Budget   The **selling expense budget** is a plan listing the types and amounts of selling expenses expected during the budget period. Its initial responsibility usually rests with the vice president of marketing or an equivalent sales manager. The selling expense budget is normally created to provide sufficient selling expenses to meet sales goals reflected in the sales budget. Predicted selling expenses are based on both the sales budget and the experience of previous periods. After some or all of the master budget is prepared, management might decide that projected sales volume is inadequate. If so, subsequent adjustments in the sales budget can require corresponding adjustments in the selling expense budget.

To illustrate, HD's selling expense budget is in Exhibit 23.9. The firm's selling expenses consist of commissions paid to sales personnel and a $2,000 monthly salary paid to the sales manager. Sales commissions equal 10% of total sales and are paid in the month sales occur. Sales commissions are variable with respect to sales volume, but the sales manager's salary is fixed. No advertising expenses are budgeted for this particular quarter.

EXHIBIT 23.9

Selling Expense Budget

HOCKEY DEN Selling Expense Budget October 2011–December 2011	October	November	December	Totals
Budgeted sales	$100,000	$80,000	$140,000	$320,000
Sales commission percent	× 10%	× 10%	× 10%	× 10%
Sales commissions	10,000	8,000	14,000	32,000
Salary for sales manager	2,000	2,000	2,000	6,000
Total selling expenses	$ 12,000	$10,000	$ 16,000	$ 38,000

Example: If sales commissions in Exhibit 23.9 are increased, which budgets are affected? *Answer:* Selling expenses budget, cash budget, and budgeted income statement.

General and Administrative Expense Budget   The **general and administrative expense budget** plans the predicted operating expenses not included in the selling expenses budget. General and administrative expenses can be either variable or fixed with respect to sales volume. The office manager responsible for general administration often is responsible for preparing the initial general and administrative expense budget.

Exhibit 23.10 shows HD's general and administrative expense budget. It includes salaries of $54,000 per year, or $4,500 per month (paid each month when they are earned). Using information in Exhibit 23.5, the depreciation on equipment is computed as $18,000 per year [($200,000 − $20,000)/10 years], or $1,500 per month ($18,000/12 months).

EXHIBIT 23.10

General and Administrative Expense Budget

HOCKEY DEN General and Administrative Expense Budget October 2011–December 2011				
	October	November	December	Totals
Administrative salaries	$4,500	$4,500	$4,500	$13,500
Depreciation of equipment	1,500	1,500	1,500	4,500
Total general and administrative expenses	$6,000	$6,000	$6,000	$18,000

Interest expense and income tax expense are often classified as general and administrative expenses in published income statements but normally cannot be planned at this stage of the budgeting process. The prediction of interest expense follows the preparation of the cash budget and the decisions regarding debt. The predicted income tax expense depends on the budgeted amount of pretax income. Both interest and income taxes are usually beyond the control of the office manager. As a result, they are not used in comparison to the budget to evaluate that person's performance.

Example: In Exhibit 23.10, how would a rental agreement of $5,000 per month plus 1% of sales affect the general and administrative expense budget? (Budgeted sales are in Exhibit 23.6.) *Answer: Rent expense:* Oct. = $6,000; Nov. = $5,800; Dec. = $6,400; Total = $18,200; *Revised total general and administrative expenses:* Oct. = $12,000; Nov. = $11,800; Dec. = $12,400; Total = $36,200.

Decision Insight

No Biz Like Snow Biz   Ski resorts' costs of making snow are in the millions of dollars for equipment alone. Snowmaking involves spraying droplets of water into the air, causing them to freeze and come down as snow. Making snow can cost more than $2,000 an hour. Snowmaking accounts for 40 to 50 percent of the operating budgets for many ski resorts. ■

Quick Check   Answers — p. 968

5. What is a master budget?

6. A master budget (*a*) always includes a manufacturing budget specifying the units to be produced; (*b*) is prepared with a process starting with the operating budgets and continues with the capital expenditures budget and then financial budgets; or (*c*) is prepared with a process ending with the sales budget.

7. What are the three primary categories of budgets in the master budget?

8. In preparing monthly budgets for the third quarter, a company budgeted sales of 120 units for July and 140 units for August. Management wants each month's ending inventory to be 60% of next month's sales. The June 30 inventory consists of 50 units. How many units of product for July acquisition should the merchandise purchases budget specify for the third quarter? (*a*) 84, (*b*) 120, (*c*) 154, or (*d*) 204.

9. How do the operating budgets for merchandisers and manufacturers differ?

10. How does a just-in-time inventory system differ from a safety stock system?

Capital Expenditures Budget

The **capital expenditures budget** lists dollar amounts to be both received from plant asset disposals and spent to purchase additional plant assets to carry out the budgeted business activities. It is usually prepared after the operating budgets. Since a company's plant assets determine its productive capacity, this budget is usually affected by long-range plans for the business. Yet the process of preparing a sales or purchases budget can reveal that the company requires more (or less) capacity, which implies more (or less) plant assets.

Capital budgeting is the process of evaluating and planning for capital (plant asset) expenditures. This is an important management task because these expenditures often involve long-run commitments of large amounts, affect predicted cash flows, and impact future debt and equity financing. This means that the capital expenditures budget is often linked with management's evaluation of the company's ability to take on more debt. We describe capital budgeting in Chapter 25.

Hockey Den does not anticipate disposal of any plant assets through December 2011, but it does plan to acquire additional equipment for $25,000 cash near the end of December 2011. This is the only budgeted capital expenditure from October 2011 through January 2012. Thus, no separate budget is shown. Hockey Den's cash budget will reflect this $25,000 planned expenditure.

Financial Budgets

After preparing its operating and capital expenditures budgets, a company uses information from these budgets to prepare at least three financial budgets: the cash budget, budgeted income statement, and budgeted balance sheet.

P2 Link both operating and capital expenditures budgets to budgeted financial statements.

Cash Budget   After developing budgets for sales, merchandise purchases, expenses, and capital expenditures, the next step is to prepare the **cash budget,** which shows expected cash inflows and outflows during the budget period. It is especially important to maintain a cash balance necessary to meet ongoing obligations. By preparing a cash budget, management can prearrange loans to cover anticipated cash shortages before they are needed. A cash budget also helps management avoid a cash balance that is too large. Too much cash is undesirable because it earns a relatively low (if any) return. Exhibit 23.11 shows the general formula for the cash budget.

EXHIBIT 23.11

General Formula for
Cash Budget

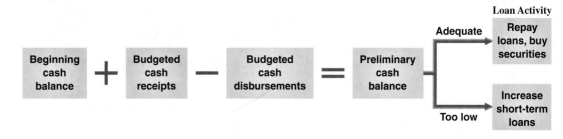

When preparing a cash budget, we add expected cash receipts to the beginning cash balance and deduct expected cash disbursements. If the expected (preliminary) ending cash balance is too low, additional cash requirements appear in the budget as planned increases from short-term loans. If the expected ending cash balance exceeds the desired balance, the excess is used to repay loans or to acquire short-term investments. Information for preparing the cash budget is mainly taken from the operating and capital expenditures budgets.

Cash Receipts from Sales   To illustrate, Exhibit 23.12 presents HD's budgeted cash receipts.

EXHIBIT 23.12

Computing Budgeted Cash
Receipts

	September	October	November	December
Sales...	$70,000	$100,000	$80,000	$140,000
Less ending accounts receivable (60%).........	42,000	60,000	48,000	84,000
Cash receipts from				
Cash sales (40% of sales).....................		40,000	32,000	56,000
Collections of prior month's receivables		42,000	60,000	48,000
Total cash receipts		$ 82,000	$92,000	$104,000

We begin with reference to HD's budgeted sales (Exhibit 23.6). Analysis of past sales indicates that 40% of the firm's sales are for cash. The remaining 60% are credit sales; these customers are expected to pay in full in the month following the sales. We now can compute the budgeted cash receipts from customers as shown in Exhibit 23.12. October's budgeted cash receipts consist of $40,000 from expected cash sales ($100,000 × 40%) plus the anticipated collection of $42,000 of accounts receivable from the end of September.

Cash Disbursements for Merchandise   Next, we see that HD's merchandise purchases are entirely on account. It makes full payment during the month following its purchases. Therefore, cash disbursements for purchases can be computed from the September 30, 2011, balance sheet (Exhibit 23.5), for October disbursements, and the merchandise purchases budget (Exhibit 23.8), for November and December disbursements. This is shown in Exhibit 23.13.

	October	November	December
Purchases (from Exhibit 23.8)	$49,200	$80,400	$57,000
Cash disbursements for			
Current month purchases (0%)	0	0	0
Prior month purchases (100%)	58,200*	49,200	80,400
Total cash disbursements for purchases	$58,200	$49,200	$80,400

*From September 30 balance sheet (Exhibit 23.5)

EXHIBIT 23.13

Computing Cash Disbursements for Purchases

The schedule above can be modified for alternative payment timing. For example, if Hockey Den paid for 20% of its purchases in the month of purchase, and paid the remaining 80% of a month's purchases in the following month, its cash disbursements in December would equal $75,720, computed as (20% × $57,000) plus (80% × $80,400).

Exhibit 23.14 shows the full cash budget for Hockey Den, beginning with information on budgeted cash receipts from Exhibit 23.13 and budgeted cash purchases for merchandise from Exhibit 23.13. Next we discuss HD's other cash disbursements and loan activity on its cash budget.

HOCKEY DEN
Cash Budget
October 2011–December 2011

	October	November	December
Beginning cash balance	$ 20,000	$ 20,000	$ 22,272
Cash receipts from customers (Exhibit 23.12)	82,000	92,000	104,000
Total cash available	102,000	112,000	126,272
Cash disbursements			
Payments for merchandise (Exhibit 23.13)	58,200	49,200	80,400
Sales commissions (Exhibit 23.9)	10,000	8,000	14,000
Salaries			
Sales (Exhibit 23.9)	2,000	2,000	2,000
Administrative (Exhibit 23.10)	4,500	4,500	4,500
Income taxes payable (Exhibit 23.5)	20,000		
Dividends ($150,000 × 2%)		3,000	
Interest on bank loan			
October ($10,000 × 1%)*	100		
November ($22,800 × 1%)		228	
Purchase of equipment			25,000
Total cash disbursements	94,800	66,928	125,900
Preliminary cash balance	$ 7,200	$ 45,072	$ 372
Loan activity			
Additional loan from bank	12,800		19,628
Repayment of loan to bank		22,800	
Ending cash balance	$ 20,000	$ 22,272	$ 20,000
Loan balance, end of month	$ 22,800	$ 0	$ 19,628

* Beginning loan balance from Exhibit 23.5

EXHIBIT 23.14

Cash Budget

Example: If the minimum ending cash balance in Exhibit 23.14 is changed to $25,000 for each month, what is the projected loan balance at Dec. 31, 2011?
Answer:

Loan balance, Oct. 31.......	$27,800
November interest	278
November payment........	25,022
Loan balance, Nov. 30	2,778
December interest	28
Additional loan in Dec.	21,928
Loan balance, Dec. 31.......	$24,706

The monthly budgeted cash disbursements for sales commissions and salaries are taken from the selling expense budget (Exhibit 23.9) and the general and administrative expense budget (Exhibit 23.10). The cash budget is unaffected by depreciation as reported in the general and administrative expenses budget.

Cash Disbursements for Other Items   Income taxes are due and payable in October as shown in the September 30, 2011, balance sheet (Exhibit 23.5). The cash budget in Exhibit 23.14 shows this $20,000 expected payment in October. Predicted income tax expense for the quarter ending December 31 is 40% of net income and is due in January 2012. It is therefore not reported in the October–December 2011 cash budget but in the budgeted income statement as income tax expense and on the budgeted balance sheet as income tax liability.

Hockey Den also pays a cash dividend equal to 2% of the par value of common stock in the second month of each quarter. The cash budget in Exhibit 23.14 shows a November payment of $3,000 for this purpose (2% of $150,000; see Exhibit 23.5).

Loan Activity   Analyzing Hockey Den's loan activity is necessary in computing its budgeted cash disbursements for interest. Hockey Den has an agreement with its bank that promises additional loans at each month-end, if necessary, to keep a minimum cash balance of $20,000. If the cash balance exceeds $20,000 at a month-end, HD uses the excess to repay loans. Interest is paid at each month-end at the rate of 1% of the beginning balance of these loans. For October, this payment is 1% of the $10,000 amount reported in the balance sheet of Exhibit 23.5. For November, HD expects to pay interest of $228, computed as 1% of the $22,800 expected loan balance at October 31. No interest is budgeted for December because the company expects to repay the loans in full at the end of November. Exhibit 23.14 shows that the October 31 cash balance declines to $7,200 (before any loan-related activity). This amount is less than the $20,000 minimum. Hockey Den will bring this balance up to the minimum by borrowing $12,800 with a short-term note. At the end of November, the budget shows an expected cash balance of $45,072 before any loan activity. This means that HD expects to repay $22,800 of debt. The equipment purchase budgeted for December reduces the expected cash balance to $372, far below the $20,000 minimum. The company expects to borrow $19,628 in that month to reach the minimum desired ending balance.

Decision Insight

Cash Cushion   Why do some companies maintain a minimum cash balance when the budget shows extra cash is not needed? For example, iPhone sales have pushed Apple's cash and investments balance to over $40 billion. Per CEO Steve Jobs the cushion provides "flexibility and security," important in navigating uncertain economic times. ∎

Budgeted Income Statement   One of the final steps in preparing the master budget is to summarize the income effects. The **budgeted income statement** is a managerial accounting report showing predicted amounts of sales and expenses for the budget period. Information needed for preparing a budgeted income statement is primarily taken from already prepared budgets. The volume of information summarized in the budgeted income statement is so large for some companies that they often use spreadsheets to accumulate the budgeted transactions and classify them by their effects on income. We condense HD's budgeted income statement and show it in Exhibit 23.15. All information in this exhibit is taken from earlier budgets. Also, we now can predict the amount of income tax expense for the quarter, computed as 40% of the budgeted pretax income. This amount is included in the cash budget and/or the budgeted balance sheet as necessary.

Budgeted Balance Sheet   The final step in preparing the master budget is summarizing the company's financial position. The **budgeted balance sheet** shows predicted amounts for the

Point: Lenders often require potential borrowers to provide cash budgets, budgeted income statements, and budgeted balance sheets, as well as data on past performance.

EXHIBIT 23.15

Budgeted Income Statement

HOCKEY DEN Budgeted Income Statement For Three Months Ended December 31, 2011		
Sales (Exhibit 23.6, 3,200 units @ $100)		$320,000
Cost of goods sold (3,200 units @ $60)		192,000
Gross profit		128,000
Operating expenses		
Sales commissions (Exhibit 23.9)	$32,000	
Sales salaries (Exhibit 23.9)	6,000	
Administrative salaries (Exhibit 23.10)	13,500	
Depreciation on equipment (Exhibit 23.10)	4,500	
Interest expense (Exhibit 23.14)	328	56,328
Income before income taxes		71,672
Income tax expense ($71,672 × 40%)		28,669
Net income		$ 43,003

company's assets, liabilities, and equity as of the end of the budget period. HD's budgeted balance sheet in Exhibit 23.16 is prepared using information from the other budgets. The sources of amounts are reported in the notes to the budgeted balance sheet.[1]

EXHIBIT 23.16

Budgeted Balance Sheet

HOCKEY DEN Budgeted Balance Sheet December 31, 2011		
Assets		
Cash[a]...........................		$ 20,000
Accounts receivable[b]		84,000
Inventory[c]		48,600
Equipment[d]	$225,000	
Less accumulated depreciation[e]........	40,500	184,500
Total assets		$337,100
Liabilities and Equity		
Liabilities		
Accounts payable[f]	$ 57,000	
Income taxes payable[g]	28,669	
Bank loan payable[h]	19,628	$105,297
Stockholders' equity		
Common stock[i]	150,000	
Retained earnings[j]	81,803	231,803
Total liabilities and equity		$337,100

[a] Ending balance for December from the cash budget in Exhibit 23.14.

[b] 60% of $140,000 sales budgeted for December from the sales budget in Exhibit 23.6.

[c] 810 units in budgeted December ending inventory at the budgeted cost of $60 per unit (from the purchases budget in Exhibit 23.8).

[d] September 30 balance of $200,000 from the beginning balance sheet in Exhibit 23.5 plus $25,000 cost of new equipment from the cash budget in Exhibit 23.14.

[e] September 30 balance of $36,000 from the beginning balance sheet in Exhibit 23.5 plus $4,500 expense from the general and administrative expense budget in Exhibit 23.10.

[f] Budgeted cost of purchases for December from the purchases budget in Exhibit 23.8.

[g] Income tax expense from the budgeted income statement for the fourth quarter in Exhibit 23.15.

[h] Budgeted December 31 balance from the cash budget in Exhibit 23.14.

[i] Unchanged from the beginning balance sheet in Exhibit 23.5.

[j] September 30 balance of $41,800 from the beginning balance sheet in Exhibit 23.5 plus budgeted net income of $43,003 from the budgeted income statement in Exhibit 23.15 minus budgeted cash dividends of $3,000 from the cash budget in Exhibit 23.14.

---

[1] An eight-column spreadsheet, or work sheet, can be used to prepare a budgeted balance sheet (and income statement). The first two columns show the ending balance sheet amounts from the period prior to the budget period. The budgeted transactions and adjustments are entered in the third and fourth columns in the same manner as adjustments are entered on an ordinary work sheet. After all budgeted transactions and adjustments have been entered, the amounts in the first two columns are combined with the budget amounts in the third and fourth columns and sorted to the proper Income Statement (fifth and sixth columns) and Balance Sheet columns (seventh and eighth columns). Amounts in these columns are used to prepare the budgeted income statement and balance sheet.

Decision Insight

Plan Ahead Most companies allocate dollars based on budgets submitted by department managers. These managers verify the numbers and monitor the budget. Managers must remember, however, that a budget is judged by its success in helping achieve the company's mission. One analogy is that a hiker must know the route to properly plan a hike and monitor hiking progress. ■

Quick Check

Answers — p. 968

11. In preparing a budgeted balance sheet, (*a*) plant assets are determined by analyzing the capital expenditures budget and the balance sheet from the beginning of the budget period, (*b*) liabilities are determined by analyzing the general and administrative expense budget, or (*c*) retained earnings are determined from information contained in the cash budget and the balance sheet from the beginning of the budget period.
12. What sequence is followed in preparing the budgets that constitute the master budget?

GLOBAL VIEW

Royal Phillips Electronics of the Netherlands is a diversified company. Preparing budgets and evaluating progress helps the company achieve its goals. In a recent annual report the company reports that it expects sales to grow at a faster pace than overall economic growth. Based on this sales target, company managers prepare detailed operating, capital expenditure, and financial budgets.

Decision Analysis

Activity-Based Budgeting

A1 Analyze expense planning using activity-based budgeting.

Activity-based budgeting (ABB) is a budget system based on expected activities. Knowledge of expected activities and their levels for the budget period enables management to plan for resources required to perform the activities. To illustrate, we consider the budget of a company's accounting department. Traditional budgeting systems list items such as salaries, supplies, equipment, and utilities. Such an itemized budget informs management of the use of the funds budgeted (for example, salaries), but management cannot assess the basis for increases or decreases in budgeted amounts as compared to prior periods. Accordingly, management often makes across-the-board cuts or increases. In contrast, ABB requires management to list activities performed by, say, the accounting department such as auditing, tax reporting, financial reporting, and cost accounting. Exhibit 23.17 contrasts a traditional budget with an activity-based budget for a company's accounting department. An understanding of the resources required to perform the activities, the costs associated with these resources, and the way resource use changes with

EXHIBIT 23.17

Activity-Based Budgeting versus Traditional Budgeting (for an accounting department)

Activity-Based Budget		Traditional Budget	
Auditing	$ 58,000	Salaries	$152,000
Tax reporting	71,000	Supplies	22,000
Financial reporting	63,000	Depreciation	36,000
Cost accounting	32,000	Utilities	14,000
Total	$224,000	Total	$224,000

changes in activity levels allows management to better assess how expenses will change to accommodate changes in activity levels. Moreover, by knowing the relation between activities and costs, management can attempt to reduce costs by eliminating nonvalue-added activities.

Decision Maker   Answer — p. 968

Environmental Manager   You hold the new position of environmental control manager for a chemical company. You are asked to develop a budget for your job and identify job responsibilities. How do you proceed? ■

DEMONSTRATION PROBLEM

Wild Wood Company's management asks you to prepare its master budget using the following informa-tion. The budget is to cover the months of April, May, and June of 2011.

WILD WOOD COMPANY
Balance Sheet
March 31, 2011

Assets		Liabilities and Equity	
Cash	$ 50,000	Accounts payable	$156,000
Accounts receivable	175,000	Short-term notes payable	12,000
Inventory	126,000	Total current liabilities	168,000
Total current assets	351,000	Long-term note payable	200,000
Equipment, gross	480,000	Total liabilities	368,000
Accumulated depreciation	(90,000)	Common stock	235,000
Equipment, net	390,000	Retained earnings	138,000
		Total stockholders' equity	373,000
Total assets	$741,000	Total liabilities and equity	$741,000

Additional Information

a. Sales for March total 10,000 units. Each month's sales are expected to exceed the prior month's results by 5%. The product's selling price is $25 per unit.

b. Company policy calls for a given month's ending inventory to equal 80% of the next month's expected unit sales. The March 31 inventory is 8,400 units, which complies with the policy. The purchase price is $15 per unit.

c. Sales representatives' commissions are 12.5% of sales and are paid in the month of the sales. The sales manager's monthly salary will be $3,500 in April and $4,000 per month thereafter.

d. Monthly general and administrative expenses include $8,000 administrative salaries, $5,000 depreciation, and 0.9% monthly interest on the long-term note payable.

e. The company expects 30% of sales to be for cash and the remaining 70% on credit. Receivables are collected in full in the month following the sale (none is collected in the month of the sale).

f. All merchandise purchases are on credit, and no payables arise from any other transactions. One month's purchases are fully paid in the next month.

g. The minimum ending cash balance for all months is $50,000. If necessary, the company borrows enough cash using a short-term note to reach the minimum. Short-term notes require an interest payment of 1% at each month-end (before any repayment). If the ending cash balance exceeds the minimum, the excess will be applied to repaying the short-term notes payable balance.

h. Dividends of $100,000 are to be declared and paid in May.

i. No cash payments for income taxes are to be made during the second calendar quarter. Income taxes will be assessed at 35% in the quarter.

j. Equipment purchases of $55,000 are scheduled for June.

Required

Prepare the following budgets and other financial information as required:

1. Sales budget, including budgeted sales for July.
2. Purchases budget, the budgeted cost of goods sold for each month and quarter, and the cost of the June 30 budgeted inventory.
3. Selling expense budget.
4. General and administrative expense budget.
5. Expected cash receipts from customers and the expected June 30 balance of accounts receivable.
6. Expected cash payments for purchases and the expected June 30 balance of accounts payable.
7. Cash budget.
8. Budgeted income statement.
9. Budgeted statement of retained earnings.
10. Budgeted balance sheet.

PLANNING THE SOLUTION

- The sales budget shows expected sales for each month in the quarter. Start by multiplying March sales by 105% and then do the same for the remaining months. July's sales are needed for the purchases budget. To complete the budget, multiply the expected unit sales by the selling price of $25 per unit.

- Use these results and the 80% inventory policy to budget the size of ending inventory for April, May, and June. Add the budgeted sales to these numbers and subtract the actual or expected beginning inventory for each month. The result is the number of units to be purchased each month. Multiply these numbers by the per unit cost of $15. Find the budgeted cost of goods sold by multiplying the unit sales in each month by the $15 cost per unit. Compute the cost of the June 30 ending inventory by multiplying the expected units available at that date by the $15 cost per unit.

- The selling expense budget has only two items. Find the amount of the sales representatives' commissions by multiplying the expected dollar sales in each month by the 12.5% commission rate. Then include the sales manager's salary of $3,500 in April and $4,000 in May and June.

- The general and administrative expense budget should show three items. Administrative salaries are fixed at $8,000 per month, and depreciation is $5,000 per month. Budget the monthly interest expense on the long-term note by multiplying its $200,000 balance by the 0.9% monthly interest rate.

- Determine the amounts of cash sales in each month by multiplying the budgeted sales by 30%. Add to this amount the credit sales of the prior month (computed as 70% of prior month's sales). April's cash receipts from collecting receivables equals the March 31 balance of $175,000. The expected June 30 accounts receivable balance equals 70% of June's total budgeted sales.

- Determine expected cash payments on accounts payable for each month by making them equal to the merchandise purchases in the prior month. The payments for April equal the March 31 balance of accounts payable shown on the beginning balance sheet. The June 30 balance of accounts payable equals merchandise purchases for June.

- Prepare the cash budget by combining the given information and the amounts of cash receipts and cash payments on account that you computed. Complete the cash budget for each month by either borrowing enough to raise the preliminary balance to the minimum or paying off short-term debt as much as the balance allows without falling below the minimum. Show the ending balance of the short-term note in the budget.

- Prepare the budgeted income statement by combining the budgeted items for all three months. Determine the income before income taxes and multiply it by the 35% rate to find the quarter's income tax expense.

- The budgeted statement of retained earnings should show the March 31 balance plus the quarter's net income minus the quarter's dividends.

- The budgeted balance sheet includes updated balances for all items that appear in the beginning balance sheet and an additional liability for unpaid income taxes. Amounts for all asset, liability, and equity accounts can be found either in the budgets, other calculations, or by adding amounts found there to the beginning balances.

SOLUTION TO DEMONSTRATION PROBLEM

1. Sales budget

	April	May	June	July
Prior period's unit sales	10,000	→10,500	→11,025	→11,576
Plus 5% growth	500	525	551	579
Projected unit sales	10,500	11,025	11,576	12,155

	April	May	June	Quarter
Projected unit sales	10,500	11,025	11,576	
Selling price per unit	× $25	× $25	× $25	
Projected sales	$262,500	$275,625	$289,400	$827,525

2. Purchases budget

	April	May	June	Quarter
Next period's unit sales (part 1)	11,025	11,576	12,155	
Ending inventory percent	× 80%	× 80%	× 80%	
Desired ending inventory	8,820	9,261	9,724	
Current period's unit sales (part 1)	10,500	11,025	11,576	
Units to be available	19,320	20,286	21,300	
Less beginning inventory	8,400	8,820	9,261	
Units to be purchased	10,920	11,466	12,039	
Budgeted cost per unit	× $15	× $15	× $15	
Projected purchases	$163,800	$171,990	$180,585	$516,375

Budgeted cost of goods sold

	April	May	June	Quarter
This period's unit sales (part 1)	10,500	11,025	11,576	
Budgeted cost per unit	× $15	× $15	× $15	
Projected cost of goods sold	$157,500	$165,375	$173,640	$496,515

Budgeted inventory for June 30

Units (part 2)	9,724
Cost per unit	× $15
Total	$145,860

3. Selling expense budget

	April	May	June	Quarter
Budgeted sales (part 1)	$262,500	$275,625	$289,400	$827,525
Commission percent	× 12.5%	× 12.5%	× 12.5%	× 12.5%
Sales commissions	32,813	34,453	36,175	103,441
Manager's salary	3,500	4,000	4,000	11,500
Projected selling expenses	$ 36,313	$ 38,453	$ 40,175	$114,941

4. General and administrative expense budget

	April	May	June	Quarter
Administrative salaries	$ 8,000	$ 8,000	$ 8,000	$24,000
Depreciation	5,000	5,000	5,000	15,000
Interest on long-term note payable (0.9% × $200,000)	1,800	1,800	1,800	5,400
Projected expenses	$14,800	$14,800	$14,800	$44,400

5. Expected cash receipts from customers

	April	May	June	Quarter
Budgeted sales (part 1)	$262,500	$275,625	$289,400	
Ending accounts receivable (70%)	$183,750	$192,938	$202,580	
Cash receipts				
Cash sales (30% of budgeted sales)	$ 78,750	$ 82,687	$ 86,820	$248,257
Collections of prior month's receivables	175,000	183,750	192,938	551,688
Total cash to be collected	$253,750	$266,437	$279,758	$799,945

6. Expected cash payments to suppliers

	April	May	June	Quarter
Cash payments (equal to prior month's purchases)	$156,000	$163,800	$171,990	$491,790
Expected June 30 balance of accounts payable (June purchases)			$180,585	

7. Cash budget

	April	May	June
Beginning cash balance	$ 50,000	$ 89,517	$ 50,000
Cash receipts (part 5)	253,750	266,437	279,758
Total cash available	303,750	355,954	329,758
Cash payments			
Payments for merchandise (part 6)	156,000	163,800	171,990
Sales commissions (part 3)	32,813	34,453	36,175
Salaries			
Sales (part 3)	3,500	4,000	4,000
Administrative (part 4)	8,000	8,000	8,000
Interest on long-term note (part 4)	1,800	1,800	1,800
Dividends		100,000	
Equipment purchase			55,000
Interest on short-term notes			
April ($12,000 × 1.0%)	120		
June ($6,099 × 1.0%)			61
Total cash payments	202,233	312,053	277,026
Preliminary balance	101,517	43,901	52,732
Loan activity			
Additional loan		6,099	
Loan repayment	(12,000)		(2,732)
Ending cash balance	$ 89,517	$ 50,000	$ 50,000
Ending short-term notes	$ 0	$ 6,099	$ 3,367

8.

WILD WOOD COMPANY
Budgeted Income Statement
For Quarter Ended June 30, 2011

Sales (part 1)		$827,525
Cost of goods sold (part 2)		496,515
Gross profit		331,010
Operating expenses		
Sales commissions (part 3)	$103,441	
Sales salaries (part 3)	11,500	
Administrative salaries (part 4)	24,000	
Depreciation (part 4)	15,000	
Interest on long-term note (part 4)	5,400	
Interest on short-term notes (part 7)	181	
Total operating expenses		159,522
Income before income taxes		171,488
Income taxes (35%)		60,021
Net income		$111,467

9.

WILD WOOD COMPANY
Budgeted Statement of Retained Earnings
For Quarter Ended June 30, 2011

Beginning retained earnings (given)	$138,000
Net income (part 8)	111,467
	249,467
Less cash dividends (given)	100,000
Ending retained earnings	$149,467

10.

WILD WOOD COMPANY
Budgeted Balance Sheet
June 30, 2011

Assets		
Cash (part 7)		$ 50,000
Accounts receivable (part 5)		202,580
Inventory (part 2)		145,860
Total current assets		398,440
Equipment (given plus purchase)	$535,000	
Less accumulated depreciation (given plus expense)	105,000	430,000
Total assets		$828,440
Liabilities and Equity		
Accounts payable (part 6)		$180,585
Short-term notes payable (part 7)		3,367
Income taxes payable (part 8)		60,021
Total current liabilities		243,973
Long-term note payable (given)		200,000
Total liabilities		443,973
Common stock (given)		235,000
Retained earnings (part 9)		149,467
Total stockholders' equity		384,467
Total liabilities and equity		$828,440

23A

Production and Manufacturing Budgets

P3 Prepare production and manufacturing budgets.

Unlike a merchandising company, a manufacturer must prepare a **production budget** instead of a merchandise purchases budget. A production budget, which shows the number of units to be produced each month, is similar to merchandise purchases budgets except that the number of units to be purchased each month (as shown in Exhibit 23.8) is replaced by the number of units to be manufactured each month. A production budget does not show costs; it is *always expressed in units of product.* Exhibit 23A.1 shows the production budget for **Toronto Sticks Company (TSC),** a manufacturer of hockey sticks. TSC is an exclusive supplier of hockey sticks to Hockey Den, meaning that TSC uses HD's budgeted sales figures (Exhibit 23.6) to determine its production and manufacturing budgets.

EXHIBIT 23A.1

Production Budget

TSC Production Budget October 2011–December 2011	October	November	December
Next period's budgeted sales (units)	800	1,400	900
Ratio of inventory to future sales	× 90%	× 90%	× 90%
Budgeted ending inventory (units)	720	1,260	810
Add budgeted sales for the period (units)	1,000	800	1,400
Required units of available production	1,720	2,060	2,210
Deduct beginning inventory (units)	(900)	(720)	(1,260)
Units to be produced	820	1,340	950

A **manufacturing budget** shows the budgeted costs for direct materials, direct labor, and overhead. It is based on the budgeted production volume from the production budget. The manufacturing budget for most companies consists of three individual budgets: direct materials budget, direct labor budget, and overhead budget. Exhibits 23A.2–23A.4 show these three manufacturing budgets for TSC. These budgets yield the total expected cost of goods to be manufactured in the budget period.

The *direct materials budget* is driven by the budgeted materials needed to satisfy each month's production requirement. To this we must add the desired ending inventory requirements. The desired ending inventory of direct materials as shown in Exhibit 23A.2 is 50% of next month's budgeted materials requirements of wood. For instance, in October 2011, an ending inventory of 335 units of material is desired (50% of November's 670 units). The desired ending inventory for December 2011 is 225 units, computed from the direct material requirement of 450 units for a production level of 900 units in January 2012. The total materials requirements are computed by adding the desired ending inventory figures to that month's budgeted production material requirements. For October 2011, the total materials requirement is 745 units (335 + 410). From the total materials requirement, we then subtract the units of

EXHIBIT 23A.2

Direct Materials Budget

TSC Direct Materials Budget October 2011–December 2011	October	November	December
Budget production (units)	820	1,340	950
Materials requirements per unit	× 0.5	× 0.5	× 0.5
Materials needed for production (units)	410	670	475
Add budgeted ending inventory (units)	335	237.5	225
Total materials requirements (units)	745	907.5	700
Deduct beginning inventory (units)	(205)	(335)	(237.5)
Materials to be purchased (units)	540	572.5	462.5
Material price per unit	$ 20	$ 20	$ 20
Total cost of direct materials purchases	$10,800	$11,450	$9,250

materials available in beginning inventory. For October 2011, the materials available from September 2011 are computed as 50% of October's materials requirements to satisfy production, or 205 units (50% of 410). Therefore, direct materials purchases in October 2011 are budgeted at 540 units (745 − 205). See Exhibit 23A.2.

TSC's *direct labor budget* is shown in Exhibit 23A.3. About 15 minutes of labor time is required to produce one unit. Labor is paid at the rate of $12 per hour. Budgeted labor hours are computed by multiplying the budgeted production level for each month by one-quarter (0.25) of an hour. Direct labor cost is then computed by multiplying budgeted labor hours by the labor rate of $12 per hour.

TSC Direct Labor Budget October 2011–December 2011			
	October	**November**	**December**
Budgeted production (units)	820	1,340	950
Labor requirements per unit (hours)	× 0.25	× 0.25	× 0.25
Total labor hours needed	205	335	237.5
Labor rate (per hour)	$ 12	$ 12	$ 12
Labor dollars	$2,460	$4,020	$2,850

EXHIBIT 23A.3

Direct Labor Budget

TSC's *factory overhead budget* is shown in Exhibit 23A.4. The variable portion of overhead is assigned at the rate of $2.50 per unit of production. The fixed portion stays constant at $1,500 per month. The budget in Exhibit 23A.4 is in condensed form; most overhead budgets are more detailed, listing each overhead cost item.

TSC Factory Overhead Budget October 2011–December 2011			
	October	**November**	**December**
Budgeted production (units)	820	1,340	950
Variable factory overhead rate	× $2.50	× $2.50	× $2.50
Budgeted variable overhead	2,050	3,350	2,375
Budgeted fixed overhead	1,500	1,500	1,500
Budgeted total overhead	$3,550	$4,850	$3,875

EXHIBIT 23A.4

Factory Overhead Budget

Summary

C1 **Describe the importance and benefits of budgeting and the process of budget administration.** Planning is a management responsibility of critical importance to business success. Budgeting is the process management uses to formalize its plans. Budgeting promotes management analysis and focuses its attention on the future. Budgeting also provides a basis for evaluating performance, serves as a source of motivation, is a means of coordinating activities, and communicates management's plans and instructions to employees. Budgeting is a detailed activity that requires administration. At least three aspects are important: budget committee, budget reporting, and budget timing. A budget committee oversees the budget preparation. The budget period pertains to the time period for which the budget is prepared such as a year or month.

C2 **Describe a master budget and the process of preparing it.** A master budget is a formal overall plan for a company. It consists of plans for business operations and capital expenditures, plus the financial results of those activities. The budgeting process begins with a sales budget. Based on expected sales volume, companies can budget purchases, selling expenses, and administrative expenses. Next, the capital expenditures budget is prepared, followed by the cash budget and budgeted financial statements. Manufacturers also must budget production quantities, materials purchases, labor costs, and overhead.

A1 **Analyze expense planning using activity-based budgeting.** Activity-based budgeting requires management to identify activities performed by departments, plan necessary activity levels, identify resources required to perform these activities, and budget the resources.

P1 **Prepare each component of a master budget and link each to the budgeting process.** The term *master budget* refers to a collection of individual component budgets. Each component budget is designed to guide persons responsible for activities covered by that component. A master budget must reflect the components of a company and their interaction in pursuit of company goals.

P2 **Link both operating and capital expenditures budgets to budgeted financial statements.** The operating budgets, capital expenditures budget, and cash budget contain much of the information to prepare a budgeted income statement for the budget period and a budgeted balance sheet at the end of the budget period. Budgeted financial statements show the expected financial consequences of the planned activities described in the budgets.

P3 **Prepare production and manufacturing budgets.** A manufacturer must prepare a *production budget* instead of a purchases budget. A *manufacturing budget* shows the budgeted production costs for direct materials, direct labor, and overhead.

Guidance Answers to Decision Maker and Decision Ethics

Budget Staffer Your superior's actions appear unethical because she is using private information for personal gain. As a budget staffer, you are low in the company's hierarchical structure and probably unable to confront this superior directly. You should inform an individual with a position of authority within the organization about your concerns.

Entrepreneur You must deal with two issues. First, because fashions and designs frequently change, you cannot heavily rely on previous budgets. As a result, you must carefully analyze the market to understand what designs are in vogue. This will help you plan the product mix and estimate demand. The second issue is the budgeting

period. An annual sales budget may be unreliable because tastes can quickly change. Your best bet might be to prepare monthly and quarterly sales budgets that you continuously monitor and revise.

Environmental Manager You are unlikely to have data on this new position to use in preparing your budget. In this situation, you can use activity-based budgeting. This requires developing a list of activities to conduct, the resources required to perform these activities, and the expenses associated with these resources. You should challenge yourself to be absolutely certain that the listed activities are necessary and that the listed resources are required.

Guidance Answers to Quick Checks

1. Major benefits include promoting a focus on the future; providing a basis for evaluating performance; providing a source of motivation; coordinating the departments of a business; and communicating plans and instructions.

2. The budget committee's responsibility is to provide guidance to ensure that budget figures are realistic and coordinated.

3. Budget periods usually coincide with accounting periods and therefore cover a month, quarter, or a year. Budgets can also be prepared for longer time periods, such as five years.

4. Rolling budgets are budgets that are periodically revised in the ongoing process of continuous budgeting.

5. A master budget is a comprehensive or overall plan for the company that is generally expressed in monetary terms.

6. *b*

7. The master budget includes operating budgets, the capital expenditures budget, and financial budgets.

8. *c*; Computed as (60% × 140) + 120 − 50 = 154.

9. Merchandisers prepare merchandise purchases budgets; manufacturers prepare production and manufacturing budgets.

10. A just-in-time system keeps the level of inventory to a minimum and orders merchandise or materials to meet immediate sales demand. A safety stock system maintains an inventory that is large enough to meet sales demands plus an amount to satisfy unexpected sales demands and an amount to cover delayed shipments from suppliers.

11. *a*

12. (a) Operating budgets (such as sales, selling expense, and administrative budgets), (b) capital expenditures budget, (c) financial budgets: cash budget, budgeted income statement, and budgeted balance sheet.

Key Terms

mhhe.com/wildFAP20e

Activity-based budgeting (ABB) (p. 960)
Budget (p. 946)
Budgeted balance sheet (p. 958)
Budgeted income statement (p. 958)
Budgeting (p. 946)
Capital expenditures budget (p. 956)

Cash budget (p. 956)
Continuous budgeting (p. 949)
General and administrative expense budget (p. 955)
Manufacturing budget (p. 966)
Master budget (p. 950)

Merchandise purchases budget (p. 953)
Production budget (p. 966)
Rolling budgets (p. 949)
Safety stock (p. 953)
Sales budget (p. 952)
Selling expense budget (p. 954)

Additional Quiz Questions are available at the book's Website.

1. A plan that reports the units or costs of merchandise to be purchased by a merchandising company during the budget period is called a
   a. Capital expenditures budget.
   b. Cash budget.
   c. Merchandise purchases budget.
   d. Selling expenses budget.
   e. Sales budget.

2. A hardware store has budgeted sales of $36,000 for its power tool department in July. Management wants to have $7,000 in power tool inventory at the end of July. Its beginning inventory of power tools is expected to be $6,000. What is the budgeted dollar amount of merchandise purchases?
   a. $36,000
   b. $43,000
   c. $42,000
   d. $35,000
   e. $37,000

3. A store has the following budgeted sales for the next five months.

May	$210,000
June	186,000
July	180,000
August	220,000
September	240,000

   Cash sales are 25% of total sales and all credit sales are expected to be collected in the month following the sale. The total amount of cash expected to be received from customers in September is

   a. $240,000
   b. $225,000
   c. $ 60,000
   d. $165,000
   e. $220,000

4. A plan that shows the expected cash inflows and cash outflows during the budget period, including receipts from loans needed to maintain a minimum cash balance and repayments of such loans, is called
   a. A rolling budget.
   b. An income statement.
   c. A balance sheet.
   d. A cash budget.
   e. An operating budget.

5.ᴬThe following sales are predicted for a company's next four months.

	September	October	November	December
Unit sales . .	480	560	600	480

   Each month's ending inventory of finished goods should be 30% of the next month's sales. At September 1, the finished goods inventory is 140 units. The budgeted production of units for October is
   a. 572 units.
   b. 560 units.
   c. 548 units.
   d. 600 units.
   e. 180 units.

ᴬ *Superscript letter A denotes assignments based on Appendix 23A.*
🔲 Icon denotes assignments that involve decision making.

Discussion Questions

1. 🔲 Identify at least three roles that budgeting plays in helping managers control and monitor a business.

2. What two common benchmarks can be used to evaluate actual performance? Which of the two is generally more useful?

3. 🔲 What is the benefit of continuous budgeting?

4. Identify three usual time horizons for short-term planning and budgets.

5. 🔲 Why should each department participate in preparing its own budget?

6. 🔲 How does budgeting help management coordinate and plan business activities?

7. 🔲 Why is the sales budget so important to the budgeting process?

8. What is a selling expense budget? What is a capital expenditures budget?

9. Budgeting promotes good decision making by requiring managers to conduct _____ and by focusing their attention on the _____.

10. **Nokia** prepares a cash budget. What is a cash budget? Why must operating budgets and the capital expenditures budget be prepared before the cash budget?   **NOKIA**

11.ᴬ What is the difference between a production budget and a manufacturing budget?

12. 🔲 Would a manager of an **Apple** retail store participate more in budgeting than a manager at the corporate offices? Explain.   Apple

13. 🔲 Does the manager of a **Research In Motion** distribution center participate in long-term budgeting? Explain.   **RIM**

14. 🔲 Assume that **Palm**'s smartphone division is charged with preparing a master budget. Identify the participants—for example, the sales manager for the sales budget—and describe the information each person provides in preparing the master budget.   Palm

QUICK STUDY

QS 23-1
Budget motivation   C1

The motivation of employees is one goal of budgeting. Identify three guidelines that organizations should follow if budgeting is to serve effectively as a source of motivation for employees.

QS 23-2
Budgeting process   C1

Good management includes good budgeting. (1) Explain why the bottom-up approach to budgeting is considered a more successful management technique than a top-down approach. (2) Provide an example of implementation of the bottom-up approach to budgeting.

QS 23-3
Components of a master budget
C2

Which one of the following sets of items are all necessary components of the master budget?
1. Operating budgets, historical income statement, and budgeted balance sheet.
2. Sales budget, operating budgets, and historical financial budgets.
3. Operating budgets, financial budgets, and capital expenditures budget.
4. Prior sales reports, capital expenditures budget, and financial budgets.

QS 23-4
Purchases budget   P1

Rockgate Company's July sales budget calls for sales of $400,000. The store expects to begin July with $40,000 of inventory and to end the month with $50,000 of inventory. Gross margin is typically 30% of sales. Determine the budgeted cost of merchandise purchases for July.

QS 23-5
Computing budgeted accounts receivable
P2

Treehouse Company anticipates total sales for June and July of $420,000 and $398,000, respectively. Cash sales are normally 60% of total sales. Of the credit sales, 10% are collected in the same month as the sale, 70% are collected during the first month after the sale, and the remaining 20% are collected in the second month. Determine the amount of accounts receivable reported on the company's budgeted balance sheet as of July 31.

QS 23-6
Cash budget
P1

Use the following information to prepare a cash budget for the month ended on March 31 for Sosa Company. The budget should show expected cash receipts and cash disbursements for the month of March and the balance expected on March 31.
   a. Beginning cash balance on March 1, $82,000.
   b. Cash receipts from sales, $300,000.
   c. Budgeted cash disbursements for purchases, $120,000.
   d. Budgeted cash disbursements for salaries, $80,000.
   e. Other budgeted cash expenses, $55,000.
   f. Cash repayment of bank loan, $30,000.

QS 23-7
Activity-based budgeting
A1

Activity-based budgeting is a budget system based on *expected activities*. (1) Describe activity-based budgeting, and explain its preparation of budgets. (2) How does activity-based budgeting differ from traditional budgeting?

QS 23-8[A]
Production budget
P3

Goldenlock Company manufactures watches and has a JIT policy that ending inventory must equal 20% of the next month's sales. It estimates that October's actual ending inventory will consist of 95,000 watches. November and December sales are estimated to be 350,000 and 400,000 watches, respectively. Compute the number of watches to be produced that would appear on the company's production budget for the month of November.

QS 23-9[A]
Factory overhead budget   P3

Refer to information from QS 23-8[A]. Goldenlock Company assigns variable overhead at the rate of $1.75 per unit of production. Fixed overhead equals $5,000,000 per month. Prepare a factory overhead budget for November.

QS 23-10
Sales budget   P1

Turks sells miniature digital cameras for $400 each. 900 units were sold in May, and it forecasts 5% growth in unit sales each month. Determine (a) the number of camera sales and (b) the dollar amount of camera sales for the month of June.

Refer to information from QS 23-10. Turks pays a sales manager a monthly salary of $4,000 and a commission of 10% of camera sales (in dollars). Prepare a selling expense budget for the month of June.

QS 23-11
Selling expense budget P1

Refer to information from QS 23-10. Assume 20% of Turks's sales are for cash. The remaining 80% are credit sales; these customers pay in the month following the sale. Compute the budgeted cash receipts for June.

QS 23-12
Cash budget P1

Following are selected accounts for a company. For each account, indicate whether it will appear on a budgeted income statement (BIS) or a budgeted balance sheet (BBS). If an item will not appear on either budgeted financial statement, label it NA.

QS 23-13
Budgeted financial statements
P2

Sales	_____	Interest paid on bank loan	_____
Administrative salaries paid	_____	Cash dividends paid	_____
Accumulated depreciation	_____	Bank loan owed	_____
Depreciation expense	_____	Cost of goods sold	_____

The Candy Shoppe reports the following sales forecast: August, $110,000; September, $120,000. Cash sales are normally 25% of total sales and all credit sales are expected to be collected in the month following the date of sale. Prepare a schedule of cash receipts for September.

QS 23-14
Cash receipts P1

Zen Den reports the following sales forecast: September, $25,000; October, $36,000; and November, $30,000. All sales are on account. Collections of credit sales are received as follows: 15% in the month of sale, 60% in the first month after sale, 20% in the second month after sale, and 5% is uncollectible. Prepare a schedule of cash receipts for November.

QS 23-15
Cash receipts P1

T-Mart purchased $100,000 of merchandise in August and expects to purchase $120,000 in September. Merchandise purchases are paid as follows: 25% in the month of purchase and 75% in the following month. Compute cash disbursements for merchandise for September.

QS 23-16
Cash disbursements for merchandise P1

Jam Co. forecasts merchandise purchases of $11,600 in January, $11,800 in February, and $15,400 in March; 40% of purchases are paid in the month of purchase and 60% are paid in the following month. At December 31 of the prior year, the balance of Accounts Payable (for December purchases) is $8,000. Prepare a schedule of cash disbursements for merchandise for each of the months of January, February, and March.

QS 23-17
Cash disbursements for merchandise
P1

Splinter Company forecasts sales of 6,000 units for April. Beginning inventory is 1,000 units. The desired ending inventory is 30% higher than the beginning inventory. How many units should Splinter purchase in April?

QS 23-18
Computing purchases
P1

Li Company forecasts unit sales of 640,000 in April, 720,000 in May, 780,000 in June, and 620,000 in July. Beginning inventory on April 1 is 192,000 units, and the company wants to have 30% of next month's sales in inventory at the end of each month. Prepare a merchandise purchases budget for the months of April, May, and June.

QS 23-19
Computing purchases
P1

Kyoto, Inc. predicts the following sales in units for the coming three months:

	May	June	July
Sales in units	280	300	240

QS 23-20[A]
Production budget
P3

Each month's ending inventory of finished units should be 60% of the next month's sales. The April 30 finished goods inventory is 168 units. Compute Kyoto's budgeted production (in units) for May.

Zyton Corp. budgets production of 292 units in January and 264 units in February. Each finished unit requires five pounds of raw material Z, which costs $6 per pound. Each month's ending inventory of raw materials should be 30% of the following month's budgeted production. The January 1 raw materials inventory has 438 pounds of Z. Prepare a direct materials budget for January.

QS 23-21[A]
Direct materials budget
P3

QS 23-22ᴬ
Direct labor budget   P3

Tek Co. plans to produce 620 units in July. Each unit requires two hours of direct labor. The direct labor rate is $16 per hour. Prepare a direct labor budget for July.

QS 23-23
Sales budget   P1

Shay, Inc., is preparing its master budget for the quarter ending March 31. It sells a single product for $25 per unit. Budgeted sales for the next four months follow. Prepare a sales budget for the months of January, February, and March.

	January	February	March	April
Sales in units	1,200	1,000	1,600	1,400

QS 23-24
Cash receipts budget   P1

Refer to information in QS 23-23. In addition, sales are 40% cash and 60% on credit. All credit sales are collected in the month following the sale. The January 1 balance in accounts receivable is $10,000. Prepare a schedule of budgeted cash receipts for January, February, and March.

QS 23-25
Selling expense budget   P1

Refer to information in QS 23-23. In addition, sales commissions are 10% of sales and the company pays a sales manager a salary of $5,000 per month. Sales commissions and salaries are paid in the month incurred. Prepare a selling expense budget for January, February, and March.

QS 23-26
Budgeted loan activity
P1

Mink Company is preparing a cash budget for February. The company has $30,000 cash at the beginning of February and anticipates $75,000 in cash receipts and $96,250 in cash disbursements during February. What amount, if any, must the company borrow during February to maintain a $10,000 cash balance? The company has no loans outstanding on February 1.

QS 23-27
Operating budgets
P1

Royal Phillips Electronics of the Netherlands reports sales of €23,200 million for a recent year. Assume that the company expects sales growth of 3 percent for the next year. Also assume that selling expenses are typically 20 percent of sales, while general and administrative expenses are 4 percent of sales.

Required

1. Compute budgeted sales for the next year.
2. Assume budgeted sales for next year is €24,000 million, and then compute budgeted selling expenses and budgeted general and administrative expenses for the next year. Round amounts to one decimal.

Mc Graw Hill **connect**

EXERCISES

Exercise 23-1
Preparation of merchandise purchases budgets (for three periods)
P1

Formworks Company prepares monthly budgets. The current budget plans for a September ending inventory of 15,000 units. Company policy is to end each month with merchandise inventory equal to a specified percent of budgeted sales for the following month. Budgeted sales and merchandise purchases for the three most recent months follow. (1) Prepare the merchandise purchases budget for the months of July, August, and September. (2) Compute the ratio of ending inventory to the next month's sales for each budget prepared in part 1. (3) How many units are budgeted for sale in October?

	Sales (Units)	Purchases (Units)
July	120,000	138,000
August	210,000	204,000
September	180,000	159,000

Exercise 23-2
Preparation of cash budgets (for three periods)
P1

Kasik Co. budgeted the following cash receipts and cash disbursements for the first three months of next year.

	Cash Receipts	Cash Disbursements
January	$500,000	$450,000
February.........	300,000	250,000
March	400,000	500,000

According to a credit agreement with the company's bank, Kasik promises to have a minimum cash balance of $30,000 at each month-end. In return, the bank has agreed that the company can borrow up to $150,000 at an annual interest rate of 12%, paid on the last day of each month. The interest is computed based on the beginning balance of the loan for the month. The company has a cash balance of $30,000 and a loan balance of $60,000 at January 1. Prepare monthly cash budgets for each of the first three months of next year.

Check January ending cash balance, $30,000

Use the following information to prepare the July cash budget for Sanchez Co. It should show expected cash receipts and cash disbursements for the month and the cash balance expected on July 31.

a. Beginning cash balance on July 1: $50,000.

b. Cash receipts from sales: 30% is collected in the month of sale, 50% in the next month, and 20% in the second month after sale (uncollectible accounts are negligible and can be ignored). Sales amounts are: May (actual), $1,720,000; June (actual), $1,200,000; and July (budgeted), $1,400,000.

c. Payments on merchandise purchases: 60% in the month of purchase and 40% in the month following purchase. Purchases amounts are: June (actual), $430,000; and July (budgeted), $600,000.

d. Budgeted cash disbursements for salaries in July: $211,000.

e. Budgeted depreciation expense for July: $12,000.

f. Other cash expenses budgeted for July: $150,000.

g. Accrued income taxes due in July: $80,000.

h. Bank loan interest due in July: $6,600.

Exercise 23-3
Preparation of a cash budget
P1

Check Ending cash balance, $434,400

Use the information in Exercise 23-3 and the following additional information to prepare a budgeted income statement for the month of July and a budgeted balance sheet for July 31.

a. Cost of goods sold is 44% of sales.

b. Inventory at the end of June is $80,000 and at the end of July is $64,000.

c. Salaries payable on June 30 are $50,000 and are expected to be $40,000 on July 31.

d. The equipment account balance is $1,600,000 on July 31. On June 30, the accumulated depreciation on equipment is $280,000.

e. The $6,600 cash payment of interest represents the 1% monthly expense on a bank loan of $660,000.

f. Income taxes payable on July 31 are $124,320, and the income tax rate applicable to the company is 30%.

g. The only other balance sheet accounts are: Common Stock, with a balance of $600,000 on June 30; and Retained Earnings, with a balance of $1,072,000 on June 30.

Exercise 23-4
Preparing a budgeted income statement and balance sheet
P2

Check Net income, $290,080; Total assets, $3,026,400

Powerdyne Company's cost of goods sold is consistently 60% of sales. The company plans to carry ending merchandise inventory for each month equal to 40% of the next month's budgeted cost of good sold. All merchandise is purchased on credit, and 50% of the purchases made during a month is paid for in that month. Another 35% is paid for during the first month after purchase, and the remaining 15% is paid for during the second month after purchase. Expected unit sales are: August (actual), 150,000; September (actual), 350,000; October (estimated), 200,000; November (estimated), 300,000. Use this information to determine October's expected cash payments for purchases. (*Hint:* Use the layout of Exhibit 23.8, but revised for the facts given here.)

Exercise 23-5
Computing budgeted cash payments for purchases
P1

Check Budgeted purchases: August, $138,000; October, $144,000

Sand Dollar Company purchases all merchandise on credit. It recently budgeted the following month-end accounts payable balances and merchandise inventory balances. Cash payments on accounts payable during each month are expected to be: May, $1,300,000; June, $1,450,000; July, $1,350,000; and August, $1,400,000. Use the available information to compute the budgeted amounts of (1) merchandise purchases for June, July, and August and (2) cost of goods sold for June, July, and August.

Exercise 23-6
Computing budgeted purchases and costs of goods sold
P1

	Accounts Payable	Merchandise Inventory
May 31	$120,000	$250,000
June 30	170,000	400,000
July 31	200,000	300,000
August 31	160,000	330,000

Check June purchases, $1,500,000; June cost of goods sold, $1,350,000

Exercise 23-7

Computing budgeted accounts payable and purchases—sales forecast in dollars

P1 P2

Check July purchases, $199,500; Sept. payments on accts. pay., $183,225

Sound Check, a merchandising company specializing in home computer speakers, budgets its monthly cost of goods sold to equal 70% of sales. Its inventory policy calls for ending inventory in each month to equal 25% of the next month's budgeted cost of goods sold. All purchases are on credit, and 20% of the purchases in a month is paid for in the same month. Another 50% is paid for during the first month after purchase, and the remaining 30% is paid for in the second month after purchase. The following sales budgets are set: July, $300,000; August, $240,000; September, $270,000; October, $240,000; and November, $210,000. Compute the following: (1) budgeted merchandise purchases for July, August, September, and October; (2) budgeted payments on accounts payable for September and October; and (3) budgeted ending balances of accounts payable for September and October. (*Hint:* For part 1, refer to Exhibits 23.7 and 23.8 for guidance, but note that budgeted sales are in dollars for this assignment.)

Exercise 23-8ᴬ

Preparing production budgets (for two periods) P3

Check Second quarter production, 240,000 units

Nascar Company manufactures an innovative automobile transmission for electric cars. Management predicts that ending inventory for the first quarter will be 37,500 units. The following unit sales of the transmissions are expected during the rest of the year: second quarter, 225,000 units; third quarter, 262,500 units; and fourth quarter, 237,500 units. Company policy calls for the ending inventory of a quarter to equal 20% of the next quarter's budgeted sales. Prepare a production budget for both the second and third quarters that shows the number of transmissions to manufacture.

Exercise 23-9ᴬ

Direct materials budget

P3

Refer to information from Exercise 23-8ᴬ. Each transmission requires 0.60 pounds of a key raw material. Nascar Company aims to end each quarter with an ending inventory of direct materials equal to 50% of next quarter's budgeted materials requirements. Direct materials cost $175 per unit. Prepare a direct materials budget for the second quarter.

Exercise 23-10ᴬ

Direct labor budget P3

Refer to information from Exercise 23-8ᴬ. Each transmission requires 4 direct labor hours, at a cost of $9 per hour. Prepare a direct labor budget for the second quarter.

Exercise 23-11

Budgeted cash disbursements

P1

Jake Company reports the following:

	July	August	September
Sales	$24,000	$32,000	$36,000
Purchases	14,400	19,200	21,600

Payments for purchases are made in the month after purchase. Selling expenses are 15% of sales, administrative expenses are 10% of sales, and both are paid in the month of sale. Rent expense of $2,400 is paid monthly. Depreciation expense is $1,300 per month. Prepare a schedule of budgeted cash disbursements for August and September.

Exercise 23-12

Budgeted cash receipts

P1

Emily Company has sales on account and for cash. Specifically, 60% of its sales are on account and 40% are for cash. Credit sales are collected in full in the month following the sale. The company forecasts sales of $525,000 for April, $535,000 for May, and $560,000 for June. The beginning balance of Accounts Receivable is $300,000 on April 1. Prepare a schedule of budgeted cash receipts for April, May, and June.

Exercise 23-13

Cash budget

P1

Kaizen Corp. requires a minimum $8,000 cash balance. If necessary, loans are taken to meet this requirement at a cost of 1% interest per month (paid monthly). Any excess cash is used to repay loans at month-end. The cash balance on July 1 is $8,400 and the company has no outstanding loans. Forecasted cash receipts (other than for loans received) and forecasted cash payments (other than for loan or interest payments) are:

	July	August	September
Cash receipts	$24,000	$32,000	$40,000
Cash disbursements	28,000	30,000	32,000

Prepare a cash budget for July, August, and September. Round interest payments to the nearest whole dollar.

Fabrice Corp. requires a minimum $6,000 cash balance. If necessary, loans are taken to meet this requirement at a cost of 1% interest per month (paid monthly). Any excess cash is used to repay loans at month-end. The cash balance on October 1 is $6,000 and the company has an outstanding loan of $2,000. Forecasted cash receipts (other than for loans received) and forecasted cash payments (other than for loan or interest payments) follow. Prepare a cash budget for October, November, and December. Round interest payments to the nearest whole dollar.

Exercise 23-14
Cash budget
P1

	October	November	December
Cash receipts	$22,000	$16,000	$20,000
Cash disbursements	24,000	15,000	16,000

Cambridge, Inc. is preparing its master budget for the quarter ended June 30. Budgeted sales and cash payments for merchandise for the next three months follow:

Exercise 23-15
Cash budget
P1

	April	May	June
Budgeted sales	$32,000	$40,000	$24,000
Budgeted cash payments for merchandise...................	20,200	16,800	17,200

Sales are 60% cash and 40% on credit. All credit sales are collected in the month following the sale. The March 30 balance sheet includes balances of $12,000 in cash, $12,000 in accounts receivable, $11,000 in accounts payable, and a $2,000 balance in loans payable. A minimum cash balance of $12,000 is required. Loans are obtained at the end of any month when a cash shortage occurs. Interest is 1% per month based on the beginning of the month loan balance and is paid at each month-end. If an excess balance of cash exists, loans are repaid at the end of the month. Operating expenses are paid in the month incurred and consist of sales commissions (10% of sales), shipping (3% of sales), office salaries ($3,000 per month) and rent ($5,000 per month). Prepare a cash budget for each of the months of April, May, and June (round all dollar amounts to the nearest whole dollar).

Kool-Ray is preparing its master budget for the quarter ended September 30. Budgeted sales and cash payments for merchandise for the next three months follow:

Exercise 23-16
Cash budget
P1

	July	August	September
Budgeted sales	$64,000	$80,000	$48,000
Budgeted cash payments for merchandise...................	40,400	33,600	34,400

Sales are 20% cash and 80% on credit. All credit sales are collected in the month following the sale. The June 30 balance sheet includes balances of $12,000 in cash; $45,000 in accounts receivable; $4,500 in accounts payable; and a $2,000 balance in loans payable. A minimum cash balance of $12,000 is required. Loans are obtained at the end of any month when a cash shortage occurs. Interest is 1% per month based on the beginning of the month loan balance and is paid at each month-end. If an excess balance of cash exists, loans are repaid at the end of the month. Operating expenses are paid in the month incurred and consist of sales commissions (10% of sales), office salaries ($4,000 per month), and rent ($6,500 per month). (1) Prepare a cash receipts budget for July, August, and September. (2) Prepare a cash budget for each of the months of July, August, and September. (Round all dollar amounts to the nearest whole dollar.)

Exercise 23-17
Budgeted balance sheet
P2

The following information is available for Zhao Company:

a. The cash budget for March shows an ending bank loan of $10,000 and an ending cash balance of $48,000.

b. The sales budget for March indicates sales of $120,000. Accounts receivable are expected to be 70% of the current-month sales.

c. The merchandise purchases budget indicates that $89,000 in merchandise will be purchased on account in March. Purchases on account are paid 100% in the month following the purchase. Ending inventory for March is predicted to be 600 units at a cost of $35 each.

d. The budgeted income statement for March shows net income of $48,000. Depreciation expense of $1,000 and $26,000 in income tax expense were used in computing net income for March. Accrued taxes will be paid in April.

e. The balance sheet for February shows equipment of $84,000 with accumulated depreciation of $30,000, common stock of $25,000, and ending retained earnings of $8,000. There are no changes budgeted in the equipment or common stock accounts.

Prepare a budgeted balance sheet for March.

Exercise 23-18
Budgeted income statement
P2

Zulu, Inc., is preparing its master budget for the first quarter. The company sells a single product at a price of $25 per unit. Sales (in units) are forecasted at 40,000 for January, 60,000 for February, and 50,000 for March. Cost of goods sold is $14 per unit. Other expense information for the first quarter follows. Prepare a budgeted income statement for this first quarter.

Commissions	10% of sales
Rent	$20,000 per month
Advertising	15% of sales
Office salaries	$75,000 per month
Depreciation	$50,000 per month
Interest	15% annually on a $250,000 note payable
Tax rate.	40%

Exercise 23-19[A]
Direct labor budget
P3

The production budget for Zink Company shows units to be produced as follows: July, 620; August, 680; September, 540. Each unit produced requires two hours of direct labor. The direct labor rate is currently $16 per hour but is predicted to be $16.75 per hour in September. Prepare a direct labor budget for the months July, August, and September.

Exercise 23-20[A]
Production budget
P3

Rad Co. provides the following sales forecast for the next four months:

	April	May	June	July
Sales (units)	500	580	530	600

The company wants to end each month with ending finished goods inventory equal to 20% of next month's sales. Finished goods inventory on April 1 is 174 units. Assume July's budgeted production is 540 units. Prepare a production budget for the months of April, May, and June.

Exercise 23-21[A]
Direct materials budget
P3

Refer to the information in Exercise 23-20[A]. In addition, assume each finished unit requires five pounds of raw materials and the company wants to end each month with raw materials inventory equal to 30% of next month's production needs. Beginning raw materials inventory for April was 663 pounds.
Prepare a direct materials budget for April, May, and June.

Match the definitions 1 through 9 with the term or phrase a through i.

A. Master budget

B. General and administrative expense budget

C. Budget

D. Safety stock

E. Budgeted income statement

F. Budgeted balance sheet

G. Sales budget

H. Cash budget

I. Merchandise purchases budget

_____ **1.** A plan that shows the units or costs of merchandise to be purchased by a merchandising company during the budget period.

_____ **2.** An accounting report that presents predicted amounts of the company's assets, liabilities, and equity balances at the end of the budget period.

_____ **3.** A plan showing the units of goods to be sold and the sales to be derived; the usual starting point in the budgeting process.

_____ **4.** An accounting report that presents predicted amounts of the company's revenues and expenses for the budgeting period.

_____ **5.** A quantity of inventory or materials over the minimum to reduce the risk of running short.

_____ **6.** A comprehensive business plan that includes specific plans for expected sales, the units of product to be produced, the merchandise or materials to be purchased, the expenses to be incurred, the long-term assets to be purchased, and the amounts of cash to be borrowed or loans to be repaid, as well as a budgeted income statement and balance sheet.

_____ **7.** A formal statement of a company's future plans, usually expressed in monetary terms.

_____ **8.** A plan that shows predicted operating expenses not included in the selling expenses budget.

_____ **9.** A plan that shows the expected cash inflows and cash outflows during the budget period, including receipts from any loans needed to maintain a minimum cash balance and repayments of such loans.

Exercise 23-22
Master budget definitions
C2

Participatory budgeting can sometimes lead to negative consequences. Identify three potential negative outcomes that can arise from participatory budgeting.

Exercise 23-23
Budget consequences   C1

Kirk Co. CPA is preparing activity-based budgets for 2011. The partners expect the firm to generate billable hours for the year as follows:

Data entry	1,100 hours
Auditing	2,400 hours
Tax	2,150 hours
Consulting	375 hours

The company pays $8 per hour to data-entry clerks, $40 per hour to audit personnel, $50 per hour to tax personnel, and $50 per hour to consulting personnel. Prepare a schedule of budgeted labor costs for 2011 using activity-based budgeting.

Exercise 23-24
Activity-based budgeting
A1

Connect

Pinsetter's Supply is a merchandiser of three different products. The company's February 28 inventories are footwear, 15,500 units; sports equipment, 70,000 units; and apparel, 40,000 units. Management believes that excessive inventories have accumulated for all three products. As a result, a new policy dictates that ending inventory in any month should equal 40% of the expected unit sales for the following month. Expected sales in units for March, April, May, and June follow.

	Budgeted Sales in Units			
	March	April	May	June
Footwear	10,000	20,000	30,000	33,000
Sports equipment	66,000	85,000	90,000	80,000
Apparel	36,000	30,000	30,000	18,000

PROBLEM SET A

Problem 23-1A
Preparation and analysis of merchandise purchases budgets

C2 P1

mhhe.com/wildFAP20e

Required

1. Prepare a merchandise purchases budget (in units) for each product for each of the months of March, April, and May.

Analysis Component

2. The purchases budgets in part 1 should reflect fewer purchases of all three products in March compared to those in April and May. What factor caused fewer purchases to be planned? Suggest business conditions that would cause this factor to both occur and impact the company in this way.

Problem 23-2A

Preparation of cash budgets (for three periods)

C2 P2

mhhe.com/wildFAP20e

During the last week of August, Apache Arts Company's owner approaches the bank for an $80,000 loan to be made on September 2 and repaid on November 30 with annual interest of 12%, for an interest cost of $2,400. The owner plans to increase the store's inventory by $60,000 during September and needs the loan to pay for inventory acquisitions. The bank's loan officer needs more information about Apache Arts' ability to repay the loan and asks the owner to forecast the store's November 30 cash position. On September 1, Apache Arts is expected to have a $3,000 cash balance, $135,000 of accounts receivable, and $100,000 of accounts payable. Its budgeted sales, merchandise purchases, and various cash disbursements for the next three months follow.

Budgeted Figures*	September	October	November
Sales	$220,000	$300,000	$380,000
Merchandise purchases	210,000	180,000	220,000
Cash disbursements			
Payroll	16,000	17,000	18,000
Rent	6,000	6,000	6,000
Other cash expenses	64,000	8,000	7,000
Repayment of bank loan			80,000
Interest on the bank loan			2,400

* Operations began in August; August sales were $180,000 and purchases were $100,000.

The budgeted September merchandise purchases include the inventory increase. All sales are on account. The company predicts that 25% of credit sales is collected in the month of the sale, 45% in the month following the sale, 20% in the second month, 9% in the third, and the remainder is uncollectible. Applying these percents to the August credit sales, for example, shows that $81,000 of the $180,000 will be collected in September, $36,000 in October, and $16,200 in November. All merchandise is purchased on credit; 80% of the balance is paid in the month following a purchase, and the remaining 20% is paid in the second month. For example, of the $100,000 August purchases, $80,000 will be paid in September and $20,000 in October.

Required

Prepare a cash budget for September, October, and November for Apache Arts Company. Show supporting calculations as needed.

Problem 23-3A

Preparation and analysis of cash budgets with supporting inventory and purchases budgets

C2 P2

Abacus Company sells its product for $125 per unit. Its actual and projected sales follow.

	Units	Dollars
April (actual)	8,000	$1,000,000
May (actual)	4,000	500,000
June (budgeted)	12,000	1,500,000
July (budgeted)............	6,000	750,000
August (budgeted).........	7,600	950,000

All sales are on credit. Recent experience shows that 20% of credit sales is collected in the month of the sale, 30% in the month after the sale, 48% in the second month after the sale, and 2% proves to be uncollectible. The product's purchase price is $100 per unit. All purchases are payable within 12 days. Thus, 60% of purchases made in a month is paid in that month and the other 40% is paid in the next month. The company has a policy to maintain an ending monthly inventory of 25% of the next month's unit sales plus a safety stock of 100 units. The April 30 and May 31 actual inventory levels are consistent with this policy. Selling and administrative expenses for the year are $1,200,000 and are paid evenly throughout the year in cash. The company's minimum cash balance at month-end is $60,000. This minimum is maintained, if necessary, by borrowing cash from the bank. If the balance exceeds $60,000, the company repays as much of the loan as it can without going below the minimum. This type of loan carries an annual 9% interest rate. On May 31, the loan balance is $32,000, and the company's cash balance is $60,000.

Required

1. Prepare a table that shows the computation of cash collections of its credit sales (accounts receivable) in each of the months of June and July.

2. Prepare a table that shows the computation of budgeted ending inventories (in units) for April, May, June, and July.

3. Prepare the merchandise purchases budget for May, June, and July. Report calculations in units and then show the dollar amount of purchases for each month.

4. Prepare a table showing the computation of cash payments on product purchases for June and July.

5. Prepare a cash budget for June and July, including any loan activity and interest expense. Compute the loan balance at the end of each month.

Analysis Component

6. Refer to your answer to part 5. Abacus's cash budget indicates the company will need to borrow more than $40,000 in June and will need to borrow $60,000 in July. Suggest some reasons that knowing this information in May would be helpful to management.

Check   (1) Cash collections: June, $930,000; July, $840,000

(3) Budgeted purchases: May, $600,000; June, $1,050,000

(5) Budgeted ending loan balance: June, $72,240; July, $136,782

Lilliput, a one-product mail-order firm, buys its product for $60 per unit and sells it for $130 per unit. The sales staff receives a 10% commission on the sale of each unit. Its December income statement follows.

Problem 23-4A
Preparation and analysis of budgeted income statements

C2 P2

LILLIPUT COMPANY	
Income Statement	
For Month Ended December 31, 2011	
Sales	$1,300,000
Cost of goods sold	600,000
Gross profit	700,000
Expenses	
Sales commissions (10%)	130,000
Advertising	200,000
Store rent	24,000
Administrative salaries	40,000
Depreciation	50,000
Other expenses	12,000
Total expenses	456,000
Net income	$ 244,000

Management expects December's results to be repeated in January, February, and March of 2012 without any changes in strategy. Management, however, has an alternative plan. It believes that unit sales will increase at a rate of 10% *each* month for the next three months (beginning with January) if the item's selling price is reduced to $115 per unit and advertising expenses are increased by 25% and remain at that level for all three months. The cost of its product will remain at $60 per unit, the sales staff will continue to earn a 10% commission, and the remaining expenses will stay the same.

Required

1. Prepare budgeted income statements for each of the months of January, February, and March that show the expected results from implementing the proposed changes. Use a three-column format, with one column for each month.

Check   (1) Budgeted net income: January, $102,500; February, $150,350; March, $202,985

Analysis Component

2. Use the budgeted income statements from part 1 to recommend whether management should implement the proposed changes. Explain.

Problem 23-5A
Preparation of a complete master budget

C2 P1 P2

Near the end of 2011, the management of Simid Sports Co., a merchandising company, prepared the following estimated balance sheet for December 31, 2011.

SIMID SPORTS COMPANY
Estimated Balance Sheet
December 31, 2011

Assets

Cash		$ 18,000
Accounts receivable		262,500
Inventory		75,000
Total current assets		355,500
Equipment	$270,000	
Less accumulated depreciation	33,750	236,250
Total assets		$591,750

Liabilities and Equity

Accounts payable	$180,000	
Bank loan payable	7,500	
Taxes payable (due 3/15/2012)	45,000	
Total liabilities		$232,500
Common stock	236,250	
Retained earnings	123,000	
Total stockholders' equity		359,250
Total liabilities and equity		$591,750

To prepare a master budget for January, February, and March of 2012, management gathers the following information.

a. Simid Sports' single product is purchased for $30 per unit and resold for $55 per unit. The expected inventory level of 2,500 units on December 31, 2011, is more than management's desired level for 2012, which is 20% of the next month's expected sales (in units). Expected sales are: January, 3,500 units; February, 4,500 units; March, 5,500 units; and April, 5,000 units.

b. Cash sales and credit sales represent 25% and 75%, respectively, of total sales. Of the credit sales, 60% is collected in the first month after the month of sale and 40% in the second month after the month of sale. For the December 31, 2011, accounts receivable balance, $62,500 is collected in January and the remaining $200,000 is collected in February.

c. Merchandise purchases are paid for as follows: 20% in the first month after the month of purchase and 80% in the second month after the month of purchase. For the December 31, 2011, accounts payable balance, $40,000 is paid in January and the remaining $140,000 is paid in February.

d. Sales commissions equal to 20% of sales are paid each month. Sales salaries (excluding commissions) are $30,000 per year.

e. General and administrative salaries are $72,000 per year. Maintenance expense equals $1,000 per month and is paid in cash.

f. Equipment reported in the December 31, 2011, balance sheet was purchased in January 2011. It is being depreciated over eight years under the straight-line method with no salvage value. The following amounts for new equipment purchases are planned in the coming quarter: January, $18,000; February, $48,000; and March, $14,400. This equipment will be depreciated under the straight-line method over eight years with no salvage value. A full month's depreciation is taken for the month in which equipment is purchased.

g. The company plans to acquire land at the end of March at a cost of $75,000, which will be paid with cash on the last day of the month.

h. Simid Sports has a working arrangement with its bank to obtain additional loans as needed. The interest rate is 12% per year, and interest is paid at each month-end based on the beginning balance. Partial or full payments on these loans can be made on the last day of the month. The company has agreed to maintain a minimum ending cash balance of $12,500 in each month.

i. The income tax rate for the company is 40%. Income taxes on the first quarter's income will not be paid until April 15.

Required

Prepare a master budget for each of the first three months of 2012; include the following component budgets (show supporting calculations as needed, and round amounts to the nearest dollar):

1. Monthly sales budgets (showing both budgeted unit sales and dollar sales).
2. Monthly merchandise purchases budgets.
3. Monthly selling expense budgets.
4. Monthly general and administrative expense budgets.
5. Monthly capital expenditures budgets.
6. Monthly cash budgets.
7. Budgeted income statement for the entire first quarter (not for each month).
8. Budgeted balance sheet as of March 31, 2012.

Check   (2) Budgeted purchases:
January, $57,000; February, $141,000
        (3) Budgeted selling expenses:
January, $41,000; February, $52,000

        (6) Ending cash bal.: January,
$15,050; February, $105,150

        (8) Budgeted total assets at
March 31, $784,325

Diamond Slope Company produces snow skis. Each ski requires 2 pounds of carbon fiber. The company's management predicts that 7,000 skis and 10,000 pounds of carbon fiber will be in inventory on June 30 of the current year and that 120,000 skis will be sold during the next (third) quarter. Management wants to end the third quarter with 4,000 skis and 5,000 pounds of carbon fiber in inventory. Carbon fiber can be purchased for $12 per pound.

Problem 23-6A[A]
Preparing production and direct materials budgets

C2 P3

Required

1. Prepare the third-quarter production budget for skis.
2. Prepare the third-quarter direct materials (carbon fiber) budget; include the dollar cost of purchases.

Check   (1) Units manuf., 117,000;
        (2) Cost of carbon fiber
purchases, $2,748,000

H20 Company is a merchandiser of three different products. The company's March 31 inventories are water skis, 40,000 units; tow ropes, 90,000 units; and life jackets, 250,000 units. Management believes that excessive inventories have accumulated for all three products. As a result, a new policy dictates that ending inventory in any month should equal 10% of the expected unit sales for the following month. Expected sales in units for April, May, June, and July follow.

PROBLEM SET B

Problem 23-1B
Preparation and analysis of merchandise purchases budgets

C2 P1

	Budgeted Sales in Units			
	April	May	June	July
Water skis	70,000	90,000	130,000	140,000
Tow ropes	100,000	90,000	110,000	100,000
Life jackets	300,000	260,000	310,000	260,000

Required

1. Prepare a merchandise purchases budget (in units) for each product for each of the months of April, May, and June.

Check   (1) April budgeted
purchases: Water skis, 39,000; Tow
ropes, 19,000; Life jackets, 76,000

Analysis Component

2. The purchases budgets in part 1 should reflect fewer purchases of all three products in April compared to those in May and June. What factor caused fewer purchases to be planned? Suggest business conditions that would cause this factor to both occur and affect the company as it has.

During the last week of March, Siro Stereo's owner approaches the bank for a $125,000 loan to be made on April 1 and repaid on June 30 with annual interest of 10%, for an interest cost of $3,125. The owner plans to increase the store's inventory by $100,000 in April and needs the loan to pay for inventory acquisitions. The bank's loan officer needs more information about Siro Stereo's ability to repay the loan and asks the owner to forecast the store's June 30 cash position. On April 1, Siro Stereo is expected to have a $12,000 cash balance, $121,500 of accounts receivable, and $90,000 of accounts

Problem 23-2B
Preparation of cash budgets (for three periods)

C2 P2

payable. Its budgeted sales, merchandise purchases, and various cash disbursements for the next three months follow.

File Edit View Insert Format Tools Data Window Help			
Budgeted Figures*	**April**	**May**	**June**
Sales	$350,000	$500,000	$550,000
Merchandise purchases	250,000	200,000	190,000
Cash disbursements			
Payroll	22,500	30,000	37,500
Rent	12,000	12,000	12,000
Other cash expenses	9,000	13,500	16,500
Repayment of bank loan			125,000
Interest on the bank loan.........			3,125

*Operations began in March; March sales were $135,000 and purchases were $90,000.

The budgeted April merchandise purchases include the inventory increase. All sales are on account. The company predicts that 10% of credit sales is collected in the month of the sale, 60% in the month following the sale, 25% in the second month, 3% in the third, and the remainder is uncollectible. Applying these percents to the March credit sales, for example, shows that $81,000 of the $135,000 will be collected in April, $33,750 in May, and $4,050 in June. All merchandise is purchased on credit; 80% of the balance is paid in the month following a purchase and the remaining 20% is paid in the second month. For example, of the $90,000 March purchases, $72,000 will be paid in April and $18,000 in May.

Check Budgeted cash balance: April, $137,500; May, $157,750; June, $200,175

Required

Prepare a cash budget for April, May, and June for Siro Stereo. Show supporting calculations as needed.

Problem 23-3B
Preparation and analysis of cash budgets with supporting inventory and purchases budgets

C2 P2

LaRocca Company sells its product for $20 per unit. Its actual and projected sales follow.

	Units	Dollars
January (actual)	18,000	$360,000
February (actual)	27,000	540,000
March (budgeted)	15,000	300,000
April (budgeted)	27,000	540,000
May (budgeted)	33,000	660,000

All sales are on credit. Recent experience shows that 40% of credit sales is collected in the month of the sale, 30% in the month after the sale, 25% in the second month after the sale, and 5% proves to be uncollectible. The product's purchase price is $12 per unit. All purchases are payable within 21 days. Thus, 30% of purchases made in a month is paid in that month and the other 70% is paid in the next month. The company has a policy to maintain an ending monthly inventory of 30% of the next month's unit sales plus a safety stock of 300 units. The January 31 and February 28 actual inventory levels are consistent with this policy. Selling and administrative expenses for the year are $1,440,000 and are paid evenly throughout the year in cash. The company's minimum cash balance for month-end is $45,000. This minimum is maintained, if necessary, by borrowing cash from the bank. If the balance exceeds $45,000, the company repays as much of the loan as it can without going below the minimum. This type of loan carries an annual 12% interest rate. At February 28, the loan balance is $12,000, and the company's cash balance is $45,000.

Required

Check (1) Cash collections: March, $372,000; April, $441,000

1. Prepare a table that shows the computation of cash collections of its credit sales (accounts receivable) in each of the months of March and April.

2. Prepare a table showing the computations of budgeted ending inventories (units) for January, February, March, and April.

(3) Budgeted purchases: February, $280,800; March, $223,200

3. Prepare the merchandise purchases budget for February, March, and April. Report calculations in units and then show the dollar amount of purchases for each month.

4. Prepare a table showing the computation of cash payments on product purchases for March and April.

(5) Ending cash balance: March, $45,000, April, $82,204

5. Prepare a cash budget for March and April, including any loan activity and interest expense. Compute the loan balance at the end of each month.

Analysis Component

6. Refer to your answer to part 5. LaRocca's cash budget indicates whether the company must borrow additional funds at the end of March. Suggest some reasons that knowing the loan needs in advance would be helpful to management.

Computa-Cations buys its product for $20 and sells it for $50 per unit. The sales staff receives a 10% commission on the sale of each unit. Its June income statement follows.

Problem 23-4B
Preparation and analysis of budgeted income statements

C2 P2

COMPUTA-CATIONS COMPANY	
Income Statement	
For Month Ended June 30, 2011	
Sales	$1,000,000
Cost of goods sold	400,000
Gross profit	600,000
Expenses	
Sales commissions (10%)	100,000
Advertising	100,000
Store rent	10,000
Administrative salaries	20,000
Depreciation	12,000
Other expenses	24,000
Total expenses	266,000
Net income	$ 334,000

Management expects June's results to be repeated in July, August, and September without any changes in strategy. Management, however, has another plan. It believes that unit sales will increase at a rate of 10% *each* month for the next three months (beginning with July) if the item's selling price is reduced to $45 per unit and advertising expenses are increased by 20% and remain at that level for all three months. The cost of its product will remain at $20 per unit, the sales staff will continue to earn a 10% commission, and the remaining expenses will stay the same.

Required

1. Prepare budgeted income statements for each of the months of July, August, and September that show the expected results from implementing the proposed changes. Use a three-column format, with one column for each month.

Check Budgeted net income: July, $265,000; August, $310,100; September, $359,710

Analysis Component

2. Use the budgeted income statements from part 1 to recommend whether management should implement the proposed plan. Explain.

Near the end of 2011, the management of Oasis Corp., a merchandising company, prepared the following estimated balance sheet for December 31, 2011.

Problem 23-5B
Preparation of a complete master budget

C2 P1 P2

OASIS CORPORATION		
Estimated Balance Sheet		
December 31, 2011		
Assets		
Cash		$ 160,000
Accounts receivable		400,000
Inventory		180,000
Total current assets		740,000
Equipment	$1,200,000	
Less accumulated depreciation	120,000	1,080,000
Total assets		$1,820,000

[continued on next page]

[continued from previous page]

Liabilities and Equity		
Accounts payable	$ 300,000	
Bank loan payable	20,000	
Taxes payable (due 3/15/2012)	200,000	
Total liabilities		$ 520,000
Common stock	1,500,000	
Retained earnings	(200,000)	
Total stockholders' equity		1,300,000
Total liabilities and equity		$1,820,000

To prepare a master budget for January, February, and March of 2012, management gathers the following information.

a. Oasis Corp.'s single product is purchased for $10 per unit and resold for $24 per unit. The expected inventory level of 18,000 units on December 31, 2011, is more than management's desired level for 2012, which is 40% of the next month's expected sales (in units). Expected sales are: January, 30,000 units; February, 24,000 units; March, 40,000 units; and April, 50,000 units.

b. Cash sales and credit sales represent 40% and 60%, respectively, of total sales. Of the credit sales, 70% is collected in the first month after the month of sale and 30% in the second month after the month of sale. For the $400,000 accounts receivable balance at December 31, 2011, $280,000 is collected in January 2012 and the remaining $120,000 is collected in February 2012.

c. Merchandise purchases are paid for as follows: 80% in the first month after the month of purchase and 20% in the second month after the month of purchase. For the $300,000 accounts payable balance at December 31, 2011, $240,000 is paid in January 2012 and the remaining $60,000 is paid in February 2012.

d. Sales commissions equal to 10% of sales are paid each month. Sales salaries (excluding commissions) are $288,000 per year.

e. General and administrative salaries are $336,000 per year. Maintenance expense equals $6,000 per month and is paid in cash.

f. Equipment reported in the December 31, 2011, balance sheet was purchased in January 2011. It is being depreciated over 10 years under the straight-line method with no salvage value. The following amounts for new equipment purchases are planned in the coming quarter: January, $240,000; February, $120,000; and March, $96,000. This equipment will be depreciated using the straight-line method over 10 years with no salvage value. A full month's depreciation is taken for the month in which equipment is purchased.

g. The company plans to acquire land at the end of March at a cost of $232,000, which will be paid with cash on the last day of the month.

h. Oasis Corp. has a working arrangement with its bank to obtain additional loans as needed. The interest rate is 12% per year, and interest is paid at each month-end based on the beginning balance. Partial or full payments on these loans can be made on the last day of the month. Oasis has agreed to maintain a minimum ending cash balance of $160,000 in each month.

i. The income tax rate for the company is 30%. Income taxes on the first quarter's income will not be paid until April 15.

Required

Prepare a master budget for each of the first three months of 2012; include the following component budgets (show supporting calculations as needed, and round amounts to the nearest dollar):

1. Monthly sales budgets (showing both budgeted unit sales and dollar sales).

2. Monthly merchandise purchases budgets.

3. Monthly selling expense budgets.

4. Monthly general and administrative expense budgets.

5. Monthly capital expenditures budgets.

6. Monthly cash budgets.

Check (2) Budgeted purchases: January, $216,000; February, $304,000;

(3) Budgeted selling expenses: January, $96,000; February, $81,600

(6) Ending cash bal.: January, $160,000; February, $281,578

7. Budgeted income statement for the entire first quarter (not for each month).

8. Budgeted balance sheet as of March 31, 2012.

RBI Company produces baseball bats. Each bat requires 4 pounds of aluminum alloy. Management predicts that 10,000 bats and 28,000 pounds of aluminum alloy will be in inventory on March 31 of the current year and that 100,000 bats will be sold during this year's second quarter. Management wants to end the second quarter with 3,000 finished bats and 2,000 pounds of aluminum alloy in inventory. Aluminum alloy can be purchased for $3 per pound.

Required

1. Prepare the second-quarter production budget for bats.

2. Prepare the second-quarter direct materials (aluminum alloy) budget; include the dollar cost of purchases.

Problem 23-6B[A]

Preparing production and direct materials budgets

C2 P3

Check (1) Units manuf., 93,000;
(2) Cost of aluminum purchases, $1,038,000

(8) Budgeted total assets at March 31, $2,768,880

(This serial problem began in Chapter 1 and continues through most of the book. If previous chapter segments were not completed, the serial problem can begin at this point. It is helpful, but not necessary, to use the Working Papers that accompany the book.)

SP 23 Santana Rey expects second quarter 2012 sales of her new line of computer furniture to be the same as the first quarter's sales (reported below) without any changes in strategy. Monthly sales averaged 40 desk units (sales price of $1,250) and 20 chairs (sales price of $500).

SERIAL PROBLEM
Business Solutions

P2

BUSINESS SOLUTIONS Segment Income Statement* For Quarter Ended March 31, 2012	
Sales[†]	$180,000
Cost of goods sold[‡]	115,000
Gross profit	65,000
Expenses	
Sales commissions (10%)	18,000
Advertising expenses	9,000
Other fixed expenses	18,000
Total expenses	45,000
Net income	$ 20,000

* Reflects revenue and expense activity only related to the computer furniture segment.

[†] Revenue: (120 desks × $1,250) + (60 chairs × $500) = $150,000 + $30,000 = $180,000

[‡] Cost of goods sold: (120 desks × $750) + (60 chairs × $250) + $10,000 = $115,000

Santana Rey believes that sales will increase each month for the next three months (April, 48 desks, 32 chairs; May, 52 desks, 35 chairs; June, 56 desks, 38 chairs) *if* selling prices are reduced to $1,150 for desks and $450 for chairs, and advertising expenses are increased by 10% and remain at that level for all three months. The products' variable cost will remain at $750 for desks and $250 for chairs. The sales staff will continue to earn a 10% commission, the fixed manufacturing costs per month will remain at $10,000 and other fixed expenses will remain at $6,000 per month.

Required

1. Prepare budgeted income statements for each of the months of April, May, and June that show the expected results from implementing the proposed changes. Use a three-column format, with one column for each month.

2. Use the budgeted income statements from part 1 to recommend whether Santana Rey should implement the proposed changes. Explain.

Check (1) Budgeted income (loss): April, $(660); May, $945

Beyond the Numbers

REPORTING IN ACTION

P2

RIM

BTN 23-1 Financial statements often serve as a starting point in formulating budgets. Review **Research In Motion**'s financial statements to determine its cash paid for acquisitions of property, plant and equipment in the current year and the budgeted cash needed for such acquisitions in the next year.

Required

1. Which financial statement reports the amount of cash paid for acquisitions of property, plant, and equipment? Explain where on the statement this information is reported.

2. Indicate the amount of cash (a) paid for acquisitions of property, plant, and equipment in the year ended February 27, 2010, and (b) to be paid (budgeted for) next year under the assumption that annual acquisitions of property, plant and equipment equal 60% of the prior year's net income.

Fast Forward

3. Access Research In Motion's financial statements for a year ending after February 27, 2010, from either its Website [RIM.com] or the SEC's EDGAR database [www.sec.gov]. Compare your answer for part 2 with actual cash paid for acquisitions of property, plant and equipment for that fiscal year. Compute the error, if any, in your estimate. Speculate as to why cash paid for acquisitions of property, plant and equipment was higher or lower than your estimate.

COMPARATIVE ANALYSIS

P2

RIM

Apple

BTN 23-2 One source of cash savings for a company is improved management of inventory. To illustrate, assume that **Research In Motion** and **Apple** both have $200,000 per month in sales of one model of handheld devices in Canada, and both forecast this level of sales per month for the next 24 months. Also assume that both Research In Motion and Apple have a 20% contribution margin and equal fixed costs, and that cost of goods sold is the only variable cost. Assume that the main difference between Research In Motion and Apple is the distribution system. Research In Motion uses a just-in-time system and requires ending inventory of only 10% of next month's sales in inventory at each month-end. However, Apple is building an improved distribution system and currently requires 40% of next month's sales in inventory at each month-end.

Required

1. Compute the amount by which Apple can reduce its inventory level if it can match Research In Motion's system of maintaining an inventory equal to 10% of next month's sales. (*Hint:* Focus on the facts given and only on the Canada area.)

2. Explain how the analysis in part 1 that shows ending inventory levels for both the 40% and 10% required inventory policies can help justify a just-in-time inventory system. You can assume a 15% interest cost for resources that are tied up in ending inventory.

ETHICS CHALLENGE

C1

BTN 23-3 Both the budget process and budgets themselves can impact management actions, both positively and negatively. For instance, a common practice among not-for-profit organizations and government agencies is for management to spend any amounts remaining in a budget at the end of the budget period, a practice often called "use it or lose it." The view is that if a department manager does not spend the budgeted amount, top management will reduce next year's budget by the amount not spent. To avoid losing budget dollars, department managers often spend all budgeted amounts regardless of the value added to products or services. All of us pay for the costs associated with this budget system.

Required

Write a one-half page report to a local not-for-profit organization or government agency offering a solution to the "use it or lose it" budgeting problem.

COMMUNICATING IN PRACTICE

C2

BTN 23-4 The sales budget is usually the first and most crucial of the component budgets in a master budget because all other budgets usually rely on it for planning purposes.

Required

Assume that your company's sales staff provides information on expected sales and selling prices for items making up the sales budget. Prepare a one-page memorandum to your supervisor outlining concerns with the sales staff's input in the sales budget when its compensation is at least partly tied to these budgets. More generally, explain the importance of assessing any potential bias in information provided to the budget process.

BTN 23-5 Access information on e-budgets through The Manage Mentor:
http://www.themanagementor.com/kuniverse/kmailers_universe/finance_kmailers/cfa/budgeting2.htm
Read the information provided.

TAKING IT TO THE NET
C1

Required

1. Assume the role of a senior manager in a large, multidivision company. What are the benefits of using e-budgets?
2. As a senior manager, what concerns do you have with the concept and application of e-budgets?

BTN 23-6 Your team is to prepare a budget report outlining the costs of attending college (full-time) for the next two semesters (30 hours) or three quarters (45 hours). This budget's focus is solely on attending college; do not include personal items in the team's budget. Your budget must include tuition, books, supplies, club fees, food, housing, and all costs associated with travel to and from college. This budgeting exercise is similar to the initial phase in activity-based budgeting. Include a list of any assumptions you use in completing the budget. Be prepared to present your budget in class.

TEAMWORK IN ACTION
A1

BTN 23-7 **Smathers and Branson** handcrafts needlepoint belts and other products. Company founders, Peter Smathers Carter and Austin Branson stress the importance of planning and budgeting.

ENTREPRENEURIAL DECISION
C1

Required

1. How can budgeting help the owners efficiently develop and operate their business?
2. Why would direct materials budgets and direct labor budgets be particularly important for a business like Smathers and Branson?

BTN 23-8 To help understand the factors impacting a sales budget, you are to visit three businesses with the same ownership or franchise membership. Record the selling prices of two identical products at each location, such as regular and premium gas sold at **Chevron** stations. You are likely to find a difference in prices for at least one of the three locations you visit.

HITTING THE ROAD
C2 P1

Required

1. Identify at least three external factors that must be considered when setting the sales budget. (*Note:* There is a difference between internal and external factors that impact the sales budget.)
2. What factors might explain any differences identified in the prices of the businesses you visited?

BTN 23-9 Access **Nokia's** income statement (www.Nokia.com) for the year ended December 31, 2009.

GLOBAL DECISION
P1

NOKIA

Required

1. Is Nokia's administrative and general expense budget likely to be an important budget in its master budgeting process? Explain.
2. Identify three types of expenses that would be reported as administrative and general expenses on Nokia's income statement.
3. Who likely has the initial responsibility for Nokia's administrative and general expense budget? Explain.

ANSWERS TO MULTIPLE CHOICE QUIZ

1. c
2. e; Budgeted purchases = $36,000 + $7,000 − $6,000 = $37,000
3. b; Cash collected = 25% of September sales + 75% of August sales = (0.25 × $240,000) + (0.75 × $220,000) = $225,000
4. d
5. a; 560 units + (0.30 × 600 units) − (0.30 × 560 units) = 572 units

24

Flexible Budgets and Standard Costs

A Look Back

Chapter 23 explained the master budget and its component budgets as well as their usefulness for planning and monitoring company activities.

A Look at This Chapter

This chapter describes flexible budgets, variance analysis, and standard costs. It explains how each is used for purposes of better controlling and monitoring of business activities.

A Look Ahead

Chapter 25 focuses on capital budgeting decisions. It also explains and illustrates several procedures used in evaluating short-term managerial decisions.

Learning Objectives

CAP

CONCEPTUAL

C1 Define *standard costs* and explain how standard cost information is useful for management by exception. (p. 995)

C2 Describe variances and what they reveal about performance. (p. 997)

ANALYTICAL

A1 Analyze changes in sales from expected amounts. (p. 1005)

LP24

PROCEDURAL

P1 Prepare a flexible budget and interpret a flexible budget performance report. (p. 992)

P2 Compute materials and labor variances. (p. 998)

P3 Compute overhead variances. (p. 1002)

P4 *Appendix 24A*—Prepare journal entries for standard costs and account for price and quantity variances. (p. 1012)

Behind the Curtains

"Don't back down . . . find ways to overcome problems"
—MEGAN DUCKETT

RANCHO DOMINGUEZ, CA—What do Kenny Chesney and Alice in Chains have in common? Both have played shows with custom backdrops and drapes sewed by Megan Duckett's company, **SewWhat? Inc. (SewWhatInc.com)** Megan's company has quickly become a top provider of customized stage curtains, drapes, and backdrops for the entertainment and special events industries, providing the "soft goods" for hard-edged clients like Green Day and Sonic Youth.

Founder Megan Duckett immigrated to the United States from Australia at age 19. Working as a technician for a concert production company, she started sewing in her spare time. Her first gig? Sewing fabric coffin linings for a Halloween show. "I rented a sewing machine and lined 10 coffins. I discovered I had an ability to sew, and I really enjoyed it," says Megan. The business stayed on the sidelines until Megan's husband Adam noticed she made more money "sewing on the kitchen table than at her 40-hour-per week commuter job." Megan boldly invested $2,000 in a small office and sewing machine and pursued her passion.

SewWhat? Inc. adheres to tight standards. As with many manufacturers, production problems can arise from materials, processes, or employees. Main drapes are made from cotton or synthetic material, and factors like light blockage, sound absorption, and budget are important in determining materials re-

quirements. Megan stresses the importance of "having exact specifications and controls to detect problems; we don't use any material that doesn't satisfy our requirements." As for process, the company monitors its sewing machines to ensure excessive wear does not impair production efficiency and product quality. Megan uses innovative software to guide production. "Our application calculates yardage and purchasing requirements and prints out sewing instructions both in Spanish and English. It allows us to standardize pricing," explains Megan. Employees have work quotas, and the company knows how much labor costs and how long projects should take.

Achieving high standards is the goal at SewWhat? Inc. "We've made a commitment to push ourselves in order to grow," says Megan. From modest beginnings at Megan's kitchen table, the company's sales have grown to over $4.6 million per year. Megan encourages entrepreneurs to "build a business around something you are good at and feel passionate about." After phenomenal successes with massive installations for recent Carrie Underwood and Rod Stewart tours, the company's future looks bright. Proclaims Megan, "Bring on the next one!"

[Sources: *SewWhat? Inc. Website*, January 2011; *Dell Website, Trailblazer Stories*, May 2010; *Inc.com*, May 2009; *Entreprenuer.com*, October 2007]

Budgeting helps organize and formalize management's planning activities. This chapter extends the study of budgeting to look more closely at the use of budgets to evaluate performance. Evaluations are important for controlling and monitoring business activities. This chapter also describes and illustrates the use of standard costs and variance analyses. These managerial tools are useful for both evaluating and controlling organizations and for the planning of future activities.

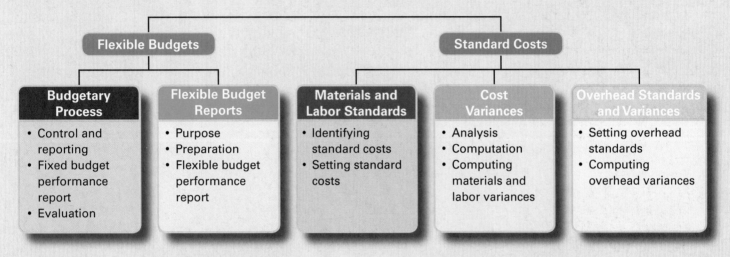

Flexible Budgets

Standard Costs

Budgetary Process	**Flexible Budget Reports**	**Materials and Labor Standards**	**Cost Variances**	**Overhead Standards and Variances**
• Control and reporting • Fixed budget performance report • Evaluation	• Purpose • Preparation • Flexible budget performance report	• Identifying standard costs • Setting standard costs	• Analysis • Computation • Computing materials and labor variances	• Setting overhead standards • Computing overhead variances

Section 1—Flexible Budgets

This section introduces fixed budgets and fixed budget performance reports. It then introduces flexible budgets and flexible budget performance reports and illustrates their advantages.

BUDGETARY PROCESS

A master budget reflects management's planned objectives for a future period. The preparation of a master budget is based on a predicted level of activity such as sales volume for the budget period. This section discusses the effects on the usefulness of budget reports when the actual level of activity differs from the predicted level.

Budgetary Control and Reporting

Budgetary control refers to management's use of budgets to monitor and control a company's operations. This includes using budgets to see that planned objectives are met. **Budget reports** contain relevant information that compares actual results to planned activities. This comparison is motivated by a need to both monitor performance and control activities. Budget reports are sometimes viewed as progress reports, or *report cards,* on management's performance in achieving planned objectives. These reports can be prepared at any time and for any period. Three common periods for a budget report are a month, quarter, and year.

Point: Budget reports are often used to determine bonuses of managers.

The budgetary control process involves at least four steps: (1) develop the budget from planned objectives, (2) compare actual results to budgeted amounts and analyze any differences, (3) take corrective and strategic actions, and (4) establish new planned objectives and prepare a new budget. Exhibit 24.1 shows this continual process of budgetary control. Budget reports and

EXHIBIT 24.1

Process of Budgetary Control

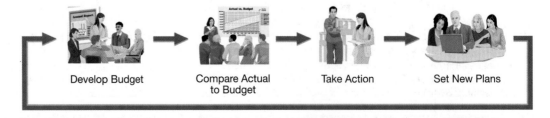

Develop Budget   Compare Actual to Budget   Take Action   Set New Plans

related documents are effective tools for managers to obtain the greatest benefits from this budgetary process.

Fixed Budget Performance Report

In a fixed budgetary control system, the master budget is based on a single prediction for sales volume or other activity level. The budgeted amount for each cost essentially assumes that a specific (or *fixed*) amount of sales will occur. A **fixed budget,** also called a *static budget,* is based on a single predicted amount of sales or other measure of activity.

One benefit of a budget is its usefulness in comparing actual results with planned activities. Information useful for analysis is often presented for comparison in a performance report. As shown in Exhibit 24.2, a **fixed budget performance report** for **Optel** compares actual results for January 2011 with the results expected under its fixed budget that predicted 10,000 (composite) units of sales. Optel manufactures inexpensive eyeglasses, frames, contact lens, and related supplies. For this report, its production volume equals sales volume (its inventory level did not change).

EXHIBIT 24.2

Fixed Budget Performance Report

OPTEL Fixed Budget Performance Report For Month Ended January 31, 2011	Fixed Budget	Actual Results	Variances*
Sales (in units)	10,000	12,000	
Sales (in dollars)	$100,000	$125,000	$25,000 F
Cost of goods sold			
Direct materials	10,000	13,000	3,000 U
Direct labor	15,000	20,000	5,000 U
Overhead			
Factory supplies	2,000	2,100	100 U
Utilities	3,000	4,000	1,000 U
Depreciation—machinery	8,000	8,000	0
Supervisory salaries	11,000	11,000	0
Selling expenses			
Sales commissions	9,000	10,800	1,800 U
Shipping expenses	4,000	4,300	300 U
General and administrative expenses			
Office supplies	5,000	5,200	200 U
Insurance expenses	1,000	1,200	200 U
Depreciation—office equipment	7,000	7,000	0
Administrative salaries	13,000	13,000	0
Total expenses	88,000	99,600	11,600 U
Income from operations	$ 12,000	$ 25,400	$13,400 F

* F = Favorable variance; U = Unfavorable variance.

This type of performance report designates differences between budgeted and actual results as variances. We see the letters *F* and *U* located beside the numbers in the third number column of this report. Their meanings are as follows:

F = **Favorable variance**   When compared to budget, the actual cost or revenue contributes to a *higher* income. That is, actual revenue is higher than budgeted revenue, or actual cost is lower than budgeted cost.

U = **Unfavorable variance**   When compared to budget, the actual cost or revenue contributes to a *lower* income; actual revenue is lower than budgeted revenue, or actual cost is higher than budgeted cost.

This convention is common in practice and is used throughout this chapter.

Example: How is it that the favorable sales variance in Exhibit 24.2 is linked with so many unfavorable cost and expense variances? *Answer:* Costs have increased with the increase in sales.

Budget Reports for Evaluation

A primary use of budget reports is as a tool for management to monitor and control operations. Evaluation by Optel management is likely to focus on a variety of questions that might include these:

- Why is actual income from operations $13,400 higher than budgeted?
- Are amounts paid for each expense item too high?
- Is manufacturing using too much direct material?
- Is manufacturing using too much direct labor?

The performance report in Exhibit 24.2 provides little help in answering these questions because actual sales volume is 2,000 units higher than budgeted. A manager does not know if this higher level of sales activity is the cause of variations in total dollar sales and expenses or if other factors have influenced these amounts. This inability of fixed budget reports to adjust for changes in activity levels is a major limitation of a fixed budget performance report. That is, it fails to show whether actual costs are out of line due to a change in actual sales volume or some other factor.

Green Budget   Budget reporting and evaluation are used at the **Environmental Protection Agency (EPA)**. It regularly prepares performance plans and budget requests that describe performance goals, measure outcomes, and analyze variances. ■

FLEXIBLE BUDGET REPORTS

Purpose of Flexible Budgets

To help address limitations with the fixed budget performance report, particularly from the effects of changes in sales volume, management can use a flexible budget. A **flexible budget,** also called a *variable budget,* is a report based on predicted amounts of revenues and expenses corresponding to the actual level of output. Flexible budgets are useful both before and after the period's activities are complete.

A flexible budget prepared before the period is often based on several levels of activity. Budgets for those different levels can provide a "what-if" look at operations. The different levels often include both a best case and worst case scenario. This allows management to make adjustments to avoid or lessen the effects of the worst case scenario.

A flexible budget prepared after the period helps management evaluate past performance. It is especially useful for such an evaluation because it reflects budgeted revenues and costs based on the actual level of activity. Thus, comparisons of actual results with budgeted performance are more likely to identify the causes of any differences. This can help managers focus attention on real problem areas and implement corrective actions. This is in contrast to a fixed budget, whose primary purpose is to assist managers in planning future activities and whose numbers are based on a single predicted amount of budgeted sales or production.

Point: A flexible budget yields an "apples to apples" comparison because budgeted activity levels are the same as the actual.

Preparation of Flexible Budgets

P1 Prepare a flexible budget and interpret a flexible budget performance report.

A flexible budget is designed to reveal the effects of volume of activity on revenues and costs. To prepare a flexible budget, management relies on the distinctions between fixed and variable costs. Recall that the cost per unit of activity remains constant for variable costs so that the total amount of a variable cost changes in direct proportion to a change in activity level. The total amount of fixed cost remains unchanged regardless of changes in the level of activity within a relevant (normal) operating range. (Assume that costs can be reasonably classified as variable or fixed within a relevant range.)

When we create the numbers constituting a flexible budget, we express each variable cost as either a constant amount per unit of sales or as a percent of a sales dollar. In the case of a fixed cost, we express its budgeted amount as the total amount expected to occur at any sales volume within the relevant range.

Exhibit 24.3 shows a set of flexible budgets for Optel for January 2011. Seven of its expenses are classified as variable costs. Its remaining five expenses are fixed costs. These classifications result from management's investigation of each expense. Variable and fixed expense categories are *not* the same for every company, and we must avoid drawing conclusions from specific cases. For example, depending on the nature of a company's operations, office supplies expense can be either fixed or variable with respect to sales.

Point: The usefulness of a flexible budget depends on valid classification of variable and fixed costs. Some costs are mixed and must be analyzed to determine their variable and fixed portions.

EXHIBIT 24.3

Flexible Budgets

			Flexible Budget			Flexible Budget for Unit Sales of 10,000	Flexible Budget for Unit Sales of 12,000	Flexible Budget for Unit Sales of 14,000
			Variable Amount per Unit	Total Fixed Cost				
Sales			$10.00			$100,000	$120,000	$140,000
Variable costs								
Direct materials			1.00			10,000	12,000	14,000
Direct labor			1.50			15,000	18,000	21,000
Factory supplies			0.20			2,000	2,400	2,800
Utilities			0.30			3,000	3,600	4,200
Sales commissions			0.90			9,000	10,800	12,600
Shipping expenses			0.40			4,000	4,800	5,600
Office supplies			0.50			5,000	6,000	7,000
Total variable costs			4.80			48,000	57,600	67,200
Contribution margin			$ 5.20			$ 52,000	$ 62,400	$ 72,800
Fixed costs								
Depreciation—machinery				$ 8,000		8,000	8,000	8,000
Supervisory salaries				11,000		11,000	11,000	11,000
Insurance expense				1,000		1,000	1,000	1,000
Depreciation—office equipment				7,000		7,000	7,000	7,000
Administrative salaries				13,000		13,000	13,000	13,000
Total fixed costs				$40,000		40,000	40,000	40,000
Income from operations						$ 12,000	$ 22,400	$ 32,800

OPTEL
Flexible Budgets
For Month Ended January 31, 2011

The layout for the flexible budgets in Exhibit 24.3 follows a *contribution margin format*—beginning with sales followed by variable costs and then fixed costs. Both the expected individual and total variable costs are reported and then subtracted from sales. The difference between sales and variable costs equals contribution margin. The expected amounts of fixed costs are listed next, followed by the expected income from operations before taxes.

Example: Using Exhibit 24.3, what is the budgeted income from operations for unit sales of (a) 11,000 and (b) 13,000? *Answers:* $17,200 for unit sales of 11,000; $27,600 for unit sales of 13,000.

The first and second number columns of Exhibit 24.3 show the flexible budget amounts for variable costs per unit and each fixed cost for any volume of sales in the relevant range. The third, fourth, and fifth columns show the flexible budget amounts computed for three different sales volumes. For instance, the third column's flexible budget is based on 10,000 units. These numbers are the same as those in the fixed budget of Exhibit 24.2 because the expected volumes are the same for these two budgets.

Recall that Optel's actual sales volume for January is 12,000 units. This sales volume is 2,000 units more than the 10,000 units originally predicted in the master budget. When differences between actual and predicted volume arise, the usefulness of a flexible budget is apparent. For instance, compare the flexible budget for 10,000 units in the third column (which is the same as the fixed budget in Exhibit 24.2) with the flexible budget for 12,000 units in the fourth

Point: Flexible budgeting allows a budget to be prepared at the *actual* output level. Performance reports are then prepared comparing the flexible budget to actual revenues and costs.

column. The higher levels for both sales and variable costs reflect nothing more than the increase in sales activity. Any budget analysis comparing actual with planned results that ignores this information is less useful to management.

To illustrate, when we evaluate Optel's performance, we need to prepare a flexible budget showing actual and budgeted values at 12,000 units. As part of a complete profitability analysis, managers could compare the actual income of $25,400 (from Exhibit 24.2) with the $22,400 income expected at the actual sales volume of 12,000 units (from Exhibit 24.3). This results in a total favorable income variance of $3,000 to be explained and interpreted. This variance is markedly lower from the $13,400 favorable variance identified in Exhibit 24.2 using a fixed budget, but still suggests good performance. After receiving the flexible budget based on January's actual volume, management must determine what caused this $3,000 difference. The next section describes a flexible budget performance report that provides guidance in this analysis.

■ Decision Maker   Answer — p. 1014

Entrepreneur   The heads of both the strategic consulting and tax consulting divisions of your financial services firm complain to you about the unfavorable variances on their performance reports. "We worked on more consulting assignments than planned. It's not surprising our costs are higher than expected. To top it off, this report characterizes our work as *poor!*" How do you respond? ■

Flexible Budget Performance Report

A **flexible budget performance report** lists differences between actual performance and budgeted performance based on actual sales volume or other activity level. This report helps direct management's attention to those costs or revenues that differ substantially from budgeted amounts. Exhibit 24.4 shows Optel's flexible budget performance report for January. We prepare this report after the actual volume is known to be 12,000 units. This report shows a $5,000 favorable variance in total dollar sales. Because actual and budgeted volumes are both 12,000 units, the $5,000 sales variance must have resulted from a higher than expected selling price.

EXHIBIT 24.4

Flexible Budget
Performance Report

OPTEL Flexible Budget Performance Report For Month Ended January 31, 2011	Flexible Budget	Actual Results	Variances*
Sales (12,000 units).....................	$120,000	$125,000	$5,000 F
Variable costs			
Direct materials	12,000	13,000	1,000 U
Direct labor	18,000	20,000	2,000 U
Factory supplies	2,400	2,100	300 F
Utilities	3,600	4,000	400 U
Sales commissions	10,800	10,800	0
Shipping expenses	4,800	4,300	500 F
Office supplies	6,000	5,200	800 F
Total variable costs	57,600	59,400	1,800 U
Contribution margin	62,400	65,600	3,200 F
Fixed costs			
Depreciation—machinery	8,000	8,000	0
Supervisory salaries	11,000	11,000	0
Insurance expense	1,000	1,200	200 U
Depreciation—office equipment	7,000	7,000	0
Administrative salaries	13,000	13,000	0
Total fixed costs	40,000	40,200	200 U
Income from operations	$ 22,400	$ 25,400	$3,000 F

* F = Favorable variance; U = Unfavorable variance.

Further analysis of the facts surrounding this $5,000 sales variance reveals a favorable sales variance per unit of nearly $0.42 as shown here:

Actual average price per unit (rounded to cents)	$125,000/12,000 = $10.42
Budgeted price per unit	$120,000/12,000 = 10.00
Favorable sales variance per unit	$5,000/12,000 = $ 0.42

The other variances in Exhibit 24.4 also direct management's attention to areas where corrective actions can help control Optel's operations. Each expense variance is analyzed as the sales variance was. We can think of each expense as the joint result of using a given number of units of input and paying a specific price per unit of input. Optel's expense variances total $2,000 unfavorable, suggesting poor control of some costs, particularly direct materials and direct labor.

Each variance in Exhibit 24.4 is due in part to a difference between *actual price* per unit of input and *budgeted price* per unit of input. This is a **price variance.** Each variance also can be due in part to a difference between *actual quantity* of input used and *budgeted quantity* of input. This is a **quantity variance.** We explain more about this breakdown, known as **variance analysis,** later in the standard costs section.

Quick Check   Answers — p. 1015

1. A flexible budget (*a*) shows fixed costs as constant amounts of cost per unit of activity, (*b*) shows variable costs as constant amounts of cost per unit of activity, or (*c*) is prepared based on one expected amount of budgeted sales or production.
2. What is the initial step in preparing a flexible budget?
3. What is the main difference between a fixed and a flexible budget?
4. What is the contribution margin?

Section 2—Standard Costs

Standard costs are preset costs for delivering a product or service under normal conditions. These costs are established by personnel, engineering, and accounting studies using past experiences and data. Management uses these costs to assess the reasonableness of actual costs incurred for producing the product or service. When actual costs vary from standard costs, management follows up to identify potential problems and take corrective actions. **Management by exception** means that managers focus attention on the most significant differences between actual costs and standard costs and give less attention to areas where performance is reasonably close to standard. Management by exception is especially useful when directed at controllable items, enabling top management to affect the actions of lower-level managers responsible for the company's revenues and costs.

C1 Define *standard costs* and explain how standard cost information is useful for management by exception.

Standard costs are often used in preparing budgets because they are the anticipated costs incurred under normal conditions. Terms such as *standard materials cost, standard labor cost,* and *standard overhead cost* are often used to refer to amounts budgeted for direct materials, direct labor, and overhead.

Point: Since standard costs are often budgeted costs, they can be used to prepare both fixed budgets and flexible budgets.

While many managers use standard costs to investigate manufacturing costs, standard costs can also help control *nonmanufacturing* costs. Companies providing services instead of products can also benefit from the use of standard costs. For example, while quality medical service is paramount, efficiency in providing that service is also important to medical professionals. The use of budgeting and standard costing is touted as an effective means to control and monitor medical costs, especially overhead.

Decision Ethics   Answer — p. 1014

Internal Auditor   You discover a manager who always spends exactly what is budgeted. About 30% of her budget is spent just before the period-end. She admits to spending what is budgeted, whether or not it is needed. She offers three reasons: (1) she doesn't want her budget cut, (2) "management by exception" focuses on budget deviations; and (3) she believes the money is budgeted to be spent. What action do you take? ■

MATERIALS AND LABOR STANDARDS

This section explains how to set materials and labor standards and how to prepare a standard cost card.

Identifying Standard Costs

Point: Business practice often uses the word *budget* when speaking of total amounts and *standard* when discussing per unit amounts.

Managerial accountants, engineers, personnel administrators, and other managers combine their efforts to set standard costs. To identify standards for direct labor costs, we can conduct time and motion studies for each labor operation in the process of providing a product or service. From these studies, management can learn the best way to perform the operation and then set the standard labor time required for the operation under normal conditions. Similarly, standards for materials are set by studying the quantity, grade, and cost of each material used. Standards for overhead costs are explained later in the chapter.

Example: What factors might be considered when deciding whether to revise standard costs? *Answer:* Changes in the processes and/or resources needed to carry out the processes.

Regardless of the care used in setting standard costs and in revising them as conditions change, actual costs frequently differ from standard costs, often as a result of one or more factors. For instance, the actual quantity of material used can differ from the standard, or the price paid per unit of material can differ from the standard. Quantity and price differences from standard amounts can also occur for labor. That is, the actual labor time and actual labor rate can vary from what was expected. The same analysis applies to overhead costs.

Decision Insight

Cruis'n Standards   The **Corvette** consists of hundreds of parts for which engineers set standards. Various types of labor are also involved in its production, including machining, assembly, painting, and welding, and standards are set for each. Actual results are periodically compared with standards to assess performance. ■

Setting Standard Costs

To illustrate the setting of a standard cost, we consider a professional league baseball bat manufactured by **ProBat.** Its engineers have determined that manufacturing one bat requires 0.90 kg. of high-grade wood. They also expect some loss of material as part of the process because of inefficiencies and waste. This results in adding an *allowance* of 0.10 kg., making the standard requirement 1.0 kg. of wood for each bat.

Point: Companies promoting continuous improvement strive to achieve ideal standards by eliminating inefficiencies and waste.

The 0.90 kg. portion is called an *ideal standard;* it is the quantity of material required if the process is 100% efficient without any loss or waste. Reality suggests that some loss of material usually occurs with any process. The standard of 1.0 kg. is known as the *practical standard,* the quantity of material required under normal application of the process.

High-grade wood can be purchased at a standard price of $25 per kg. The purchasing department sets this price as the expected price for the budget period. To determine this price, the purchasing department considers factors such as the quality of materials, future economic conditions, supply factors (shortages and excesses), and any available discounts. The engineers also decide that two hours of labor time (after including allowances) are required to manufacture a bat. The wage rate is $20 per hour (better than average skilled labor is required). ProBat assigns all overhead at the rate of $10 per labor hour. The standard costs of direct materials, direct labor, and overhead for one bat are shown in Exhibit 24.5 in what is called a *standard cost card.* These cost amounts are then used to prepare manufacturing budgets for a budgeted level of production.

EXHIBIT 24.5

Standard Cost Card

STANDARD COST CARD		
Production factor	**Cost factor**	**Total**
Direct materials (wood)	1 kg. @ $25 per kg.	$25
Direct labor	2 hours @ $20 per hour	40
Overhead	2 labor hours @ $10 per hour	20
	Total	**$85**

REMARKS:

Based on standard costs of direct materials, direct labor, and overhead for a single ProBat

SUMMARY:

Materials	$25
Labor	40
Overhead	20
Total cost	$85

COST VARIANCES

A **cost variance,** also simply called a *variance,* is the difference between actual and standard costs. A cost variance can be favorable or unfavorable. A variance from standard cost is considered favorable if actual cost is less than standard cost. It is considered unfavorable if actual cost is more than standard cost.[1] This section discusses variance analysis.

C2 Describe variances and what they reveal about performance.

Cost Variance Analysis

Variances are usually identified in performance reports. When a variance occurs, management wants to determine the factors causing it. This often involves analysis, evaluation, and explanation. The results of these efforts should enable management to assign responsibility for the variance and then to take actions to correct the situation.

To illustrate, ProBat's standard materials cost for producing 500 bats is $12,500. Assume that its actual materials cost for those 500 bats is $13,000. The $500 unfavorable variance raises questions that call for answers that, in turn, can lead to changes to correct the situation and eliminate this variance in the next period. A performance report often identifies the existence of a problem, but we must follow up with further investigation to see what can be done to improve future performance.

Exhibit 24.6 shows the flow of events in the effective management of variance analysis. It shows four steps: (1) preparing a standard cost performance report, (2) computing and analyzing variances, (3) identifying questions and their explanations, and (4) taking corrective and strategic actions. These variance analysis steps are interrelated and are frequently applied in good organizations.

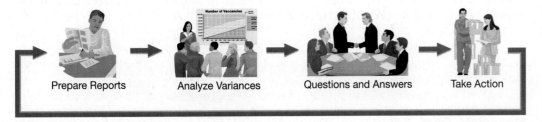

| Prepare Reports | Analyze Variances | Questions and Answers | Take Action |

EXHIBIT 24.6

Variance Analysis

Cost Variance Computation

Management needs information about the factors causing a cost variance, but first it must properly compute the variance. In its most simple form, a cost variance (CV) is computed as the difference between actual cost (AC) and standard cost (SC) as shown in Exhibit 24.7.

---

[1] Short-term favorable variances can sometimes lead to long-term unfavorable variances. For instance, if management spends less than the budgeted amount on maintenance or insurance, the performance report would show a favorable variance. Cutting these expenses can lead to major losses in the long run if machinery wears out prematurely or insurance coverage proves inadequate.

EXHIBIT 24.7

Cost Variance Formulas

> **Cost Variance (CV) = Actual Cost (AC) − Standard Cost (SC)**
> where:
> **Actual Cost (AC) = Actual Quantity (AQ) × Actual Price (AP)**
> **Standard Cost (SC) = Standard Quantity (SQ) × Standard Price (SP)**

A cost variance is further defined by its components. Actual quantity (AQ) is the input (material or labor) used to manufacture the quantity of output. Standard quantity (SQ) is the expected input for the quantity of output. Actual price (AP) is the amount paid to acquire the input (material or labor), and standard price (SP) is the expected price.

Point: Price and quantity variances for direct labor are nearly always referred to as *rate* and *efficiency variances*, respectively.

Two main factors cause a cost variance: (1) the difference between actual price and standard price results in a *price* (or rate) *variance* and (2) the difference between actual quantity and standard quantity results in a *quantity* (or usage or efficiency) *variance*. To assess the impacts of these two factors in a cost variance, we use the formulas in Exhibit 24.8.

EXHIBIT 24.8

Price Variance and Quantity Variance Formulas

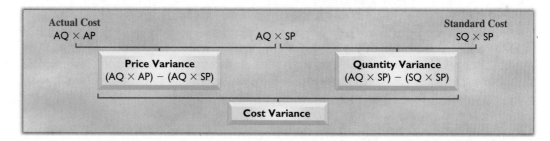

In computing a price variance, the quantity (actual) is held constant. In computing a quantity variance, the price (standard) is held constant. The cost variance, or total variance, is the sum of the price and quantity variances. These formulas identify the sources of the cost variance. Managers sometimes find it useful to apply an alternative (but equivalent) computation for the price and quantity variances as shown in Exhibit 24.9.

EXHIBIT 24.9

Alternative Price Variance and Quantity Variance Formulas

> **Price Variance (PV) = [Actual Price (AP) − Standard Price (SP)] × Actual Quantity (AQ)**
> **Quantity Variance (QV) = [Actual Quantity (AQ) − Standard Quantity (SQ)] × Standard Price (SP)**

The results from applying the formulas in Exhibits 24.8 and 24.9 are identical.

Computing Materials and Labor Variances

P2 Compute materials and labor variances.

We illustrate the computation of the materials and labor cost variances using data from **G-Max,** a company that makes specialty golf equipment and accessories for individual customers. This company has set the following standard quantities and costs for materials and labor per unit for one of its hand-crafted golf clubheads:

Direct materials (0.5 lb. per unit at $20 per lb.)	$10.00
Direct labor (1 hr. per unit at $8 per hr.)	8.00
Total standard direct cost per unit	$18.00

Materials Cost Variances   During May 2011, G-Max budgeted to produce 4,000 clubheads (units). It actually produced only 3,500 units. It used 1,800 pounds of direct materials (titanium) costing $21.00 per pound, meaning its total materials cost was $37,800. This information allows us to compute both actual and standard direct materials costs for G-Max's 3,500 units and its direct materials cost variance as follows:

Actual cost	1,800 lbs. @ $21.00 per lb. =	$37,800
Standard cost	1,750 lbs. @ $20.00 per lb. =	35,000
Direct materials cost variance (unfavorable)	=	$ 2,800

To better isolate the causes of this $2,800 unfavorable total direct materials cost variance, the materials price and quantity variances for these G-Max clubheads are computed and shown in Exhibit 24.10.

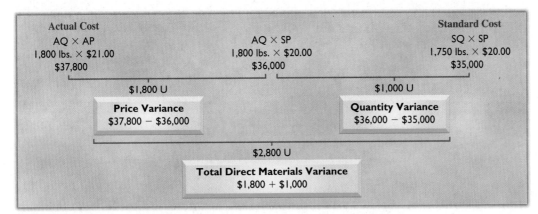

EXHIBIT 24.10

Materials Price and Quantity Variances*

*AQ is actual quantity; AP is actual price; SP is standard price; SQ is standard quantity allowed for actual output.

The $1,800 unfavorable price variance results from paying $1 more per unit than the standard price, computed as 1,800 lbs. × $1. The $1,000 unfavorable quantity variance is due to using 50 lbs. more materials than the standard quantity, computed as 50 lbs. × $20. The total direct materials variance is $2,800 and it is unfavorable. This information allows management to ask the responsible individuals for explanations and corrective actions.

The purchasing department is usually responsible for the price paid for materials. Responsibility for explaining the price variance in this case rests with the purchasing manager if a price higher than standard caused the variance. The production department is usually responsible for the amount of material used and in this case is responsible for explaining why the process used more than the standard amount of materials.

Variance analysis presents challenges. For instance, the production department could have used more than the standard amount of material because its quality did not meet specifications and led to excessive waste. In this case, the purchasing manager is responsible for explaining why inferior materials were acquired. However, the production manager is responsible for explaining what happened if analysis shows that waste was due to inefficiencies, not poor quality material.

In evaluating price variances, managers must recognize that a favorable price variance can indicate a problem with poor product quality. **Redhook Ale**, a micro brewery in the Pacific Northwest, can probably save 10% to 15% in material prices by buying six-row barley malt instead of the better two-row from Washington's Yakima valley. Attention to quality, however, has helped Redhook Ale become the first craft brewer to be kosher certified. Redhook's purchasing activities are judged on both the quality of the materials and the purchase price variance.

Example: Identify at least two factors that might have caused the unfavorable quantity variance and the unfavorable price variance in Exhibit 24.10. *Answer:* Poor quality materials or untrained workers for the former; poor price negotiation or higher-quality materials for the latter.

Labor Cost Variances   Labor cost for a specific product or service depends on the number of hours worked (quantity) and the wage rate paid to employees (price). When actual amounts for a task differ from standard, the labor cost variance can be divided into a rate (price) variance and an efficiency (quantity) variance.

To illustrate, G-Max's direct labor standard for 3,500 units of its hand-crafted clubheads is one hour per unit, or 3,500 hours at $8 per hour. Since only 3,400 hours at $8.30 per hour were actually used to complete the units, the actual and standard labor costs are

Actual cost	3,400 hrs. @ $8.30 per hr.	= $28,220
Standard cost	3,500 hrs. @ $8.00 per hr.	= 28,000
Direct labor cost variance (unfavorable)		= $ 220

This analysis shows that actual cost is merely $220 over the standard and suggests no immediate concern. Computing both the labor rate and efficiency variances reveals a different picture, however, as shown in Exhibit 24.11.

EXHIBIT 24.11

Labor Rate and
Efficiency Variances*

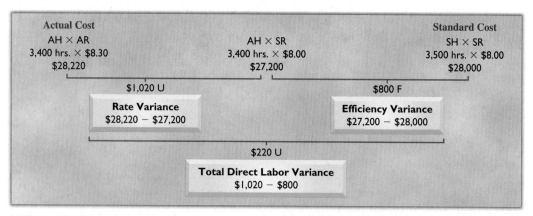

* AH is actual direct labor hours: AR is actual wage rate; SH is standard direct labor hours allowed for actual output; SR is standard wage rate.

Example: Compute the rate variance and the efficiency variance for Exhibit 24.11 if 3,700 actual hours are used at an actual price of $7.50 per hour. *Answer:* $1,850 favorable labor rate variance and $1,600 unfavorable labor efficiency variance.

The analysis in Exhibit 24.11 shows that an $800 favorable efficiency variance results from using 100 fewer direct labor hours than standard for the units produced, but this favorable variance is more than offset by a wage rate that is $0.30 per hour higher than standard. The personnel administrator or the production manager needs to explain why the wage rate is higher than expected. The production manager should also explain how the labor hours were reduced. If this experience can be repeated and transferred to other departments, more savings are possible.

One possible explanation of these labor rate and efficiency variances is the use of workers with different skill levels. If this is the reason, senior management must discuss the implications with the production manager who has the responsibility to assign workers to tasks with the appropriate skill level. In this case, an investigation might show that higher-skilled workers were used to produce 3,500 units of hand-crafted clubheads. As a result, fewer labor hours might be required for the work, but the wage rate paid these workers is higher than standard because of their greater skills. The effect of this strategy is a higher than standard total cost, which would require actions to remedy the situation or adjust the standard.

Decision Maker   Answer — p. 1014

Human Resource Manager   You receive the manufacturing variance report for June and discover a large unfavorable labor efficiency (quantity) variance. What factors do you investigate to identify its possible causes? ∎

Quick Check   Answers — p. 1015

5. A standard cost (a) changes in direct proportion to changes in the level of activity, (b) is an amount incurred at the actual level of production for the period, or (c) is an amount incurred under normal conditions to provide a product or service.

6. What is a cost variance?

7. The following information is available for York Company.

Actual direct labor hours per unit	2.5 hours
Standard direct labor hours per unit	2.0 hours
Actual production (units)	2,500 units
Budgeted production (units)	3,000 units
Actual rate per hour	$3.10
Standard rate per hour	$3.00

The labor efficiency variance is (a) $3,750 U, (b) $3,750 F, or (c) $3,875 U.

8. Refer to Quick Check 7; the labor rate variance is (a) $625 F or (b) $625 U.

9. If a materials quantity variance is favorable and a materials price variance is unfavorable, can the total materials cost variance be favorable?

OVERHEAD STANDARDS AND VARIANCES

When standard costs are used, a predetermined overhead rate is used to assign standard overhead costs to products or services produced. This predetermined rate is often based on some overhead allocation base (such as standard labor cost, standard labor hours, or standard machine hours).

Setting Overhead Standards

Standard overhead costs are the amounts expected to occur at a certain activity level. Unlike direct materials and direct labor, overhead includes fixed costs and variable costs. This results in the average overhead cost per unit changing as the predicted volume changes. Since standard costs are also budgeted costs, they must be established before the reporting period begins. Standard overhead costs are therefore average per unit costs based on the predicted activity level.

To establish the standard overhead cost rate, management uses the same cost structure it used to construct a flexible budget at the end of a period. This cost structure identifies the different overhead cost components and classifies them as variable or fixed. To get the standard overhead rate, management selects a level of activity (volume) and predicts total overhead cost. It then divides this total by the allocation base to get the standard rate. Standard direct labor hours expected to be used to produce the predicted volume is a common allocation base and is used in this section.

Point: With increased automation, machine hours are frequently used in applying overhead instead of labor hours.

To illustrate, Exhibit 24.12 shows the overhead cost structure used to develop G-Max's flexible overhead budgets for May 2011. The predetermined standard overhead rate for May is set before the month begins. The first two number columns list the per unit amounts of variable costs and the monthly amounts of fixed costs. The four right-most columns show the costs expected to occur at four different levels of production activity. The predetermined overhead rate per labor hour is smaller as volume of activity increases because total fixed costs remain constant.

EXHIBIT 24.12

Flexible Overhead Budgets

G-MAX Flexible Overhead Budgets For Month Ended May 31, 2011	Variable Amount per Unit	Total Fixed Cost	Flexible Budget at 70% Capacity	Flexible Budget at 80% Capacity	Flexible Budget at 90% Capacity	Flexible Budget at 100% Capacity
Production (in units)	1 unit		3,500	4,000	4,500	5,000
Factory overhead						
Variable costs						
Indirect labor	$0.40/unit		$1,400	$1,600	$1,800	$2,000
Indirect materials	0.30/unit		1,050	1,200	1,350	1,500
Power and lights	0.20/unit		700	800	900	1,000
Maintenance	0.10/unit		350	400	450	500
Total variable overhead costs	$1.00/unit		3,500	4,000	4,500	5,000
Fixed costs (per month)						
Building rent		$1,000	1,000	1,000	1,000	1,000
Depreciation—machinery		1,200	1,200	1,200	1,200	1,200
Supervisory salaries		1,800	1,800	1,800	1,800	1,800
Total fixed overhead costs		$4,000	4,000	4,000	4,000	4,000
Total factory overhead			$7,500	$8,000	$8,500	$9,000
Standard direct labor hours 1 hr./unit . .			3,500 hrs.	4,000 hrs.	4,500 hrs.	5,000 hrs.
Predetermined overhead rate per standard direct labor hour			$ 2.14	$ 2.00	$ 1.89	$ 1.80

G-Max managers predicted an 80% activity level for May, or a production volume of 4,000 clubheads. At this volume, they budget $8,000 as the May total overhead. This choice implies a $2 per unit (labor hour) average overhead cost ($8,000/4,000 units). Since G-Max has a standard of one direct labor hour per unit, the predetermined standard overhead rate for May is $2 per standard direct labor hour. The variable overhead rate remains constant at $1 per direct labor hour regardless of the budgeted production level. The fixed overhead rate changes according to the budgeted production volume. For instance, for the predicted level of 4,000 units of production, the fixed rate is $1 per hour ($4,000 fixed costs/4,000 units). For a production level of 5,000 units, however, the fixed rate is $0.80 per hour ($4,000 fixed costs/5,000 units).

When choosing the predicted activity level, management considers many factors. The level can be set as high as 100% of capacity, but this is rare. Factors causing the activity level to be less than full capacity include difficulties in scheduling work, equipment under repair or maintenance, and insufficient product demand. Good long-run management practices often call for some plant capacity in excess of current operating needs to allow for special opportunities and demand changes.

Decision Insight

Measuring Up   In the spirit of continuous improvement, competitors compare their processes and performance standards against benchmarks established by industry leaders. Those that use **benchmarking** include Precision Lube, Jiffy Lube, All Tune and Lube, and Speedee Oil Change and Tune-Up. ■

Total Overhead Cost Variance

P3 Compute overhead variances.

EXHIBIT 24.13

Overhead Cost Variance

When standard costs are used, the cost accounting system applies overhead to the good units produced using the predetermined standard overhead rate. At period-end, the difference between the total overhead cost applied to products and the total overhead cost actually incurred is called an **overhead cost variance** (total overhead variance), which is defined in Exhibit 24.13.

> **Overhead cost variance (OCV) = Actual overhead incurred (AOI) − Standard overhead applied (SOA)**

The standard overhead applied is based on the predetermined overhead rate and the standard number of hours that should have been used, based on the actual production. To illustrate, G-Max produced 3,500 units during the month, which should have used 3,500 direct labor hours. From Exhibit 24.12, G-Max's predetermined overhead rate at the predicted capacity level of 4,000 units was $2.00 per direct labor hour, so the standard overhead applied is $7,000 (computed as 3,500 × $2.00). Additional data from cost reports show that the actual overhead cost incurred in the month is $7,650. G-Max's total overhead variance is thus $650, computed as $7,650 − $7,000. This variance is unfavorable, as G-Max's actual overhead was higher than it should have been based on budgeted amounts.

Controllable and Volume Variances   To help identify factors causing the overhead cost variance, managers analyze this variance separately for controllable and volume variances, as illustrated in Exhibit 24.14. The results provide information useful for taking strategic actions to improve company performance.

EXHIBIT 24.14

Framework for Understanding Total Overhead Variance

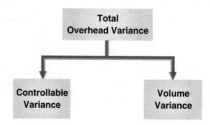

The **controllable variance** is the difference between actual overhead costs incurred and the budgeted overhead costs based on a flexible budget. The controllable variance is so named because it refers to activities usually under management control. A **volume variance** occurs when there is a difference between the actual volume of production and the standard volume of production. The budgeted fixed overhead amount is the same regardless of the volume of production (within the relevant range). This budgeted amount is computed based on the standard direct labor hours that the budgeted production volume allows. The applied fixed overhead is based, however, on the standard direct labor hours allowed for the actual volume of production, using the flexible budget. When a company operates at a capacity different from what it expected, the volume variance will differ from zero.

Returning to the G-Max data, the flexible budget in Exhibit 24.12 shows budgeted factory overhead of $7,500 at the production volume of 3,500 units during the month. The controllable variance is then computed as:

Actual total overhead (given)	$7,650
Applied total overhead (from flexible budget)	7,500
Controllable variance (unfavorable)	$ 150

We then compute the volume variance. It is important to note that the volume variance is based solely on *fixed* overhead. G-Max's budgeted fixed overhead at the predicted capacity level for the month was $4,000. Recall from Exhibit 24.12 that G-Max's predetermined fixed overhead at the predicted capacity level of 4,000 units was $1 per hour. Thus, G-Max's applied fixed overhead was $3,500, computed as 3,500 units × $1.00 per unit. G-Max's volume variance is then computed as:

Budgeted fixed overhead (at predicted capacity)	$4,000
Applied fixed overhead (3,500 × $1.00)	3,500
Volume variance (unfavorable)	$ 500

Analyzing Controllable and Volume Variances How should the top management of G-Max interpret the unfavorable controllable and volume variances? An unfavorable volume variance implies that the company did not reach its predicted operating level. In this case, 80% of manufacturing capacity was budgeted but only 70% was used. Management needs to know why the actual level of production differs from the expected level. The main purpose of the volume variance is to identify what portion of the total overhead variance is caused by failing to meet the expected production level. Often the reasons for failing to meet this expected production level are due to factors, for example customer demand, that are beyond employees' control. This information permits management to focus on explanations for the controllable variance, as we discuss next.

Overhead Variance Reports To help management isolate the reasons for the $150 unfavorable controllable variance, an *overhead variance report* can be prepared. A complete overhead variance report provides managers information about specific overhead costs and how they differ from budgeted amounts. Exhibit 24.15 shows G-Max's overhead variance report for May. It reveals that (1) fixed costs and maintenance costs were incurred as expected, (2) costs for indirect labor and power and lights were higher than expected, and (3) indirect materials cost was less than expected.

"Well, according to the books, you've got too much overhead."

EXHIBIT 24.15

Overhead Variance Report

G-MAX
Overhead Variance Report
For Month Ended May 31, 2011

Volume Variance

Expected production level	80% of capacity	
Production level achieved.	70% of capacity	
Volume variance	$500 (unfavorable)	

Controllable Variance	Flexible Budget	Actual Results	Variances*
Variable overhead costs			
Indirect labor	$1,400	$1,525	$125 U
Indirect materials	1,050	1,025	25 F
Power and lights	700	750	50 U
Maintenance	350	350	0
Total variable overhead costs	3,500	3,650	150 U
Fixed overhead costs			
Building rent	1,000	1,000	0
Depreciation—machinery	1,200	1,200	0
Supervisory salaries	1,800	1,800	0
Total fixed overhead costs	4,000	4,000	0
Total overhead costs	$7,500	$7,650	$150 U

* F = Favorable variance; U = Unfavorable variance.

    The total controllable variance amount is also readily available from Exhibit 24.15. The overhead variance report shows the total volume variance as $500 unfavorable (shown at the top) and the $150 unfavorable controllable variance (reported at the bottom right). The sum of the controllable variance and the volume variance equals the total overhead variance of $650 unfavorable.

    Appendix 24A describes an expanded analysis of overhead variances.

Quick Check   Answers – p. 1015

10. Under what conditions is an overhead volume variance considered favorable?

11. To use management by exception, a company (a) need not study fixed overhead variances, (b) should compute variances from flexible budget amounts to allow management to focus its attention on significant differences between actual and budgeted results, or (c) should analyze only variances for direct materials and direct labor.

GLOBAL VIEW

    BMW, a German automobile manufacturer, uses concepts of standard costing and variance analysis. Production begins with huge rolls of steel and aluminum, which are then cut and pressed by large machines. Material must meet high quality standards, and the company sets standards for each of its machine operations. In the Assembly department, highly-trained employees complete the assembly of the painted car chassis, often to customer specifications. Again, BMW sets standards for how much labor should be used and monitors its employee performance.

Sales Variances   **Decision Analysis**

This chapter explained the computation and analysis of cost variances. A similar variance analysis can be applied to sales. To illustrate, consider the following sales data from G-Max for two of its golf products, Excel golf balls and Big Bert® drivers.

A1 Analyze changes in sales from expected amounts.

	Budgeted	Actual
Sales of Excel golf balls (units)	1,000 units	1,100 units
Sales price per Excel golf ball.	$10	$10.50
Sales of Big Bert® drivers (units)	150 units	140 units
Sales price per Big Bert® driver.	$200	$190

Using this information, we compute both the *sales price variance* and the *sales volume variance* as shown in Exhibit 24.16. The total sales price variance is $850 unfavorable, and the total sales volume variance is $1,000 unfavorable. Neither total variance implies anything positive about these two products. However, further analysis of these total sales variances reveals that both the sales price and sales volume variances for Excel golf balls are favorable, meaning that both the unfavorable total sales price variance and the unfavorable total sales volume variance are due to the Big Bert driver.

EXHIBIT 24.16

Computing Sales Variances*

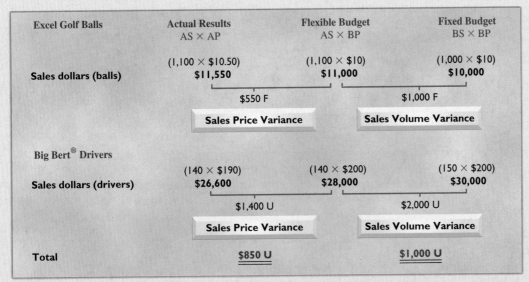

* AS = actual sales units; AP = actual sales price; BP = budgeted sales price; BS = budgeted sales units (fixed budget).

Managers use sales variances for planning and control purposes. The sales variance information is used to plan future actions to avoid unfavorable variances. G-Max sold 90 total combined units (both balls and drivers) more than planned, but these 90 units were not sold in the proportion budgeted. G-Max sold fewer than the budgeted quantity of the higher-priced driver, which contributed to the unfavorable total sales variances. Managers use such detail to question what caused the company to sell more golf balls and fewer drivers. Managers also use this information to evaluate and even reward their salespeople. Extra compensation is paid to salespeople who contribute to a higher profit margin. Finally, with multiple products, the sales volume variance can be separated into a *sales mix variance* and a *sales quantity variance*. The sales mix variance is the difference between the actual and budgeted sales mix of the products. The sales quantity variance is the difference between the total actual and total budgeted quantity of units sold.

Decision Maker   Answer — p. 1014

Sales Manager   The current performance report reveals a large favorable sales volume variance but an unfavorable sales price variance. You did not expect to see a large increase in sales volume. What steps do you take to analyze this situation? ■

DEMONSTRATION PROBLEM

Pacific Company provides the following information about its budgeted and actual results for June 2011. Although the expected June volume was 25,000 units produced and sold, the company actually produced and sold 27,000 units as detailed here:

	Budget (25,000 units)	Actual (27,000 units)
Selling price	$5.00 per unit	$5.23 per unit
Variable costs (per unit)		
Direct materials........................	1.24 per unit	1.12 per unit
Direct labor	1.50 per unit	1.40 per unit
Factory supplies*.......................	0.25 per unit	0.37 per unit
Utilities*...............................	0.50 per unit	0.60 per unit
Selling costs	0.40 per unit	0.34 per unit
Fixed costs (per month)		
Depreciation—machinery*...............	$3,750	$3,710
Depreciation—building*	2,500	2,500
General liability insurance	1,200	1,250
Property taxes on office equipment	500	485
Other administrative expense..............	750	900

* Indicates factory overhead item; $0.75 per unit or $3 per direct labor hour for variable overhead, and $0.25 per unit or $1 per direct labor hour for fixed overhead.

Standard costs based on expected output of 25,000 units

	Per Unit of Output	Quantity to Be Used	Total Cost
Direct materials, 4 oz. @ $0.31/oz...........	$1.24/unit	100,000 oz.	$31,000
Direct labor, 0.25 hrs. @ $6.00/hr.	1.50/unit	6,250 hrs.	37,500
Overhead.............................	1.00/unit		25,000

Actual costs incurred to produce 27,000 units

	Per Unit of Output	Quantity Used	Total Cost
Direct materials, 4 oz. @ $0.28/oz...........	$1.12/unit	108,000 oz.	$30,240
Direct labor, 0.20 hrs. @ $7.00/hr.	1.40/unit	5,400 hrs.	37,800
Overhead.............................	1.20/unit		32,400

Standard costs based on expected output of 27,000 units

	Per Unit of Output	Quantity to Be Used	Total Cost
Direct materials, 4 oz. @ $0.31/oz...........	$1.24/unit	108,000 oz.	$33,480
Direct labor, 0.25 hrs. @ $6.00/hr.	1.50/unit	6,750 hrs.	40,500
Overhead.............................			26,500

Required

1. Prepare June flexible budgets showing expected sales, costs, and net income assuming 20,000, 25,000, and 30,000 units of output produced and sold.

2. Prepare a flexible budget performance report that compares actual results with the amounts budgeted if the actual volume had been expected.

3. Apply variance analysis for direct materials and direct labor.

4. Compute the total overhead variance, and the controllable and volume variances.

5. Compute spending and efficiency variances for overhead. (Refer to Appendix 24A.)

6. Prepare journal entries to record standard costs, and price and quantity variances, for direct materials, direct labor, and factory overhead. (Refer to Appendix 24A.)

PLANNING THE SOLUTION

- Prepare a table showing the expected results at the three specified levels of output. Compute the variable costs by multiplying the per unit variable costs by the expected volumes. Include fixed costs at the given amounts. Combine the amounts in the table to show total variable costs, contribution margin, total fixed costs, and income from operations.

- Prepare a table showing the actual results and the amounts that should be incurred at 27,000 units. Show any differences in the third column and label them with an *F* for favorable if they increase income or a *U* for unfavorable if they decrease income.

- Using the chapter's format, compute these total variances and the individual variances requested:
  - Total materials variance (including the direct materials quantity variance and the direct materials price variance).
  - Total direct labor variance (including the direct labor efficiency variance and rate variance).
  - Total overhead variance (including both controllable and volume overhead variances and their component variances).

SOLUTION TO DEMONSTRATION PROBLEM

1.

PACIFIC COMPANY
Flexible Budgets
For Month Ended June 30, 2011

	Flexible Budget		Flexible Budget for Unit Sales of 20,000	Flexible Budget for Unit Sales of 25,000	Flexible Budget for Unit Sales of 30,000
	Variable Amount per Unit	Total Fixed Cost			
Sales	$5.00		$100,000	$125,000	$150,000
Variable costs					
Direct materials.....................	1.24		24,800	31,000	37,200
Direct labor	1.50		30,000	37,500	45,000
Factory supplies	0.25		5,000	6,250	7,500
Utilities	0.50		10,000	12,500	15,000
Selling costs	0.40		8,000	10,000	12,000
Total variable costs	3.89		77,800	97,250	116,700
Contribution margin	$1.11		22,200	27,750	33,300
Fixed costs					
Depreciation—machinery		$3,750	3,750	3,750	3,750
Depreciation—building		2,500	2,500	2,500	2,500
General liability insurance		1,200	1,200	1,200	1,200
Property taxes on office equipment		500	500	500	500
Other administrative expense		750	750	750	750
Total fixed costs		$8,700	8,700	8,700	8,700
Income from operations			$ 13,500	$ 19,050	$ 24,600

2.

PACIFIC COMPANY Flexible Budget Performance Report For Month Ended June 30, 2011			
	Flexible Budget	Actual Results	Variance*
Sales (27,000 units)	$135,000	$141,210	$6,210 F
Variable costs			
Direct materials	33,480	30,240	3,240 F
Direct labor	40,500	37,800	2,700 F
Factory supplies	6,750	9,990	3,240 U
Utilities.	13,500	16,200	2,700 U
Selling costs	10,800	9,180	1,620 F
Total variable costs	105,030	103,410	1,620 F
Contribution margin	29,970	37,800	7,830 F
Fixed costs			
Depreciation—machinery	3,750	3,710	40 F
Depreciation—building	2,500	2,500	0
General liability insurance	1,200	1,250	50 U
Property taxes on office equipment	500	485	15 F
Other administrative expense	750	900	150 U
Total fixed costs	8,700	8,845	145 U
Income from operations	$ 21,270	$ 28,955	$7,685 F

* F = Favorable variance; U = Unfavorable variance.

3. Variance analysis of materials and labor costs.

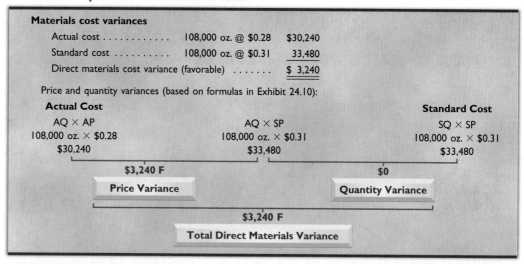

Materials cost variances

Actual cost	108,000 oz. @ $0.28	$30,240
Standard cost	108,000 oz. @ $0.31	33,480
Direct materials cost variance (favorable)	$ 3,240

Price and quantity variances (based on formulas in Exhibit 24.10):

Actual Cost
AQ × AP
108,000 oz. × $0.28
$30,240

AQ × SP
108,000 oz. × $0.31
$33,480

Standard Cost
SQ × SP
108,000 oz. × $0.31
$33,480

$3,240 F → **Price Variance**
$0 → **Quantity Variance**

$3,240 F
Total Direct Materials Variance

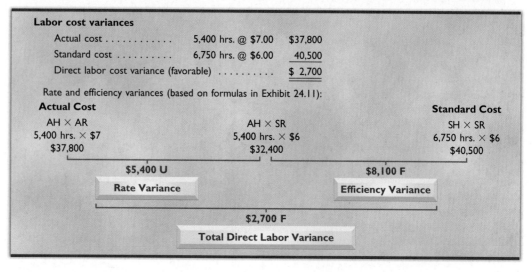

Labor cost variances

Actual cost	5,400 hrs. @ $7.00	$37,800
Standard cost	6,750 hrs. @ $6.00	40,500
Direct labor cost variance (favorable)	$ 2,700

Rate and efficiency variances (based on formulas in Exhibit 24.11):

Actual Cost
AH × AR
5,400 hrs. × $7
$37,800

AH × SR
5,400 hrs. × $6
$32,400

Standard Cost
SH × SR
6,750 hrs. × $6
$40,500

$5,400 U → **Rate Variance**
$8,100 F → **Efficiency Variance**

$2,700 F
Total Direct Labor Variance

4. Total, controllable, and volume variances for overhead.

Overhead cost variances			
Total overhead cost incurred	27,000 units @ $1.20	$32,400	
Total overhead applied	27,000 units @ $1.00	27,000	
Overhead cost variance (unfavorable)		$ 5,400	
Controllable variance			
Actual overhead (given)		$32,400	
Applied overhead (from flexible budget for 27,000 units)		26,500	
Controllable variance (unfavorable)		$ 5,900	
Volume variance			
Budgeted fixed overhead (at predicted capacity)		$ 6,250	
Applied fixed overhead (6,750 × $1.00)		6,750	
Volume variance (favorable)		$ 500	

5. Variable and fixed overhead spending and efficiency variances.

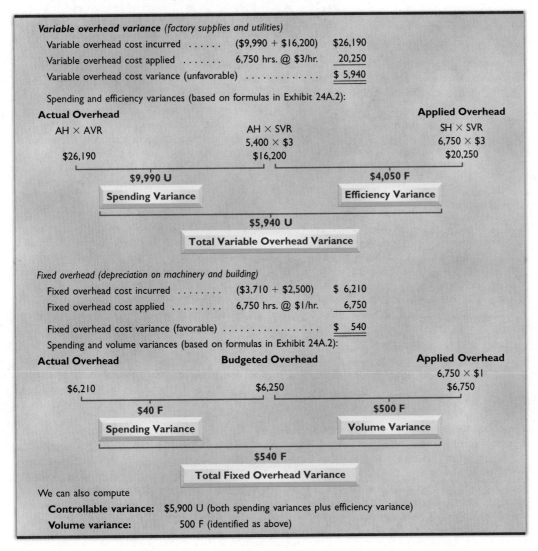

We can also compute

Controllable variance: $5,900 U (both spending variances plus efficiency variance)

Volume variance: 500 F (identified as above)

6.

Goods in Process Inventory	33,480	
Direct Materials Price Variance		3,240
Raw Materials Inventory		30,240
Goods in Process Inventory	40,500	
Direct Labor Rate Variance	5,400	
Direct Labor Efficiency Variance		8,100
Factory Payroll............................		37,800
Goods in Process Inventory*	27,000	
Variable Overhead Spending Variance	9,990	
Variable Overhead Efficiency Variance		4,050
Fixed Overhead Spending Variance		40
Fixed Overhead Volume Variance		500
Factory Overhead†........................		32,400

* $20,250 + $6,750   †$26,190 + $6,210

24A

Expanded Overhead Variances and Standard Cost Accounting System

Expanded Overhead Variances   Similar to analysis of direct materials and direct labor, overhead variances can be more completely analyzed. Exhibit 24A.1 shows an expanded framework for understanding these component overhead variances. This framework uses classifications of overhead costs as either variable or fixed. A **spending variance** occurs when management pays an amount different than the standard price to acquire an item. For instance, the actual wage rate paid to indirect labor might be higher than the standard rate. Similarly, actual supervisory salaries might be different than expected. Spending variances such as these cause management to investigate the reasons that the amount paid differs from the standard. Both variable and fixed overhead costs can yield their own spending variances. Analyzing variable overhead includes computing an **efficiency variance,** which occurs when standard direct labor hours (the allocation base) expected for actual production differ from the actual direct labor hours used. This efficiency variance reflects on the cost-effectiveness in using the overhead allocation base (such as direct labor).

Exhibit 24A.1 shows that we can combine the variable overhead spending variance, the fixed overhead spending variance, and the variable overhead efficiency variance to get the controllable variance.

EXHIBIT 24A.1

Expanded Framework for Total Overhead Variance

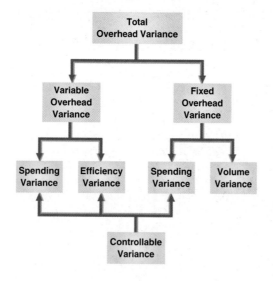

Computing Variable and Fixed Overhead Cost Variances   To illustrate the computation of more detailed overhead cost variances, we return to the G-Max data. We know that G-Max produced 3,500 units when 4,000 units were budgeted. Additional data from cost reports show that the actual overhead cost incurred is $7,650 (the variable portion of $3,650 and the fixed portion of $4,000). Recall from Exhibit 24.12 that each unit requires 1 hour of direct labor, that variable overhead is applied at a rate of $1.00 per direct labor hour, and that the predetermined fixed overhead rate is $1.00 per direct labor hour. Using this information, we can compute overhead variances for both variable and fixed overhead as follows:

Actual variable overhead (given)	$3,650
Applied variable overhead (3,500 × $1.00)	3,500
Variable overhead variance (unfavorable)	$ 150

Actual fixed overhead (given)	$4,000
Applied fixed overhead (3,500 × $1.00)	3,500
Fixed overhead variance (unfavorable)	$ 500

Management should seek to determine the causes of these unfavorable variances and take corrective action. To help better isolate the causes of these variances, more detailed overhead variances can be used, as shown in the next section.

Expanded Overhead Variance Formulas   Exhibit 24A.2 shows formulas to use in computing detailed overhead variances that can better identify reasons for variable and fixed overhead variances.

EXHIBIT 24A.2

Variable and Fixed
Overhead Variances

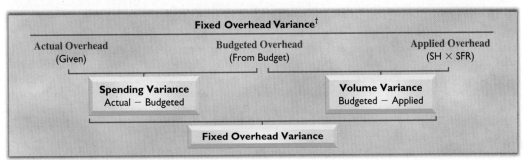

* AH = actual direct labor hours; AVR = actual variable overhead rate; SH = standard direct labor hours; SVR = standard variable overhead rate.

†SH = standard direct labor hours; SFR = standard fixed overhead rate.

Variable Overhead Cost Variances   Using these formulas, Exhibit 24A.3 offers insight into the causes of G-Max's $150 unfavorable variable overhead cost variance. Recall that G-Max applies overhead based on direct labor hours as the allocation base. We know that it used 3,400 direct labor hours to produce 3,500 units. This compares favorably to the standard requirement of 3,500 direct labor hours at one labor hour per unit. At a standard variable overhead rate of $1.00 per direct labor hour, this should have resulted in variable overhead costs of $3,400 (middle column of Exhibit 24A.3).

EXHIBIT 24A.3

Computing Variable Overhead
Cost Variances

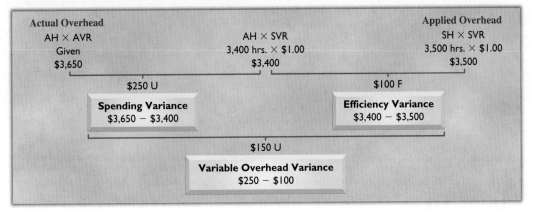

G-Max's cost records, however, report actual variable overhead of $3,650, or $250 higher than expected. This means G-Max has an unfavorable variable overhead spending variance of $250 ($3,650 − $3,400). On the other hand, G-Max used 100 fewer labor hours than expected to make 3,500 units, and its actual variable overhead is lower than its applied variable overhead. Thus, G-Max has a favorable variable overhead efficiency variance of $100 ($3,400 − $3,500).

Fixed Overhead Cost Variances   Exhibit 24A.4 provides insight into the causes of G-Max's $500 unfavorable fixed overhead variance. G-Max reports that it incurred $4,000 in actual fixed overhead; this amount equals the budgeted fixed overhead for May at the expected production level of 4,000 units (see Exhibit 24.12). Thus, the fixed overhead spending variance is zero, suggesting good control of fixed overhead costs. G-Max's budgeted fixed overhead application rate is $1 per hour ($4,000/4,000 direct labor hours), but the actual production level is only 3,500 units. Using this information, we can compute the fixed overhead volume variance shown in Exhibit 24A.4. The applied fixed overhead is computed by multiplying 3,500 standard hours allowed for the actual production by the $1 fixed overhead allocation rate. The volume variance of $500 occurs because 500 fewer units are produced than budgeted; namely, 80% of the manufacturing capacity is budgeted but only 70% is used.

EXHIBIT 24A.4

Computing Fixed Overhead Cost Variances

Standard Cost Accounting System   We have shown how companies use standard costs in management reports. Most standard cost systems also record these costs and variances in accounts. This practice simplifies recordkeeping and helps in preparing reports. Although we do not need knowledge of standard cost accounting practices to understand standard costs and their use, we must know how to interpret the accounts in which standard costs and variances are recorded. The entries in this section briefly illustrate the important aspects of this process for G-Max's standard costs and variances for May.

The first of these entries records standard materials cost incurred in May in the Goods in Process Inventory account. This part of the entry is similar to the usual accounting entry, but the amount of the debit equals the standard cost ($35,000) instead of the actual cost ($37,800). This entry credits Raw Materials Inventory for actual cost. The difference between standard and actual direct materials costs is recorded with debits to two separate materials variance accounts (recall Exhibit 24.10). Both the materials price and quantity variances are recorded as debits because they reflect additional costs higher than the standard cost (if actual costs were less than the standard, they are recorded as credits). This treatment (debit) reflects their unfavorable effect because they represent higher costs and lower income.

Assets	= Liabilities +	Equity
+35,000		−1,000
−37,800		−1,800

May 31			
	Goods in Process Inventory	35,000	
	Direct Materials Price Variance*	**1,800**	
	Direct Materials Quantity Variance	**1,000**	
	Raw Materials Inventory		37,800
	To charge production for standard quantity of materials used (1,750 lbs.) at the standard price ($20 per lb.), and to record material price and material quantity variances.		

* Many companies record the materials price variance when materials are purchased. For simplicity, we record both the materials price and quantity variances when materials are issued to production.

The second entry debits Goods in Process Inventory for the standard labor cost of the goods manufactured during May ($28,000). Actual labor cost ($28,220) is recorded with a credit to the Factory Payroll account. The difference between standard and actual labor costs is explained by two variances (see Exhibit 24.11). The direct labor rate variance is unfavorable and is debited to that account. The direct labor efficiency variance is favorable and that account is credited. The direct labor efficiency variance is favorable because it represents a lower cost and a higher net income.

May 31	Goods in Process Inventory	28,000	
	Direct Labor Rate Variance	1,020	
	Direct Labor Efficiency Variance		800
	Factory Payroll		28,220
	To charge production with 3,500 standard hours of direct labor at the standard $8 per hour rate, and to record the labor rate and efficiency variances.		

Assets = Liabilities + Equity
+28,000   +28,220
                    − 1,020
                    +   800

The entry to assign standard predetermined overhead to the cost of goods manufactured must debit the $7,000 predetermined amount to the Goods in Process Inventory account. Actual overhead costs of $7,650 were debited to Factory Overhead during the period (entries not shown here). Thus, when Factory Overhead is applied to Goods in Process Inventory, the actual amount is credited to the Factory Overhead account. To account for the difference between actual and standard overhead costs, the entry includes a $250 debit to the Variable Overhead Spending Variance, a $100 credit to the Variable Overhead Efficiency Variance, and a $500 debit to the Volume Variance (recall Exhibits 24A.3 and 24A.4). An alternative (simpler) approach is to record the difference with a $150 debit to the Controllable Variance account and a $500 debit to the Volume Variance account (recall from Exhibit 24A.1 that controllable variance is the sum of both variable overhead variances and the fixed overhead spending variance).

May 31	Goods in Process Inventory	7,000	
	Volume Variance	500	
	Variable Overhead Spending Variance	250	
	Variable Overhead Efficiency Variance		100
	Factory Overhead		7,650
	To apply overhead at the standard rate of $2 per standard direct labor hour (3,500 hours), and to record overhead variances.		

Assets = Liabilities + Equity
+7,000   +7,650
                    − 250
                    − 500
                    + 100

The balances of these different variance accounts accumulate until the end of the accounting period. As a result, the unfavorable variances of some months can offset the favorable variances of other months.

These ending variance account balances, which reflect results of the period's various transactions and events, are closed at period-end. If the amounts are *immaterial,* they are added to or subtracted from the balance of the Cost of Goods Sold account. This process is similar to that shown in the job order costing chapter for eliminating an underapplied or overapplied balance in the Factory Overhead account. (*Note:* These variance balances, which represent differences between actual and standard costs, must be added to or subtracted from the materials, labor, and overhead costs recorded. In this way, the recorded costs equal the actual costs incurred in the period; a company must use actual costs in external financial statements prepared in accordance with generally accepted accounting principles.)

Point: If variances are material they can be allocated between Goods in Process Inventory, Finished Goods Inventory, and Cost of Goods Sold. This closing process is explained in advanced courses.

Quick Check

Answers — p. 1015

12. A company uses a standard cost accounting system. Prepare the journal entry to record these direct materials variances:

Direct materials cost actually incurred..................	$73,200
Direct materials quantity variance (favorable)	3,800
Direct materials price variance (unfavorable)	1,300

13. If standard costs are recorded in the manufacturing accounts, how are recorded variances treated at the end of an accounting period?

Summary

C1 **Define *standard costs* and explain how standard cost information is useful for management by exception.** Standard costs are the normal costs that should be incurred to produce a product or perform a service. They should be based on a careful examination of the processes used to produce a product or perform a service as well as the quantities and prices that should be incurred in carrying out those processes. On a performance report, standard costs (which are flexible budget amounts) are compared to actual costs, and the differences are presented as variances. Standard cost accounting provides management information about costs that differ from budgeted (expected) amounts. Performance reports disclose the costs or areas of operations that have significant variances from budgeted amounts. This allows managers to focus attention on the exceptions and less attention on areas proceeding normally.

C2 **Describe variances and what they reveal about performance.** Management can use variances to monitor and control activities. Total cost variances can be broken into price and quantity variances to direct management's attention to those responsible for quantities used and prices paid.

A1 **Analyze changes in sales from expected amounts.** Actual sales can differ from budgeted sales, and managers can investigate this difference by computing both the sales price and sales volume variances. The *sales price variance* refers to that portion of total variance resulting from a difference between actual and budgeted selling prices. The *sales volume variance* refers to that portion of total variance resulting from a difference between actual and budgeted sales quantities.

P1 **Prepare a flexible budget and interpret a flexible budget performance report.** A flexible budget expresses variable costs in per unit terms so that it can be used to develop budgeted amounts for any volume level within the relevant range. Thus, managers compute budgeted amounts for evaluation after a period for the volume that actually occurred. To prepare a flexible budget, we express each variable cost as a constant amount per unit of sales (or as a percent of sales dollars). In contrast, the budgeted amount

of each fixed cost is expressed as a total amount expected to occur at any sales volume within the relevant range. The flexible budget is then determined using these computations and amounts for fixed and variable costs at the expected sales volume.

P2 **Compute materials and labor variances.** Materials and labor variances are due to differences between the actual costs incurred and the budgeted costs. The price (or rate) variance is computed by comparing the actual cost with the flexible budget amount that should have been incurred to acquire the actual quantity of resources. The quantity (or efficiency) variance is computed by comparing the flexible budget amount that should have been incurred to acquire the actual quantity of resources with the flexible budget amount that should have been incurred to acquire the standard quantity of resources.

P3 **Compute overhead variances.** Overhead variances are due to differences between the actual overhead costs incurred and the overhead applied to production. An overhead spending variance arises when the actual amount incurred differs from the budgeted amount of overhead. An overhead efficiency (or volume) variance arises when the flexible overhead budget amount differs from the overhead applied to production. It is important to realize that overhead is assigned using an overhead allocation base, meaning that an efficiency variance (in the case of variable overhead) is a result of the overhead application base being used more or less efficiently than planned.

P4^A **Prepare journal entries for standard costs and account for price and quantity variances.** When a company records standard costs in its accounts, the standard costs of materials, labor, and overhead are debited to the Goods in Process Inventory account. Based on an analysis of the material, labor, and overhead costs, each quantity variance, price variance, volume variance, and controllable variance is recorded in a separate account. At period-end, if the variances are material, they are allocated among the balances of the Goods in Process Inventory, Finished Goods Inventory, and Cost of Goods Sold accounts. If they are not material, they are simply debited or credited to the Cost of Goods Sold account.

Guidance Answers to Decision Maker and Decision Ethics

Entrepreneur From the complaints, this performance report appears to compare actual results with a fixed budget. This comparison is useful in determining whether the amount of work actually performed was more or less than planned, but it is not useful in determining whether the divisions were more or less efficient than planned. If the two consulting divisions worked on more assignments than expected, some costs will certainly increase. Therefore, you should prepare a flexible budget using the actual number of consulting assignments and then compare actual performance to the flexible budget.

Internal Auditor Although the manager's actions might not be unethical, this action is undesirable. The internal auditor should report this behavior, possibly recommending that for the purchase of such discretionary items, the manager must provide budgetary requests using an activity-based budgeting process. The internal auditor would then be given full authority to verify this budget request.

Human Resource Manager As HR manager, you should investigate the causes for any labor-related variances although you may not be responsible for them. An unfavorable labor efficiency variance occurs because more labor hours than standard were used during the period. There are at least three possible reasons for this: (1) materials quality could be poor, resulting in more labor consumption due to rework; (2) unplanned interruptions (strike, breakdowns, accidents) could have occurred during the period; and (3) the production manager could have used a different labor mix to expedite orders. This new labor mix could have consisted of a larger proportion of untrained labor, which resulted in more labor hours.

Sales Manager The unfavorable sales price variance suggests that actual prices were lower than budgeted prices. As the sales manager, you want to know the reasons for a lower than expected price. Perhaps your salespeople lowered the price of certain products by offering quantity discounts. You then might want to know what prompted them to offer the quantity discounts (perhaps competitors were offering discounts). You want to break the sales volume variance into both the sales mix and sales quantity variances. You could find that although the sales quantity variance is favorable, the sales mix variance is not. Then you need to investigate why the actual sales mix differs from the budgeted sales mix.

Guidance Answers to Quick Checks

1. *b*

2. The first step is classifying each cost as variable or fixed.

3. A fixed budget is prepared using an expected volume of sales or production. A flexible budget is prepared using the actual volume of activity.

4. The contribution margin equals sales less variable costs.

5. *c*

6. It is the difference between actual cost and standard cost.

7. *a*; Total actual hours: $2{,}500 \times 2.5 = 6{,}250$

Total standard hours: $2{,}500 \times 2.0 = 5{,}000$

Efficiency variance $= (6{,}250 - 5{,}000) \times \$3.00$
$= \$3{,}750$ U

8. *b*; Rate variance $= (\$3.10 - \$3.00) \times 6{,}250 = \$625$ U

9. Yes, this will occur when the materials quantity variance is more than the materials price variance.

10. The overhead volume variance is favorable when the actual operating level is higher than the expected level.

11. *b*

12.

Goods in Process Inventory	75,700	
Direct Materials Price Variance	1,300	
Direct Materials Quantity Variance		3,800
Raw Materials Inventory		73,200

13. If the variances are material, they should be prorated among the Goods in Process Inventory, Finished Goods Inventory, and Cost of Goods Sold accounts. If they are not material, they can be closed to Cost of Goods Sold.

Key Terms

mhhe.com/wildFAP20e

Benchmarking (p. 1002)

Budget report (p. 990)

Budgetary control (p. 990)

Controllable variance (p. 1003)

Cost variance (p. 997)

Efficiency variance (p. 1010)

Favorable variance (p. 991)

Fixed budget (p. 991)

Fixed budget performance report (p. 991)

Flexible budget (p. 992)

Flexible budget performance report (p. 994)

Management by exception (p. 995)

Overhead cost variance (p. 1002)

Price variance (p. 995)

Quantity variance (p. 995)

Spending variance (p. 1010)

Standard costs (p. 995)

Unfavorable variance (p. 991)

Variance analysis (p. 995)

Volume variance (p. 1003)

Multiple Choice Quiz

Answers on p. 1033   mhhe.com/wildFAP20e

Additional Quiz Questions are available at the book's Website.

1. A company predicts its production and sales will be 24,000 units. At that level of activity, its fixed costs are budgeted at $300,000, and its variable costs are budgeted at $246,000. If its activity level declines to 20,000 units, what will be its fixed costs and its variable costs?

  a. Fixed, $300,000; variable, $246,000

  b. Fixed, $250,000; variable, $205,000

  c. Fixed, $300,000; variable, $205,000

  d. Fixed, $250,000; variable, $246,000

  e. Fixed, $300,000; variable, $300,000

2. Using the following information about a single product company, compute its total actual cost of direct materials used.

  • Direct materials standard cost: 5 lbs. × $2 per lb. = $10.

  • Total direct materials cost variance: $15,000 unfavorable.

  • Actual direct materials used: 300,000 lbs.

  • Actual units produced: 60,000 units.

  a. $585,000

  b. $600,000

  c. $300,000

  d. $315,000

  e. $615,000

3. A company uses four hours of direct labor to produce a product unit. The standard direct labor cost is $20 per hour. This period the company produced 20,000 units and used 84,160 hours of direct labor at a total cost of $1,599,040. What is its labor rate variance for the period?

  a. $83,200 F

  b. $84,160 U

  c. $84,160 F

  d. $83,200 U

  e. $ 960 F

4. A company's standard for a unit of its single product is $6 per unit in variable overhead (4 hours × $1.50 per hour). Actual data for the period show variable overhead costs of $150,000 and production of 24,000 units. Its total variable overhead cost variance is
    a. $ 6,000 F.
    b. $ 6,000 U.
    c. $114,000 U.
    d. $114,000 F.
    e. $ 0.

5. A company's standard for a unit of its single product is $4 per unit in fixed overhead ($24,000 total/6,000 units budgeted). Actual data for the period show total actual fixed overhead of $24,100 and production of 4,800 units. Its volume variance is
    a. $4,800 U.
    b. $4,800 F.
    c. $ 100 U.
    d. $ 100 F.
    e. $4,900 U.

---

^A *Superscript letter A denotes assignments based on Appendix 24A.*

Icon denotes assignments that involve decision making.

Discussion Questions

1. What limits the usefulness to managers of fixed budget performance reports?

2. Identify the main purpose of a flexible budget for managers.

3. Prepare a flexible budget performance report title (in proper form) for Spalding Company for the calendar year 2011. Why is a proper title important for this or any report?

4. What type of analysis does a flexible budget performance report help management perform?

5. In what sense can a variable cost be considered constant?

6. What department is usually responsible for a direct labor rate variance? What department is usually responsible for a direct labor efficiency variance? Explain.

7. What is a price variance? What is a quantity variance?

8. What is the purpose of using standard costs?

9. **Nokia** monitors its fixed overhead. In an analysis of fixed overhead cost variances, what is the volume variance?   **NOKIA**

10. What is the predetermined standard overhead rate? How is it computed?

11. In general, variance analysis is said to provide information about _____ and _____ variances.

12. **Research In Motion** monitors its overhead. In an analysis of overhead cost variances, what is the controllable variance and what causes it?   *RIM*

13. What are the relations among standard costs, flexible budgets, variance analysis, and management by exception?

14. How can the manager of handheld devices at an **Apple** retail store use flexible budgets to enhance performance?   Apple

15. Is it possible for a retail store such as **Apple** to use variances in analyzing its operating performance? Explain.   Apple

16. Assume that **Palm** is budgeted to operate at 80% of capacity but actually operates at 75% of capacity. What effect will the 5% deviation have on its controllable variance? Its volume variance?   Palm

---

connect

QUICK STUDY

QS 24-1
Flexible budget performance report
P1

Santana Company sold 100,000 units of its product in May. For the level of production achieved in May, the budgeted amounts were: sales, $850,000; variable costs, $675,000; and fixed costs, $150,000. The following actual financial results are available for May. Prepare a flexible budget performance report for May.

Sales (100,000 units)	$837,500
Variable costs	656,250
Fixed costs	150,000

QS 24-2
Management by exception
C1

Managers use *management by exception* for control purposes. (1) Describe the concept of management by exception. (2) Explain how standard costs help managers apply this concept to monitor and control costs.

QS 24-3
Standard cost card   C1

BatPro makes metal baseball bats. Each bat requires 1 kg. of aluminum at $20 per kg. and 0.50 direct labor hours at $16 per hour. Overhead is assigned at the rate of $40 per labor hour. What amounts would appear on a standard cost card for BatPro?

QS 24-4
Cost variances   C2

Refer to information in QS 24-3. Assume the actual cost to manufacture one metal bat was $54. Compute the cost variance and classify it as favorable or unfavorable.

Jacomo Company's output for the current period was assigned a $300,000 standard direct materials cost. The direct materials variances included a $44,000 favorable price variance and a $6,000 favorable quantity variance. What is the actual total direct materials cost for the current period?

QS 24-5
Materials cost variances   P2

Reflection Company's output for the current period results in a $40,000 unfavorable direct labor rate variance and a $20,000 unfavorable direct labor efficiency variance. Production for the current period was assigned an $800,000 standard direct labor cost. What is the actual total direct labor cost for the current period?

QS 24-6
Labor cost variances   P2

For the current period, Kawaga Company's manufacturing operations yield a $4,000 favorable price variance on its direct materials usage. The actual price per pound of material is $77; the standard price is $77.50. How many pounds of material are used in the current period?

QS 24-7
Materials cost variances   P2

Hewitt Company's output for the current period yields a $30,000 favorable overhead volume variance and a $50,400 unfavorable overhead controllable variance. Standard overhead charged to production for the period is $225,000. What is the actual total overhead cost incurred for the period?

QS 24-8
Overhead cost variances   P3

Refer to the information in QS 24-8. Hewitt records standard costs in its accounts. Prepare the journal entry to charge overhead costs to the Goods in Process Inventory account and to record any variances.

QS 24-9^A
Preparing overhead entries   P4

Masters Company applies overhead using machine hours and reports the following information. Compute the total variable overhead cost variance.

Actual machine hours used	4,950 hours
Standard machine hours	5,000 hours
Actual variable overhead rate per hour	$4.10
Standard variable overhead rate per hour	$4.00

QS 24-10^A
Overhead cost variances

P3

Refer to the information from QS 24-10. Compute the variable overhead spending variance and the variable overhead efficiency variance.

QS 24-11^A
Overhead spending and efficiency variances   P3

VanWay, Inc. specializes in selling used SUVs. During the first six months of 2011, the dealership sold 100 trucks at an average price of $10,000 each. The budget for the first six months of 2011 was to sell 90 trucks at an average price of $10,500 each. Compute the dealership's sales price variance and sales volume variance for the first six months of 2011.

QS 24-12
Computing sales price and volume variances   A1

Based on predicted production of 12,000 units, a company anticipates $150,000 of fixed costs and $123,000 of variable costs. If the company actually produces 10,000 units, what are the flexible budget amounts of fixed and variable costs?

QS 24-13
Flexible budget   P1

Beck Company expects to produce 10,000 units for the year ending December 31. A flexible budget for 10,000 units of production reflects sales of $200,000; variable costs of $40,000; and fixed costs of $75,000. If the company instead produces and sells 13,000 units for the year, calculate the expected level of income from operations.

QS 24-14
Flexible budget

P1

Refer to information in QS 24-14. Assume that actual sales are $265,000, actual variable costs for the year are $59,000, and actual fixed costs for the year are $73,400. Prepare a flexible budget performance report for the year.

QS 24-15
Flexible budget performance report   P1

TenPro reports the following on one of its products. Compute the direct materials price and quantity variances.

Direct materials standard (4 lbs. @ $2/lb.)	$8 per finished unit
Actual direct materials used	150,000 lbs.
Actual finished units produced	30,000 units
Actual cost of direct materials used	$267,500

QS 24-16
Materials variances

P2

QS 24-17
Direct labor variances
P2

The following information describes a company's usage of direct labor in a recent period. Compute the direct labor rate and efficiency variances for the period.

Actual direct labor hours used	45,000
Actual direct labor rate per hour	$15
Standard direct labor rate per hour	$14
Standard direct labor hours for units produced	47,000

QS 24-18
Controllable overhead variance
P3

Funk Co. expects to produce 48,000 units for the year. The company's flexible budget for 48,000 units of production shows variable overhead costs of $72,000 and fixed overhead costs of $64,000. For the year, the company incurred actual overhead costs of $122,800 while producing 40,000 units. Compute the controllable overhead variance.

QS 24-19
Controllable overhead variance
P3

Aigne Corp. reports the following for November. Compute the controllable overhead variance for November.

Actual total factory overhead incurred	$28,175
Standard factory overhead:	
Variable overhead	$3.10 per unit produced
Fixed overhead	
($12,000/6,000 predicted units to be produced)	$2 per unit
Predicted units produced	6,000 units
Actual units produced	4,800 units

QS 24-20
Volume variance   P3

Refer to information in QS 24-19. Compute the volume variance for November.

QS 24-21
Sales variances   A1

In a recent year, **BMW** sold 216,944 of its 1 Series cars. Assume the company expected to sell 225,944 of these cars during the year. Also assume the budgeted sales price for each car was $30,000, and the actual sales price for each car was $30,200. Compute the sales price variance and the sales volume variance.

EXERCISES

Exercise 24-1
Preparation of flexible budgets
P1

Mesa Company's fixed budget for the first quarter of calendar year 2011 reveals the following. Prepare flexible budgets following the format of Exhibit 24.3 that show variable costs per unit, fixed costs, and three different flexible budgets for sales volumes of 7,500, 10,000, and 12,500 units.

Sales (10,000 units)		$3,000,000
Cost of goods sold		
Direct materials	$320,000	
Direct labor	680,000	
Production supplies	264,000	
Plant manager salary	60,000	1,324,000
Gross profit		1,676,000
Selling expenses		
Sales commissions	120,000	
Packaging	210,000	
Advertising	100,000	430,000
Administrative expenses		
Administrative salaries	80,000	
Depreciation—office equip.	30,000	
Insurance	18,000	
Office rent	24,000	152,000
Income from operations		$1,094,000

Check Income (at 7,500 units), $742,500

KMAR Company manufactures and sells mountain bikes. It normally operates eight hours a day, six days a week. Using this information, classify each of the following costs as fixed or variable. If additional information would affect your decision, describe the information.

a. Incoming shipping expenses

b. Office supplies

c. Depreciation on tools

d. Taxes on property

e. Bike tires

f. Gas used for heating

g. Bike frames

h. Direct labor

i. Screws for assembly

j. Repair expense for tools

k. Management salaries

Exercise 24-2
Classification of costs as fixed or variable

P1

Cimarron Company's fixed budget performance report for July follows. The $630,000 budgeted expenses include $588,000 variable expenses and $42,000 fixed expenses. Actual expenses include $54,000 fixed expenses. Prepare a flexible budget performance report that shows any variances between budgeted results and actual results. List fixed and variable expenses separately.

	Fixed Budget	Actual Results	Variances
Sales (in units)	8,400	10,800	
Sales (in dollars)	$840,000	$1,080,000	$240,000 F
Total expenses	630,000	756,000	126,000 U
Income from operations ..	$210,000	$ 324,000	$114,000 F

Exercise 24-3
Preparation of a flexible budget performance report

P1

Check   Income variance, $42,000 F

Daytec Company's fixed budget performance report for June follows. The $440,000 budgeted expenses include $300,000 variable expenses and $140,000 fixed expenses. Actual expenses include $130,000 fixed expenses. Prepare a flexible budget performance report showing any variances between budgeted and actual results. List fixed and variable expenses separately.

	Fixed Budget	Actual Results	Variances
Sales (in units)	6,000	4,800	
Sales (in dollars)	$480,000	$422,400	$57,600 U
Total expenses	440,000	394,000	46,000 F
Income from operations ..	$ 40,000	$ 28,400	$11,600 U

Exercise 24-4
Preparation of a flexible budget performance report

P1

Check   Income variance, $24,400 F

After evaluating Zero Company's manufacturing process, management decides to establish standards of 1.5 hours of direct labor per unit of product and $11 per hour for the labor rate. During October, the company uses 3,780 hours of direct labor at a $45,360 total cost to produce 2,700 units of product. In November, the company uses 4,480 hours of direct labor at a $47,040 total cost to produce 2,800 units of product. (1) Compute the rate variance, the efficiency variance, and the total direct labor cost variance for each of these two months. (2) Interpret the October direct labor variances.

Exercise 24-5
Computation and interpretation of labor variances P2

Check   (1) October rate variance, $3,780 U

Sonic Company set the following standard costs for one unit of its product for 2011.

Direct material (20 lbs. @ $2.50 per lb.)	$ 50.00
Direct labor (15 hrs. @ $8.00 per hr.)	120.00
Factory variable overhead (15 hrs. @ $2.50 per hr.)	37.50
Factory fixed overhead (15 hrs. @ $0.50 per hr.)	7.50
Standard cost	$215.00

Exercise 24-6ᴬ
Computation of total variable and fixed overhead variances

P3

The $3.00 ($2.50 + $0.50) total overhead rate per direct labor hour is based on an expected operating level equal to 75% of the factory's capacity of 50,000 units per month. The following monthly flexible budget information is also available.

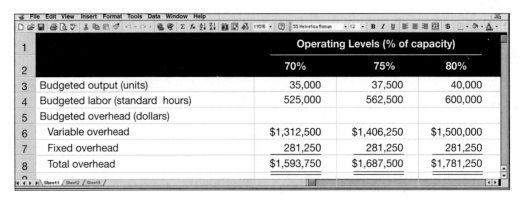

	Operating Levels (% of capacity)		
	70%	**75%**	**80%**
Budgeted output (units)	35,000	37,500	40,000
Budgeted labor (standard hours)	525,000	562,500	600,000
Budgeted overhead (dollars)			
Variable overhead	$1,312,500	$1,406,250	$1,500,000
Fixed overhead	281,250	281,250	281,250
Total overhead	$1,593,750	$1,687,500	$1,781,250

During the current month, the company operated at 70% of capacity, employees worked 500,000 hours, and the following actual overhead costs were incurred.

Variable overhead costs	$1,267,500
Fixed overhead costs	285,000
Total overhead costs	$1,552,500

Check (2) Variable overhead cost variance, $45,000 F

(1) Show how the company computed its predetermined overhead application rate per hour for total overhead, variable overhead, and fixed overhead. (2) Compute the variable and fixed overhead variances.

Exercise 24-7[A]

Computation and interpretation of overhead spending, efficiency, and volume variances P3

Check (1) Variable overhead: Spending, $17,500 U; Efficiency, $62,500 F

Refer to the information from Exercise 24-6. Compute and interpret the following.

1. Variable overhead spending and efficiency variances.
2. Fixed overhead spending and volume variances.
3. Controllable variance.

Exercise 24-8

Computation and interpretation of materials variances

Check Price variance, $8,800 F

BTS Company made 6,000 bookshelves using 88,000 board feet of wood costing $607,200. The company's direct materials standards for one bookshelf are 16 board feet of wood at $7 per board foot. (1) Compute the direct materials variances incurred in manufacturing these bookshelves. (2) Interpret the direct materials variances.

Exercise 24-9[A]

Materials variances recorded and closed

P4

Check (2) Cr. to Cost of Goods Sold, $64,800

Refer to Exercise 24-8. BTS Company records standard costs in its accounts and its material variances in separate accounts when it assigns materials costs to the Goods in Process Inventory account. (1) Show the journal entry that both charges the direct materials costs to the Goods in Process Inventory account and records the materials variances in their proper accounts. (2) Assume that BTS's material variances are the only variances accumulated in the accounting period and that they are immaterial. Prepare the adjusting journal entry to close the variance accounts at period-end. (3) Identify the variance that should be investigated according to the management by exception concept. Explain.

Exercise 24-10

Computation of total overhead rate and total overhead variance

P3

Check (1) Variable overhead rate, $7.00 per hour

Earth Company expects to operate at 80% of its productive capacity of 25,000 units per month. At this planned level, the company expects to use 40,000 standard hours of direct labor. Overhead is allocated to products using a predetermined standard rate based on direct labor hours. At the 80% capacity level, the total budgeted cost includes $40,000 fixed overhead cost and $280,000 variable overhead cost. In the current month, the company incurred $340,000 actual overhead and 39,000 actual labor hours while producing 19,500 units. (1) Compute its overhead application rate for total overhead. (2) Compute its total overhead variance.

Exercise 24-11

Computation of volume and controllable overhead variances

P3

Check (2) $27,000 U

Refer to the information from Exercise 24-10. Compute the (1) overhead volume variance and (2) overhead controllable variance.

Comp Wiz sells computers. During May 2011, it sold 500 computers at a $900 average price each. The
May 2011 fixed budget included sales of 550 computers at an average price of $850 each. (1) Compute the
sales price variance and the sales volume variance for May 2011. (2) Interpret the findings.

Exercise 24-12
Computing and interpreting
sales variances

A1

Match the terms a–e with their correct definition 1–5.

a. Standard cost
b. Practical standard
c. Standard cost card
d. Ideal standard
e. Management by
exception

1. Record that accumulates standard cost information.
2. Quantity of input required if a production process is 100% efficient.
3. Managing by focusing on large differences from standard costs.
4. Quantity of input required under normal conditions.
5. Preset cost for delivering a product or service under normal conditions.

Exercise 24-13
Standard costs

C1

Presented below are terms preceded by letters a through j and a list of definitions 1 through 10. Enter the
letter of the term with the definition, using the space preceding the definition.

a. Cost variance
b. Volume variance
c. Price variance
d. Quantity variance
e. Standard costs
f. Controllable variance
g. Fixed budget
h. Flexible budget
i. Variance analysis
j. Management by
exception

_____ **1.** The difference between the total budgeted overhead cost and the
overhead cost that was allocated to products using the predetermined fixed overhead rate.

_____ **2.** A planning budget based on a single predicted amount of sales
or production volume; unsuitable for evaluations if the actual
volume differs from the predicted volume.

_____ **3.** Preset costs for delivering a product, component, or service under normal conditions.

_____ **4.** A process of examining the differences between actual and budgeted sales or costs and describing them in terms of the amounts
that resulted from price and quantity differences.

_____ **5.** The difference between actual and budgeted sales or cost caused
by the difference between the actual price per unit and the budgeted price per unit.

_____ **6.** A budget prepared based on predicted amounts of revenues and
expenses corresponding to the actual level of output.

_____ **7.** The difference between actual and budgeted cost caused by the
difference between the actual quantity and the budgeted quantity.

_____ **8.** The combination of both overhead spending variances (variable
and fixed) and the variable overhead efficiency variance.

_____ **9.** A management process to focus on significant variances and give
less attention to areas where performance is close to the standard.

_____ **10.** The difference between actual cost and standard cost, made up
of a price variance and a quantity variance.

Exercise 24-14
Cost variances

C2

Dee-Daw Co. provides the following results of April's operations: F indicates favorable and U indicates
unfavorable. Applying the management by exception approach, which of the variances are of greatest
concern? Why?

Exercise 24-15
Analyzing variances

C1

Direct materials price variance	$ 400 F
Direct materials quantity variance	2,000 U
Direct labor rate variance	100 U
Direct labor efficiency variance	1,200 F
Controllable overhead variance	400 U
Fixed overhead volume variance	600 F

Exercise 24-16
Direct materials and direct
labor variances

P2

The following information describes production activities of Truzor Manufacturing for the year:

Actual raw materials used	16,000 lbs. at $4.05 per lb.
Actual factory payroll	5,545 hours for a total of $72,085
Actual units produced	30,000

Budgeted standards for each unit produced are 0.50 pounds of raw material at $4.15 per pound and 10 minutes of direct labor at $12.50 per hour. (1) Compute the direct materials price and quantity variances. Round to the nearest whole dollar. (2) Compute the direct labor rate and efficiency variances. Indicate whether each variance is favorable or unfavorable.

McGraw Hill **connect**

PROBLEM SET A

Problem 24-1A
Computation of materials, labor,
and overhead variances

P2 P3

mhhe.com/wildFAP20e

Tuna Company set the following standard unit costs for its single product.

Direct materials (25 lbs. @ $4 per lb.)	$100.00
Direct labor (6 hrs. @ $8 per hr.)	48.00
Factory overhead—variable (6 hrs. @ $5 per hr.)	30.00
Factory overhead—fixed (6 hrs. @ $7 per hr.)	42.00
Total standard cost	$220.00

The predetermined overhead rate is based on a planned operating volume of 80% of the productive capacity of 60,000 units per quarter. The following flexible budget information is available.

	Operating Levels		
	70%	80%	90%
Production in units	42,000	48,000	54,000
Standard direct labor hours	252,000	288,000	324,000
Budgeted overhead			
Fixed factory overhead	$2,016,000	$2,016,000	$2,016,000
Variable factory overhead	$1,260,000	$1,440,000	$1,620,000

During the current quarter, the company operated at 70% of capacity and produced 42,000 units of product; actual direct labor totaled 250,000 hours. Units produced were assigned the following standard costs:

Direct materials (1,050,000 lbs. @ $4 per lb.)	$4,200,000
Direct labor (252,000 hrs. @ $8 per hr.)	2,016,000
Factory overhead (252,000 hrs. @ $12 per hr.)	3,024,000
Total standard cost	$9,240,000

Actual costs incurred during the current quarter follow:

Direct materials (1,000,000 lbs. @ $4.25)	$4,250,000
Direct labor (250,000 hrs. @ $7.75)	1,937,500
Fixed factory overhead costs	1,960,000
Variable factory overhead costs	1,200,000
Total actual costs	$9,347,500

Check   (1) Materials variances: Price,
$250,000 U; Quantity, $200,000 F.
          (2) Labor variances: Rate,
$62,500 F; Efficiency, $16,000 F

Required

1. Compute the direct materials cost variance, including its price and quantity variances.
2. Compute the direct labor variance, including its rate and efficiency variances.
3. Compute the overhead controllable and volume variances.

Problem 24-2A^A
Expanded overhead variances

P3

Refer to information in Problem 24-1A.

Required

Compute these variances: (a) variable overhead spending and efficiency, (b) fixed overhead spending and volume, and (c) total overhead controllable.

Pebco Company's 2011 master budget included the following fixed budget report. It is based on an expected production and sales volume of 20,000 units.

Problem 24-3A
Preparation and analysis
of a flexible budget   P1

PEBCO COMPANY		
Fixed Budget Report		
For Year Ended December 31, 2011		
Sales		$3,000,000
Cost of goods sold		
Direct materials........................	$1,200,000	
Direct labor	260,000	
Machinery repairs (variable cost)	57,000	
Depreciation—plant equipment	250,000	
Utilities ($50,000 is variable)	200,000	
Plant management salaries	140,000	2,107,000
Gross profit		893,000
Selling expenses		
Packaging	80,000	
Shipping	116,000	
Sales salary (fixed annual amount)	160,000	356,000
General and administrative expenses		
Advertising expense	81,000	
Salaries.............................	241,000	
Entertainment expense	90,000	412,000
Income from operations		$ 125,000

Required

1. Classify all items listed in the fixed budget as variable or fixed. Also determine their amounts per unit or their amounts for the year, as appropriate.

2. Prepare flexible budgets (see Exhibit 24.3) for the company at sales volumes of 18,000 and 24,000 units.

3. The company's business conditions are improving. One possible result is a sales volume of approximately 28,000 units. The company president is confident that this volume is within the relevant range of existing capacity. How much would operating income increase over the 2011 budgeted amount of $125,000 if this level is reached without increasing capacity?

4. An unfavorable change in business is remotely possible; in this case, production and sales volume for 2011 could fall to 14,000 units. How much income (or loss) from operations would occur if sales volume falls to this level?

Refer to the information in Problem 24-3A. Pebco Company's actual income statement for 2011 follows.

Problem 24-4A
Preparation and analysis
of a flexible budget
performance report

P1 P2 A1

PEBCO COMPANY		
Statement of Income from Operations		
For Year Ended December 31, 2011		
Sales (24,000 units)		$3,648,000
Cost of goods sold		
Direct materials........................	$1,400,000	
Direct labor	360,000	
Machinery repairs (variable cost)	60,000	
Depreciation—plant equipment	250,000	
Utilities (fixed cost is $154,000)	218,000	
Plant management salaries................	155,000	2,443,000
Gross profit		1,205,000
Selling expenses		
Packaging	90,000	
Shipping	124,000	
Sales salary (annual)....................	162,000	376,000
General and administrative expenses		
Advertising expense	104,000	
Salaries.............................	232,000	
Entertainment expense	100,000	436,000
Income from operations		$ 393,000

Required

1. Prepare a flexible budget performance report for 2011.

Analysis Component

2. Analyze and interpret both the (a) sales variance and (b) direct materials variance.

Problem 24-5A
Flexible budget preparation;
computation of materials, labor,
and overhead variances; and
overhead variance report

P1 P2 P3 C2

Kwikeze Company set the following standard costs for one unit of its product.

Direct materials (4.5 lbs. @ $6 per lb.)	$27.00
Direct labor (1.5 hrs. @ $12 per hr.)	18.00
Overhead (1.5 hrs. @ $16 per hr.)	24.00
Total standard cost.......................	$69.00

The predetermined overhead rate ($16 per direct labor hour) is based on an expected volume of 75% of the factory's capacity of 20,000 units per month. Following are the company's budgeted overhead costs per month at the 75% level.

Overhead Budget (75% Capacity)		
Variable overhead costs		
Indirect materials	$22,500	
Indirect labor	90,000	
Power	22,500	
Repairs and maintenance	45,000	
Total variable overhead costs		$180,000
Fixed overhead costs		
Depreciation—building	24,000	
Depreciation—machinery	72,000	
Taxes and insurance	18,000	
Supervision	66,000	
Total fixed overhead costs		180,000
Total overhead costs		$360,000

The company incurred the following actual costs when it operated at 75% of capacity in October.

Direct materials (69,000 lbs. @ $6.10 per lb.)		$ 420,900
Direct labor (22,800 hrs. @ $12.30 per hr.)		280,440
Overhead costs		
Indirect materials	$21,600	
Indirect labor	82,260	
Power	23,100	
Repairs and maintenance	46,800	
Depreciation—building	24,000	
Depreciation—machinery	75,000	
Taxes and insurance	16,500	
Supervision	66,000	355,260
Total costs		$1,056,600

Required

1. Examine the monthly overhead budget to (a) determine the costs per unit for each variable overhead item and its total per unit costs, and (b) identify the total fixed costs per month.

2. Prepare flexible overhead budgets (as in Exhibit 24.12) for October showing the amounts of each variable and fixed cost at the 65%, 75%, and 85% capacity levels.

3. Compute the direct materials cost variance, including its price and quantity variances.

4. Compute the direct labor cost variance, including its rate and efficiency variances.

5. Prepare a detailed overhead variance report (as in Exhibit 24.15) that shows the variances for individual items of overhead.

(4) Labor variances: Rate, $6,840 U; Efficiency, $3,600 U

Kudos Company has set the following standard costs per unit for the product it manufactures.

Problem 24-6A[A]
Materials, labor, and overhead variances; and overhead variance report

C2 P2 P3

Direct materials (10 lbs. @ $3 per lb.)	$30.00
Direct labor (4 hrs. @ $6 per hr.)	24.00
Overhead (4 hrs. @ $2.50 per hr.)	10.00
Total standard cost	$64.00

The predetermined overhead rate is based on a planned operating volume of 80% of the productive capacity of 10,000 units per month. The following flexible budget information is available.

	Operating Levels		
	70%	80%	90%
Production in units	7,000	8,000	9,000
Standard direct labor hours	28,000	32,000	36,000
Budgeted overhead			
Variable overhead costs			
Indirect materials	$ 8,750	$10,000	$11,250
Indirect labor	14,000	16,000	18,000
Power	3,500	4,000	4,500
Maintenance	1,750	2,000	2,250
Total variable costs	28,000	32,000	36,000
Fixed overhead costs			
Rent of factory building	12,000	12,000	12,000
Depreciation—machinery	20,000	20,000	20,000
Supervisory salaries	16,000	16,000	16,000
Total fixed costs	48,000	48,000	48,000
Total overhead costs	$76,000	$80,000	$84,000

During May, the company operated at 90% of capacity and produced 9,000 units, incurring the following actual costs.

Direct materials (92,000 lbs. @ $2.95 per lb.)		$271,400
Direct labor (37,600 hrs. @ $6.05 per hr.)		227,480
Overhead costs		
Indirect materials	$10,000	
Indirect labor	16,000	
Power	4,500	
Maintenance	3,000	
Rent of factory building	12,000	
Depreciation—machinery	19,200	
Supervisory salaries	17,000	81,700
Total costs		$580,580

Required

1. Compute the direct materials variance, including its price and quantity variances.

2. Compute the direct labor variance, including its rate and efficiency variances.

Check (1) Materials variances: Price, $4,600 F; Quantity, $6,000 U
(2) Labor variances: Rate, $1,880 U; Efficiency, $9,600 U

3. Compute these variances: (a) variable overhead spending and efficiency, (b) fixed overhead spending and volume, and (c) total overhead controllable.

4. Prepare a detailed overhead variance report (as in Exhibit 24.15) that shows the variances for individual items of overhead.

Problem 24-7A[A]
Materials, labor, and overhead
variances recorded and analyzed

C1   P4

Loretto Company's standard cost accounting system recorded this information from its December operations.

Standard direct materials cost	$130,000
Direct materials quantity variance (unfavorable)	5,000
Direct materials price variance (favorable)	1,500
Actual direct labor cost	65,000
Direct labor efficiency variance (favorable).............	7,000
Direct labor rate variance (unfavorable)	500
Actual overhead cost	250,000
Volume variance (unfavorable)...........................	12,000
Controllable variance (unfavorable).....................	8,000

Required

Check (1) Dr. Goods in Process
Inventory (for overhead), $230,000

1. Prepare December 31 journal entries to record the company's costs and variances for the month. (Do not prepare the journal entry to close the variances.)

Analysis Component

2. Identify the areas that would attract the attention of a manager who uses management by exception. Explain what action(s) the manager should consider.

PROBLEM SET B

Problem 24-1B
Computation of materials, labor,
and overhead variances

P2   P3

Sabates Company set the following standard unit costs for its single product.

Direct materials (5 lbs. @ $10 per lb.)	$ 50.00
Direct labor (3 hrs. @ $15 per hr.)......................	45.00
Factory overhead—variable (3 hrs. @ $5 per hr.)	15.00
Factory overhead—fixed (3 hrs. @ $3 per hr.)	9.00
Total standard cost	$119.00

The predetermined overhead rate is based on a planned operating volume of 90% of the productive capacity of 100,000 units per quarter. The following flexible budget information is available.

	Operating Levels		
	80%	90%	100%
Production in units	32,000	36,000	40,000
Standard direct labor hours	96,000	108,000	120,000
Budgeted overhead			
Fixed factory overhead	$324,000	$324,000	$324,000
Variable factory overhead	480,000	540,000	600,000

During the current quarter, the company operated at 80% of capacity and produced 32,000 units of product; direct labor hours worked were 100,000. Units produced were assigned the following standard costs:

Direct materials (160,000 lbs. @ $10 per lb.)	$1,600,000
Direct labor (96,000 hrs. @ $15 per hr.)	1,440,000
Factory overhead (96,000 hrs. @ $8 per hr.)	768,000
Total standard cost	$3,808,000

Actual costs incurred during the current quarter follow:

Direct materials (155,000 lbs. @ $10.20)	$1,581,000
Direct labor (100,000 hrs. @ $14)	1,400,000
Fixed factory overhead costs	370,000
Variable factory overhead costs	480,000
Total actual costs	$3,831,000

Required

1. Compute the direct materials cost variance, including its price and quantity variances.
2. Compute the direct labor variance, including its rate and efficiency variances.
3. Compute the total overhead controllable and volume variances.

Check (1) Materials variances:
Price, $31,000 U; Quantity, $50,000 F
(2) Labor variances: Rate, $100,000 F;
Efficiency, $60,000 U

Refer to information in Problem 24-1B.

Required

Compute these variances: (a) variable overhead spending and efficiency, (b) fixed overhead spending and volume, and (c) total overhead controllable.

Problem 24-2B[A]
Expanded overhead variances
P3

Razorback Company's 2011 master budget included the following fixed budget report. It is based on an expected production and sales volume of 10,000 units.

Problem 24-3B
Preparation and analysis of a flexible budget P1 A1

RAZORBACK COMPANY Fixed Budget Report For Year Ended December 31, 2011		
Sales		$250,000
Cost of goods sold		
Direct materials	$100,000	
Direct labor	20,000	
Machinery repairs (variable cost)	3,000	
Depreciation—machinery	11,920	
Utilities (80% is variable cost)	8,000	
Plant manager salaries	6,000	148,920
Gross profit		101,080
Selling expenses		
Packaging	9,000	
Shipping	30,000	
Sales salary (fixed annual amount)	18,000	57,000
General and administrative expenses		
Advertising	4,000	
Salaries	9,360	
Entertainment expense	10,000	23,360
Income from operations		$ 20,720

Required

1. Classify all items listed in the fixed budget as variable or fixed. Also determine their amounts per unit or their amounts for the year, as appropriate.
2. Prepare flexible budgets (see Exhibit 24.3) for the company at sales volumes of 8,000 and 12,000 units.
3. The company's business conditions are improving. One possible result is a sales volume of approximately 14,400 units. The company president is confident that this volume is within the relevant range of existing capacity. How much would operating income increase over the 2011 budgeted amount of $20,720 if this level is reached without increasing capacity?
4. An unfavorable change in business is remotely possible; in this case, production and sales volume for 2011 could fall to 5,000 units. How much income (or loss) from operations would occur if sales volume falls to this level?

Check (2) Budgeted income at 12,000 units, $37,040

(4) Potential operating loss, $(20,080)

Problem 24-4B

Preparation and analysis of a flexible budget performance report

P1 A1

Refer to the information in Problem 24-3B. Razorback Company's actual income statement for 2011 follows.

RAZORBACK COMPANY Statement of Income from Operations For Year Ended December 31, 2011		
Sales (12,000 units)		$288,000
Cost of goods sold		
Direct materials	$95,000	
Direct labor	16,000	
Machinery repairs (variable cost)	3,300	
Depreciation—machinery	11,920	
Utilities (variable cost, $7,160)	8,520	
Plant manager salaries	6,720	141,460
Gross profit		146,540
Selling expenses		
Packaging	10,800	
Shipping	37,200	
Sales salary (annual)	19,200	67,200
General and administrative expenses		
Advertising expense	4,200	
Salaries	9,360	
Entertainment expense	10,000	23,560
Income from operations		$ 55,780

Required

Check   (1) Variances: Fixed costs, $1,880 U; Income, $18,740 F

1. Prepare a flexible budget performance report for 2011.

Analysis Component

2. Analyze and interpret both the (a) sales variance and (b) direct materials variance.

Problem 24-5B

Flexible budget preparation; computation of materials, labor, and overhead variances; and overhead variance report

P1 P2 P3 C2

Sunburst Company set the following standard costs for one unit of its product.

Direct materials (48 kgs. @ $4 per kg.)	$192.00
Direct labor (12 hrs. @ $9 per hr.)	108.00
Overhead (12 hrs. @ $4.50 per hr.)	54.00
Total standard cost........................	$354.00

The predetermined overhead rate ($4.50 per direct labor hour) is based on an expected volume of 50% of the factory's capacity of 10,000 units per month. Following are the company's budgeted overhead costs per month at the 50% level.

Overhead Budget (50% Capacity)		
Variable overhead costs		
Indirect materials	$40,000	
Indirect labor	80,000	
Power	20,000	
Repairs and maintenance	30,000	
Total variable overhead costs		$170,000
Fixed overhead costs		
Depreciation—building	20,000	
Depreciation—machinery	30,000	
Taxes and insurance	10,000	
Supervision	40,000	
Total fixed overhead costs		100,000
Total overhead costs		$270,000

The company incurred the following actual costs when it operated at 40% of capacity in December.

Direct materials (196,000 kgs. @ $4.00)		$ 784,000
Direct labor (46,000 hrs. @ $9.15)		420,900
Overhead costs		
Indirect materials	$30,000	
Indirect labor	66,000	
Power	15,600	
Repairs and maintenance	21,000	
Depreciation—building	20,000	
Depreciation—machinery	30,000	
Taxes and insurance	9,600	
Supervision	39,600	231,800
Total costs		$1,436,700

Required

1. Examine the monthly overhead budget to (a) determine the costs per unit for each variable overhead item and its total per unit costs, and (b) identify the total fixed costs per month.

2. Prepare flexible overhead budgets (as in Exhibit 24.12) for December showing the amounts of each variable and fixed cost at the 40%, 50%, and 60% capacity levels.

3. Compute the direct materials cost variance, including its price and quantity variances.

4. Compute the direct labor cost variance, including its rate and efficiency variances.

5. Prepare a detailed overhead variance report (as in Exhibit 24.15) that shows the variances for individual items of overhead.

Check (2) Budgeted total overhead at 6,000 units, $304,000

(3) Materials variances: Price, $0 U; Quantity, $16,000 U

(4) Labor variances: Rate, $6,900 U; Efficiency, $18,000 F

Carlsbad Company has set the following standard costs per unit for the product it manufactures.

Direct materials (40 oz. @ $0.75 per oz.)	$ 30.00
Direct labor (2 hr. @ $20 per hr.)	40.00
Overhead (2 hr. @ $53.50 per hr.)	107.00
Total standard cost	$177.00

Problem 24-6B[A]
Materials, labor, and overhead variances; and overhead variance report

C2   P2   P3

The predetermined overhead rate is based on a planned operating volume of 60% of the productive capacity of 3,000 units per month. The following flexible budget information is available.

	Operating Levels		
	50%	60%	70%
Production in units	1,500	1,800	2,100
Standard direct labor hours	3,000	3,600	4,200
Budgeted overhead			
Variable overhead costs			
Indirect materials	$ 18,000	$21,600	$25,200
Indirect labor	10,500	12,600	14,700
Power	7,500	9,000	10,500
Maintenance	4,500	5,400	6,300
Total variable costs	40,500	48,600	56,700
Fixed overhead costs			
Rent of factory building	48,000	48,000	48,000
Depreciation—machinery	44,000	44,000	44,000
Taxes and insurance	20,000	20,000	20,000
Supervisory salaries	32,000	32,000	32,000
Total fixed costs	144,000	144,000	144,000
Total overhead costs	$184,500	$192,600	$200,700

During March, the company operated at 70% of capacity and produced 2,100 units, incurring the following actual costs.

Direct materials (88,000 oz. @ $0.70 per oz.)		$ 61,600
Direct labor (4,000 hrs. @ $19.50 per hr.)		78,000
Overhead costs		
Indirect materials.	$23,600	
Indirect labor	14,800	
Power.	10,000	
Maintenance.	3,200	
Rent of factory building	48,000	
Depreciation—machinery	44,000	
Taxes and insurance	24,000	
Supervisory salaries.	31,600	199,200
Total costs		$338,800

Required

1. Compute the direct materials cost variance, including its price and quantity variances.
2. Compute the direct labor variance, including its rate and efficiency variances.
3. Compute these variances: (a) variable overhead spending and efficiency, (b) fixed overhead spending and volume, and (c) total overhead controllable.
4. Prepare a detailed overhead variance report (as in Exhibit 24.15) that shows the variances for individual items of overhead.

Problem 24-7B[A]
Materials, labor, and overhead
variances recorded and analyzed

C1   P4

Kincaid Company's standard cost accounting system recorded this information from its June operations.

Standard direct materials cost	$220,500
Direct materials quantity variance (favorable)	20,250
Direct materials price variance (favorable)	14,500
Actual direct labor cost	335,000
Direct labor efficiency variance (favorable)	26,700
Direct labor rate variance (unfavorable)	3,500
Actual overhead cost	359,000
Volume variance (unfavorable)	1,650
Controllable variance (unfavorable)	32,500

Required

1. Prepare journal entries dated June 30 to record the company's costs and variances for the month. (Do not prepare the journal entry to close the variances.)

Analysis Component

2. Identify the areas that would attract the attention of a manager who uses management by exception. Describe what action(s) the manager should consider.

SERIAL PROBLEM
Business Solutions

P1

(This serial problem began in Chapter 1 and continues through most of the book. If previous chapter segments were not completed, the serial problem can begin at this point. It is helpful, but not necessary, to use the working papers that accompany the book.)

SP 24 Business Solutions' second quarter 2012 fixed budget performance report for its computer furniture operations follows. The $156,000 budgeted expenses include $108,000 in variable expenses for desks and $18,000 in variable expenses for chairs, as well as $30,000 fixed expenses. The actual expenses include $31,000 fixed expenses. Prepare a flexible budget performance report that shows any variances between budgeted results and actual results. List fixed and variable expenses separately.

	Fixed Budget	Actual Results	Variances
Desk sales (in units).............	144	150	
Chair sales (in units)	72	80	
Desk sales (in dollars)	$180,000	$186,000	$6,000 F
Chair sales (in dollars)..........	$ 36,000	$ 41,200	$5,200 F
Total expenses.................	$156,000	$163,880	$7,880 U
Income from operations	$ 60,000	$ 63,320	$3,320 F

Check   Variances: Fixed expenses, $1,000 U

Beyond the Numbers

BTN 24-1   Analysis of flexible budgets and standard costs emphasizes the importance of a similar unit of measure for meaningful comparisons and evaluations. When **Research In Motion** compiles its financial reports in compliance with GAAP, it applies the same unit of measurement, U.S. dollars, for most measures of business operations. One issue for Research In Motion is how best to adjust account values for its subsidiaries that compile financial reports in currencies other than the U.S. dollar.

REPORTING IN ACTION

C1

RIM

Required

1. Read Research In Motion's Note 1 in Appendix A and identify the financial statement where it reports the annual adjustment (remeasurement) for foreign currency translation.
2. Translating financial statements requires the use of a currency exchange rate. For each of the following three financial statement items, explain the exchange rate the company would apply to translate into U.S. dollars.
   a. Cash
   b. Sales revenue
   c. Property, plant and equipment

BTN 24-2   The usefulness of budgets, variances, and related analyses often depends on the accuracy of management's estimates of future sales activity.

COMPARATIVE ANALYSIS

A1

RIM

Apple

Palm

Required

1. Identify and record the prior three years' sales (in dollars) for **Research In Motion, Apple**, and **Palm** using their financial statements in Appendix A.
2. Using the data in part 1, predict all three companies' sales activity for the next two to three years. (If possible, compare your predictions to actual sales figures for these years.)

BTN 24-3   Setting materials, labor, and overhead standards is challenging. If standards are set too low, companies might purchase inferior products and employees might not work to their full potential. If standards are set too high, companies could be unable to offer a quality product at a profitable rate and employees could be overworked. The ethical challenge is to set a high but reasonable standard. Assume that as a manager, you are asked to set the standard materials price and quantity for the new 1,000 CKB Mega-Max chip, a technically advanced product. To properly set the price and quantity standards, you assemble a team of specialists to provide input.

ETHICS CHALLENGE

C1

Required

Identify four types of specialists that you would assemble to provide information to help set the materials price and quantity standards. Briefly explain why you chose each individual.

COMMUNICATING IN PRACTICE

P4   C2

BTN 24-4   The reason we use the words *favorable* and *unfavorable* when evaluating variances is made clear when we look at the closing of accounts. To see this, consider that (1) all variance accounts are closed at the end of each period (temporary accounts), (2) a favorable variance is always a credit balance, and (3) an unfavorable variance is always a debit balance. Write a one-half page memorandum to your instructor with three parts that answer the three following requirements. (Assume that variance accounts are closed to Cost of Goods Sold.)

Required

1. Does Cost of Goods Sold increase or decrease when closing a favorable variance? Does gross margin increase or decrease when a favorable variance is closed to Cost of Goods Sold? Explain.
2. Does Cost of Goods Sold increase or decrease when closing an unfavorable variance? Does gross margin increase or decrease when an unfavorable variance is closed to Cost of Goods Sold? Explain.
3. Explain the meaning of a favorable variance and an unfavorable variance.

TAKING IT TO THE NET

C1

BTN 24-5   Access **iSixSigma**'s Website (**iSixSigma.com**) to search for and read information about *benchmarking* to complete the following requirements.

Required

1. Write a one-paragraph explanation (in layperson's terms) of benchmarking.
2. How does standard costing relate to benchmarking?

TEAMWORK IN ACTION

C2

BTN 24-6   Many service industries link labor rate and time (quantity) standards with their processes. One example is the standard time to board an aircraft. The reason time plays such an important role in the service industry is that it is viewed as a competitive advantage: best service in the shortest amount of time. Although the labor rate component is difficult to observe, the time component of a service delivery standard is often readily apparent—for example, "Lunch will be served in less than five minutes, or it is free."

Required

Break into teams and select two service industries for your analysis. Identify and describe all the time elements each industry uses to create a competitive advantage.

ENTREPRENEURIAL DECISION

C1   C2

BTN 24-7   **SewWhat? Inc.**, as discussed in the chapter opener, uses a costing system with standard costs for direct materials, direct labor, and overhead costs. Two comments frequently are mentioned in relation to standard costing and variance analysis: "Variances are not explanations" and "Management's goal is not to minimize variances."

Required

Write a short memo to Megan Duckett, SewWhat? Inc.'s CEO, (no more than 1 page) interpreting these two comments.

HITTING THE ROAD

C1

BTN 24-8   Training employees to use standard amounts of materials in production is common. Typically large companies invest in this training but small organizations do not. One can observe these different practices in a trip to two different pizza businesses. Visit both a local pizza business and a national pizza chain business and then complete the following.

Required

1. Observe and record the number of raw material items used to make a typical cheese pizza. Also observe how the person making the pizza applies each item when preparing the pizza.
2. Record any differences in how items are applied between the two businesses.
3. Estimate which business is more profitable from your observations. Explain.

BTN 24-9 Access the annual report of **Nokia** (at www.Nokia.com) for the year ended December 31, 2009. The usefulness of its budgets, variances, and related analyses depends on the accuracy of management's estimates of future sales activity.

GLOBAL DECISION

A1

NOKIA

Required

1. Identify and record the prior two years' sales (in € millions) for Nokia from its income statement.
2. Using the data in part 1, predict sales activity for Nokia for the next two years. Explain your prediction process.

ANSWERS TO MULTIPLE CHOICE QUIZ

1. c; Fixed costs remain at $300,000; Variable costs = ($246,000/24,000 units) × 20,000 units = $205,000.

2. e; Budgeted direct materials + Unfavorable variance = Actual cost of direct materials used; or, 60,000 units × $10 per unit = $600,000 + $15,000 U = $615,000.

3. c; (AH × AR) − (AH × SR) = $1,599,040 − (84,160 hours × $20 per hour) = $84,160 F.

4. b; Actual variable overhead − Variable overhead applied to production = Variable overhead cost variance; or $150,000 − (96,000 hours × $1.50 per hour) = $6,000 U.

5. a; Budgeted fixed overhead − Fixed overhead applied to production = Volume variance; or $24,000 − (4,800 units × $4 per unit) = $4,800 U.

25

Capital Budgeting and Managerial Decisions

A Look Back

Chapter 24 discussed flexible budgets, variance analysis, and standard costs. It explained how management uses each to control and monitor business activities.

A Look at This Chapter

This chapter focuses on evaluating capital budgeting decisions. It also explains several tools and procedures used in making and evaluating short-term managerial decisions.

Learning Objectives

CAP

CONCEPTUAL

C1 Describe the importance of relevant costs for short-term decisions. (p. 1047)

ANALYTICAL

A1 Evaluate short-term managerial decisions using relevant costs. (p. 1048)

A2 Analyze a capital investment project using break-even time. (p. 1055)

LP25

PROCEDURAL

P1 Compute payback period and describe its use. (p. 1037)

P2 Compute accounting rate of return and explain its use. (p. 1039)

P3 Compute net present value and describe its use. (p. 1041)

P4 Compute internal rate of return and explain its use. (p. 1043)

Top Dog!

"Always improve your product . . ."
—MARCO GIANNINI

SAN FRANCISCO, CA—Bothered by dealing with his dog's painful health problems, Marco Giannini started **Dogswell LLC (Dogswell.com),** a company devoted to developing foods to fight disease in dogs. The company combines natural ingredients with nutritional supplements like flaxseed, glucosamine, and taurine to make Happy Hips™, Mellow Mut™, and Biscuits with Benefits™.

Marco started with $30,000 of his own money and insight into the benefits of nutritional supplements after the failure of his venture into nutritional beverages. His first product was cage-free chicken jerky sold from plastic bags hanging from grocery store hooks. "The treat was very cost-effective, and it was easy to get shelf space for a small product that provided good contribution margins for retailers," explains Marco. Focusing on contribution margins also helps Marco and his Dogswell team make decisions on sales mix and whether to eliminate certain products. "Not all of our products have been successful, but we quickly push the successful ones and we take the bottom ones out of the market," admits Marco. Focusing on relevant costs and incremental revenues guides these important business decisions.

Marco applies high standards to his production process. Unlike some companies that might be able to rework substandard materials into a viable product, Marco says "raw materials that do not meet our specifications never enter our processing facilitities." Assessing payback periods, rates of return, and break-even points helps Marco make decisions on what, and when, to buy. While capital budgeting decisions are important, Marco stresses the importance of employees— "We didn't bring on human capital fast enough," he admits. And, says Marco, don't ignore factors such as employee morale and the company's image in making decisions.

Marco advises would-be entrepreneurs to develop the best product they can. He stresses "simplicity" as one key to success. "Make everything easy for the customer," says Marco. "We have a simple product line with easy-to-read ingredients. People appreciate that." With projected sales of over $21 million, that recipe is working.

[Sources: *Dogswell Company Website*, January 2011; *Los Angeles Business Journal*, November 2008; *Entrepeneur.com*, August 2008; *Pet Business,* September 2008]

Making business decisions involves choosing between alternative courses of action. Many factors affect business decisions, yet analysis typically focuses on finding the alternative that offers the highest return on investment or the greatest reduction in costs. Some decisions are based on little more than an intuitive understanding of the situation because available information is too limited to allow a more systematic analysis. In other cases, intangible factors such as convenience, prestige, and environmental considerations are more important than strictly quantitative factors. In all situations, managers can reach a sounder decision if they identify the consequences of alternative choices in financial terms. This chapter explains several methods of analysis that can help managers make those business decisions.

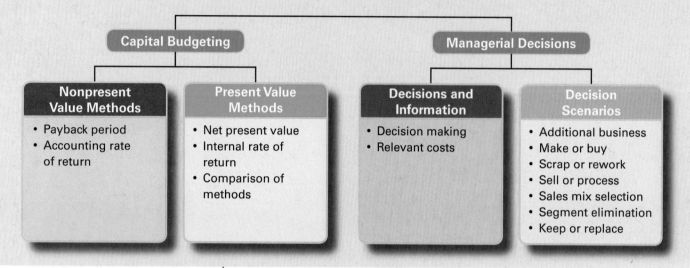

Capital Budgeting

Nonpresent Value Methods	Present Value Methods
• Payback period • Accounting rate of return	• Net present value • Internal rate of return • Comparison of methods

Managerial Decisions

Decisions and Information	Decision Scenarios
• Decision making • Relevant costs	• Additional business • Make or buy • Scrap or rework • Sell or process • Sales mix selection • Segment elimination • Keep or replace

Section 1—Capital Budgeting

The capital expenditures budget is management's plan for acquiring and selling plant assets. **Capital budgeting** is the process of analyzing alternative long-term investments and deciding which assets to acquire or sell. These decisions can involve developing a new product or process, buying a new machine or a new building, or acquiring an entire company. An objective for these decisions is to earn a satisfactory return on investment.

Capital budgeting decisions require careful analysis because they are usually the most difficult and risky decisions that managers make. These decisions are difficult because they require predicting events that will not occur until well into the future. Many of these predictions are tentative and potentially unreliable. Specifically, a capital budgeting decision is risky because (1) the outcome is uncertain, (2) large amounts of money are usually involved, (3) the investment involves a long-term commitment, and (4) the decision could be difficult or impossible to reverse, no matter how poor it turns out to be. Risk is especially high for investments in technology due to innovations and uncertainty.

Managers use several methods to evaluate capital budgeting decisions. Nearly all of these methods involve predicting cash inflows and cash outflows of proposed investments, assessing the risk of and returns on those flows, and then choosing the investments to make. Management often restates future cash flows in terms of their present value. This approach applies the time value of money: A dollar today is worth more than a dollar tomorrow. Similarly, a dollar tomorrow is worth less than a dollar today. The process of restating future cash flows in terms of their present value is called *discounting*. The time value of money is important when evaluating capital investments, but managers sometimes apply evaluation methods that ignore present value. This section describes four methods for comparing alternative investments.

Point: The nature of capital spending has changed with the business environment. Budgets for information technology have increased from about 25% of corporate capital spending 20 years ago to an estimated 35% today.

METHODS NOT USING TIME VALUE OF MONEY

All investments, whether they involve the purchase of a machine or another long-term asset, are expected to produce net cash flows. *Net cash flow* is cash inflows minus cash outflows. Sometimes managers perform simple analyses of the financial feasibility of an investment's net cash flow without using the time value of money. This section explains two of the most common methods in this category: (1) payback period and (2) accounting rate of return.

Payback Period

An investment's **payback period (PBP)** is the expected time period to recover the initial investment amount. Managers prefer investing in assets with shorter payback periods to reduce the risk of an unprofitable investment over the long run. Acquiring assets with short payback periods reduces a company's risk from potentially inaccurate long-term predictions of future cash flows.

P1 Compute payback period and describe its use.

Computing Payback Period with Even Cash Flows To illustrate use of the payback period for an investment with even cash flows, we look at data from FasTrac, a manufacturer of exercise equipment and supplies. (*Even cash flows* are cash flows that are the same each and every year; *uneven cash flows* are cash flows that are not all equal in amount.) FasTrac is considering several different capital investments, one of which is to purchase a machine to use in manufacturing a new product. This machine costs $16,000 and is expected to have an eight-year life with no salvage value. Management predicts this machine will produce 1,000 units of product each year and that the new product will be sold for $30 per unit. Exhibit 25.1 shows the expected annual net cash flows for this asset over its life as well as the expected annual revenues and expenses (including depreciation and income taxes) from investing in the machine.

EXHIBIT 25.1

Cash Flow Analysis

FASTRAC Cash Flow Analysis—Machinery Investment January 15, 2011	Expected Accrual Figures	Expected Net Cash Flows
Annual sales of new product	$30,000	$30,000
Deduct annual expenses		
Cost of materials, labor, and overhead (except depreciation)	15,500	15,500
Depreciation—Machinery	2,000	
Additional selling and administrative expenses	9,500	9,500
Annual pretax accrual income	3,000	
Income taxes (30%)	900	900
Annual net income	$ 2,100	
Annual net cash flow		$4,100

The amount of net cash flow from the machinery is computed by subtracting expected cash outflows from expected cash inflows. The cash flows column of Exhibit 25.1 excludes all noncash revenues and expenses. Depreciation is FasTrac's only noncash item. Alternatively, managers can adjust the projected net income for revenue and expense items that do not affect cash flows. For FasTrac, this means taking the $2,100 net income and adding back the $2,000 depreciation.

Point: Annual net cash flow in Exhibit 25.1 equals net income plus depreciation (a noncash expense).

The formula for computing the payback period of an investment that yields even net cash flows is in Exhibit 25.2.

$$\text{Payback period} = \frac{\text{Cost of investment}}{\text{Annual net cash flow}}$$

EXHIBIT 25.2

Payback Period Formula with Even Cash Flows

The payback period reflects the amount of time for the investment to generate enough net cash flow to return (or pay back) the cash initially invested to purchase it. FasTrac's payback period for this machine is just under four years:

$$\text{Payback period} = \frac{\$16,000}{\$4,100} = 3.9 \text{ years}$$

Example: If an alternative machine (with different technology) yields a payback period of 3.5 years, which one does a manager choose? Answer: The alternative (3.5 is less than 3.9).

The initial investment is fully recovered in 3.9 years, or just before reaching the halfway point of this machine's useful life of eight years.

Decision Insight

Payback Phones   Profits of telecoms have declined as too much capital investment chased too little revenue. Telecom success depends on new technology, and communications gear is evolving at a dizzying rate. Consequently, managers of telecoms often demand short payback periods and large expected net cash flows to compensate for the investment risk. ■

Computing Payback Period with Uneven Cash Flows   Computing the payback period in the prior section assumed even net cash flows. What happens if the net cash flows are uneven? In this case, the payback period is computed using the *cumulative total of net cash flows*. The word *cumulative* refers to the addition of each period's net cash flows as we progress through time. To illustrate, consider data for another investment that FasTrac is considering. This machine is predicted to generate uneven net cash flows over the next eight years. The relevant data and payback period computation are shown in Exhibit 25.3.

EXHIBIT 25.3

Payback Period Calculation with Uneven Cash Flows

Period*	Expected Net Cash Flows	Cumulative Net Cash Flows
Year 0	$(16,000)	$(16,000)
Year 1	3,000	(13,000)
Year 2	4,000	(9,000)
Year 3...........	4,000	(5,000)
Year 4	4,000	(1,000)
Year 5	5,000	4,000
Year 6	3,000	7,000
Year 7	2,000	9,000
Year 8	2,000	11,000
		Payback period = 4.2 years

* All cash inflows and outflows occur uniformly during the year.

Example: Find the payback period in Exhibit 25.3 if net cash flows for the first 4 years are:
Year 1 = $6,000; Year 2 = $5,000;
Year 3 = $4,000; Year 4 = $3,000.
Answer: 3.33 years

Year 0 refers to the period of initial investment in which the $16,000 cash outflow occurs at the end of year 0 to acquire the machinery. By the end of year 1, the cumulative net cash flow is reduced to $(13,000), computed as the $(16,000) initial cash outflow plus year 1's $3,000 cash inflow. This process continues throughout the asset's life. The cumulative net cash flow amount changes from negative to positive in year 5. Specifically, at the end of year 4, the cumulative net cash flow is $(1,000). As soon as FasTrac receives net cash inflow of $1,000 during the fifth year, it has fully recovered the investment. If we assume that cash flows are received uniformly *within* each year, receipt of the $1,000 occurs about one-fifth of the way through the year. This is computed as $1,000 divided by year 5's total net cash flow of $5,000, or 0.20. This yields a payback period of 4.2 years, computed as 4 years plus 0.20 of year 5.

Using the Payback Period   Companies desire a short payback period to increase return and reduce risk. The more quickly a company receives cash, the sooner it is available for other uses and the less time it is at risk of loss. A shorter payback period also improves the company's ability to respond to unanticipated changes and lowers its risk of having to keep an unprofitable investment.

Payback period should never be the only consideration in evaluating investments. This is so because it ignores at least two important factors. First, it fails to reflect differences in the timing of net cash flows within the payback period. In Exhibit 25.3, FasTrac's net cash flows in the first five years were $3,000, $4,000, $4,000, $4,000, and $5,000. If another investment had predicted cash flows of $9,000, $3,000, $2,000, $1,800, and $1,000 in these five years, its payback period would also be 4.2 years, but this second alternative could be more desirable because it provides cash more quickly. The second important factor is that the payback period ignores *all* cash flows after the point where its costs are fully recovered. For example, one investment might pay back its cost in 3 years but stop producing cash after 4 years. A second investment might require 5 years to pay back its cost yet continue to produce net cash flows for another 15 years. A focus on only the payback period would mistakenly lead management to choose the first investment over the second.

"So what if I underestimated costs and overestimated revenues? It all averages out in the end."

Quick Check

Answers — p. 1061

1. Capital budgeting is (*a*) concerned with analyzing alternative sources of capital, including debt and equity, (*b*) an important activity for companies when considering what assets to acquire or sell, or (*c*) best done by intuitive assessments of the value of assets and their usefulness.
2. Why are capital budgeting decisions often difficult?
3. A company is considering purchasing equipment costing $75,000. Future annual net cash flows from this equipment are $30,000, $25,000, $15,000, $10,000, and $5,000. The payback period is (*a*) 4 years, (*b*) 3.5 years, or (*c*) 3 years.
4. If depreciation is an expense, why is it added back to an investment's net income to compute the net cash flow from that investment?
5. If two investments have the same payback period, are they equally desirable? Explain.

Accounting Rate of Return

The **accounting rate of return,** also called *return on average investment,* is computed by dividing a project's after-tax net income by the average amount invested in it. To illustrate, we return to FasTrac's $16,000 machinery investment described in Exhibit 25.1. We first compute (1) the after-tax net income and (2) the average amount invested. The $2,100 after-tax net income is already available from Exhibit 25.1. To compute the average amount invested, we assume that net cash flows are received evenly throughout each year. Thus, the average investment for each year is computed as the average of its beginning and ending book values. If FasTrac's $16,000 machine is depreciated $2,000 each year, the average amount invested in the machine for each year is computed as shown in Exhibit 25.4. The average for any year is the average of the beginning and ending book values.

P2 Compute accounting rate of return and explain its use.

	Beginning Book Value	Annual Depreciation	Ending Book Value	Average Book Value
Year 1	$16,000	$2,000	$14,000	$15,000
Year 2	14,000	2,000	12,000	13,000
Year 3	12,000	2,000	10,000	11,000
Year 4	10,000	2,000	8,000	9,000
Year 5	8,000	2,000	6,000	7,000
Year 6	6,000	2,000	4,000	5,000
Year 7	4,000	2,000	2,000	3,000
Year 8	2,000	2,000	0	1,000
All years				$ 8,000

EXHIBIT 25.4

Computing Average Amount Invested (Book Value)

Next we need the average book value for the asset's entire life. This amount is computed by taking the average of the individual yearly averages. This average equals $8,000, computed as $64,000 (the sum of the individual years' averages) divided by eight years (see last column of Exhibit 25.4).

If a company uses straight-line depreciation, we can find the average amount invested by using the formula in Exhibit 25.5. Because FasTrac uses straight-line depreciation, its average

Point: General formula for *annual average investment* is the sum of individual years' average book values divided by the number of years of the planned investment.

amount invested for the eight years equals the sum of the book value at the beginning of the asset's investment period and the book value at the end of its investment period, divided by 2, as shown in Exhibit 25.5.

EXHIBIT 25.5

Computing Average Amount
Invested under Straight-Line
Depreciation

$$\text{Annual average investment} = \frac{\text{Beginning book value} + \text{Ending book value}}{2}$$
(straight-line case only)

$$= \frac{\$16,000 + \$0}{2} = \$8,000$$

If an investment has a salvage value, the average amount invested when using straight-line depreciation is computed as (Beginning book value + Salvage value)/2.

Once we determine the after-tax net income and the average amount invested, the accounting rate of return on the investment can be computed from the annual after-tax net income divided by the average amount invested, as shown in Exhibit 25.6.

EXHIBIT 25.6

Accounting Rate of
Return Formula

$$\text{Accounting rate of return} = \frac{\text{Annual after-tax net income}}{\text{Annual average investment}}$$

This yields an accounting rate of return of 26.25% ($2,100/$8,000). FasTrac management must decide whether a 26.25% accounting rate of return is satisfactory. To make this decision, we must factor in the investment's risk. For instance, we cannot say an investment with a 26.25% return is preferred over one with a lower return unless we recognize any differences in risk. Thus, an investment's return is satisfactory or unsatisfactory only when it is related to returns from other investments with similar lives and risk.

When accounting rate of return is used to choose among capital investments, the one with the least risk, the shortest payback period, and the highest return for the longest time period is often identified as the best. However, use of accounting rate of return to evaluate investment opportunities is limited because it bases the amount invested on book values (not predicted market values) in future periods. Accounting rate of return is also limited when an asset's net incomes are expected to vary from year to year. This requires computing the rate using *average* annual net incomes, yet this accounting rate of return fails to distinguish between two investments with the same average annual net income but different amounts of income in early years versus later years or different levels of income variability.

Quick Check

Answers – p. 1062

6. The following data relate to a company's decision on whether to purchase a machine:

Cost $180,000
Salvage value 15,000
Annual after-tax net income 40,000

The machine's accounting rate of return, assuming the even receipt of its net cash flows during the year and use of straight-line depreciation, is (a) 22%, (b) 41%, or (c) 21%.

7. Is a 15% accounting rate of return for a machine a good rate?

METHODS USING TIME VALUE OF MONEY

This section describes two methods that help managers with capital budgeting decisions and that use the time value of money: (1) net present value and (2) internal rate of return. *(To apply these methods, you need a basic understanding of the concept of present value. An expanded explanation of present value concepts is in Appendix B near the end of the book. You can use the present value tables at the end of Appendix B to solve many of this chapter's assignments that use the time value of money.)*

Net Present Value

Net present value analysis applies the time value of money to future cash inflows and cash outflows so management can evaluate a project's benefits and costs at one point in time. Specifically, **net present value (NPV)** is computed by discounting the future net cash flows from the investment at the project's required rate of return and then subtracting the initial amount invested. A company's required return, often called its hurdle rate, is typically its **cost of capital,** which is the rate the company must pay to its long-term creditors and shareholders.

To illustrate, let's return to FasTrac's proposed machinery purchase described in Exhibit 25.1. Does this machine provide a satisfactory return while recovering the amount invested? Recall that the machine requires a $16,000 investment and is expected to provide $4,100 annual net cash inflows for the next eight years. If we assume that net cash flows from this machine are received at each year-end and that FasTrac requires a 12% annual return, net present value can be computed as in Exhibit 25.7.

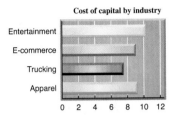

	Net Cash Flows*	Present Value of 1 at 12%†	Present Value of Net Cash Flows
Year 1	$ 4,100	0.8929	$ 3,661
Year 2	4,100	0.7972	3,269
Year 3	4,100	0.7118	2,918
Year 4	4,100	0.6355	2,606
Year 5	4,100	0.5674	2,326
Year 6	4,100	0.5066	2,077
Year 7	4,100	0.4523	1,854
Year 8	4,100	0.4039	1,656
Totals	$32,800		20,367
Amount invested			(16,000)
Net present value			$ 4,367

EXHIBIT 25.7

Net Present Value Calculation with Equal Cash Flows

* Cash flows occur at the end of each year.

† Present value of 1 factors are taken from Table B.1 in Appendix B.

The first number column of Exhibit 25.7 shows the annual net cash flows. Present value of 1 factors, also called *discount factors,* are shown in the second column. Taken from Table B.1 in Appendix B, they assume that net cash flows are received at each year-end. *(To simplify present value computations and for assignment material at the end of this chapter, we assume that net cash flows are received at each year-end.)* Annual net cash flows from the first column of Exhibit 25.7 are multiplied by the discount factors in the second column to give present values shown in the third column. The last three lines of this exhibit show the final NPV computations. The asset's $16,000 initial cost is deducted from the $20,367 total present value of all future net cash flows to give this asset's NPV of $4,367. The machine is thus expected to (1) recover its cost, (2) provide a 12% compounded return, and (3) generate $4,367 above cost. We summarize this analysis by saying the present value of this machine's future net cash flows to FasTrac exceeds the $16,000 investment by $4,367.

Net Present Value Decision Rule The decision rule in applying NPV is as follows: When an asset's expected cash flows are discounted at the required rate and yield a *positive* net present value, the asset should be acquired. This decision rule is reflected in the graphic below. When comparing several investment opportunities of about the same cost and same risk, we prefer the one with the highest positive net present value.

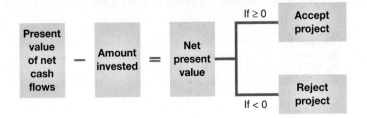

Point: The assumption of end-of-year cash flows simplifies computations and is common in practice.

Point: The amount invested includes all costs that must be incurred to get the asset in its proper location and ready for use.

Example: What is the net present value in Exhibit 25.7 if a 10% return is applied? *Answer:* $5,873

Simplifying Computations   The computations in Exhibit 25.7 use separate present value of 1 factors for each of the eight years. Each year's net cash flow is multiplied by its present value of 1 factor to determine its present value. The individual present values for each of the eight net cash flows are added to give the asset's total present value. This computation can be simplified in two ways if annual net cash flows are equal in amount. One way is to add the eight annual present value of 1 factors for a total of 4.9676 and multiply this amount by the annual $4,100 net cash flow to get the $20,367 total present value of net cash flows.[1] A second simplification is to use a calculator with compound interest functions or a spreadsheet program. We show how to use Excel functions to compute net present value in this chapter's Appendix. Whatever procedure you use, it is important to understand the concepts behind these computations.

■ Decision Ethics   Answer — p. 1061

Systems Manager   Top management adopts a policy requiring purchases in excess of $5,000 to be submitted with cash flow projections to the cost analyst for capital budget approval. As systems manager, you want to upgrade your computers at a $25,000 cost. You consider submitting several orders all under $5,000 to avoid the approval process. You believe the computers will increase profits and wish to avoid a delay. What do you do? ■

Uneven Cash Flows   Net present value analysis can also be applied when net cash flows are uneven (unequal). To illustrate, assume that FasTrac can choose only one capital investment from among projects A, B, and C. Each project requires the same $12,000 initial investment. Future net cash flows for each project are shown in the first three number columns of Exhibit 25.8.

EXHIBIT 25.8

Net Present Value Calculation with Uneven Cash Flows

	Net Cash Flows			Present Value of 1 at 10%	Present Value of Net Cash Flows		
	A	**B**	**C**		**A**	**B**	**C**
Year 1	$ 5,000	$ 8,000	$ 1,000	0.9091	$ 4,546	$ 7,273	$ 909
Year 2	5,000	5,000	5,000	0.8264	4,132	4,132	4,132
Year 3	5,000	2,000	9,000	0.7513	3,757	1,503	6,762
Totals	$15,000	$15,000	$15,000		12,435	12,908	11,803
Amount invested					(12,000)	(12,000)	(12,000)
Net present value					$ 435	$ 908	$ (197)

The three projects in Exhibit 25.8 have the same expected total net cash flows of $15,000. Project A is expected to produce equal amounts of $5,000 each year. Project B is expected to produce a larger amount in the first year. Project C is expected to produce a larger amount in the third year. The fourth column of Exhibit 25.8 shows the present value of 1 factors from Table B.1 assuming 10% required return.

Computations in the right-most columns show that Project A has a $435 positive NPV. Project B has the largest NPV of $908 because it brings in cash more quickly. Project C has a $(197) *negative* NPV because its larger cash inflows are delayed. If FasTrac requires a 10% return, it should reject Project C because its NPV implies a return *under* 10%. If only one project can be accepted, project B appears best because it yields the highest NPV.

---

[1] We can simplify this computation using Table B.3, which gives the present value of 1 to be received periodically for a number of periods. To determine the present value of these eight annual receipts discounted at 12%, go down the 12% column of Table B.3 to the factor on the eighth line. This cumulative discount factor, also known as an *annuity* factor, is 4.9676. We then compute the $20,367 present value for these eight annual $4,100 receipts, computed as 4.9676 × $4,100.

Salvage Value and Accelerated Depreciation FasTrac predicted the $16,000 machine to have zero salvage value at the end of its useful life (recall Exhibit 25.1). In many cases, assets are expected to have salvage values. If so, this amount is an additional net cash inflow received at the end of the final year of the asset's life. All other computations remain the same.

Depreciation computations also affect net present value analysis. FasTrac computes depreciation using the straight-line method. Accelerated depreciation is also commonly used, especially for income tax reports. Accelerated depreciation produces larger depreciation deductions in the early years of an asset's life and smaller deductions in later years. This pattern results in smaller income tax payments in early years and larger payments in later years. Accelerated depreciation does not change the basics of a present value analysis, but it can change the result. Using accelerated depreciation for tax reporting affects the NPV of an asset's cash flows because it produces larger net cash inflows in the early years of the asset's life and smaller ones in later years. Being able to use accelerated depreciation for tax reporting always makes an investment more desirable because early cash flows are more valuable than later ones.

Use of Net Present Value In deciding whether to proceed with a capital investment project, we approve the proposal if the NPV is positive but reject it if the NPV is negative. When considering several projects of similar investment amounts and risk levels, we can compare the different projects' NPVs and rank them on the basis of their NPVs. However, if the amount invested differs substantially across projects, the NPV is of limited value for comparison purposes. One means to compare projects, especially when a company cannot fund all positive net present value projects, is to use the **profitability index,** which is computed as:

$$\text{Profitability index} = \frac{\text{Net present value of cash flows}}{\text{Investment}}$$

A higher profitability index suggests a more desirable project. To illustrate, suppose that Project X requires a $1 million investment and provides a $100,000 NPV. Project Y requires an investment of only $100,000 and returns a $75,000 NPV. Ranking on the basis of NPV puts Project X ahead of Y, yet X's profitability index is only 0.10 ($100,000/$1,000,000) whereas Y's profitability index is 0.75. We must also remember that when reviewing projects with different risks, we computed the NPV of individual projects using different discount rates. The higher the risk, the higher the discount rate.

Inflation Large price-level increases should be considered in NPV analyses. Hurdle rates already include investor's inflation forecasts. Net cash flows can be adjusted for inflation by using *future value* computations. For example, if the expected net cash inflow in year 1 is $4,100 and 5% inflation is expected, then the expected net cash inflow in year 2 is $4,305, computed as $4,100 × 1.05 (1.05 is the future value of $1 (Table B.2) for 1 period with a 5% rate).

Internal Rate of Return

Another means to evaluate capital investments is to use the **internal rate of return (IRR),** which equals the rate that yields an NPV of zero for an investment. This means that if we compute the total present value of a project's net cash flows using the IRR as the discount rate and then subtract the initial investment from this total present value, we get a zero NPV.

To illustrate, we use the data for FasTrac's Project A from Exhibit 25.8 to compute its IRR. Exhibit 25.9 shows the two-step process in computing IRR.

EXHIBIT 25.9

Computing Internal Rate of Return
(with even cash flows)

Step 1: Compute the present value factor for the investment project.

$$\text{Present value factor} = \frac{\text{Amount invested}}{\text{Net cash flows}} = \frac{\$12,000}{\$5,000} = 2.4000$$

Step 2: Identify the discount rate (IRR) yielding the present value factor

Search Table B.3 for a present value factor of 2.4000 in the three-year row (equaling the 3-year project duration). The 12% discount rate yields a present value factor of 2.4018. This implies that the IRR is approximately 12%.*

* Since the present value factor of 2.4000 is not exactly equal to the 12% factor of 2.4018, we can more precisely estimate the IRR as follows:

Discount rate	Present Value Factor from Table B.3
12%	2.4018
15%	2.2832
	0.1186 = difference

$$\text{Then, IRR} = 12\% + \left[(15\% - 12\%) \times \frac{2.4018 - 2.4000}{0.1186} \right] = \underline{\underline{12.05\%}}$$

When cash flows are equal, as with Project A, we compute the present value factor (as shown in Exhibit 25.9) by dividing the initial investment by its annual net cash flows. We then use an annuity table to determine the discount rate equal to this present value factor. For FasTrac's Project A, we look across the three-period row of Table B.3 and find that the discount rate corresponding to the present value factor of 2.4000 roughly equals the 2.4018 value for the 12% rate. This row is reproduced here:

Present Value of an Annuity of 1 for Three Periods

	Discount Rate				
Periods	1%	5%	10%	12%	15%
3	2.9410	2.7232	2.4869	2.4018	2.2832

The 12% rate is the Project's IRR. A more precise IRR estimate can be computed following the procedure shown in the note to Exhibit 25.9. Spreadsheet software and calculators can also compute this IRR. We show how to use an Excel function to compute IRR in this chapter's appendix.

Uneven Cash Flows   If net cash flows are uneven, we must use trial and error to compute the IRR. We do this by selecting any reasonable discount rate and computing the NPV. If the amount is positive (negative), we recompute the NPV using a higher (lower) discount rate. We continue these steps until we reach a point where two consecutive computations result in NPVs having different signs (positive and negative). Because the NPV is zero using IRR, we know that the IRR lies between these two discount rates. We can then estimate its value. Spreadsheet programs and calculators can do these computations for us.

▐ Decision Insight

Fun-IRR   Many theme parks use both financial and nonfinancial criteria to evaluate their investments in new rides and activities. The use of IRR is a major part of this evaluation. This requires good estimates of future cash inflows and outflows. It also requires risk assessments of the uncertainty of the future cash flows. ■

Use of Internal Rate of Return   When we use the IRR to evaluate a project, we compare it to a predetermined **hurdle rate,** which is a minimum acceptable rate of return and is applied as follows.

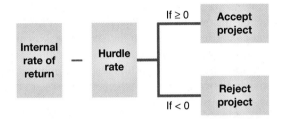

Top management selects the hurdle rate to use in evaluating capital investments. Financial formulas aid in this selection, but the choice of a minimum rate is subjective and left to management. For projects financed from borrowed funds, the hurdle rate must exceed the interest rate paid on these funds. The return on an investment must cover its interest and provide an additional profit to reward the company for its risk. For instance, if money is borrowed at 10%, an average risk investment often requires an after-tax return of 15% (or 5% above the borrowing rate). Remember that lower-risk investments require a lower rate of return compared with higher-risk investments.

If the project is internally financed, the hurdle rate is often based on actual returns from comparable projects. If the IRR is higher than the hurdle rate, the project is accepted. Multiple projects are often ranked by the extent to which their IRR exceeds the hurdle rate. The hurdle rate for individual projects is often different, depending on the risk involved. IRR is not subject to the limitations of NPV when comparing projects with different amounts invested because the IRR is expressed as a percent rather than as an absolute dollar value in NPV.

Example: How can management evaluate the risk of an investment? *Answer:* It must assess the uncertainty of future cash flows.

Point: A survey reports that 41% of top managers would reject a project with an internal rate of return *above* the cost of capital, *if* the project would cause the firm to miss its earnings forecast. The roles of benchmarks and manager compensation plans must be considered in capital budgeting decisions.

Decision Maker   Answer — p. 1061

Entrepreneur   You are developing a new product and you use a 12% discount rate to compute its NPV. Your banker, from whom you hope to obtain a loan, expresses concern that your discount rate is too low. How do you respond? ∎

Comparison of Capital Budgeting Methods

We explained four methods that managers use to evaluate capital investment projects. How do these methods compare with each other? Exhibit 25.10 addresses that question. Neither the payback period nor the accounting rate of return considers the time value of money. On the other hand, both the net present value and the internal rate of return do.

EXHIBIT 25.10

Comparing Capital Budgeting Methods

	Payback Period	Accounting Rate of Return	Net Present Value	Internal Rate of Return
Measurement basis	• Cash flows	• Accrual income	• Cash flows • Profitability	• Cash flows • Profitability
Measurement unit	• Years	• Percent	• Dollars	• Percent
Strengths	• Easy to understand	• Easy to understand	• Reflects time value of money	• Reflects time value of money
	• Allows comparison of projects	• Allows comparison of projects	• Reflects varying risks over project's life	• Allows comparisons of dissimilar projects
Limitations	• Ignores time value of money	• Ignores time value of money	• Difficult to compare dissimilar projects	• Ignores varying risks over life of project
	• Ignores cash flows after payback period	• Ignores annual rates over life of project		

The payback period is probably the simplest method. It gives managers an estimate of how soon they will recover their initial investment. Managers sometimes use this method when they have limited cash to invest and a number of projects to choose from. The accounting rate of return yields a percent measure computed using accrual income instead of cash flows. The accounting rate of return is an average rate for the entire investment period. Net present value considers all estimated net cash flows for the project's expected life. It can be applied to even and uneven cash flows and can reflect changes in the level of risk over a project's life. Since it yields a dollar measure, comparing projects of unequal sizes is more difficult. The internal rate of return considers all cash flows from a project. It is readily computed when the cash flows are even but requires some trial and error estimation when cash flows are uneven. Because the IRR is a percent measure, it is readily used to compare projects with different investment amounts. However, IRR does not reflect changes in risk over a project's life.

Decision Insight

And the Winner Is . . . How do we choose among the methods for evaluating capital investments? Management surveys consistently show the internal rate of return (IRR) as the most popular method followed by the payback period and net present value (NPV). Few companies use the accounting rate of return (ARR), but nearly all use more than one method. ■

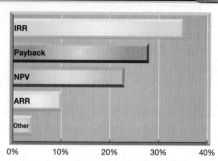

Company Usage of Capital Budgeting Methods

Quick Check

Answers — p. 1062

8. A company can invest in only one of two projects, A or B. Each project requires a $20,000 investment and is expected to generate end-of-period, annual cash flows as follows:

	Year 1	Year 2	Year 3	Total
Project A	$12,000	$8,500	$4,000	$24,500
Project B	4,500	8,500	13,000	26,000

Assuming a discount rate of 10%, which project has the higher net present value?

9. Two investment alternatives are expected to generate annual cash flows with the same net present value (assuming the same discount rate applied to each). Using this information, can you conclude that the two alternatives are equally desirable?

10. When two investment alternatives have the same total expected cash flows but differ in the timing of those flows, which method of evaluating those investments is superior, (a) accounting rate of return or (b) net present value?

Section 2—Managerial Decisions

This section focuses on methods that use accounting information to make several important managerial decisions. Most of these involve short-term decisions. This differs from methods used for longer-term managerial decisions that are described in the first section of this chapter and in several other chapters of this book.

DECISIONS AND INFORMATION

This section explains how managers make decisions and the information relevant to those decisions.

Decision Making

Managerial decision making involves five steps: (1) define the decision task, (2) identify alternative courses of action, (3) collect relevant information and evaluate each alternative, (4) select the preferred course of action, and (5) analyze and assess decisions made. These five steps are illustrated in Exhibit 25.11.

Define Task and Goal   Identify Alternative Actions   Collect Relevant Information   Select Course of Action   Analyze and Assess Decision

EXHIBIT 25.11

Managerial Decision Making

Both managerial and financial accounting information play an important role in most management decisions. The accounting system is expected to provide primarily *financial* information such as performance reports and budget analyses for decision making. *Nonfinancial* information is also relevant, however; it includes information on environmental effects, political sensitivities, and social responsibility.

Relevant Costs

Most financial measures of revenues and costs from accounting systems are based on historical costs. Although historical costs are important and useful for many tasks such as product pricing and the control and monitoring of business activities, we sometimes find that an analysis of *relevant costs,* or *avoidable costs,* is especially useful. Three types of costs are pertinent to our discussion of relevant costs: sunk costs, out-of-pocket costs, and opportunity costs.

> **C1** Describe the importance of relevant costs for short-term decisions.

A *sunk cost* arises from a past decision and cannot be avoided or changed; it is irrelevant to future decisions. An example is the cost of computer equipment previously purchased by a company. Most of a company's allocated costs, including fixed overhead items such as depreciation and administrative expenses, are sunk costs.

An *out-of-pocket cost* requires a future outlay of cash and is relevant for current and future decision making. These costs are usually the direct result of management's decisions. For instance, future purchases of computer equipment involve out-of-pocket costs.

An *opportunity cost* is the potential benefit lost by taking a specific action when two or more alternative choices are available. An example is a student giving up wages from a job to attend summer school. Companies continually must choose from alternative courses of action. For instance, a company making standardized products might be approached by a customer to supply a special (nonstandard) product. A decision to accept or reject the special order must consider not only the profit to be made from the special order but also the profit given up by devoting time and resources to this order instead of pursuing an alternative project. The profit given up is an opportunity cost. Consideration of opportunity costs is important. The implications extend to internal resource allocation decisions. For instance, a computer manufacturer must decide between internally manufacturing a chip versus buying it externally. In another case, management of a multidivisional company must decide whether to continue operating or close a particular division.

Example: Depreciation and amortization are allocations of the original cost of plant and intangible assets. Are they out-of-pocket costs? *Answer:* No; they are sunk costs.

Point: Opportunity costs are not entered in accounting records. This does not reduce their relevance for managerial decisions.

Besides relevant costs, management must also consider the relevant benefits associated with a decision. **Relevant benefits** refer to the additional or *incremental* revenue generated by selecting a particular course of action over another. For instance, a student must decide the relevant benefits of taking one course over another. In sum, both relevant costs and relevant benefits are crucial to managerial decision making.

MANAGERIAL DECISION SCENARIOS

A1 Evaluate short-term managerial decisions using relevant costs.

Managers experience many different scenarios that require analyzing alternative actions and making a decision. We describe several different types of decision scenarios in this section. We set these tasks in the context of FasTrac, an exercise supplies and equipment manufacturer introduced earlier. *We treat each of these decision tasks as separate from each other.*

Additional Business

FasTrac is operating at its normal level of 80% of full capacity. At this level, it produces and sells approximately 100,000 units of product annually. Its per unit and annual total costs are shown in Exhibit 25.12.

EXHIBIT 25.12

Selected Operating Income Data

	Per Unit	Annual Total
Sales (100,000 units)	$10.00	$1,000,000
Direct materials	(3.50)	(350,000)
Direct labor	(2.20)	(220,000)
Overhead	(1.10)	(110,000)
Selling expenses	(1.40)	(140,000)
Administrative expenses	(0.80)	(80,000)
Total costs and expenses	(9.00)	(900,000)
Operating income	$ 1.00	$ 100,000

A current buyer of FasTrac's products wants to purchase additional units of its product and export them to another country. This buyer offers to buy 10,000 units of the product at $8.50 per unit, or $1.50 less than the current price. The offer price is low, but FasTrac is considering the proposal because this sale would be several times larger than any single previous sale and it would use idle capacity. Also, the units will be exported, so this new business will not affect current sales.

To determine whether to accept or reject this order, management needs to know whether accepting the offer will increase net income. The analysis in Exhibit 25.13 shows that if management relies on per unit historical costs, it would reject the sale because it yields a loss. However, historical costs are *not* relevant to this decision. Instead, the relevant costs are the additional costs, called **incremental costs.** These costs, also called *differential costs,* are the additional costs incurred if a company pursues a certain course of action. FasTrac's incremental costs are those related to the added volume that this new order would bring.

EXHIBIT 25.13

Analysis of Additional Business Using Historical Costs

	Per Unit	Total
Sales (10,000 additional units)	$ 8.50	$ 85,000
Direct materials	(3.50)	(35,000)
Direct labor	(2.20)	(22,000)
Overhead	(1.10)	(11,000)
Selling expenses	(1.40)	(14,000)
Administrative expenses	(0.80)	(8,000)
Total costs and expenses	(9.00)	(90,000)
Operating loss	$(0.50)	$(5,000)

To make its decision, FasTrac must analyze the costs of this new business in a different manner. The following information regarding the order is available:

● Manufacturing 10,000 additional units requires direct materials of $3.50 per unit and direct labor of $2.20 per unit (same as for all other units).

- Manufacturing 10,000 additional units adds $5,000 of incremental overhead costs for power, packaging, and indirect labor (all variable costs).
- Incremental commissions and selling expenses from this sale of 10,000 additional units would be $2,000 (all variable costs).
- Incremental administrative expenses of $1,000 for clerical efforts are needed (all fixed costs) with the sale of 10,000 additional units.

We use this information, as shown in Exhibit 25.14, to assess how accepting this new business will affect FasTrac's income.

EXHIBIT 25.14

Analysis of Additional Business Using Relevant Costs

	Current Business	Additional Business	Combined
Sales	$1,000,000	$ 85,000	$1,085,000
Direct materials	(350,000)	(35,000)	(385,000)
Direct labor	(220,000)	(22,000)	(242,000)
Overhead	(110,000)	(5,000)	(115,000)
Selling expenses	(140,000)	(2,000)	(142,000)
Administrative expense	(80,000)	(1,000)	(81,000)
Total costs and expenses	(900,000)	(65,000)	(965,000)
Operating income	$ 100,000	$ 20,000	$ 120,000

The analysis of relevant costs in Exhibit 25.14 suggests that the additional business be accepted. It would provide $85,000 of added revenue while incurring only $65,000 of added costs. This would yield $20,000 of additional pretax income, or a pretax profit margin of 23.5%. More generally, FasTrac would increase its income with any price that exceeded $6.50 per unit ($65,000 incremental cost/10,000 additional units).

An analysis of the incremental costs pertaining to the additional volume is always relevant for this type of decision. We must proceed cautiously, however, when the additional volume approaches or exceeds the factory's existing available capacity. If the additional volume requires the company to expand its capacity by obtaining more equipment, more space, or more personnel, the incremental costs could quickly exceed the incremental revenue. Another cautionary note is the effect on existing sales. All new units of the extra business will be sold outside FasTrac's normal domestic sales channels. If accepting additional business would cause existing sales to decline, this information must be included in our analysis. The contribution margin lost from a decline in sales is an opportunity cost. If future cash flows over several time periods are affected, their net present value also must be computed and used in this analysis.

The key point is that *management must not blindly use historical costs, especially allocated overhead costs*. Instead, the accounting system needs to provide information about the incremental costs to be incurred if the additional business is accepted.

Decision Maker Answer — p. 1061

Partner You are a partner in a small accounting firm that specializes in keeping the books and preparing taxes for clients. A local restaurant is interested in obtaining these services from your firm. Identify factors that are relevant in deciding whether to accept the engagement. ■

Make or Buy

The managerial decision to make or buy a component for one of its current products is commonplace and depends on incremental costs. To illustrate, FasTrac has excess productive capacity it can use to manufacture Part 417, a component of the main product it sells. The part is currently purchased and delivered to the plant at a cost of $1.20 per unit. FasTrac estimates that making Part 417 would cost $0.45 for direct materials, $0.50 for direct labor, and an undetermined amount for overhead. The task is to determine how much overhead to add to these costs so we can decide whether to make or buy Part 417. If FasTrac's normal predetermined overhead application rate is 100% of direct labor cost, we might be tempted to conclude that overhead cost is $0.50 per unit, computed as 100% of the $0.50 direct labor cost. We would then mistakenly conclude that total cost is $1.45 ($0.45 of materials + $0.50 of labor + $0.50 of overhead). A wrong decision in this case would be to conclude that the company is better off buying the part at $1.20 each than making it for $1.45 each.

Instead, as we explained earlier, only incremental overhead costs are relevant in this situation. Thus, we must compute an *incremental overhead rate.* Incremental overhead costs might include, for example, additional power for operating machines, extra supplies, added cleanup costs, materials handling, and quality control. We can prepare a per unit analysis in this case as shown in Exhibit 25.15.

EXHIBIT 25.15

Make or Buy Analysis

	Make	Buy
Direct materials	$0.45	—
Direct labor	0.50	—
Overhead costs	[?]	—
Purchase price	—	$1.20
Total incremental costs	$0.95 + [?]	$1.20

We can see that if incremental overhead costs are less than $0.25 per unit, the total cost of making the component is less than the purchase price of $1.20 and FasTrac should make the part. FasTrac's decision rule in this case is that any amount of overhead less than $0.25 per unit yields a total cost for Part 417 that is less than the $1.20 purchase price. FasTrac must consider several nonfinancial factors in the make or buy decision, including product quality, timeliness of delivery (especially in a just-in-time setting), reactions of customers and suppliers, and other intangibles such as employee morale and workload. It must also consider whether making the part requires incremental fixed costs to expand plant capacity. When these added factors are considered, small cost differences may not matter.

Decision Insight

Make or Buy Services   Companies apply make or buy decisions to their services. Many now outsource their payroll activities to a payroll service provider. It is argued that the prices paid for such services are close to what it costs them to do it, and without the headaches. ■

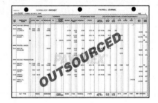

Scrap or Rework

Managers often must make a decision on whether to scrap or rework products in process. Remember that costs already incurred in manufacturing the units of a product that do not meet quality standards are sunk costs that have been incurred and cannot be changed. Sunk costs are irrelevant in any decision on whether to sell the substandard units as scrap or to rework them to meet quality standards.

To illustrate, assume that FasTrac has 10,000 defective units of a product that have already cost $1 per unit to manufacture. These units can be sold as is (as scrap) for $0.40 each, or they can be reworked for $0.80 per unit and then sold for their full price of $1.50 each. Should FasTrac sell the units as scrap or rework them?

To make this decision, management must recognize that the already incurred manufacturing costs of $1 per unit are sunk (unavoidable). These costs are *entirely irrelevant* to the decision. In addition, we must be certain that all costs of reworking defects, including interfering with normal operations, are accounted for in our analysis. For instance, reworking the defects means that FasTrac is unable to manufacture 10,000 *new* units with an incremental cost of $1 per unit and a selling price of $1.50 per unit, meaning it incurs an opportunity cost equal to the lost $5,000 net return from making and selling 10,000 new units. This opportunity cost is the difference between the $15,000 revenue (10,000 units $\times$ $1.50) from selling these new units and their $10,000 manufacturing costs (10,000 units $\times$ $1). Our analysis is reflected in Exhibit 25.16.

	Scrap	Rework
Sale of scrapped/reworked units	$ 4,000	$15,000
Less costs to rework defects		(8,000)
Less opportunity cost of not making new units		**(5,000)**
Incremental net income	$4,000	$ 2,000

EXHIBIT 25.16

Scrap or Rework Analysis

The analysis yields a $2,000 difference in favor of scrapping the defects, yielding a total incremental net income of $4,000. If we had failed to include the opportunity costs of $5,000, the rework option would have shown an income of $7,000 instead of $2,000, mistakenly making the reworking appear more favorable than scrapping.

Quick Check   Answers — p. 1062

11. A company receives a special order for 200 units that requires stamping the buyer's name on each unit, yielding an additional fixed cost of $400 to its normal costs. Without the order, the company is operating at 75% of capacity and produces 7,500 units of product at the following costs:

Direct materials	$37,500
Direct labor	60,000
Overhead (30% variable)	20,000
Selling expenses (60% variable)	25,000

The special order will not affect normal unit sales and will not increase fixed overhead and selling expenses. Variable selling expenses on the special order are reduced to one-half the normal amount. The price per unit necessary to earn $1,000 on this order is (a) $14.80, (b) $15.80, (c) $19.80, (d) $20.80, or (e) $21.80.

12. What are the incremental costs of accepting additional business?

Sell or Process

The managerial decision to sell partially completed products as is or to process them further for sale depends significantly on relevant costs. To illustrate, suppose that FasTrac has 40,000 units of partially finished Product Q. It has already spent $0.75 per unit to manufacture these 40,000 units at a $30,000 total cost. FasTrac can sell the 40,000 units to another manufacturer as raw material for $50,000. Alternatively, it can process them further and produce finished products X, Y, and Z at an incremental cost of $2 per unit. The added processing yields the products and revenues shown in Exhibit 25.17. FasTrac must decide whether the added revenues from selling finished products X, Y, and Z exceed the costs of finishing them.

Product	Price	Units	Revenues
Product X	$4.00	10,000	$ 40,000
Product Y	6.00	22,000	132,000
Product Z	8.00	6,000	48,000
Spoilage	—	2,000	0
Totals		40,000	$220,000

EXHIBIT 25.17

Revenues from Processing Further

Exhibit 25.18 shows the two-step analysis for this decision. First, FasTrac computes its incremental revenue from further processing Q into products X, Y, and Z. This amount is the difference between the $220,000 revenue from the further processed products and the $50,000 FasTrac will give up by not selling Q as is (a $50,000 opportunity cost). Second, FasTrac computes its incremental costs from further processing Q into X, Y, and Z. This amount is $80,000 (40,000 units × $2 incremental cost). The analysis shows that FasTrac can earn incremental net income of $90,000 from a decision to further process Q. (Notice that the earlier incurred $30,000 manufacturing cost for the 40,000 units of Product Q does not appear in Exhibit 25.18 because it is a sunk cost and as such is irrelevant to the decision.)

EXHIBIT 25.18

Sell or Process Analysis

Revenue if processed	$220,000
Revenue if sold as is	(50,000)
Incremental revenue	170,000
Cost to process	(80,000)
Incremental net income	**$90,000**

Quick Check

Answers — p. 1062

13. A company has already incurred a $1,000 cost in partially producing its four products. Their selling prices when partially and fully processed follow with additional costs necessary to finish these partially processed units:

Product	Unfinished Selling Price	Finished Selling Price	Further Processing Costs
Alpha	$300	$600	$150
Beta	450	900	300
Gamma	275	425	125
Delta	150	210	75

Which product(s) should *not* be processed further, (a) Alpha, (b) Beta, (c) Gamma, or (d) Delta?

14. Under what conditions is a sunk cost relevant to decision making?

Sales Mix Selection

When a company sells a mix of products, some are likely to be more profitable than others. Management is often wise to concentrate sales efforts on more profitable products. If production facilities or other factors are limited, an increase in the production and sale of one product usually requires reducing the production and sale of others. In this case, management must identify the most profitable combination, or *sales mix* of products. To identify the best sales mix, management must know the contribution margin of each product, the facilities required to produce each product, any constraints on these facilities, and its markets.

To illustrate, assume that FasTrac makes and sells two products, A and B. The same machines are used to produce both products. A and B have the following selling prices and variable costs per unit:

	Product A	Product B
Selling price per unit	$5.00	$7.50
Variable costs per unit	3.50	5.50
Contribution margin per unit	$1.50	$2.00

The variable costs are included in the analysis because they are the incremental costs of producing these products within the existing capacity of 100,000 machine hours per month. We consider three separate cases.

Demand Is Unlimited and Products Use Same Inputs   Assume that (1) each product requires 1 machine hour per unit for production and (2) the markets for these products are unlimited. Under these conditions, FasTrac should produce as much of Product B as it can because of its larger contribution margin of $2 per unit. At full capacity, FasTrac would produce $200,000 of total contribution margin per month, computed as $2 per unit times 100,000 machine hours.

Demand Is Unlimited and Products Use Different Inputs   Assume that (1) Product A requires 1 machine hour per unit, (2) Product B requires 2 machine hours per unit, and (3) the markets for these products are unlimited. Under these conditions, FasTrac should produce as much of Product A as it can because it has a contribution margin of $1.50 per machine hour compared with only $1 per machine hour for Product B. Exhibit 25.19 shows the relevant analysis.

	Product A	Product B
Selling price per unit	$5.00	$7.50
Variable costs per unit	3.50	5.50
Contribution margin per unit	$1.50	$2.00
Machine hours per unit	1.0	2.0
Contribution margin per machine hour	**$1.50**	**$1.00**

EXHIBIT 25.19

Sales Mix Analysis

At its full capacity of 100,000 machine hours, FasTrac would produce 100,000 units of Product A, yielding $150,000 of total contribution margin per month. In contrast, if it uses all 100,000 hours to produce Product B, only 50,000 units would be produced yielding a contribution margin of $100,000. These results suggest that when a company faces excess demand and limited capacity, only the most profitable product per input should be manufactured.

Example: If Product B's variable costs per unit increase to $6, Product A's variable costs per unit decrease to $3, and the same machine hours per unit are used, which product should FasTrac produce? *Answer:* Product A. Its contribution margin of $2 per machine hour is higher than B's $.75 per machine hour.

Demand Is Limited   The need for a mix of different products arises when market demand is not sufficient to allow a company to sell all that it produces. For instance, assume that (1) Product A requires 1 machine hour per unit, (2) Product B requires 2 machine hours per unit, and (3) the market for Product A is limited to 80,000 units. Under these conditions, FasTrac should produce no more than 80,000 units of Product A. This would leave another 20,000 machine hours of capacity for making Product B. FasTrac should use this spare capacity to produce 10,000 units of Product B. This sales mix would maximize FasTrac's total contribution margin per month at an amount of $140,000.

Decision Insight

Companies such as **Gap**, **Abercrombie & Fitch**, and **American Eagle** must continuously monitor and manage the sales mix of their product lists. Selling their products in hundreds of countries and territories further complicates their decision process. The contribution margin of each product is crucial to their product mix strategies. ■

Segment Elimination

When a segment such as a department or division is performing poorly, management must consider eliminating it. Segment information on either net income (loss) or its contribution to overhead is not sufficient for this decision. Instead, we must look at the segment's avoidable expenses and unavoidable expenses. **Avoidable expenses,** also called *escapable expenses,* are amounts the company would not incur if it eliminated the segment. **Unavoidable**

Point: FasTrac might consider buying another machine to reduce the constraint on production. A strategy designed to reduce the impact of constraints or bottlenecks, on production, is called the *theory of constraints.*

expenses, also called *inescapable expenses,* are amounts that would continue even if the segment is eliminated.

To illustrate, FasTrac considers eliminating its treadmill division because its $48,300 total expenses are higher than its $47,800 sales. Classification of this division's operating expenses into avoidable or unavoidable expenses is shown in Exhibit 25.20.

EXHIBIT 25.20

Classification of Segment Operating Expenses for Analysis

	Total	Avoidable Expenses	Unavoidable Expenses
Cost of goods sold	$ 30,000	$ 30,000	—
Direct expenses			
Salaries expense	7,900	7,900	—
Depreciation expense—Equipment	200	—	$ 200
Indirect expenses			
Rent and utilities expense	3,150	—	3,150
Advertising expense	400	400	—
Insurance expense	400	300	100
Service department costs			
Share of office department expenses	3,060	2,200	860
Share of purchasing expenses	3,190	1,000	2,190
Total	**$48,300**	**$41,800**	**$6,500**

Example: How can insurance be classified as either avoidable or unavoidable? *Answer:* Depends on whether the assets insured can be removed and the premiums canceled.

FasTrac's analysis shows that it can avoid $41,800 expenses if it eliminates the treadmill division. Because this division's sales are $47,800, eliminating it will cause FasTrac to lose $6,000 of income. *Our decision rule is that a segment is a candidate for elimination if its revenues are less than its avoidable expenses.* Avoidable expenses can be viewed as the costs to generate this segment's revenues.

When considering elimination of a segment, we must assess its impact on other segments. A segment could be unprofitable on its own, but it might still contribute to other segments' revenues and profits. It is possible then to continue a segment even when its revenues are less than its avoidable expenses. Similarly, a profitable segment might be discontinued if its space, assets, or staff can be more profitably used by expanding existing segments or by creating new ones. Our decision to keep or eliminate a segment requires a more complex analysis than simply looking at a segment's performance report. Such reports provide useful information, but they do not provide all the information necessary for this decision.

Example: Give an example of a segment that a company might profitably use to attract customers even though it might incur a loss. *Answer:* Warranty and post-sales services.

Keep or Replace Equipment

Businesses periodically must decide whether to keep using equipment or replace it. Advances in technology typically mean newer equipment can operate more efficiently and at lower cost than older equipment. In making the decision to keep or replace equipment, managers must decide whether the reduction in *variable* manufacturing costs with the new equipment over its useful life is greater than the net purchase price of the equipment. In this setting, the net purchase price of the equipment is its total cost minus any trade-in allowance or cash receipt for the old equipment.

For example, FasTrac has a piece of manufacturing equipment with a book value (cost minus accumulated depreciation) of $20,000 and a remaining useful life of four years. At the end of four years the equipment will have a salvage value of zero. The market value of the equipment is currently $25,000.

FasTrac can purchase a new machine for $100,000 and receive $25,000 in return for trading in its old machine. The new machine will reduce FasTrac's variable manufacturing costs by $18,000 per year over the four-year life of the new machine. FasTrac's incremental analysis is shown in Exhibit 25.21.

EXHIBIT 25.21

Keep or Replace Analysis

	Increase or (Decrease) in Net Income
Cost to buy new machine	$(100,000)
Cash received to trade in old machine	25,000
Reduction in variable manufacturing costs*	72,000
Total increase (decrease) in net income	$ (3,000)

*18,000 × 4 years

The analysis in Exhibit 25.21 shows that FasTrac should not replace the old equipment with this newer version as it will decrease income by $3,000. Note, the book value of the old equipment ($20,000) is not relevant to this analysis. Book value is a sunk cost, and it cannot be changed regardless of whether FasTrac keeps or replaces this equipment.

Qualitative Decision Factors

Managers must consider qualitative factors in making managerial decisions. Consider a decision on whether to buy a component from an outside supplier or continue to make it. Several qualitative decision factors must be considered. For example, the quality, delivery, and reputation of the proposed supplier are important. The effects from deciding not to make the component can include potential layoffs and impaired worker morale. Consider another situation in which a company is considering a one-time sale to a new customer at a special low price. Qualitative factors to consider in this situation include the effects of a low price on the company's image and the threat that regular customers might demand a similar price. The company must also consider whether this customer is really a one-time customer. If not, can it continue to offer this low price in the long run? Clearly, management cannot rely solely on financial data to make such decisions.

Quick Check   Answers — p. 1062

15. What is the difference between avoidable and unavoidable expenses?

16. A segment is a candidate for elimination if (a) its revenues are less than its avoidable expenses, (b) it has a net loss, (c) its unavoidable expenses are higher than its revenues.

 GLOBAL VIEW

Siemens AG is a global electrical engineering and electronics company headquartered in Germany. Recently, the company announced plans to invest £80 million to build a wind turbine plant in the United Kingdom. Net present value analyses support such decisions. In this case, Siemens foresees strong future cash flows based on increased demand for clean sources of energy, like wind power.

Break-Even Time   **Decision Analysis**

The first section of this chapter explained several methods to evaluate capital investments. Break-even time of an investment project is a variation of the payback period method that overcomes the limitation of not using the time value of money. **Break-even time (BET)** is a time-based measure used to evaluate a capital investment's acceptability. Its computation yields a measure of expected time, reflecting the

A2 Analyze a capital investment project using break-even time.

time period until the *present value* of the net cash flows from an investment equals the initial cost of the investment. In basic terms, break-even time is computed by restating future cash flows in terms of present values and then determining the payback period using these present values.

To illustrate, we return to the FasTrac case described in Exhibit 25.1 involving a $16,000 investment in machinery. The annual net cash flows from this investment are projected at $4,100 for eight years. Exhibit 25.22 shows the computation of break-even time for this investment decision.

EXHIBIT 25.22

Break-Even Time Analysis*

Year	Cash Flows	Present Value of I at 10%	Present Value of Cash Flows	Cumulative Present Value of Cash Flows
0	$(16,000)	1.0000	$(16,000)	$(16,000)
1	4,100	0.9091	3,727	(12,273)
2	4,100	0.8264	3,388	(8,885)
3	4,100	0.7513	3,080	(5,805)
4	4,100	0.6830	2,800	(3,005)
5	4,100	0.6209	2,546	(459)
6	4,100	0.5645	2,314	1,855
7	4,100	0.5132	2,104	3,959
8	4,100	0.4665	1,913	5,872

* The time of analysis is the start of year 1 (same as end of year 0). All cash flows occur at the end of each year.

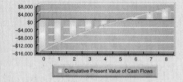

The right-most column of this exhibit shows that break-even time is between 5 and 6 years, or about 5.2 years—also see margin graph (where the line crosses the zero point). This is the time the project takes to break even after considering the time value of money (recall that the payback period computed without considering the time value of money was 3.9 years). We interpret this as cash flows earned after 5.2 years contribute to a positive net present value that, in this case, eventually amounts to $5,872.

Break-even time is a useful measure for managers because it identifies the point in time when they can expect the cash flows to begin to yield net positive returns. Managers expect a positive net present value from an investment if break-even time is less than the investment's estimated life. The method allows managers to compare and rank alternative investments, giving the project with the shortest break-even time the highest rank.

Decision Maker   Answer — p. 1061

Investment Manager   Management asks you, the investment manager, to evaluate three alternative investments. Investment recovery time is crucial because cash is scarce. The time value of money is also important. Which capital budgeting method(s) do you use to assess the investments? ■

DEMONSTRATION PROBLEM

Determine the appropriate action in each of the following managerial decision situations.

1. Packer Company is operating at 80% of its manufacturing capacity of 100,000 product units per year. A chain store has offered to buy an additional 10,000 units at $22 each and sell them to customers so as not to compete with Packer Company. The following data are available.

Costs at 80% Capacity	Per Unit	Total
Direct materials	$ 8.00	$ 640,000
Direct labor	7.00	560,000
Overhead (fixed and variable)	12.50	1,000,000
Totals	$27.50	$2,200,000

In producing 10,000 additional units, fixed overhead costs would remain at their current level but incremental variable overhead costs of $3 per unit would be incurred. Should the company accept or reject this order?

2. Green Company uses Part JR3 in manufacturing its products. It has always purchased this part from a supplier for $40 each. It recently upgraded its own manufacturing capabilities and has enough excess capacity (including trained workers) to begin manufacturing Part JR3 instead of buying it. The company prepares the following cost projections of making the part, assuming that overhead is allocated to the part at the normal predetermined rate of 200% of direct labor cost.

Direct materials	$11
Direct labor	15
Overhead (fixed and variable) (200% of direct labor)	30
Total	$56

The required volume of output to produce the part will not require any incremental fixed overhead. Incremental variable overhead cost will be $17 per unit. Should the company make or buy this part?

3. Gold Company's manufacturing process causes a relatively large number of defective parts to be produced. The defective parts can be (a) sold for scrap, (b) melted to recover the recycled metal for reuse, or (c) reworked to be good units. Reworking defective parts reduces the output of other good units because no excess capacity exists. Each unit reworked means that one new unit cannot be produced. The following information reflects 500 defective parts currently available.

Proceeds of selling as scrap	$2,500
Additional cost of melting down defective parts	400
Cost of purchases avoided by using recycled metal from defects	4,800
Cost to rework 500 defective parts	
Direct materials	0
Direct labor	1,500
Incremental overhead	1,750
Cost to produce 500 new parts	
Direct materials	6,000
Direct labor	5,000
Incremental overhead	3,200
Selling price per good unit	40

Should the company melt the parts, sell them as scrap, or rework them?

4. White Company can invest in one of two projects, TD1 or TD2. Each project requires an initial investment of $100,000 and produces the year-end cash inflows shown in the following table. Use net present values to determine which project, if any, should be chosen. Assume that the company requires a 10% return from its investments.

	Net Cash Flows	
	TD1	**TD2**
Year 1	$ 20,000	$ 40,000
Year 2	30,000	40,000
Year 3	70,000	40,000
Totals	$120,000	$120,000

PLANNING THE SOLUTION

● Determine whether Packer Company should accept the additional business by finding the incremental costs of materials, labor, and overhead that will be incurred if the order is accepted. Omit fixed costs that the order will not increase. If the incremental revenue exceeds the incremental cost, accept the order.

● Determine whether Green Company should make or buy the component by finding the incremental cost of making each unit. If the incremental cost exceeds the purchase price, the component should be purchased. If the incremental cost is less than the purchase price, make the component.

● Determine whether Gold Company should sell the defective parts, melt them down and recycle the metal, or rework them. To compare the three choices, examine all costs incurred and benefits received from the alternatives in working with the 500 defective units versus the production of 500 new units. For the scrapping alternative, include the costs of producing 500 new units and subtract the $2,500 proceeds from selling the old ones. For the melting alternative, include the costs of melting the defective units, add the net cost of new materials in excess over those obtained from recycling, and add the direct labor and overhead costs. For the reworking alternative, add the costs of direct labor and incremental overhead. Select the alternative that has the lowest cost. The cost assigned to the 500 defective units is sunk and not relevant in choosing among the three alternatives.

● Compute White Company's net present value of each investment using a 10% discount rate.

SOLUTION TO DEMONSTRATION PROBLEM

1. This decision involves accepting additional business. Since current unit costs are $27.50, it appears initially as if the offer to sell for $22 should be rejected, but the $27.50 cost includes fixed costs. When the analysis includes only *incremental* costs, the per unit cost is as shown in the following table. The offer should be accepted because it will produce $4 of additional profit per unit (computed as $22 price less $18 incremental cost), which yields a total profit of $40,000 for the 10,000 additional units.

Direct materials	$ 8.00
Direct labor	7.00
Variable overhead (given)	3.00
Total incremental cost	$18.00

2. For this make or buy decision, the analysis must not include the $13 nonincremental overhead per unit ($30 − $17). When only the $17 incremental overhead is included, the relevant unit cost of manufacturing the part is shown in the following table. It would be better to continue buying the part for $40 instead of making it for $43.

Direct materials	$11.00
Direct labor	15.00
Variable overhead	17.00
Total incremental cost	$43.00

3. The goal of this scrap or rework decision is to identify the alternative that produces the greatest net benefit to the company. To compare the alternatives, we determine the net cost of obtaining 500 marketable units as follows:

Incremental Cost to Produce 500 Marketable Units	Sell as Is	Melt and Recycle	Rework Units
Direct materials			
New materials	$ 6,000	$6,000	
Recycled metal materials		(4,800)	
Net materials cost		1,200	
Melting costs		400	
Total direct materials cost	6,000	1,600	
Direct labor	5,000	5,000	$1,500
Incremental overhead	3,200	3,200	1,750
Cost to produce 500 marketable units	14,200	9,800	3,250
Less proceeds of selling defects as scrap	(2,500)		
Opportunity costs*			5,800
Net cost	$11,700	$9,800	$9,050

* The $5,800 opportunity cost is the lost contribution margin from not being able to produce and sell 500 units because of reworking, computed as ($40 − [$14,200/500 units]) × 500 units.

The incremental cost of 500 marketable parts is smallest if the defects are reworked.

4. TD1:

	Net Cash Flows	Present Value of 1 at 10%	Present Value of Net Cash Flows
Year 1	$ 20,000	0.9091	$ 18,182
Year 2	30,000	0.8264	24,792
Year 3	70,000	0.7513	52,591
Totals	$120,000		95,565
Amount invested			(100,000)
Net present value			$ (4,435)

TD2:

	Net Cash Flows	Present Value of 1 at 10%	Present Value of Net Cash Flows
Year 1	$ 40,000	0.9091	$ 36,364
Year 2	40,000	0.8264	33,056
Year 3	40,000	0.7513	30,052
Totals	$120,000		99,472
Amount invested			(100,000)
Net present value			$ (528)

White Company should not invest in either project. Both are expected to yield a negative net present value, and it should invest only in positive net present value projects.

APPENDIX

25A

Using Excel to Compute Net Present Value and Internal Rate of Return

Computing present values and internal rates of return for projects with uneven cash flows is tedious and error prone. These calculations can be performed simply and accurately by using functions built into Excel. Many calculators and other types of spreadsheet software can perform them too. To illustrate, consider FasTrac, a company that is considering investing in a new machine with the expected cash flows shown in the following spreadsheet. Cash outflows are entered as negative numbers, and cash inflows are entered as positive numbers. Assume FasTrac requires a 12% annual return, entered as 0.12 in cell C1.

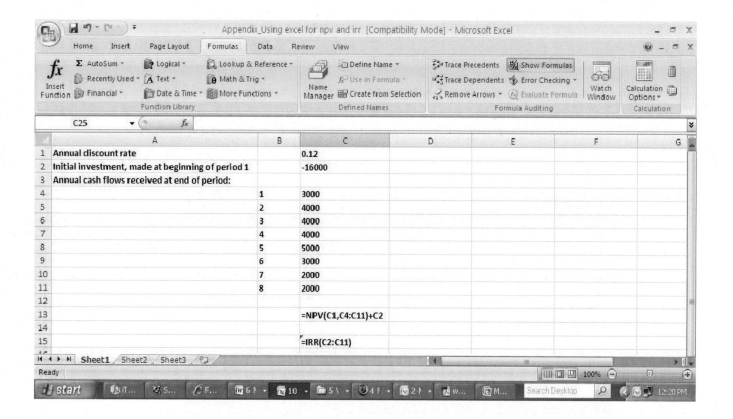

To compute the net present value of this project, the following is entered into cell C13:

$$=NPV(C1,C4:C11)+C2.$$

This instructs Excel to use its NPV function to compute the present value of the cash flows in cells C4 through C11, using the discount rate in cell C1, and then add the amount of the (negative) initial investment. For this stream of cash flows and a discount rate of 12%, the net present value is $1,326.03.

To compute the internal rate of return for this project, the following is entered into cell C15:

$$=IRR(C2:C11).$$

This instructs Excel to use its IRR function to compute the internal rate of return of the cash flows in cells C2 through C11. By default, Excel starts with a guess of 10%, and then uses trial and error to find the IRR. The IRR equals 14% for this project.

Summary

C1 **Describe the importance of relevant costs for short-term decisions.** A company must rely on relevant costs pertaining to alternative courses of action rather than historical costs. Out-of-pocket expenses and opportunity costs are relevant because these are avoidable; sunk costs are irrelevant because they result from past decisions and are therefore unavoidable. Managers must also consider the relevant benefits associated with alternative decisions.

A1 **Evaluate short-term managerial decisions using relevant costs.** Relevant costs are useful in making decisions such as to accept additional business, make or buy, and sell as is or process further. For example, the relevant factors in deciding whether to produce and sell additional units of product are incremental costs and incremental revenues from the additional volume.

A2 **Analyze a capital investment project using break-even time.** Break-even time (BET) is a method for evaluating capital investments by restating future cash flows in terms of their present values (discounting the cash flows) and then calculating the payback period using these present values of cash flows.

P1 **Compute payback period and describe its use.** One way to compare potential investments is to compute and compare their payback periods. The payback period is an estimate of the expected time before the cumulative net cash inflow from the investment equals its initial cost. A payback period analysis fails to reflect risk of the cash flows, differences in the timing of cash flows within the payback period, and cash flows that occur after the payback period.

P2 **Compute accounting rate of return and explain its use.** A project's accounting rate of return is computed by dividing the expected annual after-tax net income by the average amount of investment in the project. When the net cash flows are received evenly throughout each period and straight-line depreciation is used, the average investment is computed as the average of the investment's initial book value and its salvage value.

P3 **Compute net present value and describe its use.** An investment's net present value is determined by predicting the future cash flows it is expected to generate, discounting them at a rate that represents an acceptable return, and then by subtracting the investment's initial cost from the sum of the present values. This technique can deal with any pattern of expected cash flows and applies a superior concept of return on investment.

P4 **Compute internal rate of return and explain its use.** The internal rate of return (IRR) is the discount rate that results in a zero net present value. When the cash flows are equal, we can compute the present value factor corresponding to the IRR by dividing the initial investment by the annual cash flows. We then use the annuity tables to determine the discount rate corresponding to this present value factor.

Guidance Answers to Decision Maker and Decision Ethics

Systems Manager Your dilemma is whether to abide by rules designed to prevent abuse or to bend them to acquire an investment that you believe will benefit the firm. You should not pursue the latter action because breaking up the order into small components is dishonest and there are consequences of being caught at a later stage. Develop a proposal for the entire package and then do all you can to expedite its processing, particularly by pointing out its benefits. When faced with controls that are not working, there is rarely a reason to overcome its shortcomings by dishonesty. A direct assault on those limitations is more sensible and ethical.

Entrepreneur The banker is probably concerned because new products are risky and should therefore be evaluated using a higher rate of return. You should conduct a thorough technical analysis and obtain detailed market data and information about any similar products available in the market. These factors might provide sufficient information to support the use of a lower return. You must convince yourself that the risk level is consistent with the discount rate used.

You should also be confident that your company has the capacity and the resources to handle the new product.

Partner You should identify the differences between existing clients and this potential client. A key difference is that the restaurant business has additional inventory components (groceries, vegetables, meats, etc.) and is likely to have a higher proportion of depreciable assets. These differences imply that the partner must spend more hours auditing the records and understanding the business, regulations, and standards that pertain to the restaurant business. Such differences suggest that the partner must use a different "formula" for quoting a price to this potential client vis-à-vis current clients.

Investment Manager You should probably focus on either the payback period or break-even time because both the time value of money and recovery time are important. Break-even time method is superior because it accounts for the time value of money, which is an important consideration in this decision.

Guidance Answers to Quick Checks

1. *b*

2. A capital budgeting decision is difficult because (1) the outcome is uncertain, (2) large amounts of money are usually involved, (3) a long-term commitment is required, and (4) the decision could be difficult or impossible to reverse.

3. *b*

4. Depreciation expense is subtracted from revenues in computing net income but does not use cash and should be added back to net income to compute net cash flows.

5. Not necessarily. One investment can continue to generate cash flows beyond the payback period for a longer time period than the other. The timing of their cash flows within the payback period also can differ.

6. *b;* Annual average investment = ($180,000 + $15,000)/2
$$= \$97,500$$
Accounting rate of return = $40,000/$97,500 = 41%

7. For this determination, we need to compare it to the returns expected from alternative investments with similar risk.

8. Project A has the higher net present value as follows:

Year	Present Value of 1 at 10%	Project A Net Cash Flows	Project A Present Value of Net Cash Flows	Project B Net Cash Flows	Project B Present Value of Net Cash Flows
1	0.9091	$12,000	$10,909	$ 4,500	$ 4,091
2	0.8264	8,500	7,024	8,500	7,024
3	0.7513	4,000	3,005	13,000	9,767
Totals		$24,500	$20,938	$26,000	$20,882
Amount invested			(20,000)		(20,000)
Net present value			**$ 938**		**$ 882**

9. No, the information is too limited to draw that conclusion. For example, one investment could be riskier than the other, or one could require a substantially larger initial investment.

10. *b*

11. *e;* Variable costs per unit for this order of 200 units follow:

Direct materials ($37,500/7,500)	$ 5.00
Direct labor ($60,000/7,500)	8.00
Variable overhead [(0.30 × $20,000)/7,500]	0.80
Variable selling expenses [(0.60 × $25,000 × 0.5)/7,500]	1.00
Total variable costs per unit	$14.80

Cost to produce special order: (200 × $14.80) + $400
$$= \$3,360.$$
Price per unit to earn $1,000: ($3,360 + $1,000)/200 = 21.80.

12. They are the additional (new) costs of accepting new business.

13. *d;*

	Incremental benefits		Incremental costs
Alpha	$300 ($600 − $300)	>	$150 (given)
Beta	$450 ($900 − $450)	>	$300 (given)
Gamma	$150 ($425 − $275)	>	$125 (given)
Delta	$ 60 ($210 − $150)	<	$ 75 (given)

14. A sunk cost is *never* relevant because it results from a past decision and is already incurred.

15. Avoidable expenses are ones a company will not incur by eliminating a segment; unavoidable expenses will continue even after a segment is eliminated.

16. *a*

Key Terms   mhhe.com/wildFAP20e

Accounting rate of return (p. 1039)
Avoidable expense (p. 1053)
Break-even time (BET) (p. 1055)
Capital budgeting (p. 1036)
Cost of capital (p. 1041)

Hurdle rate (p. 1045)
Incremental cost (p. 1048)
Internal rate of return (IRR) (p. 1043)
Net present value (NPV) (p. 1041)
Payback period (PBP) (p. 1037)

Profitability index (p. 1043)
Relevant benefits (p. 1047)
Unavoidable expense (p. 1053)

Multiple Choice Quiz   Answers on p. 1078   mhhe.com/wildFAP20e

Additional Quiz Questions are available at the book's Website.

1. A company inadvertently produced 3,000 defective MP3 players. The players cost $12 each to produce. A recycler offers to purchase the defective players as they are for $8 each. The production manager reports that the defects can be corrected for $10 each, enabling them to be sold at their regular market price of $19 each. The company should:
   a. Correct the defect and sell them at the regular price.
   b. Sell the players to the recycler for $8 each.
   c. Sell 2,000 to the recycler and repair the rest.
   d. Sell 1,000 to the recycler and repair the rest.
   e. Throw the players away.

2. A company's productive capacity is limited to 480,000 machine hours. Product X requires 10 machine hours to produce; and Product Y requires 2 machine hours to produce. Product X

sells for $32 per unit and has variable costs of $12 per unit; Product Y sells for $24 per unit and has variable costs of $10 per unit. Assuming that the company can sell as many of either product as it produces, it should:
   a. Produce X and Y in the ratio of 57% and 43%.
   b. Produce X and Y in the ratio of 83% X and 17% Y.
   c. Produce equal amounts of Product X and Product Y.
   d. Produce only Product X.
   e. Produce only Product Y.

3. A company receives a special one-time order for 3,000 units of its product at $15 per unit. The company has excess capacity and it currently produces and sells the units at $20 each to its regular customers. Production costs are $13.50 per unit, which includes $9 of variable costs. To produce the special order, the

company must incur additional fixed costs of $5,000. Should the company accept the special order?

a. Yes, because incremental revenue exceeds incremental costs.

b. No, because incremental costs exceed incremental revenue.

c. No, because the units are being sold for $5 less than the regular price.

d. Yes, because incremental costs exceed incremental revenue.

e. No, because incremental cost exceeds $15 per unit when total costs are considered.

4. A company is considering the purchase of equipment for $270,000. Projected annual cash inflow from this equipment is $61,200 per year. The payback period is:

a. 0.2 years

b. 5.0 years

c. 4.4 years

d. 2.3 years

e. 3.9 years

5. A company buys a machine for $180,000 that has an expected life of nine years and no salvage value. The company expects an annual net income (after taxes of 30%) of $8,550. What is the accounting rate of return?

a. 4.75%

b. 42.75%

c. 2.85%

d. 9.50%

e. 6.65%

I Icon denotes assignments that involve decision making.

Discussion Questions

1. What is capital budgeting?

2. **I** Identify four reasons that capital budgeting decisions by managers are risky.

3. Capital budgeting decisions require careful analysis because they are generally the _____ _____ and _____ decisions that management faces.

4. Identify two disadvantages of using the payback period for comparing investments.

5. **I** Why is an investment more attractive to management if it has a shorter payback period?

6. What is the average amount invested in a machine during its predicted five-year life if it costs $200,000 and has a $20,000 salvage value? Assume that net income is received evenly throughout each year and straight-line depreciation is used.

7. If the present value of the expected net cash flows from a machine, discounted at 10%, exceeds the amount to be invested, what can you say about the investment's expected rate of return? What can you say about the expected rate of return if the present value of the net cash flows, discounted at 10%, is less than the investment amount?

8. Why is the present value of $100 that you expect to receive one year from today worth less than $100 received today? What is the present value of $100 that you expect to receive one year from today, discounted at 12%?

9. **I** Why should managers set the required rate of return higher than the rate at which money can be borrowed when making a typical capital budgeting decision?

10. **I** Why does the use of the accelerated depreciation method (instead of straight line) for income tax reporting increase an investment's value?

11. **Palm** has many types of costs. What is an out-of-pocket cost? What is an opportunity cost? Are opportunity costs recorded in the accounting records?   **Palm**

12. **I** **Nokia** must confront sunk costs. Why are sunk costs irrelevant in deciding whether to sell a product in its present condition or to make it into a new product through additional processing?   **NOKIA**

13. **I** Identify the incremental costs incurred by **Apple** for shipping one additional iPod from a warehouse to a retail store along with the store's normal order of 75 iPods.   **Apple**

14. **I** **Apple** is considering expanding a store. Identify three methods management can use to evaluate whether to expand.   **Apple**

15. **I** Assume that **Research In Motion** manufactures and sells 500,000 units of a product at $30 per unit in domestic markets. It costs $20 per unit to manufacture ($13 variable cost per unit, $7 fixed cost per unit). Can you describe a situation under which the company is willing to sell an additional 25,000 units of the product in an international market at $15 per unit?   **RIM**

---

connect

Ting Company is considering two alternative investments. The payback period is 3.5 years for investment A and 5 years for investment B. (1) If management relies on the payback period, which investment is preferred? (2) Why might Ting's analysis of these two alternatives lead to the selection of B over A?

QUICK STUDY

QS 25-1

Analyzing payback periods   **P1**

QS 25-2
Payback period   P1

Fabiano Brothers Co. is considering an investment that requires immediate payment of $550,000 and provides expected cash inflows of $100,000 annually for eight years. What is the investment's payback period?

QS 25-3
Computation of
net present value   P3

If Kelsey K. Company invests $250,000 today, it can expect to receive $50,000 at the end of each year for the next seven years, plus an extra $32,000 at the end of the seventh year. What is the net present value of this investment assuming a required 8% return on investments?

QS 25-4
Computation of
accounting rate of return   P2

Cardinal Company is considering an investment expected to generate an average net income after taxes of $1,300 for three years. The investment costs $30,000 and has an estimated $4,000 salvage value. Compute the accounting rate of return for this investment; assume the company uses straight-line depreciation. Hint: Use the formula in Exhibit 25.5 when computing the average annual investment.

QS 25-5
Internal rate of return   P4

A company is considering investing in a new machine that requires a cash payment of $15,982 today. The machine will generate annual cash flows of $7,000 for the next three years. What is the internal rate of return if the company buys this machine?

QS 25-6
Relevant costs

C1

Label each of the following statements as either true ("T") or false ("F").

1. An opportunity cost is the potential benefit that is lost by taking a specific action when two or more alternative choices are available.

2. A sunk cost will change with a future course of action.

3. An out-of-pocket cost requires a current and/or future outlay of cash.

4. Relevant costs are also known as unavoidable costs.

5. Incremental costs are also known as differential costs.

QS 25-7
Analysis of incremental costs

A1

Mo-Kan Company incurs a $6 per unit cost for Product A, which it currently manufactures and sells for $9 per unit. Instead of manufacturing and selling this product, the company can purchase Product B for $5 per unit and sell it for $8 per unit. If it does so, unit sales would remain unchanged and $5 of the $6 per unit costs assigned to Product A would be eliminated. Should the company continue to manufacture Product A or purchase Product B for resale?

QS 25-8
Selection of sales mix

A1

Memory Lane Company can sell all units of computer memory X and Y that it can produce, but it has limited production capacity. It can produce four units of X per hour *or* three units of Y per hour, and it has 8,000 production hours available. Contribution margin is $10 for product X and $8 for product Y. What is the most profitable sales mix for this company?

QS 25-9
Decision to accept additional
business

A1

Kirk Company sells bikes for $600 each. The company currently sells 7,500 bikes per year and could make as many as 10,000 bikes per year. The bikes cost $450 each to make; $300 in variable costs per bike and $150 of fixed costs per bike. Kirk received an offer from a potential customer who wants to buy 1,500 bikes for $500 each. Incremental fixed costs to make this order are $100,000. No other costs will change if this order is accepted. Compute Kirk's additional income (ignore taxes) if it accepts this order.

QS 25-10
Scrap or rework

A1

Z-Tech mistakenly produced 10,000 defective cell phones. The phones cost $60 each to produce. A salvage company will buy the defective phones as they are for $30 each. It would cost Z-Tech $80 per phone to rework the phones. If the phones are reworked, Z-Tech could sell them for $125 each. Compute the incremental net income from reworking the phones.

QS 25-11
Sell or process decision

A1

Bartel Company produces a product that can either be sold as is or processed further. Bartel has already spent $10,000 to produce 250 units that can be sold now for $13,500 to another manufacturer. Alternatively, Bartel can process the units further at an incremental cost of $36 per unit. If Bartel processes further, the units can be sold for $100 each. Compute the incremental income if Bartel processes further.

A guitar manufacturer is considering eliminating its electric guitar division because its $76,000 expenses are higher than its $72,000 sales. The company reports the following expenses for this division. Should the division be eliminated?

QS 25-12
Segment elimination
A1

	Avoidable Expenses	Unavoidable Expenses
Cost of goods sold	$55,000	
Direct expenses	6,250	$2,250
Indirect expenses	470	3,600
Service department costs	7,000	1,430

Tak Company has a machine with a book value of $50,000 and a remaining five-year useful life. A new machine is available at a cost of $75,000, and Tak can also receive $40,000 for trading in its old machine. The new machine will reduce variable manufacturing costs by $12,000 per year over its five-year useful life. Should the machine be replaced?

QS 25-13
Keep or replace decision
A1

Soles, a shoe manufacturer, is evaluating the costs and benefits of new equipment that would custom fit each pair of athletic shoes. The customer would have his or her foot scanned by digital computer equipment; this information would be used to cut the raw materials to provide the customer a perfect fit. The new equipment costs $100,000 and is expected to generate an additional $35,000 in cash flows for five years. A bank will make a $100,000 loan to the company at a 10% interest rate for this equipment's purchase. Use the following table to determine the break-even time for this equipment. (Round the present value of cash flows to the nearest dollar.)

QS 25-14
Computation of break-even time
A2

Year	Cash Flows*	Present Value of 1 at 10%	Present Value of Cash Flows	Cumulative Present Value of Cash Flows
0	$(100,000)	1.0000		
1	35,000	0.9091		
2	35,000	0.8264		
3	35,000	0.7513		
4	35,000	0.6830		
5	35,000	0.6209		

* All cash flows occur at year-end.

Jester Company is considering two alternative projects. Project 1 requires an initial investment of $500,000 and has a net present value of cash flows of $1,200,000. Project 2 requires an initial investment of $3,500,000 and has a net present value of cash flows of $1,900,000. Compute the profitability index for each project. Based on the profitability index, which project should the company prefer? Explain.

QS 25-15
Profitability index
P3

Siemens AG invests €80 million to build a manufacturing plant to build wind turbines. The company predicts net cash flows of €16 million per year for the next 8 years. Assume the company requires an 8% rate of return from its investments. (1) What is the payback period of this investment? (2) What is the net present value of this investment?

QS 25-16
Capital budgeting methods
P1 P3

connect

Compute the payback period for each of these two separate investments (round the payback period to two decimals):

EXERCISES

a. A new operating system for an existing machine is expected to cost $260,000 and have a useful life of five years. The system yields an incremental after-tax income of $75,000 each year after deducting its straight-line depreciation. The predicted salvage value of the system is $10,000.

b. A machine costs $190,000, has a $10,000 salvage value, is expected to last nine years, and will generate an after-tax income of $30,000 per year after straight-line depreciation.

Exercise 25-1
Payback period computation;
even cash flows
P1

Exercise 25-2

Payback period computation; uneven cash flows

P1

Check 3.167 years

Wenro Company is considering the purchase of an asset for $90,000. It is expected to produce the following net cash flows. The cash flows occur evenly throughout each year. Compute the payback period for this investment.

	Year 1	Year 2	Year 3	Year 4	Year 5	Total
Net cash flows	$30,000	$20,000	$30,000	$60,000	$19,000	$159,000

Exercise 25-3

Payback period computation; declining-balance depreciation

P1

Check 2.265 years

A machine can be purchased for $300,000 and used for 5 years, yielding the following net incomes. In projecting net incomes, double-declining balance depreciation is applied, using a 5-year life and a $50,000 salvage value. Compute the machine's payback period (ignore taxes). (Round the payback period to two decimals.)

	Year 1	Year 2	Year 3	Year 4	Year 5
Net incomes	$20,000	$50,000	$100,000	$75,000	$200,000

Exercise 25-4

Accounting rate of return   P2

A machine costs $500,000 and is expected to yield an after-tax net income of $15,000 each year. Management predicts this machine has a 10-year service life and a $100,000 salvage value, and it uses straight-line depreciation. Compute this machine's accounting rate of return.

Exercise 25-5

Payback period and accounting rate of return on investment

P1 P2

K2B Co. is considering the purchase of equipment that would allow the company to add a new product to its line. The equipment is expected to cost $240,000 with a 12-year life and no salvage value. It will be depreciated on a straight-line basis. The company expects to sell 96,000 units of the equipment's product each year. The expected annual income related to this equipment follows. Compute the (1) payback period and (2) accounting rate of return for this equipment.

Sales	$150,000
Costs	
Materials, labor, and overhead (except depreciation)	80,000
Depreciation on new equipment	20,000
Selling and administrative expenses	15,000
Total costs and expenses...............................	115,000
Pretax income	35,000
Income taxes (30%)	10,500
Net income	$ 24,500

Check (1) 5.39 years (2) 20.42%

Exercise 25-6

Computing net present value   P3

After evaluating the risk of the investment described in Exercise 25-5, K2B Co. concludes that it must earn at least a 8% return on this investment. Compute the net present value of this investment. (Round the net present value to the nearest dollar.)

Exercise 25-7

Computation and interpretation of net present value and internal rate of return

P3 P4

Kase Company can invest in each of three cheese-making projects: C1, C2, and C3. Each project requires an initial investment of $190,000 and would yield the following annual cash flows.

	C1	C2	C3
Year 1.........	$ 10,000	$ 80,000	$150,000
Year 2	90,000	80,000	50,000
Year 3	140,000	80,000	40,000
Totals	$240,000	$240,000	$240,000

Check (1) C2 net present value, $2,152

(1) Assuming that the company requires a 12% return from its investments, use net present value to determine which projects, if any, should be acquired. (2) Using the answer from part 1, explain whether the internal rate of return is higher or lower than 12% for project C2. (3) Compute the internal rate of return for project C2.

Exercise 25-8

NPV and profitability index   P3

Following is information on two alternative investments being considered by Jin Company. The company requires a 10% return from its investments.

	Project A	Project B
Initial investment	$(175,000)	$(145,000)
Expected net cash flows in year:		
1.......................	40,000	32,000
2.......................	56,000	50,000
3.......................	80,295	66,000
4.......................	90,400	72,000
5.......................	55,000	29,000

For each alternative project compute the (a) net present value, and (b) profitability index. If the company can only select one project, which should it choose? Explain.

Refer to the information in Exercise 25-8. Create an Excel spreadsheet to compute the internal rate of return for each of the projects. Round the percentage return to two decimals.

Exercise 25-9^A
Using Excel to compute IRR   P4

Fill in each of the blanks below with the correct term.

1. Relevant costs are also known as _____.

2. An _____ requires a future outlay of cash and is relevant for current and future decision making.

3. An _____ is the potential benefit lost by taking a specific action when two or more alternative choices are available.

4. A _____ arises from a past decision and cannot be avoided or changed; it is irrelevant to future decisions.

5. _____ refer to the incremental revenue generated from taking one particular action over another.

Exercise 25-10
Relevant costs

C1

A company must decide between scrapping or reworking units that do not pass inspection. The company has 15,000 defective units that cost $6 per unit to manufacture. The units can be sold as is for $2.50 each, or they can be reworked for $4.50 each and then sold for the full price of $9 each. If the units are sold as is, the company will have to build 15,000 replacement units at a cost of $6 each, and sell them at the full price of $9 each. (1) What is the incremental income from selling the units as scrap? (2) What is the incremental income from reworking and selling the units? (3) Should the company sell the units as scrap or rework them?

Exercise 25-11
Scrap or rework

A1

Xu Company is considering replacing one of its manufacturing machines. The machine has a book value of $45,000 and a remaining useful life of 4 years, at which time its salvage value will be zero. It has a current market value of $55,000. Variable manufacturing costs are $34,000 per year for this machine. Information on two alternative replacement machines follows. Should Xu keep or replace its manufacturing machine? If the machine should be replaced, which alternative new machine should Xu purchase?

Exercise 25-12
Keep or replace

A1

	Alternative A	Alternative B
Cost......................................	$115,000	$125,000
Variable manufacturing costs per year.........	22,000	12,000

Feist Co. expects to sell 200,000 units of its product in the next period with the following results.

Exercise 25-13
Decision to accept additional business or not

A1

Sales (200,000 units)	$3,000,000
Costs and expenses	
Direct materials.................	400,000
Direct labor	800,000
Overhead.......................	200,000
Selling expenses...............	300,000
Administrative expenses	514,000
Total costs and expenses...........	2,214,000
Net income	$ 786,000

The company has an opportunity to sell 20,000 additional units at $12 per unit. The additional sales would not affect its current expected sales. Direct materials and labor costs per unit would be the same for the additional units as they are for the regular units. However, the additional volume would create the following incremental costs: (1) total overhead would increase by 15% and (2) administrative expenses would increase by $86,000. Prepare an analysis to determine whether the company should accept or reject the offer to sell additional units at the reduced price of $12 per unit.

Exercise 25-14

Make or buy decision

A1

Check $10,000 increased costs to buy

Santos Company currently manufactures one of its crucial parts at a cost of $3.40 per unit. This cost is based on a normal production rate of 50,000 units per year. Variable costs are $1.50 per unit, fixed costs related to making this part are $50,000 per year, and allocated fixed costs are $45,000 per year. Allocated fixed costs are unavoidable whether the company makes or buys the part. Santos is considering buying the part from a supplier for a quoted price of $2.70 per unit guaranteed for a three-year period. Should the company continue to manufacture the part, or should it buy the part from the outside supplier? Support your answer with analyses.

Exercise 25-15

Sell or process decision

A1

Cantrell Company has already manufactured 20,000 units of Product A at a cost of $20 per unit. The 20,000 units can be sold at this stage for $500,000. Alternatively, the units can be further processed at a $300,000 total additional cost and be converted into 4,000 units of Product B and 8,000 units of Product C. Per unit selling price for Product B is $75 and for Product C is $50. Prepare an analysis that shows whether the 20,000 units of Product A should be processed further or not.

Exercise 25-16

Analysis of income effects from eliminating departments

A1

Suresh Co. expects its five departments to yield the following income for next year.

	Dept. M	Dept. N	Dept. O	Dept. P	Dept. T
Sales	$31,500	$17,500	$28,000	$21,000	$ 14,000
Expenses					
Avoidable	4,900	18,200	11,200	7,000	18,900
Unavoidable	25,900	6,300	2,100	14,700	4,900
Total expenses	30,800	24,500	13,300	21,700	23,800
Net income (loss)	$ 700	$ (7,000)	$14,700	$ (700)	$ (9,800)

Recompute and prepare the departmental income statements (including a combined total column) for the company under each of the following separate scenarios: Management (1) does not eliminate any department, (2) eliminates departments with expected net losses, and (3) eliminates departments with sales dollars that are less than avoidable expenses. Explain your answers to parts 2 and 3.

Exercise 25-17

Sales mix determination and analysis

A1

Bethel Company owns a machine that can produce two specialized products. Production time for Product TLX is two units per hour and for Product MTV is five units per hour. The machine's capacity is 2,200 hours per year. Both products are sold to a single customer who has agreed to buy all of the company's output up to a maximum of 3,750 units of Product TLX and 2,000 units of Product MTV. Selling prices and variable costs per unit to produce the products follow. Determine (1) the company's most profitable sales mix and (2) the contribution margin that results from that sales mix.

	Product TLX	Product MTV
Selling price per unit	$12.50	$7.50
Variable costs per unit	3.75	4.50

Exercise 25-18

Comparison of payback and BET

P1 A2

This chapter explained two methods to evaluate investments using recovery time, the payback period and break-even time (BET). Refer to QS 25-14 and (1) compute the recovery time for both the payback period and break-even time, (2) discuss the advantage(s) of break-even time over the payback period, and (3) list two conditions under which payback period and break-even time are similar.

connect

Elite Company is planning to add a new product to its line. To manufacture this product, the company needs to buy a new machine at a $300,000 cost with an expected four-year life and a $20,000 salvage value. All sales are for cash, and all costs are out of pocket except for depreciation on the new machine. Additional information includes the following.

Expected annual sales of new product	$1,150,000
Expected annual costs of new product	
Direct materials	300,000
Direct labor	420,000
Overhead excluding straight-line depreciation on new machine	210,000
Selling and administrative expenses	100,000
Income taxes	30%

Required

1. Compute straight-line depreciation for each year of this new machine's life. (Round depreciation amounts to the nearest dollar.)
2. Determine expected net income and net cash flow for each year of this machine's life. (Round answers to the nearest dollar.)
3. Compute this machine's payback period, assuming that cash flows occur evenly throughout each year. (Round the payback period to two decimals.)
4. Compute this machine's accounting rate of return, assuming that income is earned evenly throughout each year. (Round the percentage return to two decimals.)
5. Compute the net present value for this machine using a discount rate of 7% and assuming that cash flows occur at each year-end. (*Hint:* Salvage value is a cash inflow at the end of the asset's life. Round the net present value to the nearest dollar.)

Pleasant Company has an opportunity to invest in one of two new projects. Project Y requires a $700,000 investment for new machinery with a four-year life and no salvage value. Project Z requires a $700,000 investment for new machinery with a three-year life and no salvage value. The two projects yield the following predicted annual results. The company uses straight-line depreciation, and cash flows occur evenly throughout each year.

	Project Y	Project Z
Sales	$700,000	$560,000
Expenses		
Direct materials	98,000	70,000
Direct labor...........................	140,000	84,000
Overhead including depreciation	252,000	252,000
Selling and administrative expenses	50,000	50,000
Total expenses	540,000	456,000
Pretax income	160,000	104,000
Income taxes (30%)	48,000	31,200
Net income	$112,000	$ 72,800

Required

1. Compute each project's annual expected net cash flows. (Round the net cash flows to the nearest dollar.)
2. Determine each project's payback period. (Round the payback period to two decimals.)
3. Compute each project's accounting rate of return. (Round the percentage return to one decimal.)
4. Determine each project's net present value using 8% as the discount rate. For part 4 only, assume that cash flows occur at each year-end. (Round the net present value to the nearest dollar.)

Analysis Component

5. Identify the project you would recommend to management and explain your choice.

PROBLEM SET A

Problem 25-1A
Computation of payback period, accounting rate of return, and net present value

P1 P2 P3

mhhe.com/wildFAP20e

Check   (4) 21.88%

(5) $70,915

Problem 25-2A
Analysis and computation of payback period, accounting rate of return, and net present value

P1 P2 P3

Check   For Project Y: (2) 2.44 years, (3) 32%, (4) $250,573

Problem 25-3A

Computation of cash flows and net present values with alternative depreciation methods

P3

Angiletta Corporation is considering a new project requiring a $30,000 investment in test equipment with no salvage value. The project would produce $12,000 of pretax income before depreciation at the end of each of the next six years. The company's income tax rate is 40%. In compiling its tax return and computing its income tax payments, the company can choose between the two alternative depreciation schedules shown in the table.

	Straight-Line Depreciation	MACRS Depreciation*
Year 1	$ 3,000	$ 6,000
Year 2	6,000	9,600
Year 3	6,000	5,760
Year 4	6,000	3,456
Year 5	6,000	3,456
Year 6	3,000	1,728
Totals	$30,000	$30,000

* The modified accelerated cost recovery system (MACRS) for depreciation is discussed in Chapter 10.

Required

1. Prepare a five-column table that reports amounts (assuming use of straight-line depreciation) for each of the following for each of the six years: (a) pretax income before depreciation, (b) straight-line depreciation expense, (c) taxable income, (d) income taxes, and (e) net cash flow. Net cash flow equals the amount of income before depreciation minus the income taxes. (Round answers to the nearest dollar.)

2. Prepare a five-column table that reports amounts (assuming use of MACRS depreciation) for each of the following for each of the six years: (a) pretax income before depreciation, (b) MACRS depreciation expense, (c) taxable income, (d) income taxes, and (e) net cash flow. Net cash flow equals the income amount before depreciation minus the income taxes. (Round answers to the nearest dollar.)

Check Net present value: (3) $10,041, (4) $10,635

3. Compute the net present value of the investment if straight-line depreciation is used. Use 10% as the discount rate. (Round the net present value to the nearest dollar.)

4. Compute the net present value of the investment if MACRS depreciation is used. Use 10% as the discount rate. (Round the net present value to the nearest dollar.)

Analysis Component

5. Explain why the MACRS depreciation method increases this project's net present value.

Problem 25-4A

Analysis of income effects of additional business

A1

mhhe.com/wildFAP20e

Cayman Products manufactures and sells to wholesalers approximately 300,000 packages per year of underwater markers at $4 per package. Annual costs for the production and sale of this quantity are shown in the table.

Direct materials	$384,000
Direct labor	96,000
Overhead	288,000
Selling expenses	120,000
Administrative expenses	80,000
Total costs and expenses	$968,000

A new wholesaler has offered to buy 50,000 packages for $3.44 each. These markers would be marketed under the wholesaler's name and would not affect Cayman Products' sales through its normal channels. A study of the costs of this additional business reveals the following:

● Direct materials costs are 100% variable.

● Per unit direct labor costs for the additional units would be 50% higher than normal because their production would require overtime pay at one-and-one-half times the usual labor rate.

● 25% of the normal annual overhead costs are fixed at any production level from 250,000 to 400,000 units. The remaining 75% of the annual overhead cost is variable with volume.

● Accepting the new business would involve no additional selling expenses.

● Accepting the new business would increase administrative expenses by a $4,000 fixed amount.

Required

Prepare a three-column comparative income statement that shows the following:

1. Annual operating income without the special order (column 1).

2. Annual operating income received from the new business only (column 2).

3. Combined annual operating income from normal business and the new business (column 3).

Check Operating income:
(1) $232,000, (2) $44,000

Ortiz Company is able to produce two products, G and B, with the same machine in its factory. The following information is available.

Problem 25-5A

Analysis of sales mix strategies

A1

	Product G	Product B
Selling price per unit	$120	$160
Variable costs per unit.	40	90
Contribution margin per unit	$ 80	$ 70
Machine hours to produce I unit	0.8 hours	2.0 hours
Maximum unit sales per month.	400 units	350 units

The company presently operates the machine for a single eight-hour shift for 22 working days each month. Management is thinking about operating the machine for two shifts, which will increase its productivity by another eight hours per day for 22 days per month. This change would require $6,500 additional fixed costs per month.

Required

1. Determine the contribution margin per machine hour that each product generates.

2. How many units of Product G and Product B should the company produce if it continues to operate with only one shift? How much total contribution margin does this mix produce each month?

3. If the company adds another shift, how many units of Product G and Product B should it produce? How much total contribution margin would this mix produce each month? Should the company add the new shift? Explain.

4. Suppose that the company determines that it can increase Product G's maximum sales to 440 units per month by spending $2,000 per month in marketing efforts. Should the company pursue this strategy and the double shift? Explain.

Check Units of Product G: (2) 220,
(3) 400, (4) 440

Home Decor Company's management is trying to decide whether to eliminate Department 200, which has produced losses or low profits for several years. The company's 2011 departmental income statement shows the following.

Problem 25-6A

Analysis of possible elimination of a department

A1

HOME DECOR COMPANY Departmental Income Statements For Year Ended December 31, 2011	Dept. 100	Dept. 200	Combined
Sales	$872,000	$580,000	$1,452,000
Cost of goods sold	524,000	414,000	938,000
Gross profit	348,000	166,000	514,000
Operating expenses			
Direct expenses			
Advertising	34,000	24,000	58,000
Store supplies used	8,000	7,600	15,600
Depreciation—Store equipment.	10,000	6,600	16,600
Total direct expenses	52,000	38,200	90,200

[continued on next page]

[continued from previous page]

Allocated expenses			
Sales salaries	130,000	78,000	208,000
Rent expense..........................	18,880	9,440	28,320
Bad debts expense	19,800	16,200	36,000
Office salary	37,440	24,960	62,400
Insurance expense	4,000	2,200	6,200
Miscellaneous office expenses	4,800	3,200	8,000
Total allocated expenses	214,920	134,000	348,920
Total expenses........................	266,920	172,200	439,120
Net income (loss)	$ 81,080	$ (6,200)	$ 74,880

In analyzing whether to eliminate Department 200, management considers the following:

a. The company has one office worker who earns $1,200 per week, or $62,400 per year, and four sales-clerks who each earn $1,000 per week, or $52,000 per year.

b. The full salaries of two salesclerks are charged to Department 100. The full salary of one salesclerk is charged to Department 200. The salary of the fourth clerk, who works half-time in both departments, is divided evenly between the two departments.

c. Eliminating Department 200 would avoid the sales salaries and the office salary currently allocated to it. However, management prefers another plan. Two salesclerks have indicated that they will be quitting soon. Management believes that their work can be done by the other two clerks if the one office worker works in sales half-time. Eliminating Department 200 will allow this shift of duties. If this change is implemented, half the office worker's salary would be reported as sales salaries and half would be reported as office salary.

d. The store building is rented under a long-term lease that cannot be changed. Therefore, Department 100 will use the space and equipment currently used by Department 200.

e. Closing Department 200 will eliminate its expenses for advertising, bad debts, and store supplies; 70% of the insurance expense allocated to it to cover its merchandise inventory; and 25% of the miscellaneous office expenses presently allocated to it.

Required

Check (1) Total expenses:
(a) $1,377,120, (b) $568,140

(2) Forecasted net income without Department 200, $63,020

1. Prepare a three-column report that lists items and amounts for (a) the company's total expenses (including cost of goods sold)—in column 1, (b) the expenses that would be eliminated by closing Department 200—in column 2, and (c) the expenses that will continue—in column 3.

2. Prepare a forecasted annual income statement for the company reflecting the elimination of Department 200 assuming that it will not affect Department 100's sales and gross profit. The statement should reflect the reassignment of the office worker to one-half time as a salesclerk.

Analysis Component

3. Reconcile the company's combined net income with the forecasted net income assuming that Department 200 is eliminated (list both items and amounts). Analyze the reconciliation and explain why you think the department should or should not be eliminated.

PROBLEM SET B

Problem 25-1B
Computation of payback period, accounting rate of return, and net present value

P1 P2 P3

Concorde Company is planning to add a new product to its line. To manufacture this product, the company needs to buy a new machine at a $100,000 cost with an expected five-year life and a $25,000 salvage value. All sales are for cash and all costs are out of pocket, except for depreciation on the new machine. Additional information includes the following.

Expected annual sales of new product	$350,000
Expected annual costs of new product	
Direct materials.......................................	150,000
Direct labor	50,000
Overhead excluding straight-line depreciation on new machine	100,000
Selling and administrative expenses	23,000
Income taxes	20%

Required

1. Compute straight-line depreciation for each year of this new machine's life. (Round depreciation amounts to the nearest dollar.)

2. Determine expected net income and net cash flow for each year of this machine's life. (Round answers to the nearest dollar.)

3. Compute this machine's payback period, assuming that cash flows occur evenly throughout each year. (Round the payback period to two decimals.)

4. Compute this machine's accounting rate of return, assuming that income is earned evenly throughout each year. (Round the percentage return to two decimals.)

5. Compute the net present value for this machine using a discount rate of 12% and assuming that cash flows occur at each year-end. (*Hint:* Salvage value is a cash inflow at the end of the asset's life.)

Check (4) 15.36%

(5) $2,862

Micelli Company has an opportunity to invest in one of two projects. Project A requires a $480,000 investment for new machinery with a three-year life and no salvage value. Project B also requires a $480,000 investment for new machinery with a four-year life and no salvage value. The two projects yield the following predicted annual results. The company uses straight-line depreciation, and cash flows occur evenly throughout each year.

Problem 25-2B
Analysis and computation of payback period, accounting rate of return, and net present value

P1 P2 P3

	Project A	Project B
Sales	$750,000	$800,000
Expenses		
Direct materials	125,000	250,000
Direct labor	130,000	80,000
Overhead including depreciation	330,000	276,000
Selling and administrative expenses	120,000	120,000
Total expenses	705,000	726,000
Pretax income	45,000	74,000
Income taxes (30%)	13,500	22,200
Net income	$ 31,500	$ 51,800

Required

1. Compute each project's annual expected net cash flows. (Round net cash flows to the nearest dollar.)
2. Determine each project's payback period. (Round the payback period to two decimals.)
3. Compute each project's accounting rate of return. (Round the percentage return to one decimal.)
4. Determine each project's net present value using 10% as the discount rate. For part 4 only, assume that cash flows occur at each year-end. (Round net present values to the nearest dollar.)

Check For Project A: (2) 2.5 years, (3) 13.1%, (4) $(3,759)

Analysis Component

5. Identify the project you would recommend to management and explain your choice.

Cologne Corporation is considering a new project requiring a $25,000 investment in an asset having no salvage value. The project would produce $15,000 of pretax income before depreciation at the end of each of the next six years. The company's income tax rate is 30%. In compiling its tax return and computing its income tax payments, the company can choose between two alternative depreciation schedules as shown in the table.

Problem 25-3B
Computation of cash flows and net present values with alternative depreciation methods

P3

	Straight-Line Depreciation	MACRS Depreciation*
Year 1	$ 2,500	$ 5,000
Year 2	5,000	8,000
Year 3	5,000	4,800
Year 4	5,000	2,880
Year 5	5,000	2,880
Year 6	2,500	1,440
Totals	$25,000	$25,000

* The modified accelerated cost recovery system (MACRS) for depreciation is discussed in Chapter 10.

Required

1. Prepare a five-column table that reports amounts (assuming use of straight-line depreciation) for each of the following items for each of the six years: (a) pretax income before depreciation, (b) straight-line depreciation expense, (c) taxable income, (d) income taxes, and (e) net cash flow. Net cash flow equals the amount of income before depreciation minus the income taxes. (Round answers to the nearest dollar.)

2. Prepare a five-column table that reports amounts (assuming use of MACRS depreciation) for each of the following items for each of the six years: (a) income before depreciation, (b) MACRS depreciation expense, (c) taxable income, (d) income taxes, and (e) net cash flow. Net cash flow equals the amount of income before depreciation minus the income taxes. (Round answers to the nearest dollar.)

Check Net present value:
(3) $19,437, (4) $19,914

3. Compute the net present value of the investment if straight-line depreciation is used. Use 15% as the discount rate. (Round the net present value to the nearest dollar.)

4. Compute the net present value of the investment if MACRS depreciation is used. Use 15% as the discount rate. (Round the net present value to the nearest dollar.)

Analysis Component

5. Explain why the MACRS depreciation method increases the net present value of this project.

Problem 25-4B
Analysis of income effects of additional business

A1

Windtrax Company manufactures and sells to local wholesalers approximately 200,000 units per month at a sales price of $1 per unit. Monthly costs for the production and sale of this quantity follow.

Direct materials	$ 30,000
Direct labor	12,000
Overhead	50,000
Selling expenses	7,500
Administrative expenses	31,500
Total costs and expenses	$131,000

A new out-of-state distributor has offered to buy 20,000 units next month for $0.80 each. These units would be marketed in other states and would not affect Windtrax's sales through its normal channels. A study of the costs of this new business reveals the following:

- Direct materials costs are 100% variable.
- Per unit direct labor costs for the additional units would be 100% higher than normal because their production would require double overtime pay to meet the distributor's deadline.
- Eighty percent of the normal annual overhead costs are fixed at any production level from 120,000 to 300,000 units. The remaining 20% is variable with volume.
- Accepting the new business would involve no additional selling expenses.
- Accepting the new business would increase administrative expenses by a $750 fixed amount.

Required

Prepare a three-column comparative income statement that shows the following:

Check Operating income:
(1) $69,000, (2) $8,850

1. Monthly operating income without the special order (column 1).
2. Monthly operating income received from the new business only (column 2).
3. Combined monthly operating income from normal business and the new business (column 3).

Problem 25-5B
Analysis of sales mix strategies

A1

Digits Company is able to produce two products, 22 and 44, with the same machine in its factory. The following information is available.

	Product 22	Product 44
Selling price per unit	$175	$200
Variable costs per unit	100	150
Contribution margin per unit	$ 75	$ 50
Machine hours to produce 1 unit	0.8 hours	0.5 hours
Maximum unit sales per month	525 units	450 units

The company presently operates the machine for a single eight-hour shift for 23 working days each month. Management is thinking about operating the machine for two shifts, which will increase its productivity by another eight hours per day for 23 days per month. This change would require $5,000 additional fixed costs per month.

Required

1. Determine the contribution margin per machine hour that each product generates.

2. How many units of Product 22 and Product 44 should the company produce if it continues to operate with only one shift? How much total contribution margin does this mix produce each month?

3. If the company adds another shift, how many units of Product 22 and Product 44 should it produce? How much total contribution margin would this mix produce each month? Should the company add the new shift? Explain.

4. Suppose that the company determines that it can increase Product 44's maximum sales to 500 units per month by spending $500 per month in marketing efforts. Should the company pursue this strategy and the double shift? Explain.

Check   Units of Product 44: (2) 368, (3) 450, (4) 500

Turftime Company's management is trying to decide whether to eliminate Department Z, which has produced low profits or losses for several years. The company's 2011 departmental income statement shows the following.

Problem 25-6B
Analysis of possible elimination of a department

A1

TURFTIME COMPANY Departmental Income Statements For Year Ended December 31, 2011	Dept. A	Dept. Z	Combined
Sales	$350,000	$87,500	$437,500
Cost of goods sold	230,650	62,550	293,200
Gross profit	119,350	24,950	144,300
Operating expenses			
Direct expenses			
Advertising	13,500	1,500	15,000
Store supplies used	2,800	700	3,500
Depreciation—Store equipment	7,000	3,500	10,500
Total direct expenses	23,300	5,700	29,000
Allocated expenses			
Sales salaries	35,100	11,700	46,800
Rent expense	11,040	2,760	13,800
Bad debts expense	10,500	2,000	12,500
Office salary	10,400	2,600	13,000
Insurance expense	2,100	700	2,800
Miscellaneous office expenses	850	1,250	2,100
Total allocated expenses	69,990	21,010	91,000
Total expenses	93,290	26,710	120,000
Net income (loss)	$ 26,060	$(1,760)	$ 24,300

In analyzing whether to eliminate Department Z, management considers the following items:

a. The company has one office worker who earns $250 per week or $13,000 per year and four sales-clerks who each earn $225 per week or $11,700 per year.

b. The full salaries of three salesclerks are charged to Department A. The full salary of one salesclerk is charged to Department Z.

c. Eliminating Department Z would avoid the sales salaries and the office salary currently allocated to it. However, management prefers another plan. Two salesclerks have indicated that they will be quitting soon. Management believes that their work can be done by the two remaining clerks if the one office worker works in sales half-time. Eliminating Department Z will allow this shift of duties. If this change is implemented, half the office worker's salary would be reported as sales salaries and half would be reported as office salary.

d. The store building is rented under a long-term lease that cannot be changed. Therefore, Department A will use the space and equipment currently used by Department Z.

e. Closing Department Z will eliminate its expenses for advertising, bad debts, and store supplies; 65% of the insurance expense allocated to it to cover its merchandise inventory; and 30% of the miscellaneous office expenses presently allocated to it.

Required

Check   (1) Total expenses:
(a) $413,200, (b) $90,980

       (2) Forecasted net income
without Department Z, $27,780

1. Prepare a three-column report that lists items and amounts for (a) the company's total expenses (including cost of goods sold)—in column 1, (b) the expenses that would be eliminated by closing Department Z—in column 2, and (c) the expenses that will continue—in column 3.

2. Prepare a forecasted annual income statement for the company reflecting the elimination of Department Z assuming that it will not affect Department A's sales and gross profit. The statement should reflect the reassignment of the office worker to one-half time as a salesclerk.

Analysis Component

3. Reconcile the company's combined net income with the forecasted net income assuming that Department Z is eliminated (list both items and amounts). Analyze the reconciliation and explain why you think the department should or should not be eliminated.

SERIAL PROBLEM
Business Solutions

P1   P2

(This serial problem began in Chapter 1 and continues through most of the book. If previous chapter segments were not completed, the serial problem can begin at this point. It is helpful, but not necessary, to use the Working Papers that accompany the book.)

SP 25   Santana Rey is considering the purchase of equipment for Business Solutions that would allow the company to add a new product to its computer furniture line. The equipment is expected to cost $300,000 and to have a six-year life and no salvage value. It will be depreciated on a straight-line basis. Business Solutions expects to sell 100 units of the equipment's product each year. The expected annual income related to this equipment follows.

Sales	$375,000
Costs	
Materials, labor, and overhead (except depreciation)	200,000
Depreciation on new equipment	50,000
Selling and administrative expenses	37,500
Total costs and expenses	287,500
Pretax income	87,500
Income taxes (30%)	26,250
Net income	$ 61,250

Required

Compute the (1) payback period and (2) accounting rate of return for this equipment. (Record answers as percents, rounded to one decimal.)

Beyond the Numbers

REPORTING IN ACTION

P3

RIM

BTN 25-1   Assume **Research In Motion** invested $834 million to expand its manufacturing capacity. Assume that these assets have a seven-year life, and that Research In Motion requires a 12% internal rate of return on these assets.

Required

1. What is the amount of annual cash flows that Research In Motion must earn from these projects to have a 12% internal rate of return? (*Hint:* Identify the seven-period, 12% factor from the present value of an annuity table, and then divide $834 million by this factor to get the annual cash flows necessary.)

Fast Forward

2. Access RIM's financial statements for fiscal years ended after February 27, 2010, from its Website (**RIM.com**) or the SEC's Website (**SEC.gov**).

  a. Determine the amount that RIM invested in capital assets for the most recent year. (*Hint:* Refer to the statement of cash flows.)

  b. Assume a seven-year life and a 12% internal rate of return. What is the amount of cash flows that RIM must earn on these new projects?

BTN 25-2   Research In Motion, Apple, and **Palm** sell several different products; most are profitable but some are not. Teams of employees in each company make advertising, investment, and product mix decisions. A certain portion of advertising for both companies is on a local basis to a target audience.

Required

1. Find one major advertisement of a product or group of products for each company in your local newspaper. Contact the newspaper and ask the approximate cost of this ad space (for example, cost of one page or one-half page of advertising).

2. Estimate how many products this advertisement must sell to justify its cost. Begin by taking the product's sales price advertised for each company and assume a 20% contribution margin.

3. Prepare a one-half page memorandum explaining the importance of effective advertising when making a product mix decision. Be prepared to present your ideas in class.

COMPARATIVE ANALYSIS

A1

RIM

Apple

Palm

BTN 25-3   A consultant commented that "too often the numbers look good but feel bad." This comment often stems from estimation error common to capital budgeting proposals that relate to future cash flows. Three reasons for this error often exist. First, reliably predicting cash flows several years into the future is very difficult. Second, the present value of cash flows many years into the future (say, beyond 10 years) is often very small. Third, it is difficult for personal biases and expectations not to unduly influence present value computations.

Required

1. Compute the present value of $100 to be received in 10 years assuming a 12% discount rate.

2. Why is understanding the three reasons mentioned for estimation errors important when evaluating investment projects? Link this response to your answer for part 1.

ETHICS CHALLENGE

P3

BTN 25-4   Payback period, accounting rate of return, net present value, and internal rate of return are common methods to evaluate capital investment opportunities. Assume that your manager asks you to identify the type of measurement basis and unit that each method offers and to list the advantages and disadvantages of each. Present your response in memorandum format of less than one page.

COMMUNICATING IN PRACTICE

P1 P2 P3 P4

BTN 25-5   Many companies must determine whether to internally produce their component parts or to outsource them. Further, some companies now outsource key components or business processes to international providers. Access the Website **BizBrim.com** and review the available information on outsourcing—especially as it relates to both the advantages and the negative effects of outsourcing.

Required

1. What does Bizbrim identify as the major advantages and the major disadvantages of outsourcing?

2. Does it seem that Bizbrim is generally in favor of or opposed to outsourcing? Explain.

TAKING IT TO THE NET

A1

BTN 25-6   Break into teams and identify four reasons that an international airline such as **Southwest, Delta**, or **American** would invest in a project when its direct analysis using both payback period and net present value indicate it to be a poor investment. (*Hint:* Think about qualitative factors.) Provide an example of an investment project supporting your answer.

TEAMWORK IN ACTION

P1 P3

ENTREPRENEURIAL DECISION

P1   P2   P3   P4

BTN 25-7   Read the chapter opener about Marco Giannini and his company, **Dogswell**. Marco is considering building a new, massive warehousing center to make his business more efficient and reduce costs. He expects that an efficient warehouse could reduce his costs by 20%.

Required

1. What are some of the management tools that Marco can use to evaluate whether the new warehousing center will be a good investment?
2. What information does Marco need to use the tools that you identified in your answer to part 1?
3. What are some of the advantages and disadvantages of each tool identified in your answer to part 1?

HITTING THE ROAD

P3

BTN 25-8   Visit or call a local auto dealership and inquire about leasing a car. Ask about the down payment and the required monthly payments. You will likely find the salesperson does not discuss the cost to purchase this car but focuses on the affordability of the monthly payments. This chapter gives you the tools to compute the cost of this car using the lease payment schedule in present dollars and to estimate the profit from leasing for an auto dealership.

Required

1. Compare the cost of leasing the car to buying it in present dollars using the information from the dealership you contact. (Assume you will make a final payment at the end of the lease and then own the car.)
2. Is it more costly to lease or buy the car? Support your answer with computations.

GLOBAL DECISION

C1

NOKIA

BTN 25-9   Access **Nokia**'s 2009 annual report dated December 31, 2009, from its Website **www.Nokia.com**. Identify and read the section on *Environment—Corporate Responsibility*.

Required

Nokia reports that up to 80 percent of a Nokia mobile device can be recycled and the remainder can be recovered as energy or materials so that nothing goes to a landfill. These recycling efforts are costly. Why would a company like Nokia pursue these costly efforts?

ANSWERS TO MULTIPLE CHOICE QUIZ

1. a; Reworking provides incremental revenue of $11 per unit ($19 − $8); and, it costs $10 to rework them. The company is better off by $1 per unit when it reworks these products and sells them at the regular price.
2. e; Product X has a $2 contribution margin per machine hour [($32 − $12)/ 10 MH]; Product Y has a $7 contribution margin per machine hour [($24 − $10)/2 MH]. It should produce as much of Product Y as possible.
3. a; Total revenue from the special order = 3,000 units × $15 per unit = $45,000; and, Total costs for the special order = (3,000 units × $9 per unit) + $5,000 = $32,000. Net income from the special order = $45,000 − $32,000 = $13,000. Thus, yes, it should accept the order.
4. c; Payback = $270,000/$61,200 per year = 4.4 years.
5. d; Accounting rate of return = $8,550/[($180,000 + $0)/2] = 9.5%.

Appendix

Financial Statement Information

This appendix includes financial information for (1) **Research In Motion**, (2) **Apple**, (3) **Palm**, and (4) **Nokia**. This information is taken from their annual 10-K reports (20-F for Nokia) filed with the SEC. An **annual report** is a summary of a company's financial results for the year along with its current financial condition and future plans. This report is directed to external users of financial information, but it also affects the actions and decisions of internal users.

A company often uses an annual report to showcase itself and its products. Many annual reports include photos, diagrams, and illustrations related to the company. The primary objective of annual reports, however, is the *financial section,* which communicates much information about a company, with most data drawn from the accounting information system. The layout of an annual report's financial section is fairly established and typically includes the following:

- Letter to Shareholders
- Financial History and Highlights
- Management Discussion and Analysis
- Management's Report on Financial Statements and on Internal Controls
- Report of Independent Accountants (Auditor's Report) and on Internal Controls
- Financial Statements
- Notes to Financial Statements
- List of Directors and Officers

This appendix provides the financial statements for Research In Motion (plus selected notes), Apple, Palm, and Nokia. The appendix is organized as follows:

- **Research In Motion A-2** through **A-18**
- **Apple A-19** through **A-23**
- **Palm A-24** through **A-28**
- **Nokia A-29** through **A-33**

RIM
Apple
Palm
NOKIA

Many assignments at the end of each chapter refer to information in this appendix. We encourage readers to spend time with these assignments; they are especially useful in showing the relevance and diversity of financial accounting and reporting.

Special note: The SEC maintains the EDGAR (**E**lectronic **D**ata **G**athering, **A**nalysis, and **R**etrieval) database at **www.sec.gov**. (Over the next few years, the SEC will be moving to IDEA, short for Interactive Data Electronic Applications, which will eventually replace the EDGAR system.) The **Form 10-K** is the annual report form for most companies. It provides electronically accessible information. The **Form 10-KSB** is the annual report form filed by small businesses. It requires slightly less information than the Form 10-K. One of these forms must be filed within 90 days after the company's fiscal year-end. (Forms 10-K405, 10-KT, 10-KT405, and 10-KSB405 are slight variations of the usual form due to certain regulations or rules.)

Research In Motion Financial Report

Research In Motion Limited
Summary Data—Management's Discussion and Analysis of Financial Condition and Results of Operations

As at and for the Fiscal Year Ended	February 27, 2010	February 28, 2009	March 1, 2008	March 3, 2007	March 4, 2006
	(in thousands, except for per share amounts)				
Revenue	$ 14,953,224	$ 11,065,186	$ 6,009,395	$ 3,037,103	$ 2,065,845
Cost of sales	8,368,958	5,967,888	2,928,814	1,379,301	925,598
Gross margin	6,584,266	5,097,298	3,080,581	1,657,802	1,140,247
Operating expenses					
Research and development	964,841	684,702	359,828	236,173	158,887
Selling, marketing and administration	1,907,398	1,495,697	881,482	537,922	314,317
Amortization	310,357	194,803	108,112	76,879	49,951
Litigation	163,800	—	—	—	201,791
Total operating expenses	3,346,396	2,375,202	1,349,422	850,974	724,946
Income from operations	3,237,870	2,722,096	1,731,159	806,828	415,301
Investment income	28,640	78,267	79,361	52,117	66,218
Income before income taxes	3,266,510	2,800,363	1,810,520	858,945	481,519
Provision for income taxes	809,366	907,747	516,653	227,373	106,863
Net income	$ 2,457,144	$ 1,892,616	$ 1,293,867	$ 631,572	$ 374,656
Earnings per share					
Basic	$ 4.35	$ 3.35	$ 2.31	$ 1.14	$ 0.66
Diluted	$ 4.31	$ 3.30	$ 2.26	$ 1.10	$ 0.64
Weighted-average number of shares outstanding (000's)					
Basic	564,492	565,059	559,778	556,059	566,742
Diluted	569,759	574,156	572,830	571,809	588,468
Total asset	$ 10,204,409	$ 8,101,372	$ 5,511,187	$ 3,088,949	$ 2,314,349
Total liabilities	$ 2,601,746	$ 2,227,244	$ 1,577,621	$ 605,449	$ 318,934
Total long-term liabilities	$ 169,969	$ 111,893	$ 103,190	$ 58,874	$ 34,709
Shareholders' equity	$ 7,602,663	$ 5,874,128	$ 3,933,566	$ 2,483,500	$ 1,995,415

REPORT OF
INDEPENDENT REGISTERED PUBLIC ACCOUNTING FIRM

To the Shareholders of **Research In Motion Limited**

We have audited the accompanying consolidated balance sheets of **Research In Motion Limited** [the "Company"] as at February 27, 2010 and February 28, 2009, and the related consolidated statements of operations, shareholders' equity and cash flows for the years ended February 27, 2010, February 28, 2009 and March 1, 2008. These financial statements are the responsibility of the Company's management. Our responsibility is to express an opinion on these financial statements based on our audits.

We conducted our audits in accordance with Canadian generally accepted auditing standards and the standards of the Public Company Accounting Oversight Board (United States). Those standards require that we plan and perform the audit to obtain reasonable assurance about whether the financial statements are free of material misstatement. An audit includes examining, on a test basis, evidence supporting the amounts and disclosures in the financial statements. An audit also includes assessing the accounting principles used and significant estimates made by management, as well as evaluating the overall financial statement presentation. We believe that our audits provide a reasonable basis for our opinion.

In our opinion, the consolidated financial statements referred to above present fairly, in all material respects, the financial position of the Company as at February 27, 2010 and February 28, 2009, and the results of its operations and its cash flows for the years ended February 27, 2010, February 28, 2009 and March 1, 2008, in conformity with United States generally accepted accounting principles.

We also have audited, in accordance with the standards of the Public Company Accounting Oversight Board (United States), the Company's internal control over financial reporting as of February 27, 2010, based on criteria established in Internal Control-Integrated Framework issued by the Committee of Sponsoring Organizations of the Treadway Commission and our report dated April 1, 2010 expressed an unqualified opinion thereon.

Ernst & Young LLP

Kitchener, Canada,
April 1, 2010.

Chartered Accountants
Licensed Public Accountants

RESEARCH IN MOTION

REPORT OF
INDEPENDENT REGISTERED PUBLIC ACCOUNTING FIRM
ON INTERNAL CONTROL OVER FINANCIAL REPORTING

To the Shareholders of **Research In Motion Limited**

We have audited **Research In Motion Limited's** [the "Company"] internal control over financial reporting as of February 27, 2010, based on criteria established in Internal Control — Integrated Framework issued by the Committee of Sponsoring Organizations of the Treadway Commission ["the COSO criteria"]. The Company's management is responsible for maintaining effective internal control over financial reporting, and for its assessment of the effectiveness of internal control over financial reporting. Our responsibility is to express an opinion on the Company's internal control over financial reporting based on our audit.

We conducted our audit in accordance with the standards of the Public Company Accounting Oversight Board (United States). Those standards require that we plan and perform the audit to obtain reasonable assurance about whether effective internal control over financial reporting was maintained in all material respects. Our audit included obtaining an understanding of internal control over financial reporting, assessing the risk that a material weakness exists, testing and evaluating the design and operating effectiveness of internal control based on the assessed risk, and performing such other procedures as we considered necessary in the circumstances. We believe that our audit provides a reasonable basis for our opinion.

A company's internal control over financial reporting is a process designed to provide reasonable assurance regarding the reliability of financial reporting and the preparation of financial statements for external purposes in accordance with generally accepted accounting principles. A company's internal control over financial reporting includes those policies and procedures that [1] pertain to the maintenance of records that, in reasonable detail, accurately and fairly reflect the transactions and dispositions of the assets of the company; [2] provide reasonable assurance that transactions are recorded as necessary to permit preparation of financial statements in accordance with generally accepted accounting principles, and that receipts and expenditures of the company are being made only in accordance with authorizations of management and directors of the company; and [3] provide reasonable assurance regarding prevention or timely detection of unauthorized acquisition, use or disposition of the company's assets that could have a material effect on the financial statements.

Because of its inherent limitations, internal control over financial reporting may not prevent or detect misstatements. Also, projections of any evaluation of effectiveness to future periods are subject to the risk that controls may become inadequate because of changes in conditions, or that the degree of compliance with the policies or procedures may deteriorate.

In our opinion, the Company maintained, in all material respects, effective internal control over financial reporting as of February 27, 2010, based on the COSO criteria.

We also have audited, in accordance with the standards of the Public Company Accounting Oversight Board (United States), the consolidated balance sheets of the Company as at February 27, 2010 and February 28, 2009, and the consolidated statements of operations, shareholders' equity and cash flows for the years ended February 27, 2010, February 28, 2009 and March 1, 2008 of the Company and our report dated April 1, 2010 expressed an unqualified opinion thereon.

Ernst & Young LLP

Kitchener, Canada,
April 1, 2010.

Chartered Accountants
Licensed Public Accountants

Research In Motion Limited
Consolidated Balance Sheets

($US, in thousands)	February 27, 2010	February 28, 2009
Assets		
Current		
Cash and cash equivalents	$ 1,550,861	$ 835,546
Short-term investments	360,614	682,666
Accounts receivable, net	2,593,742	2,112,117
Other receivables	206,373	157,728
Inventories	621,611	682,400
Other current assets	285,539	187,257
Deferred income tax asset	193,916	183,872
Total current assets	5,812,656	4,841,586
Long-term investments	958,248	720,635
Property, plant and equipment, net	1,956,581	1,334,648
Intangible assets, net	1,326,363	1,066,527
Goodwill	150,561	137,572
Deferred income tax asset	—	404
Total assets	$10,204,409	$8,101,372
Liabilities		
Current		
Accounts payable	$ 615,620	$ 448,339
Accrued liabilities	1,638,260	1,238,602
Income taxes payable	95,650	361,460
Deferred revenue	67,573	53,834
Deferred income tax liability	14,674	13,116
Total current liabilities	2,431,777	2,115,351
Deferred income tax liability	141,382	87,917
Income taxes payable	28,587	23,976
Total liabilities	2,601,746	2,227,244
Shareholders' Equity		
Capital stock		
Preferred shares, authorized unlimited number of non-voting, cumulative, redeemable and retractable	—	—
Common shares, authorized unlimited number of non-voting, redeemable, retractable Class A common shares and unlimited number of voting common shares. Issued — 557,328,394 voting common shares (February 28, 2009 — 566,218,819)	2,207,609	2,208,235
Treasury stock		
February 27, 2010 — 1,458,950 (February 28, 2009 — nil)	(94,463)	—
Retained earnings	5,274,365	3,545,710
Additional paid-in capital	164,060	119,726
Accumulated other comprehensive income	51,092	457
Total shareholders equity	7,602,663	5,874,128
Total liabilities and shareholders' equity	$10,204,409	$8,101,372

RESEARCH IN MOTION

Research In Motion Limited
Consolidated Statements of Operations

($US, in thousands, except per share data)

For the Year Ended	February 27, 2010	February 28, 2009	March 1, 2008
Revenue			
Devices and other	$12,535,998	$ 9,410,755	$4,914,366
Service and software	2,417,226	1,654,431	1,095,029
Total revenue	$14,953,224	11,065,186	6,009,395
Cost of sales			
Devices and other	7,979,163	5,718,041	2,758,250
Service and software	389,795	249,847	170,564
Total cost of sales	8,368,958	5,967,888	2,928,814
Gross margin	6,584,266	5,097,298	3,080,581
Operating expenses			
Research and development	964,841	684,702	359,828
Selling, marketing and administration	1,907,398	1,495,697	881,482
Amortization	310,357	194,803	108,112
Litigation	163,800	—	—
Total operating expenses	3,346,396	2,375,202	1,349,422
Income from operations	3,237,870	2,722,096	1,731,159
Investment income	28,640	78,267	79,361
Income before income taxes	3,266,510	2,800,363	1,810,520
Provision for income taxes	809,366	907,747	516,653
Net income	$ 2,457,144	$ 1,892,616	$1,293,867
Earnings per share			
Basic	$ 4.35	$ 3.35	$ 2.31
Diluted	$ 4.31	$ 3.30	$ 2.26

Research In Motion Limited

Consolidated Statements of Shareholders' Equity

($US, in thousands)	Capital Stock	Additional Paid-In Capital	Treasury Stock	Retained Earnings	Accumulated Other Comprehensive Income (Loss)	Total
Balance as at March 3, 2007	$2,099,696	$ 36,093	$ —	$ 359,227	$(11,516)	$2,483,500
Comprehensive income (loss):						
Net income	—	—	—	1,293,867	—	1,293,867
Net change in unrealized gains on available-for-sale investments	—	—	—	—	13,467	13,467
Net change in fair value of derivatives designated as cash flow hedges during the year	—	—	—	—	37,564	37,564
Amounts reclassified to earnings during the year	—	—	—	—	(9,232)	(9,232)
Other paid-in capital	—	9,626	—	—	—	9,626
Shares issued:						
Exercise of stock options	62,889	—	—	—	—	62,889
Transfers to capital stock from stock option exercises	7,271	(7,271)	—	—	—	—
Stock-based compensation	—	33,700	—	—	—	33,700
Excess tax benefits from stock-based compensation	—	8,185	—	—	—	8,185
Balance as at March 1, 2008	$2,169,856	$ 80,333	$ —	$1,653,094	$ 30,283	$3,933,566
Comprehensive income (loss):						
Net income	—	—	—	1,892,616	—	1,892,616
Net change in unrealized gains on available-for-sale investments	—	—	—	—	(7,161)	(7,161)
Net change in fair value of derivatives designated as cash flow hedges during the year	—	—	—	—	(6,168)	(6,168)
Amounts reclassified to earnings during the year	—	—	—	—	(16,497)	(16,497)
Shares issued:						
Exercise of stock options	27,024	—	—	—	—	27,024
Transfers to capital stock from stock option exercises	11,355	(11,355)	—	—	—	—
Stock-based compensation	—	38,100	—	—	—	38,100
Excess tax benefits from stock-based compensation	—	12,648	—	—	—	12,648
Balance as at February 28, 2009	$2,208,235	$119,726	$ —	$3,545,710	$ 457	$5,874,128
Comprehensive income:						
Net income	—	—	—	2,457,144	—	2,457,144
Net change in unrealized gains on available-for-sale investments	—	—	—	—	6,803	6,803
Net change in fair value of derivatives designated as cash flow hedges during the year	—	—	—	—	28,324	28,324
Amounts reclassified to earnings during the year	—	—	—	—	15,508	15,508
Shares issued:						
Exercise of stock options	30,246	—	—	—	—	30,246
Transfers to capital stock from stock option exercises	15,647	(15,647)	—	—	—	—
Stock-based compensation	—	58,038	—	—	—	58,038
Excess tax benefits from stock-based compensation	—	1,943	—	—	—	1,943
Purchase of treasury stock	—	—	(94,463)	—	—	(94,463)
Common shares repurchased	(46,519)	—	—	(728,489)	—	(775,008)
Balance as at February 27, 2010	$2,207,609	$164,060	$(94,463)	$5,274,365	$ 51,092	$7,602,663

RESEARCH IN MOTION

Research In Motion Limited
Consolidated Statements of Cash Flows

For the Year Ended ($US, in thousands)	February 27, 2010	February 28, 2009	March 1, 2008
Cash flows from operating activities			
Net income	$ 2,457,144	$ 1,892,616	$ 1,293,867
Adjustments to reconcile net income to net cash provided by operating activities:			
Amortization	615,621	327,896	177,366
Deferred income taxes	51,363	(36,623)	(67,244)
Income taxes payable	4,611	(6,897)	4,973
Stock-based compensation	58,038	38,100	33,700
Other	8,806	5,867	3,303
Net changes in working capital items	(160,709)	(769,114)	130,794
Net cash provided by operating activities	3,034,874	1,451,845	1,576,759
Cash flows from investing activities			
Acquisition of long-term investments	(862,977)	(507,082)	(757,656)
Proceeds on sale or maturity of long-term investments	473,476	431,713	260,393
Acquisition of property, plant and equipment	(1,009,416)	(833,521)	(351,914)
Acquisition of intangible assets	(421,400)	(687,913)	(374,128)
Business acquisitions, net of cash acquired	(143,375)	(48,425)	(6,200)
Acquisition of short-term investments	(476,956)	(917,316)	(1,249,919)
Proceeds on sale or maturity of short-term investments	970,521	739,021	1,325,487
Net cash used in investing activities	(1,470,127)	(1,823,523)	(1,153,937)
Cash flows from financing activities			
Issuance of common shares	30,246	27,024	62,889
Additional paid-in capital	—	—	9,626
Excess tax benefits from stock-based compensation	1,943	12,648	8,185
Purchase of treasury stock	(94,463)	—	—
Common shares repurchased	(775,008)	—	—
Repayment of debt	(6,099)	(14,305)	(302)
Net cash provided by (used in) financing activities	(843,381)	25,367	80,398
Effect of foreign exchange gain (loss) on cash and cash equivalents	(6,051)	(2,541)	4,034
Net increase (decrease) in cash and cash equivalents for the year	715,315	(348,852)	507,254
Cash and cash equivalents, beginning of year	835,546	1,184,398	677,144
Cash and cash equivalents, end of year	$ 1,550,861	$ 835,546	$ 1,184,398

RIM—<u>SELECTED</u> Notes to the Consolidated Financial Statements

$US in thousands, except share and per share data, and where otherwise indicated

1. RESEARCH IN MOTION LIMITED AND SUMMARY OF SIGNIFICANT ACCOUNTING POLICIES

Research In Motion Limited ("RIM" or the "Company") is a leading designer, manufacturer and marketer of innovative wireless solutions for the worldwide mobile communications market. Through the development of integrated hardware, software and services that support multiple wireless network standards, RIM provides platforms and solutions for seamless access to time-sensitive information including email, phone, short messaging service (SMS), Internet and intranet-based applications. RIM technology also enables a broad array of third party developers and manufacturers to enhance their products and services with wireless connectivity to data. RIM's portfolio of award-winning products, services and embedded technologies are used by thousands of organizations and millions of consumers around the world and include the BlackBerry wireless solution, and other software and hardware. The Company's sales and marketing efforts include collaboration with strategic partners and distribution channels, as well as its own supporting sales and marketing teams, to promote the sale of its products and services.

Basis of presentation and preparation

The consolidated financial statements include the accounts of all subsidiaries of the Company with intercompany transactions and balances eliminated on consolidation. All of the Company's subsidiaries are wholly-owned. These consolidated financial statements have been prepared by management in accordance with United States generally accepted accounting principles ("U.S. GAAP") on a basis consistent for all periods presented except as described in note 2. Certain of the comparative figures have been reclassified to conform to the current year presentation. The Company's fiscal year end date is the 52 or 53 weeks ending on the last Saturday of February, or the first Saturday of March. The fiscal years ended February 27, 2010, February 28, 2009, and March 1, 2008 comprise 52 weeks.

The significant accounting policies used in these U.S. GAAP consolidated financial statements are as follows:

Use of estimates

The preparation of the consolidated financial statements requires management to make estimates and assumptions with respect to the reported amounts of assets, liabilities, revenues and expenses and the disclosure of contingent assets and liabilities. Significant areas requiring the use of management estimates relate to the determination of reserves for various litigation claims, provisions for excess and obsolete inventories and liabilities for purchase commitments with contract manufacturers and suppliers, fair values of assets acquired and liabilities assumed in business combinations, royalties, amortization expense, implied fair value of goodwill, provision for income taxes, realization of deferred income tax assets and the related components of the valuation allowance, provisions for warranty and the fair values of financial instruments. Actual results could differ from these estimates.

Foreign currency translation

The U.S. dollar is the functional and reporting currency of the Company. Foreign currency denominated assets and liabilities of the Company and all of its subsidiaries are translated into U.S. dollars. Accordingly, monetary assets and liabilities are translated using the exchange rates in effect at the consolidated balance sheet date and revenues and expenses at the rates of exchange prevailing when the transactions occurred. Remeasurement adjustments are included in income. Non-monetary assets and liabilities are translated at historical exchange rates.

Cash and cash equivalents

Cash and cash equivalents consist of balances with banks and liquid investments with maturities of three months or less at the date of acquisition.

Accounts receivable, net

The accounts receivable balance which reflects invoiced and accrued revenue is presented net of an allowance for doubtful accounts. The allowance for doubtful accounts reflects estimates of probable losses in accounts receivables. The Company is dependent on a number of significant customers and on large complex contracts with respect to sales of the majority of its products, software and services. The Company expects the majority of its accounts receivable balances to continue to come from large customers as it sells the majority of its devices and software products and service relay access through network carriers and resellers rather than directly.

The Company evaluates the collectability of its accounts receivables based upon a combination of factors on a periodic basis such as specific credit risk of its customers, historical trends and economic circumstances. The Company, in the normal course of business, monitors the financial condition of its customers and reviews the credit history of each new

$US in thousands, except share and per share data, and where otherwise indicated

customer. When the Company becomes aware of a specific customer's inability to meet its financial obligations to the Company (such as in the case of bankruptcy filings or material deterioration in the customer's operating results or financial position, and payment experiences), RIM records a specific bad debt provision to reduce the customer's related accounts receivable to its estimated net realizable value. If circumstances related to specific customers change, the Company's estimates of the recoverability of accounts receivables balances could be further adjusted. The allowance for doubtful accounts as at February 27, 2010 is $2.0 million (February 28, 2009- $2.1 million).

Investments

The Company's investments, other than cost method investments of $2.5 million and equity method investments of $4.1 million, consist of money market and other debt securities, and are classified as available-for-sale for accounting purposes. The Company does not exercise significant influence with respect to any of these investments.

Investments with maturities one year or less, as well as any investments that management intends to hold for less than one year, are classified as short-term investments. Investments with maturities in excess of one year are classified as long-term investments.

The Company determines the appropriate classification of investments at the time of purchase and subsequently reassesses the classification of such investments at each balance sheet date. Investments classified as available-for-sale are carried at fair value with unrealized gains and losses recorded in accumulated other comprehensive income (loss) until such investments mature or are sold. The Company uses the specific identification method of determining the cost basis in computing realized gains or losses on available-for-sale investments which are recorded in investment income.

The Company assesses individual investments in an unrealized loss position to determine whether the unrealized loss is other-than-temporary. The Company makes this assessment by considering available evidence, including changes in general market conditions, specific industry and individual company data, the length of time and the extent to which the fair value has been less than cost, the financial condition, the near-term prospects of the individual investment and the Company's intent and ability to hold the investments. In the event that a decline in the fair value of an investment occurs and the decline in value is considered to be other-than-temporary, an impairment charge is recorded in investment income equal to the difference between the cost basis and the fair value of the individual investment at the balance sheet date of the reporting period for which the assessment was made. The fair value of the investment then becomes the new cost basis of the investment.

Effective in the second quarter of fiscal 2010, if a debt security's market value is below its amortized cost and the Company either intends to sell the security or it is more likely than not that the Company will be required to sell the security before its anticipated recovery, the Company records an other-than-temporary impairment charge to investment income for the entire amount of the impairment. For other-than-temporary impairments on debt securities that the Company does not intend to sell and it is not more likely than not that the entity will be required to sell the security before its anticipated recovery, the Company would separate the other-than-temporary impairment into the amount representing the credit loss and the amount related to all other factors. The Company would record the other-than-temporary impairment related to the credit loss as a charge to investment income and the remaining other-than-temporary impairment would be recorded as a component of accumulated other comprehensive income.

Derivative financial instruments

The Company uses derivative financial instruments, including forward contracts and options, to hedge certain foreign currency exposures. The Company does not use derivative financial instruments for speculative purposes.

Inventories

Raw materials are stated at the lower of cost and replacement cost. Work in process and finished goods inventories are stated at the lower of cost and net realizable value. Cost includes the cost of materials plus direct labour applied to the product and the applicable share of manufacturing overhead. Cost is determined on a first-in-first-out basis.

Property, plant and equipment, net

Property, plant and equipment is stated at cost less accumulated amortization. No amortization is provided for construction in progress until the assets are ready for use. Amortization is provided using the following rates and methods:

Buildings, leaseholds and other	Straight-line over terms between 5 and 40 years
BlackBerry operations and other information technology	Straight-line over terms between 3 and 5 years
Manufacturing equipment, R&D equipment and tooling	Straight-line over terms between 2 and 8 years
Furniture and fixtures	Declining balance at 20% per annum

$US in thousands, except share and per share data, and where otherwise indicated

Intangible assets, net

Intangible assets are stated at cost less accumulated amortization and are comprised of acquired technology, licenses, and patents. Acquired technology consists of purchased developed technology arising from the Company's business acquisitions. Licenses include licenses or agreements that the Company has negotiated with third parties upon use of third parties' technology. Patents comprise trademarks, internally developed patents, as well as individual patents or portfolios of patents acquired from third parties. Costs capitalized and subsequently amortized include all costs necessary to acquire intellectual property, such as patents and trademarks, as well as legal defense costs arising out of the assertion of any Company-owned patents.

Intangible assets are amortized as follows:

Acquired technology	Straight-line over 2 to 5 years
Licenses	Straight-line over terms of the license agreements or on a per unit basis based upon the anticipated number of units sold during the terms, subject to a maximum of 5 years
Patents	Straight-line over 17 years or over estimated useful life

Goodwill

Goodwill represents the excess of the purchase price of business acquisitions over the fair value of identifiable net assets acquired. Goodwill is allocated as at the date of the business combination. Goodwill is not amortized, but is tested for impairment annually, or more frequently if events or changes in circumstances indicate the asset may be impaired.

Impairment of long-lived assets

The Company reviews long-lived assets such as property, plant and equipment and intangible assets with finite useful lives for impairment whenever events or changes in circumstances indicate that the carrying amount may not be recoverable. If the total of the expected undiscounted future cash flows is less than the carrying amount of the asset, a loss is recognized for the excess of the carrying amount over the fair value of the asset.

Income taxes

The Company uses the liability method of tax allocation to account for income taxes. Deferred income tax assets and liabilities are recognized based upon temporary differences between the financial reporting and tax bases of assets and liabilities, and measured using enacted tax rates and laws that will be in effect when the differences are expected to reverse. The Company records a valuation allowance to reduce deferred income tax assets to the amount that is more likely than not to be realized. The Company considers both positive evidence and negative evidence, to determine whether, based upon the weight of that evidence, a valuation allowance is required. Judgment is required in considering the relative impact of negative and positive evidence.

Revenue recognition

The Company recognizes revenue when it is realized or realizable and earned. The Company considers revenue realized or realizable and earned when it has persuasive evidence of an arrangement, the product has been delivered or the services have been provided to the customer, the sales price is fixed or determinable and collectability is reasonably assured. In addition to this general policy, the following paragraphs describe the specific revenue recognition policies for each major category of revenue.

Devices

Revenue from the sales of BlackBerry devices is recognized when title is transferred to the customer and all significant contractual obligations that affect the customer's final acceptance have been fulfilled. For hardware products for which software is deemed not to be incidental, the Company recognizes revenue in accordance with industry specific software revenue recognition guidance. The Company records reductions to revenue for estimated commitments related to price protection and for customer incentive programs, including reseller and end-user rebates. The estimated cost of the incentive programs are accrued based on historical experience, as a reduction to revenue in the period the Company has sold the product and committed to a plan. Price protection is accrued as a reduction to revenue based on estimates of future price reductions and certain agreed customer inventories at the date of the price adjustment. In addition, provisions are made at the time of sale for warranties and royalties.

Service

Revenue from service is recognized rateably on a monthly basis when the service is provided. In instances where the Company bills the customer prior to performing the service, the prebilling is recorded as deferred revenue.

Software

Revenue from licensed software is recognized at the inception of the license term and in accordance with industry

RESEARCH IN MOTION

$US in thousands, except share and per share data, and where otherwise indicated

specific software revenue recognition guidance. When the fair value of a delivered element has not been established, the Company uses the residual method to recognize revenue if the fair value of undelivered elements is determinable. Revenue from software maintenance, unspecified upgrades and technical support contracts is recognized over the period that such items are delivered or that services are provided.

Other

Revenue from the sale of accessories is recognized when title is transferred to the customer and all significant contractual obligations that affect the customer's final acceptance have been fulfilled. Technical support ("T-Support") contracts extending beyond the current period are recorded as deferred revenue. Revenue from repair and maintenance programs is recognized when the service is delivered which is when the title is transferred to the customer and all significant contractual obligations that affect the customer's final acceptance have been fulfilled. Revenue for non-recurring engineering contracts is recognized as specific contract milestones are met. The attainment of milestones approximates actual performance.

Shipping and handling costs

Shipping and handling costs charged to income are included in cost of sales where they can be reasonably attributed to certain revenue; otherwise they are included in selling, marketing and administration.

Multiple-element arrangements

The Company enters into transactions that represent multiple-element arrangements which may include any combination of hardware and/or service or software and T-Support. These multiple-element arrangements are assessed to determine whether they can be separated into more than one unit of accounting or element for the purpose of revenue recognition. When the appropriate criteria for separating revenue into more than one unit of accounting is met and there is vendor specific objective evidence of fair value for all units of accounting or elements in an arrangement, the arrangement consideration is allocated to the separate units of accounting or elements based on each unit's relative fair value. When the fair value of a delivered element has not been established, the Company uses the residual method to recognize revenue if the fair value of undelivered elements is determinable. This vendor specific objective evidence of fair value is established through prices charged for each revenue element when that element is sold separately. The revenue recognition policies described above are then applied to each unit of accounting.

Research and development

Research costs are expensed as incurred. Development costs for BlackBerry devices and licensed software to be sold, leased or otherwise marketed are subject to capitalization beginning when a product's technological feasibility has been established and ending when a product is available for general release to customers. The Company's products are generally released soon after technological feasibility has been established and therefore costs incurred subsequent to achievement of technological feasibility are not significant and have been expensed as incurred.

Comprehensive income (loss)

Comprehensive income (loss) is defined as the change in net assets of a business enterprise during a period from transactions and other events and circumstances from non-owner sources and includes all changes in equity during a period except those resulting from investments by owners and distributions to owners. The Company's reportable items of comprehensive income are cash flow hedges and changes in the fair value of available-for-sale investments. Realized gains or losses on available-for-sale investments are reclassified into investment income using the specific identification basis.

Earnings per share

Earnings per share is calculated based on the weighted-average number of shares outstanding during the year. The treasury stock method is used for the calculation of the dilutive effect of stock options.

Stock-based compensation plans

The Company has stock-based compensation plans.

Warranty

The Company provides for the estimated costs of product warranties at the time revenue is recognized. BlackBerry devices are generally covered by a time-limited warranty for varying periods of time. The Company's warranty obligation is affected by product failure rates, differences in warranty periods, regulatory developments with respect to warranty obligations in the countries in which the Company carries on business, freight expense, and material usage and other related repair costs. The Company's estimates of costs are based upon historical experience and expectations of future return rates and unit warranty repair cost. If the Company experiences increased or decreased warranty activity, or increased or decreased costs associated with servicing those obligations, revisions to the estimated warranty liability would be recognized in the reporting period when such revisions are made.

Advertising costs

The Company expenses all advertising costs as incurred. These costs are included in selling, marketing and administration.

$US in thousands, except share and per share data, and where otherwise indicated

4. CASH, CASH EQUIVALENTS AND INVESTMENTS
The components of cash, cash equivalents and investments were as follows:

	Cost Basis	Unrealized Gains	Unrealized Losses	Recorded Basis	Cash and Cash Equivalents	Short-term Investments	Long-term Investments
As at February 27, 2010							
Bank balances	$ 535,445	$ —	$ —	$ 535,445	$ 535,445	$ —	$ —
Money market fund	3,278	—	—	3,278	3,278	—	—
Bankers acceptances and term deposits/certificates	377,596	—	—	377,596	377,596	—	—
Commercial paper and corporate notes/bonds	855,145	6,528	(49)	861,624	472,312	187,369	201,943
Treasury bills/notes	203,514	129	(12)	203,631	92,272	50,786	60,573
Government sponsored enterprise notes	447,131	2,590	(13)	449,708	69,958	111,977	267,773
Asset-backed securities	393,751	5,280	(50)	398,981	—	10,482	388,499
Auction-rate securities	40,527	—	(7,688)	32,839	—	—	32,839
Other investments	6,621	—	—	6,621	—	—	6,621
	$2,863,008	$14,527	$ (7,812)	$2,869,723	$1,550,861	$360,614	$958,248

Realized gains and losses on available-for-sale securities comprise the following:

For the year ended	February 27, 2010	February 28, 2009	March 1, 2008
Realized gains	$439	$ 158	$ 10
Realized losses	(17)	(1,801)	(410)
Net realized gains (losses)	$422	$(1,643)	$(400)

The contractual maturities of available-for-sale investments at February 27, 2010 were as follows:

	Cost Basis	Fair Value
Due in one year or less	$1,371,047	$1,372,752
Due in one to five years	773,471	783,451
Due after five years	173,146	168,176
No fixed maturity date	3,278	3,278
	$2,320,942	$2,327,657

5. FAIR VALUE MEASUREMENTS
The Company defines fair value as the price that would be received to sell an asset or paid to transfer a liability in an orderly transaction between market participants at the measurement date. When determining the fair value measurements for assets and liabilities required to be recorded at fair value, the Company considers the principal or most advantageous market in which it would transact and considers assumptions that market participants would use in pricing the asset or liability such as inherent risk, non-performance risk and credit risk. The Company applies the following fair value hierarchy, which prioritizes the inputs used in the valuation methodologies in measuring fair value into three levels:

• Level 1 — Unadjusted quoted prices at the measurement date for identical assets or liabilities in active markets.

• Level 2 — Observable inputs other than quoted prices included in Level 1, such as quoted prices for similar assets and liabilities in active markets; quoted prices for identical or similar assets and liabilities in markets that are not active; or other inputs that are observable or can be corroborated by observable market data.

• Level 3 — Significant unobservable inputs which are supported by little or no market activity.

The fair value hierarchy also requires the Company to maximize the use of observable inputs and minimize the use of unobservable inputs when measuring fair value. The carrying amounts of the Company's cash and cash equivalents, accounts receivable, other receivables, accounts payable and accrued liabilities, approximate fair value due to their short maturities. When determining the fair value of its investments held, the Company primarily relies on an independent third party valuator for the fair valuation of securities.

$US in thousands, except share and per share data, and where otherwise indicated

6. INVENTORIES

Inventories were comprised as follows:

	February 27, 2010	February 28, 2009
Raw materials	$ 490,063	$464,497
Work in process	231,939	250,728
Finished goods	17,068	35,264
Provision for excess and obsolete inventories	(117,459)	(68,089)
	$ 621,611	$682,400

7. PROPERTY, PLANT AND EQUIPMENT, NET

Property, plant and equipment were comprised of the following:

February 27, 2010	Cost	Accumulated amortization	Net book value
Land	$ 104,254	$ —	$ 104,254
Buildings, leaseholds and other	926,747	115,216	811,531
BlackBerry operations and other information technology	1,152,637	484,180	668,457
Manufacturing equipment, research and development equipment, and tooling	347,692	182,228	165,464
Furniture and fixtures	346,641	139,766	206,875
	$2,877,971	$921,390	$1,956,581

As at February 27, 2010, the carrying amount of assets under construction was $254.3 million (February 28, 2009 — $88.9 million). Of this amount, $110.9 million (February 28, 2009 — $50.0 million) was included in buildings, leaseholds and other; $102.5 million (February 28, 2009 - $35.8 million) was included in BlackBerry operations and other information technology; and $40.9 million (February 28, 2009 — $3.2 million) was included in manufacturing equip-

ment, research and development equipment, and tooling. As at February 27, 2010, $31.7 million has been classified as an asset held for sale and accordingly has been reclassified from property, plant and equipment to other current assets. For the year ended February 27, 2010, amortization expense related to property, plant and equipment was $344.5 million (February 28, 2009 — $203.4 million; March 1, 2008 — $133.1 million).

8. INTANGIBLE ASSETS, NET

Intangible assets were comprised of the following:

February 27, 2010	Cost	Accumulated amortization	Net book value
Acquired technology	$ 165,791	$ 70,777	$ 95,014
Licenses	711,969	196,618	515,351
Patents	889,467	173,469	715,998
	$1,767,227	$440,864	$1,326,363

For the year ended February 27, 2010, amortization expense related to intangible assets was $271.1 million (February 28, 2009 — $124.5 million; March 1, 2008 — $44.3 million). Total additions to intangible assets in fiscal 2010 were $531.0 million (2009 — $721.1 million). Based on the carrying value of the identified intangible assets as at February 27, 2010 and assuming no subsequent impairment of the

underlying assets, the annual amortization expense for the next five fiscal years is expected to be as follows: 2011 — $324 million; 2012 — $275 million; 2013 — $227 million; 2014 — $139 million; and 2015 — $61 million. The weighted-average remaining useful life of the acquired technology is 3.4 years (2009 – 3.7 years).

$US in thousands, except share and per share data, and where otherwise indicated

10.   INCOME TAXES

The difference between the amount of the provision for income taxes and the amount computed by multiplying income before income taxes by the statutory Canadian tax rate is reconciled as follows:

For the year ended	February 27, 2010	February 28, 2009
Statutory Canadian tax rate	32.8%	33.4%
Expected income tax provision	$1,072,395	$935,881
Differences in income taxes resulting from:		
Impact of Canadian U.S. dollar functional currency election	(145,000)	—
Investment tax credits	(101,214)	(81,173)
Manufacturing and processing activities	(52,053)	(49,808)
Foreign exchange	2,837	99,575
Foreign tax rate differences	5,291	(16,273)
Non-deductible stock compensation	9,600	10,500
Adjustments to deferred tax balances for enacted changes in tax laws and rates	7,927	1,260
Other differences	9,583	7,785
	$ 809,366	$907,747

11.   CAPITAL STOCK

(a) Capital stock

The Company is authorized to issue an unlimited number of non-voting, redeemable, retractable Class A common shares, an unlimited number of voting common shares and an unlimited number of non-voting, cumulative, redeemable, retractable preferred shares. At February 27, 2010 and February 28, 2009, there were no Class A common shares or preferred shares outstanding. The Company declared a 3-for-1 stock split of the Company's outstanding common shares on June 28, 2007. The stock split was implemented by way of a stock dividend. Shareholders received an additional two common shares of the Company for each common share held. The stock dividend was paid on August 20, 2007 to common shareholders of record at the close of business on August 17, 2007. All share, earnings per share and stock option data have been adjusted to reflect this stock dividend.

The following details the changes in issued and outstanding common shares for the year ended February 27, 2010:

	Capital Stock		Treasury Stock	
	Stock Outstanding (000's)	Amount	Stock Outstanding (000's)	Amount
Common shares outstanding as at February 28, 2009	566,219	2,208,235	—	—
Exercise of stock options	3,408	30,246	—	—
Conversion of restricted share units	2	—	—	—
Transfers to capital stock resulting from stock option exercises	—	15,647	—	—
Restricted share unit plan purchase of shares	—	—	1,459	(94,463)
Common shares repurchased	(12,300)	(46,519)	—	—
Common shares outstanding as at February 27, 2010	557,329	$2,207,609	1,459	$(94,463)

On November 4, 2009, the Company's Board of Directors authorized a Common Share Repurchase Program for the repurchase and cancellation, through the facilities of the NASDAQ Stock Market, common shares having an aggregate purchase price of up to $1.2 billion, or approximately 21 million common shares based on trading prices at the time of the authorization. This represents approximately 3.6% of the outstanding common shares of the Company at the time of the authorization. All common shares repurchased by the Company pursuant to the Common Share Repurchase Program have been cancelled. The Common Share Repurchase Program will remain in place for up to 12 months from November 4, 2009 or until the purchases are completed or the program is terminated by the Company.

(b) Stock-based compensation

Stock Option Plan

The Company recorded a charge to income and a credit to paid-in-capital of $37.0 million in fiscal 2010 (fiscal 2009 — $38.1 million; fiscal 2008 — $33.7 million) in relation to stock-based compensation expense.

The Company has not paid a dividend in the previous twelve fiscal years and has no current expectation of paying cash dividends on its common shares.

Restricted Share Unit Plan

During fiscal 2010, the trustee purchased 1,458,950 common shares for total consideration of approximately $94.5 million

$US in thousands, except share and per share data, and where otherwise indicated

to comply with its obligations to deliver shares upon vesting. These purchased shares are classified as treasury stock for accounting purposes and included in the shareholders' equity section of the Company's consolidated balance sheet. The Company recorded compensation expense with respect to RSUs of $21.0 million in the year ended February 27, 2010 (February 28, 2009 — $196; March 1, 2008 — $33).

Deferred Share Unit Plan

The Company issued 14,593 DSUs in the year ended February 27, 2010. There are 34,801 DSUs outstanding as at February 27, 2010 (February 28, 2009 — 20,208). The Company had a liability of $2.5 million in relation to the DSU plan as at February 27, 2010 (February 28, 2009 — $834).

12.   COMMITMENTS AND CONTINGENCIES

(a) Credit Facility

The Company has $150.0 million in unsecured demand credit facilities (the "Facilities") to support and secure operating and financing requirements. As at February 27, 2010, the Company has utilized $6.9 million of the Facilities for outstanding letters of credit, and $143.1 million of the Facilities are unused.

(b) Lease commitments

The Company is committed to future minimum annual lease payments under operating leases as follows:

For the years ending	Real Estate	Equipment and other	Total
2011	$ 35,088	$1,917	$ 37,005
2012	30,611	1,202	31,813
2013	27,841	163	28,004
2014	26,178	—	26,178
2015	21,755	—	21,755
Thereafter	63,631	—	63,631
	$205,104	$3,282	$208,386

For the year ended February 27, 2010, the Company incurred rental expense of $39.6 million (February 28, 2009 — $22.7 million; March 1, 2008 — $15.5 million).

(c) Litigation

The Company is involved in litigation in the normal course of its business, both as a defendant and as a plaintiff. The Company may be subject to claims (including claims related to patent infringement, purported class actions and derivative actions) either directly or through indemnities against these claims that it provides to certain of it partners.

13.   PRODUCT WARRANTY

The Company estimates its warranty costs at the time of revenue recognition based on historical warranty claims experience and records the expense in cost of sales. The warranty accrual balance is reviewed quarterly to establish that it materially reflects the remaining obligation based on the anticipated future expenditures over the balance of the obligation period. Adjustments are made when the actual warranty claim experience differs from estimates. The change in the Company's warranty expense and actual warranty experience from March 3, 2007 to February 27, 2010 as well as the accrued warranty obligations as at February 27, 2010 are set forth in the following table:

Accrued warranty obligations as at March 3, 2007	$ 36,669
Actual warranty experience during fiscal 2008	(68,166)
Fiscal 2008 warranty provision	116,045
Accrued warranty obligations as at March 1, 2008	84,548
Actual warranty experience during fiscal 2009	(146,434)
Fiscal 2009 warranty provision	258,757
Adjustments for changes in estimate	(12,536)
Accrued warranty obligations as at February 28, 2009	184,335
Actual warranty experience during fiscal 2010	(416,393)
Fiscal 2010 warranty provision	462,834
Adjustments for changes in estimate	21,541
Accrued warranty obligations as at February 27, 2010	$ 252,317

$US in thousands, except share and per share data, and where otherwise indicated

14. EARNINGS PER SHARE
The following table sets forth the computation of basic and diluted earnings per share:

For the year ended	February 27, 2010	February 28, 2009	March 1, 2008
Net income for basic and diluted earnings per share available to common shareholders	$2,457,144	$1,892,616	$1,293,867
Weighted-average number of shares outstanding (000's) — basic	564,492	565,059	559,778
Effect of dilutive securities (000's) — stock-based compensation	5,267	9,097	13,052
Weighted-average number of shares and assumed conversions (000's) — diluted	569,759	574,156	572,830
Earnings per share — reported			
Basic	$ 4.35	$ 3.35	$ 2.31
Diluted	$ 4.31	$ 3.30	$ 2.26

15. COMPREHENSIVE INCOME (LOSS)
The components of comprehensive income (loss) are shown in the following table:

For the year ended	February 27, 2010	February 28, 2009	March 1, 2008
Net income	$2,457,144	$1,892,616	$1,293,867
Net change in unrealized gains (losses) on available-for-sale investments	6,803	(7,161)	13,467
Net change in fair value of derivatives designated as cash flow hedges during the year, net of income taxes of $13,190 (February 28, 2009 - tax recovery of $8,641; March 1, 2008 - income taxes of $19,238)	28,324	(6,168)	37,564
Amounts reclassified to earnings during the year, net of income tax recovery of $6,079 (February 28, 2009 - income taxes of $4,644; March 1, 2008 - income taxes of $5,142)	15,508	(16,497)	(9,232)
Comprehensive income	$2,507,779	$1,862,790	$1,335,666

The components of accumulated other comprehensive income (loss) are as follows:

	February 27, 2010	February 28, 2009	March 1, 2008
Accumulated net unrealized gains (losses) on available- for-sale investments	$ 6,715	$ (88)	$ 7,073
Accumulated net unrealized gains on derivative instruments designated as cash flow hedges	44,377	545	23,210
Total accumulated other comprehensive income	$51,092	$457	$30,283

16. SUPPLEMENTAL INFORMATION
(a) Cash flows resulting from net changes in working capital items are as follows:

For the year ended	February 27, 2010	February 28, 2009	March 1, 2008
Accounts receivable	$(480,610)	$(936,514)	$(602,055)
Other receivables	(44,719)	(83,039)	(34,515)
Inventories	60,789	(286,133)	(140,360)
Other current assets	(52,737)	(50,280)	(26,161)
Accounts payable	167,281	177,263	140,806
Accrued liabilities	442,065	506,859	383,020
Income taxes payable	(266,517)	(113,868)	401,270
Deferred revenue	13,739	16,598	8,789
	$(160,709)	$(769,114)	$ 130,794

(b) Certain statement of cash flow information related to interest and income taxes paid is summarized as follows:

For the year ended	February 27, 2010	February 28, 2009	March 1, 2008
Interest paid during the year	$ —	$ 502	$ 518
Income taxes paid during the year	$1,081,720	$946,237	$216,095

RESEARCH IN MOTION

RESEARCH IN MOTION

$US in thousands, except share and per share data, and where otherwise indicated

(c) The following items are included in the accrued liabilities balance:

	February 27, 2010	February 28, 2009
Marketing costs	$ 91,554	$ 91,160
Vendor inventory liabilities	125,761	18,000
Warranty	252,316	184,335
Royalties	383,939	279,476
Rebates	146,304	134,788
Other	638,386	530,843
	$1,638,260	$1,238,602

Other accrued liabilities as noted in the above chart, include, among other things, salaries, payroll withholding taxes and incentive accruals, none of which are greater than 5% of the current liability balance.

(d) Additional information

Advertising expense, which includes media, agency and promotional expenses totalling $790.8 million (February 28, 2009 — $718.9 million; March 1, 2008 — $336.0 million) is included in selling, marketing and administration expense.

Selling, marketing and administration expense for the fiscal year includes $58.4 million with respect to foreign exchange losses (February 28, 2009 – loss of $6.1 million; March 1, 2008 – loss of $5.3 million). For the year ended February 27, 2010, the Company recorded a $54.3 million charge primarily relating to the reversal of foreign exchange gains previously recorded in fiscal 2009 on the revaluation of Canadian dollar denominated tax liability balances.

17. DERIVATIVE FINANCIAL INSTRUMENTS

The Company uses derivative instruments to manage exposures to foreign exchange risk resulting from transactions in currencies other than its functional currency, the U.S. dollar. The Company's risk management objective in holding derivative instruments is to reduce the volatility of current and future income as a result of changes in foreign currency. To limit its exposure to adverse movements in foreign currency exchange rates, the Company enters into foreign currency forward and option contracts.

18. SEGMENT DISCLOSURES

The Company is organized and managed as a single reportable business segment. The Company's operations are substantially all related to the research, design, manufacture and sales of wireless communications products, services and software. Selected financial information is as follows:

Revenue, classified by major geographic segments in which our customers are located, was as follows:

For the year ended	February 27, 2010	February 28, 2009	March 1, 2008
Revenue			
Canada	$ 843,762	$ 887,005	$ 438,302
United States	8,619,762	6,967,598	3,528,858
United Kingdom	1,447,417	711,536	461,592
Other	4,042,283	2,499,047	1,580,643
	$14,953,224	$11,065,186	$6,009,395

	February 27, 2010	February 28, 2009
Total assets		
Canada	$ 4,502,522	$3,218,640
United States	4,059,174	2,646,783
United Kingdom	1,195,534	1,931,387
Other	447,179	304,562
	$10,204,409	$8,101,372

Apple Financial Report

APPLE

APPLE INC.
CONSOLIDATED BALANCE SHEETS
(in millions, except share amounts)

	September 26, 2009	September 27, 2008
ASSETS		
Current assets		
Cash and cash equivalents	$ 5,263	$11,875
Short-term marketable securities	18,201	10,236
Accounts receivable, less allowances of $52 and $47, respectively	3,361	2,422
Inventories	455	509
Deferred tax assets	1,135	1,044
Other current assets	3,140	3,920
Total current assets	31,555	30,006
Long-term marketable securities	10,528	2,379
Property, plant and equipment, net	2,954	2,455
Goodwill	206	207
Acquired intangible assets, net	247	285
Other assets	2,011	839
Total assets	$47,501	$36,171
LIABILITIES AND SHAREHOLDERS' EQUITY		
Current liabilities		
Accounts payable	$ 5,601	$ 5,520
Accrued expenses	3,852	4,224
Deferred revenue	2,053	1,617
Total current liabilities	11,506	11,361
Deferred revenue – non-current	853	768
Other non-current liabilities	3,502	1,745
Total liabilities	15,861	13,874
Shareholders' equity		
Common stock, no par value; 1,800,000,000 shares authorized; 899,805,500 and 888,325,973 shares issued and outstanding, respectively	8,210	7,177
Retained earnings	23,353	15,129
Accumulated other comprehensive income/(loss)	77	(9)
Total shareholders' equity	31,640	22,297
Total liabilities and shareholders' equity	$47,501	$36,171

APPLE INC.
CONSOLIDATED STATEMENTS OF OPERATIONS
(in millions, except share amounts which are reflected in thousands and per share amounts)

For fiscal year ended	September 26, 2009	September 27, 2008	September 29, 2007
Net sales	$ 42,905	$ 37,491	$ 24,578
Cost of sales	25,683	24,294	16,426
Gross margin	17,222	13,197	8,152
Operating expenses			
Research and development	1,333	1,109	782
Selling, general and administrative	4,149	3,761	2,963
Total operating expenses	5,482	4,870	3,745
Operating income	11,740	8,327	4,407
Other income and expense	326	620	599
Income before provision for income taxes	12,066	8,947	5,006
Provision for income taxes	3,831	2,828	1,511
Net income	$ 8,235	$ 6,119	$ 3,495
Earnings per common share:			
Basic	$ 9.22	$ 6.94	$ 4.04
Diluted	$ 9.08	$ 6.78	$ 3.93
Shares used in computing earnings per share:			
Basic	893,016	881,592	864,595
Diluted	907,005	902,139	889,292

APPLE

APPLE

APPLE INC.
CONSOLIDATED STATEMENTS OF SHAREHOLDERS' EQUITY
(in millions, except share amounts which are reflected in thousands)

	Common Stock		Retained Earnings	Accumulated Other Comprehensive Income	Total Share-holders' Equity
	Shares	Amount			
Balances as of September 30, 2006	855,263	$ 4,355	$ 5,607	$ 22	$ 9,984
Components of comprehensive income:					
Net income	—	—	3,495	—	3,495
Change in foreign currency translation	—	—	—	51	51
Change in unrealized loss on available-for-sale securities, net of tax	—	—	—	(7)	(7)
Change in unrealized gain on derivative instruments, net of tax	—	—	—	(3)	(3)
Total comprehensive income					3,536
Stock-based compensation	—	251	—	—	251
Common stock issued under stock plans, net of shares withheld for employee taxes	17,066	364	(2)	—	362
Tax benefit from employee stock plan awards	—	398	—	—	398
Balances as of September 29, 2007	872,329	5,368	9,100	63	14,531
Cumulative effect of change in accounting principle	—	45	11	—	56
Components of comprehensive income:					
Net income	—	—	6,119		6,119
Change in foreign currency translation	—	—	—	(28)	(28)
Change in unrealized loss on available-for-sale securities, net of tax	—	—	—	(63)	(63)
Change in unrealized gain on derivative instruments, net of tax	—	—	—	19	19
Total comprehensive income					6,047
Stock-based compensation	—	513	—	—	513
Common stock issued under stock plans, net of shares withheld for employee taxes	15,888	460	(101)	—	359
Issuance of common stock in connection with an asset acquisition	109	21	—	—	21
Tax benefit from employee stock plan awards	—	770	—	—	770
Balances as of September 27, 2008	888,326	7,177	15,129	(9)	22,297
Components of comprehensive income:					
Net income	—	—	8,235	—	8,235
Change in foreign currency translation	—	—	—	(14)	(14)
Change in unrealized loss on available-for-sale securities, net of tax	—	—	—	118	118
Change in unrealized gain on derivative instruments, net of tax	—	—	—	(18)	(18)
Total comprehensive income					8,321
Stock-based compensation	—	707	—	—	707
Common stock issued under stock plans, net of shares withheld for employee taxes	11,480	404	(11)	—	393
Tax benefit from employee stock plan awards, including transfer pricing adjustments	—	(78)	—	—	(78)
Balances as of September 26, 2009	899,806	$ 8,210	$23,353	$ 77	$31,640

APPLE INC.
CONSOLIDATED STATEMENTS OF CASH FLOWS
(in millions)

For fiscal year ended	September 26, 2009	September 27, 2008	September 29, 2007
Cash and cash equivalents, beginning of the year	$ 11,875	$ 9,352	$ 6,392
Operating Activities			
Net income	8,235	6,119	3,495
Adjustments to reconcile net income to cash generated by operating activities			
Depreciation, amortization and accretion	734	496	327
Stock-based compensation expense	710	516	242
Deferred income tax expense	1,040	398	73
Loss on disposition of property, plant and equipment	26	22	12
Changes in operating assets and liabilities			
Accounts receivable, net	(939)	(785)	(385)
Inventories	54	(163)	(76)
Other current assets	749	(274)	(1,279)
Other assets	(902)	289	285
Accounts payable	92	596	1,494
Deferred revenue	521	718	566
Other liabilities	(161)	1,664	716
Cash generated by operating activities	10,159	9,596	5,470
Investing Activities			
Purchases of marketable securities	(46,724)	(22,965)	(11,719)
Proceeds from maturities of marketable securities	19,790	11,804	6,483
Proceeds from sales of marketable securities	10,888	4,439	2,941
Purchases of other long-term investments	(101)	(38)	(17)
Payments made in connection with business acquisitions, net of cash acquired	—	(220)	—
Payment for acquisition of property, plant and equipment	(1,144)	(1,091)	(735)
Payment for acquisition of intangible assets	(69)	(108)	(251)
Other	(74)	(10)	49
Cash used in investing activities	(17,434)	(8,189)	(3,249)
Financing Activities			
Proceeds from issuance of common stock	475	483	365
Excess tax benefits from stock-based compensation	270	757	377
Cash used to net share settle equity awards	(82)	(124)	(3)
Cash generated by financing activities	663	1,116	739
(Decrease)/increase in cash and cash equivalents	(6,612)	2,523	2,960
Cash and cash equivalents, end of the year	$ 5,263	$11,875	$ 9,352
Supplemental cash flow disclosures:			
Cash paid for income taxes, net	$ 2,997	$ 1,267	$ 863

APPLE

Palm Financial Report

Palm, Inc.

Consolidated Balance Sheets

(In thousands, except par value amounts)

	May 31, 2009	May 31, 2008
ASSETS		
Current assets		
Cash and cash equivalents	$ 152,400	$ 176,918
Short-term investments	102,733	81,830
Accounts receivable, net of allowance for doubtful accounts of $350 and $1,169, respectively	66,452	116,430
Inventories	19,716	67,461
Deferred income taxes	174	82,011
Prepaids and other	12,104	15,436
Total current assets	353,579	540,086
Restricted investments	9,496	8,620
Non-current auction rate securities	6,105	29,944
Deferred costs	14,896	—
Property and equipment, net	31,167	39,636
Goodwill	166,320	166,332
Intangible assets, net	48,914	61,048
Deferred income taxes	331	318,850
Other assets	12,428	15,746
Total assets	$ 643,236	$1,180,262
LIABILITIES AND STOCKHOLDERS' EQUITY (DEFICIT)		
Current liabilities		
Accounts payable	$ 105,628	$ 161,642
Income taxes payable	475	1,088
Deferred revenues	18,429	4,080
Accrued restructuring	6,090	8,058
Current portion of long-term debt	4,000	4,000
Other accrued liabilities	207,820	232,478
Total current liabilities	342,442	411,346
Non-current liabilities		
Long-term debt	390,000	394,000
Non-current deferred revenues	13,077	—
Non-current tax liabilities	5,783	6,127
Other non-current liabilities	—	2,098
Series B redeemable convertible preferred stock, $0.001 par value, 325 shares authorized and outstanding; aggregate liquidation value: $325,000	265,412	255,671
Series C redeemable convertible preferred stock, $0.001 par value, 100 shares authorized; outstanding: 51 shares and 0 shares, respectively; aggregate liquidation value: $51,000 and $0, respectively	40,387	—
Stockholders' equity (deficit)		
Preferred stock, $0.001 par value, 125,000 shares authorized:		
Series A: 2,000 shares authorized, none outstanding	—	—
Common stock, $0.001 par value, 2,000,000 shares authorized; outstanding: 139,687 shares and 108,369 shares, respectively	140	108
Additional paid-in capital	854,649	659,141
Accumulated deficit	(1,269,672)	(537,484)
Accumulated other comprehensive income (loss)	1,018	(10,745)
Total stockholders' equity (deficit)	(413,865)	111,020
Total liabilities and stockholders' equity (deficit)	$ 643,236	$1,180,262

PALM

Palm, Inc.

Consolidated Statements of Operations

(In thousands, except per share amounts)

Years Ended May 31	2009	2008	2007
Revenues	$ 735,872	$1,318,691	$1,560,507
Cost of revenues	576,113	916,810	985,369
Gross profit	159,759	401,881	575,138
Operating expenses			
Sales and marketing	174,052	229,702	248,685
Research and development	177,210	202,764	190,952
General and administrative	55,923	60,778	59,762
Amortization of intangible assets	3,054	3,775	1,981
Restructuring charges	16,134	30,353	—
Casualty recovery	(268)	—	—
Patent acquisition cost (refund)	(1,537)	5,000	—
Gain on sale of land	—	(4,446)	—
In-process research and development	—	—	3,700
Total operating expenses	424,568	527,926	505,080
Operating income (loss)	(264,809)	(126,045)	70,058
Impairment of non-current auction rate securities	(35,885)	(32,175)	—
Interest (expense)	(25,299)	(20,397)	(1,970)
Interest income	5,840	21,860	25,958
Loss on series C derivative	(2,515)	—	—
Other income (expense), net	(5,255)	(1,471)	(1,619)
Income (loss) before income taxes	(327,923)	(158,228)	92,427
Income tax provision (benefit)	404,265	(52,809)	36,044
Net income (loss)	(732,188)	(105,419)	56,383
Accretion of series B and series C redeemable convertible preferred stock	21,285	5,516	—
Net income (loss) applicable to common shareholders	$(753,473)	$ (110,935)	$ 56,383
Net income (loss) per common share:			
Basic	$ (6.51)	$ (1.05)	$ 0.55
Diluted	$ (6.51)	$ (1.05)	$ 0.54
Shares used to compute net income (loss) per common share:			
Basic	115,725	105,891	102,757
Diluted	115,725	105,891	104,442

PALM

Palm, Inc.
Consolidated Statements of Stockholders' Equity (Deficit) and Comprehensive Income (Loss)
(In thousands)

	Common Stock	Additional Paid-In Capital	Unamortized Deferred Stock-Based Compensation	Accumulated Deficit	Accumulated Other Comprehensive Income (Loss)	Total
Balances, May 31, 2006	$ 103	$1,475,319	$ (2,752)	$ (488,081)	$ (684)	$ 983,905
Components of comprehensive income:						
Net income	—	—	—	56,383	—	56,383
Net unrealized gains on available-for-sale investments	—	—	—	—	1,522	1,522
Recognized gains included in results of operations	—	—	—	—	(110)	(110)
Accumulated translation adjustments	—	—	—	—	915	915
Total comprehensive income	—	—	—	—	—	58,710
Common stock issued under stock plans, net	3	21,923	—	—	—	21,926
Stock-based compensation expense	—	21,503	2,752	—	—	24,255
Tax benefit from employee stock options	—	4,578	—	—	—	4,578
Shares repurchased and retired	(2)	(30,961)				(30,963)
Balances, May 31, 2007	104	1,492,362	—	(431,698)	1,643	1,062,411
Components of comprehensive loss:						
Net loss	—	—	—	(105,419)	—	(105,419)
Net unrealized losses on available-for-sale investments	—	—	—	—	(1,261)	(1,261)
Net unrealized losses in value of non-current auction rate securities	—	—	—	—	(44,706)	(44,706)
Net recognized losses on non-current auction rate securities included in results of operations	—	—	—	—	32,175	32,175
Net recognized gains on available-for-sale investments included in results of operations	—	—	—	—	(68)	(68)
Accumulated translation adjustments	—	—	—	—	1,472	1,472
Total comprehensive loss	—	—	—	—	—	(117,807)
Common stock issued under stock plans, net	4	28,433	—	—	—	28,437
Stock-based compensation expense	—	32,181	—	—	—	32,181
Tax deficiency from employee stock options	—	(3,663)	—	—	—	(3,663)
Cash distribution to stockholders	—	(949,691)	—	—	—	(949,691)
Discount recognized on issuance of series B redeemable convertible preferred stock	—	65,035	—	—	—	65,035
Accretion of series B redeemable convertible preferred stock	—	(5,516)	—	—	—	(5,516)
Adjustment to accumulated deficit due to adoption of FIN No. 48 (see Note 16)	—	—	—	(367)	—	(367)
Balances, May 31, 2008	108	659,141	—	(537,484)	(10,745)	111,020
Components of comprehensive loss:						
Net loss	—	—	—	(732,188)	—	(732,188)
Net unrealized losses on available-for-sale investments	—	—	—	—	(1,649)	(1,649)
Net unrealized losses in value of non-current auction rate securities	—	—	—	—	(23,354)	(23,354)
Net recognized losses on non-current auction rate securities included in results of operations	—	—	—	—	35,885	35,885
Net recognized losses on available-for-sale investments included in results of operations	—	—	—	—	3,594	3,594
Accumulated translation adjustments	—	—	—	—	(2,713)	(2,713)
Total comprehensive loss	—	—	—	—	—	(720,425)
Common stock issued under stock plans, net	5	15,531	—	—	—	15,536
Stock-based compensation expense	—	23,853	—	—	—	23,853
Tax benefit from employee stock options	—	1,924	—	—	—	1,924
Distribution liability related to canceled shares of restricted stock	—	34	—	—	—	34
Accretion of series B and series C redeemable convertible preferred stock	—	(21,285)	—	—	—	(21,285)
Warrants recorded in connection with issuance of series C units	—	21,966	—	—	—	21,966
Conversion of series C units and issuance of additional common stock, net	27	101,544	—	—	—	101,571
Discount recognized on issuance of series C redeemable convertible preferred stock	—	51,941	—	—	—	51,941
Balances, May 31, 2009	$ 140	$ 854,649	$ —	$ (1,269,672)	$ 1,018	$ (413,865)

PALM

Palm, Inc.

Consolidated Statements of Cash Flows

(In thousands)

Years Ended May 31	2009	2008	2007
Cash flows from operating activities			
Net income (loss)	$(732,188)	$(105,419)	$ 56,383
Adjustments to reconcile net income (loss) to net cash flows from operating activities			
Depreciation	19,677	19,699	13,316
Stock-based compensation	23,853	32,181	24,255
Amortization of intangible assets	12,134	16,510	8,315
Amortization of debt issuance costs	3,139	1,834	—
In-process research and development	—	—	3,700
Deferred income taxes	401,670	(58,227)	11,313
Realized (gain) loss on short-term investments	3,594	(68)	(110)
Excess tax benefit related to stock-based compensation	(142)	(40)	(5,241)
Realized loss (gain) on disposition of property and equipment and sale of land	619	(4,446)	—
Impairment of non-current auction rate securities	35,885	32,175	—
Loss on series C derivative	2,515	—	—
Changes in assets and liabilities			
Accounts receivable	48,425	89,312	2
Inventories	47,571	(28,147)	18,842
Prepaids and other	4,542	736	1,790
Accounts payable	(54,883)	(35,840)	11,654
Income taxes payable	(346)	3,033	16,421
Accrued restructuring	(361)	6,303	(1,803)
Deferred revenues/costs, net	12,530	—	—
Other accrued liabilities	(16,746)	12,866	9,354
Net cash provided by (used in) operating activities	(188,512)	(17,538)	168,191
Cash flows from investing activities			
Purchase of brand name intangible asset	—	(1,500)	(44,000)
Purchase of property and equipment	(13,452)	(22,999)	(24,651)
Proceeds from sale of land	—	64,446	—
Cash paid for business acquisitions	—	(495)	(19,000)
Purchase of short-term investments	(112,385)	(517,104)	(682,882)
Sales/maturities of short-term investments	88,109	777,917	671,623
Purchase of restricted investments	(2,000)	(8,951)	—
Sale of restricted investments	1,124	331	—
Proceeds related to investments in non-current auction rate securities	485	250	—
Net cash provided by (used in) investing activities	(38,119)	291,895	(98,910)
Cash flows from financing activities			
Proceeds from issuance of common stock, net	104,049	—	—
Proceeds from issuance of common stock, employee stock plans	15,536	28,437	21,926
Purchase and subsequent retirement of common stock	—	—	(30,963)
Excess tax benefit related to stock-based compensation	142	40	5,241
Proceeds from issuance of redeemable convertible preferred stock and series C units, net	99,173	315,190	—
Proceeds from issuance of debt, net	—	381,107	—
Repayment of debt	(14,446)	(3,089)	(50,816)
Cash distribution to stockholders	(439)	(948,949)	—
Net cash provided by (used in) financing activities	204,015	(227,264)	(54,612)
Effects of exchange rate changes on cash and cash equivalents	(1,902)	1,695	—
Change in cash and cash equivalents	(24,518)	48,788	14,669
Cash and cash equivalents, beginning of period	176,918	128,130	113,461
Cash and cash equivalents, end of period	$ 152,400	$ 176,918	$ 128,130
Supplemental cash flow information:			
Cash paid for income taxes	$ 3,402	$ 3,391	$ 8,900
Cash paid for interest	$ 21,828	$ 18,042	$ 1,741
Non-cash investing and financing activities:			
Liability for property and equipment acquired	$ —	$ 3,334	$ 2,309

PALM

Nokia Financial Report

Nokia Corporation and Subsidiaries
Consolidated Statements of Financial Position

December 31	2009 EURm	2008 EURm
ASSETS		
Non-current assets		
Capitalized development costs	143	244
Goodwill	5 171	6 257
Other intangible assets	2 762	3 913
Property, plant and equipment	1 867	2 090
Investments in associated companies	69	96
Available-for-sale investments	554	512
Deferred tax assets	1 507	1 963
Long-term loans receivable	46	27
Other non-current assets	6	10
	12 125	15 112
Current assets		
Inventories	1 865	2 533
Accounts receivable, net of allowances for doubtful accounts (2009: EUR 391 million, 2008: EUR 415 million)	7 981	9 444
Prepaid expenses and accrued income	4 551	4 538
Current portion of long-term loans receivable	14	101
Other financial assets	329	1 034
Investments at fair value through profit and loss, liquid assets	580	—
Available-for-sale investments, liquid assets	2 367	1 272
Available-for-sale investments, cash equivalents	4 784	3 842
Bank and cash	1 142	1 706
	23 613	24 470
Total assets	35 738	39 582
SHAREHOLDERS' EQUITY AND LIABILITIES		
Capital and reserves attributable to equity holders of the parent		
Share capital	246	246
Share issue premium	279	442
Treasury shares, at cost	(681)	(1 881)
Translation differences	(127)	341
Fair value and other reserves	69	62
Reserve for invested non-restricted equity	3 170	3 306
Retained earnings	10 132	11 692
	13 088	14 208
Minority interests	1 661	2 302
Total equity	14 749	16 510
Non-current liabilities		
Long-term interest-bearing liabilities	4 432	861
Deferred tax liabilities	1 303	1 787
Other long-term liabilities	66	69
	5 801	2 717
Current liabilities		
Current portion of long-term loans	44	13
Short-term borrowings	727	3 578
Other financial liabilities	245	924
Accounts payable	4 950	5 225
Accrued expenses	6 504	7 023
Provisions	2 718	3 592
	15 188	20 355
Total shareholders' equity and liabilities	35 738	39 582

Nokia Corporation and Subsidiaries
Consolidated Income Statements

Financial Year Ended December 31	2009 EURm	2008 EURm	2007 EURm
Net sales	**40 984**	50 710	51 058
Cost of sales	**(27 720)**	(33 337)	(33 781)
Gross profit	**13 264**	17 373	17 277
Research and development expenses	**(5 909)**	(5 968)	(5 636)
Selling and marketing expenses	**(3 933)**	(4 380)	(4 379)
Administrative and general expenses	**(1 145)**	(1 284)	(1 165)
Impairment of goodwill	**(908)**	—	—
Other income	**338**	420	2 312
Other expenses	**(510)**	(1 195)	(424)
Operating profit	**1 197**	4 966	7 985
Share of results of associated companies	**30**	6	44
Financial income and expenses	**(265)**	(2)	239
Profit before tax	**962**	4 970	8 268
Tax	**(702)**	(1 081)	(1 522)
Profit	**260**	3 889	6 746
Profit attributable to equity holders of the parent	**891**	3 988	7 205
Loss attributable to minority interests	**(631)**	(99)	(459)
	260	3 889	6 746

	2009 EUR	2008 EUR	2007 EUR
Earnings per share			
(for profit attributable to the equity holders of the parent)			
Basic	**0.24**	1.07	1.85
Diluted	**0.24**	1.05	1.83

	2009	2008	2007
Average number of shares (000's shares)			
Basic	**3 705 116**	3 743 622	3 885 408
Diluted	**3 721 072**	3 780 363	3 932 008

Nokia Corporation and Subsidiaries
Consolidated Statements of Comprehensive Income

Financial Year Ended December 31	2009 EURm	2008 EURm	2007 EURm
Profit	**260**	3 889	6 746
Other comprehensive income			
Translation differences	**(563)**	595	(151)
Net investment hedge gains (losses)	**114**	(123)	51
Cash flow hedges	**25**	(40)	(7)
Available-for-sale investments	**48**	(15)	49
Other increase (decrease), net	**(7)**	28	(46)
Income tax related to components of other comprehensive income	**(44)**	58	(12)
Other comprehensive income (expense), net of tax	**(427)**	503	(116)
Total comprehensive income (expense)	**(167)**	4 392	6 630
Total comprehensive income (expense) attributable to:			
Equity holders of the parent	**429**	4 577	7 073
Minority interests	**(596)**	(185)	(443)
	(167)	4 392	6 630

NOKIA

Nokia Corporation and Subsidiaries
Consolidated Statements of Changes in Shareholders' Equity

	Number of shares (000's)	Share capital	Share issue premium	Treasury shares	Translation differences	Fair value and other reserves	Reserve for invested non-restrict. equity	Retained earnings	Before minority interests	Minority interests	Total
Balance at December 31, 2007	**3 845 950**	**246**	**644**	**(3 146)**	**(163)**	**23**	**3 299**	**13 870**	**14 773**	**2 565**	**17 338**
Translation differences					595				595		595
Net investment hedge gains, net of tax					(91)				(91)		(91)
Cash flow hedges, net of tax						42			42	(67)	(25)
Available-for-sale investments, net of tax						(3)			(3)	(2)	(5)
Other increase, net								46	46	(17)	29
Profit								3 988	3 988	(99)	3 889
Total comprehensive income		**—**	**—**	**—**	**504**	**39**	**—**	**4 034**	**4 577**	**(185)**	**4 392**
Stock options exercised	3 547							51	51		51
Stock options exercised related to acquisitions			1						1		1
Share-based compensation			74						74		74
Excess tax benefit on share-based compensation			(117)						(117)	(6)	(124)
Settlement of performance and restricted shares	5 622		(179)	154			(44)		(69)		(69)
Acquisition of treasury shares	(157 390)			(3 123)					(3 123)		(3 123)
Reissuance of treasury shares	143			2					2		2
Cancellation of treasury shares			0	4 232				(4 232)	—		
Dividend								(1 992)	(1 992)	(35)	(2 027)
Acquisitions and other change in minority interests										(37)	(37)
Vested portion of share-based payment awards related to acquisitions			19						19		19
Acquisition of Symbian								12	12		12
Total of other equity movements		**—**	**(202)**	**1 265**	**—**	**—**	**7**	**(6 212)**	**(5 142)**	**(78)**	**(5 220)**
Balance at December 31, 2008	**3 697 872**	**246**	**442**	**(1 881)**	**341**	**62**	**3 306**	**11 692**	**14 208**	**2 302**	**16 510**
Translation differences					(552)				(552)	(9)	(561)
Net investment hedge gains, net of tax					84				84		84
Cash flow hedges, net of tax						(35)			(35)	49	14
Available-for-sale investments, net of tax						42			42	2	44
Other decrease, net								(1)	(1)	(7)	(8)
Profit								891	891	(631)	260
Total comprehensive income		**—**	**—**	**—**	**(468)**	**7**	**—**	**890**	**429**	**(596)**	**(167)**
Stock options exercised	7						—				
Stock options exercised related to acquisitions			(1)						(1)		(1)
Share-based compensation			16						16		16
Excess tax benefit on share-based compensation			(12)						(12)	(1)	(13)
Settlement of performance and restricted shares	10 352		(166)	230			(136)		(72)		(72)
Acquisition of treasury shares									—		
Reissuance of treasury shares	31			1					1		1
Cancellation of treasury shares				969				(969)	—		
Dividend								(1 481)	(1 481)	(44)	(1 525)
Total of other equity movements		**—**	**(163)**	**1 200**	**—**	**—**	**(136)**	**(2 450)**	**(1 549)**	**(45)**	**(1 594)**
Balance at December 31, 2009	**3 708 262**	**246**	**279**	**(681)**	**(127)**	**69**	**3 170**	**10 132**	**13 088**	**1 661**	**14 749**

Dividends declared per share were EUR 0.40 for 2009 (EUR 0.40 for 2008 and EUR 0.53 for 2007), subject to shareholders' approval.

Nokia Corporation and Subsidiaries
Consolidated Statements of Cash Flows

Financial Year Ended December 31	2009 EURm	2008 EURm	2007 EURm
Cash flow from operating activities			
Profit attributable to equity holders of the parent	**891**	3 988	7 205
Adjustments, total	**3 390**	3 024	1 159
Change in net working capital	**140**	(2 546)	605
Cash generated from operations	**4 421**	4 466	8 969
Interest received	**125**	416	362
Interest paid	**(256)**	(155)	(59)
Other financial income and expenses, net received	**(128)**	250	67
Income taxes paid, net received	**(915)**	(1 780)	(1 457)
Net cash from operating activities	**3 247**	3 197	7 882
Cash flow from investing activities			
Acquisition of Group companies, net of acquired cash	**(29)**	(5 962)	253
Purchase of current available-for-sale investments, liquid assets	**(2 800)**	(669)	(4 798)
Purchase of investments at fair value through profit and loss, liquid assets	**(695)**	—	—
Purchase of non-current available-for-sale investments	**(95)**	(121)	(126)
Purchase of shares in associated companies	**(30)**	(24)	(25)
Additions to capitalized development costs	**(27)**	(131)	(157)
Long-term loans made to customers	**—**	—	(261)
Proceeds from repayment and sale of long-term loans receivable	**—**	129	163
Proceeds from (+) / payment of (-) other long-term receivables	**2**	(1)	5
Proceeds from (+) / payment of (-) short-term loans receivable	**2**	(15)	(119)
Capital expenditures	**(531)**	(889)	(715)
Proceeds from disposal of shares in associated companies	**40**	3	6
Proceeds from disposal of businesses	**61**	41	—
Proceeds from maturities and sale of current available-for-sale investments, liquid assets	**1 730**	4 664	4 930
Proceeds from maturities and sale of investments at fair value through profit and loss, liquid assets	**108**	—	—
Proceeds from sale of non-current available-for-sale investments	**14**	10	50
Proceeds from sale of fixed assets	**100**	54	72
Dividends received	**2**	6	12
Net cash used in investing activities	**(2 148)**	(2 905)	(710)
Cash flow from financing activities			
Proceeds from stock option exercises	**—**	53	987
Purchase of treasury shares	**—**	(3 121)	(3 819)
Proceeds from long-term borrowings	**3 901**	714	115
Repayment of long-term borrowings	**(209)**	(34)	(16)
Proceeds from (+) / repayment of (-) short-term borrowings	**(2 842)**	2 891	661
Dividends paid	**(1 546)**	(2 048)	(1 760)
Net cash used in financing activities	**(696)**	(1 545)	(3 832)
Foreign exchange adjustment	**(25)**	(49)	(15)
Net increase (+) / decrease (-) in cash and cash equivalents	**378**	(1 302)	3 325
Cash and cash equivalents at beginning of period	**5 548**	6 850	3 525
Cash and cash equivalents at end of period	**5 926**	5 548	6 850
Cash and cash equivalents comprise of:			
Bank and cash	**1 142**	1 706	2 125
Current available-for-sale investments, cash equivalents	**4 784**	3 842	4 725
	5 926	5 548	6 850

NOKIA

B

Time Value of Money

Learning Objectives

CAP

CONCEPTUAL

C1 Describe the earning of interest and the concepts of present and future values. (p. B-1)

PROCEDURAL

P1 Apply present value concepts to a single amount by using interest tables. (p. B-3)

P2 Apply future value concepts to a single amount by using interest tables. (p. B-4)

P3 Apply present value concepts to an annuity by using interest tables. (p. B-5)

P4 Apply future value concepts to an annuity by using interest tables. (p. B-6)

The concepts of present and future values are important to modern business, including the preparation and analysis of financial statements. The purpose of this appendix is to explain, illustrate, and compute present and future values. This appendix applies these concepts with reference to both business and everyday activities.

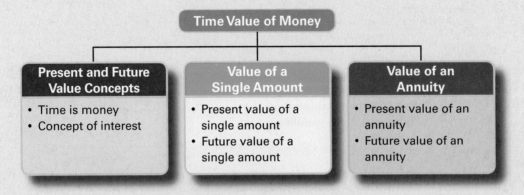

Time Value of Money

Present and Future Value Concepts	**Value of a Single Amount**	**Value of an Annuity**
• Time is money • Concept of interest	• Present value of a single amount • Future value of a single amount	• Present value of an annuity • Future value of an annuity

PRESENT AND FUTURE VALUE CONCEPTS

The old saying "Time is money" reflects the notion that as time passes, the values of our assets and liabilities change. This change is due to *interest*, which is a borrower's payment to the owner of an asset for its use. The most common example of interest is a savings account asset. As we keep a balance of cash in the account, it earns interest that the financial institution pays us. An example of a liability is a car loan. As we carry the balance of the loan, we accumulate interest costs on it. We must ultimately repay this loan with interest.

Present and future value computations enable us to measure or estimate the interest component of holding assets or liabilities over time. The present value computation is important when we want to know the value of future-day assets *today*. The future value computation is important when we want to know the value of present-day assets *at a future date*. The first section focuses on the present value of a single amount. The second section focuses on the future value of a single amount. Then both the present and future values of a series of amounts (called an *annuity*) are defined and explained.

C1 Describe the earning of interest and the concepts of present and future values.

Decision Insight

Keep That Job Lottery winners often never work again. Kenny Dukes, a recent Georgia lottery winner, doesn't have that option. He is serving parole for burglary charges, and Georgia requires its parolees to be employed (or in school). For his lottery winnings, Dukes had to choose between $31 million in 30 annual payments or $16 million in one lump sum ($10.6 million after-tax); he chose the latter. ■

PRESENT VALUE OF A SINGLE AMOUNT

We graphically express the present value, called *p*, of a single future amount, called *f*, that is received or paid at a future date in Exhibit B.1.

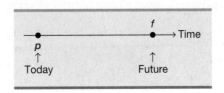

EXHIBIT B.1

Present Value of a Single Amount Diagram

The formula to compute the present value of a single amount is shown in Exhibit B.2, where p = present value; f = future value; i = rate of interest per period; and n = number of periods. (Interest is also called the *discount,* and an interest rate is also called the *discount rate.*)

EXHIBIT B.2

Present Value of a Single
Amount Formula

$$p = \frac{f}{(1 + i)^n}$$

To illustrate present value concepts, assume that we need $220 one period from today. We want to know how much we must invest now, for one period, at an interest rate of 10% to provide for this $220. For this illustration, the p, or present value, is the unknown amount—the specifics are shown graphically as follows:

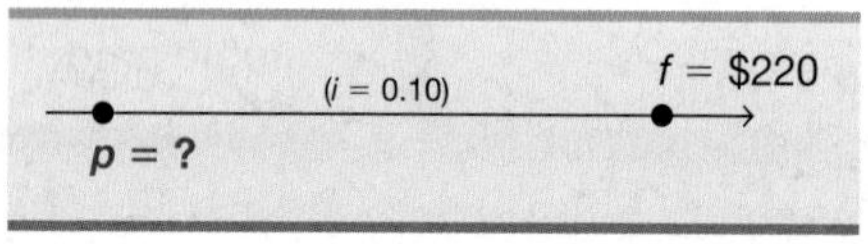

$$(i = 0.10) \qquad f = \$220$$
$$p = ?$$

Conceptually, we know p must be less than $220. This is obvious from the answer to this question: Would we rather have $220 today or $220 at some future date? If we had $220 today, we could invest it and see it grow to something more than $220 in the future. Therefore, we would prefer the $220 today. This means that if we were promised $220 in the future, we would take less than $220 today. But how much less? To answer that question, we compute an estimate of the present value of the $220 to be received one period from now using the formula in Exhibit B.2 as follows:

$$p = \frac{f}{(1 + i)^n} = \frac{\$220}{(1 + 0.10)^1} = \$200$$

We interpret this result to say that given an interest rate of 10%, we are indifferent between $200 today or $220 at the end of one period.

We can also use this formula to compute the present value for *any number of periods.* To illustrate, consider a payment of $242 at the end of two periods at 10% interest. The present value of this $242 to be received two periods from now is computed as follows:

$$p = \frac{f}{(1 + i)^n} = \frac{\$242}{(1 + 0.10)^2} = \$200$$

I will pay your allowance at the end of the month. Do you want to wait or receive its present value today?

Together, these results tell us we are indifferent between $200 today, or $220 one period from today, or $242 two periods from today given a 10% interest rate per period.

The number of periods (n) in the present value formula does not have to be expressed in years. Any period of time such as a day, a month, a quarter, or a year can be used. Whatever period is used, the interest rate (i) must be compounded for the same period. This means that if a situation expresses n in months and i equals 12% per year, then i is transformed into interest earned per month (or 1%). In this case, interest is said to be *compounded monthly.*

A present value table helps us with present value computations. It gives us present values (factors) for a variety of both interest rates (i) and periods (n). Each present value in a present value table assumes that the future value (f) equals 1. When the future value (f) is different from 1, we simply multiply the present value (p) from the table by that future value to give us the estimate. The formula used to construct a table of present values for a single future amount of 1 is shown in Exhibit B.3.

EXHIBIT B.3

Present Value of 1 Formula

$$p = \frac{1}{(1 + i)^n}$$

This formula is identical to that in Exhibit B.2 except that *f* equals 1. Table B.1 at the end of this appendix is such a present value table. It is often called a **present value of 1 table**. A present value table involves three factors: *p*, *i*, and *n*. Knowing two of these three factors allows us to compute the third. (A fourth is *f*, but as already explained, we need only multiply the 1 used in the formula by *f*.) To illustrate the use of a present value table, consider three cases.

Case 1   (solve for *p* when knowing *i* and *n*). To show how we use a present value table, let's look again at how we estimate the present value of $220 (the *f* value) at the end of one period (*n* = 1) where the interest rate (*i*) is 10%. To solve this case, we go to the present value table (Table B.1) and look in the row for 1 period and in the column for 10% interest. Here we find a present value (*p*) of 0.9091 based on a future value of 1. This means, for instance, that $1 to be received one period from today at 10% interest is worth $0.9091 today. Since the future value in this case is not $1 but $220, we multiply the 0.9091 by $220 to get an answer of $200.

Case 2   (solve for *n* when knowing *p* and *i*). To illustrate, assume a $100,000 future value (*f*) that is worth $13,000 today (*p*) using an interest rate of 12% (*i*) but where *n* is unknown. In particular, we want to know how many periods (*n*) there are between the present value and the future value. To put this in context, it would fit a situation in which we want to retire with $100,000 but currently have only $13,000 that is earning a 12% return and we will be unable to save any additional money. How long will it be before we can retire? To answer this, we go to Table B.1 and look in the 12% interest column. Here we find a column of present values (*p*) based on a future value of 1. To use the present value table for this solution, we must divide $13,000 (*p*) by $100,000 (*f*), which equals 0.1300. This is necessary because *a present value table defines f equal to 1, and p as a fraction of 1*. We look for a value nearest to 0.1300 (*p*), which we find in the row for 18 periods (*n*). This means that the present value of $100,000 at the end of 18 periods at 12% interest is $13,000; alternatively stated, we must work 18 more years.

Case 3   (solve for *i* when knowing *p* and *n*). In this case, we have, say, a $120,000 future value (*f*) worth $60,000 today (*p*) when there are nine periods (*n*) between the present and future values, but the interest rate is unknown. As an example, suppose we want to retire with $120,000, but we have only $60,000 and we will be unable to save any additional money, yet we hope to retire in nine years. What interest rate must we earn to retire with $120,000 in nine years? To answer this, we go to the present value table (Table B.1) and look in the row for nine periods. To use the present value table, we must divide $60,000 (*p*) by $120,000 (*f*), which equals 0.5000. Recall that this step is necessary because a present value table defines *f* equal to 1 and *p* as a fraction of 1. We look for a value in the row for nine periods that is nearest to 0.5000 (*p*), which we find in the column for 8% interest (*i*). This means that the present value of $120,000 at the end of nine periods at 8% interest is $60,000 or, in our example, we must earn 8% annual interest to retire in nine years.

Quick Check   Answer — p. B-7

1. A company is considering an investment expected to yield $70,000 after six years. If this company demands an 8% return, how much is it willing to pay for this investment?

FUTURE VALUE OF A SINGLE AMOUNT

We must modify the formula for the present value of a single amount to obtain the formula for the future value of a single amount. In particular, we multiply both sides of the equation in Exhibit B.2 by $(1 + i)^n$ to get the result shown in Exhibit B.4.

$$f = p \times (1 + i)^n$$

EXHIBIT B.4

Future Value of a Single Amount Formula

The future value (f) is defined in terms of p, i, and n. We can use this formula to determine that $200 ($p$) invested for 1 ($n$) period at an interest rate of 10% (i) yields a future value of $220 as follows:

$$f = p \times (1 + i)^n$$
$$= \$200 \times (1 + 0.10)^1$$
$$= \$220$$

P2 Apply future value concepts to a single amount by using interest tables.

This formula can also be used to compute the future value of an amount for *any number of periods* into the future. To illustrate, assume that $200 is invested for three periods at 10%. The future value of this $200 is $266.20, computed as follows:

$$f = p \times (1 + i)^n$$
$$= \$200 \times (1 + 0.10)^3$$
$$= \$266.20$$

A future value table makes it easier for us to compute future values (f) for many different combinations of interest rates (i) and time periods (n). Each future value in a future value table assumes the present value (p) is 1. As with a present value table, if the future amount is something other than 1, we simply multiply our answer by that amount. The formula used to construct a table of future values (factors) for a single amount of 1 is in Exhibit B.5.

EXHIBIT B.5

Future Value of 1 Formula

$$f = (1 + i)^n$$

Table B.2 at the end of this appendix shows a table of future values for a current amount of 1. This type of table is called a **future value of 1 table**.

There are some important relations between Tables B.1 and B.2. In Table B.2, for the row where $n = 0$, the future value is 1 for each interest rate. This is so because no interest is earned when time does not pass. We also see that Tables B.1 and B.2 report the same information but in a different manner. In particular, one table is simply the *inverse* of the other. To illustrate this inverse relation, let's say we invest $100 for a period of five years at 12% per year. How much do we expect to have after five years? We can answer this question using Table B.2 by finding the future value (f) of 1, for five periods from now, compounded at 12%. From that table we find $f = 1.7623$. If we start with $100, the amount it accumulates to after five years is $176.23 ($100 \times 1.7623$). We can alternatively use Table B.1. Here we find that the present value (p) of 1, discounted five periods at 12%, is 0.5674. Recall the inverse relation between present value and future value. This means that $p = 1/f$ (or equivalently, $f = 1/p$). We can compute the future value of $100 invested for five periods at 12% as follows: $f = \$100 \times (1/0.5674) = \$176.24$ (which equals the $176.23 just computed, except for a 1 cent rounding difference).

A future value table involves three factors: f, i, and n. Knowing two of these three factors allows us to compute the third. To illustrate, consider these three possible cases.

Case 1 (solve for f when knowing i and n). Our preceding example fits this case. We found that $100 invested for five periods at 12% interest accumulates to $176.24.

Case 2 (solve for n when knowing f and i). In this case, we have, say, $2,000 ($p$) and we want to know how many periods (n) it will take to accumulate to $3,000 ($f$) at 7% ($i$) interest. To answer this, we go to the future value table (Table B.2) and look in the 7% interest column. Here we find a column of future values (f) based on a present value of 1. To use a future value table, we must divide $3,000 ($f$) by $2,000 ($p$), which equals 1.500. This is necessary because *a future value table defines* p *equal to 1, and* f *as a multiple of 1*. We look for a value nearest to 1.50 (f), which we find in the row for six periods (n). This means that $2,000 invested for six periods at 7% interest accumulates to $3,000.

Case 3 (solve for i when knowing f and n). In this case, we have, say, $2,001 ($p$), and in nine years ($n$) we want to have $4,000 ($f$). What rate of interest must we earn to accomplish this? To answer that, we go to Table B.2 and search in the row for nine periods. To use a future value table, we must divide $4,000 ($f$) by $2,001 ($p$), which equals 1.9990. Recall that this is necessary because a future value table defines p equal to 1 and f as a multiple of 1. We look for a value nearest to 1.9990 (f), which we find in the column for 8% interest (i). This means that $2,001 invested for nine periods at 8% interest accumulates to $4,000.

Quick Check   Answer — p. B-7

2. Assume that you win a $150,000 cash sweepstakes. You decide to deposit this cash in an account earning 8% annual interest, and you plan to quit your job when the account equals $555,000. How many years will it be before you can quit working?

PRESENT VALUE OF AN ANNUITY

An *annuity* is a series of equal payments occurring at equal intervals. One example is a series of three annual payments of $100 each. An *ordinary annuity* is defined as equal end-of-period payments at equal intervals. An ordinary annuity of $100 for three periods and its present value (p) are illustrated in Exhibit B.6.

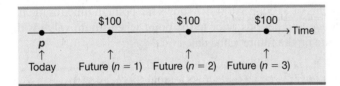

EXHIBIT B.6

Present Value of an Ordinary Annuity Diagram

One way to compute the present value of an ordinary annuity is to find the present value of each payment using our present value formula from Exhibit B.3. We then add each of the three present values. To illustrate, let's look at three $100 payments at the end of each of the next three periods with an interest rate of 15%. Our present value computations are

P3 Apply present value concepts to an annuity by using interest tables.

$$p = \frac{\$100}{(1 + 0.15)^1} + \frac{\$100}{(1 + 0.15)^2} + \frac{\$100}{(1 + 0.15)^3} = \$228.32$$

This computation is identical to computing the present value of each payment (from Table B.1) and taking their sum or, alternatively, adding the values from Table B.1 for each of the three payments and multiplying their sum by the $100 annuity payment.

A more direct way is to use a present value of annuity table. Table B.3 at the end of this appendix is one such table. This table is called a **present value of an annuity of 1 table**. If we look at Table B.3 where $n = 3$ and $i = 15\%$, we see the present value is 2.2832. This means that the present value of an annuity of 1 for three periods, with a 15% interest rate, equals 2.2832.

A present value of an annuity formula is used to construct Table B.3. It can also be constructed by adding the amounts in a present value of 1 table. To illustrate, we use Tables B.1 and B.3 to confirm this relation for the prior example:

From Table B.1		From Table B.3	
$i = 15\%, n = 1$	0.8696		
$i = 15\%, n = 2$	0.7561		
$i = 15\%, n = 3$	0.6575		
Total	2.2832	$i = 15\%, n = 3$	2.2832

We can also use business calculators or spreadsheet programs to find the present value of an annuity.

Quick Check   Answer — p. B-7   ☑

3. A company is considering an investment paying $10,000 every six months for three years. The first payment would be received in six months. If this company requires an 8% annual return, what is the maximum amount it is willing to pay for this investment?

FUTURE VALUE OF AN ANNUITY

The future value of an *ordinary annuity* is the accumulated value of each annuity payment with interest as of the date of the final payment. To illustrate, let's consider the earlier annuity of three annual payments of $100. Exhibit B.7 shows the point in time for the future value (f). The first payment is made two periods prior to the point when future value is determined, and the final payment occurs on the future value date.

EXHIBIT B.7

Future Value of an Ordinary Annuity Diagram

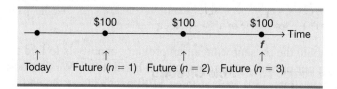

One way to compute the future value of an annuity is to use the formula to find the future value of *each* payment and add them. If we assume an interest rate of 15%, our calculation is

$$f = \$100 \times (1 + 0.15)^2 + \$100 \times (1 + 0.15)^1 + \$100 \times (1 + 0.15)^0 = \$347.25$$

This is identical to using Table B.2 and summing the future values of each payment, or adding the future values of the three payments of 1 and multiplying the sum by $100.

A more direct way is to use a table showing future values of annuities. Such a table is called a **future value of an annuity of 1 table**. Table B.4 at the end of this appendix is one such table. Note that in Table B.4 when $n = 1$, the future values equal 1 ($f = 1$) for all rates of interest. This is so because such an annuity consists of only one payment and the future value is determined on the date of that payment—no time passes between the payment and its future value. The future value of an annuity formula is used to construct Table B.4. We can also construct it by adding the amounts from a future value of 1 table. To illustrate, we use Tables B.2 and B.4 to confirm this relation for the prior example:

	From Table B.2		From Table B.4	
$i = 15\%, n = 0$	1.0000			
$i = 15\%, n = 1$	1.1500			
$i = 15\%, n = 2$	1.3225			
Total	3.4725	$i = 15\%, n = 3$	3.4725	

Note that the future value in Table B.2 is 1.0000 when $n = 0$, but the future value in Table B.4 is 1.0000 when $n = 1$. Is this a contradiction? No. When $n = 0$ in Table B.2, the future value is determined on the date when a single payment occurs. This means that no interest is earned

P4   Apply future value concepts to an annuity by using interest tables.

because no time has passed, and the future value equals the payment. Table B.4 describes annuities with equal payments occurring at the end of each period. When $n = 1$, the annuity has one payment, and its future value equals 1 on the date of its final and only payment. Again, no time passes between the payment and its future value date.

Quick Check   Answer — p. B-7

4. A company invests $45,000 per year for five years at 12% annual interest. Compute the value of this annuity investment at the end of five years.

Summary

C1 **Describe the earning of interest and the concepts of present and future values.** Interest is payment by a borrower to the owner of an asset for its use. Present and future value computations are a way for us to estimate the interest component of holding assets or liabilities over a period of time.

P1 **Apply present value concepts to a single amount by using interest tables.** The present value of a single amount received at a future date is the amount that can be invested now at the specified interest rate to yield that future value.

P2 **Apply future value concepts to a single amount by using interest tables.** The future value of a single amount invested

at a specified rate of interest is the amount that would accumulate by the future date.

P3 **Apply present value concepts to an annuity by using interest tables.** The present value of an annuity is the amount that can be invested now at the specified interest rate to yield that series of equal periodic payments.

P4 **Apply future value concepts to an annuity by using interest tables.** The future value of an annuity invested at a specific rate of interest is the amount that would accumulate by the date of the final payment.

Guidance Answers to Quick Checks

1. $70,000 × 0.6302 = $44,114 (use Table B.1, $i = 8\%$, $n = 6$).

2. $555,000/$150,000 = 3.7000; Table B.2 shows this value is not achieved until after 17 years at 8% interest.

3. $10,000 × 5.2421 = $52,421 (use Table B.3, $i = 4\%$, $n = 6$).

4. $45,000 × 6.3528 = $285,876 (use Table B.4, $i = 12\%$, $n = 5$).

connect

Assume that you must make future value estimates using the *future value of 1 table* (Table B.2). Which interest rate column do you use when working with the following rates?

1. 8% compounded quarterly
2. 12% compounded annually
3. 6% compounded semiannually
4. 12% compounded monthly

QUICK STUDY

QS B-1
Identifying interest
rates in tables
C1

Ken Francis is offered the possibility of investing $2,745 today and in return to receive $10,000 after 15 years. What is the annual rate of interest for this investment? (Use Table B.1.)

QS B-2
Interest rate
on an investment **P1**

Megan Brink is offered the possibility of investing $6,651 today at 6% interest per year in a desire to accumulate $10,000. How many years must Brink wait to accumulate $10,000? (Use Table B.1.)

QS B-3
Number of periods
of an investment **P1**

Flaherty is considering an investment that, if paid for immediately, is expected to return $140,000 five years from now. If Flaherty demands a 9% return, how much is she willing to pay for this investment?

QS B-4
Present value of an amount **P1**

CII, Inc., invests $630,000 in a project expected to earn a 12% annual rate of return. The earnings will be reinvested in the project each year until the entire investment is liquidated 10 years later. What will the cash proceeds be when the project is liquidated?

QS B-5
Future value of an amount **P2**

QS B-6 Present value of an annuity P3	Beene Distributing is considering a project that will return $150,000 annually at the end of each year for six years. If Beene demands an annual return of 7% and pays for the project immediately, how much is it willing to pay for the project?
QS B-7 Future value of an annuity P4	Claire Fitch is planning to begin an individual retirement program in which she will invest $1,500 at the end of each year. Fitch plans to retire after making 30 annual investments in the program earning a return of 10%. What is the value of the program on the date of the last payment?

McGraw Hill connect

EXERCISES

Exercise B-1 Number of periods of an investment P2	Bill Thompson expects to invest $10,000 at 12% and, at the end of a certain period, receive $96,463. How many years will it be before Thompson receives the payment? (Use Table B.2.)
Exercise B-2 Interest rate on an investment P2	Ed Summers expects to invest $10,000 for 25 years, after which he wants to receive $108,347. What rate of interest must Summers earn? (Use Table B.2.)
Exercise B-3 Interest rate on an investment P3	Jones expects an immediate investment of $57,466 to return $10,000 annually for eight years, with the first payment to be received one year from now. What rate of interest must Jones earn? (Use Table B.3.)
Exercise B-4 Number of periods of an investment P3	Keith Riggins expects an investment of $82,014 to return $10,000 annually for several years. If Riggins earns a return of 10%, how many annual payments will he receive? (Use Table B.3.)
Exercise B-5 Interest rate on an investment P4	Algoe expects to invest $1,000 annually for 40 years to yield an accumulated value of $154,762 on the date of the last investment. For this to occur, what rate of interest must Algoe earn? (Use Table B.4.)
Exercise B-6 Number of periods of an investment P4	Kate Beckwith expects to invest $10,000 annually that will earn 8%. How many annual investments must Beckwith make to accumulate $303,243 on the date of the last investment? (Use Table B.4.)
Exercise B-7 Present value of an annuity P3	Sam Weber finances a new automobile by paying $6,500 cash and agreeing to make 40 monthly payments of $500 each, the first payment to be made one month after the purchase. The loan bears interest at an annual rate of 12%. What is the cost of the automobile?
Exercise B-8 Present value of bonds P1 P3	Spiller Corp. plans to issue 10%, 15-year, $500,000 par value bonds payable that pay interest semiannually on June 30 and December 31. The bonds are dated December 31, 2011, and are issued on that date. If the market rate of interest for the bonds is 8% on the date of issue, what will be the total cash proceeds from the bond issue?
Exercise B-9 Present value of an amount P1	McAdams Company expects to earn 10% per year on an investment that will pay $606,773 six years from now. Use Table B.1 to compute the present value of this investment. (Round the amount to the nearest dollar.)
Exercise B-10 Present value of an amount and of an annuity P1 P3	Compute the amount that can be borrowed under each of the following circumstances: **1.** A promise to repay $90,000 seven years from now at an interest rate of 6%. **2.** An agreement made on February 1, 2011, to make three separate payments of $20,000 on February 1 of 2012, 2013, and 2014. The annual interest rate is 10%.
Exercise B-11 Present value of an amount P1	On January 1, 2011, a company agrees to pay $20,000 in three years. If the annual interest rate is 10%, determine how much cash the company can borrow with this agreement.

Find the amount of money that can be borrowed today with each of the following separate debt agreements *a* through *f.* (Round amounts to the nearest dollar.)

Exercise B-12
Present value
of an amount   P1

Case	Single Future Payment	Number of Periods	Interest Rate
a.	$40,000	3	4%
b.	75,000	7	8
c.	52,000	9	10
d.	18,000	2	4
e.	63,000	8	6
f.	89,000	5	2

C&H Ski Club recently borrowed money and agrees to pay it back with a series of six annual payments of $5,000 each. C&H subsequently borrows more money and agrees to pay it back with a series of four annual payments of $7,500 each. The annual interest rate for both loans is 6%.

Exercise B-13
Present values of annuities
P3

1. Use Table B.1 to find the present value of these two separate annuities. (Round amounts to the nearest dollar.)
2. Use Table B.3 to find the present value of these two separate annuities. (Round amounts to the nearest dollar.)

Otto Co. borrows money on April 30, 2011, by promising to make four payments of $13,000 each on November 1, 2011; May 1, 2012; November 1, 2012; and May 1, 2013.

Exercise B-14
Present value with semiannual compounding

C1 P3

1. How much money is Otto able to borrow if the interest rate is 8%, compounded semiannually?
2. How much money is Otto able to borrow if the interest rate is 12%, compounded semiannually?
3. How much money is Otto able to borrow if the interest rate is 16%, compounded semiannually?

Mark Welsch deposits $7,200 in an account that earns interest at an annual rate of 8%, compounded quarterly. The $7,200 plus earned interest must remain in the account 10 years before it can be withdrawn. How much money will be in the account at the end of 10 years?

Exercise B-15
Future value
of an amount   P2

Kelly Malone plans to have $50 withheld from her monthly paycheck and deposited in a savings account that earns 12% annually, compounded monthly. If Malone continues with her plan for two and one-half years, how much will be accumulated in the account on the date of the last deposit?

Exercise B-16
Future value
of an annuity   P4

Starr Company decides to establish a fund that it will use 10 years from now to replace an aging production facility. The company will make a $100,000 initial contribution to the fund and plans to make quarterly contributions of $50,000 beginning in three months. The fund earns 12%, compounded quarterly. What will be the value of the fund 10 years from now?

Exercise B-17
Future value of
an amount plus
an annuity   P2 P4

Catten, Inc., invests $163,170 today earning 7% per year for nine years. Use Table B.2 to compute the future value of the investment nine years from now. (Round the amount to the nearest dollar.)

Exercise B-18
Future value of
an amount   P2

For each of the following situations, identify (1) the case as either (*a*) a present or a future value and (*b*) a single amount or an annuity, (2) the table you would use in your computations (but do not solve the problem), and (3) the interest rate and time periods you would use.

Exercise B-19
Using present and future
value tables

C1 P1 P2 P3 P4

a. You need to accumulate $10,000 for a trip you wish to take in four years. You are able to earn 8% compounded semiannually on your savings. You plan to make only one deposit and let the money accumulate for four years. How would you determine the amount of the one-time deposit?

b. Assume the same facts as in part (*a*) except that you will make semiannual deposits to your savings account.

c. You want to retire after working 40 years with savings in excess of $1,000,000. You expect to save $4,000 a year for 40 years and earn an annual rate of interest of 8%. Will you be able to retire with more than $1,000,000 in 40 years? Explain.

d. A sweepstakes agency names you a grand prize winner. You can take $225,000 immediately or elect to receive annual installments of $30,000 for 20 years. You can earn 10% annually on any investments you make. Which prize do you choose to receive?

Market Rate w/ Tables (handwritten)

TABLE B.1

Present Value of 1

$$p = 1/(1 + i)^n$$

						Rate						
Periods	1%	2%	3%	4%	5%	6%	7%	8%	9%	10%	12%	15%
1	0.9901	0.9804	0.9709	0.9615	0.9524	0.9434	0.9346	0.9259	0.9174	0.9091	0.8929	0.8696
2	0.9803	0.9612	0.9426	0.9246	0.9070	0.8900	0.8734	0.8573	0.8417	0.8264	0.7972	0.7561
3	0.9706	0.9423	0.9151	0.8890	0.8638	0.8396	0.8163	0.7938	0.7722	0.7513	0.7118	0.6575
4	0.9610	0.9238	0.8885	0.8548	0.8227	0.7921	0.7629	0.7350	0.7084	0.6830	0.6355	0.5718
5	0.9515	0.9057	0.8626	0.8219	0.7835	0.7473	0.7130	0.6806	0.6499	0.6209	0.5674	0.4972
6	0.9420	0.8880	0.8375	0.7903	0.7462	0.7050	0.6663	0.6302	0.5963	0.5645	0.5066	0.4323
7	0.9327	0.8706	0.8131	0.7599	0.7107	0.6651	0.6227	0.5835	0.5470	0.5132	0.4523	0.3759
8	0.9235	0.8535	0.7894	0.7307	0.6768	0.6274	0.5820	0.5403	0.5019	0.4665	0.4039	0.3269
9	0.9143	0.8368	0.7664	0.7026	0.6446	0.5919	0.5439	0.5002	0.4604	0.4241	0.3606	0.2843
10	0.9053	0.8203	0.7441	0.6756	0.6139	0.5584	0.5083	0.4632	0.4224	0.3855	0.3220	0.2472
11	0.8963	0.8043	0.7224	0.6496	0.5847	0.5268	0.4751	0.4289	0.3875	0.3505	0.2875	0.2149
12	0.8874	0.7885	0.7014	0.6246	0.5568	0.4970	0.4440	0.3971	0.3555	0.3186	0.2567	0.1869
13	0.8787	0.7730	0.6810	0.6006	0.5303	0.4688	0.4150	0.3677	0.3262	0.2897	0.2292	0.1625
14	0.8700	0.7579	0.6611	0.5775	0.5051	0.4423	0.3878	0.3405	0.2992	0.2633	0.2046	0.1413
15	0.8613	0.7430	0.6419	0.5553	0.4810	0.4173	0.3624	0.3152	0.2745	0.2394	0.1827	0.1229
16	0.8528	0.7284	0.6232	0.5339	0.4581	0.3936	0.3387	0.2919	0.2519	0.2176	0.1631	0.1069
17	0.8444	0.7142	0.6050	0.5134	0.4363	0.3714	0.3166	0.2703	0.2311	0.1978	0.1456	0.0929
18	0.8360	0.7002	0.5874	0.4936	0.4155	0.3503	0.2959	0.2502	0.2120	0.1799	0.1300	0.0808
19	0.8277	0.6864	0.5703	0.4746	0.3957	0.3305	0.2765	0.2317	0.1945	0.1635	0.1161	0.0703
20	0.8195	0.6730	0.5537	0.4564	0.3769	0.3118	0.2584	0.2145	0.1784	0.1486	0.1037	0.0611
25	0.7798	0.6095	0.4776	0.3751	0.2953	0.2330	0.1842	0.1460	0.1160	0.0923	0.0588	0.0304
30	0.7419	0.5521	0.4120	0.3083	0.2314	0.1741	0.1314	0.0994	0.0754	0.0573	0.0334	0.0151
35	0.7059	0.5000	0.3554	0.2534	0.1813	0.1301	0.0937	0.0676	0.0490	0.0356	0.0189	0.0075
40	0.6717	0.4529	0.3066	0.2083	0.1420	0.0972	0.0668	0.0460	0.0318	0.0221	0.0107	0.0037

TABLE B.2

Future Value of 1

$$f = (1 + i)^n$$

						Rate						
Periods	1%	2%	3%	4%	5%	6%	7%	8%	9%	10%	12%	15%
0	1.0000	1.0000	1.0000	1.0000	1.0000	1.0000	1.0000	1.0000	1.0000	1.0000	1.0000	1.0000
1	1.0100	1.0200	1.0300	1.0400	1.0500	1.0600	1.0700	1.0800	1.0900	1.1000	1.1200	1.1500
2	1.0201	1.0404	1.0609	1.0816	1.1025	1.1236	1.1449	1.1664	1.1881	1.2100	1.2544	1.3225
3	1.0303	1.0612	1.0927	1.1249	1.1576	1.1910	1.2250	1.2597	1.2950	1.3310	1.4049	1.5209
4	1.0406	1.0824	1.1255	1.1699	1.2155	1.2625	1.3108	1.3605	1.4116	1.4641	1.5735	1.7490
5	1.0510	1.1041	1.1593	1.2167	1.2763	1.3382	1.4026	1.4693	1.5386	1.6105	1.7623	2.0114
6	1.0615	1.1262	1.1941	1.2653	1.3401	1.4185	1.5007	1.5869	1.6771	1.7716	1.9738	2.3131
7	1.0721	1.1487	1.2299	1.3159	1.4071	1.5036	1.6058	1.7138	1.8280	1.9487	2.2107	2.6600
8	1.0829	1.1717	1.2668	1.3686	1.4775	1.5938	1.7182	1.8509	1.9926	2.1436	2.4760	3.0590
9	1.0937	1.1951	1.3048	1.4233	1.5513	1.6895	1.8385	1.9990	2.1719	2.3579	2.7731	3.5179
10	1.1046	1.2190	1.3439	1.4802	1.6289	1.7908	1.9672	2.1589	2.3674	2.5937	3.1058	4.0456
11	1.1157	1.2434	1.3842	1.5395	1.7103	1.8983	2.1049	2.3316	2.5804	2.8531	3.4785	4.6524
12	1.1268	1.2682	1.4258	1.6010	1.7959	2.0122	2.2522	2.5182	2.8127	3.1384	3.8960	5.3503
13	1.1381	1.2936	1.4685	1.6651	1.8856	2.1329	2.4098	2.7196	3.0658	3.4523	4.3635	6.1528
14	1.1495	1.3195	1.5126	1.7317	1.9799	2.2609	2.5785	2.9372	3.3417	3.7975	4.8871	7.0757
15	1.1610	1.3459	1.5580	1.8009	2.0789	2.3966	2.7590	3.1722	3.6425	4.1772	5.4736	8.1371
16	1.1726	1.3728	1.6047	1.8730	2.1829	2.5404	2.9522	3.4259	3.9703	4.5950	6.1304	9.3576
17	1.1843	1.4002	1.6528	1.9479	2.2920	2.6928	3.1588	3.7000	4.3276	5.0545	6.8660	10.7613
18	1.1961	1.4282	1.7024	2.0258	2.4066	2.8543	3.3799	3.9960	4.7171	5.5599	7.6900	12.3755
19	1.2081	1.4568	1.7535	2.1068	2.5270	3.0256	3.6165	4.3157	5.1417	6.1159	8.6128	14.2318
20	1.2202	1.4859	1.8061	2.1911	2.6533	3.2071	3.8697	4.6610	5.6044	6.7275	9.6463	16.3665
25	1.2824	1.6406	2.0938	2.6658	3.3864	4.2919	5.4274	6.8485	8.6231	10.8347	17.0001	32.9190
30	1.3478	1.8114	2.4273	3.2434	4.3219	5.7435	7.6123	10.0627	13.2677	17.4494	29.9599	66.2118
35	1.4166	1.9999	2.8139	3.9461	5.5160	7.6861	10.6766	14.7853	20.4140	28.1024	52.7996	133.1755
40	1.4889	2.2080	3.2620	4.8010	7.0400	10.2857	14.9745	21.7245	31.4094	45.2593	93.0510	267.8635

$$p = \left[1 - \frac{1}{(1 + i)^n}\right]/i$$

TABLE B.3

Present Value of an Annuity of 1

| Periods | \multicolumn{12}{c}{Rate} |
	1%	2%	3%	4%	5%	6%	7%	8%	9%	10%	12%	15%
1	0.9901	0.9804	0.9709	0.9615	0.9524	0.9434	0.9346	0.9259	0.9174	0.9091	0.8929	0.8696
2	1.9704	1.9416	1.9135	1.8861	1.8594	1.8334	1.8080	1.7833	1.7591	1.7355	1.6901	1.6257
3	2.9410	2.8839	2.8286	2.7751	2.7232	2.6730	2.6243	2.5771	2.5313	2.4869	2.4018	2.2832
4	3.9020	3.8077	3.7171	3.6299	3.5460	3.4651	3.3872	3.3121	3.2397	3.1699	3.0373	2.8550
5	4.8534	4.7135	4.5797	4.4518	4.3295	4.2124	4.1002	3.9927	3.8897	3.7908	3.6048	3.3522
6	5.7955	5.6014	5.4172	5.2421	5.0757	4.9173	4.7665	4.6229	4.4859	4.3553	4.1114	3.7845
7	6.7282	6.4720	6.2303	6.0021	5.7864	5.5824	5.3893	5.2064	5.0330	4.8684	4.5638	4.1604
8	7.6517	7.3255	7.0197	6.7327	6.4632	6.2098	5.9713	5.7466	5.5348	5.3349	4.9676	4.4873
9	8.5660	8.1622	7.7861	7.4353	7.1078	6.8017	6.5152	6.2469	5.9952	5.7590	5.3282	4.7716
10	9.4713	8.9826	8.5302	8.1109	7.7217	7.3601	7.0236	6.7101	6.4177	6.1446	5.6502	5.0188
11	10.3676	9.7868	9.2526	8.7605	8.3064	7.8869	7.4987	7.1390	6.8052	6.4951	5.9377	5.2337
12	11.2551	10.5753	9.9540	9.3851	8.8633	8.3838	7.9427	7.5361	7.1607	6.8137	6.1944	5.4206
13	12.1337	11.3484	10.6350	9.9856	9.3936	8.8527	8.3577	7.9038	7.4869	7.1034	6.4235	5.5831
14	13.0037	12.1062	11.2961	10.5631	9.8986	9.2950	8.7455	8.2442	7.7862	7.3667	6.6282	5.7245
15	13.8651	12.8493	11.9379	11.1184	10.3797	9.7122	9.1079	8.5595	8.0607	7.6061	6.8109	5.8474
16	14.7179	13.5777	12.5611	11.6523	10.8378	10.1059	9.4466	8.8514	8.3126	7.8237	6.9740	5.9542
17	15.5623	14.2919	13.1661	12.1657	11.2741	10.4773	9.7632	9.1216	8.5436	8.0216	7.1196	6.0472
18	16.3983	14.9920	13.7535	12.6593	11.6896	10.8276	10.0591	9.3719	8.7556	8.2014	7.2497	6.1280
19	17.2260	15.6785	14.3238	13.1339	12.0853	11.1581	10.3356	9.6036	8.9501	8.3649	7.3658	6.1982
20	18.0456	16.3514	14.8775	13.5903	12.4622	11.4699	10.5940	9.8181	9.1285	8.5136	7.4694	6.2593
25	22.0232	19.5235	17.4131	15.6221	14.0939	12.7834	11.6536	10.6748	9.8226	9.0770	7.8431	6.4641
30	25.8077	22.3965	19.6004	17.2920	15.3725	13.7648	12.4090	11.2578	10.2737	9.4269	8.0552	6.5660
35	29.4086	24.9986	21.4872	18.6646	16.3742	14.4982	12.9477	11.6546	10.5668	9.6442	8.1755	6.6166
40	32.8347	27.3555	23.1148	19.7928	17.1591	15.0463	13.3317	11.9246	10.7574	9.7791	8.2438	6.6418

$$f = [(1 + i)^n - 1]/i$$

TABLE B.4

Future Value of an Annuity of 1

| Periods | \multicolumn{12}{c}{Rate} |
	1%	2%	3%	4%	5%	6%	7%	8%	9%	10%	12%	15%
1	1.0000	1.0000	1.0000	1.0000	1.0000	1.0000	1.0000	1.0000	1.0000	1.0000	1.0000	1.0000
2	2.0100	2.0200	2.0300	2.0400	2.0500	2.0600	2.0700	2.0800	2.0900	2.1000	2.1200	2.1500
3	3.0301	3.0604	3.0909	3.1216	3.1525	3.1836	3.2149	3.2464	3.2781	3.3100	3.3744	3.4725
4	4.0604	4.1216	4.1836	4.2465	4.3101	4.3746	4.4399	4.5061	4.5731	4.6410	4.7793	4.9934
5	5.1010	5.2040	5.3091	5.4163	5.5256	5.6371	5.7507	5.8666	5.9847	6.1051	6.3528	6.7424
6	6.1520	6.3081	6.4684	6.6330	6.8019	6.9753	7.1533	7.3359	7.5233	7.7156	8.1152	8.7537
7	7.2135	7.4343	7.6625	7.8983	8.1420	8.3938	8.6540	8.9228	9.2004	9.4872	10.0890	11.0668
8	8.2857	8.5830	8.8923	9.2142	9.5491	9.8975	10.2598	10.6366	11.0285	11.4359	12.2997	13.7268
9	9.3685	9.7546	10.1591	10.5828	11.0266	11.4913	11.9780	12.4876	13.0210	13.5795	14.7757	16.7858
10	10.4622	10.9497	11.4639	12.0061	12.5779	13.1808	13.8164	14.4866	15.1929	15.9374	17.5487	20.3037
11	11.5668	12.1687	12.8078	13.4864	14.2068	14.9716	15.7836	16.6455	17.5603	18.5312	20.6546	24.3493
12	12.6825	13.4121	14.1920	15.0258	15.9171	16.8699	17.8885	18.9771	20.1407	21.3843	24.1331	29.0017
13	13.8093	14.6803	15.6178	16.6268	17.7130	18.8821	20.1406	21.4953	22.9534	24.5227	28.0291	34.3519
14	14.9474	15.9739	17.0863	18.2919	19.5986	21.0151	22.5505	24.2149	26.0192	27.9750	32.3926	40.5047
15	16.0969	17.2934	18.5989	20.0236	21.5786	23.2760	25.1290	27.1521	29.3609	31.7725	37.2797	47.5804
16	17.2579	18.6393	20.1569	21.8245	23.6575	25.6725	27.8881	30.3243	33.0034	35.9497	42.7533	55.7175
17	18.4304	20.0121	21.7616	23.6975	25.8404	28.2129	30.8402	33.7502	36.9737	40.5447	48.8837	65.0751
18	19.6147	21.4123	23.4144	25.6454	28.1324	30.9057	33.9990	37.4502	41.3013	45.5992	55.7497	75.8364
19	20.8109	22.8406	25.1169	27.6712	30.5390	33.7600	37.3790	41.4463	46.0185	51.1591	63.4397	88.2118
20	22.0190	24.2974	26.8704	29.7781	33.0660	36.7856	40.9955	45.7620	51.1601	57.2750	72.0524	102.4436
25	28.2432	32.0303	36.4593	41.6459	47.7271	54.8645	63.2490	73.1059	84.7009	98.3471	133.3339	212.7930
30	34.7849	40.5681	47.5754	56.0849	66.4388	79.0582	94.4608	113.2832	136.3075	164.4940	241.3327	434.7451
35	41.6603	49.9945	60.4621	73.6522	90.3203	111.4348	138.2369	172.3168	215.7108	271.0244	431.6635	881.1702
40	48.8864	60.4020	75.4013	95.0255	120.7998	154.7620	199.6351	259.0565	337.8824	442.5926	767.0914	1,779.0903

Glossary

Absorption costing Costing method that assigns both variable and fixed costs to products. *(p. 915)*

Accelerated depreciation method Method that produces larger depreciation charges in the early years of an asset's life and smaller charges in its later years. *(p. 400)*

Account Record within an accounting system in which increases and decreases are entered and stored in a specific asset, liability, equity, revenue, or expense. *(p. 51)*

Account balance Difference between total debits and total credits (including the beginning balance) for an account. *(p. 55)*

Account form balance sheet Balance sheet that lists assets on the left side and liabilities and equity on the right. *(p. 18)*

Account payable Liability created by buying goods or services on credit; backed by the buyer's general credit standing. *(p. 50)*

Accounting Information and measurement system that identifies, records, and communicates relevant information about a company's business activities. *(p. 4)*

Accounting cycle Recurring steps performed each accounting period, starting with analyzing transactions and continuing through the post-closing trial balance (or reversing entries). *(p. 146)*

Accounting equation Equality involving a company's assets, liabilities, and equity; Assets = Liabilities + Equity; also called *balance sheet equation*. *(p. 14)*

Accounting information system People, records, and methods that collect and process data from transactions and events, organize them in useful forms, and communicate results to decision makers. *(p. 272)*

Accounting period Length of time covered by financial statements; also called *reporting period*. *(p. 94)*

Accounting rate of return Rate used to evaluate the acceptability of an investment; equals the after-tax periodic income from a project divided by the average investment in the asset; also called *rate of return on average investment*. *(p. 1039)*

Accounts payable ledger Subsidiary ledger listing individual creditor (supplier) accounts. *(p. 277)*

Accounts receivable Amounts due from customers for credit sales; backed by the customer's general credit standing. *(p. 360)*

Accounts receivable ledger Subsidiary ledger listing individual customer accounts. *(p. 277)*

Accounts receivable turnover Measure of both the quality and liquidity of accounts receivable; indicates how often receivables are received and collected during the period; computed by dividing net sales by average accounts receivable. *(p. 375)*

Accrual basis accounting Accounting system that recognizes revenues when earned and expenses when incurred; the basis for GAAP. *(p. 95)*

Accrued expenses Costs incurred in a period that are both unpaid and unrecorded; adjusting entries for recording accrued expenses involve increasing expenses and increasing liabilities. *(p. 101)*

Accrued revenues Revenues earned in a period that are both unrecorded and not yet received in cash (or other assets); adjusting entries for recording accrued revenues involve increasing assets and increasing revenues. *(pp. 103 & 960)*

Accumulated depreciation Cumulative sum of all depreciation expense recorded for an asset. *(p. 97)*

Acid-test ratio Ratio used to assess a company's ability to settle its current debts with its most liquid assets; defined as quick assets (cash, short-term investments, and current receivables) divided by current liabilities. *(p. 196)*

Activity-based budgeting (ABB) Budget system based on expected activities. *(p. 960)*

Activity-based costing (ABC) Cost allocation method that focuses on activities performed; traces costs to activities and then assigns them to cost objects. *(p. 861)*

Activity cost driver Variable that causes an activity's cost to go up or down; a causal factor. *(p. 861)*

Activity cost pool Temporary account that accumulates costs a company incurs to support an activity. *(p. 861)*

Adjusted trial balance List of accounts and balances prepared after period-end adjustments are recorded and posted. *(p. 106)*

Adjusting entry Journal entry at the end of an accounting period to bring an asset or liability account to its proper amount and update the related expense or revenue account. *(p. 96)*

Aging of accounts receivable Process of classifying accounts receivable by how long they are past due for purposes of estimating uncollectible accounts. *(p. 368)*

Allowance for Doubtful Accounts Contra asset account with a balance approximating uncollectible accounts receivable; also called *Allowance for Uncollectible Accounts*. *(p. 365)*

Allowance method Procedure that (a) estimates and matches bad debts expense with its sales for the period and/or (b) reports accounts receivable at estimated realizable value. *(p. 364)*

Amortization Process of allocating the cost of an intangible asset to expense over its estimated useful life. *(p. 409)*

Annual financial statements Financial statements covering a one-year period; often based on a calendar year, but any consecutive 12-month (or 52-week) period is acceptable. *(p. 94)*

Annual report Summary of a company's financial results for the year with its current financial condition and future plans; directed to external users of financial information. *(p. A-1)*

Annuity Series of equal payments at equal intervals. *(p. 571)*

Appropriated retained earnings Retained earnings separately reported to inform stockholders of funding needs. *(p. 525)*

Asset book value (See *book value*.)

Assets Resources a business owns or controls that are expected to provide current and future benefits to the business. *(p. 14)*

Audit Analysis and report of an organization's accounting system, its records, and its reports using various tests. *(p. 12)*

Auditors Individuals hired to review financial reports and information systems. *Internal auditors* of a company are employed to assess and evaluate its system of internal controls, including the resulting reports. *External auditors* are independent of a company and are hired to assess and evaluate the "fairness" of financial statements (or to perform other contracted financial services) *(p. 13)*.

Authorized stock Total amount of stock that a corporation's charter authorizes it to issue. *(p. 511)*

Available-for-sale (AFS) securities Investments in debt and equity securities that are not classified as trading securities or held-to-maturity securities. *(p. 600)*

Average cost See *weighted average*.

Avoidable expense Expense (or cost) that is relevant for decision making; expense that is not incurred if a department, product, or service is eliminated. *(p. 1053)*

Bad debts Accounts of customers who do not pay what they have promised to pay; an expense of selling on credit; also called *uncollectible accounts*. *(p. 363)*

Balance column account Account with debit and credit columns for recording entries and another column for showing the balance of the account after each entry. *(p. 58)*

Balance sheet Financial statement that lists types and dollar amounts of assets, liabilities, and equity at a specific date. *(p. 19)*

Balance sheet equation (See *accounting equation*.)

Balanced scorecard A system of performance measurement that collects information on several key performance indicators within each of four perspectives: customer, internal processes, innovation and learning, and financial. *(p. 874)*

Bank reconciliation Report that explains the difference between the book (company) balance of cash and the cash balance reported on the bank statement. *(p. 331)*

Bank statement Bank report on the depositor's beginning and ending cash balances, and a listing of its changes, for a period. *(p. 330)*

Basic earnings per share Net income less any preferred dividends and then divided by weighted-average common shares outstanding. *(p. 527)*

Batch processing Accumulating source documents for a period of time and then processing them all at once such as once a day, week, or month. *(p. 286)*

Bearer bonds Bonds made payable to whoever holds them (the *bearer*); also called *unregistered bonds*. *(p. 566)*

Benchmarking Practice of comparing and analyzing company financial performance or position with other companies or standards. *(p. 1002)*

Betterments Expenditures to make a plant asset more efficient or productive; also called *improvements*. *(p. 405)*

Bond Written promise to pay the bond's par (or face) value and interest at a stated contract rate; often issued in denominations of $1,000. *(p. 552)*

Bond certificate Document containing bond specifics such as issuer's name, bond par value, contract interest rate, and maturity date. *(p. 554)*

Bond indenture Contract between the bond issuer and the bondholders; identifies the parties' rights and obligations. *(p. 554)*

Book value Asset's acquisition costs less its accumulated depreciation (or depletion, or amortization); also sometimes used synonymously as the *carrying value* of an account. *(p. 100)*

Book value per common share Recorded amount of equity applicable to common shares divided by the number of common shares outstanding. *(p. 528)*

Book value per preferred share Equity applicable to preferred shares (equals its call price [or par value if it is not callable] plus any cumulative dividends in arrears) divided by the number of preferred shares outstanding. *(p. 528)*

Bookkeeping (See *recordkeeping*.)

Break-even point Output level at which sales equals fixed plus variable costs; where income equals zero. *(p. 915)*

Break-even time (BET) Time-based measurement used to evaluate the acceptability of an investment; equals the time expected to pass before the present value of the net cash flows from an investment equals its initial cost. *(p. 1055)*

Budget Formal statement of future plans, usually expressed in monetary terms. *(p. 946)*

Budget report Report comparing actual results to planned objectives; sometimes used as a progress report. *(p. 990)*

Budgetary control Management use of budgets to monitor and control company operations. *(p. 990)*

Budgeted balance sheet Accounting report that presents predicted amounts of the company's assets, liabilities, and equity balances as of the end of the budget period. *(p. 958)*

Budgeted income statement Accounting report that presents predicted amounts of the company's revenues and expenses for the budget period. *(p. 958)*

Budgeting Process of planning future business actions and expressing them as formal plans. *(p. 946)*

Business An organization of one or more individuals selling products and/or services for profit. *(p. 10)*

Business entity assumption Principle that requires a business to be accounted for separately from its owner(s) and from any other entity. *(p. 11)*

Business segment Part of a company that can be separately identified by the products or services that it provides or by the geographic markets that it serves; also called *segment*. *(p. 710)*

C corporation Corporation that does not qualify for nor elect to be treated as a proprietorship or partnership for income tax purposes and therefore is subject to income taxes; also called *C corp*. *(p. 482)*

Call price Amount that must be paid to call and retire a callable preferred stock or a callable bond. *(p. 521)*

Callable bonds Bonds that give the issuer the option to retire them at a stated amount prior to maturity. *(p. 566)*

Callable preferred stock Preferred stock that the issuing corporation, at its option, may retire by paying the call price plus any dividends in arrears. *(p. 521)*

Canceled checks Checks that the bank has paid and deducted from the depositor's account. *(p. 331)*

Capital budgeting Process of analyzing alternative investments and deciding which assets to acquire or sell. *(p. 1036)*

Capital expenditures Additional costs of plant assets that provide material benefits extending beyond the current period; also called *balance sheet expenditures*. *(p. 404)*

Capital expenditures budget Plan that lists dollar amounts to be both received from disposal of plant assets and spent to purchase plant assets. *(p. 956)*

Capital leases Long-term leases in which the lessor transfers substantially all risk and rewards of ownership to the lessee. *(p. 577)*

Capital stock General term referring to a corporation's stock used in obtaining capital (owner financing). *(p. 511)*

Capitalize Record the cost as part of a permanent account and allocate it over later periods.

Carrying (book) value of bonds Net amount at which bonds are reported on the balance sheet; equals the par value of the bonds less any unamortized discount or plus any unamortized premium; also called *carrying amount or book value*. *(p. 556)*

Cash Includes currency, coins, and amounts on deposit in bank checking or savings accounts. *(p. 321)*

Cash basis accounting Accounting system that recognizes revenues when cash is received and records expenses when cash is paid. *(p. 95)*

Cash budget Plan that shows expected cash inflows and outflows during the budget period, including receipts from loans needed to maintain a minimum cash balance and repayments of such loans. *(p. 956)*

Cash disbursements journal Special journal normally used to record all payments of cash; also called *cash payments journal*. *(p. 284)*

Cash discount Reduction in the price of merchandise granted by a seller to a buyer when payment is made within the discount period. *(p. 183)*

Cash equivalents Short-term, investment assets that are readily convertible to a known cash amount or sufficiently close to their maturity date (usually within 90 days) so that market value is not sensitive to interest rate changes. *(p. 321)*

Cash flow on total assets Ratio of operating cash flows to average total assets; not sensitive to income recognition and measurement; partly reflects earnings quality. *(p. 650)*

Cash Over and Short Income statement account used to record cash overages and cash shortages arising from errors in cash receipts or payments. *(p. 323)*

Cash receipts journal Special journal normally used to record all receipts of cash. *(p. 281)*

Change in an accounting estimate Change in an accounting estimate that results from new information, subsequent developments, or improved judgment that impacts current and future periods. *(pp. 403 & 525)*

Chart of accounts List of accounts used by a company; includes an identification number for each account. *(p. 54)*

Check Document signed by a depositor instructing the bank to pay a specified amount to a designated recipient. *(p. 328)*

Check register Another name for a cash disbursements journal when the journal has a column for check numbers. *(pp. 284 & 340)*

Classified balance sheet Balance sheet that presents assets and liabilities in relevant subgroups, including current and noncurrent classifications. *(p. 147)*

Clock card Source document used to record the number of hours an employee works and to determine the total labor cost for each pay period. *(p. 782)*

Closing entries Entries recorded at the end of each accounting period to transfer end-of-period balances in revenue, gain, expense, loss, and withdrawal (dividend for a corporation) accounts to the capital account (to retained earnings for a corporation). *(p. 143)*

Closing process Necessary end-of-period steps to prepare the accounts for recording the transactions of the next period. *(p. 142)*

Columnar journal Journal with more than one column. *(p. 278)*

Committee on Sponsoring Organizations (COSO) Committee devoted to improving the quality of financial reporting through effective internal controls, consisting of five interrelated components, along with other mechanisms (www.COSO.org). *(p. 315)*

Common stock Corporation's basic ownership share; also generically called *capital stock*. *(pp. 12 & 510)*

Common-size financial statement Statement that expresses each amount as a percent of a base amount. In the balance sheet, total assets is usually the base and is expressed as 100%. In the income statement, net sales is usually the base. *(p. 693)*

Comparative financial statement Statement with data for two or more successive periods placed in side-by-side columns, often with changes shown in dollar amounts and percents. *(p. 688)*

Compatibility principle Information system principle that prescribes an accounting system to conform with a company's activities, personnel, and structure. *(p. 273)*

Complex capital structure Capital structure that includes outstanding rights or options to purchase common stock, or securities that are convertible into common stock. *(p. 527)*

Components of accounting systems Five basic components of accounting systems are source documents, input devices, information processors, information storage, and output devices. *(p. 273)*

Composite unit Generic unit consisting of a specific number of units of each product; unit comprised in proportion to the expected sales mix of its products. *(p. 922)*

Compound journal entry Journal entry that affects at least three accounts. *(p. 61)*

Comprehensive income Net change in equity for a period, excluding owner investments and distributions. *(p. 604)*

Computer hardware Physical equipment in a computerized accounting information system.

Computer network Linkage giving different users and different computers access to common databases and programs. *(p. 286)*

Computer software Programs that direct operations of computer hardware.

Conceptual framework A written framework to guide the development, preparation, and interpretation of financial accounting information. *(p. 9)*

Conservatism constraint Principle that prescribes the less optimistic estimate when two estimates are about equally likely. *(p. 238)*

Consignee Receiver of goods owned by another who holds them for purposes of selling them for the owner. *(p. 228)*

Consignor Owner of goods who ships them to another party who will sell them for the owner. *(p. 228)*

Consistency concept Principle that prescribes use of the same accounting method(s) over time so that financial statements are comparable across periods. *(p. 237)*

Consolidated financial statements Financial statements that show all (combined) activities under the parent's control, including those of any subsidiaries. *(p. 603)*

Contingent liability Obligation to make a future payment if, and only if, an uncertain future event occurs. *(p. 448)*

Continuous budgeting Practice of preparing budgets for a selected number of future periods and revising those budgets as each period is completed. *(p. 949)*

Continuous improvement Concept requiring every manager and employee continually to look to improve operations. *(p. 748)*

Contra account Account linked with another account and having an opposite normal balance; reported as a subtraction from the other account's balance. *(p. 99)*

Contract rate Interest rate specified in a bond indenture (or note); multiplied by the par value to determine the interest paid each period; also called *coupon rate, stated rate,* or *nominal rate. (p. 555)*

Contributed capital Total amount of cash and other assets received from stockholders in exchange for stock; also called *paid-in capital. (p. 13)*

Contributed capital in excess of par value Difference between the par value of stock and its issue price when issued at a price above par.

Contribution margin Sales revenue less total variable costs.

Contribution margin income statement Income statement that separates variable and fixed costs; highlights the contribution margin, which is sales less variable expenses.

Contribution margin per unit Amount that the sale of one unit contributes toward recovering fixed costs and earning profit; defined as sales price per unit minus variable expense per unit. *(p. 914)*

Contribution margin ratio Product's contribution margin divided by its sale price. *(p. 914)*

Control Process of monitoring planning decisions and evaluating the organization's activities and employees. *(p. 733)*

Control principle Information system principle that prescribes an accounting system to aid managers in controlling and monitoring business activities. *(p. 272)*

Controllable costs Costs that a manager has the power to control or at least strongly influence. *(pp. 737 & 875)*

Controllable variance Combination of both overhead spending variances (variable and fixed) and the variable overhead efficiency variance. *(p. 1003)*

Controlling account General ledger account, the balance of which (after posting) equals the sum of the balances in its related subsidiary ledger. *(p. 277)*

Conversion costs Expenditures incurred in converting raw materials to finished goods; includes direct labor costs and overhead costs. *(p. 743)*

Conversion costs per equivalent unit The combined costs of direct labor and factory overhead per equivalent unit. *(p. 829)*

Convertible bonds Bonds that bondholders can exchange for a set number of the issuer's shares. *(p. 566)*

Convertible preferred stock Preferred stock with an option to exchange it for common stock at a specified rate. *(p. 520)*

Copyright Right giving the owner the exclusive privilege to publish and sell musical, literary, or artistic work during the creator's life plus 70 years. *(p. 410)*

Corporation Business that is a separate legal entity under state or federal laws with owners called *shareholders* or *stockholders.* *(pp. 12 & 508)*

Cost All normal and reasonable expenditures necessary to get an asset in place and ready for its intended use. *(p. 395)*

Cost accounting system Accounting system for manufacturing activities based on the perpetual inventory system. *(p. 776)*

Cost-based transfer pricing A form of pricing transfers between divisions of the same company based on costs to the transferring division; typically used when the transferring division has excess capacity. *(p. 883)*

Cost-benefit constraint Notion that only information with benefits of disclosure greater than the costs of disclosure need be disclosed. *(p. 12)*

Cost-benefit principle Information system principle that prescribes the benefits from an activity in an accounting system to outweigh the costs of that activity. *(p. 273)*

Cost center Department that incurs costs but generates no revenues; common example is the accounting or legal department. *(p. 865)*

Cost object Product, process, department, or customer to which costs are assigned. *(p. 737)*

Cost of capital Rate the company must pay to its long-term creditors and shareholders; also called *hurdle rate. (p. 1041)*

Cost of goods available for sale Consists of beginning inventory plus net purchases of a period.

Cost of goods manufactured Total manufacturing costs (direct materials, direct labor, and factory overhead) for the period plus beginning goods in process less ending goods in process; also called *net cost of goods manufactured* and *cost of goods completed. (p. 827)*

Cost of goods sold Cost of inventory sold to customers during a period; also called *cost of sales. (p. 180)*

Cost principle Accounting principle that prescribes financial statement information to be based on actual costs incurred in business transactions. *(p. 10)*

Cost variance Difference between the actual incurred cost and the standard cost. *(p. 997)*

Cost-volume-profit (CVP) analysis Planning method that includes predicting the volume of activity, the costs incurred, sales earned, and profits received. *(p. 908)*

Cost-volume-profit (CVP) chart Graphic representation of cost-volume-profit relations. *(p. 916)*

Coupon bonds Bonds with interest coupons attached to their certificates; bondholders detach coupons when they mature and present them to a bank or broker for collection. *(p. 566)*

Credit Recorded on the right side; an entry that decreases asset and expense accounts, and increases liability, revenue, and most equity accounts; abbreviated Cr. *(p. 55)*

Credit memorandum Notification that the sender has credited the recipient's account in the sender's records. *(p. 189)*

Credit period Time period that can pass before a customer's payment is due. *(p. 183)*

Credit terms Description of the amounts and timing of payments that a buyer (debtor) agrees to make in the future. *(p. 183)*

Creditors Individuals or organizations entitled to receive payments. *(p. 52)*

Cumulative preferred stock Preferred stock on which undeclared dividends accumulate until paid; common stockholders cannot receive dividends until cumulative dividends are paid. *(p. 519)*

Current assets Cash and other assets expected to be sold, collected, or used within one year or the company's operating cycle, whichever is longer. *(p. 148)*

Current liabilities Obligations due to be paid or settled within one year or the company's operating cycle, whichever is longer. *(p. 149 & 437)*

Current portion of long-term debt Portion of long-term debt due within one year or the operating cycle, whichever is longer; reported under current liabilities. *(p. 445)*

Current ratio Ratio used to evaluate a company's ability to pay its short-term obligations, calculated by dividing current assets by current liabilities. *(p. 150)*

Curvilinear cost Cost that changes with volume but not at a constant rate. *(p. 910)*

Customer orientation Company position that its managers and employees be in tune with the changing wants and needs of consumers. *(p. 747)*

Cycle efficiency (CE) A measure of production efficiency, which is defined as value-added (process) time divided by total cycle time. *(p. 750)*

Cycle time (CT) A measure of the time to produce a product or service, which is the sum of process time, inspection time, move time, and wait time; also called *throughput time*. *(p. 749)*

Date of declaration Date the directors vote to pay a dividend. *(p. 515)*

Date of payment Date the corporation makes the dividend payment. *(p. 515)*

Date of record Date directors specify for identifying stockholders to receive dividends. *(p. 515)*

Days' sales in inventory Estimate of number of days needed to convert inventory into receivables or cash; equals ending inventory divided by cost of goods sold and then multiplied by 365; also called days' *stock on hand. (p. 241)*

Days' sales uncollected Measure of the liquidity of receivables computed by dividing the current balance of receivables by the annual credit (or net) sales and then multiplying by 365; also called *days' sales in receivables. (p. 335)*

Debit Recorded on the left side; an entry that increases asset and expense accounts, and decreases liability, revenue, and most equity accounts; abbreviated Dr. *(p. 55)*

Debit memorandum Notification that the sender has debited the recipient's account in the sender's records. *(p. 184)*

Debt ratio Ratio of total liabilities to total assets; used to reflect risk associated with a company's debts. *(p. 69)*

Debt-to-equity ratio Defined as total liabilities divided by total equity; shows the proportion of a company financed by non-owners (creditors) in comparison with that financed by owners. *(p. 567)*

Debtors Individuals or organizations that owe money. *(p. 51)*

Declining-balance method Method that determines depreciation charge for the period by multiplying a depreciation rate (often twice the straight-line rate) by the asset's beginning-period book value. *(p. 400)*

Deferred income tax liability Corporation income taxes that are deferred until future years because of temporary differences between GAAP and tax rules. *(p. 460)*

Degree of operating leverage (DOL) Ratio of contribution margin divided by pretax income; used to assess the effect on income of changes in sales. *(p. 924)*

Departmental accounting system Accounting system that provides information useful in evaluating the profitability or cost effectiveness of a department. *(p. 864)*

Departmental contribution to overhead Amount by which a department's revenues exceed its direct expenses. *(p. 871)*

Depletion Process of allocating the cost of natural resources to periods when they are consumed and sold. *(p. 408)*

Deposit ticket Lists items such as currency, coins, and checks deposited and their corresponding dollar amounts. *(p. 328)*

Deposits in transit Deposits recorded by the company but not yet recorded by its bank. *(p. 331)*

Depreciable cost Cost of a plant asset less its salvage value.

Depreciation Expense created by allocating the cost of plant and equipment to periods in which they are used; represents the expense of using the asset. *(pp. 99 & 397)*

Diluted earnings per share Earnings per share calculation that requires dilutive securities be added to the denominator of the basic EPS calculation. *(p. 527)*

Dilutive securities Securities having the potential to increase common shares outstanding; examples are options, rights, convertible bonds, and convertible preferred stock. *(p. 527)*

Direct costs Costs incurred for the benefit of one specific cost object. *(p. 737)*

Direct expenses Expenses traced to a specific department (object) that are incurred for the sole benefit of that department. *(p. 865)*

Direct labor Efforts of employees who physically convert materials to finished product. *(p. 742)*

Direct labor costs Wages and salaries for direct labor that are separately and readily traced through the production process to finished goods. *(p. 742)*

Direct material Raw material that physically becomes part of the product and is clearly identified with specific products or batches of product. *(p. 742)*

Direct material costs Expenditures for direct material that are separately and readily traced through the production process to finished goods. *(p. 742)*

Direct method Presentation of net cash from operating activities for the statement of cash flows that lists major operating cash receipts less major operating cash payments. *(p. 638)*

Direct write-off method Method that records the loss from an uncollectible account receivable at the time it is determined to be uncollectible; no attempt is made to estimate bad debts. *(p. 363)*

Discount on bonds payable Difference between a bond's par value and its lower issue price or carrying value; occurs when the contract rate is less than the market rate. *(p. 555)*

Discount on note payable Difference between the face value of a note payable and the (lesser) amount borrowed; reflects the added interest to be paid on the note over its life.

Discount on stock Difference between the par value of stock and its issue price when issued at a price below par value. *(p. 513)*

Discount period Time period in which a cash discount is available and the buyer can make a reduced payment. *(p. 183)*

Discount rate Expected rate of return on investments; also called *cost of capital, hurdle rate,* or *required rate of return.* *(p. B-2)*

Discounts lost Expenses resulting from not taking advantage of cash discounts on purchases. *(p. 341)*

Dividend in arrears Unpaid dividend on cumulative preferred stock; must be paid before any regular dividends on preferred stock and before any dividends on common stock. *(p. 519)*

Dividends Corporation's distributions of assets to its owners.

Dividend yield Ratio of the annual amount of cash dividends distributed to common shareholders relative to the common stock's market value (price). *(p. 528)*

Double-declining-balance (DDB) depreciation Depreciation equals beginning book value multiplied by 2 times the straight-line rate.

Double taxation Corporate income is taxed and then its later distribution through dividends is normally taxed again for shareholders.

Double-entry accounting Accounting system in which each transaction affects at least two accounts and has at least one debit and one credit. *(p. 55)*

Earnings (See *net income.*)

Earnings per share (EPS) Amount of income earned by each share of a company's outstanding common stock; also called *net income per share.* *(p. 527)*

Effective interest method Allocates interest expense over the bond life to yield a constant rate of interest; interest expense for a period is found by multiplying the balance of the liability at the beginning of the period by the bond market rate at issuance; also called *interest method.* *(p. 572)*

Efficiency Company's productivity in using its assets; usually measured relative to how much revenue a certain level of assets generates. *(p. 687)*

Efficiency variance Difference between the actual quantity of an input and the standard quantity of that input. *(p. 1010)*

Electronic funds transfer (EFT) Use of electronic communication to transfer cash from one party to another. *(p. 329)*

Employee benefits Additional compensation paid to or on behalf of employees, such as premiums for medical, dental, life, and disability insurance, and contributions to pension plans. *(p. 445)*

Employee earnings report Record of an employee's net pay, gross pay, deductions, and year-to-date payroll information. *(p. 456)*

Enterprise resource planning (ERP) software Programs that manage a company's vital operations, which range from order taking to production to accounting. *(p. 287)*

Entity Organization that, for accounting purposes, is separate from other organizations and individuals.

EOM Abbreviation for *end of month;* used to describe credit terms for credit transactions. *(p. 183)*

Equity Owner's claim on the assets of a business; equals the residual interest in an entity's assets after deducting liabilities; also called *net assets.* *(p. 14)*

Equity method Accounting method used for long-term investments when the investor has "significant influence" over the investee. *(p. 602)*

Equity ratio Portion of total assets provided by equity, computed as total equity divided by total assets. *(p. 701)*

Equity securities with controlling influence Long-term investment when the investor is able to exert controlling influence over the investee; investors owning 50% or more of voting stock are presumed to exert controlling influence. *(p. 603)*

Equity securities with significant influence Long-term investment when the investor is able to exert significant influence over the investee; investors owning 20 percent or more (but less than 50 percent) of voting stock are presumed to exert significant influence. *(p. 602)*

Equivalent units of production (EUP) Number of units that would be completed if all effort during a period had been applied to units that were started and finished. *(p. 821)*

Estimated liability Obligation of an uncertain amount that can be reasonably estimated. *(p. 445)*

Estimated line of cost behavior Line drawn on a graph to visually fit the relation between cost and sales. *(p. 912)*

Ethics Codes of conduct by which actions are judged as right or wrong, fair or unfair, honest or dishonest. *(pp. 8 & 736)*

Events Happenings that both affect an organization's financial position and can be reliably measured. *(p. 15)*

Expanded accounting equation Assets = Liabilities + Equity; Equity equals [Owner capital − Owner withdrawals + Revenues − Expenses] for a noncorporation; Equity equals [Contributed capital + Retained earnings + Revenues − Expenses] for a corporation where dividends are subtracted from retained earnings. *(p. 14)*

Expense recognition (or **matching) principle** (See *matching principle.*) *(pp. 11 & 96)*

Expenses Outflows or using up of assets as part of operations of a business to generate sales. *(p. 14)*

External transactions Exchanges of economic value between one entity and another entity. *(p. 15)*

External users Persons using accounting information who are not directly involved in running the organization. *(p. 5)*

Extraordinary gains or losses Gains or losses reported separately from continuing operations because they are both unusual and infrequent. *(p. 710)*

Extraordinary repairs Major repairs that extend the useful life of a plant asset beyond prior expectations; treated as a capital expenditure. *(p. 405)*

Factory overhead Factory activities supporting the production process that are not direct material or direct labor; also called *overhead and manufacturing overhead.* *(p. 742)*

Factory overhead costs Expenditures for factory overhead that cannot be separately or readily traced to finished goods; also called *overhead costs.* *(p. 742)*

Fair value option Reporting option that permits a company to use fair value in reporting certain assets and liabilities, which is presently based on a 3-level system to determine fair value. *(p. 565)*

Favorable variance Difference in actual revenues or expenses from the budgeted amount that contributes to a higher income. *(p. 991)*

Federal depository bank Bank authorized to accept deposits of amounts payable to the federal government. *(p. 453)*

Federal Insurance Contributions Act (FICA) Taxes Taxes assessed on both employers and employees; for Social Security and Medicare programs. *(p. 442)*

Federal Unemployment Taxes (FUTA) Payroll taxes on employers assessed by the federal government to support its unemployment insurance program. *(p. 444)*

FIFO method (See *first-in, first-out.*) *(pp. 233 & 833)*

Financial accounting Area of accounting aimed mainly at serving external users. *(p. 5)*

Financial Accounting Standards Board (FASB) Independent group of full-time members responsible for setting accounting rules. *(p. 9)*

Financial leverage Earning a higher return on equity by paying dividends on preferred stock or interest on debt at a rate lower than the return earned with the assets from issuing preferred stock or debt; also called *trading on the equity.* *(p. 521)*

Financial reporting Process of communicating information relevant to investors, creditors, and others in making investment, credit, and business decisions. *(p. 687)*

Financial statement analysis Application of analytical tools to general-purpose financial statements and related data for making business decisions. *(p. 686)*

Financial statements Includes the balance sheet, income statement, statement of owner's (or stockholders') equity, and statement of cash flows.

Financing activities Transactions with owners and creditors that include obtaining cash from issuing debt, repaying amounts borrowed, and obtaining cash from or distributing cash to owners. *(p. 634)*

Finished goods inventory Account that controls the finished goods files, which acts as a subsidiary ledger (of the Inventory account) in

which the costs of finished goods that are ready for sale are recorded. *(pp. 741 & 779)*

First-in, first-out (FIFO) Method to assign cost to inventory that assumes items are sold in the order acquired; earliest items purchased are the first sold. *(p. 233)*

Fiscal year Consecutive 12-month (or 52-week) period chosen as the organization's annual accounting period. *(p. 95)*

Fixed budget Planning budget based on a single predicted amount of volume; unsuitable for evaluations if the actual volume differs from predicted volume. *(p. 991)*

Fixed budget performance report Report that compares actual revenues and costs with fixed budgeted amounts and identifies the differences as favorable or unfavorable variances. *(p. 991)*

Fixed cost Cost that does not change with changes in the volume of activity. *(p. 736)*

Flexibility principle Information system principle that prescribes an accounting system be able to adapt to changes in the company, its operations, and needs of decision makers. *(p. 273)*

Flexible budget Budget prepared (using actual volume) once a period is complete that helps managers evaluate past performance; uses fixed and variable costs in determining total costs. *(p. 992)*

Flexible budget performance report Report that compares actual revenues and costs with their variable budgeted amounts based on actual sales volume (or other level of activity) and identifies the differences as variances. *(p. 994)*

FOB Abbreviation for *free on board;* the point when ownership of goods passes to the buyer; *FOB shipping point* (or *factory*) means the buyer pays shipping costs and accepts ownership of goods when the seller transfers goods to carrier; *FOB destination* means the seller pays shipping costs and buyer accepts ownership of goods at the buyer's place of business. *(p. 185)*

Foreign exchange rate Price of one currency stated in terms of another currency. *(p. 610)*

Form 940 IRS form used to report an employer's federal unemployment taxes (FUTA) on an annual filing basis. *(p. 453)*

Form 941 IRS form filed to report FICA taxes owed and remitted. *(p. 453)*

Form 10-K (or 10-KSB) Annual report form filed with SEC by businesses (small businesses) with publicly traded securities. *(p. A-1)*

Form W-2 Annual report by an employer to each employee showing the employee's wages subject to FICA and federal income taxes along with amounts withheld. *(p. 455)*

Form W-4 Withholding allowance certificate, filed with the employer, identifying the number of withholding allowances claimed. *(p. 458)*

Franchises Privileges granted by a company or government to sell a product or service under specified conditions. *(p. 410)*

Full disclosure principle Principle that prescribes financial statements (including notes) to report all relevant information about an entity's operations and financial condition. *(p. 11)*

GAAP (See *generally accepted accounting principles.*)

General accounting system Accounting system for manufacturing activities based on the *periodic* inventory system. *(p. 776)*

General and administrative expenses Expenses that support the operating activities of a business. *(p. 193)*

General and administrative expense budget Plan that shows predicted operating expenses not included in the selling expenses budget. *(p. 955)*

General journal All-purpose journal for recording the debits and credits of transactions and events. *(pp. 56 & 276)*

General ledger (See *ledger*.) *(p. 51)*

General partner Partner who assumes unlimited liability for the debts of the partnership; responsible for partnership management. *(p. 481)*

General partnership Partnership in which all partners have mutual agency and unlimited liability for partnership debts. *(p. 481)*

Generally accepted accounting principles (GAAP) Rules that specify acceptable accounting practices. *(p. 8)*

Generally accepted auditing standards (GAAS) Rules that specify auditing practices.

General-purpose financial statements Statements published periodically for use by a variety of interested parties; includes the income statement, balance sheet, statement of owner's equity (or statement of retained earnings for a corporation), statement of cash flows, and notes to these statements. *(p. 687)*

Going-concern assumption Principle that prescribes financial statements to reflect the assumption that the business will continue operating. *(p. 11)*

Goods in process inventory Account in which costs are accumulated for products that are in the process of being produced but are not yet complete; also called *work in process inventory*. *(pp. 741 & 778)*

Goodwill Amount by which a company's (or a segment's) value exceeds the value of its individual assets less its liabilities. *(p. 411)*

Gross margin (See *gross profit*.)

Gross margin ratio Gross margin (net sales minus cost of goods sold) divided by net sales; also called *gross profit ratio*. *(p. 196)*

Gross method Method of recording purchases at the full invoice price without deducting any cash discounts. *(p. 341)*

Gross pay Total compensation earned by an employee. *(p. 442)*

Gross profit Net sales minus cost of goods sold; also called *gross margin*. *(p. 180)*

Gross profit method Procedure to estimate inventory when the past gross profit rate is used to estimate cost of goods sold, which is then subtracted from the cost of goods available for sale. *(p. 252)*

Held-to-maturity (HTM) securities Debt securities that a company has the intent and ability to hold until they mature. *(p. 600)*

High-low method Procedure that yields an estimated line of cost behavior by graphically connecting costs associated with the highest and lowest sales volume. *(p. 912)*

Horizontal analysis Comparison of a company's financial condition and performance across time. *(p. 688)*

Hurdle rate Minimum acceptable rate of return (set by management) for an investment. *(pp. 873 & 1045)*

Impairment Diminishment of an asset value. *(pp. 404 & 410)*

Imprest system Method to account for petty cash; maintains a constant balance in the fund, which equals cash plus petty cash receipts.

Inadequacy Condition in which the capacity of plant assets is too small to meet the company's production demands. *(p. 397)*

Income (See *net income*.)

Income statement Financial statement that subtracts expenses from revenues to yield a net income or loss over a specified period of time; also includes any gains or losses. *(p. 19)*

Income Summary Temporary account used only in the closing process to which the balances of revenue and expense accounts (including any gains or losses) are transferred; its balance is transferred to the capital account (or retained earnings for a corporation). *(p. 143)*

Incremental cost Additional cost incurred only if a company pursues a specific course of action. *(p. 1048)*

Indefinite life Asset life that is not limited by legal, regulatory, contractual, competitive, economic, or other factors. *(p. 409)*

Indirect costs Costs incurred for the benefit of more than one cost object. *(p. 737)*

Indirect expenses Expenses incurred for the joint benefit of more than one department (or cost object). *(p. 865)*

Indirect labor Efforts of production employees who do not work specifically on converting direct materials into finished products and who are not clearly identified with specific units or batches of product. *(p. 742)*

Indirect labor costs Labor costs that cannot be physically traced to production of a product or service; included as part of overhead. *(p. 742)*

Indirect material Material used to support the production process but not clearly identified with products or batches of product. *(p. 740)*

Indirect method Presentation that reports net income and then adjusts it by adding and subtracting items to yield net cash from operating activities on the statement of cash flows. *(p. 638)*

Information processor Component of an accounting system that interprets, transforms, and summarizes information for use in analysis and reporting. *(p. 274)*

Information storage Component of an accounting system that keeps data in a form accessible to information processors. *(p. 274)*

Infrequent gain or loss Gain or loss not expected to recur given the operating environment of the business. *(p. 710)*

Input device Means of capturing information from source documents that enables its transfer to information processors. *(p. 274)*

Installment note Liability requiring a series of periodic payments to the lender. *(p. 562)*

Institute of Management Accountants (IMA) A professional association of management accountants. *(p. 736)*

Intangible assets Long-term assets (resources) used to produce or sell products or services; usually lack physical form and have uncertain benefits. *(pp. 149 & 409)*

Interest Charge for using money (or other assets) loaned from one entity to another. *(p. 370)*

Interim financial statements Financial statements covering periods of less than one year; usually based on one-, three-, or six-month periods. *(pp. 94 & 251)*

Internal controls or **Internal control system** All policies and procedures used to protect assets, ensure reliable accounting, promote efficient operations, and urge adherence to company policies. *(pp. 272 & 736)*

Internal rate of return (IRR) Rate used to evaluate the acceptability of an investment; equals the rate that yields a net present value of zero for an investment. *(p. 1043)*

Internal transactions Activities within an organization that can affect the accounting equation. *(p. 15)*

Internal users Persons using accounting information who are directly involved in managing the organization. *(p. 6)*

International Accounting Standards Board (IASB) Group that identifies preferred accounting practices and encourages global acceptance; issues International Financial Reporting Standards (IFRS). *(p. 9)*

International Financial Reporting Standards (IFRS) International Financial Reporting Standards (IFRS) are required or allowed by over 100 countries; IFRS is set by the International Accounting Standards Board (IASB), which aims to develop a single set of global standards, to promote those standards, and to converge national and international standards globally. *(p. 9)*

Inventory Goods a company owns and expects to sell in its normal operations. *(p. 181)*

Inventory turnover Number of times a company's average inventory is sold during a period; computed by dividing cost of goods sold by average inventory; also called *merchandise turnover*. *(p. 241)*

Investing activities Transactions that involve purchasing and selling of long-term assets; includes making and collecting notes receivable and investments in other than cash equivalents. *(p. 634)*

Investment center Center of which a manager is responsible for revenues, costs, and asset investments. *(p. 865)*

Investment center residual income The net income an investment center earns above a target return on average invested assets. *(p. 873)*

Investment center return on total assets Center net income divided by average total assets for the center. *(p. 873)*

Investment turnover The efficiency with which a company generates sales from its available assets; computed as sales divided by average invested assets. *(p. 878)*

Invoice Itemized record of goods prepared by the vendor that lists the customer's name, items sold, sales prices, and terms of sale. *(p. 339)*

Invoice approval Document containing a checklist of steps necessary for approving the recording and payment of an invoice; also called *check authorization*. *(p. 339)*

Job Production of a customized product or service. *(p. 776)*

Job cost sheet Separate record maintained for each job. *(p. 778)*

Job lot Production of more than one unit of a customized product or service. *(p. 777)*

Job order cost accounting system Cost accounting system to determine the cost of producing each job or job lot. *(pp. 778 & 817)*

Job order production Production of special-order products; also called *customized production*. *(p. 776)*

Joint cost Cost incurred to produce or purchase two or more products at the same time. *(p. 883)*

Journal Record in which transactions are entered before they are posted to ledger accounts; also called *book of original entry*. *(p. 56)*

Journalizing Process of recording transactions in a journal. *(p. 56)*

Just-in-time (JIT) manufacturing Process of acquiring or producing inventory only when needed. *(p. 748)*

Known liabilities Obligations of a company with little uncertainty; set by agreements, contracts, or laws; also called *definitely determinable liabilities*. *(p. 438)*

Land improvements Assets that increase the benefits of land, have a limited useful life, and are depreciated. *(p. 396)*

Large stock dividend Stock dividend that is more than 25% of the previously outstanding shares. *(p. 516)*

Last-in, first-out (LIFO) Method to assign cost to inventory that assumes costs for the most recent items purchased are sold first and charged to cost of goods sold. *(p. 233)*

Lean business model Practice of eliminating waste while meeting customer needs and yielding positive company returns. *(p. 747)*

Lease Contract specifying the rental of property. *(pp. 411 & 576)*

Leasehold Rights the lessor grants to the lessee under the terms of a lease. *(p. 411)*

Leasehold improvements Alterations or improvements to leased property such as partitions and storefronts. *(p. 411)*

Least-squares regression Statistical method for deriving an estimated line of cost behavior that is more precise than the high-low method and the scatter diagram. *(p. 913)*

Ledger Record containing all accounts (with amounts) for a business; also called *general ledger*. *(p. 51)*

Lessee Party to a lease who secures the right to possess and use the property from another party (the lessor). *(p. 411)*

Lessor Party to a lease who grants another party (the lessee) the right to possess and use its property. *(p. 411)*

Liabilities Creditors' claims on an organization's assets; involves a probable future payment of assets, products, or services that a company is obligated to make due to past transactions or events. *(p. 14)*

Licenses (See *franchises.*) *(p. 410)*

Limited liability Owner can lose no more than the amount invested. *(p. 11)*

Limited liability company Organization form that combines select features of a corporation and a limited partnership; provides limited liability to its members (owners), is free of business tax, and allows members to actively participate in management. *(p. 482)*

Limited liability partnership Partnership in which a partner is not personally liable for malpractice or negligence unless that partner is responsible for providing the service that resulted in the claim. *(p. 481)*

Limited life (See *useful life.*)

Limited partners Partners who have no personal liability for partnership debts beyond the amounts they invested in the partnership. *(p. 481)*

Limited partnership Partnership that has two classes of partners, limited partners and general partners. *(p. 481)*

Liquid assets Resources such as cash that are easily converted into other assets or used to pay for goods, services, or liabilities. *(p. 321)*

Liquidating cash dividend Distribution of assets that returns part of the original investment to stockholders; deducted from contributed capital accounts. *(p. 516)*

Liquidation Process of going out of business; involves selling assets, paying liabilities, and distributing remainder to owners.

Liquidity Availability of resources to meet short-term cash requirements. *(pp. 321 & 687)*

List price Catalog (full) price of an item before any trade discount is deducted. *(p. 182)*

Long-term investments Long-term assets not used in operating activities such as notes receivable and investments in stocks and bonds. *(pp. 149 & 596)*

Long-term liabilities Obligations not due to be paid within one year or the operating cycle, whichever is longer. *(pp. 149 & 437)*

Lower of cost or market (LCM) Required method to report inventory at market replacement cost when that market cost is lower than recorded cost. *(p. 237)*

Maker of the note Entity who signs a note and promises to pay it at maturity. *(p. 370)*

Management by exception Management process to focus on significant variances and give less attention to areas where performance is close to the standard. *(p. 995)*

Managerial accounting Area of accounting aimed mainly at serving the decision-making needs of internal users; also called *management accounting*. *(pp. 6 & 732)*

Manufacturer Company that uses labor and operating assets to convert raw materials to finished goods.

Manufacturing budget Plan that shows the predicted costs for direct materials, direct labor, and overhead to be incurred in manufacturing units in the production budget. *(p. 966)*

Manufacturing statement Report that summarizes the types and amounts of costs incurred in a company's production process for a period; also called *cost of goods manufacturing statement*. *(p. 745)*

Margin of safety Excess of expected sales over the level of break-even sales. *(p. 920)*

Market-based transfer price The market price of a good or service being transferred between divisions within a company; typically used when the transferring division does not have excess capacity. *(p. 883)*

Market prospects Expectations (both good and bad) about a company's future performance as assessed by users and other interested parties. *(p. 687)*

Market rate Interest rate that borrowers are willing to pay and lenders are willing to accept for a specific lending agreement given the borrowers' risk level. *(p. 555)*

Market value per share Price at which stock is bought or sold. *(p. 511)*

Master budget Comprehensive business plan that includes specific plans for expected sales, product units to be produced, merchandise (or materials) to be purchased, expenses to be incurred, plant assets to be purchased, and amounts of cash to be borrowed or loans to be repaid, as well as a budgeted income statement and balance sheet. *(p. 950)*

Matching (or expense recognition) principle Prescribes expenses to be reported in the same period as the revenues that were earned as a result of the expenses. *(pp. 11 & 364)*

Materiality constraint Prescribes that accounting for items that significantly impact financial statement and any inferences from them adhere strictly to GAAP. *(pp. 12 & 364)*

Materials consumption report Document that summarizes the materials a department uses during a reporting period; replaces materials requisitions. *(p. 818)*

Materials ledger card Perpetual record updated each time units are purchased or issued for production use. *(p. 780)*

Materials requisition Source document production managers use to request materials for production; used to assign materials costs to specific jobs or overhead. *(p. 781)*

Maturity date of a note Date when a note's principal and interest are due. *(p. 370)*

Measurement principle Accounting information is based on cost with potential subsequent adjustments to fair value; see also *cost principle*. *(p. 10)*

Merchandise (See *merchandise inventory*.) *(p. 180)*

Merchandise inventory Goods that a company owns and expects to sell to customers; also called *merchandise* or *inventory*. *(p. 181)*

Merchandise purchases budget Plan that shows the units or costs of merchandise to be purchased by a merchandising company during the budget period. *(p. 953)*

Merchandiser Entity that earns net income by buying and selling merchandise. *(p. 180)*

Merit rating Rating assigned to an employer by a state based on the employer's record of employment. *(p. 444)*

Minimum legal capital Amount of assets defined by law that stockholders must (potentially) invest in a corporation; usually defined as par value of the stock; intended to protect creditors. *(p. 511)*

Mixed cost Cost that behaves like a combination of fixed and variable costs. *(p. 909)*

Modified Accelerated Cost Recovery System (MACRS) Depreciation system required by federal income tax law. *(p. 402)*

Monetary unit assumption Principle that assumes transactions and events can be expressed in money units. *(p. 11)*

Mortgage Legal loan agreement that protects a lender by giving the lender the right to be paid from the cash proceeds from the sale of a borrower's assets identified in the mortgage. *(p. 564)*

Multinational Company that operates in several countries. *(p. 610)*

Multiple-step income statement Income statement format that shows subtotals between sales and net income, categorizes expenses, and often reports the details of net sales and expenses. *(p. 192)*

Mutual agency Legal relationship among partners whereby each partner is an agent of the partnership and is able to bind the partnership to contracts within the scope of the partnership's business. *(p. 480)*

Natural business year Twelve-month period that ends when a company's sales activities are at their lowest point. *(p. 95)*

Natural resources Assets physically consumed when used; examples are timber, mineral deposits, and oil and gas fields; also called *wasting assets*. *(p. 408)*

Negotiated transfer price A price, determined by negotiation between division managers, to record transfers between divisions; typically lies between the variable cost and the market price of the item transferred. *(p. 883)*

Net assets (See *equity*.)

Net income Amount earned after subtracting all expenses necessary for and matched with sales for a period; also called *income, profit,* or *earnings*. *(p. 14)*

Net loss Excess of expenses over revenues for a period. *(p. 14)*

Net method Method of recording purchases at the full invoice price less any cash discounts. *(p. 341)*

Net pay Gross pay less all deductions; also called *take-home pay*. *(p. 442)*

Net present value (NPV) Dollar estimate of an asset's value that is used to evaluate the acceptability of an investment; computed by discounting future cash flows from the investment at a satisfactory rate and then subtracting the initial cost of the investment. *(p. 1041)*

Net realizable value Expected selling price (value) of an item minus the cost of making the sale. *(p. 228)*

Noncumulative preferred stock Preferred stock on which the right to receive dividends is lost for any period when dividends are not declared. *(p. 519)*

Noninterest-bearing note Note with no stated (contract) rate of interest; interest is implicitly included in the note's face value.

Nonparticipating preferred stock Preferred stock on which dividends are limited to a maximum amount each year. *(p. 520)*

Nonsufficient funds (NSF) check Maker's bank account has insufficient money to pay the check; also called *hot check*.

Non-value-added time The portion of cycle time that is not directed at producing a product or service; equals the sum of inspection time, move time, and wait time. *(p. 750)*

No-par value stock Stock class that has not been assigned a par (or stated) value by the corporate charter. *(p. 511)*

Not controllable costs Costs that a manager does not have the power to control or strongly influence. *(p. 737)*

Note (See *promissory note*.)

Note payable Liability expressed by a written promise to pay a definite sum of money on demand or on a specific future date(s).

Note receivable Asset consisting of a written promise to receive a definite sum of money on demand or on a specific future date(s).

Objectivity principle Principle that prescribes independent, unbiased evidence to support financial statement information. *(p. 9)*

Obsolescence Condition in which, because of new inventions and improvements, a plant asset can no longer be used to produce goods or services with a competitive advantage. *(p. 397)*

Off-balance-sheet financing Acquisition of assets by agreeing to liabilities not reported on the balance sheet. *(p. 577)*

Online processing Approach to inputting data from source documents as soon as the information is available. *(p. 286)*

Operating activities Activities that involve the production or purchase of merchandise and the sale of goods or services to customers, including expenditures related to administering the business. *(p. 633)*

Operating cycle Normal time between paying cash for merchandise or employee services and receiving cash from customers. *(p. 147)*

Operating leases Short-term (or cancelable) leases in which the lessor retains risks and rewards of ownership. *(p. 576)*

Operating leverage Extent, or relative size, of fixed costs in the total cost structure. *(p. 924)*

Opportunity cost Potential benefit lost by choosing a specific action from two or more alternatives. *(p. 738)*

Ordinary repairs Repairs to keep a plant asset in normal, good operating condition; treated as a revenue expenditure and immediately expensed. *(p. 404)*

Organization expenses (costs) Costs such as legal fees and promoter fees to bring an entity into existence. *(pp. 509 & 514)*

Other comprehensive income Equals net income less comprehensive income; includes unrealized gains and losses on available-for-sale securities, foreign currency adjustments, and pension adjustments. *(p. 604)*

Out-of-pocket cost Cost incurred or avoided as a result of management's decisions. *(p. 738)*

Output devices Means by which information is taken out of the accounting system and made available for use. *(p. 275)*

Outsourcing Manager decision to buy a product or service from another part of a *make-or-buy* decision; also called *make or buy*.

Outstanding checks Checks written and recorded by the depositor but not yet paid by the bank at the bank statement date. *(p. 331)*

Outstanding stock Corporation's stock held by its shareholders.

Overapplied overhead Amount by which the overhead applied to production in a period using the predetermined overhead rate exceeds the actual overhead incurred in a period. *(p. 787)*

Overhead cost variance Difference between the total overhead cost applied to products and the total overhead cost actually incurred. *(p. 1002)*

Owner, Capital Account showing the owner's claim on company assets; equals owner investments plus net income (or less net losses) minus owner withdrawals since the company's inception; also referred to as *equity*. *(p. 14)*

Owner investment Assets put into the business by the owner. *(p. 14)*

Owner's equity (See *equity*.)

Owner, withdrawals Account used to record asset distributions to the owner. (See also *withdrawals*.) *(p. 14)*

Paid-in capital (See *contributed capital*.) *(p. 512)*

Paid-in capital in excess of par value Amount received from issuance of stock that is in excess of the stock's par value. *(p. 513)*

Par value Value assigned a share of stock by the corporate charter when the stock is authorized. *(p. 511)*

Par value of a bond Amount the bond issuer agrees to pay at maturity and the amount on which cash interest payments are based; also called *face amount* or *face value* of a bond. *(p. 552)*

Par value stock Class of stock assigned a par value by the corporate charter. *(p. 511)*

Parent Company that owns a controlling interest in a corporation (requires more than 50% of voting stock). *(p. 603)*

Participating preferred stock Preferred stock that shares with common stockholders any dividends paid in excess of the percent stated on preferred stock. *(p. 520)*

Partner return on equity Partner net income divided by average partner equity for the period. *(p. 492)*

Partnership Unincorporated association of two or more persons to pursue a business for profit as co-owners. *(pp. 11 & 480)*

Partnership contract Agreement among partners that sets terms under which the affairs of the partnership are conducted; also called *articles of partnership*. *(p. 480)*

Partnership liquidation Dissolution of a partnership by (1) selling noncash assets and allocating any gain or loss according to partners' income-and-loss ratio, (2) paying liabilities, and (3) distributing any remaining cash according to partners' capital balances. *(p. 489)*

Patent Exclusive right granted to its owner to produce and sell an item or to use a process for 20 years. *(p. 410)*

Payback period (PBP) Time-based measurement used to evaluate the acceptability of an investment; equals the time expected to pass before an investment's net cash flows equal its initial cost. *(p. 1037)*

Payee of the note Entity to whom a note is made payable. *(p. 370)*

Payroll bank account Bank account used solely for paying employees; each pay period an amount equal to the total employees' net pay is deposited in it and the payroll checks are drawn on it. *(p. 458)*

Payroll deductions Amounts withheld from an employee's gross pay; also called *withholdings*. *(p. 442)*

Payroll register Record for a pay period that shows the pay period dates, regular and overtime hours worked, gross pay, net pay, and deductions. *(p. 455)*

Pension plan Contractual agreement between an employer and its employees for the employer to provide benefits to employees after they retire; expensed when incurred. *(p. 578)*

Period costs Expenditures identified more with a time period than with finished products costs; includes selling and general administrative expenses. *(p. 738)*

Periodic inventory system Method that records the cost of inventory purchased but does not continuously track the quantity available or sold to customers; records are updated at the end of each period to reflect the physical count and costs of goods available. *(p. 182)*

Permanent accounts Accounts that reflect activities related to one or more future periods; balance sheet accounts whose balances are not closed; also called *real accounts*. *(p. 142)*

Perpetual inventory system Method that maintains continuous records of the cost of inventory available and the cost of goods sold. *(p. 182)*

Petty cash Small amount of cash in a fund to pay minor expenses; accounted for using an imprest system. *(p. 326)*

Planning Process of setting goals and preparing to achieve them. *(p. 732)*

Plant asset age Estimate of the age of a company's plant assets, computed by dividing accumulated depreciation by depreciation expense. *(p. 413)*

Plant assets Tangible long-lived assets used to produce or sell products and services; also called *property, plant and equipment (PP&E)* or *fixed assets*. *(pp. 99 & 394)*

Pledged assets to secured liabilities Ratio of the book value of a company's pledged assets to the book value of its secured liabilities.

Post-closing trial balance List of permanent accounts and their balances from the ledger after all closing entries are journalized and posted. *(p. 146)*

Posting Process of transferring journal entry information to the ledger; computerized systems automate this process. *(p. 56)*

Posting reference (PR) column A column in journals in which individual ledger account numbers are entered when entries are posted to those ledger accounts. *(p. 58)*

Predetermined overhead rate Rate established prior to the beginning of a period that relates estimated overhead to another variable, such as estimated direct labor, and is used to assign overhead cost to production. *(p. 784)*

Preemptive right Stockholders' right to maintain their proportionate interest in a corporation with any additional shares issued. *(p. 510)*

Preferred stock Stock with a priority status over common stockholders in one or more ways, such as paying dividends or distributing assets. *(p. 518)*

Premium on bonds Difference between a bond's par value and its higher carrying value; occurs when the contract rate is higher than the market rate; also called *bond premium*. *(p. 558)*

Premium on stock (See *contributed capital in excess of par value*.) *(p. 513)*

Prepaid expenses Items paid for in advance of receiving their benefits; classified as assets. *(p. 97)*

Price-earnings (PE) ratio Ratio of a company's current market value per share to its earnings per share; also called *price-to-earnings*. *(p. 527)*

Price variance Difference between actual and budgeted revenue or cost caused by the difference between the actual price per unit and the budgeted price per unit. *(p. 995)*

Prime costs Expenditures directly identified with the production of finished goods; include direct materials costs and direct labor costs. *(p. 743)*

Principal of a note Amount that the signer of a note agrees to pay back when it matures, not including interest. *(p. 370)*

Principles of internal control Principles prescribing management to establish responsibility, maintain records, insure assets, separate record-keeping from custody of assets, divide responsibility for related transactions, apply technological controls, and perform reviews. *(p. 317)*

Prior period adjustment Correction of an error in a prior year that is reported in the statement of retained earnings (or statement of stockholders' equity) net of any income tax effects. *(p. 525)*

Pro forma financial statements Statements that show the effects of proposed transactions and events as if they had occurred. *(p. 142)*

Process cost accounting system System of assigning direct materials, direct labor, and overhead to specific processes; total costs associated with each process are then divided by the number of units passing through that process to determine the cost per equivalent unit. *(p. 817)*

Process cost summary Report of costs charged to a department, its equivalent units of production achieved, and the costs assigned to its output. *(p. 826)*

Process operations Processing of products in a continuous (sequential) flow of steps; also called *process manufacturing* or *process production*. *(p. 814)*

Product costs Costs that are capitalized as inventory because they produce benefits expected to have future value; include direct materials, direct labor, and overhead. *(p. 738)*

Production budget Plan that shows the units to be produced each period. *(p. 966)*

Profit (See *net income.*)

Profit center Business unit that incurs costs and generates revenues. *(p. 865)*

Profit margin Ratio of a company's net income to its net sales; the percent of income in each dollar of revenue; also called *net profit margin.* *(pp. 109 & 878)*

Profitability Company's ability to generate an adequate return on invested capital. *(p. 687)*

Profitability index A measure of the relation between the expected benefits of a project and its investment, computed as the present value of expected future cash flows from the investment divided by the cost of the investment; a higher value indicates a more desirable investment, and a value below 1 indicates an unacceptable project. *(p. 1043)*

Promissory note (or **note**) Written promise to pay a specified amount either on demand or at a definite future date; is a *note receivable* for the lender but a *note payable* for the lendee. *(p. 370)*

Proprietorship (See *sole proprietorship.*) *(p. 11)*

Proxy Legal document giving a stockholder's agent the power to exercise the stockholder's voting rights. *(p. 509)*

Purchase discount Term used by a purchaser to describe a cash discount granted to the purchaser for paying within the discount period. *(p. 183)*

Purchase order Document used by the purchasing department to place an order with a seller (vendor). *(p. 338)*

Purchase requisition Document listing merchandise needed by a department and requesting it be purchased. *(p. 338)*

Purchases journal Journal normally used to record all purchases on credit. *(p. 283)*

Quantity variance Difference between actual and budgeted revenue or cost caused by the difference between the actual number of units and the budgeted number of units. *(p. 995)*

Ratio analysis Determination of key relations between financial statement items as reflected in numerical measures. *(p. 688)*

Raw materials inventory Goods a company acquires to use in making products. *(p. 740)*

Realizable value Expected proceeds from converting an asset into cash. *(p. 365)*

Receiving report Form used to report that ordered goods are received and to describe their quantity and condition. *(p. 339)*

Recordkeeping Part of accounting that involves recording transactions and events, either manually or electronically; also called *bookkeeping.* *(p. 4)*

Registered bonds Bonds owned by investors whose names and addresses are recorded by the issuer; interest payments are made to the registered owners. *(p. 566)*

Relevance principle Information system principle prescribing that its reports be useful, understandable, timely, and pertinent for decision making. *(p. 272)*

Relevant benefits Additional or incremental revenue generated by selecting a particular course of action over another. *(p. 1047)*

Relevant range of operations Company's normal operating range; excludes extremely high and low volumes not likely to occur. *(p. 917)*

Report form balance sheet Balance sheet that lists accounts vertically in the order of assets, liabilities, and equity.

Responsibility accounting budget Report of expected costs and expenses under a manager's control. *(p. 876)*

Responsibility accounting performance report Responsibility report that compares actual costs and expenses for a department with budgeted amounts. *(p. 876)*

Responsibility accounting system System that provides information that management can use to evaluate the performance of a department's manager. *(p. 864)*

Restricted retained earnings Retained earnings not available for dividends because of legal or contractual limitations. *(p. 524)*

Retail inventory method Method to estimate ending inventory based on the ratio of the amount of goods for sale at cost to the amount of goods for sale at retail. *(p. 251)*

Retailer Intermediary that buys products from manufacturers or wholesalers and sells them to consumers. *(p. 180)*

Retained earnings Cumulative income less cumulative losses and dividends. *(p. 512)*

Retained earnings deficit Debit (abnormal) balance in Retained Earnings; occurs when cumulative losses and dividends exceed cumulative income; also called *accumulated deficit.* *(p. 515)*

Return Monies received from an investment; often in percent form. *(p. 26)*

Return on assets (See *return on total assets*) *(p. 22)*

Return on equity Ratio of net income to average equity for the period.

Return on total assets Ratio reflecting operating efficiency; defined as net income divided by average total assets for the period; also called *return on assets* or *return on investment.* *(p. 605)*

Revenue expenditures Expenditures reported on the current income statement as an expense because they do not provide benefits in future periods. *(p. 404)*

Revenue recognition principle The principle prescribing that revenue is recognized when earned. *(p. 10)*

Revenues Gross increase in equity from a company's business activities that earn income; also called *sales.* *(p. 14)*

Reverse stock split Occurs when a corporation calls in its stock and replaces each share with less than one new share; increases both market value per share and any par or stated value per share. *(p. 518)*

Reversing entries Optional entries recorded at the beginning of a period that prepare the accounts for the usual journal entries as if adjusting entries had not occurred in the prior period. *(p. 154)*

Risk Uncertainty about an expected return. *(p. 26)*

Rolling budget New set of budgets a firm adds for the next period (with revisions) to replace the ones that have lapsed. *(p. 949)*

S corporation Corporation that meets special tax qualifications so as to be treated like a partnership for income tax purposes. *(p. 482)*

Safety stock Quantity of inventory or materials over the minimum needed to satisfy budgeted demand. *(p. 953)*

Sales (See *revenues*.)

Sales budget Plan showing the units of goods to be sold or services to be provided; the starting point in the budgeting process for most departments. *(p. 952)*

Sales discount Term used by a seller to describe a cash discount granted to buyers who pay within the discount period. *(p. 183)*

Sales journal Journal normally used to record sales of goods on credit. *(p. 278)*

Sales mix Ratio of sales volumes for the various products sold by a company. *(p. 921)*

Salvage value Estimate of amount to be recovered at the end of an asset's useful life; also called *residual value* or *scrap value*. *(p. 397)*

Sarbanes-Oxley Act (SOX) Created the *Public Company Accounting Oversight Board*, regulates analyst conflicts, imposes corporate governance requirements, enhances accounting and control disclosures, impacts insider transactions and executive loans, establishes new types of criminal conduct, and expands penalties for violations of federal securities laws. *(pp. 12 & 316)*

Scatter diagram Graph used to display data about past cost behavior and sales as points on a diagram. *(p. 911)*

Schedule of accounts payable List of the balances of all accounts in the accounts payable ledger and their totals. *(p. 284)*

Schedule of accounts receivable List of the balances of all accounts in the accounts receivable ledger and their totals. *(p. 279)*

Section 404 (of SOX) Section 404 of SOX requires that company management document and assess the effectiveness of all internal control processes that can affect financial reporting; company auditors express an opinion on whether management's assessment of the effectiveness of internal controls is fairly stated. *(p. 317)*

Secured bonds Bonds that have specific assets of the issuer pledged as collateral. *(p. 566)*

Securities and Exchange Commission (SEC) Federal agency Congress has charged to set reporting rules for organizations that sell ownership shares to the public. *(p. 9)*

Segment return on assets Segment operating income divided by segment average (identifiable) assets for the period. *(p. 288)*

Selling expense budget Plan that lists the types and amounts of selling expenses expected in the budget period. *(p. 954)*

Selling expenses Expenses of promoting sales, such as displaying and advertising merchandise, making sales, and delivering goods to customers. *(p. 193)*

Serial bonds Bonds consisting of separate amounts that mature at different dates. *(p. 566)*

Service company Organization that provides services instead of tangible products.

Shareholders Owners of a corporation; also called *stockholders*. *(p. 12)*

Shares Equity of a corporation divided into ownership units; also called *stock*. *(p. 12)*

Short-term investments Debt and equity securities that management expects to convert to cash within the next 3 to 12 months (or the operating cycle if longer); also called *temporary investments* or *marketable securities*. *(p. 596)*

Short-term note payable Current obligation in the form of a written promissory note. *(p. 439)*

Shrinkage Inventory losses that occur as a result of theft or deterioration. *(p. 190)*

Signature card Includes the signatures of each person authorized to sign checks on the bank account. *(p. 328)*

Simple capital structure Capital structure that consists of only common stock and nonconvertible preferred stock; consists of no dilutive securities. *(p. 527)*

Single-step income statement Income statement format that includes cost of goods sold as an expense and shows only one subtotal for total expenses. *(p. 193)*

Sinking fund bonds Bonds that require the issuer to make deposits to a separate account; bondholders are repaid at maturity from that account. *(p. 566)*

Small stock dividend Stock dividend that is 25% or less of a corporation's previously outstanding shares. *(p. 516)*

Social responsibility Being accountable for the impact that one's actions might have on society. *(p. 8)*

Sole proprietorship Business owned by one person that is not organized as a corporation; also called *proprietorship*. *(p. 11)*

Solvency Company's long-run financial viability and its ability to cover long-term obligations. *(p. 687)*

Source documents Source of information for accounting entries that can be in either paper or electronic form; also called *business papers*. *(p. 50)*

Special journal Any journal used for recording and posting transactions of a similar type. *(p. 276)*

Specific identification Method to assign cost to inventory when the purchase cost of each item in inventory is identified and used to compute cost of inventory. *(p. 231)*

Spending variance Difference between the actual price of an item and its standard price. *(p. 1010)*

Spreadsheet Computer program that organizes data by means of formulas and format; also called *electronic work sheet*.

Standard costs Costs that should be incurred under normal conditions to produce a product or component or to perform a service. *(p. 995)*

State Unemployment Taxes (SUTA) State payroll taxes on employers to support its unemployment programs. *(p. 444)*

Stated value stock No-par stock assigned a stated value per share; this amount is recorded in the stock account when the stock is issued. *(p. 512)*

Statement of cash flows A financial statement that lists cash inflows (receipts) and cash outflows (payments) during a period; arranged by operating, investing, and financing. *(pp. 19 & 632)*

Statement of owner's equity Report of changes in equity over a period; adjusted for increases (owner investment and net income) and for decreases (withdrawals and net loss). *(p. 19)*

Statement of partners' equity Financial statement that shows total capital balances at the beginning of the period, any additional investment by partners, the income or loss of the period, the partners' withdrawals, and the partners' ending capital balances; also called *statement of partners' capital*. *(p. 485)*

Statement of retained earnings Report of changes in retained earnings over a period; adjusted for increases (net income), for decreases (dividends and net loss), and for any prior period adjustment.

Statement of stockholders' equity Financial statement that lists the beginning and ending balances of each major equity account and describes all changes in those accounts. *(p. 525)*

Statements of Financial Accounting Standards (SFAS) FASB publications that establish U.S. GAAP.

Step-wise cost Cost that remains fixed over limited ranges of volumes but changes by a lump sum when volume changes occur outside these limited ranges. *(p. 910)*.

Stock (See *shares*.) *(p. 12)*

Stock dividend Corporation's distribution of its own stock to its stockholders without the receipt of any payment. *(p. 516)*

Stock options Rights to purchase common stock at a fixed price over a specified period of time. *(p. 525)*

Stock split Occurs when a corporation calls in its stock and replaces each share with more than one new share; decreases both the market value per share and any par or stated value per share. *(p. 518)*

Stock subscription Investor's contractual commitment to purchase unissued shares at future dates and prices.

Stockholders (See *shareholders*.) *(p. 12)*

Stockholders' equity A corporation's equity; also called *shareholders' equity* or *corporate capital*. *(p. 512)*

Straight-line depreciation Method that allocates an equal portion of the depreciable cost of plant asset (cost minus salvage) to each accounting period in its useful life. *(pp. 99 & 398)*

Straight-line bond amortization Method allocating an equal amount of bond interest expense to each period of the bond life. *(p. 556)*

Subsidiary Entity controlled by another entity (parent) in which the parent owns more than 50% of the subsidiary's voting stock. *(p. 603)*

Subsidiary ledger List of individual subaccounts and amounts with a common characteristic; linked to a controlling account in the general ledger. *(p. 276)*

Sunk cost Cost already incurred and cannot be avoided or changed. *(p. 738)*

Supplementary records Information outside the usual accounting records; also called *supplemental records*. *(p. 186)*

Supply chain Linkages of services or goods extending from suppliers, to the company itself, and on to customers.

T-account Tool used to show the effects of transactions and events on individual accounts. *(p. 55)*

Target cost Maximum allowable cost for a product or service; defined as expected selling price less the desired profit. *(p. 777)*

Temporary accounts Accounts used to record revenues, expenses, and withdrawals (dividends for a corporation); they are closed at the end of each period; also called *nominal accounts*. *(p. 142)*

Term bonds Bonds scheduled for payment (maturity) at a single specified date. *(p. 566)*

Throughput time (See *cycle time*.)

Time period assumption Assumption that an organization's activities can be divided into specific time periods such as months, quarters, or years. *(pp. 11 & 94)*

Time ticket Source document used to report the time an employee spent working on a job or on overhead activities and then to determine the amount of direct labor to charge to the job or the amount of indirect labor to charge to overhead. *(p. 782)*

Times interest earned Ratio of income before interest expense (and any income taxes) divided by interest expense; reflects risk of covering interest commitments when income varies. *(p. 450)*

Total asset turnover Measure of a company's ability to use its assets to generate sales; computed by dividing net sales by average total assets. *(p. 413)*

Total quality management (TQM) Concept calling for all managers and employees at all stages of operations to strive toward higher standards and reduce number of defects. *(p. 748)*

Trade discount Reduction from a list or catalog price that can vary for wholesalers, retailers, and consumers. *(p. 182)*

Trademark or **trade (brand) name** Symbol, name, phrase, or jingle identified with a company, product, or service. *(p. 411)*

Trading on the equity (See *financial leverage*.)

Trading securities Investments in debt and equity securities that the company intends to actively trade for profit. *(p. 599)*

Transfer price The price used to record transfers of goods or services between divisions in the same company. *(p. 882)*

Transaction Exchange of economic consideration affecting an entity's financial position that can be reliably measured.

Treasury stock Corporation's own stock that it reacquired and still holds. *(p. 522)*

Trial balance List of accounts and their balances at a point in time; total debit balances equal total credit balances. *(p. 65)*

Unadjusted trial balance List of accounts and balances prepared before accounting adjustments are recorded and posted. *(p. 106)*

Unavoidable expense Expense (or cost) that is not relevant for business decisions; an expense that would continue even if a department, product, or service is eliminated. *(p. 1053)*

Unclassified balance sheet Balance sheet that broadly groups assets, liabilities, and equity accounts. *(p. 147)*

Uncontrollable costs Costs that a manager does not have the power to determine or strongly influence. *(p. 875)*

Underapplied overhead Amount by which overhead incurred in a period exceeds the overhead applied to that period's production using the predetermined overhead rate. *(p. 787)*

Unearned revenue Liability created when customers pay in advance for products or services; earned when the products or services are later delivered. *(pp. 52 & 100)*

Unfavorable variance Difference in revenues or costs, when the actual amount is compared to the budgeted amount, that contributes to a lower income.

Unit contribution margin Amount a product's unit selling price exceeds its total unit variable cost.

Units-of-production depreciation Method that charges a varying amount to depreciation expense for each period of an asset's useful life depending on its usage. *(p. 399)*

Unlimited liability Legal relationship among general partners that makes each of them responsible for partnership debts if the other partners are unable to pay their shares. *(p. 481)*

Unrealized gain (loss) Gain (loss) not yet realized by an actual transaction or event such as a sale. *(p. 599)*

Unsecured bonds Bonds backed only by the issuer's credit standing; almost always riskier than secured bonds; also called *debentures*. *(p. 566)*

Unusual gain or loss Gain or loss that is abnormal or unrelated to the company's ordinary activities and environment. *(p. 710)*

Useful life Length of time an asset will be productively used in the operations of a business; also called *service life* or *limited life*. *(p. 397)*

Value-added time The portion of cycle time that is directed at producing a product or service; equals process time. *(p. 750)*

Value chain Sequential activities that add value to an entity's products or services; includes design, production, marketing, distribution, and service. *(p. 748)*

Variable cost Cost that changes in proportion to changes in the activity output volume. *(p. 736)*

Variable costing income statement An income statement which reports variable costs and fixed costs separately; also called a *contribution margin income statement*. *(p. 915)*

Variance analysis Process of examining differences between actual and budgeted revenues or costs and describing them in terms of price and quantity differences. *(p. 995)*

Vendee Buyer of goods or services. *(p. 339)*

Vendor Seller of goods or services. *(p. 338)*

Vertical analysis Evaluation of each financial statement item or group of items in terms of a specific base amount. *(p. 688)*

Volume variance Difference between two dollar amounts of fixed overhead cost; one amount is the total budgeted overhead cost, and the other is the overhead cost allocated to products using the predetermined fixed overhead rate. *(p. 1003)*

Voucher Internal file used to store documents and information to control cash disbursements and to ensure that a transaction is properly authorized and recorded. *(p. 325)*

Voucher register Journal (referred to as *book of original entry*) in which all vouchers are recorded after they have been approved. *(p. 340)*

Voucher system Procedures and approvals designed to control cash disbursements and acceptance of obligations. *(p. 324)*

Wage bracket withholding table Table of the amounts of income tax withheld from employees' wages. *(p. 458)*

Warranty Agreement that obligates the seller to correct or replace a product or service when it fails to perform properly within a specified period. *(p. 446)*

Weighted average Method to assign inventory cost to sales; the cost of available-for-sale units is divided by the number of units available to determine per unit cost prior to each sale that is then multiplied by the units sold to yield the cost of that sale. *(pp. 234 & 824)*

Weighted-average contribution margin Contribution margin for a multiproduct company; computed based on each products' percentage of the company's sales mix. *(p. 922)*

Weighted-average method (See *weighted average*.)

Wholesaler Intermediary that buys products from manufacturers or other wholesalers and sells them to retailers or other wholesalers. *(p. 180)*

Withdrawals Payment of cash or other assets from a proprietorship or partnership to its owner or owners. *(p. 14)*

Work sheet Spreadsheet used to draft an unadjusted trial balance, adjusting entries, adjusted trial balance, and financial statements. *(p. 138)*

Working capital Current assets minus current liabilities at a point in time. *(p. 697)*

Working papers Analyses and other informal reports prepared by accountants and managers when organizing information for formal reports and financial statements. *(p. 138)*

Credits

Note: Page numbers followed by *n* indicate information found in footnotes; **boldface** entries indicate defined terms.

A Rose by Any Other Name

The same financial statement sometimes receives different titles. Following are some of the more common aliases.*

Balance Sheet	Statement of Financial Position Statement of Financial Condition
Income Statement	Statement of Income Operating Statement Statement of Operations Statement of Operating Activity Earnings Statement Statement of Earnings Profit and Loss (P&L) Statement
Statement of Cash Flows	Statement of Cash Flow Cash Flows Statement Statement of Changes in Cash Position Statement of Changes in Financial Position
Statement of Owner's Equity	Statement of Changes in Owner's Equity Statement of Changes in Owner's Capital Statement of Shareholders' Equity[†] Statement of Changes in Shareholders' Equity[†] Statement of Stockholders' Equity and Comprehensive Income[†] Statement of Changes in Capital Accounts[†]

* The term **Consolidated** often precedes or follows these statement titles to reflect the combination of different entities, such as a parent company and its subsidiaries.
[†] For corporations only.

We thank Dr. Louella Moore from Arkansas State University for suggesting this listing.

Chart of Accounts

Following is a typical chart of accounts, which is used in several assignments. Every company has its own unique accounts and numbering system.

Assets

Current Assets

101 Cash
102 Petty cash
103 Cash equivalents
104 Short-term investments
105 Fair value adjustment, _____ securities (S-T)
106 Accounts receivable
107 Allowance for doubtful accounts
108 Legal fees receivable
109 Interest receivable
110 Rent receivable
111 Notes receivable
119 Merchandise inventory
120 _____ inventory
121 _____ inventory
124 Office supplies
125 Store supplies
126 _____ supplies
128 Prepaid insurance
129 Prepaid interest
131 Prepaid rent
132 Raw materials inventory
133 Goods in process inventory, _____
134 Goods in process inventory, _____
135 Finished goods inventory

Long-Term Investments

141 Long-term investments
142 Fair value adjustment, _____ securities (L-T)
144 Investment in _____
145 Bond sinking fund

Plant Assets

151 Automobiles
152 Accumulated depreciation—Automobiles
153 Trucks
154 Accumulated depreciation—Trucks
155 Boats
156 Accumulated depreciation—Boats
157 Professional library
158 Accumulated depreciation—Professional library
159 Law library
160 Accumulated depreciation—Law library
161 Furniture
162 Accumulated depreciation—Furniture
163 Office equipment
164 Accumulated depreciation—Office equipment
165 Store equipment

166 Accumulated depreciation—Store equipment
167 _____ equipment
168 Accumulated depreciation—_____ equipment
169 Machinery
170 Accumulated depreciation—Machinery
173 Building _____
174 Accumulated depreciation—Building _____
175 Building _____
176 Accumulated depreciation—Building _____
179 Land improvements _____
180 Accumulated depreciation—Land improvements _____
181 Land improvements _____
182 Accumulated depreciation—Land improvements _____
183 Land

Natural Resources

185 Mineral deposit
186 Accumulated depletion—Mineral deposit

Intangible Assets

191 Patents
192 Leasehold
193 Franchise
194 Copyrights
195 Leasehold improvements
196 Licenses
197 Accumulated amortization—_____

Liabilities

Current Liabilities

201 Accounts payable
202 Insurance payable
203 Interest payable
204 Legal fees payable
207 Office salaries payable
208 Rent payable
209 Salaries payable
210 Wages payable
211 Accrued payroll payable
214 Estimated warranty liability
215 Income taxes payable
216 Common dividend payable
217 Preferred dividend payable
218 State unemployment taxes payable
219 Employee federal income taxes payable
221 Employee medical insurance payable

222 Employee retirement program payable
223 Employee union dues payable
224 Federal unemployment taxes payable
225 FICA taxes payable
226 Estimated vacation pay liability

Unearned Revenues

230 Unearned consulting fees
231 Unearned legal fees
232 Unearned property management fees
233 Unearned _____ fees
234 Unearned _____ fees
235 Unearned janitorial revenue
236 Unearned _____ revenue
238 Unearned rent

Notes Payable

240 Short-term notes payable
241 Discount on short-term notes payable
245 Notes payable
251 Long-term notes payable
252 Discount on long-term notes payable

Long-Term Liabilities

253 Long-term lease liability
255 Bonds payable
256 Discount on bonds payable
257 Premium on bonds payable
258 Deferred income tax liability

Equity

Owner's Equity

301 _____, Capital
302 _____, Withdrawals
303 _____, Capital
304 _____, Withdrawals
305 _____, Capital
306 _____, Withdrawals

Paid-In Capital

307 Common stock, $ _____ par value
308 Common stock, no-par value
309 Common stock, $ _____ stated value
310 Common stock dividend distributable
311 Paid-in capital in excess of par value, Common stock

CA

312 Paid-in capital in excess of stated value,
    No-par common stock
313 Paid-in capital from retirement of common stock
314 Paid-in capital, Treasury stock
315 Preferred stock
316 Paid-in capital in excess of par value,
    Preferred stock

Retained Earnings

318 Retained earnings
319 Cash dividends (or Dividends)
320 Stock dividends

Other Equity Accounts

321 Treasury stock, Common
322 Unrealized gain—Equity
323 Unrealized loss—Equity

Revenues

401 _____ fees earned
402 _____ fees earned
403 _____ services revenue
404 _____ services revenue
405 Commissions earned
406 Rent revenue (or Rent earned)
407 Dividends revenue (or Dividend earned)
408 Earnings from investment in _____
409 Interest revenue (or Interest earned)
410 Sinking fund earnings
413 Sales
414 Sales returns and allowances
415 Sales discounts

Cost of Sales

Cost of Goods Sold

502 Cost of goods sold
505 Purchases
506 Purchases returns and allowances
507 Purchases discounts
508 Transportation-in

Manufacturing

520 Raw materials purchases
521 Freight-in on raw materials
530 Factory payroll
531 Direct labor
540 Factory overhead
541 Indirect materials
542 Indirect labor
543 Factory insurance expired
544 Factory supervision
545 Factory supplies used
546 Factory utilities
547 Miscellaneous production costs
548 Property taxes on factory building
549 Property taxes on factory equipment
550 Rent on factory building
551 Repairs, factory equipment
552 Small tools written off
560 Depreciation of factory equipment
561 Depreciation of factory building

Standard Cost Variance

580 Direct material quantity variance
581 Direct material price variance
582 Direct labor quantity variance
583 Direct labor price variance
584 Factory overhead volume variance
585 Factory overhead controllable variance

Expenses

Amortization, Depletion, and Depreciation

601 Amortization expense—_____
602 Amortization expense—_____
603 Depletion expense—_____
604 Depreciation expense—Boats
605 Depreciation expense—Automobiles
606 Depreciation expense—Building _____
607 Depreciation expense—Building _____
608 Depreciation expense—Land
    improvements _____
609 Depreciation expense—Land
    improvements _____
610 Depreciation expense—Law library
611 Depreciation expense—Trucks
612 Depreciation expense—_____ equipment
613 Depreciation expense—_____ equipment
614 Depreciation expense—_____
615 Depreciation expense—_____

Employee-Related Expenses

620 Office salaries expense
621 Sales salaries expense
622 Salaries expense
623 _____ wages expense
624 Employees' benefits expense
625 Payroll taxes expense

Financial Expenses

630 Cash over and short
631 Discounts lost
632 Factoring fee expense
633 Interest expense

Insurance Expenses

635 Insurance expense—Delivery equipment
636 Insurance expense—Office equipment
637 Insurance expense—_____

Rental Expenses

640 Rent expense
641 Rent expense—Office space
642 Rent expense—Selling space
643 Press rental expense
644 Truck rental expense
645 _____ rental expense

Supplies Expenses

650 Office supplies expense
651 Store supplies expense
652 _____ supplies expense
653 _____ supplies expense

Miscellaneous Expenses

655 Advertising expense
656 Bad debts expense
657 Blueprinting expense
658 Boat expense
659 Collection expense
661 Concessions expense
662 Credit card expense
663 Delivery expense
664 Dumping expense
667 Equipment expense
668 Food and drinks expense
671 Gas and oil expense
672 General and administrative expense
673 Janitorial expense
674 Legal fees expense
676 Mileage expense
677 Miscellaneous expenses
678 Mower and tools expense
679 Operating expense
680 Organization expense
681 Permits expense
682 Postage expense
683 Property taxes expense
684 Repairs expense—_____
685 Repairs expense—_____
687 Selling expense
688 Telephone expense
689 Travel and entertainment expense
690 Utilities expense
691 Warranty expense
695 Income taxes expense

Gains and Losses

701 Gain on retirement of bonds
702 Gain on sale of machinery
703 Gain on sale of investments
704 Gain on sale of trucks
705 Gain on _____
706 Foreign exchange gain or loss
801 Loss on disposal of machinery
802 Loss on exchange of equipment
803 Loss on exchange of _____
804 Loss on sale of notes
805 Loss on retirement of bonds
806 Loss on sale of investments
807 Loss on sale of machinery
808 Loss on _____
809 Unrealized gain—Income
810 Unrealized loss—Income
811 Impairment gain
812 Impairment loss

Clearing Accounts

901 Income summary
902 Manufacturing summary

SELECTED TRANSACTIONS AND RELATIONS

① Merchandising Transactions Summary

Merchandising Transactions		Merchandising Entries	Dr.	Cr.
Purchases	Purchasing merchandise for resale.	• Merchandise Inventory .... Cash or Accounts Payable	#	#
	Paying freight costs on purchases; FOB shipping point.	• Merchandise Inventory .... Cash	#	#

	Paying within discount period.	• Accounts Payable ....
		    Merchandise Inventory ....
		    Cash ....
			#	#
				 #

	Recording purchase returns or allowances.	• Cash or Accounts Payable .... Merchandise Inventory	#	#

Sales	Selling merchandise.	• Cash or Accounts Receivable ....
		    Sales ....
		 • Cost of Goods Sold ....
		    Merchandise Inventory ....
			#
			
			 #
				#
				
				 #

	Receiving payment within discount period.	• Cash ....
		    Sales Discounts ....
		    Accounts Receivable ....
			#
			 #
				#

	Granting sales returns or allowances.	• Sales Returns and Allowances..........
		    Cash or Accounts Receivable ....
		 • Merchandise Inventory ....
		    Cost of Goods Sold ....
			#
			
			 #
				#
				
				 #

	Paying freight costs on sales; FOB destination.	• Delivery Expense .... Cash	#	#

Merchandising Events		Adjusting and Closing Entries		
Adjusting	Adjusting due to shrinkage (occurs when recorded amount larger than physical inventory).	Cost of Goods Sold .... Merchandise Inventory	#	#
Closing	Closing temporary accounts with credit balances.	Sales .... Income Summary	#	#

	Closing temporary accounts with debit balances.	Income Summary ....
		    Sales Returns and Allowances ....
		    Sales Discounts ....
		    Cost of Goods Sold ....
		    Delivery Expense ....
		    "Other Expenses" ....
			#	#
				 #
				 #
				 #
				 #

② Merchandising Cash Flows

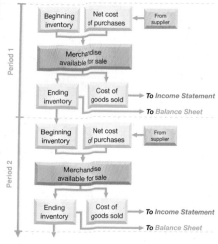

③ Credit Terms and Amounts

*Discount refers to a purchase discount for a buyer and a sales discount for a seller.

④ Bad Debts Estimation

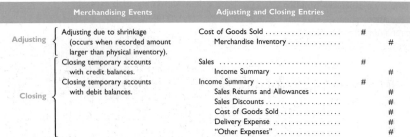

⑤ Bond Valuation

Bond Sets	Market Sets	Bond Price Determined	
Contract rate	Market rate	Contract rate > Market rate	Bond sells at Premium
		Contract rate = Market rate	Bond sells at Par
		Contract rate < Market rate	Bond sells at Discount

⑦ Dividend Transactions

Account Affected	Type of Dividend		
	Cash Dividend	Stock Dividend	Stock Split
Cash	Decrease	—	—
Common Stock	—	Increase	—
Retained Earnings ..	Decrease	Decrease	—

⑥ Stock Transactions Summary

Stock Transactions		Stock Entries	Dr.	Cr.
Issue Common Stock	Issue par value common stock at par (par stock recorded at par).	Cash .... Common Stock	#	#

	Issue par value common stock at premium (par stock recorded at par).	Cash ....
		    Common Stock ....
		    Paid-In Capital in Excess of
		      Par Value, Common Stock .....
			#	#
				
				 #

	Issue no-par value common stock (no-par stock recorded at amount received).	Cash .... Common Stock	#	#
	Issue stated value common stock at stated value (stated stock recorded at stated value).	Cash .... Common stock	#	#

	Issue stated value common stock at premium (stated stock recorded at stated value).	Cash ....
		    Common stock ....
		    Paid-In Capital in Excess of
		      Stated Value, Common Stock ....
			#	#
				
				 #

Issue Preferred Stock	Issue par value preferred stock at par (par stock recorded at par).	Cash .... Preferred Stock	#	#

	Issue par value preferred stock at premium (par stock recorded at par).	Cash ....
		    Preferred Stock ....
		    Paid-In Capital in Excess of
		      Par Value, Preferred Stock .....
			#	#
				
				 #

Reacquire Common Stock	Reacquire its own common stock (treasury stock recorded at cost).	Treasury Stock, Common .... Cash	#	#
Reissue Common Stock	Reissue its treasury stock at cost (treasury stock removed at cost).	Cash .... Treasury Stock, Common	#	#

	Reissue its treasury stock above cost (treasury stock removed at cost).	Cash ....
		    Treasury Stock, Common........
		    Paid-In Capital, Treasury ....
			#	#
				 #

	Reissue its treasury stock below cost (treasury stock removed at cost; if paid-in capital is insufficient to cover amount below cost, retained earnings is debited for remainder).	Cash ....
		 Paid-In Capital, Treasury ....
		    Treasury Stock, Common ....
		    Retained Earnings (if necessary) ...
			#
			 #
				#
				 #

⑧ A Rose by Any Other Name

The same financial statement sometimes receives different titles. Following are some of the more common aliases.*

Balance Sheet	Statement of Financial Position Statement of Financial Condition
Income Statement	Statement of Income Operating Statement Statement of Operations Statement of Operating Activity Earnings Statement Statement of Earnings Profit and Loss (P&L) Statement
Statement of Cash Flows	Statement of Cash Flow Cash Flows Statement Statement of Changes in Cash Position Statement of Changes in Financial Position
Statement of Owner's Equity	Statement of Changes in Owner's Equity Statement of Changes in Owner's Capital Statement of Shareholders' Equity† Statement of Changes in Shareholders' Equity† Statement of Stockholders' Equity and Comprehensive Income† Statement of Changes in Capital Accounts†

*The term **Consolidated** often precedes or follows these statement titles to reflect the combination of different entities, such as a parent company and its subsidiaries.
† Corporation only.

MANAGERIAL ANALYSES AND REPORTS

① Cost Types

Variable costs: Total cost changes in proportion to volume of activity
Fixed costs: Total cost does not change in proportion to volume of activity
Mixed costs: Cost consists of both a variable and a fixed element

② Cost Sources

Direct materials: Raw materials costs directly linked to finished product
Direct labor: Employee costs directly linked to finished product
Overhead: Costs indirectly linked to finished product

③ Costing Systems

Job order costing: Costs assigned to each unique unit or batch of units
Process costing: Costs assigned to similar products that are mass-produced in a continuous manner

④ Costing Ratios

Contribution margin ratio = (Net sales − Variable costs)/Net sales
Predetermined overhead rate = Estimated overhead costs/Estimated activity base
Break-even point in units = Total fixed costs/Contribution margin per unit

⑤ Planning and Control Metrics

Cost variance = Actual cost − Standard (budgeted) cost
Sales (revenue) variance = Actual sales − Standard (budgeted) sales

⑥ Capital Budgeting

Payback period = Time expected to recover investment cost
Accounting rate of return = Expected annual net income/Average annual investment
Net present value (NPV) = Present value of future cash flows − Investment cost
NPV rule: 1. Compute net present value (NPV in $)
2. If NPV ≥ 0, then accept project; If NPV < 0, then reject project
Internal rate 1. Compute internal rate of return (IRR in %)
of return rule: 2. If IRR ≥ hurdle rate, accept project; If IRR < hurdle rate, reject project

⑦ Costing Terminology

Relevant range: Organization's normal range of operating activity.
Direct cost: Cost incurred for the benefit of one cost object.
Indirect cost: Cost incurred for the benefit of more than one cost object.
Product cost: Cost that is necessary and integral to finished products.
Period cost: Cost identified more with a time period than with finished products.
Overhead cost: Cost not separately or directly traceable to a cost object.
Relevant cost: Cost that is pertinent to a decision.
Opportunity cost: Benefit lost by choosing an action from two or more alternatives.
Sunk cost: Cost already incurred that cannot be avoided or changed.
Standard cost: Cost computed using standard price and standard quantity.
Budget: Formal statement of an organization's future plans.
Break-even point: Sales level at which an organization earns zero profit.
Incremental cost: Cost incurred only if the organization undertakes a certain action.
Transfer price: Price on transactions between divisions within a company.

⑧ Standard Cost Variances

| Total materials variance | = | Materials price variance | + | Materials quantity variance |

| Total labor variance | = | Labor (rate) variance | + | Labor efficiency (quantity) variance |

| Total overhead variance | = | Overhead controllable variance | + | Fixed overhead volume variance |

Overhead controllable variance = Actual total overhead − Applied total overhead from flexible budget

Fixed overhead volume variance = Budgeted fixed overhead − Applied fixed overhead

Variable overhead variance = Variable overhead spending variance + Variable overhead efficiency variance

Fixed overhead variance = Fixed overhead spending variance + Fixed overhead volume variance

$\Bigr\}$ = Total overhead variance

Materials price variance	= [AQ × AP] − [AQ × SP]
Materials quantity variance	= [AQ × SP] − [SQ × SP]
Labor (rate) variance	= [AH × AR] − [AH × SR]
Labor efficiency (quantity) variance	= [AH × SR] − [SH × SR]

Variable overhead spending variance = [AH × AVR] − [AH × SVR]
Variable overhead efficiency variance = [AH × SVR] − [SH × SVR]
Fixed overhead spending variance = Actual fixed overhead − Budgeted fixed overhead

where AQ is actual quantity of materials; AP is actual price of materials; AH is actual hours of labor; AR is actual rate of wages; AVR is actual variable rate of overhead; SQ is standard quantity of materials; SP is standard price of materials; SH is standard hours of labor; SR is standard rate of wages; SVR is standard variable rate of overhead.

⑨ Sales Variances

| **Sales price variance** | = [AS × AP] − [AS × BP] |
| **Sales volume variance** | = [AS × BP] − [BS × BP] |

where AS = actual sales units; AP = actual sales price; BP = budgeted sales price;
BS = budgeted sales units (fixed budget)

Manufacturing Statement
For _period_ Ended _date_

Direct materials		
Raw materials inventory, Beginning	$	#
Raw materials purchases		#
Raw materials available for use		#
Raw materials inventory, Ending		(#)
Direct materials used		#
Direct labor		#
Overhead costs		
Total overhead costs		#
Total manufacturing costs		#
Add goods in process inventory, Beginning		#
Total cost of goods in process		#
Deduct goods in process inventory, Ending		(#)
Cost of goods manufactured	$	#

Contribution Margin Income Statement
For _period_ Ended _date_

Net sales (revenues)	$	#
Total variable costs		#
Contribution margin		#
Total fixed costs		#
Net income	$	#

Flexible Budget
For _period_ Ended _date_

	Flexible Budget		Flexible Budget for Unit Sales of #
	Variable Amount per Unit	Fixed Cost	
Sales (revenues)	$ #		$ #
Variable costs			
Examples: Direct materials, Direct labor,			
Other variable costs	#		#
Total variable costs	#		#
Contribution margin	$ #		#
Fixed costs			
Examples: Depreciation, Manager		$ #	
salaries, Administrative salaries		#	#
Total fixed costs		$ #	#
Income from operations			$ #

Fixed Budget Performance Report
For _period_ Ended _date_

	Fixed Budget	Actual Performance	Variances†
Sales: In units	#	#	
In dollars	$ #	$ #	$ # F or U
Cost of sales			
Direct costs	#	#	# F or U
Indirect costs	#	#	# F or U
Selling expenses			
Examples: Commissions,	#	#	# F or U
Shipping expenses	#	#	# F or U
General and administrative expenses			
Examples: Administrative salaries	#	#	# F or U
Total expenses	$ #	$ #	$ # F or U
Income from operations	$ #	$ #	$ # F or U

†F = Favorable variance; U = Unfavorable variance.

Master Budget Sequence

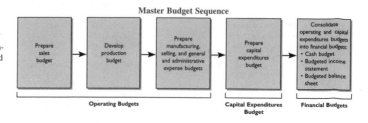

FUNDAMENTALS

① Accounting Equation

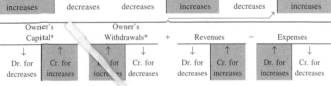

| Assets | = | Liabilities | + | Equity |

| Debit for increases ↑ | Credit for decreases ↓ | Debit for decreases ↓ | Credit for increases ↑ | Debit for decreases ↓ | Credit for increases ↑ |

Owner's Capital* | Owner's Withdrawals* | + | Revenues | − | Expenses

| Dr. for decreases ↓ | Cr. for increases ↑ | Dr. for increases ↑ | Cr. for decreases ↓ | Dr. for decreases ↓ | Cr. for increases ↑ | Dr. for increases ↑ | Cr. for decreases ↓ |

☐ Indicates normal balance.

*Comparable corporate accounts are Common Stock (Paid-In Capital) and Dividends.

② Accounting Cycle

1. Analyze transactions
2. Journalize
3. Post
4. Prepare unadjusted trial balance
5. Adjust
6. Prepare adjusted trial balance
7. Prepare statements
8. Close
9. Prepare post-closing trial balance
10. Reverse (Optional)

Accounting Cycle

③ Adjustments and Entries

Type	Adjusting Entry	
Prepaid Expenses	Dr. Expense	Cr. Asset*
Unearned Revenues	Dr. Liability	Cr. Revenue
Accrued Expenses	Dr. Expense	Cr. Liability
Accrued Revenues	Dr. Asset	Cr. Revenue

*For depreciation, credit Accumulated Depreciation (contra asset).

④ 4-Step Closing Process

1. Transfer revenue and gain account balances to Income Summary.
2. Transfer expense and loss account balances to Income Summary.
3. Transfer Income Summary balance to Owner's Capital.
4. Transfer Withdrawals balance to Owner's Capital.

⑤ Accounting Concepts

Characteristics	Assumptions	Principles	Constraints
Relevance	Business entity	Historical cost	Cost-benefit
Reliability	Going concern	Revenue recognition	Materiality
Comparability	Monetary unit	Expense recognition	Industry practice
Consistency	Periodicity	Full disclosure	Conservatism

⑥ Ownership of Inventory

	Ownership Transfers When Goods Passed To	Transportation Costs Paid By
FOB Shipping Point	Carrier	Buyer
FOB Destination	Buyer	Seller

⑦ Inventory Costing Methods

- Specific Identification
- First-In, First-Out (FIFO)
- Weighted-Average
- Last-In, First-Out (LIFO)

⑧ Depreciation and Depletion

Straight-Line: $\dfrac{\text{Cost} - \text{Salvage value}}{\text{Useful life in periods}} \times \text{Periods expired}$

Units-of-Production: $\dfrac{\text{Cost} - \text{Salvage value}}{\text{Useful life in units}} \times \text{Units produced}$

Declining-Balance: Rate* × Beginning-of-period book value
*Rate is often double the straight-line rate, or 2 × (1/Useful life)

Depletion: $\dfrac{\text{Cost} - \text{Salvage value}}{\text{Total capacity in units}} \times \text{Units extracted}$

⑨ Interest Computation

Interest = Principal (face) × Rate × Time

⑩ Accounting for Investment Securities

Classification*	Accounting
Short-Term Investment in Securities	
Held-to-maturity (debt) securities	**Cost** (without any discount or premium amortization)
Trading (debt and equity) securities	**Fair value** (with fair value adjustment to income)
Available-for-sale (debt and equity) securities	**Fair value** (with fair value adjustment to equity)
Long-Term Investment in Securities	
Held-to-maturity (debt) securities	**Cost** (with any discount or premium amortization)
Available-for-sale (debt and equity) securities	**Fair value** (with fair value adjustment to equity)
Equity securities with significant influence	Equity method
Equity securities with controlling influence	Equity method (with consolidation)

*A *fair value option* allows companies to report HTM and AFS securities much like trading securities.

ANALYSES

① Liquidity and Efficiency

Current ratio $= \dfrac{\text{Current assets}}{\text{Current liabilities}}$ — p. 148

Working capital = Current assets − Current liabilities — p. 697

Acid-test ratio $= \dfrac{\text{Cash} + \text{Short-term investments} + \text{Current receivables}}{\text{Current liabilities}}$ — p. 196

Accounts receivable turnover $= \dfrac{\text{Net sales}}{\text{Average accounts receivable, net}}$ — p. 375

Credit risk ratio $= \dfrac{\text{Allowance for doubtful accounts}}{\text{Accounts receivable, net}}$ — p. 375

Inventory turnover $= \dfrac{\text{Cost of goods sold}}{\text{Average inventory}}$ — p. 241

Days' sales uncollected $= \dfrac{\text{Accounts receivable, net}}{\text{Net sales}} \times 365*$ — p. 335

Days' sales in inventory $= \dfrac{\text{Ending inventory}}{\text{Cost of goods sold}} \times 365*$ — p. 241

Total asset turnover $= \dfrac{\text{Net sales}}{\text{Average total assets}}$ — p. 413

Plant asset useful life $= \dfrac{\text{Plant asset cost}}{\text{Depreciation expense}}$ — p. 413

Plant asset age $= \dfrac{\text{Accumulated depreciation}}{\text{Depreciation expense}}$ — p. 413

Days' cash expense coverage $= \dfrac{\text{Cash and cash equivalents}}{\text{Average daily cash expenses}}$ — p. 322

*360 days is also commonly used.

② Solvency

Debt ratio $= \dfrac{\text{Total liabilities}}{\text{Total assets}}$ Equity ratio $= \dfrac{\text{Total equity}}{\text{Total assets}}$ — pp. 69 & 701

Debt-to-equity $= \dfrac{\text{Total liabilities}}{\text{Total equity}}$ — p. 567

Times interest earned $= \dfrac{\text{Income before interest expense and income taxes}}{\text{Interest expense}}$ — p. 450

Cash coverage of growth $= \dfrac{\text{Cash flow from operations}}{\text{Cash outflow for plant assets}}$ — p. 651

Cash coverage of debt $= \dfrac{\text{Cash flow from operations}}{\text{Total noncurrent liabilities}}$ — p. 646

③ Profitability

Profit margin ratio $= \dfrac{\text{Net income}}{\text{Net sales}}$ — p. 109

Gross margin ratio $= \dfrac{\text{Net sales} - \text{Cost of goods sold}}{\text{Net sales}}$ — p. 196

Return on total assets $= \dfrac{\text{Net income}}{\text{Average total assets}}$ — p. 22

$= \text{Profit margin ratio} \times \text{Total asset turnover}$ — p. 703

Return on common stockholders' equity $= \dfrac{\text{Net income} - \text{Preferred dividends}}{\text{Average common stockholders' equity}}$ — p. 703

Book value per common share $= \dfrac{\text{Stockholders' equity applicable to common shares}}{\text{Number of common shares outstanding}}$ — p. 528

Basic earnings per share $= \dfrac{\text{Net income} - \text{Preferred dividends}}{\text{Weighted-average common shares outstanding}}$ — p. 527

Cash flow on total assets $= \dfrac{\text{Cash flow from operations}}{\text{Average total assets}}$ — p. 650

Payout ratio $= \dfrac{\text{Cash dividends declared on common stock}}{\text{Net income}}$ — p. 528

④ Market

Price-earnings ratio $= \dfrac{\text{Market value (price) per share}}{\text{Earnings per share}}$ — p. 527

Dividend yield $= \dfrac{\text{Annual cash dividends per share}}{\text{Market price per share}}$ — p. 528

Residual income = Net income − Target net income